William Manchester is the author of fourteen other books which include *The Death of a President* (1967), *American Caesar: Douglas MacArthur 1880–1964* (1978) and *Goodbye Darkness* (1980).

He is currently Adjunct Professor of History at the Wesleyan University of Connecticut.

'Mr Manchester is hospitable to every pro and con, every admiring or malicious comment, every shred of damning or vindicating evidence. As he did in his MacArthur biography, he demonstrates that he is unperturbed by the sharpest and most contrary judgements of his subject.'

Alistair Cooke, *The New Yorker*

The Last Lion:
Winston Spencer Churchill
Visions of Glory 1874–1932

WILLIAM MANCHESTER

SPHERE BOOKS LIMITED
30–32 Gray's Inn Road, London WC1X 8JL

To
MARY
and
CHARTWELL

The credit belongs to the man who is actually in the arena, whose face is marred by dust and sweat and blood, who knows the great enthusiasms, the great devotions, and spends himself in a worthy cause; who at best, if he wins, knows the thrills of high achievement, and, if he fails, at least fails daring greatly, so that his place shall never be with those cold and timid souls who know neither victory nor defeat.

—JOHN F. KENNEDY *on Theodore Roosevelt*
New York City, December 5, 1961

CONTENTS

CHRONOLOGY

1874	*WSC born November 20 at Blenheim*
1886	*His father becomes chancellor of the Exchequer*
	His mother is now a great Victorian courtesan
1888	WSC enters Harrow; gets lowest marks in school
1893	Admitted to Sandhurst on third try
1894	Commissioned cavalry subaltern, Fourth Hussars
1895	His father dies
	WSC covers the guerrilla warfare in Cuba
1896	Educates himself in India; discovers Macaulay and Gibbon
	Writes first book
1897	Sees heavy fighting in Khyber Pass
1898	Omdurman: WSC in the last cavalry charge
1899	WSC runs for Parliament; loses
	Captured in the Boer War
	His sensational escape
1900	Recommended for VC
	Elected to Parliament
	Tours United States, Canada
1901	Queen Victoria dies
	WSC's maiden speech
1904	Quits Tories for Liberals
1905	Becomes colonial under secretary
1907	Tours East Africa
1908	Promoted to cabinet
	Marries Clementine Hozier
	His alliance with Lloyd George
	They declare war on House of Lords
1910	WSC becomes home secretary
	His welfare state programmes
1911	Battle of Sidney Street
	WSC becomes first lord of the Admiralty
	Father of the tank
1912–14	Irish Home Rule crisis
1913	WSC learns to fly, founds Royal Naval Flying Corps
1914	Outbreak of the Great War
	WSC commands defence of Antwerp
1915	The Dardanelles tragedy
	WSC dismissed from the Admiralty
	Learns to paint
	Commissioned and sent to the front

PREAMBLE

THE LION AT BAY

The French had collapsed. The Dutch had been overwhelmed. The Belgians had surrendered. The British army, trapped, fought free and fell back towards the Channel ports, converging on a fishing town whose name was then spelled Dunkerque.

Behind them lay the sea.

It was England's greatest crisis since the Norman conquest, vaster than those precipitated by Philip II's Spanish Armada, Louis XIV's triumphant armies, or Napoleon's invasion barges massed at Boulogne. This time Britain stood alone. If the Germans crossed the Channel and established uncontested beachheads, all would be lost, for it is a peculiarity of England's island that its southern weald is indefensible against disciplined troops. In A.D. 61, Queen Boudicca of the Iceni rallied the tribes of East Anglia and routed the Romans at Colchester, Saint Albans, and London (then Londinium), cutting the Ninth Legion to pieces and killing seventy thousand. But because the nature of the southern terrain was unsuitable for the construction of strongpoints, new legions under Paulinus, arriving from Gaul, crushed the revolt, leaving the grief-stricken queen to die by her own hand.

Now the 220,000 Tommies at Dunkirk, Britain's only hope, seemed doomed. On the Flanders beaches they stood around in angular, existential attitudes, like dim purgatorial souls awaiting disposition. There appeared to be no way to bring more than a handful of them home. The Royal Navy's vessels were inadequate. King George VI has been told that they would be lucky to save 17,000. The House of Commons was warned to prepare for 'hard and heavy tidings.'[1] Then, from the streams and estuaries of Kent and Dover, a strange fleet appeared: trawlers and tugs, scows and fishing sloops, lifeboats and pleasure craft, smacks and coasters; the island ferry *Gracie Fields*; Tom Sopwith's America's Cup challenger *Endeavour;* even the London fire brigade's fire-float *Massey Shaw* – all of them manned by civilian volunteers: English fathers, sailing to rescue England's exhausted, bleeding sons.

Even today what followed seems miraculous. Not only were Britain's soldiers delivered; so were French support troops: a total of 338,682 men. But wars are not won by fleeing from the enemy. And British morale was still unequal to the imminent challenge. These were the same people who, less than a year earlier, had rejoiced in the fake peace bought by the betrayal of Czechoslovakia at Munich. Most of their leaders and most of the press remained craven. It had been over a thousand years since Alfred the Great had made himself and his countrymen one and sent them into battle transformed.

Now in this new exigency, confronted by the mightiest conqueror Europe had ever known, England looked for another Alfred, a figure cast in a mould which, by the time of the Dunkirk deliverance, seemed to have been forever lost.

England's new leader, were he to prevail, would have to stand for everything England's decent, civilized Establishment had rejected. They viewed Adolf Hitler as the product of complex social and historical forces. Their successor would have to be a passionate Manichaean who saw the world as a medieval struggle to the death between the powers of good and the powers of evil, who held that individuals are responsible for their actions and that the German dictator was therefore wicked. A believer in martial glory was required, one who saw splendour in the ancient parades of victorious legions through Persepolis and could rally the nation to brave the coming German fury. An embodiment of fading Victorian standards was wanted: a tribune for honour, loyalty, duty, and the supreme virtue of action; one who would never compromise with iniquity, who would create a sublime mood and thus give men heroic visions of what they were and might become. Like Adolf Hitler he would have to be a leader of intuitive genius, a born demagogue in the original sense of the word, a believer in the supremacy of his race and his national destiny, an artist who knew how to gather the blazing light of history into his prism and then distort it to his ends, an embodiment of inflexible resolution who could impose his will and his imagination on his people – a great tragedian who understood the appeal of martyrdom and could tell his followers the worst, hurling it to them like great hunks of bleeding meat, persuading them that the year of Dunkirk would be one in which it was 'equally good to live or to die' – who could if necessary be just as cruel, just as cunning, and just as ruthless as Hitler but who could win victories without enslaving populations, or preaching supernaturalism, or foisting off myths of his infallibility, or destroying, or even warping, the libertarian institutions he had sworn to preserve. Such a man, if he existed, would be England's last chance.[2]

In London there was such a man.

Now at last, at last, his hour had struck. He had been waiting in Parliament for forty years, had grown bald and grey in his nation's service, had endured slander and calumny only to be summoned when the situation seemed hopeless to everyone except him. His youngest daughter, seventeen-year-old 'Mary the Mouse' – her family nickname – had been sunning herself at Chartwell, their country home in Kent, during the first hours of the German breakthrough, when the music on her portable radio had been interrupted by a BBC bulletin: 'His Majesty the King has sent for Mr Winston Churchill and asked him to form a government.' Mary, who adored her father, prayed for him and assumed that he would save England. So, of course, did he. But among those who fully grasped the country's plight, that was a minority view. The Conservative party leadership, the men of Munich, still controlled the Government

– Lord Halifax, Sir Horace Wilson, Sir Kingsley Wood, Sir John Simon, Sir Samuel Hoare, and, of course, Churchill's predecessor as prime minister, Neville Chamberlain, who detested him and everything he represented. Even George VI hadn't wanted Chamberlain to quit No. 10 Downing Street; he thought his treatment had been 'grossly unfair.' The King suggested Halifax as his successor. Labour's erratic Stafford Cripps had already come out for Halifax. That suited the Tory hierarchy, but only a coalition could govern the nation, and the National Executive of the Labour party, meeting in a basement room of the Highcliff Hotel in Bournemouth, sent word that they would serve under no Conservative except Churchill. So Chamberlain persuaded the reluctant King to choose the man neither wanted.[3]

Not that it seemed to matter much. Churchill had said that 'the Germans are always either at your throat or at your feet,' and as a hot May melted into a hotter June it appeared that their stranglehold was now unbreakable. Hitler was master of Europe. No one, not even Caesar, had stood so securely upon so glittering a pinnacle. The Führer told Göring: 'The war is finished. I'll come to an understanding with England.' On May 28, the first day of the Dunkirk evacuation, Halifax, speaking for the Conservative leadership, had told Churchill that a negotiated peace was England's only alternative. Now, as the new prime minister's foreign secretary and a member of his War Cabinet, the Yorkshire noblemen was quoted by the United Press as inviting 'Chancellor Hitler to make a new and more generous peace offer.' It was, he said, the only reasonable course, the only decision a stable man of sound judgement could reach.[4]

He was quite right. But Winston Churchill was not a reasonable man. He was about as sound as the Maid of Orleans, a comparison he himself once made – 'It's when I'm Joan of Arc that I get excited.' Even more he was an Elijah, an Isaiah; a prophet. Deep insight, not stability, was his forte. To the War Cabinet he said, 'I have thought carefully in these last days whether it was part of my duty to consider entering into negotiations with that man,' and concluded: 'If this long island story of ours is to end at last, let it end only when each one of us lies choking in his own blood upon the ground.' He spoke to them, to the House, and then to the English people as no one had before or ever would again. He said: 'I have nothing to offer but blood, toil, tears, and sweat.' Another politician might have told them; 'Our policy is to continue the struggle; all our forces and resources will be mobilized.' This is what Churchill said:

Even though large tracts of Europe and many old and famous states have fallen or may fall into the grip of the Gestapo and all the odious apparatus of Nazi rule, we shall not flag or fail. We shall go on to the end. We shall fight in France, we shall fight on the seas and oceans, we shall fight with growing confidence and growing strength in the air, we shall defend our island, whatever the cost may be, we shall fight on the beaches, we shall fight on the landing grounds, we shall fight in the fields and in the streets, we shall fight in the hills; we shall never surrender.

'Behind us,' he said, '. . . gather a group of shattered states and bludgeoned races: the Czechs, the Poles, the Danes, the Norwegians, the Belgians, the Dutch – upon all of whom a long night of barbarism will descend, unbroken even by a star of hope, unless we conquer, as conquer we must, as conquer we shall.' That was the language of the Elizabethans, and of a particular Elizabethan, the greatest poet in history: 'This England never did, nor never shall, /Lie at the proud foot of a conqueror.'[5]

Now, fired by the conviction which could only belong to one who had faced down inner despair, Churchill defied the 'celestial grins' of Britain's enemies, said peace feelers would 'be viewed with the greatest disfavour by me,' and said he contemplated the future 'with stern and tranquil gaze.' Free Englishmen, he told his people, would be more than a match for the 'deadly, drilled, docile, brutish mass of the Hun soldiery plodding on like a swarm of crawling locusts.' But he warned his family to prepare for invaders. His son's bride Pamela protested: 'But Papa, what can *I* do?' He growled: 'You can always get a carving knife from the kitchen and take one with you, can't you?' To the demoralized French he declared: 'Whatever you may do, we shall fight on forever and ever and ever.' General Maxime Weygand replied by asking what would happen if a hundred Nazi divisions landed at Dover. Churchill told him: '*Nous les frapperons sur la tête*' – they would be hit on the head as they crawled ashore. Visiting Harrow, he heard the boys sing an old school song rewritten in his honour:

> *Not less we praise in darker days*
> *The Leader of our Nation,*
> *And Churchill's name shall win acclaim*
> *From each new generation.*

He suggested a change. 'Darker,' he said, should be 'sterner.' These were no dark days, he told them. Indeed, they would be remembered as great days, provided this 'island race' followed his watchword: 'Never, never, never, never give in.'[6]

And so he saved Western civilization when men considered its redemption worth any price. The Nazi stain was spreading into the Balkans, into the Middle East, into Brazil; the German-American Bund was staging mass rallies in Madison Square Garden; the *New York Times* reported in front-page headlines: URUGUAY ON GUARD FOR FIFTH COLUMN, NAZIS TAKE BOLD TONE IN ECUADOR, and ARGENTINE NAZIS RALLY. Men who think of themselves as indispensable are almost always wrong, but Winston Churchill was surely that then. He was like the lion in Revelation, 'the first beast,' with 'six wings about him' and 'full of eyes within.' In an uncharacteristically modest moment on his eightieth birthday he said: 'It was the nation and the race dwelling all round the globe that had the lion's heart; I had the luck to be called upon to give the roar.' It wasn't that simple. The spirit, if indeed within them, lay dormant until he became prime minister and they, kindled by his soaring prose, came to see themselves as he saw them and emerged a people transformed, the admiration of free men everywhere.[7]

At the height of the Battle of Britain, when Hitler tried to win in the air over London what he had expected to gain in a negotiated peace, the prime minister's headquarters lay in a drab brick bunker two blocks south of Downing Street, beneath a stone government building which bears the plaque CABINET OFFICE/CENTRAL STATISTICAL OFFICE. The bunker is still there – nothing in it, not even the pins in the maps, has been changed since V-E Day – and you can descend a cellar stair into the past, emerging into what was known as 'the Annexe,' or 'the CWR,' short for 'Cabinet War Room.' In fact there are many rooms, including a rather barren cell containing a desk bearing the microphone which the prime minister used for his broadcasts and the bed into which his wife could tuck him at night. All messages reached him here through the No 10 switchboard; an aide could be put through anywhere in England by dialling the magic number: Rapid Falls 4466.

Churchill hated the Annexe's cramped quarters. Donning his zippered blue Siren Suit, as he called it (it looked like a workman's boiler suit; the staff called it his 'Rompers'), he would mount the stairs to visit his family in their ground-floor flat, or stroll over to No. 10, or cross the street into St James's Park to feed the ducks and pelicans in the lake despite reports, taken seriously, that German agents lurked there. At night he was even more incautious. During raids he would dart out after close hits to see the damage. Sometimes he climbed up to the roof and squatted there on a hot-air vent, counting the Heinkel IIIs as the searchlights picked them up. He wanted to be wherever the bombs were falling. It is a lie that he knew Coventry would be destroyed on November 14, 1940, and didn't alert the city because the Germans would have known their code had been broken. Sir John Martin was with him that evening. They were driving out of the capital when a motor-cyclist stopped them; word had just arrived that the Luftwaffe was headed for London. So the prime minister ordered the car turned around. It was early morning before he knew that the real target had been Coventry.

All his life he was a man of extraordinary personal courage. As a youth he sought danger in Cuba, on India's North-West Frontier, on the Nile, and in South Africa. Each battle found him recklessly exposing himself to gunfire. In the Sudan in 1898 he was a subaltern and Herbert Kitchener was Anglo-Egyptian commander in chief (Sirdar), but he attacked Kitchener, in print, for 'the inhuman slaughter of the wounded' and the desecration of the tomb of the Mahdi, the natives' idol. Then, in Natal, the Boers captured Churchill. He escaped and later rode a bicycle in civilian clothes through the Boer stronghold of Johannesburg, risking execution as a spy had he been caught. Elected to Parliament at the age of twenty-five, he defended the enemy in his maiden speech – and then savaged Britain's war minister, a senior statesman of his own party. At sea in 1943 he awoke Averell Harriman to tell him that a U-boat had them in its sights. He said: 'I won't be captured. The finest way to die is in the excitement of fighting the enemy.' After a moment's thought he added: 'It might not be so nice if one were in the water and they tried to pick me up.' Harriman, frightened, said, 'I thought you told me that the worst a torpedo could do to this ship . . . was to knock out one engine room.' Churchill grinned and replied, 'Ah, but they might put two torpedoes in us. You must come with me . . . and see the fun.'[8]

The harder question is whether he enjoyed war too much. He denied it. He called it a 'dirty, shoddy business, . . . disguise it as you may.' On September 4, 1898, after he had survived the dreadful battle of Omdurman on the Nile, he wrote his mother that the scenes he had witnessed 'made me anxious and worried during the night and I speculated on the shoddiness of war. You cannot gild it. The raw comes through.' At Tehran in 1943 he said to his daughter Sarah: 'War is a game played with a smiling face, but do you think there is laughter in my heart?' And he said: 'War, which used to be cruel and magnificent, has now become cruel and squalid. In fact it has been completely spoilt.'[9]

But this assumes that there was something magnificent to spoil. The implication is ineluctable: he saw chivalric, Arthurian, *brioso* aspects of war; it was to him, as life was to Peter Pan, 'an awfully big adventure.' As a young war correspondent he reported the death of a young peer in battle as 'a sad item, for which the only consolation is that the Empire is worth the blood of the noblest of its citizens.' In 1914, the diarist Frances Stevenson, Lloyd George's mistress, noted that the outbreak of war found the British cabinet sunk in gloom, whereupon 'in burst Churchill, radiant, smiling, a cigar in his mouth and satisfaction upon his face. "Well!" he exclaimed, "the deed is done!"' Lloyd George, who was also there, told Margot Asquith that 'Winston was radiant, his face bright, his manner keen . . . You could see he was a really happy man,' and Churchill himself wrote his wife: 'I am interested, geared up and happy. Is it not horrible to be built up like that?' During World War II he liked to cap his day by watching captured German combat films. After the second Quebec conference in 1944 he told the press that he would visit the battlefronts soon because he did not wish to miss any of the 'fun' of 'the good things.' The *New Statesman* acidly commented that these were 'strange words for a process whereby human beings are being disembowelled, roasted to death, drowned, blown into fragments, or are dying slowly of agonizing wounds.' But the prime minister was unchastened. Six months later he stood on Xanten hilltop, watching British regiments cross the Rhine. The spectacle, he complained, was insufficiently dramatic. He said: 'I should have liked to have deployed my men in red coats on the plain down there and ordered them to charge.'[10]

Red coats, which the army had doffed for khaki in the late 1890s, obviously belonged to the wars of earlier times. But so did he. He liked panoply, bugles, drums, battle flags, British squares. He said: 'It is a shame that War should have flung all this aside in its greedy, base, opportunistic march, and should turn instead to chemists in spectacles, and chauffeurs pulling the levers of aeroplanes or machine guns.' At times he believed it a shame that technology had altered peace, too. 'In the nineteenth century,' he observed, 'Jules Verne wrote *Round the World in Eighty Days.* It seemed a prodigy. Now you can get around it in four, but you do not see much of it on the way.' He thought that 'the substitution of the internal combustion machine for the horse marked a very gloomy milestone in the progress of mankind' and that it was 'arguable whether the human race have been the gainers by the march of science beyond the steam engine.' The real point here was that steam had opened up the British Empire; air power, and then the atom, had closed it down. Lord Moran, his physician, wrote that 'Winston is a proud man, and it hurts him to think how vulnerable, in the atomic age, a small, densely populated island like Britain has become.' It was to Moran that Churchill said glumly: 'I wish flying had never been invented. The world has shrunk since the Wrights got into the air; it was an evil hour for poor England.' And addressing England as though it were a colleague – he was apt to do this – he said: 'You came into big things as an accident of naval power when you were an island. The world had confidence in you. You became the workshop of the world. You populated the island beyond its capacity. Through an accident of airpower you will probably cease to exist.'[11]

In a thousand little ways he revealed his preference for the past and his reluctance to part with it. Victorian expressions salted his speech: 'I venture to say,' 'I am greatly distressed,' 'I rejoice,' and 'I pray'; so many of his memos began 'Pray do,' 'Pray do not,' or 'Pray give me the facts on half a sheet of paper' that they became known among his staff as 'Churchill's prayers.' If it was time to leave Chartwell for London, and he wanted to know if his chauffeur was behind the wheel, he would ask: 'Is the coachman on his box?' After the House of Commons snuffbox was destroyed in the Blitz, he replaced it with one from his family's ancestral home of Blenheim, explaining, 'I confess myself to be a great admirer of tradition.' He frankly preferred 'the refinements of Louis XIV' to the modern 'age of clatter and buzz, of gape and gloat.' He also thought that 'bad luck always pursues peoples who change the names of their cities. Fortune is rightly malignant to those who break with the customs of the past.' Accordingly, Istanbul was Constantinople to him; Ankara was Angora; Sevastopol was Sebastopol; and in a directive to his minister of information dated August 29, 1941, he wrote: 'Do try to blend in without causing trouble the word Persia instead of Iran.' As for Cambodia and Guatemala, they didn't exist for him; he had got this far without having heard of them and saw no need to change now. He spoke of Sir Walter Raleigh, Henry VIII, and James I as though they were his contemporaries. Anthony Montague Browne recalls walking into Churchill's office after Harold Macmillan had been chosen over R.A. ('Rab') Butler as the new Conservative leader. Churchill was muttering, 'Intelligent, yes. Good looking, yes. Well-meaning, yes. But not the stuff of which Prime Ministers are made.' Montague Browne asked: 'But would Rab have been any better?' Churchill looked at him blankly. He said: 'I was thinking of Melbourne.'[12]

Like Melbourne and all other Victorian prime ministers, Churchill never attended Parliament, or called at Buckingham Palace, wearing anything but a frock coat. It was sometimes difficult for those around him to remember that he had fought his first election in the nineteenth century and had been, by the time of the old Queen's death, one of the highest paid newspaper reporters in the world. Some thought his viewpoint and attitudes reached even farther back in history; Harold Laski called him 'a gallant and romantic relic of eighteenth-century imperialism.' Churchill replied: 'I like to live in the past. I don't think people are going to get much fun in the future.' The older he grew, the stronger the bond he felt between himself and others who had reached manhood before the turn of the century. When he was told that a Londoner over seventy-five years of age had been arrested in Hyde Park for making improper advances towards a young girl in subzero weather, he chortled: 'Over seventy-five and below zero! Makes you *proud* to be an Englishman!'[13]

But to those who chided him for being preoccupied with earlier ages, he answered: 'The longer you look back, the farther you can look forward. This is not a philosophical or political argument – any oculist can tell you it is true.' Certainly it was true of him. He was no mere fogy. Clement Attlee, his great Labour adversary, compared him to a layer cake: 'One layer was certainly seventeenth century. The eighteenth century in him is obvious. There was the nineteenth century, and a large slice, of course, of the twentieth century; and another, curious, layer which may possibly have been the twenty-first.'[14] Churchill may have lacked sympathy for inventive contributions to warfare, but he understood them and even anticipated them. In World War I he was the father of the tank. As early as 1917 he conceived of vessels which would serve as landing craft for tanks. In the late 1930s he became interested in rockets and showed friends graphs illustrating their ballistic characteristics. And in the war against Hitler his genius was responsible for 'Window,' strips of tinfoil dropped by bombers to confuse enemy radar; 'Pluto,' a pipeline under the ocean; 'Gee,' a device for guiding pilots; and the artificial harbours used at Normandy.

All these, of course, were weapons. Martial strains reverberated throughout his career as a kind of background score. In the House his rhetorical metaphors were those of the battlefield – events marched, political flanks were turned, legislative skirmishes fought, ultimata delivered, and opponents told to surrender, to strike their colours, to lay down their arms. More than half of the fifty-six books he published were about war and warriors; the two he most regretted not having found time to write were biographies of Caesar and Napoleon. Partly this was because he knew that peace hath not her heroes, and he meant to be heroic. In part it was because of his combative spirit. He agreed with George Meredith: 'It is a terrific decree in life that they must act who would prevail.' There is no doubt that he enjoyed peril and delighted in battle.

In his last days he said that 1940 and 1941 had been the best years of his life, despite the fact that for other Englishmen they had been incomparably the worst.

It is equally true that throughout his life he retained the small boy's glee in making mischief, in dressing up, in showing off. He was probably the only man in London who owned more hats than his wife – top hats, Stetsons, seamen's caps, his hussar helmet, a privy councillor's cocked hat, homburgs, an astrakhan, an Irish 'paddy hat,' a white pith helmet, an Australian bush hat, a fez, the huge beplumed hat he wore as a Knight of the Garter, even the full headdress of a North American Indian chieftain. He had closets full of costumes. When his grandchildren visited him, he appeared as an ape, snarling. Dressing for dinner when he travelled abroad, he wore the decorations awarded him by whatever country he was visiting – his favourite was the Danish Order of the Elephant – together with his sash. If nothing else was suitable, he would don his uniforms as RAF air commodore, as colonel of the Queen's Own Fourth Hussars, as Lord Warden of the Cinque Ports, or as Elder Brother of Trinity House, England's first lighthouse and pilotage authority, chartered by Henry VIII in 1514. His fame had eclipsed the medals; his figure had outgrown the uniforms; it didn't matter. Once in Strasbourg Lord Boothby entered wearing a Légion d'Honneur rosette. Churchill glared, pointed at it, and demanded: 'What's that in your buttonhole?' Told, he scowled, then brightened. 'I've got something better than that,' he said. He disappeared and reappeared, proudly wearing the *médaille militaire*.[15]

In the House he expressed this side of himself by thumbing his nose at the Opposition, or sticking out his tongue, or, when he had enraged them and they looked apoplectic, by blowing them a kiss. He once wrote of his childhood that he had been 'so happy in my nursery with all my toys.' He still was; the imp lurked within. As home secretary before World War I he refused to prohibit roller-skating on sidewalks; pedestrians might be bowled over, but boys must not be deprived of their fun. Once during World War II, vacationing in Florida, he disguised himself as 'a Mr Lobb, an invalid requiring quiet.' His principal private secretary, Sir John Martin, was registered as the invalid's butler. Security officers, after thinking it over, encouraged the prime minister to use pseudonyms when phoning. So he used Martin's name, with the consequence, Sir John wryly recalls, that 'I received a rocket from Censorship.' Despairing, the security men begged Churchill at least to keep his movements secret. He then telephoned Franklin Roosevelt before a Washington summit meeting: 'They won't let me tell you how I'm going to travel. You know security measures. So all I can say is that I'm coming by puff-puff. Got it? *Puff-puff*.' Once during the height of the Blitz, Mrs Kathleen Hill, one of the prime minister's secretaries, was visited by her son Richard, an army private on leave. She sent him out on a personal errand for the prime minister – buying an electric train for his first grandson. Hill had just finished assembling it on the rug of a first-floor room at No. 10 when he became aware of an august presence hovering over him. 'You've got two locomotives,' Churchill rumbled. 'Have you got two transformers?' Private Hill nodded dumbly. 'Good!' boomed Churchill, clapping his hands together. 'Let's have a crash!'[16]

That, too, was a part of him, but to leave it there would be to trivialize him. On a deeper level his aggressive, let's-have-a-crash manner was rooted in his vision of statesmanship. That vision is difficult to grasp today. It is wholly at odds with a central doctrine of his contemporaries, sanctified by the conventional wisdom of generations since. They hold that peace is the norm and war a primitive aberration. Churchill held otherwise. As a youth he concluded that the great issues of his time would be decided on the battlefield, that Nietzsche, Carlyle, and Gobineau had been right: that war was a legitimate political instrument, that it was by no means the worst that could happen; that conflict, not amity, would be the customary relationship between great states. He reconciled himself to it – as did Hitler, Stalin, Mao Tse-tung, and the Zionists – and began a lifelong study of strategy.

Although he was diametrically opposed to the prevailing attitudes in Western Europe and the United States, it is arguable that events have vindicated him. In this century every world power has been engulfed by war in Europe, Asia, the Middle East, and Africa. Latin America has not known a year of silent guns. Australia was threatened by Japanese invasion. Indians have fought Pakistanis, Arabs have fought Israelis, Danes and Norwegians have fought Germans; Spaniards have fought Spaniards and Burmese, Burmese. Emerging nations have acquired independence only to cross the frontiers of their newly independent neighbours. Cuba became a missile base, then a port serving Soviet submarines. Even the remote, barren Falkland Islands saw Britons and Argentinians slay one another. The United States has seen no fighting on its mainland, but American soldiers and airmen have died in France, Belgium, the Netherlands, Germany, Sicily, Italy, North Africa, China, the Pacific islands, Japan, Korea, Vietnam, and Cambodia, and US warships lie rusting on the bottom of every ocean. Russia and the West are locked in a truce of terror held in check only by the fear of mutual annihilation.

Having accepted what was unacceptable to others, Churchill devoted his remarkable gifts to martial arts at an early age. His aim was always victory, but victory at the least possible cost in suffering, at the lowest price in casualties. The proper course for Britain, he reasoned, was to follow the principle of Chatham – the Elder Pitt – and hold continental enemies in the grip of English sea power, sapping their strength at the distant fringes of their dominions. In 1915 this led to the most controversial, most misunderstood decision of Churchill's career. He meant to break the stalemate in France by forcing the Dardanelles, the narrow strait between the Sea of Marmara and the Aegean which separates Europe and Asia, knocking Turkey out of the war and joining British and French forces with their Russian ally. Because of blunders in the field, the stratagem failed. That failure, which drove him from office and nearly ended his career, haunted him all his years. Today the wisdom of his plan then is obvious. 'In the whole of the First World War,' Attlee has written, there was 'only one brilliant strategical idea – and that was Winston's: the Dardanelles.'[17]

Still, in the age of nuclear weapons, which Churchill did not anticipate, even the most humane of warriors is suspect. The London *Observer* declared in 1951: 'Any consideration of Mr Churchill's career as a whole brings one up against the extraordinary fact that, for all its majestic scope, it remains to this day tragically unfulfilled and fragmentary. His political role has not been meteoric and disastrous, like Napoleon's or Hitler's. But neither has it been linked to a definite achievement, like Richelieu's or Chatham's, Washington's or Lincoln's, Bismarck's or Lenin's.' An American is struck by the facility with which so many British intellectuals slight the man who saved their country. In fact, Churchill was more than an exponent of Mars. His ultimate goal was the 'broad, sunlit uplands' of a time when all swords became ploughshares. Even in the grim days after Dunkirk he looked westward and saw hope. If the British Isles were conquered by the Germans, he said, then the struggle would continue abroad 'until, in God's good time, the new world, with all its power and might, steps forth to the rescue and liberation of the old.' He had faith in eventual peace, and he believed he knew how it could be achieved: by combining the might of the English-speaking peoples in so strong a defence of the United States and the Commonwealth that the rest of the world would be held at bay, as it had been held by the British Empire in the relatively quiescent nineteenth century. Then, from that absolute base, freedom would expand outward. He cherished the possibility of a world order, a kind of Renaissance pageant to be accomplished, not by emerging states squabbling on United Nations Plaza in Manhattan, but by the Americans and the great powers of Europe, including Germany but not, significantly, the Russians, whom he 'always looked on,' in Sir Isaiah Berlin's words, 'as a formless, quasi-Asiatic mass.' His dreams of a tranquil global civilization in many ways resembled the exotic mysticism of Cecil Rhodes, Alfred Milner, and Joseph Chamberlain, but they never turned westward. To Churchill, the 'Great Republic,' as he called it, was the key. This, as he readily acknowledged, was partly because of his origins. The blood in his veins was as American as English. His mother was a New Yorker. He always kept a cast of her hand, moulded in copper, on his desk. It was an exact replica of his own.[18]

He adored her and she neglected him. He later wrote: 'She shone for me like the Evening Star. I loved her dearly – but at a distance.' She later told friends she ignored Winston until he grew older and became 'interesting.' That was an improvement on the attitude of her husband, who didn't even like his son, but young Winston's happiness among his nursery toys derived from neither parent but from his nanny, Elizabeth Everest – 'Woom.' He recalled: 'My nurse was my confidante . . . . [At her death she was] my dearest and most

13

intimate friend.' Wrenched from her while still a child, he was sent to a brutal boarding school in Ascot, where the sadistic headmaster caned him until his back was a mass of welts. His treatment at the hands of the other boys was, if anything, worse. Towards the end of his life, in halting tones, he told his doctor about it. Sickly, an uncoordinated weakling with the pale fragile hands of a girl, speaking with a lisp and a slight stutter, he had been at the mercy of bullies. They beat him, ridiculed him, and pelted him with cricket balls. Trembling and humiliated, he hid in a nearby wood. This was hardly the stuff of which gladiators are made. His only weapons were an unconquerable will and an incipient sense of immortality. Already he was memorizing Macaulay's tale of a man with two comrades barring a bridge to an army:[19]

> *Then out spake brave Horatius,*
> *The Captain of the Gate:*
> *'To every man upon this earth*
> *Death cometh soon or late.*
> *And how can man die better*
> *Than facing fearful odds,*
> *For the ashes of his fathers,*
> *And the temples of his gods?'*

Beginning at the age of seven, Churchill deliberately set out to change his nature, to prove that biology need *not* be destiny. Anthony Storr, the English psychiatrist and author of *Human Aggression*, concludes that he 'was, to a marked extent, forcing himself to go against his own inner nature.'[20] As a Victorian, Churchill believed he could be master of his fate, and that faith sustained him, but everything we have learned about human motivation since then underscores the immensity of his undertaking. W. H. Sheldon has delineated three dominant physiques, each with its concomitant personality traits. Of the three – ectomorphic (slight), mesomorphic (muscular), and endomorphic (fat) – Churchill clearly fell in the third category. His head was ponderous, his limbs small, his belly tumescent, his chest puny. His skin was so sensitive that he broke into a rash unless he slept naked at night between silk sheets. By day he could wear only silk underwear against his skin. Endomorphs are characteristically lazy, calculating, easygoing, and predictable. Churchill was none of these. He altered his emotional constitution to that of an athlete, projecting the image of a valiant, indomitable bulldog.

At times along the way he despaired. In 1893 he wrote, 'I am cursed with so feeble a body, that I can hardly support the fatigues of the day.' Yet he was determined to prove just as hardy as any mesomorph. In his teens he nearly killed himself while leaping from a bridge during a game of tag; he pitched down almost thirty feet and lay unconscious for three days. He fell again steeplechasing at Aldershot, and yet again when disembarking at Bombay, where he permanently injured a shoulder; for the rest of his active life he played polo, off and on, with his arm bound to his side. As a child he caught pneumonia. He suffered from chest ailments the rest of his life. He was allergic to anaesthetics and periodically erupted in boils. Nevertheless, he refused to yield to human frailty. In his inner world there was no room for concessions to weakness. He never complained of fatigue. In his seventieth year he flew to councils of war overseas sprawled across a tick mattress on the floor of an unheated World War II bomber. During the ten years after V-E Day he suffered a heart attack, three bouts of pneumonia, two strokes, and two operations. Nevertheless, he continued to build the image of a tireless embodiment of machismo who ate, smoked, and drank, all to excess. It survives to this day. Actually, most of the stories about his alcohol intake are myth. It is true that he started each day with a scotch and soda. What is not generally known is that he made that drink last until lunch, and that the amount of liquor he put away over a twenty-four-hour day was surprisingly modest. You would never have known it to hear him talk. He wanted to be remembered as a two-bottle man, like Pitt, and he cultivated the yarns about his drinking with characteristic aplomb. Once he asked Frederick Lindemann – 'the Prof,' a scientific wizard who later became Lord Cherwell – how many boxcars could be filled with the champagne he had drunk in his lifetime. The Prof replied: 'Only part of one.' Churchill sighed. He said: 'So little time and so much to achieve.'[21]

In his most famous photograph he is seen glaring at the camera, his jaw jutting like the butt end of a ham, the incarnation of defiant Britain. The Canadian photographer Yousuf Karsh, who understood him, caught the expression by a trick. Just before he triggered the shutter, he reached out and yanked Churchill's cigar from his mouth. What you really see in that picture is an endomorph rudely deprived of his pacifier. If you look closely, however, you may catch a glimpse of something else: a man ruled by his instincts. In triumphing over his physiognomy Churchill had become an aggressive extrovert, but at the same time he had developed into a rare type – C. G. Jung called it the 'extroverted intuitive' – and it was that, not his surface toughness, which changed the history of the world. Jung wrote: 'The intuitive is never to be found among the generally recognized reality values, but is always present where possibilities exist. He has a keen nose for things in the bud, pregnant with future promise . . . Thinking and feeling, the indispensable components of conviction, are, with him, inferior functions, possessing no decisive weight: hence they lack the power to offer any lasting resistance to the force of intuition.' That, or something like it, was what C. P. Snow had in mind when he wrote: 'Judgement is a fine thing: but it is not all that uncommon. Deep insight is much rarer. Churchill had flashes of that kind of insight. . . . When Hitler came to power Churchill did not use judgement but one of his deep insights . . . *That* was what we needed . . . Plenty of people on the left could see the danger; but they did not know how the country had to be seized and unified.' The answer was found by an extroverted intuitive. In Jung's description of the type, 'his capacity to inspire his fellow-men with courage, or to kindle enthusiasm for something new, is unrivalled.' Field Marshal Alanbrooke, Churchill's chief of the Imperial General Staff, was constantly astonished by his 'method of suddenly arriving at some decision as it were by intuition, without any kind of logical examination of the problem. . . . He preferred to work by intuition and by impulse.' Jan Christiaan Smuts said: 'That is why Winston is indispensable.' A colleague described it as his 'zigzag streak of lightning in the brain.'[22]

Political genius, said Bismarck, consists of hearing the distant hoofbeat of the horse of history and leaping to catch the passing horseman by the coattails. The difficulty is that one may hear the wrong horse, or lunge for the wrong horseman. As Jung pointed out, the extroverted intuitive lacks judgement. Churchill was right about the Dardanelles, right about Ireland, right about Munich, right about stripping England of tanks to defend the Suez Canal in 1940, and, as the Third Reich crumbled, supremely right about the menace of the rising Russian empire in Eastern Europe. However, he had not been right about fascism; at first, his conservative instincts and his allegiance to tradition had led him to apologias for strong men who posed as defenders of the established order. In 1926 he told Italian journalists that he had been 'charmed . . . by Signor Mussolini's gentle and simple bearing.' Resisting British opposition to Franco, he recommended instead that England 'send charitable aid under the Red Cross to both sides.' And while loathing Nazism, he once remarked that he 'admired' Hitler for being a 'champion' of his nation's pride. As his friend F. E. Smith put it, 'Winston was often right, but when he was wrong, well, my God.'[23]

Despite his versatility, vitality, and fertile mind, his belligerent instincts led him to fight Gandhi's campaign for Indian independence, to oppose the abdication of Edward VIII, and, in the heat of the 1945 political campaign, to predict that a Labour party victory would bring Britain 'a Gestapo apparatus.' In January 1938 he wrote: 'The air menace against properly armed and protected ships of war will not be of a decisive character.' This conviction, stubbornly held, led to the sinking of the *Prince of Wales* and *Repulse* by the Twenty-second Japanese Air Flotilla on December 10, 1941. In the opening months of the war, when he was first lord of the Admiralty, he was responsible for England's intervention in Norway, a fiasco which was mercifully over-looked when he became prime minister. Anzio was his idea; later he admitted that 'I had hoped that we were hurling a wildcat onto the shore, but all we got was a stranded whale.' Diversionary attacks, however impractical, always had his support. Late in the war he still wanted to land in Norway. At his insistence amphibious assaults were attempted on Rhodes and other Greek islands. All failed. In 1944 he even wanted to seize the tip of Sumatra, which was wholly without strategic value. George C. Marshall said, 'His planning was all wishing and guessing.' Actually, it wasn't. Had the combined chiefs adopted his grand proposal to sail up the Adriatic and invade Europe through the Ljubljana Gap, some military historians believe, British Tommies and

American GIs, not Russians, would have been the liberators of Budapest, Prague, Vienna, and Warsaw, with all that would have entailed for the postwar world. But by then his stock had fallen because he had championed so many impractical schemes.[24]

That had been the story of much of his public life. His career passed through three stages: from 1900 to 1915, when his star rose to a dizzy height; from then until 1940, when he achieved little and failed often; and from Dunkirk to the end, when he became a legend. The legend obscures what was a patchy record. Again and again he was rejected by his countrymen; he never won their love and confidence until they faced disaster. His following was limited to a few personal friends. He lost more elections than any other British politician of his time. Twice he switched parties, and although he wound up leader of the Conservatives, he spent three-quarters of his political life battling Tory leaders. His brilliance was recognized from the first, but he was regarded as erratic, unreliable, shallow, impetuous, a hatcher of 'wildcat schemes.' In 1915, Liberal Prime Minister Herbert Asquith observed of Churchill that 'to speak with the tongue of men and angels, and to spend laborious days and nights in administration, is no good if a man does not inspire trust.' Instead, he inspired suspicion. His love of adventure, it was said, ran away with his discretion. He was put down as an opportunist, a swashbuckler, a man who was 'jaywalking through life.' He was labelled a man incapable of party loyalty. In the House of Commons he wasn't even a good listener; he 'lacked antennae.' Once his mind was set, he wouldn't budge an inch. Nor could he judge men. He was easily taken in by quacks and charlatans; in the words of Air Chief Marshal Charles Portal, 'Winston was a bad picker.' By the 1930s it was generally felt that the people were wise to him at last, that he was a figure from the past, out of touch with reality. A newspaper editorial described him as a 'genius without judgement.' Prime Minister Stanley Baldwin, who watched Germany rearm and crushed all proposals for British military expenditures, said that although Churchill had a 'hundred-horsepower brain,' he didn't know how to harness it. Harold Begbie wrote: 'Mr Churchill carries great guns, but his navigation is uncertain. His effect on men is one of interest and curiosity, not of admiration and loyalty. His power is the power of gifts, not character. Men watch him but do not follow him. He beguiles their reason but never warms their emotions.'[25]

Margot Asquith had sized him up in 1908 as a man of 'transitory convictions.' Later, the Tories reached the same conclusion; they accused him of inconstancy, of veering opinions. In fact, it was the other way round. It was Baldwin and Chamberlain who were the trimmers, switching their policies when public opinion shifted. Except in the 1920s – when, as Baldwin's chancellor of the Exchequer, he withheld criticism of some questionable policies – Churchill never changed at all. He could misjudge others, but his own principles were a rock. This, in fact, is what offended traditional party politicians. If one reads the letters he wrote as a subaltern, his dispatches as a war correspondent, his speeches as a young MP, his cabinet papers, his books,

17

and his 'Action-This-Day' memoirs of the early 1940s, it will be clear that his views, once formed, were immutable. Here and there one encounters surprises. In the Edwardian era he and David Lloyd George were the most effective champions of the working class in the cabinet. Churchill's sympathy for workmen had been engaged by the humble circumstances of Mrs Everest, who had given him the love his mother withheld, and by reading early sociological studies of the desperate poverty in the lower classes. Despite his wealthy friends and relatives and his allegiance to the Empire, he denounced 'our unbridled Imperialists who have no thought but to pile up armaments, taxation, and territory.' He invented the excess-profits tax. Yet more than thirty years later he bitterly fought Labour's cradle-to-grave welfare legislation. The explanation is intriguing. He wasn't opposed to the substance of Labour's bills; what he found objectionable was the *way* the thing was being done. Labour held that the people had an absolute right to these comprehensive benefits. Churchill thought they should be gifts from a benign upper class to grateful lower classes. It was characteristic of him that in 1944, when Harold Laski proposed raising a fund as a token of the nation's gratitude to him, he demurred, then added: 'If, however, when I am dead people think of commemorating my services, I should like to think that a park was made for the children of London's poor on the south bank of the Thames, where they have suffered so grimly from the Hun.' Subscriptions were admirable. Taxes were an affront.[26]

His concept of magnanimity is among his more fascinating and, if you disregard the overtones of noblesse oblige, more endearing traits. He was always being excoriated in print or on the platform, and one of his sources of income was damage suits for libel or slander. He always won, and he always felt genuine pity for the loser. He wrote: 'I have always urged fighting wars and other contentions with might and main till overwhelming victory, and then offering the hand of friendship to the vanquished. Thus I have always been against the Pacifists during the quarrel, and against the Jingoes at its close.' It was a pattern with him. Defeat had to precede conciliation. He refused to negotiate until his adversary had capitulated. Revenge afterwards, however, was to him unmanly and ungentlemanly. It was Kitchener's vindictiveness on the Nile, his total lack of generosity towards the routed natives, which infuriated young Churchill. After Chamberlain's fall, which was swiftly followed by his death, Churchill rose in the House of Commons to pay him tribute. He said Chamberlain's hopes had been foiled by events, then asked: 'But what were these hopes in which he was disappointed?. . . They were surely among the most noble and benevolent instincts of the human heart – the love of peace, the pursuit of peace, even at great peril.' He was a ferocious enemy of Germany in both world wars, yet after each he begged the British government – in vain – to dispatch emergency shipments of food to its starving people. However high he rose, the man who as a boy had been bullied and bruised could always identify with the underdog.[27]

*　　*　　*

In a profound sense, he himself always remained the underdog. All his life he suffered spells of depression, sinking into the brooding depths of melancholia, an emotional state which, though little understood, resembles the passing sadness of the normal man as a malignancy resembles a canker sore. The depressive knows what Dante knew: that hell is an endless, hopeless conversation with oneself. Every day he chisels his way through time, praying for relief. The etiology of the disease is complex, but is thought to include family history, childhood influences, biological deficiencies, and – particularly among those of aggressive temperament – feelings of intense hostility which the victim, lacking other targets, turns inward upon himself. Having chosen to be macho, Churchill became the pugnacious, assertive fighter ready to cock a snook at anyone who got in his way. That was why he began carrying a Bren gun in his car when he became prime minister, then took bayonet lessons, and insisted that his lifeboat on the wartime *Queen Mary* be equipped with a mounted machine gun. But in peacetime he often lacked adequate outlets for his aggression. The deep reservoir of vehemence he carried within him backed up, and he was plunged into fathomless gloom.

Depression is common among the great; it may balance their moods of omnipotence. Among its sufferers have been Goethe, Lincoln, Bismarck, Schumann, Tolstoy, Robert E. Lee, and Martin Luther. To these should be added Churchill's father and five of the seven dukes of Marlborough, his ancestors, for it should be remembered that genes, too, play a depressive role. The personality traits are unmistakable; it is impossible to imagine Franklin Roosevelt offering blood, toil, tears, and sweat, but the expression would have come naturally from Lincoln. We first encounter Churchill's awareness of his illness in a letter, written when he was twenty, complaining of 'mental stagnation' and a 'slough of despond.' The note is sounded again in his second book, a novel. The hero drops into a chair and asks himself: 'Was it worth it? The struggle, the labour, the constant rush of affairs, the sacrifice of so many things that make life easy, or pleasant – for what?' Later, 'a sense of weariness, of disgust with struggling, of desire for peace filled [the hero's] soul. The object for which he had toiled so long was now nearly attained and it seemed of little worth.' An echo of this is heard more than a half-century later. It was Churchill's birthday. Glasses were raised to honour his accomplishments. He muttered to his daughters Diana and Sarah: 'I have achieved a great deal to achieve nothing in the end.'[28]

'What a creature of strange moods he is,' Max Aitken, later Lord Beaverbrook, wrote, 'always at the top of the wheel of confidence or at the bottom of an intense depression.' In times of disappointment, rejection, or bereavement, feelings of hopelessness overwhelmed him. Thoughts of self-destruction were never far away. He told his doctor: 'I don't like standing near the edge of a platform when an express train is passing through. I like to stand back and if possible to get a pillar between me and the train. I don't like to stand by the side of a ship and look down into the water. A second's action would end everything.' He also disliked sleeping near a balcony. He ex-

19

plained: 'I've no desire to quit this world, but thoughts, desperate thoughts, come into the head.'[29]

To a remarkable degree he coped successfully with 'Black Dog,' as he called his depressive spells. He sought flamboyant, stimulating, zestful company. He avoided hospitals. And like Cuchulain, the Hound of Ulster, he found solace in incessant activity. He told Violet Asquith* that unless he was perpetually active he relapsed into 'dark moments of impatience and frustration.' Sir George Riddell wrote in his diary in January 1915 that Churchill 'is one of the most industrious men I have ever known. He is like a wonderful piece of machinery with a flywheel which occasionally makes unexpected movements.' He would tell his family, 'A change is as good as a rest,' and then set about laying bricks at Chartwell or painting landscapes at Marrakesh. After the Dardanelles he crossed into France, fought in the trenches as a battalion commander, and set up his easel just behind the front line. And he always pursued acclaim. Depressives, more than most people, are dependent upon external sources of self-esteem. Churchill was never bashful about soliciting applause. As a youth, mailing a manuscript to his mother, he sought from her what she had not given him in childhood. He wrote: 'Write to me at great length about the book and be nice about it. Don't say what you think, but what I . . . should like you to think.' If friends suggested that this book or that speech might be improved, he reproached them: 'You are not on my side.' He expected total, uncritical loyalty. And he reciprocated. Brendan Bracken, one of the few who stood by him in the 1930s, said: 'He would go to the stake for a friend.'[30]

Nothing, however, could match the satisfaction of directing his hostility outward, towards a great antagonist, a figure worthy of massive enmity. But as the years rolled by and he approached old age, the possibilities of finding such an object became remote. The strain began to tell. Anthony Storr writes: 'In day-to-day existence, antagonists are not wicked enough, and depressives suffer from pangs of conscience about their own hostility.'[31] Then Churchill's prospects were dramatically altered. Adolf Hitler entered his life. It would be fatuous to suggest that the Nazi dictator's only significance for Churchill was as an answer to an emotional longing. Churchill was no warmonger. He was a statesman, a humanitarian, a thinker in cosmic terms; he would have been profoundly grateful if Hitler had strangled on his own venom. But the Führer's repeated lunges across the borders of peaceful neighbouring states did arouse a Churchillian belligerence far beyond the capacity of ordinary men. His basic weakness became his basic strength. Here, at last, was pure evil, a monster who deserved no pity, a tyrant he could claw and maim without admonishment from his scruples. By provoking his titanic wrath, the challenge from central Europe released enormous stores of long-suppressed

*The prime minister's daughter. In November 1915 she became Violet Bonham Carter, but since she was single during the years when she knew Churchill best, her maiden name is used in this volume.

vitality within him. In the beginning Hitler responded in kind. He, too, was a hoarder of rage, and he was a great hater. He may have felt that Britain's prime minister met an ache in him, too. As it turned out, he needed Churchill the way a murderer needs a noose.

Hitler's archenemy was not a man of small ego. It is an egalitarian fiction that the great are modest. They haven't any right to be, and they aren't. He said to Attlee: 'Of course I am an egotist. Where do you get if you aren't?' In 1940 he believed that he had been destined for the extraordinary role he must now play. He declared to Lord Moran: 'This cannot be accident, it must be design. I was kept for this job.' It didn't surprise him. Determined to prove himself unworthy of parental neglect, he had lived much of his life in a world of fantasy centred on the conviction that something special lay ahead for him. He wasn't vain; merely self-centred. As a young war correspondent in the midst of combat he called to the soldiers around him: 'Keep cool, men! This will make great copy for my paper!' Later, he liked to lie in bed listening to recordings of his speeches. Once he and his valet had words. Afterwards Churchill rumbled: 'You were rude.' His manservant, forgetting his station, said, 'You were rude, too.' Churchill pouted. After a moment he said: 'But I am a great man.' His idea of a good dinner, he said, was to dine well and then 'to discuss a good topic – with myself as chief conversationalist.' After one meal his son, Randolph, was trying to make a point. Churchill broke in with a comment of his own. Randolph tried to pick up the thread of his argument. His father barked: 'Don't interrupt me when I am interrupting!' In 1945, after the collapse of the Third Reich and his electoral defeat, he said: 'For my part, I consider that it will be found much better by all parties to leave the past to history, especially as I propose to write that history myself.'[32]

Some of the most moving passages in his historical accounts pay tribute to England's common man, but he never really understood his constituents' minds, and in fact he didn't much care. During one campaign he described his audience as 'a sea of hard little hats on hard little heads.' Lloyd George, who cared very much about the voters' dreams, was saturated with class consciousness; Churchill, as Attlee once observed, would have been content in a feudal society. He never grasped the revolution of rising expectations in the Birmingham mills and the bazaars of New Delhi. He thought Labour unfit to govern, and his early appeals for labourers' votes were almost absurd in their condescension. (In 1900 he told them: 'I like the British working man and so did my father before me.') This insensitivity is one explanation for the periodic eclipse of his political fortunes. It is indeed singular that a man so remote from commonality, so completely out of touch with his times, could have become a national hero. Eventually he became beloved for his courage, his humour, his bulldog image, and such touches as his V-for-Victory sign, his ritualistic circumcision of cigars, and his deliberate mispronunciation of *Nazis* – it came out of the Churchill euphonium as 'Nahrzees.' But he never mastered the British political mood. Instead, he repeatedly misjudged it. Except in national emergencies, at the hour of fate or the crack of doom, he

was largely ignored. People didn't identify with him because he never reciprocated.[33]

In his personal life he was the complete patrician. F. E. Smith said:
'Winston is a man of simple tastes. He is always prepared to put up with the
best of everything.' Churchill's wife, Clementine, told Lord Moran that at
home 'Winston is a pasha.' If no servant responded when he clapped his hands
upon entering the house, he would immediately call for his valet. The valet
dressed him right down to the pulling on of his socks, and ran his bath – twice a
day – almost to the brim, at a precise temperature. Churchill's nanny had
begun ministering to him; she had been succeeded by his manservants,
batman, wife, secretaries, footmen, doctors, and attendants. He was inconsiderate of them; impatient, arrogant, unfeeling. Why did they put up with it?
Dr. Storr suggests that 'men who demand and need a great deal of attention
from others are manifesting a kind of childlike helplessness, which evokes an
appropriate response, however difficult they may be.' Churchill could be very
difficult. When a plane was preparing to land and the NO SMOKING sign
flashed on, he would light up a cigar. If he found himself driving in a traffic
jam, he wheeled his car out on the shoulder or sidewalk and drove to the head
of the line. He rarely travelled with fewer than sixteen pieces of matched
baggage. Once, according to Vincent Sheean, he arrived by himself at Maxine
Elliott's Riviera villa and told her: 'My dear Maxine, you have no idea how
easy it is to travel without a servant. I came here all the way from London alone
and it was quite simple.' She murmured: 'Winston, how brave of you.'[34]

Reminiscing, he once said: 'I was not twenty at the time of the Cuban War,
and was only a Second Lieutenant, but I was taken to an inspection at West
Point and treated as if I had been a General. I was brought up in that state of
civilization when it was everywhere accepted that men are born unequal.' This
explains, in foreign affairs, the ferocity of his attacks on bolshevism well into
the 1920s, long after his intransigence had become embarrassing to the
government, and in domestic politics it accounts for his distrust of Labour.
Late in life he read that Christopher Mayhew, one of Attlee's junior ministers,
had walked out during the arena scene in the film *Quo Vadis*. Winston ordered
the picture screened at Chartwell and intently watched the scenes of mayhem
in the arena. After it was over, he rose and told his family: 'Do you know why
Mr Mayhew walked out? It was because his socialist, egalitarian principles
were outraged. There was one poor lion who hadn't got a Christian.'[35]

But if Churchill's blind spots are often attributable to his aristocratic
heritage, so are many of his successes. His career would have been impossible
without preferential treatment. His name, not academic competence, got him
through Harrow and Sandhurst. Then his mother, finally taking an interest in
his affairs, began pulling strings for him. There were a great many available to
her. She had been intimate with many influential men in America, on the
Continent, in the British establishment; even in the royal family. Theoretically, her son was subject to army discipline in his youth. Actually, he moved
around the world as he pleased. There is a stunning line in his book *The River*

Wars: 'With the design of thereafter writing this account, I moved to a point on the ridge which afforded a view of both armies.' Here are two mighty forces preparing to do battle, and here is a lowly subaltern riding off to get the best perspective. A fellow war correspondent in South Africa pointed out that Churchill had the assurance, arrogance, and bravado that one found in the British ruling classes, 'the conviction that he belongs to the best group in the world.' He never doubted it. Nor did his mother. In 1900 other English-women yearned to see their sons, off fighting the Boers. Jennie Churchill simply outfitted a hospital ship and sailed down to Cape Town to see how Winston was doing.[36]

She didn't pay for the vessel herself. She raised the funds by subscription. Her name wasn't even among the subscribers'. She couldn't afford it. She was always just a jump ahead of her creditors. So, for most of his life, was her son. To be sure, neither of them ever came close to a soup kitchen. Winston often complained of being broke, but that did not mean to him what it meant to most of his countrymen. He had expensive tastes, and he always indulged them. Consequently, he was often short of funds. In the desperate 1930s he was reduced to writing, for *Collier's* and other popular magazines on both sides of the Atlantic, such pieces as 'The American Mind and Ours,' 'Is There Life on the Moon?' and 'Under the Microscope.' (His most striking idea was an article to be titled 'Will There Be a Woman Prime Minister?' Editors vetoed it on the ground that it was too fantastic.) He would ask editors for payment, 'if possible, by Monday morning.' Six months before Munich, when he was waiting in the wings to stride out on the stage of history, he was so deep in red ink that he contemplated resigning from Parliament. He – and all he repre-sented – was saved only when a wealthy friend settled his debts. On August 31, 1939, he wrote his publisher, 'I am, as you know, concentrating every minute of my spare life and strength upon completing our contract. These distractions are trying.' The distractions were German troop movements along the Reich's eastern border. That night, as he stood at his high desk in Chartwell, correcting proofs, Hitler invaded Poland.[37]

At Harrow he had first learned that he had a remarkable memory. Aged thirteen, he recited, without a slip, the twelve hundred lines of Macaulay's *Lays of Rome.* And once he had committed something to memory, he rarely forgot it. In the autumn of his life he quoted verses he had read in *Punch* as a boy. Riding through the Maryland countryside, during World War II, he declaimed the whole of Whittier's 'Barbara Frietchie.' In 1953, after he had suffered a stroke, he recited the thirty-four lines of Longfellow's 'King Robert of Sicily,' which he had last read fifty years earlier, while his doctor followed the text. Moran found that 'here and there he got a word wrong: priests became monks and lamps candles; perhaps half a dozen words out of three hundred and fifty.' The writer met him that same year – my stateroom was next to his suite on the *Queen Mary* – and when he learned that I was a fledgling foreign correspondent on my way to Egypt and India, he reeled off amazingly detailed accounts of his own experiences as a correspondent there in the 1890s. At about the same time he asked Sir David Hunt: 'Can you look up the exact words of this quotation from Aristophanes: "The qualities required for writing tragedy and comedy are the same, and a tragic genius must also be a comic genius"?' Hunt told him he must mean Aristotle. Churchill indignantly denied it. 'Light began to dawn,' Hunt recalls. He checked the Loeb Classical Library in the Cabinet Room at No. 10 and found the line at the end of the *Symposium,* in Plato's imaginary dialogue with Aristophanes. Awed, he asked the prime minister how recently he had read it. In Bangalore, Churchill said, in 1896. Hunt notes: 'He was then twenty-two; at the time he recalled these words with perfect accuracy he was seventy-eight.' Hunt was among those who suffered through the showing of *Quo Vadis* but thought it worth it when, later that evening, Churchill recited the entire fourteenth chapter of Gibbon's *Decline and Fall of the Roman Empire.* That, too, had been among the books he had read at Bangalore.[38]

He had also discovered at Harrow that he had a flair for the language. Although rated the stupidest boy in the school, he scribbled off essays for classmates who had difficulty writing. His later years as a newspaperman, and his early books, showed him that he could make a good living with his pen. His work was not universally admired; in *English Prose Style,* published in 1928, the eminent Oxford literary critic Sir Herbert Read declared that it revealed 'aggrandisation of the self,' that 'such eloquence is false because it is artificial . . . the images are stale, the metaphors violent,' and that a typical passage 'exhales a false dramatic atmosphere . . . a volley of rhetorical imperatives.' But Churchill wasn't writing for critics. He was addressing the world, and to that end he had fashioned a soaring, resonant style, sparkling with eighteenth-century phrases, derivative of Gibbon, Johnson, Macaulay, and Thomas Peacock, throbbing with classical echoes of Demosthenes and Cicero, but uniquely his own. It is impossible to imagine him employing a ghost writer. No one but Churchill could write Churchillian prose. The stamp of the man is on everything he wrote or uttered, whether pondering the lessons of the past ('the grievous inquest of history'), or describing Roosevelt's polio ('his lower limbs refused their office'), or those who feigned contempt for public affairs because they dared not commit themselves ('flaccid sea anemones of virtue who can hardly wobble an antenna in the waters of negativity'). It made Sir Herbert wince, but its author won the Nobel Prize in literature.[39]

Churchill's feeling for the English tongue was sensual, almost erotic; when he coined a phrase he would suck it, rolling it around his palate to extract its full flavour. On first meeting Violet Asquith he told her that words had 'a magic and a music' all their own. That was what troubled Lloyd George, another critic of his rhetoric; he protested that to call Mussolini's conduct in Ethiopia 'at once obsolete and reprehensible,' as Winston had, was meaning-less. Unchastened, Churchill replied, 'Ah, the b's in those words: "obsolete, reprehensible." You must pay attention to euphony.' He said, 'I like short words and vulgar fractions.' When short words hit hard he used them. Needing military equipment after Dunkirk, he told the United States, 'Give us the tools and we will finish the job.' He did not declare that the Allies had 'consented to a coalition' or 'agreed to cooperate.' Instead, they had 'joined hands.' But on other occasions he did not hesitate to dip into his enormous vocabulary. Once he dictated a note to the Admiralty: 'Must we have this lugubrious ingemination of the news of our shipping losses?' At first the sea lords thought his secretary had mistyped 'insemination.' Then they consulted the *Oxford English Dictionary* and found that *ingemination* means 'redundancy.'[40]

Like all writers, he had his favourite words: *unflinching, austere, sombre, squalid.* He said *aircraft*, not *aeroplane*, and *airfield*, never *aerodrome.* He also liked to gather his adjectives in squads of four. Bernard Montgomery was 'austere, severe, accomplished, tireless'; Joe Chamberlain was 'lively, sparkling, insurgent, compulsive.' He would open a speech with a sluggish largo tempo, apparently unsure of himself; then he would pull out his organ's Grand Swell and the Vox Humana, and the essence of his prose would be revealed; a bold, ponderous, rolling, pealing, easy rhythm, broken by vivid stabbing strokes. It gained force by its participatory character. He himself was part of the great events he described; he could say, with Aeneas, *'Quorum pars magna fui.'* It is an advantage given to few, and those few have usually bungled it, resorting, among other things, to euphemisms, which Churchill scorned. He derided bureaucrats who called the poor the 'lower income group,' or lorries 'commercial vehicles,' or homes 'accommodation units' – once he astonished the House of Commons by bursting into song: 'Accommodation unit, sweet accommodation unit, / There's no place like accommodation unit.' One of his first acts when he took over as prime minister in 1940 was to change the name of the 'Local Defence Volunteers' to the 'Home Guard.' Words like *adumbrated* and *coordination* do not appear in his work. Of an MP who strung together phrases of jargon, Churchill said: 'He can best be described as one of those orators who, before they get up, do not know what they are going to say; when they are speaking, do not know what they are saying; and when they have sat down, do not know what they have said.' Of another, who had been defeated at the polls, he said, 'Thank God we've seen the last of that Wuthering Height.'[41]

He loved books and wrote of them: 'If you cannot read all your books, at any rate handle, or, as it were, fondle them – peer into them, let them fall open where they will, read from the first sentence that arrests the eye, set them back on their shelves with your own hands, arrange them on your own plan so that if you do not know what is in them, you will at least know where they are. Let them be your friends; let them at any rate be your acquaintances.' But he hated verbosity. 'This paper, by its very length,' he told a cabinet meeting, 'defends itself against the risk of being read.' And he despised pedants. A junior civil servant had tortuously reworded a sentence to avoid ending with a preposition. The prime minister scrawled across the page: 'This is nonsense up with which I will not put.' His profound knowledge of Latin and Greek was acquired through translations; he had been a miserable classics student. Labour MPs, most of whom lacked public-school educations, objected to classical phrases in the House for the very sensible reason that they couldn't understand them. During a discussion of this Churchill rose to a point and began, 'As to the chairman of this committee, he should be not *facile princeps*, but *primus inter pares*, which for the benefit of any . . .' He paused while the Opposition MPs, anticipating insult, struggled to their feet. Then he broke up the House by continuing, '. . . for the benefit of any Old Etonians present, I should, if very severely pressed, venture to translate.' His insularity, his feigned ignorance of all foreign tongues, was a source of popularity with the masses and served as antidote to his elitism. He told Jack Seely, later Lord Mottistone, 'Jack, when you cross Europe you land at Marsai, spend a night at Lee-on and another in Paree and, crossing by Callay, eventually reach Londres. *I* land at Marsales, spend a night in Lie-ons, and another in Paris, cross by Calase, and come home to London.' He believed that of all languages, English was incomparably superior. On his tongue, it was.[42]

Throughout his youth, he once said, 'it was my only ambition to be master of the spoken word.' He glittered as a young MP, speaking after elaborate preparation but – like his father before him – without a note. Then one spring evening, in the middle of an address on a trade-union bill, he discovered that he couldn't recall a word of his peroration. Speechless, he sank down on the bench and buried his head in his hands. Thereafter, when delivering a major speech, he came armed with everything he was going to say, including the pauses and the pretended fumbling for the right phrase in the first few sentences and anticipating 'Cheers, "Hear, hears," ' 'Prolonged cheering,' and even 'Standing ovation.' He said accurately, 'I am not an orator. An orator is spontaneous.' William Hazlitt wrote that the first duty of an orator is to echo back the feelings of his audience. Pitt translated a Latin epigram: 'Eloquence is like a flame: it requires fuel to feed it, motion to excite it, and it brightens as it burns.' But Churchill was no echo; he needed neither fuel, motion, nor reflected glow. His speeches were one-way. Their lustre owed nothing to his listeners. F. E. Smith said: 'Winston has spent the best years of his life writing impromptu speeches.' Many of them were written in the bathtub. Norman McGowan, one of his valets, was surprised on his first day to hear his master's voice rumbling from the bathroom. He put his head in and asked: 'Do you want me?' Churchill rumbled, 'I wasn't talking to you, Norman. I was addressing the House of Commons.' Harold Nicolson congratulated him upon a remark to a small audience, apparently improvised as he left the podium. Churchill snapped, 'Improvised be damned! I thought of it this morning in my bath and I wish now I hadn't wasted it on this little crowd.'[43]

He estimated that the preparation of a forty-minute speech took between six and eight hours. The actual writing of it wasn't writing at all, at least not by him. He made his living, he said, 'from mouth to hand.' He prowled back and forth in his study, head down, hands clasped behind his back, dictating to a secretary at a typewriter. That became the first of several drafts, the basis for his preliminary revisions. Scissoring and pasting came next. He despised the thump of staplers – the only sound he hated more was whistling – so in fastening pages he used a paper punch and threaded tape through the holes. He called the punch his 'klop' or 'klopper.' 'Bring me my klop,' he would tell a secretary. (There was a memorable day at Chartwell when a new girl left and returned staggering under the weight of Onno Klopp's fourteen-volume *Der Fall des Hauses Stuart*.) Eventually, when the address reached its penultimate form, he would add the asides and 'RHGs' (Right Honourable Gentlemen), underlining certain sentences, capitalizing others, and spacing the lettering to indicate words which were to be stressed or spoken slowly. In the last stage a special typewriter with large type was wheeled out. The speech was ready to be set down in what the staff called 'psalm form' because it looked as though it were being pointed for singing. This is what Churchill would see when he stood in the House, arranged his two pairs of spectacles, and glanced down at the final draft:[44]

> *We cannot yet see how deliverance will come*
> *or when it will come.*
>
> *but nothing is more certain*
> *than tt every trace of Hitler's footsteps,*
>
> *every strain of his infected*
> *and corroding fingers,*
>
> *will be sponged and purged*
> *and, if need be, blasted*
> *fr the surface of the earth.*

He was never a man for small talk, and during his early, awkward years, the cut and thrust of House debates found him wanting. Painfully aware of this weakness, he blamed it on his lack of a university education, during which such skills would have been developed and honed. His manner, haughty even then, invited merciless attack. Arthur Balfour taunted him: 'The Right Honourable Gentleman's artillery is very powerful but not very mobile.' Slowly Churchill realized that while he was a born writer, he would have to make himself a great parliamentarian. He did it by practising endlessly in front of mirrors, fashioning ripostes to this or that parry. He would never be comfortable listening to others speak, but over the years he came to relish Question Time in the House. And though his monologues were always more brilliant than his exchanges across the aisle, he developed a wit which has become an authentic part of his legend. It was not always good for him. As Harold Laski pointed out, people were so anxious to remember what he said that they didn't drive him to defend his positions. Yet we can only be grateful to them for setting down his gibes. He shone and would have shone in any company – Falstaff in Eastcheap, say, or Ben Jonson at the Mermaid, or Johnson and Burke at the Mitre. Watching him build up to a quip was an entertainment in itself. Hugh Massingham recalls: 'One always knew it was coming. His own laughter began somewhere in the region of his feet. Then a leg would twitch; the bubble of mirth was slowly rising through the body. The stomach would swell; a shoulder heave. By this time, the audience would also be convulsed, although it had no idea what the joke was going to be. Meanwhile, the bubble had ascended a little further and had reached the face; the lips were as mobile and expressive as a baby's. The rich, stumbling voice would become even more hesitant. And finally there would be the explosion, the triumphant sentence of ridicule.'[45]

Like all true wits, he knew the tickling quality of the unexpected. One day in the White House, according to Harry Hopkins, Churchill stepped naked from his bathroom just as Roosevelt was wheeling his chair into the room. This was always happening to him; the maids in his household at No. 10 had grown accustomed to his nudity. In this case FDR apologized and turned to go, but Churchill held up a detaining hand. He said solemnly: 'The Prime Minister of Great Britain has nothing to hide from the President of the United States.' Before the battle of El Alamein, he summoned General Montgomery and suggested that he study logistics. Montgomery doubted that he should become involved in such technical matters. 'After all, you know,' he said, 'they say that familiarity breeds contempt.' Churchill replied: 'I would like to remind you that without a degree of familiarity we could not breed anything.' On his seventy-fifth birthday a photographer said: 'I hope, sir, that I will shoot your picture on your hundredth birthday.' Churchill answered: 'I don't see why not, young man. You look reasonably fit and healthy.' On his eighty-fifth birthday a back-bencher in the House, assuming that Churchill was out of earshot, told the MP beside him: 'They say the old man's getting gaga.' Without turning, Winston said: 'Yes, and they say he's getting deaf, too.'[46]

More in character, his wit was usually aggressive. Sometimes he chose the rapier. Lady Astor neither gave nor asked for quarter, and she got none from him. At a dinner party she told him: 'Winston, if I were your wife I'd poison your soup.' He replied, 'Nancy, if I were your husband, I'd drink it.' But he was at his best baiting public men who crossed broadswords with him. It was Churchill who called John Foster Dulles 'the only bull who brings his own china shop with him,' and who coined the progression, 'dull, duller, Dulles.' The austere Sir Stafford Cripps was a favourite target. In North Africa in World War II the prime minister said: 'Here we are, marooned in all these miles of sand – not one blade of grass or drop of water or a flower. How Cripps would love it.' After Cripps gave up smoking cigars, Churchill remarked that he was sorry to hear it: 'The cigar was his last contact with humanity.' As leader of the Opposition, Attlee could hardly escape, though the Labour leader, with his strong ego, enjoyed Churchill's jabs at him. When Attlee was in Moscow, Churchill said of the Labour MPs he had left behind, 'When the mouse is away, the cats will play.' He called Attlee 'a sheep in sheep's clothing,' and 'a modest man with much to be modest about,' and he drove a sharp needle into Labour policy one day when he met him in the House's men's room. Attlee, arriving first, had stepped up to the urinal trough when Churchill strode in on the same mission, glanced at him, and stood at the trough as far away from him as possible. Attlee said, 'Feeling standoffish today, are we, Winston?' Churchill said: 'That's right. Every time you see something big, you want to nationalize it.'[47]

His niche in history – it is a big one – is secure. And so is his place in our affections. He will be remembered as freedom's champion in its darkest hour, but he will be cherished as a man. He was a feast of character, a figure emanating parochial grandeur like King David, and he also belonged to that rare species, the cultivated man of action, the engagé intellectual. Attlee said: 'Energy and poetry . . . sum him up.' But nothing sums him up. He was too many people. If ever there was a renaissance man, he was it. In the age of the specialist, he was the antithesis, our Leonardo. As a writer he was a reporter, novelist, essayist, critic, historian, and biographer. As a statesman he served, before becoming His Majesty's first magistrate, as a minister for the colonies and for trade, home affairs, finance, and all three of the armed forces. Away from his desk he was at various times an aeroplane pilot, artist, farmer, fencer, hunter, breeder of racehorses, polo player, collector of tropical fish, and shooter of wild animals in Africa. One felt he could do anything. That was why he seemed inevitable in 1940. Bernard Shaw said: 'The moment we got a good fright, and had to find a man who could and would do something, we were on our knees to Winston Churchill.'[48]

It is pointless to expect balance and consistency in genius. Churchill was not made like other men. Among his many traits was a kind of built-in shock absorber which permitted him to survive his repeated defeats and concomitant depressions. Going through his papers one is struck by his resilience, his pounding energy, his volatility, his dogged determination, and his utter lack of humility. He said: 'I am not usually accused, even by my friends, of being of a modest or retiring disposition.'[49] In the thousands of photographs of his face you will find every expression but one. He never looked apologetic. He had the temperament of a robber baron. As Walter Bagehot said of Palmerston, 'His personality was a power.' In World War I John Maynard Keynes singled out as his most striking virtue his intense concentration on the matter at hand – precisely the quality which, in the opinion of William James, identifies men of genius. In games he was a consistent winner. Like his distant cousin Douglas MacArthur, he was satisfied by nothing short of victory.

He was formidable, but he was also cherubic. That was what made him lovable even to those who recoiled from his benevolent despotism. He said, 'All babies look like me.' They did, and he looked like, and sometimes acted like, them. He enjoyed a child's anthropomorphism – finishing a book, he would put it aside and say: 'I don't want to see his face again.' His chief playthings were his seven-inch cigars, Romeo y Julietas and La Aroma de Cubas. Most of the time they were unlit; he liked to chew and suck them anyway, and when an end grew soggy, he would fashion mouthpieces – 'bellybandos,' he called them – from paper and glue. Mornings he worked in bed wearing a scarlet and green-dragon silk bed jacket, with papers strewn around him, and his play in the bath was an important part of his daily ritual; on long flights his luggage included a portable canvas bathtub. Dictating, or just puttering around his study, he wore a bright quilted dressing gown, which had been originally designed for a character playing Pooh-Bah in a production of *The Mikado,* and gold-embroidered slippers bearing his initials, a gift from Lady Diana Cooper. In his Siren Suit, Lady Diana recalls, he looked 'exactly like the good little pig building his house with bricks.'[50]

He was the absolute romantic. His paintings reflect this. There are no monotones – each stroke of his brush added shimmering light and colour. And everything he painted or wrote, his very gestures, was invested with emotionalism. 'I've always been blubbery,' he said. No man wept more easily. His tears flowed at the mention of gallantry in battle, the thought of 'invincible knights in olden days,' victims of anti-Semitism, Canadian loyalty to the Empire, the death of George VI, Elizabeth II's kindnesses towards him, or the name of Franklin Roosevelt – 'the best friend Britain ever had.' He never tried to hold back the teardrops because he never knew any inhibitions. In the middle of a 3:00 A.M. wartime conference at Chequers, the prime minister's country home, his generals took a smoking break. One started playing 'The Blue Danube' on a piano, and to their amazement their host, all alone, started waltzing dreamily around the floor. His feelings about his family were laced with sentimentality. His home was an independent kingdom, with its own laws, its own customs, even its own language. 'Wow!' one of them would say in greeting another. When Churchill entered the front door he would cry: 'Wow! Wow!' and his wife would call back an answering 'Wow!' Then the children would rush into his arms and his eyes would mist over. Except when they lived at Chequers, their closest moments were at Chartwell. He tried never to miss a weekend there. It says much for his belief in privilege, and for his staff's unquestioning acceptance of it, that No.10 observed two distinct standards at Christmas, 1940. He was asked if the staff would have any time off. He said, 'Yes, an hour for divine services.' Then they all applauded as he flourished his V sign and left to spend a working holiday with his family.[51]

The Churchill children were never spanked. The worst that could happen to them, according to Sarah, was banishment from his presence. Like many another great captain who has sent thousands of men to their deaths, he shrank from personal violence. This was most striking in his treatment of animals, even of insects. Since he detested fresh air – he had his bedroom windows sealed with putty – it was hard for bugs to get at him. But sometimes a bee, wasp, or moth flew in from another part of the house. 'Don't kill him,' he would tell his valet. 'Make sure you put him out of the window.' Once, during a division in the House, Anthony Head, the first man out of the chamber, spied a ladybird on the carpet. Realizing that a thunder of MP feet would soon pass this way, he bent down to rescue it. At that moment the prime minister arrived and instantly grasped the situation. Taking charge, he said, 'Put her out the window.' But since the introduction of air conditioning the windows had been permanently locked. 'Use the Chancellor's office,' he said, 'and report back to me.' Head did, but when he returned Churchill was in conference with the French foreign minister. The secretary told him he could look in for a moment. Head did and told Churchill: 'She escaped. I let her out through Macmillan's window. Nobody touched her.' 'Good, good!' the prime minister boomed. To this day Head wonders what must have passed through the foreign minister's mind.[52]

'Poor fox,' Churchill said brokenly when an MFH presented him with a mounted fox head. En route to Chartwell one night, his car ran over a badger. He ordered the car stopped, picked up the shattered animal, and carried the dead, bleeding body home in the lap of his striped pants. He would cry over the death of a swan or a cat; would leave the House chamber to telephone Chartwell, asking about the health of his goldfish. But his favourite pet was his little poodle Rufus. More accurately, there were two of them, Rufus I and Rufus II; the first was run down when a maid left him off his leash. (Churchill never spoke to her again.) Sometimes the Rufuses slept with him. After taking dictation – it might be 3:00 or 4:00 A.M. – his secretary would take the dog for his nightly walk. As Winston was about to drift off he would ask, 'Did Rufus do his business?' and, assured that he had, would sleepily congratulate him. The poodle ate in the dining room with the rest of the family. A cloth was laid for him on the Persian carpet beside the head of the household, and no one else ate until the butler had served Rufus's meal. One evening at Chequers the film was *Oliver Twist*. Rufus, as usual, had the best seat in the house, on his master's lap. At the point when Bill Sikes was about to drown his dog to put the police off his track, Churchill covered Rufus's eyes with his hand. He said, 'Don't look now, dear. I'll tell you all about it afterwards.'[53]

Predictably, Churchill's taste in entertainment was unpredictable. In literature it was excellent, though of course he preferred British authors. Music was another matter; aged eleven, he had asked his parents for cello lessons, had been turned down, and had developed instead a fondness for what his daughter Mary calls 'somewhat primitive' tunes – such music hall favourites as 'Daddy Wouldn't Buy Me a Bow-wow,' 'Ta-ra-ra-boom-de-ay,' 'Hang Out the Washing on the Siegfried Line,' and a curious ballad about a husband who discovers that his bride has a wooden leg: 'I Married Half a Woman and Half a Tree.' He enjoyed any movie about the Royal Navy; otherwise, his preference in films was less discriminating than one might expect. When he learned that Rudolf Hess had parachuted into Scotland, for example, he was watching the Marx Brothers. His favourite star was Deanna Durbin. His favourite motion picture – he must have seen it twenty times – was *Lady Hamilton* with Laurence Olivier playing Lord Nelson and Vivien Leigh as his mistress. He

31

was always lachrymose at the end of it. But probably the trashiest movie he ever watched was a sentimental pastiche based on a novel by Paul Gallico. Entitled *Never Take No for an Answer*, its chief character was a little Italian orphan whose donkey, named Violetta, helped him run a grocery stand. Violetta sickened. She could be healed, the boy believed, if he could take her to that hub of miracles, the Shrine of Saint Francis. So the orphan embarked on a journey, appealing in vain to a series of clerics: priests, archdeacons, bishops, archbishops, cardinals. Each time the boy was turned down the camera would flash back to Violetta, sprawled in her stable, ready for the last rites. Churchill wept inconsolably. 'Oh, the donkey's dead!' he would sob. The others would reassure him: 'No, no, Prime Minister, she's still alive.' Churchill would recover and declare firmly: 'If the donkey dies, I shan't stay. I shall go out.' Finally the boy, in his finest hour, was granted an audience with the pope. The pontiff reversed the lower rulings and made an appointment at the shrine for Violetta. In the last scene a blazing cone of light, slanting down from heaven, revealed the donkey, bursting with health, beside her loyal, trudging little friend. The prime minister arose slowly from his chair, his eyes luminous and his cheeks streaming.[54]

Joyously human, anachronistic and wise, capable of wilful misjudgement and blinding vision, dwarfing all those around him, he was the most benevolent of statesmen and the most gifted. Today the ordinary Englishman lives a better life than his fathers did, and for that he is largely indebted to Labour. But the extraordinary man has a harder time of it. He is trapped in regulations, his rise is impeded; his country pays a price. And even the masses seem to sense that while the socialists love ideas, Churchill, the unrepentant Victorian Tory, loved life. Since that love was balanced by a hatred of injustice, the average Briton owes him more than a higher standard of living. He owes him his very liberty.

'History,' wrote Aristotle, 'is what Alcibiades did and suffered.' Social scientists impeach that, but Churchill never doubted it. Because the man was matched by his times, he achieved immortality and changed the world, for good or for ill – though not as he had expected or would have wanted, for he was not the only giant in the century. In the long reach of events the impact of the Churchillian era upon his island was decidedly mixed. Hitler lost the war but he didn't lose it to Britain alone. Churchill, in desperate need of allies, forged a coalition with the United States and the Soviet Union and then had to make concession after concession to them. They emerged in 1945 as superpowers, while Britain, formerly Great Britain, lost its Empire, lost its independent and decisive role in world affairs, and sank to the level of a second-rate power. Of course, that, too, was Aristotelian. Alcibiades routed the Spartans, but in the end he was dismissed and fled to Asia Minor, where he was murdered by Spartan agents. Tragedy is the wasting shadow always cast, sooner or later, by towering heroism. Therein lay the terrible grandeur in

Churchill's funeral, a quarter-century after Dunkirk. The nation was bidding farewell both to a great Englishman and to the greatness of England. When his flag-draped coffin moved slowly across the old capital, drawn by naval ratings, and bareheaded Londoners stood trembling in the cold, they mourned, not only him and all he had meant, but all that they had been, and were no longer, and would never be again.

PROLOGUE

LAND OF HOPE AND GLORY

On February 4, 1874 – the year of Winston Churchill's birth – British troops led by General Sir Garnet Wolseley entered the small African city of Kumasi, now part of central Ghana, and put it to the torch, thereby ending the Second Ashanti War and winning the general a handsome spread on the weekly page devoted to the Empire in the *Illustrated London News*. He had worked for it. A melancholy martinet with spaniel eyes and a long drooping moustache rather like that of Lord Randolph Churchill, Winston's father, Wolseley had joined Victoria's army – 'putting on the widow's uniform,' as they later said – while still in his teens. Convinced that the surest way to glory lay in courting death at every opportunity, he had been felled by a severe thigh wound in the Second Burmese War, lost an eye to a bursting shell in the Crimea, and survived hairbreadth escapes while relieving Lucknow in the Indian Mutiny, capturing the Ta-ku Forts and Peking during Britain's 1860 dispute with the Chinese, and suppressing an insurrection in Canada. After finishing off the Ashantis he fought Zulus and dervishes, and organized campaigns against Boer guerrillas. His concern for soldiers' welfare won him a reputation among England's upper classes as a dangerous radical. London's cockneys loved him, however; their expression for top-notch was 'all Sir Garnet.' His great ambition was to die a heroic death in action against the French. That failing, the general, who ended up a viscount, planned to enrich his heirs by writing his memoirs after his retirement. Unfortunately, by then he had completely lost his memory. Visitors who mentioned his conquests to him were met by blank stares. He died in 1913, the last year of England's golden age.

Wolseley was one of the country's imperial heroes – others included Clive, Stamford Raffles, Chinese Gordon, Richard Burton, and, of course, Cecil Rhodes – whose feats were held up to the nation as examples of how men of courage and determination could shape the destiny of that noblest achievement of mankind, the Empire. If their lives were metaphors of the Empire's rise, that of Churchill, their rapt pupil, was the other way around. He entered the world in 1874, when the royal domain was approaching flood tide, and left it in 1965, as the last rays of imperial splendour were vanishing. That is one way of summing him up; it is, in fact, one of the ways he saw himself. Towards the end of his life he told Lord Boothby: 'History judges a man, not by his victories or defeats, but by their results.'[1] Yet the vitiation of the Empire does not diminish his stature. Alexander was driven out of India; Genghis Khan was undone by his sons; Napoleon lost everything, including France. Indeed, it may be argued that the greater the fall, the greater was a man's height. If that is true, then Churchill's stature rises above that of all other statesmen, for no realm, past or present, can match the grandeur of imperial Britain at its sublime peak.

It was the Tory journalist John Wilson of *Blackwood's Magazine* who first observed, in 1817, that 'the sun never sets upon the Union Jack.' At any given moment, wherever dawn was breaking, Britain's colours were rippling up some flagpole. If one could have ascended high enough in one of those balloons which fascinated Jules Verne and were actually used in the Franco-Prussian War, the view of Britain's colonial sphere would have been breath-taking. Victoria reigned over most of Africa, both ends of the Mediterranean, virtually all that mattered in the Middle East; the entire Indian subcontinent, from Afghanistan to Thailand, including Ceylon, which on a map appeared to be merely the dot below India's exclamation mark but which was actually the size of Belgium; Malaya, Singapore, Australia, islands spread all over the Pacific and the Atlantic, and Canada. The Canadians, proud of their loyalty to the Queen, issued a stamp depicting a world map with the Empire's lands coloured red. It was a study in crimson splotches. Although the British Isles themselves were dwarfed by czarist Russia, and were smaller than Sweden, France, Spain, or Germany, their inhabitants ruled a quarter of the world's landmass and more than a quarter of its population – thrice the size of the Roman Empire, far more than the Spanish Empire at full flush, or, for that matter, than the United States or the Soviet Union today.

To its classically educated patricians, London was what Rome had once been: *caput mundi,* the head of the world. The popular aristocrat Lord Palmerston said that colonies were multiplying so rapidly that he had to 'keep looking the damned places up on the map.' Disraeli said: 'No Caesar or Charlemagne ever presided over a dominion so peculiar. Its flag floats on many waters, it has provinces in every zone, they are inhabited by persons of different races, . . . manners, customs.' All this had been acquired by imperial conquest, and young Winston Churchill, writing for the *Morning Post* from a colonial battlefield on September 12, 1898, took note of 'the odd and bizarre potentates against whom the British arms continually are turned. They pass in a long procession. The Akhund of Swat, Cetewayo brandishing an assegai as naked as himself, Kruger singing a Psalm of Victory, Osman Digna, the Immortal and the Irrepressible, Theebaw with his umbrella, the Mahdi with his banner, Lobengula gazing fondly at the pages of *Truth*, Prompeh abasing himself in the dust, the Mad Mullah on his white ass and, latest of all, the Khalifa in his Coach of State. It is like a pantomime scene at Drury Lane.'[2]

All these suzerains lost, and all England rejoiced – loudly. The British were very vocal in their allegiance to their Empire. In public schools and public houses boys and men responded to 'Three cheers for India!' and roared, to the music of 'Pomp and Circumstance,' Edward Elgar's patriotic hymn, composed in the last weeks of the old Queen's reign:

> *Land of hope and glory, mother of the free,*
> *How shall we extol thee, who art born of thee?*
> *Wider still and wider shall thy bounds be set;*
> *God who made thee mighty, make thee mightier yet;*
> *God who made thee mighty, make thee mightier yet!*

On declamation days children recited, from Kipling:

> *Dear-bought and clear, a thousand year,*
> *Our fathers' title runs.*
> *Make we likewise their sacrifice,*
> *Defrauding not our sons.*

Music hall favourites were 'The Death of Nelson,' by S. J. Arnold and John B. Raham; 'Annie Laurie,' the great hit of the Crimean War; and, later, the rousing 'Soldiers of the Queen.' Today their great-grandsons wince at the public displays of patriotism, but the Victorians responded quickly to calls of Duty, the Flag, the Race, the White Man's Burden; the lot. Far from feeling manipulated – which they were; most Victorians gained nothing from the nation's foreign conquests – they memorized lines from W. E. Henley, the balladeer of England's colonial wars:

> *What if the best our wages be*
> *An empty sleeve, a stiff-set knee,*
> *A crutch for the rest of life – who cares,*
> *So long as One Flag floats and dares?*
> *So long as One Race dares and grows?*
> *Death – what is death but God's own rose?*

Her Britannic Majesty was 'by the Grace of God of the United Kingdom of Great Britain and Ireland and of the British Dominions beyond the Seas, Queen, Defender of the Faith, Empress of India.' In thatch-roofed villages of British North Borneo and the steamy jungles of Sierra Leone, her primitive vassals regarded her as divine and slit the throats of propitiatory goats before her image, usually a drab statue of a dowdy woman wearing a tiny crown and holding an orb and sceptre. Elsewhere Anglican missionaries prevailed and read their Book of Common Prayer in hundreds of languages and dialects, from Swahili to Urdu, from Maori to Bugi, from Kikuyu to Mandarin, and even, in remote valleys on the Isle of Man, the ancient tongue of Manx. Information from Victoria's twenty-five turbulent tribal possessions in the Middle East reached Britain from their only contact with the outside world, Aden, on the tip of the Arabian Peninsula, which had been acquired as a coaling station for the British fleet. There an Englishman perspiring beneath a gyrating punkah sent the Queen all the news she needed from the sheikhs: 'They are content to be governed from London.' No one in Whitehall paid much attention. The only resource the Arabs could offer the Empire was an unpleasant liquid, of limited value, called oil.

Most Englishmen were familiar with scattered facts about the Empire.

They had only the haziest idea of where Borneo was, but they had seen its Wild Man exhibited in a travelling cage. They knew the silhouette of lion-shaped Gibraltar, knew the legend that if Gibraltar's monkeys vanished from its caves, the Empire was finished. (In the midst of World War II Churchill found time to replenish the Rock's supply of monkeys.) They were proud of the Suez Canal, then considered an engineering marvel, and they were under the impression that all Egypt belonged to them, too. That wasn't strictly true; Egypt still flew its own flag and paid homage to the sultan of Turkey, but after the Queen's fleet had pounded Alexandria into submission, the country was run by the British agent and consul general. Thomas Cook and Son, booking clerks for the Empire, reserved Shepheard's Hotel's best rooms for English-men on official business. Cook's also ran steamers up the Nile for English tourists, though pilots turned back short of the Sudan border in 1885, after fanatic tribesmen of the Mahdi butchered Chinese Gordon in Khartoum. This tiresome restriction ended in 1898 when Kitchener routed and humiliated the tribesmen under the critical eye of young Churchill.

The British public was aware of the tiny island of Saint Helena, in the middle of the Atlantic, because that was where imprisoned Napoleon spent his last years, but such possessions as Ascension isle, Saint Helena's neighbour, which provided the turtles for the turtle soup at the traditional banquets of London's Lord Mayor, and Tristan da Cunha, the most isolated of the Empire's outposts, twelve hundred miles south of Saint Helena, in the broadest and most desolate reaches of the Atlantic, were virtually unknown outside the Colonial Office. Yet if ordinary Englishmen were confused about details of their realm, they can scarcely be blamed. The Empire itself was the vaguest of entities. Legally, under the British constitution, it did not exist. It was a kind of stupendous confidence trick. By arms or by arrogance, English-men had persuaded darker races that Britain was the home of a race meant to dominate the world. Therefore they ruled by consent. So successful was this bluff that the Mother Country held its possessions with an extraordinarily thin line of bwanas and sahibs; in India, for example, the rule of the Raj was administered by roughly one member of the Indian Civil Service for every 200,000 subjects.

Unless one counts Ireland, England's first imperial conquest was New-foundland, discovered by John Cabot in 1497. The East India Company was chartered in 1600, and thereafter explorers like Captain James Cook, roaming the South Pacific, were followed by missionaries and merchants who ruled and exploited the new lands. It is true that the newcomers introduced natives to law, sanitation, hospitals, and, eventually, to self-government, but Dickens's Mrs Jellyby, neglecting her family while 'educating natives of Borrioboola-Gha, on the left bank of the Niger,' was deceiving herself about her country's chief imperial motive. Palmerston, under no such illusion, said it was the government's goal to 'open and secure the roads for the merchant,' and Joseph Chamberlain said Whitehall must 'find new markets and defend old ones.'[3] Expansion of Britain's maritime strength had led to settlements on America's east coast and the hoisting of the Union Jack over the West Indies. The conquest of India had begun with a small trading station at Surat, on the west coast. Canada had been an acquisition of the Hudson's Bay Company, a firm just as zealous in its pursuit of profits as the East India Company. Victorian Australia was built on the need for cargoes of gold and wool. And each new territory meant a further boost of England's entrepôt trade, expansion of markets for the coal of Wales, the textiles of Lancashire and Yorkshire, and the steel of Sheffield and Birmingham. By Churchill's youth the nation's foreign trade had reached the astounding total of £669,000,000 a year.

As James Morris pointed out in his masterful *Pax Britannica*, the Empire's growth had been 'a jerky process,' a formless, piecemeal advance which leapfrogged across continents and was never static. Sometimes imperial possessions were lost – Manila and Java were once British, and so, of course, were the American colonies – but the realm always waxed more than it waned. The great prize, 'the brightest jewel in the imperial crown,' as Englishmen said then, was the Indian Empire, comprising the modern nations of India, Burma, Pakistan, Sri Lanka, and Bangladesh. It was the need to secure their ties to India which, they said, justified holding the southern tip of Africa, Gibraltar, Malta, Cyprus, Port Said, and Aden. But the brightest jewel could also be approached from the other direction, so they had to have Sarawak, the Straits Settlements, and Malaya, too. The fact is that just as all roads had once led to Rome, so did all sea-lanes lead to India. When that argument seemed strained, as in Africa, the Queen's statesmen explained that they had to move in before other great powers did. With this excuse, Victoria's Lord Salisbury gobbled up the lion's share of Africa without igniting a European war.

Imperial unity was a fiction proclaimed every time colonial officials visited London. Usually all they had in common were hats bought in St James's Street and gloves and spats from Dents'. Each possession had its own degree of freedom, its own language and customs, its own vision of God. The stable Dominions, Canada, Australia, and New Zealand, governed themselves, and Australia even ran its own colonies, the Cook Islands in the Pacific. Most possessions of the Queen were protectorates, territories, or Crown Colonies. Running these was the responsibility of His Excellency, the local governor, who had all the trappings of royalty. On ceremonial occasions he wore a gaudy uniform with a cocked hat sprouting ostrich feathers; he was entitled to a seventeen-gun salute; men bowed to him; and women, including his own wife, curtsied as he led a party into his dining room, where he was served before anyone else. His reward for good and faithful service was inclusion on the Honours List at home. (The irreverent said that CMG stood for 'Call Me God,' KCMG for 'Kindly Call Me God,' and GCMG for 'God Calls Me God.') This, subscriptions to *The Times*, the stiff upper lip, the legends of Nelson and the Charge of the Light Brigade, faith in the pound sterling, 'Abide with Me,' and a passion for cricket were among the frail linchpins linking imperial lands. Yet even on the administrative level there were exceptions to the colonial pattern. One Asian state was governed from a private office at 37 Threadneedle Street in London. Another, Sarawak, in Borneo, was an independent, third-generation despotism whose 600,000 people were ruled by an Englishman, the 'White Raja.' The White Raja, Charles Brooke, had his own flag; national anthem; newspaper, the *Sarawak Gazette;* and army, the Sarawak Rangers. Since he accepted British 'protection' – permitting Whitehall to handle his foreign affairs – Sarawak was considered part of the Empire. Similarly, Nepal had a native sovereign, but the Nepalese cavalry pledged allegiance to the British Resident and bore his personal crest. Native sultans and rajas were accepted as aristocrats and were usually addressed as 'Your Exalted Highness.' For diplomatic reasons, however, the islands of Tonga were recognized as an independent kingdom. Tonga's queen was greeted as 'Your Majesty.' When Edward VII, who took the matter of royal blood very seriously, was told that he was about to meet the sovereign of Tonga, he asked suspiciously, 'Is she a real queen or just another damned nigger?'[4]

By then the Empire was on an ebb tide, but even at its peak it was a lurching, reeling contraption, riddled with contradictions and inequities. Matthew Arnold knew how vulnerable it was:

> . . . she
> The weary Titan, with deaf
> Ears, and labour-dimm'd eyes,
> Regarding neither to right
> Nor left, goes passively by.
> Staggering on to her goal;
> Bearing on shoulders immense,
> Atlantean, the load,
> Well-nigh not to be borne,
> Of the too vast orb of her fate.

And yet the thing worked. In those days before the Wright brothers began the annihilation of distance, sea power was everything, and no other nation could match Britain's. Altogether there were 330 imperial warships, manned by over 92,000 tars, policing the world's waterways and keeping trade free. Spangling all oceans with their coaling stations and strategic forts, they were the strongest guarantee of the Empire's integrity, and their men spoke of its far-flung domains with the affectionate familiarity of men supremely confident of their national strength: the sacred Swami Rock in Ceylon was 'Sammy Rock'; Barbados was 'Bimshire'; Kuala Lumpur was 'K.L.'; Johannesburg was 'Joburg'; Alexandria was simply 'Alex.' When the mighty British Mediterranean Fleet sighted Malta, the whole population turned out for the spectacle. The ships were painted silver, with tars in white in rigid formation on the decks; the procession was led by destroyers, followed by cruisers and then the battleships. Royal Marine bands played 'Hearts of Oak' and the ships anchored with their prows pointing seaward, baring their teeth to any challenger.

Britannia ruled the waves, and Britons knew how important that was; every family with the means clothed its children in sailor suits and sailor dresses, their caps bearing the name of the Queen's latest battleship. And the warships were only part of it. The other part was the merchant marine. At the peak of its glory, England was launching a thousand merchant ships every year, most of them on the Clyde. More than half the world's maritime vessels flew the red ensign of British merchantmen; at any given moment they were carrying 200,000 passengers. The Peninsula and Oriental Steam Navigation Company's four-week voyage between the Mother Country and Calcutta, then India's capital, had become a legend. The worst part of the passage was the crossing of the Red Sea. Those who could afford relative comfort bought – for fifty pounds each way, not counting deck-chair rental – port-side cabins going out to India and starboard cabins for the trip home; in time 'Port Out, Starboard Home' became the acronym *POSH*. Unfortunately the service was anything but posh. Kipling wrote that P & O crewmen behaved 'as though twere a favour to allow you to embark.'[5]

But if the crews seemed high-handed to their British passengers, all Britons had that reputation in other nations. Robert Laird Collier, an American touring England in the 1880s, wrote: 'No people are so disliked out of their own country . . . They assume superiority, and this manner is far from pleasant to other people . . . They are overbearing, and haughty . . . . I have never seen among any people such rudeness and violation of good breeding . . . As a nation they are intensely selfish and arrogant.' In their 'Splendid Isolation' – isolationism was British before it became American – Englishmen looked disdainfully across their Channel and said: 'The wogs begin at Calais.' Thomas Cook lectured the French on the cancan as a sign of national decadence, performed with 'an unnatural and forced abandon,' and when a dispatch from Africa reported a French colonial claim, Joe Chamberlain, the very model of an imperial statesman, scrawled in the margin: 'Cheek!' England issued the first postage stamp, the 'Penny Black,' in 1847, and in an act of conceit undiminished by the fact that it was unintentional, the stamp bore a cameo of the Queen and nothing else – identification of the country seemed superfluous. Yet sometimes British contempt could be magnificent. Dressed to the nines, buttons glittering and collar starched, Captain William Packenham went ashore to deal with a gang of cutthroats who were massacring Armenians. The leaders of the pogrom gathered around him, glowering and fingering the edges of their bloody knives. Packenham stroked his beard and told the interpreter: 'Let us begin. Tell these ugly bastards that I am not going to tolerate any more of their bestial habits.'[6]

Britons were so sure of themselves. Like today's Americans, who are also disliked abroad, their dominance was the consequence of a cluster of accidents, among them their tremendous deposits of coal and iron ore – one-third of all the miners on earth were British – and England's role as the birthplace of the Industrial Revolution. Thus, Britain had naturally become the world's manufacturer, merchant, shipper, and banker – 'the workshop of the world.'

Not only were Britons certain that they would keep all they had; they expected more and more – 'wider still and wider.' Already English economists were managing Siam's foreign trade. There were two British colonies, British Honduras and British Guiana, in Latin America. More important, Hong Kong and Weihaiwei were on the Chinese coast; in London, men speculated over when Victoria's other titles would be joined by 'Empress of China.' They also dreamed of a Cape-to-Cairo railway, just as Germans looked towards a Berlin-to-Baghdad railway. Englishmen had expelled officious Chinese from Tibet, and the Indian Ocean was already an English lake. Southeast Asia's future was pretty much settled. The Bank of Persia was a British firm. In Italy, the cable car route up Mount Vesuvius was owned outright by Cook's. Constantinople had its own judge and jail for Englishmen. The Inspector General of Chinese Customs was Irish, and the military adviser to the sultan of Morocco was a Scot. Foreign governments were told where and when to build new lighthouses, and if they weren't prompt, the British solved the problem in their own way; the P & O put one up in the Red Sea on Dardalus Reef – foreign soil – and hired Englishmen to man it.

London was not only the capital of the world; it was the largest metropolis history had ever known, bigger than most imperial possessions or even some European powers. As we shall see, in matters of sex the Victorians should be judged, not by what they said, but by what they did; during the century before Churchill's birth the population of the island tripled – then a reproductive record – and London grew from two million souls to five million. (It was also the favourite of expatriates. Over thirty thousand Germans lived there, over fifteen thousand Americans, and more Irishmen than in Dublin.) The advent of trains and steamships had seen London rise as England's greatest port and the largest exporter on earth. The clocks of the world were measured from Greenwich. The Near East and the Far East were so called because they were near and far from London. Lloyd's was the world's insurance agent, and had been for two hundred years. In the vaults beneath the City's banks, gold bars rose in gleaming stacks; British securities were worth an astounding £11,333,000,000. The interest on foreign investments alone exceeded £100,000,000 a year. The gold sovereign was the strongest currency on earth; the City, the world's centre of finance, commerce, and banking. London was the centre of much else. Here, at the time of Churchill's birth, Joseph Lister was pioneering antiseptic surgery. Here Bessemer had perfected his process. Here Darwin, Tennyson, Browning, and Trollope were at the height of their careers. Dickens had been in his grave only four years; John Stuart Mill less than one. And if distant natives became restless, British ingenuity could be counted on to solve the problem:

> Whatever happens, we have got
> The Maxim gun and they have not.

In London there were ten mail deliveries a day. 'Communications,' Morris wrote, 'were the first concern of [the] late Victorian rulers.'[7] Letters reached Melbourne in four weeks, and British lines of communication, which had begun with cables to India and the United States in 1866 and were now spanning Australia, would soon gird the entire world. Distant outposts still depended upon native runners, trotting through jungles or over highlands with forty-five-pound leather pouches slung over their shoulders, but the days of isolation for months or sometimes years were past. Lebensraum was one of the Empire's driving forces; millions of Englishmen lived under its mandates, and serving them was a major industry. If you were posted near one of the population centres, the free ports of Aden, Gibraltar, Singapore, or Hong Kong, for example, you lived in style. The ubiquitous Cook's would provide you with poultry, vegetables, rowboats, donkeys, servants wearing Cook's livery, and even the Oxford Marmalade of which Victorians were so fond. Cook's made the arrangements for Gordon's and Kitchener's military expeditions on the Nile and also for troops fighting on India's frontiers. Cook's planned Moslem pilgrimages to Mecca and arranged Queen Victoria's own travels. On one occasion Cook's mapped out a European trip for an Indian maharaja whose baggage train included twenty chefs, ten elephants, thirty-three tigers, and a Krupp cannon.

Except for the time lag for news from home, which the cables would soon close, Englishmen in the Empire's settled possessions were well informed about the world's goings-on. In Cairo, say, you could read the *Egyptian Gazette,* or in Lahore the *Civil and Military Gazette,* subedited by young Kipling. The reading room of your club carried *Punch,* the *Book of Horse, Blackwood's, Wisden,* and *Country Life.* The favourite London paper was the archimperialist *Daily Mail,* which, typically, said of lascars: 'It is because there are people like this in the world that there is an Imperial Britain. This sort of creature has to be ruled, so we rule him, for his good and our own.' Doing so required preservation of the myth of white supremacy; of what we call racism. (Significantly, there was no such word then.) Conditions had improved since pre-Victorian days, when a native could be castrated for striking a white man or hanged for the theft of one shilling and sixpence. Certainly the average Indian or African toiling beneath the Union Jack was far better off than the average Chinese under his warlords, but British colonial hotels still found it necessary to display notices reading: 'Gentlemen are requested not to strike the servants.' English soldiers arriving in imperial cantonments were coached in how to avoid inflicting blows on the face, where the bruises would show. And Africans were caned frequently, like unruly boys.[8]

Playing the role of an *Übermensch* wasn't always pleasant. You paid the price of the myth. In Calcutta it meant wearing a frock coat and top hat in the punishing heat. Even the white linen suits and cork topees worn inland could be cruelly uncomfortable. Emotional discomfort could be worse. For loving parents the hardest moment came when a boy reached his seventh birthday, time for him to be sent home to school, never again to be seen as a child.

Health was also a problem. Every newcomer could expect to be laid low by diarrhoea – 'Delhi Belly.' Old-timers suggested Cockle's Pills, and they seemed to work for some. Others suffered from intestinal upsets, off and on, throughout their colonial years, attended by the native 'wet sweepers' who serviced the privies known as 'gulkskhanas' or, more vulgarly, as 'thunder boxes.' It didn't help that snakes were said to slither inside sometimes and lurk within the thunder box, coiled there, waiting to bite the next visitor.

The penultimate sin for an Englishman, in all imperial possessions, was to go broke. If it happened, the hat was passed for passage home, and the penniless offender was dumped on the dock like trash, which was how he was regarded. Only cowardice was worse than indigence. Showing a yellow streak was the greatest threat to rule by consent of the ruled, the surest way to shatter the image, and the man guilty of it was lucky to escape unflogged. Absolute fearlessness was assumed. Death in battle was the noblest of ends. In Africa, men's eyes misted over and their voices grew husky in speaking of Major Allen Wilson's Last Stand on the bank of the Shangani River during the wars against the Matabele tribesmen in 1896. When Wilson and his thirty-two men had run out of ammunition, the story ran, they shook hands, sang 'God Save the Queen,' and stood shoulder to shoulder to meet their doom. There were many similar examples. The Last Stand – resistance to the last man – was in fact a kind of rite, a tableau vivant celebrated in Victorian yarns and ballads, and in Wilson's case by a famous painting, Allan Stewart's *There Was No Survivor*, depicting dauntless men veiled in gunsmoke, surrounded by their dead horses, with their leader stage front, bareheaded, a sublime expression on his face. Such accounts were particularly popular in *Chatterbox*, a magazine favoured by genteel children; they were probably a secular expression of the evangelical Christianity which swept England in the 1870s and 1880s.

Chinese Gordon was the most heroic martyr. His hour of glory struck on January 28, 1885, when Winston was ten. According to one popular account, Gordon waited until the Arabs were storming his Khartoum palace. Then, knowing all was lost, it was said, he changed into his white uniform at daybreak and took up a position at the head of the stairs, 'standing in a calm and dignified manner, his left hand resting on the hilt of his sword.' Racing upward, one sneering Arab shouted, 'O cursed one, your time has come!' Gordon, according to this version, 'made a gesture of scorn and turned away.' Moments later he was impaled upon a half-dozen spears. Queen Victoria wrote his sister: '*How* shall I write to you, or how shall I attempt to express *what I feel?* To *think* of your dear, noble, heroic Brother, who served his Country and his Queen so truly, so heroically, with a self-sacrifice so edifying to the World . . . is to me *grief inexpressible!*' What is peculiar about this is that Gordon's garrison, like Wilson's, had been wiped out. As there were no survivors, there had been no one to tell the world how either had actually ended.[9]

In India, Last Stand immortality was attained in Burma or on the North-West Frontier, among the Afghans and the warring tribes of the Waziris, the

Mahsuds, and the Afridis. It was in Kabul, on September 3,1879 – the year Winston began reading *Chatterbox* – that Arabs invaded the British legation and put Sir Louis Cavagnari and his staff to the sword. Disraeli had assured the Commons that the position was impregnable, and Gladstone never let him forget it. Yet turning the brittle pages of old newspapers one has the distinct impression that the sentimental Victorians enjoyed their sobs. They erected statues of Sir Louis and went about rejuvenated. The following year they put up another after a gallant young officer named Thomas Rice Henn and eleven men forfeited their lives while covering the retreat of an entire British brigade. Wolseley wrote of Henn: 'I envy the manner of his death . . . . If I had ten sons, I should indeed be proud if all ten fell as he fell.'[10] Horatius had held the Sublician Bridge over the Tiber to the last, or so Macaulay had said, and now, over two thousand years later, soldiers of the Queen were inspired by a similar code of valour:

> *The sand of the desert is sodden red*
> *Red with the wreck of a square that broke –*
> *The Gatling's jammed and the Colonel dead,*
> *And the regiment blind with dust and smoke,*
> *The river of death has brimmed his banks,*
> *And England's far, and honour a name,*
> *But the voice of a schoolboy rallies the ranks:*
> *'Play up! play up! and play the game!'*

This famous stanza strikes an odd note. The typical British soldier, if he had any education at all, had attended a 'Ragged School' for the poor, where there were no games and certainly no concept of fair play. Those were the legacy of the public schools – Eton, Harrow, Winchester, Westminster, Charterhouse, Rugby, Shrewsbury – in whose forms the future rulers of the Empire were trained. The Victorian age was the Indian summer of homage, before wars, depressions, and nuclear horrors had destroyed faith in all establishments. The social contract was everywhere honoured. England was guided by the self-assured men of the upper classes. They thought themselves better than the middle and lower classes, just as those classes assumed that they were better than the *fellahin* and the *dukawallahs*. In both cases the presumption was rarely challenged.

The selection of the Queen's proconsuls in the colonies was oligarchic, a product of what later generations would call 'the old-boy network' or – to use an allusion they would have understood – a philosophic vision not unlike that of Er the Pamphylian in Plato's *Republic,* who, watching the souls choosing their destiny, saw the noblest pick power. There were two ways to enter the autocracy of colonial Britain. If you were recommended by your tutor at Oxford, say, or at Cambridge or Edinburgh, and were between the ages of twenty-one and twenty-three, you could make an appointment at the India Office, situated along one side of the Foreign Office quadrangle at the corner of Whitehall and Downing Street. There you were given the Indian Civil

Service examination on subjects ranging from Sanskrit to English literature, and if you passed you were tested on another spectrum of topics, including Asian languages and horsemanship, a year later. Candidates who were accepted were off to Calcutta, Bombay, or Madras on the P & O, probably for good. The 'Indian Civil,' or 'ICS,' was a much stiffer hurdle than that at the Colonial Office, on another side of the quadrangle. Applicants there needn't be brilliant; indeed, those with a first-class degree were suspect. The emphasis was on 'character' and the 'all-rounder,' on being 'steel-true and blade-straight.' You were interviewed by the colonial secretary's assistant private secretary, who never saw a British colony in his life. The atmosphere in his homey office was convivial, clublike, manly. One talked of mutual acquaintances, friends, headmasters, tutors, and engaged in similar rituals of self-reference. In this crucial stage it was important to have the backing of someone whom the interviewer considered a keen judge of men – someone like Benjamin Jowett, the cherubic master of Balliol College, Oxford. Jowett's maxims tell us much about his protégés. He said: 'Never retract. Never explain. Get it done and let them howl.' And: 'We are all dishonest together, and therefore we are all honest.' And, on Darwin's *Descent of Man:* 'I don't believe a word of it.' He was partial to peers and noble families on the ground that 'social eminence is an instrument wherewith, even at the present day, the masses may be moved.' If Jowett or his sort approved, a stripling just out of the university might find himself ruling a territory twice the size of Great Britain, acting as magistrate, veterinarian, physician, resolver of family quarrels, and local expert on crop blight. The similarity of officials' backgrounds gave the realm a certain cohesiveness. Morris observed: 'All over the Empire these administrators, like members of some scattered club, shared the same values, were likely to laugh at the same jokes, very probably shared acquaintances at home . . . Place them all at a dinner table, and they would not feel altogether strangers to each other.'[11]

It was collusion, of course, and it could lead to highly unsuitable appointments, particularly when a great family wanted to rid itself of a black sheep. But most of the youths grew into shrewd men; the level of performance was very high. And many of them could scarcely be envied. Often they started out living in leaky mud huts, rarely seeing anything of their countrymen except for an occasional trader or missionary with whom, under other circumstances, they would have had nothing in common. They often had only the vaguest idea of the boundaries defining their territories, or the size of the populations for which they were responsible. In Uganda, six months was added to home leave because an Englishman had to walk eight hundred miles to reach civilization. While on leave he had to choose an English wife in a hurry, because it might be years before he saw another white woman. With grit, that quality much prized among the Victorians, he stuck it out, sometimes leaving a benign stamp on his tract of the wild. In Nyasaland, England's deepest penetration into Africa, you can still find natives who, because their overlord was Scottish, recite Christian prayers with a Scot's burr: 'The Lor-r-r-d is my shepherd . . .'[12] It is difficult to condemn men who followed their star when the temptation to slacken was immense, who daily wore their quaint little uniform of white shorts and white stockings into which the traditional pipe was stuffed, but dressed for dinner whenever possible, to keep a sense of order, and carried collapsible little flagpoles wherever they went, so that the fluttering Union Jack would always remind their wards of their distant Queen.

Uganda and Nyasaland were hardship posts. Elsewhere life was more agreeable. In Kenya, British residents stocked streams with trout, and all the great imperial cities had racecourses and polo fields. John Stuart Mill called the whole Empire 'a vast system of outdoor relief for the British upper classes.'[13] That was misleading – by their sheer numbers, non-U voices were more audible than the accents of the U – but it was the highborn British who set the tone, which, by the time young Winston Churchill reached India, had become disturbingly insular. In the beginning white men had adopted local ways, learning that in Kerala, for example, it was polite to cover one's mouth when talking to an Indian of high caste. In 1859 Samuel Shepheard, who built Shepheard's Hotel, was photographed on an Egyptian divan, wearing a fez, with a glittering brass hookah at one elbow and a parrot at the other. Then, with the invasion of English wives, the memsahibs, all this began to change. Potted plants arrived, and whatnots, and acres of that printed fabric so popular among the natives that its admirers gave it the Hindi name of chintz. The metamorphosis reached its culmination in the hill station of Simla, the cool summer capital of the Raj, in the foothills of the Himalayas, with its Scottish-baronial palace for the viceroy and his vicereine; tea shops; bandstands where Gilbert and Sullivan airs were played; and the Anglican tower of Christ Church, whose bell had been fashioned from mortar seized in the Second Sikh War.

Churchill, writing from Bangalore, told his brother Jack: 'Labour here is cheap and plentiful – existence costs but little and luxury can be easily obtained. The climate is generous and temperate. The sun – even in the middle of the day – is not unbearable and if you wear a "Solar topee" or a cork hat – you can walk out at any time.' And then he reported: 'I have just been to luncheon at the Western India Club – a fine large building where every convenience can be obtained.'[14] The Raj was beginning to sink its hooks into him. He had been disarmed 'up at the Club,' a phrase familiar all over the Empire. There, surrounded by panelled walls, deep leather chairs, and cut-glass decanters, a fresh subaltern like Winston could step up to the bar and find himself, if not among friends, at least among friends of friends. It was an important moment in Churchill's life. Only by understanding the spell of the Empire, and particularly the Raj, can one begin to grasp the Churchillian essence.

It is a way of life which has vanished, and now, in the heyday of liberal piety, it is considered disreputable, even shameful. Yet there was an attractive side to the Raj, and its vitality is preserved in our language, in such words as *bazaar, bungalow, pyjamas, punch, dinghy, khaki, veranda, sàndals, gingham, shampoo, jodhpurs,* and *chit.* For young patricians who had passed the Indian Civil, or, like Churchill, had passed out of Sandhurst, the adventure began in London, with a shopping expedition in Oxford Street. There you bought your topee, in white or tan, at Henry Heath's Well Known Shoppe for Hattes. Also available were clever contrivances for coping with the tropics – Churchill had been wrong about the heat, and soon acknowledged it ('Imagine . . . a sun 110 in the shade!').[15] Among these were antitermite matting, mosquito netting, thorn-proof linen, canvas baths, and patent ice machines. Quinine was essential, but the thrifty postponed ordering tropical clothing until they docked in India, where they would also hire a tropical servant, the first of as many as twenty-five servants. Help was cheap, as Churchill had observed; a lower-middle-class mem who had slaved over a washtub at home would supervise a whole staff, and even British privates had bearers who polished their brass and boots and blancoed their webbing. Once ready for the next leg of his journey, the tyro would travel by train, chugging along at twenty miles per hour, his blinds securely locked at night, telegraphing ahead for a light breakfast (which he would learn to call *chota hazri*) and for lunch (tiffin). Detraining, he might cover as much as a hundred miles on horseback before reaching his appointed bungalow or, if he were a serving officer, his canton-ment. By then he might be ready for his first trip to the thunder box, but if he still felt fit he would be introduced to the more welcome ritual of the 'sun-downer.' This was the daily drink, and it was served in style by a bearer in a gown and turban. His tray would support a variety of paraphernalia: a carafe, linen napkin, gasogene, and ice bucket. Seasoned sahibs might add a nip of their quinine, as insurance against fever. Indeed, that is how the sundowner custom had begun, when men believed that alcohol was preventive medicine in the tropics.

It was an exotic, colourful life, and at a time when masculinity was valued, its greatest appeal was to men. The mems established their own conventions, their weekly At Homes and dances, their solemn talks with the C of E vicar, and, during the lawn tennis craze of the 1870s, a little exercise. But it was their husbands and the bachelors who thrived in India. They could retreat to their club, where women were of course forbidden, and they had polo, tiger hunting, golf, and all the glory, fireworks, and bunting that were manifes-tations of virile patriotism. If they were lucky and industrious, one day their names would appear on an Honours List. They were absolutely incorrupt, and the best of them were devoted to the natives in their charge. They adored their Queen, they knew that God was an Anglican, they believed in courage, in honour, in heroes. They could no more have identified with an antihero than with the Antichrist. In retrospect they all appear to have been gallant figures in one of history's greatest Last Stands. Of course, they didn't think of it that way. It never occurred to them that they, and all they represented, would one day be disowned, as the result of a national *défaillance,* within the lifetime of young Lieutenant Churchill, the polo star in Bangalore.

If you were passed back through a time warp and set down in Victorian London, your first impressions would depend upon where in the city you were, and under what circumstances. Henry James saw it at its most inhospitable, while riding in a 'greasy four-wheeler to which my luggage had compelled me to commit myself ' from the Euston train station to Morley's Hotel in Trafalgar Square. Night had fallen. It was a cold, damp March Sunday. Recalling the scene in 1888, James wrote: 'The weather had turned wet . . . The low black houses were as inanimate as so many rows of coal-scuttles, save where at frequent corners, from a gin-shop, there was a flare of light more brutal still than the darkness.' He felt 'a sudden horror of the whole place . . . like a tiger-pounce of homesickness which had been watching its moment. London was hideous, vicious, cruel, and above all overwhelming.'[16]

The city itself was also overwhelmed, engulfed by changes with which it had not learned to cope, and which were scarcely understood. Some were inherent in the trebling of the population, some consequences of the Industrial Revolution. Particles of grime from factory smokestacks, blending with the cold fogs that crept down from the North Sea channel, produced impenetrable pea-soupers which could reduce visibility to a few feet – 'London particulars,' Dickens called them in *Bleak House*. They could be dangerous; it was in one of them that Soames Forsyte's wife's lover was run down by horses and killed. Much of London stank. The city's sewage system was at best inadequate and in the poorer of neighbourhoods nonexistent. Buildings elsewhere had often been constructed over cesspools which, however, had grown so vast that they formed ponds, surrounding homes with moats of effluvia. Thoroughfares were littered with animal excrement. Gaslight was not yet the clear piped white light which arrived with the invention of the incandescent mantle in the 1890s. It was smokier, smellier, and yellower; some smudged lanterns dating from the reigns of George IV and William IV may still be found in Regent's Park. And the narrow, twisted streets were neither sealed nor asphalted. Victorians are often mocked for locking their windows, even in summer, but they had a lot to keep out: odours; dust; gusts of wind that could turn the open flames of candles or kerosene lamps into disastrous conflagrations.

In affluent neighbourhoods windows were barred during most of the Queen's reign, for no policemen pounded beats until late in the century. James recoiled from the gin shops, but he didn't see the worst of it. The worst was in the blackened, brooding slums of Bluegate Fields, Cheapside, Wapping Docks, Bleeding Heart Yard, Mile End Road, Maiden Lane, Paddington; St Giles's, along Saffron Hill; Westminster ('the Devil's Acre'); Granby Street, beneath what is now Waterloo Station, with its bolt-holes for criminals; and Whitechapel, where the heaviest concentration of London's eighty thousand prostitutes lived and Jack the Ripper stalked his prey. At night the East End was eerie. Here the bricks which built the rising city were hardened in kilns like those in *Bleak House* and in Trollope's *Last Chronicle of Barset*, where fugitives found warmth at night. Workingmen were no longer paid in pubs, but that was where many headed when they had their money. There cheap gin, the curse of their class, fuelled murderous fights and, by blurring judgement, converted men into easy recruits for criminal schemes – burglaries, typically, or pocket picking in Piccadilly. London's vast slums terrified respectable Londoners. Even the huskiest gentlemen refused to enter them without a heavy police escort.

The centre of London was a hive of hyperactivity. If, like Henry James, you were an American who had spent his first night beneath Nelson's column and rose in the morning for a stroll along the Embankment, you might first become aware of a familiar quickness in the air. *'Mon Dieu, ces anglais, comme ils travaillent!'* wrote a French tourist.[17] London then had the push and bustle foreign visitors began to note in New York in the 1920s. You could hear it; Londoners called it 'the Hum.' This was the busiest metropolis in the world; men were all in a hurry, doing the world's work. And in this part of the city they *were* men. If you wanted to see women you would have to stroll towards the shopping district and its centre, Piccadilly Circus, then named Regent Circus, with its beguiling statue, now called *Eros* but then, more primly, *Charity*. Wealthy ladies would be accompanied by servants carrying their parcels and followed, at a respectful distance, by their carriages (hence 'the carriage trade'), which, if they were upper class, bore heraldic crests on the doors and were driven by coachmen wearing livery. Middle-class women hired their 'Parcels Men' by the hour and usually shopped in pairs. An extraordinary number of them were pregnant, though propriety forbade them from venturing out in public after their third month. Whatever their condition, they would be tightly corseted in armour of whalebone and steel, a cruel fashion which was responsible for internal injuries even among women not carrying children. The point was to show the world that your husband had a comfortable income, that you didn't have to work. So styles were wildly impractical: great loops of ribbon, hoopskirts, lacy caps, silken parasols, dangling ringlets, blunt bustles, frills, petticoats, and layers of silk and satin heavily trimmed with bugles and beads.

None of them made women attractive to men. That was, or was thought to be, their last objective. Men were 'the coarser sex'; women, as Janet Horowitz Murray found in her study of gender attitudes in nineteenth-century England, were thought to be 'softer, more moral and pure.' The very existence of sexual desire was denied. It says much about the Victorians that none of them recognized the Ripper murders as sex crimes. This was part of what O. R. MacGregor calls 'the Victorian conspiracy of silence about sex.' Occasional male lubricity was grudgingly accepted for the future of the race, though men who lacked it were reassured by William Acton, a distinguished surgeon of the day: 'No feeble or nervous young man need . . . be deterred from marriage by any exaggerated notion of the duties required of him.' For a wife, her husband's animal drive was a cross to be borne. Dr. Acton wrote: 'As a general rule, a modest woman seldom desires any sexual gratification for herself. She submits to her husband but only to please him; and, but for the desire for maternity, would far rather be relieved of his attentions.' A Victorian mother prepared her daughter for the marriage bed with the advice: 'Lie still, and think of England.' It was in this spirit that Thomas Bowdler, earlier in the century, had published *The Family Shakespeare*, bearing the subtitle: 'In which nothing is added to the Text; but those Words and Expressions are omitted which cannot with Propriety be read aloud in a Family.' By contrast, the distributors of a pamphlet which advised couples not ready for children to practice douching were indicted for scheming 'to vitiate and corrupt the morals of youth as well as of divers other subjects of the Queen and to incite . . . to indecent, obscene, unnatural, and immoral practices' by publishing an 'indecent, lewd, filthy, bawdy, and obscene book.' During the year before their trial, the pamphlet, which the jury agreed was salacious, had sold 700 copies. In the four months of notoriety, sales leapt to 125,000. The issue, it should be noted, was a middle-class issue. Sex was one of the few pleasures not denied to working-class women, and they hadn't the slightest intention of abandoning it. (Their word for lustful was *gay*.) As for the patricians – ladies like Winston's mother – the upper class had, as it had always had, a moral code all its own.[18]

Identifying a stranger's class has always been a social challenge for Londoners. Today it is not so clear cut. In those days it was far easier, and would usually be accomplished by a glance. J. M. Bailey, an American visitor to London in the 1870s, wrote that he could find 'traces of nobility' in an aristocrat's 'very step and bearing.' He asked mischievously: 'Can you conceive of a bowlegged duke? Or is it possible for you to locate a pimple on the nose of a viscount? And no one, however diseased his imagination, ever pictured a baron with an ulcerated leg, or conceived of such a monstrous impossibility as a cross-eyed duchess.'[19] That was Yankee wit, but the plain fact was that you *could* tell. At least you could tell the difference between a gentleman and a man who was not. Partly it was a matter of genes. The Normans had introduced high cheekbones, Roman noses, an abundance of equine chin, and hooded, sardonic eyes to the Anglo-Saxon nobility. Diet was more important. Generations of malnutrition and, more recently, of stooping in mines or bending over looms had given workmen's descendants slight stature, poor posture, and coarse complexion. They aged prematurely; they needed the attention of doctors they could seldom afford. The gentry were tall, fair, and erect. Although they may not have been godlike, they were certainly far healthier than their social inferiors, and by today's standards, even the genteel were sick a great deal. The groaning tables on Victorian Christmas cards groaned beneath platters of food that would be condemned as unfit by modern public health officials. Preventive medicine was in its infancy. The twentieth-century visitor to the Strand would be startled by the number of pitted faces there. Smallpox was still rife. There were far more pocked features among the workmen, however. They simply lacked the resistance to affliction. They also lacked running water. Cholera hit them harder; so did diphtheria; so did infant mortality. In all of London, more babies died than adults. We cannot even guess at the toll in the slums, but it must have been appalling.

Gentlemen, no less than ladies, could be identified by their clothing. They wore top hats, indoors and out, except in homes or churches. Cuffs and collars were starched, cravats were affixed with jewelled pins, waistcoats were white, wide tubular trousers swept the ground at the heel but rose in front over the instep, black frock coats were sombre and exquisitely cut. Swinging their elegant, gold-headed canes, gentlemen swaggered when crossing the street, dispensing coins to fawning men who swept the dung from their paths. (These men were followed by nimble boys with pans and brushes, who collected the ordure and sold it in the West End for fertilizer.) Bowlers were worn by clerks and shopkeepers and caps by those below them. Switching hats wouldn't have occurred to them, and it wouldn't have fooled anyone anyway. Despite advances in the mass production of menswear, dry cleaning was unknown in the London of the time. Suits had to be picked apart at the seams, washed, and sewn back together. Patricians wore new clothes or had tailors who could resew the garments they had made in the first place. The men in bowlers and caps couldn't do it; their wives tried but were unskilful, which accounts for their curiously wrinkled Sabbath-suit appearance in old photographs. Towards the end of Victoria's reign games and cycling modified gentlemen's dress. The Prince of Wales introduced the lounge coat. Short loose breeches and Norfolk jackets were worn on bikes, football players and runners and jumpers appeared in shorts, and cricketers and tennis players adopted long pants of white flannel. Except at regattas, none of this was matched in feminine fashions. Not only were bustles worn on the tennis court; a woman had to use her free hand to hold her trailing skirt off the ground. And the lower classes were unaffected because they had neither the money for fashions nor the time for sports.

Social mobility, as we understand it today, was not only unpursued by the vast majority; it had never existed. For centuries an Englishman's fate had been determined at birth. The caste system was almost as rigid as India's. Obedience to the master had been bred in childhood, and those who left the land for the mills as the agricultural class seeped into the cities were kept in line by custom and the example of all around them. Successful merchants were an exception, and a significant one. They built mansions, bought coaches, and hired servants, yet they were never fully accepted by the patriciate. As late as the spring of 1981 a *New Yorker* writer attributed Britain's sagging economy to the fact that a stigma was still attached to men 'in trade.' Similarly, the British trade unions' twentieth-century truculence may arise from the lower classes' inability to transfer their allegiance from aristocrats to merchants. In Victorian England, the chimney sweeps, ragpickers, chip sellers, dustmen, coachmen, and sandwich-board men who hired out at one-and-six a day were no more rebellious than the serfs from whom they were descended. They did what they did well, and that was enough for them. Richard Harding Davis wrote from England: 'In America we hate uniforms because they have been twisted into meaning badges of servitude; our housemaids will not wear caps, nor will our coachmen shave their moustaches. This tends to make every class of citizen look more or less alike. But in London you can always tell a 'bus-driver from the driver of a four-wheeler, whether he is on his box or not. The Englishman recognizes that if he is in a certain social grade he is likely to remain there, and so, instead of trying to dress like some one else in a class to which he will never reach, he "makes up" for the part in life he is meant to play, and the 'bus-driver buys a high white hat, and the barmaid is content to wear a turned-down collar and turned-back cuffs, and the private coachman would as soon think of wearing a false nose as a moustache. He accepts his position and is proud of it, and the butcher's boy sits up in his cart just as smartly, and squares his elbows and straightens his legs and balances his whip with just as much pride, as any driver of a mail-cart in the Park.'[20]

London's massed horsepower made a lively spectacle, bewildering and even frightening to visitors. Each morning some twenty thousand vehicles drawn by steeds lumbered and surged over the toll-free London Bridge – Tower Bridge would not be ready until 1894 – and fanned out into the wakening city. The rigs varied. At this hour, in this tumult, you would see few private carriages. They sat parked in the West End and could be seen in large numbers only when they assembled for such liturgical upper-class ceremonies as the annual Eton-Harrow cricket match at Lord's, in St John's Wood, where over six hundred of them were counted in 1871. Much of the bridge traffic carried essentials. There were convoys of carts bearing galvanized tanks, headed for neighbourhoods which still had no running water. Produce and livestock accompanied them, including, once a year, sheep on their way to an enclosure near Kensington Palace. A contemporary account tells of the annual sheepshearing: 'Thousands of sheep are brought from Scotland and distributed over London wherever grazing can be obtained. After the shearing, the sheep are kept awhile in the park for fattening, and thence gradually find their way to the butchers' shops.'[21]

In the city these wagons mingled with public transport and cabs. The first electric tramcar was built in 1883 – electric lights had made their appearance two years earlier, for the Savoy Theatre's premiere of Gilbert and Sullivan's *Patience* – but London wasn't introduced to trolleys until 1900. Before that, horse-drawn streetcars crawled along tracked paths in the centre of the streets, maddening obstacles to the faster hansoms, growlers, and flys. Flys were usually rented. The Coupé and Dunlop Brougham Company in Regent Street would hire one out at seven shillings and sixpence for the first two hours. But the smartest and fastest way to travel was in the two-wheeled hansom cabs, 'the gondolas of London,' as Disraeli called them. Harnesses jingling, horses trotting briskly, and lamps and brass work polished to a blazing finish, there were over three thousand hansoms in London, charging a shilling for two miles and sixpence a mile over that, though the driver could charge more if he travelled beyond the 'Four Mile Radius' from Charing Cross, which was (and still is) the geographic centre of the city. The cabman sat high in the back, holding reins which passed through a support on the front of the roof, and the front of the cab was open except for two folding doors which came halfway up and protected the passenger from dust and mud. This feature was important. Trains had been so successful that other forms of transportation had hardly changed since Victoria's coronation. Country roads were surfaced with grass, earth, and stones. Downtown London's streets were cobbled, but unless you were in an enclosed coach you were lucky to arrive at your destination unstained.

Alighting at Charing Cross, a visitor from the 1980s would quickly become aware of a gamy tang in the air – blended aromas of saddle soap, leather, brass polish, and strong tobacco; scents of wood fires; the fragrance of baking bread and roasting meat manipulated by street chefs. All sorts of entrepreneurs were active on the pavements, and they fascinated Gustave Doré, who executed a series of engravings of them in the early 1870s: dog sellers, flower girls, flypaper merchants (who wore fly-studded samples on their dilapidated top hats), hardware dealers, tinkers, ragmen, knife grinders, ginger-beer men, apple sellers, oyster men, match vendors, 'lemonade' men who mixed their chemicals on the spot in portable tubs, and some four thousand hawkers of oranges. The popularity of oranges was due less to their taste than to their smell. Even where sanitation existed, not all street odours were pleasant. Deodorants were unknown. The poor reeked, which was why they were unwelcome in Victorian churches. Nell Gwyn had carried oranges to cut the stench of sweat, vermin, and manure. Before that, the Elizabethans had used pomanders, small balls of pierced metal packed with fragrant herbs. To this day, London judges mount their benches wearing nosegays – hence the name – and once a year herbs are scattered in courtrooms.

Among the other peddlars were salesmen exhibiting great bolts of black broadcloth. The Victorians were very open about death. Today people die in hospitals, where children are 'shielded' or 'protected' from them; graveyards are landscaped like parks, and mourning is seldom worn. In those days a demise was an important, fascinating event. Typically it occurred in the home, in bed, with the whole family in attendance and little ones held up for a final embrace from the departing parent or grandparent. The pavement chapmen made garments of deep mourning available to the lower classes. Patricians bought their black, grey, and deep purple clothes and black ostrich feathers in Oxford Street shops devoted solely to that trade. Men draped sashed crepe 'weepers' around their hats. Even cousins sewed black armbands on their sleeves. Englishmen were more preoccupied with death then than we are, partly because there was much more of it. In 1842 a royal commission had found that the average professional man lived thirty years; the average labourer, seventeen. By the year of Churchill's birth about fifteen years had been added to these, but it was still not unusual for a middle-class man to die at thirty-nine, as Arthur Sullivan's brother Fred did in 1877, inspiring Sullivan to write 'The Lost Chord.' Another reason for bereavement had nothing to do with delicacy of feeling. The loss of a father was disastrous. There was seldom any financial net beneath the survivors of a wage earner. Jobs were at a premium; artisans provided or rented their own tools, and one mill outdid Scrooge, issuing the notice: 'A stove is provided for the clerical staff. It is recommended that each member of the clerical staff bring four pounds of coal each day during cold weather.'[22] Except for the thriftiest of savers, however, no class was immune to the catastrophe which followed the passing of a head of household. If a man had been a successful physician, say, or a respectable barrister, his family might have belonged to the upper middle class as long as he was alive, living in the Wordsworthian tranquillity of a leafy Georgian square, with a coach in the mews and a boy at Winchester. All that vanished with his last breath. The family was evicted from the house; the son took a job as a clerk; his mother made what she could as a seamstress, or, in that bitterest refuge of shabby gentility, as a governess in a bourgeois home.

Prosperous homes could be identified by their bay windows, as much a status symbol as the eight-paned window had been a century earlier. The skyline was dominated by St Paul's, Wren's fifty other baroque churches, Big Ben, and the Gothic Houses of Parliament. In Pall Mall were the Athenaeum and the Reform Club, the home of the Liberal party; the Conservatives' Carlton Club; and the great imperial clubs: the Oriental, the East India, and the Omar Khayyam. The city was a mass of poles and crossbars that bore telegraph wires and the boisterous excesses of Victorian advertising. Napoleon had scorned England as *un pays de marchands.* Actually, it was more a nation of hucksters. Billboards, or 'sky-signs,' celebrated the virtues of Salada Tea, Waltham Watches, Cook's Tours, Thurston's Billiard Tables, Brinstead Pianos, and Gooddall's Yorkshire Relish. Bumping down London's streets came remarkable vehicles shaped like Egyptian obelisks, cabbages, and huge top hats, each of them bearing a brand name. The front of opticians' shops looked like the lenses of gigantic spectacles. Of all the forms of ads, the cheapest and wildest was the 'fly-poster,' which could be plastered on any 'dead wall' in public view. Gangs pasted these up at night, so that early risers would be greeted, typically, with: 'Good morning! Have you used Pears' Soap?' Sometimes householders would find their windows, even their doors, papered over. Other times gangs from different agencies would clash in the dark, tearing down the others' posters or obliterating them with buckets of black tar.

Optical illusions, red puzzle signs, posters gummed to public monuments or the hulls of ships anchored in the Thames – anything went. A young advertising man said: 'Any fool can make soap. It takes a clever man to sell it.' One innovation, still with us, was the endorsement of a product by a celebrity, which in those days meant such notables as Eugene Sandow, the German strong man, and Captain Webb, the Channel swimmer. Ambitious copywriters aimed even higher than that. We think of the Victorians as deferential towards the royal family. So they were, but some admen, who weren't, exploited that deference. The Queen was depicted holding a cup of Mazawattee

Tea or presiding over the legend: ' "The Subject's Best Friend" – HUDSON'S DRY SOAP – Home and Clothes as Sweet as a Rose.' The Prince of Wales was shown handing a glass of Bushmills Whiskey to the shah of Persia at the Paris Exhibition in 1889, and saying: *This, your Majesty, is the celebrated Bushmills Whiskey which you tasted in England and liked so much. I feel sure it will win the gold medal.*' A florist, pushing corsages, quoted the Duchess of York – without her approval; none of the luminaries were consulted – 'She thinks the Flower Shield a most ingenious invention and wishes it success.' Even the pontiff was identified as an admirer of a popular drink: 'Two Infallible Powers. The Pope and Bovril.' The soap manufacturers knew no shame. Sir John Millais, a successful artist, painted a portrait of a boy making soap bubbles with a clay pipe. The boy's bar of soap lay on the ground. To Sir John's astonishment, the picture was reproduced all over the country with 'Pears' painted on the bar. In Berlin, Heinrich von Treitschke told a class: 'The English think soap is civilization.'[23]

One device the advertisers missed was the jingle, and this is puzzling, because Victorians loved melodies. Garibaldian organ-grinders stood on every downtown London street corner, bawling ballads. Gilbert and Sullivan were national figures. Not counting the Salvation Army and the military, there were over five thousand bands in the country, and on holidays Londoners crowded around the bandstands in their parks. This was the golden age of the music halls. Between 1850 and 1880 about five hundred new ones were built – with the city's fifty theatres, this meant that 350,000 Londoners were entertained every night – of which the most famous were the Alhambra, the London Pavilion, the Empire, and the Tivoli. Each hall had its portentous chairman, with his candle, his gavel, and his vast expanse of shirtfront; each encouraged its audience to join the choruses. The stars were famous enough to endorse soap and whiskey, though unlike the eminent they expected their cut and got it. (Lillie Langtry got it and lost it; her signature was reproduced in an ad, and a forger copied it and cleaned her out.) High on the lists of sightseers arriving from the far reaches of the Empire were evenings hearing the 'lion comiques': Harry Clifton singing 'Knees Up, Mother Brown,' George Layborne leading 'Champagne Charlie Is My Name,' Jenny Valmore whispering 'So Her Sister Says,' and Marie Lloyd:

> *Only fancy if Gladstone's there,*
> *And falls in love with me;*
> *If I run across Labouchère*
> *I'll ask him home to tea.*
> *I shall say to a young man gay,*
> *If he treads upon my frock,*
> *'Randy pandy, sugardy pandy,*
> *Buy me some Almond Rock.'*

Henry du Pré Labouchère was an advocate of Home Rule for Ireland. And 'Randy pandy' was Lord Randolph Churchill. Music hall performers were keenly aware of politicians and public events, of England's power around the world, of London's role as an imperial capital. Britain was hardly a democracy, at least as we understand it; only 16.4 per cent of the people could vote But Britain's people counted because they, like the distant races toiling beneath the same flag, consented to be ruled as they were. Not the Queen, not peers, not the Commons, and not public school men wrote the ditties that celebrated the nation's glory and defied those who sought to curb the growth of an Empire which they believed belonged to them. It was G. H. 'the Great' Macdermott, the most celebrated of the music hall performers, who, singing the lyrics of George William Hunt, gave voice to their determination in the 1878 crisis which arose during the Russo-Turkish War:

> *We don't want to fight, but by jingo, if we do,*
> *We've got the ships, we've got the men, we've got the money, too.*
> *We've fought the Bear before,*
> *And while Britons shall be true,*
> *The Russians shall not have*
> *Constantinople.*

The British soldier was given a small island for his birthplace and the whole world as his grave. Including Indian sepoys, there were about 356,000 soldiers in the army – at the time of Marcus Ulpius Trajanus, Rome's legions had numbered 300,000 men – including 55 line battalions scattered about India, Ireland, Hong Kong, Bermuda, Ceylon, Malta, Egypt, Gibraltar, Canada, Singapore, the West Indies, South Africa, Barbados, and Mauritius. Their epitaph may be found today on sinking gravestones: 'For Queen and Empire.' It is inadequate. They died for more than that. So vast an Empire, so vigorous a society, could have been neither built nor held without staunch ideological support, a complex web of powerful beliefs, powerfully held. Alfred North Whitehead defined a civilization in spiritual terms, and Christopher Dawson, in *The Dynamics of World History*, said: 'Behind every great civilization there is a vision.' What was the vision of imperial Britain?

Jingoism was part of it, or rather one of its outward manifestations, and it wasn't confined to the music halls. On the slightest excuse, Londoners in the city's rookeries hung out bunting and gay streamers, criss-crossing mews and alleys where washing was usually hung to dry. Behind the calls to honour, duty, and glory lay the Victorians' firm belief in obedience – absolute obedience to God, the Queen, and one's superiors, in the family as much as in the army. It was a time of pervasive authoritarianism. The Baptist preacher C.H. Spurgeon wrote of the Victorian wife that her husband 'has many objects in life which she does not quite understand; but she believes in them all, and anything which she can do to promote them, she delights to perform.'[24] Unquestioning submission to orders was taught to schoolboys as soon as they reached the age of awareness; they recited 'The Death of Nelson,' 'Drake's Drum,' 'The Boy Stood on the Burning Deck,' 'The Wreck of the Hesperus,' and 'The Charge of the Light Brigade.' Every story for Victorian children had a point, a moral; usually one of dutifulness. Winston Churchill was four years old when the most popular glorifier of discipline, G. A. Henty, published the first of his eighty novels for children. With loyalty went courage, as witness Red Riding Hood, Hansel and Gretel, Alice, the Ugly Duckling, and Tom Thumb.

War was Henleyized, and such ancient institutions as the Crown, the aristocracy, and the Church of England were venerated. This allegiance to tradition accounts for the immense popularity of Tennyson's *Idylls of the King* and the flood of best-selling historical novels: Scott's *Ivanhoe,* Bulwer-Lytton's *Last Days of Pompeii,* Robert Louis Stevenson's *Kidnapped,* Charles Reade's *Cloister and the Hearth,* Stanley Weyman's *Under the Red Robe,* Charles Kingsley's *Westward Ho!* and Harrison Ainsworth's *Old St. Paul's.* Reverence for the past was especially strong in the church. The devout took the Bible literally, assumed the existence of an afterlife, and believed that the only significance of life on earth was as a preparation for eternity. That blind faith could have flourished in an age of intellectual ferment may be puzzling, but the Victorians could rationalize anything; for them, doubts raised by evolution, for example, were resolved by Tennyson's *In Memoriam.* By the time a youth of good family had reached manhood, he had heard more than a thousand sermons. He could not matriculate at Oxford, or graduate from Cambridge, until he had signed the church's Thirty-Nine Articles. Days of Humiliation, such as the one commemorating the Mutiny martyrs, signified national atonement. The Sabbath was sacred. To be sure, half the population stayed away from weekly services – when the Archbishop of Canterbury grieved that the church was losing the working people, Disraeli replied; 'Your Grace, it has never had them' – but this was a matter of propriety, not piety.[25] The poor were only too well aware that they were unwelcome. Nevertheless, they knew their Bible, knew their hymns; the ancestors of workmen who read nothing today were familiar with *Pilgrim's Progress* and *Paradise Lost* and could quote from them.

The middle classes, who were always in their pews, if not singing in choirs, cultivated evangelical seriousness, Arnoldian earnestness, and the eagerness of Bagehot. They loved maxims. 'Attend church, abstain from drink, read a serious newspaper, put your money in the bank,' they told one another. And:

> Staid Englishmen, who toil and save
> From your first childhood to your grave,
> And seldom spend and always save –
> And do your duty all your life
> By your young family and wife.

Carlyle impored them to devote themselves to work, which was sending coals to Newcastle. They had already made a cult of toil. It dominated their lives, and not just in London. A French visitor to the Midlands in the 1870s wrote: 'On entering an office, the first thing you see written up is: "You are requested to speak of business only." ' *Bradshaw's Handbook to the Manufac-*

turing Districts described 'the utmost order and regularity' in the enormous textile mills of Ancoats and Chorlton, and said that visitors were discouraged because they 'occupy the time of an attendant, and disturb the attention of operatives throughout the mill. The loss accruing from this cause is frequently more than can be readily estimated.' Until the year of Churchill's birth, working-class children started in the mills on their ninth birthday; then the age was raised to ten. When Parliament passed a 'short-time' bill limiting workers to a sixty-hour week, employers were outraged. Safety measures, as the term is understood today, were unknown. This led to what Professor Geoffrey Best calls 'Death's continuing Dance around the scene of labour.' Toilers in phosphorus factories suffered from 'fossy jaw.' A thousand miners were killed each year, and more than three thousand railway workers killed or maimed. The proliferation of moving parts was lethal, but mill owners airily dismissed the problem: 'Workers *will* be careless.' Protests were few and unheard. Writing in *The Uncommercial Traveller*, Dickens quoted a Shoreditch woman: 'Better be ulcerated and paralyzed for eighteenpence a day . . . than see the children starve.' Yet, astonishingly, she made no complaint. Like her Queen, she believed that all work, even drudgery, was sacred. The Victorians were never more Victorian than when they stood in church, or around a Salvation Army band, belting out 'Art Thou Weary?'[26]

Though safer than mill hands, the middle classes drove themselves just as hard in pursuit of 'respectability,' which was not, as Shaw acidly noted, the same thing as morality. Gilbert's Pirate King sang that piracy was more honest than respectability, and in *H.M.S. Pinafore* the reproachful Captain Rackstraw tells Buttercup that it would have been 'more respectable' if she had gone ashore before nightfall. Respectability, in short, was largely a matter of appearances. It was fragile; the slightest lapse could shatter it. Those who retained it were, in G. M. Young's words, forever fearful that 'an unguarded look, a word, a gesture, a picture, or a novel, might plant a seed of corruption in the most innocent heart, and the same word or gesture might betray a lingering affinity with the class below.' Ridiculing the Victorians is easy, and nearly everyone who has written of them since their departure has done it. They were hypocritical, snobbish, maudlin, fanatical about 'moral rectitude' and the superiority of the British 'race,' devoted to Augustan 'order, regularity, and refinement of life.'[27] The books on their shelves told you that they played their games according to Hoyle, toured England as directed by *Bradshaw's Weekly Guide to the Railways*, were instructed in housekeeping by Mrs Beeton and guided abroad by Baedeker and Cook. Always deferential (Bagehot's favourite word), they dreamed that their daughters might marry someone in *Who's Who* or, even better, in Burke's *Peerage* and *Baronetage*. At the table they watched their tongues. Legs were 'limbs,' and anyone wanting to use such words as 'disembowelled' or 'pelvis' employed another language or remained silent.

Palmerston had pointed the way for those who obeyed the rules; he extolled the nation's social system as one 'in which every class of society accepts with cheerfulness the lot which providence has assigned to it; while at the same time each individual is constantly trying to raise himself, not by violence and illegality, but by preserving good conduct and by the steady and energetic exertion of the moral and intellectual faculties with which his creator has endowed him.' This sent them to public reading rooms, Mechanics Institutes, mutual improvement groups, and public lectures and displays. Not only did they intend to better themselves; they insisted that the lower classes follow their example, until Dickens protested: 'The English are, so far as I know, the hardest worked people on whom the sun shines. Be content if in their wretched intervals of leisure they read for amusement and do no worse. They are born at the oar, and they live and die at it. Good God, what would we have of them!'[28]

Yet even Dickens believed that true love and marriage led to a horse and carriage – that respectability was rewarded by a rise in social standing. The nouveaux riches Victorians, with their sudden access to prosperity and power, were certainly naive, and often vulgar. They worshipped false gods (the theme of *Dombey and Son*) and they failed to meet the standards they set for themselves. But certainly that is loftier than the abandonment of all standards. The stars of social navigation which they tried to follow were stars – genuine ideals, even if unattainable. Their 'civilizing mission' in far lands was not only well-meant; at its best it was also noble. The English way of life, which they believed was exportable, was at least as estimable as the way of life the Americans tried to export a century later, with less success. When the Romans conquered a province, the glories of Roman citizenship were slow to follow. The moment the Union Jack raced up a colonial flagstaff, speech was free and habeas corpus the right of all. Among distant people a parliament became a status symbol, like having a national airline today, but more admirable. And if the Victorians' system was flawed, they knew it. Believing in individual and collective reform, the best of their intellectuals, like the Americans who followed them, practised vigorous, often savage, self-criticism. In the fine arts, London was a suburb of Paris and Berlin, but in literature it led the way. Carlyle, Dickens, John Ruskin, Samuel Butler, Herbert Spencer, and the contributors to *Yellow Book* were all Victorian rebels.

The chief difference between rebels then and rebels now is that they saw the world as rational, harmonious, teleological. Cartesians to a man, they believed that life was rational and mechanical and that progress was as inevitable as evolution and moved in the same direction. Their world, in Hans Koning's happy phrase, was 'an unthreatened world.' The earth seemed to be on the verge of being totally understood. Its flora, fauna, tides, and mountain ranges had been catalogued, measured, and minutely described. Some parts were still unexplored, but steamships would soon fix that. So the Victorian intellectuals felt a sense of confidence and optimism. They never doubted that the globe would always be dominated by Caucasian men. If the white masters differed among themselves, their governments would resort to arms. That prospect didn't alarm them. 'Unwarlike,' indeed, was a pejorative. It signified vitiation. The prime weakness of the darker races was their lack of martial spirit. Kipling urged England's youth: 'Bite the bullet, old man, and don't let them think you're afraid.' Not that there was much to fear; the Industrial Revolution had not yet caught up with weaponry. The Gatling and the Maxim were clever gadgets but, it was thought, without potential. Bloodshed in Britain's little colonial wars was relatively light. The eleventh edition of the *Encyclopaedia Britannica* actually told its readers that 'losses in battle are . . . almost insignificant when compared with the fearful carnage wrought by sword and spear.'[29]

If any Victorian institution was cherished above all others, it was the home. 'Home Sweet Home' – which sold 100,000 copies in its first year – was the most popular song of the century, even among workingmen who sang it in pubs because their own homes were unbearable. When an Englishman crossed his threshold he was in his castle, with almost absolute power over everyone within. That wasn't true of his wife, but if diaries and letters are to be trusted, she enjoyed their hearth even more than he did. It was a good thing they liked it. They hadn't much choice. Divorce usually meant ruin. It was almost impossible to obtain; a woman had to prove, not only that her husband was an adulterer, but that he was also guilty of desertion, cruelty, incest, rape, sodomy, or bestiality. Simple infidelity on his wife's part was all a man need show. However, the moment he picked up his decree, he was an outcast. Victoria dismissed one divorced member of her court even though he was the injured party. Often families turned a divorced relative's picture to the wall and spoke of him, if at all, as though he were dead.

Home was sanctuary, a place of peace and stability with sturdy furniture, in which evenings were spent reading aloud, whence the family departed for church and reunions with grandparents, uncles, aunts, and cousins, and where children were trained to assure the continuity of generations to come:

sic fortis Etruria crevit,
scilicet et facta est rerum pulcherrima Roma.

Keeping the Empire growing 'strong and most beautiful' would be the solemn legacy of these children. Middle-class Victorian parents had no Rousseauistic illusions about youthful innocence; their young were never allowed to stray from adult supervision. The inference of repression is not necessarily justified. Children were taken to Punch-and-Judy shows, 'suitable' plays in Drury Lane, and summer holidays at the seashore. But their lives revolved around the family. London evenings found them in the parlour, the boys in Norfolk jackets and the girls in beribboned bonnets and buttoned boots, joining in indoor games, handicrafts, watercolours, tableaux vivants, and, most colourfully, standing around the cheap upright pianos which began to be mass-produced in the 1870s, singing ballads. Over seven hundred publishers thrived in the city selling sheet music, including such favourites as 'Danny Boy,' 'I Dreamt I Dwelt in Marble Halls,' 'Yes, Let Me Like a Soldier Fall,' 'I'll Sing Three Songs of Araby,' 'Annie Laurie,' 'Oft in the Stilly Night,' 'Come into the Garden, Maud' (from Tennyson), selections from Handel's *Messiah* and Mendelssohn's *Elijah*, and Sullivan's 'Onward, Christian Soldiers' and 'The Lost Chord,' which sold a half-million copies before Victoria's death.

The music would be read – and everyone with social aspirations could read music – by gaslight. By the 1880s gas had been installed in most middle-class neighbourhoods. (Lower-class illumination was still provided by wax, oil, and tallow; penny-in-the-slot meters did not arrive until 1892.) The light flickered on gleaming brass coal scuttles and much that would seem stifling today: heavy repp curtains; reproductions of pre-Raphaelite paintings; patterned carpets, patterned wallpaper, even patterned ceilings; overstuffed Tavistock chairs with the new coiled springs; ebonized Chippendale music stools; and almost unbelievable clutter, with whatnots displaying bric-a-brac, ostrich feathers in vases, fans fastened to the walls, and marble-topped tables crowded with family photographs, china nodding cats, vases of flowers, and, on the mantel, a 'Madeleine' clock in black marble with bronze columns from Oetzmann's which cost thirty-two shillings and sixpence.

All this required a great deal of dusting. That was the point of it. Keeping it clean, and polishing the brass knockers, bedsteads, taps, and andirons, required servants, and the number of servants was a sign of status. They were cheap. A clerk making seventy or eighty pounds a year could afford a charwoman or a scullery maid ('skivvy') at twelve pounds a year, less than five shillings a week, plus such fringe benefits as broken dishes and cast-off clothes. At the very least, a middle-class family would have a staff of four – cook, housemaid, parlourmaid, and kitchen maid – and many homes would have six or seven bustling around in their lavender-print dresses and freshly laundered Breton caps. There were also butlers, footmen, and coachmen, but most domestic servants were young women. In 1881 there were 1,545,000 Englishwomen 'in service'; one of every three girls between fifteen and twenty years of age was waiting on someone. Their employers complained endlessly about their dishonesty, their incompetence, and the expense of them. (A first-class cook made nineteen pounds a year, though experienced lady's maids earned more.) *Punch* was always having fun with them, depicting them as insolent and pretentious. Actually, they were almost pathetically servile. They had little choice. To be dismissed without a reference was a girl's nightmare. Moreover, in her situation she was learning domestic arts and might attract the eye of a promising footman. If that led to matrimony it meant a step up. It was the responsibility of the butler, or the housekeeper, to see that it led nowhere else, though sometimes it did. One's heart is wrung by the plea of a maid begging her mistress to let her keep her illegitimate baby: 'It's only a little one, ma'm.'

Doubtless many of them did steal from the pantry. They would have been inhuman not to have done it; outside in the dark and cold were relatives who had left the land, like them, and had found no jobs. These were the drifting poor who could not even afford a twopence Whitechapel breakfast and whom Shaw and H. G. Wells would soon discover. During the day they lived in London's parks, but when the parks closed at sunset they would shuffle out and huddle in doorways or on Embankment benches, wrapped in rags and newspapers against the cold, until 4:15 A.M., when the gates of the first to open, Green Park, were unbolted. Primitive as street life was, it was considered preferable to the desperate workhouses. Now and then these institutions created by the Poor Law were humane; Maggie, Little Dorrit's protégée, was so thankful for her treatment in a workhouse hospital that she called all kindness 'hospitality.' But to most of the suffering masses they meant pitilessness and terror and were a major reason for the emigration of nearly three million Englishmen between 1853 and 1880. The system was against them. The purpose of law enforcement was the protection of property. Policemen deferred to top-hatted gentlemen and hounded wretches in ragged clothes. Under the Master and Servant Law, employees could be arrested in the dead of night for disobeying the most outrageous of orders, and under the Prevention of Poaching Act, suspicious constables could stop and search anyone in 'streets, highways, and public places.' The woman in a middle-class servant's hall, warm and well fed, not only knew her place but was grateful for it.

Her mistress had solved the middle-class woman's greatest challenge just by reaching the altar. With so many men of her social standing abroad in the Empire, the supply of bachelors was limited, and marriage was the only respectable occupation open to her. Failing that, she was doomed to lifelong submissiveness in her parents' home, serving as an unpaid servant. There were many like her. Indeed, W. L. Burn noted in *The Age of Equipoise* that 'the dependent daughter was one of the fundamentals on which the mid-Victorian home was based.' Not all daughters suffered in silence; Florence Nightingale denounced 'the petty grinding tyranny of a good English family. What I complain of . . . is the degree to which they have raised the claims upon women of "Family." It is a kind of Fetishism.'[30] Miss Nightingale is one of the few women whose names have survived, an outrider of twentieth-century feminism. Another, who was actually more useful to her sisters, was Isabella Beeton, born within the sound of London's Bow Bells and therefore a cockney. Like Florence, Isabella was a human dynamo. Before her death at twenty-eight of puerperal fever, that assassin of Victorian mothers, she had given birth to four children, served as fashion editor for her husband's periodical, the *British Domestic Magazine*, and produced a tremendously successful volume of her own, her 1,111-page *Household Management*, with fourteen colour plates and hundreds of black-and-white illustrations. (It weighed two pounds and cost seven shillings and sixpence.) By 1871, six years after her funeral, two million copies had been sold.

'Mrs Beeton,' as Englishwomen called the book, was to them what 'Dr

Spock' became for American mothers four generations later. The needs it filled tell us a great deal about their circumstances. As wealth poured into England from its colonial possessions abroad, the waves of growing influence enriched and complicated life in a nation arriviste. Brides had no precedents for orchestrating sophisticated social skills; their mothers, having lived in simpler times, were of little help. So Mrs Beeton explained when to wear gloves, how to manoeuvre on the pavement so that gentlemen escorts walked on the street side, and what the French names for courses of food meant. The British were still an insular people. (A headline of the period was FOG IN THE CHANNEL, CONTINENT CUT OFF.) And serving as hostess at dinner parties was a wife's most important role. Ladies did not eat out until the Savoy Hotel opened in 1889, with César Ritz as the headwaiter. Entertaining was done at private residences only. Mrs Beeton told her readers, in extraordinary detail, which wines to serve with meat and fish, when the ladies should leave the gentlemen to their brandy, and how to cope with a party of three dozen, counting the coachmen who had to wait for their masters and mistresses. She provided recipes, information on how much to order, and what to do with the leftovers. One entry was: 'Bill of Fare for a Picnic for Forty Persons.' It recommended, among other things, 122 bottles of refreshment for the entire group, including servants, coachmen, and lady's maids. The food was absurdly cheap, but the logistics were staggering. Moreover, this was a *middle-class* affair. The upper class entertained on a scale unmatched today. It was expected of them, which sometimes presented difficulties. Winston Churchill, born to a noble family, simply could not afford it. He had to live by his wits most of his life.

Upper-class hostesses had no need to plan picnics in the country. They were already there. They had London mansions, too, but the soul of the leisure class was in the land. It always had been. Chaucer wrote of his medieval franklin, or landowner, that 'It snewed in his hous of mete and drinke, / Of alle deyntees men coude thinke.' Arundel Castle, in Sussex, goes back even farther. It is mentioned in the will of King Alfred, who reigned eleven centuries ago. An ancestor of the present tenant, the sixteenth Duke of Norfolk, won it when an arrow from the bow of one of his archers pierced the eye of Harold in the Battle of Hastings. Socially a duke in the country has always had the best of all possible worlds. In the British aristocracy the twenty-seven dukes are outranked only by members of the British royal family; the College of Arms advised a hostess, who was worried about seating arrangements for her dinner party, that 'the Aga Khan is held to be a direct descendant of God,' but 'an English Duke takes precedence.' The other degrees of the British peerage, in descending order, are marquess, earl, viscount, and baron, and though these don't carry as much weight as they once did, in Victoria's time to be titled, in most instances, still meant to be landed. On the estates of the nobility stood the great country houses, where

England's three hundred ruling families celebrated the weekly three-night British holiday, which is popularly thought to have been a brainchild of the Queen's hedonistic Prince of Wales, but which was actually created by, of all people, Oliver Cromwell; in 1899 one of Cromwell's biographers, S. R. Gardiner, found that 'Oliver . . . may be regarded as the inventor of that modified form of enjoyment to which hard-worked citizens have, in our day, given the name of "week-end." '[31]

But upper-class Victorians weren't hard-worked. Most of them didn't work at all. That was what set the upper class apart from the upper-middle class. The two mingled, but never as equals; as Lady Warwick explained to Elinor Glyn, 'Doctors and solicitors might be invited to garden parties, though never of course to luncheon or dinner.' The elite kept themselves to themselves. This small, select, homogeneous patriciate, this 'brilliant and powerful body,' in Churchill's admiring phrase, passed most of their time by passing the port, sherry, and claret; by discussing cricket; by playing billiards, admiring their horses, and shooting grouse – a thousand grouse were felled in a single shoot attended by Churchill's mother. Unlike the French, they did not cultivate tête-à-têtes; Robert Laird Collier found that 'they are poor talkers as a rule and conversation seems to be a labour to most of them,' that they 'never express the least feeling in their social intercourse,' and that 'all the social talk is stupid and insipid.' In an age which cherished the Latin motto *laborare est orare*, when Samuel Smile's *Self-Help* could be found in almost every middle-class home, an idle nobility seemed an affront to social critics. In Edward Lear's *Book of Nonsense* the likeable figures are Floppy Fly and Daddy Long Legs, who are ejected from court because their legs are ill-made. Lewis Carroll depicted patricians as tyrants and muddlers. Gilbert and Sullivan's *Iolanthe* described the House of Lords as a body that 'did nothing in particular and did it very well.' But the ruling class was unperturbed. Ideas bored them. 'As a class,' Lady Warwick said, 'we did not like brains.' A contemporary work, *Kings, Courts and Society*, saw Britain comprising 'a small, select aristocracy, booted and spurred to ride, and a large, dim mass, born, saddled and bridled to be ridden.' On Sunday the weekenders gathered in the chapels found under every country-house roof and sang:[32]

> *The rich man in his castle*
> *The poor man at his gate*
> *God made them high and lowly*
> *And orders their estate.*

Later Churchill wrote: 'The old world in its sunset was fair to see.' It doesn't seem very fair to us. In their portraits titled Victorians, particularly the men, seem to be oozing complacency and self-esteem, wholly indifferent to the fact that 30 percent of the inhabitants of their capital city were undernourished while they feasted, at a typical lunch for six, on cold pheasant, a brace of partridges, a pair of roast fowls, steak, salmon, and a choice of two soups. As late as 1940 Clare Boothe Luce, though an anglophile, fumed: 'Sometimes they are so insolent, so sure of themselves, so smug, I feel as though it would do them good for once to be beaten.' But by then they had become an anachronism, and the brightest among them knew it. To put them in context is to see them against the background of nineteenth-century Eurasia. From the Barents Sea to the Mediterranean, from the Rhine to Vladivostok, monarchs not only reigned but ruled through bewildering hierarchies of grand dukes, archdukes, princelings, and other hereditary nobles – twenty-two dynasties in Germany alone. The masses having accepted the saddles and bridles, threadbare commoners also sang about God making men high and lowly. It was, James Laver writes, 'probably the last period in history when the fortunate thought they could give pleasure to others by displaying their good fortune before them.' Bagehot wrote: 'The fancy of the mass of men is incredibly weak; it can see nothing without a visible symbol . . . . Nobility is a symbol of mind.' So ingrained was the habit of forelock-tugging that by 1875, when Trollope wrote *The Way We Live Now,* that society accepted the exploitation of titles by impecunious nobles who sold their prestige by consenting to serve as directors of businesses in wobbly shape.[33]

This did not declass them. Their social status was their birthright, and nothing could deprive them of it. Even if a peer committed murder, he was entitled to a trial by the House of Lords, and if sentenced to the gallows he was hanged with a silken rope. Of course, most of the upper class were merely related to peers. Given primogeniture, with all property going to the eldest son, including the title, the patriciate was heavily populated with younger sons who had inherited nothing and usually entered the navy, army, church, or diplomatic corps – the traditional order of preference. (Two generations passed before a descendant became a commoner. The firstborn son of the seventh Duke of Marlborough was his heir. The second son was called Lord Randolph Churchill. Randolph's wife was Lady Randolph Churchill. *Their* son was simply Mr Winston Churchill.) Yet all retained the life-style of the aristocracy. Characteristically, members of the upper class never lifted an unnecessary finger. It was said of Lady Ida Sitwell that she not only did not know how to lace up her own shoes; she would have been humiliated by the knowledge. Churchill's cousin, the ninth duke, while visiting friends and travelling without his valet, or 'man,' complained that his toothbrush didn't 'froth properly.'[34] He had to be told gently that toothpaste had to be applied to the brush before it would foam. His man had always done that, and he hadn't realized it. Winston himself lived ninety years without once drawing his own bath or riding on a bus. He took the tube just once. His wife had to send a party to rescue him; helpless, he was whirling round and round the tunnels under London. And all his life he was dressed and undressed by someone else, usually a valet, though during one period by a secretary in her twenties. There are those among his friends who believe that this sort of thing taught him how to use people properly.

It was during the London 'Season' – from the Queen Charlotte's Ball in mid-spring to the Goodwood races in midsummer – that the great peers were to be found in their town houses. These were surrounded by barbered gardens, high walls, and gates manned by gatekeepers who fought off beggars and other street people. Sometimes they shot them. This aroused neighbours, who knew their station but believed a line should be drawn short of homicide. Actually, the very sites of many of the huge homes were outrageous. In Mayfair, Belgravia, Marylebone and St Pancras, streets maintained at public expense had been included within such walls, which meant that fire engines were blocked and buildings burned down. All attempts at legislation outlawing this extraordinary practice were defeated in Parliament.

In London the upper classes had their stylized rituals, most of them frivolous. Every morning after breakfast processions of victorias – low four-wheeled carriages with folding tops – debouched from the West End and trotted along Park Lane, gay harnesses tinkling and erect postilions wearing uniforms, glistening high boots, and varnished, high-crowned hats. Daughters were presented at court; the ladies, *en grande toilette,* wore three ostrich feathers in their hats if married, two feathers if not. Wasp-waisted, their gowns off the shoulder, skirts voluminous and rustling, the debutantes would be waited upon by uniformed members of the Corps Diplomatique, Gentlemen of the Household in full court dress, and Yeomen of the Guard in scarlet and gold. The fathers of the girls being brought out would be absent, loitering in their clubs: the Athenaeum, White's, the Carlton, the Reform, and the rest. They did not care to be 'seen' then. But the sexes did mingle on other public occasions. Everyone enjoyed the royal enclosure at Ascot, gorging on champagne, strawberries, and lobster mousse. And – rowing being considered manly – it was rather a good thing to turn out for the Henley Regatta. Dress there was about as informal as it ever got for that class. Ladies appeared in blouses and long linen skirts; their husbands, in straw boaters, blazers, and flannels.

The best club in London was Parliament, which, by no coincidence, held its key sessions between Easter and August – in effect, the Season. At the time of Winston Churchill's birth, MPs were not only unpaid; they were expected to contribute generously to charities in their constituencies. So the upper class controlled both the Lords *and* the House of Commons. B. Cracroft, analysing the House in his *Essays on Reform,* found that 326 members were patricians, including 226 sons or grandsons of peers, and a hundred others 'connected with the peerage by marriage or descent.' Over a hundred more belonged 'substantially to the same class,' which meant that three out of every four MPs were linked to each other and to the older generation in the Lords by blood as well as by conservative outlook. Between a third and a half of all cabinet members were from the upper house – six of Disraeli's thirteen ministers, five of Gladstone's fourteen. As we have seen, their hold on key posts in the Empire was even greater. Every viceroy of India was a peer by inheritance. In *Little Dorrit* Dickens wrote caustically of the Barnacle 'clan, or clique, or family, or connection' that 'there was not a list, in all the Circumlocution Office, of places that might fall vacant anywhere within half a century, from a

Lord of the Treasury to a Chinese Consul, and up again to a Governor-General of India, but, as applicants for such places, the names of some or every one of these hungry and adhesive Barnacles were down.'[35]

So the opening of Parliament, or a heralded debate in the Commons, was not unlike a family reunion. Broughams, landaus, barouches, victorias, and hansoms tingling their unmistakable bells clattered over the cobblestones of New Palace Yard and drew up in front of the Westminster Hall entrance. Men in striped trousers and frock coats descended carrying bulky red leather boxes stuffed with state papers, then disappeared into lobbies brightened by flaring gas jets. In the Strangers' Dining Room wives and daughters awaited them, wearing flowing skirts of tulle and hats as large as the displays at the Chelsea Flower Show. Gossip was exchanged, outcomes predicted, Liberals scorned by Tories or Tories by Liberals – it scarcely mattered, since their interests and social positions were virtually identical. The mighty seemed completely secure. Yet there were those who worried. Macaulay had warned against 'the encroachments of despotism and the licentiousness of democracy.' Bagehot said 'sensible men of substantial means are what we wish to be ruled by' and cautioned that 'a political combination of the lower classes . . . is an evil of the first magnitude . . . So long as they are not taught to act together there is a chance of this being averted, and it can only be averted by the greater wisdom and foresight in the higher classes.' The Queen, alarmed, let it be known that 'a democratic monarchy is what she will never belong to.'[36] Skittish patricians held their breath when the franchise bill of 1884 swept away 216 seats in rotten boroughs and increased the electorate. One man in five now had the vote – but at the next election the Conservatives were returned to power, with Lord Salisbury succeeding Disraeli. Salisbury was eminently a patrician of his time. A descendant of the two Cecils who had been Elizabeth I's and James I's chief ministers, he was a towering, massive man – acerbic, gauche, preoccupied, disdainful, and possessed of a penetrating intellect. He declined to live at 10 Downing Street, preferring his own more elegant London home, in the chapel of which he prayed each morning upon arising. He suffered spells of depression which he described as 'nerve storms.' It was Salisbury's firm belief that only uncontentious legislation should be brought before Parliament. If it was controversial, England wasn't ready for it.

In one of those little paragraphs that illumine the era, *The Times,* reporting on a public trial, noted that 'Viscount Raynham, MP, and other gentlemen present were accommodated with seats on the bench.'[37] Given the system, it is unsurprising that the judge moved over for men whose social rank was equal to, or more likely greater than, his own. The key word is 'gentlemen.' What was a gentleman? Even then the term was inexact, and it has been the despair of sociologists ever since. Some cases were easy. Phileas Fogg in Jules Verne's *Around the World in Eighty Days* was almost an archetype. In 1872 he lived in Burlington Gardens, in the house at No. 7 Savile Row – flats didn't become respectable till the mid-1870s – and he was a member of the Reform Club. His financial independence permitted him to be indifferent to public opinion (though not to his conscience and his fellow gentlemen) and his arrogance and eccentricity arose naturally from his absolute security. Other cases were marginal. You could be a gentleman in one place but not in another. In a small community the word would be applied to a physician, a lawyer, a country squire, a master of foxhounds, or just a man who had a little money and good manners. In London, or in the great country homes, that wasn't enough. Samuel Smiles to the contrary, the mantle did not fall upon every responsible, brave, selfless Englishman. If gentlemen were those who were treated as such – the best definition – the standards were usually higher than that.

The high-born and members of the landed gentry were gentlemen by birthright. Stupidity – even illiteracy – did not disqualify them. But they were exceptions. It was generally understood that a 'gentleman's education' meant Oxford or Cambridge, admittance to which was still largely limited to public school boys. During their heyday, roughly from Waterloo to the outbreak of World War I, the self-contained public schools were the ruling class's boot camps. Their autocratic headmasters, Church of England clerics, taught austerity, loyalty, honour, and the virtue of 'service.' Theoretically this meant serving those not lucky enough to see the inside of a public school; in practice it came down to defending the established order. Since the tuition exceeded the annual income of the huskiest workman, the pool of applicants was limited, as it was meant to be, to the affluent. The teaching of Latin and Greek was thought useful in disciplining young minds, but the playing fields were at least as important. The Duke of Wellington had said that the schools should produce the kind of youth who could go straight from his sixth form to a convict ship and, with the help of two sergeants and fifteen privates, transport a shipload of convicted criminals to Australia without incident. Thomas Arnold of Rugby told his faculty: 'What we must look for . . . is, first religious and moral principles; secondly, gentlemanly conduct; thirdly, intellectual ability.' At Harrow it was said that a boy might spend fifteen hours a week at cricket or, if he took 'every opportunity,' twenty hours. Sports were believed to be peculiarly suitable to the building of character. A small boy learned to submit to the authority of older boys because they were physically stronger than he. As he moved up through the higher forms, it was reasoned, he himself matured and became a 'natural ruler,' a self-reliant gentleman, disciplined by what Irving Babbitt later called the 'inner check.' Thus, though his family may have had no aristocratic connections, he joined the gentry and was accepted as a member of the ruling class. Merchants couldn't make it, but their sons could.[38]

In a revealing aside, John Buchan wrote: 'In the conventional sense, I never went to school at all.' In fact, he had received an excellent education in a Glasgow day school, but socially that didn't count. Yet Buchan rose to become Lord Tweedsmuir, governor-general of Canada. So it was possible to bypass the Etons and Harrows. Even an American could do it; in 1879 Henry James dined out 107 times. There were a thousand little ways, some of them extraordinarily petty, by which one gentleman identified another. One's vocabulary was important. Mantelpieces were 'chimney-pieces,' notepaper was 'writing paper,' mirrors were 'looking glasses.' But there was a catch. If you worried about such things, your concern showed, and you were dismissed as a swot. The true gentleman emanated a kind of mystique. He always belonged wherever he was. If he was intellectual he did not hide it; in *Paracelsus* Browning had told him: 'Measure your mind's height by the shadow it casts.' And somehow he always recognized his equals, whatever the circumstances or attire. When two strangers meet in *Doctor Thorne*, Trollope says of one: 'In spite of his long absence, he knew an English gentleman when he saw one.' Even penury was no obstacle. At the end of Trollope's *Last Chronicle of Barset* Josiah Crawley meets Archdeacon Grantley. The archdeacon is about to become Crawley's daughter's father-in-law. Crawley is wearing seedy clothes and 'dirty broken boots.' He is suspected of being a thief. He is quirky and perverse. But he was a scholar at Oxford and has 'good connections,' and when he apologizes because he is too impoverished to provide a dowry, the archdeacon replies: 'My dear Crawley, I have enough for both.' Crawley says: 'I wish we stood on equal grounds.' Rising from his chair, the archdeacon tells him: 'We stand on the only perfect level on which such men can meet each other. We are both gentlemen.' Crawley, also rising, replies: 'Sir, from the bottom of my heart I agree with you. I could not have spoken such words; but coming from you who are rich to me who am poor, they are honourable to the one and comfortable to the other.'[39]

The Barsetshire novels are set outside London, which was one reason for their popularity in the upper class. Out of season, thoroughbreds found the capital's social life stifling. They felt more comfortable in their country houses, surrounded by parks landscaped in the eighteenth century, where fountains danced, deer darted, and, in the case of Blenheim, peacocks strutted. On foxhunts they galloped past villages whose inhabitants' forebears had toiled as serfs for their own ancestors – ancestors who now lay in village churchyards beneath marble armour with marble Basset hounds at their feet. And the great houses were communities unto themselves, where servants might be waited upon by their own servants and hospitality was almost a secular religion. Chatsworth, seat of the Duke of Devonshire, accommodated almost five hundred guests, but the finest view in England was found at Blenheim, set among the thousand-year-old oaks of what was once a royal forest. When George III saw Turner's painting of its great lake, its poplared island, and the hanging beeches beyond, he said: 'We have nothing to equal this!'[40]

This was the home of the Duke of Marlborough, head of the Churchill family. Winston once described it as 'an Italian palace in an English park.'[41] A stupendous castle of almost ominous power, buttressed by massive towers, it is surrounded by courtyards, formal gardens, and 2,700 acres of parkland. Beneath its roof – which covers an incredible 7 acres – lie 320 rooms: bedrooms, salons, cabinets, state apartments, drawing rooms, a conservatory, the obligatory chapel, and a library 183 feet long. The lock on the main door, copied from one on the old Warsaw Gate, is turned by a brass key weighing 3 pounds. Within, busts of deceased dukes and duchesses stand in a grand hall whose 67-foot-high ceiling, supported by Corinthian columns, is embellished by a remarkable allegorical painting showing the first duke, John Churchill, kneeling before a figure of Britannia, who is seated on a globe, one hand resting on a lance as the other extends a wreath to him, while a figure holds fire and sword at John's feet, a white horse prances alongside, and trumpeters hover all around him.

Today Blenheim and other such shrines of the advantaged, with their marble halls and vast distances, seem intimidating. Their inhabitants didn't feel that way. On the contrary, they found them warm and convivial, bright, for some of them, with the promise of the greatest social gift they could imagine. It was illicit love. Here, too, the privileged enjoyed special privileges. Seen through the prism of a long century, they are hard to comprehend. Nineteenth-century sex, between thoroughbred lovers, was extremely complex, but like everything else they enjoyed, it had its precedents. The British aristocracy had always gloried in its sexual prowess. Exceptional concupiscence was rewarded; John Churchill, the first Duke of Marlborough, first rose to prominence because his sister Arabella, maid of honour to the Duchess of York, became the duke's most passionate mistress. When Marlborough returned from European battlefields at an advanced age, his wife Sarah proudly wrote: 'Today the Duke returned from the war and pleasured me twice in his top boots.' Had she sought lovers during his absence, the social risk would have been slight. For generations before Victoria's coronation the patriciate had tolerated promiscuity among its more hot-blooded members. Byron wrote his shortest and most eloquent poem as a testament to a titled woman who had taken leave of her husband for a nine-month romp with him:

> *Caroline Lamb,*
> *Goddamn.*

The Duke of Wellington had his pick of ladies when he returned from his various triumphs, and two of his bedmates expressed their appreciation to him in their memoirs. The duke's sister-in-law, Lady Charlotte Wellesley, the mother of four young children, left them to sleep with Lord Paget, himself the father of four children by his wife, Lady Caroline Villiers, daughter of Lady Jersey, who was the former 'favourite,' as it was then put, of the Prince of Wales. At Waterloo the duke made Paget his chief of cavalry. An aide protested: 'Your Grace cannot have forgotten the affair with Lady Charlotte Wellesley?' The duke: 'Oh, no! I have not forgotten that.' Aide: 'That is not the only case, I am afraid. At any rate [he] has a reputation of running away with everybody he can.' Duke: 'I'll take good care he don't run away with me. I don't care about anybody else.'*[42] During the Regency, upper-class sexual

* Apocrypha has it that the two commanders did not speak during the battle. Actually, they were mounted side by side when a ball passed over the neck of Wellington's horse and hit Paget. 'By God, sir,' Paget cried, 'I've lost my leg!' Wellington

73

conduct became particularly flagrant. It was then that ladies diverted themselves with the best-selling *Memoirs of Harriet Smith,* which opened with the gripping line: 'I will not relate the exact circumstances by which at the age of thirteen I became the mistress of the Earl of Croydon.'

The tradition has continued to flourish in the twentieth century, a colourful example being the beautiful and wanton Edwina Ashley, Lady Mountbatten. When Lord Louis Mountbatten was viceroy of India, negotiating the terms for Indian independence, the sessions went much more smoothly because the vicereine, with her husband's resigned knowledge, was sleeping with Jawaharlal Nehru. Earlier she had been even more headstrong. At one point she vanished from London society for four months. Friends in Park Lane found Louis extremely vague when asked about his wife's whereabouts. Actually, he didn't know. Later he learned that Edwina had shipped aboard a fifty-ton trading schooner, bound for the South Seas, as an ordinary seaman. Night after night, she cruised among the lush islands oblivious of her anxious husband.

Victoria's reign was a hiatus, not in extracurricular upper-class ardour, but in the flagrant practice of it. Her ascent saw the triumph of the puritans – of what Melbourne called 'that d—— morality.' In the 1840s and 1850s debauchery went underground. By the time of Winston Churchill's childhood and early youth it had become prudent to keep mum about your love affairs. Gladstone in a candid moment said he had known 'eleven prime ministers and ten were adulterers'; nevertheless, he joined in the persecution of Charles Stewart Parnell, an Irish MP who had been the lover of Kitty O'Shea with Mrs O'Shea's husband's consent. In 1887 Sir Charles Dilke, at one time regarded as a future prime minister, was ruined by a divorce trial. He lost his cabinet post, then lost his seat, and eventually became a social pariah. One modern British scholar is convinced that 'Disraeli slept his way to the top,' but Dizzy was too crafty to be caught. Gladstone made a curious practice of prowling the London streets at night and holding long, intimate conversations with prostitutes. Sometimes he brought them home and Mrs Gladstone gave them hot chocolate. It was assumed that he was trying to convince them to mend their ways. If so, he doesn't appear to have been discouraged by his failure to produce a single convert. Indeed, after these talks he always appeared beaming, animated, and flushed. No one thought that odd. Nor could anyone pass judgement on affairs of which they knew nothing. The key to successful extramarital sex, therefore, was discretion. Mrs Patrick Campbell, perhaps the most outspoken woman in polite society, said dryly: 'It doesn't matter what you do in the bedroom, as long as you don't do it in the street and frighten the horses.'[43]

The difficulty lay in finding the bedroom. Mrs Campbell also said, after manoeuvring one man out of his marriage to a Churchill and up the aisle with her: 'Ah, the peace of the double bed after the hurly-burly of the chaise looked over and replied: 'By God, sir, so you have!' (From *Waterloo: Day of Battle* by David Howarth [New York, 1968], page 186.)

74

longue!' It was all very well for a Forsyte to tuck away a common mistress in Chelsea, but that couldn't be done with a lady. In the city she was under observation all the time. Her gown, her coif, her bearing, gestures, and diction testified to her class, and she couldn't be seen outside her aerie. Her very presence in a hotel lobby would invite scandal. Thus the preference of the aristocracy and gentry for their homes in the country. London society was too ritualized; there was little privacy, unless you were an unmarried bachelor, like young Freud, who informed his housekeeper that he expected a woman for tea and was told: 'Right, sir, I'll change the sheets on the bed.'[44]

The servants knew of most dalliances. They even understood why there was one standard for their masters and mistresses and another for the rest of England. Victorian morality arose from the needs of the new middle class. As the lord chancellor explained when divorce courts were established in 1857, a woman lost nothing by her husband's infidelity and could absolve him 'without any loss of caste,' while 'no one would venture to suggest' that he could pardon her adultery, which 'might be the means of palming spurious children upon him.' This was important; such children shared a middle-class legacy. In titled families it was meaningless. Only the legitimacy of the first patrician child counted. Professor McGregor writes: 'The sexual waywardness of aristocrats . . . did not endanger the integrity or succession of family properties regulated by primogeniture and entail. Countless children of the mist played happily in Whig and Tory nurseries where they were no threat to the security of family property or to the interests of the heirs.' Pamela Harriman, a Digby who was Winston Churchill's daughter-in-law before she married New York's former governor, takes the traditional light view of such sex: 'They went to bed a lot with each other, but they were all cousins, so it didn't really count.' It was their insularity that largely limited them to cousins; among the great families, Barbara Tuchman notes, 'everyone knew or was related to everyone else . . . People who met each other every day, at each other's homes, at race meetings and hunts, at Cowes, for the Regatta, at the Royal Academy, at court and in Parliament, were more often than not meeting their second cousins or brother-in-law's uncle or stepfather's sister or aunt's nephew on the other side.'[45]

One area of scholarly inquiry being explored by today's sexologists is how the voluptuaries of the Victorian upper class led such colourful sex lives and produced so little issue. The average British wife then conceived ten times during her childbearing years. But the great thoroughbred beauties, who treasured their figures, carried far less often. After giving birth to Winston, Jennie Churchill was in and out of lovers' beds all her life, yet she bore only one more child. And she was not exceptional.

It is worth noting that these small victories of desire were achieved, not by men, but by prudent women. One would expect that Victorian gentlemen, proud of their protective instincts, would have shielded their mistresses from impregnation. The means were at hand. Condoms, originally thin sheaths made from the visceral tissue of sheep, had been used for two centuries;

Casanova mentions them, and so does Boswell. ('French letter' was the term used in England; across the Channel it was *la capote anglaise.*') But Victorian males were also romantics, and they found condoms distasteful. Therefore their partners turned to faithful douching with a solution of sulphate of zinc or alum, rigid austerity during their ripe periods each month, beeswax discs which blocked the entrance to the uterus, sponges moistened with diluted lemon juice and inserted into the vagina, and, increasingly, the Dutch cap, a primitive diaphragm designed to fit longitudinally in the vagina with the forward end under the pubic bone and the back end in the posterior fornix. Aletta Jacobs introduced this device in the Netherlands in the early 1880s. The cap comprised a steel ring with rubber stretched across it – a painful expedient, but passion overrode the discomfort. Mere possession of a Dutch cap was a sign of privilege in London. The vast majority of Englishwomen didn't know they existed and would have had difficulty acquiring one anyhow; the caps were available, only to those who furnished respectable references, at a Mayfair bookshop.

Partly because they bred less, ladies flourished. They were so much healthier and more active than their unprivileged sisters that they almost seem to have belonged to a different species. Lower-class women weren't envious; they adored them. An article in *Graphic Magazine* described in the saccharine prose of the time how such social celebrities were regarded:

> For the fashionable beauty, life is an endless carnival, and dress a round of disguises. She does everything and the wings of Mercury might be attached to her tiny bottines, so rapid are her changes of scene and character. She is a sportswoman, a huntress, a bold and skillful swimmer; she drives a pair of horses like a charioteer, mounts the roof of a four-in-hand, plays lawn tennis, is at home on a race course or the deck of a fast yacht. She is aware of the refinements of dining and has a pretty taste in vintages. She is a power at the theatre or the Opera; and none is more brilliant at a supper party. Of the modern young lady a la mode, who wields alike the fiddle-bow, the billiard-cue, and the etching-needle, who climbs mountains and knows the gymnasium, none but herself can be the prototype.[46]

Among the most sophisticated of these women, often bored partners in arranged marriages, the affairs which were joyously celebrated during weekends were sometimes launched in wife-to-wife conversations. 'Tell Charles I have designs on him,' one would tell Charles's lady, who would acknowledge the proposal with a nod and an amused smile; she herself already had a lover or had designs of her own on someone else's husband. But you had to be very secure to take that approach – had to be, say, one of that select circle of ladies who took turns sleeping with Victoria's eldest son. More often an understanding would have been reached in advance between the primary partners. Some affairs were known to everyone. General Sir Neville Bowles Chamberlain, for example, always slept with the Duchess of Manchester, and the Duke of Marlborough with Lady Colin Campbell. Of course, they didn't cross a bedroom threshold together. On Thursdays each of the hundred-odd guests was assigned a room; a tiny brass frame on the door held a card with his or her name written on it. Wise and worldly hostesses knew who should be paired with whom. Vita Sackville-West later described how they served as accomplices to Victorian and later Edwardian intrigue: 'This question of the disposition of bedrooms always gave the . . . hostesses cause for anxious thought. It was so necessary to be tactful, and at the same time discreet. The professional Lothario would be furious if he found himself in a room surrounded by ladies who were all accompanied by their husbands. Tommy Brand, on one such occasion, had been known to leave the house on the Sunday morning. . . . Tommy's motto was "Chacun à sa chacune." Then there were the recognised lovers to be considered; the duchess herself would have been greatly annoyed had she gone to stay at the same party as Harry Tremaine, only to find that he had been put at the other end of the house. . . . It was part of a good hostess' duty to see to such things; they must be made easy, though not too obvious.' After lights were out, shadowy figures would glide through the darkened hall and everyone would settle in for the night's pleasure. An hour before dawn the butler would appear in the hall bearing a gong. He would strike it once and depart. The same tiptoeing figures would reappear. Presently they would all meet at the breakfast table.[47]

Breakfast could be bewildering to outsiders. At the table you were expected to be brusque, even rude, to your companion of the night. 'Pass the toast,' you would say crossly, or 'I want the salt.' The upper class was always very direct ('I want to pee'), but this went beyond that. It was important to sort out your different roles, to let it be known that you weren't going to break the rules by being demonstrative, or eloping, or doing anything else rash. One-night stands were very rare, but now and then they happened. The story of one, involving a young Frenchwoman, survives. During an evening musicale a handsome gentleman propositioned her. She accepted, and a memorable night followed. Two hours later she was cracking a soft-boiled egg downstairs when he appeared, took a seat, and arranged his napkin. Still aglow with romance, she bestowed a tender smile upon him. He glowered and growled: 'Are you going to hog the butter all day?' She was shocked, then enraged. Hurling the butter in his face, she flew upstairs, summoned her maid, packed, and demanded that she be driven to the station at once. She told their stunned hostess that she would never again visit *atroce* England. She didn't. She wasn't invited.[48]

The casual promiscuity of the English patriciate over the centuries suggests the need for caution in tracing the bloodlines of Winston Churchill. He himself, while researching his biography of the great duke – the income from which went far towards supporting his family in the 1930's, when pleas for resistance to Hitler made him a political pariah – found 'disquieting' evidence of 'a rather shady phase' in the 1500s, when the duke's great-grandmother so forgot herself in the early years of her marriage that she presented the family blacksmith with a sturdy son. On a loftier scale, the duke's sister gave birth to

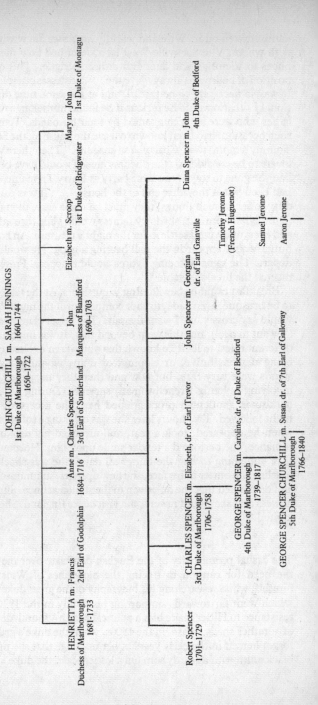

THE CHURCHILL FAMILY

John Churchill m. Sarah
of Wootton Glanville   dr. of Sir Henry Winston

SIR WINSTON CHURCHILL m. ELIZABETH DRAKE
1620–1688   of Ashe, Devon

JOHN CHURCHILL m. SARAH JENNINGS
1st Duke of Marlborough   1660–1744
1650–1722

HENRIETTA m. Francis
Duchess of Marlborough   2nd Earl of Godolphin
1681–1733

Anne m. Charles Spencer
1684–1716   3rd Earl of Sunderland

John
Marquess of Blandford
1690–1703

Elizabeth m. Scroop
1st Duke of Bridgwater

Mary m. John
1st Duke of Montagu

Robert Spencer
1701–1729

CHARLES SPENCER m. Elizabeth, dr. of Earl Trevor
3rd Duke of Marlborough
1706–1758

Diana Spencer m. John
4th Duke of Bedford

John Spencer m. Georgina
dr. of Earl Granville

Timothy Jerome
(French Huguenot)

Samuel Jerome

Aaron Jerome

GEORGE SPENCER m. Caroline, dr. of Duke of Bedford
4th Duke of Marlborough
1739–1817

GEORGE SPENCER CHURCHILL m. Susan, dr. of 7th Earl of Galloway
5th Duke of Marlborough
1766–1840

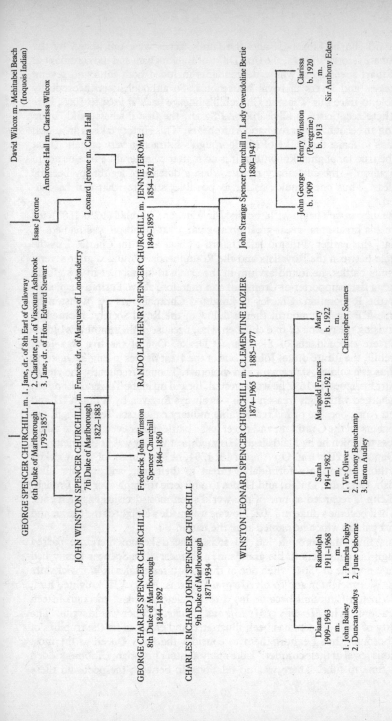

David Wilcox m. Mehitabel Beach
(Iroquois Indian)

Isaac Jerome

Ambrose Hall m. Clarissa Wilcox

Leonard Jerome m. Clara Hall

GEORGE SPENCER CHURCHILL m. 1. Jane, dr. of 8th Earl of Galloway
6th Duke of Marlborough   2. Charlotte, dr. of Viscount Ashbrook
1793–1857   3. Jane, dr. of Hon. Edward Stewart

JOHN WINSTON SPENCER CHURCHILL m. Frances, dr. of Marques of Londonderry
7th Duke of Marlborough
1822–1883

RANDOLPH HENRY SPENCER CHURCHILL m. JENNIE JEROME
1849–1895   1854–1921

John Strange Spencer Churchill m. Lady Gwendoline Bertie
1880–1947

GEORGE CHARLES SPENCER CHURCHILL
8th Duke of Marlborough
1844–1892

Frederick John Winston
Spencer Churchill
1846–1850

CHARLES RICHARD JOHN SPENCER CHURCHILL
9th Duke of Marlborough
1871–1934

WINSTON LEONARD SPENCER CHURCHILL m. CLEMENTINE HOZIER
1874–1965   1885–1977

John George
b. 1909

Henry Winston
(Peregrine)
b. 1913

Clarissa
b. 1920
m.
Sir Anthony Eden

Diana
1909–1963
m.
1. John Bailey
2. Duncan Sandys

Randolph
1911–1968
m.
1. Pamela Digby
2. June Osborne

Sarah
1914–1982
m.
1. Vic Oliver
2. Anthony Beauchamp
3. Baron Audley

Marigold Frances
1918–1921

Mary
b. 1922
m.
Christopher Soames

a bastard son of James II, and the family genes were quickened by the passionate George Villiers, the first Duke of Buckingham and the confidant of two Stuart sovereigns, whose descendants included both Pitts and several mistresses and lovers in royal households. So although it is theoretically possible to trace our Winston Churchill's lineage back at least to 1066, here and there scepticism is advisable. As Sarah, the first duchess, said, upon reading an account of her husband's forebears, 'This History takes a great deal of Pains to make the Duke of Marlborough's Extraction very ancient. That may be true for aught I know. But it is no matter whether it be true or not in my opinion' – the customary riposte when a defense of legitimacy became hopeless. Thus one should, as far as possible, stick to what can be confirmed.[49]

One may as well begin with the first Sir Winston Churchill (1620-1688), for whom his great-great-great-great-great-great-great-grandson was named. A scholar, this earlier Winston left Oxford to bear arms for Charles I in the struggle between the Royalists and the Roundheads. Wounded after several ferocious battles, he found asylum in the castle of his mother-in-law, Lady Drake, a firm supporter of Cromwell and therefore above Puritan suspicion. After the Restoration, Charles II knighted Churchill. As Sir Winston he became MP for Weymouth, then a fellow of the Royal Society, meanwhile supervising the raising of five children who, because of their mother's bloodline, were descendants of Sir Francis Drake. One of the five was John Churchill, the future duke. John is one of the great figures in English history, glorious as a soldier, statesman, and diplomat. Though frequently the victim of court intrigue – in 1692 he was arrested, locked up in the Tower of London, and charged with high treason – he was always forgiven by William III and Queen Anne because of his remarkable military conquests. John fought ten campaigns on the Continent and never lost a battle, never even failed to take a fortress to which he had laid siege. His mightiest victory was at Blenheim, on the Danube, in Bavaria. On August 13, 1704, he and Eugene of Savoy risked everything, ignoring a formidable threat to their rear, and led the allied English, Germans, Dutch, and Danes to a historic triumph over the French. Blenheim is regarded as one of the world's ten most decisive engagements. John had become a duke in 1702. Now he was made a Knight of the Garter and given a palace, which he named after the battle.

This first Marlborough left no sons. The dukedom therefore passed through his daughters to his grandson, a Spencer. The Spencer family had become notable in 1504, when one of them acquired estates in Warwickshire and at Wormleighton and received a grant in arms. Henry VIII knighted him; our Winston Churchill became his direct male descendant through fifteen generations. In his *Memoirs of My Life and Writings*, Gibbon would write: 'The nobility of the Spencers has been illustrated and enriched by the trophies of Marlborough; but I exhort them to consider the Fairy Queen as the most precious jewel of their coronet.' Like many another historian, Gibbon skidded from time to time. There was no relationship between the poet and these

Spencers. But they were remarkable in other ways. One served as ambassador to Spain and France. Another, a contemporary of Robert Walpole, England's first prime minister, was first lord of the Treasury between 1718 and 1721. A third, the second Earl Spencer, was first lord of the Admiralty in Nelson's great years. The next earl was one of the authors of the reform bill of 1832, and his son became viceroy of Ireland and then Gladstone's first lord.

In 1817, by royal licence, the fifth Duke of Marlborough changed his family name to Spencer-Churchill. The arms were quartered beneath two crests, a griffin's head for the Spencers and a lion for the Churchills. The lion is the traditional symbol of England's greatness, and a duke outranks an earl, but for over a century the Spencers had outperformed the Churchills as servants of the Crown. One Duke of Marlborough became a mere brigadier of foot guards; another, during his fifty-eight years as master of Blenheim, simply collected pictures. During the Regency, two dukes succumbed to that gambling fever which afflicted so many members of the aristocracy in those raffish years. Rees Howell Gronow, a gossip writer of the early nineteenth century, told of a coach ride with a Marquess of Blandford (the title of the elder son of the Duke of Marlborough before his succession). The marquess produced a wad of fifty thousand-pound notes. He had just borrowed them. He said: 'You see, Gronow, how the immense fortune of my family will be frittered away; but I can't help it; I must live. My father inherited five hundred thousand pounds in ready money and seventy thousand pounds a year in land; and in all probability when it comes my turn to live at Blenheim I shall have nothing left but the annuity of five thousand pounds a year on the Post Office.' When he did become duke, we are told, 'he lived in one remote corner of his magnificent Palace, a melancholy instance of extravagance.'[50]

It was his son, John Winston, who began restoration of the Churchill pride. He and his successors added such lustre to the family's reputation that recent generations have used Spencer only as a middle name or dropped it altogether. John Winston entered politics, was elected MP for Woodstock, and sat in the Commons for fifteen years. Becoming the seventh duke, he moved to the Lords and served as a cabinet minister under Lord Derby and then Disraeli. His elder son, George, was a disappointment. So, at first, was George's brother Randolph. Randolph was a poor student at Eton. He failed his first examinations at Oxford. But then he picked up. At Merton College he left a creditable record, marred only by an arrest for drunkenness and assault. After the ceremonial grand tour of Europe which had become customary for upper-class youths, and after a brief period as an idler and carouser, he stood for Parliament in 1874 and was elected to his father's old seat. His first speech went well; Disraeli wrote the Queen: 'Lord Randolph said many imprudent things, which is not very important in the maiden speech of a young member and a young man, but the House was surprised, and then captivated, by his energy, and his natural flow, and his impressive manners. With self-control and study he might mount. It was a speech of great promise.'[51]

Dizzy's unerring eye had caught the flaws, however. Randolph was 'impru-

dent,' lacking in 'self-control.' Later, after disaster had overwhelmed him –
after he had first been marked as a future prime minister and had then lost
everything – that was all which would be remembered. It is easy to withhold
sympathy from him. Surviving pictures do not help. His most striking feature
was his eyes. They were not attractive; he suffered from exophthalmos, and
his protruding eyeballs seem to have surveyed the world with a supercilious,
offensive stare. His walrus moustache draws attention to a large head set on a
short, frail body. He looks pompous, curt, and rude. And so he was, to those
who bored him. Yet his friends have left eloquent testaments to his jauntiness,
wittiness, and charm. He was an enthusiastic foxhunter, a splendid horseman.
His mind and tongue were quick. He was courtly with the ladies. He had little
money; Disraeli, who made it his business to know such things, told the
Queen in another letter that Randolph's father was 'not rich for a Duke,' and
virtually everything would pass to the new MP's elder brother anyhow.[52]
Nevertheless, 'Randy,' as he was known to the whispering galleries and
sounding boards of London society, was a popular member of the 'fast' set
headed by the Prince of Wales. Randy's chief attractions were his social
standing, his eligibility, and his faultless dress, for he was very much the
dandy. And he enjoyed his kaleidoscopic social role. He detested dancing, yet
he never turned down an invitation to a ball.

In time he might have overcome his youthful impetuosity, but time was
denied him. His greatest misfortune, though he didn't know it then, was a
consequence of what was surely the cruellest of all Oxford pranks. Years later
he described it to Louis Jennings, a close friend, and Jennings passed it along
to another of Randy's friends, Frank Harris, editor of the *Fortnightly Review*.
One evening at Merton a small group of students were discussing a favourite
undergraduate topic: the relationship between masters and servants. Randy
had firm views on this. He believed the aristocracy knew instinctively how to
handle menials and that the rising merchants – he once told Harris that he
regarded them as 'jumped-up grocers from Ballarat and shopkeepers from
Sydney' – would never learn. That evening he was eloquent; he was
applauded; a fellow student handed him an enormous stirrup cup of champagne; he drank it off. It had been drugged. He awoke at daybreak with a
ghastly taste in his mouth. He was in a strange room. The wallpaper, in his
words, was 'hideous – dirty.' He turned his head and sat bolt upright, gasping.
There was an old woman lying beside him; 'one thin strand of dirty grey hair'
lay on the pillow. His hopeless questions to Jennings evoked the chilling
horror and the pathos of his plight: 'How had I got there? What had happened
to bring me to such a den?' Did he remember anything? *Pas trop;* the stirrup
cup, and now this. Rising quietly, he slid into his trousers. Abruptly, the hag
awoke and grinned. She asked hoarsely: 'Oh, Lovie, you're not going to leave
me like that?'[53]

Randolph vividly recalled that she had 'one long yellow tooth in her top jaw
that waggled as she spoke.' Obviously, she expected to be paid – this was the
ultimate master-servant relationship. Emptying his pockets, he threw all the

money he had on the bed. Her leer grew. Speechless, he struggled into his waistcoat and coat and bolted. As he slammed the door he heard her call, 'Lovie, you're not kind!' Then, said Randolph, 'Downstairs I fled in livid terror.'*He knew his peril; he made for the nearest doctor's office. There he was treated with a strong disinfectant, but three weeks later a venereal sore appeared on his genitals, followed by lesions elsewhere. He returned to the physician, who treated him with mercury, warned him to abstain from alcohol, and told him he had nothing to worry about. It was a lie. Victorian medicine, confronted with such symptoms, was helpless. Thus it was that at the height of the 1873 Season, even before his entrance into public life, the elegant twenty-four-year-old bachelor son of a duke, the cynosure of aspiring debutantes and their ambitious mothers, was a doomed syphilitic.[54]

To meet
Randolph
Their Royal Highnesses the Prince and Princess of Wales
and
Their Imperial Russian Highnesses the
Grand Duke Cesarewitch and Grand Duchess Cesarevna.

Captain Carpenter and the Officers of H.M.S. "Ariadne"
request the honour of the Company of
Mr & Mrs Jerome

On board, on Tuesday, August 12th, from 3.30 to 7.30, p m.

Boats will be in attendance at the R.Y.C. Landing Place.

DANCING.

R.S.V.P.

On this deckle-edged invitation – it still exists; the Churchills, the biographer ardently notes, saved everything – a feminine hand later wrote, below 'To meet,' the name 'Randolph.' Certainly Clarissa ('Clara') Jerome hoped that she and her three daughters would meet *someone* interesting. Lately Europe had been a disappointment to them. Clara had begun to long for Newport, or even the Jeromes' New York mansion on Madison Square. She

---

* In his *Lord Randolph Churchill* (Oxford, 1981) R. F. Foster discounts Harris's 'almost completely unlikely assertion of the manner in which he [Randolph] contracted syphilis.' Foster does not say why. The account does not seem unlikely to this writer, and Harris, as Foster concedes, enjoyed a relationship with both Lord Randolph and Winston which 'was both genuine and appreciably close' (page 389).

took the Franco-Prussian War as a personal affront. She and her daughters – Clarita, Leonie, and Jeanette ('Jennie') – had adored the Paris of the Second Empire. Beginning in 1858 they had lived in a palatial apartment on the Champs-Elysées. Clarita had made her debut at the Tuileries and had been the guest of Napoleon III and Eugénie at Compiègne. Jennie had been scheduled to come out in 1870. She had already been fitted for her gown when Louis Napoleon sent Wilhelm a rude note. Wilhelm of Prussia replied – at Bismarck's urging – with the ruder Ems telegram, and suddenly the two armies were lunging at each other. In the beginning Clara saw no need for alarm. French confidence was boundless. And neutral observers thought it fully justified. The *Pall Mall Gazette* of July 29, 1870, predicted that the first Napoleon's triumphs were about to be repeated. *The Times* felt an Englishman would be justified in laying his 'last shilling on Casquette against Pumpernickel.' The élan of Louis Napoleon's soldiery could scarcely have been higher. They pored over the maps of Prussia which had been issued to them, studied German phrase books, and eagerly looked forward to heroic attacks gallantly carried out by them and their comrades crying *'En avant! A la baïonnette! A Berlin!'* to the strains of 'La Marseillaise.'[55]

It was 'unthinkable,' the *London Standard* said, for the Prussians 'to take the offensive.'[56] General Helmuth von Moltke and his general staff disagreed. They had built their railroad grid with war in mind, had profited by William T. Sherman's brilliant use of railways in Tennessee, and had mastered the coordination of telegraph lines and troop trains. Three weeks after war had been declared, Moltke had efficiently mobilized 1,183,000 Germans, backed by more than 1,440 Krupp cast-steel cannon. The French, who regarded efficiency as a pedestrian virtue, weren't ready. They collided with massed battalions wearing spiked helmets and uniforms of Prussian blue singing 'Die Wacht am Rhein' and 'Deutschland über Alles' and chanting *'Nach Paris!'* While their deadly artillery, outranging Louis Napoleon's obsolete bronze guns, flung shattering barrages ahead of them, they blazed a trail which would be followed by their grandsons in 1914 and their great-grandsons in 1940. Suddenly news reached the Champs-Elysées that half the French army was bottled up in the mighty fortress of Metz. At Sedan the other half, led by Louis Napoleon himself, laid down their arms and accepted humiliating surrender terms. Paris lay open to the invader.

Clara and her daughters fled to Cowes, the fashionable British seaside resort on the Isle of Wight. They moved back to Paris the following spring, taking a house in the boulevard Haussman, but the city had been devastated by the Commune, the leftist regime which had defied the Prussians and their own countrymen until starved into submission. Returning to Cowes, the Jeromes leased what Clara called a 'sweet little cottage' and were frequently seen there and in London, attending balls, recitals, receptions, and musicales, and other highlights of the Season. Most weekends found them on the great country estates. Unlike the Frenchwoman whose naiveté spoiled a perfectly good English breakfast, they were not shocked by careless interpretations of the marriage sacrament. Clara's husband slept with many women in New York; she knew it, knew that he had sired several illegitimate children, and was indifferent. Her grandson Winston relished telling of a meeting between Clara and one of Leonard Jerome's mistresses; Clara said: 'My dear, I understand how you feel. He is *so* irresistible.' But a lady's sexual emancipation was possible only after matrimony. As long as the Misses Jerome remained single, they must also be maidens. At least one of them was straining at the leash. A photograph of the mother and her daughters, taken at about this time, shows her seated, facing left, regarding the world with a resolute jaw and eyes like raisins. Clarita, also seated, is holding her mother's hand and searching her face, as though for guidance. Leonie, standing, leans on her mother's shoulder for support. Jennie, however, doesn't seem even to be a part of the group. She was already known as 'a great show-off.' Here the show is well worth watching. Dark, vivacious, and magnificent, she stands alone, staring boldly at the photographer, her left arm outflung, the hand atop a furled umbrella, her hips cocked saucily. It is almost a wanton pose, the posture of a virgin who can hardly wait to assume another position.[57]

Their Cowes home was a 'cottage' in the sense that the sprawling Newport châteaux were called cottages. Leonard was seldom there, but when he crossed the Atlantic – usually at the helm of his own yacht – he expected to find his family living in style. He was an American type peculiar to his time, a vigorous, handsome man, a brokerage partner of William R. Travers and a member of the New York Stock Exchange who repeatedly amassed, and then spent, enormous portfolios of wealth. As Winston told the story, 'My grandfather would devote himself to work and in a short time make a fortune. Then he would give up the life completely, disappearing for a year or two, generally to Europe. When he came back to New York he might have lost the fortune he had made, and at once set about piling up another. Money poured through his fingers. He generally had an income of about £10,000, perhaps equal to £40,000 now. My grandfather thought nothing of spending $70,000 on a party, where each lady found a gold bracelet, inset with diamonds, wrapped in her napkin.'[58]

In his careening career, Leonard seems to have succeeded at almost everything he tried. He founded the American Jockey Club, built a racetrack in the Bronx, supported an opera house, was for a time a part-owner of the *New York Times*, participated in politics, spent eighteen months as American consul in Trieste, gambled heavily and successfully, and was the first man to drive a team of racing horses four-in-hand down Broadway. Like many other Wall Street millionaires of that period, he held mixed feelings about the English aristocracy. He envied their power; Britain was a mightier nation than the United States, and an English peer was a great figure throughout the Empire and beyond. But Americans were also proud, especially self-made men. Having reached the top of a mobile society, they scorned those whose future had been assured at birth. After all, Britain's patricians and New York's financiers came from the same stock. Leonard was the great-great-grandson of a Huguenot who had arrived in what were then the American colonies in 1710. Leonard's wife's family had settled in Connecticut by 1650. There was one faint blemish in Clara's otherwise pure Anglo-Saxon blood, one which later delighted Winston: her grandmother had been an Iroquois Indian. But that merely made her more colourful. Both Leonard and Clara were descended from American officers who had fought in the War of Independence. One, a major in the Fourth Massachusetts Regiment, had served with Washington at Valley Forge. To be sure, the Jeromes would be unlikely to place obstacles in the path of a titled British son-in-law. Palmerston had predicted: 'Before the century is out, these clever and pretty women from New York will pull the strings in half the chancelleries in Europe.'[59] Louisa Caton, the daughter of a Baltimore merchant, had been Lady Hervey-Bathurst and then, after her first husband's death, Duchess of Leeds. Minnie Stevens became Lady Paget; Mrs Arthur Post, Lady Barrymore; Mary Leiter of Chicago, Lady Curzon and vicereine of India. And Consuelo del Valle, who had been Jennie's schoolmate, would soon be Duchess of Manchester. So a Jerome girl wouldn't find herself in altogether unfamiliar company. Leonard and Clara might have been pleased by the thought. At the same time, they would have bridled at the suggestion that she was marrying up.

The shipboard dance at Cowes aboard the cruiser *Ariadne* was considered a major social event and even a historic occasion, for the guests of honour were the future Czar Alexander III and his czarina, Maria Feodorovna. Today they are forgotten, part of the legacy which was destroyed with the last of the Romanovs, but one question asked that evening by an acquaintance of the Jeromes, by an obscure dandy named Frank Bertie, is memorable. Although Jennie had a full dance card, she happened to be standing alone, watching the bobbing Chinese lanterns and the entwined British and Russian flags overhead and listening to the Royal Marine band, when Bertie appeared at her elbow with a pale youth. Bertie said: 'Miss Jerome, may I present an old friend of mine who has just arrived in Cowes, Lord Randolph Churchill.' Jennie inclined her lovely head. Randolph stared. She was nineteen, at the height of her glory, bare-shouldered and sheathed below in a flowing white gown with flowers pinned to the bosom. After some hesitation, he invited her to dance. The quadrille proved to be beyond him; he tripped and suggested they sit this one out. They did. Her dance card notwithstanding, they sat out the next one, and then the next, talking of horses and mutual friends until Clara, wondering uneasily where her daughter might be among all these virile naval officers, sought her out. Before leaving, Jennie persuaded her mother to invite Randolph to dinner the following evening, accompanied by a British colonel for the sake of appearances. At the dinner Randolph seems to have tried hard to be clever, without much success. Afterwards Jennie and Clarita played piano duets. Randolph whispered to the startled colonel: 'If I can, I mean to make the dark one my wife.' They left, and Jennie asked her sister what she thought of Randolph. Clarita wasn't impressed. She thought his manner pretentious and his moustache absurd. She doubted she could learn to like him. Jennie said: 'Please try to, Clarita, because I have the strangest feeling that he's going to ask me to marry him.' If he did, she said, 'I'm going to say "yes."'' Her sister laughed, but in three days, during a stroll in the Cowes garden, the two became engaged.[60]

Leonard's first response was apprehension. When Jennie wrote him the news he replied, 'You quite startle me. I shall feel very anxious till I hear more. If it has come to that – that *he* only "waits to consult his family" you are pretty far gone. . . I fear if anything goes wrong you will make a dreadful shipwreck of your affections. I always thought if you ever did fall in love it would be a very dangerous affair.' Letters from her and her mother brought him round, however. Once persuaded, his optimism was irrepressible. In Wall Street the panic of '73 was at its peak. He had been all but wiped out. But he never doubted that he would win it all back – as he did – and on September 11, giving the marriage his blessing, he wrote Jennie: 'I must say I have been very happy all day long. I have thought of nothing else. I telegraphed your mother immediately that I was "delighted" and that I would arrange £2,000 a year for you which she says in her letter will do. The letter I recd from you the other day only filled me with anxiety. I feared nothing would come of it and that you would be left shipwrecked. The situation as related by you today leaves no reasonable doubt of the accomplishment of your hopes. The consent of his paternal [sic] I should say must follow when he learns that moderate provision can be made for you and that our family is entirely respectable – all that can be said for any American family.'[61]

It wasn't enough. At Blenheim the duchess was muttering angrily about 'dollars and impudence.' On August 25 Randolph's brother had written him: 'I tell you that you are mad simply mad. I don't care if *la demoiselle* was the incarnation of all moral excellences & physical beauties on God's earth. My opinion is the same.' If he wanted to run off with a married woman, George said, that would be one thing. 'But my friend *le mariage*! It is a delusion and a snare like all the rest, and in this disagreeable addition [sic], that it is irrevocable . . . You really only want to marry because you are in love with *an idea "une phantasie* . . ."' Meanwhile, Randolph had written his father of his plans. He told him: 'I love her better than life itself,' then added with exasperating vagueness: 'Mr Jerome is a gentleman who is obliged to live in New York to look after his business. I do not know what it is.'[62]

The duke meant to find out. He wrote Randolph: 'I can't say that what you have told me is reassuring. . . . This Mr J. seems to be a sporting, and I should think vulgar kind of man. I hear he drives about 6 and 8 horses in N.Y. (one may take this as a kind of indication of what the man is). I hear he and his two brothers are stock brokers, one of them bears a *bad* character in commercial judgement in *this* country, but which of them it is, I do not know, but it is evident he is of the class of speculators; he has been bankrupt once; and may be so again; and when we come to think of N.Y. speculators & their deeds look at Fisk and *hoc genus omne*.'[63]

Randolph besieged Blenheim. A month later he wrote Clara that although his father still deplored 'the suddenness & rapidity of the attachment formed . . . he wld give his consent if we were of the same mind in a year hence.' Neither Randolph nor Jennie would agree to wait. They were both hot-blooded and impatient; with each passing day they wanted each other more. Weeks dragged on, and then months. Randolph's election to Parliament in February seems to have improved his standing in his father's eyes, and presently the duke, mollified if not reconciled, was getting down to the bedrock issue. It was money. He had decided to give Randolph £1,000 a year, which, with the £2,000 from Leonard, seemed ample for the couple. The issue was who should control it. Lawyers were consulted. The Churchill family's solicitors took the position that settling any money on the bride was inconsistent with English practice. The groom, they said, should get everything. Leonard offered a split between husband and wife, writing: 'My daughter although not a *Russian* princess is an American and ranks precisely the same and you have doubtless seen that the Russian settlement recently published' – this was between the Grand Duchess Marie Alexandrovna and Victoria's second son, the Duke of Edinburgh – 'claims *everything* for the bride.' It was now April 7, and Jennie and Randolph could scarcely control themselves. Indeed, as we shall see, they probably couldn't, and didn't. A compromise was reached involving settlements on children to be born of the union. On April 14, 1874, Randolph wrote to his mother: 'Things are now going as merrily as a marriage bell. I expect the settlements over tonight and they will be signed tomorrow.'[64]

They were. The next day, Wednesday, April 15, the Reverend Dr Edward Forbes united them during a ceremony in the British embassy in Paris – Paris, which had become civilized once more, having been Clara's suggestion. Present were the bride's parents, the groom's brother George, and Francis Knollys, private secretary to the Prince of Wales. Absent were the Duke and Duchess of Marlborough. This was an extraordinary snub, for Randolph was their favourite son. But they had made it quite clear that they had no intention of attending the service. Leonard had sent the duke a chilly note the previous Tuesday. ('I am very sorry you are not able to come over for the wedding. We had all hoped to have had the pleasure of seeing both yourself & the Duchess.') There is no record of a reply. But the inhabitants of Woodstock – which lies outside Blenheim's grounds and was the new constituency of Randolph Churchill, MP – were overjoyed. When the couple arrived there on Monday, May 25, the station was decorated with bunting and crowded with well-wishers. Cheering broke out as Jennie appeared carrying a lacy parasol mounted on a tortoiseshell rod trimmed with gold, a present from her father. ('Just the sort of bit of nonsense you like,' he had said.) The parasol was inadequate that day. A heavy rain was falling, split by bolts of lightning. Nevertheless, the throng, undaunted, unhitched the horses from the carriage which had been sent from the palace and pulled it through the narrow streets. They paused at the Bear Hotel, where the mayor spoke briefly, telling them that Woodstock 'cannot be unmindful of anything which concerns the happiness of the noble house of Churchill,' and wishing them many years of 'unclouded' joy. Then they were off again, through the triumphant arch dividing the town from the palace grounds. 'As we passed through the entrance archway and the lovely scenery burst upon me,' Jennie later wrote, 'Randolph said with pardonable pride, "This is the finest view in England." Looking at the lake, the bridge, the miles of magnificent park studded with old oaks . . . and the huge and stately palace, I confess I felt awed. But my American pride forbade the admission.'[65]

Another admission, which she preferred to keep from her husband's family, was that she was bearing their grandchild. Indeed, it is virtually certain that she had been pregnant for three months, and soon it would begin to show. Randolph had leased a house in Mayfair, at 48 Charles Street, off Berkeley Square; they planned to return to London and await the delivery there, explaining, when invited to Blenheim, that his political duties required his presence in town. But when Parliament rose, the duke and duchess would hear no excuses. Having accepted the marriage grimly, they wanted a long close look at their new daughter-in-law. As the weeks passed, they were pleasantly surprised. They found her charming. The increase in her girth appears to have been slight; the time for consulting the calendar hadn't yet arrived. Ironically, she no longer cared. Free of her cloying mother, she also felt free of her in-laws. By October she was her own woman, independent and headstrong. She would never change again. It would be characteristic of her that she would always do exactly as she pleased, flouting convention and tossing her head when met by disapproval. Expectant mothers – she was very heavy by now – were supposed to remain quiet and, so far as was possible, immobile. But she was her father's daughter; she had always been lively; she loathed inactivity, and gave it the back of her hand now. On Tuesday, November 24, she left the palace on a shooting party, stumbled in a field, and fell. Shaking off anxious hands, she said she was fine. On Saturday, as Randolph later wrote Clara, she took 'a rather imprudent & rough drive in a pony carriage.' That evening the annual St. Andrew's Ball was held in the palace. To the astonishment of everyone, including her husband, she appeared in a loose gown, holding a dance card. She was actually on the floor, pirouetting, when the pains started. Randolph wrote his mother-in-law: 'We tried to stop them, but it was no use.' It was, in fact, time to choose a birthplace. Her grandniece, Ann Leslie, afterwards described Jennie's search for one. Attended by servants and by Randolph's aunt Clementina, Lady Camden, she stumbled away from the party – which seems to have proceeded gaily without her – and lurched 'past the endless suite of drawing-rooms, through the library, "the longest room in England,"' towards her bedroom.[66]
    She didn't make it. She fainted and was carried into a little room just off Blenheim's great hall. Once it had belonged to the first duke's chaplain; tonight it was the ladies' cloakroom. Sprawling, she lay on velvet capes and

feather boas, which were deftly drawn from beneath her when the ball ended and the merry guests departed. It was a long night, with servants hurrying in and out with poultices and towels. The pains, Randolph told Clara, 'went on all Sunday.' He had telegraphed the London obstetrician Jennie had consulted, but, Sunday train schedules being what they were, the doctor couldn't arrive until Monday. Thus, the historic role of delivering England's greatest prime minister fell to Frederic Taylor, a Woodstock physician. 'The country Dr is . . . a clever man,' Randolph reported, '& the baby was safely born at 1.30 this morning after about 8 [sic] hrs labour. She suffered a good deal poor darling, but was vy plucky & had no chloroform. The boy is wonderfully pretty so everybody says dark eyes and hair & vy healthy considering its prematureness.'[67]

Premature? *The Times* bought it. At the head of its birth notices it reported: 'On the 30th Nov., at Blenheim Palace, the Lady Randolph Churchill, prematurely, of a son.' But no one believed it, not the patrician friends of the family, chuckling over the announcement, nor even the yeomen of Woodstock who, the *Oxford Times* reported, rang 'a merry peal on the church bells . . . in honour of the event.' Winston was full-term. It was generally believed that sometime the previous February, during the maddening negotiations over the marriage settlement, Jennie had eluded her mother, divested herself of the incredible layers of clothing then worn by young ladies, and received Randolph's seed. Indeed, it was thought the duke and duchess had known Jennie was pregnant at the time of the wedding; that was why they had boycotted it. Sly allusions to the circumstances of his birth followed Winston all his life. He enjoyed them. He would reply: 'Although present on the occasion, I have no clear recollection of the events leading up to it.'[68] Of course, it is possible that his parents have been slandered. Periods of gestation do vary. He may have been premature. It would have been just like him. He never could wait his turn.

ONE

HEADWATERS
1874 – 1895

Winston's early appearance, despite its implications, actually improved Jennie's relationship with her mother-in-law. Frances, Duchess of Marlborough – the 'Duchess Fanny' – was a formidable, domineering woman, at the rustle of whose skirt all Blenheim trembled. Had she elected to make an issue of Winston's conception, life would have been difficult for the young couple. She did the exact opposite. Jennie was now accepted as a full-fledged member of the family. Like many another grandmother the duchess had taken one adoring look at her grandson and capitulated. The infant was no beauty – he had an upturned nose, red curls, and what his daughter Sarah later called 'strange pallid eyes' – but Fanny thought him stunning, and she briskly set about seeing to his needs. Someone had to see to them. There had been no preparation for his advent: no diapers, no cradle, nothing. Fanny borrowed these from the wife of the village solicitor, whose baby was not expected until late in January, and dispatched orders for others from London. At the end of the first week Randolph wrote Clara: 'The *layette* has given great satisfaction but the little shawls with *capuchons* have not arrived. Jennie says they are much wanted, also the pillow cases have not come.'[1] By Christmas the crisis was past, however. On December 27 the duke's chaplain baptized the infant in the palace chapel, naming him Winston Leonard Spencer Churchill.

New Year's Day found the Randolph Churchills back in Charles Street. Ladies did not feed their babies then, and one of Fanny's first tasks had been to hire a wet nurse. The nurse was swiftly followed by Elizabeth Anne Everest. Plump, calm, vehemently Low Church, and proud of her origins in Kent, 'the garden of England,' as she called it, 'Mrs' Everest – she had no husband; nannies, like cooks, received the honorific as a courtesy – entered Winston's life when he was a month old. That was the custom. 'I had him from the month' was a nanny's equivalent of 'He is my own child.' Violet Asquith wrote: 'In his solitary childhood and unhappy school days Mrs Everest was his comforter, his strength and stay, his one source of unfailing human understanding. She was the fireside at which he dried his tears and warmed his heart. She was the night light by his bed. She was security.' Except at bedtime, when mother appeared for good-night kisses, nurseries, like kitchens, were rarely visited by upper-class parents then. Like popes granting audiences, they received their children at appointed times, when the small ones, scrubbed and suitably dressed, presented themselves for inspection while their nannies reported on their deportment. Randolph and Jennie appear to have omitted even these token meetings. They had no time for them.

Every hour appears to have been devoted to the pursuit of pleasure. Randolph all but abandoned politics; in two years he delivered just two speeches in Parliament. Thirty years afterwards Jennie wrote in *The Century:* 'We seemed to live in a whirl of gaieties and excitement. Many were the delightful balls I went to, which, unlike those of the present day, lasted till five o'clock in the morning.' The Churchills were also lavish hosts. In Winston's words, 'They continued their gay life on a somewhat more generous scale than their income warranted. Fortified by an excellent French cook, they entertained with discrimination. The Prince of Wales, who from the beginning had shown them much kindness, dined sometimes with them.'[2]

In London, His Royal Highness, the Prince of Wales, was the key to social success. Since the Queen had withdrawn from fashionable gatherings after her husband's death, His Royal Highness and Alexandra, Princess of Wales, had assumed the social duties of royalty. Great prestige therefore accompanied acceptance into HRH's entourage. The 'Marlborough House Set,' to which the Randolph Churchills belonged, was simply a clique of HRH's friends and their wives or, in several instances, HRH's mistresses and their husbands. In their dissipation of leisure they seem to have been both vigorous and inane. They studied the finer points of the Venetian quadrille, the Van Dyke quadrille, and – Jennie's favourite – the cancan. At fancy balls, prolonged discussions examined the merits of holding one's partner's hand high, in the polonaise fashion. In Mayfair the Churchills gave grand dinners, hired expensive orchestras, spent fifteen pounds on masked-ball costumes, journeyed to Hurlingham to watch the pigeon shooting, and attended the Derby and races at Goodwood and Ascot. Later Jennie would remember how dinners, balls, and parties succeeded one another without intermission, and 'how we all laughed at M. de Soveral, because he looked like a blue monkey and was always called the blue monkey,' and laughed again when 'the Grand Duke poured the chocolate sauce over his head,' and applauded HRH's spectacular attire: 'The doublet and cloak were of light maroon satin embroidered in gold, the large black felt hat . . . had a white feather, and the dress was completed with loose buff boots, steel spurs, and a long sword. On the left shoulder was a diamond star, and the Prince wore the Order of the Garter hanging from a blue riband round his neck. Fair cavalier curls flowing down his shoulder somewhat distinguished H.R.H. [and] were the finishing touch to a very splendid and perfect costume.' In those giddy years, Jennie later recalled, they were confronted by only one serious misfortune: 'it was no less than the sudden illness of the greatest hairdresser of his day.'[3]

But a genuine crisis loomed in 1876. What HRH gave, HRH could take away. It was in his power to consign any member of his set to social oblivion. It happened to the Churchills. In his biography of his father, Winston wrote: 'Engaging in his brother's quarrels with fierce and reckless partisanship, Lord Randolph incurred the displeasure of a great personage . . . London became odious to him.'[4] Or vice versa. The fact is that Randolph had acted badly, as a consequence of his brother George's having acted badly, which was a result of

Lady Aylesford's having acted badly and the Prince of Wales, impetuously. All of them had broken the thin membrane of contrived deceit which permitted adultery and civility to coexist. Since the details became public in subsequent divorce proceedings, it is possible to reconstruct the chain of events which led to the Churchills' exile and meant that Winston's first childhood memories would be of Dublin.

On October 11, 1875, when Lord Heneage, Earl of Aylesford, left England with the Prince of Wales to hunt in India, his wife, Edith, Countess of Aylesford, moved to Packingham, the family seat, with their two daughters. George Churchill was living in a nearby inn. As heir to the dukedom, George bore the title Marquess of Blandford and lived more or less independently. Each evening he entered an unused wing of the hall, using a key which, in the words of the divorce court, he 'had obtained . . . with the knowledge and sanction of Lady Aylesford, with whom he passed many nights.' There was nothing indiscreet here. As a marquess, George was a suitable lover for a lonely countess. Unfortunately, the two of them couldn't leave it at that. In February they decided to leave the children with Edith's mother-in-law and elope. Edith imprudently wrote her husband, telling him this, and he hurried home from India. Meanwhile, the Duke of Marlborough sent one of his sons-in-law to persuade his son to abandon the impossible affair. The emissary reported: 'I think that any steps you may take to influence Blandford to give up Lady Aylesford would be for the present at any rate entirely thrown away.'[5]

Edith's brother then challenged George to a duel, and that brought Randolph, as George's brother, into the drama. Randolph told all interested parties that his brother could be called out by Lord Aylesford and no one else. Then he hired private detectives to watch both George and his challenger, 'to prevent,' he said, 'a breach of the peace.' Had he stopped there, his social position would have remained intact. But Randolph discovered that George's predecessors in Edith's bed included none other than the Prince of Wales. The breakdown in decorum was complete; Edith had saved HRH's love letters, which she turned over to Randolph. Incredibly, Randolph then called upon Alexandra, Princess of Wales, asking her to use her influence with the prince and see to it that Lord Aylesford cancelled plans to divorce his erring wife. Whether he showed her the love letters is unknown, but he did tell friends about them, boasting that 'I have the Crown of England in my pocket.' Victoria heard of this; indignant, she wrote her son: 'What a dreadful disgraceful business!' But her anger was a moonshadow on that of the prince. Enraged, HRH arrived home and wrote the Earl of Beaconsfield – Disraeli – that 'Ld B. and Ld R.C.' were spreading lies about him and that 'it is a pity that there is no desert island to which these young gentlemen (?) could be banished.' He then settled for the next best thing. Lord Blandford and Lord Randolph Churchill, he announced, were in Coventry. Not only would he refuse to see them; he would not enter the home of anyone who had entertained them. Socially they had ceased to exist. Jennie was grief-stricken. She wrote her husband: *C'est trop fort* – my own darling dear Randolph I shd give anything to have you here tonight I feel so wretchedly.' As for Randolph, Winston wrote, 'The fashionable world no longer smiled. Powerful enemies were anxious to humiliate him. His own sensitiveness and pride magnified every coldness into an affront. . . . A nature originally genial and gay contracted a stern and bitter quality, a harsh contempt for what is called "Society," and an abiding antagonism to rank and authority.'[6]

Even Randolph realized that he had gone too far, however. He turned the letters over to a royal emissary, Lord Hartington, later Duke of Devonshire. Hartington – who himself had been sleeping with another duke's duchess for thirty years – burned them in Randolph's presence. But HRH was unappeased. To untangle the mess, he sent another letter to Disraeli, the wisest man in the kingdom, begging his advice. Dizzy told Duchess Fanny, 'My dear Lady, there's but one way: make your husband take the Lord Lieutenancy of Ireland and take Lord Randolph with him. It will put an end to it all.' Randolph, he said, could leave Parliament to serve as his father's unpaid secretary. At first the duke said no. He was loath to move from Blenheim to Dublin, which he regarded as a primitive outpost of Empire, and an expensive one at that, but he had never been able to deny Disraeli anything. As Winston once said, 'He always did whatever Lord Beaconsfield told him to do.' On July 22 he wrote Beaconsfield from his town house in St. James's Square: 'The acceptance of such a high office, is as you say a matter of much moment, and the change, I may almost say the sacrifice of one's ordinary habits and engagements in England is not an insignificant one, but as you have again done me the honour to repeat the offer you previously made, I should not feel it my duty on the present occasion to stand aloof, and I shall be therefore happy to place myself at the disposal of the Queen's service.'[7]

That settled it. On a bitter morning the following winter the duke, Fanny, Randolph, Jennie, and various other relatives – *The Times* incorrectly identified the youngest of them as 'Lord Winston Spencer Churchill' – left London in a private saloon carriage attached to the Irish Mail. At Holyhead they boarded the mail steamer *Connaught* and crossed to Kingstown, where a delegation greeted them and led them to a special train. In Dublin the duke was greeted by a salute of twenty-one guns, invested with the Collar and Insignia of the Order of Saint Patrick, and installed in the Vice Regal Lodge. The Randolph Churchills moved into the Little Lodge nearby. Back in London the bad Aylesfords left England forever. Lord Aylesford sailed off to America, bought twenty-seven thousand acres at Big Spring, Texas, and flourished as a dude rancher until his death, at thirty-five, of cirrhosis of the liver. As Miss Edith Williams – her divorce had gone through – Lady Aylesford emigrated to Paris, where she bore George's child. She had wanted to marry him, but he had grown weary of her, and she died an unwed mother.

Volatile Ireland was enjoying one of its periods of quiescence. The problems were there, and Randolph, for whom these were maturing years, began a serious study of the social unrest. Jennie didn't. During her three years there it is doubtful that she saw a typical Irishman, except when trampling potato fields beneath the hooves of her favourite stallion. The Dublin she beheld was a creation of the Anglo-Irish aristocracy. To her surprise and delight, she found it very like Mayfair: balls, theatres, dinner parties every evening, amusing friends to be made, and splendid steeplechasing, point-to-points, and foxhunting. Winston's picture of her in Ireland was 'in a riding habit, fitting like a skin and often beautifully spotted with mud. She and my father hunted continually on their large horses; and sometimes there were great scares because one or other did not come back for many hours after they were expected.'[8]

His mother was only in her early twenties, approaching the height of her beauty. Viscount D'Abernon, seeing her for the first time in the Vice Regal Lodge, wrote that although the duke sat at one end of the room on a dais, 'eyes were turned not on him or on his consort, but on a dark, lithe figure, standing somewhat apart and appearing to be of another texture to those around her, radiant, translucent, intense. A diamond star in her hair, her favourite ornament – its lustre dimmed by the flashing glory of her eyes. More of the panther than of the woman in her look, but with a cultivated intelligence unknown to the jungle.' Later Margot Asquith met her at a racecourse and thought: 'She had a forehead like a panther's and great wild eyes that looked through you.' Pantherlike women do not project maternal images, and two notes she wrote Randolph when he was absent from Dublin reinforce the impression that she had grown no closer to her son. In the first she reported: 'Winston is flourishing tho' rather X the last 2 days more teeth I think. Everest has been bothering me about some clothes for him saying that it was quite a disgrace how few things he has & how shabby at that.' In the second she wrote: 'Winston has just been with me – such a darling he is – "I can't have my Mama go – & if she does I will run after the train & jump in" he said to me. I have told Everest to take him out for a drive tomorrow if it is fine – as it is better the stables shd have a little work.'[9]

The shabby clothes are insignificant, except in revealing what came first for Jennie; she wore a diamond in her hair but didn't see to it that her son was dressed properly. But childish fears of being abandoned are easily aroused. Staying away on horseback until the entire household is fearful of an accident, and telling a little boy that you are about to leave on a train – information he does not need – are bound to unsettle him and leave scars afterwards. It is in this context that his relationship with his nanny assumed such importance. Her role in his childhood cannot be overemphasized. She was the dearest figure in his life until he was twenty; her picture hung in his bedroom until he died. He wrote: 'Mrs Everest it was who looked after me and tended all my wants. It was to her I poured out my many troubles.' After reading Gibbon's memoirs he wrote: 'When I read his reference to his old nurse: "If there be any, as I trust there are some, who rejoice that I live, to that dear and excellent woman their gratitude is due," I thought of Mrs Everest; and it shall be her epitaph.' An even more revealing tribute appeared in his second book, the novel *Savrola*. He wrote of the hero's nanny:

She had nursed him from his birth up with a devotion and care which knew no break. It is a strange thing, the love of these women. Perhaps it is the only disinterested affection in the world. The mother loves her child; that is maternal nature. The youth loves his sweetheart; that, too, may be explained. The dog loves his master, he feeds him; a man loves his friend, he has stood by him perhaps at doubtful moments. In all these are reasons; but the love of a foster-mother appears absolutely irrational.[10]

Why irrational? Childless women have maternal feelings, too; surely it is understandable that they should lavish affection on other women's children entrusted to them. Anthony Storr comments upon this passage: 'Churchill is showing surprise at being loved, as if he had never felt he was entitled to it.' This is part of the depressive syndrome. Most infants are loved for themselves; they accept that love as they accept food and warmth. But in Winston's case, as his son later observed, 'The neglect and lack of interest in him shown by his parents were remarkable, even judged by the standards of late Victorian and Edwardian days.' That anyone should love him became a source of wonder. The uncritical devotion of 'Woom' (derived from an early attempt to say 'woman') was inadequate. He could hardly have failed to sense that the woman was a servant. Affection from others had to be earned; eventually he would win it by doing great things. At the same time – and this would cripple his schooling – the deprivation of parental attachment bred resentment of authority. One might expect that his mother and father, the guilty parties, would be the targets of his hostility. Not so. The deprived child cherishes the little attention his parents do give him; he cannot risk losing it. Moreover, he blames himself for his plight. Needing outlets for his own welling adoration, he enshrines his parents instead, creating images of them as he wishes they were, and the less he sees of them, the easier that transformation becomes. By this devious process Lord Randolph became Winston's hero, and his mother, as he wrote, 'always seemed to me a fairy princess: a radiant being possessed of limitless riches and power.' His resentment had to be directed elsewhere. Therefore he became in his own words, 'a troublesome boy.' His mother called him 'a most difficult child to manage.' Towards the end of their years in Ireland Jennie engaged a governess for him. He couldn't stand her. He kicked, he screamed, he hid. There is a story that one day a parlourmaid was summoned to the Little Lodge room where he was having his lessons. The maid asked the governess why she had rung. Winston said: '*I* rang. Take Miss Hutchinson away. She is very cross.'[11]

That was precocious. He was just approaching the age of assertiveness, with consequences which would not be realized until he was ready for boarding school. Most of his Irish memories were passive. There was the mist and the rain and the red-coated British soldiers and the breathtaking emerald greenery. There was the time in Phoenix Park when he ran away into the woods, or what he thought were woods; actually, he had just crept under some shrubbery. Once Woom organized an expedition to a pantomime show. When they arrived at the Theatre Royal it had burned down; the mournful manager said all he had left was the key to the front door. Already insatiably curious, Winston demanded to see the key and was awarded a black look. Another day the duke unveiled a statue of Lord Gough, and his grandson would remember 'a great black crowd, scarlet soldiers on horseback, strings pulling away a brown shiny sheet, the old Duke, the formidable grandpapa, talking loudly to the crowd. I even recall a phrase he used: "And with a withering volley he shattered the enemy's line." '* Woom dressed him in a sailor suit and took him to a photographer. Freckled, redheaded, and pug-nosed, the likeness gives the impression of violent motion suddenly arrested, and in fact he was already hyperactive; from the time he had learned to talk his lips had been moving almost incessantly. Woom, the nanny-cum-chauvinist, kept him quiet with chilly tales about the 'wicked Fenians.' They were not wholly fanciful. The ancestors of the Irish Republican Army were active, and they were a murderous gang; two years after the duke's successor arrived in Dublin, his under secretary and a companion were hacked to death with long surgical knives within sight and hearing of the Vice Regal Lodge. Mrs Everest had good reason to be wary, and she was. One afternoon when Winston was riding a donkey beside her she saw some soldiers in the distance and mistook them for Irish rebels; she screamed and frightened the donkey, which reared up, unseating its young mount. Winston recalled: 'I was thrown off and had concussion of the brain. This was my first introduction to Irish politics.'[12]

In the early 1880s the Churchills' banishment ended. Randolph had laid low when visiting in London, but he had never really abandoned politics; three years earlier he had slipped across the Irish Sea and spoken to his Woodstock constituency, attacking Disraeli's lacklustre Irish policy. ('The only excuse I can find for Randolph,' his mortified father had written a Tory leader, 'is that he must either be mad or have been singularly affected with local champagne or claret.') Now he ran for Parliament again in the family borough and was elected by 60 votes – something of a triumph, for there were only 1,071 voters in the borough, compared with today's typical constituency of 50,000. Moreover, he was bucking the tide; Gladstone had overthrown Disraeli and would be prime minister for the next five years. That meant a new viceroy in Dublin. Back in London, Randolph moved his small family into a new house at 29 St. James's Place, next door to Sir Stafford Northcote, the leader of the Conservative opposition in the House, and opened negotiations for his re-entry into the Prince of Wales's favour. Victoria approved. She had already told her son that she could not continue to exclude Randolph from court festivities. Sir Stafford approached Disraeli and wrote in his diary: 'I asked him whether Randolph Churchill was forgiven yet in high quarters. He said he was all right as far as the Queen was concerned, but that the Prince of

---

* That was close. The actual line was: 'And with a crashing volley the enemy was fiercely beaten back.' Winston was five years old at the time. Actually, his version is an improvement on the original.

Wales had not yet made it up with him.' Four years were to pass before HRH and Randolph sat at table together, at a dinner given by Sir Henry James, MP (the future Lord James of Hereford), in March 1884. Afterwards the prince sent word to Sir Henry that 'R. Churchill's manner was *just* what it ought to have been.' Yet all bygones were not to be bygones. *Vanity Fair* reported the 'full and formal reconciliation' between the two but added: 'It is understood, however, that while Lord Randolph feels much satisfaction at being again on friendly terms with the Heir-Apparent, he does not propose to become intimate with all the Prince's friends.' Randolph would never forgive those Tories who had turned their backs when HRH had ostracized him. He would remain a member of the Conservative party, but would be a rebel within it. After his death his son would step into the same role. Thus, in a sense, one source of Winston's rebellious stand against Neville Chamberlain in the 1930s lay in Lady Aylesford's bed.[13]

Randolph's brief but spectacular political career was just beginning when Winston reached the age of full awareness, first at St. James's Place, then at Beech Lodge in Wimbledon after Randolph and Jennie had toured the United States, and, finally, at 2 Connaught Place, a block from Hyde Park and Marble Arch and the first house in Mayfair to be equipped with electricity. All three homes had large nursery wings; Winston lost himself in fantasy there, playing with his steam engine, his magic lantern, and his toy soldiers. Already he had more than a thousand lead soldiers. Year by year the collection would grow. It is not clear who first gave them to him – Randolph, perhaps, or perhaps Mrs Everest, who was provided with cash to be used at her discretion – but relatives learned that, when in doubt about presents, a gift of tiny dragoons or lancers would be prized by him. He now had a brother, or half-brother, Jack. Six years separated them, however, and there appears to have been no attempt to find playmates for Winston. Woom took him to pantomimes, Drury Lane, Madame Tussaud's, and for walks in the park. But mostly he was alone. He loved it. The time flew – 'It is the brightest hours,' he wrote of these years, 'that flash away the fastest.'[14]

In *Cradles of Eminence*, their study of childhood patterns found in the lives of men who later distinguished themselves, Victor Goertzel and Mildred George Goertzel found that Winston's family provided 'multiple examples of the qualities in parents and other relatives which seem to be related to the production of an eminent man. There was respect for learning, an experimental attitude, failure-proneness, a plenitude of opinionated relatives, and turbulence in the family life as a result of the erratic behaviour of his irrepressible uncle and father. During the time that Winston was thought dull, he was, like other boys, evidencing qualities which presaged ability.' But that was hindsight. It was no consolation to Woom. She worried about her charge. When not lost in thought, he was in constant motion, jumping up and down, leaping from chair to chair, rushing about, and falling and hurting himself. He seemed to have no sense of personal safety. His love of martial poetry was obsessive. He had a speech defect, and one miserable cold after another. But his interest in politics was, for a boy his age, decidedly precocious. When Disraeli sickened in March 1881 and died six weeks later, Winston could talk of nothing else. He later recalled: 'I followed his illness from day to day because everyone said what a loss he would be to his country.'[15] In one way, his anxiety for Disraeli was a boon to Woom. It gave him an incentive to read. She had given Winston a book, *Reading Without Tears*. Soon he was forming letters. His first letter, undated, was to his mother:

My dear mama bathe in the
I am so glad sea to day.
you are coming love to papa
to see us I had your loving
such a nice winston

His second, also to her, was written on January 4, 1882, at Blenheim, where he was visiting his grandmother:

My dear Mamma
I hope you are quite
well I thank you
very very much
for the beautiful
presents those
Soldiers and you my love
Flags and Castle and a great
they are so nice many kisses
it was so kind Your loving
of you and dear Winston
Papa I send

101

Still at Blenheim – Jennie was in a frenzy of preparation for the Season – he learned on March 20 that his father was afflicted with a serious infection. He wrote another note: 'My dear Papa, I hope you are getting better. I am enjoying myself very much. I find a lot of primroses every day. I bought a basket to put them in. I saw three little Indian children on Saturday, who came to see the house. Best love to you and dear Mamma. I am, Yr loving son Winston.' Very likely Woom helped guide his hand in these first attempts; his subsequent childhood correspondence, scrawled while he was away from her, is peppered with misspellings. But writing already came easily to him; his fluency would grow year by year, undiscouraged by the infrequency of replies from his parents. Arithmetic was another matter. His struggles with it seemed hopeless, and led to his only real battle with his nurse. He remembered afterwards: 'Letters after all had only got to be known, and when they stood together in a certain way one recognized their formation and that it meant a certain sound. But the figures were tied into all sorts of tangles and did things to one another which it was extremely difficult to forecast with complete accuracy. You had to say what they did each time they were tied up together. It was not any use being "nearly right." In some cases these figures got into debt with one another: you had to borrow one or carry one, and afterwards you had to pay back the one you borrowed.' He tried, he tried again, and again; he gave up, threw down his pad and paper and stamped on them. Patiently Woom explained. Impatiently he shook his head. He fled; she pursued him. He threatened to attack her with his toy soldiers. She wasn't intimidated by that, but she did surrender when he shouted that unless she quit he would bow down and worship graven images. In time his grasp of numbers improved, yet he never fully mastered them, as England would learn to its sorrow when he became chancellor of the Exchequer.[16]

He was seven years old and his parents decided it was time he left home. On November 3, 1882, five weeks after the start of the autumn term, he was enrolled as a boarder at St George's School near Ascot, a place famous for its women and horses. St George's was an expensive school – fifty-two pounds for the first month, payable in advance – which prepared boys for Eton. Winston wept when told he must go. 'I had been so happy in my nursery,' he wrote later; '. . . now it was to be all lessons.' Precisely how he travelled there is unclear. Jennie rode with him to Paddington Station in Randolph's private hansom, but on the train platform they parted; she gave him three half crowns and sent him on alone. He lost the coins, panicked, found them, and arrived trembling. It was late afternoon, and dark. A master led him to a desk, handed him a thin, brown-green Latin grammar, told him to memorize the declension of *mensa*, and departed. When the teacher returned, Winston reeled off a perfect recitation. The man seemed satisfied, and Winston, encouraged, asked, 'What does it mean, sir?' He was told, *'Mensa* means a table.' Winston pointed out that according to the book, one of the forms would then be translated as 'O table.' He asked why. The master explained that this was the vocative case, that 'you would use that in addressing a table.' Astonished, the boy blurted out: 'But I never do.' The master snapped: 'If you are impertinent, you will be punished, and punished, let me tell you, very severely.'[17]

That was the quintessential St George's, the school in microcosm. Churchill would remember 'how I hated this school, and what a life of anxiety I lived there for more than two years. I made very little progress at my lessons, and none at all at games. I counted the days and the hours to the end of every term, when I should return home from this hateful servitude and range my soldiers in line of battle on the nursery floor.' However, he did not tell his parents that. At the end of his first month there he wrote his father, 'I am very happy at [s]chool. You will be very plesed to hear I spent a very happy birthday,' and the same day he wrote Jennie, 'I hope you are quite well. I am very happy at school.' But this is unsurprising. Boarding-school boys who feel wretched and badly treated seldom mention it in letters home. They think the flaw is in them, and they hide it. He doubtless assumed that his father would have snorted had he complained, and he was probably right. Like all Victorian children of his class, he had been taught to keep a stiff upper lip, so he did. Now and then he hinted at his immense yearning to quit St George's. In March he wrote: '30 days [sic] more and the *Holidays* will be *Here*.' Then; 'Only 18 more days.' And then, on the eve of his next vacation: 'I am comeinge home *In a month*.' He dragged out the end of his letters, as though he could not bear to break this frail tie with his family:[18]

. . .W. . .I. . .T. . .H
love & kisses
I
Remain
your
loveing
Son
W.L.S. Churchill

Mostly he wrote of trivia. 'We went to hampton cort palace.' 'We went to see the picture gallry.' 'Give my love to my ants.' He had caught another cold, but wrote, 'My cough is nearly well now.' Still another cold followed six

103

months later; it hung on and on before he could report: 'I am all wright and well. I have been allowed to go back into my own room.' It is doubtful that his mother had known he had a room. Certainly she didn't know what it looked like. She never came. And he mourned her absence. That is the one thread that runs through his pathetic little correspondence: he desperately wanted visitors. 'It was so kind of you to let Everest come,' he wrote in the summer of 1883, but Woom, and then Woom and Jack, seem to have been the only ones who came. Ascot was a short hansom ride from Mayfair – trains from Paddington were even quicker – but neither Jennie nor Randolph found the trip convenient. So his pathetic pleas were unanswered. He begged his mother to 'come and see me soon,' to 'Come & see me soon dear Mamma.' He wrote, 'I am wondering when you are coming to see me?' and, 'You must send somebody to see me.' The least she could have done was reply. She seldom did. On June 8, 1884, when he was nine, his accumulating resentment flared briefly: 'It is very unkind of you not to write to me before this, I have only had one letter from you this term.' The back of one of his notes tells us something about her priorities. On it are scribbled lists of guests for two dinner parties. She had time to entertain 'Sir R. Peel,' 'Consuelo,' 'Duke of Portland,' 'Ld Marcus,' and sixteen others, but she couldn't spare a few minutes to slake her small son's thirst for a line or two of love. She planned feasts for her friends. Winston asked for bread, and she gave him a stone.[19]

Randolph, surprisingly, did send him a gift that year. It was a copy of *Treasure Island*. Winston devoured it and promised to be worthy of it: 'I will try to be a good boy.' Most boys at St George's tried to be good, though, and without incentives from home. The penalties for failure were dire. Since the Churchills were not the only influential family to be gulled into sending their son there, we know a good deal about the school. It was an upper-class version of Dotheboys Hall in *Nicholas Nickleby*. The regimen was fierce: eight hours a day of lessons, followed by football and cricket. There was fagging, and there were floggings almost every day, the chief whipper being the Reverend H. W. Sneyd-Kynnersley, a sadistic headmaster who would lay as many as twenty strokes of birch on a boy's bare rump. Given Winston's extremely sensitive skin, this must have been excruciating. Yet he became, and remained, the school's chief rebel. He excelled in history, but refused to learn Latin verse he did not understand; in his words, 'Where my reason, imagination or interest were not engaged, I would not or I could not learn.' Pitted against authority for the first time in his life, he defied it, refused to curry favour, and was, as a consequence, beaten until he shrieked. He later wrote: 'My teachers saw me at once backward and precocious, reading books beyond my years and yet at the bottom of the Form. They were offended. They had large resources of compulsion at their disposal, but I was stubborn.'[20]

His rebelliousness did not arise from the dignified resolution of a mature man standing on principle. Principles were indeed at stake, but he couldn't have known that. He was less than ten years old. His behaviour was intuitive. To others he simply seemed a disobedient, mischievous little boy. Maurice

Baring, who entered St George's shortly after Winston left it, wrote: 'Dreadful legends were told about Winston Churchill, who had been taken away from the school. His naughtiness appeared to have surpassed anything. He had been flogged for taking sugar from the pantry, and so far from being penitent, he had taken the Headmaster's sacred straw hat from where it hung over the door and kicked it to pieces. His sojourn at this school had been one long feud with authority.' His masters and even his schoolmates, with the conformity of youth, were appalled. Baring said: 'The boys did not seem to sympathise with him. Their point of view was conventional and priggish.'[21]

One afternoon Sir Henry Drummond Wolff, a political ally of Randolph's and a founder of the Tory Primrose League, called at Connaught Place and asked Jack if he was good. Jack said, 'Yes, but brother is teaching me to be naughty.' Actually, Jack would never be naughty. Though he was born of the same mother and shared the same family life, his development was the opposite of Winston's. He resisted nothing, accepted what he was given, turned inward, and grew up to be an inoffensive man from whom little was expected or given. Boys like Jack create no difficulties for their parents. He was the kind of son Jennie wanted, and the contrast with his sibling pained her. As early as December 26, 1882, she wrote Randolph at Monte Carlo – the familiar Christmas rites, so beloved by other Victorians, seem never to have been celebrated at Connaught Place – 'As to Winston's improvement I am sorry to say I see none. Perhaps there has not been enough time. He can read very well, but that is all, and the first two days he came home he was terribly slangy and loud. Altogether I am disappointed.' Sneyd-Kynnersley, she said, had assured her that the masters intended 'to be more strict with him.' She meant to try her own hand anyhow; 'it appears that he is afraid of me.' That was an odd admission from a mother, but perhaps it was true; a fearsome mother was at any rate preferable to maternal indifference. But she failed. Nothing intimidated him, certainly not St George's. One riffles through his report cards there with mounting rage and amazement. It seems to have occurred to no one that a fresh approach might improve the behaviour of this very difficult child. In his first accounting to Jennie the headmaster noted that Winston 'has been *very* naughty.' Then: 'He is still troublesome.' Next: 'He is, I hope, *beginning* to realize that school means work and discipline.' And then: 'He is rather greedy at meals' – a peculiar description of a youthful appetite. After that, according to Sneyd-Kynnersley's comments, it was all downhill. His conduct was 'very bad'; he was 'a constant trouble to everybody and is always in some scrape or other'; he could not 'be trusted to behave himself anywhere'; he had 'no ambition'; he gave 'a great deal of trouble.' There is a sense of impending crisis in all this, and it crystallized when Winston, flayed beyond endurance, fled home to Mrs Everest. Woom undressed him and recoiled when she saw his back and bottom crisscrossed with welts. She summoned Jennie, and the sight of his wounds told her what he, in the mute, tortuous language of a child, had been trying to tell her for two years. She immediately removed him from St. George's and entered him in a small school run by two maiden sisters in Brunswick Road, Brighton. It is unclear what, if anything, passed between her and the headmaster. Very likely Randolph knew nothing of the incident; his own letters show that he did not even know how old Winston was. But it is satisfying to report that two years later Mr Sneyd-Kynnersley, aged thirty-eight, dropped dead of a heart attack.[22]

Brighton, with its sea air, chalybeate springs, colourful architecture, and general atmosphere of freedom, was a distinct improvement on St. George's, but Winston continued to play the imp. Any form of discipline still incensed him. The word *permissiveness* cannot be found in any dictionary of the time; as a concept it did not exist. Even if it had, Kate and Charlotte Thomson would have condemned it. They expected docility from their wards, and the record shows that they did not get it from their new boy; in his first term, when he passed his tenth birthday, his conduct was ranked twenty-sixth in a class of thirty-two. By the next term he was at the bottom, and there he remained. Charlotte Thomson wrote Jennie in her first report that 'frequent absence from the schoolroom made competition with other boys very difficult.' His dancing teacher, Vera Moore, later depicted him as 'a small, red-haired pupil, the naughtiest boy in the class; I used to think he was the naughtiest small boy in the world.' Even the indulgent Duchess Fanny, in whose Grosvenor Square home he spent his holidays from time to time, wrote to Randolph: 'Winston is going back to school today. Entre nous I do not feel very sorry for he certainly is a handful.'[23]

Yet the Thomson sisters treated him with kindness and understanding, and he began to respond. At the end of his second term they noted 'very satisfactory progress,' and, after the third, 'very marked progress.' He was first in his classics class and near the top in English, French, and Scripture knowledge. He began to enjoy school: 'We are learning Paradise Lost for Elocution, it is very nice.' He was 'getting on capitally in Euclid. I and another boy are top of the school in it we have got up to the XXX Proposition.' In French they were rehearsing 'Molière's *"Médecin Malgré lui."* I take the part of "Martine." ' In Greek, he wrote, 'I have at last begun the verbs in " " of which the first is " " ' He proudly wrote his mother: 'I have got two prizes one for English Subjects & one for Scripture.' He even wrote Jack, aged six: 'When I come home I must try and teach you the rudiments of Latin.' In later life he recalled: 'At this school I was allowed to learn things which interested me: French, History, lots of Poetry by heart, and above all Riding and Swimming. The impressions of those years make a pleasant picture in my mind, in strong contrast to my earlier schoolday memories.'[24]

Collecting stamps, autographs, and goldfish, he began to share the interests of the other boys. He even tried sports – 'We had a game of Cricket this afternoon, I hit a twoer, as the expression goes, my first runs this year' – though that didn't last long. He was now reading every newspaper he could find, poring over accounts of the Belgian conquest of the Congo, the Haymarket riot in Chicago, the death of Chinese Gordon, the erecting of the Statue of Liberty, and, in Germany, Gottlieb Daimler's invention of the first practical automobile. (These years also saw the founding of the Fabian Society and the Indian National Congress, both of which were to play major roles in his life, but London editors had dismissed them as insignificant.) In the spring of 1885 he was aroused by the uproar in Paris over whether or not Victor Hugo should receive a Christian burial and wrote his mother: 'Will you send me the paper with Victor Hugo's funeral in it?' *King Solomon's Mines,* published during his first year in Brighton, held him mesmerized. He begged Jennie to send him everything Rider Haggard wrote, and was transported when her elder sister Leonie, who knew the author, took the boy out of school to meet him. Afterwards he wrote Haggard: 'Thank you so much for sending me *Allan Quartermain*; it was so good of you. I like *A.Q.* better than *King Solomon's Mines;* it is more amusing. I hope you will write a good many more books.'[25]

The visit with Haggard, though unusual, was not unique; teachers and relatives were taking the restless boy off the school grounds on frequent trips. He saw what he described as 'a Play called "Pinafore" ' with Leonie's daughter Olive, and, with Randolph's sister Cornelia, heard Samuel Brandram recite *Twelfth Night.* Then came electrifying news. 'Buffalo Bill,' he wrote home, was bringing his show to London; Bill was a friend of Clarita Jerome's husband, Moreton Frewen, who owned a Montana ranch. Queen Victoria's Golden Jubilee was to be celebrated the Monday after that weekend, and Winston was determined to see both of them. He wanted to come home to Connaught Place on Saturday and stay until Wednesday. The Thomsons discouraged him, explaining that there would be no place for him in Westminster Abbey and his mother would be far too busy to look after him. Predictably, Jennie agreed with the sisters; she rejected his first appeal. He wouldn't give up: 'I can think of nothing else but Jubilee. Uncertainty is at all times perplexing write to me by return post please!!! I love you so much dear Mummy and I know you love me too much to disappoint me. Do write to tell me what you intend to do. I must come home, I feel I must . . . Please, as you love me, do as I have begged you.' Before she could reply, he wrote again: 'Miss Thomson says that she will let me go if you write to ask for me. For my sake write before it is too late. Write to Miss Thomson by return post please!!!' In the end, his mother relented. A seat for him in the abbey was in fact out of the question – though Jennie had a good one – but he did see Buffalo Bill and all the rest. Thus it was that Winston Churchill stood among the cheering throngs on June 21, 1887, as the old Queen rode by, crowned by a coronet-shaped bonnet of lace studded with diamonds, her hands folded, her head bowed, her cheeks glistening with tears. Afterwards Jennie and the Prince of Wales took him for a ride on the royal yacht, where he met the future King George V. It would be pleasant to report that his conduct was exceptional. It wasn't. He was loud, he stunted, he showed off. Back in Brighton he apologized to his mortified mother: 'I hope you will soon forget my bad behaviour

. . . and not . . . make it alter . . . my summer Holidays.'[26]

He feared a summer tutor. One tutor had spoiled a seaside holiday at Cromer, then as now a watering place on the North Sea coast; Winston had complained that she was 'very unkind, so strict and stiff, I can't enjoy myself at all.' But the reports of improvements in Brighton had lifted that threat. He was free to play, and in his choice of games we see the growth of his combative instincts. Once he talked Woom into taking him and his cousins to the Tower of London, where he delivered, with great relish, a lecture on medieval tortures. Pencil sketches of cannon and soldiers adorned the margins of his letters. His cousin Clare Frewen recalled in her memoirs that when the Churchills rented a summer house in Banstead, Winston erected a log fort with the help of the gardener's children, dug a moat around it, and, with Jack's help, built a drawbridge that could be raised and lowered. Then, she said, the children were divided into two rival groups and 'the fort was stormed. I was hurriedly removed from the scene of the action as mud and stones began to fly with effect. But the incident impressed me and Winston became a very important person in my estimation.' Shane Leslie, Leonie's son, remembered that 'we thought he was wonderful, because he was always leading us into danger.' There were the fort struggles, fights with the village children, and raids on the nests of predatory birds. In Connaught Place he had converted the entire nursery into a battlefield. According to Clare Frewen, 'His playroom contained from one end to the other a plank table on trestles, upon which were thousands of lead soldiers arrayed for battle. He organized wars. The lead battalions were manoeuvred into action, peas and pebbles committed great casualties, forts were stormed, cavalry charged, bridges were destroyed. . . . Altogether it was a most impressive show, and played with an interest that was no ordinary child game.' It impressed Lord Randolph. One day he put his head in the door and studied the intricate formations. He asked his son, then in his early teens, if he would like to enter the army. In Winston's words: 'I thought it would be splendid to command an Army, so I said "Yes" at once: and immediately I was taken at my word. For years I thought my father with his experience and flair had discerned in me the qualities of military genius. But I was told later that he had only come to the conclusion that I was not clever enough to go to the Bar.'[27]

On such slender evidence was so weighty a verdict reached. Winston was clearly ready for intellectual stimulation, and one might expect that he would have found it in the home of a lord who was also a member of Parliament and a charismatic MP at that. Instead, the boy's mind was fired by, of all people, Mrs Everest's brother-in-law, John Balaam, a senior warden at Parkhurst Prison. British workmen in the nineteenth century, undiverted by mass media, often read deeply and thoughtfully. The family of Woom's sister Mary lived in the coastal town of Ventnor, on the Isle of Wight, and she took him there on holiday. It was the first time Winston had seen a humble English home. The experience was worthwhile for that alone, but the old warden, after holding the boy spellbound with tales of prison mutinies, produced a worn copy of Macaulay's *History of England*. He read passages aloud; Winston listened, rapt, to the cadences of the majestic prose. Later in India he remembered those evenings in the cottage on the sea. He acquired his own Macaulay and, in his words, 'voyaged with full sail in a strong wind.'[28]

Woom never let him down, but her health did. During the Christmas holidays at the end of 1887, while Jennie and Randolph were abroad, she contracted diphtheria, then a fearsome disease and often fatal. Dr Robson Roose found two bad patches of false membrane in her throat and moved the two boys from Connaught Place to his own home. 'It is very hard to bear – we feel so destitute,' Winston wrote. 'I feel very dull – worse than school.' Duchess Fanny whisked them off to Blenheim, and Leonie telegraphed the news to their parents. Fanny, very much in charge, wrote to Randolph: 'I fear you will have been bothered about this misfortune of Everest having diphtheria but she appears to be recovering & the 2 children are here safe & well.' Blandford (George) offered to take them into his London house. Fanny wrote: 'They leave here & go to Grovr Sq tomorrow so you might write (or Jennie might in your name) a line to B for having had them. It has done them good & I keep Winston in good order as I know you like it. He is a clever Boy & not really naughty but he wants a firm hand. Jack requires *no* keeping in order. They will stay at 46 till you return.'[29]

By January 12 Winston could write his mother: 'Everest is much better – thanks to Dr Roose. My holidays have chopped about a good deal but . . . I do not wish to complain. It might have been so much worse if Woomany had died.'[30] There seems to have been a tacit acceptance by the relatives of both parents that Randolph and Jennie were not really responsible for their children. As a consequence, Winston's awareness of his grandparents, uncles, aunts, and cousins deepened; they move in and out of his early life like characters in a Pirandello play. Had his immediate family been more self-sufficient, he might have been less conscious of his Marlborough heritage on one side and his American roots on the other. Jennie, by now, was indistinguishable from the titled Englishwomen of her social circle. She had no interest in Buffalo Bill. But her sisters were vibrant with the US chauvinism of the time. Jennie, a purebred American, had become indifferent to the fact. Her son was half American, was constantly reminded of it by his maternal aunts, and never forgot it.

Winston's own illnesses, with one important exception, were normal for children of the time. He caught mumps ('My mumps are getting smaller every day the very thought of going home is enough to draw them away') and, later, measles, which – to his mother's intense annoyance – he passed along to her current lover, the dashing Austrian sportsman Count Charles Kinsky. The important exception was double pneumonia. All his life he would be plagued by recurrences of bronchial infections; his consequent indispositions would play a role in World War II. He was first stricken in his twelfth year, on Saturday, March 13, 1886. The danger was clear from the outset; Jennie and Randolph arrived separately in Brighton, and Dr Roose, who kept a house there, remained by the boy's side, sending them bulletins after they had departed. These survive. At 10:15 P.M. Sunday he scrawled: 'Temp. 104.3 right lung generally involved. . . . This report may appear grave yet it merely indicates the approach of the crisis which, please God, will result in an improved condition should the left lung remain free. I am in the next room and shall watch the patient during the night – for I am anxious.' Infection of the left lung swiftly followed. At 6:00 A.M. Monday he wrote: 'The high temp indicating exhaustion I used stimulants, by the mouth and rectum . . . I shall give up my London work and stay by the boy today.' Then, at 1:00 P.M.: 'We are still fighting the battle for your boy . . . As long as I can fight the temp and keep it under 105 I shall not feel anxious.' At 11:00 P.M.: 'Your boy, in my opinion, on his perilous path is holding his own well, right well!' Tuesday: 'We have had a very anxious night but have managed to hold our own. . . On the other hand we have to realise that we may have another 24 hours of this critical condition, to be combatted with all our vigilant energy.' By Wednesday the worst was over. At 7:00 A.M. Roose scribbled: 'I have a very good report to make. *Winston has had 6 hours quiet sleep*. Delirium has now ceased.' Later in the day he wrote from Brighton station: 'Forgive my troubling you with these lines to impress upon you the absolute necessity of quiet and sleep for Winston and that Mrs Everest should not be allowed in the sick room today – even the excitement of pleasure at seeing her might do harm! and I am so fearful of relapse knowing that we are not quite out of the wood yet.'[31]

But they were, and the suggestion that Woom might constitute a threat is curious. Duchess Fanny agreed. 'I hope Everest will be sensible,' she wrote Jennie, 'and not gushing so as to excite him. This certainly is not wise.' His nurse was entrusted with his love, but not his health. In an emergency, it was thought, women of her class could not be depended upon to remain stoical. A display of affection could endanger him; only patricians could be counted on to remain poised. Jennie, certainly no gusher, was admitted to the sickroom (Randolph sent her sandwiches and sherry) while the woman who had saved him from emotional starvation was deliberately excluded. A child of the aristocracy was in jeopardy, and the Churchills' peers were closing ranks. Because Randolph was at the pinnacle of his career that year, powerful men were concerned for Winston's survival. Sir Henry James prayed for him; so did Sir Michael Hicks-Beach. Lord Salisbury, who had succeeded Disraeli as the Tory leader, wrote of his anxiety from Monte Carlo, and Moreton Frewen told Jennie that the Prince of Wales had 'stopped the whole line at the levée' to ask after Winston. In a sense, the boy's recovery was an affair of England's ruling families, and the humble people whose lives had touched his did not belong.[32]

At Brighton, in his later words, 'I got gradually stronger in that bracing air and gentle surroundings.' Meanwhile, his relatives sententiously vowed to cherish him the more now that he had been saved and urged Jennie to do the same. Frewen thought of 'poor dear Winny, & I hope it will leave no troublesome after effects, but even if it leaves him delicate for a long time to come you will make the more of him after being given back to you from the very threshold of the unknown.' Duchess Fanny was 'so thankful for God's Goodness for preserving your dear Child,' and Jennie's own mother, in London but sick herself, wrote her, 'I can't tell you how anxious we have all been about poor little Winston. And how delighted & thankful now that he is better. And what a relief for you my dear child. Yr whole life has been one of good fortune & this the crowning blessing that little Winston has been spared to you. You can't be too *grateful* dear Jennie.'[33]

Jennie had been scared, and was doubtless relieved, but if gratitude meant changing her life-style, she wouldn't have it. These were the busiest years of her life, and she was enjoying them immensely. In those days an ambitious woman – and she was very ambitious – could express her drive only by advancing her husband's career. In the year of Winston's pneumonia, Anita Leslie writes, 'Jennie took it for granted that her husband would reach the post of Prime Minister,' but she was leaving nothing to chance.[34] She was active in the Primrose League; she campaigned for Randolph in a smart tandem with the horses beribboned in pink and chocolate, his racing colours; she gave endless dinner parties. No one declined her invitations, for she had become a celebrity in her own right. In the England of the 1880s and 1890s beautiful young genteel ladies diverted the public as film stars do now; their photographs were displayed in shop windows and sold as pinups. Jennie's was among the most popular. She was also recognized as a gifted amateur pianist, always in demand for charity concerts. In addition there were her social schedules. It was a grand thing to leave each autumn on her annual tour of Scotland's country houses, grand to receive the Order of the Crown of India from the Queen's own hands, grand to be courted by Europe's elegant gallants. There were hazards, to be sure, but they merely added to the excitement. Ironically, the only public embarrassment to arise from Jennie's catholicity of friendships among the eminent had nothing to do with her role as a romantic adventuress. She cultivated both Oscar Wilde and Sir Edward Carson. Later this proved awkward when Wilde and Carson faced each other in the Old Bailey with the ugly charge of sodomy facing Wilde.

In short, Jennie had her priorities to consider, and while the frail child in Brighton was not at the bottom of the list, he scarcely led it. She wrote him, but except when he lay at death's door and propriety gave her no choice, she avoided the school. Pleas continued to pepper his letters: 'Will you come and see me?' 'When are you coming to see me?' 'It was a great pity you could not come down Sunday,' '*I want you to come down on some fine day and see me,*' he would give her billions of kisses if she came. She never found time. He had the chief role in a class entertainment, and he wanted her in the audience – 'Whatever you do come Monday please. I shall be miserable if you don't.' He was miserable. Another entertainment was planned – 'I shall expect to see you and shall be very disappointed indeed if I do not see you, so do come.' He was very disappointed. They were going to perform *The Mikado* – 'It would give me tremendous pleasure, do come please.' He forwent tremendous pleasure. He ached for the sight of her – 'Please do do do do do do come down to see me . . . Please do come I have been disappointed so many times.' He was disappointed once more. Learning that a dinner party at Connaught Place conflicted with a school play, he begged her to cancel the dinner – 'Now you know I was always your darling and you can't find it in your heart to give me a denial.' Nevertheless, she found it in her heart to do just that.[35]

At times the breakdown in communications was total. He made elaborate plans for Christmas in 1887, only to discover at the last minute that both his parents were away on a seven-week tour of Russia. Jennie's sister Clarita – now called 'Clara,' like her mother – invited him to her home but then fell ill, so he spent the holiday with his brother, Woom, Leonie, and his uncle Jack Leslie. Once he wanted to write his mother but didn't have her address, didn't even know which country she was visiting. He was too young to travel in London alone, yet he couldn't even be sure there would be anyone to greet his train when he arrived: 'We have 19 days holiday at Easter. I hope you will send some one to meet me at the station.' Astonishingly, Randolph met an appointment in Brighton a short walk from the school but didn't bother to cross the street and call on his son. Winston found out about it. 'My dear Papa,' he wrote, 'You never came to see me on Sunday when you were in Brighton.' It happened again: 'I cannot think why you did not come to see me, while you were in Brighton, I was very disappointed but I suppose you were too busy to come.'[36] There was a note of resignation here. He was disappointed, but he was not surprised. His father was too busy. His father would always be too busy. Indeed, unlike his wife, he rarely wrote Winston. Jennie was a lax mother, but later, when her situation altered, she became a loving one. In Randolph's case that was impossible. Randolph actually disliked his son.

It is impossible to say exactly when a diagnostician told Lord Randolph Churchill that he was hopelessly afflicted with veneral infection and could not possess his wife without risking her health, too. Before meeting her he had passed through the first two stages of syphilis – the penile chancre and the body rash. After his wedding, according to Frank Harris, he told Louis Jennings that he had followed the physicians' medical advice for a while, 'but I was young and heedless and did not stop drinking in moderation and soon got reckless. Damn it, one can't grieve forever. Yet I have had few symptoms since.' He added, 'The Oxford doctor and the London man said I was quite clear of all weakness and perfectly cured.' Frank Harris asked Jennings if he thought Randolph's optimism unfounded. Jennings said, 'I'm sure of it. He has fits of excessive irritability and depression which I don't like. In spite of what he told me, I don't think he took much care. He laughed at the secondary symptoms.'[37]

Randolph's assumption that he had emerged from the sinister shadow of the disease was shattered in 1881, when, at the age of thirty-two, he suffered his first paralytic attack. His speech and gait were affected, though at first almost imperceptibly. The following year, however, he was mysteriously absent from London for seven months, and when he returned in October, gaunt and grim, he evaded all questions about where or why he had gone. The fact was that he had entered the third phase of syphilis; the deadly spirochetes had begun their invasion of his blood vessels and internal organs. Less than two months later, on December 12, the London newspapers announced that on the advice of his doctors he was sailing off again, to stay in Algeria and Monte Carlo until February. A remission brought him back, outwardly healthy, apparently his old self.

By now, however, Jennie, too, knew everything. Her source may have been Randolph; it could have been their family physician, Dr. Roose, who had made his own examination of her husband. Henry Pelling of St. John's College, Cambridge, observes: 'The nature of Randolph's illness, once it had been diagnosed, was such that he could no longer claim his conjugal rights, and it is not surprising that Jennie began to seek the company of other men.'[38] She may have begun to seek it earlier in their marriage. Indeed, one of her first admirers, Lieutenant Colonel John Strange Jocelyn, had found her receptive when the Churchills were still in Ireland. Jennie was Jocelyn's guest on his 8,900-acre Irish estate. She became pregnant in the summer of 1879, and when Winston's brother was born in Dublin the following February 4, he was christened John Strange Spencer Churchill.

That would not do; it was not done. Back in England, older and more experienced women counselled her in discretion. One disguise for affairs was to affect a lively interest in the arts and so encounter others similarly inclined. So she joined an artistic set called 'the Souls.' Reporting one of their parties at the Bachelor's Club, the London *World* told its readers: 'This highest and most aristocratic cult comprises only the youngest, most beautiful and most exclusive of married women in London.' Lady Warwick thought they were 'more pagan than soulful.' Sir William Harcourt said, 'All I know about The Souls is that some of them have very beautiful bodies,' and George Curzon wrote an ode to them called 'The Belles' – a parody of 'The Bells' by Poe – which ended: 'How delicious and delirious are the curves / With which their figure swells / Voluptuously and voluminously swells / To what deed the thought impels.' Marriage vows were certainly broken, but the fact was not advertised. After Ireland, Jennie never flaunted her lovers. Neither, however, was she furtive. She had superb legs, and she found a way to display them; *Town Topics* quoted a footman who had seen her dance the cancan at a ball: 'She suddenly touched the mantelpiece with her foot, making a dreadful exposé.' *Town Topics* also wrote that 'Society has invented a new name for Lady R. Her fondness for the exciting sport of husband-hunting and fiancé-fishing has earned her the title "Lady Jane Snatcher." ' Later she herself published an article slyly observing that some aristocratic wives could 'live down scandals, whereas the less-favoured go under, emphasising the old saying, "One may steal a horse while another may not look over the wall." '[39]

She was a cunning thief, and at times piratical, but she learned to observe the rules. If a prospect was happy in marital harness, she did not tempt him to leave it. She was careful to point out that at the time she was meeting Paul Bourget he was 'then unmarried.' When another Frenchman married an American girl, she left his bed, though only temporarily; he implored her not to be puritanical, and perhaps because he was charming and a magnificent horseman, she returned. He was a diplomat, with a reputation to guard. That was important. She had an instinct for men who were dangerous. Sir Charles Dilke was attractive, engaging, and apparently on his way to high office. He seemed to have his pick of Souls. When Mrs J. Comyns-Carr told Lady Lindsay that she was interested in Dilke, she was told: 'There's a waiting list, you know.' But Jennie wasn't on it. He sank to his knees and beseeched her to become his mistress. She refused, and described the preposterous scene to Lord Rosebery, who put it in his papers. Afterwards, when Dilke was trapped in a public scandal woven of testimony about brothels, exotic sex, and some of Jennie's friends, her foresight was remembered. She always knew just when to stop. It was one of her many rare traits. Shane Leslie recalled: 'She didn't seem to be like other women at all.'[40]

Towards the end of her life, the novelist George Moore said that she had slept with two hundred men. That is absurd. She was far too fastidious for that, and only she would have known the figure anyhow. But though far from promiscuous, she had certainly led an active romantic life. Her lovers are known to include Kinsky, Henri Breteuil, Thomas Trafford, Baron Hirsch, Sir Edgar Vincent (later Viscount D'Abernon), Lord Dunraven, Herbert von Bismarck, Henri le Tonnelie, Norman Forbes Robertson, Hugh Warrender of the Grenadier Guards, a cavalry officer named Kinkaid Smith, the American Bourke Cockran, Bourget, William Waldorf Astor, Harry Cust, a soldier named Taylor, a man called Simon, an Italian named Casati, and Albert Edward of the house of Saxe-Coburg, eldest son of Queen Victoria, Prince of Wales and later King Edward VII.

Jennie was one of those favoured ladies who, invited to dinner by his Royal Highness, found that she was the only guest. HRH usually made his royal conquests in a private dining room over a fashionable restaurant; one panelled wall swung down at the touch of a button, exposing a double bed. There was also a settee on one side which was adequate for most lovers, but HRH needed more room; Rudyard Kipling described him as 'a corpulent voluptuary.' Jennie was more than paramour to him. He granted her the rare privilege of using Buckingham Palace's private garden entrance. According to Ralph G. Martin, 'she had a significant and lasting influence on him because he respected her judgement. He also knew he could rely on her. If he wanted a small private party arranged, he often asked her to oversee the compiling of the guest list and decide on the menu. Jennie knew his particular friends as well as his favourite foods. She knew what kind of music he liked. She knew the level of his impatience and boredom, the danger point of his anger, and what to do about them. In return, he was lavish in his gifts and in his open affection for her.'[41] On his coronation in Westminster Abbey, she sat in the King's Box with the other women he loved, including Mrs George Keppel, his current mistress, all wearing diamond tiaras. Edward saw to it that pleasure was not sin's only reward. So did his wife; like Jennie's mother, Princess Alexandra understood and forgave her husband. She was on the best of terms with Mrs Keppel, and always kind to Jennie.

Randolph had been less forgiving. He had put up with a lot from the prince; first Ireland, and now this. In 1889, when he had nothing left to lose, he ordered HRH out of his Mayfair house. On another occasion, after hearing from Rosebery that Dilke had propositioned Jennie, Randolph attacked him with his fists. This was rather hard on Dilke, who hadn't even made it into Jennie's arms, but he seems to have been a chronic loser. So was the man who hit him. And apart from these two episodes, Randolph, at least in his marriage, appears to have accepted his lot. He dined with men who had lain between his wife's thighs; he played cards with them; he rode to hounds with them and entertained them in his club. There were those who wondered why. Some speculated that he had become homosexual. That might explain his ant-agonism towards Winston, but there is no evidence of it. All we can say with certainty is that Winston knew about Jennie's affairs. The question is when. There is a story, probably apocryphal, that he first learned of her waywardness as a small boy because of a flaw in one of her stockings. In the late 1870s fashionable women in London wore red hose. Red was his favourite colour. As she left home one noon, according to this account, he noticed a blemish in her left stocking, just above her shoe, and when she returned several hours later he saw the imperfection had moved from her left ankle to her right. But he would have become aware of her lovers anyhow. He could not have avoided it. In one of his schoolboy letters to his brother he wrote that upon arriving in London for a weekend, 'I went, as Mamma had told me to Aldford Street, where I found Mamma & Count Kinsky Breakfasting.' Visiting France, he was enter-tained by three of his mother's gallants: Trafford, Hirsch, and Breteuil. In *Savrola* the character based on Jennie is presented as an adulteress whose husband saw her less and less frequently. Not all this should be entered in the debit column: Jennie's men, including Edward VII, were to help Winston enormously during his struggle to establish himself. But his knowledge of her guilt undoubtedly contributed to his adolescent turmoil. Even in his early thirties he would have difficulty establishing relationships with young women. 'Ambitions I still have: I have always had them,' says *Savrola*'s hero, 'but love I am not to know, or to know it only to my vexation and despair.'[42]

His knowledge of romantic love came later, and it was glorious. Because Jennie lived until his late forties, he resolved his relationship with her. It was otherwise with his father. Here the grave denied him any opportunity for reconciliation; his image of Randolph was arrested in time. The crucial years were 1884 to 1886, roughly from Winston's tenth to twelfth birthdays, when he was in Brighton and beginning to take a serious interest in current events. Randolph was in the news constantly. Paresis, which progresses very slowly, had only just begun to cripple him. Outwardly he was vigorous, witty, powerful; the most spectacular man of the day. Newspapers called him 'Gladstone's great adversary,' and described workmen smiling at his moustache and doffing their caps as his carriage passed by. Winston clipped these stories and cartoons of his father and pasted them in scrapbooks. He next memorized his speeches verbatim. To his father he wrote: 'I have been out riding with a gentleman who thinks that Gladstone is a brute and thinks that "the one with the curly moustache ought to be Premier." The driver of the Electric Railway said "that Lord R. Churchill would be Prime Minister." . . . Everybody wants your Autograph but I can only say I will try, and I should like you to sign your name in full at the end of your letter. I only want a scribble as I know that you are very busy indeed.'[43]

Long afterwards he recalled that his father seemed to him 'to own the key to everything or almost everything worth having.' He could imagine nothing more exalted than to stand in the House of Commons, guiding the course of England and Empire. Taken to Marylebone swimming baths, he asked the attendant whether he was a Liberal or a Conservative. The unfortunate man replied that he didn't 'bother myself about politics.' Winston was outraged. 'What?' he cried. 'You pay rates and taxes and you don't bother yourself about politics?' He broke off his friendship with a playmate. The playmate's father asked his son why. The boy answered, 'Winston says you're one of those damned Radicals and he's not coming over here again.' Probably the man believed in nothing more rabid than Gladstonian liberalism, and possibly the bath attendant wasn't even allowed to vote, but a boy couldn't be expected to know that. He was his father's staunchest supporter. He yearned to battle for him. He was obsessed with his image. He had placed him on a high pedestal. He worshipped at the altar of a man he did not, in fact, even know.[44]

He tried to know him; tried, in his childish way, to draw Randolph into the family. 'We had a Christmas tree and party here this year,' he wrote, 'which went off very well. My Stamp Book is gradually getting filled . . . Jack had such a beautiful box of soldiers sent him from Lady de Clifford.' Winston might have been a foreign correspondent sending word of developments from abroad, and indeed at times Randolph was a stranger to Connaught Place. Once he arrived home with a full beard – 'a horrid beard so raged [ragged],' Jack wrote his brother at Brighton, and Jennie wrote that 'his beard is a "terror." I think I shall have to bribe him to shave it off.' Most of the time Winston could keep track of him in the newspapers. Apparently he did not find it peculiar that Randolph, who had been too occupied to visit him in Brighton, should have journeyed to speak to another school: 'I went to see Grandmamma a fortnight ago, & she read me your speech on the Distribution of Prizes at the school of Art, it was just the sort of speech for school boys.' Then, wistfully: 'You had great luck in Salmon fishing. I wish I had been with you I should have liked to have seen you catch them.'[45]

To a ten-year-old English boy in the 1880s, India was enthralling, and Winston was transported by news that his father was actually on his way there. 'Will you write and tell me all about your voyage, was it rough at all?' he asked. 'I wrote to you once when the ship stopped at Gibralter. How nice for sailing all over the sea.' Then, six weeks later: 'I hear you have been out shooting at Calcutta and shot some animals. When are you coming home again. I hope it will not be long. I am at school now and am getting on pretty well. Will you write and tell me about India what it's like . . . Will you go out on a tiger Hunt while you are there? Are the Indians very funny? . . . Try and get me a few stamps for my stamp album, Papa. Are there many *ants* in India if so, you will have a nice time, what with *ants mosquitos* [sic]. . . . I am longing to see you so much.'[46]

At the end of this letter he again raised the question of autographs, asking, 'Every body wants to get your signature will you send me a few to give away?' How anxious the other boys were is moot. We do know that later, at Harrow, subjects which interested schoolmates and those Winston thought should interest them were not always identical. It seems unlikely that many could have shared his passion for politics. Boys aren't like that now; they weren't then. But Winston was rapt in the world he had fashioned for himself, surrounded by scrapbooks, pastepots, scissors, and cuttings. His father thought he would have to go for a soldier, that he was too stupid for anything else. Yet politics already had him in its spell. He wrote his mother: 'I am very glad Papa got in for South Paddington by so great a majority' – Randolph had polled 77 per cent of the vote – 'I think that was a victory. I hope the Conservatives will get in, do you think they will?' And three months later, on October 19, 1886, he wrote his father, 'I hope you will [be] as successful in your speech at Bradford as you were at Dartford, and regularly "cut the ground from under the feet of the Liberals." ' That winter he campaigned tirelessly among the other boys, bullying them or cajoling them into making a Conservative commitment, and a handful yielded. The following May 24 he jubilantly informed Jennie that 'about a dozen boys have joined the Primrose League since yesterday. I am among the number & intend to join the one down here, and also the one which you have in London. Would you send me a nice badge as well as a paper of Diploma, for I want to belong to yours most tremendously.'[47]

It was an act of faith in his father's destiny, and it came too late. Not for the last time in his life, Winston had boarded a sinking ship. Randolph's political career had ended five months earlier.

Disraeli, whose memory the Primrose League was meant to perpetuate – it had been his favourite flower – had in his last days pointed Randolph out to a young colleague and said: 'He can have anything he asks for, and will soon make them take anything he will give them.' Gladstone had called him the greatest Conservative since Pitt. Lord Hartington had said that Randolph knew the House of Commons better than it knew itself; it always filled to hear him speak. Harris thought that 'from his entrance into the House till 1886, it was Randolph's courage chiefly that commended him to the House of Commons. It may have been mainly aristocratic *morgue*, but Englishmen liked it none the less on that account.' After a century which has seen countless changes in oratorical style, it is difficult to account for his appeal, but men of all political persuasions testified to it. He wrote his speeches out and learned them by heart; then he spoke at great speed, with daunting vehemence and compelling intensity. In debate his acid tongue set the House roaring. Once the Liberals thought he was napping. They introduced a specious motion, concealing a trap. He said: 'Surely in vain is the net spread in the sight of any bird.' In a typical thrust he attacked George Sclater-Booth, a ponderous Liberal minister: 'I don't object to the Head of the Local Government Board dealing with such grave questions as the salaries of inspectors of nuisances. But I have the strongest possible objection to his coming down here with all the appearance of a great law-giver to repair, according to his small ideas and in his little way, breaches in the British Constitution.' Then, almost as though speaking to himself, he added: 'Strange, strange how often we find mediocrity dowered with a double-barrelled name.'[48]

He was at his sharpest when he took the offensive. At Blackpool, early in 1884, he turned one of Gladstone's endearing little traits into a sharp jab at the Grand Old Man. The GOM and his son enjoyed felling trees together. Randolph told his audience how a delegation of workingmen arrived at Gladstone's home and were led out into the grounds, where 'all around them' lay 'the rotting trunks of once umbrageous trees; all around them, tossed by the winds, were boughs and bark and withered shoots. They came suddenly on the Prime Minister and Master Herbert, in scanty attire and profuse perspiration, engaged in the destruction of a gigantic oak, just giving its last dying groan.' The workmen were 'permitted to gaze and worship and adore'; then each was 'presented with a few chips as a memorial of that memorable scene.' Randolph swiftly developed his theme, which was that the GOM had given the delegation exactly what he had given the Empire: 'Chips to the faithful allies in Afghanistan, chips to the trusting native races of South Africa, chips to the Egyptian fellah, chips to the manufacturer and the artisan, chips to the agricultural labourer, chips to the House of Commons itself. To all who leaned on Mr Gladstone, who trusted him, and who hoped for something from him – chips, nothing but chips – hard, dry, unnourishing, indigestible chips.'[49]

The self-righteous GOM was particularly vulnerable to satirical oratory, and it was Randolph's great good fortune that the Liberals should have been in power when he returned from Dublin to make his way in the House as a Tory MP. Gadflies like him flourish in opposition. It was Winston's boyhood impression, he later wrote, that 'Dizzy had been thoroughly beaten by Mr Gladstone, so we were all flung out into Opposition and the country began to be ruined very rapidly. Everyone said it was "going to the dogs."' Afterwards, looking back, he wrote that the position of the Conservatives, as a result of that beating, had 'become weak and miserable in the extreme . . . Outmatched in debate, outnumbered in division, the party was pervaded by a feeling of gloom.' Dispirited, many stopped attending Parliament altogether. But for Randolph, the moment and his mood were matched. His resentment of the men who had cut him after his row with HRH had infused him with a Jacobin spirit. The membership of the House was divided into Liberals, Conservatives, and Irish Nationalists; Randolph, without relinquishing his Tory label, founded what he called 'the Fourth Party.' There were four members: himself, Sir Henry Wolff, Sir John Gorst, and Arthur Balfour. Salisbury picked up the torch of Conservative leadership after Disraeli's death, but in his grasp it flickered low. The four freelances concentrated their fire on Gladstone and his ministers, but they did not spare the Tories' shadow government. They dubbed Tory insiders 'the Old Gang'; Salisbury's weaker colleagues were 'the Goats.' Nothing was sacred to the four, not even Disraeli's spirit. Dizzy's policy had been *Imperium* abroad and *Libertas* at home. Randolph challenged both. He attacked Gladstone's occupation of Egypt and embarrassed both Gladstone and Salisbury by squaring off against Charles Bradlaugh, a professed atheist who, when elected to Parliament by Northampton, refused to take the religious oath of allegiance. There was a fiery scene in the House on February 21, 1882, when Bradlaugh appeared, produced a book, identified it as 'a Testament,' and swore himself in. Randolph bounded up from his corner seat below the gangway and called the oath a farce. The book could have been anything, he said; 'it might have been *Fruits of Philosophy*' – an appeal for birth control of which Bradlaugh was coauthor. After a series of complicated parliamentary manoeuvres, Randolph persuaded the House to expel the member from Northampton. It was a brilliant coup, but it left a bad taste. Disraeli, wiser men knew, would never have permitted it. Then they remembered that Randolph, unlike his father, had never deferred to Disraeli – had, in fact, scarred him with the same rapier he was brandishing now.[50]

The week after his 'chips' speech, Randolph stunned England by announcing that in the next election he would contest John Bright's Birmingham seat. This was carrying the battle into the very stronghold of liberalism, the home ground of the mighty Joe Chamberlain.* He had no chance of winning, but his audacity invigorated his party and brought it recruits in workmen's pubs, where spirit was admired. Winston, of course, was too young to appreciate this strategy. He wrote Jennie from Ascot: 'Mrs Kynnersley went to Birmingham this week. And she heard they were betting two to one that Papa would get in for Birmingham.' In fact, he polled 4,216 votes to Bright's 4,989. It was an impressive moral victory, and the next day an admirer stepped down in

---

* Father of Neville, Winston's great adversary. This marked the beginning of the on-and-off feud between the Chamberlains and the Churchills – a dispute which, in the tradition of British politics, was conducted with great civility.

South Paddington, giving Randolph his seat. Randolph, by now, was the fighting heart of his party. As he moved from triumph to triumph, the House came to realize that eventually he would challenge Salisbury's role as Conservative leader. He was still in his thirties, his following in the country was growing, and he had a rallying cry: 'Tory democracy.' The party, he argued, needed new blood and wider popular appeal. *Democracy* was less than a charmed word among entrenched Tory diehards. The mere mention of it made Salisbury shudder, and he rejected Randolph's proposal to bring more rank-and-file members into the party's inner councils. The two split in 1884 in a struggle for control of the National Union of Conservative Associations. Winston, aged nine, wrote to Jennie, 'Has Papa got in I hope he has. You must let me know if he does.' Papa did get in; he and Salisbury then staged a public reconciliation, each giving a little. Salisbury was still the leader, but the challenger was inching closer. 'Trust the people, and the people will trust you!' Randolph told an enthusiastic crowd in Birmingham that same year. It sounded selfless. It wasn't. Randolph had become a shrewd campaigner. The Liberals were winning elections, he concluded, because the workmen felt closer to them than to the aristocratic Conservatives. 'But,' he said, 'my feeling is that this earl or marquis is much more in sympathy with the working man than the greedy nonconformist butcher or baker or candlestick maker. I want you to seize my point because it explains what I have always meant when I speak of myself as a Tory-democrat. The best class and the lowest class in England come together naturally. They like and esteem each other. They are not greasy hypocrites talking of morality and frequenting the Sunday school while sanding the sugar. They are united in England in the bonds of a frank immorality.'[51]

If this was devious, it wasn't a patch on his Irish policy, which had ripened slowly during the early 1880s and was held in abeyance, to be revealed at the right moment. As Randolph's gibes wore Gladstone down, Home Rule became the key issue in Parliament. In a close election between the two major parties, the Irish Nationalists would hold the balance of power. It says much for England's ignorance of Ireland that Randolph's three years in Dublin made him an expert on the country in the eyes of Parliament, even though his knowledge of the people was largely confined to glimpses from the saddle while foxhunting. Thus his exile there, which had been looked upon as a punishment, turned out to be a political asset. Gladstone, whose whole career would eventually hinge on this one question, had spent only three weeks in Ireland. Yet he was on good terms with Parnell, the Nationalists' militant leader, and he regarded that as his trump card when, on June 8, 1885, his government fell over a minor budget bill. Salisbury formed a caretaker government, but both sides knew that was of small consequence. The main event was the imminent general election.

Gladstone had miscalculated. Unable to pry an acceptable Home Rule pledge from him, Parnell issued a 'Vote Tory' manifesto. Salisbury, meanwhile, had appointed Randolph to his first office. Denying him a post was impractical; his strength had been evident for a year. He had been told in camera that he would become secretary of state for India – hence his trip there, to get ready – but a problem now arose, and it was revealing. Randolph was sulking. He refused to be sworn in until he had been assured that a rival, Sir Stafford Northcote, would be denied the office of leader of the House in the caretaker government. The Queen was shocked. She wired Salisbury: 'With due consideration to Lord R., do not think he should be allowed to dictate entirely his own terms, especially as he has never held office before.'[52] Salisbury sought a meeting. Randolph refused; he had taken his stand, and that was that. Yielding, the new prime minister sent the rival to the House of Lords as the Earl of Iddesleigh, and Randolph received his seals of office from the Queen, Then, to the astonishment of all London, the man who had denounced imperialism in Egypt launched the Third Burmese War and annexed the country. Aristocratic disdain for consequences was common, but this went beyond that. The first rumours about Randolph's unreliability and bad judgement spread through Parliament and beyond.

In effect, the election was a dead heat. The voters returned 335 Liberals, 249 Conservatives, and 86 Irish Nationalists. Salisbury and Parnell could lock the GOM in stalemate. But after the results were in, Gladstone's youngest son revealed that his father did in fact favour Home Rule. The Irish then swung behind him, and he was again prime minister. Randolph now played a deep game. He courted the support of Irishmen on both sides of the Home Rule issue. His fight against Bradlaugh had won him the admiration of Catholics; that was one reason he had fought it. Privately, he assured Parnell that he favoured Irish self-government on the local level and would oppose the coercion bill, which permitted the arrest and detention of Irish suspects without trial. Publicly, however, he became the most eloquent of Unionists; that is, opponents of Home Rule. Speaking in Belfast's Ulster Hall, he told Irish Unionists – Protestants – that he would stick with them to the end. By now he had had a great deal of experience in demagoguery and had got into the way of it. He compared Gladstone to Macbeth before the murder of Duncan and predicted that if politicians 'should be so utterly lost to every feeling and dictate of honour and courage as to hand over coldly . . . the lives and liberties of the Loyalists of Ireland to their hereditary and most bitter foes, make no doubt on this point: Ulster at the proper moment will resort to the supreme arbitrament of force; *Ulster will fight, Ulster will be right.*'[53] This mischievous slogan was to be his chief contribution to history. It outlived him and his son. People are still dying for it in Northern Ireland.

Parliament rejected Gladstone's Home Rule bill in June 1886 – a quarter of his Liberals defected – and the country went to the polls again. This time the result was a Conservative landslide. The Tories held a clear majority of 118 seats over the Liberals, Irish Nationalists, and Unionists combined. Salisbury was now prime minister with a clear mandate, but as Randolph's grandson wrote, 'It had been Lord Randolph's victory. He had pioneered it, engineered it and executed it. His exceptional services to the Party had to be recognized.

He was indispensable to it.' Harris observed, 'When the House met again Lord Randolph's power had grown: he had deposed Gladstone, had won a greater position in the House than Gladstone himself.' Sir Michael Hicks-Beach, offered the post of party leader of the House by Salisbury, insisted on stepping aside for the Tories' most brilliant campaigner. He wrote: 'I felt that Lord Randolph Churchill was superior in eloquence, ability and influence to myself; that the position of Leader in name, but not in fact, would be intolerable; and that it was better for the party and the country that the Leader in fact should also be Leader in name.' Randolph was good in the job. He was always in his seat, always informed, always an able tactician. And he could be charming when he chose. Margot Asquith boldly invited both him and Gladstone to her Grosvenor Square home. Randolph, she recalled afterwards, 'had made himself famous by attacking and abusing the Grand Old Man with such virulence that everyone thought it impossible that they could ever meet in intimacy . . . I was not awed by this but asked them to a luncheon-party; and they both accepted. I need hardly say that when they met they talked with fluency and interest, for it was as impossible for Mr Gladstone to be gauche or rude as it was for anyone to be ill at ease with Lord Randolph Churchill. The news of their lunching with us spread all over London; and the West End buzzed round me with questions: all the political ladies, including the Duchess of Manchester, were torn with curiosity to know whether Randolph was going to join the Liberal Party.'[54]

And yet . . .

Everyone who had worked closely with Randolph knew that he had a dark underside. Certainly Salisbury was aware of it. He would have disputed Mrs Asquith; he was always ill at ease with Churchill. He had found him rude, peevish, temperamental, and, much of the time, unapproachable. The four crosses he bore, he said, were 'the Prime Ministership, the Foreign Office, the Queen, and Randolph Churchill – and the burden of them increases in that order.' Randolph had been an exasperating colleague in the India Office the year before. Salisbury's friends were appalled, therefore, when he appointed him chancellor of the Exchequer, the second most powerful position in the government. Even Randolph's friends were apprehensive. Lord Rosebery wrote that the new chancellor had displayed 'certain defects of brain and character which are inconsistent with the highest statesmanship.' And the Exchequer was the last place where he might succeed. Commenting on the columns of decimals in his budget, he growled, 'I could never make out what those damned dots meant.' But Salisbury knew what he was doing. He owed his landslide to Randolph. No one could say he was ungrateful now. At the same time, he was alert to the fact that Randolph was after his job. So he had put him in an impossible position and then sat back, waiting for him to destroy himself.[55]

It took six months. 'Very soon,' Harris heard, 'there were rumours of disputes in the Cabinet.'[56] Churchill was restive in harness; being a critic had been more fun. Tiring of the damned dots, he took a subversive interest in the affairs of other ministers. On October 3, without consulting Salisbury, he delivered a sensational speech before fourteen thousand people at Oakfield Park, Dartford, demanding more sovereignty for local governments in England, close ties with Germany and Austria-Hungary, and stiff protests against Russian influence in the Balkans – all at odds with the prime minister's programmes. Next he submitted a startling budget to the cabinet. He proposed to reduce taxes and military spending: a plank right out of Gladstone's platform. Salisbury calmly rejected it. Churchill then decided to force his hand. He did it in the worst possible way.

His relationship with the Queen had been improving steadily. Victoria admired success. And he had been courting her. She disliked the patronizing Gladstone – 'He always addresses me as though I were a public meeting,' she complained – and was pleased by Randolph's more graceful approach. He wrote to her constantly, explaining political developments without a flicker of condescension. On September 22 she had expressed her gratitude to him: 'Now that the session is over, the Queen wishes to write and thank Lord Randolph Churchill for his regular and full and interesting reports of the debates in the House of Commons, which must have been most trying. Lord Randolph has shown much skill and judgement in his leadership during the exceptional session of Parliament.' She asked him to dine with her at Windsor Castle on December 20. He was immensely pleased; it was his first royal invitation since the row over her son's love letters to Lady Aylesford. The dinner went exceptionally well. On his return he glowed. Victoria, he told Harris, had called him 'a true statesman.' He in return felt that she was 'a great woman, one of the wisest and best of women.' What he did not tell Harris was that he had used the Queen's letter paper to write a letter of resignation from the cabinet. He had shown it to a fellow guest at the castle, Lord George Hamilton, the first lord of the Admiralty. Hamilton had remonstrated: 'You cannot send a letter like that to Salisbury. Won't you consult somebody?' Randolph had replied, 'No, I won't consult anybody.' Nor had he. By Tuesday, December 21, the letter was in the prime minister's hands.[57]

On Wednesday evening, while Churchill was dining at the Carlton Club with Sir Henry Wolff, a messenger handed him Salisbury's reply. His resignation had been accepted. As Winston later wrote, Salisbury was doubtless 'glad to have the whole power in his hands, instead of dividing it with a restless rival, entrenched in the leadership of the House of Commons and the control of the public purse.' Randolph hadn't expected this – he had come to think of himself as indispensable – but he wasn't dejected. Indeed, he seemed strangely euphoric. Taking a cab to Connaught Place, he and Sir Henry picked up Jennie, and the three of them proceeded to the Strand Theatre. The play was Sheridan's *School for Scandal*, a theme of special interest to Jennie. She knew nothing of his letter. As they settled in the stalls, she mentioned the guest list for an official reception she was planning. He said enigmatically, 'Oh, I shouldn't worry about that if I were you. It probably will never take place.' Before she could ask him what he meant, the curtain rose, and when it fell on the first act, he excused himself, saying that he was returning to the club.[58]

Actually, he went to *The Times* and gave the editor copies of his correspondence with the prime minister, including a final, savage note from him to Salisbury. The editor read this last and said, 'You can't send that.' Lord Randolph said, 'It has already gone.' He then said he expected, in exchange for the scoop, editorial support from *The Times*. Nothing doing, the editor replied; indeed, the paper would attack him. That jarred Randolph, but not much; he was under the illusion that the party would rise up, depose Salisbury, and make him Salisbury's successor. He told a friend, 'There is only one place, that is Prime Minister. I like to be boss. I like to hold the reins.' In the morning he welcomed Harris to Connaught Place with the merry cry: 'What do you think of it? More than two hundred and fifty Tory members come to attest their allegiance to me. I've won! The Old Gang will have to give in.' But when Harris returned a few days later, Randolph said gloomily, 'The rats desert the sinking ship.'[59]

In fact, he had come closer to bringing Salisbury down than most commentators realized. It took the prime minister twelve days to find another Conservative willing to serve as chancellor. But with that, the crisis was over. Randolph was finished. In a moment of arrogance and folly he had gambled everything and lost. He was thirty-seven years old. He would never hold office again.* Jennie was bitter: 'It was gall and wormwood,' she said, 'to hear Randolph abused in every quarter,' often by men who owed 'their political existence to him.' Randolph himself wrote vainly, 'What a fool Lord S. was to let me go so easily.' For a time he affected gaiety. His appearances on the back benches became infrequent. He was seen more often at racecourses, where he entered horses from his own stable and bet heavily. He won often. 'People smiled,' wrote Harris, 'as at the aberrations of a boy.'[50]

'Did you go to Harrow or Eton?' Winston wrote Randolph the following October. 'I should like to know.' It is extraordinary that he did not know already. Since 1722, Churchill boys – six generations of them – had been Etonians. But Dr Roose urged a break in the tradition. Eton, hard by Windsor Castle, often cloaked and soaked in the fogs rolling off the Thames, was highly unsuitable for a boy with a weak chest. Randolph's brother had sent his son Charles ('Sunny') to Winchester. The cousins had been playmates; Sunny liked the school; it seemed the logical choice for Winston. On May 30, 1885, when he was ten, Winston wrote that he was 'rather backward with Greek, but

---

* Writing of this in 1930, his son commented: 'It is never possible for a man to recover his lost position. He may recover another position in the fifties or sixties, but not the one he lost in the thirties or forties' (*Roving Commission,* page 47). Perhaps Winston was thinking of himself. He had been dismissed as first lord of the Admiralty in 1915, when he was forty-one. But *never* is a treacherous word. In 1939 Winston was again appointed first lord.

I suppose I must know it to get into Winchester so I will try and work it up,' and as late as the summer of 1887 he was still bearing down on Greek because it was 'my weak point & I cannot get into Winchester without it.' But then Randolph and his brother quarrelled. Their father had died. George was duke. Like his predecessors, he was improvident; to pay his debts he sold the family library, paintings, and jewels. Randolph denounced George with his customary venom and the two stopped speaking. Dr Roose then recommended Harrow – 'Harrow-on-the-Hill' – as best for Winston's health, and the boy was piloted in that direction. On October 8 Winston wrote his father: 'I am very glad to hear that I am going to Harrow & not Winchester. I think I shall pass the Entrance Examination, which is not so hard as Winchester.'[61]

It was characteristic of him in his teens that he always approached tests of his learning with breezy confidence and, in the breach, always performed wretchedly. In this instance Brighton may have been partly responsible for his failure. He had just won two more prizes there, in English and Scripture, but the level of instruction was perhaps not all it might have been: 'A master here is going to give a lecture on Chemistry, is it not wonderful to think that water is made up of two gases namely hydrogen and nitrodgen. I like it, only it seems funny that two gases should make water.' But to scapegoat the Thomson sisters would be unfair. The pattern continued until the end of his school days. He was not, as many have assumed, a victim of dyslexia. Nor could he have been as stupid as he seemed. Confronted with the testing ritual, he seemed stricken by the kind of paralysis that can afflict men in moments of unbearable stress, when the mind seems fathoms down, like some poor land creature entangled in the weeds of the sea. Later he would write poignantly of his entrance into 'the inhospitable regions of examinations, through which, for the next seven years, I was destined to journey. These examinations were a great trial to me. The subjects which were dearest to the examiners were almost invariably those I fancied least . . . I should have liked to be asked to say what I knew. They always tried to ask what I did not know. When I would have willingly displayed my knowledge, they sought to expose my ignorance. This sort of treatment had only one result: I did not do well in examinations.'[62]

The explanation, of course, was hostility, and it angered his parents, who never dreamed that they themselves, by their rejection of him, might have been responsible for it. They assumed that he was lazy. But he really wanted to get into Harrow. He boned up weeks in advance; on February 28, 1888, he wrote Jennie, 'I am working hard for Harrow,' and a week later he wrote his father, 'I am working hard for my examination which is a very Elementary one, so there is all the more reason to be careful & not to miss in the easy things.' On Friday, March 16, a day of shocking weather – the roads, in his words, 'were in a horrible condition mud & water & in some places the road was covered with water which reached up to the carriage step and extended for over 200 yrd' – Charlotte Thomson accompanied him to Harrow, where they were received by the headmaster, J. E. C. Welldon. Winston thought Welldon 'very nice,' but then he was led into a classroom and the ordeal was upon him. There were no questions about the subjects he felt he had mastered: grammar, history, French, geography. Instead, he was asked to translate passages in Greek and Latin. His mind went blank. He couldn't even remember the Greek alphabet. Then as he recalled afterwards, he found himself 'unable to answer a single question in the Latin paper. I wrote my name at the top of the page. I wrote down the number of the question, "I." After much reflection I put a bracket round it, thus, "(I)." But thereafter I could not think of anything connected with it that was either relevant or true. Incidentally there arrived from nowhere in particular a blot and several smudges. I gazed for two whole hours at this sad spectacle; and then merciful ushers collected up my piece of foolscap and carried it up to the Headmaster's table.'[63]

In the corridor he was near hysteria. He told Miss Thomson that he had never been asked to render Latin into English before. She knew he had been translating Virgil for a year and Caesar longer, but, wisely, did not contradict him. To their mutual astonishment, Harrow accepted him. She wrote Randolph, 'I hear from Mr Welldon today that Winston passed the examination yesterday.' She didn't try to camouflage the truth: 'My worst fears were realized with regard to the effect the nervous excitement would produce on his work: and he had only scraped through . . . He had a severe attack of sickness after we left Harrow and we only reached Victoria in time for the 7.5 train. If Mr Welldon would allow him to try again on the 18th April, I believe that Winston would do himself more justice; but I think the permission would be difficult to obtain.' It was, in fact, denied. Winston didn't think it mattered. He wrote: 'I have passed, but it was far harder than I expected . . . However I am through, which is the great thing.'[64]

It wasn't that simple. Had he been another boy, he would have been automatically rejected. His sole qualification was that he was the son of a former cabinet minister. Thus, even before he was enrolled, the masters at Harrow regarded him as a special problem. On April 17, after a holiday at Blenheim with Duchess Fanny, he arrived at the school with his baggage and wrote his mother: 'I will write tomorrow evening to say what form I'm in. It is going to be read out in the speech room tomorrow.' The news was crushing. He was assigned to the lowest form. Only two boys in all Harrow were below him, and when both withdrew he was left as the school dunce. On visitors' days, the roll ('Bill') was called outside the Old School, and boys filed past in the order of their scholastic record. Other parents, curious about the son of the famous Lord Randolph, would await Winston's appearance and then whisper to one another: 'Why, he's the last of all!'[65]

Today Harrow is part of Greater London, but in the 1880s it stood in open country. Peering towards the city from Headmaster's House you saw nothing but green fields, and the churchyard provided an unbroken view of rolling English landscape as far as Windsor, which could be seen on a clear day. Old Boys muttered indignantly about the Metropolitan Railway, which had begun to inch this way, and the new bicycle craze, which, in the phrase of the day, was 'annihilating distance.' Proud of their school, conscious of its role in English history, which to them meant the history of the world, they wanted nothing to change there. Strangers were shown the flat churchyard tombstone where Byron had brooded beneath the elms and the Fourth Form Room, dating from 1609, whose walls were inscribed with the names of Harrow boys who had made their mark. The Bill was followed closely for pupils of promise; already two of Winston's contemporaries, John Galsworthy and Stanley Baldwin, had been marked for future greatness. Harrovian traditions, encrusted by generations of observance, were considered sacred. Some seem odd. The food was inedible. Boys needed generous allowances to survive; such delicacies as eggs and sardines were available only in the private 'tuck-shops' in High and West Streets. If you wanted to read anything but classical literature, you had to buy it in J. F. Moore's bookshop. And masters were regarded as the natural enemies of boys, though Welldon, then in his third year as head of the school, was personally popular. In appearance he resembled the twentieth-century British actor Jack Hawkins. One of Winston's classmates later wrote that the headmaster's 'great massive form, as he swung into Fourth Form Room or Speech Room to take prayers or introduce a lecturer or ascended the pulpit to deliver one of his impressive sermons, produced a feeling of confidence.'[66] Most important, in tracing Harrovian influences on Winston, were the school's patriotic songs:

> *So today – and oh! if ever*
> *Duty's voice is ringing clear*
> *Bidding men to brave endeavour –*
> *Be our answer, 'We are here.'*

And:

> *God give us bases to guard or beleaguer,*
> *Games to play out whether earnest or fun;*
> *Fights for the fearless and goals for the eager,*
> *Twenty and thirty and forty years on.*

In 1940 Churchill revisited Harrow and heard these stanzas again from another generation. Afterwards he said: 'Listening to those boys singing all those well-remembered songs I could see myself fifty years before, singing with them those tales of great men and wondering with intensity how I could ever do something glorious for my country.' Here his memory was perhaps selective – songfests were not typical of his Harrow experience – but that is true of most Old Boy memories. Moreover, when one of their number becomes famous, many former schoolmates tend to edit their recollections, or even to distort them. It happens to old retainers, too. In the aftermath of Dunkirk, when Churchillian rhetoric seemed Britain's only shield against Nazi conquest, a reporter interviewed Wright Cooper, whose confectioner's store had been Harrow's most popular tuck-shop of the 1880s and 1890s. Cooper said:

Churchill was an extraordinarily good boy. He was honest and generous in a day when robust appetites were not always accompanied by well-lined pockets. My family lived over the shop, and when Churchill was downstairs we all knew it. Boys crowded round his table. . . . He was witty and critical and kept the other boys in roars of laughter. He was exceedingly popular and even the seniors sought his company. He was well behaved and had the ear of everyone. When his father or his mother came to see him, he used to book a table in the tuck shop, and that was a great occasion for him. He was extremely happy at Harrow and full of high spirits. I knew him well in the tuck-shop days and it is one of the proudest memories of my life that I should have known the Prime Minister when he was preparing for his great career.[67]

So much for the infallibility of eyewitnesses. It would be difficult to find a statement more riddled with falsehood. He wasn't a good boy; he was a disciplinary problem. He wasn't generous; he couldn't afford to be – 'I am afraid I shall want more money,' he wrote on his third day at the school, and he never had enough to cover his debts. Other boys disliked him; Sir Gerald Wollaston, a classmate, later recalled that those who 'had not met him personally soon heard about him, and what we heard created a somewhat unfavourable opinion.' Most seniors sought his company only when they wanted him to black their boots or make their beds; he had to fag for three years, performing menial tasks until he was nearly seventeen. Each of his parents visited him but once, and were never there together. And he was wretched most of the time. He himself said later that he was, 'on the whole, considerably discouraged' during his Harrow years, and in another reminiscence he wrote that he had been 'just a pack-horse that had to crop what herbage he could find by the roadside in the halts of long marches, a bit here and there.'[68]

'High spirits,' however, rings true. His letters attest to his misery, but he concealed it from his masters and the other boys. They saw him as an energetic, abrasive, insolent miscreant who, in Sir Gerald's words, 'broke almost every rule made by masters or boys, was quite incorrigible, and had an unlimited vocabulary of "backchat" which he produced with dauntless courage on every occasion of remonstrance.' The most frequent target of his back talk was Harrow's ultimate authority figure, the headmaster. Once Welldon told him sternly, 'Churchill, I have grave reason to be displeased with you.' Winston instantly replied, 'And I, sir, have grave reason to be displeased with you.' Another time the headmaster, hearing reports that the boy was using bad language, called him on the carpet. He said: 'Now, my boy, when was the last time you used bad language.' Winston had developed a stammer – which should have triggered suspicions that his self-confidence was frailer than it seemed – and he replied: 'W-ell, sir, as I en-entered this r-room, I tr-tr-tripped over the do-do-or m-mat, and I am afr-fr-aid I s-s-said D-d-damn.' Pets were strictly forbidden, but he kept two dogs in a kennel on West Street. Parts of the town were out-of-bounds for Harrovians. He made it a point to trespass there. Once he tried to blow up an out-of-bounds building, Roxreth House on Bessborough Road, which was said to be haunted. Using gunpowder, a stone ginger-beer bottle, and a home-made fuse, Winston built a bomb, lit it, and lowered it into the gloomy cellar. When nothing happened, he peered down. At that instant it exploded. His face scorched and his eyebrows singed, he was rescued by a neighbour; she bathed him and sent him back to school. As he left he cheerily told her, 'I expect this will get me the bag.' He wasn't expelled, but he was birched. It wasn't the first time for him. Harrow wasn't Ascot, and Welldon was no sadist, but all public schools practised corporal punishment then. Guilty Harrovians were birched before breakfast in the Fourth Form Room. In most cases it didn't come to that. Usually it was enough for the headmaster to warn a boy that unless he mended his ways, 'It might become my painful duty to swish you.' Winston, however, ignored these threats and was a frequent swishee. He didn't seem to care. Perhaps the Reverend Sneyd-Kynnersley had hardened him to beatings.[69]

Once he had a bad accident while playing and had to be confined to bed. Lord Salisbury heard about it from the father of another Harrow boy and asked how it happened. 'It was during a game of "Follow the Leader,"' he was told. Salisbury muttered, 'He doesn't take after his father.' But that is precisely what he *was* trying to do. During his first day at the school he tried to engage a master in political debate. The master may have been embarrassed; by then Randolph had tumbled into public disgrace. But Randolph was still his son's idol. During his infrequent visits home, Winston begged his mother to introduce him to men prominent in Parliament. This, at least, was something Jennie could enjoy doing for her son. Invitations went out, and among the guests Winston met were three future prime ministers: Rosebery, Balfour, and Asquith. He later wrote: 'It seemed a very great world where these men lived; a world in which high rules reigned and every trifle in public conduct counted; a duelling ground where although business might be ruthless, and the weapons loaded with ball, there was ceremonious personal courtesy and mutual respect.' During the convalescence after his fall, Sir Edward Carson, one of Jennie's beaux, took Winston to dinner and then to the Strangers' Gallery overlooking the House of Commons. There the boy peered down and listened, in his later words, to 'the great parties ranged on each side fighting the Home Rule controversy.' Gladstone, he thought, resembled 'a great white eagle, at once fierce and splendid.' He also witnessed the Grand Old Man's tribute to Joe Chamberlain after the maiden speech of Joe's son Austen. 'It was,' the Grand Old Man said, 'a speech which must have been dear and refreshing to a father's heart.' The boy saw how moved Joe was: 'He was hit as if a bullet had struck him.' Winston was touched, too. He thought how proud his own father would be if he were elected to Parliament and spoke well. Back at Harrow, he stood before a mirror, trying to imitate Randolph's style and delivery. Except for his stammer, a speech impediment which was just becoming evident, and a certain guttural quality which was developing in his reedy adolescent voice, it went well.[70]

It went too well. He was modelling his tone and phrases after those of an embittered man who denounced 'a government which has boycotted and slandered me' and used the language to inflict painful wounds on the men who, he thought, had betrayed him. In the mouth of an adolescent who was already thought odd by his peers, Randolph's studied invective and biting sarcasm were bound to alienate other boys. During his entire time at Harrow he made but one friend, an older boy, John – later Sir John – Milbanke. Even those who admired his nerve were put off by his truculence; one of them would recall in his memoirs how 'this small red-haired snub-nosed jolly-faced youngster' darted up 'during a house debate, against all rules, before he had been a year in the house, to refute one of his seniors.' He was also becoming cheeky at home. In the kitchen he taunted Rosa Ovenden, the Churchills' cook, until she took a broom to him, shouting, 'What the devil are you messing about here for? Hop it, copper-nob.' Clara Jerome came to see her grandson and left describing him as 'a naughty, sandy-haired little bulldog.'[71]

In his first letter to Jennie from Harrow, he had told her: 'I want to learn Gymnastics and carpentering.' Later he also became interested in fencing, but most of the time he was alone, sawing and hammering with the intensity of purpose he would later show in laying bricks; collecting mulberry leaves for a colony of silkworms he kept; poring over his stamp album; or going on long walks with his dogs, sometimes accompanied by a town detective he had befriended. He hated cricket, hated football, hated field days. He liked boxing in the gym and swimming in Ducker, the school swimming pool, and might have developed warm relationships with other boys there, but he would only box with a master, and his manner elsewhere discouraged intimacy. After Churchill had become prime minister, J. E. B. Seely, by then Lord Mottistone, recalled setting eyes on him for the first time at Ducker. Winston was trying unsuccessfully to push a floating log towards the bank. A Sixth Former said, 'You see that little red-headed fellow having a row with the log? That's young Churchill.' His companion called, 'Hi, Churchill, I bet you two buns to one you don't get it out.' Winston, said Seely, 'bent his head down and appeared to be thinking deeply,' as he later did 'in the House of Commons.' Then he turned his back on Seely, thereby snubbing a popular boy who could have helped him. On another occasion at Ducker, he sneaked up behind a slight figure and pushed him into the water. As the indignant boy climbed out, another swimmer said, 'Now you're for it. That's Leo Amery, a Sixth Former.' Realizing that he had gone too far this time, Winston apologized ineptly: 'I thought you were a Fourth Former because you are so small.' Sensing his blunder, he bit his tongue and added what, for him, was the supreme compliment: 'My father is small, too, and he is a great man.'[72]

As editor of the school paper, the *Harrovian*, Amery got even. Using the pseudonym 'Junius Junior,' Winston sent, as a letter to the editor, an attack on the school's gym policy. Amery thought part of it too abusive to print. He cut it, adding the note: 'We have omitted a portion of our correspondent's letter, which seemed to us to exceed the limits of fair criticism.' Winston was in tears; his best paragraphs, he protested, had been deleted. Actually, he should have been grateful for the blue-pencilling. Even expurgated, the letter aroused Welldon; he resented its implied criticism of his authority. Amery quite properly refused to identify 'Junius Junior.' The headmaster knew his boys, however; Winston was summoned and threatened with another swishing. By now he was regarded as the school subversive, a hoarder of grievances and defier of conventions. But some of his grievances were justified. Unreasonably, the school insisted upon listing him alphabetically under *S* – Spencer-Churchill instead of Churchill. Before his arrival, he had been promised a room in Welldon's house; he had to wait a year for it. And in at least one instance his defiance was admirable. Public school boys then were ashamed of their nannies. They would no sooner have invited one to Harrow than an upper-class American boy today would bring his teddy bear to his boarding school. Winston not only asked Woom to come; he paraded his old nurse, immensely fat and all smiles, down High Street, and then unashamedly kissed her in full view of his schoolmates. One of them was Seely, who later became a cabinet colleague of Winston's and won the DSO in France. Seely called that kiss 'one of the bravest acts I have ever seen.'[73]

Churchillian stubbornness, which would become the bane of Britain's enemies, was the despair of his teachers. He refused to learn unless it suited him. Welldon put him in what today would be called a remedial reading class, where slow boys were taught English. He stared out the window. Maths, Latin, Greek, and French were beneath his contempt. Questions 'about these Cosines or Tangents in their squared or even cubed condition,' as he later called them, were in his opinion unworthy of answers. He repeated Horace's *Odes* four times and remained ignorant of it. Looking back on those days, the man Churchill would write: 'If the reader has ever learned any Latin prose he will know that at quite an early stage one comes across the Ablative Absolute . . . I was often uncertain whether the Ablative Absolute should end in "e" or "i" or "is" or "ibus," to the correct selection of which great importance was attached. Dr Welldon seemed to be physically pained by a mistake being made in any of these letters . . . It was more than annoyance; it was a pang.' His French accent was atrocious. It would *always* be atrocious. During World War II he remarked that one of the greatest ordeals of the French Resistance was hearing him address them in their own tongue over the BBC.★[74]

He had scarcely settled in at Harrow when he was put 'on reports.' That meant that he had to acquire weekly accounts of his progress in each subject and discuss them with the headmaster. He begged his mother to come and 'jaw Welldon about keeping me on reports for such a long time.' For once Jennie came, but the headmaster was immune to her charm; Winston's status remained unchanged. The following week he wrote her: 'It is a most shameful thing that he should keep me on like this . . . I am awfully cross because now I

★ *'Prenez garde!* I am going to speak to you in French, a formidable undertaking and one which will put great demands upon your friendship for Great Britain.'

am not able to come home for an absit [overnight leave] on Thursday which I very much wanted to do. I hope you don't imagine I am happy here. It's all very well for monitors & Cricket Captains but it is quite a different thing for fourth form boys. Of course what I should like best would be to leave this *hell of a* [italicized phrase underlined, then struck out] place but I cannot expect that at present.'[75]

One member of the faculty who looked forward to seeing the last of Winston was H.O.D. Davidson, who, as his housemaster, was responsible for discipline and therefore his natural enemy. On July 12, when Winston had been enrolled less than three months, Davidson sent his mother an extraordinary complaint. He was a seasoned teacher, and had been a champion shot-putter at Oxford, but this thirteen-year-old boy was clearly beyond his competence. 'After a good deal of hesitation and discussion with his form-master,' he wrote Jennie, 'I have decided to allow Winston to have his exeat ['day out']; but I must own that he has not deserved it. I do not think, nor does Mr [Robert] Somervell, that he is in any way *wilfully* troublesome; but his forgetfulness, carelessness, unpunctuality, and irregularity in every way, have really been so serious, that I write to ask you, when he is at home to speak very gravely to him on the subject.' New boys, he conceded, needed 'a week or two' to adjust to Harrow. But 'Winston, I am sorry to say, has, if anything got worse as the term passed. Constantly late for school, losing his books, and papers and various other things into which I need not enter – he is so regular in his irregularity that I really don't know what to do; and sometimes think he cannot help it. But if he is unable to conquer his slovenliness . . . he will never make a success of a public school. . . As far as ability goes he ought to be at the top of his form, whereas he is at the bottom. Yet I do not think he is idle; only his energy is fitful, and when he gets to his work it is generally too late for him to do it well.' Davidson thought it 'very serious that he should have acquired such phenomenal slovenliness.' He felt 'sure that unless a very determined effort is made it will grow upon him.' Winston, he concluded, 'is a remarkable boy in many ways, and it would be a thousand pities if such good abilities were made useless by habitual negligence. I ought not to close without telling you that I am very much pleased with some history work he has done for me.'[76]

Clearly there was something odd here. Winston, Davidson had conceded, was the ablest boy in his form. He was, in fact, remarkable. His grasp of history was outstanding. Yet he was considered a hopeless pupil. It occurred to no one that the fault might lie, not in the boy, but in the school. Samuel Butler defined genius as 'a supreme capacity for getting its possessors into trouble of all kinds,' and it is ironic that geniuses are likeliest to be misunderstood in classrooms. Studies at the University of Chicago and the University of Minnesota have found that teachers smile on children with high IQs and frown upon those with creative minds. Intelligent but uncreative students accept conformity, never rebel, and complete their assignments with dispatch and to perfection. The creative child, on the other hand, is manipulative, imaginative, and intuitive. He is likely to harass the teacher. He is regarded as wild, naughty, silly, undependable, lacking in seriousness or even promise. His behaviour is distracting; he doesn't seem to be trying; he gives unique answers to banal questions, touching off laughter among the other children. E. Paul Torrance of Minnesota found that 70 per cent of pupils rated high in creativity were rejected by teachers picking a special class for the intellectually gifted. The Goertzels concluded that a Stanford study of genius, under which teachers selected bright children, would have excluded Churchill, Edison, Picasso, and Mark Twain.

None of this was known to Welldon and his staff, but as term succeeded term an awareness grew among them that Winston was a baffling boy. He couldn't, or wouldn't, learn the ablative absolute – a minor feat of memory – but he could recite twelve hundred lines of Macaulay without missing a word, and at no one's urging he memorized whole scenes from three Shakespeare plays: *A Midsummer Night's Dream, Henry VIII,* and *The Merchant of Venice.* There are learned men who do not know that *byss* is the opposite of *abyss.* He knew it; he had been haunting J.F. Moore's bookshop and the school library. Teachers who misquoted English poets were corrected by him. He sat rapt through a lecture on the battle of Waterloo and delivered a stunning critique of it, citing sources which were unknown to the lecturer but which, when checked, were confirmed. This merely convinced his masters that he could do the work if he wanted to and didn't do it because he was obstinate. One of them would recall, 'I formed the highest opinion of his abilities and never ceased to wonder why he did not rise higher in the School. But he hated the Classics, and in his time that kept him down . . .On one field-day he came and asked me to let him act as my *aide-de-camp,* and his alertness and zeal for action were amazing.' Another wrote: 'He was plainly uninterested in the academic subjects.' A third teacher came close to the truth; with a fine disregard for prepositional precedence he observed that 'he was not an easy boy to deal with. Of course he had always a brilliant brain, but he would only work when he chose to and for the matters he approved of.'[77]

That would have been the solution: to put him under the spell of gifted teachers who, shunning pedantry, could engage his interest and persuade him that the challenge of some courses, at least, deserved his best response. It was pointless to scold him, as Jennie did in her letters: 'Your report which I enclose is as you see a *very* bad one. You work in such a fitful inharmonious way, that you are bound to come out last – look at your place in the form! . . . If only you had a better place in your form, & were a little more methodical I would *try* & find an excuse for you. Dearest Winston you make me very unhappy. . . Your work is an insult to your intelligence.' He could only reply: 'I will not try to excuse myself for not working hard, because I know that what with one thing & another I have been rather lazy. Consequently when the month ended the crash came I got a bad report & got put on reports etc etc. . . My own Mummy I can tell you your letter cut me up very much. . . I knew that work however hard at Mathematics I could not pass in that. All other boys going in were taught these things & I was not, so they said it was useless.' Such sterile exchanges merely led him farther down the low road. Luckily there were three masters at Harrow who knew how to guide him upward. One taught maths, the very subject Winston thought hopeless. In afterlife Churchill wrote: 'All my life from time to time I have had to get up disagreeable subjects at short notice, but I consider my triumph, moral and technical, was in learning Mathematics in six months . . . I owe this achievement not only to my own "back-to-the-wall" resolution – for which no credit is too great; but to the very kindly interest taken in my case by a much respected Harrow master, Mr C. H. P. Mayo. He convinced me that Mathematics was not a hopeless bog of nonsense, and that there were meanings and rhythms behind the comical hieroglyphics.'[78]

Robert Somervell deserves a footnote in history. When Winston was about to go down for the third time, this perceptive young master – 'a most delightful man, to whom my debt is great,' Winston said of him – took over the remedial English class. His pupils were considered dolts too simple to learn Latin and Greek. They must continue to try, but Harrow would be satisfied if they mastered their own language. Usually such assignments fall to teachers who are inept themselves, and had that been true of Somervell, Winston's life might have taken a different turn. But not only was he not dull; he thought English inspiring, and his enthusiasm was infectious. In the words of Churchill: 'He knew how to do it. He taught it as no one else has ever taught it.' First they learned to parse sentences thoroughly. Then they practised continuing grammatical analysis, using a system of Somervell's which appealed to the playful instinct in every boy: using a spectrum of inks, he would score a long sentence, breaking it up into subject, verb, object; relative clauses, conditional clauses, conjunctive and disjunctive clauses. Each had its colour and its bracket. 'It was a kind of drill,' Churchill recalled. 'We did it almost daily.' Since Winston remained obdurate in his refusal to study the classics, he remained in Somervell's class for three terms. As a man he would write that he went through the drills 'three times as long as anyone else. I had three times as much of it. I learned it thoroughly. Thus I got into my bones the essential structure of the ordinary British sentence – which is a noble thing. And when in after years my schoolfellows who had won prizes and distinction for writing such beautiful Latin poetry and pithy Greek epigrams had to come down again to common English, to earn their living or make their way, I did not feel myself at any disadvantage.'[79]

At Harrow his lifelong fascination with words grew. He was thirteen, and Somervell was introducing him to literature. Except for best-sellers like Wilkie Collins's *Moonstone*, few Harrovians read for pleasure. Winston was soon deep in Thackeray, Dickens, Wordsworth, and every biography he could lay his hands on. He knew what was good and found he liked it. Inevitably his vocabulary increased. In his letters he wrote of a toy given him by his aunts as 'a source of unparalleled amusement,' his funds needed 'replenishing,' welcome news was 'pleasing intelligence.' The bookseller Moore, who saw him almost daily, noticed that he was displaying 'evidences of his unusual command of words. He would argue in the shop on any subject, and, as a result of this, he was, I am afraid, often left in sole possession of the floor.'[80] At this point another teacher, L. M. Moriarty, Winston's fencing master, suggested that he drop in on him evenings at home to discuss essays and history. They talked, not only of content, but also of form, particularly essay techniques then being developed by Stevenson, Ruskin, Huxley, and Cardinal Newman. None of this was reflected in the report cards sent to Connaught Place, but the autodidactic pattern was forming. Winston was being taught to teach himself. He would always be a dud in the classroom and a failure in examinations, but in his own time, on his own terms, he would become one of the most learned statesmen of the coming century.

Aware of his growing intellect and increasing flair for expression, he was exasperated by his dismal marks. Welldon was also frustrated, and for the same reason. Shortly after Winston's fourteenth birthday, the headmaster told Seely that he had never seen a boy with 'such a love and veneration for the English language.'[81] When he received a sparkling paper from a Sixth Former who was a brilliant classicist but clumsy with his native tongue, Welldon called the boy in. He told him he didn't believe he had written the theme. Churchill, he said, was the only pupil who wrote that well. Confession followed. Welldon had uncovered a conspiracy. The Sixth Former had been translating Winston's elementary Latin assignments. Then he had sat at his desk with paper and pencil while Winston, pacing back and forth, dictated the theme. There is no record of disciplinary action, but the incident is striking. It is the first known instance of the technique Churchill would use in writing his greatest books. And it is a devastating comment on public school values. Eloquent and lucid in living English, Winston was a scholastic failure because of his disdain for two languages which would be almost useless to him.

He was writing now, submitting further contributions to the school paper as 'Junius Junior.' They seldom appeared. He didn't fit here, either. A fellow Old Boy recalled: 'From time to time he sent notes on current events to *The Harrovian*; these could not always be printed, but they were extraordinarily witty and well expressed, and often caused the editors to roar with laughter.' This is reminiscent of the nineteenth-century Krupp cannon which was sent to Saint Petersburg as a sample in the hope of stimulating sales. It fired so well that the Russians put it in a museum. Laughing editors spiked Winston's copy because they felt that passing their amusement along to their readers would be undignified. Of his contributions which were accepted, only one survives, a lugubrious poem inspired by an epidemic of influenza raging on the Continent:[82]

> And now Europe groans aloud
> And 'neath the heavy thunder-cloud
> Husked in both song and dance:
> The germs of illness wend their way
> To westward each succeeding day
> And enter merry France.

*   *   *

The flu hit Winston during his first Christmas holidays from Harrow. On December 30 Randolph peevishly wrote his sister-in-law, 'Of course the boys have made themselves ill with their Christmassing, & yesterday both were in bed with [Dr] Roose and [Dr] Gordon hopping in & out of the house. Jack is better this morning but Winston has a sore throat & some fever. I hope it is nothing but biliousness & indigestion.' He and Jennie didn't hover around to find out. They left that day on a vacation of their own. Meanwhile, Winston worsened. Two days later he wrote his mother: 'My throat is still painful & swelled – I get very hot in the night – & have very little appetite to speak of . . . It is awful "rot" spending ones holidays in bed or one room.' Another letter followed a few days later. He was 'tired of bed and slops.' His new magic lantern didn't work. The 'Dr says I ought to go to the seaside, & then I *shan't see you at all.*' He calculated that '1 week at the seaside leaves 1 week & that 1 week you will be away. It is an awful pity. I don't know what to do.' Woom knew. She bundled him off to her brother-in-law's cottage at Ventnor. Back at Harrow he wired her: 'Am quite well.'[83]

But he wasn't. Suffering a relapse the following month, he wrote his mother that he was 'still far from well & am in bed because I can hardly stand. I am so weak I have had very [little] food for 4 days.' Woom had come, and Mrs Davidson had told him that 'she hopes you will let Woomany come [again] tomorrow, because she says the company will do me good. I do not know how the day would have passed but for Woomany. I have had another big poultice on my liver to-day to make it worse [sic]. I hope you will allow Woomany to come tomorrow as I shall certainly be very disappointed if she does not turn up.' His need for his nurse is a thread running through his correspondence with his mother: 'Thank you so much for letting Woom come down.' 'Do let Woom come down tomorrow.' 'Thanks awfully for letting Woom come down today.' Mrs Everest, for her part, wrote him faithfully, but she couldn't grasp his adolescent problems; she still thought of him as a small boy. She sent him 'some fine flannel shirts to sleep in' and a new suit: 'Winny dear do try to keep the new suit expressly for visiting, the brown one will do for everyday wear, please do this to please me. I hope you will not take cold my darling take care not to get wet or damp.' And: 'I hope you have recovered from the effects of your dental operation deary. . . I hope you wear your coat in this wet weather & change your Boots when they are damp, that is what gives you tooth ache sitting in wet boots.'[84]

Woom alone attended to his errands. She was anxious about his well-being and missed him terribly; in her long, gushing letters she told him again and again that she was always at his beck and call. She asked, 'Did you get your luggage alright to Harrow this time it is always best to take it with you from the Station. . . Have sent you 3 Black Waistcoats let me know dear also if you receive a small parcel of 2 shirts &c I sent off yesterday. I am sending you 1 dozen new Handkerchiefs on Monday with the hamper. Are you always going to have the room to yourself or is it only temporary. Old Mr Wickes sent me a lot of lovely grapes from Ventnor out of his green house. I am so glad you are well my sweet mind & try to get through the exam my precious loving darling old lamb – much love & kisses from Your old Woom.' If he neglected to write to her, she was reproachful: 'My darling Lamb, I have been looking for a letter from you all last week. I never heard anything about you for a whole week. Are you well dear. . . Did you get a Pocket Book or a Memorandum Book from me I sent you one . . . Do send me a line there's a dear Boy & tell me what you are going to do. Did Mamma bring you a Birthday present. I have no news to tell you so with fondest love to you my darling. I am ever your loving W.'[85]

His mother had not brought him a present. Unlike her husband, Jennie remembered Winston's age, but she doesn't appear to have been much more thoughtful. 'His Lordship has postponed his arrival for a fortnight, so you will not see him,' Woom wrote in a typical midweek letter to Winston; 'Mamma has been away since Saturday.' Except for two years when Randolph rented a house at Banstead – it was here that Winston built his great fort, together with a homemade catapult which hurled green apples at a nearby cow – Winston and Jack spent their long holidays with Woom, often in the Balaam cottage at Ventnor. Even at Banstead, Woom was usually in loco parentis, the only adult on the spot. She wrote Jennie from there in 1891: 'I hope you got Master Winston's letter he wrote last evening. They are both so happy & delighted & in towering spirits . . . They are so happy and well I should like to keep Master Jack here until Mr Winston returns from Canford . . . It is so much better for them than London. I am desired to enclose drawings of last night with their best love & kisses. Your ladyship's obednt servant E. A. Everest.'[86]

Lord Randolph was usually to be found these days at the Jockey Club. His most successful horse was a yearling he named 'Abbess' after a French novel Jennie happened to be reading at the time. Abbess won, among other races, the Oaks at Epsom, the Manchester Cup, and the Hardwicke Stakes – over £10,000 in prize money. Unfortunately for her owner, when she won the Oaks at twenty-to-one, Randolph, convinced she couldn't do it, had bet all his money on another horse. The story went around the London clubs; it was regarded as characteristic of his recidivous disloyalty. He was down now, and his critics were kicking him mercilessly. The *Spectator* reported that parliamentary debates showed 'that Lord Randolph's power to impress, if not to interest the House of Commons, is dwindling rapidly. The House watch his gyrations with languid curiosity or mild amusement . . . Most of them probably think that it was indeed a memorable, a very memorable, mistake to put so feather-headed a politician as Lord Randolph Churchill in the position in which he was expected to counsel gentlemen on the Ministerial side of the House, and did counsel them with more or less cleverness for a few weeks.' To escape this sort of thing – and perhaps to flee from the winks of London society, which saw Jennie openly reaching for younger and younger men – Randolph decided to try his hand at journalism. He sailed to Cape Town for three months, after reaching an agreement with the *Daily Graphic*, which would publish his letters from there. Even these pieces vexed the *Review of Reviews:* 'Lord Randolph Churchill in his time has played many parts, but not

137

even in the famous somersault which terminated his career as leader of the House of Commons and possible leader of the Conservative party has he afforded the public a more unseemly exhibition of irresponsibility than in his letters from South Africa. They furnish the culminating evidence, if further evidence were necessary, as to the impossibility of Lord Randolph Churchill as the leader of men.'[87]

Such a man, in such straits, is ever alert for slights. When Abbess won the Manchester Cup, again at twenty-to-one, Randolph harvested £2,202 in prize money plus his enormous winnings from his bets. He sent Winston a five-pound note. When instant gratitude was not forthcoming from Harrow, he was furious. Jennie wrote: 'Your Father is very angry with you for not acknowledging the gift of the £5 for a whole week, and then writing an offhand careless letter.' Of course, money wasn't what Winston wanted from his father. Welldon knew that, and he wrote Lord Randolph, tactfully suggesting that it might 'perhaps not be disagreeable' to His Lordship and Her Ladyship to come to Harrow sometime and take 'at least the opportunity of seeing what Winston's school life is like.' Winston hoped they would come for Speech Day, when he would be honoured for his feat of memory with Macaulay's *Lays*. He checked timetables and wrote his father: 'If you take the 11.7 from Baker Street you will get to Harrow at 11.37. I shall meet you at the station with a fly, if I can get one . . . You have never been to see me & so everything will be new to you.' He wrote his mother: 'Do try to get Papa to come. He has never been.' Papa refused. The relationship between these two had long been doomed. Randolph had sent him a bicycle, but Welldon wrote Jennie the following month: 'I am sorry to say Winston has fallen off his bicycle and hurt himself . . . The Doctor calls it "slight concussion." ' Later Winston wrote his mother that he had decided to have the bike fixed and then exchange it for a bulldog. Jennie didn't care – 'Do as you like about yr bicycle' – but Woom foresaw trouble if Randolph found out: 'What on earth is the good of your having a Bull Dog unless it is to keep us all in terror of our lives . . . Besides His Lordship gave you the Bicycle & he would not like you to part with it.' Winston found her argument persuasive. Offending his father was the last thing he intended. Randolph's African journey excited him. He wrote him in Johannesburg: 'Have you shot a lion yet?' He was still Randolph's most loyal partisan.[88]

His father's criticisms of conditions in South Africa, brought on by commercial exploitation, were appearing in the *Daily Graphic*. Savage rebuttals of them had spread from the *Spectator* and the *Review of Reviews* to virtually every serious newspaper. Winston excitedly wrote him: 'You cannot imagine what vials of wrath you have uncorded [sic]. All the papers simply rave. Shareholders, friends of the company, and directors from Sir Donald Currie to the lowest Bottle Washer are up in arms. *Truth*, the *Speaker*, *Standard* and others including even the *Harrow Gazette* devote a column to "Lord Randolph's Grumbles." The *Standard* quotes the *Speaker* & is particularly offensive. It states that – but oh I will not bore you with the yapping of these curs hungry for their money bags.' Winston's vows of filial loyalty seem to have brought father and son to the brink of cordiality. Randolph replied to one of them, 'You cannot think how pleased I was to get your interesting & well written letter.' But the moment swiftly passed. It was like that flash of green in tropical sunsets just before the sun vanishes over the horizon. It lasts but a microsecond and is followed by total darkness. Randolph was approaching the last stages of his terrible disease. Ahead, for his family, lay horror.[89]

Jennie flourished during her husband's South African absence. She was deeply in love with Count Kinsky, and when not sleeping with him she spent virtually every moment entertaining friends. No. 2 Connaught Place was always full. Then, to her annoyance, the annual Eton-Harrow cricket match rolled around. Cricket still bored Winston, but the match at Lord's was an annual social ritual, a great occasion for the boys at both schools to wear top hats, ride around in glittering coaches with the aristocracy, and feast on strawberries and cream. To Winston's consternation, his mother told him that her social calendar was full; there was no room for him at the Connaught Place house. Indeed, there was no room for *her*. She had invited so many guests that she had been obliged to move in with her sister Clara at 18 Aldford Street. Unappeased, he wrote her: 'Think how unhappy I should be being left at Harrow when 90 out of every hundred boys are enjoying themselves. You promised I should come . . . I was terribly frightened when I got your letter this morning. The Possibility of my not being able to come being to my mind entirely out of the question. Could you not ask Grandmamma Marlborough to let me come stay with her (at least) . . . My darling Mummy I am sure you have not been very much troubled about me this term. I have asked for no visits & I forfeited the pleasure of seeing you on Speech Day therefore I do hope you will endeavour not to disappoint me utterly with regard to July 11th and 12th.' Two days later she replied: 'Oh! dear oh! You silly old boy I did not mean that you would have to remain at Harrow only that I cld not have you here.' She suggested that Clara might 'put you up.' That proved impossible, and Woom wrote him the next day: 'Well my dearest the reason Mamma cannot have you at home is the house is to be full of visitors for the race week which commences on the Tuesday tomorrow week. But I don't see why you could not go from Friday till Monday because you could go by yourself.' Since she herself would be billeted elsewhere, he could stay with her 'and then perhaps Aunt Clara or some one would see you off to Harrow.' That evening it was settled. He would stay with Duchess Fanny on Grosvenor Square.[90]

Actually, it turned out to be Winston's most memorable boyhood weekend. Despite Jennie's lack of maternal instincts, her strong erotic drive assured a constant string of sensitive suitors, some of whom sensed Winston's loneliness, understood his yearning for an affectionate father figure, and were eager to give him strong arms to lean on. On the morning of Friday, July 10, 1891, sixteen-year-old Winston arrived at Baker Street Station, watched the early innings at Lord's, took a hansom to Grosvenor Square, and lunched with

Duchess Fanny. That evening John Milbanke took him to dinner at the Isthmian Club; afterwards they attended the Naval Exhibition. 'Most beautiful models & guns of every description,' Winston wrote Jack. 'Got home at 11.45.')[91] His great treat, however, came the following day. Kaiser Wilhelm II, emperor of Germany's Second Reich and now in the fourth year of his reign, was visiting Queen Victoria, his grandmother. All London knew he would be appearing at the Crystal Palace, where a special exhibition awaited him, and that the public was invited. Count Kinsky decided to take Winston.

Charles Andreas Kinsky, son of an Austrian prince and a Liechtenstein princess, was then thirty-five, two years younger than Jennie. In appearance he was the apotheosis of what a man of the world should be. Tall, powerfully built, handsome, with a bristling moustache, he wore his top hat at a jaunty angle and, superbly tailored, glided across drawing rooms with effortless grace. Nine years earlier, riding against heavy odds, he had become the first amateur to win the Grand National. Disdainful of danger, he repeatedly risked his life steeplechasing. In 1881, the year he met Jennie, he had been appointed honorary attaché at the Austro-Hungarian embassy. Since then he had become an imperial chamberlain. Impetuous and hot-tempered, he was as much in love with Jennie as she with him. Now he meant to charm her son. Back at Harrow afterwards, Winston would write Jack, for whom he set down all his experiences on that glorious day, that he spent part of the morning at Lord's. 'Of course you know Harrow won by five wickets. I could not "smash an Eton hat" as I had to leave the ground early to go to the Crystal Palace.' Then Kinsky picked him up and 'drove me in his phaeton.'[92]

The palace, a glass-and-iron conception of Joseph Paxton and Victoria's Albert, had been built in Hyde Park for the Great Exhibition of 1851 and then moved to Penge, in South London. From Lord's it was an eight-mile ride, but Kinsky had brought a copy of the July *Strand Magazine,* which carried 'A Scandal in Bohemia,' the first of Conan Doyle's Sherlock Holmes short stories. Winston thought it a capital yarn and Kinsky a capital fellow. After he had finished the tale of Irene Adler's ingenuity, they sang that year's most popular song, already a hit though still only in rehearsal at London's Gaiety Theatre:

> *Ta-ra-ra-boom-de-ay:*
> *Did you see my wife today?*
> *No, I saw her yesterday:*
> *Ta-ra-ra-boom-de-ay!*

And then they were there. The first sight to greet Winston was a menagerie of 'Wild Beasts. (wonderful never seen anything like them.)' Next came a parade, before the seated spectators, of two thousand firemen and a hundred engines, marching past the kaiser and his kaiserin to the music of a military band. Winston was especially interested in the guest of honour. He had brought a sketchbook, and there, in the crowd beside Kinsky, he made his first surviving attempt in the arts. He wrote Jack: 'I must describe the Emperor's uniform. A helmet of bright Brass surmounted by a white eagle nearly 6 inches high.' Wilhelm also wore 'a polished steel cuirass & a perfectly white uniform with high boots.'[93]

After 'the Engines trotted past & finally all the lot Galloped past as hard as they could go,' the count took Winston to dinner. The maître d' told them the restaurant was full, that he couldn't possibly seat them, but 'Count K. spoke German to him & it had a wonderful effect.' The dinner was 'very tolerable,' with 'lots of champagne which pleased your loving brother very much.' More fun lay ahead. The major event that evening was to be a display of fireworks for Wilhelm. Finding time on their hands before it began, Kinsky took Winston to another exhibition, which, when they arrived, turned out to be closed. Instead, they visited a nearby feature attraction, an 'Aerial Car,' which raced along a wire rope 'nearly 300 yards in length & awfully high.' They waited in line ten minutes. Then the car broke down, and a distant cannon signalled the start of the fireworks. The count led Winston over a rail and was preparing to leave when 'a half breed sort of Kaffir who was in charge' tried to stop them by grabbing Kinsky's coattails. The count, 'whom you know is immensely strong,' grabbed 'the blackguards hand' and crushed his fingers. At that 'the Mulatto' dropped the coattails, swore, and told Kinsky he should think himself ' "d—— lucky" ' that he wasn't pitched over the banisters. ' "By——" ' said Count Kinsky "I should like to see you touch me." "You go and learn manners," retorted the cad. "But not from you" said Count K.' Then the crowd howled down 'the scoundrel' and 'we went on our way angry but triumphant.' It is an incident right out of *Chatterbox*, Nick Carter, or Karl May. The uppity ruffian of inferior race accosts our hero, is defied by him, and slinks away. Boys of Winston's class believed that sort of thing happened all the time, that it was the classic confrontation between the wicked and the just. And because Winston never entirely put away childish things, part of him would go on believing it to the end.[94]

The kaiser, whose image would later alter in Winston's eyes, was in all his splendour that night. Pyrotechnists opened their display with volleys of rockets. Next came 'two great pieces of Cornflowers & Roses (the Emperors Favourit Flowers) which afterwards changed to the heads of the Emperor and Empress.' Then the battle of the Nile was refought in the sky. 'The ships actually moved & the cannonading was terrific. Finally L'Orient blew up.' It was an ironic moment, though they did not appreciate it. That was how they saw war then: brilliant girandoles, flares, Catherine wheels, candlebombs, and whizzbangs, celebrating the feats of daring of the intrepid Nelson and his 'band of brothers' aboard the *Vanguard* while honouring the gallant French squadron who went down nobly – and apparently bloodlessly – when thirteen of Napoleon's men-of-war were annihilated and strewn across the waters of Abukir Bay. No horror, no agony, no bestiality; just puffs and streaks of blinding colour against the serene night sky. No spectator was more deceived than the guest of honour, and Winston, grown to manhood, would be among those who had to cope with the consequences of his deception. But he himself had been dazzled, that evening; he too had believed in what the French called *la Gloire*. The day, he thought, had been perfect, and when the display ended 'we went & got our coat & had each an American drink & then we went to our carriage. Count K. drives beautifully & we passed with our fast pair of horses everything on the road.'[95]

If that was the high point of his Harrow years, the low point came five months later. Jennie was becoming increasingly exasperated with the reports from Welldon. Again and again she tried to convince Winston that his record now could affect his whole life, pleading with him to 'stop and think it out for yourself and take a good pull before it is too late.' Now from Paris, now from Monte Carlo, now from Mayfair ('I would go down to you – but I have so many things to arrange about the Ascot party next week that I can't manage it'), she implored him to tackle and master languages, his biggest bugbear. He was by turns contrite, confident that next term his marks would soar (which they never did), or teasing. His sense of timing was poor. When he learned that her purse had been snatched at Monte Carlo, he wrote carelessly: 'C'est Dommage, because at the same moment I must put in a request for "un peu plus d'argent." . . . Don't go to that Casino. Invest your money in me, its safer . . . You are a bird.' She was not amused. She had also begun to find his company irritating. He was an awkward teenager; in a letter she described him as 'just at the "ugly" stage – slouchy and tiresome.' Something drastic, she decided, must be done. A hint of what it would be came in a letter she wrote Randolph during Winston's Kinsky weekend: 'Welldon says W should have special help for the French this summer.'[96]

He was to be taught a lesson, and not just in French. Jennie and Welldon worked it out together. He would be sent across the Channel to learn the language by speaking with Frenchmen. The first plan was to board him with a family in Rouen. Winston objected violently: 'No family! No family! Ugh!' he wrote Jennie. 'I beg and Pray that you will not send me to a vile, nasty, fusty, beastly French "Family," ' adding – a sign that he knew the company his mother was keeping – that 'even if the worst comes to the worst you could send me to some of your friends & not to "respectable creatures." ' That was in July, when he assumed that the distasteful experience would be behind him by autumn. Then the blow fell. He was told he would spend Christmas at the Versailles home of one of Harrow's French masters. He was accustomed, if by no means reconciled, to his parents' absence over the year-end holiday. But at least he could count on the company of Woom, Jack, his aunts, and his grandmother. Now he would be alone, in a foreign country, trying to cope with a language he detested. He fought back with everything he had. 'Darling Mummy,' he wrote on December 6, 'I shall think it will be very unkind and unnatural of you . . . to do me out of my Christmas. Out of all this school not 5 boys are going away at all . . . Mummy don't be so unkind and make me unhappy . . . If you in spite of my entreaties force me to go I will do as little as I can and the holidays will be one continual battle.'[97]

Jennie struck back savagely: 'Quite apart from other considerations, the tone of your letter is not calculated to make one over lenient. When one wants something in this world, it is not by delivering ultimatums that one is likely to get it.' She told him that he was 'old enough not to play the fool' for 'the sake of a few days pleasure,' and that 'you can be quite certain my darling that I will decide for what is best, but I tell you frankly that *I* am going to decide not *you*.' Replying, he reproached her for being 'so sarcastic to me since it is I not you who have to make the sacrifice . . . You say it is for you to decide. I am required to give up my holidays – not you. I am forced to go to people who bore me excessively – not you. You were asked to give up a short part of the year to take me abroad – you promised – refused & I did not press the point . . . Please do have a little regard for my happiness.'[98]

She returned this note without comment. He wrote again, asking why, and she told him: 'I have read only one page of yr letter and I send it back to you – as its style does not please me . . . My dear you won't gain anything by taking this line.' It was now December 16, and he was close to panic. 'Never,' he wrote her, 'would I have believed that you would have been so unkind. I am utterly miserable. That you should refuse to read my letter is most painful to me. There was nothing in it to give you grounds for rejecting it . . . Oh my Mummy!' Next: 'I am more unhappy than I can possibly say . . . Darling Mamma if you want me to do anything for you, especially so great a sacrifice don't be so cruel to Your loving son Winny.' Then, the next day: 'Please don't be so unkind. Do answer my letter.' Then, the day after that – with Christmas a week away – he made his last pitiful effort: 'Darling Mummy do attend to my letter. I am so wretched. Even now I weep. Please my darling Mummy be kind to your loving son. Don't let my silly letters make you angry. Let me at least think you love me. – Darling Mummy I despair. I am so wretched. I don't know what to do. Don't be angry I am so miserable . . . Please write something kind to me. I am very sorry if I have "riled" you before I did only want to explain things from my point of view. Good Bye my darling Mummy. With best love I remain, Ever your loving son Winston.' It availed him nothing. Jennie was adamant. She booked second-class passage for him for a December 21 crossing and wrote Randolph, 'I can't tell you what trouble I have had with Winston this last fortnight he has bombarded me with letters, cursing his fate and everyone. Of course it is a great disappointment to him not being home for Xmas but he makes as much fuss as tho' he were going to Australia for 2 years.'[99]

Debarking, he telegraphed Woom: 'Arrived safe. Good passage.' Putting a brave face on what remained a desolate business, he jauntily wrote his mother, to convince her that his French needed no improvement: 'We arrived at Dieppe où nous partook of de bon Café au lait. Le chemin de fer etait très incommode. Pour quatres heures I waited having nothing to do. Nous arrivames au gare St Lazare. J'ai déclaré ma boite des cigarettes. But they did not charge me anything nor did they open mon mal.' He rode three hours on hired hacks ('chevaux de louage'); then his host, M. Minssen, met him with a spare mount and led him to his Versailles home at 18, rue de Provence. 'M.M. rides very well & very hard at full gallop on the 'ard 'igh road. Les chevaux ne sont pas mal. Ils son véritablement rossés. Mme Monsieur M's mère ne dit rien que "Son progrés est marveilleux." "N'est ce pas extraordinaire" etc etc' Christmas was quiet at Versailles, but Minssen *mère* turned out to be English, so they had turkey and plum pudding. 'Also,' Winston acknowledged, 'a little fun on Christmas Eve.' He went to the theatre to see Michel Stroghoff, learned to skate, rode a great deal – once, with M.M., for three hours: 'The horses are very good considering.' But his chief excitement was the 'Bon Marche,' which sold toy soldiers. He wrote Jack that the shop carried French and Russian infantrymen, artillerymen, and black cannon. 'They were all in positions for loading & firing. Ramming home, etc. Only 7 francs=5/-.' The soldiers were two francs for a dozen. 'When I return we will have much fun and great games with the army.' He was 'longing to return . . . I count the hours. I won't travel 2nd again by Jove.'[100]

He wrote his mother daily, heard nothing from her, and protested: 'It seems to me that with you "out of sight is out of mind" indeed. Not a line from anybody. You promised to write 3 times a week – I have recd 1 letter.' Jennie didn't even acknowledge his present to her. The fact was that she couldn't have received either letters or gift; she was away at Penn, the ancestral home of Lord and Lady Howe, preparing a party for the Prince of Wales. Winston's one letter had been from Mrs Everest. He had picked a good time to be away, Woom said; the electricity had failed, there was no gas, so for five days she and Jack had lived in utter darkness 'in this room with a candle until I am half blind.' On Christmas Day she and the servants, in the tradition of the time, 'drank to the health and the happiness of Mamma and Papa'; then, after supper, 'we went into the kitchen & they put aside the table & danced for dear life. There was no music, so Edney [the butler] whistled & I played the comb with a piece of paper & comb like we used to do in our good old nursery days.' Of Winston's present to her she wrote: 'It is very kind of you but you know my Lamb I would rather you did not spend your money on me.' Woom had mailed him a gift and hoped his spirits picked up: 'Cheer up old Boy enjoy yourself try & feel contented you have much to be thankful for if you only consider & fancy how nice it will be to be able to parlez vous francais.' His glumness troubled her, and, nannylike, she suspected an earthy cause: 'I should buy plenty of fruit & eat it if I were you keep you *regular you know dear*.'[101]

Lack of congeniality, not constipation, was Winston's chief complaint. Before leaving England he had extracted from his mother a pledge that he would be entertained by three of her continental admirers. He wanted another Kinsky. Unaware that she was absent from London, he had written her on Christmas Eve: 'Write to Baron Hirsch. Do! I have not heard a word from those "friends" you spoke about.' Three days later he sent another reminder: 'Not a word from Baron Hirsch – not a line from M. de Breteuil – Not a sound from Mr Trafford. I don't know any of their addresses, so what can I do?' He waited two more days and wrote again: 'I wish you would try my mummy to fulfill your promise. Baron Hirsch may be in Jericho for all I know.' He needn't have worried. Jennie was an adroit manipulator of men. Approaching her fortieth birthday, she still had the figure of a young girl, coupled with extraordinary social skills, and when she gave her lovers marching orders, they leapt to obey. At the bottom of a letter to Jack, Winston scrawled: 'N.B. Invitations have come. Baron Hirsch Friday last Mr Trafford Sat yesterday. Baron Hirsch Tomorrow M. de Breteuil Tuesday.' They moved in a Paris unknown to Winston's French master; they entertained him at the best restaurants, taught him wines, and introduced him to the recherché society of continental gentlemen. He also saw his first corpses: 'Last Monday I went to M. de B. and B. Hirsch after. He took me to the morgue. I was much interested. Only 3 Macabres – not a good bag.' One suspects adolescent bravado here. At the age of seventeen he could scarcely have coped with massed cadavers. [102]

Another pledge from his mother was of a different order. Jennie had given him her word that upon his return from Versailles he would be kept out of school for a week to provide him a decent vacation at Connaught Place. He wrote her from France on December 27: 'I will remind you of the promise you made me at Harrow of an extra week [at home] if I gave up my Christmas. A promise is a promise & as I have fulfilled my part I rely on you my darling mummy to do the rest. I know you won't chuck me like that.' On January 13 he again told her that he meant to hold her to her commitment: 'I am of course counting, my Mummy, on you to fulfil your promise which was more than anything the reason of my coming here willingly.' He was nailing her to her vow, and his very vehemence suggests an uneasiness, a growth of doubt. But cutting even a day of classwork was a serious matter for a boy with his academic record. Mothers in Victorian families lacked the authority to make so grave a decision, and Winston, sensing that, decided to lay the matter before Randolph. He pointed out to him that 'I have missed everything this year. Christmas, New Years Day etc.' Then he wrote: 'The chief inducement Mamma held out for me to go to France was the promise of an extra week. Please do see what you can arrange for me.' [103]

His father was in no mood to arrange any such thing. He was in a foul temper. The party at Penn had collapsed because the Duke of Clarence had chosen this extremely inconvenient moment to die, causing HRH to cancel all his social engagements. But even if Randolph had been in the best of spirits, he believed he had the best of reasons for pulling the rug from under his wife. He wrote Winston, 'I think I will not try and get you an extra week because really every moment is of value to you now before you go up for your examination in June. The loss of a week now may mean your not passing, which I am sure you will admit would be very discreditable and disadvantageous . . . I do pray you my dear boy to make the most of every hour of your time so as to render your passing a certainty . . . I hope you will work like a little dray horse right up to the summer examination, only about four months off.' Winston was bitter. He wrote: 'How I have been tricked!' Jennie wrote him: 'Papa showed me his letter to you. He won't hear of yr asking for an extra week. I am very sorry.' So she should have been. Robert Rhodes James concludes that 'behind Lady Randolph's vivid beauty and warm vivacity there lay an essentially selfish and frivolous character.'[104] That is hard but just. Winston rightly felt betrayed. Yet his affection for her did not diminish. And such is the wonder of human relationships that soon she would reciprocate. Jennie was not a faithful wife, but in other ways she was a loyal one. As the final stages of Randolph's paresis overtook him – as he became less endearing each day – she would slowly transfer her devotion to her brilliant, eccentric elder son. Her passion would run deep and strong, and it would be of immeasurable benefit to him, though it could never be mistaken for maternal love.

The examination, a screening of candidates for admission to the Royal Military College at Sandhurst, had been looming before Winston ever since his father's decision, based on a display of toy soldiers in a nursery, to make his son an army officer. Other Harrovians were following the same star – so many, indeed, that Welldon had created a special Army Class. Winston had joined it in September 1889, when he was fourteen. In effect these boys were cramming for military exams. Moriarty and another master decided early that Winston's maths was too poor for Woolwich, the academy that prepared cadets for commissions in the artillery and engineers. Instead, they piloted him towards Sandhurst, which turned out subalterns of infantry and cavalry.

After four months in the Army Class, Winston had written his mother, 'I am getting along capitally. . . I am going up for my "preliminary Exam" for "Sandhurst" in June.' His confidence, here as so often before, was wholly unjustified. Welldon withdrew his name, explaining to him that he wasn't ready for the test; among other things, his grasp of geometrical drawing was hopelessly deficient. But the headmaster gave him the green light six months later, and then Winston had three pieces of good luck. This was the last Sandhurst preliminary in which Latin was an optional subject. Second, an essay question dealt with the American Civil War, and Jennie's mother had seen to it that he knew a great deal about that long before he entered Harrow. The third stroke of fortune was remarkable. He had known there would be a map question, but did not know of which country. Therefore, he wrote the names of twenty-five countries on scraps of paper the night before the exam, put them in a hat, and drew one. He had picked New Zealand. He memorized it. And in the morning the geographical problem was: 'Draw a map of New Zealand.' So he passed all subjects, becoming one of twelve out of the twenty-nine Harrow candidates to succeed. He wrote his mother: 'I have received congratulations from scores of boys and many masters. Dudley' – Dudley Marjoribanks, the son of Randolph's sister Fanny – 'has not spoken to me. Vive la joie! He has not passed and is furious.' Jennie wrote her husband:

'I think you might make him a present of a gun as a reward. He is pining for one, and ought to have a little encouragement.'[105]

No gun arrived, there was no pat on the back from Randolph, and the edge of Winston's enthusiasm for a military career was briefly blunted. He toyed with the notion of taking holy orders. In a postscript home he wrote: 'Really I feel less keen about the Army every day. I think the church would suit me better.' Looking back long afterwards, he reflected that 'I might have gone into the Church and preached orthodox sermons in a spirit of audacious contradiction to the age.' But it had been a preposterous notion; while Churchill can easily be pictured in a pulpit, one cannot imagine him on his knees. As a boy, he would say in later life, he had to go to church every week and 'this was very good. I had accumulated in those years so fine a surplus in the Bank of Observance that I have been drawing confidently upon it ever since. Weddings, christenings, and funerals have brought in a steady annual income, and I have never made too close enquiries about the state of my account. It might well even be that I should find an overdraft.' He wrote trenchantly of World War I: 'Religion, having discreetly avoided conflict on the fundamental issues, offered its encouragement and consolations through all its forms impartially to all the combatants.' Towards the end of his life he said: 'I am ready to meet my Maker. Whether my Maker is ready to meet me is another question.' To those who pressed him, he quoted Disraeli: 'Sensible men are all of the same religion.' Asked what that was, he quoted him again: 'Sensible men never tell.'[106]

But Disraeli had also said that 'what we anticipate seldom occurs, what we least expected generally happens,' and this was Winston's immediate problem in the summer of 1892, when he was seventeen. Having leapt over the preliminary hurdle, he assumed that he was as good as accepted by Sandhurst. Thus he was rudely shaken when, having taken the main entrance examination, he learned that he had flunked, and flunked badly. Not only had he failed to qualify for an infantry cadetship; his marks were also inadequate for the cavalry, which accepted lower performances. He had scored 39 per cent in freehand drawing, 30 per cent in Latin, and 28 per cent in maths, and had excelled only in English composition. Counting French, English history, chemistry, and geometry, he was 300 marks below the minimum and 700 below his cousin Dudley, who had caught up with the other successful applicants. Moriarty consoled Winston – 'I think your marks and place very creditable for your first try' – but Welldon was brusque: 'I feel it essential that in coming back to school you should come resolved to work not by fits and starts but with regular persistent industry.' The headmaster considered recommending a freelance tutor, then decided against it. Randolph, predictably, was disgusted. He was also unsurprised. On the few occasions he had questioned his son about his education, he had been distinctly unimpressed. Once he had turned on him and suddenly asked: 'What was the Grand Remonstrance against Charles I?' This had been a complicated issue in 1641, turning on parliamentary influence in the monarch's court and the Anglican church. Winston's reply was: 'Parliament beat the king and cut his head off.' (Decapitation 'seemed to me,' he later said wistfully, 'the grandest remonstrance imaginable.') But his father had sworn to himself and turned away. Now, with the results from Sandhurst, Randolph felt confirmed. He glumly awaited Winston's second attempt to matriculate, writing Duchess Fanny that his 'next try is on Nov. 24th. If he fails again I shall think about putting him in business.' Trade would have been even less suitable for Winston than the ministry, and he knew it. Thus, his last term at Harrow was clouded by the possibility of an aborted career. Welldon kept giving him pep talks and seems to have convinced himself that they were justified; on the eve of the second exam he wrote Randolph that the boy's 'work this term has been excellent. He understands now the need of taking trouble, and the way to take it. . . It is due him to say that of late he has done all that could be asked of him.'[107]

One bright spot for Winston that fall was that Jack was now a twelve-year-old Harrovian, and the brothers were allowed to share a room. ('We have now quite settled down,' he wrote home. 'The room is very beautiful. We purchased in London sufficiency of ornaments to make it look simply magnificent.') Moreover, Winston had finally mastered skills which won him the admiration of his peers. He made the swimming team, led the School Rifle Corps, starred in boxing, and became the fencing champion of Harrow. 'I have won the fencing,' he wrote his mother, then in Monte Carlo. 'A very fine cup. I was far and away first. Absolutely untouched in the finals.' Then he accomplished something spectacular. He was chosen to stand for Harrow in a tournament at Aldershot, the winner to be England's public-school fencing champion. He wrote excitedly: 'My fencing is now my great employment out of school as now that I represent the School it behoves me to "sweat up."' On the great day he crossed foils with boys from Eton, Winchester, Bradfield, and Tonbridge and beat them all. His victory, the *Harrovian* reported, 'was chiefly due to his quick and dashing attack which quite took his opponents by surprise.' The school paper commented: 'Churchill must be congratulated on his success over all his opponents in the fencing line, many of whom must have been much taller and more formidable than himself.'[108]

He ought to have left Harrow on a rising tide of hope. Instead, he departed in despair. The second Sandhurst examination had not gone well. Traditionally, seniors passing out entertained their friends at a 'Leaving Breakfast' in Hance's Tuck Shop: mutton cutlets, steak and onions, ham, mushrooms, eggs, sausages, and devilled kidneys – all for sixpence. Winston wouldn't have it. In December he quietly bade farewell to Jack and then slunk off to the station alone, like a fugitive. Sandhurst posted the exam results the next month; they then appeared in *The Times*. As he feared, he had failed again. His performance had actually worsened in Latin, French, and – the cruellest cut – English composition. It is astonishing that in this, of all subjects, the boy who would become one of the greatest masters of his native language scored 53 per cent. Randolph pondered putting him out as a commercial apprentice to Rothschild, Farquharson, or Cassel, but relented when Welldon told him that he felt certain Winston would make it on the third try. The headmaster urged tutoring. There was no disgrace in this. In 1870 Lord Dufferin's Royal Commission on Military Education had 'earnestly' deprecated 'the irregular system of "cramming" ' because, as one member explained, they feared that the acceptance 'of such a large proportion of crammed candidates would cause the Army to lose its "tone." ' Nevertheless, in Winston's day seven out of every ten successful candidates for admission to Sandhurst had been rigorously tutored. Spencer Coyle, in Henry James's story 'Owen Wingrave,' was a typical Victorian crammer. The character was inspired by Captain Walter H. James, who, Welldon wrote Lord Randolph, was 'the most successful "crammer" for the Sandhurst Examination.' Randolph approved, and James then wrote him from 5 Lexham Gardens, London: 'I shall be very happy to receive your son and should be pleased to see you at 12:30 on Monday next.'[109]

Winston didn't keep the appointment. He was near death. In their study of boys marked for future greatness, the Goertzels found that among adventurous youths 'there is almost always a history of accident-proneness.' Sometimes the youthful Winston seemed to move from crisis to crisis, risking his life in pointless adventures. That was true of him that year. His second failure as a Sandhurst candidate had left him tense and distraught, which probably contributed to his flirtation with disaster. Randolph's sister-in-law, the 'Duchess Lily,' had given his family the run of Deepdene, her estate at Branksome Dene, near Bournemouth, for the winter. Its fifty acres of pine forest, sloping down to the Channel, offered endless opportunities for the daring games Winston loved to play in the woods. Each morning he briefed Jack and a fourteen-year-old cousin on his newest game plan while the servants, Woom among them, wrung their hands and prayed for the children's safety. In the wildest corner of the estate, a thicket was split by a deep cleft called the 'chine.' The chine was bridged by a crude fifty-yard bridge. The boys were playing fox and hare, with Winston the hare, when he found himself in the middle of the bridge with a foe at either end. He contemplated jumping down into the cleft. It was thick with fir trees; he thought he might leap to one and slide down, snapping off tiers of branches as he descended and thus breaking his fall. In his words: 'I looked at it. I computed it. I meditated. Meanwhile I climbed over the balustrade. My young pursuers stood wonderstruck at either end of the bridge. To plunge or not to plunge, that was the question! In a second I had plunged, throwing out my arms to embrace the summit of the fir tree. The argument was correct; the data was absolutely wrong.' He tumbled twenty-nine feet to hard ground and lay insensible. Jack and their cousin ran back to the mansion, crying, 'He won't speak to us!' This was real trouble, and it brought his parents flying. Jennie arrived first; Randolph, who had been spending Christmas at one of Lord Fitzgibbon's interminable wild parties in Ireland, took the next express from Dublin. Dr Roose appeared with Dr John Rose, a Harley Street specialist. They found, among other things, that Winston had ruptured a kidney. He did not recover consciousness for three days. The physicians recommended three months in bed, Rose adding that 'young Mr Churchill should not return to hard study any more than he should take vigorous exercise.'[110]

Unfortunately, abstinence from study was out of the question. Winston's last chance at Sandhurst loomed in June, and in Lexham Gardens Captain James sat waiting, pencils sharpened, textbooks open. Some forty years later Winston decided that he understood why this obscure half-pay officer had stood at the top of his small, curious profession. James, he wrote, had studied the minds of the men who drew up civil service examinations and could predict 'with almost Papal infallibility the sort of questions which that sort of person would be bound on the average to ask on any of the selected subjects.' His skill lay in anticipating such questions and how best to answer them. He was 'really the ingenious forerunner of the inventors of the artillery barrages of the Great War,' Churchill wrote. 'He fired from carefully selected positions upon the areas which he knew must be tenanted by large bodies of enemy troops. . . He did not need to see the enemy soldiers. Drill was all he had to teach his gunners. Thus year by year for at least two decades he held the Blue Ribbon among the Crammers.'[111]

But he had never dealt with anyone remotely like Winston. The crammer represents everything the creative youth despises: drill, contempt for intuition, slavish fixation on meaningless, unrelated facts. Winston, in his own words, found himself in 'an "Alice-in-Wonderland" world, at the portals of which stood "A Quadratic Equation," ' followed by the 'dim chambers' inhabited by the 'Differential Calculus' and then a 'strange corridor' of sines and cosines 'in a highly square-rooted condition.' Of mathematical skills he wrote: 'I am assured they are most helpful in engineering, astronomy and things like that. It is important to build bridges and canals and to comprehend all the stresses and potentialities of matter, to say nothing of counting all the stars and even universes and measuring how far off they are, and foretelling eclipses, the arrival of comets and such like. I am glad there are quite a number of people born with a gift and a liking for all this.' He, however, was not one of them. The Goertzels found that most boys pregnant with genius have serious problems with school curricula and dull, irrational teachers. James was a distillate of these. He was concentrating on the courses Winston had found pointless, using the very methods Winston hated most. By March he must have wished that this exasperating boy had killed himself in his fall. Reporting to Randolph on March 7, he deplored his pupil's 'casual manner.' Winston was 'distinctly inclined to be inattentive and to think too much of his abilities.' He had been 'rather too much inclined up to the present to teach his instructors instead of endeavouring to learn from them.' In fact, 'he suggested to me that his knowledge of history was such that he did not want any more teaching in it! . . . What he wants,' he concluded, 'is very firm handling.' Unfortunately, James could not provide it for the moment. He was literally sick of Winston, 'confined to my room.'[112]

Staggering to his feet, he plodded on. But he deceived neither himself nor his ward's father. He was making little progress. In an April 29 report he gloomily warned his employer: 'I do not think that his work is going on satisfactorily.' Although the boy 'has good abilities he does not apply himself with sufficient earnestness to his reading' and 'I doubt his passing if he does not do this.' James delicately hinted at one difficulty. Randolph was making his last attempt at a political comeback, and his son could think of little else. The crammer realized that 'at a time like the present it is difficult for him not to take an interest in current political topics, but if this be done to an extent which takes his mind away from his studies, the result is bad for the latter.' Every attempt must be made to impress upon him 'the absolute necessity of single-minded devotion to the immediate object before him, and the extreme desirability of thoroughness and detail [sic] attention to all he attempts.'[113]

The break came sometime in May. Winston gave ground. He yielded as little as possible, but he knew what was at stake, and though the job revolted him, he set his jaw and made some progress. Not much; just enough. On June 19, James wrote: 'Without saying that your son is a certainty I think he ought to pass this time. He is working well and I think doing his best to get on but, as you know, he is at times inclined to take the bit in his teeth and go his own course.' The exam was upon them then, and this time Winston squeaked by. He came in too low to become an infantry cadet, but was admitted to the cavalry. He hadn't changed much, even under his crammer's pressure; most of the spring, when he should have been doing James's lessons, he had been reading English history for pleasure, with the jarring effect – jarring for James, who had abandoned attempts to drill him in history – that he far out-scored every other candidate in that subject. When the list of those who had passed was announced, Winston had left on a hiking trip in Switzerland with Jack and J.D.G. Little, a young Eton master. He was in Lucerne when he learned he had made it. Immediately he wired his father and then wrote him from the Schweizerhof Hotel: 'I was so glad to be able to send you the good news on Thursday. I did not expect that the list would be published so soon & was starting off in the train, when Little congratulated me on getting in. I looked in the paper & found this to be true.' It was only fitting, he thought, that he should celebrate his achievement in such 'a splendid hotel – lifts, electric light, & fireworks (every Saturday).'[114]

Other congratulations arrived from grandparents, aunts, uncles, and cousins, but there was an ominous silence from Bad Kissingen, where Lord Randolph and Jennie were taking the cure. Unknown to his son, Randolph had been counting heavily on an infantry cadetship. That would have relieved him of the cost of horses. It would also have brought a social dividend; a friend of his, the aged, royal Duke of Cambridge, commander in chief of the army, had promised, once Winston had been commissioned, to find a place for him in the crack Sixtieth Rifles. Now the humiliated father had to tell His Grace that his boy was too stupid to become an infantry officer. Jennie saw the storm gathering in her husband. She sent a warning to Lucerne: 'I am glad of course that you have got into Sandhurst but Papa is not pleased at yr getting in by the skin of yr teeth & missing the Infantry by 18 marks. He is not as pleased by yr exploits as you seem to be!'[115] That was putting it gently. A week later, in Milan, Winston received an extraordinary letter from his father.

Randolph was surprised that he had expressed 'exultation over your inclusion in the Sandhurst list' instead of being ashamed of 'your slovenly happy-go-lucky harum scarum style of work.' It was the same old story: 'Never have I received a really good report of your conduct in your work from any master or tutor you had from time to time to do with. Always behind-hand, never advancing in your class, incessant complaints of total want of application, and this character which was constant in yr reports has shown the natural results clearly in your last army examination.' Thus 'you have failed to get into the "60th Rifles" one of the finest regiments in the army.' Further-more, as a cavalry cadet, 'you have imposed on me an extra charge of some £200 a year.' It got worse: 'Do not think I am going to take the trouble of writing to you long letters after every failure you commit and undergo . . . I no longer attach the slightest weight to anything you may say about your own acquirements & exploits.' Randolph predicted that 'if you cannot prevent yourself from leading the idle useless unprofitable life you have had during your schooldays & later months, you will become a mere social wastrel one of the hundreds of the public school failures, and you will degenerate into a shabby unhappy & futile existence. If that is so you will have to bear all the blame for such misfortunes yourself.' He ended venomously: 'Your mother sends her love.'[116]

Little wrote Randolph that Winston had showed him this letter and 'was a good deal depressed.' Actually, he was stunned. It never occurred to him that this philippic might be the work of an unstable mind. He considered his father's judgement above reproach, and believed that he had failed him again. In his reply he wrote that he was 'very sorry indeed that you are displeased with me,' that he would 'try to modify your opinion of me by my work at Sandhurst,' that 'my extremely low place in passing *in* will have *no* effect whatever on my chance there,' and that Randolph needn't worry about expenses there because 'all the necessary equipment & outfit are supplied at Sandhurst at a charge of £30.' Here he erred. All cadets were charged £120 tuition, in addition to the costs of their mounts, to screen out applicants who were not considered suitable. But in a larger sense he was right. Sandhurst fees were a pittance when set against the costs Randolph's own father had paid for his Oxford education; Randolph had raised the issue only to justify his wrath. Winston closed his own letter pathetically: 'Thank you very much for writing to me.' And, once again, 'I am very sorry indeed that I have done so badly.' Yet on a deeper level he may have smouldered. At the bottom he wrote: 'P.S. Excuse smudge &c as pens & blotting paper are awfully bad.' The page was a mess. Hostility, though repressed, must have been there. By now it should have been clear that the relationship between father and son would be abrasive for both until one of them lay in his grave.[117]

Winston almost died first. His second skirting of the Styx immediately followed the posting of this response. He and a companion hired a boat on the shore of Lake Geneva and rowed out a mile. Stripping, they dove in for a swim. Suddenly a breeze sprang up and carried the boat away from them. Striking out desperately, Winston just managed to reach the hull, hoist himself aboard, and return for his friend. Afterwards he wrote that he had seen Death 'as near as I believe I have ever seen Him. He was swimming in the water, whispering from time to time in the rising wind.' Either because of this or because of Randolph's tirade, he was still upset when he returned to London and found that the row over his poor showing in the exam had been entirely unnecessary. At 50 Grosvenor Square a letter from the military secretary awaited him, disclosing that several boys with higher scores than his had dropped out, so he needn't go into the cavalry. He wrote his father: 'I have no doubt that you will be pleased to find that I have got an Infantry cadetship and shall be able, after all, to enter the 60th.' Randolph's pride enjoined an acknowledgment, but he wrote Duchess Fanny – as he had grown apart from Jennie, his mother had become the only woman he fully trusted – that 'I am very glad Winston has got an infantry cadetship. It will save me £200 a year.'[118]

On the afternoon of Friday, September 1, 1893, Winston switched from train to carriage in the village of Camberley and rode into the grounds of the Royal Military College, passing through a forest of pine, birch, and larch before debouching on the plain where, every year since 1812, young members of England's upper classes had been certified as 'officers and gentlemen.' The landscape was inviting: two lakes, athletic fields, rifle and revolver ranges, and, of course, parade grounds. As a 'junior,' or plebe, he was assigned to 'E' Company, led to the long, low, white stone building which would be his barracks for the next sixteen months, and measured for his cadet uniform, a gaudy costume featuring gold lace, pantaloons, and a pillbox cap. He studied the daily schedule he would be expected to meet, worried about his physical frailty, and wrote his mother, with a confidence he did not feel: 'I suppose I shall get stronger during my stay here.'[119] His physique was in fact unimpressive. He was only five feet, six and a half inches tall, and his chest measured but thirty-one inches, with an expansion of two and a half inches – inadequate, unless he could improve upon it, for a commission. To succeed at Sandhurst he would summon strengths which, until now, had been unrevealed.

Even before the tailor had finished outfitting him, he had again incurred his father's displeasure. Lord Randolph had decided to give him a ten-pound monthly allowance and little leave. 'I wont have any running backwards & forwards to London,' he wrote Duchess Fanny. 'He shall be kept to his work so that he may acquire the elementary principles of a military education.' But since his arrival on the post, Winston had discovered that his financial expectations required revision. He needed a batman to black his boots, pipe-clay his belt, clean his rifle, and carry away slops. He thought he ought to have a horse; other cadets had them. His room needed furnishing, and he not

153

only wanted to visit the capital regularly – 'going up to town,' as they said at Sandhurst – he also meant to join clubs there. His father would have none of it. To Duchess Fanny, Randolph explained: 'I have demurred to "unrestricted leave," and have told him he can come to town when his mother is there. I have declined paying for horses . . . Winston's letters are generally full of requests for unnecessary things and articles.' The youth begged his mother to intervene. Without a horse, he said, he would be excluded from polo classes. 'As to leave – it is very hard that Papa cannot grant me the same liberty that other boys in my position are granted. It is only a case of trusting *me*. As my company officer said, he "liked to know the boys whom their parents could trust" – and therefore recommended me to get the permission I asked for. However, it is no use trying to explain to Papa, & I suppose I shall go on being treated as "that boy" till I am 50 years old.'[120] Actually, it would be only a short time longer. But Winston had been kept at such a distance from his family that he knew nothing of the tensions within it. He couldn't understand the niggling over money. He was keenly aware of his father's reentry into politics. He did not, however, grasp the futility of it.

In the summer of 1892, when Winston was beginning his struggle to enter Sandhurst, the voters narrowly rejected Salisbury's Conservatives, giving Gladstone the chance to form his last government. His position in the House of Commons was fragile. Even with the support of eighty Irish Nationalists, the Liberal majority was only forty. In 1886 Joe Chamberlain had deserted the Grand Old Man on the question of Home Rule and joined the Ulster Unionists, whom he would eventually leave to become a full-fledged Tory. The cabinet differed sharply among themselves on key issues. Obviously the Tories would soon return. But Randolph didn't see it that way. He thought they needed his help. When Parliament met the following summer – the summer Winston scraped through his third examination – the political configuration looked like 1885 all over again. The GOM sat on the government bench, and Churchill, the master of invective, was preparing to display his brilliant talent once more. In Winston's words, 'It was thought that he would in Opposition swiftly regain the ascendancy in Parliament and in his party which had been destroyed by his resignation six years before. No one cherished these hopes more ardently than I . . . We all looked forward to his reconquest of power . . . Although he was only a private member and quite isolated, everything he said even at the tiniest bazaar was reported verbatim in all the newspapers, and every phrase was scrutinized and weighed. Now it seemed that his chance had come again.'[121]

Only rarely could Winston observe the parliamentary manoeuvring from the Strangers' Gallery, and even then he deferred to his father's wishes, asking his permission to attend: 'I have had a letter from Mr Carson inviting me to dine with him at the House on Friday evening. I have accepted as I have very little work on Saturday. If you would rather I would not go Please send me a line.' He was fascinated by the civility between adversaries; at table 'not only colleagues, but opponents, amicably interchanged opinions on the burning topics of the hour.' Apart from newspapers, his sources of information on what was happening behind the scenes in the House were his mother and his father's brother-in-law Edward Marjoribanks, who, as Gladstone's chief whip, was on the other side. Political civility also prevailed within the family, though Winston enjoyed trying to pin Marjoribanks down. He wrote his father: 'Uncle Edward has been here to dinner. He spent nearly half an hour after dinner explaining to me the methods by which the Opposition of the House of the Lords were going to be overcome. I wish you had been there to answer him, as I am sure there was an answer though I could not think of it.'[122]

Jennie and Uncle Edward gave him accounts of Randolph's progress. They said he was doing well, and in the beginning they were right. Even the *Spectator*, the Conservative organ, which had abused him so cruelly, reported: 'The chief feature of this Session . . . has been the return of Lord Randolph Churchill to active political life, and his successful reassertion of himself as a force to be reckoned with in party warfare. Lord Randolph has seen his opportunity in the crusade against the Home-rule Bill . . . we rejoice that the party has recovered the services of a man with such excellent fighting qualities . . . More than any of the Unionist leaders, Lord Randolph possesses the faculty of speaking to uneducated men in the style which they understand and admire . . . We wish Lord Randolph every success.'[123]

Suddenly it was all over. Although Home Rule passed the Commons, it was rejected by the Lords. The Grand Old Man, half blind and half deaf at eighty-five, rode up Birdcage Walk to the Queen who had never liked him and resigned. Randolph had been deprived of his prey. But even before then it had become evident that he, like Gladstone, was not the man he had been. Winston noted: 'I could not help feeling that my father's speeches were not as good as they used to be. There were some brilliant successes; yet on the whole he seemed to be hardly holding his own. I hoped of course that I should grow up in time to come to his aid . . . I thought of Austen Chamberlain who was allowed to fight at his father's side, and Herbert Gladstone who had helped the Grand Old Man to cut down the oak trees and went everywhere with him, and I dreamed of days to come when Tory democracy would dismiss the "Old Gang" with one hand and defeat the Radicals with the other.' Randolph, however, found the very thought of a mature relationship between himself and Winston repellent. 'If ever I began to show the slightest idea of comradeship,' Winston wrote, 'he was immediately offended.' Once, when 'I suggested that I might help his private secretary to write some of his letters, he froze me into stone.'[124]

Now that we have the son's life spread before us, the father's behaviour seems monstrous. But Randolph could not hold a mirror up to the future. He only saw what was there to be seen, and it was anything but encouraging. His letter from Bad Kissingen had been unforgivably brutal, but it had not been an exercise in fantasy. Winston's school records *were* a catalogue of misconduct and scholastic failure. Even when seen through the kind eyes – those, say, of Mrs Everest – he was a redheaded, puny little swaggerer who was always in trouble, always disobedient, always making and breaking promises. Unquestionably parental negligence had contributed to his many fiascos. Undoubtedly his father bore a thinly veiled animosity towards him. But Randolph had his own troubles. Although stricken with a vile disease through no fault of his own, he had achieved a certain position in public life. He was, in fact, the most successful Churchill since the first duke. A proud man, he yearned for parental pride and was thwarted. If he had little faith in his son's potential, there was precious little there to inspire faith. He wrote Duchess Fanny in August 1893: 'I have told you often & you would never believe me that he has little [claim] to cleverness, to knowledge or any capacity for settled work. He has great talent for show off exaggeration & make believe.'[125] Sending his son to a military academy was the wisest decision he ever made, but he had no way of knowing that then. At one point he even asked a friend about career opportunities in South America. Winston, he was convinced, would never make good in England.

Recognizing that an upper-class father had certain obligations to a son who had become a gentleman cadet, responsibilities which could not be slighted without offending society, he invited Winston to join him for weekends with his racing cronies and fellow MPs. Winston enjoyed the company of the friends and parliamentarians, but the man he really wanted to talk to was his father. That was not possible. Randolph could write Duchess Fanny: 'He has much smartened up,' but the closest he came to a public compliment was in introducing Winston to Bram Stoker, Sir Henry Irving's secretary and the future author of *Dracula*. 'He's not much yet,' he told Stoker, 'but he's a good 'un.' Winston, immensely pleased, hoped that intimacy would follow. It didn't. He felt that 'I would far rather have been apprenticed as a bricklayer's mate, or run errands as a messenger boy, or helped my father to dress the front windows of a grocer's shop. It would have been real; it would have been natural; it would have taught me more; and I should have got to know my father, which would have been a joy to me.' Later, when Herbert Asquith was prime minister, his daughter Violet quoted Asquith's views on issues and public men to Winston. Winston was amazed. He said: 'Your father told you that? He talks to you about such things quite freely? I wish I could have had such talks with mine.' In middle age he told his own son, home from Eton, 'I have talked to you more in this holiday than my father talked to me in his whole life.' He wrote of Lord Randolph that 'only once did he lift his visor in my sight.' Vacationing with his family in the country, Winston fired a double-barrelled gun at a rabbit which had appeared beneath his father's window. Randolph raged at him; then, seeing that he had upset him, backed down and explained that old people, absorbed in their own affairs, sometimes spoke rudely to their children. He said: 'Do remember things do not always go right with me. My every action is misjudged and every word distorted . . .So make some allowance.'[126]

156

Winston's later view of Lord Randolph was ambivalent. To Violet Asquith he spoke of him with 'glowing pride.' He liked to call on Lord Rosebery, encouraging him to reminisce about Randolph, whom Rosebery had known well and Winston hardly at all, and Winston's two-volume biography *Lord Randolph Churchill* is a tribute to filial devotion. Yet he was bitter when he told Frank Harris that whenever he tried to open serious conversations with his father, he was snubbed pitilessly. He recalled: 'He wouldn't listen to me or consider anything I said. There was no companionship with him possible and I tried so hard and so often. He was so self-centred no one else existed for him.' Harris asked: 'You didn't like him?' Winston replied: 'How could I? . . . He treated me as if I had been a fool; barked at me whenever I questioned him. I owe everything to my mother; to my father, nothing.' Actually, he owed him a great deal, much of which he could have done without, for when he himself entered politics he felt obliged to pay off Randolph's old scores. But there was no real love lost between them. In Winston's books one may trace a steady theme: great men are frequently products of boyhood loneliness. Three years after his father's death he wrote of the Mahdi, leader of Sudanese tribesmen: 'Solitary trees, if they grow at all, grow strong; and a boy deprived of a father's care often develops, if he escapes the perils of youth, an independence and vigour of thought which may restore in after life the heavy loss of early days.' And in his biography of the first Duke of Marlborough he observed that 'famous men are usually the product of an unhappy childhood. The stern compression of circumstances, the twinges of adversity, the spur of slights and taunts in early years, are needed to evoke that ruthless fixity of purpose and tenacious mother wit without which great actions are seldom accomplished.'[127]

It is difficult to resist the tide of Churchillian eloquence. Yet every author, as Cicero observed, is wise and forbearing in his own eyes. The fact is that at Sandhurst, as at Harrow, Winston could be a vexing son, though now his growing flair for seizing command of situations – and perhaps a ripening imagination – added a lively touch to his explanations. These were summed up in the remarkable case of the gold watch. When Winston settled in at the military academy, his father presented him with a fine watch, made by Dents'. Later, dropping into the London shop to see about his own timepiece, Randolph was 'annoyed and vexed,' in his words, to learn that Winston's watch had twice been sent back for repairs, first after it had been 'dropped . . . on a stone pavement & broken,' and, second, when it had been immersed in water, with the result that 'the whole of the works were horribly rusty & that every bit of the watch had had to be taken to pieces.' Mending it after it had been dropped had cost three pounds, seventeen shillings. At the time of Randolph's infelicitous visit it was still in the shop from the submersion. He scribbled off a furious note to Sandhurst. He 'could not believe that you could be such a young stupid. It is clear you are not to be trusted with a valuable watch & when I get it back from Mr Dent I shall not give it back to you.' Then he wrote the details to Jennie in Paris, adding that Winston 'wont forget my

157

letter for some time & it will be a long time before I give him anything worth having. I wanted you to know this as he may tell you a vy different story.'[18]

Winston told a vy different story indeed. 'The first accident,' he wrote, 'was not my fault at all.' He hadn't been careless; quite the contrary. Shielding the Dent watch from harm had, it seemed, been a major concern of his, almost a mission. To that end, he had had a special leather case made for it. He was holding it in this protective case when a rude cadet ran into him, dislodging it from his grasp with such force that, to his horror, it crashed on the surface of the parade ground, emitting a discordant tintinnabulation, a knell of ruin. The dunking had been more complicated. Cadets' tunics, unlike waistcoats, lacked deep pockets. He had been strolling along the bank of Sandhurst's Wish Stream when he stooped to pick up a stick. Out popped the watch, sinking into six feet of water, 'the only deep place for miles.' Instantly he stripped and dove after it, trying again and again until exhaustion raised the possibility that he might drown. 'The next day I had the pool dredged – but without result,' he wrote. Therefore, obtaining official permission for a major effort, he borrowed twenty-three infantrymen, 'dug a new course for the stream,' rerouted it, acquired a fire engine from the nearest village, 'pumped the pool dry and so recovered the watch.' It was irresistible. Jennie wrote: 'Oh! Winny what a harum scarum fellow you are!' Even Randolph relented: 'You need not trouble any more about the watch. It is quite clear that the rough work of Sandhurst is not suitable for a watch made by Dent.' He sent an inexpensive substitute.[129]

Bills, Winston's allowance, expenses – throughout 1893 Randolph was increasingly preoccupied with the disagreeable subject of money. To trim his budget, he sold the Connaught Place house and moved his family in with his mother at the ducal mansion on Grosvenor Square. With Jack away at Harrow, Elizabeth Everest stepped into a new role, becoming Duchess Fanny's housekeeper. Randolph continued to write for the *Daily Graphic*, but he still couldn't make ends meet. On October 6, when his elder son was entering his sixth week as a cadet, he wrote Jennie that 'I am vy sorry but I have no money at the present moment & balance overdrawn at bank.' He had some South African mining shares for which he had paid £10,000 two years earlier, and was putting them on the market, 'but it is vy difficult to get 4½ for them now, & I must not sell more than £500. I will try & send you £105 to Hotel Scribe.' He turned to his mother for help. The duchess, however, was having financial difficulties of her own. She, too, had to economize. She decided she needed less domestic help. She fired Mrs Everest.[130]

If ever a servant was a member of a family, Woom was she. She had been with the Churchills for nineteen years, and she had few savings. Randolph knew that, because she had entrusted them to him; he had driven her down to the City in his private hansom and turned them over to Lord Rothschild at New Court for investment. The return was a pittance. By the time Winston learned of her dismissal, she had been gone for three months. Aghast, he wrote his mother, who replied that it was none of his business and she would refuse to read anything further he wrote her about it. He begged her to listen to him out of 'common decency.' He felt that if he allowed Woom 'to be cut adrift without protest' he would be 'extremely ungrateful – besides I should be very sorry not to have her at Grosvenor Square – because she is in my mind associated – more than anything else with home.' She was an old woman; to be 'packed off' in this way 'would possibly, if not probably break her down altogether . . . At her age she is invited to find a new place & practically begin over again . . . I think such proceedings cruel & rather mean.' Of course, the duchess had 'every right to discharge a servant for whom she has "no further use." ' But at the very least Woom should be kept on until she found another job or 'be given a pension – which would be sufficient to keep her from want – & which should continue during her life.' He told Jennie: 'It is in your power to explain to the Duchess that she *cannot* be sent away until she has got a good place.' He posted this letter on October 29. There was no reply. Randolph sent Woom seventeen pounds. Other 'presents' followed from time to time, but apart from that, she had been discarded like a shabby cradle. Her sisters kept her from destitution. In the little time left to her, she continued to write Winston and Jack faithfully, and to remember them with little gifts on their birthdays and Christmas.[131]

Winston had entered Sandhurst ninety-second in a class of 102. Immediately he had trouble with parade-ground drill – his officers were dumbfounded to find that he wanted to argue about commands – and was put in the awkward squad. But within a fortnight he had grown to love the life. He felt himself 'growing up every week.' Gone, he later wrote, were Harrow's 'unending spell of worries that did not then seem petty, and of toil uncheered by fruition; a time of discomfort, restriction and purposeless monotony . . . At Sandhurst I had a new start. I was no longer handicapped by past neglect of Latin, French or Mathematics.' Instead, there were just five subjects to master: fortification, tactics, topography, military law, and military administration. In retrospect it seems inadequate preparation for England's greatest war leader. 'We were never taught anything about bombs or hand-grenades,' he would recall, 'because of course these weapons were known to be long obsolete. They had gone out of use in the eighteenth century, and would be quite useless in modern war.' And though Winston would be disdainful of the U.S. Military Academy when he visited there two years later, West Point without maths would have been unthinkable even then.[132]

But Sandhurst was *fun*. He particularly liked the exercises in field fortification. They dug trenches, built breastworks, and revetted parapets with sandbags, heather, fascines, and 'Jones' iron-band gabions' – cylinders filled with earth. Chevaux-de-frise were constructed, and *fougasses*, a kind of primitive land mine in which the charge was overlaid with stones. Using slabs of guncotton, they blew up simulated railroad tracks and masonry bridges; then they erected pontoon or timber substitutes. All the hills around

Camberley were mapped. Roads were reconnoitred. Picket lines were established and advance and rear guards posted. It was like being back at Banstead with Jack and their cousins, building the castle with its moat and drawbridge and using the homemade elastic catapult to hurl green apples at the cow. In a revealing comment on his cadet days, Winston later said he thought it 'a pity that it all had to be makebelieve, and that the age of wars between civilized nations had come to an end for ever. If only it had been 100 years earlier what splendid times we should have had! Fancy being nineteen in 1793 with more than twenty years of war against Napoleon in front of one!'[133]

Sandhurst, like West Point, divided cadets into companies. There were six, each commanded by a commissioned officer, regular army NCOs, and cadet corporals; each with its own quarters, mess, and billiard room; each fielding athletic teams against the others. The year after he was commissioned, Winston wrote an article about the academy for the *Pall Mall Magazine*. He used the pseudonym 'Cornet of Horse,'* and he described a typical day at Sandhurst. Reveille sounded at 6:00 A.M. and forty-five minutes later the study halls were filled with cadets in immaculate blue uniforms, 'deep in the wiles of tactics or the eccentricities of fortification.'[134] Breakfast was served at 8:00 A.M. Morning parade came an hour later, followed by gymnastics, the formation of skirmishers beyond the cricket pavilion, bayonet practice, lectures on outposts and attacking enemy positions, and lunch. Riding school was held in the early afternoon and was mandatory, even for infantry cadets; those who lacked mounts, like Winston, hired 'screws' at the local livery stables. Sports began at 4:00 P.M. Tea and study preceded mess, the school's only formal meal. Evenings were devoted to reading, talking, playing whist and billiards, and, sometimes, watching a boxing match between cadets. The bugler played 'lights out' at 11:00 P.M.

Winston became a passionate horseman. He was the liveryman's steadiest customer. Gradually, he wrote, he developed 'a tolerably firm seat,' learning to saddle his mount, to ride without stirrups or reins, to ride bareback, to leap fences, and to mount and dismount while his horse was trotting, a 'feat very easily performed.' He became Sandhurst's second-best rider. 'I enjoyed the riding-school thoroughly,' he wrote, 'and got on – and off – as well as most . . . Horses were the greatest of my pleasures . . . Young men have often been ruined through owning horses, or through backing horses, but never through riding them; unless of course they break their necks, which, if taken at a gallop, is a very good death to die.' In idle hours he organized races and point-to-points. His sole complaint about Sandhurst was that 'polo for the last two years had been relegated to the limbo of prohibited pleasures,' despite the fact that 'if there is a game which could prepare a youth for a soldier's life, that game is polo.' The argument against it was that some officers would be

---

* The rank held by Chatham (the elder Pitt). Sir Robert Walpole, his political adversary, said, 'We must muzzle this terrible young Cornet of Horse,' and Chatham was expelled by the army.

unable to afford it. 'This levelling-down doctrine,' he concluded, 'is pure Socialism.' Thus, in the first piece he sold to a newspaper, he identified his parliamentary enemies of the coming century.[135]

He was now an eager student of war. Lord Randolph had instructed his bookseller to send Winston any books he needed for his studies, and presently the young cadet was devouring Maine's *Infantry Fire Tactics*, Prince Kraft's *Letters on Infantry, Cavalry and Artillery*, and Sir Edward Bruce Hamley's 1866 classic, *Operations of War*. Days passed pleasantly. He was surrounded by his peers. As Byron Farwell observes in *Mr Kipling's Army*, a youth arriving at Sandhurst or Woolwich 'found himself surrounded by others with backgrounds similar to his own . . . Officer-instructors and cadets spoke the same language in the same accents, possessed similar vocabularies, had the same set of attitudes and beliefs.' Lieutenant General Brian Horrocks, looking back, wrote: 'We regular army officers of those days might all have come out of the same mould. We had been to identical public schools . . . We . . . were, I'm afraid, terribly dull.' Winston, though his social position was loftier than most, didn't think them at all dull. After the long dreadful years of being bullied and taunted, he was accepted here as a comrade, and rejoiced.[136]

In his early cadet days his father had written him: 'Mind you if you do well at Sandhurst *&* get good reports good positions in your classes *&* even the good conduct medal you would go to your regiment so much higher in credit *&* more thought of. So if you feel at times like giving way or falling off "Don't." ' Winston had been getting these goads for twelve years. They hadn't worked then, and now they were unnecessary. In the examinations at the end of his first term, he scored near the top of his class, his strongest subjects being tactics and military law. Under 'Conduct' the official verdict was 'Good but unpunctual.' He would always be unpunctual, always missing trains, ships, and, later, planes, until he reached a station so exalted that they all waited for him. But he excelled so in every other Sandhurst course that his tardiness was overlooked. His earlier status of public-school dolt was forgotten now that he was an admirable young soldier with a brilliant career ahead of him. This showed, he wrote, 'that I could learn quickly enough the things that mattered.' He was growing stronger physically. Furthermore, he was popular with his fellow cadets. Randolph, astounded by all this, lifted the restrictions on his leave, and Winston began entraining for Waterloo Station in London with his new friends.[137]

The imperial capital was then approaching its prime, and for privileged youths who knew they would inherit it one day, the city was a source of endless wonder and ebullience. The metropolis of the 1870s, when Winston had played in Mayfair and Hyde Park, had been transformed. London was gay; it was, by earlier Victorian standards, permissive. These were the 1890s, the Naughty Nineties, the Mauve Decade, the best time, Churchill would later write, in his entire life: 'Twenty to twenty-five – those are the years!'[138] It was almost as though the capital were preparing for the momentous events which lay ahead. Popular institutions which would flourish in the next century, and which later generations of Englishmen would come to regard as the very essence of the British way of life, were just then arriving on the national stage. The first white-fronted J. Lyon's Teashop had just opened at 213 Piccadilly, Harrods had newly installed display windows. Marks and Spencer had opened their Penny Bazaar ('Don't ask the price, it's a penny') at Cheetham Hill, Manchester, and were building a branch in London. Londoners of the upper and middle classes had plenty to spend; that year the capital of England's limited liability companies exceeded £1,000,000,000 – one and a third times that of France and Germany combined. At the five-year-old Savoy, Auguste Escoffier had created the Peach Melba, honouring Dame Nellie Melba, who was singing Wagner's *Lohengrin* at Covent Garden. Piccadilly Circus was acquiring its fountain. In Langham Place, Queen's Hall had replaced old St. James's Hall as the home of the capital's orchestral music; it would be famous for its Promenade Concerts until Nazi bombers levelled it in 1941. The Tower Bridge had just been completed. Strolling along the Embankment from Westminster Bridge, the cadets from Sandhurst could see New Scotland Yard rising, a creation of the architect Norman Shaw, who contrived to give the police station the appearance of a French Renaissance château transplanted from the Seine to the Thames.

If they were in the mood for a play, the Sandhurst cadets could see Oscar Wilde's *A Woman of No Importance* at the Haymarket Theatre, George Bernard Shaw's *Arms and the Man* at the Avenue, *Charley's Aunt* at the Royalty, and, at the St James's, Arthur Wing Pinero's *The Second Mrs Tanqueray*, starring that acrobat of the chaise longue, Mrs Patrick Campbell. The hit songs likeliest to be hummed by passersby in the street were Dvořák's 'Humoresque'; or 'Happy Birthday to You,' a curious tune composed by a Kentucky kindergarten teacher; or, if the pedestrian had just returned from Paris, the theme of Debussy's *Après-midi d'un faune*. Lounge suits, worn with bowlers in winter and boaters in summer, were frequently seen here in the centre of town, but in the West End cadets' fathers were loyal to their frock coats and toppers. Women's fashions were another matter. The bustle had disappeared four years earlier. Leg-of-mutton sleeves had arrived, and so had separate blouses and skirts, a by-product of lawn tennis's popularity, though the blouses were worn with stiff collars. Hems were higher, always a source of pleasure for the coarser sex, and boys who could divert chaperons and make exceptional progress with a cooperative girl were delighted to find that knickers had replaced thick petticoats. This was a tribute, not to sexual emancipation, but to the bicycle craze, which dated from J.K. Starley's invention of the Rover 'Safety' bike and J.B. Dunlop's patenting of the pneumatic tyre. The most startling switch in women's appearance, which did nothing for anyone, was in hair and hats. During Jennie's youth, hair had been plaited and coiled in a knob at the back of the neck; bonnets were then arched over the knob and tied under the chin. Now hair was brushed forward from the back of the neck and massed on top. Hatpins became indispensable. Hatpin hats, floating on top of coiffures, might be toques, miniature straw hats, or wide-brimmed picture hats. Many pins were required to anchor them. Keeping them in place discouraged motion, a handicap to a youth intent upon exploring his date's knickers, and the pins themselves were long and deadly, which, if push came to shove on a park bench, could be lethal.

Had Winston but known it, the change with the greatest significance for his future was the appearance on London streets of W.H. Smith's newsstands. Once Richard Hoe's steam-powered rotary 'lightning' press had replaced flatbed presses, vast supplies of fodder were needed to feed it. The answer, a German discovered, was cheap groundwood pulp. Readers were ready. W.E. Forster's Compulsory Education Act of 1870, followed by compulsory schooling ten years later, had raised the entire nation's level of literacy. In 1858 only 5 per cent of the army's recruits had been able to read and write. But by Churchill's time the figure was 85.4 per cent. Civilians had made similar progress. Reading materials began to be available to them. The 1880s had brought free libraries; Parliament had then abolished the newspaper tax and the excise duty on paper. That cleared the way for what can only be called an explosion in journalism. W.T. Stead's *Pall Mall Gazette,* which was founded in 1892 and cost a penny, was one of the first eruptions. Others were the *Daily Chronicle,* the *Daily Mail,* George Newnes's *Tid-bits,* and, from the Harmsworth Brothers, *Answers to Correspondents, Comic Cuts* (for children), the *Evening News,* and, the year after Winston left Sandhurst, the *Daily News,* which, at a halfpenny, would reach a circulation of a half-million, twice as high as that of any other paper. Five years later Alfred Harmsworth would become Lord Northcliffe, and three years after that he would acquire *The Times* and begin trumpeting the danger of war with Germany.

Because of this print revolution, Winston would reach millions of the newly literate, like Mrs Everest's brother-in-law, and, with cheques from editors and book royalties, support his political career. He would also become a lifelong omnivorous reader of newspapers and one of the most well-informed men in the world on the events of his time. At Sandhurst, as at Brighton, he was scanning column after column of newsprint every evening. Among his discoveries, during his three terms at the school, were the passage of woman suffrage in New Zealand, the election of Keir Hardie as the first MP to represent Britain's workingmen, and the court-martial conviction, in France, of Captain Alfred Dreyfus, after which a mob outside chanted, 'Death to the Jews!' Winston approved of none of these. He was more pleased by the West African explorations of the English naturalist Mary Kinsley, who travelled through cannibal country protected by Fan tribesmen, and by the expansion of French imperialism in Laos, French Guiana, and Dahomey; by Belgian imperialism in the Congo; by American imperialism in Hawaii; and by British imperialism in South Africa, where Cecil Rhodes and Leander Starr Jameson had just suppressed a native revolt. (Already they were plotting the fateful Jameson Raid, to be carried out a few months after young Churchill had passed out of Sandhurst.) Czar Nicholas II had succeeded his father in Russia and seemed to be settling in for a long, stable reign. Winston liked that, too, and because he was fascinated by the trivial as well as the momentous, he was gratified by descriptions of the new Winchester rifle; by the first striptease, at the Bal des Quatre Arts in Paris; by the defeat of John L. Sullivan by James Corbett; and by the invention of the safety razor by an American bottle-stopper salesman named King Gillette.

Hubert Gough, recalling his own early days in uniform, wrote that on weekends he and his friends rode by 'coach, with four horses and two men, all taken from the ranks, to almost every race meeting round London.'[139] Winston liked horses, but he was developing other interests. On each excursion to the city he browsed through bookstores. The expansion of the publishing industry, he found, had not been confined to penny dailies. New magazines were also flourishing, from the popular *Strand Magazine* and the *Review of Reviews* through W.E. Henley's *National Observer* and C.H. Pearson's *National Life and Character*, both journals of imperialist thought, to the avant-garde *Yellow Book*, which carried Aubrey Beardsley's black-and-white 'art nouveau' drawings. The book counters offered a feast: Thomas Hardy's *Tess of the D'Urbervilles* and *Jude the Obscure*, Marie Corelli's *Sorrows of Satan*, Kipling's *Jungle Book*, Robert Louis Stevenson's *Ebb-Tide*, Anthony Hope's *Prisoner of Zenda*, H.G. Wells's *Time Machine*, volumes of poems by A.E. Housman, Yeats, and Hardy; Robert Blatchford's *Merrie England*, which sold over a million copies; A. Conan Doyle's *Memoirs of Sherlock Holmes* (in the December 1893 issue of the *Strand*, Conan Doyle had contrived to kill Holmes in the Reichenbach Falls, but his public successfully demanded a resurrection); and, if you were more fluent in continental languages than Winston was, Emile Zola's *Débâcle*, just off the Paris presses, and thirty-nine-year-old Sigmund Freud's *Studien über Hysterie*.

In knowledgeable circles *Yellow Book*, Oscar Wilde, and *fin de siècle* were code words. They signalled flagrant vice in the West End and, among most educated Englishmen, a collapse of morals. In the upper classes extramarital coitus was acceptable, but sodomy and fellatio were literally unmentionable. Everyone knew that certain public school boys became confused about sexual roles. You didn't talk about that. You didn't let the side down. But these new people were advertising it. 'Art for Art's Sake' meant more than it said. Polite critics called it decadence, which was accurate, though hedonism, a broader term, was more applicable. What few grasped was that this was one of but three new forces which, by the 1890s, had evolved from the religious evangelism of Victoria's prime years. The other two were Anglo-Catholicism – 'High Church,' or 'Ritualistic,' Christianity – and rationalism. Rationalism was the wave of the future. Charles Booth had begun his nine-volume inquiry into London poverty when eleven-year-old Winston caught double pneumonia in Brighton. Booth was still at it, and now, while Cadet Churchill was galloping across the meadows around Camberley, Sidney and Beatrice Webb brought out their *History of Trade Unionism*. Conscience, until now the province of men of the cloth, had found secular forms of expression. When Randolph had gone up to Oxford, the brightest students had been preparing for the ministry. Hardly any were now. Church attendance had dropped sharply all over England. Family prayers in upper-class households, though still prevalent, began to decline. One casualty of this shift was the Victorian Sabbath. Sunday papers were frowned upon, and public restaurants were closed on that day, but it was difficult to defend the old values when all London knew of the Prince of Wales's showy Sunday dinner parties. Throughout the decade society receded from the old Sabbath observance. Museums and art galleries were thrown open on Sunday afternoon. The National Sunday League urged healthy Sunday recreation and organized Sunday railway excursions at cheap rates. The railroads, unwilling to haggle over old values when profits loomed, accommodated them.

The lower classes couldn't afford the excursions, even at half price. Instead, they crowded into the music halls, which, responding to the new moral climate, permitted their comedians' humour to grow broader and broader. This was the halls' Augustan age. The stars, like their audiences, were mostly cockneys: Marie Lloyd, George Robey, Albert Chevalier, Little Titch, Dan Leno, Harry Champion. They sang 'My Old Dutch,' 'Don't Dilly Dally,' 'Two Lovely Black Eyes,' 'Oh, Mr Porter,' 'One of the Ruins That Cromwell Knocked About a Bit,' and England's greatest hit of 1892:

> *After the Ball is over, after the break of morn;*
> *After the dancers' leaving, after the stars are gone;*
> *Many a heart is aching, if you could read them all;*
> *Many the hopes that have vanished, After the Ball.*

Sometimes celebrities paraded across the stage; Eugene Sandow, the German strong man; Blondin, the tightrope walker; Captain Webb, the Channel swimmer. Audiences were intensely patriotic, cheering every glimpse of the Union Jack and, when the chairman thumped his gavel and gave them their cue, belting out 'Tommy, Tommy Atkins,' and 'The Union Jack of Dear Old England.' The best of the halls were in the heart of London. The Eagle, the Alhambra, and the Empire in Leicester Square were the most popular. It was in the Empire, of all places, that Winston Churchill delivered his first speech. The date was Saturday, November 3, 1894. He was defending prostitution.

Mrs Ormiston Chant, a crusader against vice, had been eyeing the theatre with disapproval for some time. The management, like those of most of the halls, had built a promenade beside the men's bar, and it was along this walk, as patrons emptied their glasses, that elegant doxies strolled back and forth, describing their specialties and citing their prices in stage whispers. Winston, now a Sandhurst senior, was not among their customers. He, like many of his peers, sublimated his sex drive and idealized women. He had a crush on Mabel Love, a performer at the Lyric, and at his written request she had sent him an autographed photograph; but his feelings for her were nothing if not chaste.

His band of cadets regularly toured all London's great music halls, however, and he was stung when he read that, at Mrs Chant's insistence, a 'barricade' had been erected between the Empire and its promenade. Instinctively hostile towards authority, he wanted to lash out. He wrote, and then thrice rewrote, a speech which, Churchill the man would recall, was 'a serious constitutional argument upon the inherent rights of British subjects; upon the dangers of State interference with the social habits of law-abiding persons; and upon the evil consequences which inevitably follow upon repression not supported by healthy public opinion.' Reading in the *Daily Telegraph* that champions of the harlots were forming an 'Entertainments Protective League' to defend their dishonour, he resolved to join up. The meeting was held in a seedy London hotel. When he arrived by hansom, he found there was only one other member. The man said sadly, 'It's very difficult to get people to do anything in England now. They take everything lying down, I do not know what's happened to the country; they seem to have no spirit left.'[140]

Winston felt that someone had to speak for freedom. But organization needed funds. In the Strand he spotted the three golden balls hanging over Attenborough's celebrated moneylending shop and hocked his watch, reflecting that, 'after all, the Crown Jewels of great kingdoms [have] been pawned on hard occasions.' Three days later he rounded up fellow cadets out for lark, led them to the Empire, and found that the 'barricade' was merely a canvas screen supported by a wooden framework. He had come prepared to incite a riot. The elements were there. The men already in the bar agreed with him and his friends that the barrier was a bloody shame. A silence spread among them, like the thickening in the air before a storm. One man poked a hole through the screen with his cane. A cadet gave it a shove. Someone else kicked it, and it moved. In a flash the whole crowd, suddenly excited and infuriated, rushed at the flimsy encumbrance and demolished it. Amid the din Winston shouted: 'Ladies of the Empire! I stand for Liberty!' It turned out that there were no ladies present, soiled or otherwise; the prostitutes had prudently decamped. That ought to have been a letdown, but he felt flushed with victory. Leaping on a chair – his text, revised, was in his hand – he cried: 'Where does the Englishman in London always find a welcome? Where does he first go when, battle-scarred and travel-worn, he reaches home? Who is always there to greet him with a smile and join him with a drink? Who is ever faithful, ever true? The ladies of the Empire promenade!'[141]

It was in vain. The London County Council, as licensing authority for the music halls, supported Mrs Chant. Trollops were banned from all of them. Nonetheless, Winston felt a sense of achievement. He wrote to Jack, at Harrow: 'It was I who led the rioters – and made a speech to the crowd. I enclose a cutting from one of the papers so that you may see.' After the council had acted he wrote a formal denunciation of its decision and sent it to his father, who, though he didn't know it, had strong personal reasons for favouring the suppression of tarts. 'I am sure,' Winston wrote to him, 'you will disapprove of so coercive and futile a measure.' He wrote to his aunt Leonie:

'It is hard to say whether one dislikes the prudes or the weak-minded creatures who listen to them most. Both to me are extremely detestable. In trying to be original they have merely lapsed into the aboriginal. The "new woman" is merely the old Eve in a divided skirt.' He also wrote an open letter to the *Westminster Gazette*, submitting that the only way to lasting reform lay in 'educating the mind of the individual and improving the social conditions under which he lives,' but the editor refused to print it, hoping, perhaps, to conceal the identity of the crowd's ringleader. If so, he failed. Mandel Creighton, the bishop of London, found out. He wrote to *The Times*: 'I never expected to see an heir of Marlborough greeted by a flourish of strumpets.'[142]

Winston, satisfied that he had at least drawn blood, continued to drop into music halls whenever he had a free evening. Shortly after he had been commissioned, he was at the Alhambra with a fellow officer when a flag-waving entertainer, inspired by a disagreement between Salisbury and the new czar over the Armenian crisis of 1896, sang:

> *Cease your preaching! Load your guns!*
> *Their roar our mission tells,*
> *The day is come for Britain's sons*
> *To seize the Dardanelles!*

Winston leaned towards his friend and asked: 'Where are the Dardanelles exactly?'[143]

He reached the pinnacle of his Sandhurst days on December 2, 1894. Fifteen of the 127 seniors who had qualified to receive the Queen's commission were chosen to compete for the school's annual riding prize, and he was among them. He wrote to his father, who was abroad with Jennie, 'Well we rode – jumped with & without stirrups & with out reins – hands behind back & various other tricks. Then 5 were weeded out leaving only ten of us. Then we went in the field & rode over the numerous fences several times. 6 more were weeded out leaving only 4 in. I was wild with excitement and rode I think better than I have ever done before but failed to win the prize by 1 mark being 2nd with 199 out of 200 marks. I am awfully pleased with the result, which in a place where everyone rides means a great deal, as I shall have to ride before the Duke and also as it makes it very easy to pick regts when the Colonels know you can ride. I hope you will be pleased.'[144]

It was unlikely. By the time this letter reached Randolph he was in no condition to express pleasure or displeasure. Winston knew, however, that his riding skills had reopened the sore subject of whether he should enter the cavalry or the infantry. Earlier in the year, when they had last exchanged views on the subject through Jennie, his father had still been strong for the Sixtieth Rifles. But Winston now wanted nothing to do with foot soldiering. The man responsible for this view was, ironically, an old friend of Randolph's, Colonel John Brabazon, an impoverished Irish landlord who had seen action during the Afghan War in 1878 and 1879 and during the fierce fighting around Suakin, on the Red Sea, in 1884. Brabazon now commanded the Fourth Queen's Own Hussars – light cavalry. During Winston's first months at Sandhurst, this regiment had been transferred from Ireland to Aldershot, and Brabazon had invited Winston to ride over and dine with him in the regimental mess. The young cadet was dazzled. Some thirty officers, magnificently uniformed in blue and gold, gathered around a table which bore the shining plate and trophies won by the Fourth Hussars during two hundred years of campaigning. In Winston's words: 'It was like a State banquet. In an all-pervading air of glitter, affluence, ceremony and veiled discipline, an excellent and lengthy dinner was served to the strains of the regimental string band.' Even the imperfections were charming; the colonel's lisp, he was delighted to find, was worse than his own. By the time the vintage port was passed, he had lost his heart to his hosts. Brabazon invited him back several times. Early in 1894 Winston had decided that he wanted a commission in the regiment. He had asked his mother to write to the Duke of Cambridge, requesting that he be released from his commitment to the Sixtieth Rifles. The duke, however, had been incensed by the threat of defection, and Randolph had sent word to him that 'Brabazon, who I know is one of the finest soldiers in the army, had no business to go and turn that boy's head about going to the 4th Hussars.'[145]

But turned it was, and it wouldn't be turned back. When Jennie had reproached him for continuing to accept invitations to the regimental mess, he had replied: 'I should not think that Papa would object to my having stayed with Col Brab at Aldershot. How I wish I were going into the 4th instead of those old Rifles. It would not cost a penny more & the regiment goes to India in 3 years which is just right for me. I hate the Infantry – in which physical weaknesses will render me nearly useless on service & the only thing I am showing an aptitude for athletically – riding – will be no good to me.' There was another reason. Ambition was beginning to flame in him. 'Promotions much quicker in Cavalry than in Infantry (60th Rifles slowest regiment in the army).' Nevertheless, his father, unconvinced, had closed the subject in May. Now, seven months later, he passed out of Sandhurst with honours, twentieth in a class of 130. He wrote afterwards that he passed out 'into the world. It opened like Aladdin's Cave . . . an endless moving picture in which one was an actor . . . All the days were good and each day better than the other. Ups and downs, risks and journeys, but always the sense of motion, and the illusion of hope.'[146]

What is baffling about this passage is that the weeks after he left Sandhurst were among the most terrible of his life. His parents were away; he had no home. He drifted from his aunt Leonie's London house at 53 Seymour Street to Deepdene, his aunt's estate; to his grandmother at Blenheim; to the home of a friend at Bayham; to the estate of Lord Hindlip, another friend; and then back to Deepdene. He had not yet been commissioned. That would come only when he had been gazetted. Eventually he was to serve in nine different

British regiments – the Fourth Hussars, the Thirty-first Punjab Infantry, the Twenty-first Lancers, the South African Light Horse, the Oxfordshire Hussars, the Oxfordshire Yeomanry, the Grenadier Guards, the Royal Scots Fusiliers, and the Oxfordshire Artillery – but in that winter of his twenty-first year he was an upper-class vagabond, a wanderer with no place to hang his top hat. Not that it much mattered. He was in a state of shock, trying to come to terms with the shattering fact that his father, whom he cherished despite the sad history of their relationship, was about to die.

By 1885, when Winston was ten, his father had entered the fourth syphilitic stage, the slow invasion of the nervous system, in which the micro-organisms successively attack the membranes, the spinal cord, and, finally, the brain, producing general paresis – total paralysis. Lord Rosebery began to notice physical impairment in his friend early in the year. That summer other friends became disturbed. Dilke, Chamberlain, and Lord James put their heads together in September, shared observations, and broke up after realizing that it was beyond them. Labouchère sent Rosebery a note: 'R. Churchill is in a very bad way . . . He says he cannot sleep after 6 in the morning and breaks down if he does not go to bed early.' In August and again in November Randolph was confined to his bed. He confided to Lord Dufferin that sessions in the House entailed strain 'and the constant necessity of trying to say something new makes one a drivelling idiot.'[147]

By now Dr Roose had thrown in his hand. Although chiefly known in the West End for his successful treatment of gout, Roose had also researched neurasthenic diseases and was, for his time, an accomplished diagnostician. He had bluntly told Randolph that he believed his disease to be incurable, then sent him to Dr Thomas Buzzard, a VD specialist, for another opinion. Buzzard shared Roose's pessimism. In the 1880s anyone who had reached the quaternary stage of syphilis was beyond hope. The two doctors proscribed alcohol and tobacco, and prescribed early bedtimes and doses of potassium iodide, mercury, and digitalis. They might as well have done nothing. Except for the digitalis, which fought the cardiac weakness accompanying the affliction, their drugs merely produced embarrassing side effects: hoarseness, dizziness, darkened skin, and progressive deafness – all of which were observed by Randolph's acquaintances in subsequent years and noted in their diaries and letters.

Paresis, though fatal in the end, is interrupted by frequent remissions, thereby encouraging false hope. It is also characterized by spells of feverish energy alternating with despair; by poor judgement, violent rages, and moodiness. In 1892, as general paralysis slowly approached, these were joined, in Randolph's case, by palpitations and slurred speech. Jennie was in torment. She was nursing her husband, keeping up a brave front, trying to pretend that life was normal, and wondering what to tell the children. Her sons were not only unaware that their father had an irremediable social disease; they didn't even know he was seriously ill. On the face of it this is inexplicable. Others watched Randolph's deterioration for ten years. But the boys rarely saw him. Most of what Winston knew about his father's activities now came from his mother. Randolph did write to him from time to time, and with hindsight we can trace his deterioration in those letters. Winston didn't, or couldn't. There had always been a wild streak in his father's scrawled notes to him anyhow. Those who saw Randolph more frequently, however, had long since despaired of him. It had been more than a year since his friends had been able to endure hearing him speak in Parliament. 'R.C. terrible,' James wrote to Chamberlain after one scene in the House. After another, *The Times* parliamentary correspondent wrote that 'nothing more tragical has been seen in the House of Commons in our generation.' Randolph became completely unpredictable. In a shrewd moment he drafted an amendment to the Parnell Report, shifting responsibility for the witch-hunt from the government to one of his favourite bêtes noires, *The Times*. Louis Jennings was to speak first; Randolph was to follow. The House was full. Before the Speaker could recognize Jennings, Randolph was on his feet, denouncing the government in the crudest language members had heard there. Jennings never spoke to him again. Others left the chamber whenever he rose, not out of anger, but because they knew they could not suffer what they knew would follow. Rosebery said: 'There was no curtain, no retirement. He died by inches in public.'[148]

The final symptoms were now evident. As his brain and spinal cord rotted, he became subject to unexpected attacks, facial tremors, tremors of the lip and tongue, abrupt changes in the pupils of his eyes, impaired vision, splitting headaches, lapses of memory, delusions, depressions, and dementia. At times he could not engage in coherent conversation. William H. Rideing, who sat at his right during a dinner party, later recalled: 'Lord Randolph was plainly a doomed man. He shook as if in a palsy; his voice was woolly and stuttering, almost unintelligible.' On May 27, 1894, Wilfrid Scawen Blunt wrote in his diary: 'Wednesday I called on Randolph Churchill in Grosvenor Square (his mother's house) and had some political talk with him. He is terribly altered, poor fellow, having some disease, paralysis, I suppose, which affects his speech, so that it is painful to listen to him. He makes prodigious efforts to express himself clearly, but these are only too visible . . . As he came to the door with me he tried again to explain to me what he wanted to tell me about Egypt, but broke down and said, almost in tears, "I know what I want to say, but damn it, I can't say it." ' Frank Harris, another caller at 50 Grosvenor Square, wrote of Randolph that he was 'appalled by his appearance. In a couple of years he had changed out of character, had become an old man instead of a young one. His face was haggard; his hair greyish and very thin on top; his thick beard, also half-grey, changed him completely . . . As I took his hand and looked at him I felt sick: the deep lines on his face, the heavy gummy bags under his miserable eyes, the shaking hand . . . A moment later he put his hand over his eyes and sat down heavily. "I have slept badly and I don't feel well today," he went on in trembling, indistinct tones . . . He filled me with pity and regret – such an end to such a great career!'[149]

Shortly afterwards, Harris was a guest at one of Sir Henry Thompson's 'octave' dinners, so called because of the number of guests. He sat almost opposite Randolph. 'His face was drawn and his skin leaden grey,' he wrote; 'there were gleams of hate, anger, and fear in his eyes, the dreadful fear of those who have learned how close madness is.' After one course Randolph pointed at grouse on the sideboard and squealed, as if in pain, 'E-e-e-e-e-e!' Sir Henry asked quietly, 'What is it, Lord Randolph?' Randolph squealed 'E-e-e-e!' again, pointing at the footman who was carving. 'I want that – e-e-e! Some of that – e-e!' Sir Henry said, 'It shall be brought back. I'm very glad you like it.' Served, Randolph ate greedily, then suddenly dropped his knife and fork and glared at each face in turn around the table. Harris was convinced he had seen 'what I called "the malignant monkey stage" of insanity. His shrill prolonged squeal is always in my ears when I think of him.' But Harris, though a gifted editor and confidant of gentlemen, was a native of Ireland and a naturalized American. In a word, he was not British. The distinction became apparent to him when, after the dinner, he approached a fellow guest and asked whether he had noticed the incident with the game. The man replied, 'No, I didn't remark anything, but the grouse was excellent.' Harris then asked another man whether he had thought anything strange in Randolph's behaviour. 'No,' he was told, 'except that he seems to be in a d—d bad temper.' Harris persisted: 'Didn't you notice how he squealed and pointed? He's mad!' The man chuckled and asked lightly, 'Was he ever sane?'[150]

If Randolph's friends refused to discuss his deterioration with one another, they certainly weren't going to acknowledge it in front of his son. The fact that others, including Jennie, treated his conduct as normal, and that Winston apparently never witnessed one of his father's seizures, contributed to the boy's inability to grasp the gravity of his illness until the end approached. He was solicitous, but not alarmed, when Jennie told him that his father's doctors had recommended that he take a long sea voyage, and that she would accompany him. Actually, there was more to it than that. The doctors' chief concern had been persuading Randolph to give up politics for a year, and this was the solution. At the last minute they worried about losing touch for so long. Therefore, a young physician, Dr George Keith, would accompany the Churchills. The family was worried for another reason. Jennie's presence at his side troubled them; as Marjoribanks wrote to Rosebery, she 'always grates on his nerves.' Nevertheless, she was going. Her marriage to this strange man had become a brittle shell, but she felt she owed him this. They would circumnavigate the globe via the United States, Canada, Japan, Burma, India, and the P & O route home, with frequent stops along the way. Winston, Jack, and Rosebery, now prime minister, saw them off at the station, and they sailed aboard the S.S. *Majestic* on June 27, 1894. Their first stop was New York, where reporters met them. One observed that Randolph, who had appeared 'gay, clever and vivacious' when he had visited the city a decade earlier, was now 'restless, nervous and irritable, and walks feebly, with jerky steps, like a

171

man uncertain of where he is putting his feet. His whole manner indicates a painful nervousness and mental irritation, from the querulous tones of his voice to his compressed lips, which he keeps drawn over his teeth in an apparent effort to control their trembling.' After that it was all downhill. By the time they reached Asia, *Harper's Weekly* reported, it was the opinion of his fellow passengers 'that he would not leave Japan alive. He grew very much worse on the voyage. At the outset he was petulant and irritable, but soon an ominous calmness, at times almost a lethargic quietness, grew upon him. His malady was one of the forms of softening of the brain, and this change was called a very bad symptom. His face, thin and wrinkled, was pitiful to look upon.' Sometimes, behind closed doors, his lethargy vanished. Jennie later told Leonie that her husband, now paranoid, had come to believe that she was his persecutor. Once in their cabin he produced a loaded revolver and threatened her; she grabbed it, shoved him on his berth, and left, locking the door behind her. She later said: 'At first, when he was practically a maniac and very strong, it was bad, but as soon as he became weak and idiotic, I didn't mind.'[151]

She minded very much. The trip was a six-month ordeal for her. She wrote to her sister Clara aboard ship on the Bay of Bengal, after a week in Rangoon: 'I can't tell you how I pine for a little society . . . And yet the worst of it is that I dread the chance even of seeing people for his sake. He is quite unfit for society . . . One never knows what he may do. At Govt House Singapore he was very bad for 2 days and it was quite dreadful being with strangers. Since then he has become quieter & sometimes is quite apathetic but Keith thinks it a bad sign.' She felt that it was 'quite impossible for us to go travelling about in India. It means staying with people all the time & R is too unfit for it . . . Dearest Clarinette I cannot go into all the details of his illness but you cannot imagine anything *more* distracting & desperate than to watch it & see him as he is.' As if this weren't enough, she had received a further jolt in Burma. Of all her men, the one she had loved most deeply was Charles Kinsky. For years he had remained single, hoping that one day she would be free. Now he had given up; he had found another woman, a countess twenty years younger than Jennie: 'I had a telegraph from Charles at Rangoon telling me of his engagement. *I hate it.*'[152]

Dr Keith blew the whistle in Madras. On November 24 he wired Roose that their patient had begun to sink and the party would return to London as soon as possible. Six days later Keith wrote to Randolph's sister Cornelia from Bombay: 'I regret extremely that we have to come home but for everyone's sake I know it is the only thing to do. Lord Randolph is in no condition to continue his journey: it is the worst thing for him, he gets no pleasure out of it, and did he understand how he is he would be the last person to wish it . . . It may seem that rather a cruel way has been taken to prevail on Lord Randolph to return but he really does not think about it much and it does not strike him in the way it would do if he were well. We ought to reach Marseilles on the 20th of next month and our subsequent movements must be entirely guided by

Lord Randolph's condition. He stood the journey from Madras very well, it certainly did him no harm. I will write to you again from Port Said.'[153]

Winston's awareness of what was happening seems to have come to him in fits and starts. He would accept the situation, reject it, accept it again, and reject it again – the cycle was repeated over and over. Nearly a month earlier, before his parents had even reached Yokohama on the *Empress of Japan*, he had confronted Roose and demanded to know the facts about the state of his father's health. He wrote to his mother on November 2, 'I thought it was only right that I should know exactly how he was progressing. You see I only hear through grandmamma Jerome who does not take a very sanguine view of things – or through the Duchess who is at one extreme one minute and at the other the next. So I asked Dr Roose and he showed me the medical reports. . . . I need not tell you how anxious I am. I had never realised how ill Papa had been and had never until now believed that there was anything serious the matter. I do trust & hope as sincerely as human beings can that the relapse Keith spoke of in his last report was only temporary and that the improvement of the few months [sic] has been maintained. Do, my darling mamma when you write let me know *exactly* what you think.' He suggested that she and Keith 'write nothing but good to the Duchess' because 'she lives, thinks, and cares for nothing in the world but to see Papa again.'[154]

Six days later, after Keith had sent Roose his report from Japan, Winston had written to Jennie: 'I am very very sorry to hear that so little improvement has been made, and that apparently there is not much chance of improvement.' Yet a few lines later he suggested, 'If I were you I would always try and look on the bright side of things and endeavour perpetually to derive interest from everything.' In addition, as we have seen, he had not only sent his father a cheery report on the Sandhurst riding competition but felt the world opening for him 'like Aladdin's cave.' And by then he had known the worst. Upon receiving Keith's Madras telegram, Roose had summoned Winston from Hindlip Hall and informed him that his father's life was approaching its end. On Christmas Eve his parents reached London. 'For a month,' Winston wrote in his biography of Randolph, 'he lingered pitifully.' Most of the time he was in a stupor. His son had by now become reconciled to the inevitable. He saw his father only as 'a swiftly-fading shadow.' In the early hours of Thursday, January 24, 1895, Winston was roused in the mansion of a neighbour, where he had been sleeping. 'I ran in the darkness,' he wrote, 'across Grosvenor Square, then lapped in snow.' It was all over. Three days later Randolph was buried in Bladon churchyard – the bells overhead, which had pealed merrily at Winston's birth, now tolled slowly – and a memorial service was held in Westminster Abbey.[155]

Behind him Randolph left disorder. His career had been one long strife, and it did not end at the Bladon grave. He had his defenders. The *Saturday Review* thought him 'the greatest elemental force in English politics since Cromwell,' and Sir Herbert Maxwell wrote in the *National Review*: 'Reckless beyond all men's reckoning in prosperity, he was wont to be swift and dangerous when hard pressed . . . Lord Randolph remained, to the last, first favourite among his party with a very large section of the people. No one can doubt that, who was in London during the closing weeks of his life, for one had only to lend an ear . . . to hear anxious discussion of the latest bulletins about "Randy," as he was affectionately called.' But *de mortuis nil nisi bonum* was not observed by his enemies. Other obituaries described him as a man lacking in delicacy, subtlety, or decency – the *Outlook* said that he represented 'the coarser qualities of his race . . . his defect was his lack of power of subordination.' An officious young man from the Treasury even appeared at the Grosvenor Square portal and demanded the return of the robes Randolph had worn as chancellor of the Exchequer. His widow replied superbly – and prophetically – 'I am saving them for my son.' Jennie's demeanour was the subject of much comment. *Harper's Weekly* had reported on the fateful last trip: 'Lady Churchill's devotion to her husband won for her the admiration of all who saw them abroad. Vigorous and active, and still a great beauty, she gave up every other pleasure to give him constant and loving care.' That wasn't the half of it. She had vowed that the nature of his disease should remain forever secret. To Leonie she wrote that 'up to now the General Public and even Society does not know the real truth, and after *all* my sacrifice and the misery of these 6 months it would be hard if it got out. It would do incalculable harm to his political reputation and memory and be a dreadful thing for all of us.'[156] Nevertheless, there was some ill feeling towards her in her husband's family. Duchess Fanny felt that her mourning for Randolph was inadequate. There was some truth in this. Jennie was grief-stricken, but it was for Count Kinsky, who had been married just two weeks before she returned to England. The duchess extended her resentment to Winston, however, and that was unjust, for he was, and would continue to be, obsessed with the memory of his father. Seldom, indeed, has a man invested so little affection in a son and reaped such dividends of posthumous loyalty.

It is clear now that Randolph, had he lived, would have been a crushing burden for Winston's parliamentary ambitions. But the boy did not see it that way. He never would. At the funeral he felt that his task was 'to lift again the flag I found lying on a stricken field.' Over thirty years later he would write: 'All my dreams of comradeship with him, of entering Parliament at his side and in his support, were ended. There remained for me only to pursue his aims and vindicate his memory.' Unfortunately, aspiring politicians needed money – even ambitious cavalry officers needed it – and although his father had left an estate of £75,951, debts claimed most of that. Winston's pay as a subaltern would be £120 a year. Fortunately Jennie received $10,000 a year from the rental of the Jerome family home on Madison Square in New York, and she told Winston she would provide him with another £300. It wasn't nearly enough, but a dim plan was forming in his mind. He must take his father's place in Parliament. To be elected he would have to become famous. The quickest way to popular acclaim, he believed, was to acquire a reputation for military heroism. This, he knew, would be difficult. He wrote afterwards: 'In the closing decade of the Victorian era the Empire had enjoyed so long a spell of almost unbroken peace, that medals and all they represented in experience and adventure were becoming extremely scarce in the British Army.' Still, there were always small wars here and there. Someone was always fighting someone else. He would shop around. There was nothing to stop him. Here, at least, he was realistic about Randolph's death: 'I was now in the main the master of my fortunes.'[157]

Among his father's last words to him had been: 'Have you got your horses?' Winston interpreted this to mean an end to talk of the Sixtieth Rifles and approval of the cavalry. Jennie agreed. Their relationship had changed. 'My mother was always at hand to help and advise,' he later recalled, 'but I was now in my twenty-first year and she never sought to exercise parental control. Indeed, she soon became an ardent ally, furthering my plans and guarding my interests with all her influence and boundless energy. She was still at forty young, beautiful and fascinating. We worked together on even terms, more like brother and sister than mother and son.' Jennie had been indifferent towards him in his childhood, but she knew men. Now she wired Brabazon, who suggested she reopen negotiations with the Duke of Cambridge, which she did. In less than two weeks Winston's orders were cut. On February 18 he reported to the Fourth Hussars, and two days later he was awarded his commission, informing him: 'VICTORIA by the grace of God of the United Kingdom of Great Britain and Ireland, Queen, Defender of the Faith, Empress of India, & To Our Trusty and well beloved Winston Leonard Spencer Churchill, Gentleman, Greeting: We, reposing especial Trust and Confidence in your Loyalty, Courage and Good Conduct, do by these Presents Constitute and Appoint you to be an Officer in Our Land Forces from the twentieth day of February 1895. You are therefore carefully and diligently to discharge your Duty as such in the Rank of 2nd Lieutenant . . .'[158]

Discomfort has always been the lot of men being initiated into professional soldiering, and Sandhurst graduates were not exempt. Winston's first six months were to be spent in the company of enlisted recruits, drilling under the command of the regimental riding master, a fiery tyrant nicknamed 'Jocko.' After the glamour of the regimental mess, this was a comeuppance. The life, Winston wrote to Jennie, 'is fearfully severe and I suffer terribly from stiffness – but what with hot baths and *massage* I hope soon to be better. At present I can hardly walk. I have however been moved up in the 2nd Class recruits which is extremely good. The horses are very different to [sic] the Sandhurst screws. Rather too broad I think for me.' Jocko's taunts were humiliating for a green officer, and were meant to be. Early in the course Winston strained a thigh muscle, necessary for gripping a horse; the choice was to suffer tortures or be thought wet, so he suffered, and sometimes fell. He later wrote: 'Many a time did I pick myself up shaken and sore . . . and don again my little gold braided pork-pie cap, fastened on the chin by a boot-lace strap, with what

175

appearance of dignity I could command, while twenty recruits grinned furtively but delightedly to see their Officer suffering the same misfortunes which it was their lot so frequently to undergo.' But he was a good horseman, and it began to show. In a break with precedent, his time of indoctrination was cut to three months. He began to like Jocko, though not the drill, 'which as usual I loathe and abominate.'[159]

He was still drilling, and still under Jocko's eye, when older officers invited him to ride in the regiment's annual point-to-point for subalterns. Jennie had tried to discourage him from steeplechasing – Kinsky had nearly come to grief that way – telling him it was 'idiotic' and could be 'fatal.' As yet he had no horse of his own, and had therefore reassured her that his participation was out of the question, but when another subaltern offered to lend him a charger, he couldn't resist. Afterwards he wrote to his brother: 'It was very exciting, and there is no doubt about it being dangerous. I had never jumped a regulation fence before and they are pretty big things as you know. Everybody in the regiment was awfully pleased by my riding, more especially as I came in third. They thought it very sporting. I thought so too.' Jennie was reproachful. So was Woom, and for the same reason. She wrote to him: 'I hope you will take care of yourself my darling. I hear of your exploits at steeple chasing. I do so dread to hear of it. Remember Count Kinsky broke his nose once at that.'[160]

His mother had scarcely recovered from this, and he had hardly seen the last of the bull-lunged Jocko, when real trouble loomed, a scandal which could have ruined him. Alan Bruce, a Sandhurst classmate, was about to join the Fourth Hussars. He had been an unpopular cadet, as ill-adjusted there as Winston had been at Harrow. Winston and his new confreres in the officers' mess decided they didn't want him; they took him to dinner at the Nimrod Club in London and told him that his father's allowance of £500 would be inadequate. That was preposterous, and he said so. Since he had failed to take their hint, they discouraged him in other ways. The details are unclear, but it is not a pretty story. Bruce was accused of using foul language, of being familiar with enlisted men, of abusing regimental sergeants. The upshot was that he was asked to resign from the army. His infuriated father, A.C. Bruce-Pryce, persuaded the weekly review *Truth* to mount a press crusade against an 'undisguised conspiracy formed against this subaltern before he joined to have him out of the regiment unless he consented to go voluntarily.' That was the last way to engage the affections of those who had manoeuvred Bruce's dismissal, and the incident would have been swiftly forgotten if Bruce-Pryce hadn't taken leave of his senses. He charged that Winston Churchill had been guilty of 'acts of gross immorality of the Oscar Wilde type.'[161]

Winston moved fast. He hired the Holborn solicitors Lewis and Lewis, who, four days later, issued a writ demanding damages of £20,000. Within a month he got £500, an apology, and a complete withdrawal: 'I unreservedly withdraw all and every imputation against your character complained of by

176

you in paragraph 2 of your Statement of Claim and I hereby express my regret for having made the same.' *Truth* howled on, now charging that the point-to-point had been rigged, but the great reef had been skirted. Except for an absurd remark by Lord Beaverbrook – that Winston had told him he once went to bed with a man to see what it was like – nothing in Churchill's life offers the remotest ground for intimations of homosexuality. At the time, however, the barest rumour of it, unless instantly suppressed, could have been calamitous. As Brabazon wrote to him, expressing 'very great relief' at the outcome, 'one cannot touch pitch without soiling one's hands however clean they may originally have been and the world is so ill natured and suspicious that there would always have been found some ill natured sneak or perhaps some d—d good natured friend to hem & ha! & wink over it – perhaps in years to come, when everyone even yourself had forgotten all about the disagreeable incident. You took the only line possible . . . For malignant, preposterous as it was, it would have been impossible to have left such a charge unchallenged.' Thus, with the colonel's sanction, the regiment regarded Winston as a martyr. The triumph of irony was complete. The Harrovian who had been at odds with his peers and a rebel against school authority was now accepted, and content with his acceptance, in an authoritarian sodality.[162]

Hubert Gough, later recalling his days at Aldershot as a subaltern in the Sixteenth Lancers, said: 'We led a cheerful, care-free life; what duties we had to do . . . did not call for much mental effort. Afternoons were usually free for most officers.' Winston's life there followed a relaxed routine. His batman brought him breakfast in bed. A subaltern's only obligations in a typical day were to spend two hours riding, an hour with the horses in the stables, and ninety minutes drilling. The rest of his time was his own. If he remained in barracks, Winston might play bezique for threepence a point, 'a shocking descent from the shillings at Deepdene,' he wrote, or whist, 'a most uninteresting game and one at which I have but little luck.' He liked games he could win. He described golf, one of his failures, as 'a curious sport whose object is to put a very small ball in a very small hole with implements ill-designed for the purpose.' Polo and steeplechasing occupied him more and more, though he paid for his recklessness; after one fall, which confined him to bed for three days, he explained to his mother that at a jump 'the animal refused and swerved. I tried to cram him in and he took the wings. Very nearly did he break my leg, but as it is I am only bruised and stiff.' Another young officer might have kept that information to himself. Winston didn't; he was still an egotistical, bumptious, rude youth. But these traits were common among young Victorian officers. Besides, he was witty, daring, generous, entertaining. Jennie had found the right word for him. He was *interesting*.[163]

Because Aldershot was only thirty-two miles from London, celebrities often visited to take the salute. Once the hussars rehearsed in the Long Valley under the scrutiny of a rising cavalryman, Captain Douglas Haig. It was 'a very fine thing,' Winston wrote, to see 'a cavalry division of thirty or forty squadrons' manoeuvred 'as if it were one single unit . . . When the line was finally formed

177

and the regiment or brigade was committed to the charge, one could hardly help shouting in joyous wrath.' As the grandson of a duke, Winston was chosen to escort the Prince of Wales, the Duke of Cambridge, the Duke of Connaught, Field Marshal Lord Roberts, and the Duke and Duchess of York (later King George V and Queen Mary). Best of all were the 'splendid parades when Queen Victoria sat in her carriage at the saluting point and . . . the whole Aldershot garrison, perhaps 25,000 strong, blue and gold, scarlet and steel, passed before her, Horse, Foot, and Artillery . . . in a broad and scintillating flood.' The purpose of all this was obscure. Winston later wrote: 'Certainly no Jingo Lieutenant or Fire-eating Staff Officer in the Aldershot Command in 1895, even in his most sanguine moments, would have believed that our little army would ever again be sent to Europe.'[164]

Any member of England's ruling families was, by that very fact, welcome in the London mansions and country homes of the aristocracy. Even Lord Randolph, diseased and mad, had not been excluded. And his son was not only a Churchill; he was also an eligible bachelor. 'A gay and lordly life,' he wrote, 'now opened upon me.' He had 'a great many invitations and could go to a ball every night should I wish to.' The greatest affairs that Season were held in Stafford House and Devonshire House, and he was always present. 'Everywhere one met friends and kinfolk,' he wrote. 'The leading figures of Society were in many cases the leading statesmen in Parliament.' Present were 'all the elements which made a gay and splendid social circle in close relation to the business of Parliament, the hierarchies of the Army and Navy, and the policy of the State.' It was almost always urbane; only once was he obliged to step between two men lunging at each other, one a participant in the Jameson Raid then on trial in Bow Street, the other a former Liberal minister who regarded the raid as an outrage. Neither thought it incongruous that a mere subaltern should step between them. It was Winston's social standing, not his rank, which counted.[165]

In his regiment, he was glad to find, virtually all the officers were Conservatives, and since the country was going to the polls that summer, there was much talk of politics. Rosebery, though a Liberal, was personally popular, particularly with Winston, for he had been a good friend to the Churchills. But everyone agreed that he had fallen among bad companions; as prime minister he owed his office to the Irish Nationalists and hence was tainted with the Fenian brush. His government fell in June because, it was said, he had permitted the country's stocks of cordite to run low. Why England needed cordite just then was unmentioned, and it wasn't true anyway, but there were cheers in Aldershot when Salisbury was returned with a majority of 150. Winston attended a party at Devonshire House and found that the other guests included Salisbury's new ministers, looking smart in their new blue-and-gold uniforms. 'These uniforms were not so magnificent as ours,' he wrote, 'but they had a style about them which commended them to my eye.' He fell into conversation with George Curzon, the new under secretary for foreign affairs. Curzon outlined his duties. In the House of Commons he would explain and defend Britain's foreign policy. More important, in Whitehall he would share in making that policy. Specifically, he expected to guide Britain's conduct towards other European powers. That was very different from galloping about and parading in an army which, everyone agreed, would never see action on the Continent. The difference between him and Curzon, Winston reflected gloomily, had nothing to do with braid and frogging. One had power and the other only the illusion of it. He studied the under secretary as he listened to him, looked around at the other ministerial uniforms, and 'felt free to give rein to jealousy.'[166]

It was a year of funerals. His father had slipped away in January, his grandmother Clara died in April, and as hot weather approached he learned that Elizabeth Everest lay stricken with peritonitis. They had kept in touch; she was living with her sister Emma at 15 Crouch Hill in the Islington district of North London. On April 1 she had written to him: 'My darling Precious Boy, I have just recd £2.10s from Cox & Co. Charing Cross on your account. I thank you very much indeed dearest it is awfully kind & thoughtful of you. My dear dear Boy you are one in ten thousand but I am afraid you will find your income not any too much for your expenses dear. It really is too good & kind of you I don't know how to thank you enough. I am afraid Her Ladyship will think me a terrible imposter [sic].'[167]

Late in June her sister wrote to him that Woom was ill, and he hurried to Islington. She knew her condition was grave, but Woom's only anxiety was for him. He had passed through a heavy shower, his jacket was wet; she told him he might catch cold and would not rest until he spread out the jacket to dry. He had to return to Aldershot by the midnight train for an early parade, and he was there when a telegram arrived from Emma. His old nurse's end was very near. Winston fetched Dr Keith, engaged a private nurse, and hurried to Woom's side. She recognized him, but as she spoke she sank into a coma. He sat there, holding her hand, until she died at 2:15 the following morning. He wrote: 'Death came very easily to her. She had lived such an innocent and loving life of service to others and held such a simple faith, that she had no fears at all, and did not seem to mind very much.'[168]

He organized the funeral. Knowing that she had nursed the children of an archdeacon in Cumberland, he wired him, and the clergyman agreed to come and read the service. Winston didn't want to telegraph Jack; he went to Harrow and told him, and they travelled together to London's Manor Park cemetery. Jennie was in Paris and saw no reason to return, but Winston ordered a wreath in her name. He was surprised at the number of mourners. He wrote to his mother: 'All her relations were there – a good many of whom had travelled from Ventnor overnight – and I was quite surprised to find how many friends she had made in her quiet and simple life. The coffin was covered with wreaths & everything was as it should be.' Afterwards he paid for a headstone:

Erected in Memory
of
Elizabeth Anne Everest
who died 3rd July 1895
Aged 62
by
Winston Spencer Churchill
Jack Spencer Churchill

Then he made arrangements with the local florist for the upkeep of the grave. 'I feel very low,' he wrote to Jennie, 'and find that I never realized how much poor old Woom was to me.' It was 'indeed another link with the past gone – & I look back with regret to the old days at Connaught Place when fortune still smiled.' Depressed, he made a pilgrimage to his father's grave in Bladon and wrote to his mother, who had never been there, that he 'was so struck by the sense of quietness & peace as well as by the old world air of the place – that my sadness was not unmixed with solace . . . I think it would make you happier to see it.'[169] The real source of his solace, although he could not have recognized it, was that all his links with the past were well broken. Except for his hours in the nursery with Woom, his early years had brought him very little pleasure and much pain. But they had fashioned him into a strong young man possessed of immense drive, ready to mount the steep slopes of challenge ahead.

TWO

STREAM
1895 – 1901

QUEEN Victoria's army, which would leave a lasting impression upon Churchill, was an eccentric, insular institution that had changed little since Waterloo, a battle some men still alive could remember clearly. The troops were led by patricians: Wellington had decreed that English gentlemen made 'the best officers in the world, and to compose the officers from a lower class would cause the Army to deteriorate.' Military leaders, it was held, should be men with 'a stake in the country.' Only WASPs need apply; there were few Disraelis or Rothschilds wearing epaulets. Apart from that, public school boys were accepted if they were 'sound,' were 'of the right sort,' and came from 'good families.' (You could quickly identify those with classical educations; they swore 'By Jove,' an oath never heard in Other Ranks.) In endorsing an application, one colonel scrawled across it, 'The son of a good soldier, his mother is a lady.' It was common to note on reports as a recommendation: 'A good man to hounds.' Lord Roberts always checked the bloodlines of a man applying for an appointment, and according to the career officer Ian Hamilton, if Roberts thought the candidate 'owned a good grandmother he would give him a trial.'[1] Gentlemen were expected to guard zealously their regiment's 'tone,' a Victorian word freighted with class consciousness. The army counted on them to live by the gentleman's code, and if they didn't know what that was, they weren't commissioned in the first place. In some ways the code was peculiar. Gambling debts were always settled promptly, but those to tradesmen weren't. Six years after joining the Fourth Hussars, Churchill still hadn't paid the tailor who made his first uniforms. But once you were in, you could stay in forever. Some officers who had reached their eighties retained their commands. Nor were crippling wounds disqualifying. Two generals, Roberts and Wolseley, were one-eyed. Hamilton's wrist had been shattered at Majuba.* Lord Raglan had been one-armed. So was Samuel Browne, who invented the Sam Browne belt so he could draw his sword swiftly with his remaining hand.

By continental standards, the number of men in uniform was tiny. Asked what he would do if the British army landed in Prussia, Bismarck replied: 'Send a policeman and have it arrested.' There were no corps, no divisions, nor even brigades. Everything was built around the regiment. An infantry regiment might have a single battalion of seven hundred men divided into five or six companies. An entire cavalry regiment like Winston's – hussars,

---

* On February 27, 1881, Boer troops fighting for their independence had defeated a British force under Sir George Colley and killed Sir George at Majuba Hill.

dragoons, or lancers – numbered from three hundred to five hundred men, led by its colonel, four majors, eight captains, and fourteen or fifteen subalterns. There were just thirty-one cavalry regiments in the whole of the British Empire. Seniority – which determined which outfit was stationed on the right in an attack – was jealously guarded in both the cavalry and the infantry. The Coldstream Guards went back to 1661, the Grenadier Guards to 1656, the Scots Guards to 1633, the Buffs to 1572, and the Honourable Artillery Company, which was neither a company nor confined to ordnance, to 1537. Each of them cherished drums and flags captured in battles, some long forgotten, and each dressed officers and ranks in absurd uniforms. *The Times* had reported on the regalia of the Eleventh Hussars: 'The brevity of their jackets, the irrationality of their headgear, the incredible tightness of their cherry-coloured pants altogether defy description.' The man responsible was George IV, who had never been near a battlefield but who, as Prince Regent, had designed uniforms so tight that men could hardly get into them. In his opinion, 'A wrinkle is unpardonable.'[2]

These zany costumes had become preposterous with the invention of smokeless gunpowder in 1886, but the British didn't like smokeless powder, and wouldn't accept it until their enemies had shown them how effective it could be. It was new; therefore, it was suspect. So were the breech-loading fieldpieces Krupp had introduced; Britain was the last European power to abandon muzzle-loading cannon. So were carbines; those issued to one cavalry regiment were dumped on the stable manure pile. The Duke of Cambridge protested that he wasn't against change. He favoured it, he said, when there was no alternative. But encroachments on tradition, if avoidable, were fiercely resisted. Enlisted men were called Tommy Atkins because that was the name of the private Wellington had picked for a specimen signature on an army identity card. Officers drank wine, brandy, and whisky, and Other Ranks drank gin and beer, because it had always been that way. Regulation bugle calls, though difficult for some buglers, were defended on the ground that they were quintessentially British, though in fact they had been composed by Franz Joseph Haydn.

The citadel of custom, charmingly described in Byron Farwell's *Mr Kipling's Army*, was the regimental mess. This, thought Captain R.W. Campbell, was 'the school for courage, honour, and truth'; there, Hamilton wrote, one understood the 'Chivalry of Arms'; there, in the opinion of Major General George Younghusband, 'The prig ceases to be priggish: it isn't good enough. The cad, if by chance he has slipped in, ceases to be caddish: it isn't good enough. The real "bad hat," or "untamable bounder" quietly disappears.'[3] Meals were rituals. You wore a proper mess jacket, which varied from one regiment to another. New subalterns did not speak until spoken to, never expressed opinions, and, in at least one regiment, did not stand on the hearthrug in front of the fire until they had completed three years' service. The first toast of the evening was to the Queen. Thereafter the port was passed from right to left, and no one smoked until the decanter had circulated twice, or, as they put it, 'when the cloth was removed.' Those who broke the rules were fined, and the rules were so numerous, and so divorced from reality, that one wonders when they had time to ponder the profession of arms. Not at mess; shoptalk was forbidden there. So were discussions of politics, religion, and women. Therefore, they rambled on about sport and horses, particularly hunting, where they shot hares, plover, quail, stags, grouse, partridges, ducks, snipe, woodcocks, pigeons, and, occasionally, through error, one another.

What did their countrymen think of them? It is difficult to say. 'Victorian England,' Brian Bond writes, 'was simultaneously jingoistic and anti-militarist.' A visiting foreigner observed: 'How this blind glorification and worship of the Army continues to co-exist with the contemptuous dislike felt towards the members of it, must remain a problem of the national psychology.' They were paid almost nothing. Regimental rates, established in 1806, varied from £95 for a subaltern to £365 for a lieutenant colonel – less than half the wages of War Office clerks – and they would remain unchanged until 1914. No man could afford a commission unless he possessed a private income of at least £150 a year for an infantry office and as much as £700 in the cavalry. Enlisted men received eleven shillings and fourpence per week, twopence less than the most exploited rural labourer in England. Edward Spiers quotes a recruiting sergeant: 'It was only in the haunts of dissipation or inebriation, and among the very lowest dregs of society, that I met with anything like success.'[4]

Yet these men had conquered an Empire. Under Victoria one regiment or another had been in action every year, somewhere on five continents, fighting from Aden and Afghanistan to Zululand and the Zhor Valley. They were almost always victorious. One reason was their sublime, unfathomable courage. Braver officers never led men into battle. They marched at the head of their columns, disdaining weapons for themselves, brandishing only cigars or swagger sticks. At the battle of Isandhlwana every officer had a horse and could have escaped with his life. Not one did; all remained and died with their men. Under fire, they refused to 'bob' – to duck bullets and shells. An astonishing number actually enjoyed courting death. Of his first wound Wolseley wrote: 'What a supremely delightful moment that was!' A captain in the First Royal Dragoons wrote to his mother: 'I *adore* war. It is like a big picnic. I have never been so well or happy.' Chinese Gordon, seeing combat for the first time in the Crimea, found it 'indescribably exciting.'[5] If officers found themselves in peaceful billets, they looked for war elsewhere, took leave to get there, and paid their own expenses. The colonel commanding the Fourth Dragoon Guards enlisted as a private in the King's Own Scottish Borderers so he could join the storming of the Malakand Pass. The commander of the Tenth Hussars fought under the Turkish and Egyptian flags. Younghusband, having vanished from his post, was next seen standing rapturously in the middle of a Philippine bloodletting. And in November 1895 Second Lieutenant Winston Churchill went to embattled Cuba via the United States.

His motives were mixed. He wanted to see a real war. He was curious about New York, his mother's home. And he was bored. Anticipating its move to India, the Fourth Hussars had been giving its officers ten weeks' leave. They were expected to spend it yachting, racing, steeplechasing, and riding to hounds. The War Office assumed that, as gentlemen, they all had independent incomes and could afford such diversions. Being broke was bad form. The Manchester Regiment had the lowest status in the army because it was said that its officers could live on their pay. But a young cavalry subaltern needed a charger, two hunters, and three polo ponies. Buying them had exhausted Churchill's funds and his mother's patience. Therefore, as he put it, he 'searched the world for some scene of adventure or excitement.'[6] Spain was making its last attempt to quell the insurrection led by José Martí and Máximo Gómez, and 200,000 Spanish troops were tied down in Cuba. Both sides were murdering civilians and putting towns to the torch. That, and its proximity to America, appealed to Churchill. Moreover, he could manage some of the expenses. The *Daily Graphic*, which had published Randolph's letters from Africa in 1891, agreed to pay Winston five guineas for every dispatch from the front. He persuaded one of his regiment's senior subalterns, Reginald Barnes, to accompany him.

At that time there were no restrictions on officers writing for the press. Brabazon had no objections to the trip. Neither had Jennie. She sent ninety pounds and wrote: 'I understand all right – & of course darling it is natural that you shd want to travel & I won't throw cold water on yr little plans.' Next Winston wrote to Lord Randolph's old friend Sir Henry Wolff, now the British ambassador in Madrid, applying for permission from the Spanish military authorities to visit the war zone. It was granted instantly, almost eagerly. The fighting in Cuba had given Spain a terrible image. The press in both England and the United States ardently supported the rebels. This briefly became an issue. Churchill needed one more endorsement, from the War Office. He called on the commander in chief, Wolseley, who seemed embarrassed by the request and hinted that it would be better if Winston went without asking him; newspapermen might misinterpret his sanction of two British officers marching with the Spanish troops. But he couldn't deny a Churchill. He sighed, nodded, and, Winston wrote, added that 'if I worked at the military profession he would help me in every way he could & that I was always to come and ask when I wanted anything.' Then Wolseley sent Winston to his director of military intelligence. This officer, unlike his commander, saw no need for discretion. He provided Churchill with maps and a full briefing. In addition, Winston wrote, he and Barnes were 'requested to collect information and statistics on various points and particularly as to the effect of the new bullet – its penetration and striking power. This invests our mission with almost an official character & cannot fail to help one in the future.'[7]

On November 2 they sailed aboard the Cunard Royal Mail Steamship *Etruria*. The voyage was 'tedious and uncomfortable . . . & I shall always look upon journeys by sea as necessary evils.' But in New York they forgot their grievances. Originally they had scheduled three days in the city, and, aboard ship, had considered cutting this in half. Actually, they were there a week. The man responsible for this revision in plans was Bourke Cockran, a wealthy Irish-American lawyer, congressman, and power in the Tammany wigwam. Cockran was one of Jennie's men – at one time he had been her favourite – and like the rest he cut a remarkable figure, towering, leonine, with deep-set eyes and a massive forehead. His mobile features gave a contemporary the impression of 'something Spanish, Celtiberian as well as Celtic.'[8] His oratory was remarkable. Twice, in 1884 and 1892, his deep, resonant brogue had held Democratic national conventions spellbound. Churchill was to be one of his early conquests. Among the last was Adlai Stevenson, who modelled his rhetoric on Cockran's. In the early 1950s Churchill would astound Stevenson by quoting long passages from Cockran speeches.

Churchill and Barnes were Cockran's guests in his sprawling apartment at 763 Fifth Avenue, on the corner of Fifty-eighth Street. Jennie had written to him that they would be calling, and he made wonderful things happen. Her son wrote to her that he had 'engagements for the next few days about three deep. It is very pleasant staying here as the rooms are beautifully furnished and fitted with every convenience & also as Mr Cockran is one of the most charming hosts and interesting men I have met.' Twelve judges, including a Supreme Court justice, came to dine with them the first evening. The two young English officers dined out at the Waldorf, were entertained at Koster and Bial's, toured the harbour in a tugboat, attended the annual horse show, were shown around the iron-clad cruiser *New York*, attended five fires with the fire commissioner, were received by the Cornelius Vanderbilts – whose niece would be the next Duchess of Marlborough – and visited West Point. Winston wrote: 'We are members of all the Clubs and one person seems to vie with another in trying to make our time pleasant.'[9]

He was not an uncritical tourist. To Jack he wrote that West Point discipline was so strict as to be 'positively disgraceful.' He wrote to his aunt Leonie that he had paid his fare across the eleven-year-old Brooklyn Bridge 'with a paper dollar,' which he thought 'abominable currency.' It seemed to him that 'the essence of American journalism is vulgarity divested of truth.' Considering the character of Pulitzer's *World* and Hearst's new *Journal*, this was not unjust. Besides, he qualified it: 'I think mind you that vulgarity is a sign of strength. A great, crude, strong, young people are the Americans – like a boisterous healthy boy among enervated but well bred ladies and gentlemen.' And New Yorkers, by their treatment of him, won his heart. 'What an extraordinary people the Americans are! Their hospitality is a revelation to me and they make you feel at home and at ease in a way that I have never before experienced.' He adored America's most popular song that year:[10]

> *When you hear dem a bells go ding, ling ling,*
> *All join 'round and sweetly you must sing,*
> *And when the verse am through, in the chorus all join in,*
> *There'll be a hot time in the old town tonight!*

But there is no doubt about which New Yorker impressed him most. He wrote: 'I have great discussions with Mr Cockran on every conceivable subject from Economics to yacht racing. He is a clever man and one from whose conversation much is to be learned.' Night after night, long after Barnes had retired, they sat in the flat's large library, sipping brandy, smoking cigars – Churchill's first – and talking, talking, talking. Jennie's intimate admirer introduced her son to the works of Edmund Burke. He told him: 'Burke mastered the English language as a man masters the horse. He was simple, direct, eloquent, yet there is a splendour in his phrases that even in cold type reveals how forcibly he must have enthralled his visitors.' Churchill was enthralled by his host's fire, vision, vigour, and, most of all, by his own mastery of English. In speaking, Cockran advised him, one should avoid scurrility, affectations, and cant. He said: 'What people really want to hear is the truth – it is the exciting thing – speak the simple truth.' All his life Winston would remember, and frequently quote, some of the phrases he heard by the fire in that Fifth Avenue apartment. Cockran said: 'The earth is a generous mother. She will provide in plentiful abundance food for all her children, if they will but cultivate her soil in justice and peace.' He also said: 'In a society where there is democratic tolerance and freedom under the law, many kinds of evils will crop up, but give them a little time and they usually breed their own cure.' Thirty-seven years later Churchill would write of Cockran: 'I have never seen his like or, in some respects, his equal. His conversation, in point, in pith, in rotundity, in antithesis and in comprehension, exceeded anything I have ever heard.'[11] By then Winston knew scores of great men. But even in 1895 he had met Rosebery, Salisbury, and Balfour. The difference was that they had all regarded him as his father's misfit son. In New York, for the first time, he found himself in the company of a distinguished man who treated him as a peer. Today Bourke Cockran's papers gather dust in the New York Public Library. He is forgotten in his own city. Yet a man who aroused young Churchill, and inspired Stevenson's gallant campaign in 1952, deserves remembrance.

Cockran seemed omnipotent in New York. At a word from him, the two English lieutenants had a private compartment for the thirty-six-hour train trip through Philadelphia, Washington, Savannah, Tampa Bay, and Key West, where they boarded the steamer *Olivette*. In the early hours of Wednesday, November 20, they sighted Havana and the rugged coast outlined against the deep blue horizon. Winston felt 'delicious yet tremulous . . . I felt as if I sailed with Long John Silver and first gazed on Treasure Island. Here was a place where anything might happen. Here was a place where something would certainly happen. Here I might leave my bones.' In his first dispatch as a war correspondent he wrote:

High up on the cliffs, as the ship enters the narrows, one sees the fortress of El Moro, formerly a place of great strength, and commanding the channel to the port. It is now only used as a prison for political and military offenders, and an occasional place for execution. Here it was that the sentence of death on Lieutenant Gallegos was carried out in May last. This officer had the charge of a small post with some fifty soldiers, and was unfortunate enough to be breakfasting in a café when the insurgents happened to pass.[12]

A carriage carried them to the Gran Hotel Inglaterra and then to the office of Alexander Gollan, the British consul general. Everything had been arranged. In the morning they would leave the capital for a twelve-hour train trip to Santa Clara, the headquarters of Captain General Arsenio Martínez de Campos. Unfortunately, they could not be guaranteed a safe passage. Rebels frequently used passing trains for target practice. Sometimes they set them afire, or blew up the tracks. Winston was excited. He told readers of the *Graphic* that the train preceding theirs, carrying a Spanish general, 'had been thrown off the line a few miles beyond Santo Domingo, and . . . fifteen of its occupants had been severely injured.' Their train, however, completed the trip without incident. 'Marshal Campos, to whose headquarters we went, received us very kindly, and readily gave us the necessary passes and letters.'[13]

Campos turned them over to Lieutenant Juan O'Donnell, son of the Duke of Tetuán. The lieutenant was fluent in English. Unfortunately, he had a sad tale to tell. Churchill was introduced to the most exasperating problem of correspondents covering a guerrilla war – finding the front. A Spanish mobile column was camped twenty miles away, pursuing a force of four thousand insurgents, but the jungle between here and there was 'infested by the enemy.' To get there, Churchill and Barnes must take another train to Cienfuegos, proceed by steamer to Tuna, and then travel, again by train, to Sancti Spiritu. 'Though this route forms two sides of a triangle, it is – Euclid notwithstanding – shorter than the other, and we shall catch the column there.'[14]

Altogether he filed five 'Letters from the Front' for the *Graphic*, each of which ran under the head 'The Insurrection in Cuba,' was by-lined 'From Our Own Correspondent,' and concluded with the initials 'WSC.' They show a keen eye for detail, a gift for clarity, and a sure grasp of tactics. The fourth was the best. By November 30 – his twenty-first birthday – he had joined troops commanded by General Juarez Valdez in the fortified village of Arroyo Blanco. At 5:00 A.M., wearing his British uniform, he accompanied two battalions, seventeen hundred men, who were feeling their way towards a band of rebels led by Gómez. 'No sooner had we got clear of the town than we heard the sound of firing.' To deceive Gómez's scouts, the Spaniards retraced their steps and approached from a different direction, 'through swampy meadows of coarse grass traversed by frequent water-courses.' At 10:00 A.M., to his astonishment, they halted and everyone except sentries slept for four hours. This was his introduction to the siesta, a custom which he would appropriate and use during both world wars to turn one working day into two. Rising, they advanced and came upon a rebel encampment; the enemy's line of march could be traced 'by broken branches and trampled grass, and this line the column followed.' At 5:00 P.M. the Spaniards found rebel campfires 'still smouldering, and signs of a hasty departure were to be seen on every side.' Here they dug in for the night, with four companies of infantry posted as sentinels. 'The whole scene, bathed in brilliant moonlight – in strong contrast to which the tall palm trees and the surrounding woods showed in deepest black' – was compared with 'the numerous watch fires, against whose glaze the figures of the soldiers were silhouetted.'[15]

At 5:15 A.M. they were off again. 'The sun had not yet risen, and a mist hung over all the low-lying ground.' The path ahead 'lay through the thickest and most impenetrable forest.' Until now Valdez's plan had been to throw one battalion ahead, with two extended companies guarding each flank, but here the flank guards had to be abandoned; the dense jungle confined them to a narrow path. 'Daylight slowly broadened, and the long Spanish column insinuated itself like a snake into the endless forests and undulations of a vast, lustrous landscape dripping with moisture and sparkling with sunshine.' Their siesta was interrupted by rebel sharpshooters. Back on the trail Winston lit a Cuban cigar – he had the habit now – and noted that the bush here 'gave place to a forest of extraordinary palm trees of all possible sizes and most peculiar shapes.' The column forded a river and camped at a place called Las Grullas, where he persuaded two officers to join him in a swim. As they were dressing, 'suddenly we heard a shot fired. Another and another followed; then came a volley. The bullets whistled over our heads.' Like Chinese Gordon and George Washington, he found it thrilling to be under fire: 'There is nothing more exhilarating than to be shot at without result.' He coolly observed that while Valdez's men carried Mausers, the enemy used Remingtons, 'and the deep note of their pieces contrasted strangely with the shrill rattle of the magazine rifles of the Spaniards.'[16]

That night a bullet passed through the thatched hut in which he was sleeping and another wounded an orderly just outside. Battle – the battle of La Reforma – was joined in the morning. The Spanish column debouched into open country, and the general, scanning the field through his field glasses, saw the enemy's main position. He ordered an attack. His infantry advanced three hundred yards in silence; then 'from the distant crest line came a lot of little puffs of smoke, followed immediately by the report of the insurgent rifles.' The Spaniards' rifles replied as the infantrymen continued their advance. 'The firing on both sides became heavy.' There was 'a sound in the air sometimes like a sigh, sometimes like a whistle, and at others like the buzz of an offended hornet.' Valdez, 'in his white uniform and gold lace, mounted on a grey horse, was a mark for every sharpshooter,' yet he rode up to within fifty yards of the firing line, urging his men on while bullets felled staff officers riding on either side of him. 'Presently the sound of the Mauser volleys began to predominate and the rebel fire to slacken, till finally it ceased altogether.' Churchill saw 'figures scurrying to the shelter of the woods,' then silence. Spanish troops occupied the enemy's position. They had but one day's rations left, however, and pursuit of the insurgents 'was impossible owing to the impenetrable nature of the woods.' Valdez, triumphant but foiled, returned to his base in Cienfuegos. [17]

Campos – who was about to be relieved by Veleriano Weyler, whose suppression of rebellious Cuban civilians helped precipitate the Spanish-American War – awarded Churchill and Barnes the Red Cross, a Spanish decoration for officers. In London the War Office announced that they wouldn't be permitted to wear it, however; sympathy for the insurrection was still strong on both sides of the Atlantic. New York newspapers reported that Winston had fought under the Spanish colours. In Tampa he hotly denied it: 'I have not even fired a revolver. I am a member of General Valdez's staff by courtesy only.' But in England the *Newcastle Leader*, ignoring British army precedents, observed that 'spending a holiday in fighting other people's battles is rather an extraordinary proceeding even for a Churchill,' and the *Eastern Morning News* predicted that 'difficulties are certain to arise and Lord Wolseley will probably order him to return at once and report himself.' Wolseley did no such thing; if he reprimanded officers for serving in foreign armies, he would lose his best men. American editors were more cutting; the two subalterns were described as 'emissaries of the British Government sent to teach Campos how to whip the secessionists' and proof that England was 'throwing more bricks at the Monroe doctrine.' [18]

Back in Cockran's flat, Churchill, stung, held his first press conference. Some of his remarks were foolish. If Campos took two Cuban strongholds before spring, he said, 'he will, in my judgement, break the back of the revolution.' The rebels might then 'carry on the war for a year or two longer, but ultimately they will be forced to accept virtually dictated terms.' Campos was, 'in my judgement, one of the most distinguished men that Spain has ever produced,' a leader of 'rare judgement and great humanity.' The rebels were 'not good soldiers, but as runners would be hard to beat.' That inspired derisive headlines across the United States. He was described as a 'pleasant faced young officer' wholly lacking in judgement. Yet he had qualified his predictions. If the Cubans held their present gains, he said, they would 'be in a position to demand more favourable terms in the event of any attempt at settlement or arbitration.' The Spaniards were valiant and energetic, 'but the nature of the country is against them, and, furthermore, there is too little combination in the movements of their various columns.' This could turn the tide. Indeed, 'If the insurgents hold out until the spring rains set in, they may yet win.' [19]

He and Barnes sailed home on the *Etruria*, but the Cuban dilemma still weighed heavily upon him. He dashed off a piece for the *Saturday Review* denouncing rebel cruelty and adding, 'They neither fight bravely nor do they use their weapons effectively.' Bad as the Spanish administration was, 'a Cuban Government would be worse, equally corrupt, more capricious, and far less stable. Under such a Government revolutions would be periodic, property insecure, equity unknown.' The best solution, he wrote to Cockran, would be an American takeover of the island: 'I hope the United States will not force Spain to give up Cuba – unless you are prepared to accept responsibility.' If the rebels won, the government would be dominated by 'the negro element among the insurgents,' who would 'create renewed and even more bitter conflict of a racial kind.'[20]

Cuba had been the first test of his courage and his sagacity. He had handled himself well under fire, inviting death near the firing line when, as a non-belligerent, he might honourably have sought safety in the rear. His reportorial skills were already remarkable. On the other hand, he had failed to grasp the essential nature of guerrilla warfare, so important to an understanding of the century ahead. He had been, and in some respects always would be, a defender of the established order. *Imperialism* would never be a pejorative for him. Of the infamous Jameson Raid, which took place a week after his return from New York, he later wrote, 'I was all for Dr Jameson and his men. I understood fairly well the causes of the dispute on both sides. I longed for the day on which we should "avenge Majuba." I was shocked to see our Conservative Government act so timidly in this crisis. I was ashamed to see them truckling to a misguided Liberal Opposition and even punishing these brave raiders, many of whom I knew so well.' His forecasts of Cuba's immediate future would soon be discredited. But in the long run his pessimism about the island would be vindicated. He had just reached his majority. He had been growing in acumen since his father's death, and was continually revising his judgements. Little more than a year after his return from embattled Cuba, he expressed misgivings over his first interpretation of the revolution there. 'I reproach myself somewhat,' he wrote, 'for having written a little uncandidly and for having perhaps done injustice to the insurgents. I rather tried to make out, and in some measure succeeded in making out, a case for Spain. It was politic and did not expose me to the charge of being ungrateful to my hosts, but I am not quite clear whether it was right . . . I am aware that what I wrote did not shake thrones or upheave empires – but the importance of principles do not [sic] depend on the importance of what involves them.' One principle was clear. It was inconceivable to him that a colony could survive as a sovereign state. After the *Maine* blew up, he told a reporter that 'America can give the Cubans peace, and perhaps prosperity will then return. American annexation is what we must all urge, but possibly we shall not have to urge long.' To him the very thought of Cuban independence was as absurd as, say, an independent India.[21]

*   *   *

India now loomed. The Fourth Hussars marched from Aldershot to Hounslow, paraded past the retiring Brabazon for the last time, and began packing leisurely for the long voyage eastward in the autumn. Churchill later recalled: 'I now passed a most agreeable six months; in fact they formed almost the only idle spell I have ever had.' It was the year of Victoria's Diamond Jubilee; fashionable London celebrated with balls, receptions, recitals, and dinner parties. Jennie was back after nine months of dalliance on the Continent, including a marathon romp with Bourke Cockran in a Champs-Elysées apartment, and vexed only by pursuing, jealous little notes from the Prince of Wales, who typically speculated on 'where your next loved victim is . . . ?' Winston had also missed her. 'My darling Mamma,' he had written to her from Aldershot, 'I am longing for the day when you will be able to have a little house of your own and when I can really feel that there is such a place as home.' Now she had taken, not a little house, but a seven-storey Georgian mansion at 35A Great Cumberland Place, near Hyde Park and within sight of Marble Arch, and using London's six-year-old 'electric deep-level' subway, the precursor of the modern tube, he commuted between there and Waterloo, taking the train on to his barracks. Once Duchess Lily invited him to join a weekend party at Deepdene given for the prince. Colonel Brabazon would also be present. Churchill realized, he wrote, that 'I must be upon my best behaviour: punctual, subdued, reserved, in short display all the qualities with which I am least endowed.' Unforgivably, he missed the six o'clock train to Dorking. That delayed him by an hour and a quarter. In his railway compartment, he frantically changed to full dress – to the dismay of the man who shared it – and a servant, meeting him at the station with a brougham, lashed the horses into a gallop. Nevertheless, he was late. He hoped to slip into the dining room unnoticed and apologize afterwards. Instead, he found the entire company assembled in the drawing room. Without him there were only thirteen in the party, and the royal family was superstitious about that. As Winston bowed, HRH said shirtily with his German accent: 'Don't they teach you to be punctual in your regiment, Winston?' He glared at Brabazon, who glared at Winston, who was, for once, mute.[22]

It didn't last. Before the meal ended he was chatting amiably with the prince. Duchess Lily reproachfully called him incorrigible; he cheerfully acknowledged it. Among the other guests he had met Sir Bindon Blood, an influential veteran of colonial wars, so he counted the weekend a triumph. In his letters of those months one has the feeling that skies were always blue. He danced, he hunted, he devised clever masquerades for fancy-dress balls, and he evaded creditors. His means during this period are in fact mysterious. Messrs E. Tautz, breeches and trousers makers, were dunning him for nearly forty guineas. He now had 'five quite good ponies' and owed payment for them. Wine bills, book bills, saddler's bills – they accumulated, were stuffed away and ignored. His attitude towards them was insouciant. He left a note for his mother: 'Our finance is indeed involved! If I had not been so foolish as to pay a lot of bills I should have the money now.'[23]

She wrote to him tautly: 'I assure you unless something extraordinary turns up I see ruin staring me in the face.' Jennie was as improvident as Winston – she would spend £200 on a ball dress – but after he left she would be in London to face the consequences of his extravagance, and her alarm mounted. She borrowed from friends. She borrowed £17,000 from a bank, using her life insurance as collateral. She raised money on her jewels and juggled balances. Still the drain continued. She wrote: 'My darling boy, you can't think how all this worries me. I have so many money problems of my own I feel I cannot take on any others'; and, 'What an extraordinary boy you are as regards yr business affairs.' Her annual income had fallen to £900, out of which she had to provide allowances for both her sons. She explained this to Winston, and he replied: 'The situation as described by your letter is appalling. As you say it is of course impossible for you to live in London on such a pittance.' Then he hinted unscrupulously: 'I hate the idea of your marrying – but that of course would be a solution.' It was indeed the eventual solution. Meanwhile, she made ends meet by taking over houses, redecorating them, and selling them for a profit. Winston remained indifferent to her struggle. Once one of his cheques actually bounced. She told him: 'I marvel at their allowing you to overdraw as you do. Neither the Westminster or the National Bank will let me overdraw £5 without telling me at once.' She sounded envious.[24]

He remitted thirty pounds of the forty-five she had paid on his account and vaguely assured her he would send the rest 'when my ship comes home.' He did not mean the ship to India. He had decided that he wanted to miss that one. The Fourth Hussars would be there nine years, and the more he thought about that, the less he liked it. The fact was that he wasn't really cut out to be a professional officer. His father's impression that he was, fragilely based on a boyhood infatuation with toy soldiers, had been whimsical. Winston was brave, and would distinguish himself in battle, but the long droughts of peacetime service could only frustrate him. He wanted to get on. Barracks life in the East would be dull, confining, dispiriting – Harrow all over again. England was the place to be; here he could find a constituency and run for office. Money would be necessary, of course, but he was an experienced journalist now; surely some newspaper would pay for his by-line. Crete was going through one of its periodic upheavals. He approached the *Daily Chronicle* with the suggestion that the paper send him there as its correspondent. The editor replied that they would pay him 'at the rate of ten guineas a letter' if he got there on his own. He couldn't afford it. In Fleet Street he floated other proposals. He offered to cover the Nile expedition Kitchener was organizing, or Sir Frederick Carrington's expedition in Matabeleland, or the Ninth Lancers' adventures in Rhodesia. There were no takers. He urged relatives and powerful friends to intercede on his behalf. They failed, and Lord Lansdowne, the secretary of state for war, wrote to Jennie that Winston's importuning was causing talk. His duty, Lansdowne said, lay with his regiment. There were rumours that he was trying to dodge it. 'There are plenty of ill natured people about,' Lansdowne wrote, 'and it is just conceivable that an attempt might be made to misrepresent his action.'[25]

Churchill was unchastened. By now it was August, and they would be sailing for Bombay in a month. He leaned on his mother. He leaned hard. Perhaps he sensed that she, ashamed of her early neglect of him, was vulnerable to pressure. Surely, he felt, one of her many contacts could solve his problem. Writing from Hounslow he begged her to find 'places where I could gain experience and derive advantage – rather than to [sic] the tedious land of India.' If he went he would be losing a 'golden opportunity' and 'guilty of an indolent folly that I shall regret all my life. A few months in South Africa would earn me the SA medal and in all probability the company's star. Thence hot foot to Egypt – to return with two more decorations in a year or two – and beat my sword into an iron despatch box.' He turned the screw: 'I cannot believe that with all the influential friends you possess and all those who would do something for me for my father's sake' something could not be done. It was 'useless to preach the gospel of patience to me. Others as young are making the running now and what chance have I of ever catching up. I put it down here – definitely on paper – that you really ought to leave no stone unturned to help me at such a period.' He begged her: 'Three months leave is what I want & you could get it for me.'[26]

She couldn't, or at any rate didn't; no reply from her survives. The army had been lenient with him, and what he was asking of her was probably impossible. Later she would move mountains for him, but he could not avoid India now. On September 11, 1896, he and a hundred other officers sailed from Southampton aboard the SS *Britannia*. Twelve days later, at Balmoral, Queen Victoria celebrated the sixtieth year of her reign. Churchill, who would do more to preserve and protect the Victorian legacy than any of her other subjects, was on the Red Sea, at mid-point in the twenty-three-day voyage. He played chess with a fellow officer that afternoon and listened to a string band that evening. His spirits were low. He wrote home: 'The weather is beginning to get hot and the troop decks are awful.' His only good news was that he had reached the semifinal of a shipboard chess tournament: 'I have improved greatly since the voyage began, and I think I shall try to get really good while I am in India.' But that was the limit of his expectations there. He had no inkling that India, far from dooming his future, would be the first crucial experience of his youth.[27]

In 1896 the British Raj had reached flood tide. It lay halfway between the Mutiny forty years earlier, which had seen the transfer of power from the Honourable East India Company to the Crown, and the great days of that improbable, bespectacled nationalist who wore only a homespun dhoti and was known as Mahatma Gandhi. In the interval English dominance over the subcontinent flourished. The Indian Empire was a jigsaw of 602 states, ranging in size from Kashmir and Hyderabad to tiny holdings of a few acres. All were ruled from London under the principle of 'paramountcy.' This was paternalism at best, and at worst, dictatorship, but the British argued, not unreasonably, that India had never been democratic, had never even been a country, and had always been governed by rajas, whose rights were respected by the Queen's viceroy. As Englishmen saw it, they had rescued the people from pagans and savagery and introduced them to a better way of life. This was not entirely hypocritical. At the time of the Mutiny they had founded three Indian universities. Qualified natives, though few in number, had been admitted to the Indian Civil Service since 1864. Irrigation, railroads, newspapers, and the concept of Western justice and its quaint trimmings had been introduced and accepted. Solicitors wore white collar-tabs, like lawyers in Lincoln's Inn; barristers wore wigs; judges wore imperial ermine. Hospitals, physicians, and public-health officials treated black and white patients alike.

Nevertheless, the Union Jack flew over all public buildings. Englishmen could, with impunity, strike natives who offended them. The pukka sahib and the burra sahib were masters to be respected and feared. By no means did all of them abuse their privileges. Those who came to love India, and they were many, treated its people with respect and civility. To them the Raj was a gigantic humming chromoscope providing endless, delightful, exotic sights and sounds: the sullen red glow growing in the bazaars and the little compounds crayoned with light at dawn, and equestrian statues of British generals staring blankly at the alien sunshine; the rhinestone eyes of plodding bullocks, and chuprassies fussing busily about in their gold-frogged *chamras*, and red *tikkas* on the foreheads of Brahmin women; dholl *banyas* beating their gongs and chewing blood-red pan supari; the fierce *dadu* wind blowing down the Himalayas and the contrasting hot puff of a sultry *loo* breeze; the fabrics of Mysore silk and Travancore coir and khuskhus screening from Bombay; the strumming of sitars, the quiet green maidans, the pye-dogs, the *ita'at* festivals of holy sadhus, the *did-you-do-it did-you-do-it* of lapwings perched on the branches of gigantic haldu trees, and the choruses of doves weeping piteously in scented foliage overhead, throbbing like a fever in the night. Britons who had found a home here ('Ah India, my country, my country,' Kipling had scribbled in the middle of an essay) rejoiced in the land's eccentricities: the sacred elephants with their embroidered howdahs, the big fruit bats which flapped home at daybreak and hung upside down in trees by day; the fields of steaming white where dhobis' sheets lay drying; the native railway engineers who rode around seated beneath umbrellas on their little inspection trolleys; the paddle-wheelers of the Ganges; the '*kala* memsahibs,' or black ladies, who could be just as arrogant as the most insensitive English mems; and the obscene carvings on the Nepalese temple of Benares, of which *Murray's Handbook* chastely observed, 'visitors need not see them if the attendant is discouraged from pointing them out.' Visits to rajas' palaces could be stunning; one might see strutting peacocks, figures of four-armed goddesses in marble courtyards, gardens of brilliant melon-flowers, displays of star rubies, Kashmir sapphires, and emeralds like eggs – visions of the ancient, merciless India of priceless jewels and slave girls. Performing scorpions were to be found in the streets. So were snake-charmers, and fakirs, and freak shows, and the indescribable scent of communal India, a complex compound of kerosene, burned ghee, rose, dung, and dahlia. Excitement could be found in just sitting on your veranda at teatime, sipping whisky in the heat, your legs propped up on the long arms of your wicker chair, awaiting the first mango showers and watching the fading of daylight, so unlike the long blue twilights of England, when the sun plunged behind the Arabian Sea with dramatic swiftness, and darkness fell on the vast Hindustan plain before you could grope your way inside.

This was the India Kipling loved, but it was known to too few of the new arrivals of the 1890s. A majority of them ignored the magic of India, eschewed curry, tried to re-create English suburbs in their cantonments, and watched regimental cricket matches while bands played Gilbert and Sullivan airs. Among themselves they laughed heartily, slapped one another on the back, and called each other 'old chap' while completely ignoring the Indians, or, as they called them, the 'wogs.'* They travelled like lords. Short distances were covered in horse-drawn tongas, in coolie-drawn rickshas, or in sedan chairs, where you sat on a *dholi*, a small stool suspended from poles carried on the shoulders of two natives. Long trips were by train, in coaches reserved for the English; at stations there were rest rooms for First Class Gents, even special ones for Officers. On Saturday evenings subalterns got drunk, played rugger for regimental trophies, and sobered up in the morning over mulligatawny soup – all without leaving the post to explore the mysteries beyond the gate. It was assumed that the greatest possible achievement of an Indian youth would be to be accepted by a British public school. Natives believed it, too. Jawaharlal Nehru, Gandhi's greatest protégé, became, and remained, a loyal Harrovian.

That did not, however, entitle him to enter a Raj club. It was said that the only difference between the Bengal Club and the Bombay Club was that one excluded Indians and dogs while the other admitted dogs. These were sahib bastions. A member sat at a little table, rang a silver bell with the reproduction of a cobra as a handle, and ordered a chota peg, a small whisky, secure in the knowledge that no one of inferior blood could approach. Reading matter was all from home: *Punch*, *Country Life*, the *Book of the Horse*, *The Times*, *Blackwood's Magazine*, and, of course, the *Queen's Regulations*, *Hart's Army List*, and, later, *Jane's Fighting Ships*. In the clubs, members of the ascendant race planned war memorials, fountains, and statues honouring great Anglo-Indians. Memsahibs concentrated on converting hill stations – cooler because of their altitude, and therefore summer refuges – into a bit of the Mother Country. Naini Tal, Mussoorie, Ootacamund, and Darjeeling were popular hill stations, but the greatest was Simla, to which the viceroy and his court repaired when thermometers began to soar. Simla's English parks and its half-timbered cluttered homes, shrines of Victorian materialism, testified to

* Originally an acronym of Worthy Oriental Gentlemen.

the insularity of the Raj. There one could sit by evening fires, breathe deeply of moist, cool air, ride bridle paths, and pretend that the real India did not exist.

Architecture reflected the confusion of disparate cultures, no more so than in Bombay, the destination of the Fourth Hussars before they moved south to permanent quarters outside Bangalore in the Madras Presidency. Here, where Kipling was born nine years before Churchill, you could find Moslem and Hindu and Occidental architectural principles warring with one another in the Municipality, erected in 1893, and in the Victoria Terminus, the central train station, which Nicholas Wollaston called 'pure imported ingenuity, a fantasy of spikes and pillars full of grime and purple gloom.'[28] The Mint was Ionic. The Town Hall was Doric outside and Corinthian inside. The Old Secretariat was Venetian Gothic. The university library and clock tower, fourteenth-century Gothic, were the work of Sir Gilbert Scott, who had built the Albert Memorial. You couldn't miss the similarity; it was awesome. University Hall, fifteenth-century French Decorative, was named, appropriately, after Sir Cowasjee Jehangir Readymoney, an Indian who had met the standards of success recognized in the Victorian Midlands. The telegraph office was Romanesque; the High Court, Early English. Various monuments, in indescribable styles, saluted the military virtues, commerce, and equity. The identity of the designer of Bombay's Sassoon Dock has not survived, luckily for his reputation. It is a triumph of incompetence, so ill-suited to disembarkation that impatient immigrants often chose to come ashore in skiffs, a risky procedure which could cripple a man before he set foot on Indian soil.

It happened to Churchill. Let him tell it: 'We came alongside of a great stone wall with dripping steps and iron rings for hand-holds. The boat rose and fell four or five feet with the surges. I put out my hand and grasped at a ring; but before I could get my feet on the steps the boat swung away, giving my right shoulder a sharp and peculiar wrench. I scrambled up all right, making a few remarks of a general character, mostly beginning with the earlier letters of the alphabet, hugged my shoulder and soon thought no more about it.' He was reminded of it in Poona, where the regiment spent the night under double-fly tents and then tried out the polo ponies of the Poona Light Horse. On his mount he found he could not swing a polo stick unless his right arm was strapped to his side. He procured a leather harness. That would come and go, but tennis was out forever. Indeed, his injury was to plague him in various maddening ways all his life. His shoulder would go out at unexpected moments, while he was taking a book from a shelf, swimming, sleeping with his arm under a pillow, or slipping on a stairway. Once the capsule that held the joint together nearly tore loose during an expansive gesture in Parliament, and he thought 'how astonished the members would have been to see the speaker to whom they were listening, suddenly for no reason throw himself upon the floor in an instinctive effort to take the strain and leverage off the displaced arm bone.'[29]

But he reflected little then on what seemed a temporary disability. He was too caught up in the new life that lay before him. India, 'that famous appanage of the Bwitish Cwown,' as Brabazon had called it, overwhelmed him. He thought he might have landed on 'a different planet.' That first morning he acquired his staff, or, as he came to call it, his 'Cabinet.' All salaamed and presented recommendations from the homeward-bound regiment the Fourth Hussars was replacing. For a few pice he hired a dressing boy, who would be responsible for his uniform and clothing; a butler, who would manage his money; a syce, or groom, who would handle his ponies; various bearers; a wet sweeper; and, to be shared with two officers, two gardeners, three water carriers, four dhobis, and a watchman. 'Princes,' he wrote, 'could live no better than we.' That noon, after he had completed his only official task of the day – reprimanding troopers who weren't wearing their cork helmets in the beating heat – he and another subaltern were approached by a messenger in a red-and-gold frock coat carrying an envelope with a puissant crest. It was an invitation to dine with William Mansfield, Baron Sandhurst, governor of Bombay.* At the table Winston, cocky as ever, over-rode his host and dominated the conversation. Afterwards he put it charmingly: 'There were indeed moments when he seemed willing to impart his own views; but I thought it would be ungracious to put him to so much trouble. He kindly sent his aide-de-camp with us to make sure we found our way back to camp all right. On the whole, after forty-eight hours of intensive study, I formed a highly favourable opinion about India.' Hugo Baring, the young officer who had accompanied him, told the tale to the regimental mess. Their comrades were amused but unsurprised. They had grown accustomed to the strutting, slim, freckle-faced, irrepressible youth so quick to resent a slight, but quicker to offer the hand of friendship. Their favourite word for him was, and would continue to be, *bumptious*. Repeatedly, and unsuccessfully, they had tried to put him in his place. Once, aboard the *Britannia*, they had shoved him, struggling, under a huge couch, and then piled themselves upon it, but while they were still sorting themselves out he crept from beneath, rumpled but crowing: 'You can't keep me down like *that!*'[30]

Darkness still lay over Poona the following morning when the bugles sounded reveille, rousing them in time to catch the 5:10 for a thirty-six-hour, twenty-mile-per-hour trip aboard a typical troop train 'where the 'eat,' as Kipling wrote, 'would make your bloomin' eyebrows crawl.' But Bangalore, on the great triangular plateau of southern India, was worth the discomfort. It was a coveted station, three thousand feet above sea level. Days were fierce, but nights, except in the months preceding the annual monsoon flowering, were fresh and cool. The cantonment lay six miles from the city. Troops were housed in spacious, colonnaded barracks. Officers were paid a lodging allowance and left to find their own quarters. Churchill, Barnes, and Baring rented an enormous bungalow, a pink-and-white structure with a heavy tile

* Lady Sandhurst was a daughter of the fourth Earl Spencer, and thus great-great-great-great-grandmother of Lady Diana, who became Princess of Wales in 1981.

roof supported by white plaster columns and broad verandas, the whole enlaced with purple bougainvillea and surrounded by two acres of gardens. He wrote to his mother: 'My writing table at which I now am – is covered with photographs and memories of those in England. The house is full of you – in every conceivable costume and style. My cigarette box that you brought me from Japan – my books – and the other Lares and Penates lie around and I quite feel at home – though 6,000 miles away.'[31]

Days began just before dawn, when, he wrote, one was 'awakened by a dusky figure with a clammy hand adroitly lifting one's chin and applying a gleaming razor to a lathered and defenceless throat.'[32] Morning parade formed at 6:00 A.M. Mounted, they drilled and manoeuvred for an hour and a half. Baths followed, and then breakfast. After that they were free until 5:00 P.M., the hour of polo. Despite his shoulder, he rode in every chukker, or playing period, he could find. As shadows crossed the field they broke up, bathed again, and dined at 8:30 P.M. to the strains of the regimental band. Subalterns fortunate enough to avoid being drafted for after-dinner whisky by garrulous senior officers smoked and talked until 11:00 P.M. and lights out.

Every reveille found him ready for the new day. He was a keen soldier. His troop sergeant later recalled in the regimental history that 'after a field day Mr Churchill would arrive at stables with rolls of foolscap and lots of lead pencils of all colours, and tackle me on the movements we had done at the exercise.' Both sergeant and subaltern were detailed to attend a course on musketry; Churchill passed out first in the class. He was happy, at least in the beginning, to be ignorant of political crises and social gossip. Long afterwards he would say: 'If you liked to be waited on and relieved of home worries, India thirty years ago was perfection.' He seldom gave money a thought. In addition to his lodging allowance, he was paid fourteen shillings a day, and three pounds a month to keep two horses. This, with his allowance from Jennie, constituted his income. Each month the paymaster handed him a string bag about the size of a turnip, filled with silver rupees. He immediately turned it over to his butler and forgot about it. This lofty disdain was irresponsible; his mother, her sister Clara, and several friends had just been defrauded of over £4,000 by an American confidence man. Jennie wrote, begging him to practise thrift. Instead, he lived beyond his means, borrowing from native moneylenders. He would recall: 'Every officer was warned against these gentlemen. I found them most agreeable; very fat, very urbane, quite honest and mercilessly rapacious. All you had to do was to sign little bits of paper, and produce a polo pony as if by magic. The smiling financier rose to his feet, covered his face with his hands, replaced his slippers, and trotted off contentedly till that day three months.'[33] Somehow Jennie managed to cover their debts. Her admirers were still many, and rich.

Romance first reared its violin-shaped head in Winston's life on November 3, 1896. He wrote home from Trimulgherry that he had just been introduced 'to Miss Pamela Plowden – who lives here. I must say that she is the most beautiful girl I have ever seen – "Bar none" as the Duchess Lily says. We are going to try and do the City of Hyderabad together – on an elephant.' Pamela would be in and out of his life for years. Other girls did not attract him. Returning from a racecourse he reported that he had seen 'a lot of horrid Anglo-Indian women' there, and that 'nice people in India are few & far between. They are like oases in the desert . . . I have lived the life of a recluse out here. The vulgar Anglo-Indians have commented on my not "calling" as is the absurd custom of the country . . . I know perhaps three people who are agreeable and I have no ambitions to extend my acquaintance.' But there were other diversions. For a time he collected butterflies in the gardens around his bungalow – swallowtails, white admirals, purple emperors, and rare species. He sent home for nets, collecting boxes, pins, boards, and a killing tin. Barnes and Baring protested that he was turning the house into a taxidermist's shop. Then disaster struck. 'My butterfly collection,' he mournfully wrote to Jack, 'which included upwards of 65 different sorts, has been destroyed by the malevolence of a rat who crawled into the cabinet and devoured all the specimens.' Undaunted, he cultivated roses: Maréchal Niel, La France, Gloire de Dijon – 'over 50 different kinds of roses,' he wrote to his mother, adding, 'if it would not worry you I would like you very much to send a few English seeds – Wallflowers, Stocks, Tulips etc.'[34]

Winston's one great passion in those first months continued to be polo. His fellow officers shared it, and they concocted a plan. Never in the history of the Raj had a cavalry regiment from southern India won the Indian Empire's Regimental Cup. But the officers of the Fourth Hussars, pooling their resources, helped to break this precedent. Their scheme was to approach the Poona Light Horse. Because this regiment was permanently stationed in the country, the Poona sepoys, largely officered by Britons, had a clear advantage in securing the Arabian ponies so prized by polo players. Specifically, they had first choice of mounts arriving at the Byculla stables in Bombay, where Arab steeds were imported. During the Fourth Hussars' pause in Maharashtra, Churchill and his comrades had admired these animals. Now they bought an entire stud of twenty-five ponies from the Poona Light Horse. Ordinarily two or three years' practice was believed essential before a regiment could field a passable team, but six weeks after their landing they challenged the Nineteenth Hussars for the Golconda Cup in Hyderabad. Although the match was considered a joke – and the laughter grew when the crowd saw that one subaltern from Bangalore had to ride one-armed – it was preceded by customary ceremonies. The native army of the nizam of Hyderabad paraded in full dress. The British troops followed. Elephants hauling cannon raised their trunks in salute as they passed the reviewing stand. After tiffin the game began, and the lithe, darting Nineteenth Hussars, as expected, quickly scored three goals. They were held to that, however, while the Fourth Hussars, with the one-armed officer leading them, scored nine times, thus establishing a record, never broken, of a regiment's winning a major tournament within fifty days of landing in India. One of Churchill's contemporaries, Patrick Thompson, believed that if you wanted to understand him, you had to see him play polo. 'He rides in the game,' Thompson said, 'like heavy cavalry getting into position for the assault. He trots about, keenly watchful, biding his time, a master of tactics and strategy. Abruptly he sees his chance, and he gathers his pony and charges in, neither deft nor graceful, but full of tearing physical energy – and skilful with it, too. He bears down opposition by the weight of his dash and strikes the ball. Did I say "strikes"? He *slashes* the ball.'[35]

Apart from polo, he had acquired a taste for horse racing, with himself as jockey. Duchess Lily had promised him a pony, and he had expected to find it waiting for him in Bombay. It wasn't there. He wrote to Jennie of his disappointment. She was unsympathetic: 'It may be dead for all I know, but if it is not I want you to promise me to sell it.' She and the Prince of Wales had discussed it, '& he begged me to tell you that you ought not to race . . . it is next to impossible to race in India & keep clean hands.' Winston bridled: 'I do not at all want to sell it – and I cannot see that it is unwise of me to keep it . . . Everyone out here possesses an animal of one sort or another which they race in the numerous local meetings . . . Now I cannot believe that all who race – *on this small scale* – must necessarily soil their hands.' He scoffed at HRH: 'He always loves "glittering generalities" and it is so easy to say, "They are all cheats in India." Such a statement is of course nonsense and I am sure you will not believe it.' His mother shot back, 'They all tell me that the racing in India is a very shifty unsatisfactory thing.' He boldly retorted: 'You should tell His Royal Highness, if he says anything further about racing in India, that I intend to be just as much an example to the Indian turf as he is to the English as far as fair play goes.'[36] Anticlimax followed. The pony, which arrived in November, was a lemon. Riding it, he came in third three times, and, of course, even second place would have been unacceptable to him. But in London his second cousin, the Marquess of Londonderry, put him up for the Turf Club; Brabazon seconded the nomination, and he was in. Loyally he registered his father's old racing colours, chocolate and pink.

Comradeship, ease, butterflies, roses, horses – obviously his new life was enchanting. But a new hunger was growing within him. That appetite, and the means he took to satisfy it, marks the end of his youth and the incipient signs of his emergence as an exceptional man. The transformation began with early pangs of intellectual curiosity. He found that he had 'a liking for words and for the feel of words fitting and falling into their places like pennies in the slot. I caught myself using a good many words the meaning of which I could not define precisely. I admired these words, but was afraid to use them for fear of being absurd.' On the day his troopship left Southampton a friend had told him, 'Christ's gospel was the last word in ethics.' Churchill had been puzzled. What, he wondered, were ethics? Judging from the context, he assumed they meant the Public School Spirit, Playing the Game, honourable behaviour, or patriotism. Then someone else remarked to him that ethics dealt, not merely with what you ought to do, but with why it ought to be done, and that there was a vast literature on the subject. He knew tactics, he had some grasp of politics, but 'here in Bangalore there was no one to tell me about Ethics for love or money.' Next he remembered his father's gibe about the Grand Remonstrance during the reign of Charles I. It occurred to him that his knowledge of history was limited and something ought to be done about it. He overheard a man using the phrase 'the Socratic method.' Churchill wondered who Socrates was, or had been. He made inquiries. They were unsatisfactory. He was told that Socrates was a contentious Greek, hounded by a nagging wife, who became so troublesome that he was forced to take his own life. But Winston knew there must have been more to it than that. More than twenty-three hundred years had passed since the Greek's death, and people were still arguing about it. 'Such antagonisms,' Churchill reasoned, 'do not spring from petty issues. Evidently Socrates had called something into being long ago which was very explosive. Intellectual dynamite! A moral bomb! But there was nothing about it in *The Queen's Regulations*.'[37]

In the winter of 1896, as he approached his twenty-second birthday, he 'resolved to read history, philosophy, economics, and things like that; and I wrote to my mother asking for such books as I had heard of on these topics.' He began with Gibbon's eight-volume *Decline and Fall of the Roman Empire*. At Harrow his history text had been *The Student's Hume*, and he had found it dull. Now, 'all through the glistening middle hours of the Indian day, from when we quitted stables till the evening shadows proclaimed the hour of Polo, I devoured Gibbon. I rode triumphantly through it . . . and enjoyed it all. I scribbled all my opinions on the margins of the pages.' On January 14, 1897, we find him writing to Jennie, 'The eighth volume of Gibbon is still unread as I have been lured from its completion by [Winwood Reade's] *The Martyrdom of Man* & a fine translation of the Republic of Plato: both of which are fascinating.' Then, remembering Woom's brother-in-law by the fire at Ventnor, he tackled twelve volumes of Macaulay. On March 17 he wrote, 'I have completed Macaulay's History and very nearly finished his Essays.' He thought that Macaulay 'is easier reading than Gibbon and in quite a different style. Macaulay crisp and forcible, Gibbon stately and impressive. Both are fascinating and show what a fine language English is since it can be pleasing in styles so different.' He was covering 'fifty pages of Macaulay and twenty-five of Gibbon every day. There are only 100 of the latter's 4,000 odd left now.'[38]

The scope of his explorations was broadening – 'I read three or four books at a time to avoid tedium' – and he was poring over Schopenhauer, Malthus, Darwin, Aristotle (on politics only), Henry Fawcett's *Political Economy*, William Lecky's *European Morals* and *Rise and Influence of Rationalism*, Pascal's *Provincial Letters*, Adam Smith's *Wealth of Nations*, Bartlett's *Familiar Quotations*, Liang's *Modern Science and Modern Thought*, Victor-Henri Rochefort's *Memoirs*, the memoirs of the Duc de Saint Simon, and Henry Hallam's *Constitutional History*. Incredibly, he asked his mother to send him all one hundred volumes of the *Annual Register*, the record of British public events founded by Burke. He explained that he wanted to know 'the detailed Parliamentary history (Debates, Divisions, Parties, cliques & caves)* of the last 100 years.' Jennie balked at the expense – fourteen shillings a volume – but she did send twenty-seven. In using them, he first set down his opinion of an issue, then studied the debates. By this practice he hoped 'to build up a scaffolding of logical and consistent views which will perhaps tend to the creation of a logical and consistent mind. Of course the *Annual Register* is valuable only for its facts. A good knowledge of these would arm me with a sharp sword. Macaulay, Gibbon, Plato etc must train the muscles to wield that sword to the greatest effect.'[39]

He was scrawling letters to Jennie, Jack, Welldon, and Cockran, rekindling issues which had fired Parliaments of the past but were now resolved or at least dormant. Disraeli's support for the popular election of Scottish clergymen won his approval; Gladstone's opposition to parliamentary reform, his disapproval. He thought Lord Northbrook right in banning the export of Indian grain during the famine of 1873-1874. He favoured the Irish Coercion Laws, advocated the establishment of a criminal appeals court in England, came down hard on the side of slum clearance, death duties, compulsory vaccination, and capital punishment in public ('Justice in every form should not shrink from publicity'), and rejected the charge that newspapers fanned the flames of war – a curious inference from one who knew the role of Pulitzer's *World* and Hearst's *Journal* in Cuba. What sort of education, he asked rhetorically, could a pupil anticipate in a tax-supported school? 'Reading and writing, the knowledge of sufficient arithmetic to enable the individual to keep his accounts; the singing of patriotic songs and a gymnastic course is all that he may expect.' Woman suffrage was ridiculous, 'contrary to natural law and the practice of civilized states.' Wives were 'adequately represented by their husbands.' Spinsters would back religious intolerance and 'every kind of hysterical fad.' Admit females to the polls and 'all power passes to their hands.' Indeed, 'if you give women votes you must ultimately allow women to sit as members of Parliament.' It was, he darkly prophesied, 'only the thin end of the wedge.'[40]

His autodidactism precipitated a religious crisis. At Harrow he had attended daily prayers and Sunday services; in the army he participated in church parades. Until now he had never doubted their value. The anticipation of a hereafter, he had assumed, justifiably disciplined the lower classes and served as an incentive for middle-class morality. Indian sects were similarly useful, provided they did not degenerate into fanaticism. But the books he was now reading challenged the underpinning of everything he had learned since childhood. Gibbon, Reade, and Lecky convinced him that he had been gulled, and as a consequence he 'passed through a violent and aggressive anti-religious phase which, had it lasted, might have made me a nuisance.' This, of course, is a common experience among the self-educated. But

* In British politics a cave is a group of MPs who quit their party. Here Churchill was anticipating himself.

Churchill's resolution of it was unusual. In moments of danger in Cuba and later, he instinctively recited prayers he had learned at Woom's knee. He survived. He asked for lesser gifts, 'and nearly always in these years, and indeed throughout my life, I got what I wanted. This practice seemed perfectly natural, and just as real as the reasoning process which contradicted it so sharply.' In a book of quotations he had read: '*Le coeur a ses raisons que la raison ne connaît point.*' Why, he asked himself, should he discard the reasons of the heart for those of the head? Why not enjoy both? He therefore adopted 'quite early in life a system of believing whatever I wanted to believe, while at the same time leaving reason to pursue unfettered whatever paths she was capable of treading.'[41]

'I have hardly looked at a novel,' he wrote on March 31, 1897. He was sticking to tough reading and writing letters meshed with abstruse allusions. His brother officers wondered how he did it. The climate was punishing. This was the Raj in its heroic period, without air conditioning, refrigerators, or even electric fans. One thinks of Kipling in the Punjab only a few years earlier, sweating and scribbling under the same sun through long afternoons in his darkened bungalow, struggling to immortalize the age. Churchill was writing, too, but his was a genius of a different order, and he had not found his medium. He was writing his first book, and only novel, *Savrola*, though he had not yet settled on that title. Once it had begun to take shape he wrote to Jennie: 'I think you will be surprised when you get the MS. It is far and away the best thing that I have ever done. I have only written 80 MS pages – but I find a fertility of ideas that surprises me . . . It is called "Affairs of State," a political romance. Scene Plot a hypothetical Republic . . . I am quite enthusiastic about it. All my philosophy is put into the mouth of the hero. But you must see for yourself. It is full of adventure.'[42]

He added a postscript: 'Do try to get me up to the war if you can possibly.' He meant the imminent clashes along India's North-West Frontier, but it is clear from his correspondence that year that the prospect of fighting anywhere would have been welcome. The first flush of his enthusiasm for Bangalore had faded. He had become restless; his temperament cried for action. India had become 'an abominable country to live long in. Comfort you get – company you miss . . . There is every temptation to relapse into a purely animal state of existence.' He and Baring had spent Christmas in Bengal, but he had concluded that 'Calcutta is full of supremely uninteresting people endeavouring to assume an air of heartiness'; he was glad to have seen it only because 'it will be unnecessary ever to see it again.' Yearning for a stimulating environment, he wrote that if he could 'only get hold of the right people my stay here might be of value. If I had come to India as an MP – however young & foolish, I could have had access to all who know and can convey. As a soldier . . . I vegetate.' Without his books, he felt, he would stagnate. 'The Indian press is despicable – being chiefly advertisements.' All sorts of complaints crowded his letters now. 'My face is blistered by the sun so badly that I have had to see a doctor,' he wrote after one field exercise, and when he was appointed acting adjutant he had to write 'so many memos etc that to touch a pen is an effort.'[43]

His first chance to break free from this oppression came in the spring of 1897. The Greeks had sent a small expeditionary force to fight rebellious Turks on Crete. The British Mediterranean fleet, joining those of five other nations, was blockading the island to prevent the landing of Greek reinforcements. Churchill was indignant: 'What an atrocious crime the Government have committed in Crete! That British warships should lead the way in protecting the blood bespattered Turkish soldiery from the struggles of their victims is horrible to contemplate.' His mother disagreed: 'The Concert of Europe were *obliged* to act as they did altho' they certainly were slow in making up their minds.' He was unconvinced: 'We are doing a very wicked thing in firing on the Cretan insurgents . . . so that she [Greece] cannot succour them.' He saw the whole thing as a devious Salisbury plot to strengthen the Turks and thereby deny Constantinople to the Russians. He was right there, but wrong in an aside which, in the light of subsequent events, has a haunting ring: Salisbury's policy was 'foolish because, as surely as night follows day – the Russians are bound to get Constantinople. We could never stop them even if we wished. Nor ought we to wish for anything that could impede the expulsion from Europe of the filthy Oriental.'[44]

All this laid the groundwork for his letter to Jennie of April 21. 'I am afraid you will regard this letter somewhat in the aspect of a bombshell,' he began. He proposed to cover the Cretan fighting as a war correspondent, and he didn't care which side accepted his credentials. 'Of course all my sympathies are entirely with the Greeks, but on the other hand the Turks are bound to win – are in enormous strength & will be on the offensive the whole time.' It didn't matter, really; 'if you can get me good letters to the Turks – to the Turks I will go. If to the Greeks – to the Greeks.' He thought her close friend Sir Edgar Vincent 'could probably do everything for me in Constantinople & could get me attached to some general's staff etc as in Cuba. On the other hand you know the King of Greece and could of course arrange matters in that quarter.' Jennie, he was confident, could also find a newspaper which would hire him. He expected to be paid ten or fifteen pounds for each piece but would meet his own expenses, and he asked her to manage a loan – 'Lord Rothschild would be the person to arrange this for me as he knows every one.' His mother, he felt certain, would 'not stand in my way in this matter but will facilitate my going just as you did in the case of Cuba.' He misjudged her. In London she described his design to friends as 'a wild scheme' and told Jack that the men she knew in the Foreign Office thought the war would end soon anyhow. This being true, his plan, far from being a bombshell, would end rather 'like a damp firework,' which is precisely what happened.[45]

He had been checked. But not mated. Considering the powerful men who had been enticed by his mother's beauty – the Prince of Wales, the Duke of Cambridge, Salisbury, Vincent, Sir Evelyn Wood, Kitchener, Lord Cromer, Sir Bindon Blood – Winston concluded that she could surely exploit at least one of her relationships to his advantage. He had no compunction about twisting her arm, thereby persuading her to twist theirs. But he could not do it from six thousand miles away. Luckily he would soon be at her side. As the hot season of 1897 approached, the officers of the Fourth Hussars were offered what was called 'three months' accumulated privilege leave' in England. Most declined on the ground that they had just settled in, but 'I,' Churchill would recall, 'thought it was a pity that such good things should go a-begging, and I therefore volunteered to fill the gap.' On May 8 he sailed from Bombay aboard the *Ganges*. The trip was an ordeal: 'sweltering heat, rough weather and fearful seasickness.' At Aden he was greeted by bitter news. The Greeks had sued for peace. His disappointment was shared by a fellow passenger, Colonel Ian Hamilton, a romantic who dreamed of Greece's past glories and would later encounter Churchill again and yet again, but Winston, unconsoled, left the ship when it reached Naples, dawdled in Pompeii, Rome, and Paris, and reached home only just in time to attend society's annual fancy-dress ball at Devonshire House in Piccadilly. Jennie went as Theodora. Of Winston we know only that he wore a sword. He had, he said, returned to enjoy 'the gaieties of the London Season,' but he had other matters on his mind.[46] War, any war, was one. Politics was another. After the ball he dropped into the St Stephen's Chambers office of Fitzroy Stewart, secretary of the Conservative Central Office and a distant cousin, and told him he wanted to stand for Parliament as a Conservative.

No seats were vacant, Stewart explained, but he wrote to Henry Skrine, the party's agent in Bath, asking: 'Will you allow the late Lord Randolph Churchill's son, Mr Winston S. Churchill . . . to speak at your gathering on the 26th? He is very keen about politics and about the Primrose League and has told us he would like to address a few political meetings before rejoining his regiment . . . He is a clever young man and his presence would no doubt be of some interest to the Bath Conservatives.' Thus it was that Churchill delivered his first political address at Claverton Manor, now England's American Museum, in a park near Bath, in the high summer of 1897. Newspapers then devoted roughly the same space to politics that they give to sports today, and both the *Bath Daily Chronicle* and London's *Morning Post* ran full accounts of his performance. The speech was enthusiastically received – he was interrupted by cheers forty-one times – but that may have arisen in part from sympathy for his inexperience; he began by telling his audience that the timeworn 'unaccustomed as I am to public speaking' should be pardoned in this instance, because this was, in fact, his maiden effort.[47]

Not much was happening in politics just now, he said, which was dull for the politicians but probably a relief to the people. Then he launched into a spirited defence of the Conservative party and an attack on its critics. Liberals were 'always liberal with other people's money.' Radicals – 'the dried-up drain-pipe of Radicalism' – reminded him of 'the man who, on being told that ventilation was an excellent thing, went and smashed every window in his house, and died of rheumatic fever.' Conservative policy, on the other hand, was 'a look-before-you-leap policy . . . a policy of don't leap at all if there is a ladder.' He praised the Tories' bill to compensate workers injured in industrial accidents, regretted a recent strike, and took the position, always popular with politicians courting the average voter, of damning both labour and capital. Ultimately, he believed, 'the labourer will become, as it were, a shareholder in the business in which he works,' though he hastily added that this solution would become practical only 'in the distant future.' The greatest achievement of the Conservatives, he said, had been teaching 'the people of Great Britain the splendour of their Empire, the nature of their Constitution, and the importance of their fleet.' This was the heart of his message, a paean to imperialism, and his peroration, throbbing with the rhythms of Gibbon, is both a tribute to his imperial faith and a demonstration of his beginning struggle towards eloquence:

There are not wanting those who say that in this Jubilee year our Empire has reached the height of its glory and power, and that we now should begin to decline, as Babylon, Carthage, and Rome declined. Do not believe these croakers, but give the lie to their dismal croaking by showing by our actions that the vigour and vitality of our race is unimpaired and that our determination is to uphold the Empire that we have inherited from our fathers as Englishmen, that our flag shall fly high upon the sea, our voice be heard in the councils of Europe, our Sovereign supported by the love of her subjects, then shall we continue to pursue that course marked out for us by an all-wise hand and carry out our mission of bearing peace, civilization, and good government to the uttermost ends of the earth.[48]

On the day that Churchill spoke in Bath, news reached England of a Pathan uprising in the Swat Valley, on India's North-West Frontier. This had been smouldering for some time, and was a direct consequence of Whitehall's policy in that harsh, craggy corner of Asia. The British, having conquered the plains of India, had paused at the foothills of the Himalayas and turned back to develop the lands they had taken. The mountains formed a natural barrier as definite, and as unbridgeable, as the English Channel. But in the northwest the peaks trailed off. There, in 1893, an Anglo-Afghan frontier had been demarcated; Britain intended to build Afghanistan up as a buffer between the Raj and the Russians, Asia's other great power. Meanwhile, they went about enrolling the tribesmen on their side of the frontier as subjects of the Queen. And there lay the rub. These clansmen – Pathans, Swatis, Waziris, Mahsuds, Afridis, Bunerwalis, Chitralis, and Gilgitis – had lived in remote independence since the dawn of time. Now bands of pale aliens were moving among them, building roads, putting up signs, establishing outposts and blockhouses. They were bewildered, then angry. They knew almost nothing of what was happening in the rest of the world, but now they were being informed, and misinformed, by a Moslem rabble-rouser whom the British called the Mad Fakir and Churchill later described as 'a priest of great age and of peculiar holiness.'[49] This mullah told the tribesmen of victories by their fellow Moslems – the Turks on Crete and the Mahdi in the Sudan – and spread wild tales. Turks had captured the Suez Canal, he said, explaining what it was, and he assured them that the British bullets could not harm men faithful to Mohammed, displaying as proof a small bruise on his leg which, he said, was the only consequence of a direct hit by an English cannonball. The viceregal staff in Calcutta was not unaware of this agitation. Word of it came to them through networks of – readers of *Kim* will have guessed – informers. Punitive expeditions were organized; reinforcements of Tommies were on their way from other parts of the Empire. London was particularly worried by the isolation of the Raj's key frontier fort, Chitral, far to the north, a miniature Gibraltar situated on an eminence commanding the great passes into Afghanistan. A Swati revolt threatened the British garrison holding the Malakand Pass and, specifically, a long wire-rope *jhula*, or swinging bridge, needed to provision Chitral. Whitehall reacted by announcing that a field force of three brigades would put down the uprising. It would be led by General Sir Bindon Blood.

Churchill was standing on the lawn at the Goodwood races, enjoying balmy weather and winning money, when the report of this decision buzzed through the crowd. He was electrified. On meeting Sir Bindon at Deepdene the year before he had extracted a promise that, should the general take the field again, Winston would join him. Churchill had three weeks of leave left, but he instantly wired Blood, reminding him of his pledge, and caught the next boat to India, the SS *Rome*, leaving behind, in his haste, a batch of new books, his polo sticks, his pet dog Peas, a Primrose League badge old Mr Skrine had lent him in Bath, and, of course, a sheaf of bills. At each port of call he looked, in vain, for a reply from Blood. This P & O voyage was even worse than the last, particularly on the Red Sea: 'The temperature is something like over 100° and as it is damp heat – it is equal to a great deal more . . . It is like being in a vapour bath. The whole sea is steamy and there is not a breath of air – by night or day.' Finally, at Bombay, a telegram from Upper Swat awaited him: 'Very difficult. No vacancies. Come as correspondent. Will try to fit you in. B.B.'[50]

A four-day detour to Bangalore was necessary; he needed his colonel's permission to join Blood. Newspaper credentials came next. Jennie tried *The Times*, without success, but the *Daily Telegraph* contracted to pay Winston five pounds a column, and in India the Allahabad *Pioneer*, which had published much of Kipling's early work, agreed to run a three-hundred-word telegram from him every day and pay accordingly. At the Bangalore train station he pushed a small sack of rupees across the counter and asked, out of curiosity, how far north his journey would take him. The ticket babu checked a timetable and told him 2,028 miles – a five-day trip through the worst of the summer heat. But there were compensations. He had bought a bag of books, and the first-class, leather-lined, heavily shuttered railway compartment carried a circular wheel of wet straw which the passenger could turn from time to time. Thus, he proceeded, as he put it, 'in a dark padded moving cell, reading mostly by lamplight or by some jealously admitted ray of glare.'[51] He broke his trip at Rawalpindi to visit a friend in the Fourth Dragoon Guards.

The dragoons were preparing to be sent to the front; officers expected the order to grind their swords any day. That evening he joined a sing-along in the sergeants' mess. Long afterwards he would remember roaring out:

> *And England asks the question*
> *When danger's nigh*
> *Will the sons of India do or die?*

And:

> *Great White Mother, far across the sea,*
> *Ruler of the Empire may she ever be.*
> *Long may she reign, glorious and free,*
> *In the Great White Motherland!*

A photograph of Churchill taken at the time shows him faultlessly turned out in the romantic uniform of that period: spurred cavalry boots, whipcord jodhpurs, and military tunic with choker collar, Sam Browne belt, and the swooping khaki topee which will forever be identified with Victorian colonial wars. Wearing it, with a Wolseley valise for paper and pencils slung over his shoulder, he stood on the platform at Nowshera, the railhead of Blood's Malakand Field Force, and arranged for transportation for the last leg of his journey: forty miles across a scorching plain and then up the steep, winding ascent to Malakand Pass, the general's headquarters. Upon arrival Winston learned that Blood himself was off with a flying column, putting down a local mutiny by the Bunerwal tribe. Yellow with dust, Churchill was provided with a tent, a place in the staff mess, and a tumbler of whisky. He took this last only to be polite. He had long enjoyed the taste of wine and brandy, but until this moment the smoky taste of whisky had turned his stomach. Here, however, he faced a choice of tepid water, tepid water with lime juice, and tepid water with whisky. As he put it, he 'grasped the larger hope.' In the five days Blood was away he conquered his aversion. 'Nor was this a momentary acquirement,' he later wrote. 'Once one got the knack of it, the very repulsion of the flavour developed an attraction of its own . . . I have never shrunk when occasion warranted it from the main basic refreshment of the white officer in the East.' Thus fortified, he contemplated his immediate future. He cherished few illusions about warfare; he had, after all, come under fire in Cuba. Aboard the train to Nowshera he had warned his mother that danger lay ahead for him. Nevertheless, 'I view every possibility with composure. It might not have been worth my while, who am really no soldier, to risk so many fair chances on a war which can only help me directly in a profession I mean to discard.' That, at least, was settled. 'But I have considered everything and I feel that the fact of having seen service with British troops while still a young man must give me more weight politically – must add to my claims to be listened to and may perhaps improve my prospects of gaining popularity with the country.' Now he wrote to her again, more sombrely: 'By the time this reaches you everything will be over so that I do not mind writing about it. I have faith in my star – that is that I am intended to do something in the world. If I am mistaken – what does it matter? My life has been a pleasant one and though I should regret to leave it – it would be a regret that perhaps I should never know.'[52]

General Blood returned, magnificently erect on his charger, moustache bristling, snorting with triumph. The Bunerwalis were vanquished. Moreover, during his absence the Eleventh Bengal Lancers and the Guides Cavalry had driven the Swatis from Chakdara and chased the tribesmen up and down the valley. Everyone was ready for more action. Several officers had been killed in local skirmishes, and their effects, in accordance with Anglo-Indian campaigning custom, had been auctioned off. Winston had bought two horses, hired a groom, and acquired a kit. He was now fully equipped. In the morning Blood welcomed him, motioned him to his side, and then led an expedition of twelve thousand men and four thousand animals over the bridge, into the valleys where lurking tribesmen, armed with long rifles, lay in wait. In describing the enemy's practice of hiding in the hills and firing down at the moving British column, Churchill introduced his readers to a new word. Such a rifleman, he wrote, was 'a "sniper," as they are called in the Anglo-Indian army.'[53]

While pursuing tribesmen, the Malakand Field Force also carried out punitive missions: destroying crops, driving off cattle, putting huts to the torch. The Pathans were a pitiless foe, but the British perpetrated atrocities, too. Winston wrote to Reggie Barnes in Bangalore: 'After today we begin to burn villages. Every one. And all who resist will be killed without quarter. The [tribesmen] need a lesson – and there is no doubt we are a very cruel people. At Malakand the Sikhs put a wounded man into the cinerator & burnt him alive. This was hushed up. However I will tell you more stories – some queer ones I have heard too – when we meet.' He wrote to his mother: 'The danger & difficulty of attacking these active – fierce hill men is extreme. They can get up the hills twice as fast as we can – and shoot wonderfully well . . . It is a war without quarter. They kill and mutilate everyone they catch and we do not hesitate to finish their wounded off. I have seen several things wh. have not been very pretty since I have been up here – but as you will believe I have not soiled my hands with any dirty work – though I recognise the necessity of some things.' Long afterwards he recalled that 'it was all very exciting and, for those who did not get killed or hurt, very jolly.' His newspaper dispatches do not reflect this. Even less so do his letters. He was ill. It cannot have been pleasant to remain on the line at Inayat Kila with a 103-degree fever. 'Here I am,' he wrote miserably, 'lying in a hole – dug two feet deep in the ground – to protect me against the night firing – on a mackintosh with an awful headache – and the tent & my temperature getting hotter every moment as the sun climbs higher and higher.'[54]

Most war correspondents hover around headquarters, writing dispatches based on communiqués; in World War II they reported the fighting on the island of Okinawa, in the Pacific, while sitting at typewriters on Guam, fourteen hundred miles away. Churchill went into the field. Indeed, as Sir Bindon's officers fell, he found himself leading troops. At one point he commanded a company of the Thirty-first Punjab Infantry, sepoys whose language he didn't even speak. (He learned two words, *maro* ['kill'] and *chalo* ['get on'], and introduced them to an English one, 'Tallyho!') There can be no doubt that he was remarkably brave, at times even rash. After closing within forty yards of the enemy he wrote, 'I felt no excitement and very little fear.' Like Nelson, he freely admitted that he was chiefly driven, not by patriotism, but by ambition. He wrote to Jennie: 'I rode on my grey pony all along the skirmish line where everyone else was lying down in cover. Foolish perhaps but I play for high stakes and given an audience there is no act too daring or too noble. Without the gallery things are different.' This, he was convinced, was advancing him another step towards the House of Commons. 'I shall get a medal and perhaps a couple of clasps,' he wrote at one point, and, at another, 'I should like to come back and wear my medals at some big dinner or some other function.' The awful thought crossed his mind that no medal might be struck for this expedition. He told Jennie, 'Here out of one brigade we have lost in a fortnight 245 killed and wounded and nearly 25 officers,' suggested a comparison with 'actions like Firket in Egypt – wh are cracked up as great battles and wh are commemorated by clasps & medals etc etc,' and concluded, 'I hope you will talk about this to the Prince and others.' But apart from its political value, physical courage had an intrinsic value in his eyes, and the lack of it was shameful. To his 'intense mortification' he saw men of the Royal West Kents 'run and leave their officer on the ground.' He added: 'I know the Buffs wd never have done this.' Despite the heavy casualties, when he thought of 'what the Empire might have lost I am relieved.'[55]

He wrote to Reggie: 'It is bloody hot.' You could 'lift the heat with your hands, it sat on your shoulders like a knapsack, it rested on your head like a nightmare.' The worst scorcher was Thursday, September 16. It also saw the heaviest fighting – '16th was biggest thing in India since Afgan [sic] war,' he wrote to his mother. Judging from his letters and dispatches, it was a harrowing day for him. On its eve Sir Bindon ordered Brigadier Patrick Jeffreys, commanding his Second Brigade, to enter the Mamund Valley, a cul-de-sac, and clear it out. Swinging around in his saddle, the general told Churchill, 'If you want to see a fight, you may ride back and join Jeffreys.' A troop of Bengal Lancers was headed that way, so Winston mounted and accompanied them as they gingerly picked their way through the ten miles of broken ground between the general's camp and the brigadier's. They reached Jeffreys at dusk. 'All night long the bullets flew across the camp; but everyone now had good holes to lie in, and the horses and mules were protected to a large extent.'[56]

At the instant of dawn the entire brigade, preceded by a squadron of lancers, moved in warlike formation into the valley, Lee-Enfields at the ready. The Mamund basin widened as they entered it, and when they fanned out in three separate detachments, Churchill chose to ride with the centre column. As they advanced not an enemy shot was fired. The slopes above were silent, watchful. But the natives were there. Approaching the far end of the valley,

Churchill raised his field glasses and saw 'a numerous force of tribesmen on the terraced hillsides . . . they appeared seated in long lines, each with his weapon upright beside him . . . The sun threw back at intervals bright flashes of steel as the tribesmen waved their swords.' At 7:30 A.M. the lancers, trotting a hundred yards forward, opened fire with their carbines. Martini-Henrys immediately replied. Churchill wrote: 'From behind rocks and slopes of ground, on spurs, and from stone houses, little puffs of smoke darted. A brisk skirmish began.' He accompanied about fifteen men around him who rode up, dismounted, and opened fire at seven hundred yards. They, too, came under fire. Then the British infantry, the bulk of Jeffreys's brigade, toiled up and reached them. The Thirty-fifth Sikhs split into small parties and attacked various hills, hummocks, and a village. Churchill picked the one heading for the village. Enemy fire died away; they reached their objective without incident. But once there, he looked back and saw no brigade. He searched the valley with his glasses. Jeffreys's force had simply disappeared. Although he did not realize it then, they were in fact enveloped in folds of the vast terrain. He and his people were equally invisible to the brigade; geography was the Pathans' great ally. It occurred to Winston that his was a very small troop: five officers, including him, and eighty-five Sikhs. He recalled Sandhurst warnings about 'dispersion of forces,' and was grateful when the company commander relayed word from a lieutenant colonel down below to withdraw because 'we are rather up in the air here.' Churchill noted on his pad that this was 'a sound observation.' Then the officer said: 'You stay here and cover our retirement till we take up a fresh position on that knoll below the village.'[57]

Winston's small rear guard waited uneasily for ten minutes. They were about to depart when the mountain above them sprang to life. Sabres flashed, gun muzzles erupted, bright flags appeared, and figures dressed in white and blue began dropping down from ledges hundreds of feet overhead, shrieking, 'Yi! Yi! Yi!' A group of Pathans began to assemble in a clump of rocks about a hundred yards from Churchill, and as they fired, Winston, borrowing the rifle of a Sikh, squeezed off answering shots while the Sikh handed him cartridges. This continued for five minutes; then the battalion adjutant scrambled up and panted: 'Come on back now. There is no time to lose. We can cover you from the knoll.' Churchill pocketed his ammunition – it was a standing order to let no bullets fall into the hands of the tribesmen – and was about to leave when an enemy fusillade killed the man beside him and hit five others, one of whom 'was spinning around just behind me, his face a mass of blood, his right eye cut out.' Recovering wounded was a point of honour; torture was the lot of those who fell into the hands of the Pathans. Carrying their casualties, they were halfway down the slope when a force of thirty tribesmen charged them. Chaos followed. More Sikhs fell. The adjutant was hit; Churchill stayed behind to rescue him, but a Pathan swordsman, getting there first, butchered the dying officer. At this point Winston remembered that he had won the public school fencing championship. He drew his cavalry sabre. 'I resolved on personal combat *à l'arme blanche*.' But he was all alone, and other clansmen were

213

hurrying up. These were not public school boys. 'I changed my mind about cold steel.' Instead, 'I fired nine shots from my revolver' and leapt down the hill, gratefully finding refuge with the Sikhs on the knoll nearest the plain.[58]

But they were being outflanked. And they were demoralized. As Winston wrote to his 'Uncle Bill,' Lord William Beresford, a winner of the Victoria Cross, 'The men were completely out of hand. The wounded were left to be cut up. We could do nothing . . . Of course I had no legal status but the urgency was such that I felt bound to see the affair out . . . Martini rifles at 80 yards make excellent practice and there were lots of bullets. At last we got to the bottom in great disorder, dragging some wounded with us, and the men loosing off wildly in all directions – utterly out of hand with a crowd of Ghazis at our heels.' During the descent, he himself got off thirty or forty shots ('I am sure I never fired without taking aim') before they joined the battalion. There the lieutenant colonel drew them up two deep, shoulder to shoulder, while hundreds of firing Pathans, 'frenzied with excitement,' streamed around their flanks. In that formation the Sikhs presented a tremendous target, but anything was preferable to scattering. British officers shouted above the din: 'Volley firing. Ready. Present. Fire!' Tribesmen were toppling, but their numbers were overwhelming. The lieutenant colonel told Churchill: 'The Buffs are not more than half a mile away. Go and tell them to hurry or we shall all be wiped out.' Winston was turning away when he had a vision of himself as the sole, fleeing survivor of a massacre. That was *not* the way to Parliament. He turned back and said, 'I must have the order in writing, sir.' Startled, the commander fumbled in his tunic and began to write. Then they heard the distant notes of a bugler sounding the Charge. 'Everyone shouted. The crisis was over, and here, Praise be to God, were the leading files of the Buffs.'[59]

His ranks swollen, the lieutenant colonel ordered a counterattack to recover the wounded, the adjutant's body, and his own prestige. They retook the knoll (all the wounded had been slain and mutilated) but not till 5:00 P.M. Then they fell back. In the confusion Winston had lost his mount, 'but I borrowed a mule – I was too blown to walk and rode up again. We were attacked coming down but the Buffs were steady as rocks and hence lost very little.' Meanwhile, another company of Sikhs, on their right, had been driven to the plain with even heavier casualties. 'Well then we found the [brigadier Jeffreys] had split up his force and that odd companies were cut off and being cut up etc and it got pitch dark and poured with rain.' It had been a calamitous day, and it wasn't over. Winston had been in action for thirteen hours, but before he could fall asleep he heard the boom of a fieldpiece three miles away, followed by twenty more booms, followed by silence. It had to be Jeffreys; he had the only battery in the valley. But why should his cannon be fired at night? There was only one explanation – he, his staff, his sappers, and miscellaneous headquarters personnel must be fighting at very close quarters. The battalion officers, including Churchill, conferred. Sending a rescue party in the dark would be an invitation to disaster. The brigadier and those with him must fight it out where they were with what they had. At daybreak a squadron of lancers galloped across the open pan of the valley and found them dug in around the battery. They had taken heavy casualties in hand-to-hand fighting. Jeffreys himself had been wounded in the head, though not seriously; he reported by heliograph to Sir Bindon Blood. Sir Bindon and the brigade with him had also been heavily engaged. Blood ordered that the valley be laid waste. 'So long as the villages were in the plain, this was quite easy,' Winston wrote. 'The tribesmen sat on the mountains and sullenly watched the destruction of their homes and means of livelihood. When however we had to attack the villages on the sides of the mountains they resisted fiercely, and we lost for every village two or three British officers and fifteen or twenty native soldiers.' He commented dryly: 'Whether it was worth it, I cannot tell. At any rate, at the end of a fortnight the valley was a desert, and honour was satisfied.'[60]

He saw action again with Jeffreys's brigade at Domodoloh, with the Buffs at Zagia, with the Mohmands in a minor engagement, and, after Sir Bindon had succeeded in getting his leave from the Fourth Hussars extended for two more weeks, at Agrah and then with the Thirty-first Punjab Infantry. Twice more he rode his grey pony along skirmish lines. Jeffreys mentioned him in dispatches, praising 'the courage and resolution of Lieutenant W.L.S. Churchill, 4th Hussars, the correspondent of the *Pioneer* newspaper with the force who made himself useful at a critical moment,' and Sir Bindon wrote to Brabazon predicting that Winston 'if he gets a chance will have the VC or a DSO.' He received neither, partly because his reports were creating considerable discomfort at the highest levels of the Indian army in Simla. In a cable from Nowshera he had commented that 'the power of the Lee-Metford rifle with the new dum-dum bullet – as it is called, though officially, the "ek dum" bullet – is tremendous,' a fact Simla would have preferred not to see in print. And he grew increasingly free with his criticisms of the British military establishment, condemning the manner in which sympathetic civilians were put in jeopardy, the failure to cover retreating soldiers with continuous fire, the 'short service' system of recruitment, and the lack of proper rations for soldiers on long marches. Defiant of the wrath he knew this would arouse, he wrote: 'There will not be wanting those who will remind me that in this matter my opinion finds no support in age or experience. To such I shall reply that if what is written is false or foolish, neither age nor experience should fortify it; and if it is true, it needs no such support.'[61]

On October 12 he wrote to his mother 'one line to let you know that I am across the frontier and rejoining my regiment,' and nine days later he followed this with news that 'once again I write to you from my old table and my own room here in Bangalore.' His first impression, when he leafed through back copies of the *Daily Telegraph*, was that his vivid reporting had been wasted in England. His stories had carried the anonymous by-line, 'From a Young Officer.' A letter from Jennie explained that the editor had 'begged me not to sign yr name. He said it was very unusual & might get you into trouble.'

Winston indignantly replied: 'I will not conceal my disappointment at their not being signed. I had written them with the design, a design which took form as the correspondence advanced, of bringing my personality before the electorate.' He believed that 'if I am to do anything in the world, you will have to make up your mind to publicity and also to my doing unusual things. Of course a certain number of people will be offended. I am afraid some people like Brab will disapprove . . . But I recognise the fact that certain elements must always be hostile and I am determined not to allow them to interfere with my actions. I regard an excellent opportunity of bringing my name before the country in a correct and attractive light – by means of graphic & forcible letters, as lost.'[62]

It was not lost. Jennie was more experienced in these matters than her son, and she had seen that everyone who mattered, from the Prince of Wales down, learned the identity of the Young Officer writing in the distant passes and gorges of the North-West Frontier. They even knew at Harrow. Welldon wrote her: 'I have been much interested in seeing Winston's articles. I think he possesses in a high degree the special correspondent's art of seizing the picturesque and interesting features of a campaign. Really he is very clever, and must make a mark in the world.' Voyages to India took over three weeks, and it was November before Churchill realized how deep an impression he had made. 'I am very gratified to hear that my follies have not been altogether unnoticed,' he wrote. His flair for the language was responsible, but he persisted in his belief that his valour, implicit in the pieces, would count far more among the Tory elders. He told his brother: 'Being in many ways a coward – particularly at school – there is no ambition I cherish so keenly as to gain a reputation of personal courage.'*[63]

Despite his daring and acclaim, Winston's standing in the army was not enhanced by all this. Generals were not alone in their disapproval. In the Fourth Hussars his brother officers were civil but cool. There was a vague feeling that what he had done was, by Victorian standards, 'ungentlemanly.' Regimental messes elsewhere put him down as a 'medal-hunter,' 'self-advertiser,' and 'thruster.' One officer would note in his memoirs that Churchill 'was widely regarded in the Army as super-precocious, indeed by some as insufferably bumptious.' Why, it was asked, should a subaltern praise or deprecate his seniors? Why should he write for newspapers while wearing the uniform? How did he get so much leave? Who was indulging him? The resentment was real, and became an obstacle to his plans. Sir Bindon asked that he be made his orderly officer. The adjutant general in Simla refused. Surely, Churchill thought, Lord Roberts could clear this up. The omnipotent

* To the end of his life Churchill would believe that men who had performed well in combat held a great political advantage. In 1945 he urged Conservative friends to campaign in uniform and persuaded holders of the Victoria Cross and the Distinguished Service Order to stand for office. According to his son, Randolph, those who wore uniforms and won were convinced that it had made no difference. The heroes, almost without exception, were rejected at the polls.

Roberts, now in Ireland, had been a friend of his father's, and now Jennie, at his urging, wrote to the field marshal, reminding him of past favours. But the old man declined to intervene. Churchill wrote bitterly: 'I don't understand Lord Roberts' refusal. A good instance of ingratitude in a fortunate and much overrated man.' Spurred by his mother, the *Daily Telegraph* appointed him a permanent correspondent, but the high command continued to deny him access to all battlefields. He complained to her: 'The Simla authorities have been very disagreeable to me. They did all they could to get me sent down to my regiment . . . I . . . invite you to consider what a contemptible position it is for high military officers to assume – to devote so much time and energy to harrying an insignificant subaltern. It is indeed a vivid object lesson in the petty social intrigue that makes or prevents appointments in this country.' He added: 'Talk to the prince about it.' She did. Ian Hamilton also got busy, and finally, the morning after a polo match in Meerut, Churchill was gazetted to the staff of Sir William Lockhart. Sir William was organizing a punitive expedition into the Tirah, where the Afridi and Orzkzai tribes had risen. 'Red tabs sprouted on the lapels of my coat,' Winston wrote. For once, 'I behaved and was treated as befitted my youth and subordinate station. I sat silent at meals or only rarely asked a tactful question.' It was all for nothing. The tribesmen begged for peace; the expedition was abandoned; he boarded a train for the long ride back to Bangalore.[64]

Calling him a 'publicity hound' – another epithet heard in the messes – seemed cruel. It was not, however, inaccurate. His correspondence admits of no other explanation. He had no interest in a military career, and meant to use the service to advance his prospects in public life. Peace having broken out on the frontier, he returned to his pen. He had several projects in mind: finishing his novel, writing a biography of Garibaldi, a 'short & dramatic' history of the American Civil War, and a volume of short stories to be called, obscurely, 'The Correspondent of the *New York Examiner*.' He wanted recognition, but he also expected to be paid. The *Telegraph* had sent him five pounds an article, and he felt that wasn't enough. 'The pinch of the whole matter is we are damned poor,' he wrote to his mother. He sent her a short story 'wh I want you to sell, signed, to one of the magazines. I think the *Pall Mall* wd like it & would pay my price. You should not get less than £20 for it, as it is a very good story – in my opinion. So don't sell it without a good offer.' Financial relief was on its way, however. His first major effort to reach the British public was, in fact, ready: an account of his frontier adventures with Sir Bindon Blood, largely a paste-up of his frontier dispatches. This has become a common journalistic practice today, but he became one of its pioneers with *The Story of the Malakand Field Force*. Working five hours a day, he had dashed off a draft in two months before his posting to Sir William in Peshawar, where, he confessed, it had occupied his thoughts 'more than . . . anything else.' He had 'affected the style of Macaulay and Gibbon, the staccato antitheses of the former and the rolling sentences and genitival endings of the latter; and I stuck in a bit of my own from time to time.' Later he would say that writing a book 'is an adventure. To begin with it is a toy and an amusement. Then it becomes a mistress, then it becomes a master, then it becomes a tyrant. The last phase is that just as you are about to be reconciled to your servitude, you kill the monster and fling him to the public.' This monster was almost ready to be flung on December 22, 1897, when he wrote to his mother: 'I hope you will like it. I am pleased with it chiefly because I have discovered a great power of application which I did not think I possessed.' Nine days later he mailed her the manuscript – 'Herewith the book' – accompanied by maps and, for the frontispiece, a photograph of Sir Bindon Blood.[65]

There were details, as there always are, to be cleared up before publication. Quotations had to be verified; some sentences were awkward; here and there he had repeated himself. But 'I don't want anything modified or toned down in any way. I will stand or fall by what I have written.' Revisions and proofreading, he decided, would be entrusted to his uncle Moreton, who, on the frail strength of a monograph on bimetalism, was the only member of the family with literary pretensions. Churchill told his mother that he thought he ought to get at least £300 for the first edition, with royalties, 'but if the book hits the mark I might get much more.' There was one problem. Another author was writing a book on the same subject. That called for haste: 'Do not I beg you lose one single day in taking the MS to some publisher. [Lord] Fincastle's book may for all I know be ready now.' On reflection he decided to 'recommend Moreton's treating with the publishers, it is so much easier for a man.' Here he misjudged both uncle and mother. The first edition, to Winston's horror, would contain some two hundred misprints. 'A mad printer's reader,' one reviewer would write, and Winston would add sadly, 'As far as Moreton is concerned, I now understand why his life has been a failure in the city and elsewhere.' Jennie, on the other hand, had very sensibly gone to Arthur Balfour, who had referred her to A.P. Watt, the literary agent. Watt negotiated the terms with Longmans. *Malakand*, appearing in March 1898, sold eighty-five hundred copies in nine months. It was priced at six shillings; the royalty was 15 per cent. Winston had earned more in a few weeks (£382) than he could in four years as a subaltern.[66]

But far more welcome was the book's enthusiastic reception. Moreton's disgraceful performance did not pass unnoticed: the *Athenaeum* observed that 'one word is printed for another, words are defaced by shameful blunders, and sentence after sentence ruined by the punctuation of an idiot or of a school-boy in the lowest form.' But the same reviewer predicted that the author might become as great a soldier as the first Marlborough and 'a straighter politician.' The *Pioneer* found 'a wisdom and comprehension far beyond his years.' The *Spectator* agreed. It was hailed as a minor classic, the debut of an exciting new talent, and, in the *Times of India*, the *Madras Mail*, and Delhi's *Morning Post*, a penetrating study of Raj policy. Churchill's response to all this is curiously moving. He was 'filled with pride and pleasure . . . I had never been praised before. The only comments which had ever been made upon my work at school had been "Indifferent," "Slovenly," "Bad," "Very bad," etc. Now here was the great world with its leading literary newspapers and vigilant erudite critics, writing whole columns of praise!'[67]

The Prince of Wales read *Malakand*, sent a copy to his sister, the Empress Dowager Victoria of Germany, and wrote 'My dear Winston' on April 22: 'I cannot resist writing a few lines to congratulate you on the success of your book! I have read it with the greatest possible interest and I think the descriptions and the language generally excellent. Everybody is reading it, and I only hear it spoken of with praise.' HRH thought Churchill probably wanted to see more combat, and he approved: 'You have plenty of time before you, and should certainly stick to the Army before adding MP to your name.' He had, of course, misread the author. Winston wanted to be where the fighting was thickest, but as a correspondent, not as a junior officer. He had vowed to 'free myself from all discipline and authority, and set up in perfect independence in England with nobody to give me orders or arouse me by bell or trumpet.' Besides, the struggle on the Indian frontier was over. Everyone knew that the next excitement would be in Africa. Sir Herbert Kitchener's campaign to reconquer the Sudan had begun two years earlier; he had been moving slowly, building a railroad as he went, but now in April 1898 his major victory over sixteen thousand dervishes on the Atbara River signalled the beginning of the end. Churchill longed to be at his side. Once more he implored his mother to yank strings. 'You must work Egypt for me,' he told her. 'You have so many lines of attack . . . Now I beg you – have no scruples but worry right and left and take no refusal.' He wanted her to 'stimulate the Prince into writing to Kitchener.' Two months later he wrote: 'Oh how I wish I could work you up over Egypt! I know you could do it with all your influence – and all the people you know. It is a pushing age and we must shove with the best.'[68]

Unfortunately Kitchener, at that time, detested Churchill. He had been outraged by his book; it was bad for discipline, he believed, for subalterns to chide their superiors. In any event, he felt that Winston already had had a good run for his money in India; the Nile was out of bounds for him. 'It was,' Churchill later said, 'a case of dislike before first sight.' Jennie and her influential friend Mary, Lady Jeune, were wining and cajoling everyone in the War Office – Winston later said that they 'left no wire unpulled, no stone unturned, no cutlet uncooked' – but while guests were susceptible to petticoat diplomacy, Kitchener, as Egyptian commander in chief, or Sirdar, had the final say, and in Winston's case he said it over and over. It was *no*. Lady Jeune wired him: 'Hope you will take Churchill. Guarantee he wont write.' She couldn't guarantee it, and the Sirdar knew it. Sir Evelyn Wood, the adjutant general and an admirer of Lady Jeune's, was recruited to the Churchill cause. Lady Jeune and Jennie lunched with Wood and the Prince of Wales, and Wood then cabled the Sirdar: 'Personage asked me personally desires you take Churchill.' Kitchener was adamant: 'Do not want Churchill as no room.' Jennie knew Kitchener, of course; she knew everyone. Winston asked her to write to him directly: 'Strike while the iron is hot and the ink wet.' She did,

219

and he replied with elaborate courtesy. He had too many officers as it was, he was overwhelmed with applications from men more qualified than her son, but if at some future time an opportunity arose he would be pleased, et cetera, et cetera. Really challenged now, she decided to go to Egypt herself. Winston wrote: 'I hope you may be successful. I feel almost certain you will. Your wit & tact & beauty – should overcome all obstacles.' They didn't. Setting up headquarters in Cairo's Continental Hotel with her current lover, Major Caryl John Ramsden, she bombarded the Sirdar with letters. The best reply she got was: 'I have noted your son's name and I hope I may be able to employ him later in the Sudan.' All Jennie had to show for her pains was humiliation, from Kitchener and then, unexpectedly, from Major Ramsden, who jilted her; returning to her hotel room on an impulse after she had left it for Port Said, she found Ramsden in bed with Lady Robert Maxwell, the wife of another army officer. HRH sent her a teasing note: 'You had better have stuck to your old friends than gone on your Expedition to the Nile! Old friends are the best!'[69]

On June 18 Churchill sailed from Bombay, taking leave to plead his cause in person. But at the War Office he found several hundred officers on similar errands. He ran up against one blank wall after another. Kitchener's general advance on Khartoum was scheduled for early August. Time was short, and Winston seemed beaten when, out of the blue, he received a note from the prime minister's private secretary. Lord Salisbury had read *Malakand* with great pleasure and wanted to discuss it. An appointment was set for the following Tuesday, July 12. Salisbury received him at the Foreign Office with elaborate old-world courtesy and led him to a small sofa. He praised the book, 'not only for its manner but for its style,' told him that it had provided him with greater insight into the frontier fighting than any parliamentary debate, and said, as he saw him to the door, 'If there is anything at any time that I can do which would be of assistance to you, pray do not fail to let me know.'[70]

Back at Great Cumberland Place, Churchill seized the opportunity. He wrote to Salisbury: 'I am vy anxious to go to Egypt and to proceed to Khartoum with the Expedition. It is not my intention, under any circumstances to stay in the army long.' He wanted to cover the Sirdar's battles as he had covered Sir Bindon's. Sir Evelyn had written a letter approving his plan. Churchill enclosed it, explaining that Sir Evelyn had 'tried his best – so he assures me – on my behalf. My mother has exerted what influence she can for two years. Even HRH has allowed his name to be used as a recommendation. All have failed.' One hope remained: Lord Cromer, British agent and consul general in Egypt. Winston was 'convinced,' he told the prime minister, 'that if you will write a letter to Lord Cromer and say that on personal grounds you wish me to go – the affair will be immediately arranged.' He was 'loth to afflict you with this matter. Yet the choice lies between doing so, and abandoning a project which I have set my heart on for a long time . . . The affair is after all of extreme insignificance to any but me.'[71]

Salisbury saw nothing wrong in this brazen manipulation; it was common among 'young men with suitable introductions,' to use Churchill's delicate phrase. The prime minister wrote to Cromer, suggesting that he approach Kitchener, but as he told Winston in his reply, 'I cannot advise you to rely too confidently on the result of his letter.' Wheels were turning in the bureaucracy. Salisbury's role, here as in so much else, is unclear. All we know is that nothing happened before Churchill's visit to the Foreign Office and that something happened soon afterwards. Sir Evelyn told Lady Jeune that the Sirdar was going too far in picking his officers and ignoring recommendations from London. He could do as he liked with his Egyptian troops, but British regiments remained under the control of the War Office. Lady Jeune repeated this to Winston, who asked: 'Have you told him that the Prime Minister has telegraphed personally on my behalf?' She hadn't. 'Do so,' he said, 'and let us see whether he will stand up for his prerogatives.' Conveniently, a young officer in the Twenty-first Lancers, a regiment of English cavalry, died in Cairo that day. The Sirdar routinely informed the War Office of the vacancy, and the War Office routinely replied that another officer would be on his way. It was left to Cromer to suggest Churchill as the replacement. Kitchener, we are told, 'simply shrugged his shoulders and passed on to what were after all matters of greater concern.' Meanwhile, fresh orders had been delivered to Winston by courier at 35A Great Cumberland Place. He had been 'attached as a supernumerary Lieutenant to the 21st Lancers for the Soudan Campaign' and would report to the Abbasiya barracks, Cairo. It was understood that he would pay his own expenses and that the government would not be liable if he were killed or wounded. He immediately took a hansom to his solicitors, Lumley and Lumley, and then, with their approval, borrowed £3,500 at 4½ per cent interest from the Norwich Union Society, using as collateral an insurance policy bequeathed him by his grandfather. Then he called on Oliver Borthwick of the *Morning Post*. Borthwick agreed to pay him £15 apiece – his value was rising – for a series of Nile dispatches which, to avoid ruffling Kitchener further, would be disguised as letters to 'Dear Oliver.' Winston told Aylmer Haldane, a friend, 'If you look at the *Morning Post* it is possible that you will see that one of my friends has committed and continues to commit an unpardonable breach of confidence by publishing letters of mine. Don't give away the pious fraud as I do not want to be recalled.'[72]

He was not yet in the clear. He needed official permission from the Fourth Hussars. But that didn't trouble him; his future didn't lie there. It lay in public life, and so, while packing, he decided to deliver a political address. He spoke at Bradford and wrote afterwards: 'The meeting was a complete success. The hall was not a vy large one – but it was closely packed. I was listened to with the greatest attention for 55 minutes at the end of which time there were loud & general cries of "Go on." . . . All of which was very gratifying . . . The conclusions I form are these – with practice I shall obtain great power on a public platform. My impediment is no hindrance. My voice sufficiently powerful, and – this is vital – my ideas & modes of thought are pleasing to men.' R.B. (later Lord) Haldane, a leading Liberal MP, read the speech in the *Morning Post* the next day and wrote to Jennie: 'I thought it very good – broad in tone – fresh & vigorous. I hope he will soon be in the House.'[73]

After Bradford, Churchill vanished. Once in Cairo, he reasoned, he would be beyond reach of the Fourth Hussars. Indeed, unless the War Office proved uncharacteristically helpful, Bangalore wouldn't even know where he was. Ignoring the swift, comfortable steamers of the P & O and Australian Lloyd, he took the train to Marseilles and boarded the freighter *Sindh*, 'a filthy tramp,' he wrote in a note on July 30, manned by 'detestable French sailors.' On August 2 he reached Cairo and took a carriage to the cavalry barracks. 'All was hustle and bustle' there. 'Two squadrons of the 21st Lancers had already started up the Nile.' He paid forty pounds for a charger and paraded that evening with 'A' Squadron, to which he was attached, in the uniform of the day: khakis, topee, Sam Browne belt, field glasses, revolver – he had forgotten his regular one, with its lucky silk lanyard, and had to buy a new Mauser pistol – and Stohwasser gaiters. The band struck up 'Auld Lang Syne,' and they were off. That was on a Tuesday. On Friday he was 'toiling slowly up the rising river – against a 6 knot current with only a balance of speed of 4 miles an hour,' pausing briefly in Luxor, on the east bank of the Nile, where he paid 'a flying visit' to the ancient temple and was reminded of Rider Haggard's *Cleopatra*. He felt like a fugitive from the Fourth Hussars, which he was. He had 'heard nothing definite about my leave being sanctioned by India – but as there has been no cancelling order & a fortnight has already passed I think I may now conclude . . . that "silence has given consent." ' The trip was proving 'delightful,' though the boat was a strange troop transport, one of Cook's, painted alabaster white, with chintz curtains in the saloon windows and flowered toiletries in every cabin. Winston, interested in everything, noted that it was powered by steam-driven pistons which turned 'a great paddle-wheel which protrudes from the stern. The appearance is peculiar.' He had found 'many old friends in the regiment.' He had also learned that never, in its entire history, had the Twenty-first Lancers seen action. Indeed, other regiments gibed that its motto was 'Thou Shalt Not Kill.' The taunt was of long standing, but in a month it would be forgotten.[74]

What were the British doing on the Nile? To the public at home, and to Churchill, who wrote ardently of Queen, Empire, and Flag, the answer was obvious. They were there, he wrote, to assure the destruction of an autocracy, 'a state of society which had long become an anachronism – an insult as well as a danger to civilisation; the liberation of the great waterway; perhaps the foundation of an African India; certainly the settlement of a long account.' That long account was the martyrdom of Chinese Gordon in Khartoum at the hands of the Mahdi's howling dervishes. After Khartoum had been retaken, Churchill thought, it would be rather a good thing to 'tell some stonemason to bring his hammer and chisel and cut on the pedestal of Gordon's statue in Trafalgar Square the significant, the sinister, yet the somehow satisfactory word, "Avenged." '[75]

But over thirteen years had passed since Gordon had been butchered. The Mahdi, as inscrutable as his victim, had died suddenly (and mysteriously) five months later. Before his death he had chosen Abdullah Ibn Mohammed as Khalifa – literally 'successor' – to lead the forces in Mahdism. Under the Khalifa the Sudanese situation had been transformed. After suppressing a conspiracy by the Mahdi's relatives and disarming the forces of other leading emirs, he had sought to accomplish the Mahdi's dream of a universal jihad, or holy war, reforming Islam throughout the Moslem world. Although the Sudanese people were of mixed Arab, Hamitic, and Negro ancestry, all of them were, and are, commonly called Arabs, and their devotion to the Prophet Mohammed approached the absolute. The Khalifa's hordes attacked north, south, east, and west. They were checked everywhere, notably by the Belgians in the Congo and the British in Egypt. Then the Mahdist Sudan entered a three-year period of great suffering. Almost no rain fell. Crops shrivelled, herds grew emaciated, dervishes starved, epidemics broke out, thousands died. Eventually the rains returned; improved harvests brought prosperity. The Khalifa became a popular leader. He was an autocrat, but his people had never known democracy, and in any event the charge of autocracy was hardly one to be flung about carelessly by a twenty-three-year-old youth who was deftly exploiting his own membership in a privileged class to build popular support among his fellow countrymen.

England's real enemy on the Nile was France. Now that the British held Egypt, they wanted to insulate the length of the river, without which Egypt could not survive. 'The Nile is Egypt,' said Roberts, 'and Egypt is the Nile.' The Italians, the Belgians, and the Germans agreed to stay out of the river's valley. The French declined. Instead, they sent an expedition to Africa under Captain Jean-Baptiste Marchand, whose orders were to land on the continent's west coast, march inland, and seize Fashoda (now Kodok) on the upper Nile, where, it was believed, a dam could be built to shut off Egypt's water. Fashoda, not the ruins of Gordon's Khartoum, would be Kitchener's ultimate destination. The Khalifa's tribesmen merely lay between him and his objective. Since all this was beyond Churchill, it was probably beyond the Khalifa, too. All he knew was that an army of British and Egyptian troops, led by the Sirdar, was coming after him. He sat in the Mahdist capital of Omdurman, built opposite Khartoum after Gordon's death, and plotted the movements of his sixty-thousand-man army. His confidence was sky-high. Kitchener, after all, had only twenty thousand men, counting his Egyptian Camel Corps and the disaffected Sudanese he had enlisted. What the Khalifa did not realize was that the new technological superiority of European armies – resulting from such innovations as shrapnel, magazine rifles, and Maxim guns – had rendered his passionate masses, clad in their patched blue-and-white jibbas, or smocks, waving their obsolete weapons and their banners inscribed with passages from the Koran, almost meaningless. And logistics, another technological development, solved the Sirdar's supply problems, permitting him to plan the orderly arrival of reinforcing troops like the Twenty-first

Lancers, setting out from Cairo, fourteen hundred miles away.

The journey took two weeks: by steamer to Aswân, where they led their horses around the cascading water at Philae and reembarked; on to Wadi Halfa, a four-day trip by boat; then four hundred miles by military railroad to Kitchener's main camp, where the waters of the Atbara flow into the vast, brown, muddy, fifteen-hundred-foot-wide Nile. Many of the place-names in Churchill's dispatches are meaningless today: Shellal, Metemmeh, Wad Habeshi, Wad Bishara, and, nine miles above the main camp, the Shabluka gorge and cataract, beyond which long, low heights overlooked Omdurman

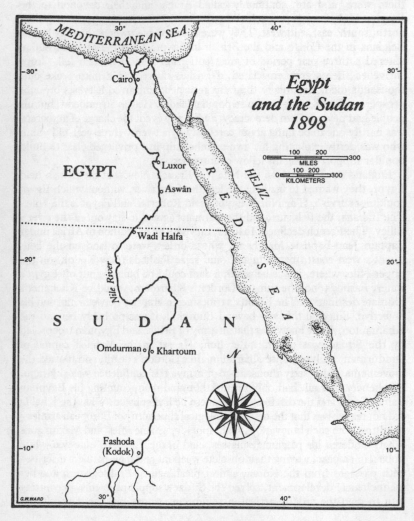

Egypt
and the Sudan
1898

and the ruins of Khartoum. But Winston's reportorial skills were growing. A *khor*, he carefully explained to his readers, 'is a watercourse, usually dry. In India it would be called a *nullah*; in South Africa a *donga*; in Australia a *gully*.' A *zareba* was a hedgehog. He described the lovely gazelles running along the riverbanks, and the Sirdar's telegraph wires, strung above them; how, where the Nile narrowed to two hundred yards, 'great swirls and eddies disturb its surface'; the disembarkation of an entire division – with fifteen hundred horses, mules, camels, and donkeys – and how, when ashore, 'our line of march lay partly in the desert and partly along the strip of vegetation by the Nile, to which we returned every evening to water, and by which we camped at night.'[76]

It was serene, hardly like war at all, and he commented on that. Ordinarily one might expect patrols, sniping, skirmishing, preludes to a major operation: 'Usually the game gets warmer by degrees.' The enemy lurked near Omdurman but had sent no one, except perhaps lone horsemen, to investigate the British approach. Not a shot had been heard. The British and Egyptian camps were 'as peaceful as Aldershot or Bisley.' And yet they knew that one day the guns would 'begin to fire and a big battle open.' At Wad Habeshi he wrote to his mother: 'We are but 60 miles from Khartoum and on the 27th we march 21 miles putting us in front of the infantry and in full contact. Within the next ten days there will be a general action – perhaps a vy severe one. I may be killed. I do not think so.' He was more worried about his other enemy, the Sirdar. Nothing could be easier for the commander than to send Churchill back and say, 'Let him come on with the remounts after the battle.' At every stage along the way Winston half expected to be detained by a staff officer. 'I suppose,' he wrote, 'a criminal flying from justice goes through the same emotions at every stopping-point.' Towards the end hope replaced fear, though he knew his presence was resented at the top. He wrote home that Frank Rhodes, the *Times* correspondent, had 'talked to the Sirdar about me. Kitchener said he had known I was not going to stay in the army – was only making a convenience of it; that he had disapproved of my coming in place of others whose professions were at stake & that E. Wood had acted wrongly & had annoyed him by sending me. But that I was quite right to try my best.' Churchill concluded that Kitchener 'may be a general – but never a gentleman.' That was arrogant. But Churchillian swagger was almost always redeemed by his boyish charm and the quickness with which he could laugh at himself. He captured an Arab who turned out to be a British intelligence agent. Lionel James of Reuters wanted to write a story about it, 'but I prevailed on him not to do so,' Winston wrote, 'having a detestation of publicity.'[77]

Before they even reached the battlefield he had a bad fright. From Atbara the Twenty-first Lancers marched to Shabluka, bandoliers filled, lances with pennons tightly rolled, ready for action. Various duties kept Winston behind on the river's east bank; he had been told to join the column that evening at its first camp, fifteen miles away. His chores took longer than he had expected, and it was late afternoon before the ferry steamer *Tahra* carried him over to the west shore. He asked for directions and was told: 'It is perfectly simple. You just go due south until you see the campfires and then turn towards the river.' He nodded and left. An hour later the sun sank; darkness enveloped him. To avoid the thorny bushes on the Nile bank he struck inland and rode down through the desert, steering southward by keeping his back to the North Star. After two hours of trotting he paused for a drink and rations. To his dismay, clouds drifted across the star, and the pointers of the Great Bear became invisible. He was lost. Unless the overcast lifted, he would have no choice but to wait. Picking a spot, he passed the reins around his waist, leaned against a rock, and tried to sleep. The night was sultry; 'a hot, restless, wearing wind blew continuously with a mournful sound'; slumber was impossible. Then, at 3:30 A.M., the sky cleared and 'the beautiful constellation of Orion came into view. Never did the giant look more splendid.' He rode towards it, and after two hours he found the Nile. He and his mount drank deeply. But it was broad daylight before he found the lancers' camp, and the regiment had gone. Nearby villagers spoke no English; he made himself understood, indicating hunger by pointing to his mouth and stomach, but nothing happened until he uttered the magical Arabic word *baksheesh*. Now that they knew he was going to give them money, everything changed; 'all difficulties melted.' Three women appeared to serve him dates and milk. His pony was fed *doura*. What he now needed was information. Using the point of his sword, he sketched a profile of a lancer on the red mud wall. A man wearing a fez nodded excitedly, made lapping motions with his tongue to convey the fact that the troopers had watered their horses here, and pointed southward. 'Then he gazed hard at me, and, with an expression of ferocious satisfaction, pronounced the word "Omdurman." ' Thus Churchill first learned where battle would be joined.[78]

He caught up with the column at its camp that evening. By August 27 all Anglo-Egyptian forces, both the army in the desert and the gunboats on the Nile, were concentrated south of the Shabluka Hills. The following morning they began their final advance, covering only eight to ten miles a day to save their strength. The heat was 'intense. In spite of thick clothes, spine pads, broad-brimmed pith helmets, one felt the sun leaning down upon one and piercing our bodies with its burning rays.' But that was the only enemy Churchill saw. Omdurman seemed undefended. He began to doubt the villager in the fez. The crisp surface of the desert plain, through which the Nile meandered in its broad sweeps, stretched wide and vacant: 'Everyone in the British cavalry had made up his mind that there was to be no battle,' that ' "we shall be marching like this towards the Equator for months and months." ' At nine o'clock on the morning of September 1, the Twenty-first Lancers, riding ahead as scouts, sighted Omdurman. If the Khalifa meant to fight, he would fight here. Winston was studying the city's mud huts and the dome of the Mahdi's tomb – and trying to ignore a hundred vultures circling overhead, which made him extremely uncomfortable ('It would be difficult,' he told readers of the *Morning Post*, 'to assign limitations to the possibilities of instinct') – when another subaltern motioned towards a ridge ahead and cried: 'Enemy in sight! They haven't bolted!'[79]

Churchill squinted at the ridge. It lay three miles away, between them and the city. At first he saw only 'a long black line with white spots.' The white spots appeared to be dervishes, perhaps 'three thousand men behind a high dense zareba of thorn bushes.' They thought this 'better than nothing. There would in any case be a skirmish.' They rode closer for a better view. At 11:00 A.M., to his astonishment, 'the whole black line, which seemed to be zareba, began to move. It was made of men not bushes. Behind it other immense masses and lines of men appeared over the crest, and while we watched, amazed by the wonder of the sight, the whole face of the slope became black with swarming savages.' It crossed his mind that this was what the Crusaders had seen. The Khalifa's army, five miles from end to end, advanced while the sun, glinting on over forty thousand spear points, 'spread a sparkling cloud. It was, perhaps, the impression of a lifetime, nor do I expect ever again to see such an awe-inspiring and formidable sight.'[80]

'Mr Churchill!' called Colonel Rowland Martin, the Twenty-first's commander. Winston cantered up and was told to first take a long look 'and then go back as quickly as you can without knocking up your horse and report personally to the Sirdar. You will find him marching with the infantry.' So there it was. He was going to meet Kitchener after all. After further scrutiny of the enemy position, it took him forty minutes to cover the six miles separating his advance party from the main body of the army, and on the way he appraised the Anglo-Egyptian formation: five solid brigades in open columns, with the grey and chocolate mass of the Camel Corps on his left below the rocky Kerrari Hills, and, to his right, seven or eight large white British gunboats on the river. He found the Sirdar riding between the Union Jack and the flag of the Egyptian khedive. Reining in, he identified himself as an officer from the Twenty-first – but gave no name – and described the situation. Kitchener said: 'You say the Dervish Army is advancing. How long do you think I have got?' In a rough calculation, Churchill estimated that the enemy was jog-trotting at four miles an hour and had another seven miles to cover. He said, 'You have got at least an hour – probably an hour and a half, sir, even if they come on at their present rate.'[81]

There followed an interval which would have been impossible for any youth who was not a member of the Victorian privileged class. Kitchener gave no sign of knowing who Winston was, but his chief of intelligence, Sir Reginald Wingate, recognized him and invited him to lunch. They dined on a white picnic cloth with knives and forks and what was, under the circumstances, remarkable nonchalance. The outcome of the imminent battle was by no means certain. Dervishes had overwhelmed Egyptian troops in several encounters. At Abu Klea and Tamai they had broken British squares, and only seven thousand of the Sirdar's bayonets were British anyway. Moreover, the enemy was armed with more than spears; twenty thousand of the Khalifa's men were equipped with old Martini-Henrys. Yet Sir Reginald and his guests were, Winston wrote, 'in the highest spirits and the best of tempers. It was like a race luncheon before the Derby.' They watched, as interested but detached spectators, while the infantry formed a defensive arc and the leading brigade built a thorn-bush zareba. A young lieutenant on a passing gunboat shouted: 'How are you off for drinks? We have got everything in the world on board here. Can you catch?' It was David Beatty – like Ian Hamilton he would play a larger role in Churchill's later career – and he tossed Winston a large bottle of champagne.[82]

No engagement was fought that day. The dervishes halted. Kitchener's howitzers pounded Omdurman, and Churchill returned to his regiment, which pitched camp that night inside the zareba, under the steep bank of the river. Reports, considered reliable, predicted that the enemy would attack that night. They were wrong, but the threat was real. Churchill defied it, strolling around in the moonlight to inspect the Sirdar's defences, and when the Twenty-first's buglers blew at 4:30 A.M., he swung into his saddle, ready to join the spray of officers' patrols which would serve as Kitchener's eyes at dawn. Daybreak arrived and revealed the enemy. Churchill was delighted. 'This,' he wrote, 'is an hour to live.' He mounted a ridge which had been christened Heliograph Hill. Afterwards, writing to Ian Hamilton of that morning's events, he said that he believed he was 'the first to see the enemy – certainly the first to hear their bullets . . . I and my little patrol felt very lonely.' At 5:50 A.M., kneeling, he scribbled in his field service notebook the first of two messages to the Sirdar, both of which survive.

Dervish army, strength unchanged, occupies last nights [sic] position with their left well extended. Their patrols have reported the advance and loud cheering is going on. There is no *zeriba*.

Nothing hostile is between a line drawn from Heliograph Hill to the Mahdi's tomb, and river. Nothing is within three miles from the camp.

> WINSTON S. CHURCHILL
> Lieut 4th Hussars
> attd 21st Lancers

Handing this to a corporal, he climbed for a better view. The sun was high now. Scarcely four hundred yards away he beheld the humps and squares of the Khalifa's multitude, bright with glittering weapons and iridescent standards. He wrote: 'Talk of fun! Where will you beat this? On horseback, at daybreak, within shot of an advancing army, seeing everything, and corresponding direct with Headquarters.' He was a target now; enemy bullets were swatting sand around him. The corporal, spurring his weary horse to a full gallop, returned with a request from the Sirdar's chief of staff for word of new developments. It was 6:20 A.M. Winston scrawled his second report:

About ¼ Dervish army is on their right which they have refused at present. Should this force continue to advance it would come the South side of Heliograph Hill.

Most of the Cavalry are with this force.

Duplicate to Col Martin

WINSTON S. CHURCHILL
Lieut 4th Hussars

By now, he wrote to Hamilton, 'the fire was for the time being as hot as anything I have seen – barring only those 10 minutes with the 35th Sikhs – a year ago today.' An enemy patrol of three horsemen approached him: 'They were dark, cowled figures, like monks on horseback – ugly, sinister brutes with long spears. I fired a few shots at them from the saddle, and they sheered off.' But the enemy mass was coming on like a sea. 'The tide was rising fast. One rock, one mound of sand after another was submerged by that human flood. It was time to go.' Still he was reluctant. Then a major appeared and ordered him to withdraw; the British infantry was about to open fire. Back he scampered then, to watch, from the flank, the Sirdar's response to the challenge and, opposite him, 'all the pride and might of the Dervish Empire . . . on this last great day of its existence.'[83]

Unlike twentieth-century warfare, nearly everything at Omdurman was visible, if distorted, to the naked eye. As Churchill wrote, 'the whole scene lay revealed in minute detail, curiously twisted, blurred, and interspersed with phantom waters by the mirage.' It quickly became apparent that the Khalifa had now committed every man he had, including his reserves, hoping to overwhelm the infidels. His sacred black flag floated above the bright banners of lesser emirs and the white standards bearing Mohammed's most stirring passages in Arabic script. Shrieking as they ran, these troops dipped beneath a swell of ground which briefly concealed the main bodies of the rival armies from one another and then swept up, over, and down into the arena where the invaders of their soil stood shoulder to shoulder, braced to receive them. But the two never met. Lashed and scythed by storms of Lee-Enfield dumdums, by four batteries of howitzers, and by shells from at least seventy big guns on the Nile bank and in the gunboats, the dervishes faltered seven hundred yards from their objective, the last of them stumbling and sprawling over the bodies of seven thousand of their fallen comrades. Kitchener then wheeled his five brigades into echelon formation and prepared to move on Omdurman. That would cut the enemy off from his base and force him into the desert. The fifty-three thousand remaining dervishes regrouped and attacked again. This time they came within a hundred yards of the Anglo-Egyptian lines, but at the appalling cost of twenty thousand men. The Sirdar's force was virtually unblooded. The city was still accessible to the Khalifa's survivors, however, and despite their casualties, numbers were still on their side. Kitchener believed that he had to occupy Omdurman before the enemy could flee there. His army, as Churchill noted, 'could fight as many Dervishes as cared to come in the plain; among the houses it was different.' But before the Anglo-

Egyptian infantry could advance, the Arabs must be driven from the intervening ground. That was a cavalry task. The Twenty-first Lancers, on the spot, waiting in a little hollow, stood to their horses. Then the heliograph at Kitchener's side instructed them, in flashes of reflected sunlight: 'Advance – clear the left flank – use every effort to prevent the enemy entering Omdurman.' The stage was set for Britain's last great cavalry charge, and Churchill, leading twenty-five troopers, would be in the thick of it.[84]

Scrambling into their saddles, the massed lancers walked forward at a deliberate pace, stepping over the crisp desert towards the city, stirred by what Churchill called 'a high state of excitement.' Presently they noticed, three hundred yards away and parallel to their course, a long row of blue-black objects, two or three yards apart. At that moment the bugles sounded Trot, and the regiment began to jingle and clatter across the front of these crouching dervishes. It was a lull in the battle. Except for the sound of the harnesses, silence was near perfect. Abruptly the Arabs broke it, firing a volley; three horses and several lancers toppled to the ground. Until then the colonel had intended to swing around the flank of the enemy riflemen, but now he decided to attack them head-on. The bugles sounded Right Wheel into Line. There was no further order. As Winston wrote to Hamilton: 'Gallop & Charge were understood.'[85] In a solid line, the regiment lunged towards what appeared to be 150 dervish riflemen.

At this critical moment, Winston became preoccupied with a personal problem. He had every confidence in his grey polo pony, but until the regiment wheeled he, like the other officers, had been carrying a drawn sword. Because of his bad shoulder, he had decided early in the campaign that if hand-to-hand combat loomed, he would rely on his pistol. At full gallop, he had to return his sword to its scabbard and fumble for his wooden holster. He explained to Hamilton: 'I drew my Mauser pistol – a ripper – and cocked it. Then I looked to my front. Instead of the 150 riflemen who were still blazing I saw a line nearly (in the middle) – 12 deep . . . of closely jammed spearmen – all in a *nullah* with steep sloping sides 6 foot deep & 20 foot broad.'[86] The lancers found themselves heading into a mob of nearly three thousand dervishes led by mounted emirs waving bright flags. What had happened? The Khalifa's black flag, which had moved to within five hundred yards of this dry watercourse, should have told them. He had anticipated the flanking movement and reinforced the *khor*. Thus, the 310 shouting lancers, plunging furiously ahead in crescent formation, their overlapping flanks curving inward like the horns of a moon, their helmets bowed against the enemy musketry like the cuirassiers at Waterloo, were hurtling towards a wall of human flesh.

The collision was tremendous. Nearly thirty lancers and their horses, Churchill wrote, 'fell knocked A.O.T. [arse over tip!].' Some two hundred dervishes were down. Winston himself had passed between two riflemen; both had fired at him, missed, and hit the trooper just behind him, who was immediately stabbed to death as he slid from his mount. But most of the dervishes – and the British – were too stunned to fight. 'For perhaps ten wonderful seconds no man heeded his enemy.' Terrified horses were wedged in the mob. Bruised men lay in heaps, dazed and astonished. Several lancers, unhorsed but alert, had time to remount. Then the Arabs began to come to their senses. They threw spears at their enemies, swung heavy swords, cut reins and stirrup leathers, and tried to hamstring horses. Troopers jabbed back with their lances, officers with their sabres. Churchill saw his men being 'dragged from their horses and cut to pieces by the infuriated foe.' Finding himself 'surrounded by what seemed to be dozens of men,' he 'rode up to individuals firing my pistol in their faces and killing several – 3 for certain – 2 doubtful – one very doubtful.' One was swinging a gleaming, curved sword, trying to hamstring the pony. Another wore a steel helmet and chain-mail hangings. A third came at him 'with uplifted sword. I raised my pistol and fired. So close were we that the pistol itself actually struck him.' The dervish mass, he saw, was re-forming. At this point, he later recalled, 'The whole scene seemed to flicker.' He looked around. His troop was gone. His squadron was gone. He could not see a single British officer or trooper within a hundred yards. Instead, 'I saw two or three [dervish] riflemen crouching and aiming their rifles at me.'[87]

In a letter to his mother two days later (headed 'Khartoum and be damned to it') he wrote: 'I never felt the slightest nervousness and felt as cool as I do now.' But in another account he was more candid. Staring at the Martini-Henry muzzles, he wrote, 'for the first time that morning I experienced a sudden sensation of fear.' And he told Hamilton: 'I looked at them stupidly for what may have been 2 seconds.' He thought: 'What a fool I was to loiter in the midst of the enemy.' The dervish riflemen fired together and missed. Hunching down over his pommel, he spurred his pony free and found his squadron two hundred yards away, faced about and already forming up. His own troop had just finished sorting itself out, but as he joined it a dervish sprang out of a hole in the ground and into the midst of his men, lunging about with a spear. They thrust at him with their lances; he dodged, wheeled, and charged Churchill. 'I shot him at less than a yard. He fell on the sand, and lay there dead. How easy to kill a man! But I did not worry about it. I found I had fired the whole magazine of my Mauser pistol, so I put in a new clip of ten cartridges before thinking of anything else.' It occurred to him that if he hadn't injured his shoulder in Bombay, he would have had to defend himself with a sword and might now be dead. Afterwards he reflected: 'One must never forget when misfortunes come that it is quite possible they are saving one from something much worse.' He wrote to Jennie: 'The pistol was the best thing in the world.'[88]

He was ready to charge again; they all were; several of his troopers asked permission to discard their lances and draw their swords. Then they looked back at where they had been, and their blood cooled. Winston saw, coming from the direction of the enemy, 'a succession of grisly apparitions; horses spouting blood, struggling on three legs, men staggering on foot, men bleeding from terrible wounds, fish-hook spears stuck right through them, arms and faces cut to pieces, bowels protruding, men gasping, crying, collapsing, expiring.'[89] Attending to these came first. As they finished improvising bandages, the colonel, apparently for the first time in the action, remembered that his men carried carbines. Bugles sounded and they trotted off to the flank, where they could enfilade the *khor* from three hundred yards. This forced the dervishes to retreat towards the ridge where the Khalifa's black flag still waved. Twenty minutes after the British had wheeled into line and charged, they occupied the watercourse and were breakfasting there, in sole possession of the field.

The question is whether it was worth it. Churchill wrote to Hamilton: 'It was I suppose the most dangerous 2 minutes I shall live to see. Out of 310 officers & men we lost – 1 officer and 20 men killed – 4 officers and 45 men wounded and 119 horses of which 56 were bullet wounds. All this in 120 seconds!' He told his mother that he was 'about the only officer whose clothes, saddlery, or horse were uninjured.' In the final reckoning it was found that Kitchener had lost fewer than 3 per cent of his troops in the entire battle of Omdurman. Yet the Twenty-first Lancers' casualties, in their brief encounter, had exceeded 22 per cent. Churchill conceded in the *Morning Post* that this isolated engagement 'did not greatly influence the fortunes of the battle.'[90] Actually, it had no impact whatever. The Sirdar's fears of house-to-house fighting in the city proved groundless. To be sure, the Khalifa did everything he could to arouse his people there. He ordered the Mahdi's great war drum beaten, the martial *ombya* blown, and his sole Krupp gun wheeled into position and fired, while exhorting the inhabitants to prepare for a last stand. But his troops wanted none of it. They had seen enough of pointless slaughter. Disregarding his summons and the pleas of their emirs, they faded into the desert or surrendered. As the Sirdar approached Omdurman's walls, three men emerged, knelt before him, and presented him with the keys to the city. British soldiers then marched through it, end to end. All this would have happened without the lancers' charge. The evidence is overwhelming: the blood of Colonel Martin's men had bought nothing.

The survivors of heavy fighting always try to justify the cost, however, and Churchill was no exception. He reasoned in his dispatches that the regiment had faced 'no choice but to charge or gallop away. The definite orders excluded the latter alternative. In any case there was no time to argue. At that close range it was impossible so heavy a fire could be ineffective.' Actually, the lancers had proceeded to outflank the position after the charge, which proves that the enemy could have been outmanoeuvred without it. Churchill offered his readers other arguments, which, though irrational, tell much about the era and his enthusiasm for its values. The regiment's feat, he said, 'was of perhaps as great value to the Empire as the victory itself.' It was important that untested British troops show 'those intrinsic fighting virtues without which no race can long continue to rule.' Because of the Twenty-first Lancers at

Omdurman, he concluded, England 'may rise refreshed and, contemplating the past with calmness, may feel confidence in the present and high hope in the future. We can still produce soldiers worthy of their officers – and there has hitherto been no complaint about the officers.'[91]

There was more of this, most of it, by today's standards, deplorable. He rejoiced to see that the Union Jack hoisted over the ashes of Khartoum was four times the size of the Egyptian khedive's flag. He wept over the new English graveyard on an eminence overlooking the desert, with its 'protecting crosses which the living raised as a last tribute to those who had paid the bill for all the fun and glory of the game.' To Hamilton he wrote that after his experience in the *khor*, 'my faith in our race & blood was much strengthened.' 'Perhaps,' he told his readers with heavy humour, 'to these savages with their vile customs and brutal ideas, we appeared as barbarous aggressors' – which is, of course, precisely how they were regarded, and understandably so. After the guns had fallen silent he wrote in the *Morning Post*, 'I raised my voice and helmet in honour of that persevering British people who, often affronted, usually get their own way in the end.' And although he had assured his mother that war could not be gilded, he tried to do it himself; brave deeds, he told his newspaper's subscribers, 'brighten the picture of war with beautiful colours, till from a distance it looks almost magnificent, and the dark background and dirty brown canvas are scarcely seen.' David Beatty's eye was clearer. He had watched the lancers' charge from his gunboat. Years later he told Churchill he had seen it, and Churchill eagerly asked him what his impression had been. 'It looked,' Beatty said, 'like plum duff: brown currants scattered about in a great deal of suet.'[92]

Churchill's impressions of the dervish rout were melodramatic because he was, and always would be, a romantic. In this he was a man of his time. He was no more persuaded of war's ennobling virtues than Sir Henry Newbolt or Tennyson in *Maud* ('. . . hail once more to the banner of battle unroll'd!'), or Thomas Hughes. *Fighting*, to Hughes, was one of the most honourable words in the language, 'the real, highest, honestest business of every son of man.' As late as August 24, 1914, when the British cavalry flung itself against a sleet of German bullets, John Buchan felt exalted. He knew that this suicidal act was 'as futile and gallant as any other like attempt in history on unbroken infantry and guns in position. But it proved to the world that the spirit which inspired the Light Brigade at Balaclava . . . was still alive in the cavalry of today.' Somehow carnage had been transformed by concepts of Saint George, the Holy Grail, and 'playing the game,' as though butchery were a manlier form of rugby. 'Victorian and Edwardian chivalry,' Mark Girouard notes, 'produced its own world of myth and legend, just as much as medieval chivalry.'[93]

Young Winston had fallen under this dark enchantment, and he would never be entirely free of it. But even at Omdurman he was his own man, undazzled by rank and quick to accuse those who betrayed the code of honour, which, he realized, must be observed by all or none. Kitchener soon discovered this. Despite his lordly bearing and his impeccable guardsman's moustache, the Sirdar was a man of primitive, inclement instincts. On his orders the Mahdi's tomb was desecrated, the corpse ripped from its shroud, and the head lopped off and dumped in a kerosene can to be 'preserved for future disposal' – an official phrase which, the outraged Churchill wrote, could only be interpreted as meaning that it would be 'passed from hand to hand till it reached Cairo,' where it would be treated as 'an interesting trophy.'[94]

Lord Cromer read this and had the gruesome relic sent back for reinterment. Kitchener seethed. Then Churchill found evidence of battlefield atrocities. He wrote to his mother that the triumph had been 'disgraced' by atrocities, and that 'Kitchener is responsible for this.' Most of the guilty had been Egyptians and Sudanese fighting under the khedive's colours, but some had been Englishmen. No blind chauvinist would have acknowledged that. Winston accepted it and wrote about it, and that took courage. 'The sentiment that the British soldier is incapable of brutality,' he told his readers, 'is one which never fails to win the meed of popular applause; but there are in fact a considerable proportion of cruel men in any army.' Kitchener now erupted. Winston wrote to Hamilton: 'I am in great disfavour with the authorities here . . . Generally things have been a little unpleasant.' The Sirdar tried to punish him by putting him in charge of a band of sick camels limping wearily back to Cairo. Churchill tore up the orders, took the next launch north, and reached England in time to join the lancers' triumphant London parade. A 'general officer' testily wrote to the *Army and Navy Gazette*: 'What is the position of Lieut Spencer Churchill in Her Majesty's Army?' Here he was, a subaltern with less than four years' service, 'acting as special correspondent here, there, and everywhere. Now, as a special correspondent he has, as a matter of course, to criticise general officers highly placed in authority and to influence public opinion. Can it be for the good of the Service . . . ?' Even the Prince of Wales was offended. He wrote to Winston: 'I fear that in matters of discipline I may be considered old fashioned – and I must say that I think an officer serving in a campaign should not write letters for newspapers or express strong opinions of how the operations were carried out.' HRH said he now realized why the Sirdar 'viewed your joining his force with dislike – it is I am sure merely because he knows you write, for which he has the greatest objection I understand – and I cannot help agreeing with him.'[95]

Winston was unruffled. This was one test for which his pathetic school years had prepared him. He knew how to stand alone. As for the controversy and evidence of his independence, he welcomed them; they would be useful in Parliament. At the same time, he was developing political acumen in other, subtler ways. Earlier he had missed the significance of the French troops on the upper Nile, but now, as Kitchener led a force there, he noted 'rumours about Fashoda' in a dispatch and predicted that 'the Battle of Fashoda will be fought in Westminster, that tempers rather than lives will be lost, and ink rather than blood expended.' And so it happened. Five days later the Sirdar confronted Captain Marchand and demanded he leave. Paris was furious, but the deputies were split by the growing Dreyfus crisis, and Théophile Delcassé, the foreign minister, ordered Marchand to withdraw. As compensation, the British generously gave France an expanse of Sahara Desert. That was how the Empire did things under Victoria, and Churchill would go to his grave believing that it was the best way, not just for England, but for all mankind. He could hardly wait to get his own hands on the reins of some of this vast power. The lancers' charge had been less than forty-eight hours old when, itching to reach the hustings, he had written to Jennie: 'Arrange me some good meetings in October, Bradford & Birmingham. Sunny will help.' He was still obsessed with medals. After he had left Kitchener's command, to the vast relief of both, he wrote to a superior: 'I naturally want to wear my medals while I still have a uniform to wear them on. They have already sent me the Egyptian one. I cannot think why the Frontier one has not arrived. Young Life Guardsmen on Sir B. Blood's staff in Buner have already got theirs. Do try and get mine for me as soon as possible.'[96]

In Egypt he felt he had mounted another rung on his ladder to the House of Commons. He had even acquired a sort of vicarious wound. Having floated down the Nile with the Grenadier Guards, he had encountered a fellow officer in Cairo, a subaltern who had charged the *khor* with him and had emerged with a severe sword cut above his right wrist. A doctor, coming to dress the wound, said a skin graft would be necessary. Winston rolled up his sleeve. The doctor warned him that he would feel as though he were being flayed alive, and Churchill later recalled, 'My sensations as he sawed the razor slowly to and fro fully justified his description of the ordeal.' At the end of it Winston was missing a piece of skin about the size of a shilling with a thin layer of flesh attached to it. 'This precious fragment was then grafted on to my friend's wound. It remains there to this day and did him lasting good in many ways. I for my part keep the scar as a souvenir.' One has the distinct impression that he believed that this, like his decorations, would win votes.[97]

Ironically, he had overlooked his greatest achievement on the Nile, a propitious sign of what was to come. It lay in the sinew of his dispatches. His mastery of the language was growing. The fruits of his formal schooling had been negligible. He had entered the army an ignorant youth. Now, less than four years later, his command of English distinguished him from every other correspondent in the field and won the admiration of readers accustomed to the finest Victorian prose. He had arrived in Bangalore without knowing who Sophocles was or what ethics were, yet he could write, speculating about the Khalifa's men meeting Kitchener's first storm of fire: 'What must the Dervishes have heard? Only those who were with the Prussian Guard on the glacis of St Privat, or with Skobeleff in front of the Grivica Redoubt, can know.' He could capture, as few writers can, moments of utter horror. Of a sergeant trying to collect his troop after the charge, he wrote: 'His face was cut to pieces, and as he called on his men to rally, the whole of his nose, cheeks, and lips flapped amid red bubbles.' He described the abandoned battlefield as looking 'like a place where rubbish is thrown, or where a fair has recently been held. White objects, like dirty bits of newspaper, lay scattered here and there – the bodies of the enemy. Brown objects, almost the colour of the earth, like bundles of dead grass or heaps of manure, were also dotted about – the bodies of soldiers. Among these were goat-skin water-bottles, broken weapons, torn and draggled flags, cartridge-cases. In the foreground lay a group of dead horses and several dead or dying donkeys. It was all litter.'[98]

As magnanimous to the enemy as he was rebellious towards his commander, he paid tribute to the slain Arabs:

When the soldier of a civilised power is killed in action his limbs are composed and his body is borne by friendly arms reverently to the grave. The wail of the fifes, the roll of the drums, the triumphant words of the Funeral Service, all divest the act of its squalor, and the spectator sympathises with, perhaps almost envies, the comrade who has found this honourable exit. But there was nothing *dulce et decorum* about the Dervish dead. Nothing of the dignity of unconquerable manhood. All was filthy corruption. Yet these were as brave men as ever walked the earth. The conviction was borne in on me that their claim beyond the grave in respect of a valiant death was as good as that which any of our countrymen could make . . . There they lie, those valiant warriors of a false faith and of a fallen domination, their only history preserved by their conquerors, their only monument their bones – and these the drifting sand of the desert will bury in a few short years. Three days before I had seen them rise eager, confident, resolved. The roar of their shouting had swelled like the surf on a rocky shore. The flashing of their blades and points had displayed their numbers, their vitality, their ferocity. They were confident in their strength, in the justice of their cause, in the support of their religion. Now only the heaps of corruption in the plain and fugitives dispersed and scattered in the wilderness remained. The terrible machinery of scientific war had done its work. The Dervish host was scattered and destroyed. Their end, however, only anticipates that of the victors, for Time, which laughs at Science, as Science laughs at Valour, will in due course contemptuously brush both combatants away.[99]

The Prince of Wales, though he felt his rebuke justified, added thoughtfully: 'Your writing a book with an account of the campaign is quite another matter.' Such a work, HRH said, would have his blessing, and he hoped Winston would 'come & see me & tell me all about the recent campaign & about your future plans.' Then, revising his earlier advice, he observed: 'I cannot help feeling that Parliamentary & literary life is what would suit you best.'[100] Winston agreed, of course. And he was in a hurry. He had reached the odd conclusion that he was destined to die, like his father, at forty-six, that whatever he did must be done by 1920. He had already anticipated the prince's literary advice and was at work on a new manuscript. Its working title was *The War for the Waterway*. He believed it would be ready for publication in a year, and he was right. What he did not anticipate was that he would be unable to read the reviews, because by then, still racing the calendar, he would be a prisoner of war in another part of Africa.

Back in England he was all business. In Rotherhithe, Dover, and Southsea he addressed cheering Tories. 'To keep the Empire you must have the imperial spark,' he said. And: 'To keep our Empire we must have a free people, an educated and well fed people.' And: 'The great game will go on until we are come through all the peril and trial, and rule in majesty and tranquillity by merit as well as by strength over the fairest and happiest regions of the world in which we live.' Turning a room at 35A Great Cumberland Place into a study, he started the new book; then, taking a break, he finished his novel, *Savrola*, and sent the completed manuscript to his grandmother for comment. Duchess Fanny thought it had 'much merit and originality,' but she noted shrewdly that the character based on Jennie 'is a weak and uninteresting personality. It is clear you have not yet attained a knowledge of Women – and it is evident you have (I am thankful to see) no experience of Love!'[101]

Pamela Plowden could have told her that. As the daughter of Sir Trevor John Chichele-Plowden and granddaughter of a general, Pamela was eminently suitable for Winston, and he had written to his mother that he thought her 'the most beautiful girl' he had 'ever seen,' but although they had been meeting and corresponding for two years now, their relationship was going nowhere. One has the feeling that Miss Plowden, like Eliza Doolittle, was ready for action and was becoming exasperated as she got only words, words, words. She as much as told him so. He admitted it and promised to 'try and take your advice,' telling her that he had met a girl 'nearly as clever & wise as you,' which meant 'I rank her one above Plato.' Pamela, who plainly did not relish a comparison with Plato, at least not in this situation, accused him of lacking ardour, thus offering him a classic opening. But Winston was merely wounded: 'Why do you say I am incapable of affection? Perish the thought. I love one above all others. And I shall be constant. I am no fickle gallant capriciously following the fancy of the hour. My love is deep and strong. Nothing will ever change it.'[102]

In a sense this was true, but the object of his designs was not the marriage bed but political office. Pamela can scarcely be blamed if she found this unflattering. In retrospect Winston appears to have been a very eligible bachelor. Yet vaunting ambition can be unattractive in a young man. It can even be unpleasant for him. In a revealing note, Churchill wrote that though tempted, 'I have no right to dally in the pleasant valleys of amusement.' Then, in gnawing terror: 'What an awful thing it will be if I don't come off. It will break my heart for I have nothing else but ambition to cling to.' So he turned from arms which would have welcomed him and sought hands that could help him up. He lunched at the Carlton Club with rising Tories of his generation: Ian Malcolm, Lord Hugh Cecil, Lord Percy, and Lord Balcarres. The discussion was sharper and far more clever than anything he had heard in his regimental mess; he felt like an 'earthen pot among the brass' and considered attending Oxford or Cambridge – until he learned he must first pass examinations in Latin and Greek. Then he discovered that companions at the Tory club possessed another political asset he lacked. They were rich. At Conservative party headquarters Fitzroy Stewart introduced him to Richard Middleton, 'the Skipper,' or party manager. Middleton greeted him warmly.

He said the party would certainly find him a seat, and soon. Then he delicately raised the question of money. How much could Churchill pay for a constituency? Winston, taken aback, replied that he could meet his campaign expenses and no more. The Skipper grew distant. Safe seats, he said, cost MPs as much as £1,000 a year; 'forlorn hopes' were cheap, but few were free. Churchill had already decided that he could not afford to serve HRH's mother as an army officer – 'Her Majesty was so stinted by Parliament,' he later said, 'that she was not able to pay even a living wage' – and this strengthened his resolve. His pen had already brought him five times as much as his soldier's salary. His Sudan dispatches alone had produced £300. Now the *Pioneer* was offering him £3 a week for letters from London. That in itself would be more than the income of a subaltern. As he wrote to Duchess Fanny: 'I can live cheaper & earn more as a writer, special correspondent or journalist: and this work is moreover more congenial and more likely to assist me in pursuing the larger ends of life.'[103]

He would have quit the army then, while his *Morning Post* pieces were still the talk of Fleet Street, had it not been for India's annual Inter-Regimental Tournament, now imminent. It may seem strange that a young man afire with ambition should journey halfway around the world to play a game, but to Churchill polo was 'the emperor of games,' almost a religion. So he sailed the first week in December aboard the SS *Osiris* and rejoined the Fourth Hussars just before Christmas. The trip north from Bangalore to the tournament ground at Meerut was another fourteen hundred miles by special train, with a two-week pause spent as guests of Sir Pertab Singh, regent of Jodhpur. They practised there with local players, though it was eerie; the field was constantly enveloped in clouds of red dust, through which turbaned figures galloped at full speed, following the ball by the sound of its whistle. Then, the night before they were to leave for Meerut, calamity befell them. Churchill slipped on a stone staircase, and out went his shoulder. The team was dismayed. He was their No. 1. They had brought along an extra player, and he suggested a substitution, but they voted to keep him in, his elbow bound to his side. The weather was fine, the crowd huge, and their opponents, in the final, the formidable Fourth Dragoon Guards. In a close, furious match, the Fourth Hussars won the cup, 4–3. And Churchill, despite his disability, was the star. He wrote to his mother from Calcutta on March 3: 'I hit three goals out of four in the winning match so that my journey to India was not futile as far as the regiment was concerned.'[104]

After a week in Calcutta as the guest of the new viceroy (the vicereine, Lady Curzon, wrote to Jennie, 'People in India have an immense opinion of Winston & his book'), he returned to Bangalore, forwarded his resignation papers to London, and sat misty-eyed while his fellow officers drank his health for the last time. 'Discipline and comradeship' were the lessons he had learned in the regiment, he wrote, and 'perhaps after all they are just as valuable as the lore of the universities. Still,' he added, 'one would like to have both.' His university continued to be his books – he could now read at great speed – and his writing had become his livelihood. *Macmillan's Magazine* was paying a hundred pounds for serial rights to *Savrola*. For *The River War*, as he now called his new manuscript, he had even greater expectations. He had worked on it during the voyage over, in Jodhpur, in Meerut, and Calcutta; he continued writing it in Bangalore and on the trip home. To his mother he wrote that he was at it 'all day & every day . . . My hand gets so cramped. I am writing every word twice & some parts three times. It ought to be good since it is the best I can do.'[105]

He was still learning. Macaulay was the real architect of *The River War*, and the balanced and ironical apothegms which appeared from time to time were borrowed from Gibbon. But his own style was nearly formed now. It was evident, not only on paper, but also in conversation, a fact noted during his trip homeward by a fellow passenger, the gifted G.W. Steevens of the *Daily Mail*. When they docked, Steevens filed a story about him, prophesying that he might become 'a great popular leader, a great journalist, or the founder of a great advertising business.' He said Churchill was 'born a demagogue, and he happens to know it. The master strain in his character is the rhetorician. Platform speeches and leading articles flow from him almost against his will. At dinner he talks and talks, and you can hardly tell when he leaves off quoting his one idol, Macaulay, and begins his other, Winston Churchill . . . We shall hear more about this in the course of ten years . . . At the rate he goes there will hardly be room for him in Parliament at thirty or in England at forty.'[106]

Kitchener tried to see to it that there was hardly room for him in Cairo, where he broke his journey to deepen his research on the Nile. The Sirdar had forbidden Major James Watson, his aide-de-camp in the Sudan, to furnish Churchill with any documents. Winston solved the problem, as many another writer has, by simply interviewing Watson. He also lunched with Lord Cromer, who 'afterwards did me the honour of talking to me about the Soudan, its past and its future with reference to my book for more than two hours and a half.' Cromer saw him twice more, provided him with letters of introduction to everyone of importance in Egypt, and introduced him to the khedive. Winston's letter to Jennie written at Cairo's Savoy Hotel immediately afterwards serves as a vintage example of the British contempt which outraged the Empire's darker subjects. 'I was much amused,' he told her, 'by observing the relations between the British Agent and the *de jure* Ruler of Egypt. The Khedive's attitude reminded me of a school-boy who is brought to see another school-boy in the presence of the head-master. But he seemed to me to be an amiable young man who tries to take an intelligent interest in the affairs of his kingdom, which, since they have passed entirely beyond his control is, to say the least, very praiseworthy.'[107]

He finished the manuscript – now destined to be two fat volumes, running, with maps, to nearly a thousand pages – in Great Cumberland Place. On May 3, 1899, he noted: 'Miss P. has been vy much impressed with the Proofs of the first two chapters of *The River War*.' Pamela was still trying. Jennie, on the other hand, was busy pursuing literary ambitions of her own, launching a competitor to *Yellow Book* called the *Anglo-Saxon Review*, which, at a price of five dollars in the United States and a guinea in England, was destined to last eleven issues before she ran out of money. Winston's own finances were unchanged. He had high and, as it turned out, justifiable hopes for his new work, but nothing in hand except the *Macmillan's* cheque. Nevertheless, he was determined to stand for office now. He would, of course, run as a Conservative. It didn't matter that Gibbon had been a protégé of a renegade Tory and Macaulay a Whig, a precursor of the Liberals, or that all the indignation over Kitchener's profanation of the Mahdi's remains lay on the Liberal side of the House of Commons, while the Conservatives, as he noted from the Strangers' Gallery, seemed to think it 'rather a lark.' The explanation, of course, is that to desert the Tories would have been to betray his father's memory. He couldn't do that, at least not in 1899.[108]

The constituency chosen for him was Oldham, a working-class district in Lancashire, and the chooser, at the outset, was Robert Ascroft, one of the two Tory MPs who represented it. Ascroft wanted Churchill to run with him. Suddenly he died. Oldham's other MP resigned. That called for a double by-election. The Skipper expected to lose both seats, hoping he would win them back on the rebound in the next general election, and he picked Winston and a radical Conservative for the sacrifice. Winston knew how small his chances were, but reasoned that any fight was better than none. On June 20 he wrote to Miss Plowden: 'I have just returned from Oldham overnight. The whole thing is in my hands as far as the Tory Party there go.' He wanted her to campaign with him. She refused; reading proofs was one thing, sweaty politics quite another. She sent him encouragement, a charm, and word that she would remain in London. In his reply he said he understood; 'it would perhaps have been a mistake – but I shall be sorry nevertheless.' He was still drawn to her, and kept her posted with bulletins on his progress. His left tonsil became inflamed; Dr Roose, ever reliable, put a throat spray in the mail. On June 28 Winston wrote that 'the big meeting was a great success and although I spoke for fifty minutes my throat is no worse – but rather better. We are now in the middle of the fight.' Four days later he reported, 'A vy busy week has closed. I now make speeches involuntarily. Yesterday I delivered no fewer than eight.' He felt he was improving: 'At each meeting I am conscious of growing powers and facilities of speech, and it is in this that I shall find my consolation should the result be, as is probable, unfortunate. But I still wear your charm – so who can tell. Write to me Pamela – I have had you in my mind more perhaps this week than ever.' The London papers had predicted his defeat. He didn't doubt it, or resent it; 'after all,' he told her, 'the battle in the end must be to the strong.'[109]

This Nietzschean sloganeering, though in high favour at the time – Winston was actually quoting John Davidson, a popular poet of the 1890s – begs the question. The fact is that while he spoke well, he was not yet a competent politician. Disraeli had warned Conservatives never to neglect social issues when soliciting blue-collar votes; so, in fact, had Lord Randolph Churchill. Winston was addressing undernourished, underpaid textile workmen, most of whom still wore wooden clogs. He told them: 'Never before were there so many people in England, and never before have they had so much to eat.' He praised the status quo, the Conservatives, Irish policy, 'pride in our Empire,' and 'love for the ancient traditions of the realm.' Although he also urged provisions for the poor – Woom was not forgotten – he was vulnerable to the charge that he represented the vested interests, despite the fact that both Liberal candidates were wealthy men. He even ran afoul of his own party. Salisbury had introduced a bill increasing government support of the Anglican church. Three days before the election Churchill announced that, if elected, he would vote against it. His words were flung at the embarrassed Tories in Parliament. Arthur Balfour, the Conservative leader in the Commons – 'the divine Arthur' of the fashionable Panshanger set – said, 'I thought he was a young man of promise, but it appears he is a young man of promises.'[110]

To Winston's delight, his mother appeared on polling day, 'dressed entirely in blue,' according to a newspaperman, '. . . in a landau and pair with gaily ribboned and rosetted postillions.' Pamela Plowden might recoil from electioneering, but for Jennie it evoked memories of the early years of her marriage. Nevertheless, Winston lost. She was at his side when the returns came in. The Liberals had taken both seats; his margin of defeat was 1,293 votes out of 48,672 cast. The *Manchester Courier* reported that Churchill 'looked upon the process of counting with amusement, and the result of the election did not disturb him. He might have been defeated, but he was conscious that in this fight he had not been disgraced.' He had, however, been wounded. Tory newspapers concluded that it had been a mistake to field a green youth in a working-class district. Word reached him that in the Carlton Club members were shaking their heads over the fact that he had run in tandem with a radical: 'Serves him right for standing with a Socialist. No man of any principle would have done such a thing!' He later wrote dryly: 'Everyone threw the blame on me. I have noticed that they nearly always do. I suppose it is because they think I shall be able to bear it best . . . I returned to London with those feelings of deflation which a bottle of champagne or even soda-water represents when it has been half emptied and left uncorked for the night. No one came to see me on my return to my mother's house.'[111]

He did, however, receive a letter. It was from Balfour, who regretted his slight and was now 'very sorry to hear of your ill success at Oldham, as I had greatly hoped to see you speedily in the House where your father and I fought many a good battle side by side in days gone by. I hope however you will not be discouraged . . . This small reverse will have no permanent ill effect upon your political fortunes.' And later in July, Lady Jeune brought Churchill and Joe Chamberlain together in her home on the Thames. They talked of South Africa. Now secretary of state for the colonies, 'Pushful Joe' was negotiating the government's growing dispute with the Boers, the Dutch farmers in South

Africa. At one point he offered Winston a bit of political advice. He told him: 'It's no use blowing the trumpet for the charge and then looking around to find nobody following.'[112]

Chamberlain and Sir Alfred Milner, the British high commissioner in Cape Town, were preparing to blow the trumpet for a showdown with South Africa's Boers, and they wanted the backing of all England. Over the next two months, while Churchill was making his final changes in *The River War*, they carefully built it. By the end of September hostilities were imminent. Obviously Winston would go as a war correspondent. Harmsworth's *Daily Mail* and Borthwick's *Morning Post* were bidding for him, but in the end he stayed with Borthwick, who offered him unprecedented terms: expenses, protection of his copyright, and £250 a month. He wired news of his coming departure to Chamberlain, who replied from Birmingham on October 4: 'I have your telegraph & will write to Milner tonight asking his good offices for the son of my old friend . . . I shall be in London on Monday but I gather that you leave before then. If so good luck & best wishes!' In fact, Milner was to receive two letters recommending Winston; Chamberlain's, which was tepid ('He has the reputation of being bumptious. Put him on the right lines.'), and a warmer one from George Wyndham, the under secretary of state for war: 'He is a very clever fellow & is bringing out an unprejudiced mind.'[113] mind.'[113]

Actually, Winston wasn't due to sail until Saturday, so he saw Chamberlain once more. The autocratic colonial secretary invited him to share his morning hansom ride from the Chamberlain house at Prince's Gardens to Parliament. That morning he was the very quiddity of Joe, 'Joe the Brummagem screw-maker,' the self-made manufacturer from the Midlands: the diamond pin in his stock, the homegrown orchid in his buttonhole, his monocle in his eye, and, with the inevitable cigar in his teeth, as calm and self-assured as a slab of his Birmingham steel. 'Buller,' he said of General Sir Redvers Buller, the new commander in chief for South Africa, who was still in England, 'would have been wiser to have gone out earlier. Now, if the Boers invade Natal, Sir George White with his 16,000 men may easily settle the whole thing.' Sir George was in Ladysmith, which, with Kimberley and Mafeking, was regarded as one of the three keys to English defence. Churchill asked about Mafeking, close to the border. 'Ah, Mafeking, that may be besieged,' Chamberlain said airily, 'but if they cannot hold out for a few weeks, what is one to expect?' He added prudently, 'Of course, I have to base myself on the War Office opinion. They are all quite confident. I can only go by what they say.'[114]

On Thursday, when the first Boer shots were fired at Kraajpan, Churchill was packing his black tin steamer trunks with Thomas Walden, who had been Lord Randolph's valet and was now his son's. Winston had just submitted his first expense account, for £30 18s. 6d. Clearly he had no intention of living a Spartan life at the front. In addition to a compass, a new saddle fitted with a pigskin case, and his Ross telescope and Voigtlander field glass, repaired at Borthwick's expense, he was taking thirty bottles of 1887 Vin d'Ay Sec, eighteen bottles of St Emilion, eighteen of ten-year-old scotch, a dozen bottles of Rose's Cordial Lime Juice, six bottles of light port, six of French vermouth, and six of Very Old Eau de Vie 1866.* Every evening that week he attended a dinner party in his honour. Since the election he had been trying, without much success, to grow a guardsman's moustache, and his touchiness about it inspired what may have been the first faint flash of Churchillian wit in London society. A friend of Jennie's, seated next to him at one of the dinners, told him she liked neither his politics nor his moustache. He replied, 'Madame, I see no earthly reason why you should come in contact with either.'[115]

The Royal Mail steamer *Dunottar Castle* was to sail at 6:00 P.M. Saturday, October 14, 1899, from Southampton docks. Churchill arrived early, jaunty in a yachting cap, but the huge crowd, perched on roofs and cranes, hadn't gathered for him. It was there to cheer his most distinguished fellow passenger, Buller, and Buller's staff. A fleet of civilian liners would follow with forty-seven thousand volunteers, but Sir Redvers was the man of the hour. The general's special train arrived at the wharf two hours before the *Castle* weighed anchor. Everyone was ready to follow Chamberlain's trumpet now. The throng sang 'Rule Britannia,' 'For He's a Jolly Good Fellow,' and 'God Save the Queen.' Men shouted, 'Remember Majuba!' 'Pull old Krojer's whiskers!' and 'Give it to the Boers!' The ship's foghorn blew. A pioneer newsreel cameraman from the Biograph Company cranked his camera. From the head of the gangplank Sir Redvers thanked everyone and said he hoped he would not be away long. His hope was to be dashed. So were their hopes in him.

Eight years earlier Lord Randolph, during his own trip to South Africa for the *Daily Graphic*, had acquired five thousand shares in Rand Mines. They had been sold to cover his debts, but had he held them their value would have been increased by twenty times at his death, and, shortly thereafter, by fifty or sixty times. That was the key to the Boer issue. After Majuba, Gladstone had negotiated the London treaty of 1884, which had granted limited self-government to the two Boer republics, the Transvaal and the Orange Free State; the two South African colonies, Natal and Cape Colony, were to remain British. Then gold had been discovered in the Transvaal – diamonds had already been found near Kimberley – and Empire builders like Cecil Rhodes wanted the Transvaal and the Orange Free State back. At that time the world's monetary systems, chiefly British, were dependent on gold. The Empire builders thought they saw a way to regain power over the Boer lands. The gold rush of the 1880s had brought the Transvaal a tremendous influx of Englishmen, or Uitlanders ('Outlanders' – foreigners), as the Boers called them: so many that by the mid-1890s they probably formed a majority of the

---

* This seems extraordinary today. It was less remarkable then. In the Sudan campaign Major Haig's personal pack train had included 'one camel, laden with claret.'

243

republic's inhabitants. To British imperialists they seemed exploitable.

President Paul Kruger – 'Oom Paul,' that strong Brueghel peasant whom Chamberlain had called an 'ignorant, dirty, cunning' old man – was uncowed. He refused to give these British immigrants the vote. That was what the Jameson Raid had been all about; the raiders had hoped to spark an uprising by the English settlers. Badly planned, the plot had failed. Nevertheless, Rhodes and Chamberlain, who had been implicated in it, were determined to answer the Uitlanders' *cri de coeur*. The fact that this was a violation of the 1884 pact, in which the British had agreed not to intervene in the Transvaal's domestic affairs, was ignored. Imperialists continued to speak ominously of 'consolidating the Empire.' On the eve of the first Boer crisis Gladstone had warned against 'the fascinations of passion and of pride,' but his voice had been stilled in 1898. Thousands of young Englishmen agreed with the more strident advocates of expansion; in India, Churchill had written: 'Imperial aid

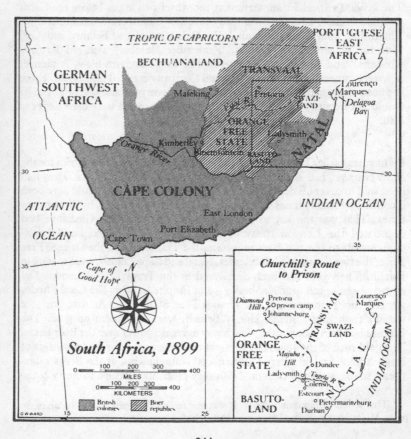

South Africa, 1899

must redress the wrongs of the Outlanders. Imperial troops must curb the insolence of the Boers.' He thought the issue was the persecution of his countrymen, not gold. Chamberlain himself regretted that there was 'too much of "money-bags" about the whole business.' Still, he and Milner kept nagging Oom Paul in Pretoria. The Boers refused their demands, and when the British began pouring reinforcements into Cape Colony and Natal, became alarmed. Unless the Afrikaners struck back, they realized, their forces would soon be outnumbered. Kruger, who understood the impact of technology on warfare, decided to put his faith in 'God and the Mauser' – the Mauser, his Krupp howitzers and 75-millimetre field guns from the Ruhr, his 155-millimetre 'Long Toms' from Schneider-Creusot in France, and, from Britain itself, his Maxim 'pom-poms.' He issued an ultimatum. If Chamberlain didn't stop his troop buildup, the Transvaal would fight. On October 11, 1899, three days before the *Dunottar Castle* sailed, the ultimatum expired and the war began.[116]

At the last minute the Orange Free State Boers had thrown in their lot with their Transvaal brothers. The British were surprised, but undaunted. Supremely self-confident, they were sure it would all be over by Christmas. *The Times* thought the ultimatum an 'infatuated step' by a 'petty republic,' the *Globe* was irked by this 'trumpery little state' and its 'impudent burghers,' the *Daily Telegraph* was 'in doubt whether to laugh or weep.' Since Victoria's coronation two generations earlier, her subjects had been swaggering down the highways of the world, fighting short, relatively bloodless colonial wars at almost no cost; the army had fought only two engagements since the Indian Mutiny of 1857 in which more than a hundred men had been lost. The rewards for this insignificant sacrifice had been immense; Rosebery had told an Edinburgh audience that during the past twelve years 2,600,000 square miles had been added to the Empire, chiefly in Africa. That might be called the end of the red-coat era. Now, at the end of the 1890s, the army was about to fight its first big conflict in its new khaki uniforms. Churchill and the *Dunottar Castle* were heading for the last of the Victorian wars, England's costliest struggle between Waterloo and Sarajevo, which would drain the Empire of half a million men and bring down upon London the opprobrium of the civilized world. 'If there was a good case for the Boer War,' Margot Asquith would later write in her diary, 'it was indifferently put, and I doubt if a single nation understood it.' The war was about to give England, in Kipling's phrase, 'no end of a lesson.'[117]

Plunging through high seas and what Churchill called 'grey storms' – as usual he was ill – the *Dunottar Castle* lurched towards the Canary Islands. Cut off from the world, they endured more than two weeks of what Winston called a 'heavy silence'; it was, he wrote to his mother, 'a long time in war, especially in the beginning.' At Madeira they learned nothing, which was 'very hard to understand. Why did they declare war if they had nothing up their sleeves? Why do they waste time now?' On their sixteenth day they passed a tramp steamer, the *Australian*, whose crew held aloft a crude white-on-black sign:

They took this to mean that the enemy had been routed in three engagements, though the loss of Symonds, a Natal general, was difficult to reconcile with victory. Winston heard an aide tell Buller, 'It looks as if it will be over, sir.' Sir Redvers replied, 'I dare say there will be enough left to give us a fight outside Pretoria.' The soundness of this military judgement was confirmed when, two days later, on October 31, they anchored in Table Bay and a launch sped out bearing, in Winston's words, a 'Man Who Knew.' All the tidings were grim. Mafeking and Kimberley were surrounded by Boers – had been, in fact, since the *Dunottar Castle* left Southampton. After Symonds's death General Sir George White had begun retreating into Ladysmith, which was itself threatened with encirclement. The enemy had been defeated nowhere. So much for the reliability of tramp steamers as news media. Ashore, Winston interviewed a distraught Milner and sent off a report: 'We have greatly underestimated the military strength and spirit of the Boers. I vy much doubt whether one army Corps will be enough to overcome their resistance.' Moreover, Kruger wasn't the only man with troublesome immigrants. Milner had told Winston that the Boers who lived here in Cape Colony under the Union Jack were 'trembling on the verge of rebellion.' Winston concluded that the British government could, 'for the moment, be sure of nothing beyond the gunshot of the Navy.'[119]

Buller intended to remain in Cape Town, pondering his choices and awaiting the arrival of his troop transports. At home, Salisbury was telling a Guildhall audience that his confidence in the British soldier 'is only equalled by my confidence in Sir Redvers Buller.' Churchill wasn't so sure. The general struck him as the kind of man who plodded 'on from blunder to blunder and from one disaster to another.' It was, Winston felt, time to leave him. During the voyage he and J.B. Atkins of the *Manchester Guardian* had agreed to knit their fortunes; now they decided to reach Ladysmith before the enemy slammed the door. On inquiry at the Mount Nelson Hotel they learned that by taking a train to East London, seven hundred miles away, and continuing by small mail boat or tug to Durban, they could beat other correspondents to the front by four days. It would be risky; the railroad skirted Boer strongpoints and was undefended. They caught the last express to get through safely and reached Durban, but the sea leg was an ordeal. Their ship, a steamer of about 150 tons, had to fight its way through a howling Antarctic gale. Between waves Winston could see 'rocks which showed their black teeth endlessly a bare mile away upon our port beam.' The seasickness, however, was far worse. He lay in his bunk 'in an extreme of physical misery while our tiny ship bounded and reeled, and kicked and pitched, and fell and turned almost over and righted itself again . . . through an endless afternoon, a still longer evening and an eternal night.'[120]

Arriving at midnight, they slept six hours and awoke only to be told that they were too late; Ladysmith was invested. The disappointment was deep, but they resolved to get as close to it as possible. Another train, zigzagging up and down hills and negotiating hairpin curves, took them sixty miles to Pietermaritzburg and on to Estcourt, a town of about three hundred stone-walled houses roofed with corrugated iron. Estcourt was the end of the line. They could hear the Ladysmith cannonade from there. While his valet pitched his tent, Winston uncapped his pen and began to write. All along the way he had been interviewing everyone who had fought or seen the Boers, beginning, in Durban, with Reggie Barnes, his companion in Cuba and polo teammate later. Barnes had been wounded in the groin storming a hill at Elandslaagte; his colonel had fallen beside him; sixty-seven of their men had been killed or wounded in the assault. He had said: 'All these colonials tell you that the Boers only want one good thrashing to satisfy them. Don't you believe it. They mean going through with this to the end.' Again, Churchill's instincts told him Barnes was right. They betrayed him, however, when he talked to Uitlander refugees. On November 5 he reported 'the fullest confirmation of the horrible barbarities perpetrated by the Boers,' telling of a woman who had been flogged across the breasts and commenting: 'Such is the Boer – gross, fierce, and horrid – doing the deeds of the devil with the name of the Lord on his lips. It is quite true that he is brave, but so are many savage tribes.'[121]

One is struck, in reading Churchill's accounts from the South African battlefields, by the frequency with which he encountered old friends and acquaintances. Barnes was one. Ian Hamilton commanded troops nearby. Brabazon, back in uniform, was on his way. Leo Amery, Winston's fellow Harrovian, was the *Times* correspondent in Estcourt, and among the officers there was Captain Aylmer Haldane, whom he had known in India. On the night of November 14 the captain was ordered by his commanding officer, Colonel Charles Long, to lead two companies aboard an armoured train and probe the Boer lines. As he later wrote in his memoirs, he was leaving headquarters when he noticed Churchill 'hanging about to pick up such crumbs of information for his newspaper as might be available.' Haldane described his mission to Winston and 'suggested that he might care to accompany me next day. Although he was not at all keen he consented to do so, and arranged to be at the station in time for the start.'[122]

Churchill's lack of enthusiasm was sensible. Buller, when he heard of Long's decision, called it 'inconceivable stupidity.' Winston had already described the armoured train. It was 'cloaked from end to end with thick plates and slabs of blue-grey iron.' Slits permitted soldiers aboard to fire out. It looked formidable but was, as Thomas Pakenham puts it, 'a parody of modern mobile war: an innovation that was already obsolete.' All the Boers had to do was blow up a bridge or sabotage the rails; the locomotive would then be immobile and helpless. Winston should have turned Haldane down. He didn't, he wrote afterwards, 'because I thought it was my duty to gather as much information as I could for the *Morning Post*' and he was 'eager for trouble.' On those grounds it was justified. The trip would produce plenty of news and danger. It would do more; before the adventure was over, his name would be a household word throughout England. Although it almost cost him his life the decision was, by the light of his flaming ambition, well worth the risk. He would have but one regret. Only yesterday he had posted a letter to the War Office in London, and before he saw another sunset he would wish he had left it unmailed. He had written: 'There has been a great deal too much surrendering in this war, and I hope people who do so will not be encouraged.'[123]

Louis Botha, the swarthy Boer general besieging Ladysmith, overestimated the number of British troops in Estcourt. Apprehensive that they might be preparing to break his grip on the town, Botha, on the day Churchill agreed to join Haldane, led a column of five hundred mounted raiders southward to investigate, and the next morning, standing in his stirrups atop a ridge, he sighted the armoured train steaming north. After the lumbering monstrosity had passed, he ordered rocks strewn on the rails just around a curve and then awaited its return. As the engine reappeared, headed back towards the British lines, his gunner fired two shells at it. Peering out from inside his car, or truck, as they were called, Churchill had just spotted a clump of Boers on a nearby knoll. At that instant he was dazzled by a flash of light and jarred by the sound of steel fragments rattling on the train's iron shield: 'It was shrapnel,' he later wrote – 'the first I had seen in war.' He thought the train might be headed into a trap and turned to Haldane to say so. Simultaneously the engineer up ahead, frightened by the shells, rocketed around the curve at full throttle and crashed into the rocks. Before Churchill could speak 'there was a tremendous shock, and [Captain Haldane] and I and all the soldiers in the truck were pitched head over heels on to its floor.'[124]

Scrambling up, Winston saw scores of Boers lying on the grass outside, delivering heavy and accurate rifle fire upon one side of the train. He and Haldane ducked and put their heads together. The captain, they agreed, should move to the rear and order his troops to pin down the Boer riflemen while Churchill inspected the damage and tried to repair it. Winston found the locomotive still on the rails. The next three cars had been derailed, however, and the civilian engineer, bleeding from a superficial face wound, was on the verge of hysteria. Churchill lectured him on duty. Then he congratulated him. This, he told him, was the chance of a lifetime. He might even be rewarded for 'distinguished gallantry.' Besides, he assured him, no man could be hit twice in one battle. This absurd fiction quieted the driver and they went to work.

It was the subsequent recollection of all the survivors, including the Boers, that Winston was under intermittent fire for the next seventy minutes. He himself would remember the 'soft kisses' of bullets as they 'sucked in the air' around him, but he was completely engrossed in 'the heat and excitement of the work'; his choice, he felt, lay between 'danger, captivity and shame on the one hand, and safety, freedom and triumph on the other.' It was just possible, he thought, that the engine could be used as a ram to clear the wrecked cars from the line. He darted back and forth, straining at car couplings, conferring with Haldane, and calling for volunteers from the troops in the cars behind. Few responded. His own conduct is best described in Haldane's official report, written after he and Winston had fallen out. The captain noted that 'owing to the urgency of the circumstances,' he formally placed Churchill on duty. He added: 'I would point out that while engaged on the work of saving the engine, for which he was mainly responsible, he was frequently exposed to the full fire of the enemy. I cannot speak too highly of his gallant conduct.' As a good valet, Walden was on the spot. Afterwards he wrote to Jennie: 'the driver was one of the first wounded, and he said to Mr Winston: "I am finished." So Mr Winston said to him: "Buck up a bit, I will stick to you," and he threw off his revolver and field-glasses and helped the driver . . . knock the iron trucks off the road by running into them with the engine.'[125]

It proved impossible to link the locomotive and the rear cars. Yet the situation wasn't entirely hopeless. Just ahead lay a railroad trestle and, beyond that, safety. Churchill herded Walden and forty Tommies, many of them wounded, aboard the engine and its tender, and took up a position behind the engineer until they had crossed the bridge. There he left them. He was returning to Haldane, on foot, trying to think how he might bring more men out, when two men in mufti arose from the bushes beside the tracks, 'tall figures,' he would later remember, 'full of energy, clad in dark, flapping clothes, with slouch, storm-driven hats, poising on their levelled rifles hardly a hundred yards away.' His mind flashed: 'Boers!' He tried to climb the railroad embankment; they fired and missed. Next he turned to dash back to the bridge. A Boer horseman came galloping from that direction, shaking a rifle and shouting. Churchill decided to kill him. He reached for his pistol – and realized that he had left it on the locomotive. The horseman – it was Botha himself – now had him in his sights. Winston remembered a quotation from Napoleon: 'When one is alone and unarmed, a surrender may be pardoned.' He raised his hands and stepped forward, a prisoner of war.[126]

He was prodded towards Haldane and the cowering British troops, who had already been rounded up. Churchill blurted out to Atkins when next he met him that the soldiers had indeed been rounded up 'like cattle,' and that this had been 'the greatest indignity of my life.' A heavy rain had begun to fall, and Churchill was drenched, wading through a patch of high grass, when 'a disquieting and timely reflection' crossed his mind. In the breast pocket of his khaki jacket were two clips of Mauser ammunition from Omdurman, politely known in army quartermaster manifests as 'MK IV and MK V issue' but notorious to the public as dumdum cartridges – soft-nosed or expanding bullets which disintegrated when they hit a man's body. Dumdums had been outlawed at the Hague Conference the previous July, and Churchill knew it. As his guard turned to open an umbrella he managed to drop one clip unseen. He had the other in his fist when the Boer, looking down from his horse, said sharply in English: 'What have you got there?' Winston opened his hand and asked, 'What is it? I just picked it up.' Botha took the clip, glanced at it, and tossed it in the grass. It is sad to note that the following March 9 Churchill indignantly informed his *Morning Post* readers that the Boers were using 'expansive' bullets and piously commented that 'the character of these people reveals in stress a dark and spiteful underside. A man, I use the word in its fullest sense, does not wish to lacerate his foe, however earnestly he may desire his death.'[127]

Even without the dumdums he was anxious about his fate. He ranged himself in line with the other prisoners but was brusquely picked out by the Boers and told to stand apart. It was an ominous order. He 'had enough military law,' as he put it, 'to know that a civilian in a half uniform who has taken an active and prominent part in a fight, even if he has not fired a shot himself, is liable to be shot at once by drumhead court martial.' Then, just as curtly, he was directed to rejoin the others; an enemy officer came over and told him they knew who he was and regarded him as a prize: 'We don't catch the son of a lord every day.' Churchill, in his own phrase, felt 'quite joyful' at the realization that he would live. His euphoria lasted during the subsequent three-day trek north, on foot sixty miles around the booming cannons pounding Ladysmith and then by train from Elandslaagte to their prisoner-of-war camp in Pretoria's State Model Schools. Once there behind wire, however, he forgot his gratitude for escaping a firing squad and he convinced himself that his captivity was illegal.[128]

Winston's response to imprisonment tells a great deal about him. He felt disgust, despair, rage. This is not a universal reaction to restraint. Many public men have adjusted to it without great difficulty; it has served as a temporary refuge for them, a place for reflection, study, and writing. Mohandas Gandhi, now toiling in South Africa as a leader of Indian stretcher-bearers, would later flourish in British prisons. But not Churchill. He found, he wrote, 'no comfort in any of the philosophical ideas which some men parade in their hours of ease and strength and safety.' His wrath and tremendous frustration probably arose from his depressive nature. He needed outer stimuli, the chances for excitement and achievement which were his lifelong defences against melancholia. The prisoner-of-war camp was like being back in the harness of school. It was worse; their long tin POW dormitory was enclosed by a ten-foot corrugated iron fence rimmed by barbed wire, watched by armed guards fifty yards apart, and brilliantly illuminated at night by searchlights on tall standards. Elsewhere the war continued, great events were in progress, but here he was penned in, entirely in the power of the Boers. He owed his life to their mercy, his daily bread to their compassion, his movements to their indulgence. In this atmosphere he found himself picking quarrels with other British officer inmates over trivial matters – he couldn't tolerate their whistling – and took no pleasure from their company. He felt, he wrote, 'webbed about with a tangle of regulations and restrictions. I certainly hated every minute of my captivity more than I have ever hated any other period in my whole life.'[129]

At the end of his first week behind wire he wrote to the Transvaal authorities, demanding his release as 'a non-combatant and a Press correspondent.' He argued disingenuously that he had taken 'no part in the defence of the armoured train,' had been 'quite unarmed,' and had merely done 'all I could to escape from so perilous a situation and to save my life.' Unfortunately, his fellow war correspondents had interviewed survivors of the wreck, and British newspapers were reporting details of his audacity under fire; the Natal *Witness* of November 17 had carried a statement by the railwaymen expressing their 'admiration of the coolness and pluck displayed by Mr Winston Churchill . . . who accompanied the train, and to whose efforts . . . is due the fact that the armoured train and tender were brought successfully out.' Churchill, it was reported, was being considered for the Victoria Cross. Under these circumstances, the Kruger government endorsed the recommendation of their commandant-general, Piet Joubert, who, upon hearing of. his application, urged that he be 'guarded and watched as dangerous for our war; otherwise he can still do us a lot of harm. In a word, he must not be released during the war. It is through his active part that one section of the armoured train got away.' Winston protested that because he was well known the world would regard him 'as a kind of hostage' and that this would 'excite criticism and even ridicule.' If given his freedom, he said, he would 'withdraw altogether from South Africa during the war.' The Boers were unimpressed. He wrote to his mother and the Prince of Wales, begging for help. They could do nothing. In a darker mood he wrote to Pamela ('Not a vy satisfactory address to write from – although it begins with P. . . I write you this line to tell you that among new and vivid scenes I think often of you') and, on November 30, to Bourke Cockran: 'I am 25 today – it is terrible to think how little time remains!'[130]

His weeks in prison would have been limited, whatever happened. Somehow, one feels, powerful friends of Jennie's, HRH's, or even Cockran's found a way to intervene successfully on his behalf. There is simply no other explanation for the extraordinary judgement Joubert rendered on December 12, completely reversing himself. Pondering Winston's denial that he played an active role in the events which followed the train wreck, and having decided (he didn't say why) that he was an honourable English gentleman and could therefore be only truthful, the commandant-general wrote: 'I have to accept his word in preference to all the journalists and reporters.' Their accounts, he said, must have been 'exaggerated.' He therefore concluded: 'I have no further objections to his being set free.'[131]

Had it ended there, the incident would have had little effect on Churchill's political fortunes at home. But before this order could reach the POW camp, he had taken matters into his own hands. Like his lie about the wreck, the story of his breakout from Pretoria is not entirely creditable, but a special tolerance has always been extended to prisoners of war bent on freedom, and there is no reason to withhold it from him, particularly in light of the courage and imagination with which he carried out the escape plan. The plan was not, however, his. It was the brainchild of Haldane and one A. Brockie, a regimental sergeant major, who, to get better quarters, had passed himself off as

before the moon rose, Haldane and I both got into the
roundhouse and waited for a chance of climbing over; but
after much hesitation we thought it too dangerous; and
came back to the veranda. Brockie then came up and
asked us why we had not got over. Haldane explained
the difficulty of the sentry's position, and Brockie
said; "You're afraid". Haldane replied: "You can go
and see for yourself". Brockie then went across the
yard, got into the roundhouse, and remained there some
time. Then I said: "I will go back again". I went
across the yard, and at the entrance to the roundhouse
I met Brockie coming out, but we dare not speak to each

From Churchill's later version of the escape

an officer. In the back of the enclosure, shielded from the searchlights, stood a
circular toilet. The night sentry there seemed lax. Brockie spoke both
Afrikaans, developed from seventeenth-century Dutch, and the native Bantu
language. If he and Haldane could jump the wall there unobserved, he might
be able to talk their way across the countryside to Portuguese East Africa –
'Portuguese East' – and freedom. Churchill, overhearing them, insisted that
they take him with them. He would see to it, he said, that Haldane's name
appeared in headlines all over the world. Brockie didn't want him; he thought
him unpredictable and believed another fugitive would increase their risks.
But although the key to the scheme, the sergeant major was an enlisted man;
his opinion didn't count for much. Haldane, having invited Winston aboard
the train, felt a certain responsibility for his plight. He would include him, he
said, provided he 'conform to orders.'[132]

Their chances of success were slight, and were to become slighter, but
Winston, ever confident, wrote an impudent letter to the Boer under secretary
of war on Monday, December 11, and left it in his bunk. It was headed 'p.p.c.'
– *pour prendre congé* (to take furlough). 'I do not concede,' he began, 'that your
Government was justified in holding me . . . and I have consequently resolved
to escape.' Friends 'outside,' he said, were 'making this possible.' Before
leaving he wanted to 'place on record my appreciation of the kindness which
has been shown to me,' promised to 'set forth a truthful and impartial account

252

of my experiences in Pretoria,' expressed the hope that 'this most grievous and unhappy war' would end the enmity between the Boers and British 'races,' and ended: 'Regretting the circumstances have not permitted me to bid you a personal farewell, believe me, Yours vy sincerely, Winston S. Churchill.'[133]

Tuesday night, unaware of Joubert's order, which had gone out that afternoon, the three donned civilian suits acquired by barter and awaited their chance. Haldane and Churchill entered the latrine and returned, discouraged by the sentinel's unexpected vigilance. Brockie accused them of timidity, but when he went in, he, too, was thwarted. Churchill reentered alone, passing Brockie coming out. Once inside, he saw his chance – the guard had turned to light a pipe – and leaping to the top of the wall he dropped into a garden on the other side. There he crouched, awaiting the others. But they were luckless. At one moment Haldane was in the toilet, ready to jump, when the sentry stirred and levelled his rifle at him. Churchill waited for an hour and a half, then decided to go on alone. He left behind two very resentful countrymen. The idea, after all, had been theirs. Haldane was 'bitterly disappointed to find that Winston had gone,' he would later write in his memoirs, adding, 'I resist the temptation of stating what Brockie had to say on the subject.'[134] Yet it is difficult to see what else Winston could have done. A ledge on the outer side of the wall prevented him from climbing back. His prospects in any case were extremely dim. Ahead of him lay three hundred miles of wild and hostile country. He didn't know the language. He lacked a compass and a map – Brockie had those. His pockets contained seventy-five pounds in British money, four slabs of chocolate, and a few biscuits. Believing he had no other choice, he rose from the garden, making no attempt at concealment, and strode past another sentry, unchallenged, into the moonlit evening.

Pretoria was crowded with burghers. He strode right through them, humming to himself until he reached the suburbs, where he sat on a little bridge to reflect. At dawn he would be missed; pursuit would be immediate. At any rate he was free, 'if only for an hour.' Wandering about, he found a railroad track and followed it to the nearest station. There he waited in a ditch until the next train arrived. It paused five minutes and started moving again. He had no idea where it was going, but it offered the only way out of town. As the locomotive passed him he saw the engineer 'silhouetted against the furnace,' the 'black profile of the engine,' and 'clouds of steam.' His moment was now. Twice he hurled himself at cars and fell back; on the third try he found a handhold and vaulted into a mass of empty coal bags. Burrowing into them, he fell asleep.[135]

The sky was still dark when he awoke. Remaining aboard till daybreak was out of the question; his presence would be betrayed when the bags were unloaded. He had to alight quickly, find water, and hide, awaiting the return of night and another train. Springing from the speeding car, he took two gigantic strides and sprawled in a shallow trench. Then, finding a pool in a nearby gully, he forced himself to drink all he could hold because he had no way of knowing when he would find more. Dawn broke and he felt jubilant: the train tracks ran straight towards the sunrise and Portuguese territory.

That day was spent huddled in a ravine, nibbling at chocolate; his sole companion was 'a gigantic vulture, who manifested an extravagant interest in my condition, and made hideous and ominous gurglings from time to time.'[136] As dusk deepened he crawled out and made his way to a point where the tracks lay uphill and on a curve, reasoning that a train would slow there, permitting him to hop aboard. But no train came. Sometime after midnight, having waited six hours in vain, he struck out on foot, hoping to put ten or fifteen miles of track behind him before another day dawned. Presently he saw the flaw in this plan. Every railroad bridge was guarded by armed men. To avoid them he had to creep across the moonlit veld or detour through bogs, swamps, and streams. A station loomed. On a siding lay three long strings of freight cars. He was studying their markings, hoping to learn their destinations and then hide in one which seemed promising, when loud voices came towards him, scaring him away and driving him out into the grass of the boundless plain.

By now he was exhausted, wandering aimlessly. Out in the darkness to his left gleamed what appeared to be the fires of a Kaffir kraal, a native village. It occurred to him that the Kaffirs, who were said to be disillusioned with the Boers, might be cooperative. He spoke no Bantu tongues, but perhaps sign language would do; it had worked when he was lost in the Sudanese desert. There seemed to be no alternative, so he turned that way. As he approached the settlement, he saw he had been mistaken. It wasn't a kraal at all. The lights came from furnace fires outside several stone houses clustered around what could be identified, by the wheel of a winding gear, as a coal mine. He felt a flicker of hope. In the POW pen he had heard that a few Englishmen, needed by the Boers for their skills, had been permitted to remain in some of the Witbank and Middelburg mining districts, seventy-five miles east of Pretoria. This might be one of them. But which houses would be British, and which Boer? He would have to guess. If he picked a wrong one he would produce his bank notes, explain who he was, and promise to pay anyone who would help him another thousand pounds later. Striding out of the veld and past the furnace fires, he chose a darkened home at random and knocked. A light sprang up. A man's voice called, '*Wie is daar?*'*

Churchill's heart sank. He spoke no Afrikaans. He said, 'I want help; I have had an accident.' The door opened and he saw a tall, pale, moustachioed figure, hastily attired and holding a revolver. The man said in English, 'What do you want?' Winston improvised a story: he was a burgher en route to join his commando at Komati Poort, on the Portuguese frontier; he and some friends had been skylarking on their train; he had fallen off and dislocated his shoulder. Obviously the man didn't buy it. He stared hard, backed into the house, and roughly demanded details. Winston decided to throw in the towel. Stepping inside he said, 'I think I had better tell you the truth,' and, after his

---

* In his subsequent accounts, Churchill wrote that he had heard '*Wer ist da?*' But that is German. The above is Afrikaans.

host had nodded grimly, 'I am Winston Churchill, war correspondent for the *Morning Post*. I am making my way to the frontier' – as he said it, he reflected bitterly on how wretchedly he had done – 'and I have plenty of money. Will you help me?'[137]

A silence grew, and grew uncomfortable. The tall man continued to stare, as though struggling to make up his mind. Suddenly he closed the door behind them, thrust out his hand, and blurted: 'Thank God you have come here! It is the only house for twenty miles where you would not have been handed over. But we are all British here, and we will see you through.' Churchill sagged with relief. Wringing the man's hand he felt, as he later put it, 'like a drowning man pulled out of the water and informed he has won the Derby.' His saviour introduced himself as John Howard, manager of the Transvaal Collieries. He led the way to the kitchen, produced whisky and a leg of mutton, and explained their situation. Within were his British secretary, a mechanic from Lancaster, and two Scottish miners. All four had given the Boers their parole to observe strict neutrality. Howard himself was a Transvaal citizen; if caught harbouring an escaped prisoner, he would be shot for treason. But the prospect didn't seem to alarm him. He vanished while Winston ate, consulted the others, and returned to say that the five of them had agreed that the best course, for the time being, was to hide their fugitive in the mine. Howard led him out to the winding wheel. There, to Churchill's astonishment, the mechanic introduced himself as a prospective constituent – Dan Dewsnap of Oldham. Gripping his arm, Dewsnap whispered: 'They'll all vote for you next time.'[138]

The Scotsmen were waiting at the bottom of the shaft with a mattress and blankets. By lantern light Howard gave Winston two candles, cigars, and the whisky bottle. He warned him not to move until they returned the next night; blacks would be around during the day, and if they saw him, they would talk. Winston, weary but elated, 'saw myself once more rejoining the Army with a real exploit to my credit.' Then he had misgivings. He was putting these men in real danger. He offered to move on alone; he asked only for food, a pistol, a guide, and, if possible, a pony. He wouldn't have a chance, the departing Howard told him. Only that afternoon a Boer officer had been there, asking about him. 'They have got the hue and cry out all along the line,' he said, 'and all over the district.'[139]

Back at the camp the previous morning Churchill's absence had been discovered, his letter found. Its reference to friends 'outside' had led his guards to believe, as he had meant them to, that he had accomplices in Pretoria. Warrants were issued, houses searched; nothing was found. This being the capital of the republic, correspondents from neutral countries heard of the hunt. Then the name of the missing man leaked out. Borthwick sent Jennie word: 'Just received the following from Reuter, "Churchill escaped." ' The *Daily Telegraph* speculated: 'If Mr Churchill is caught the Boers won't let him

255

have the privileges of being a prisoner-of-war again. He cannot be shot unless he uses arms to resist capture, but he may be subjected to confinement rigorous enough to control the innate daring and resourcefulness of which he inherits his full share.' He wasn't expected to reach the frontier; within forty-eight hours two papers reported he had been seized, first at Waterval-Boven and then at Komati Poort. The Boers were certainly determined to find him. Joubert felt betrayed. He furiously wired Kruger's state secretary: 'With reference to Churchill's escape I [wonder] whether it would not be a good thing to make public the correspondence about the release of Churchill to show the world what a scoundrel he is.'[140]

Despite the *Daily Telegraph*, a newsman in Pretoria cabled that on recapture he 'may probably be shot,' and one London paper, the *Phoenix*, actually thought that reasonable, commenting that 'the Boer General cannot be blamed should he order his execution. A non-combatant has no right to carry arms. In the Franco-Prussian War all non-combatants who carried arms were promptly executed.' A.E. Brofman, the Boer deputy superintendent of police, posted notices all over the Transvaal describing the fugitive as: 'Englishman 25 years old, about 5 ft 8 in tall, average build, walks with a slight stoop, pale appearance, red brown hair, almost invisible small moustache, speaks through the nose, cannot pronounce the letter "S", cannot speak Dutch, during long conversations occasionally makes a rattling noise [*voggeld*] in his throat, was last seen in a brown suit of clothes.' Boers were asked 'to remain on the alert and in case aforementioned Churchill appears to arrest him at once.' Presses were rolling with a police photograph of him, and a price was set on his head.[141]

Brofman's quarry awoke the following afternoon, reached for the candles, and found nothing. It would be dangerous, he knew, to blunder around the shaft in the dark, so he lay still until, several hours later, a faint gleam of lantern light heralded the return of Howard, bearing a chicken and several books. The chicken, he explained, came from the home of an English physician who lived twenty miles away. It was a necessary precaution; Howard's Boer servants had been inquisitive about the missing mutton. Policemen were knocking on every door here. The presence of English residents in the mining district made it a natural focus of suspicion. But he assured Churchill he was safe. He could pass the time reading. Where, by the way, were his candles? Winston told him they had vanished. His host gave him half a dozen replacements and apologized; he should have warned him to keep them under the mattress. If left out, he explained, they would be devoured by the swarms of savage white rats in the mine.

Fortunately Churchill did not share the common revulsion for rats. During his three days in the mine they were his biggest problem, pulling at his pillow when he stored the candles beneath it, scurrying around him whenever he blew the flame out, and even wakening him from a doze by running across his face. Once the two miners came down and led him on a tour of the shaft's subterranean tunnels and galleries; Winston, ever interested in new experiences, questioned them closely about their work. But mostly he glared at rats and read. On the fourth day Howard visited him and said the manhunt seemed to be losing its momentum. The police were combing Pretoria again, convinced he could not have left the town, that a British sympathizer there must be harbouring him. He was brought up for a walk on the veld that night and then moved into new quarters behind packing cases in Howard's office. There he remained for three more days, and was frightened but once, when intermittent rifle fire broke out in the neighbourhood. A Boer police officer was in fact there, but the shots had been the result of a ruse of Howard's. To draw the man away from the house, he had challenged him to a rifle match, shooting bottles. The gullible policeman had won and left no wiser.

Howard now had an escape plan. He had recruited another plotter, Charles Burnham, a local shipping agent.* On Tuesday, December 19, Winston's seventh day of freedom, a consignment of wool was to be loaded on the mine's railroad branch and sent, via the main line at Balmoral, to Lourenço Marques in Portuguese territory. Churchill would be hidden among the bales. At first, curiously, he balked. He said he would rather cross the veld with directions and a horse. Imprisonment, he later reflected, had warped his judgement. He was reading Stevenson's *Kidnapped* at the time, identifying with David Balfour and Alan Breck in the glens. Like them, he was a victim of his need for concealment and deception, which, he later concluded, 'breeds an actual sense of guilt very undermining to morale. Feeling that at any moment the officers of the law may present themselves or any stranger may ask the questions, "Who are you?" "Where do you come from?" "Where are you going?" – to which questions no satisfactory answer could be given – gnawed at the structure of self-confidence.' He agreed to the trip but dreaded it.[142]

Tuesday dawned. Howard led him to the car, and he squeezed through a tunnel in the wool to an enclosed space among the bales large enough for him to lie and sit. On the floor were a pistol, two roast chickens, several slices of meat, bread, a melon, and three bottles of cold tea. He had memorized the names of the train stations they would pass and hoped to follow their progress through a chink in the bales. A tarpaulin was tied over the car; they rumbled off. But Winston found his chink inadequate. He saw few signs. The couplings and uncouplings of cars, the banging and jerking in freight yards, the long waits on sidings, baffled and exasperated him.

It was just as well he knew no more. Burnham had decided to accompany the train in one of the passenger cars, and before the trip was over he felt he had aged a lifetime. Churchill would never have made it without him. At Middelburg, their second stop, a trainman wanted to shunt the wool car off on a sidetrack and leave it there overnight; at Waterval-Boven a railroad agent ordered it sidetracked because of a petty regulation; an armed Boer started to untie the tarpaulin when they paused in Kaapmuiden; and when they reached

---

* Churchill was always under the impression that Burnham was 'a Dutchman' named 'Burgener.'

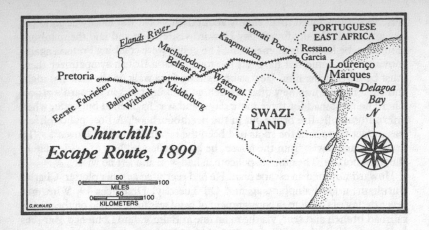

Churchill's Escape Route, 1899

MILES
50
0 ▭▭▭▭▭ 100

KILOMETERS
50
0 ▭▭▭▭▭ 100

G.W.WARD

Komanti Poort and the frontier, a detective stepped forward to search the entire train. Burnham dissuaded all of them with bribes and drinks until they had crossed the border and reached Ressano Garcia, where, for the first time, he encountered an honest man. The stationmaster, refusing his money, said the wool could not proceed with the passenger cars. The best he would do was promise it would follow within half an hour. Burnham therefore reached Lourenço first, bribed another policeman – who wanted to arrest him for 'loitering with intent' – and was waiting when his cargo arrived. According to Burnham's account in the Johannesburg *Star* twenty-four years later, 'The truck had not been stationary a minute when Churchill, black as a sweep by reason of the coal-dust which was in the bottom of the truck, sprang out.' Meanwhile, Winston, squinting through his peep-hole, had already seen a Portuguese place-name painted on a board. He was so carried away that he shoved aside the bale overhead and 'fired my revolver two or three times in the air as a *feu de joie*.'[143]

Burnham led him out of the station, around several corners, and paused. He looked up silently at the roof of a building opposite. Winston followed his gaze 'and there – blest vision! – I saw floating the gay colours of the Union Jack. It was the British Consulate.' A piece of opéra bouffe ensued. At the door a minor official took one look at his filthy clothes and snapped: 'Be off. The Consul cannot see you today. Come to his office at nine tomorrow if you want anything.' Churchill stepped back, threw back his head, and shouted at the upper storeys: 'I am Winston Bloody Churchill! Come down here at once!' An upstairs window flew open; it was the startled consul, Alexander Ross. Ross called hurried instructions to the man downstairs, and within a quarter of an hour Winston was lolling in a hot bath. In borrowed clothes he accompanied Burnham to a store, where, Burnham recalled, 'he bought a rigout and a cowboy hat.' Back at the consulate, after an enormous dinner, Churchill dispatched a sheaf of telegrams to London. At Great Cumberland Place Jennie picked up the telephone and heard a reporter shouting into the mouthpiece: 'Hurrah! Hurrah!' Miss Plowden sent a three-word telegram: 'Thank God – Pamela.'[144]

Winston meanwhile was devouring newspapers. All the news was bad. During what was being called Black Week, December 10–15, British forces had suffered appalling casualties and three staggering defeats, including a rout of an attempt by Buller to relieve Ladysmith by frontal attack up the railway line. Churchill, chagrined, wanted to rejoin the army as soon as possible. Ross was equally anxious to see him go; Lourenço Marques was a hotbed of Boer partisans, and there were rumours that his guest was about to be kidnapped and returned to the Transvaal. On December 21, nine days after Churchill's escape, a party of armed Englishmen escorted him from the consulate garden to the waterfront, where he boarded the steamer *Induna*. Two days later he docked at Durban. An enormous, cheering crowd awaited him. The entire harbour was decorated with bunting and flags; bands were playing; the mayor, an admiral, and a general leapt up the gangplank to embrace him. After Black Week, the British had been yearning for a hero, and here was a handsome young patrician who had broken out of a Boer prison and made his way across three hundred miles of hostile territory to freedom. The mob whirled him along on its shoulders, deposited him on the steps of the town hall, and demanded a speech. His remarks have not survived, but the mood of the moment, the vitality, confidence, and innocence of the English in that last month of the nineteenth century, are caught in the lively strains of the war's hit song, trumpeted by the bands as he finished:

> Goodbye, Dolly, I must leave you
> Though it breaks my heart to go
> Something tells me I am needed
> At the front to fight the foe
>
> See the boys in blue are march-ing
> And I can no longer stay
> Hark! I hear the bugle call-ing
> Goodbye, Dolly Grey!

And then, as he climbed down, they struck up that spine-tingling anthem of Victorian conquest:

> Britons always loyally declaim
> About the way we rule the waves
> Every Briton's song is just the same
> When singing of her soldiers brave . . .
>
> We're not forgetting it
> We're not letting it
> Fade away or gradually die!
>
> So when we say that England's master
> Remember who has made her so!
>
> It's the soldiers of the Queen, my lads,
> Who've been the lads, who've seen the lads

In the fight for England's glory, lads –
Of her world-wide glory let us sing!

And when we say we've always won
And when they ask us how it's done
We'll proudly point to every one
Of England's soldiers of the Queen!

That afternoon he caught a train to Pietermaritzburg, where he remained overnight as the guest of Sir Walter Hely-Hutchinson, governor of Natal, and picked up more disquieting information. The kaiser had written to his grandmother the Queen, threatening to side with the Boers. ('I cannot sit on the safety valve forever. My people demand intervention.') Buller had cabled the War Office that the investment of Ladysmith could not be lifted without further reinforcements. More troopships were on their way to him, but he had been demoted. Although he would retain command of the Natal forces, Lord Roberts was sailing down to take over as commander in chief, with Kitchener, Winston's nemesis, as chief of staff. Back at the front, Churchill celebrated Christmas Eve with the rest of the press corps, scarcely a hundred yards from the site of the armoured-train ambush. In a flush of patriotism he cabled the *Morning Post*: 'More irregular corps are wanted. Are the gentlemen of England all fox-hunting? Why not an English Light Horse? For the sake of our manhood, our devoted colonists, and our dead soldiers, we must persevere with the war.' Buller wrote to Lady Theresa Londonderry: 'Winston Churchill turned up here yesterday escaped from Pretoria. He really is a fine fellow and I must say I admire him greatly. I wish he was leading irregular troops instead of writing for a rotten paper. We are very short of good men, as he appears to be, out here.' He then sent for Churchill and questioned him closely about conditions in the Transvaal. All he got were impressions Winston had gleaned by looking through a tiny crack between bales of wool, but at the end he said: 'You have done very well. Is there anything we can do for you?'[145]

To his delight, Winston asked for a commission. The general said, 'What about poor old Borthwick?' and his face fell when Churchill replied that he couldn't possibly break his contract with the *Morning Post*. It might be a rotten paper to the general, but it paid twelve times as much as the army. That put Buller in a dilemma. After the Nile expedition, the War Office had ruled that no soldier could double as a war correspondent. Now Churchill, whose dispatches had been responsible for the ruling, was asking that he be made an exception to it. The general circled the room three times, worried an ear, and said: 'All right. You can have a commission in Bungo's regiment. You will have to do as much as you can for both jobs. But you will get no pay for ours.' Winston quickly agreed, and 'Bungo' – Colonel Julian Byng, commanding the South African Light Horse, an Uitlander regiment – appointed him assistant adjutant, with the understanding that while not actually fighting he could go where he liked. Happily stitching his badges of rank on his khaki jacket,

Churchill stuck the SALH's long plume of 'cockyolibird' feathers in his hat and headed towards the sound of the guns.[146]

In London, Borthwick raised no objection – since the escape his circulation had soared – but the arrangement was a poor one. Taken as a whole, Churchill's youthful war correspondence reveals a remarkable grasp of strategy and tactics and an admirable readiness to criticize senior officers. He felt indebted to Buller, however, and here, as in Cuba, gratitude warped his judgement. He wrote: 'If Sir Redvers Buller cannot relieve Ladysmith with his present force we do not know of any other officer in the British Service who would be likely to succeed.' That was absurd, and in moments of clarity he knew it. On January 10, after a bloody reverse on the Tugela River, he wrote to Pamela: 'Alas dearest we are again in retreat. Buller started out full of determination to do or die but his courage soon ebbed and we stood still and watched while one poor wretched brigade was pounded and hammered and we were not allowed to help them . . . And the horrible part of it all is that Ladysmith will probably fall and all our brave friends be led off to captivity and shame.' In the aftermath of another disaster – the general had delegated authority to a weak officer, then relieved him – Churchill pictured Buller at last gripping 'the whole business in his strong hands.' He failed to note that by then it was too late for the men who had died in vain.[147]

The toll was mounting. And the British, including Churchill, were shocked and bewildered. None of them had ever known anything like this slaughter. Even Majuba, fought near here, had been relatively tame. In their defeat there the British had lost just ninety-two men. The Boer bullet which had crippled Ian Hamilton's left wrist – Winston called it Hamilton's 'glorious' deformity – had been enough to distinguish him. Now, abruptly, everything had changed. This time the Boers, unlike the Pathan and Omdurman tribesmen, were armed with weapons just as modern as Buller's. Machine guns shredded the Queen's dense khaki ranks. Distant Long Toms, sited far beyond the reach of the English cavalry, fired 40-pound, 4.7-inch shrapnel shells that dismembered men or even obliterated them. Barbed wire had appeared, and sandbagged entrenchments. The Boers understood the new warfare. They told one another: 'Dig now, or they'll dig your grave later.'[148] The baffled British clung stubbornly to their Sandhurst principles. Cavalrymen like Major Douglas Haig assured one another that their *arme blanche*, the lance and sword, would winkle out the foe. They tried and failed and tried and failed and learned nothing. In British regimental accounts one finds the first pathetic strains of a theme which would be sounded throughout all the wars of the twentieth century, now less than a month old. This or that local engagement was 'imperishable,' or 'immortal'; it would 'go down in history,' 'enshrined forever' in the records of the past. So it was said in South Africa that winter of Hussar Hill, Mount Alice, Conical Hill, Aloe Knoll, and Potgeiter's Ferry. So it would be said of Broodseinde in 1917, Galloping Horse Ridge in 1942, the Punchbowl in 1951, and Pleiku in 1965. Eventually all would be forgotten, even by the descendants of those who had fought there.

261

The first of the century's butcheries was Spion Kop, or Spion Mountain, and Churchill was there, as was Gandhi with his stretcher-bearers. Abandoning the plan of forcing the Tugela at Colenso, Buller tried to turn Botha's right flank by fording the river upstream and seizing this 1,470-foot height, the hub of the range of hills between Buller and Ladysmith. On the night of January 23 his men stealthily mounted the steep slopes, scarred with huge rocks. They achieved total surprise. The enemy's defences were thin here, and a dense mist covered the flat crest; it was 4:00 A.M. before a Boer picket on the summit challenged them: '*Wie is daar?*' He was answered by hoarse yells of 'Waterloo!' and 'Majuba!,' a zigzag line of Lee-Enfield flashes, and a charge which took the kop at a cost of ten casualties. The victors held the key to the ladysmith lock. But before they could turn it they had to face the greater challenge of holding it.

Botha, roused in his tent and told 'the Khakis' were on the height, called for long-range rifle fire and salvos from his five Krupp field guns and two pom-poms. Presently Boer shells were bursting over the hilltop, seven every minute. The effect was devastating. By now the summit, an area about the size of Trafalgar Square, was packed with Uitlanders. They had no cover. One survivor later described the peak as 'the most awful scene of carnage.' Atkins, the *Guardian*'s correspondent, perched on a nearby ridge, reported that it was becoming an 'acre of massacre.'[149] Buller had expected to support this embattled force with an assault on the other Boer flank, but now the necessary men couldn't be found. One Uitlander raised a white flag; an officer furiously tore it from his hand. He was right to do so. Their position was precarious, but far from desperate. Around midnight Botha's artillery commander panicked and fled with his guns. The first wave of counterattacking Boer commandos was driven off the kop's reverse slope. At this point the obvious move for the British was to renew their drive, clearing a knoll and a spur just ahead. Their problem was that no one seemed to be in charge.

Into this muddle, out of breath but full of resolution, climbed Lieutenant Winston Churchill. He had been waiting in the vicinity with his regiment, hoping to be sent up the hill. Lacking orders and impatient, he had galloped over here on his own, tethered his horse at the bottom, and ascended on foot, gripping boulders and struggling through 'streams of wounded.' Soldiers, he wrote, were 'staggering along alone, or supported by comrades, or crawling on hands and knees, or carried on stretchers. Corpses lay here and there. Many of the wounds were of a horrible nature. The splinters and fragments of the shell [sic] had torn and mutilated in the most ghastly manner.' To Pamela he wrote: 'The scenes on Spion Kop were among the strangest and most terrible I have ever witnessed.' He had, he said, been 'continually under shell & rifle fire and once the feather in my hat was cut through by a bullet. But – in the end I came serenely through.'[150]

He came through and went back again, though hardly with serenity. He was rushing around the front in complete violation of regulations, intent on rescuing the situation by sorting everything out personally and then persuading nearby commanders to intervene. Incredibly, no one put him in his place; superior officers, distraught in the confusion, heard him out and pondered his advice. Night fell and he toiled back up the hill, which in his words was now 'hopelessly congested' with stragglers and casualties, towards 'an intermittent crackle of musketry at the top.' Battalions were intermingled. Regimental officers, he noted, were 'everywhere cool and cheery, each with a little group of men around him, all full of fight and energy. But the darkness and the broken ground paralysed everyone.' He was off again, rounding up sappers and miscellaneous troops. Finding the senior officer, a newly promoted brigadier, he explained what he had done and what he proposed be done next. The brigadier, in shock, on the verge of a complete breakdown, mumbled that it was all hopeless and he had decided to withdraw: 'Better six good battalions safely down the hill than a bloody mop-up in the morning.' Churchill insisted the gains could still be consolidated – military historians agree with him – and harangued the brigadier about 'Majuba' and 'the great British public.' It was in vain; the order to retreat went up. Down the Uitlanders came, leaving their dead three deep. In the first olive moments of dawn Churchill glowered up, his thumbs in his braces and his lower lip thrust out in that way he had, and saw two of Botha's burghers standing jubilantly on the pinnacle. They were waving their rifles and slouch hats, shouting that the Khakis had been '*kopschuw*' – routed.[151]

His bitterness over the loss of Spion Kop was relieved by the arrival in South Africa of Lady Randolph Churchill. Jennie had solicited £41,597 from wealthy Americans and commissioned a hospital ship, the *Maine*, named after the US warship lost in Havana harbour. In the forecastle were an American flag, sent by Theodore Roosevelt, and, from Queen Victoria, a Union Jack. (Jennie chose to fly the British colours.) Accompanying her on the voyage was Jack, just nineteen, whose brother had obtained a commission for him in the SALH. They had learned of Winston's escape the day before they sailed, and he met them on the Durban docks. After they had killed a bottle of '25 brandy, Jennie mounted a wild horse, tamed it, and rode it into the regiment's camp. At forty-five her beauty had reached its autumnal glory, and if she seemed determined to prove that she retained the energy of youth, there was reason: she had decided to marry George Cornwallis-West, an impecunious junior officer just Winston's age. There is no record of her sons' reaction to this. Her friends, however, were appalled. Jennie didn't care. She told one of them: 'I suppose you think I'm very foolish, but I don't care. I'm having such *fun*.'[152]

Winston's family was well represented in South Africa now. There was his mother; his brother; his bland, moustachioed cousin Sunny, the young duke, serving in Cape Town as Lord Roberts's military secretary; and, among the civilians in besieged Mafeking, his aunt Lady Sarah Wilson, Randolph's glamorous thirty-five-year-old sister, who, bored by London, had come down here for excitement and found it. Captured in the Transvaal during a clumsy attempt at spying, she had been exchanged for a Boer cattle thief and now held court in a luxurious, white-panelled bunker hewn out of Mafeking's red soil, the walls decorated with African spears from the Matabele War and a huge Union Jack. Lady Sarah was a survivor; no one seems to have been concerned about her. Winston was worried about Jack, however. He felt responsible for him, and almost immediately his fears were justified. In action for the first time on Hussar Hill, Jack was wounded in the calf. To Atkins, 'It seemed as though he had paid his brother's debts.' Winston thought it 'an instance of Fortune's caprice.' Jack, he wrote to Pamela, had been 'lying down. I was walking about without any cover – I who have tempted fortune so often. Jack was hit.' To his mother he wrote: 'It is a coincidence that one of the first patients on board the *Maine* should be your own son . . . but you may be glad with me that he is out of harm's way for a month. There will be a great battle in a few days and his presence – though I would not lift a finger to prevent him – adds much to my anxiety when there is fighting.'[153]

The great battle, for Vaal Krantz, was fought and succeeded by another, and then another. Slowly the weight of British numbers began to tell. Kimberley, 240 miles to the west, was relieved by Major General John French, while here in Natal, Botha fell back on Hlangwane Hill, then in further retreats on Inskilling Hill, Pieters Plateau, Railway Hill, and Hart's Hill. Churchill was in action almost every day, and on the historic evening of February 28, the one hundred and eighteenth day of Ladysmith's investment, he rode with the first two squadrons to enter the beleaguered town, galloping 'across the scrub-dotted plain, fired at only by a couple of Boer guns. Suddenly,' he wrote, 'from the brushwood up rose gaunt figures waving hands of welcome. On we pressed, and at the head of a battered street of tin-roofed houses met Sir George White on horseback, faultlessly attired. . . It was a thrilling moment.' That night he dined with White and Ian Hamilton on champagne and a roast from the garrison's last trek-ox, saved for this occasion. But 'better than feast or couch' was the reward, 'which was all the more splendid since it had been so long delayed – victory.'[154]

Churchill remained in Ladysmith over a month, feverishly writing a new book, *London to Ladysmith via Pretoria*. His escape had fuelled sales of his earlier works – 8,000 copies of *Savrola*, 3,000 of the two-volume *River War* at 36 shillings, and 600 of the *Malakand Field Force* – bringing him about £1,500 in royalties. This, with the cheques from Borthwick, went into his political war chest. Already Tories in Southport had invited him to run in their constituency, but he wanted vindication in Oldham. When Joe Chamberlain sent him a long letter, inviting a discussion of public affairs, he cannily replied that, while he hoped 'to find a seat before the dissolution, as I should like to record a vote on many points,' he could not return to England 'until the end of the war or at least until the Transvaal is in our hands.' His Oldham defeat had taught him the need for planning. He meant to build a financial base, at the same time cultivating readers with his vivid prose – 'Winston's graphic tongue,' as Jennie called it. Yet he could never be a cautious politician. With casualty lists lengthening, the last thing his readers wanted from him was a plea for magnanimity towards the enemy. Nevertheless, he wrote: 'Peace and happiness can only come to South Africa through the fusion and concord of the Dutch and British races, who must forever live side by side,' and 'I earnestly hope, expect and urge that a generous and forgiving policy will be followed.' Angry subscribers disagreed, and his own paper ran an editorial demanding punishment of the Boers. Hely-Hutchinson wrote to him that Boers who sought to return to Natal 'shd be tried & punished . . . You must remember that the Natal Dutch have been treated with special consideration in the past, and that if what we hear from many sources is true they have been the ringleaders in the looting & destruction that has been going on in Natal.' What looting? Winston asked. What destruction? It appeared to him that this was based on unconfirmed rumours. He refused to retract; indeed, with each Boer defeat his appeals for mercy and compassion grew stronger.[155]

As a suitor, on the other hand, he continued to be both indecisive and inept. He wrote to his mother: 'I think a great deal of Pamela; she loves me very dearly.' Yet a considerate young man would have spared his beloved the grisly details of his brushes with death. Winston kept Pamela fully informed on every bullet, every shell fragment that came his way, reminding her over and over that each breath might be his last, that even as she read this he might already be a decomposing cadaver. 'I was very nearly killed two hours ago by a shrapnel,' he wrote to her in a typical missive, and, on the eve of a battle, 'I pray to God that I may have no thoughts of myself when the time comes – but for you my darling always.' Unquestionably he missed her. Indeed, when Jennie had arrived he wrote to Pamela: 'Oh why did you not come out as secretary? Why did you not come out in the *Maine* so that I should be going to meet you now.' Then, as after her refusal to campaign in Oldham, he backed off: 'Perhaps you are wise.' He didn't understand women; he compared them with his eccentric mother and was puzzled by the variance. When Pamela, like Joe Chamberlain, hinted that he had done his part and ought to come home now, he bridled. 'I do not know whether I shall see the end or not,' he replied, raising that spectre again, 'but I am quite certain that I will not leave Africa till the matter is settled. I should forfeit my self-respect forever if I tried to shield myself behind an easily obtained reputation for courage. No possible advantage politically could compensate – besides believe me none would result.' That was the nub of it. He was convinced he was making political capital down there and was therefore content. The possibility that he might make better time with her by leaving the front seems never to have occurred to him.[156]

The limelight, which he craved more than any woman's company, now faded from Natal and shone down upon the Cape Colony, where England's shortest and most popular soldier was preparing to move through the Orange Free State and into the Transvaal. Kipling understood the popularity of the diminutive Field Marshal Lord Roberts, KCB,GCB:

> *What 'e does not know o' war,*
> *Gen'real Bobs,*

You can arst the shop next door —
can't they, Bobs?

O 'e's little but 'e's wise,
'E's a terror for 'is size,
An' — 'e — does — not advertise
Do yer, Bobs?

Churchill, forgetting his earlier bitterness, described him as 'this wonderful little man.' Bobs, however, did not reciprocate. Kitchener, bitter over Winston's criticisms at Omdurman, had deepened the field marshal's distrust of this impudent subaltern who presumed to pass judgement on his commanding officers. Moreover, Bobs had been outraged by a Churchillian critique of a church parade on the eve of the assault on Vaal Krantz. Over five thousand men had assembled, awaiting inspiration. 'The bridegroom Opportunity had come,' Winston had written. 'But the Church had her lamp untrimmed.' Instead of a rousing sermon, the chaplain 'with a raucous voice' had preached dully on Jericho, freezing the soldiers 'into apathy.' Bobs was sensitive to criticism of army chaplains, who had come to South Africa in response to a War Office call for volunteers. But Hamilton and Sir William Nicholson, another of Winston's friends from India, interceded on his behalf, and on April 11 a colonel wrote to Churchill from Bloemfontein, the Orange capital: 'Lord Roberts desires me to say that he is willing to permit you to accompany this force as a correspondent — *for your father's sake.*'[157]

Winston seethed over Bobs's 'making me accept as a favour what was already mine as a right,' as he put it in a letter home.[158] There was a marvellous inconsistency here. He had, after all, thrived on favours at every step on his journey to fame, and he continued to enjoy them by joining Hamilton, now an acting lieutenant general, and Sunny, who had become Hamilton's aide, on the flank of Bobs's drive across the Vaal River towards Pretoria. By choosing to remain among friends, he missed the relief of Mafeking by two flying columns on May 17; London's hysterical joy added a verb to the language, *maffick*, 'to indulge in extravagant demonstrations of exultation on occasion of national rejoicing,' and the release of Aunt Sarah, not to mention that of the heroic Colonel R.S.S. Baden-Powell, commander of the garrison, would have been worth columns of soaring copy which might have swung more than a few votes in Oldham. Yet he was flourishing where he was. By now he had become adept at creating his own dramas, investing skirmishes and patrols with a Churchillian aura that depended less on the news than the reporter.

The Prince of Wales, writing that he was a rapt follower of 'all yr accounts fr the front,' had permitted himself a feeble little royal joke: 'It is to be hoped you will not risk falling again into the hands of the Boers!' In fact, after attaching himself to Brabazon's brigade in the open countryside around Dewetsdorp, forty miles from Bloemfontein, Winston risked precisely that. A party of mounted British scouts decided to beat the enemy to an unoccupied white stone kopje, or hillock, and Winston impetuously joined them 'in the interests of the *Morning Post.*' They had dismounted 120 yards from the crest, and were cutting through a wire fence there, when they found they had lost the race. Over the top, Churchill wrote luridly, loomed the heads and shoulders of a dozen Boer riflemen – 'grim, hairy and terrible.' The British captain called: 'Too late; back to the other kopje. Gallop!' His scouts leapt on their mounts and bounded off, but just as Winston put his toe into his stirrup the riflemen opened fire, and his terrified horse, plunging wildly, slipped the saddle and ran off. He was alone, a mile from cover, an easy target. As he reached for his Mauser he saw a mounted British scout to his left, a tall man on a pale horse, and he thought: 'Death in Revelation, but life to me!' He ran towards him, shouting, 'Give me a stirrup!' The rider paused and Churchill vaulted up behind him. As they rode towards safety Winston wrapped his arms around his rescuer and gripped the mane. His hand came away soaked with blood. The animal had been badly hit, Churchill wrote, 'but, gallant beast, he extended himself nobly.' His rider cried: 'My horse, oh, my poor bloomin' horse; shot with a dum-dum! The bastards! Oh, my poor horse!' Churchill, realizing that they were out of range now, consoled him: 'Never mind, you saved my life.' 'Ah,' said the rider, 'but it's the horse I'm thinking about.' And that, Winston wrote, 'was the whole of our conversation.' He never saw the man again.[159]

Poring over his dispatches, one feels that war had become like that to him, a great Hentyan adventure, heightened, here and there, by breathtaking flirtations with death, threats always turned aside at the last moment. The gore on Spion Kop, though faithfully chronicled at the time, had been forgotten; it was nasty, but not so nasty as its sequel, defeat. If Englishmen showed pluck and daring, if they were loyal to their Queen and their manhood, Britain would always win through; Saint George was sure to slay the dragon in the end. The facts, however ugly, were laundered to suit the Churchillian preconception. Those who have other memories of combat turn away troubled. Yet these incidents were real. The tall man on the pale doomed horse left no version of the episode, but the captain of the scouts made a full report, and it confirmed Winston. Virtually every event he described in South Africa, as in Cuba, on the North-West Frontier, and at Omdurman, was witnessed by others whose recollections were consistent with his. The difference, of course, lay in interpretation. Winston fashioned his own reality, created his own life. 'I had thrown double sixes again,' he wrote after he had been saved from the kopje riflemen.[160] He did it over and over. He had reached the prison latrine just as the sentry was lighting his pipe, had found the one train which passed through Pretoria that night, had blindly knocked on the door of the one man in the mining district who could and would help him through to the Portuguese border, and had been spared a thousand times in battle since then while the first bullet had found poor Jack. So it would continue throughout the march with Roberts, and if his view of life under Bobs seems fantastic, one can only observe that in his case life was, and continued to be, remarkably melodramatic.

Just once was he vouchsafed a glimpse of what the South African war was all about. On the last day of May, Roberts took Johannesburg, in the heart of the Witwatersrand, the 'Rand,' that sixty-three-mile-long ridge, seamed with auriferous rock, which constitutes the world's richest goldfield. After gazing down at the grey-stockinged feet of eighteen Highlanders awaiting burial, Churchill wrote, he found himself 'scowling at the tall chimneys of the Rand.' But the moment passed. England wouldn't send men to die for *that*. He turned away and presently found himself with Hamilton, Sunny, and the exhilarating advance of the eleven-thousand-man flank force's move northward. The weather was magnificent, the scenery stunning. In later life he told his doctor, 'I loved it: all movement and riding.' He spent £1,000 of *Morning Post* expense money on a pair of horses, a team of four oxen, and a wagon whose false bottom was crammed with liquor and Fortnum and Mason groceries. They almost lost the wagon fording a stream, but naturally Winston guided the team through the current. One night they found a flock of geese on a pond. Sunny shepherded them towards his cousin, who felled one with a flying kick. They ate it that night, and they let General Hamilton have some.[161]

Counting the main force under Roberts, Johannesburg and then Pretoria were the objectives of over 200,000 British troops. The Boers never had more than 88,000 men under arms on all fronts, and they prudently prepared to abandon the Transvaal capital and withdraw eastward. On June 2 they were still there, however, standing between Hamilton's column and the main army under Roberts. Hamilton had just crushed an enemy force at Doornkop; he wanted Bobs to know of it. He was only twenty miles from the field marshal by direct route, but a courier avoiding Johannesburg would have to cover an eighty-mile detour over rough country. Churchill, as it happened, had just finished interviewing a Frenchman who had left the town only hours before on his bicycle. Boer security was lax there, said the Frenchman; he was certain Winston could safely cycle right through. He offered to lend him his bike, even volunteered to borrow another from a friend and act as his guide. If a Boer became suspicious, they would chat in French.

Here, surely, was temptation. Less than six months earlier, against all odds, Winston had fled prison just north of here. Then he had been merely a war correspondent. Now he held a Queen's commission. He would have to travel in a civilian suit. In his pocket he would be carrying an urgent report from one British commander to another. Even the debonair Frenchman – if indeed he was what he said he was; Winston, with his own atrocious French, was no judge of that, and no one else here had ever laid eyes on the man before – conceded that armed Boers were thick in the streets. A simple search by any one of them and Winston would be shoved against the nearest wall and executed by an ad hoc firing squad. Nevertheless, he agreed. He took the plan to Hamilton, who, amused, gave him a copy of the dispatch he was sending by orderlies the long way. Changing clothes, Winston shoved it into the jacket with his *Morning Post* telegrams and cycled off with his carefree guide.

In Johannesburg they had one bad moment. They were pushing their bikes up a long steep street when a slowly trotting Boer horseman drew abreast, reined in his mount, and walked alongside, carefully scrutinizing them. The rider had a rifle slung on his back, a pistol in a holster, and three bandoliers of ammunition dangling from his shoulder. Altering their pace would have been a grave mistake. Turning away, Winston said as much in French, sounding all the final consonants as usual – his companion flinched – and the Boer trotted off. Encountering no enemy picket line, another stroke of luck, they reached Roberts's advance patrols without further incident. Churchill was taken directly to Bobs. The commander in chief read the dispatch. Then he looked up and asked: 'How did you come?' 'Through Johannesburg,' Churchill said, and explained. The little man's eyes twinkled. Winston wrote gaily, 'Lord Roberts had very remarkable eyes, full of light. I remember being struck by this at the moment.' Bobs's chilliness towards him had disappeared. Kitchener remained distant, but Winston's new source of news and favours was at the very top.[162]

The first fruit of this conversion followed within seventy-two hours. Bobs permitted him to canter into Pretoria, with Sunny at his side, at the head of the lead column. They galloped towards the POW camp in the State Model Schools. It looked exactly as it had when he left nearly six months before, a long tin building surrounded by dense wire, and the Boer guards, still on watch, brought their rifles to the ready. 'Surrender!' cried Sunny, and after an uneasy pause the commandant appeared and capitulated. Prisoners had rushed to the fence. Haldane and Brockie were gone – they had finally made it to the British lines on their own – but the others were all there. One of them, Lieutenant Thomas Frankland of the Second Dublin Fusiliers, had been wondering if the sound of distant gunfire meant approaching freedom. He wrote, 'Who should I see on reaching the gate but Churchill, who, with his cousin, the Duke of Marlborough, had galloped on in front of the army to bring us the good tidings.' Another prisoner, a Yorkshire engineering officer named Melville Goodacre, recorded in his diary how he had been washing clothes in the compound 'when suddenly Winston Churchill came galloping over the hill.' Goodacre watched, astonished, a wet shirt still in his hand, as Winston pushed past the guards – Sunny was giving the commandant a receipt for their rifles – and made for the flagpole. He produced a Union Jack. Then, Goodacre's diary continues, he 'tore down the Boer flag and hoisted ours amidst cheers,' whereupon 'the Boer guards were put inside and our prisoners guard over *them*!' It was, the diarist thought, 'roarable and splendid.' It was also the first time the British colours had flown over Pretoria since April 5, 1881, immediately after Majuba.[163]

Churchill saw action once more, a week later, in the battle of Diamond Hill. Kruger, brokenhearted, was preparing to leave the country aboard a Dutch cruiser, but Botha defiantly rallied seven thousand burghers fifteen miles outside the capital and dug in on a height athwart the railroad tracks leading to Portuguese East. Roberts sent Hamilton against them. The army's elite infantry regiments, the Coldstream Guards and the Scots Guards, were bogged down on the lower slopes when Winston, according to Hamilton's memoirs, *Listening for the Drums*, saw the key to victory – a path to the crest – and realized that most of it was dead ground to the Boers because they had their heads down, seeking cover from the heavy British fire. He headed that way, having managed 'somehow,' Hamilton wrote, 'to give me the slip.' Presently the amazed British troops saw him mounting the trail alone. 'He climbed this mountain,' Hamilton recalled, 'as our scouts were trained to climb on the Indian frontier and ensconced himself in a niche not much more than a pistol shot directly below the Boer commandos – no mean feat of arms in broad daylight and one showing a fine trust in the accuracy of our own guns. Had even half a dozen of the Burghers run twenty yards over the brow they could have knocked him off his perch with a volley of stones.' Waving a handkerchief on a stick, he signalled that this was the way up. The general sent men to the path; they rushed the summit and took the hill. Citing Winston's 'conspicuous gallantry,' Hamilton recommended him for the Victoria Cross, but, he wrote, 'Bobs and K' vetoed it; Churchill 'had only been a Press Correspondent – they declared – so nothing happened.' It must have hurt. The VC was the award Winston coveted above all others. To friends, however, he assumed a philosophical air. He said of war correspondents: ' "All the danger and one-half per cent of the glory": such is our motto, and that is the reason why we expect such large salaries.'[164]

Churchill assumed that the war was over. By the rules of traditional warfare, it should have been; once the enemy's capital had fallen and his army had been beaten in the field, he was supposed to quit. Winston therefore began packing. 'I need not say how anxious I am to come back to England,' he wrote to his mother. 'Politics, Pamela, finances and books all need my attention.'[165] But the Boers disregarded the rules. Like the Cuban insurrectionists, they ignored Roberts's demand for unconditional surrender and then dispersed into guerrilla commandos, the South African conflict's last contribution to twentieth-century warfare. Their bands, brilliantly led, continued to fight for nearly two more years; one force under Jan Christiaan Smuts raided deep into the British colonies, striking within fifty miles of Cape Town. Suppressing them, and pacifying the countryside, fell to the ruthless Kitchener – Bobs had sailed back to Europe, calling the war 'practically over' – with Hamilton as his chief of staff. 'K' built blockhouses along the railways, burned the guerrillas' farms, slaughtered their livestock, and penned Boer women and children in concentration camps, where over twenty thousand died. In the end the guerrillas capitulated, bitter but helpless. The two Boer republics were dissolved and incorporated in the Empire. That action could be reversed, however, and in time it was. England's losses, on the other hand, were irreplaceable. The Boer blitz of 1899 had destroyed the myth of British invulnerability; now, in this final *fin de siècle* convulsion, Britain's moral position was also crippled.

Winston missed all this. After interviewing Milner in Cape Town and spending a day foxhunting with the Duke of Westminster, he boarded the *Dunottar Castle* and set to work on a new book, *Ian Hamilton's March*, a paste-up of his dispatches since leaving Buller. *London to Ladysmith* had appeared five days before the relief of Mafeking; the two books were to sell twenty-two thousand copies in England and the United States, the equivalent of over seventy thousand today. He was also planning his entrance into public life. He hoped his mother would tell him of the country's political temper when he docked in Southampton on July 20. To his consternation, she wasn't there; she was busy preparing for her wedding and had let the house in Great Cumberland Place, which Winston regarded as his home as well as hers. Sunny rescued him, assigning him the lease of a spacious flat at 105 Mount Street in Mayfair. Winston bought furniture at Maples and asked his aunt Leonie to redecorate the rooms – 'you cannot imagine how that kind of material arrangement irritates me; so long as my table is clear and there is plenty of paper I do not worry about the rest.'[166]

During the next seven months he was seldom there. Public interest in him was almost overwhelming. Eleven Conservative constituencies now sought him as their candidate, but he made straight for Oldham, which gave him a tremendous welcome. A band played 'See the Conquering Hero Comes' as he entered the town in the midst of a procession of ten landaus. Shopkeepers and factory hands lined the streets, some shouting, 'Young Randy!' At the Theatre Royal he addressed a full house. They wanted to hear of his escape, and when he responded, telling them of his arrival at the mine and mentioning Dan Dewsnap – British troops had occupied the Witbank colliery district, so he could name names – voices shouted: 'His wife's in the gallery!' Mrs Dewsnap took a bow, plump and blushing; Winston, bowing back, was cheered to the rafters. A chorus of mill girls stood and sang the music hall ditty sweeping England that summer:[167]

> *You've heard of Winston Churchill;*
> *This is all I need to say –*
> *He's the latest and the greatest*
> *Correspondent of the day.*

If this mood held, he would be swept into office. But it didn't hold; it couldn't. The Liberal incumbents were popular, well financed, and well organized, and when he declared his candidacy on September 19, two days after the dissolution of Parliament, it was clear that the race would be fought at concert pitch. 'The excitement is already great,' he wrote to his mother after his first day on the stump, 'and I have no doubt that before the end of the campaign the town will be in a state of frenzy.' Twice he appealed for her help ('I need not say that it would be very pleasing to me'; 'I write again to impress upon you how very useful your presence will be') but Jennie declined. She was enjoying her extended honeymoon; he would have to win by himself. Actually, no candidate in that election, 'the khaki election,' as it became known, was to be judged by his own merits. Party tactics guaranteed that. Chamberlain had set the tone with his slogan, 'Every seat lost to the Government is a seat gained to the Boers.' One poster declared: OUR BRAVE SOLDIERS IN SOUTH AFRICA EXPECT THAT EVERY VOTER WILL DO HIS DUTY . . . REMEMBER! TO VOTE FOR A LIBERAL IS A VOTE TO THE BOER. Churchill himself was not above this. One of his Oldham hoardings read: 'Be it known that every vote given to the radicals means 2 pats on the back for Kruger and 2 smacks in the face for our country.' He was stung when the Liberals retaliated with a whispering campaign, describing him as a fake and a cashiered officer. The *Daily Mail* of September 27 reported: 'In nothing does Winston Churchill show his youth more than in the way he allows slanders to affect him . . . They deeply wound him and he allows men to see it. When some indiscreet supporter brings these stories to him, his eyes flash fire, he clutches his hands angrily, and he hurries out to find opportunity of somewhere and somehow bringing his traducers to book.' He wrote the opposition in protest; their reply expressed 'extreme regret,' but added, not unreasonably, that Liberals had been exasperated by the character of the Tory campaign and 'the ill-advised attempt of your political friends to run this election on the question of your undoubted physical courage instead of upon the political issues involved.'[168]

Balfour had agreed to come and speak for him 'if I could manage it.' Now he found he couldn't. Chamberlain came, however, even though it meant a four-hour return train trip at night. They rode through Oldham together in an open carriage, with loud hurrahs rising on both sides, and afterwards Winston wrote: 'He loved the roar of the multitude . . . The blood mantled in his cheek, and his eye as it caught mine twinkled with pure enjoyment.' It is doubtless true, as Violet Asquith wrote, that at this time Joe had 'a genuine affection and admiration' for Churchill. But as party strategist he had a special interest in his campaign. In those days of 'hammer and anvil politics,' as Winston called them, England did not vote in a single day. Voters went to the polls over a period of six weeks. On October 1, Oldham's thirty thousand workmen would be almost the first to poll, and the results would affect Conservatives still on the stump. Thus, Churchill's victory – his margin was only twenty-two votes, but it represented a crossover of fifteen hundred voters, and he had won a seat from a strong Liberal – instantly put his party in his debt. Salisbury personally telegraphed his congratulations. All over the country Tories in tight contests (including a penitent Balfour) begged him to come and campaign for them before their constituents voted. He went, he received standing ovations, and he was elated when victories followed in his wake. 'I have suddenly become one of the two or three most popular speakers in this election,' he wrote to Cockran, 'and am now engaged on a fighting tour, of the kind you know – great audiences (five and six thousand people) twice & even three times a day, bands, crowds and enthusiasm of all kinds.'[169]

Politically, he had arrived. And his party still ruled England. Chamberlain's tactics, however dubious, had worked. The khaki election assured the future of Salisbury's Tory-Unionist coalition; it now held a solid majority of 134 seats over the Liberals and the Irish Nationalists combined. But when the new House of Commons met on December 3, its newest star was absent. Winston

Churchill, MP, had decided to postpone his maiden speech until next year. His finances had priority. Sunny had contributed £400 to his campaign, and would pay £100 a year towards his constituency expenses, and Winston had his royalties and the cheques from Borthwick, but he wanted more. He knew this wave of popularity would not last. He meant to cash in on it now, with lecture tours of England, the United States, and Canada. Beginning in late October, accompanied by Sunny, he covered more than half of Great Britain in a month, speaking for an hour or more almost every night except Sundays, and often twice a day, travelling ceaselessly, usually at night, seldom sleeping twice in the same bed. Because he was working with his tongue now, not his pen, he tried to master his stubborn speech between lectures by muttering under his breath such exercises as, 'The Spanish ships I cannot see for they are not in sight.' Violet Asquith has left an endearing portrait of his weary figure as he trudged from hall to hall, his magic lantern under his arm, the profile already unmistakable by virtue of 'the slightly hunched shoulders from which his head jutted forward like the muzzle of a gun about to fire.'[170] He reached his objective; by December 8, when he sailed westward on the *Luciana*, he had made £4,500 and turned it over with the rest of his savings to Sir Ernest Cassel – who had been a friend of his father's – for investment in consols.

On the whole his American tour was a disappointment. Cockran saw to it that he met President McKinley and Senator Chauncey Depew, and dined in Albany with Governor Theodore Roosevelt, the vice-president-elect. He was delighted when Mark Twain, one of his boyhood heroes, inscribed a limited edition of his works for him, writing on the first fly-leaf: 'To do good is noble; to teach others to do good is nobler, and no trouble.' But then Twain, introducing him to his first audience, in Manhattan's Waldorf-Astoria on December 12, 1900, made it clear that he thought the British treatment of the Boers ignoble. Describing the speaker as the son of an English father and an American mother, and therefore 'the perfect man,' he said bluntly: 'I think England sinned when she got herself into a war in South Africa which she could have avoided, just as we have sinned in getting into a similar war in the Philippines.' The listeners murmured in agreement, then sat on their hands when Winston described his flight across the Transvaal. Afterwards he turned to his host and growled: 'My country right or wrong.' But he was not yet Twain's match. 'Ah,' the old man nimbly replied, 'when the poor country is fighting for its life, I agree. But this was not your case.' Churchill, writing home, complained about his US lecture agent, J.B. Pond: 'First of all the interest is not what Maj Pond made out and secondly there is a strong pro-Boer feeling, which has been fomented against me by the leaders of the Dutch, particularly in New York.' Yet Baltimore and Chicago audiences were colder than New York's, and beginning in Chicago, Irish-Americans, indignant over the Tory policy towards Ireland, came to boo. To quiet them, he would describe a dramatic crisis on a South African battlefield. The British position had been desperate, he would tell them, when 'the Dublin Fusiliers arrived, trumpeters sounded the charge, and the enemy were swept from the field.' A newspaperwoman reported: 'Suddenly the balconies grew silent, then thundered with cheers.'[171]

But that was cheap, and he knew it. He wrote to his mother that the tour was 'vy unpleasant work. For instance, last week, I arrived to lecture in an American town and found Pond had not arranged any public lecture but that I was hired out for £40 to perform at an evening party in a private house – like a conjurer. Several times I have harangued in local theatres to almost empty benches. I have been horribly vulgarised by the odious advertisements Pond and Myrmidons think it necessary to circulate – and only my cynical vein has helped me go on.' He described the agent as 'a vulgar Yankee' who had 'poured a lot of very mendacious statements into the ears of the reporters.' Moreover, 'Pond's terms are vy grasping compared to Christie's.' Christie, in England, had given him a generous share of the receipts: £220 in Cheltenham, £265 6s 2d. at St James's Hall, and £273 14s. 9d. in Liverpool. Under Pond he made $330 in Boston, $175 in Baltimore, $150 in Springfield, and just $50 in Hartford. His total American earnings were $8,000, or £1,600. It was a glum start for the man who would one day become the first Honorary Citizen of the United States.[172]

Canada, on the other hand, was a ten-day triumph. In Ottawa he was the guest of the governor-general, Lord Minto – Pamela, to his surprise, appeared as a fellow guest – and in Ulster Hall, Lord Dufferin, introducing him, said: 'This young man, at an age when many of his contemporaries have hardly left their studies, has seen more active service than half the general officers in Europe.' (Winston noted, 'I had not thought of this before. It was good.') The audiences were adoring and huge. In Winnipeg alone he made $1,150 (£230). On New Year's Day he totted up his income since leaving the Fourth Hussars, deducted income tax – eleven pence to the pound, or 4.5 per cent – and wrote to his mother: 'I am very proud of the fact that there is not one person in a million who at my age could have earned £10,000 without any capital in less than two years.' She could, he told her, discontinue his allowance 'until old Papa Wests [sic] decides to give you and G more to live on.' Henceforth, as long as he remained a bachelor, he could live on dividends and interest and devote all his energy to politics.[173]

On January 22, 1901, when Victoria breathed her last at Osborne, he was still in Canada. That night he wrote to Jennie: 'So the Queen is dead. The news reached us at Winnipeg and this city far away among the snows – fourteen hundred miles from any British town of importance – began to hang its head and hoist half-masted flags.' But the sadness did not touch him. He was young, flushed with new wealth, and full of his recent accomplishments. His tone was jaunty. The end of a sixty-four-year reign was, to be sure, 'a great and solemn event, but I am curious to know about the King. Will it entirely revolutionise his way of life? Will he sell his horses and scatter his Jews or will Reuben Sassoon be enshrined among the crown jewels and other regalia? Will he become desperately serious?' Then, more delicately: 'Will he continue to be friendly with you? Will the Keppel' – Mrs Alice Keppel – 'be appointed 1st Lady of the Bedchamber?'[174]

He sailed homeward aboard the SS *Etruria* on February 2, the day five kings and forty members of Europe's royal families followed the Queen's coffin down London streets, and a week later he was in his Mount Street rooms, working on his maiden speech. Around him the city still grieved. Every shop window was streaked with a mourning shutter. Crossing sweepers carried crepe on their brooms. Women of all ages were veiled; some had gone into perpetual mourning. Even the prostitutes, whose existence Victoria had denied, were dressed in black. Churchill ignored them; all his thoughts were of the future. Steevens of the *Daily Mail* – poor Steevens, who had died of fever in besieged Ladysmith – had said of him: 'He has the twentieth century in his marrow.'[175] Winston had liked that. But Steevens had been wrong. As time would prove with growing clarity, it was the nineteenth century that was in Churchill's bones. He would become the most eloquent defender of its standards, the apotheosis of its ideals, the resolute champion of its institutions and values. They were his priceless legacy; he was their fortunate heir. His career would be inconceivable today. And it would have been equally un-thinkable before Victoria came to the throne, when England had been an agricultural island, lacking in industry and without an Empire. Native drive, wise legislation, an educated and enlightened oligarchy ingeniously harnessed to genuine democracy, sea power, skilful diplomacy, faith in the supremacy of its island race – these had made imperial Britain, which, in that first Edwardian winter, despite the stigma of South Africa, continued to glitter on its splendid pinnacle, the envy of the world's chancelleries.

Could any other nation in 1901 offer its young politicians the chance for greatness which was now his? Not the insular United States of nineteen-year-old Franklin Roosevelt, then an immature, unpromising Harvard freshman in a country of fewer than 76 million – less than a fifth of the Empire's 412 million – which largely ignored the rest of civilization. Not the vast China of thirteen-year-old Chiang Kai-shek; its few pretensions to a national identity had been shattered with the crushing of the Boxer uprising the previous summer. Certainly not the locked medieval oriental kingdom of sixteen-year-old Hideki Tojo's Japan. The domain of the Turk – the home of nineteen-year-old Mustapha Kemal – was an empire in name only. Czarist Russia seethed with anarchy, terror, despotism, nihilism, and intrigue, and was constantly menaced by uprisings in the Ukraine, the Baltic states, Finland, Poland, and Georgia, where Joseph Stalin, then Josif Vissarionovich Dzhugashvili, aged twenty-one, had just been fired from the only nonpolitical job he ever held, a clerkship in the Tiflis observatory. In Vienna, capital of the Austro-Hungarian dual monarchy, the Hapsburg emperor presided over an equally unstable polyglot of Serbs, Croats, Poles, Magyars, Czechs, Yugoslavs, and Austrians, including, in the Austrian town of Linz, a sullen eleven-year-old schoolboy named Adolf Hitler. Italy, where Benito Mussolini, seventeen, was the quarrelsome son of the Predappio blacksmith, had repeatedly tried to play the part of a world power under a recent series of ineffectual rightist premiers and had been humiliated every time. Italy was blinded by an *idée fixe*, the recovery of lost territories, *Italia irredenta*; the France of Charles de Gaulle, who had just celebrated his tenth birthday in Lille, by a yearning to settle the scores of 1871, which had marked the beginning of the Gallic decline in growth and prestige. Only Wilhelmine Germany loomed as an immediate rival to Britain, and the character of the kaiser's regime excluded any commoner from a distinguished career in public life. Thus England alone could offer young Churchill the role he sought, and its prospects seemed certain to remain unique, barring monumental English folly, or loss of will, or the abandonment of such Victorian principles as disdain for continental alliances. The mere suggestion of any of these lapses would, in 1901,have evoked global laughter.

THREE

RIVER

1901 – 1914

KING Edward VII, stout and florid, personally opened the new session of Parliament, renewing a custom his mother had discontinued after his father's death forty years earlier. It was Valentine's Day, an occasion linked with his royal presence in the hearts and loins of an astonishing number of titled Englishwomen, all of whom had turned out to see him mount his throne. They were proud of him, and he was proud of himself; having waited half a century to wear the crown, he meant to carry out the ceremony with panache. Shortly after 2:00 P.M. his huge state chariot, drawn by eight cream-coloured Hanoverians draped with trappings of morocco and gilt, emerged from Buckingham Palace accompanied by Life Guards wearing dazzling silver breastplates and by postilions in red-and-gold liveries. The monarch and his cortège rode past dense masses of roaring Londoners along the broad Mall, the Horse Guards, Whitehall, and Parliament Square, where the carriage turned in and His Majesty descended, paused in the robing room, and entered the packed House of Lords. There his eminent subjects performed their obligatory gestures of homage, the ladies with curtsies, their masters with deep curvatures of the spine. The *New York Times* correspondent noted 'the curious reversal of the customary appearance of the sexes. Here, for once, the women were sombre looking, in black . . . while the men, usually in black, were radiant with brilliant robes of scarlet and ermine.' But one lady was not drab: 'The Duchess of Marlborough was a conspicuous figure. She wore all the famous Vanderbilt pearls in ropes around her neck, a high "dog" collar of pearls and diamonds around her throat, and a tiara of diamonds with enormous diamond tips.'[1] Sunny's first duchess, the former Consuelo Vanderbilt, had never slept with HRH, now HM, and she wasn't present to honour the King. She wanted to watch Winston take the oath as a member of the House of Commons afterwards, and she meant to enter the gallery in style.

Edward tried to look disconsolate. This, he told the assembled lords and commoners, was 'a moment of national sorrow, when the whole country is mourning the irreparable loss we have so recently sustained, and which has fallen with peculiar severity on myself. My beloved mother during her long and glorious reign has set an example of what a monarch should be. It is my earnest desire to walk in her footsteps.' Then, brightening, he turned from 'this public and private grief' to other matters. The drought in his Indian Empire was over. Australia had been a commonwealth for six weeks; he planned to sail there, and to visit New Zealand and Canada. Peking having been captured, the Boxers were no more. His victorious troops were mopping up in South Africa; soon, he erroneously predicted, 'the fruitless guerrilla warfare maintained by Boer partisans in the former territories of the two republics' would end. Like his predecessors since the rout of Catholicism he assured his people that he would never be a vassal of the pope, and he entrusted the management of his crown revenues to the House of Commons.[2]

In the House, Churchill, sworn, took a back-bench seat, tilted his top hat over his forehead, and, doubling up his figure in the crouched attitude assumed by seasoned parliamentarians and plunging his hands in his pockets, studied the chamber which was to be the arena of his political life for the next sixty-three years. The House dated from 1708, and its decor had not changed since the eighteenth century. Directly beneath the timbered ceiling lay the well, with the carved chair of the Speaker, who determined which members should have the floor. On either side of him the benches, upholstered in green, rose in five tiers. Those to the Speaker's right were occupied by the party in power; the Opposition sat to his left. Each tier was separated at midpoint by an aisle, the 'gangway.' The front government bench, extending from the Speaker's chair to the gangway, was reserved for the prime minister and his cabinet; it was also called 'the Treasury Bench' because the first prime minister, Sir Robert Walpole, had also been first lord of the Admiralty and chancellor of the Exchequer. Two red stripes on the well carpet marked the point beyond which no front-bencher could advance in addressing the House; the distance between the stripes was the length of two drawn swords. There were not enough seats for all elected members; this permitted the conversational style and avoided an impression of emptiness during routine sittings. 'A crowded House' gave an air of urgency to dramatic moments.

Churchill knew all this; had known it since boyhood. He was also familiar with the customs of the House. Savage, even cruel words could be exchanged between members who, off the floor, were on the best of terms. Any speech made off the floor was said to be given 'out of doors.' The House of Lords was 'another place.' Committee meetings were held 'upstairs.' Leaders of one's own party were addressed as 'my right honourable friend'; an Opposition leader was 'the right honourable gentleman.' The dominant figures in the chamber were, for the most part, the same men who had prevailed during his father's last days here. The Tories had remained in power, and the destroyer of Lord Randolph's career, Robert Cecil, Marquess of Salisbury, was still prime minister. Salisbury's grip on the controls had in fact tightened; he had manoeuvred so many members of his family into key posts that wits called the House 'the Hotel Cecil.' No fewer than seven Salisbury sons, nephews, and cousins sat on the Conservative benches. Four were in the government, and one, Arthur J. Balfour, 'AJB,' leader of the House, was preparing to take over as prime minister when his uncle retired. As a youthful MP, AJB had belonged to Lord Randolph's Fourth Party, but now he had put all that behind him and was as rock-ribbed a supporter of Tory policies as Joseph Chamberlain. The entire Tory-Unionist hierarchy stood four-square and was prepared to defend the established order down to the last desperate inch. Leaders of the Liberals, on the other side of the House, had been split over foreign policy since the Jameson Raid. The ablest of them – Rosebery, Herbert Asquith, Edward Grey, and R.B. Haldane – had become 'Liberal Imperialists': supporters of the Boer War. But a majority of the party's MPs disagreed, remaining faithful to the Gladstonian tradition. The Liberal centre was led by Sir Henry Campbell-Bannerman ('C-B'). If the party was returned to power, C-B would become prime minister. His followers included a group of antiwar radicals from the Celtic fringe, among them the charismatic young Welshman David Lloyd George, who wanted to geld the House of Lords and follow the lodestar of *la carrière ouverte aux talents*. Since only men of means could afford to enter Parliament, the left was underrepresented. Just two workingmen, supported by union dues, sat as MPs. These 'Lib-Labs,' as they were popularly known, were identified in the House as members of the Labour Representative Committee; five years would pass before the committee was renamed the Labour party.

Mastery of the House has been given to few. Its moods arch the British spectrum, from cockney vulgarity through Midlands stolidity and Scottish scepticism to Welsh emotionalism and, in those days, Irish mysticism. It can be frivolous, irresponsible, and grave on occasions which any other body would treat with hilarity. No new member can be expected to hold it spellbound, but on the evening of February 18, 1901, when Churchill's maiden speech was scheduled, the chamber was full. Campbell-Bannerman, Asquith, and Grey faced him on the front Opposition bench. Balfour and Joe Chamberlain sat on the Treasury Bench. Mrs Chamberlain was in the gallery. So were Jennie and four of her sisters-in-law – Lady Howe, Lady Tweedmouth (Fanny Marjoribanks), Lady de Ramsey, and Lady Wimborne – and the Duchess Consuelo. Winston was known as 'Randy's Boy,' and, in his own right, as a gifted journalist and a hero of the South African war. Moreover, in his first 'division,' or vote – MPs vote by streaming from the chamber and into two different lobbies, Yes and No – he had sided with the radicals and the Irish. At home, as abroad, he was already magnetic. The *Morning Post* reported that his audience was one which 'very few new members have commanded.' The *Yorkshire Post* observed: 'In that packed assembly, everybody a critic, watching to see what sort of start he made in politics, Winston Churchill made his debut.'[3]

He had decided to speak on the war, ignoring the advice of older Tories who had warned, 'It is too soon; wait for a few months till you know the House,' and crossing the lobby he had been disconcerted to learn that, contrary to his assumption, not all these people were here just to hear him. Lloyd George was also expected to rise. He would, indeed, be Churchill's immediate predecessor. Winston suffered from a parliamentary weakness and knew it: 'I had never had the practice which comes to young men at University of speaking in small debating societies impromptu upon all sorts of subjects.' He had spent days in front of a mirror, committing every word he intended to say to memory as his father had. But a House speech cannot stand alone; it must dovetail into the previous remarks, and Lloyd George, as usual, was unpredictable.

281

He had been called to move an amendment, which would have been an easy thread for Winston to pick up. Instead, he was delivering a wide-ranging attack on the government's record in South Africa. Its truce terms were vague: 'Does anyone think the Boers will lay down their arms merely to be governed from Downing Street?' Losses were appalling: 'There have been 55,000 casualties; 30,000 men are in hospital.' Kitchener's burning of Boer barns was barbarous: 'It is not a war against men but against women and children.' Every time Winston prepared an appropriate opening, the Welsh firebrand, egged on by radicals and Irish Nationalists, switched to a new tack. Churchill felt 'a sense of alarm and even despair.' At that point an elderly member beside him whispered: 'Why don't you just say, "Instead of making his violent speech without moving his moderate amendment, he had better have moved his moderate amendment without making his violent speech"?'[4]

When Lloyd George sat down Churchill said precisely that, drawing chuckles. His spirits rising, he continued: 'I do not believe that the Boers would attach particular importance to the utterances of the hon[ourable] member. No people in the world received so much verbal sympathy and so little support. If I were a Boer fighting in the field . . .' He paused dramatically. Then: '*And if I were a Boer, I hope I should be fighting in the field* . . .' Balfour groaned; Chamberlain muttered, 'That's the way to throw away seats.'* The radicals cheered, then found he had trapped them, for he went on, 'I would not allow myself to be taken in by any message of sympathy, not even if it were signed by a hundred hon[ourable] members.' The Tories laughed – four years earlier a hundred radical MPs had sent an ineffectual cable of support to the king of Greece, immediately after which he had been obliged to capitulate to the Turks. Winston advocated a generous peace in South Africa, drawing a scowl from the Conservatives around him. Of course, he quickly added, the Boers might reject the offer 'and stand by their old cry, "Death or Independence." ' This drew applause from the Irish Nationalists. But he had set another trap: 'It is wonderful that hon[ourable] members who form the Irish party should find it in their hearts to speak and act as they do in regard to a war in which so much has been accomplished by the courage, the sacrifices, and, above all, by the military capacity of Irishmen.' Kitchener's scorched-earth policy was no worse, he said, than the German practice in the Franco-Prussian War of 'throwing shells into the dwelling houses of Paris and starving the inhabitants of that great city to the extent that they had to live upon rats and like atrocious foods in order to compel the garrison to surrender.' Indeed, the British under Kitchener had done nothing not 'justified by precedents set by European or American generals during the last fifty or sixty years.' Not that he thought Britain wholly in the right. He took a middle course: 'I do not agree very fully with the charges of treachery on the

---

* 'If I were an American, as I am an Englishman, while a foreign troop was landed in my country, I would never lay down my arms – never – never – never!' (The Earl of Chatham in Parliament, November 20, 1777.)

one side and barbarity on the other.' Having established his independence –
he had deftly said that the Boers were not traitors, that they were right to fight,
that they deserved mercy – he drew to a graceful close, evoking his father's
name by attributing 'the kindness and patience with which the House has
heard me' to 'a certain splendid memory which many hon[ourable] members
still preserve.'[5]

Older members led him to the House bar, where, in his words, 'Everyone
was very kind. The usual restoratives were applied, and I sat in a comfortable
coma till I was strong enough to go home.' Before he left, Lloyd George told
him, 'Judging from your sentiments, you are standing against the Light,' and
Churchill replied, 'You take a singularly detached view of the British Empire'
– an inauspicious opening to what would become the strongest political
friendship of Churchill's early career. Lloyd George had missed the mutinous
notes in the speech. So had most of the press. The Liberal (anti-imperialist)
Daily Chronicle dismissed the new member as 'a medium-sized, undistinguished young man, with an unfortunate lisp in his voice.' The Conservative
papers approved of his remarks. He had 'held a crowded House spellbound,'
said the *Daily Express*, had 'satisfied the highest expectations,' said the *Daily
Telegraph*, had delivered a speech 'worthy of the traditions of the House,' said
Borthwick's *Morning Post*. But Hugh Massingham noted in the Liberal
(imperialist) *Daily News* that 'this young man has kept his critical faculty
through the glamour of association with our arms.' Not only had he kept it; it
grew. As the weeks passed, and he listened to the Opposition members, he felt
himself drifting steadily to the left, feeling, as Simone Weil did, that 'one must
always be ready to change sides with justice, that fugitive from the winning
camp.' To intimate friends he confided that he now thought barn burning in
the Transvaal and Orange Free State was 'a hateful folly.' He had come to feel
'sentimental about the Boers' and was both in revolt against jingoism and
'anxious to make the Conservative party follow Liberal courses.' Outside his
circle this was unknown. In public he remained a staunch Tory back-bencher.
Yet all the while, cold as malice, unsuspected but deadly, the vengeful hand of
Lord Randolph Churchill was reaching out of the grave to smite those who had
struck him down fifteen years earlier, when his son had been twelve years old.[6]

Over the next three months Winston established himself as a rising political
star. In the House he spoke frequently, with wit and apparent ease – few knew
in those early days of the exhausting rehearsals in Mount Street, the infinite
pains that went into each polished performance – and his fame grew. He
became one of those rare celebrities who are identified by first names alone;
'Winston said,' like 'Jackie wore' in America seventy years later, brought
instant recognition. Gossips were alert to news of him. *Punch* and *Vanity Fair*
cartoons depicted him as a slight, fastidious youth with an impish smile. A
Daily Mail parliamentary reporter noted that 'he follows every important
speech delivered from the Opposition with an alertness, a mental agility,' that

he often scribbled notes and passed them forward to Tory ministers about to speak, that 'occasionally a mischievous, schoolboy grin settles over his face as he listens to some ridiculous argument.' Julian Ralph, an American journalist, prophesied: 'Already Mr Churchill's head is carried with a droop which comes to those who read and study hard. When he is thinking he drops his head forward as if it were heavy. That is how you see him at one moment, a pose prophetic of what is too likely to fasten itself upon him before he reaches middle age. But . . . the next time you look at him he has sprung to his feet with the eagerness of a boy, his pale blue eyes are sparkling, his lips are parted, he is talking a vocal torrent and hands and arms are driving home his words.' The Press Gallery delighted in his mots. Already he was displaying a puzzling contradiction which would endure throughout his public life. He could not address the House without intensive preparation. Yet no member could be quicker on his feet. He said: 'Politics is like waking up in the morning. You never know whose head you will find on the pillow.' And, in another moment, he described the plight of the *genus politicus*: 'He is asked to stand, he wants to sit, and he is expected to lie.'[7]

Diarists began to take note of him. Beatrice Webb thought him 'restless, egotistical, bumptious, shallow-minded and reactionary, but with a certain personal magnetism, great pluck and some originality – not of intellect but of character.' Dilke, who had depicted Rosebery in his diary as 'about the most ambitious man I had ever met,' now added: 'I have since known Winston Churchill.' Rosebery, ironically, found Churchill's emerging zeal distasteful. But he was far from alone; in the opinion of Robert Rhodes James, Winston was 'brash, assertive, egocentric, wholly absorbed in himself and his own career, and unashamedly on the make.' Lloyd George misjudged him, however, when he wrote that 'the applause of the House is the breath of his nostrils. He is just like an actor. He likes the limelight and the approbation of the pit.' Churchill wanted, not approval, but attention. He didn't mind boos. He expected them, for he was preparing to hoist the banner of rebellion. Wilfrid Blunt, no parliamentarian, may have sensed this in describing Winston in his diary: 'In mind and manner he is a strange replica of his father, with all his father's suddenness and assurance, and I should say more than his father's ability.' There was, he added, 'just the same *gaminerie* and contempt of the conventional.' One would think Randolph's old colleagues might have seen that. But having taught the mutinous father a lesson, they hardly expected that they would have to teach it again to the son. Besides, until now Winston had performed the rites of Tory loyalty. He had dedicated *The River War* to Salisbury, 'under whose wise direction the Conservative Party have long enjoyed power and the nation prosperity.' Lord Randolph, the insurgent, had sat below the gangway, the customary seat for independent MPs. After being sworn in, Winston had chosen a spot directly behind the front government bench.[8]

With the arrival of spring, however, he moved. The alert correspondent for the *Daily Mail* noticed that the member for Oldham was now 'sitting in the corner seat from which his father delivered his last speech in the House of Commons' and observed 'a startling resemblance' between Winston and Randolph – 'the square forehead and the full bold eye of his father,' and 'the hurried stride through the lobby.' The lobby correspondent for *Punch* wrote that the resemblance lay 'less in face than in figure, in gesture and manner of speech. When the young member for Oldham addresses the House, with hands on hips, head bent forward, right foot stretched forth, memories of days that are no more flood the brain.' The son now began to advocate tight budgets and isolation from quarrels outside the Empire. References to Secretary for War William Brodrick began to appear in his speeches – Brodrick, under secretary in 1886, had been an enemy of Randolph's – and they were caustic. He was deeply offended, and said so, when Brodrick told the House: 'It is by accident that we have become a military nation. We must endeavour to remain one.' Salisbury had grown inattentive in his seventies, but Joe Chamberlain observed Winston often conferring with Sir Francis Mowatt, who had been his father's Exchequer colleague. Winston himself wrote: 'Presently I began to criticize Mr Brodrick's Army expansion and to plead the cause of economy in Parliament. Old Mowatt said a word to me now and then and put me in touch with some younger officials, afterwards themselves eminent, with whom it was very helpful to talk.' Speaking to the Liverpool Conservative Association on April 23, Randolph's son fired his first heavy warning shot. He deplored the large sums earmarked for army expansion. 'Any danger that comes to Britain would not be on land,' he said; 'it would come on the sea. With regard to our military system we must be prepared to deal with all the little wars which occur continually on the frontiers of the Empire. We cannot expect to meet great wars . . . for I think our game essentially is to be a naval and commercial power. I cannot look upon the army as anything but an adjunct to the navy . . . I hope that in considering the lessons of the South African war we shall not be drawn from our true policy, which is to preserve the command of markets and of the seas.'[9]

At 11:00 P.M. on Monday, May 13, he opened his offensive in the House. Realizing that this would be a watershed speech for him, he had been working and reworking it for six weeks, and like his father he had sent advance copies to the press, committing himself before he rose. Reminding them of 'a half-forgotten episode' – his father's fall – he read a few lines from Randolph's letter of resignation and said he proposed 'to lift again the tattered flag of retrenchment and economy.' In less than eight years, he noted, army costs had risen from seventeen million pounds to nearly thirty million. He wryly congratulated the secretary for war. This, surely, was a triumph of acquisitiveness. But now the minister had come to the well again. The House was being asked to vote on yet another rise, this one of five million pounds. Churchill's voice rose: 'Has the wealth of the country doubled? Has the population of the Empire doubled? Have the armies of Europe doubled? Is there no poverty at home? Has the English Channel dried up and are we no longer an island?' It was time 'a Conservative by tradition, whose fortunes are linked indissolubly to the Tory party,' should protest this increase of the public burden. Brodrick wanted three army corps. Why? 'A European war can only end in the ruin of the vanquished and the scarcely less fatal commercial dislocation of the conquerors.' Besides, the minister must know that 'if we went to war with any great Power his three Army corps would scarcely serve as a vanguard. If we are hated they will not make us loved, if we are in danger they will not make us safe. They are enough to irritate; they are not enough to overawe. Yet while they cannot make us invulnerable, they may very likely make us venturesome . . . We shall make a fatal bargain if we allow the moral force which this country has so long exerted to become diminished, or perhaps even destroyed, for the sake of the costly, trumpery, dangerous military playthings on which the Secretary for War has set his heart.'[10]

His friend Atkins described him in the *Guardian* as 'a lonely but self-possessed figure as he stood there reproducing the sentiments which caused the dramatic resignation of his father.' *Punch* was jubilant. And the Opposition, of course, was elated; Massingham predicted that one day he would be prime minister. His own party was discomfited and resentful. The next day a Tory MP icily noted that it was a mistake 'to confuse filial piety with public duty.' Brodrick, scornful, observed that the party, having survived without the father, could part company with the son, too. He hoped Winston would 'grow up' to regret 'the day when he came down to the House to preach Imperialism without being able to bear the burden of Imperialism, and when the hereditary qualities he possesses of eloquence and courage may be tempered also by discarding the hereditary desire to run Imperialism on the cheap.' Some Conservatives dismissed the speech as a publicity stunt. Violet Asquith heard talk that his conduct had been 'based on an almost slavish imitation' of Lord Randolph. But the general feeling, once tempers had cooled, was that the incident was best forgotten and soon would be. A gifted young Tory had felt compelled to pay peculiar tribute to an unfortunate memory. Now that he had got it out of his system, he could move forward with his own career, unfettered by the awkward past.[11]

Not so. Churchill had believed every word in his speech. He himself insisted on pointing out that it marked 'a definite divergence of thought and sympathy from nearly all those thronging the benches around me.' The government seemed shaky to him; he was convinced he could influence it. To his mother he wrote: 'There is a good deal of dissatisfaction in the party, and a shocking lack of cohesion . . . The whole Treasury Bench appear to be sleepy and exhausted and played out.' He meant to rouse it by deliberately adopting an offensive manner, singling out a major minister, Brodrick, and baiting him. Once at Question Time the secretary for war was asked how many horses and mules had been shipped to the Boer War. He replied and Winston innocently raised a supplementary question: 'Can my right honourable friend say how many asses have been sent to South Africa?' To those who cried foul, he said: 'Criticism may not be agreeable, but it is necessary; it fulfils the same function as pain in the human body, it calls attention to the development of an unhealthy state of things.' He called Brodrick's army plan 'a humbug and a sham,' a 'total, costly, ghastly failure,' 'the Great English Fraud.' Several other young Tories joined him, and they spoke in relays. Sir James Fergusson, a die-hard Conservative, was so upset that he wrote to the *Daily Telegraph*, protesting that he had never known 'an attack upon a Government so organized, and pressed with so much bitterness and apparent determination by members elected to support it.'[12]

Sir James implied pettiness. That was unjust. Churchill's motives were noble, and so was his rhetoric. It was also extraordinarily effective. One of its strengths, the perceptive Violet Asquith thought, was his lack of formal education. His colleagues, steeped in classical erudition and experience, were intellectually jaded, but 'to Winston Churchill,' she wrote, 'everything under the sun was new – seen and appraised as on the first day of Creation. His approach to life was full of ardour and surprise. Even the eternal verities appeared to him to be an exciting personal discovery.' He was unashamed, she noted, of speaking simple truths which, from others, would have been truisms. 'Nor,' she continued, 'was he afraid of using splendid language . . . There was nothing false, inflated, artificial in his eloquence: It was his natural idiom. His world was built and fashioned in heroic lines. He spoke its language.' Other MPs, unaware how effective his eloquence would be forty years later, thought his speeches merely a last glow of Britain's Antonine age of parliamentary oratory. In fact they were mature, powerful, and, coming from a man not yet thirty, extraordinarily foresighted:

Europe is now groaning beneath the weight of armies. There is scarcely an important Government whose finances are not embarrassed; there is not a Parliament or people from whom the cry of weariness has not been wrung . . . What a pity it would be if, just at the moment when there is good hope of a change, our statesmen were to commit us to the old and vicious policy! Is it not a much more splendid dream that this realm of England . . . should be found bold enough and strong enough to send forth for the wings of honest purpose the message which the Russian Emperor tried vainly to proclaim: that the cruel and clanking struggle of armaments is drawing to a close, and that with the New Century has come a clearer and calmer sky?[13]

Astonishingly, his campaign against Brodrick succeeded. He won what was, for a new MP, a major triumph. The cabinet accepted his argument that three corps couldn't 'begin to fight Europeans.' The plan was shelved. The minister resigned and was moved to the India Office. But Churchill's victory was illusory. His premise, that 'the honour and security of the British Empire do not depend, and can never depend, on the British Army,' that 'the only weapon with which we can expect to cope with great nations is the Navy,' was rejected. In the House a senior Tory scathingly asked him if he really believed that 'in future all that would happen in the case of war with a Continental power would be our magnificent fleet pursuing an inferior fleet?' The MP said: 'Such a state of things is unthinkable and I cannot imagine a war between Britain and a Continental power in which the British Army would not be required.' Winston, irrepressible, swiftly interjected, 'Not in Europe,' but the army budget passed easily. His father's battle could not be refought on this ground and won. Wilhelm II, aged twenty-nine, had just been crowned in Königsberg when Randolph left Salisbury's cabinet. Now he was powerful, aggressive, and a clear threat to British interests.[14]

Another vernal politician would have congratulated himself for having scored an important point, counted his change, and returned to the fold. But once Churchill had taken a position, no one but himself could persuade him to abandon it. He would be among the last of the Edwardians to appreciate the menace of the kaiser. In the House he distrusted every authority except his own – as, when he finally came to power, he would ruthlessly crush everyone who revolted against *him*. Yet such was his charm and intellect, even in those early days, that he could always find recruits to his cause, sometimes against their own best interests. After Brodrick's defeat he formed a society of Conservative back-benchers in their twenties, enrolling Lord Percy, the Duke of Northumberland's heir; Ian Malcolm, Lillie Langtry's son-in-law; Arthur Stanley, a son of the Earl of Derby; and, a real coup, Lord Hugh 'Linky' Cecil, one of the prime minister's sons. They were called 'the Hooligans,' or 'Hughligans,' after Lord Hugh, but Winston was their undisputed leader. Every Thursday they dined together in the House, and he laid down their first principle: issues would not be discussed until after the meal – 'It shall be High Imperialism nourished by a devilled sardine.' Hooligans were pledged to outrageous parliamentary manners, but each week they invited a distinguished guest, and such was the prestige of their family names that no one refused them, though Salisbury insisted that they dine with him at his home in Arlington Street, a block from Green Park. Their most memorable guest was Joe Chamberlain. He joined them after a stormy House session. An English newspaperman had been imprisoned in South Africa for writing what was considered a seditious article about the war. Having served his sentence, he had been denied the right to return home on the ground, stated from the Treasury Bench, that it was 'undesirable to increase the number of persons in England who disseminated anti-British propaganda.' The Liberals had leapt to their feet, shouting objections, and the Hooligans had joined them, Winston crying, 'Where else can anti-British propaganda be less harmful at this time than in Great Britain?'[15]

Over soup Chamberlain eyed them challengingly. He growled: 'I am dining in very bad company.' They expostulated; the government's stand was arrogant, absurd, and ineptly defended. How could they be expected to support it? He shot back: 'What is the use of supporting your own party only when it is right? It is just when it is in this sort of pickle that you ought to come to its aid.' Churchill's reply is unrecorded, but he must have kept himself in check, for Joe thawed; he became mellow and then, according to Winston, 'most gay and captivating. I never remember having heard him talk better.' As he rose to leave, he turned at the door and said with great solemnity: 'You young gentlemen have entertained me royally, and in return I shall give you a priceless secret. Tariffs! There are the politics of the future, and of the near future. Study them closely and make yourselves masters of them, and you will not regret your hospitality to me.'[16]

They didn't, but he bitterly regretted his advice, for Churchill took it, studying tariffs and then rejecting them, thereby contributing heavily to Chamberlain's political ruin and the fall of the Tory government. The issue, dear to the heart of this self-made businessman, was rooted in the British economy and in his dream of Empire. Victorian prosperity had peaked in the early 1870s. Since then the country's annual growth rate had sunk below 2 per cent. The problem was foreign competition, which, with improved transport and more efficient machinery, had deeply penetrated the English market. Wheat was down ten shillings, the textile industry was in straits, and both the United States and Germany had surpassed Britain's steel production. Because of the country's heavy investments abroad, particularly in the United States, these losses had been unfelt by the public. Indeed, per capita income actually continued to grow, a tribute to the Empire's vast wealth. But the deficit could not be camouflaged indefinitely. Chamberlain believed the answer was imperial preference. After touring South Africa late in 1902 – the Boer treaty had been signed at Vereeniging in May – he returned home to propose a tariff scheme which, he was convinced, would unite the Mother Country and her colonies and Dominions in a common market. Imposing heavy taxes on imports from outside the Empire, while establishing preferential tariffs for territories within it, the union would shield imperial industry and agriculture from foreign competitors while strengthening British security and providing funds for social programmes at home.

This was logical, sensible, and political dynamite. Free Trade had been the keystone of English economic policy for half a century. Its obvious advantage, for the middle and working classes, was an abundance of cheap imported food, but to them it represented more than that; they believed that it meant peace with the rest of the world, while protective tariffs led to war. Campbell-Bannerman – who believed that Chamberlain, before turning his coat, had wrecked the Liberal party by fighting Home Rule in the 1880s – now wrote to a friend: 'This reckless criminal escapade of Joe's is the great event of our time. It is playing Old Harry with all Party relations.' The Liberal Violet Asquith thought the issue 'money for jam.'[17] The ruling coalition was deeply split; three members of the cabinet resigned in protest. A lull followed. On July 11, 1902, in the middle of a conference of colonial leaders considering the tariff proposal (they favoured it), Salisbury stepped down as prime minister. Balfour then succeeded him. The new leader needed time to settle in. Chamberlain welcomed the break; given time, he believed, he could bring the party around. And he was largely successful. The Conservative newspapers and the constituency committees rallied to him. At Sheffield a party conference voted overwhelmingly to support protectionism, backing it with almost ideological fervour as a way to bind the Empire together.

Nevertheless, there were a few important holdouts, among them Linky Cecil and his brother Robert – and Winston Churchill. At the beginning of the controversy Winston's position had been unclear. He believed colonies should stand alone economically – earlier in 1902 he had voted against a West Indian sugar subsidy because 'I object on principle to doing by legislation what properly belongs to charity' – but the following summer, in his annual report to Oldham Conservatives, he had cautiously noted that he was merely looking into 'the question of what is called Fair Trade,' adding, noncommittally, 'Time is, I think, coming near when men will have to make up their minds on this great issue, to formulate their opinions, and set them forth without hesitation or doubt.' This sounds casual. Actually, he was examining the matter with great care. He knew that his father's old friend Sir Michael Hicks-Beach, who had been Salisbury's chancellor of the Exchequer, was an ardent Free Trader. This, however, was something he had to think through for himself. 'First,' he told Violet Asquith afterwards, 'I had to learn economics. I had to learn economics in eight weeks.' She asked how he set about it. He had gone to Mowatt, he said, and Mowatt, risking dismissal as joint permanent secretary of the Treasury, 'coached and grounded me with facts and general principles and arguments and gave me half a dozen books to read. He girded on my armour and equipped me for a fight. And then,' he concluded with relish, 'I found no difficulty in doing the rest myself.' Thereafter his faith in Free Trade, Violet wrote, became 'a passionate conviction, perhaps the only economic conviction he ever held, and it was upheld and reinforced by the assurance' – given him by Hicks-Beach, Mowatt, and Sir Edward Hamilton, another elderly civil servant at the Treasury – 'that his father would have shared it.' By the autumn of 1902 his position was firm and irreversible. On November 14 he wrote to an Oldham constituent that he believed protection 'a fantastic policy to endeavour to shut the British Empire up in a ringed fence . . . Why should we deny ourselves the good and varied merchandise which the traffic of the world offers, more especially since the more we trade with others, the more they must trade with us; for it is quite clear that we give them something else back for everything they give to us.'[18]

On May 15, 1903, confident that his troops were in line, Chamberlain renewed his campaign for imperial preference with a forceful address in his political stronghold of Birmingham, dismissing Free Traders as 'a small remnant of Little Englanders, of the Manchester school.' The Cecils and other dissidents having chosen to remain silent out of loyalty to him, Joe thought himself the party's spokesman on the issue. He found otherwise when, six days later, Churchill told a crowd at Hoxton that he could not believe anyone would 'persuade the British people to abandon that system of free trade and cheap food under which they have thriven so long.' A few days later Winston rose from his House seat below the gangway to deliver a fighting speech, charging that protectionism 'means a change, not only in the historic English Parties but in the conditions of our public life. The old Conservative Party with its religious convictions and constitutional principles will disappear and a new

Jennie as drawn by John Singer Sargent

Blenheim Palace

above right:
Jennie in Ireland, about 1877

right:
Mrs Everest

Lord Randolph Churchill in his prime

Winston at Harrow in 1889

Jennie and two of her lovers
(Count Kinsky on left)

Lieutenant Winston Churchill
in India

Lieutenant Winston Churchill, Subaltern of Horse, Fourth Hussars, 1896

Jennie in her prime

Pamela Plowden, 1892

Churchill in Cairo, 1898

An artist's reconstruction of the armoured-train ambush,
in the *Daily News Weekly* of November 25, 1899

Churchill addressing the crowd at Durban

Churchill in his first,
unsuccessful, campaign
for Parliament

Churchill in 1904,
when he joined the Liberals

Spy cartoon in *Vanity Fair*,
July 10, 1900

Joseph Chamberlain

Arthur Balfour

Clementine Hozier at the time of her wedding

Churchill and
David Lloyd George,
Budget Day, 1910

Winston and Jennie, 1912

Churchill and
Kaiser Wilhelm at German
manoeuvres in 1909

Churchill at
British army manoeuvres,
September 1913

party will rise . . . perhaps like the Republican Party in the United States of America . . . rigid, materialist and secular, whose opinions will turn on tariffs and who will cause the lobbies to be crowded with the touts of protected industries.' If a European war broke out, he asked, would it not be 'very much better that the United States should be vitally interested in keeping the English market open,' rather than be indifferent to the fate of 'their present principal customer?'[19]

He now took a momentous step. In a May 25 letter to the new prime minister marked 'Most Private,' he promised 'absolute loyalty' to the party – 'I would even swallow six army corps' – if Balfour pledged support of Free Trade. 'But if on the other hand,' he added ominously, 'you have made up your mind & there is no going back, I must reconsider my position in politics.' By now, after watching Churchill in the House for two years, AJB must have known that he did not make idle threats. At the very least Winston was entitled to a frank statement of his leader's stand on this issue. So, for that matter, was the public. Balfour, incredibly, had left tariff policy to Chamberlain. Although he had been prime minister for ten months, and had urged new policies, he had taken no stand on this crucial point. Sphinxlike, leonine, outwardly a model of poise, and apparently bereft of personal ambition, Salisbury's nephew and political heir was in reality a gifted but unpredictable statesman, best remembered for a declaration in which he gave away Palestinian land Britain did not own. His answer to Winston, dictated on May 26, was tortuous and weak. Unbelievably, he wrote: 'I have never understood that Chamberlain advocated protection.' As he perceived it, his colonial secretary was recommending 'a duty on food-stuffs,' which might 'incidentally be protective in character' but whose main purpose was 'to provide an instrument for fiscal union with the colonies.' Then, absurdly: 'This is a very different thing from protection, both in theory and in practice. But undoubtedly the matter is one of difficulty, and requires the most wary walking.'[20]

Undoubtedly Balfour was wary of Churchill. Shrinking from controversy, he was inviting deeper trouble. There was another possible answer to Winston's challenge, however, and many Tory colleagues had expected him to make it before now. Traditionally, observes Colin Coote, managing editor of the *Daily Telegraph*, 'there are two ways of getting on in the House of Commons – by being very naughty, and by being very good. If you are very naughty, your party says, "Give the puppy a nice bone to keep him quiet." ' In short, the able young critic of his elders is assigned responsibility and thus silenced. Some MPs thought such a possibility was what Churchill had had in mind when he attacked Brodrick. He had shown parliamentary ability, and he had changed Salisbury's mind. But Balfour was not Salisbury. Dissent within Conservative ranks alarmed him, and he had been offended by Winston's tactics. He may also have recalled his uncle's reply when asked why, after Lord Randolph's humiliation, he had not invited him back into the government: 'When you have got rid of a boil on your neck, you don't want it back.'

In reshuffling his cabinet, Balfour had found room for one Hooligan, appointing Lord Percy under secretary of state for India, but in his view Winston was an even bigger boil than Randolph.[21]

Everyone knew Churchill was searching for a shortcut to office. Political tacticians had predicted that he would adopt one of two courses. Either he would try to talk Balfour into disowning Chamberlain, hoping to replace him as the party's strong man, or he would follow Lord Randolph's example and organize a revolt against the prime minister. His May exchange of letters with Balfour represents the failure of the first. But there is reason to believe that he had already tested the possibility of a coup. On March 4, 1905, J.L. Wanklyn, MP for Central Bradford, told an audience of constituents that more than two years earlier Winston had approached him with a scheme to unseat the Balfour leadership, replacing it with a weak ministry of Tory radicals, which in turn would be succeeded by a Churchill government. According to Wanklyn, Winston already had a list of men he would appoint to his cabinet, including Hugh Cecil as education minister. *The Times* carried Wanklyn's speech and, the next day, Winston's statement that the charge was 'devoid of the slightest foundation . . . The whole story from beginning to end is a pure invention of his own, and, if not a hallucination, can only be described as a wilful and malicious falsehood.'[22] Nevertheless, Wanklyn stuck to his guns. He invited Winston to sue him. The offer was declined, and the story credited, for by then the House believed that to reach his ends Winston would stop at nothing, that he was even prepared, if necessary, to bolt his party.

Churchill always nailed his colours to the mast, but not always to the same mast. He 'did not,' he later said, 'understand the importance of party discipline and unity, and the sacrifices of opinion which may lawfully be made in their cause.' The issue was everything. Less than forty-eight hours after receiving Balfour's squelch, he wrote another confidential letter, this time to Campbell-Bannerman. Describing his position on tariffs as 'one of great difficulty and danger,' he nevertheless proposed a joint strategy to prevent 'an immense victory for Chamberlain.' C-B swiftly agreed, and thenceforth Winston was increasingly drawn into Opposition councils. He felt comfortable there. He found John Morley, Asquith, Haldane, and Grey attractive. And he approved of their legislative programme: wider suffrage, an eight-hour day, a graduated income tax, and less expenditure on foreign and imperial affairs. Most significant, he had become an advocate of Irish Home Rule. Violet Asquith wrote that 'Irish self-government might well have stuck in his throat, for to Lord Randolph Home Rule had become anathema. But he swallowed it, apparently without effort. His filial piety had ceased to be his sole directing light. He was now charting his own course.'[23]

As early as 1901, a few months after entering Parliament, he had flirted with the thought of switching parties. His motives then had been less than lofty. Lady Warwick held a long political discussion with him at Cecil Rhodes's Scottish home on Loch Rannoch. She wrote that Winston 'had just been on a visit to Lord Rosebery, and he said he was inclined to leave the leadership to

Mr Balfour and proclaim himself a Liberal. He wanted power and the Tory road to power was blocked by the Cecils and other brilliant young Conservatives, whereas the Liberal path was open. Cecil Rhodes was all in favour of his turning Liberal.' Winston had written to his mother: 'I am a Liberal in all but name.' He was corresponding with Bourke Cockran, who was campaigning against Republican tariffs in Washington, and he knew that Cockran, still one of his heroes, had left Tammany on a matter of principle in 1896 to support McKinley for President. His aunt Cornelia begged him to cross the floor: 'Of one thing I think there is no doubt & that is that Balfour & Chamberlain are one, and that there is no future for Free Traders in the Conservative party. Why tarry?'[24]

He tarried because he wasn't so sure about Balfour's position. On this issue the man was a Hamlet. Thus far the duel had been between Churchill and Chamberlain, and in the House, Winston had more Conservative followers than Joe; when he launched his Free Food League on July 13, 1903, sixty Tory MPs signed up, while the rival Tariff Reform League enrolled only thirty. Outside Parliament, however, Chamberlain was much stronger among the party rank and file. He was a hero to the constituency committees, the men who got out the vote. That summer he crisscrossed the country, speaking fervently for imperial preference. Churchill, fighting it, made the same tour, matching him speech for speech. Both sides were still civil. Winston's sharpest barb was: 'Mr Chamberlain loves the working man. He loves to see him work.' On July 26 Sir Edward Hamilton wrote in his diary: 'W.C. is taking a very devoted line against C . . . It is the fashion to run him down – but I think there is a great deal in him and that he is bound to win in the end.' On August 12 Churchill and another MP entertained several members of the party leadership, including the prime minister, at a dinner in the House. Afterwards he wrote to his mother, 'A.B. was most amiable and very good humoured' even though 'I had been very rude to him in the House of Commons in the afternoon.' Leaving the dinner he 'ran straight into J.C. who gave me an extraordinary look of reproach as much as to say "How could you desert me" and I confess I felt very sorry for him indeed . . . I cannot help admiring Chamberlain's courage. I do not believe he means to give way an inch, and I think he is quite prepared to sacrifice his whole political position . . . for the cause in which he is so wrapped up.' Yet Winston came to regard Joe as the turncoat, the subversive, the renegade. In early September the *Pall Mall Gazette* quoted Churchill as saying: 'Some of us were born in the Tory Party and we are not going to let any aliens turn us out.' The *Gazette* reporter asked him about rumours that he would cross to the Opposition, and he replied: 'Oh, absurd. I am a Tory and must always remain a Tory.' The article concluded: 'He is a Tory by birth and inheritance. Toryism possesses him . . . It is with him something of a religion.'[25]

It wasn't, really. He was on the verge of sacrilege. The turning point came that month. On September 12, 1903, Chamberlain quit the cabinet to devote himself to his crusade. Momentarily it seemed that the prime minister might be able to ignore the issue. It was an illusion. The tension was still there, and it was growing. Two days after Joe had stepped down, Churchill wrote to his mother: 'I fancy a smash must come in a few days. Mr Balfour is coming to Balmoral on Saturday. Is he going to resign or reconstruct? . . . If he reconstructs – will it be a protectionist reconstruction of a cabinet wh does not contain the free trade Ministers, or a free trade reconstruction of a Cabinet from which J.C. has resigned? All these things are possible.' But there was no ministerial reshuffle. Two weeks later a second Conservative conference at Sheffield strongly reaffirmed imperial preference as a means of strengthening the Empire. In his speech to them, Balfour then tumbled off the fence and, with some characteristic reservations, declared himself to be on their side. This, to Winston, meant the time had come to take off his gloves. He wrote (but did not mail) a letter to Linky Cecil, declaring that 'to proceed making perfervid protestations of loyalty to the "party" & yet to trample on the dearest aspirations of the party & thwart its most popular champions is to court utter ruin.' He added, bitterly: 'I am an English Liberal. I hate the Tory party, their men, their words & their methods.' Even so, he was not yet ready to make his change of heart public: 'Nothing need happen until December at any rate, unless Oldham explodes.'[26]

But Oldham did explode. Despite promises to jump to the Tory whip, he endorsed the Liberal candidate in a Ludlow by-election on the ground that 'Free Traders of all parties should form one line of battle,' and at a Free Trade rally in Halifax he cried: 'Thank God we have a Liberal Party.' On December 23 Oldham's Tory executive committee resolved that he had 'forfeited' their confidence and could not expect their support in the next election. The resolution would be laid before the full body on January 8, 1904. In a spirited defence, Churchill wrote to them that he was responding to a higher loyalty: 'When Mr Balfour succeeded Lord Salisbury, he solemnly pledged himself at the Carlton Club that the policy of the party should be unchanged. And yet at Sheffield, only a year afterwards, he declared for a "fundamental reversal of the policy of the last fifty years." Therefore it is not against me that any charge of breaking pledges can be preferred.' He said he meant to continue representing the thirteen thousand men who had voted for him, doing his best 'to oppose all protectionist manoeuvres in Parliament and to explain to the electors of Oldham how closely Free Trade and cheap food are interwoven with the welfare of the Lancashire artisan.' The committee was unconvinced. The resolution carried with but one dissent. He offered to resign, which was crafty of him; in a by-election he would either split the vote with their candidate or win as a Liberal – a Tory loss either way. So his original Oldham sponsors fumed, impotent, while he continued to sit on the Conservative side of the House, savaging his leaders day after day.[27]

Not even the oldest MPs could remember a more brilliant, more acrimonious performance. The *Daily Mail* commented that since Sheffield 'his speeches have been almost without exception directed against the policy of the Government. They have been clever, severe, biting in their sarcasm, full of sneers and scorn for Mr Balfour and his Ministers.' The Conservative party, Churchill said, had become 'the slave of great interests.' The Tory flaw was 'a yearning for mediocrity.' The party's members were 'ready to make great sacrifices for their opinions, but they have no opinions. They are ready to die for the truth, if only they knew what the truth is.' He cried: 'To keep in office for a few more weeks and months there is no principle which the Government is not prepared to abandon, and no quantity of dust and filth they are not prepared to eat.' Balfour was guilty of 'gross, unpardonable ignorance' and a 'slipshod, slapdash, haphazard manner of doing business.' Winston said that 'the dignity of a Prime Minister, like a lady's virtue, is not susceptible of partial diminution.' Balfour, however, had 'flouted the traditions of Parliament and dishonoured the service of the Crown.' When one of the prime minister's supporters protested this outrageous language, Churchill wrote to *The Times*, accusing the man of trying to gag him, and adding: 'While Mr Balfour silences his followers in the House of Commons Mr Chamberlain is busy with their constituencies' disseminating 'protectionist propaganda.' The prime minister was only a puppet, a fool; the real Tory leader was Chamberlain, and Winston described Joe's vision of the party: 'Over all, like a red robe flung about the shoulders of a sturdy beggar, an extravagant and aggressive militarism, and at the top, installed in splendour, a party leader, half German Chancellor, half American boss.' Chamberlain's insistence that tariffs would enrich Britain was 'a downright lie.' When another Free Trader resigned from the party, Tory MPs hissed his speech explaining why. Churchill shouted: 'Mr Speaker, I rise on a point of order. I am quite unable to hear what my honourable friend is saying owing to the vulgar clamour of the Conservative Party.' Sir Trout Bartley, a Balfour supporter, leapt up, pointed at Churchill, and shrieked: 'The vulgarest expression came from this honourable gentleman!'[28]

The prime minister tut-tutted and looked away. Most of the time he ignored Churchill, but sometimes he was drawn. What galled him most was the knowledge that while the wounding slurs of other MPs arose from the heat of battle, Churchill coldly honed and barbed his insults each evening in Mount Street. It was premeditated, ungentlemanly. Once he deeply angered Balfour. In tones dripping with malice Churchill said, 'We have been told *ad nauseam* of the sacrifices which the Prime Minister makes. I do not deny there have been sacrifices. The House ought not to underrate or deny those sacrifices.' He ticked them off: 'sacrifices of leisure,' 'sacrifices of dignity,' 'the sacrifice of reputation.' He quoted the prime minister's supporters as saying that he stood 'between pride and duty.' Winston sarcastically commented: 'Pride says "go" but duty says "stay." The Right Honourable Gentleman always observes the maxim of a certain writer that whenever an Englishman takes or keeps anything he wants, it is always from a high sense of duty.' AJB rose, shaking, and accused him of poor taste. He said: 'It is not, on the whole, desirable to come down to this House with invective which is both prepared and violent. The House will tolerate, and very rightly tolerate, almost anything within the rule of order which evidently springs from genuine indignation aroused by the collision of debate; but to come down with these prepared phrases is not usually successful, and at all events, I do not think it was very successful on the present occasion. If there is preparation there should be more finish, and if there is so much violence there should certainly be more veracity of feeling.'[29]

Churchill did not hang his head. 'I fear I am still in disgrace,' he cheerfully wrote to Jennie, and, in a letter to Cockran, predicted more 'stormy times ahead.' Margot Asquith thought his problem was a lack of empathy, that he tended 'to ignore the need to feel his way about other minds,' but he didn't think he had a problem at all. He was releasing his inner aggression and enjoying it enormously. He later said: 'I did not exactly, either by my movement or my manner, invite any great continuing affection.' He didn't want it. Earl Winterton recalled: 'Churchill made no attempt to dispel the suspicion and dislike with which he was regarded by the majority of the House of Commons. He seemed to enjoy causing resentment. He appeared to have, in modern parlance, a "chip on his shoulder," when in the Chamber itself or in the Lobbies.' Winston jovially told a reporter, 'Politics are almost as exciting as war and quite as dangerous.' The newsman asked, 'Even with the new rifle?' Churchill replied, 'Well, in war you can only be killed once, but in politics many times.'[30]

Though he was to prove that repeatedly, expressions of his unpopularity in the spring of 1904 were uglier and more strident than anything his father had endured. Shouted down by his own party, he was called 'wickedly hypocritical,' the 'Blenheim Rat,' and a 'Blackleg Blueblood.' In a rare affront, the Hurlingham Polo Club blackballed his application for membership. He seemed unrepentant. And he offended men who might have befriended him. One contemporary noted in his diary on March 5: 'Went to the Speaker's Levée . . . Winston Churchill was there in a cavalry uniform with a long row of medals. He is a most astounding person. His speeches in the House this session have been very fine.' But in a fortnight the diarist changed his mind; Churchill, he had decided, was 'a most infernal nuisance.' *Punch* reported: 'His special enmity for Chamberlain and all his works is hereditary . . . Winston is a convinced Free Trader. But he enters with lighter, more fully gladdened heart into the conflict, since Protection is championed by his father's ancient adversary.' Earl Winterton thought him 'too eager to hunt down his father's old enemies.' MacCallum Scott, another contemporary, wrote that 'the followers of Mr Chamberlain repaid his [Winston's] hostility with a passionate personal hatred over which they vainly endeavoured to throw a mask of contempt. There was no better hated man in the House of Commons.' He was shunned. Only Tories who felt absolutely secure dared be seen with him. On Good Friday, Linky Cecil suggested that 'the town council of Oldham give Winston Churchill the freedom of the borough as a mark of his independence and public spirit. As he is not going to stand for Oldham again it could not be mixed up with local party politics and it would be a fitting rebuke to ill-mannered persons in the House. He is I think being abominably treated.

For he is very honest and very good-hearted.' But Linky was Lord Salisbury's son. Had this come from an MP less well connected, it could have been a note of political suicide.[31]

The beginning of the end came on March 29, 1904. At 5:00 P.M. Churchill rose to follow Lloyd George in debate. At that point Balfour left his seat and met Austen Chamberlain, Joe's son and chancellor of the Exchequer, beyond the glass door behind the Speaker's chair. Winston, offended, objected to the prime minister's departure just as he was about to speak; he called it an astonishing 'lack of deference and respect.' At that, the cabinet rose from the Treasury Bench and walked out to the smoking room, followed by almost all the back-benchers, who paused at the door to jeer and count the number of Tories left. There were fewer than a dozen, all Free Traders. One, Sir John Gorst, who had belonged to Randolph's Fourth Party, denounced his fellow Conservatives for treating Winston 'with the most marked discourtesy which I think I have ever seen.' That merely put Gorst, too, in Coventry. The morning edition of the *Daily Mail* carried the headlines: CHILLING REBUKE. UNIONISTS REFUSE TO HEAR MR CHURCHILL. STRANGE SCENE IN THE HOUSE OF COMMONS. the *Mail* reported: 'The merry jest, the sparkling epigram and the ironical sally departed . . . from Mr Churchill's oration. He never speaks unless there is a full house. The full house had melted away under his spell. It was a chilling rebuke, crushing, unanswerable. He complained bitterly at the slight, and murmured some phrases about shifty policy and evasion. There were only the crowded benches of the Liberals to cheer. Behind him was silence and desolation.' He was not yet the Winston Churchill of the 1930s; the strain of his solitary struggle had begun to tell; he was vulnerable to sudden, uncontrollable attacks of depression and had not yet learned to hide them until alone. Next day the *Pall Mall Gazette* told its readers that 'in appearance there is nothing of "the Boy" left in the white, nervous, washed-out face of the Member for Oldham. He walks with a stoop, his head thrust forward. His mouth expresses bitterness, the light eyes strained watchfulness. It is a tired face, white, worn, harassed . . . There is, indeed, little of youth left to the Member for Oldham.' He was going through the political equivalent of a divorce suit, and approaching the brink of a breakdown.[32]

On Friday, April 22, he went over the brink. He had read Benjamin Seebohm Rowntree's *Poverty: A Study of Town Life* on Morley's recommendation. The book impressed him immensely, and marked the beginning of his radical period. Trade unions, he decided, must be recognized and their rights defined. This message – 'Radicalism of the reddest type,' the *Daily Mail* called it – was the burden of his remarks for forty-five minutes that Friday, and he was approaching his peroration when calamity struck. He was speaking with his customary fire, and was about to strike his right fist into his left palm, clinching his argument, when his mind went completely blank. He had just said: 'It lies with the Government to satisfy the working classes that there is no justification . . .' His voice trailed off. He groped. The studied phrases, laboriously composed and learned by heart, had fled from his memory. He began again: 'It lies with them . . . What?' he asked, as though someone had suggested a cue. He hesitated, frowned, looked confused, and fumbled in the pockets of his frock coat, as though looking for notes. There were none; until now he hadn't carried any. The MP beside him picked some paper scraps from the floor; there was nothing on them. Winston made one more try: 'It lies with them to satisfy the electors . . .' Some members cheered encouragingly, but it was no good. He sat down abruptly, buried his face in his hands, and muttered: 'I thank honourable members for having listened to me.' The next day a headline read: MR CHURCHILL BREAKS DOWN, DRAMATIC SCENE IN THE HOUSE OF COMMONS.[33]

One name was on the lips of upper-class London: *Lord Randolph*. Less than ten years earlier Winston's father, occupying the same seat, had broken down in the same way, signalling his slide down into oblivion and death. To his family and friends the parallel was appalling. The next day Shane Leslie called at Mount Street and found his cousin huddling with his brother, Jack, and Sir Alfred Harmsworth. Winston asked Leslie to make inquiries about Pelmanism, the memory training system. It was unnecessary. His memory had been, and would again be, phenomenal; he had merely suffered a temporary lapse. In the future he would seldom speak without a text, but he rarely seemed to glance at it. Over the weekend his spirits, and his confidence, rebounded. He had passed the crisis of party renunciation. A correspondent in the Press Gallery noted the return of his 'unmistakably schoolboy grin' in House shouting matches, 'not the assumed smile so often seen in Parliament, but the real grin of one who is alive to all the fun of things.' On May 16 he delivered his last speech as a Tory, envisioning the fall of the Conservative government: 'Extravagant finance was written on the head of their indictment, and it will be written on the head of their tombstone.' The Boer War had been an 'immense public disaster.' He was partly to blame, 'tarred' in a small way 'with responsibility,' but the heavier guilt fell upon Chamberlain and his 'New Imperialism . . . that bastard Imperialism which was ground out by a party machine and was convenient for placing a particular set of gentlemen in power.' The *Manchester Guardian* reported that 'his neighbours melted away till scarcely a Protectionist was left in the House.' This time he beamed at their retreating backs.[34]

Early in April, over Easter weekend, he had been adopted by north-east Manchester as its Liberal candidate in the next election. On the last day of May he crossed the floor. It was low-key; there was no ceremony. *Punch* reported: 'House resumed to-day after Whitsun holidays. Attendance small; benches mostly empty. Winston, entering with all the world before him where to choose, strides down to his father's old quarters on the front bench below the gangway to the left of the Speaker, and sits among the ghosts of the old Fourth Party.' It was here, when the Tories were in opposition, that Randolph had stood in 1885, waving his handkerchief to cheer the downfall of Gladstone. The seat beside it was now occupied by Lloyd George, who gripped Winston's hand. Rosebery and Grey also welcomed him, none of them, of course, mentioning the invective he had once poured on their party, calling them 'prigs, prudes, and faddists,' describing liberalism as 'hiding from the public view like a toad in a hole,' and predicting that 'when it stands forth in all its hideousness the Tories will have to hew the filthy object limb from limb.'[35]

His former colleagues on the other side of the House hadn't forgotten, however. They had agreed with him then, and now regarded him as the filthiest of toads. Henry Lucy, 'Toby, MP' of *Punch* (like the *New Republic*'s later TRB), wrote in his diary: 'Winston Churchill may be safely counted upon to make himself quite as disagreeable on the Liberal side as he did on the Unionist. But he will be handicapped by the aversion that always pertains to a man who, in whatever honourable circumstances, has turned his coat.' However, Lucy had no control over another *Punch* correspondent, who wrote: ' "He's gone over at last, and good riddance," say honest hacks munching their corn in well-padded stalls of Government stables. They don't like young horses that kick out and cannot be safely counted upon to run in double harness. "Winston's gone over at last," they repeat, whinnying with decorous delight.'[36]

Afterwards they had long second thoughts. Chamberlain confided to Margot Asquith: 'He was the cleverest of all the young men. The mistake Arthur made was in letting him go.' F.E. Smith, the brilliant young Conservative who became Churchill's closest friend, wrote: ' "He can wait" has always been the Tory formula which has chilled the hopes of young and able men . . . And so chance after chance of modest promotion went by . . . Winston characteristically jumped the whole fence.' Winston himself, of course, denied that ambition had played any role in his decision. 'Some men change their party for the sake of their principles,' he said; 'others their principles for the sake of their party.' He quoted Pope: 'Sworn to no master, of no sect am I / As drives the storm, at any door I knock.'[37]

But he knew that in switching parties he was joining the future. For a generation the Liberal party had carried the cross of Home Rule. Now, in part due to him, Free Trade had replaced it as the central issue before the country. And Joe Chamberlain's exhortations to working- and middle-class audiences, his pleas to 'think imperially,' had failed. He was booed, or addressed empty halls. That debacle, public disillusionment with the Boer War, and scandalous reports that Chinese coolies were being treated as slave labour in South African mines – charges also laid at the former colonial secretary's door – had shifted England's balance of political power. The historian D.C. Somervell has concluded that 'from 1903 onwards, it seemed certain, and not only to those who wished it, that Balfour's Government would be defeated at the next election.' On December 12 of that year Churchill wrote to Cockran: 'I believe that Chamberlain will be defeated at the General Election by an overwhelming majority.'[38] And so he was. After the votes had been counted, Joe suffered a paralytic stroke and lived out his life a tragic invalid. His children carried on the family's parliamentary tradition. In subsequent governments the elder boy, Austen, went on to become foreign secretary, chancellor of the

Exchequer, and first lord of the Admiralty. The other son, Austen's half brother, was Neville Chamberlain.

It was Disraeli's cynical conviction that 'no man is regular in his attendance at the House of Commons until he is married.' Churchill had disproved that, but there were those who felt that he might have been a dash less abrasive, a shade more conciliatory, had he shared his bed. Unfortunately he continued to be an inept suitor. His romance with Pamela Plowden had died in Canada. His mother had entertained high hopes for their meeting there. 'Pamela is devoted to you,' she had written to him. His reply had been guarded, and Lord Minto, who had been their host, had written to Jennie: 'Everything seemed to me . . . platonic'; indeed, it was hard to imagine 'any other feelings than those of Plato' between them. For Pamela, that was the last straw. Back in England, she managed to get engaged to two other men in a fortnight. She chose between them and became Lady Lytton the following year.[39]

Jennie wrung her hands. She told him that if he wanted a wife he must first propose. So he did – twice. First he courted the beautiful, twenty-four-year-old American actress Ethel Barrymore; he besieged her with notes and flowers, took her to Claridge's for supper every evening after her performance, and, on July 13, 1902, entertained her at Blenheim. But Miss Barrymore, having faced the footlights since the age of fourteen, knew all the stagecraft of lovemaking. Winston had mastered none of it, and she gracefully declined his hand, explaining that she felt she 'would not be able to cope with the great world of politics.' Next he wooed Muriel Wilson, a handsome young heiress. Privately he admitted that he was after her money. Perhaps she sensed that; after an automobile tour of Italy with her and another girl in Lionel Rothschild's motorcar, he wrote glumly: 'Nothing could exceed the tranquil *banalité* of my relations with M.' Halfheartedly he pressed his suit and she, to his evident relief, rejected it. She gently told him that she didn't think he had much of a future.[40]

Part of his difficulty was inherent in his upbringing. As Lord Boothby points out, in their class 'the sexes were completely segregated from the age of ten to twenty-two.' Yet Boothby, who shared that handicap, managed to find his way into a remarkable number of beds, partly because he genuinely liked women. Winston didn't, at least not those outside his family. He was the kind of chauvinist feminists love to hate. During his bachelor days, he and Eddie Marsh, his private secretary, would arrive early at a party and watch each lady make her entrance. Recalling 'the face that launched a thousand ships,' Churchill would ask, 'How many ships do you think she would launch?' Marsh would hazard, 'Two hundred ships, or perhaps two hundred and fifty?' Winston would reply decisively: 'By no means. A small gunboat at the most.' He complained that the United States 'is too cluttered up with women. They are everywhere. They control eighty per cent of the country's wealth. They wield enormous power – and they bully their husbands.' The only person to succeed in frightening him was the American Mrs O.H.P. Belmont, who always referred to him as 'that dreadful man.' He growled that she was the least feminine woman he had ever met.[41]

But he was at a loss even with the mannequins of young Edwardian womanhood. He didn't know what to say to them. The only subject which really interested him was himself. He knew none of the delicate moves that could lead to intimacy; for example, 'peering down Pennsylvania Avenue,' as it was called – discreetly glancing down a girl's décolletage to admire her breasts. In mixed society he was a combination of Wellington and Peel – 'I have no small talk,' the great duke had said, 'and Peel has no manners.' If Churchill felt cordial, he might ask a woman her age. Sometimes he didn't even speak. In 1904, during a dance at Salisbury Hall given by Lady Crewe, Jennie introduced him to the lovely Clementine Hozier. Clementine said, 'How do you do?' In her words: 'Winston just stared. He never uttered one word and was very gauche – he never asked me for a dance, he never asked me to have supper with him. I had of course heard a great deal about him – nothing but ill. I had been told he was stuck-up, objectionable etcetera. And on this occasion he just stood and stared.' In the beginning, Violet Asquith, sitting beside him at dinner for the first time, found him equally uncommunicative. She wrote: 'For a long time he remained sunk in abstraction. Then he appeared to become suddenly aware of my existence. He turned on me a lowering gaze and asked me how old I was. I replied that I was nineteen. "And I," he said almost despairingly, "am thirty-two already." ' On reflection he added thoughtfully, 'Younger than anyone else who counts, though.' Then, savagely: 'Curse ruthless time! Curse our mortality. How cruelly short is the allotted span for all we must cram into it!' He burst into a diatribe about the brevity of life and ended: 'We are all worms. But I do believe that I am a glowworm.'[42]

Later Violet observed that his 'inner circle of friends contained no women. They had their own place in his life. His approach to women was essentially romantic . . . Their possession of all the cardinal virtues was assumed as a matter of course.' She, knowing how rare purity was in his mother's set – they openly despised 'middle-class virtue' – accused him of 'innocence.' He was offended, but he was aware that his perception of girls was flawed; comparing himself to his cousin Sunny, he wrote: 'He is quite different from me, understanding women thoroughly, getting into touch with them at once, & absolutely dependent upon feminine influence of some kind for the peace & harmony of his soul.' Later, after marriage, he developed a glorious dependence upon his wife, but outside his home he was never really comfortable in the company of women. One explanation may lie in his mother's affairs. He knew of her relationship with the King, which appears to have resumed after his coronation. In one postscript he wrote to her: 'I have been reading "An English Woman's Love Letters." Are all Mothers the same?'[43]

Certainly they weren't in the lower classes. The nine-year reign of Edward VII saw vast technological advances, but the only sexual innovations were the brassiere, invented by Charles R. Debevoise in 1902, and the perfection of the Wassermann test in Germany four years later. Few could afford, or even knew about, the expensive Dutch cap. Contraception was largely limited to withdrawal or, for the unfastidious, such abortifacients as lead-plaster. Outright abstention was surprisingly common. Paul Thompson concludes that 'the cumulative weight of three generations of Victorian puritanism, affecting the working classes directly through church and chapel teaching and indirectly through middle-class influence,' led to 'striking self-restraint among young adults.' The average bride was twenty-six. One Englishwoman in every five did not marry at all, and those who did were often parsimonious with their favours. A pioneer sex researcher, interviewing Edwardian workmen, found them bitter about their wives' unresponsiveness in bed. One wife, during the throes, kept reminding her husband not to forget to leave twopence for the gas; another chewed an apple during sexual intercourse; a third kept her clothes on (her spouse said, 'It's about as exciting . . . as posting a letter'); and a fourth, 'a sad little man, complained that not only did his wife take no interest in the proceedings, but she also insisted on a regular emolument of sixpence per session.'[44]

The liberal recommendations of the Royal Commission on Marriage and Divorce were ignored, and adultery still meant social ruin, but upper-class women, like their mothers in the 1880s – and often with their mothers' advice – had learned to manage complex intrigues. In public they were angelic. On Sundays they joined the black-bonneted, black-robed processions setting off for church. Mornings they trotted through the park in their gleaming victorias, parasols held over their heads and, on the seat opposite, card cases and pink leather address books from Dreyfous. They might sneak cigarettes in bedrooms, but in sitting rooms they merely wiggled crochet hooks or perched sedately behind teapots, and in dining rooms, their lovely faces illumined by candelabra, they sat erect and decorative, their piled hair crowned by gems and their bare, magnificent shoulders arising from clouds of tulle. An Edwardian lady in full dress was a wonder to behold, and her preparations for viewing were awesome. Silk stockings, carefully smoothed, went on first. Then she would rise in her chemise while her lady's maid fitted the long stays of pink coutil, heavily boned, around her hips, fastening the busk down the front, anchoring the garters to the stockings and tightening the silk lacings. Pads of pink satin would be affixed on the hips and under the arms, to stress the narrow waist. Drawers came next, after which the maid would spread the petticoat in a ring on the floor, and the lady, now wearing high-heeled shoes, would step into it. Buttons would be buttoned, tapes tied; then she would dive into the massive gown of taffeta and tulle and stand rigid while the maid laced up the bodice. Jewels went on last: rubies at the waist, dog collars of rubies and diamonds around the neck, and the tiara on top. As she sailed forth from her boudoir, you would never have guessed how quickly she could strip for action.

Assignations depended on circumstances. Vita Sackville-West explains in

The Edwardians: 'The code was rigid. Within the closed circle of their own set, anybody might do as they pleased, but no scandal must leak out to the uninitiated. Appearances must be respected, though morals might be neglected.' The King's mistresses had an easy time of it. No one would question a royal command, and few husbands, even in the aristocracy, were prepared to challenge His Majesty's droit du seigneur. Indeed, some women wore, pinned to their blouses, the little watches he gave them, bearing a true lover's knot of mauve enamel ribbon, and, on the back, the crown and the interlaced *E.R. VII*. 'Of course I don't *like* it,' they would say, 'but it's a good little timekeeper, and so I wear it.' Actually, HM's watches gained, on the average, about an hour a day.[45]

Amants de coeur of lesser rank had to be more discreet. Luckily transportation was slow; if His Lordship was off shooting partridge in September, or pheasant in October, or attending to fillies and paddocks, Her Ladyship could safely conclude that the coast was clear. It was then, after darkness had gathered, that a one-horse, rubber-tyred brougham would draw up outside her private entrance and her lover, using the key she had given him, would stealthily enter. (It never seems to have occurred to them that the brougham and the horse, standing there patiently throughout the evening, or even the night, were a dead giveaway.)

They were lusty in bed and rapacious at table. Meals were enormous, beginning, typically, with ortolan within quail, a truffle within the ortolan, pâté de foie gras within the truffle – on and on, until the pallor of the exhausted diners reminded one observer of the Roman vomitoria. 'Dinners,' wrote George Cornwallis-West, 'were Gargantuan affairs . . . champagne, port and old brandy were the order of the day, or, rather, night.' No one shrank from self-indulgence, and all but a few disdained work. They played tennis and auction bridge, which was invented in 1904; they attended races, amateur theatricals, elaborate teas, private recitals, and on one occasion a private circus engaged by an imaginative host. Sackville-West quotes an elderly peeress who defended all this: 'We lead the country, don't we? People who lead deserve their privileges. What would happen to the country, I should like to know, if the people at the top enjoyed no leisure? What would happen to the dressmakers, if your mother had no more pretty frocks?' Then, defending the Victorian precept that ostentation was a form of altruism, the peeress added: 'Besides, the country likes it. Don't you make any mistake about that. People must have something to look up to. It's good for 'em; gives 'em an ideal. They don't like to see a gentleman degrading himself.'[46]

That was not entirely preposterous. During Victoria's reign each new extension of the franchise to the working class had led to Tory gains at the polls. Protestant textile hands in Lancashire were particularly ardent in their conservatism, partly because Irish Catholics were Liberals but also out of loyalty to the Empire. And most of them appear to have enjoyed the ostentation of the

303

more fortunate. The addition of South Africa's 3,106-carat Cullinan diamond to the crown jewels, and the creation of twenty-seven diamond tiaras for the King's coronation by Louis Cartier, whose brother Jacques had just opened a London branch in New Bond Street, were sources of national pride.

But while the lower classes admired the glittering peak of Britain's social pyramid, and did not begrudge the lords their silks and feasts, they were not prepared to see their own children go hungry without protesting. Of course, hunger among England's poor – or the world's poor, for that matter – was nothing new. But the London press and the emerging sociological studies informed Britain's victims of their victimization. One such survey disclosed that in the bleakest neighbourhoods of the capital, the richest city in the world, one infant in four died because mothers were incapable of producing milk. Another study, in Leeds, showed that half the children of the destitute were marked by rickets, and 60 per cent had bad teeth. Workmen learned that 1 per cent of the country's population controlled 67 per cent of the nation's capital, while 87 per cent of the people were left with 8 per cent of the wealth. The average labourer earned one pound a week. At Victoria's death, Benjamin Rowntree found, 28 per cent of rural York lived in chronic poverty. In the year of her son's coronation, Charles Booth, a rich shipowner, published *The Life and Labour of the People in London*, revealing that 30 per cent of all Londoners suffered from malnutrition. The following year Jack London's *People of the Abyss* appeared; London had lived in the city's slums, and he described lodgings in which beds were let on a system of rotation, three tenants to a bed, each occupying it for eight hours. And in 1906 – the year Rolls-Royce was incorporated and Charles Nestle, a London hairdresser, introduced the permanent wave to fashionable ladies, charging £200 each – the *Daily News* exposed the perilous conditions and pitiful wages paid in England's sweated industries.

Wealthy Edwardians, like the peeress quoted by Vita Sackville-West, were untroubled by all this. It was the will of God; it was all in Malthus – the supply of food would never match population growth. They seldom visited slums. The only hunger most of them saw was that of beggars and the rheumy old women who sat under arches selling matches; to them they contributed a few coppers, a shilling, or even a half crown. Yet had they but investigated their own homes, they would have seen signs of economic distress. Butlers and lady's maids were well fed, but scullery maids and other 'under' servants were emaciated and sickly. They slept in attics, in basements, or on cots set up in pantries, and they never slept long; there was too much for them to do. Before dawn they were up raking leaves, rolling lawns, lighting fires, drawing curtains, filling vases with flowers, and bringing up breakfasts. Foreign visitors marvelled at the miracles wrought by unseen hands before 8:00 A.M., before the households' masters and mistresses arose, though one Frenchman, E.D. Gramont, found that 'this majestic silence got on my nerves. Those great mute corridors, those never-raised voices made me homesick for the Latin hurly-burly; servants shouting, banging pots and pans, slamming doors.'[47]

But Edwardian hosts enjoyed quietude. Few of them thought of the toil which made it possible. If they did discuss their menials, they were as likely as not to do it in the presence of the help. Domestics were not supposed to have feelings.

Before the ascendancy of Churchill and Lloyd George, all legislative attempts to provide relief for the unfortunate had failed. In 1905 the government established a royal commission on the Poor Law; the members included the Webbs, but both its majority and minority reports were tabled. Parliament outlawed compulsory trade-union contributions to Labour party candidates. MPs were not salaried until 1911. Financing a campaign cost about £1,000, nearly ten times the annual income of a skilled worker, so that even Liberals tended to champion the lot, not of workmen, but of the middle classes. In the radical Parliament that replaced Balfour's House, nearly half the MPs were businessmen or financiers, one in six was an Etonian, one in three was a graduate of Oxford or Cambridge, and only one in ten represented the working class. During the thirty years before 1916, half of all cabinet ministers were peers or members of peers' families. It was, for them, a splendid time, when everyone knew everybody, and gentlemen still wore toppers and ladies wore ostrich-plume bonnets, and there were always fresh strawberries in season on the House terrace, and waltz time was unthreatened by ragtime, and there were more hansoms than automobiles. A defender of Britain's oligarchic democracy wrote that MPs 'have an extraordinarily wide acquaintance with one another from one end of the land to the other. They are connected by marriage, by early association at the public schools and at Oxford or Cambridge, and they are brought constantly together by entertainments in the capital, and visits at country houses. Such a constitution gives to society great solidity and great influence, without the narrowness and rigidity that attends a purely hereditary caste.'[48]

That did not satisfy Churchill, who, despite his loyalty to his new party, would be no more a Liberal sheep than he had been a Conservative sheep. He noted that a Liberal party rule enjoined any cabinet member from serving as a director of a public company, yet thirty-one out of fifty-five Liberal ministers were directors, holding among them sixty-eight directorships – a 'laxity of principle,' he said, which 'is a sign of the degeneration of the day,' reflecting the creed of politicians 'who go about preaching the gospel of Mammon advocating the 10 per cent commandments, who raise each day the inspiring prayer, "Give cash in our time, O Lord." '[49] He raised the spectre of class warfare, and with justification. The Edwardian sky grew redder each year. In 1902 the British economist John Atkinson Hobson had published *Imperialism: A Study*, which had an immense impact on Rosa Luxemburg and Rudolf Hilferding in Germany and, through them, influenced Lenin. At the same time, the new British custom of the Pleasant Sunday Afternoon, the PSA, was providing expectant audiences for lay speakers who could entertain and divert them: journalists, humanitarians, adventurers, authors, hobbyists – and, more and more, radical propagandists intent upon exploiting forums to spread

305

a secular faith subversive of the established order.

The PSA, innocuous on the surface, was actually an institution of immense social significance. Its roots were the decline of the Victorian Sabbath and shrinking Anglican congregations – which in turn weakened the Tories, the Church of England's most ardent supporters. The solid core of agreed religious belief was gone. The Bible had lost its grip on Englishmen. People were groping for a substitute. *Fin de siècle* ideas had become unfashionable – the Boer War had tarnished Kiplingesque imperialism even as Oscar Wilde had discredited *Yellow Book* aestheticism. The new vogues were popular psychology, pragmatism, Nietzscheanism, and, towards the end of Edward's reign, the philosophy of Henri Bergson and the autosuggestivism of Emile Coué ('Every day, in every way, I'm growing better and better'). But perhaps the most influential ideological works were William James's *Varieties of Religious Experience*, appearing in 1902, and Sir James Frazer's eleven-volume *Golden Bough*, which was published intermittently, in revised editions, throughout the decade. Guided by James and Frazer, the children of nineteenth-century Christian evangelism moved towards a broadening tolerance of all creeds – which is to say, a vulnerability to radical speakers whose dogma provided hard, specific, simple answers to all complex questions.

That vulnerability was enhanced by a growing concept of a mechanistic universe – the obverse of traditional faith in the soul – which was an unanticipated by-product of the era's scientific and technological triumphs. Edwardians were bombarded by news of discoveries: glands, hormones, vitamins, genes, Einstein's $E=mc^2$, Pavlovian conditioned reflexes, Röntgen's X rays, Madame Curie's radium, and the subconscious as revealed by Freud, Adler, and Jung. Fruits of inventive genius promised more excitement to come. Because of Guglielmo Marconi, the King talked to President Roosevelt in 1903 by wireless. That same year two Americans flew the first heavier-than-air machine, and Eric S. Porter produced the first feature-length film, *The Great Train Robbery*. The British formed the Bristol Aeroplane Company; the *Daily Mail* sponsored the first international aircraft race. The Russians completed the trans-Siberian railway. Sleeping cars were introduced on Egypt's Cairo-to-Luxor Express. The production of Austin motorcars began in 1905; the following year the Royal Automobile Club turned its attention from steam-powered trucks to internal-combustion engines. In 1904 heels clicked all over Germany when the North German Lloyd steamer *Kaiser Wilhelm II* set a new transatlantic record of five days, eleven hours. Britons agreed that that would not do, and the Cunarder *Mauretania* made the trip in four days, twenty hours, and forty-one minutes. The Clyde was turning out bigger and bigger ships. The *Lusitania*, launched in 1907, was the largest yet: 31,550 tons, 790 feet long, with four screws and staterooms for 2,000 passengers. Meanwhile, the battleship HMS *Dreadnought* had been launched. She carried ten twelve-inch guns. The kaiser, chagrined, announced that he would not only match her; he would widen the Kiel Canal to permit passage of the huge new fleet he was building. *'Dem Deutschen gehört die Welt'* ('The world belongs to Germans') was the slogan of the Alldeutsche Verband (Pan-German League). The British public, however, couldn't take it seriously. To them it was as free of menace as that catchy tune written in 1908 by the English songwriters Harry Williams and Jack Judge, 'It's a Long Way to Tipperary.'

But the cumulative effect of all this change, which should have broadened the human vision, gave men a sense of confinement and helplessness. There were new powers at large, many of them incomprehensible, none in accord with the tidy, distinct images of reality they had been taught as children. Apparently there were no limits to the ways in which the world could be transformed. The Empire had provided their parents with a boundless frontier. Now, with the conquest of northern Nigeria in 1903, the map had filled up; Britain's new imperial challenge was not to get, but to hold. That stifled initiative abroad, and turned frustrated energy inward, into increased demands for innovation at home. The long peace of domestic law and order was shattered, the framework of Edwardian society shaken. Union organizers, reformers, and agitators told workmen of their plight. The mass-circulation newspapers – owned, ironically, by die-hard Tories – confirmed it. Labour struck, in the mines, on the docks, on the railroads; even in the newspaper composing rooms. In 1907 the Sinn Féin ('Ourselves Alone') was formed in Dublin, and Ireland flamed anew.

Finally, the balance between the sexes, the linchpin of the English home, came under ferocious attack. The attackers were idealistic wives. Their issue was the vote. Fewer than a third of all Edwardian Britons were entitled to go to the polls. Voters had to be heads of households, lodgers unencumbered by debts, owners of property, or educated. And they had to be male. In 1903 three militant feminists, Emmeline Pankhurst and her daughters Christabel and Sylvia, launched a crusade against sexism by founding the Women's Social and Political Union. The 'Suffragettes,' as the *Daily Mail* christened them in 1906, never attracted mass support, but they were alarmingly vocal and, in their campaign of civil disobedience, extraordinarily violent. One of them, Emily Davison, made the supreme sacrifice by throwing herself under the hooves of the King's horse at the Derby. Her comrades smashed shop windows, chained themselves to the gates of Buckingham Palace, bombed monuments, and burned down public buildings. Women like Jennie, who had flourished in the roles men had assigned them, thought that the 'female suffrage women' were, as she put it, 'too odious.' But other upper-class women were the movement's backbone. Their husbands were shocked. Some became converts, though enough remained obdurate to defeat a woman suffrage bill in the House. Churchill spoke for them when, reviving a word which had passed out of the language, he said he refused to be 'henpecked on a question of such grave importance.'[50]

* * *

These shadows cast by coming events were very real, and are defined here to qualify the general impression of the Edwardian era as one of absolute serenity. Yet they did not long darken the days of the favoured few. In his Mount Street rooms Churchill knew a tranquillity and security unavailable anywhere today. He did not appreciate it, of course; men rarely understand the sources of their strength. His inspiration continued to be the man who had abused him most. Memorabilia of his father dominated the flat. The walls were hung with pictures of Randolph, cartoons of Randolph from *Vanity Fair* and *Punch*, and a photograph of Randolph's champion horse Abbesse de Jouarre – 'Abscess of the Jaw,' the jockeys had called it. Winston sat in his father's carved oak chair behind his father's immense desk, dipped his pen in his father's brass inkwell, and toiled nearly every evening on his current work in progress, a two-volume biography entitled *Lord Randolph Churchill*.

His baths were drawn, his boots polished, his clothes laid out, and his small cellar of J. and C. Clark wines inventoried by his current valet, George Scrivings. A maid swept the grey pile carpet and dusted the gleaming, dark, heavy furniture, which, this being a typical Mayfair flat, required a lot of dusting. There were petit point chairs, a large Coromandel screen, a 'sociable' on which two people of opposite sexes might sit, facing each other but properly divided by the arm; tortured carvings of ebony, Benares brass, a red-and-gold Crown Derby tea set; and mahogany tables littered with family and polo-team photographs, silver cannon models, model soldiers, jade ashtrays, Indian and Egyptian carvings, celadon bowls, a Fabergé cigar box, twin candelabra, and a small clock. The air was exotic with the scents of wax and furniture oils. Books were everywhere. There were even bookshelves in the bathroom. Hugh Massingham, coming to call, found the occupant literally 'sleeping with encyclopaedias.' Pasted in huge scrapbooks were newspaper clippings on every public topic and on prominent men, particularly Winston S. Churchill. In an unguarded moment he mentioned these to Balfour, explaining that they were useful for reference. AJB's lip curled. He said disdainfully that he could not see the point of 'rummaging through a rubbish heap on the problematical chance of finding a cigar butt.'[51]

Impressions of Churchill at this time are varied but vivid. Wilfrid Blunt, meeting him for the first time, described him as 'a little, square headed fellow of no very striking appearance, but of wit, intelligence, and originality.' On the other hand, Leslie Hore-Belisha, who was ten years old when Churchill called on his father in Manchester, thought him very striking indeed; Winston was wearing 'a frock coat with silk facings and below his chin was a large winged collar with a black bow tie . . . I went so far as to buy – and wear in private – a large winged collar. Thus the imagination of a small boy was captured.' Directly after her first dinner-party encounter with him, Violet Asquith had gone to her father and told him that for the first time in her life she had seen genius. Asquith chuckled and said, 'Well, Winston would certainly agree with you there – but I am not sure you will find many others of the same mind.' Then he added, 'Still, I know exactly what you mean. He is not only remarkable but unique.' Jennie's new sister-in-law, Daisy Cornwallis-West, was uncharmed; her brother's marriage, she wrote, 'made Winston Churchill a connection of ours, a prospect we viewed with somewhat mixed feelings. I cannot honestly say I ever cared for him very much.' The same trait attracted and repelled: his brilliant, compulsive conversation. His critics called it 'bombast,' the 'self-advertisement' of an 'arriviste.' His admirers delighted in what they regarded as genuine wit. Lloyd George told him he was against the social order. Winston replied: 'You are only against those parts of it that get in your way.' Churchill described F.E. Smith's debating skills: 'The bludgeon for the platform; the entangling net and unexpected trident for the Courts of Law; and a jug of clear spring water for an anxious, perplexed conclave.' 'The difference between Balfour and Asquith,' he said, 'is that Arthur is wicked and moral, while Asquith is good and immoral.'[52]

Churchill's capacity for work was remarkable. His appointment book shows that in his first two weeks as an MP he dined out eight times, attended a trade conference, conducted an inquiry at the Treasury, called on the prime minister, delivered three speeches in the House, campaigned for a Conservative candidate in Manchester, and was there to congratulate him on his victory. One friend recalled in his memoirs that Winston 'gave himself to work. When he was not busy with politics, he was reading or writing. He did not lead the life of other young men in London. He may have visited political clubs, but I never met him walking in Pall Mall or Hyde Park where sooner or later one used to meet most friends. I never met him at a dinner-party that had not some public or private purpose.'[53]

Once he began writing his father's biography he attended even fewer parties, and was never seen at dances. The rest of his set hummed Franz Lehár's new waltzes; Churchill was reluctant even to learn the step. In *Anglo-American Memories*, George Smalley, a journalist from the United States, described a weekend as Churchill's fellow guest at Dunrobin, the seat of the Duke of Sutherland. Winston invited him into his bedroom, and Smalley gaped. The room, he wrote, 'had been turned into a literary workshop, strewn with books and papers and all the apparatus of the writer. He had brought with him a tin box, some three feet square, divided into closed compartments. This was his travelling companion on journeys of pleasure . . . His hostess had provided him with a large writing-table. This was covered with papers, loose and in docketed bundles, but all in exact order for ready reference . . . When we left Dunrobin we found that Winston had reserved a compartment in the railway train for himself and for his big tin case of papers. He shut himself up there, and during that long journey read and wrote and worked as if a Highland railway train were the natural and convenient laboratory in which literature of a high order was to be distilled.'[54]

Yet this view of Churchill may have been exaggerated. Like most men of affairs, he had learned to use his time efficiently, and in London he was all business. But he was not what today would be called a workaholic. Many of his leisured friends, it must be remembered, did not work at all; very little dedication was necessary to impress them. His appetite for statecraft did not prevent him from playing when he chose. He followed the races – at a Warwick Castle house party he astounded his fellow guests by reciting the names of the last fifty Derby winners and their breeding – and he always found time for polo, boar hunting, duck shooting, and holidays abroad. In Egypt he sailed up the Nile on a dahabeah with his aunt Leonie, Hicks-Beach, Sir John Gorst, the Duke and Duchess of Connaught, and Alice Keppel. In Switzerland he was the guest of Sir Ernest and Lady Cassel, and at Balmoral he stalked stags with His Majesty. ('You will see the King on Weds when he comes to Invercauld,' he wrote to his mother; 'mind you gush to him about my having written to you saying how much etc etc I had enjoyed myself here.') After observing German military manoeuvres as the guest of another personage, HM's nephew the kaiser, he travelled by stages through Breslau, Vienna, Venice, Bologna, Ravenna, Rimini, Urbino, San Marino, Perugia, Siena, and Eichorn. 'Such a lot of churches we have seen and saints and pictures "galore," ' he wrote. 'It has been vy pleasant.'⁵⁵ Similar expeditions were always available to him; indeed, he had difficulty avoiding them. He knew so many members of society, and was such an eligible bachelor, that he had to go into hiding to finish his father's biography. Sunny, not yet troubled by his growing radicalism, turned Blenheim over to him for three or four months each year. The book was completed in the palace and, when published, was well received, though Balfour found the passages mentioning him objectionable. In the first four months the set sold 5,827 copies. An American edition, and then a one-volume British edition, were equally successful.

Churchill was the most active member of every social gathering, and to the annoyance of other young men he never hesitated to take charge. As a guest at the seaside, one hostess wrote, he 'flung himself with zest into our favourite and most perilous pastime of rock climbing, revelling in the scramble up crags and cliffs, the precarious transition from ledge to ledge, with slippery seaweed underfoot and roaring seas below. Though we considered ourselves salted climbers of four weeks' experience and he was a raw novice, he always took command of every operation, decreeing strategy and tactics and even dictating the correct position of our arms and legs. He brought to every ploy the excitement of a child and, like a child, he made it seem not only exciting but serious and important.' Even more revealing was his response to a terrible fire which followed his brother's wedding. The bride and groom having departed, the rest of the party stayed in Burley-on-the-Hill, an ancient country home near Oakham famous for its panelling, tapestries, and priceless Elizabethan manuscripts. In the middle of the night a newly installed heating system burst into flames. Awakening to screams, in smoke and darkness, the guests fled to the lawn. There, Eddie Marsh wrote, 'Winston commandeered a fireman's helmet and assumed the direction of operations.' F.E. Smith's wife remembered Churchill on the roof, shouting down orders, trying to quench the blaze with a tiny fire engine which had been brought from Oakham. Unfortunately, nothing could be saved. The owners were in tears.[56]

Churchill wasn't. He wrote to Miss Hozier: 'The fire was great fun & we all enjoyed it thoroughly. It is a pity such jolly entertainments are so costly. Alas for the archives. They roared to glory in about ten minutes . . . It is a vy strange thing to be locked in deadly grapple with that cruel element. I had no conception – except from reading – of the power and majesty of a great conflagration. Whole rooms sprang into flames as if by enchantment. Chairs and tables burnt up like matches. Floors collapsed and ceilings crashed down . . . Every window spouted fire, & from the centre of the house a volcano roared skyward in a whirlwind of sparks.' As descriptive writing, this is splendid, but as a response to tragedy it is neither pleasant nor wholesome; that the others 'enjoyed it thoroughly' is doubtful – Marsh, for one, had lost his Perceval gold watch, gold chain, and three tiepins, all heirlooms. One can understand why many men distrusted Churchill. 'It is no disparagement of Winston's extraordinary qualities,' wrote Almeric Fitzroy, 'to say that his judgement is not quite equal to his abilities.' Destruction, like war, enthralled the mischievous boy in him, and he would never entirely outgrow that fascination. Yet he alone had climbed to the roof and tried to extinguish the flames.[57]

England in those years, 'lapped in the accumulated treasures of the long peace,' as he wrote, was like Burley-on-the-Hill before the fire: precious, deeply loved, apparently safe, unaware of its deadly peril.[58] The world's diplomats still set their clocks by Big Ben. Because the British government permitted it, Turkey ceded the Sinai to Egypt and Greece annexed Crete. Little importance was attached to the decision, made the year after Victoria's death, to end her policy of 'splendid isolation.' Actually, it was a move of enormous consequence. From Canning to Salisbury, isolationism had served Britain well, keeping it aloof from a whole series of continental wars. The Royal Navy was its mighty shield; for a century after Nelson's victory at Trafalgar no nation had attempted to build a competitive fleet. In 1870 Gladstone's announcement that England would intervene if Belgium's neutrality were violated had kept both the French and the Germans from crossing Belgian frontiers.

The first break with isolationist policy was made by Lord Lansdowne, the Tory foreign secretary from 1900 to 1905. Armed forces had grown all over the world, he pointed out, and at the very least England should have understandings and defined friendships with other great powers. The United States was his first choice, but America had its own isolationist tradition. Moreover, millions of new US citizens were refugees from European conflicts, and this alone made an Anglo-American alliance a political impossibility. So Lansdowne signed up Japan and, in 1904, joined France in the Entente Cordiale, an agreement to settle colonial differences between the two countries. No one, not even his fellow cabinet ministers, was informed in 1906 when Sir Edward Grey, Lansdowne's successor at the Foreign Office, assumed a 'moral obligation' to defend France should it be attacked by Germany, thus adding a

311

military dimension to the Entente. Grey had been provoked by Germany's Wilhelm II. The previous March 31 the kaiser had appeared in Tangier, the chief Moroccan port on the Mediterranean, to declare that he regarded the local sultan as an independent sovereign, thereby offending the French, who had colonial designs there. Knowing the strength of British isolationist sentiment, Grey kept his pledge from his colleagues for five years. By then the Anglo-French relationship had, with the inclusion of Russia, ripened into the Triple Entente. No promises had been made to Saint Petersburg. Still, the links had been forged, if not joined. Germany, Austria-Hungary, and Italy had been united in central Europe's Triple Alliance since 1882. The implications of this are clear now. They weren't then. An open rupture was considered inconceivable. Indeed, the balance was regarded as a guarantee of peace. The nations, Churchill wrote, 'were fitted and fastened, it seemed securely, into an immense cantilever. The two mighty European systems faced each other glittering and clanking in their panoply, but with a tranquil gaze. A polite, discrete, pacific, and on the whole sincere diplomacy spread its web of connections over both. A sentence in a dispatch, an observation by an ambassador, a cryptic phrase in a Parliament seemed sufficient to adjust from day to day the balance of the prodigious structure.'[59]

London had never seemed so secure, or so prodigious. The city's population had reached 6,600,000; New York, its closest rival, had 3,440,000; Tokyo, 1,450,000; and Los Angeles, just 103,000. Although its architecture was largely Victorian (it still is), the inhabitants believed they were leading the world into the future, literally lighting the way – the city's Inner Circle rail lines were electrified in 1905. Businessmen who wanted their firms to become household words came to London. The Italian Auguste Oddenino, determined to own the finest restaurant on earth, built it in Regent Street. In 1902 the Ritz had opened in Piccadilly, followed by Dunhill's in Duke Street, near Piccadilly Circus, Selfridge's in Oxford Street, and, in the last year of Edward's reign, the 2,500-seat London Palladium. Lord Northcliffe was Britain's most exciting press lord. Having transformed the *Daily Mail*, he turned the *Daily Mirror* into a halfpenny picture paper, drove its circulation to a million, and bought *The Times*. He introduced sports pages for a nation of innovative sportsmen. The world's affluent became small-boat enthusiasts; an English publisher gave them *The Riddle of the Sands*. Leisure time increased in industrial countries; their sportsmen turned to lawn tennis and football, both invented in Britain. A wave of nostalgia for an idealized childhood spread across Europe and North America. English writers quickly took it over. On December 27, 1904, James M. Barrie's *Peter Pan; or, The Boy Who Would Not Grow Up* opened at the Duke of York's Theatre with Maude Adams in the lead, and it has been playing in one hall or another ever since. Kipling wrote *Kim* and *Just So Stories for Little Children*; Beatrix Potter, *Peter Rabbit*; Kenneth Grahame, *The Wind in the Willows*; and Sir R.S.S. Baden-Powell, the hero of Mafeking, published *Scouting for Boys* in 1906 and founded the Boy Scout movement with the motto 'Be Prepared,' based on his initials. Boys around the globe enrolled, 11,000 of them coming to convene in the Crystal Palace.

In music and art the British were less successful. Sir Thomas Beecham was a gifted conductor and the London Symphony a distinguished orchestra, but Elgar was the only memorable composer. The best native tunes were heard in London's music halls, and the liveliest of these, 'Waltzing Matilda,' was written by an Australian, Marie Cowan, in 1903. John Singer Sargent, an American, was commissioned to paint *The Marlborough Family*; *Westminster Bridge*, *The Houses of Parliament*, and *Port of London* were the work of France's André Derain. London painters were indeed inhospitable to foreign genius. They jeered at the first major London exhibition of Postimpressionists, Derain among them; even Sargent said, 'I am absolutely sceptical as to their having any claim whatever to being works of art, with the exception of the pictures by Gauguin that strike me as admirable in colour – and in colour only.' In literature, however, the English scene glowed. The number of books published annually soared from 5,971 to 9,541. A certain sacrifice was made for wider audiences. Before the Edwardian era, authors could assume that their readers knew Latin and the Bible. The mass-circulation newspapers had altered their vocabulary for subscribers lacking a classical education, and this was reflected in the new books, including serious fiction. R.C.K. Ensor has noted that this created 'a distinct barrier of language between the modern Englishman and most of his country's greater literature from Milton down through Burke to Macaulay.'[60]

Yet the gain was greater than the loss. Edwardian writers possessed a vitality unmatched in England before or since, and this is reflected in the files of the *Times Literary Supplement*, whose first issue was dated January 17, 1902. In poetry these were the years of Masefield and Alfred Noyes's 'Highwayman' ('The wind was a torrent of darkness among the gusty trees, / The moon was a ghostly galleon tossed upon cloudy seas . . .'). Drama apart, the novel was the only popular literary form, and it glittered with the works of Kipling, George Moore, Samuel Butler (*The Way of All Flesh*, 1903), Arnold Bennett, H.G. Wells, Conrad, the early Maugham, Henry James, Saki, W.H. Hudson (*Green Mansions*, 1904), John Galsworthy (Soames Forsyte arrived in *The Man of Property*, 1906), and Bloomsbury's E.M. Forster, whose most fruitful years these were (*Where Angels Fear to Tread*, 1905; *The Longest Journey*, 1907; *A Room with a View*, 1908; and his masterpiece, *Howards End*, 1910). Fictive entertainment also flourished. This period saw the appearance of Conan Doyle's *Hound of the Baskervilles*; the first Edgar Wallace thriller, *The Four Just Men*; and the debut of P.G. Wodehouse, whose *Pothunters*, astonishingly, was published in 1902.

But it was the English stage that captivated the literary world. London's dramatic renaissance, the fruit of twenty years of brilliant criticism and experiment, reached its culmination during Edward's reign; for the first time since Shakespeare, British plays were being translated into all continental languages, and the city's little theatres were packed almost nightly throughout the decade. At His Majesty's Theatre you could see Clyde Fitch's *Last of the Dandies* and John Millington Synge's *Tinker's Wedding*. The Royal Court Theatre produced Galsworthy's *Silver Box* and seven Shaw plays: *Candida, John Bull's Other Island, Man and Superman, Major Barbara, Captain Brassbound's Conversion, The Doctor's Dilemma*, and *The Philanderer*. Shaw's *Getting Married* could be seen at the Haymarket, Masefield's *Tragedy of Man* at the New Royalty. If you liked Barrie, and he was more popular then than now, you went to the Duke of York, which staged, in addition to *Peter Pan, The Admirable Crichton, Alice Sit-by-the-Fire, What Every Woman Knows, Old Friends*, and *The Twelve-Pound Look*. The Duke of York also showed Galsworthy's *Justice* and Shaw's *Misalliance*. Quite apart from artistic merits, Edwardian playwrights dealt with the absorbing social and political issues of the time – labour unions, feminism, criminal justice, the prison system, the Irish question, imperialism, armaments, socialism, salvationism, syndicalism, property, marriage, and divorce – and they therefore found Churchill in their audiences. He met most of them and knew Shaw well. When rehearsals for *Pygmalion* ended at His Majesty's Theatre (with Mrs Patrick Campbell, Jennie's husband's mistress, playing Eliza Doolittle) GBS wired Winston: 'Am reserving two tickets for you for my premiere. Come and bring a friend – if you have one.' Churchill wired back: 'Impossible to be present for the first performance. Will attend the second – if there is one.'[61]

Winston was a Liberal back-bencher for eighteen months and, most of the time, an inconspicuous one. The larger part of his time was devoted to writing and building a Manchester constituency for the coming general election. In the House he tried to steer a careful course between the left and right wings of his new party, speaking on the safe subjects of army reform and the economy. But he was never completely himself unless in the centre of the firing line, and Balfour, dodging on and off the floor to avoid taking stands which would further split his Tories, was an irresistible target. Churchill mocked his 'miserable and disreputable shifts' of principle and 'his gross and flagrant ignorance.' *Punch* reported Balfour's reaction: 'Prince Arthur lolls on the Treasury Bench looking straight before him with studious indifference, betrayed by a countenance clouded with rare anger.' Other Conservatives were less aloof. They published an anonymous pamphlet quoting the turncoat's past attacks on his new colleagues. It was headed: 'Mr Winston Churchill on the Radical Party Before he donned their livery and Accepted their Pay.'[62]

Balfour decided to resign as prime minister before the country went to the polls. On December 4, 1905, dispirited, lacking in legislative goals, and unable to reestablish a working relationship with Chamberlain, AJB stepped down over a minor issue, and the King asked Campbell-Bannerman to form a new government. Edward gave C-B a free hand in his appointments. The new prime minister offered Churchill a choice of posts and Winston asked to be named under secretary of state for the colonies; the secretary of state would be the Earl of Elgin, and since Elgin sat in the House of Lords, Winston would handle colonial matters in the Commons. C-B agreed and it was announced. The Tories, predictably, were outraged. Now the truth was out, they cried. The renegade had changed his party to reach office; he stood exposed as 'a political adventurer who would do anything for his own advancement.' Actually, he was something of an ingrate. Members of the government were entitled to wear the uniforms of privy councillors. In those days secretaries, having ministerial rank, belonged to the first class, others were second-class, the difference between them being marked by the gold embroidery on the collar and cuffs – a plain edge for ministers and a serrated edge for the others. Sir Herbert Samuel later recalled accompanying Churchill to the investiture ceremony. 'Winston,' he wrote, 'was by no means pleased at being no more than an Undersecretary, young as he was and even as a first step in office. Suddenly, pointing to his sleeve, he said to me: "The badge of shame!" '[63]

In his first official act he picked as his private secretary Edward Marsh, a casual acquaintance who, until now, had been a well-connected but obscure clerk in the West African department. Eddie Marsh's life and Churchill's would be closely intertwined for the next thirty years. Max Beerbohm caught the essence of Eddie in one of his pencil sketches: the head cocked like a bird's, bushy eyebrows arched eagerly, monocle twinkling. He frequently removed the monocle to wipe away a tear – like Churchill, he was emotional – and his falsetto, slate-squeak voice reminded Violet Asquith of 'a high-pitched chirrup.' Eddie was nervous about his new job. He wasn't sure he liked Winston. In his memoirs he wrote that he was 'a little afraid of him' and doubted 'we could ever have anything in common.'[64]

On December 12, however, Eddie was Winston's guest in Mount Street. The next morning he wrote to Leonie Leslie: 'Such an excitement. I *must* tell you. Your nephew has asked me to be his private secretary for 6 months or so. It will be the most interesting thing I've ever done but I'm most terribly afraid of not being the right person and turning out a failure . . . I've just dined alone with Winston. He was most perfectly charming to me but made it quite clear what he would expect in the way of help and I almost *know* I can't do it – it's awful!' Churchill, however, had decided that this was his man. When he was determined to be fascinating, he could dispel virtually all misgivings. He had a way of tossing off lapidary epigrams as though they had just occurred to him, and he now flashed such a jewel before Marsh, describing the proper spirit for a great nation: 'In war, resolution; in defeat, defiance; in victory, magnanimity; in peace, good-will.' ('I wish,' Eddie wrote, 'the tones in which he spoke this could have been "recorded" – the first phrase a rattle of musketry, the second "grating harsh thunder," the third a ray of the sun through stormclouds; the last pure benediction.')* Marsh, still anxious, awoke in the morning, presented himself to Winston, and whispered worriedly, 'I'm afraid

---

* Churchill used them forty years later as the theme for his history of World War II.

I shan't be much use today, as I've lost my voice.' Churchill looked up. 'What?' he boomed. 'Is that resonant organ extinct?' By then they were firm friends. Jennie, however, remembering that ugly business at Sandhurst, was troubled by this appointment; according to Douglas Plummer, Marsh was known to be 'the centre of a large homosexual artistic colony.' But there is no evidence that his deviance was overt, and Churchill, vastly tolerant in his friendships, doubtless regarded the matter as none of his business.[65]

Three weeks later the two men checked into Manchester's Midland Hotel, which would be Winston's base for his first campaign as a Liberal candidate. That evening they toured the slums. Churchill 'looked about him,' Marsh wrote, 'and his sympathetic imagination was stirred. "Fancy," he said, "living in one of these streets, never seeing anything beautiful, never eating anything savoury, *never saying anything clever!*" ' He meant to be clever here, but not alarming. The city had become a Conservative stronghold – all nine seats were held by Tories – and apart from ringing tributes to Free Trade, he skirted controversy just twice. Courting workingmen's votes, he promised that the Liberals would remember England's 'left-out millions,' and, less honourably, assured Protestant Unionists that he would 'support no legislation which I regard as likely to injure the effective integrity of the United Kingdom.' Hecklers distributed copies of the pamphlet quoting his past scorn for his present party; one thrust it in his hands while others cried, 'Answer it!' He did: 'I said a lot of stupid things when I worked with the Conservative Party, and I left it because I did not want to go on saying stupid things.' Then, amid loud cheers, he tore the leaflet to shreds and, a newspaperman reported, 'flung it from him with a dramatic gesture, expressing . . . contempt for the cause he had once espoused.'[66]

He was the most exciting candidate in the city. 'There is no question about it,' wrote Charles E. Hands of the Tory *Daily Mail*; 'the public interest of Manchester in the General Election is centred and focussed on the personality of Mr Winston Churchill. You can hardly see the rest of the political landscape for this dominant figure.' Men discussed his alliterative rhetoric, the mammoth posters bearing his name in letters five feet high, the reviews of his new book, and the startling youthfulness of his mother, who was stumping for him every day. He was billed to speak in the Manchester Coal Exchange one afternoon at three o'clock. 'At half past two,' the *Guardian* reported, 'the hall was packed with a struggling crowd; a second crowd was struggling on the staircase leading to the hall; and a third crowd [was] jostling for standing room on the pavement in the street.' The *Mail* noted that he was 'wearing a new old-fashioned hat, a flat-topped sort of felt hat, and already the hatters are having enquiries for articles of that pattern.' In addition, 'Ladies who have been privileged to speak to him are envied of their sex.'[67]

Among the enviers of their sex were the Pankhursts. In late 1905, even before the campaign had begun, Christabel Pankhurst and her friend Annie Kenney had been arrested for disrupting a Churchill speech in northwest Manchester; Churchill had offered to pay their fifteen-shilling fine, but they chose a week's martyrdom in a cell. Emmeline Pankhurst now interrupted one of his speeches repeatedly until stewards lured her into a side room and locked the door. Winston, who thought she had left the meeting, said he had voted for the one woman suffrage bill to come before the House but deplored disturbances at political rallies. Someone shouted: 'That's right, don't be henpecked, Winston!' At St John's Schools, Gartside, he had to deal with Sylvia Pankhurst. She raised a sign bearing the slogan 'Votes for Women,' but she had it upside down, and Churchill mildly pointed that out. She called: 'Will you give us a vote?' He invited her to join him on the platform; she did, and he asked the crowd: 'Will everybody please be quiet. Let us hear what she has to say.' They refused; they chanted: 'We want to hear Churchill!' He tried again and failed. The hall was in an uproar. According to the *Guardian*, he then said: ' "We should be fair and chivalrous to ladies. They come here asking us to treat them like men." (Laughter) "That is what I particularly want to avoid. We must observe courtesy and chivalry to the weaker sex dependent upon us." (Hear hear.)' Sylvia, furious, stalked out. Like her mother, she had found that in one respect Churchill was like Arthur Balfour. He could adroitly avoid making a commitment under the wrong circumstances.[68]

Manchester voted on January 13; the results were announced two days later. All nine Liberals had won. Balfour was among the losers. Winston, whose margin of victory was over 1,200 votes, took Hands to supper at the hotel. The reporter called it 'a grand slam in doubled no trumps.'[69] Churchill agreed. Bridge was never his game, but this time he was on the money; he sensed the mood of the entire country. When the last votes were counted it was clear that the Liberals had won an historic landslide. They had swept 377 seats; of the Tories, who had gone into the fight 400 strong, only 157 survived. In addition, there were 83 Irish Nationalists, and – portentous, though few noted their significance – 53 Labour members. Campbell-Bannerman and his men could alter the face of England. Churchill confronted a personal challenge. He had been a formidable critic; now, holding office in a secure government, he must be constructive. But political tempers are slow to change. Men long in opposition cannot easily break habits of cavil, particularly when they have mastered the art, nor are they adept at the compromises and jugglery which are the plain handmaidens of responsibility. Winston was now answerable to the House for the administration of the King's colonies, and the first issue he faced would have taxed a seasoned veteran of the Treasury Bench, which he, at this time, clearly was not.

It was an ugly business. Sir Alfred Milner, last seen in this narrative being interviewed by Churchill in Cape Town, had been elevated to the peerage, and the month after the Liberal sweep he made his maiden speech in the House of Lords. A lot of men wanted to question Milner. As high commissioner in South Africa he had imported some fifty thousand Chinese coolies to work the Rand gold mines. Their contracts ran for three years; they were not permitted to bring their families, they were penned in camps, and reportedly they were subjected to corporal punishment. In one of his first acts as prime minister, Campbell-Bannerman had announced that the leasing of Chinese would be discontinued. Licences for fourteen thousand more coolies had already been issued the previous November, however, and the matter of their treatment in the past was therefore a burning question. Documents acquired by the new government revealed that mine bosses had been meting out punishments without trial, flogging the Chinese indiscriminately. This was a gross violation of London's instructions to the high commissioner and of Whitehall's assurances to authorities in China. A fellow lord asked Milner if he had sanctioned this. Milner confessed that he had, adding, 'I think, in the light of subsequent events, that I was wrong.'[70]

The Liberal press, led by Massingham and the *Guardian*, was in full cry. Radical Liberals demanded Milner's head. Churchill agreed that his conduct had been reprehensible and said: 'I should not put myself to any undue or excessive exertion to defend Lord Milner from any attacks which might be made upon him.' At Question Time, replying to Hilaire Belloc, a new Liberal MP, he added: 'Lord Milner committed a grave dereliction of public duty and at the same time an undoubted infringement of the law.' Belloc and others drafted a motion of censure. Chamberlain, whose man Milner had been, protested that it was 'despicable' to 'persecute him for a single error of judgement in a long course of public service.' Winston accused Joe of abusing the Boers, and then Free Trade. The only difference between the two, he said, was that 'whereas the first enterprise of the right honourable gentleman has had the effect of nearly ruining South Africa, the second enterprise has had the effect of politically ruining himself.' Chamberlain hotly replied that it was Churchill's duty, as 'head of a department,' to 'defend the servants of the department.' At this point senior Liberals decided to put out the fire. Milner had a large following in the country; making a martyr out of him would be both pointless and risky. Churchill had to tell the House that in the interests of peace and conciliation, he would oppose the censure motion. He was uncomfortable in this position, however, and his defence of it was deplorable. 'Lord Milner,' he said, 'has gone from South Africa, probably for ever. The public service knows him no more. Having exercised great authority he now exerts none. Having held high employment he now has no employment . . . He is today a retired Civil Servant, without pension or gratuity of any kind whatever. It is not worth while to pursue him any further.'[71]

The Conservatives were outraged, the Liberals embarrassed. Margot Asquith called the speech 'ungenerous, patronising, and tactless.' Even Eddie Marsh, who had thought it impressive in rehearsal, now concluded that his new employer 'appeared to be taunting a discredited statesman.' A Tory MP moved to reduce Winston's salary for 'embittered and empoisoned language' on coolie labour and above all for insulting Milner, 'a man whom so many of us esteem, honour, and love.' Kipling, an admirer of Milner, never forgave Winston. Sir William Anson, the warden of All Souls, Oxford, wrote that Churchill had seemed 'both pompous and impertinent. It is terrible to think what harm that young jackanapes may do with a big majority behind him and an incompetent Prime Minister to look after him.' The House of Lords passed, 170 to 35, a resolution expressing its gratitude to Milner for his service in South Africa. The King wrote to the Liberal Marquess of Crewe: 'It is a pity that Lord Elgin does not seem to be able to control the violent and objectionable language of his Parliamentary Under-Secretary.' To Lady Londonderry, a kinswoman of Churchill's, he remarked that 'the conduct of a certain relation of yours is simply scandalous. It is indeed hard on Lord Milner to be treated in such a manner.'[72]

This was hard on Elgin. The secretary of state for colonies could hardly be expected to control events in the House of Commons when, as a peer, he could not even be admitted to the chamber. A shy man, bereft of social graces – Marsh described him as 'a rugged old thane of antique virtue and simplicity' – he nevertheless possessed administrative abilities and had acquitted himself well as viceroy of India. Later he wrote: 'When I accepted Churchill as my Under Secy I knew I should have no easy task.' He had decided to show Winston all documents, let him join all policy discussions, always give him the benefit of the doubt, 'but to keep control.' Austen Chamberlain, in *Politics from Inside*, tells the story that Churchill submitted a long memorandum to his minister, ending, 'These are my views,' and Elgin sent it back with the notation, 'But not mine.' No doubt the under secretary tried the secretary's patience at times. He also bemused him. To his wife, Elgin wrote, 'Winston is a curious impulsive creature.' He described how, when he mildly criticized a paper, Churchill apologized profusely, 'seized the paper and tore it up.' It was Elgin who coined the phrase 'Winston's latest *volte face*.' The fighter of Boers had become the champion of Boers. The critic of military budgets would soon become the most ardent advocate of rearmament. The arch-Tory was now a passionate Liberal. In each instance the shift could be supported by argument, and no one ever argued more persuasively than Churchill, but those who thought him mercurial had a case.[73]

In the Colonial Office he seemed to be a combination of Pitt and Puck. Inexhaustible, frequently carried away by his own soaring rhetoric, exaggerating his importance, he was criticized by colleagues for his heavy, 'ministerial' manner. Sometimes he seemed to make work for himself and others. It is a definition of an egoist that whatever occupies his attention is, for that reason, important. The results can be hilarious. An African, one Sekgoma, had proclaimed himself chief of Batawana in Ngamiland, Bechuanaland. He was unpopular, and he was not the legal heir. When the legitimate chief came of age, the tribe crowned the youth. Sekgoma objected and was jailed. Civil servants responsible for the colony decided that the best solution was to deport Sekgoma to the Seychelles. Indeed, they seemed to have no choice. But their under secretary fiercely disagreed. To imprison or deport the deposed chief, he wrote, would be a 'flat violation of every principle of British justice.' In fact, he could not even begin to defend the lawless treatment of an innocent man upon 'an informal *lettre de cachet*.' He asked: 'If we are going to embark upon this sort of law-breaking and autocratic action, where are we going to stop? What kind of injustice is there that would not be covered by precedents of this kind?' Indeed, if men who had committed no crime could be deprived of trial by jury, exiled, and condemned to lives of penal servitude, 'why stop there? Why not poison Sekgoma by some painless drug?' Since medieval practices were to be revived, 'at least let us show medieval courage and thoroughness. Think of the expense that would be saved. A dose of laudanum, costing at the outside five shillings, is all that would be required. There would be no cost of maintenance, no charges for transportation, no legal difficulties, no need to apply to the Portuguese, no fear of the habeas corpus.' Having made his point, and believing it safe from refutation, he ended grandly: 'If however as I apprehend, Secretary of State would be averse to this procedure, the next best thing would be to obey the law, and to act with ordinary morality, however inconvenient.'[74]

Elgin was nettled. He replied shirtily that he had no intention of sending to the chemist for a five-shilling dose of laudanum. The file on Sekgoma was clear: 'This man is a savage – and is said to be contemplating proceedings in defiance of all law to disturb the peace.' In fact, he had been plotting to behead his successor. If he were released, blood would be shed, including, probably, his own. His Majesty's government could hardly encourage that. However, the minister agreed that deportation was troublesome and objectionable in principle; another African home would be found for the dethroned chief. As an episode in the history of the British Empire, this approaches the far reaches of trivia, but it is also vintage Churchill – his memo was impudent, witty, and superbly written. Ronald Hyam commented that 'Churchill exaggerated the importance of everything he touched. Every speck on the horizon, he assumed, would turn out to be a Cunarder, not a cockleshell.'[75]

If others wondered at Elgin's patience with him, they did not realize how grateful the colonial secretary was to have such a lieutenant. Tirelessly drafting answers to parliamentary questions, a gifted writer of arresting minutes, he defended colonial policy in the House with a sharpening wit; to Andrew Bonar Law, a Tory who accused him of twisting the meaning of a Tory document, he replied: 'The words which you now tell me you employed and which purport to be a paraphrase, if not an actual quotation, are separated by a small degree of inaccuracy and misrepresentation from the inaccuracy and misrepresentation of the condensed report.' He also carried a burden of day-to-day decisions which was immense because of the Empire's immensity. He negotiated with Cypriots over pledges of financial assistance, spoke up for Jewish immigrants embittered by what he regarded as a 'very harsh and quite indefensible measure,' recommended reductions of naturalization fees, advocated help for Zulu tribes mistreated by the Natal government, urged Campbell-Bannerman to invite all six of Australia's state premiers to a colonial conference, and mediated a dispute in India between Curzon, the viceroy, and

Kitchener, commander in chief of His Majesty's forces there. (He sided with Curzon, but Kitchener won.) Most of the matters brought before him were insignificant even then, but two weren't. The South African mining magnates were persuaded to repatriate their Chinese workers. And the Boers, at last, were given a just political settlement.[76]

Churchill played an active role in drafting the provisions for the Transvaal constitution, and later that of the Orange River Colony, and piloted them through the House. The former republics were to be granted self-government with universal manhood suffrage, an approach to the 'one vote, one value' principle which even England lacked. The revered name 'Orange Free State' was then restored and a limited ban on the Afrikaans language lifted; members of both Boer parliaments could address their colleagues in either English or Afrikaans. Indeed, British colonial officials posted there would be expected to master Dutch dialects, 'for,' Winston wrote, 'if the people like to talk to him in Volapuk, he must learn Volapuk. If they have a weakness for Sanskott, it must become his study. By humouring them, and understanding them, he will be able very often to make their wishes and their welfare coincide.' 'We are prepared,' he told the House, 'to make this settlement in the name of the Liberal Party. This is sufficient authority for us; but there is a higher authority which we should earnestly desire to obtain.' He asked the Tories to 'join with us to invest the grant of a free Constitution to the Transvaal with something of a national sanction. With all our majority we can only make it the gift of a Party. They can make it the gift of England.' But Balfour, who had found another seat in a by-election, wanted no part of it. He called the bill 'a dangerous, audacious and reckless experiment.' Milner condemned it in the Lords. *The Times* prophesied the doom of the Empire, and the *Daily Mail* ran the headlines: ANOTHER MAJUBA – TRANSVAAL GIVEN BACK TO THE BOERS – FRUITLESS SACRIFICES OF THE WAR – 22,000 LIVES AND £250,000,000 FOR NOTHING.[77]

Nevertheless, the measure was a triumph. Botha became prime minister, first of the self-governing Transvaal, and then after 1910 of the new Union of South Africa. When they met as fellow statesmen, he recognized Churchill as his armoured-train prisoner, whereupon Winston complained that the reward for his recapture had been stingy. In 1914 Botha and his followers chose to fight side by side with the British, something not foreseen only a few years earlier, and Churchill's fellow Liberals, among others, recognized the wisdom and generosity of his terms. His 'shame' was past; he was appointed a first-class member of the Privy Council, a rare honour for a man below cabinet rank. Now he stood in the party's front echelons. The next vacancy on the government's front bench would be his. Meanwhile, he decided to have some fun and possibly make money, too. In the summer of 1907, after a colonial conference at which he beat back appeals for imperial preference by arguing that tariffs would lead to 'a deep feeling of sullen hatred of the colonies and of colonial affairs among the poorer people in this country,' he left England for five months. He and F.E. Smith attended French military manoeuvres, joined Sunny for a partridge shoot in Moravia (now part of Czechoslovakia), and then separated, Winston making his way in easy stages, by Vienna and Syracuse, to Malta, where he rendezvoused with Eddie Marsh, George Scrivings, and a distant Churchill relative. The four of them boarded the cruiser *Venus*, which, Winston wrote, was 'lying obedient and attentive in the roads.' The Admiralty had put it at his disposal for a tour of the east African domains.[78]

On Cyprus they were greeted by a mass demonstration favouring Enosis, complete union with Greece. That was the last flicker of controversy on the journey. The rest was an idyll, impossible now and possible then only because of the unchallenged might of the Empire. The party 'threaded the long red furrow of the Suez Canal,' as Churchill wrote afterwards, and 'sweltered through the trough of the Red Sea' to Aden. Pausing in Mombasa, they travelled up-country on a special train provided by the Uganda Railway; two of them, he told his mother in a long letter home, sat 'on a seat in front of the engine with our rifles & as soon as we saw anything to shoot at – a wave of the hand brought the train to a standstill & sometimes we tried at antelope without even getting down.' They found zebras, lions, rhinoceroses, antelopes of every kind, ostriches, and giraffes. He wrote: 'On the first day I killed 1 zebra, 1 wildebeeste, two hartebeeste, 1 gazelle, 1 bustard (a giant bird),' and he had also sighted 'a vy fine kind of antelope with beautiful straight horns.' He was nearly run down by a rhino, 'a survival of prehistoric times,' whose charge was halted when he fired 'a heavy 450 rifle & hit her plumb in the chest.'[79]

Everywhere Africans waited to pay the bwana tribute: 'I was presented by the various chiefs with 108 sheep, 7 Bulls, about £100 worth of ivory, an ostrich egg, many fowls & some vy good leopard skins.' A glimpse of 'the mighty snow-clad peak of Mt Kenya' was followed by stops at Nairobi, Lake Victoria, Kampala, the Ripon Falls, Gondokoro, and, after a leisurely journey by train and steamer, Khartoum, where, to Churchill's dismay, his man-servant fell ill with choleraic diarrhoea and died. The Dublin Fusiliers, at Winston's request, gave Scrivings a military funeral; 'we all walked in procession to the cemetery as mourners, while the sun sank over the desert, and the band played that beautiful funeral march you know so well.' That put a damper on the rest of the trip; they hurried to Wadi Halfa, Aswân, Cairo, and home. But on balance the expedition had been a great success. Churchill felt fit and was in fact wealthier. After the last election he had left Mount Street and rented a small house at 12 Bolton Street, just off Piccadilly, two blocks from the Ritz, and during his absence his brother had sublet it for him. The *Strand* paid him £750 for four articles on his tour; Hodder and Stoughton advanced £500 against royalties for a book, *My African Journey*. Solvent and radiant, he was guest of honour on Saturday, January 18, 1908, at a dinner given by the National Liberal Club to welcome him home. He told them: 'I come back into the firing line in the best possible health, and with a wish to force the fighting up to the closest possible point.'[80]

That wish was swiftly granted. During his absence Campbell-Bannerman's health had deteriorated alarmingly. Aware that he had only a few weeks to live, C-B resigned on April 3. Asquith succeeded him – he crossed to Biarritz for his sovereign's permission to form a new government; Edward let nothing interrupt his holidays – and on April 8 he wrote to Churchill: 'With the King's approval, I have the great pleasure of offering you the post of President of the Board of Trade.' Thus Winston, at thirty-three, reached cabinet rank. Since the Restoration in 1660, custom had required newly appointed ministers to stand for reelection in their constituencies. The seat Winston had won two years earlier was traditionally Conservative. Now he had to run for it again. The Tories were elated. They had been waiting with red-baited breath for this chance to humiliate the 'bounder,' the 'opportunist,' the 'traitor to his class.' The suffragettes also had him in their sights. His provocative wit was partly to blame. Although he had become an ardent social reformer, he said: 'I refuse to be shut up in a soup kitchen with Mrs Sidney Webb.' And when a militant feminist asked him what should be the role of women in the future, he replied: 'The same, I trust, as it has been since the days of Adam and Eve.' She glared. Swiftly moving to recover lost ground, he assured her and her sisters that he was a convert to their cause. 'Trust me, ladies,' he begged. They refused. They would campaign against him, they said, unless he could guarantee Asquith's support of votes for women. He tried to explain that he could hardly speak for the new prime minister. They jeered; they didn't believe it; they vowed to give him no peace.[81]

And they did. 'Painful scenes,' he wrote, 'were witnessed in the Free Trade Hall when Miss Christabel Pankhurst, tragical and dishevelled, was finally ejected after having thrown the meeting into pandemonium.' This continued to be their most dramatic stratagem. His speeches were interrupted by hisses and even physical assaults, his rallies thrown into turmoil by women hurling rotten eggs and ripe fruit. Sometimes they waited until he was approaching his peroration, or the most intricate point in his argument. Then feminine voices would shriek: 'What about the women?' 'When are you going to give women the vote?' He wrote: 'It became extremely difficult to pursue connected arguments.' He toiled eighteen hours a day, organizing canvassers when he wasn't on the stump, and when the feminists allowed it, he gave the opposition as good as he got. He pictured himself arrayed against 'all the forces of reaction' and 'every discontented irresponsible element in the community,' notably 'old doddering peers, cute financial magnates, clever wirepullers, big brewers with bulbous noses . . . weaklings, sleek, smug, comfortable, self-important individuals.' The situation was complicated by a third candidate, representing the Marxist Social Democratic Federation. In an open letter, H.G. Wells, whom socialists trusted, urged workingmen to back Churchill, but the Liberal vote split. Winston lost by 529 votes. As he left the town hall a suffragette grabbed his arm and cried: 'It's the women who have done this, Mr Churchill! Now you will understand that we must have our vote.'[82]

The real victors, of course, were the Tories. In what passed for humour in Balfour's set, an ill-wisher wired him: 'What's the use of a W.C. without a seat?' The *Morning Post* rejoiced that Winston, 'though a Cabinet minister, is a political Ishmaelite wandering around as an object of compassion and commiseration. Manchester has washed its hands of him. The juveniles have for days past been singing to a popular air "Good-bye, Winnie, you must leave us," and Winnie has gone. On the whole Manchester appears to be taking the sorrowful parting with composure.' So was Churchill. Even before he left the city, telegrams had arrived offering him eight safe Liberal seats. He chose Dundee, one of whose MPs had just been elevated to the peerage. To his mother he wrote: 'It's a life seat and cheap and easy beyond all experience.' The Manchester defeat didn't rankle. He wrote to a woman friend, not a militant feminist, who mourned his loss: 'It was a real pleasure to me to get your letter & telegram. I am glad to think you watched the battle from afar with eyes sympathetic to my fortunes . . . How I should have liked you to be there. You would have enjoyed it I think. We had a jolly party and it was a whirling week. Life for all its incompleteness is rather fun sometimes.'[83]

The friend was Clementine Hozier, whom he had disconcerted with his rude, silent stare four years earlier. Now twenty-three, Clementine was at the height of her beauty. Violet Asquith, seeing her for the first time, thought she had 'a face of classical perfection' and 'a profile like the racing cutter in George Meredith's novel *Beauchamp's Career*,' or 'the prow of a Greek ship.'[84] Her social credentials were acceptable, if not spectacular. She belonged to one of those landed gentry families which lived on tight budgets. Descended from Scots whose lineage could be traced back to the twelfth century, she was a granddaughter of the Countess of Airlie. Jennie had once known her mother well; Winston's uncle Jack Leslie had been one of her godfathers. Men said she was a good hunter for a woman; women said that she had rightly decided her hair was her crowning glory, and on formal occasions she always wore it up. But there was much more to Clementine than that. The child of a shattered marriage, educated at the Sorbonne, she was a strong-minded young woman of firm likes and dislikes (she did not like Jennie), and her politics were rather to the left of the Liberal establishment. Although she never invited arrest or shouted down cabinet members, she believed women were entitled to the vote and was prepared to say so anywhere, to anyone, at any time. She was not, in short, a paradigm of an upper-class Englishwoman. Most youthful patricians would have found her a difficult wife, and she had already broken an engagement she knew was unwise. Yet there were deep reservoirs of love in her. For the right husband, she would be magnificent.

'Where does the family start?' Winston once asked rhetorically. 'It starts with a young man falling in love with a girl. No superior alternative has yet been found.' But first they must be thrown together, and both he and Clementine almost missed their second meeting. It came in March 1908, two months after his return from Africa. They had been invited separately to a dinner being given at 52 Portland Place by her aunt, Lady St Helier, formerly

Lady Jeune, who had been Winston's benefactress when he wanted to ride with Kitchener to Khartoum. At the appointed hour, however, he was in his bath. Eddie, bursting in on him, said: 'What on earth are you doing, Winston? You should be at dinner by now!' Churchill said he wasn't going, that it would be a great bore; Eddie told him he couldn't do that to Lady Jeune, and, grumbling and scowling, Winston emerged from the tub, dressed, and caught a cab. Meanwhile, at 51 Abingdon Villas in Kensington, Clementine and her mother had exchanged similar words. Clementine had spent the afternoon giving French lessons at half a crown an hour. She was tired and didn't want to go out, but Lady Blanche scolded: 'That is very ungrateful of you. Your Aunt Mary has been extremely kind to you. Let's have no more nonsense; go upstairs straight away and get dressed.'[85]

So the two unwilling guests arrived late. Seated next to Clementine, Winston was all courtesy this time, though as usual he wanted to talk about himself. He asked her if she had read his biography of Lord Randolph. She hadn't. He promised to send her a copy and then forgot. But he didn't forget Clementine. He asked his mother to invite her and her mother for a weekend at Salisbury Hall, the Cornwallis-West country home. Clementine was impressed with him; in her letter thanking Jennie, she wrote of his 'dominating charm and brilliancy.' Maddeningly, Lady Blanche, who couldn't afford it, chose this spring to take her daughter abroad for six weeks. Winston's letters pursued her. Having just called on the King to 'kiss hands' – receive royal sanction for his new office – he seized 'this fleeting hour of leisure to write & tell how much I liked our long talk on Sunday and what a comfort & pleasure it was to me to meet a girl with so much intellectual quality & such strong reserves of noble sentiment.' He wrote to her of his brother's marriage to Lady Gwendeline Bertie, or 'Goonie,' as everyone in the family called her; he wrote of politics and the fire at Burley-on-the-Hill. To this last, Clementine replied: 'I have been able to think of nothing but the fire & the terrible danger you have been in . . . My dear my heart stood still with terror.'[86]

Thus interest grew on both sides, fomented by aunts and cousins, Lady this and Lady that, until, on August 7, the Duke of Marlborough invited Clementine to a small party at Blenheim. The same mail brought a note from Winston. He hoped she would come because 'I want so much to show you that beautiful place & in its gardens we shall find lots of places to talk in, & lots of things to talk about.' His mother would act as chaperon – there were royal chuckles when the King heard that – with F.E. and Margaret Smith the only other guests. The next day he wrote to her again; he thought she would like Sunny, and would 'fascinate him with those strange mysterious eyes of yours, whose secret I have been trying so hard to learn . . . Till Monday then & may the Fates play fair.' Clementine could have had little doubt of what awaited her at the palace, and she felt, she later said, a 'sudden access of shyness.' She was down to her last clean cotton frock. The other women would have maids, and she would have to stand for fear of crumpling her skirt. Nevertheless, she arrived at Blenheim outwardly poised on Monday, August 10. That evening the stage for his proposal was set. After breakfast in the morning they would walk in the rose garden.[87]

In later years Churchill said that 'at Blenheim I took two important decisions: to be born and to marry. I am happily content with the decision I took on both those occasions.'[88] He neglected to mention that Clementine had had something to say about the second, and that his dilatoriness had nearly lost her. Always an early riser, she was prompt at breakfast on Tuesday. Winston wasn't there. She waited for him. And waited. He was fast asleep. Mortified, she considered returning to London immediately, and no one who knew her doubts that she meant it. Luckily, Sunny intervened. The duke sent his cousin a sharp note and, in his role as host, asked her to join him in a buggy ride around the grounds. They returned half an hour later to find Churchill yawning at the horizon.

The walk was postponed until late afternoon. They were in the middle of it, and Winston was just about to clear his throat, when the skies opened and wrapped them in sheets of rain. Fortunately an ornamental little Greek temple overlooking the palace's great lake offered refuge, and there, drenched and shivering, he asked her to marry him. She said yes, but swore him to secrecy until she had her mother's consent. He couldn't keep his word. The skies cleared, they strolled back to the palace, and the moment he saw his friends he broke into a run, waving his arms and shouting the news. That night in her bedroom Clementine wrote him a love letter, addressing it by drawing a heart with 'Winston' lettered inside it – the first of the endearing missives they would exchange throughout the rest of their long life together. The next day he picked a bouquet of roses for her to take home and, to make amends for breaking his pledge, wrote to his future mother-in-law asking her 'consent & blessing.' He told her, 'I am not rich nor powerfully established, but your daughter loves me & with that love I feel strong enough to assume this great & sacred responsibility; & I think I can make her happy & give her a station & career worthy of her beauty and her virtues.' He never mailed the letter – he was apt to do this – but Lady Blanche took him into her heart anyway. She wrote to Wilfrid Blunt: 'He is gentle and tender, affectionate to those he loves, much hated by those who have not come under his personal charm.' At the moment he was also busy; the wedding was scheduled for Saturday, September 12, less than three weeks after the formal announcement, and there was much to do. Congratulatory notes required answers (two were from Pamela Plowden and Muriel Wilson). He picked Linky Cecil as his best man, and asked Welldon to speak at the service. Presents had to be acknowledged. In the happy English tradition of political civility, gifts arrived from Balfour and the Chamberlains. The King sent a gold-headed walking stick; Sir Ernest Cassel, £500.[89]

On the appointed Saturday the guests, including Sir Bindon Blood, Ian Hamilton, and Lloyd George, gathered in St Margaret's Church, Westminster. Even here the groom could not elude controversy; *Tailor and Cutter* described his attire as 'one of the greatest failures as a wedding garment we have ever seen, giving the wearer a sort of glorified coachman appearance.' Blunt wrote in his diary that Churchill had 'gained in appearance since I saw him last, and has a powerful if ugly face. Winston's responses were clearly made in a pleasant voice, Clementine's inaudible.' Appropriately, the reception was held in Lady St Helier's home. In his new post Churchill had defended the right of costermongers to trade in the street, and 'Pearly Kings and Queens,' cockneys whose costumes were adorned with pearl buttons sewn in elaborate patterns, danced outside in Portland Place.[90]

Winston later wrote that he and Clementine 'lived happily ever afterwards.' It was, in fact, a great marriage, but few brides have had to adjust so quickly to their husband's careers. She was given a glimpse of the future immediately after the wedding ceremony, when she found him with Lloyd George in the church vestry, earnestly talking politics. At Blenheim, where their honeymoon began, he revised the final text of his book on Africa, and in Venice, their last stop, he was toiling away at official papers and memoranda, belying his letter to his mother from there: 'We have only loitered & loved – a good & serious occupation for which the histories furnish respectable precedents.' In Eichorn on the way back they stayed with an old friend of Winston's, the Austrian Baron Tuty de Forest, who had been educated in England. Winston and the baron had a marvellous time shooting, but Clementine found the household stiff and the baroness dull. She was glad to be headed home, and was excited by the prospect of being presented to her husband's constituents in Dundee. Her oddest experience on the wedding trip had been her first encounter with Winston's underwear. She wore cheap chemises, but his underclothes, she whispered to a wide-eyed Violet Asquith when they returned and dined at Downing Street, were made of pale pink, very finely woven silk; they came from the Army and Navy Stores and 'cost the eyes out of the head' – about eighty pounds a year, she calculated. When Violet 'taxed him with this curious form of self-indulgence, he replied: "It is essential to my well-being. I have a very delicate and sensitive cuticle which demands the finest covering." ' He invited her to examine the texture of the skin on his forearm. It was, he proudly told her, 'a cuticle without a blemish, except for one small portion of my anatomy where I sacrificed a piece of my skin to accommodate a wounded brother officer on my way back from the Sudan campaign.'[91]

Like other lovers, they invented pet names for each other. Clementine was 'Cat' or 'Kat'; Winston was 'Pug,' then 'Amber Pug,' then 'Pig.' Drawings of these animals decorated the margins of their letters to each other, and at dinner parties Winston would reach across the table, squeeze her hand, and murmur, 'Dear Cat.' After a garden luncheon, Blunt entered in his diary: 'He is *aux plus petits soins* with his wife, taking all possible care of her. They are a very happy married pair. Clementine was afraid of wasps, and one settled on her sleeve, and Winston gallantly took the wasp by the wings and thrust it into the ashes of the fire.' She became pregnant the month after the wedding. Not knowing the child's sex, they created the name 'Puppy Kitten,' then shortened it to simply 'P.K.' The imminent arrival of the P.K. made a move from the little house on Bolton Street imperative, and early in 1909 Churchill took an eighteen-year lease, at £195 a year, on a house at 33 Eccleston Square, in Pimlico, between Victoria Station and the Thames. Clementine was economizing wherever possible; on April 27 she wrote to Winston: 'I had a long afternoon with Baxter & carpets. The green carpet is lovely & will do beautifully for the library. It looks like soft green moss . . . I tried hard to make the red stair carpet do for the dining room, but it is really too shabby.' A 'green sickly looking carpet' from Bolton Street 'does Puppy Kitten's room.' One servant's room could 'be done for about £2.' She had 'written to the people who are making the blue stair carpet to ask what it will cost to cover dining room entirely with the blue – (4/6 a yard).'[92]

In May they moved in, and three months later Clementine gave birth to a girl, whom they christened Diana. Away watching army manoeuvres that September, Winston wrote to his 'dear Kat,' begging her to 'try to gather your strength. Don't spend it as it comes. Let it accumulate . . . My darling I so want your life to be a full & sweet one, I want it to be worthy of all the beauties of your nature. I am so much centered in my politics, that I often feel I must be a dull companion, to anyone who is not in the trade too. It gives me so much joy to make you happy – & often wish I were more various in my topics.' Diana was followed, less than two years later, by their son, Randolph, 'the Chumbolly.' Winston wrote from Blenheim: 'My precious pussy cat, I do trust & hope that you are being good & not sitting up or fussing yourself. The Chumbolly must do his duty and help you with your milk, you are to tell him so from me.' She replied, 'I am very happy here, contemplating the beautiful Chumbolly who grows more darling & handsome every hour, & puts on weight with every meal; so that soon he will be a little round ball of fat. Just now I was kissing him, when catching sight of my nose he suddenly fastened upon it & began to suck it, no doubt thinking it was another part of my person!'[93]

These notes are only partly attributable to his travels. She was a lark, he a nightingale; they tried having breakfast together two or three times, he later said, 'but it didn't work. Breakfast should be had in bed alone.' Since one was often bustling about while the other slept, they left hundreds of these missives for each other. All testify to a devotion that never flagged, though, like every other couple, they had their edgy moments. In the beginning his sudden and unexpected absences made her wonder if there were other women in his life. Her challenge does not survive, but we have his reply: 'Dearest, it worries me vy much that you should seem to nurse such absolutely wild suspicions wh are so dishonouring to all the love & loyalty I bear you & will please god bear you while I breathe. They are unworthy of you & me. And they fill my mind with feelings of embarrassment to wh I have been a stranger since I was a schoolboy. I know that they originate in the fond love you have for me and therefore they make me feel tenderly towards you & anxious always to deserve that most precious possession of my life. But at the same time they depress me & vex me

– & without reason. We do not live in a world of small intrigues but of serious & important affairs . . . You ought to trust me for I do not love & will never love any woman in the world but you and my chief desire is to link myself to you week by week by bonds which shall ever become more intimate & profound. Beloved I kiss your memory – your sweetness & beauty have cast a glory upon my life. You will find me always your loving & devoted husband, W.'[94]

He once said: 'It is hard, if not impossible, to snub a beautiful woman; they remain beautiful and the rebuke recoils.' Clementine's acquaintances forgot that at their peril. Her response to slights was swift and literally unanswerable, for she simply departed. Once, when they were playing bridge at Canford Manor, Ivor Guest, one of Winston's cousins, lost his temper and threw his cards at her head. She rose from the table, went to bed, and in the morning, ignoring Guest's profuse apologies, left for London with her dismayed husband in tow. Again, she was in the Green Room at Blenheim, replying to a letter from Lloyd George, when Sunny said: 'Please, Clemmie, would you mind not writing to that horrible little man on Blenheim writing-paper?' She flew upstairs and packed. Sunny begged her to stay, but she was off on the next train from Woodstock. Winston, who hadn't been with her, was tepid in his defence of her, and she resented that; she believed she had hoisted the Liberal banner against Tory spite. When she had calmed down she wrote to him: 'My sweet and Dear Pig, when I am a withered old woman how miserable I shall be if I have disturbed your life & troubled your spirit by my temper. Do not cease to love me. I could not do without it. If no one loves me, instead of being a Cat with teeth & Claws, but you will admit soft fur, I shall become like the prickly porcupine outside, & inside so raw & unhappy.' He replied that 'I loved much to read the words of your dear letter,' and this was followed by a rare Churchillian admission of self-doubt: 'At times, I think I cd conquer everything – & then again I know I am only a weak vain fool. But your love for me is the greatest glory & recognition that has or will ever befall me: & the attachment wh I feel towards you is not capable of being altered by the sort of things that happen in this world. I only wish I were more worthy of you, & more able to meet the inner needs of your soul.'[95]

Clementine was as complex as her husband, but in many ways his antithesis: less gregarious, always reserved, often lonely in the midst of people, and far more critical of others. In those days she admired Lloyd George – many women did, and he exploited them; his promiscuity was so extraordinary that it had won him the sobriquet 'Goat' – but she didn't like Guest or F.E. Smith, who went on to be Lord Birkenhead, lord chancellor of England; or the young Canadian millionaire Max Aitken. It puzzled her that 'F.E.,' as everyone called him, should be Winston's best friend. His brilliance and dazzling wit were lost on her. She saw him as simply an archconservative Tory. Yet Winston and F.E. went on summer cruises together and founded the Other Club (the House of Commons being *the* Club), where bitter political rivals dined amicably in one another's company and took up their weapons again afterwards, the constitution providing that 'nothing in the rules or intercourse of the Club shall interfere with the rancour or asperity of party politics.' Churchill later wrote of F.E. in *Great Contemporaries*: 'Never did I separate from him without having learnt something, and enjoyed myself besides.' He and F.E. were also fellow officers in the QOOH, the Queen's Own Oxfordshire Hussars, and took the field each spring in the regiment's annual camp, held in Blenheim Park. He and Clementine would engage in bantering correspondence during these gentlemanly manoeuvres. 'We are going to bathe in the lake this evening,' he told her in a typical note. 'No cats allowed! Your pug in clover, W.' And she would assure him that while he was gone, 'your lazy Kat sits purring and lapping cream and stroking her kittens.'[96]

Certainly Winston needed the exercise. In 1909 newspapers noted that his stoop had grown more pronounced, and that he was getting fat. Nevertheless, the QOOH outings made Clementine uneasy. She believed that F.E. kept her husband up late and encouraged him to play poker. Winston always stayed up late and always gambled, but her anxiety was understandable; he couldn't afford the high stakes of his rich friends. At the time of his appointment, Asquith had written him that as president of the Board of Trade he would be 'on the same level, as regards salary & status,' as a secretary of state. That would have brought in £5,000 a year, on which the family could have lived comfortably. As it turned out, he was paid only half that. The money he had invested with Cassel was gone; so were the royalties from his later books. Clementine had grown up learning to live on little money, but she became haunted by the need to make ends meet. Her husband was loving but inconsiderate. On very short notice he would send word that he was bringing friends home to dinner. If she asked what she was expected to feed them, his answer was always the same: 'Let's have Irish stew with lots of onions.' She waved handfuls of bills at him and he turned away shrugging, though once he suffered pangs of remorse. At their wedding his aunt Cornelia had given her a diamond necklace; later Winston had had rubies set around the diamonds. Beset by creditors, she impulsively sold it. When she told him, he rushed to the jeweller to buy it back, but he was too late; it was gone.[97]

Being Winston Churchill's wife was sometimes embarrassing and even dangerous. In November 1909 the Churchills, arriving at Bristol railway station, were leaving their car when a suffragette, Theresa Garnett, ran up and tried to lash his face with a whip. He grabbed her wrists and she tugged him towards the tracks and the path of a moving train. At the last moment Clementine grabbed his coat and pulled both of them back to safety. A few months later he faced another whip, this one in the hands of a suffragette's male relative who cried: 'Take that, you dirty cur!' Winston took evasive action instead. He warned his wife against opening 'suspicious parcels arriving by post without precautions . . . These harpies are quite capable of trying to burn us out.' By 1912 he would be a supporter of their cause, but as long as their assaults on public men continued, he refused to commit himself in

Parliament. Clementine's feelings were mixed. She said publicly that she was 'ardently in favour of votes for women,' and privately she believed feminism needed champions willing to break the law. On the other hand, she certainly didn't want Winston maimed or killed. No such ambiguity troubled her on other issues, however. As his advocacy of Liberal reforms grew more passionate, Tory homes were closed to the Churchills, and some die-hard acquaintances would cross the street rather than greet her. She gloried in their animosity, for in these years, when Winston's radicalism crested, his most enthusiastic supporter was Clementine Churchill.[98]

Even before he left the Colonial Office, Winston had become a thunderer on the left. He had urged the South Africans to adopt a programme of unemployment compensation, and in a letter from Africa on December 22, 1907, he had proposed parliamentary bills establishing minimum wages, insurance against sickness, and old-age pensions in England. Back in London he gave Charles Masterman, himself a reformer, the impression that he was 'full of the poor whom he had just discovered. He thinks he is called by Providence – to do something for them. "Why have I always been kept safe within a hair's breadth," he asked, "except to do something like this?" ' Writing in the *Nation* of March 7, he recommended that men without jobs be 'treated as if they were hospital patients' and that the economy be managed through a 'network of state intervention and regulation'; he saw 'little glory,' he had said, 'in an Empire which can rule the waves and is unable to flush its sewers.' In Glasgow he had delivered a historic speech, declaring that 'the fortunes and interests of Liberalism and Labour are inseparably interwoven. They rise by the same forces, they face the same enemies, they are affected by the same dangers.' The state, he said, must 'concern itself with the care of the sick and the aged, and, above all, of the children.' The government should get 'the railways of this country in our hands' and become 'the reserve employer of labour,' establishing public-works projects to 'spread a net over the abyss.'[99]

All this was breathtaking in 1908. Beatrice Webb revised her early judgement of him; she wrote: 'He is brilliantly able – more than a phrase-monger, I think.' But the upper classes, Churchill's relatives and the people he had lived among all his life, were flabbergasted. This was the man who, as a Sandhurst cadet, had approved of churchgoing for workmen on the ground that 'nothing can give them a good time here, but it makes them more contented to think that they will get one hereafter.' At heart he was a tradionalist who loved the Shakespearean 'tide of pomp/That beats upon the high shore of this world.' Except by reading, or strolling through the Manchester slum with Eddie Marsh, he knew nothing of real poverty. Clementine's small economies were hardly comparable to the destitution of jobless Britons. The Churchills always had servants. Winston never packed a bag; it was simpler to ring a bell. It never occurred to him to travel third-class. Eddie Marsh wrote that until he married, Winston had never even heard of such things as 'lodgings.' He once told Violet Asquith: 'I have always had to earn every penny I possessed, but there has never been a day in my life when I could not order a bottle of champagne for myself and offer another to a friend.'[100]

Why, then, had he chosen to become a tribune of the oppressed? Doubtless his resentment of the Tory hierarchy was one reason; as he saw it, they had ruined his father, driven Winston himself out of their party, and treated him viciously since he had crossed the House floor. He was an intuitive rebel. But being humane, he was also genuinely appalled by the plight of the down-trodden as he discovered it through reading and in talks with the Webbs, Shaw, and Wells. Another explanation is political. The Liberals, though apparently invincible, felt menaced by the burgeoning Labour party, which threatened to steal their thunder and their strong radical wing. An increase in Lib-Lab strength was the result. Asquith made their triumphs possible, though he himself was no ideologue. Silver-haired, with a small, thin-lipped, stubborn-looking mouth and a thick Yorkshire accent which had survived the City of London School and Balliol College at Oxford, he had displayed little political imagination in the past, but he grasped his party's need for movement to the left, shrewdly sensing the necessity for some official response, however limited, to the outcry over the public and private exposés of working-class destitution. One of his first acts had been to provide free meals and free medical attention for schoolchildren. Winston's combative spirit was stirred when these mild measures provoked violent Tory protests. 'Party animosity,' Lord Campion wrote nearly a half-century later, 'reached a degree of virulence which is hardly conceivable in the present generation.'[101] Finally, all these motives for the liberation of Churchill from patrician dogma were immeasurably strengthened by the charisma and leadership of his colleague Lloyd George, his senior by eleven years.

Churchill at the Board of Trade, Lloyd George at the Exchequer – this was the team which really drove the Asquith government in its first surge of reform. It was an unlikely alliance. The younger man, born to a ducal family, weaned on privilege, had been posted to fame by influential relatives and friends, including England's present King, and had, for all his brushes with death on battlefields, led a sheltered life. Lloyd George had been a penniless Welsh boy, raised by a widowed mother, articled to a solicitor at sixteen, and introduced to the practice of law by defending poachers in local courts. One wore a top hat in town, the other, except on extraordinary occasions, a crumpled fedora. Yet each was an impulsive political genius, fired by idealism, joined to the other by common goals. 'Both,' wrote Elie Halévy, 'were opposed to a policy of heavy expenditure on the Army and the Navy, both advocates of a policy of social reform which, they maintained, the Liberal Party must pursue with unprecedented daring, if the Labour Party were not to grow strong on its left. They came forward as the two leaders of the radical group of pacifists and advanced social reformers as opposed to the three Imperialists, Asquith, Grey, and Haldane.'[102]

If it is difficult to accept Churchill as the grandfather of the welfare state, it is even harder to picture him fighting plans to arm England against sabre-rattling Germans. Nevertheless, that was his position in the summer of 1908. In this he was once more his father's son, a co-conspirator with Lloyd George against military estimates. Reginald McKenna, first lord of the Admiralty, wanted to lay six keels for six dreadnoughts; Sir John Fisher, the first sea lord, wrote: '*Six in the estimates w/o any doubt is an irreducible minimum – no qualifying statement.*' Lloyd George, who regarded the navy as a toy for the rich – and called the War Office the 'Ministry of Slaughter' – thought four of the ships were enough. Winston agreed with him. Speaking to miners in south Wales on August 14, he ridiculed the notion of war with the kaiser. 'I think it is greatly to be deprecated,' he said, 'that persons should try to spread the belief in this country that war between Great Britain and Germany is inevitable. It is all nonsense.' There was nothing to fight about, he added, 'although there may be snapping and snarling in London clubs.'[103]

'What are Winston's reasons for acting as he does in this matter?' Lord Knollys later wrote to Lord Esher. 'Of course it cannot be from conviction or principle. The very idea of his having either is enough to make one laugh.' That is a fair sample of the kind of judgements Tories passed on Churchill then. Neither peer could see the obvious : money spent on warships couldn't go into social programmes. The militants in the cabinet wanted six keels, but Asquith complained to his wife: 'Winston and Ll. G. by their combined machinations have got the bulk of the Liberal press in the same camp . . . there are moments when I am disposed summarily to cashier them both.' He couldn't; his back-benchers wouldn't have stood for it; of 377 Liberal MPs, over 200 had joined the League of Liberals Against Aggression and Militarism – the 'LLAAMs,' or 'Lambs.' The issue was in doubt when Lloyd George sent Winston word 'that the Admiralty have had very serious news from their Naval attaché in Germany *since our last Cabinet Committee* & that McK is now convinced we may have to lay down *8* Dreadnoughts next year!!!' The news leaked to the press; in music halls jingoes sang a new ditty: 'We want eight and we won't wait.' They had to wait, but they got them. The two radical ministers accepted an Asquith compromise: four keels were to be laid now, and another four later if the German naval programme made it absolutely necessary. Berlin obliged. 'In the end,' Churchill therefore wrote later, 'a curious and characteristic solution was reached. The Admiralty had demanded six ships: the economists offered four and we finally compromised on eight.' He added that 'although the Chancellor of the Exchequer and I were right in the narrow sense, we were absolutely wrong in relation to the deep tides of destiny.'[104]

Despite this channelling of money into armaments, Churchill passed most of his programme through the House. A maximum workday was established for miners. Sweated labour was attacked by establishing trade boards which fixed minimum wages. In each city he set up a labour exchange where employment would be sought for the jobless, trade-union leaders could meet, and all visitors would be provided with 'facilities for washing, mending, and non-alcoholic refreshments.'[105] He also drafted an unemployment-insurance

333

bill. At the same time, Lloyd George, as chancellor, was introducing a measure providing for old-age pensions and an expanded National Health Insurance Act – his slogan was 'ninepence for fourpence,' the difference between the two figures being the contributions from employers and the government. The latter bill didn't become law until 1911, because the House of Lords balked at it. The solution which broke the legislative impasse, and which was designed by Lloyd George and Churchill, altered the historical balance between the two Houses of Parliament.

At that time the Lords, the 'upper house,' could veto bills passed by the Commons, the 'lower house,' though since 1660 money matters, by custom, had been left to the commoners. Until now there had been few confrontations between the two because members of both houses had come from the same background, and within a fairly narrow range they shared the same political convictions, regardless of party. But Asquith's Liberals were introducing new concepts of government. The burning question, said Balfour, was whether the Conservatives 'should still control, whether in power or whether in opposition, the destinies of this great Empire.' The upper house, AJB pointed out, still had a heavy Tory majority. They could block or mutilate social legislation. He urged them to do it, and they did. An education bill was so maimed by the Lords that Asquith had to drop it. A voting bill was rejected outright. A land-reform programme met the same fate, and so did a liquor-licensing bill. This last was a favourite of Winston's. Among the radical causes he had embraced – this from Churchill! – was temperance. Lucy Masterman was with him on November 26, 1908, when word arrived that the Lords had killed the measure. She wrote in her diary: 'Churchill was perfectly furious at the rejection . . . stabbed at his bread, would hardly speak: murmured perorations about "the heart of every Band of Hope in this country sinking within them." He went on: "We shall send them up a budget in June as shall terrify them, they have started a class war, they had better be careful." '[106]

Actually, the 'People's Budget' of 1909 came in April. Its essence was a revolutionary concept. Until now, with the exception of progressive death duties the taxing power had been used solely to raise revenues for the government. Now it would also redistribute the wealth. Churchill and Lloyd George drafted the budget together. On Tuesday, April 27, Winston wrote Clementine: 'Tomorrow – Sweated Trades! Thursday – the deluge [the budget]!!! Thus the world wags – good, bad, & indifferent intermingled or alternating, & only my sweet Pussy cat remains a constant darling.' The next day he reported that his minimum-wage bill had been 'beautifully received & will be passed without division,' but: 'Tomorrow is the day of wrath! I feel this budget will kill or cure. Either we shall secure ample funds for great reforms next year, or the Lords will force a Dissolution in September.' Clementine, replying from Blenheim, noted that 'Sunny is much preoccupied about the Budget.' She predicted: 'It will make politics very bitter for a long time.' She was right, but it is an astonishing fact that scarcely anyone realized the budget's implications when the chancellor introduced it in the House. He began by stating his intention to 'wage implacable warfare against poverty and squalidness' and went on for more than four hours while 'Churchill,' according to Virginia Cowles, 'watched him like an anxious nannie.' As a performance, Violet Asquith wrote, 'it was a flop. I went to the House of Commons, agog to hear it, and I failed to sit it out . . . It was read so badly that to some he gave the impression that he did not himself understand it.' Even the press missed its implications; the following day *The Times*, the trumpet of the Conservative establishment, dismissed it as 'unadventurous.'[107]

It was hardly that. Taxes were raised on everything: whisky, petrol, pub licences. But the stinger, cloaked in elaborate periphrases, provided that the rich, for the first time, be singled out for special treatment. Death duties were up, the aristocracy's great estates were assessed whether their land was used or not, capital gains were taxed if the land was sold, and everyone who received over £3,000 a year was subject to a supertax. Only some 11,500 Englishmen had that much, but they were the people who ran the country, including members in the House of Lords. The aristocracy was enraged – Winston and Sunny were estranged – and they decided that if Liberals could break precedents, so could they. Against the advice of wiser Tories, the peers vetoed the People's Budget. This created a constitutional crisis. Winston's dander was up; he relished the fight ahead. As early as June 1907 he had described the Lords as 'one-sided, hereditary, unpurged, unrepresentative, absentee. Has the House of Lords ever been right?' he had asked. 'I defy the party opposite to produce a single instance of a settled controversy in which the House of Lords was right.'[108] Until now their blunders had been borne. But never before had they usurped the lower house's power of the purse. He meant to right this wrong by taking the issue to the country, and he meant to pour it on.

So did Lloyd George, who went for the dukes, the leaders of the peerage. The economy was flourishing under the Liberal administration, he said; 'only one stock has gone down badly; there has been a great slump in dukes. A fully-equipped duke costs as much to keep up as two dreadnoughts; and the dukes are just as great a terror and they last longer.' A nobleman's elder son, he said, was merely 'the first of the litter.' Since that definition fitted Sunny, Winston was expected to curb Lloyd George's invective. Instead, he matched it. In a speech which the *Daily Express* headed HIS OWN RECORD FOR ABUSE OUTDONE, he pictured 'the small fry of the Tory party' falling back on their dukes, from whom nothing could be expected but childish behaviour. 'These unfortunate individuals,' he said, 'who ought to lead quiet, delicate, sheltered lives, far from the madding crowd's ignoble strife, have been dragged into the football scrimmage, and they have got rather roughly mauled in the process . . . Do not let us be too hard on them. It is poor sport – almost like teasing goldfish. These ornamental creatures blunder on every hook they see, and there is no sport whatever in trying to catch them. It would be barbarous to leave them gasping upon the bank of public ridicule upon which they have landed themselves. Let us put them back gently, tenderly in their fountains; and if a few bright gold scales have been rubbed off in what the Prime Minister calls the variegated handling they have received they will soon get over it. They have got plenty more.'[109]

Lloyd George was forgiven because of his background, Churchill condemned because of his. Cartoons depicted him denouncing the aristocracy and then retiring to Blenheim for the weekend. A Manchester Tory said that what was 'neither excusable nor permissable is the lack of common decency shown by vulgar abuse of the dukes on the part of a man who is the grandson of one duke, the nephew of another, and the cousin of a third; who belongs to a family which has produced nine dukes; who figures in Debrett* as boasting a dozen titled relatives; and who owes every advantage he possesses over those whom he contemptuously calls "the small fry of public life" to his aristocratic connection.' In the great country houses during that summer of 1909 venomous gossips agreed that the Churchill family, for all its power and glory, had never produced a gentleman; the first Duke of Marlborough had been a rogue, Lord Randolph a knave; Sunny's duchess had left him because he was a cad – actually, Consuelo had left him for a lover – and now Winston had revealed himself as 'utterly contemptible.' For a traditionalist like Churchill, with his great pride in his family, this was bitter medicine. Once he hesitated. He wrote to Clementine that he was working on a speech 'and am gradually getting some material together but of doubtful merit. I cannot make up my mind whether to be provocative or conciliatory and am halting between the two.' She stiffened his spine. Again and again, in these stormy years, she warned him not to be seduced by those Tories like F.E. who, even when public abuse was thickest, dined and drank with him. One morning she wrote to him: 'My Dear Darling Amber Pug – Do not let the glamour and elegance & refinement & the return of old associations blind you. The charming people you are meeting today – they do not represent Toryism, they are just the cream on the top. Below, they are ignorant, vulgar, prejudiced. They can't bear the idea of the lower classes being independent & free. They want them to sweat for them when they are well & to accept flannel & skilly [cheap clothes and thin soup] as a dole if they fall ill, & to touch their caps & drop curtsies when the great people go by – Goodbye my Darling. I love you very much. Your Radical Bristling' – here she drew an indignant cat.[110]

Probably he would have rejected propitiation anyway. Once committed to battle, he was almost incapable of restraint. Asquith complained that Winston's letters to him were all 'begotten by froth out of foam.' Asquith's wife, Margot, wrote Churchill: 'Believe me cheap scores, hen-roost phrases & all oratorical want of dignity is out of date.' He was unrepentant and untamed. 'The House of Lords,' he told his audiences, was 'not a national institution but a party dodge;' the peers had been 'tolerated all these years because they were thought to be in a comatose condition which preceded dissolution.' All they could do, 'if they go mad,' was 'to put a stone on the track and throw the train of state off the line and that is what we are told they are going to do.' He was

---

* John Debrett's *Peerage, Baronetage, Knightage and Companionage.*

ready for bloodshed, if it came to that: 'If the struggle comes, it will be between a representative assembly and a miserable minority of titled persons who represent nobody, who are responsible to nobody and who only scurry up to London to vote in their party interests, their class interests and in their own interests.' Then, savagely, to a huge crowd in Inverness: 'Just as they clutched greedily at the last sour, unpalatable dregs of the bottle before it was torn away from them at the last election, so now when they see a possible chance of obtaining power and place, they kick over the whole table in an ugly wish to jam their noses in the trough.'[111]

The King, dismayed, directed his secretary, Lord Knollys, to write to *The Times* deploring Churchill's diatribes. This was unconstitutional; flagrantly so. Winston wrote to Clementine that Edward 'must really have gone mad. The Royal Prerogative is always exercised on the advice of ministers, and ministers and not the Crown are responsible – and criticism of all debatable acts of policy should be directed to ministers . . . This looks to me like a rather remarkable Royal intervention and shows the bitterness which is felt in those circles. I shall take no notice of it. It will defeat itself.' He sent Asquith a memo: 'The time has come for the total abolition of the House of Lords.' But the prime minister wasn't prepared to do that. Indeed, he felt that under these extraordinary circumstances, he could no longer claim the Liberal victory of 1906 as a mandate. In January 1910 he called for a general election; the party slogan would be 'The People versus the Peers.' Churchill was the most popular campaigner in the election, but the results were disappointing. The Conservatives picked up 116 seats, reducing the Liberal majority to 2. The *Annual Register* called the verdict 'obscure and indecisive.' Nevertheless, with the support of Labour MPs and Irish Nationalists, the Asquith government still held the field. Then, on May 6, 1910, Edward VII suddenly died. There was just enough time for Queen Alexandra to send a brougham to fetch Mrs Keppel so she could be at the bedside of her royal lover when he breathed his last.[112]

Margot Asquith dined at Jennie's home that evening. Winston was there, and at the end of the dinner he rose and said: 'Let us drink to the health of the new King.' Lord Crewe added: 'Rather to the memory of the old.' Jennie, her face puffy from weeping, gave Crewe a grateful look. She and Edward's other mistresses knew now that their long social reign had ended. Some hoped that the younger generation would pick up their torch. Alice Keppel told Clementine that if she really wanted to advance Winston's career, she would take a wealthy, influential lover. Mrs Keppel even offered to act as a procuress and, when Clementine declined, called her 'positively selfish.' But other faded beauties realized that this was, in the words of the song they had adored, After the Ball. They stood forlornly, sobbing among a quarter-million other grievers as the gun carriage bearing Edward's coffin passed them on the Mall, between St James's Park on one side and the stately buildings, including St James's Palace, on the other, Big Ben tonguing with muffled clapper, the cortège led by the new King, George V, flanked by his uncle the Duke of Connaught and, wearing the scarlet uniform of a British field marshal, Kaiser Wilhelm II, to whom, said *The Times*, 'belongs the first place among all the foreign mourners,' because 'even when relations are most strained [he] has never lost his popularity amongst us.' Later Edward's mistresses paid him their own tribute. Jennie, Alice, Lillie Langtry, and the others celebrated that year's Ascot as Black Ascot, standing in their old box wearing black feathers and ribbons on enormous black hats – wrinkled, greying women in their late fifties, but still slender, still pert, still flirtatious, and, in Jennie's case – her marriage to Cornwallis-West was headed for the divorce court – still available.[113]

Winston's mother was not invited to the new King's coronation, but her daughter-in-law was. George sent Clementine a ticket to the Royal Box in Westminster Abbey, and when he learned that she was indisposed, he made special arrangements for her to arrive just before the crown was set on his head and then be whisked away. Her husband was another matter. Churchill tactlessly insisted that the King name a new battleship the *Cromwell,* which George flatly refused to do. Worse, when the King told him that he felt Asquith was 'not quite a gentleman,' Winston repeated it to Asquith.[114] The big issue facing the new monarch, however, was the unresolved People's Budget. The Liberals urged him to appoint enough new peers to swing the House of Lords' vote their way. He hesitated, and the country prepared to go to the polls again. Andrew Bonar Law, who would succeed Balfour as the Conservative leader, tried to exploit Churchill's gambling instincts by proposing that he and Winston run for the same constituency in Manchester, with the understanding that the loser would stay out of the next Parliament. Winston declined to abandon his safe seat, preferring to spend his time and energy campaigning for other Liberal candidates. He was a political celebrity now. Crowds gathered wherever he spoke, eager to hear his biting wit and pitiless philippics.

The second election confirmed the close results of the first. Still the Lords refused to budge. Winston wrote to Clementine: 'Things are tending to a pretty sharp crisis. What are you to do with men whose obstinacy & pride have blinded them to their interests and to every counsel of reason? It would not be surprising if we actually have to create 500. We shall not boggle about it when it comes to the pinch.' Three weeks later he wrote to her: 'If anything goes wrong we make 350 Peers at once.' It proved unnecessary. Lloyd George had derided the upper house as 'Mr Balfour's poodle,' and on this issue it was; they would take their cue from him. Asquith wrote to Balfour, telling him the King would pack the Lords with new peers. The diehards – originally a regimental nickname, the word entered the language at this time – were finished. Balfour resigned his post as party leader, signifying defeat, and in the sweltering summer of 1911 the upper house passed a parliamentary reform act, emasculating their powers, by the thin margin of 131 to 114. The Liberals, however, had paid a price. During the campaign Austen Chamberlain had predicted that Asquith's government, if kept in office, would 'establish Home Rule in

Ireland.' Churchill later wrote of Austen: 'He always played the game, and he always lost.' But this time he was right. To win the backing of the Irish MPs in the 'People versus the Peers' struggle, the Liberals had agreed to introduce a new Home Rule bill, thus reviving that old and bitter quarrel.[115]

Winston's parliamentary skills and his services to the party entitled him to a promotion – a long step towards the prime ministership which, it was generally agreed, would be his before long. Even the Tories believed it; Balfour told him: 'Winston, I believe your hour has come.' Churchill never waited for recognition. When the polls closed on the first of these two elections, he wrote to Asquith that 'Ministers should occupy positions in the Government which correspond to some extent with their influence in the country.' He wanted, he said, 'to go either to the Admiralty (assuming that place to become vacant) or to the Home Office.' He was advised that 'the First Lord could not be changed . . . without being slighted. But if you cared for the HO, no doubt it would be at your disposal.' He cared for it, and on February 14, 1910, he was appointed home secretary. He was thirty-five. Only one home secretary, Sir Robert Peel, had been younger.[116]

Churchill's salary now reached the promised £5,000, and he was working hard for it. His responsibilities included the welfare of seven million factory workers and a million miners, national security, England's police force, immigration, and law and order. Every evening when the House was in session he had to write a longhand report on its proceedings for the King. He was answerable for conservation, the censorship of stage plays, regulations governing automobile mudguards, the licensing of Italian organ-grinders – everything, in short, which directly involved the people living in the United Kingdom. His view of the office was liberal and humanitarian. He said: 'There is no finer investment for any community than putting milk into babies.'[117] Bills drafted by him limited the hours of shop assistants and introduced safety measures in the mines. Most important, at the outset, were his role in guiding Lloyd George's National Health Insurance Act through the House and his penal reforms.

On his appointment he told Violet Asquith that he was less interested in policemen than in their quarries. Memories of his POW imprisonment in Pretoria were still vivid. Prisoners, he said, must have entertainment, 'plenty of books, that's what I missed most,' and anything else which would relieve their feelings of confinement, 'except of course the chance of breaking bounds and getting out of the damned place – I suppose I mustn't give them *that!*' She said she would prefer hanging to a life sentence; he vehemently disagreed: 'Never abandon life. There is a way out of everything except death.' He soon found that the duty he liked least was signing execution warrants; after visiting him, Blunt noted in his diary that it had 'become a nightmare to him to have to exercise his power of life and death in the case of condemned criminals, on an average of one case a fortnight.' One death warrant which did not trouble him was that of Dr H.H. Crippen, who had left his wife's dismembered remains in the cellar of his London home and boarded a transatlantic steamer with his mistress, only to be intercepted on the other side by Canadian Mounties – the first fugitive to be caught by a wireless alert. Crippen was hanged at first light in Pentonville Prison on October 18, 1910. Churchill celebrated with a champagne breakfast.[118]

His predecessor, in handing over the seals of office, had told him: 'As regards prisons, it won't be a bad thing to give a harassed department some rest.' Winston gave it no rest. Beginning a series of visits to penitentiaries, he abolished floggings and introduced libraries and lecture programmes. Of Britain's 184,000 prisoners, he found, a third had been committed for drunkenness and more than a half for failure to pay fines. Imprisonment for debt, theoretically abolished, was still common: 'We are confronted annually with an ever increasing number of committals to prison and hence of failures to recover debts. A vicious system of credit, based on no real security, is increasingly involving working class families in domestic disputes, extravagance, embarrassment and ultimate disgrace, and is sapping thrift and honesty.' Here again he could identify with the men in the cells; he, too, knew the burden of debt. He instituted a 'time-to-pay' programme for debtors and replaced the jailing of drunkards with fines. The number of debtors behind bars dropped from 95,686 to 5,264; of drunks, from 62,822 to 1,670. At the same time, he moved to deprive suffragettes of their martyrdom. They were, he said, 'political prisoners.' As such they were neither searched nor forbidden to bathe; they could wear their own clothing, receive food and parcels from outside, and talk to one another. His explanation for this leniency was that 'prison rules which are suitable to criminals jailed for dishonesty or cruelty or other crimes implying moral turpitude should not be applied inflexibly to those whose general character is good and whose offences, however reprehensible, do not involve personal dishonour.'[119]

He had been impressed and influenced by John Galsworthy's *Justice*. Galsworthy now wrote the *Times*: 'These changes are one and all inspired by imagination, without which reform is deadly, and by common sense, without which it is dangerous.' But a penal official warned that England should not 'ignore the poorer classes outside the prison walls while we do so much for the worst classes of our population,' and the Tories were delighted when one case of clemency backfired. On a prison visit, accompanied by Lloyd George, Winston met the 'Dartmoor Shepherd.' This unfortunate man had been in and out of prison since 1870. Once he had been sentenced to ten years for stealing a watch and chain; another time to five years for stealing £1 6s. 6d.; and, most recently, to three years for taking two shillings from a church box. He had never been guilty of violence. At Dartmoor he tended the penitentiary's flock of sheep. Winston described him in a minute as a man who 'enjoyed a melancholy celebrity for the prodigious sentences he had endured, for his good behaviour and docility in prison, and for his unusual gift of calling individual sheep by name.' On the stump Lloyd George contrasted him with the peers, 'plunderers of the poor.' Churchill ordered him released. It was a mistake. The man was a recidivist. He promptly left the job the warden had found for him and, three months later, was arrested while breaking into a house. Winston reported to the King that the incident had received its 'mead of merriment' in the House. The Tories formally moved a reduction of £500 in his salary, and, Churchill wrote in another report to the King, 'as the Irish members were away, half the Labour ministers absent, ministers at the gala and holiday moods in the air, this flagitious proposal was rejected only by a majority of 32.'[120]

Why weren't all the Liberals and their allies there to save him from this humiliation? The answer lies in the letter's date: June 27, 1911. By then MPs on the left had begun to qualify their admiration of Churchill. Actually, it had never been wholehearted. His colleagues in the Liberal hierarchy had always had reservations about him. Asquith complained that he 'thinks with his mouth'; his wife wrote in her diary, 'Winston has a noisy mind'; Lloyd George compared him to 'a chauffeur who apparently is perfectly sane and drives with great skill for months, then suddenly takes you over a precipice.' Almeric Fitzroy thought that 'his defect is that he sees everything through the magnifying-glass of his self-confidence.' Another Liberal leader came closer to the deepest source of their misgivings when he told A.G. Gardiner: 'Don't forget that the aristocrat is still there – submerged but latent.' Charles Masterman put it bluntly a few years later: 'He desired in England a state of things where a benign upper class dispensed benefits to an industrious, *bien pensant,* and grateful working class.' There was an undefined feeling that his social legislation smacked of paternalism and had been a gesture de haut en bas; that, in Margot Asquith's words, he had merely learned 'the language of Radicalism. It was Lloyd George's native tongue, but it was not his own, and despite his efforts he spoke it "with a difference." ' In point of fact there *was* a difference. Beatrice Webb remarked upon Winston's 'capacity for quick appreciation and rapid execution of new ideas, whilst hardly comprehending the philosophy beneath them.' But in time he did comprehend the philosophy of the extremists. And when he understood it, he recoiled. He put his trust in social evolution, not upheaval. England's class distinctions suited him. He saw no need to efface them, or even blur them. Only when reactionaries refused to budge, as in the struggle with the Lords, would he endorse sweeping action. Rejected by Tories because he had betrayed his class, he was distrusted by radical reformers because his conversion had been incomplete. He couldn't win.[121]

He was likeliest to lose in the Home Office. The first duty of the home secretary was maintenance of order, and beginning in the year he took over the ministry, organized workingmen suddenly turned to violent tactics. In the beginning the prospect of labour strife didn't daunt him. Three weeks after taking over the Board of Trade he had settled a shipbuilding lockout on the Tyne to the satisfaction of both parties. But in the two years since then battle lines had been drawn between capital and labour, and as a moderate he occupied no-man's land. In union chapels his ritualistic denunciations of socialism were resented – though, curiously, Lloyd George's, just as vehement, were not – and his attempts to be evenhanded failed. He compared irresponsible workmen to irresponsible peers and succeeded only in irking the new King, who felt he had insulted the aristocracy. Replying to the sovereign, Winston said that the home secretary had received 'with deep regret the expression of YM's Displeasure wh has reached him through the PM . . . with regard to the particular phrase wh has caused YM's displeasure, wh Mr Churchill understands is "It should be remembered that there are idlers at both ends of the social scale." Mr Churchill cannot understand why this shd be thought Socialistic in character . . . To say this is not to attack the wealthy classes, most of whom as Mr Churchill knows well have done their duty in many ways: but only to point to those particular persons whose idle and frivolous conduct and lack of public spirit brings a reproach to the meritorious class to wh they belong.' George was unmollified. And the left, judging Winston by his acts, found him wanting.[122]

In the first week of November, 1910, over 25,000 coal miners walked out at Rhondda, in south Wales. Riots followed; several mines were flooded, and the disorders culminated in the battle of Glamorgan Valley, after which the miners smashed shop fronts in the town of Tonypandy. The local chief constable, unable to cope, asked for troops. Aware that sending soldiers against strikers was bad politics, Churchill kept the number of troops to a minimum of four hundred, sent three hundred London policemen, and made sure that the commanding officer was responsible to him. Afterwards the officer said: 'It was entirely due to Mr Churchill's foresight in sending a strong force of Metropolitan Police, directly he was made aware of the state of affairs in the valleys, that bloodshed was avoided.'[123] Strikers charged the bobbies, but the policemen swung rolled-up mackintoshes and beat them off. Elsewhere, however, two miners were killed, and when a unit of soldiers was stoned, they fixed bayonets and prodded the strikers into retreating.

In light of the fact that the wrecked stores in Tonypandy were looted during what *The Times* called 'an orgy of naked anarchy,' the use of force does not seem excessive. The troops had been sent in response to an appeal from the Glamorgan law-enforcement official, and Churchill had had no part in that decision. But the fact that they had been called out, and had unsheathed bayonets, infuriated union leaders. Churchill firmly told them that the soldiers now in position would remain there until he judged that troops were 'no longer necessary.' They then blamed the two deaths on him. He called this 'a cruel lie,' which it was. Keir Hardie, maddened beyond reason, declared that the Liberals 'will give you Insurance Bills, they will give you all sorts of soothing syrups to keep you quiet, but in the end your Liberal Party, just like your Tory Party, is the Party of the rich and exists to protect the rich when Labour and Capital come into conflict.'[124]

The Conservatives turned this inside out. If troops had been sent in earlier, they said in the House, there would have been no looting and no property damage. An appeal from Winston, urging the strikers to renounce violence, was ridiculed by *The Times* as showing 'a somewhat maudlin tone . . . Mr Churchill hardly seems to understand that an acute crisis has arisen, which needs decisive handling. The rosewater of conciliation is all very well in its place, but its place is not in the face of a wild mob drunk with the desire of destruction.' The *Daily Express* was even harsher: 'Nothing was ever more contemptible in childish and vicious folly than Mr Churchill's message to the miners . . . It is the last word in a policy of shameful neglect and poltroonery which may cost the country dear.' To the King, Winston reported: 'The insensate action of the rioters in wrecking shops in the town of Tonypandy, against which they had not the slightest cause for animosity, was not foreseen by anyone on the spot, and would not have been prevented by the presence of soldiers at the colliery itself.' Nevertheless, the two myths endured. Tories thought he had acted spinelessly. Labour believed he had overreacted, and for more than forty years he would be heckled by workingmen who were convinced that he had led a bloody massacre of miners at Tonypandy.[125]

Less than two months later he was in his bathtub – it is extraordinary how many crises found him bathing – when he was summoned to the telephone, 'dripping wet and shrouded in a towel,' as he later recalled, to be told that members of a gang of Latvian anarchists had been trapped at 100 Sidney Street in Whitechapel. This was welcome news, exciting and important. Churchill wanted these men badly. They were not only criminals; the Liberal government was responsible for their presence in England. The city's East End, inhabited by nearly two million poor Londoners, had always seethed with crime. But since the abortive Russian uprising of 1905 and the Liberals' refusal to restrict immigration, Whitechapel, Stepney, Shadwell, and Bethnal Green had also become asylums for political refugees from the czar's Okhrana, or secret police. Joseph Stalin had briefly lived in Whitechapel in June 1907, sharing a tiny room with Maxim Litvinov. In their homeland these anarchists – today they would be called urban guerrillas – had supported their causes by robberies, and they continued to do so here, treating bobbies as they treated the Okhrana. Among them was a band of Letts led by Peter Piaktow, alias 'Peter the Painter,' so christened because when not ambushing bank messengers or holding up shopkeepers at pistol point, he worked as a house painter. The men trapped in the Sidney Street house were part of this gang. Heavily armed, they had already murdered three policemen; Winston and Clementine had attended the funerals in St Paul's ten days earlier. Now the bobbies holding them at bay wanted the assistance of troops; hence the phone call to the home secretary. 'Use whatever force is necessary,' he said, promising that a detachment of Scots Guards from the Tower would be there within the hour. Then, dressing and donning his top hat and astrakhan-collared coat, he hurried by cab to the Home Office in search of more information. There was none there, so at noon he decided to take an official car to the scene because 'I thought it my duty to see what was going on myself . . . I must, however, admit that convictions of duty were supported by a strong sense of curiosity which perhaps it would have been well to keep in check.'[126]

In Whitechapel he found high drama. Spectators and men in uniform were crouching behind buildings on both sides of the street while the killers and their besiegers blazed away at one another – the anarchists in their hideout firing Mausers; the Scots Guards, Lee-Enfields; and the sixty policemen, obsolete Morris-tube rifles. *A Daily Chronicle* reporter perched on the roof of the Rising Sun pub estimated that in the past hour and a half several thousand bullets had been exchanged without result. Churchill realized that he had made a mistake in coming: 'It was not for me to interfere with those who were in charge on the spot. Yet . . . my position of authority, far above them all, attracted inevitably to itself direct responsibility. I saw now that I should have done much better to have remained quietly in my office. On the other hand, it was impossible to get into one's car and drive away while matters stood in such great uncertainty, and, moreover, were extremely interesting.' Crossing the street for a better view, he sheltered in a warehouse doorway. Senior officers believed the house should be stormed, and he agreed; his 'instincts,' he later wrote, 'turned at once to a direct advance up the staircase behind a steel plate or shield, and a search was made in the foundries of the neighbourhood for one of suitable size.' None was found, but the idea had lodged in his mind. In Sidney Street his concept of the tank was born.[127]

At one o'clock thin wisps of bluish smoke curled upward from a garret window of the embattled hideout, and within a half hour it was burning fiercely. The London fire brigade clattered up. Firemen and policemen argued. The bobbies refused to let the men with hoses approach the building; the firemen insisted that extinguishing the flames was their duty. At this point Churchill intervened. 'I thought it better to let the house burn down,' he explained afterwards, 'than spend good British lives in rescuing those ferocious rascals.' So it blazed for an hour. 'Then at last,' reported the *Daily News*, 'Mr Churchill stepped to the middle of the street and waved his arms . . . firemen appeared and regardless of possible bullets poured water on the burning house . . . and policemen led by Mr Churchill rushed forward to the door.' Inside they found nothing but charred bodies.[128]

All this was recorded by cameramen. Eddie Marsh, dropping into the Palace Theatre, saw flickering newsreels, captioned 'Mr Churchill directing the operations,' and heard them greeted by boos, hisses, shouts of ' 'E let the bastards in the country!' and 'Shoot 'im!' More embarrassing, Balfour rose in the House to ask caustically: 'We are concerned to observe photographs in the illustrated newspapers of the Home Secretary in the danger zone. I understand what the photographer was doing but why the Home Secretary?' The Conservative press agreed that it was absurd. Churchill noted that '*The Times* blamed me for stopping the soldiers going to Tonypandy and now blames me for sending them to Sidney Street. Their doctrine is now apparent, that soldiers should always be sent to put down British miners in trade disputes but never to apprehend alien murderers engaged in crime. This is on a par with Tory thought in other directions.' It was not only Tory thought, however, Liberals were equally troubled; his recent conduct seemed inconsistent with their serene slogan: 'Peace, Retrenchment, and Reform.' A.G. Gardiner wrote in the *Daily News:* 'He is always unconsciously playing a part – an heroic part. And he is himself his most astonished spectator. He sees himself moving through the smoke of battle – triumphant, terrible, his brow clothed in thunder, his legions looking to him for victory, and not looking in vain . . . It is not make-believe, it is not insincerity; it is that in this fervid and picturesque imagination there are always great deeds afoot, with himself cast by destiny in the Agamemnon role. Hence that portentous gravity that sits on his youthful shoulders so oddly, those impressive postures and tremendous silences, the body flung wearily in the chair, the head resting gloomily in the hand, the abstracted look.' Thus, Gardiner accounted for his 'tendency to exaggerate a situation' and dispatch 'the military hither and thither as though Armageddon was upon us.' Other Liberals believed that he had shown he lacked a sense of proportion, using 'a steamhammer to crack a nut.' Charles Masterman, returning from holiday, demanded: 'What the hell have you been doing now, Winston?' Churchill, lapsing into his lisp, replied: 'Now, Charlie. Don't be croth. It was such fun.'[129]

The 'Siege of Sidney Street,' as the press called it, was followed by the hottest summer on record, and, with it, a wave of industrial unrest. The disturbances began in June, when dockers walked out in Southampton, and swiftly spread to other ports. Then transport workers struck to show that they sided with the longshoremen. Churchill observed that 'a new force has arisen in trades unionism, whereby the power of the old leaders has proved quite ineffective, and the sympathetic strike on a wide scale is prominent. Shipping, coal, railways, dockers etc etc are all uniting and breaking out at once.' The head constable in Liverpool reported to the Home Office that rioters had built barricades of dustbins and wire entanglements in side streets, lured policemen there, and stoned them from windows and housetops. The King wired Churchill: 'Accounts from Liverpool show that situation there more like revolution than a strike . . . Strongly deprecate half-hearted employment of troops: they should not be called on except as a last resource but if called on they should be given a free hand & the mob should be made to fear them.'[130]

The immediate threat was famine. On August 9 the London meat and fruit markets shut down; they had nothing left to sell. Then, a week later, the railwaymen gave notice of a national strike. The railway companies had refused to recognize their union as a bargaining agent. Food shortages were imminent in the great quadrilateral of British industrialism, from Liverpool and Manchester in the west to Hull and Grimsby in the east, from Newcastle down to Birmingham and Coventry. Asquith offered the trainmen an enquiry by a royal commission. When they turned it down on the ground that such a commission would take too long, he reportedly said: 'Then your blood be on your own head.' That night every member of the union received a wire from its leadership: 'Your liberty is at stake, all railwaymen must strike at once.' Churchill told the House that 'no blockade by a foreign enemy' could be so perilous. If unchecked it would lead, he said, 'to the starvation of great numbers of the poorer people.'[131]

Violence erupted in Llanelly when rioters stormed a train and two were shot. The lord mayor of Liverpool telegraphed Churchill, asking him to requisition a warship and bluejackets to man the Mersey River ferries. HMS *Antrim* was dispatched. But the larger issue was the railway strike. Until August 17 the home secretary, though goaded by Tories and his sovereign, clung to the same position he had held at Tonypandy. Law enforcement was the responsibility of policemen, who were encouraged to enrol special constables. This attitude was not unappreciated; Ben Tillet, the leader of the London longshoremen, called Winston's influence moderating and responsible. In his 'History of the London Transport Workers' Strike,' a leaflet published by the transport workers' union in 1911, Tillet wrote that before the crisis he had thought of Winston as a 'ferocious man of blood and iron,' but when they met in the lobby of the House he found him 'as amiable as the gentlest shepherd on earth,' a man who 'in quite convincing manner assured us he heartily agreed with all our views.' Tillet added: 'If patience and courtesy, if anxious effort and sincerity count for respect; then Winston Churchill is entitled as a man to gratitude . . . We found an urbane young Cabinet Minister apparently fully alive to the duties and responsibilities of his office.'

Unfortunately, Churchill's approach had produced no results. He was in a dilemma. Liberal politicians, including every member of the cabinet except the chancellor of the Exchequer, shied away from the use of force, and soldiers could not be legally used in any domestic dispute without specific requests from local authorities. On August 19 Winston decided to break this precedent. He alerted fifty thousand troops and announced: 'The Army Regulation which requires a requisition for troops from a civil authority is suspended.' Asquith remained silent. Lloyd George acted; he persuaded the railroad employers to recognize the union, and the men went back to work. Churchill believed his own order had cut the knot because it proved 'that any Government must exert itself to prevent . . . catastrophe, and because it was certain that in taking such action they would be supported by the good sense and resolution of the whole mass of the people.' King George concurred; he wired him: 'Feel convinced that prompt measures taken by you prevented loss of life in different parts of the country.'[132]

Nonetheless, he had set a questionable example. In addition, he had again offended the left, whose powerful ally he had been at the Board of Trade. Masterman charged Churchill with 'whiff-of-grapeshot' tactics, even with a 'longing for blood.' Labour MP Ramsay MacDonald called the mobilization 'diabolical' and went on: 'This is not a mediaeval state, and it is not Russia. It is not even Germany . . . If the Home Secretary had just a little more knowledge of how to handle masses of men in these critical times, if he had a somewhat better instinct of what civil liberty does mean . . . we should have had much less difficulty during the last four or five days in facing and finally settling the problem.' One observer concluded that Churchill's 'reputation with organized labour suffered a severe blow.' Even the *Manchester Guardian*, until now Winston's warmest admirer in the press, was outraged when, despite the absence of any request from the lord mayor, troops appeared and occupied Manchester's railway stations.[133]

The speed with which Churchill's reforms were forgotten is puzzling. It is almost as though the radicals had felt uncomfortable with him in their midst. Henceforth he would be regarded as a conservative. He had always felt ties to the past, and there is an inevitable connection between a public man's performance and the psychic baggage which is his unshakable companion. But the politicians of the left had pushed him rightward, just as the Tories had pushed him in the opposite direction seven years earlier. His own view was evocative of Robert E. Lee's: 'True patriotism sometimes requires of men to act contrary, at one period, to that which it does another.' Essentially Churchill was unaltered. It was England which had shifted direction. The awakening of the working class, which he himself had stirred, had altered the political climate. In Victoria's reign or even during her son's early years on the throne, workmen would never have conspired to bring the country to its knees over a union issue. But neither would a chancellor have imposed a super-tax on the rich, nor a party have humiliated the peers. Social stability was wobbly, and civility diminished. The easy cordiality which had marked the rivalry between Joe Chamberlain and young Winston would soon be a rarity. Enemies were implacable. Friendships became exhausted, reservoirs of goodwill drained, public men used up. The disturbances of 1910–1911 had damaged Churchill's credibility in the Home Office, and Asquith decided to shake up his cabinet. The rift within the Liberal-Labour coalition over the use of force in industrial disputes was one reason. The other lay in Europe. The kaiser, so welcome at Edward's funeral, had been behaving outrageously. Germany was now regarded as a menace to the long European peace.

Churchill had met the kaiser on September 8, 1906, when he was still undersecretary at the Colonial Office. He had sought an invitation to the German army's military manoeuvres that year in Silesia, and as a member of Britain's ruling class he was welcome. Count von der Schulenberg, military attaché at the emperor's London embassy, informed him that an officer would meet his train in Breslau; he would stay at the Hofmarschallamt as the personal guest of *Seine Majestät*. Winston didn't speak a word of German – 'I'll never learn the beastly language,' he growled, 'until the Kaiser marches on London' – but like most upper-class Britons of the time, he assumed that every civilized man knew English.[134] His chief problem was finding an appropriate uniform. Von der Schulenberg had specified levee dress for a state dinner, and he hadn't any. He thought he could borrow the leopard skin and plume of the Oxfordshire Hussars from his brother, but Jack had turned the skin into a hearthrug six years earlier. Finally Sunny rooted around in Blenheim's attic and found his.

Winston witnessed the kaiser's 'entry into the city of Breslau at the beginning of the manoeuvres. He rode his magnificent horse at the head of a squadron of cuirassiers, wearing their white uniform and eagle-crested helmet . . . surrounded by Kings and Princes while his legions defiled before him in what seemed to be an endless procession.' On September 14 Churchill wrote to Elgin from Vienna: 'I had about 20 minutes talk with H.I.M. at the Parade dinner. He was vy friendly & is certainly a most fascinating personality.' They had bantered over a recent issue. Rebellious natives in German Southwest Africa had recently fled into the Cape Colony; German police had crossed the frontier in hot pursuit, and the kaiser, Churchill told Elgin, 'was pleased to be sarcastic about "his design of flying across the deserts to seize Cape Town" wh he suggested we attributed to him; & he said that if a native rising took place all over SA "those people (in Cape Town) would be vy glad of my troops." He enlarged on the fighting qualities of the Hereros, & said in reply that in Natal on the contrary our chief difficulty had not been to kill the rebellious natives, but to prevent our Colonists (*who so thoroughly understood native war*) from killing too many of them.' Still, Winston had been impressed by the 'massive simplicity & force' of the Prussian military machine. He told his aunt Leonie: 'I am very thankful there is a sea between that army and England.'[135]

Wilhelm remembered him, and was aware of the Churchills' prestige in England. Over a year later, in December 1907, Jennie wrote to Winston that the kaiser, meeting Leonie at a Clarence House luncheon, 'asked a great deal after me & said he remembered me in Berlin with R[andolph]. He also spoke of you.' In the summer of 1909, with his reputation growing, Churchill was asked to return to Germany for another visit. He wrote to his mother: 'The German Emperor has invited me to the Manoeuvres as his guest, and I am to be at Wurzburg, in Franconia, on the 14th of September.' He wrote to Clementine that the kaiser, who appeared 'vy sallow – but otherwise quite well,' was 'very friendly – "My dear Winston" & so on.' His imperial host warned him 'to guard against "disagreements on party politics" & chaffed about "Socialists" in a good-humoured way.' Winston was treated as an exalted guest: 'I have a vy nice horse from the Emperor's stables, & am able to ride about wherever I choose with a suitable retinue. As I am supposed to be an "Excellency" I get a vy good place.'[136]

He was troubled by the Teutonic character: 'These people are so amazingly *routinière* that anything at least [sic] out of the ordinary – anything they have not considered officially and for months – upsets them dreadfully . . . With us there are so many shades. Here it is all black & white (the Prussian colours). I think another 50 years will see a wiser and gentler world. But we shall not be spectators of it. Only the P.K. will glitter in a happier scene.' This time he was even more awed by the kaiser's martial juggernaut. He described it as 'a terrible engine. It marches sometimes 35 miles in a day. It is in number as the sands of the sea – & with all the modern conveniences . . . How easily men could make things better than they are – if they only all tried together! Much as war attracts me & fascinates my mind with its tremendous situations – I feel more deeply every year – & can measure the feeling here in the midst of arms – what vile & wicked folly & barbarism it all is.' He treasured his family all the more: 'Sweet cat – I kiss your vision as it rises before my mind. Your dear heart throbs often in my own. God bless you darling & keep you safe & sound. Kiss the P.K. for me all over. With fondest love – W.'[137]

Back in England he once more persuaded himself that war between the two empires was unthinkable; it would be too ghastly; no sane authority could countenance it. He counselled the new King to take a conciliatory line, writing to him on May 13, 1911, 'Mr Churchill thinks that Your Majesty's references on Tuesday next to the German Emperor will be very warmly welcomed by the Peace party in the country, & will do a lot of good to public sentiment here & in Germany.'[138] Then, less than seven weeks later, came Churchill's greatest volte-face, transforming him from a dove into a hawk. It was triggered that July by the incident at Agadir, an obscure port on the Atlantic coast of Morocco.

The Germans had been late entrants in the race for colonies, and by the time they reached Africa all the prizes were gone. After the Tangier incident in 1905, Germany and France had agreed that neither would annex Morocco, but unrest there spread into French Algeria, and French troops, in another hot pursuit, crossed over onto Moroccan soil. The kaiser, on the advice of his aggressive foreign minister, decided to make an issue of it. He despatched a gunboat, the *Panther*, to Agadir. Wilhelm expected the French to grab Morocco, which they did, and had no intention of contesting it; his goal was acquisition of a bargaining chip which would win him concessions in the Congo. He got them, but the arrival of the *Panther* on July 1, 1911, was destined to set off a murderous chain reaction. While Paris and Berlin were haggling, the Italians took advantage of the diversion by invading Tripoli. Tripoli was part of the Turks' Ottoman Empire. Discontented nationalities in the Balkans decided that if Italy could take on the Turks, so could they. The immediate results were the Balkan wars of 1912 and 1913, followed by the rise of Serbia, Austria-Hungary's fear of a strong Serbia, and Russia's alliance with the Serbs, a consequence of the czar's determination to preserve his credibility in the Balkans. Russia's growing military presence in the region threatened Austria-Hungary and Germany, Austria-Hungary's powerfull ally. The kaiser liked his cousin in St Petersburg, but he believed that if he ever allowed him time to mobilize and arm Russia's countless millions, they would be unbeatable. Therefore he began to contemplate pre-emptive war. Meanwhile, all the great European powers, engaging in a deadly quadrille, rearmed at a furious pace.

These sequelae were unrevealed to the Britons of 1911. No man, not even the wisest statesman, can see across the horizon, and in the barbarous 1980s the appearance of a small warship in an African harbour does not seem provocative. But it was then. Diplomacy was different in the years before 1914. A studied insult, even an unanswered note, could make governments tremble. The display of naked force – the *Panther* – had been shocking. It simply was not done. By doing it, the Germans changed a lot of minds, among them that of Lloyd George. Obviously, George told Churchill, Berlin believed that London would never intervene, whatever the kaiser did. He said, 'People think that because I was pro-Boer I am anti-war in general, and that I should faint at the mention of a cannon.' He meant to correct that impression at once, and he did, in the chancellor's annual address to the City bankers at the Mansion House. He said: 'If a situation were forced upon us in which peace could only be preserved by the surrender of the great and beneficent position Britain has won by centuries of heroism and achievement, by allowing Britain to be treated where her interests were vitally affected as if she were of no account in the Cabinet of nations, then I say emphatically that peace at that price would be a humiliation intolerable for a great country like ours to endure.' The German ambassador, who had described George as a pacifist, was recalled in disgrace.[139]

Churchill was also reappraising his position. His opposition to the Admiralty's dreadnought programme had been based upon his faith in Germany's good intentions. Now, in an undated memorandum on Home Office stationery, he set down his thoughts. 'Germany's action at Agadir,' he wrote, 'has put her in the wrong & forced us to consider her claims in the light of her policy & methods.' He believed that England must give France diplomatic support. 'If no settlement is reached between F. & G. & deadlock results we must secure Brit interests independently . . . If Germany makes war on France in the course of the discussion or deadlock (unless F. has meanwhile after full warning from us taken unjustifiable ground) we shd join with France. Germany should be told this now.' Asquith appointed him to the cabinet's Committee of Imperial Defence, formed in 1904. There Sir Edward Grey revealed his 1906 pledge to defend France. On August 30 Winston wrote to Grey that if 'decisive action' became necessary, Britian should join France and Russia in a 'triple alliance,' guarantee Belgium's frontiers, 'aid Belgium to defend Antwerp,' and plan 'a blockade of the Rhine.'[140]

Beginning that summer of 1911, after the disappointments of Tonypandy, the siege of Sidney Street, and the railway strike, preparation for war was never far from Churchill's thoughts. 'Once I got drawn in,' he later wrote, 'it dominated all other interests in my mind.'[141] He was horrified when, at a Downing Street garden party, the commissioner of police informed him that the Home Office was responsible for guarding the magazines in which all England's reserves of naval cordite were stored. Rushing from the party to the War Office, he persuaded the duty officer to post sentries at the depots until he could organize parties of constables. In mid-August he sought peace in the country. He was sitting on a hilltop, overlooking green fields, when he realized that lines from Housman's *Shropshire Lad* were running through his head:

> On the idle hill of summer,
> Sleepy with the flow of streams,
> ͞ar I hear the distant drummer
> Drumming like a noise in dreams.
> Far and near and low and louder
> On the roads of earth go by,
> Dear to friends and food for powder,
> Soldiers marching, all to die.

On August 23 he submitted a prescient memorandum to the Imperial Defence Committee. Assuming that Britain, France, and Russia were attacked by Germany and Austria-Hungary, he predicted that on the twentieth day of the war the kaiser's armies in France would break through the Meuse defence line. The French would then fall back on Paris. By the fortieth day, however, Germany would 'be extended at full strain both internally and on her war fronts,' and with each passing hour this pressure would become 'more severe and ultimately overwhelming' unless they could force an immediate decision. Denying them that would require 'heavy and hard sacrifices from France.' Whether France could make them would depend on British military support, 'and this must be known beforehand.' He proposed a contingency plan under which Britain would send 107,000 troops across the Channel at the outbreak of war, with another 100,000 men from India reaching Marseilles by the all-important fortieth day. General Henry Wilson told the committee that Winston's prediction was 'ridiculous and fantastic – a silly memorandum.' But three years later the Germans lost the battle of the Marne on the war's forty-second day.[142]

By September 1911 Churchill had tired of the Liberals' growing polarization between left and right, the internal struggle in which he was being ground up, and was again pondering the Victorian policy of Splendid Isolation. He had cherished it as part of his political legacy. But now he studied a Foreign Office paper written in 1907 by Eyre Crowe. Crowe had held that England must preserve Europe's balance of power by forging an alliance with the second-strongest nation on the Continent. Brooding over this thesis, Winston was struck by the thought that although earlier generations of Englishmen had never put it on paper, they had in fact always pursued it. This grand strategy, he believed, had been the key to the Elizabethans' rout of the Spaniards, Marlborough's defeat of Louis XIV, and Wellington's triumph over Napoleon. Following the same line of reasoning, he concluded that England must now embrace France, even hold joint manoeuvres with France. As a candidate three years earlier, he had told audiences in Manchester and Dundee that the German threat was a figment of Tory imagination. After Agadir he became the cabinet's most ardent advocate of intervention.

Another prime minister might have resented his home secretary's active interest in military issues. Asquith didn't. Indeed, he had good reason to encourage it. Churchill, one of his ablest ministers, was no longer comfortable or suitable in the Home Office, and the Royal Navy needed a forceful hand at the tiller. As first lord of the Admiralty, Reginald McKenna was far too easygoing; he had been unable to overcome the resistance of his first sea lord – the equivalent of the US chief of naval operations – to the formation of a naval war staff. Asquith pondered having them switch jobs. Apart from Churchill, the only other strong candidate for the Admiralty was the secretary for war, Lord Haldane, who had just completed a brilliant reorganization of the army. In September 1911 the prime minister invited both men and their wives to be his guests at Archerfield, his Scottish estate on the East Lothian coast. The Churchills would arrive late, because Winston had to visit Balmoral first. It was customary for each senior minister to spend a few days there with the King each year. Clementine passed those days with her grandmother in Airlie Castle – wives were not received at Balmoral on such occasions – and on September 25 she wrote: 'I hope you are happy my sweet Pug and that you are being properly petted, & that you will secure a huge stag. I am very happy here – Granny is become much kinder with age . . . She sends her love & is looking forward to seeing you on Wednesday for luncheon which is at 1:30 *to the second by Greenwich time.* Afterwards we fly away to Archerfield in the new motor.' The automobile, a £610 red Napier, had been delivered to Churchill at Balmoral. He drove over to pick Clementine up, and before they left the castle he told her he was afraid Asquith would pick Haldane. She opened her grandmother's Bible to the one hundred and seventh Psalm. 'I know it's all right about the Admiralty,' she said, and read: 'They that go down to the sea in ships, that do business in great waters; these see the works of the Lord, and his wonders in the deep.'[143]

She was right. Asquith had already made his decision. Churchill would run the navy. Asquith wrote to Haldane: 'The main and, in the longer run, the deciding factor with me has been the absolute necessity for keeping the First Lord in the Commons.' Clementine was absent at the great moment. After a round of golf with Asquith, Winston approached Violet, who was just finishing tea, and asked her to join him for a walk. In his face, she wrote, she saw 'a radiance like the sun.' Did he want tea? she asked. He shook his head. They had hardly left the house when he blurted out: 'I don't want tea, I don't want anything – anything in the world. Your father has just offered me the Admiralty.' He looked seaward, and in the fading light of evening watched the silhouettes of two battleships steaming slowly out of the Firth of Forth. It was a full moment for him. He said: 'Look at the people I've had to deal with so far. Judges and convicts! This is a big thing – the biggest thing that has ever come my way – the chance I should have chosen before all others. I shall pour into it everything I've got!' Just as Clementine had opened a Bible in Airlie Castle, so, that night at Archerfield, did he. He found himself reading from the ninth chapter of Deuteronomy: 'Hear, O Israel: Thou art to pass over Jordan this day, to go in to possess nations greater and mightier than thyself . . . Understand therefore this day that the Lord thy God is he which goeth over before thee; as a consuming fire he shall destroy them, and he shall bring them down before thy face: so shalt thou drive them out, and destroy them quickly, as the

Lord hath said unto thee.'[144]

The next day he and Clementine rode to London in the Napier, and in the morning he and McKenna changed guard. McKenna came over to the Home Office and Churchill introduced him to everyone there; then they crossed to the Admiralty, where Winston met his new board, senior officers, and departmental heads. That afternoon he convened a board meeting. The secretary read the letters patent confirming the new first lord's appointment. Thereupon Churchill, in the words of the order-in-council, became 'responsible to Crown and Parliament for all the business of the Admiralty.' In 1923 he would write: 'I was to endeavour to discharge this responsibility for the four most memorable years of my life.'[145]

His new office was accompanied by many perquisites, in all of which he revelled. There has always been a certain panache to England's service ministries, and because the Admiralty is the senior service, the navy, in an old expression, 'always travels first class.' Among other things, the first lord decides who launches ships. Seven weeks after his appointment Clementine christened the battleship *Centurion* at Devonport, and shortly thereafter Jennie baptized its sister ship, the *Benbow*. The first lord had at his disposal a luxurious steam yacht, the *Enchantress*. In Churchill's words, this vessel became 'largely my office, almost my home.' His time aboard was mostly work time; he visited every important ship and every dockyard, shipyard, and naval establishment in the British Isles and the Mediterranean. But for Clementine it was mostly fun. There was one memorable cruise up the coast of Scotland; on which her sister Nellie and her sister-in-law Goonie accompanied them. Another took them to Venice, where the crew caught a huge turtle; the cook asked, 'Which evening would madam prefer turtle soup?' and was dismayed when his mistress, as fond of pets as her husband, ordered the tortoise returned to the sea. On a third voyage, they anchored in Cardigan Bay and visited the Lloyd Georges in Criccieth, their Welsh home. Because Clementine knew that Winston hated meals at which nothing of importance was accomplished, most guests were men who could be useful to the Admiralty, and she scored a real coup by suggesting they entertain Kitchener, now a field marshal and agent-general in Egypt. 'By all means ask K to lunch,' Winston said. 'Let us just be *à trois*. I have some things to talk to him about.' So the long feud finally ended.[146]

These were golden days for Clementine. Motherhood had brought her a new tranquillity, and she had learned to suppress her objections to some of her in-laws. Winston wrote that they had received an invitation from Lady Wimborne, and asked her to accept: 'I have a great regard for her – & we have not too many friends. If however you don't want to go – I will go alone. Don't come with all your hackles up & your fur brushed the wrong way – you naughty.' She replied: 'I will write tomorrow to Aunt Cornelia – I would like to go, & I will be very good I promise you, especially if you stroke my silky tail.'

She didn't even demur when seated next to Asquith at meals, though the prime minister was a notorious peerer down Pennsylvania Avenue. Now in her late twenties, Clementine attracted many a lustful eye. After a day at Broadstairs with the Churchills, an artist friend wrote: 'Winston went off to dig castles in the sand and the rest of us bathed. It was a broiling day and the water was heavenly. Clementine came forth like the reincarnation of Venus re-entering the sea. Her form is most beautiful. I had no idea she had such a splendid body.'[147]

Yet she was jealous of Violet Asquith, feeling, according to her daughter Mary, 'an understandable reserve towards this well-ensconced friend of Winston's.' And soon Violet would be practically living next door. In addition to his yacht, the first lord was provided with a magnificent eighteenth-century residence, Admiralty House, with a superb view of St James's Park. Winston wrote to Clementine: 'I am sure you will take to it when you get there. I am afraid it all means vy hard work for you – Poor lamb.' Sir Edward Grey wanted to sublet their Eccleston Square house, but she fought the move, pleading economy. Because the government was providing them with a home, Churchill's salary was cut by £500, and Admiralty House meant increasing their servants from five to eleven or twelve. Confronted with this argument, he was, as always, vulnerable. In one helpless note he agreed with her that 'money seems to flow away.' A few days later he cheerfully wrote that he was 'preparing a scheme which will enable us to clear off our debts & bills & start on a ready money basis. We shall have to pull in our horns.' He couldn't do it, though. That same week she was off to visit France, and he wrote: 'If you have anything left out of the £40, spend it on some little thing you like in Paris.' Finally, after she had reduced the staff to nine by sealing off the first floor of Admiralty House, the move was made. Violet rejoiced. Winston, she wrote, had now become 'our nearest neighbour. Only the width of Horse Guards Parade separated the Admiralty from the garden door of No. 10 and it was often crossed hot-foot. It was a joy to see him buoyantly engaged in his new context, tasting complete fulfilment. I remember telling him that even his brooding had assumed a different quality. He travailed almost with serenity. "That is because I can now lay eggs instead of sratching around in the dust and clucking. It is a far more satisfactory occupation. I am at present in process of laying a great number of eggs – good eggs, every one of them." '[148]

He spent long days in his new nest. Eddie Marsh wrote to a friend: Winston stays until at least 8 every day . . . Even Sundays are no longer my own, as I have spent 3 out of the last 4 on the *Enchantress*. We have made a new commandment. "The seventh day is the Sabbath of the First Lord, and on it thou shalt do all manner of work." ' Officers at the Admiralty were on duty twenty-four hours a day, alert for a surprise attack. In Churchill's office hung a large chart of the North Sea with flag pins marking the position of every German warship; he studied it each morning on first entering the room 'to inculcate in myself and those working with me a sense of ever-present danger.' The *Pall Mall Gazette* described him as 'quite' a naval enthusiast, and after he had visited a submarine the *Daily Express* reported: 'He had a yarn with nearly all the lower deck men of the ship's company, asking why, wherefore, and how everything was done. All the sailors "go the bundle" on him, because he makes no fuss and takes them by surprise. He is here, there, and everywhere.' Everything about the Admiralty excited him, from the twin stone dolphins guarding the building's entrance to the furniture within, each piece of which was adorned with golden dolphins dating from Nelson's time. His delights, like Antony's, were 'dolphin-like.'[149]

Like Antony he was also accustomed to infusing his public roles with high drama. But this time it was appropriate. What had been absurd at the Colonial Office – depicting a dubious African chief as a martyr – became sublime at the Admiralty. It is arguable that the first lord's burden was greater than the prime minister's. He was answerable for England's safety. Only the fleet could protect the island from invasion, move British troops to the Continent, bring regiments home from India, replace them with territorials, and prevent what an Admiralty paper called Britain's likeliest peril: 'the interruption of our trade and destruction of merchant shipping.' Two-thirds of England's food was imported. The British merchant vessels which fetched it still accounted for over half the world's seaborne trade. Enemy sea raiders, unless held at bay, could sink every one of them. Afterwards Churchill wrote of the Royal Navy that its ships 'were all we had. On them, as we conceived, floated the might, majesty, dominion and power of the British Empire. All our long history built up century after century, all the means of livelihood and safety of our faithful, industrious, active population depended on them. Open the sea-cocks and let them sink beneath the surface . . . and in a few minutes – half an hour at the most – the whole outlook of the world would be changed. The British Empire would dissolve like a dream; each isolated community struggling by itself; the central power of union broken; mighty provinces, whole Empires in themselves, drifting hopelessly out of control, and falling a prey to others; and Europe after one sudden convulsion passing into the iron grip of the Teuton and of all that the Teutonic system meant.'[150]

He had no doubts about the identity of England's enemy. His mission, he said at the outset, was to put the fleet into 'a state of instant and constant readiness for war in case we are attacked by Germany.' Looking back, he wondered how he could ever have been gulled by Berlin's protestations of peaceful intent. In 1900, when he had been first elected to Parliament, the kaiser already presided over the most powerful army in Europe. That year *Seine Majestät* had proclaimed: 'In order to protect German trade and commerce under existing conditions, only one thing will suffice, namely, Germany must possess a battle fleet of such strength that even for the most powerful naval adversary a war would involve such risks as to make that Power's own supremacy doubtful.' Nautically, only one nation could be this 'most powerful adversary.' Since 1889 Britain had been committed to what was called the 'two-power naval standard,' meaning that England's navy must be as great as any two other navies combined. Its supremacy posed no threat to the Second Reich. England had nothing to gain on the Continent. But sea power was its lifeline, and throughout the Edwardian years the kaiser's shipbuilding programme had put it at increasing hazard. In a note to Grey on January 31, 1912, four months after taking over as first lord, Churchill wrote that while 'at present . . . several of the German Dreadnts are vy often the wrong side of the Kiel Canal wh they can't pass & therefore must make a long detour,'that consolation was only temporary: 'The deepening of the Canal by 1915 will extinguish this safety signal.' Then he submitted a formal memorandum to the Committee of Imperial Defence: 'The whole character of the German fleet shows that it was designed for aggressive and offensive action of the largest possible character in the North Sea or the North Atlantic . . . The structure of the German battleships shows clearly that they are intended for attack and for fleet action. They are not a cruiser fleet designed to protect colonies and commerce all over the world. They have been preparing for years, and continue to prepare . . . for a great trial of strength.'[151]

To end this insanity, Haldane visited Berlin early in 1912. He seemed the right man to send; a barrister with a passion for German philosophy, he was known at the War Office as 'Schopenhauer among the generals.' But the first lord was better informed about the Reich's new naval programme, due to be introduced in May. The kaiser, in the naive assumption that their friendship transcended geopolitics, had sent him a copy via Sir Ernest Cassel. On February 7, with Haldane still on the Wilhelmstrasse, the Churchills were in Victoria Station, waiting for a train, when Winston picked up the late edition of an evening newspaper and read the German emperor's speech opening the Reichstag. One sentence struck him: 'It is my constant duty and care to maintain and strengthen on land and water the power of defence of the German people, which has no lack of young men fit to bear arms.' Two days later, after comparing this with the kaiser's May plan, Churchill spoke out in Glasgow. 'This island,' he said, 'has never been, and never will be, lacking in trained and hardy mariners bred from their boyhood up in the service of the sea . . . We will face the future as our ancestors would have faced it, without disquiet, without arrogance, but in stolid and inflexible determination.' He could not understand the kaiser's motives: 'The British Navy is to us a necessity and, from some points of view, the German Navy is to them more in the nature of a luxury.'[152]

Had he understood their beastly language, he would have used another word. The German press translated it as *Luxus*, which has other implications; it denotes extravagance, or sumptuousness. In the Reich, as Churchill later wrote, it became 'an expression passed angrily from lip to lip.' In London the Tories were critical; even the *Daily News*, which had been one of his most ardent supporters, commented: 'It is difficult to reconcile Lord Haldane's mission with Mr Churchill's speech at Glasgow . . . Lord Haldane is on a mission to cultivate good feeling between the Governments and peoples of England and Germany . . . Mr Churchill will pass and be forgotten. What we trust will remain and work is Lord Haldane's mission and determination to come to an understanding with Germany which doubtless it represents.' The kaiser, told of Winston's statement, realized that he had miscalculated. Feeling betrayed by a former guest and protégé, he demanded an apology. None was forthcoming. Asquith said that although his first lord's choice of language had perhaps been unfortunate, he had nevertheless made 'a plain statement of an obvious truth.' And Haldane, upon his return from Berlin, told the cabinet that, 'so far from being a hindrance' in his negotiations, 'the Glasgow speech had been the greatest possible help.'[153]

Regrettably, he added bleakly, it had not been enough to crown his effort with success. He had talked to the emperor, to Chancellor Theobold von Bethmann-Hollweg, and to Grossadmiral Alfred von Tirpitz. Their price for accepting Britannia's rule of the waves had been exorbitant – an English pledge of neutrality in the event of war between Germany and France. Haldane had concluded that once 'the war party got into the saddle' in Berlin, they would push 'not merely for the overthrow of France or Russia but for the domination of the world.' None of them seemed to realize that the English were as sensitive on the naval issue as the French on Alsace-Lorraine. They vigorously supported the German Navy League, whose hundred thousand members, corps of paid lecturers (paid by Krupp, shipbuilders to *Seine Majestät*), and magazine *Die Flotte* were flooding the Reich with chauvinistic literature and posters with such slogans as 'England the Foe!' 'Perfidious Albion!' 'The Coming War!' 'The British Peril!' 'England's Plan to Fall on Us in 1911!' Apparently Bernard Shaw was right; the Germans were a people with contempt for common sense.[154]

Or perhaps their problem was their critical adoration of authority. Haldane was convinced that the root of it was the kaiser, *der hohe Herr*. It was he who had told them: 'Germany's future is on the water.' Apparently someone had given him a book by an American, Alfred Thayer Mahan's *Influence of Sea Power upon History*. Reading it, he had become convinced that his empire could never be truly great until it had mastered the seas. In addition, *der hohe Herr* had become paranoid. That was the explanation for his mischief-making and sabre rattling. He believed his enemies were encircling the Reich and saw a powerful German fleet as a cleaver to cut through that investment. His navy, he predicted, 'will bring the English to their senses through sheer fright,' after which they would 'submit to the inevitable, and we shall become the best friends in the world.'[155]

Winston sat stone-faced through Haldane's report and, at the end, gloomily commented that the secretary for war had confirmed his worst suspicions. The German shipbuilding programme scheduled to start in May, he pointed out to the cabinet, represented an 'extraordinary increase in the striking force, in ships of all classes,' providing Tirpitz with five fresh battle squadrons, each attended by flotillas of destroyers and submarines, each 'extremely formidable.'[156]

* * *

357

Meeting this challenge – keeping England afloat – was Churchill's responsibility, but first he had to make peace within the Admiralty, a task he compared to 'burrowing about in an illimitable rabbit-warren.' The relationship between civilian administrators and naval officers could hardly have been worse. The first called the second 'boneheads'; the second referred to the first as 'frocks' and shared the conviction of Douglas Haig, now a lieutenant general, that the word *politician* was 'synonymous with crooked dealing and wrong values.' Admiral Sir Arthur Wilson, the first sea lord, had been McKenna's undoing. Wilson was, among other things, the chief obstacle to the creation of a naval war staff. He thought it would undermine his authority. The admiral was nearly twice Churchill's age, but Winston was unintimidated. Believing that Wilson dwelt 'too much in the past' and was 'not sufficiently receptive of new ideas,' the new first lord decided to fire the old first sea lord. He didn't know whom to appoint in his place, so he sent for Lord Fisher.[157]

Admiral Sir John Arbuthnot Fisher – 'Jacky' Fisher to England's adoring masses – had retired to Lake Lucerne with a peerage four years earlier. He was a legend, 'the greatest sailor since Nelson,' and he was immensely old. In 1854, when he had joined the navy as a midshipman, British men-of-war still carried sails. He had been a captain, commanding a battleship, when Winston was born. His great period had been between 1904 and 1910, when, as first sea lord, he had scrapped ships which he said could 'neither fight nor run,' conceived the dreadnoughts, introduced submarines and 13.5-inch guns, revised the naval educational system, and built 161 warships, including 22 battleships of over 16,000 tons. Quick-tempered, emotional, with burning black eyes and a curiously Mongoloid face, he liked to portray himself as 'ruthless, relentless, and remorseless.' The description was accurate. Officers who had questioned his policies had been ruined professionally; he had branded them traitors and declared that 'their wives should be widows, their children fatherless, and their homes a dunghill.' Nevertheless, he was indisputably a genius. If Germany and England went to war, the navy Tirpitz would fight would be Fisher's creation.[158]

Churchill had met him in 1907, when both were visiting Biarritz. They had been corresponding that April, and Fisher's first letter, inspired by a sugar strike in the British West Indies, provides a fair sample of his style: 'St Lucia quite splendid! Dog eat dog! You are using niggers to fight niggers! For God's sake don't send British Bluejackets inland amongst sugar canes on this job or we shall have to set up a War Office inside the Admiralty & goodness knows *one* War Office is enough! I enclose a very secret paper. *Don't let anyone see it.* The best thing ever written in the English language bar the Bible & Robertson's Sermons & letters from a Competition Wallah. Kindly return the print with your improvements in the margin – study it closely.'[159] The enclosure has not survived. It could have been anything. The admiral was given to superlatives and overstatements; his letters were peppered with exclamation marks and words underscored two or three times. A prudent minister would have shunned him, but Winston was never that; he believed that his own vision, married to Fisher's experience, would make a brilliant union.

In the beginning he was right. The admiral came hopping home in response to Churchill's summons, and they talked for three days. Winston found him 'a veritable volcano of knowledge and inspiration; and as soon as he learnt what my main purpose was, he passed into a state of vehement eruption . . . Once he began, he could hardly stop. I plied him with questions, and he poured out ideas.' Fisher, for his part, was so excited that he ran a fever. His chief recommendations were to arm Britain's battleships with fifteen-inch guns, increase their speed, convert the entire navy from coal to oil, and shake up the senior officers: 'The argument for a War Staff is that you *may* have a d—d fool as First Sea Lord, and so you put him in commission, as it were.' Churchill adopted all these proposals, though his attempt to put the war staff under himself failed when Haldane persuaded the cabinet that a sailor, not a politician, should head it. The fuel conversion was a difficult step. Having made it, he took another, inducing the House to invest £2,000,000, later increased to £5,000,000, in the Anglo-Persian Oil Company, thus assuring adequate reserves in the event of war.[160]

Handling the admirals was easier, but more delicate. The war staff was established in January 1912 and Wilson was relieved of his post. Winston had considered bringing Fisher back as first sea lord, then rejected the idea because another retired admiral, Lord Charles Beresford, the old salt's sworn enemy, had become powerful in Parliament. At Fisher's suggestion he settled on Admiral Sir Francis Bridgeman. As second sea lord – Bridgeman's prospective successor – he chose Admiral Prince Louis of Battenberg, a relative of the royal family. It was not a foresighted move. Prince Louis was a naturalized British subject and proud of it; when one of Tirpitz's officers had reproached him at Kiel for serving under the Union Jack, he had stiffened and replied: 'Sir, when I joined the Royal Navy in 1868, the German Empire did not exist.' Still, he spoke with a heavy German accent, and the time was coming when that would be enough to discredit him. Winston appointed one friend, David Beatty of his Sudan days, to be rear admiral and his personal naval secretary. His key decision was naming Admiral Sir John Jellicoe as second in command of the Home Fleet and thus heir to England's most crucial seagoing command. Jellicoe was Fisher's candidate for Nelsonhood. The old admiral wrote to Churchill: 'He has all the Nelsonic attributes. He writes me of new designs. His *one, one, one* cry is SPEED! *Do lay that to heart!* Do remember the receipt for jugged hare in Mrs Glasse's Cookery Book! *First catch your hare!*' After leaving London he wrote to a friend: 'I'll tell you . . . the whole secret of the changes! *To get Jellicoe Commander-in-Chief of the Home Fleet prior to October 21, 1914* – which is the date of the Battle of Armageddon.' That was vintage Fisher. One moment he sounded demented and the next he came uncannily close to guessing the date of the approaching war.[161]

Back in Lucerne, he wrote of Churchill: 'So far every step he contemplates is good, *and he is brave, which is everything. Napoleonic in audacity, Cromwellian in thoroughness.*' He peppered Winston with letters signed, typically, 'Yours till Hell freezes,' 'Yours to a cinder,' and 'Till charcoal sprouts.' But he was quick to turn. Three appointments offended him, and his response was savage. 'I fear,' he wrote to Winston, 'this must be my last communication with you in any matter at all. I am sorry for it, but I consider you have betrayed the Navy.' The officers were close to the King; on no evidence whatever he blamed Clementine, saying she feared 'the social ostracism of the Court,' and called the first lord, no longer his to a cinder, 'a Royal pimp.' It is a sign of Churchill's faith in Fisher that he ignored this. In reply, he sent him a stream of flattering billets-doux and telegrams. The old man boasted to his son, 'I sent him an awful letter, and he really has replied very nicely that no matter what I say to him, he is going to stick to me and support all my schemes and always maintain that I am a genius and the greatest naval administrator, etc etc . . . However, there is no getting over the fact that he truckled to Court influence . . . and I have rubbed this into WC and he don't like it!' Doubtless he loathed it, yet he persisted in his suit. By the spring he had decided that if Fisher wouldn't come to him, he would go to Fisher. He, Asquith, and their families were planning a May cruise on the *Enchantress;* he asked Fisher to meet the yacht in Naples, where they could have 'a good talk.'[162]

The voyage was one of Churchill's working vacations. He inspected the Gibraltar defences, conferred with his admiral on Malta, and then docked at Naples. When his quarry came aboard, Violet Asquith thought Fisher's eyes, 'as always, were like smouldering charcoals.' Then 'Lord F. and W. were locked together in naval conclave . . . I'm sure they can't resist each other for long at close range.' Lord F. did. He resisted the prime minister, too. His 'advice wasn't followed,' he said, so why should he give it? Yet he stayed. Violet's next day's diary entry opened: 'Danced on deck with Lord Fisher for a very long time before breakfast . . . I reel giddily in his arms and lurch against his heart of oak.' The turning point came on Sunday. Churchill had stage-managed the church service. The chaplain riveted his eyes on the seventy-one-year-old admiral and said solemnly: 'No man still possessing all his powers and full of vitality has any right to say "I am now going to rest, as I have had a hard life," for he owes a duty to his country and fellow men.' Fisher wrote to his wife, 'It was an arrow shot at a venture [sic] like the one that killed Ahab.' The Fisher-Churchill axis was reestablished. In letters to the Admiralty, Fisher continued to protest, 'I have had my hour,' but he was slowly being drawn back from retirement, and soon the first lord would conclude that despite all arguments against it, in a crisis he would want the eccentric old prodigy at his right hand.[163]

Through dynamic energy and a genius that surpassed Fisher's, Churchill mastered the Admiralty and was ready when Armageddon, as the admiral had foreseen, arrived. By then, Winston wrote, he knew 'what everything looked like and where everything was, and how one thing fitted into another. I could put my hand on anything that was wanted and knew the current state of our naval affairs.' He had been appalled to find that no plan existed for transporting a British expeditionary force to France. He drew one up. England's Grand Fleet had no sequestered wartime anchorage. He chose Scapa Flow, a remote shelter among the Orkney Islands at the northernmost tip of the British Isles, where Britain's dreadnoughts could keep an eye on Heligoland Bight, through which Tirpitz's *Flotte* must pass in any sortie. In Parliament he won approval of his appropriation bills by vivid, lucid descriptions of abstruse technical matters. Describing the impact of a shell upon a warship, he told the House: 'If you want to make a true picture in your mind of a battle between two great modern iron-clad ships, you must not think of it as if it were two men in armour striking at each other with heavy swords. It is more like a battle between two egg-shells striking each other with hammers . . . The importance of hitting first, and hitting hardest and keeping on hitting . . . really needs no clearer proof.'[164]

His inspections of ships continued to be popular with bluejackets. After his first year in office the monthly magazine *Fleet*, which echoed forecastle views, commented: 'No First Lord in the history of the Navy has shown himself more practically sympathetic with the conditions of the Lower Deck than Winston Churchill.' The brass took another view. Churchill's predecessors had given the sea lords free rein, but he regarded them as subordinates and issued them blunt instructions. When Bridgeman rebelled, he was swiftly retired, ostensibly on grounds of poor health, with Prince Louis replacing him. Tories protested in the House, and career officers were scandalized. Rear Admiral Dudley de Chair, who succeeded Beatty as navy secretary, was shocked by the first lord's cursory judgement of men, often based on a few minutes of conversation. De Chair found him 'impulsive, headstrong and even at times obstinate.' His tours of the fleet were also controversial. He encouraged junior officers and ratings to criticize their commanding officers. When a commander dared complain of this, Churchill proposed to relieve him and was dissuaded only when the second, third, and fourth sea lords threatened to resign in protest. At the end of a strategy conference, one of the admirals accused the first lord of impugning the traditions of the Royal Navy. 'And what are they?' asked Winston. 'I shall tell you in three words. Rum, sodomy, and the lash. Good morning, gentlemen.'[165]

No profession is more wedded to the folklore of the past than the armed services. Since the last major conflict on the Continent, technology had clanked out an astonishing array of contraptions suitable for war, and the generals and admirals of Europe, regardless of national allegiance, viewed them all with deep distrust. They belonged to that generation which called electricity 'the electric,' and regarded it as newfangled. Being new was enough to make a device suspect. Haig thought the machine gun 'a much over-rated weapon,' and believed 'two per battalion should be sufficient.' Joffre of France refused to use a telephone, pretending that he did not 'understand the mechanism.' The Stokes mortar was twice rejected at the

British War Office and finally introduced by Lloyd George, who begged the money for it from an Indian maharaja and was as a consequence considered 'ungentlemanly' by British officers. Kitchener dismissed the tank as a 'toy.' It was, in fact, a pet project of Churchill's. Winston wasn't always right, however; Jellicoe was impressed by a flight in a zeppelin, and at his urging Churchill approved pilot models. Then he lost interest. As he said later, 'I rated the Zeppelin much lower as a weapon of war than almost anyone else. I believed that this enormous bladder of combustible and explosive gas would prove easily destructible.' As a result, in 1914 the navy had no reconnaissance airships. He also failed to provide adequate submarine defences in Scapa and the Firth of Forth, but that was because he became entangled in red tape; unlike H.G. Wells, who predicted that the 'blind fumblings' of U-boats would limit them to the torpedoing of hulks in harbours, he was fully aware of their minatory potential.[166]

The new weapon which fascinated him most was the aeroplane. In 1910 General Ferdinand Foch had spoken for most professional officers when he ridiculed the idea of an air force in wartime. *'Tout ça, c'est du sport,'* he said contemptuously; as far as the French army was concerned, *'l'avion c'est zéro!'* In the British navy it was otherwise. As early as February 25, 1909, when he was still at the Board of Trade, Churchill had told the cabinet that aviation would be 'most important' in the future and suggested that 'we should place ourselves in communication with Mr [Orville] Wright and avail ourselves of his knowledge.' The following year he presented a *Daily Mail* cheque for £10,000 to two airmen who had taken off from the Dominion of Newfoundland and landed on a field in, as he put it, 'the future equally happy and prosperous Dominion of Ireland' – poor political prophecy, but no other national figure had come to greet them. Arriving at the Admiralty, he had sought out the small band of adventurous officers who were the pioneers of naval aviation. In 1912 he founded the Royal Naval Air Service – a precursor of the Royal Flying Corps and, later, the Royal Air Force – to provide 'aerial protection to our naval harbours, oil tanks and vulnerable points, and also for a general strengthening of our exiguous and inadequate aviation.' A larval helicopter was built; he inspected it. In tests it proved unstable, and prone to crash, after it had risen about three hundred feet. Winston proposed a hollow propeller containing a parachute. The suggestion was completely impractical, but his encouragement of experimentation elsewhere led to breakthroughs. Because of his efforts, England became the first country to equip a plane with a machine gun, and the first to launch an airborne torpedo. He coined the words *seaplane,* and *flight* to designate a given number of aircraft, usually four.[167]

To Clementine's alarm, he decided to fly himself. He regarded his first ride, in 1912, as a matter of duty. Discovering that he enjoyed it, he made repeated ascents. The craft were primitive, the techniques slapdash. On one bumpy trip, in the teeth of a gale, nearly three hours were required to cover the sixteen miles from Gravesend to Grain, and 'after landing Churchill safely,' the pilot reported, 'my seaplane "took off" again, landing trolley and all over the sea wall, as it was being brought up the slipway, and was more or less wrecked.' The hazards whetted Winston's appetite. In October 1913, at the Eastchurch naval flying centre, he went up in three different craft. That evening he wrote Clementine: 'Darling, We have had a vy jolly day in the air . . . it has been as good as one of those old days in the S. African War, & I have lived entirely in the moment, with no care for all those tiresome party politics & searching newspapers, and awkward by-elections . . . For good luck before I started I put your locket on. It has been lying in my desk since it got bent – & as usual it worked like a charm.' She wired her dismay from the *Enchantress* and then followed up with a note: 'I hope my telegram will not have vexed you, but please be kind & don't fly any more just now.'[168]

It was a postage stamp wasted. Churchill with the bit in his teeth was incorrigible. Deeply as he loved his wife, at that moment he loved the excitement of flying more. To the consternation of the barnstormers who had been taking him up, he declared that he wanted to be a pilot himself. He was too old, they protested; thirty-two was regarded as the top age for a novice, and he was thirty-eight. He invoked his powers as first lord, ordered them to shut up, and began taking lessons in managing controls at Upavon. One of his instructors, Ivon Courtney, later recalled: 'Before our first flight together he said to me: "We are in the Stephenson age of flying. Now our machines are frail. One day they will be robust, and of value to our country." He had already done a lot of flying. "I want some more instruction," he said.' Aircraft were not equipped with headphones then; the two men sat in separate cockpits, Churchill in the rear, and shouted at each other, hoping their voices would carry above the wind. The instruments were encased in a box, but most airmen scorned them, preferring to rely on what they called 'ear.' Winston, however, was fascinated by the dials and needles. He would crouch down, peering at them, 'and,' Courtney wrote, 'he was right to do so. He saw that one day the box of instruments would be more important than the pilot's ear.'[169]

They went up as often as ten times a day. Every officer on the instruction staff worried about their eminent student. 'We were all scared stiff,' said Courtney, 'of having a smashed First Lord on our hands.' Eugene Garrard, later air commodore, said: 'WSC has had as much as twenty-five hours in the air, but no one will risk letting him solo; if anything happened to WSC the career of the man who had allowed him a solo flight would be finished.' Sir Philip Joubert de la Ferté, later air chief marshal, remembered Winston as 'a very fair pilot once he was in the air, but more than uncertain in his take-off and landing. His instructors usually took over the controls to make the final approach and touch down.' Another future RAF marshal, Hugh Trenchard, gave him lower marks. After watching him 'wallowing about the sky,' as he put it, he decided Winston was 'altogether too impatient for a good pupil.'[170]

But Churchill persevered. He spent the afternoon of Saturday, November 29, 1913, in the air with Captain Gilbert Wildman-Lushington of the Royal Marines. After they had parted, the captain wrote to his fiancée: 'I started

Winston off on his instruction about 12.15 & he got so bitten with it, I could hardly get him out of the machine, in fact except for about ¾ hour for lunch we were in the machine till about 3.30. He showed great promise, & is coming down again for further instruction & practice.' Winston himself was dissatisfied. Once he had set his mind on an objective, anything short of total conquest was unacceptable. Back in his Admiralty office that evening he wrote to Lushington: 'I wish you would clear up the question of the steering control and let me know what was the real difficulty I had in making the rudder act. Probably the explanation is that I was pushing against myself . . . Could you not go up with another flying officer and, sitting yourself in the back seat, see whether there is great stiffness and difficulty in steering, or whether it was all my clumsiness.' Then he dropped Clementine a line: 'I have been very naughty today about flying . . . With twenty machines in the air at once and thousands of flights made without mishap, it is not possible to look upon it as a vy serious risk. Do not be vexed with me.'[171]

She wasn't vexed; she was frantic. By the time this letter reached her, Lushington was dead; coming in to land at Eastchurch on Sunday, he sideslipped and crashed. F.E. wrote Winston: 'Why do you do such a foolish thing as fly repeatedly? Surely it is unfair to your family, your career & your friends.' It was; it was thoughtless, the act of a supreme egotist. H.G. Wells wrote: 'There are times when the evil spirit comes upon him and I think of him as a very intractable, a very mischievous, dangerous little boy, a knee-worthy little boy. Only thinking of him in that way can I go on liking him.' The fact is that His Majesty's first lord of the Admiralty deserved a good spanking. Despite his instructor's death and his wife's appeals, he refused to stay on the ground. At Easter Clementine wrote to him from Spain, where she and Mrs Keppel were Cassel's guests: 'I have been seized by a dreadful anxiety that you are making use of my absence to fly even more often than you do when I am there – I beg of you not to do it at all, at any rate till I can be there.' It was a shrewd guess. That very day he had not only flown; he had been shaken up when engine failure forced his new instructor to make an emergency landing. Undaunted, he took off again two days later. Clementine and the children were now staying with her mother in Dieppe, and on May 29, 1914, he wrote to her there: 'I have been at the Central Flying School for a couple of days – flying a little in good & careful hands & under perfect conditions. So I did not write you from there as I knew you would be vexed.'[172]

She replied: 'I felt what you were doing before I read about it, but I felt too weak & tired to struggle against it. It is like beating one's head against a stone wall . . . Perhaps if I saw you, I could love and pet you, but you have been so naughty that I can't do it on paper. I must be "brought round" first.' She signed the letter with the sketch of a cat, its ears down. She did see him the following week; he crossed on the *Enchantress* to spend a day with her and the children. They discussed his flying, and he assured her that the airfield he was using, at Sheerness in Kent, had every modern facility. Yet in her next letter the tension was still there: 'I cannot help knowing that you are going to fly as you go to Sheerness & it fills me with anxiety. I know nothing will stop you from doing it so I will not weary you with tedious entreaties, but don't forget that I am thinking about it all the time & so, do it as little & as moderately as you can & only with the *very best* Pilot. I feel very "ears down" about it.' Her fear haunted her; she was five months pregnant with their third child – it would be another daughter, Sarah – and thought, not unreasonably, that she was entitled to more consideration from her husband. In her next letter she described a nightmare. She had dreamed she had had her baby, but the doctor and nurse hid it. Finding the infant in a darkened room, she feverishly counted its fingers and toes only to find that it was a gaping idiot. 'And then the worst thing of all happened – I wanted the Doctor to kill it – but he was shocked & took it away & I was mad too.' The evening before, she had received a cable from Winston, telling her he was safely home. 'Every time I see a telegram now,' she wrote, 'I think it is to announce that you have been killed flying. I had a fright but went to sleep relieved; but this morning after the nightmare I looked at it again for consolation & found to my horror it was from Sheerness & not from Dover where I thought you were going first – so you are probably at it again at this very moment. Goodbye my Dear but Cruel One, Your loving Clemmie.'[173]

Winston instantly replied: 'My darling one, I will not fly any more until at any rate you have recovered from your kitten.' He had been callous, but he recognized a cry of despair when he heard it. Mulling it over, he realized that her anxiety had been fully justified. Prewar aviation was, in fact, a risky business, even for skilful airmen; only a few days earlier, Gustav Hamel, a celebrated monoplane aviator and a friend of both the Churchills, had disappeared over the Channel. Abandoning flight was 'a wrench,' Winston wrote to Clementine, 'because I was on the verge of taking my pilot's certificate; & I am confident of my ability to achieve it vy respectably. I shd greatly have liked to reach this point wh wd have made a suitable moment for breaking off. But must admit that the numerous fatalities of this year wd justify you in complaining if I continued to share the risks – as I am proud to do – of these good fellows. So I give it up decidedly for many months & perhaps for ever. This is a gift – so stupidly am I made – wh costs me more than anything wh cd be bought with money. So I am vy glad to lay it at your feet, because I know it will rejoice & relieve your heart. Anyhow I can feel I know a good deal about this fascinating new art. I can manage a machine with ease in the air, even with high winds, & only a little more practice in landings wd have enabled me to go up with reasonable safety alone. I have been up nearly 140 times, with many pilots, & all kinds of machines, so I know the difficulties the dangers & the joys of the air – well enough to appreciate them, & to understand all the questions of policy wh will arise in the near future . . . You will give me some kisses and forgive me for past distresses – I am sure. Though I had no need & perhaps no right to do it – it was an important part of my life during the last 7 months, & I am sure my nerve, my spirits & my virtue were all improved by it. But at your expense my poor pussy cat! I am so sorry.'[174]

It is astonishing to reflect that Churchill was flying over Kent before the young RAF pilots who won the Battle of Britain, dogfighting in those same skies, were even born. By then, of course, no one questioned the absolute necessity of a strong air arm. In Winston's cockpit days it was regarded as a frill, however, and he was hard put to justify it in an Admiralty budget already swollen by the need to stay ahead of Germany. Alarmed by the expensive arms race, in April 1912 he had proposed a 'Naval Holiday,' during which both nations would suspend the laying of new keels. The kaiser rejected the idea; such an agreement, he said, could be reached only between allies. But Albert Ballin, director of the Hamburg-American Steamship Line, told Cassel that the 'frankness and honesty' of Churchill's offer had 'flustered . . . the leading parties in Germany, and has caused a torrent of [comment] in the Press.' Winston wrote Cassel a conciliatory letter, meant for *der hohe Herr*'s eyes. It accomplished nothing. Ballin thought Churchill should visit Berlin; he believed he would be well received, and could 'have some useful conversation with Admiral Tirpitz.' Winston declined on the ground that 'all that could be said on our part wd be that till Germany dropped the naval challenge her policy wd be continually viewed here with deepening suspicion and apprehension; but that any slackening on her part wd produce an immediate *détente*, with much good will from England. Failing that I see little prospect but politeness and preparation.' On October 24, 1913, he again suggested a shipbuilding suspension, forwarding the recommendation to *der hohe Herr* through Ballin and advising the cabinet: 'The simultaneous building by so many powers great and small of capital ships, their general naval expansion, are causes of deep anxiety to us . . . Naval strength to other powers is a mere panache. But as the frog said to the boy in the fable "It is sport to you: it is death to us." ' This time his proposal wasn't even acknowledged.[175]

All overtures to the kaiser having failed, he and Jack Seely, who had succeeded Haldane as war minister, pushed for higher military appropriations. At the end of the year Churchill submitted his naval estimates for 1914. They were shocking: £50,694,800 – the largest in British history, the largest in the world. The chancellor of the Exchequer was stunned. Winston and Lloyd George were still friends, but they were no longer partners in political counterpoint. The first lord had become militant, even belligerent; the chancellor, whose own position was softening again, complained that Churchill was 'getting more and more absorbed in boilers.' The cabinet was divided. Asquith accepted the estimates, but Margot wrote Lloyd George: 'Don't let Winston have too much money – it will hurt our party in every way – Labour and even Liberals. If one can't be a little economical when all foreign countries are peaceful I don't know *when* we can.'[176]

The split was deep, and involved more than money. Asquith, Churchill, Seely, and Grey believed that the integrity of France was vital to England's national interest; that, as Grey put it, 'if Germany dominated the Continent it would be disagreeable to us as well as to others, for we should be isolated.' The Tories agreed, but among Liberals, even within the cabinet, it was a minority view. Their leader there, Lord Morley, believed he could count on 'eight or nine likely to agree with us' in opposing the policies being advanced by Grey with 'strenuous simplicity' and by Churchill with 'daemonic energy.' Morley described himself as 'a pacifist at heart.' He had been Gladstone's friend and biographer, and he and those who agreed with him believed they were acting on Gladstonian principles. The fights they loved were those fought for Free Trade, social reforms, Irish Home Rule, and the defeat of the arrogant dukes. They were unmoved by France. Only an appeal for help from a little country like Belgium could reach their hearts, and even that was uncertain.[177]

Thus Lloyd George had friends in power when, on New Year's Day, 1914, he told a *Daily Chronicle* reporter that Churchill's plan for 'exorbitant expenditure on armaments' violated Lord Randolph's memory. Replying, Winston rebuked him; he said he never granted newspaper interviews 'on important subjects of this character while they are under the consideration of the Cabinet.' One of the two ministers, it seemed, would have to resign. While refusing to be quoted, Churchill became the source of sensational rumours. He was pondering a return to the Conservative party; he had become doubtful about Home Rule; if he left the Admiralty, the four sea lords would quit in protest. As tempers rose, the two principals sat down for five hours of what Winston called 'polite but deadly' negotiation. The prime minister joined them, and his strong support of the estimates decided the issue. To save Lloyd George's face, 2 per cent was cut from the naval budget, further economies were promised for the following year, and expensive manoeuvres planned for the following summer were cancelled, to be replaced by a trial mobilization of the fleet. George avoided mortification by pretending that he had changed his mind. He invited Churchill to breakfast at No. 11 Downing Street, the traditional home of the chancellors. He said his wife had told him that he ought to let 'that nice Mr Churchill' have his dreadnoughts, arguing that it would be better to have too many than too few. 'So,' he said, 'I have decided to let you build them. Let's go in to breakfast.' Winston wrote to his mother: 'I think the naval estimates are now past the danger point & if so the situation will be satisfactory. But it has been a long and wearing business wh has caused me at times vy gt perplexity.'[178]

In March he presented his naval estimates to the House. The Liberals were tepid, the Conservatives enthusiastic. The *Daily Telegraph* hailed his address as 'the most weighty and eloquent speech to which the House of Commons have listened [from a first lord of the Admiralty] during the present generation.'[179] This was praise Churchill didn't need. Indeed, though Tories publicly approved of his naval expansion, behind his back they said it was inspired by a personal pursuit of glory. Winston's defection from their ranks, his humiliation of Joe Chamberlain, and his corrosive invective in political campaigns and parliamentary struggles could be neither forgotten nor forgiven. His political advancement – even survival – depended on his strength with his adopted party, where, more and more, MPs on the back benches were saying: 'He's not really a Liberal.' He had to prove that he was. In that four-year interval between the end of the Edwardian era and the outbreak of the Kaiser's War there were many disputes between the Asquith government and the Opposition, but Churchill needed a dramatic issue. One appeared. It seemed ideal: explosive, emotional, and above all a matter of principle. And it was unavoidable. The eighty-four Irish Nationalist MPs had presented their bill for services rendered in unmanning the House of Lords, and payment was now due.

By later Irish standards they were mild – 'Gentlemen first, Irishmen second' had been their muted war cry – and as gentlemen they had been patient. Their cause had been hopeless in the fourteen years between Parnell's death in Kitty O'Shea's arms and the fall of the Balfour government, but the Liberals had been in power since 1906 and had done nothing to redeem Gladstone's promise. Winston had prodded the cabinet; on February 13, 1910, Blunt had noted in his diary that Churchill had said it was 'the ambition of my life to bring in a Home Rule Bill.' But neither Asquith nor Lloyd George found the issue appealing, and even Winston, who had been offered the post of chief secretary for Ireland, had turned down what was known as the 'hoodoo job of the Cabinet.' Ireland had always been a political minefield, and it had been doubly treacherous since Lord Randolph had played what he called his 'ace of trumps, the Orange card.'[180]

Ulster – the nine counties around Belfast, in northern Ireland – was largely populated by Protestants, descendants of Scots who had settled there before the *Mayflower* sighted Plymouth. Under Home Rule, the entire island would be ruled by a parliament in Dublin. Inevitably Catholics from southern Ireland would dominate it. Before they would accept that, Ulstermen swore, they would die fighting. 'Home Rule,' they said, meant 'Rome Rule.' The differences between the northern Unionists and the southern Nationalists had been, were, and always would be irreconcilable. The southerners found the status quo intolerable. For nearly eight centuries they had been governed like serfs by English viceroys entrenched in Dublin Castle. The finest estates in what is now Eire then belonged to an Anglo-Irish aristocracy, the Protestant Ascendancy. Gladstone had told these overlords again and again that the southern yearning for freedom was an indestructible passion, but they preferred to quote Queen Victoria: 'I think it very unwise to give up what we hold.' After the coronation of George V, however, the Irish Nationalists, under pressure from home, prepared to drop their genteel manners. They wanted their own parliament, and they wanted it immediately. 'The Irish question,' Churchill wrote afterwards, 'now cut jaggedly across the British political scene.' By this time, he had completely emerged from his father's shadow and was one of the most vigorous champions of a united Ireland, governed from Dublin. Because he was Randolph's son as well as the ablest parliamentarian in the cabinet, Asquith chose him as point man for the issue. In Dundee, on October 4, 1911, Winston declared: 'Next year we propose ι_ introduce the Home Rule Bill, and we propose to carry it forward with all our strength.' The crowd, knowing he had been born and bred a Unionist, was taken aback. Someone called: 'Ulster will fight, Ulster will be right!' Churchill snapped: 'That is a slogan from which every street bully with a brickbat and every crazy fanatic fumbling with a pistol may draw inspiration.'[181]

Early the following year he announced that he had accepted an invitation from the Ulster Liberal Association to speak in Belfast's Ulster Hall, where Lord Randolph had spoken, on February 12. The Irish Unionist party erupted. 'What a man to select!' thundered Sir Edward Carson, former solicitor general and a leader of the Ulster Unionists in the House. 'The most provocative speaker in the whole party, going under the most provocative circumstances to a place where the words of his own father are still ringing in the ear!' Death threats arrived at Admiralty House by post and telephone. One Unionist warned him in an open letter: 'The heather is on fire and Belfast today is the rallying ground of the clans. The fiery cross has sped through hill and glen, and with the undying spirit of their forbears the Ulstermen are answering to the message . . . It would be well if Mr Churchill would read the writing on the wall, for there is great fear that harm may happen to him.' Clementine decided to accompany her husband, hoping that would discourage violence. At the last minute Winston's cousin Freddie Guest joined the party, carrying a revolver in his pocket.[182]

Crossing the Irish Sea, the Churchills were kept awake all night by women who stood outside their cabin window chanting: 'Votes for women! Votes for women!' Policemen patrolled, the eighteen-mile railway line from Larne, where they docked, to Belfast. Arriving at Belfast Station, Churchill was told that four infantry battalions – thirty-five hundred troops – had been called up to line his route. Even so, the risks were grave; glass had been removed from the windows of their car because demonstrators were carrying stones. The drive to the Grand Central Hotel was a tribulation in itself. Winston stared out at a burning effigy of himself. At one point, the *Guardian* reported, the mob lifted the car's back wheels eighteen inches off the ground. The *Times* correspondent wrote that 'men thrust their heads in and uttered fearful menaces and imprecations. It seemed to me that Mr Churchill was taking a greater risk than he ever expected . . . Yet he never flinched and took hostility visualised as well as vocalised calmly and no harm befell him.' This observer noted that he 'smilingly raised his hat whenever the crowd groaned.' Clementine, badly frightened herself, thought that 'the opposition and threats seemed to "ginger him up." '[183]

Nevertheless, it was clear that he had misjudged Ulster's mood. A hostile throng of ten thousand awaited them at the hotel. Businessmen in the lobby angrily shook their fists. The windows of their suite were heavily draped; when Winston tried to peek out, a roar of boos and oaths swelled up from below. Meeting in Ulster Hall was out of the question. The local Unionist Council, which had resolved to prevent his appearance 'in the centre of the loyal city of Belfast,' had occupied it with armed 'Hooligan Corner Boys,' as they were called. Evicting them would cost the lives of at least six policemen. A dozen plots were afoot to murder Churchill if he even approached the hall. The rally was therefore moved to Celtic Park in the Falls neighbourhood, a Catholic stronghold, where a heavy rain began falling at 2:00 P.M. as Winston, standing beneath a leaking canvas marquee, rose to address a drenched crowd of five thousand Irish Nationalists and a handful of Unionist hecklers. The Tories, he told them, were trying to regain office by using Ireland as a cat's-paw, but 'the flame of Irish nationality is inextinguishable.' Of his father he said: 'The reverence which I feel for his memory, and the care with which I have studied his public life, make me quite content to leave others to judge how far there is continuity or discontinuity between his work and any I have tried to do.' Then he ended audaciously, ringing a change on Lord Randolph's most famous words: 'If Ulster would fight for the honour of Ireland, for reconciliation of races and for forgiveness of ancient wrongs, for the consolidation of the Empire, then indeed Ulster will fight, and Ulster will be right.'[184]

The apologetic Liberals of Ulster presented Winston and Clementine with blackthorns, stout walking sticks – a pleasant gesture which was swiftly forgotten when, as they mounted the Larne gangplank for the journey home, dockers pelted them with rotten fish. It was a fitting farewell; in the eight centuries since Pope Adrian IV gave Ireland to Henry II, the relationship between England and Ireland had been marked by wave after wave of violence, and now new fury was rising. Churchill wasn't even safe in the House of Commons. In June, Ronald MacNeill, a prominent Unionist MP, picked up a copy of the House's standing orders from the ledge of the Speaker's chair and flung it at the first lord, cutting him in the forehead. Next day MacNeill apologized. Churchill assured him he hadn't minded at all, which was true; he was enjoying the battle, and if tempers on the other side grew frayed, he was the first to admit that his own remarks were incendiary. His treatment in Ulster, he said, was proof that Carson and Bonar Law, leader of the Tories in the House, had plotted war on the British army and had 'even suggested that this process in Ireland should be accompanied by the lynching of His Majesty's Ministers.' Captain James Craig, an Ulster MP, called him 'contemptible.' Winston replied: 'If I valued the honourable Gentleman's opinion I might get angry.' He enjoyed a studied insult, even when he was its victim, and chortled when he read that Lord Charles Beresford, during a Hyde Park rally, referred to him as a 'Lilliput Napoleon – a man with an unbalanced mind, an egomaniac whose one absorbing thought is personal vindictiveness towards Ulster.' He didn't even mind when feelings ran so high in the House that only a quick-thinking Labour MP, who started everyone singing 'Auld Lang Syne,' prevented fist-fights on the floor.[185]

He was, however, troubled by talk of Belfast's gutters running red with British blood. Abuse was tolerable only up to a certain point. Carson passed it when he called him 'Lord Randolph's renegade son, who wants to be handed down to posterity as the Belfast butcher who threatened to shoot down those who took his father's advice.' Though his language was less blistering, Law went even farther. He said: 'Ireland is two nations. The Ulster people will submit to no ascendancy, and I can imagine no lengths to which they might go in which they would not be supported by the overwhelming majority of the British people.' This was an open invitation to revolt, from the man who would be prime minister in a Conservative government. Such speeches were fanning the flame of discord in northern Ireland. Protestant volunteers were already forming insurgent regiments. Law warned the House that Ulster might explode at any moment; if blood were shed, he said, the cabinet would be answerable for it. Winston retorted that 'those who talk of revolution ought to be prepared for the guillotine.' In a letter to *The Times* he said: 'Mr Bonar Law and his lieutenant Sir Edward Carson have . . . incited the Orangemen to wage civil war . . . All this talk of violence, of bullets and bayonets, of rebellion and civil war has come from one side alone.' He wouldn't budge: 'Whatever Ulster's rights may be, she cannot stand in the way of the rest of Ireland.'[186]

One reason the Irish crisis grew is that it was given time to grow. Asquith introduced his Home Rule bill on April 11, 1912, two months after Churchill's Belfast speech, and the issue was still before the country in the summer of 1914. The House of Lords was responsible for the delay. The peers no longer possessed an absolute veto, but they retained some power to obstruct; if they stonewalled, as they did in this instance, they could force the House of Commons to pass a bill in three successive parliamentary sessions. As the seasons passed, the Orangemen's enmity hardened. For more than two years, Churchill later calculated, the question 'absorbed nine-tenths of the political field.' Meanwhile, he and his fellow ministers were struggling to find a compromise which would give Ireland both Home Rule and peace. His first proposals were naive. He saw the Transvaal constitution as a sound precedent, though it would be hard to imagine two breeds less alike than the Boers and the Irish. Lloyd George suggested a 'referendum . . . each of the Ulster counties is to have the option of exclusion from the Home Rule Bill,' which was equally impractical. The idea of partition was first mooted in June 1912, when two MPs introduced an amendment to the bill exempting four Ulster counties from Home Rule. Carson, believing that 'if Ulster were left out, Home Rule would be impossible,' supported their measure in the hope of defeating the bill in its entirety.[187]

It was rejected, but the idea remained. On August 31 Churchill wrote to John Redmond, the leader of the Irish Nationalists, that 'something should be done to afford the characteristically Protestant and Orange counties the option of several years before acceding to an Irish Parliament.' This was the first indication that he might prove receptive to partition. At the time he thought of it as a temporary measure. With the Ulster Volunteers drilling, and Carson designated head of a 'provisional government,' he appealed for a fresh approach at Dundee in October 1913. By this time Home Rule had passed the Commons twice and been spurned twice by the Lords. Its enactment was now certain. Churchill, however, was looking beyond that, to the practical problems of enforcement. The Unionists' claim for special treatment, he said, was 'very different from the claim to bar and defer Home Rule and block the path of the rest of Ireland.' He added significantly: 'Our bill is not unalterable.' The Liberals could pass it without a single Tory vote, 'but it will take more than one party to make it a lasting success. A settlement by agreement . . . would offer advantages far beyond anything now in sight. Peace is better than triumph provided it is peace with honour . . . Only one thing would make it worth while or even possible to recast a measure on which so much depends: It is a very simple thing – good will.' Redmond, afraid that his most powerful ally might be weakening, denounced the 'two-nation theory' as 'an abomination and a blasphemy.' Carson was scornful. One solitary Conservative, F.E. Smith – who, astonishingly, remained close to Winston through all this – said he had 'shown a grasp of those facts which are fundamental which none of his colleagues, at least in public, has displayed.'[188]

If his motive in entering this donnybrook had been political – and surely that was among his reasons – he had chosen the wrong arena. To be sure, he was reestablishing his credentials as a Liberal, but the cost was prohibitive. By agreeing to be Asquith's chief spokesman on Home Rule, he had added his name to that long list of English public men who had intervened in the Irish question and emerged bloodied. Other members of Asquith's cabinet could speak out in support of Winston when his decision was popular and remain silent when it wasn't. This was even true of the prime minister. Eventually Asquith would have to commit himself, but in the interim he could leave the stump to Churchill. Moreover, Winston couldn't confine himself to polemics. He had to search for a solution, a hopeless task which was bound to antagonize partisans in both Belfast and Dublin. Twice in the Autumn of 1913 he conferred with Conservative leaders in the hope of finding middle ground, talking to Bonar Law at Balmoral in September, and then to Austen Chamberlain aboard the *Enchantress* in late November. Chamberlain's memorandum on their discussion, written immediately afterwards, shows how far Churchill was prepared to go at that time to reach a settlement: 'In answer to W's opening remark I said that I had assumed that . . . he was prepared to [exempt] Ulster. He replied: "We have never excluded that possibility – never." Of course Redmond hated it, but they were not absolutely bound to R. and he was not indispensable to them. They would not allow Ulster to veto Home Rule, but they had never excluded the possibility of separate treatment for Ulster. This was repeated more than once in the course of our talk.'[189]

Winston was still not considering permanent partition. His papers leave no room for doubt on that point. He was merely contemplating a transition period for the northern counties. Yet it hardly seemed to matter. Neither side was interested in finding a middle course. Right or wrong, Ulster was preparing to fight. On September 12, 1912, Carson had drawn up a covenant, not against Home Rule for Ulster, but against any version of Home Rule, and a half-million Orangemen had signed it, some in their own blood:

Being convinced in our consciences that Home Rule would be disastrous to the material well-being of Ulster as well as the whole of Ireland, subversive to our civil and religious freedoms, destructive of our citizenship, and perilous to the unity of the Empire, we whose names are undersigned, men of Ulster, loyal subjects of His Gracious Majesty King George V, humbly relying on the God whom our fathers in days of stress and trial confidently trusted, do hereby pledge ourselves in solemn Covenant throughout this our time of threatened calamity to stand by one another in defending for ourselves and our children our cherished position of equal citizenship in the United Kingdom, and in using all means which may be found necessary to defeat the present conspiracy to set up a Home Rule Parliament in Ireland. And in the event of such a Parliament being forced upon us we further solemnly and mutually pledge ourselves to refuse to recognize its authority. In sure confidence that God will defend the right we hereto subscribe our names . . . God save the King.

Now, a year later, the deterioration of the situation was alarming. The month after the *Enchantress* conference, Belfast police reported that British army depots there might be raided. Carson publicly boasted that the soldiers would neither resist such raids nor fire on Orangemen. 'The Army,' he said, 'are with us.' General Henry Wilson, Seely's director of military operations, agreed; should the army be ordered to coerce Ulster, he said, there would be 'wholesale defections.' Law told the House: 'If Ulster does resist by force, there are stronger influences than Parliamentary majorities . . . no Government would dare to use their troops to drive them out.' Then, speaking to a massive Unionist rally at Blenheim, he declared: 'I can imagine no length of resistance to which Ulster will go in which I shall not be ready to support them.'[190]

Lloyd George warned: 'We are confronted with the gravest issue raised in this country since the days of the Stuarts.'[191] The signers of the Belfast Covenant had pledged armed resistance to the last man. And they had arms. In the early spring of 1914, a German lighter bearing 25,000 Mauser rifles and 2,500,000 rounds of ammunition had slipped out of Hamburg port and transshipped its cargo to a Norwegian tramp, the *Fanny*. Before Danish Customs officials could inspect the *Fanny* at the Kattegat, between Sweden and Denmark, the skipper had made a run for it and disappeared into the mists of the North Sea. Anchoring in a remote cove, the crew changed the steamer's appearance and renamed her the *Doreen*. Danish Customs having raised the alarm, Churchill had patrol boats searching these waters, but as the *Doreen* the renegade ship reached Yarmouth, then Lundy Island in the Bristol Channel, and finally, on the night of April 19, Tuskar Rock off county Antrim in the Irish Sea. There she rendezvoused with the *Clydevalley*, an ancient collier black with coal dust and red with rust. The two masters lashed the hulls together and ran a single set of navigation lights as crewmen heaved the deadly crates from one hold to the other. On April 25 the *Clydevalley* groaned its way into Larne, the very harbour through which the Churchills had passed. Orangemen in the town had cut telephone wires and organized a convoy of trucks. Between 11:00 P.M. and 2:30 A.M. volunteers sweating under rigged lights lugged the guns and ammunition from the collier to waiting trucks. By dawn they had fanned out all over northern Ireland. Now, if Home Rule were forced upon them, they could field an army.

By the end of the month fifty thousand Orangemen, aged seventeen to sixty-five, had joined the Ulster Volunteer Force. Their morale was excellent, and they were superbly led. England's best generals were backing them. Kitchener belonged to the Protestant Ascendancy; so did Lord Roberts. Kitchener's duties in the Middle East ruled him out, but Roberts declined the UVF command only because, at eighty-five, he was too old. More and more one heard the name of General Henry Wilson, who had been appointed Britain's chief of military operations despite the fact that as an Ulsterman he had signed the covenant. Tall, lanky, with a look of despondent fidelity which was entirely misleading, Wilson was one of many establishmentarians whose names give the incipient revolt an aura of respectability. Others included Lord Rothschild, Edward Elgar of 'Land of Hope and Glory,' and Rudyard Kipling. Kipling had contributed £30,000 to the UVF and published a poem honouring it – not in *The Times*, which supported Home Rule, but in the archconservative *Morning Post:*

> *The blood our fathers spilt,*
> *Our love, our toils, our pains,*
> *Are counted us for guilt,*
> *And only bind our chains.*
> *Before an Empire's eyes,*
> *The traitor claims his price.*
> *What need of further lies?*
> *We are the sacrifice.*

Even the King had doubts about using force against the Orangemen. He asked Bonar Law: 'Will it be wise, will it be fair to the Sovereign as head of the Army, to subject the discipline and indeed the loyalty of his troops to such a strain?' Law, a Canadian who had become an adopted Orangeman, exploited the King's discomfort. At stake, he told the monarch, was not merely Ulster, but the entire British Empire. Home Rule would be the thin end of the wedge for his Majesty's fractious subjects all over the world. He should refuse to recognize it, whatever Parliament did. Law said: 'You will save the Empire by your example.'[192]

Meanwhile, the tale of the twenty-five thousand smuggled Mausers had leaked out. The possibility of a Belfast-Berlin collaboration seemed very real, and was discussed in the House. Liberal back-benchers demanded prosecution of Orangemen negotiating with the Germans. Asquith refused; he was vacillating. Churchill spoke out: 'We have,' he said, 'been confronted with an avowed conspiracy to defy Parliament and the law, leaving a great army practising preparations for rebellion and for the setting up of a provisional Government, which would be an outrage against the realm and the Empire.' England, he said, would not be intimidated by plots to raise a revolt 'greater than the police could cope with.'[193] He was not speaking only to Belfast; Redmond and his fellow Irish Nationalists had been desperately worried about the response to all this among their own people in the south, and their nightmares were being realized. Riots were reported in Dublin. Catholic youths were flocking to join the Irish Nationalist Volunteers. Irish MPs who were counsellors of moderation were losing their followers. In 1913 a militant working-class movement had forged a tight alliance with the Sinn Féin, who regarded themselves as Irishmen first and last and gentlemen never, and wearers of the green were turning to these champions of violence.

By March 1914, with final passage of the Home Rule bill less than two months away, the strain was becoming insupportable. Asquith, with Redmond's reluctant consent, promised that Ulster would be permitted to vote itself out of Home Rule for six years, or until two successive general elections had been held. Carson angrily rejected this as 'a sentence of death with a stay of execution for six years.' Churchill decided to take his gloves off. He had been conciliatory at Dundee. Now he would swing over to the attack. At Bradford on March 14 he called Bonar Law 'a public danger seeking to terrorize the Government and to force his way into the Councils of his Sovereign' by exploiting the issue for partisan purposes. 'Behind every strident sentence which he rasps out,' he said, 'you can always hear the whisper . . . "Ulster is our best card; it is our only card." ' That was fair. The Tories had asked for it. But then, carried away by his own rhetoric, he blundered, salting the Unionists' wounds with sarcasm. Having raised troops, he said, Ulster seemed anxious for battle 'so that her volunteers could assert themselves.' But the proposed moratorium would deprive them of that test. He put words in their mouths: ' "Now the Government have had the incredible meanness to postpone all possible provocation for six long years." ' Bitterly he commented: 'Coercion for four-fifths of Ireland is a healthful, exhilarating, salutary exercise, but lay a finger on the Tory fifth – sacrilege, tyranny, murder!' The Liberals were not cowed, he said: 'There are worse things than bloodshed . . . We are not going to have the realm of Britain sunk to the condition of the Republic of Mexico.' The issue, for him, was 'whether civil and Parliamentary government in these realms is to be beaten down by the menace of armed force.' If Orangemen would extend the hand of friendship, it would be eagerly clasped by Liberals and Irish Nationalists, but 'if every effort to meet their views is only to be used as a means of breaking down Home Rule . . . if the civil and Parliamentary systems are to be brought to the crude challenge of force . . . then I can only say to you: Let us go forward and put these grave matters to the proof.' Lord Fisher wrote to him: 'I should say it's probably the best speech you ever made.' But *The Times* commented the next day that, having carried his naval estimates over the protests of rank-and-file Liberals, he 'seemed to think it necessary to show that on occasion he could shout defiance with the rest,' and another critic called his remarks redolent of 'cheap champagne made of gooseberry juice and vitriol, exhilarating at the moment but nauseating sooner or later.'[194]

It was quickly forgotten, for within a week Churchill found himself in deep trouble. He and Seely were worried about the loyalty of British soldiers in Ireland. A high proportion of them were natives of Ulster. Moreover, they were badly deployed for the approaching climax; of the twenty-three

375

thousand regulars on the island, only nine thousand were stationed in the north. Mutinous mutters had met proposals for a redistribution which would transfer troops billeted on the Curragh plain, outside Dublin, to Belfast. Even if the men remained subordinate, it was reported, Ulster officials of the Great Northern Railway might refuse to carry them northward. However, it was feasible to send them up by sea. Encouraged by Lloyd George, the two service ministers, with the approval of Asquith and the King, decided to take precautionary steps. Guards at the Ulster arms depots of Armagh, Omagh, Enniskillen, and Carrickfergus were doubled. Winston signalled the vice admiral commanding his Third Battle Squadron: 'Admiralty, 19 March 1914. Secret. Proceed at once at ordinary speed to Lamlash . . . Acknowledge and report dates of arrival. WSC.' This would put eight battleships, a cruiser, and three destroyers in Irish waters.[195]

The warships never reached the North Channel. General Henry Wilson sent word of their destination to Brigadier General Hubert Gough, commander of the Curragh garrison. Gough resigned his commission, whereupon fifty-seven of his seventy officers resigned, whereupon Sir John French, the chief of the Imperial General Staff, also resigned. The prime minister faced an army revolt. He countermanded Churchill's orders and cancelled Seely's plans to reinforce Ulster. That wasn't enough for Gough. He sent Asquith a message through Wilson: 'In the event of the present Home Rule Bill becoming law, can we be called upon to enforce it under the expression of maintaining law and order?' To make certain that his position was understood, he came to London and demanded assurances in writing. He got them. The prime minister wrote that it had all been 'a misunderstanding'; that, though His Majesty's government had the right to employ crown forces anywhere, it had 'no intention of taking advantage of this right to crush political opposition to the policy or principles of the Home Rule Bill.' Gough and his officers then withdrew their resignations. Timothy M. Healy, an Irish Nationalist MP, concluded: 'Asquith threw over Churchill, Seely and Lloyd George and refused to back up their actions.'[196]

Wilson leaked all this to Bonar Law, and there was a storm in the House. The Tory press was jubilant over Asquith's 'complete surrender'; the Liberals and Irish Nationalists were furious. Scapegoats were needed, so Seely and his two chief advisers resigned. The prime minister – who had initialled all the military arrangements – claimed ignorance of them. That left the first lord of the Admiralty to face the music. It would seem that twenty-five thousand rifles in the hands of Orangemen justified precautions of some sort, but the Tories believed that he had been trying to goad the Ulster Volunteers into open rebellion. One Conservative MP accused him of hatching a 'plot' designed to create an excuse for an 'Ulster pogrom.' Balfour added scathingly: 'There is one character disgusting to every policeman and which even the meanest criminals thinks inferior to himself in point of morals, and that character is the *agent provocateur*.'[197]

On April 28 Churchill blazed back: 'What we are now witnessing in the

House is uncommonly like a vote of censure by the criminal classes upon the police.' A Tory interjected: 'You have not arrested them.' He replied: 'Is that the complaint – that we have been too lenient?' He declared that the Conservatives, 'the party of the comfortable, the wealthy . . . who have most to gain by the continuance of the existing social order,' were now 'committed to a policy of armed violence and utter defiance of lawfully constituted authority . . . to tampering with the discipline of the Army and the Navy . . . to overpowering police, coastguards and Customs officials . . . to smuggling in arms by moonlight.' If this was an example of 'how much they care for law, how much they value order when it stands in the way of anything they like,' what would be the impact on England's impoverished millions, on 'the great audiences that watch in India,' on the Germans who believed that Britain was paralysed by factions 'and need not be taken into account as a factor in the European situation?' He said: 'I wish to make it perfectly clear that if rebellion comes we shall put it down, and if it comes to civil war, we shall do our best to conquer in the civil war. But there will be neither rebellion nor civil war unless it is of your making.'[198]

At this point he altered his tone dramatically and ended on a propitiatory note. He appealed directly to Carson: 'The right honourable Gentleman . . . is running great risks in strife. Why will he not run some risk for peace? The key is in his hands now. Why cannot the right honourable and learned Gentleman say boldly: "Give me the Amendments to this Home Rule Bill which I ask for, to safeguard the dignity and the interests of Protestant Ulster, and I in return will use all my influence and good will to make Ireland an integral unit in a federal system"?' The House was stirred. Balfour, while describing Churchill's earlier remarks as 'an outburst of demagogic rhetoric,' declared that he was 'heartily in sympathy with the First Lord's proposal,' and Carson went so far as to say that he was 'not very far from the First Lord.' Negotiations were reopened. Liberals and Irish Nationalists, who insisted that northern Ireland must yield, protested angrily. Winston's position in the party was still shaky; he wrote to Clementine that his plea for a truce was 'the biggest risk I have taken.' His cabinet colleagues, generous with their 'hear, hears' when he had taken the offensive, had sat on their hands when he offered Carson an olive branch.[199]

But the negotiations stalled and were again discontinued. The general feeling was that it was too late for one man to halt the drift towards fratricide. Churchill himself said wearily, 'A little red blood had got to flow,' though he quickly added: 'We shall give no provocation. The Ulstermen will have no excuse, and we think that public opinion will not support them if they wantonly attack.' On May 26 the Home Rule bill passed for the third and last time. Officially it was now law. The possibility of enforcing it, however, was as remote as ever. Each side was still waiting for the other to shoot first. On July 20 the King intervened, summoning an all-party conference to Buckingham Palace. The Speaker of the House presided as the delegates wrangled for four days. Winston wrote to Clementine: 'We are to go ahead with the Amending

Bill, abolishing the time limit and letting any Ulster county vote itself out if it chooses. The [southern] Irish acquiesced in this reluctantly. We must judge further events in Ulster when they occur.'[200]

Asquith's cabinet met on the afternoon of Friday, July 24, 1914, to discuss the final conclusions of the King's conference. The report was sterile; absolutely nothing had been accomplished. It was at this point that the Irish issue, foremost in everyone's mind, so certain to burst into flames at any moment, was unexpectedly deferred, destined not to reemerge for years, by which time the whole cast of characters would have changed. The ministers were about to break up when Grey began reading in quiet, grave tones a document which had just been sent in to him from the Foreign Office. It was an Austrian note to Serbia. Churchill was very tired; several minutes passed before he could disengage his mind from the tedium which had just ended. Gradually the phrases and sentences began to take shape and meaning. The foreign secretary was reading an ultimatum. Winston had never heard anything like it. He did not see how any country could accept it, or how any acceptance, however abject, could satisfy the government which had sent it. He later recalled: 'The parishes of Fermanagh and Tyrone faded back into the mists and squalls of Ireland, and a strange light began immediately, but by perceptible gradations, to fall and grow upon the map of Europe.'[201]

Churchill later blamed three men for the outbreak of the Great War: the Serb assassin, the Austrian foreign minister who had written that first ultimatum, and the kaiser, who could have stopped the chain reaction of governments bound by military alliances. But the initial culprit was an incompetent chauffeur whose name has not survived. On June 28, 1914, four weeks before the delivery of the fateful note to Serbia, Austrian Archduke Franz Ferdinand and his morganatic wife, Sophie, had been riding through the Bosnian capital of Sarajevo when the driver took a wrong turn. Realizing his mistake, he came to a dead halt—right in front of a Serbian fanatic armed with a revolver. Franz Ferdinand and Sophie were shot dead on the spot. In Vienna the toils of vengeance, like everything else in the Austro-Hungarian Empire, moved very slowly. But they were moving. Meanwhile, Britain stood aside. There was every reason to believe Britain would remain there. It had nothing at stake. Grey's 'moral obligation,' assumed eight years earlier, had been given privately and was not binding. Britain's only commitment on the Continent was to defend Belgian independence, which hardly seemed threatened then, and even that was vague. Winston didn't care for the Belgians; he thought their behaviour in the Congo disgraceful. At the Admiralty he lunched with Kitchener, on leave from Egypt and soon to be Seely's successor at the War Office. Both suspected the existence of a secret agreement between Brussels and Berlin which would permit German troops to cross Belgium on their way to France. For England, they agreed, such an 'invasion' would be an inadequate casus belli. But it was all very speculative, very remote, quite nebulous.

The Admiralty's trial mobilization had begun, as scheduled, in the middle of July, over two weeks after the Sarajevo murders. The grand review was held on July 18. Churchill called it 'incomparably the greatest assemblage of naval power ever witnessed in the world' – 223 battleships, armoured cruisers, light cruisers, destroyers, minesweepers, and submarines parading past the royal yacht and the *Enchantress* at Spithead, with the King and his first lord taking the salute. Normally, the next step would have been demobilization of all three fleets, accompanied by liberty for the regular tars and tickets home for the reservists. It wasn't taken. Churchill, concerned about rumours from central Europe, published an Admiralty notice in the newspapers of July 20: 'Orders have been given to the First Fleet, which is concentrated at Portland, not to disperse for naval leave at the present. All vessels of the Second Fleet are remaining at their home ports in proximity to their balance crews.' Yet he was confident that negotiations would settle the differences between Vienna and Belgrade. In a letter to Grey two days later, drawing an analogy between that problem and the more urgent situation in Ulster, he wrote that if the question were how to uphold British interests on the Continent, 'you wd proceed by two stages. First you wd labour to stop Austria & Russia going to war: second, if that failed, you wd try to prevent England, France, Germany & Italy being drawn in.' In either instance, mediation was the solution. The following day Lloyd George, who concurred, assured the House that 'civilization' would have no difficulty in regulating disputes which arose between nations, by means of 'some sane and well-ordered arbitrament.'[202]

After studying the note Grey had read to the cabinet, however, Churchill wrote to Clementine: 'Europe is trembling on the verge of a general war, the Austrian ultimatum to Servia [sic] being the most insolent document of its kind ever devised.' It was in fact remarkable. Serbia was required to suppress all criticism of Austria-Hungary in newspapers, magazines, societies, and schools; Serbian officials and teachers who had spoken unfavourably of Austrians were to be dismissed; certain Serbs known to be unfriendly to Austria were to be arrested at once; and Austrian officers were to enter Serbia to enforce all these demands and investigate the Sarajevo assassinations. Belgrade must reply to this ultimatum within forty-eight hours. A request for an extension was denied. In Vienna the foreign minister acknowledged that the tone of the note was 'such that we must reckon on the probability of war.'[203]

'Happily,' Asquith wrote to the King, 'there seems to be no reason why we should be anything more than spectators.' Churchill shared his view. At Overstrand, on the Norfolk coast, he had rented a little holiday house called Pear Tree Cottage for Clementine and the children – Goonie Churchill and her two young sons had taken nearby Beehive Cottage – and Friday evening he postponed an Admiralty meeting which had been scheduled for Saturday

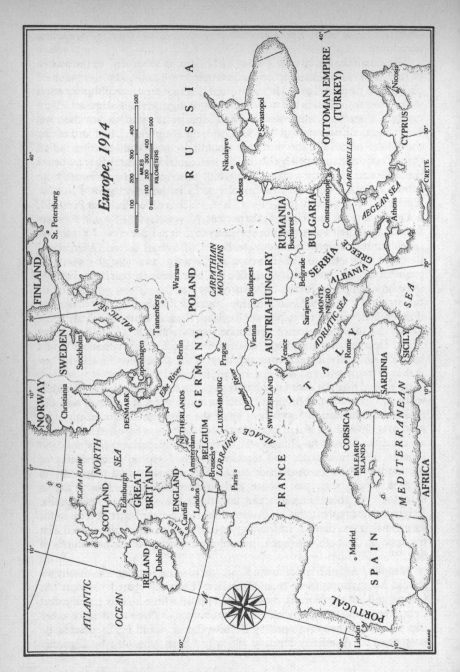

Europe, 1914

MILES
0 100 200 300 400 500
0 100 200 300 400 500
KILOMETERS

ATLANTIC OCEAN

NORWAY

Christiania

SWEDEN

Stockholm

FINLAND

St. Petersburg

BALTIC SEA

RUSSIA

Nikolayev

Odessa

Sevastopol

DENMARK

Copenhagen

Tannenberg

POLAND

Warsaw

GERMANY

Berlin

Elbe River

CARPATHIAN MOUNTAINS

NETHERLANDS

Amsterdam

BELGIUM

Brussels

LUXEMBOURG

Prague

Vienna

AUSTRIA-HUNGARY

Budapest

Danube River

RUMANIA

Bucharest

BULGARIA

Constantinople

OTTOMAN EMPIRE (TURKEY)

DARDANELLES

SCAPA FLOW

NORTH SEA

SCOTLAND

Edinburgh

GREAT BRITAIN

ENGLAND

London

Cardiff

WALES

IRELAND

Dublin

Belgrade

SERBIA

Sarajevo

MONTE-NEGRO

ALBANIA

GREECE

Athens

AEGEAN SEA

CRETE

CYPRUS

Nicosia

ADRIATIC SEA

SWITZERLAND

ALSACE

LORRAINE

Paris

FRANCE

Venice

Rome

ITALY

CORSICA

SARDINIA

SICILY

SEA

MEDITERRANEAN

BALEARIC ISLANDS

SPAIN

Madrid

PORTUGAL

Lisbon

AFRICA

G.H.WARD

380

morning, preferring to spend the weekend at the shore. He wrote: 'My darling one, I have managed to put off my naval conference and am coming to you & the kittens tomorrow by the 1 o'clock train.' Before he left London, good news arrived: Serbia had accepted all demands upon it except the supervision of compliance by Austrian officers, and Belgrade offered to submit that question to the Hague Court. Even the kaiser believed this reply had removed 'every reason for war.' Winston told Prince Louis to run the Admiralty in his absence; he would stay in touch by phone. On the beach he organized the children, distributed buckets and spades, and directed them while they built a sand castle against the rising tide. The surf levelled it. As he remembered later: 'We dammed the littled rivulets which trickled down to the sea as the tide went out. It was a very beautiful day. The North Sea sparkled to a far horizon.'[204]

Pear Tree Cottage had no telephone, but their nearest neighbour, Sir Edgar Speyer, a rich German Jew, had offered the use of his. It was here, at noon on Sunday, that Churchill heard the latest development from Prince Louis. Vienna had declared the Serbian response unsatisfactory, severed diplomatic relations with Belgrade, and ordered partial mobilization against the Serbs – who had already mobilized their army. Winston was on the next London train. There newsboys were hawking extras; Vienna had 'burst into a frenzy of delight, vast crowds parading in the streets and singing patriotic songs.' At the Admiralty he learned that the first sea lord had anticipated him; the Third Fleet had completed its test mobilization and was scheduled to disperse, but Prince Louis had ordered it to remain ready for battle, and at 4:05 P.M. he had telegraphed: 'Admiralty to C in C Home Fleets. Decypher. No ships of First Fleet or Flotillas are to leave Portland until further orders. Acknowledge.' Churchill approved and began a ten-day shuttle between his office, Whitehall, No. 10, and Admiralty House, catching sleep in brief naps. Other ministers grew wan. He thrived.[205]

The following morning, Monday, July 27, the cabinet met for the first discussion of the crisis on the Continent. Clearly the Austrians meant to invade Serbia. That might bring in Russia, the Serbs' ally, which might bring in Germany, Austria's ally, which might bring in France, Russia's ally. The kaiser, aware of the threat on his western frontier, might launch a preemptive strike into northern France. If that happened, the Liberal militants thought, England might become involved. A majority of the ministers disagreed. The Entente Cordiale of 1904 was not binding, they pointed out; it was merely 'a sentimental liaison.' Grey's assurance to the French had been unofficial. In an unpublished note Churchill wrote afterwards: 'The Cabinet was absolutely against war and would never have agreed to being committed to war at this moment.' A message arrived from Pear Tree Cottage: 'Goodnight my Dearest One. I trust the news may be better tomorrow. Surely every hour of delay must make the forces of peace more powerful. It would be a wicked war.' Winston had no intention of making it wickeder by being caught off guard. That night he telegraphed all British fleets, squadrons, and flotillas, scattered over five oceans: 'European political situation makes war between Triple Alliance and Triple Entente Powers by no means impossible. This is *not* the Warning Telegram but be prepared to shadow possible hostile men-of-war . . . Measure is purely precautionary. The utmost secrecy is to be observed and no unnecessary person is to be informed.'[206]

Austria-Hungary declared war on Tuesday, July 28, and bombed Belgrade. Both Winston and Prince Louis were worried about the position of the First Fleet, now anchored off the Isle of Wight. It was vulnerable there, and a navy's primary duty, as Mahan had written, was to remain 'a fleet in being'; Churchill pointed out that the admiral commanding the Home Fleet was the only man in Europe who could 'lose the war in the course of an afternoon.' The ships' war station was Scottish waters, where they would be secure and a deterrent to any sudden German attack, at the same time serving notice that England was prepared. Yet Winston 'feared to bring this matter before the Cabinet,' he wrote, 'lest it should be mistakenly considered a provocative action likely to damage the chances of peace.' Instead, he went to No. 10 and told Asquith he was going to act on his own authority. The prime minister, he recalled, 'looked at me with a hard stare and gave a sort of grunt. I did not require anything else.' That night, on his instructions, an eighteen-mile-long procession of darkened ships steamed through the Straits of Dover. Dawn found the battleships in Scapa Flow and the battle cruisers off Rosyth, in the Firth of Forth. 'A surprise torpedo attack,' wrote Winston, was 'at any rate one nightmare gone forever.'[207]

By Wednesday both Grey and Churchill had recommended to the cabinet, which now met daily, that England take the lead in proposing a conference of great powers to avert catastrophe. Germany had the Continent's strongest army, so Berlin was approached first. The kaiser wouldn't discuss it. Until now Winston had believed that peace was possible; Albert Ballin's biographer describes how, when he took leave of Ballin, Churchill 'implored him, almost with tears in his eyes, not to go to war.' But Thursday morning, when seventy-three-year-old Lord Fisher called at the Admiralty to see what was happening, he found the first lord in high spirits, persuading Asquith to approve the warning telegram to all warships, supervising the general alert, and swiftly retiring senior officers he felt were unfit for war service. His most controversial move, applauded by Fisher but resented by almost every other flag officer, was the replacement of Sir George Callaghan, commander in chief of the Home Fleet, by Sir John Jellicoe. Callaghan was sixty-one and in robust health. David Beatty told Churchill that dismissing him was a mistake, and Jellicoe himself sent Winston six telegrams, begging him to change his mind. He wouldn't do it. He was very sure of himself, making crucial decisions every hour and feeling remarkably euphoric. To Clementine he wrote: 'The preparations have a hideous fascination for me. I pray to God to forgive me for such fearful moods of levity. Yet I wd do my best for peace, & nothing would induce me wrongfully to strike the blow.'[208]

But the blow, he decided on Friday, must be struck. That afternoon Grey cabled Paris and Berlin, asking for formal assurances that they would respect Belgium's neutrality 'so long as no other power violates it.' France agreed; Germany did not reply. That was enough for Winston. Asquith and Kitchener joined him for lunch at the Admiralty. He listened attentively when Kitchener argued that 'if we don't back France when she is in real danger, we shall never . . . exercise real power again.' Asquith nodded in agreement. The prime minister still did not reflect the opinion of his cabinet, however. Churchill and Grey were with him – Grey intimated he would resign if they abandoned France – but the rest remained adamant. Churchill asked the cabinet to approve the final steps in naval mobilization and was refused. The strongest voice for British neutrality was Lloyd George, who had reconsidered his impulsive response to the Agadir incident three years earlier. Lord Hugh Cecil, the best man at Winston's wedding, was one of the few Tories who agreed with George. England, they said, should remain aloof. After the meeting Churchill wrote 'My dear Linky' that 'divergent views are certainly to be expected in the grt issues now afoot. But you will be wrong if you suppose that this country will be committed to any war in wh its profound national interests – among wh I include its honour – are not clearly engaged.' In a discreet letter to Arthur Ponsonby that same afternoon he revealed where he thought Britain's honour lay. 'Balkan quarrels are no vital concern of ours,' he wrote. 'But the march of events is sinister. The extension of the conflict by a German attack upon France or Belgium wd raise other issues.' And, in a third note, to Lord Robert Cecil, Linky's brother: 'If we allowed Belgian neutrality to be trampled down by Germany without exerting ourselves to aid France we shd be in a very melancholy position both in regard to our interests & our honour.'[209]

At the Admiralty he anxiously watched the moving flags and pins on his chart of the Mediterranean, now the scene of many French troop movements. The Germans had two capital ships there: the 23,000-ton battle cruiser *Goeben* and the 4,500-ton light cruiser *Breslau*. The *Goeben*, the size of a dreadnought, with a speed of 27.8 knots and immense firepower, 'would easily be able,' Winston had noted, 'to avoid the French battle squadrons and brushing aside or outstripping their cruisers, break in upon the transports and sink one after another of these vessels crammed with soldiers.' He notified his Mediterranean commander, Admiral Sir Berkeley Milne, that his first mission in the event of war would be to shield French troopships 'by covering and if possible bringing into action individual fast German ships, particularly *Goeben*.' Milne was reminded that 'the speed of your Squadrons is sufficient to enable you to choose your moment.' The first lord's tone left no doubt; if the admiral failed, his career would be over. Churchill could put it no stronger than that. If the *Goeben* survived he could not be blamed.[210]

The controversy over two Turkish warships was, however, another matter. He mentioned it casually at the end of a letter to Clementine, written that Friday evening after he had dined with Asquith. 'There is still hope although the clouds are blacker & blacker,' he began. 'Germany is realizing I think how

383

great are the forces against her & is trying tardily to restrain her idiot ally. We are all working to soothe Russia. But everybody is preparing swiftly for war and at any moment now the stroke may fall. We are ready.' A maelstrom had enveloped London's financial markets: 'The city has simply broken into chaos. The world's credit system is virtually suspended. You cannot sell stocks & shares. Quite soon it will not perhaps be possible to cash a cheque. Prices of goods are rising to panic levels.' That reminded him of the July expenses for Pear Tree; he thought £175 too high and wanted to see the bills. Almost as an afterthought he mentioned that 'I am forcibly detaining the 2 Turkish Dreadnoughts wh are ready.' It was one of the most fateful sentences written in that fateful year.[211]

Turkey had joined no alliance. In 1911 its leaders had wanted to ally themselves with the British Empire, but Churchill, with the arrogance of his class in that time, had replied that they had ideas above their station. He had merely advised them not to alienate Britain, which 'alone among European states . . . retains supremacy of the sea.' But the vigorous Young Turks, tired of hearing the Ottoman Empire scorned as the 'Sick Man' of Europe, had raised £6,000,000 by popular subscription, with every Anatolian peasant contributing at least one coin, and made a down payment for two battleships, to be built in British shipyards and armed with 13.5-inch guns. Both vessels were ready by July; they had been christened the *Sultan Osman* and the *Reshadieh*; officers and sailors from Constantinople were on hand to take delivery. Now, at 12:30 AM on the last day of the month, Churchill wrote to the King that he had 'taken the responsibility' of forbidding their departure. The Turkish commander was told his ships had been 'requisitioned.' When he threatened to lead his men aboard, Churchill ordered that they be repelled 'by armed force if necessary.' The Turkish naval minister protested. International law was moot on this point, but to the Turks it was outright piracy. Grey, as imperious as Winston, responded that England had appropriated the vessels to meet its 'own needs in this crisis.' Applications for indemnification would be given 'due consideration,' but there was no offer of compensation. The warships were summarily rechristened the *Agincourt* and the *Erin*. Turkey then turned to Germany, which eagerly grasped its hand. On August 2 the two countries signed a secret agreement. Churchill would write: 'Ah! foolish-diligent Germans, working so hard, thinking so deeply, marching and counter-marching on the parade grounds of the Fatherland . . . how many bulwarks to your peace and glory did you not, with your own hands, successively tear down!' But in this case it was the diligent Churchill, in an almost unbelievable act, who tore down what could have been a British bulwark and thereby set the stage for a disaster whose chief victim would be himself.[212]

Russia was mobilizing against Austria-Hungary. Germany, as Austria's ally, therefore proclaimed a 'threatening state of war.' At midnight on Thursday, July 30, the kaiser demanded the Russians demobilize at once, giving them twenty-four hours to stop and 'make us a distinct declaration to that effect.' In England it was Bank Holiday weekend. Saturday morning the governor of the Bank of England called on Lloyd George with the message that the City was 'totally opposed to our intervening' in the coming conflict. In the Foreign Office, Grey was reluctantly informing the French ambassador, Paul Cambon, that thus far the dispute on the Continent had been 'of no interest' to England, though 'Belgian neutrality might become a factor.' Asquith wrote in his diary: 'Of course everybody longs to stand aside.'[213]

Not everybody. His first lord of the Admiralty now relished the prospect of a fight – Jennie wrote to Leonie that he now thought war 'inevitable' – and the cabinet meeting that day was, as a consequence, tumultuous. Sir Maurice Hankey later wrote: 'Winston Churchill was a man of a totally different type from all his colleagues. He had a real zest for war. If war there must needs be, he at least could enjoy it.' Asquith described him in that session as 'very bellicose . . . It is no exaggeration to say that Winston occupied at least half the time.' When he wasn't talking, he was passing notes to Lloyd George, trying to persuade him to change his mind. Churchill wanted the cabinet to authorize full mobilization of the navy, including a call-up of all naval reserves. After what one minister called 'a sharp discussion,' he was refused on the ground that such a move might, under the circumstances, be considered incendiary. Grey suggested that preliminary plans be drawn up for the dispatch of an expeditionary force to France. He, too, was turned down.[214]

Of the eighteen ministers present, twelve went on record as being opposed to any support of France. Morley, John Burns, Sir John Simon, and Lewis Harcourt threatened to resign if they were overruled. Because of his seniority, Morley was their acknowledged leader, but the most vociferous pacifist was Lloyd George. George wasn't even sure he would fight over Belgium. If the Germans took the direct route to France, he said, they would only cross a corner of the little country; it would just be a 'little violation.' (Berlin would soon describe its earlier guarantee of Belgian neutrality as 'a scrap of paper.') Liberal back-benchers were even more vehement. That afternoon, in an informal caucus, they voted four to one for neutrality, 'whatever happens in Belgium or elsewhere.' When news of the vacillation at No. 10 reached Printing House Square, the editor of *The Times* wrote to his aunts: 'Saturday was a black day for everyone who knew what was going on – more than half the Cabinet rotten and every prospect of a complete schism or a disastrous or dishonest refusal to help France . . . Winston has really done more than anyone else to save the situation.' But in doing it he was once more alienating members of his party, who had, Hankey wrote to his wife, 'not the smallest enthusiasm for war.'[215]

Churchill had invited Bonar Law and Grey to join him for dinner that Saturday evening. The Tory leader declined and Grey then withdrew, so Winston dined alone in Admiralty House. At 9:30 P.M. F.E. Smith and Max Aitken dropped in; two Admiralty officials joinied them, and they sat down to bridge, Aitken being odd man out. The cards had just been dealt when a messenger arrived with a large red dispatch box. Winston produced his key, opened it, and drew out a single sheet of paper bearing six words: 'Germany has declared war against Russia.' Showing it to the others, he gave Aitken his cards and rang for a servant to bring him a lounge coat. He was going to No. 10. Aitken observed: 'He left the room quickly . . . He was not depressed; he was not elated; he was not surprised . . . Certainly he exhibited no fear or uneasiness. Neither did he show any signs of joy. He went straight out like a man going to a well-accustomed job.'[216]

In Downing Street he told Asquith that he intended to issue an immediate order for full naval mobilization: summoning forty thousand reservists to the colours to man the Third Fleet, putting all dockyards on a war footing, and directing cruiser squadrons and armed auxiliaries to police the world's trade routes. That was precisely what the cabinet had forbidden him to do. Once more the prime minister gave silent consent. In Churchill's words, he 'simply sat and looked at me and said no more. No doubt he felt himself bound by the morning's decision of the Cabinet. I certainly, however, sustained the impression that he would not put out a finger to stop me. I then walked back to the Admiralty and gave the order.' On the way he met Grey, who said: 'I have just done a very important thing. I have told Cambon that we shall not allow the German fleet to come into the Channel.' At 1:00 A.M., Winston wrote to Clementine; 'Cat-dear, it is all up. Germany has quenched the last hopes of peace by declaring war on Russia, & the declaration against France is momentarily expected.' He knew that she, like most Liberals, was praying for peace. 'I profoundly understand your views,' he continued. 'But the world is gone mad – & we must look after ourselves – & our friends . . . Sweet Kat – my tender love – Your devoted W.' He added a postscript: 'Kiss the kittens.'[217]

Years later, Churchill pointed out to Aitken that 'the mobilization was actually ordered against Cabinet decision and without legal authority.' On Sunday Asquith's ministers faced a hard choice. Either they ratified the actions taken by the first lord and the foreign secretary during the night, or the government fell. Reluctantly, they gave their approval, though Grey was instructed to tell the French that no British troops could be sent across the Channel. Thus England, carrying the whole Empire with it, slowly tilted towards France. No overt action was authorized – the British fleet would intervene only if the Germans tried to attack France by sea – but the Liberal rift nevertheless deepened. Morley and Burns resigned; Lloyd George abstained. Asquith said: 'We are on the brink of a split.' After they broke up, Winston, with a careless disregard for party loyalty, approached F.E. Smith and said the Liberals were seriously divided. Would the Conservatives consider the formation of a coalition government? F.E. sounded out Bonar Law, who sensibly replied that any such proposal should come from the prime minister. He did, however, empower F.E. to tell Churchill that the overwhelming majority of Tory MPs favoured backing France to the hilt.[218]

'Urgent. German ship *Goeben* at Taranto,' read a telegram to Winston from the British consul in that Italian seaport. Churchill instantly wired Milne:

'*Goeben* must be shadowed by two battle cruisers.' But the admiral bungled the job; the German ship reached Messina a few hours after Italy's declaration of neutrality, fuelled, and steamed westward towards Turkey. Everything now was being cut very fine. By a little manoeuvring the kaiser could still have kept England out of the war. Instead, he declared war on France on Monday and informed the Belgians that German troops would enter their country within twelve hours. That turned Lloyd George around. He decided that British public opinion wouldn't stand for it. If the Germans refused to withdraw their threat to Belgium, he said, England must fight. There were more resignations from the cabinet, and Morley bitterly accused George of succumbing to 'the influence of the splendid condottiere at the Admiralty,' but Redmond guaranteed the support of the Irish Nationalists, and when the prime minister, chancellor, foreign secretary, and first lord entered the House, they received a standing ovation. Pale and haggard, Grey declared that if England deserted Belgium, 'we should, I believe, sacrifice our respect and good name and reputation before the world.' As they left the Treasury Bench together, Churchill asked him, 'What happens now?' 'Now,' Grey replied, 'we shall send them an ultimatum to stop the invasion of Belgium within twenty-four hours.' Back in the House the member for Burnley, Philip Morrell, rose to protest the abandonment of neutrality. He was drowned out by shouts of 'Sit down! Sit down!' Morrell's wife, Lady Ottoline, and her lover, Bertrand Russell, glumly walked the streets of Bloomsbury, trying to console each other. Most other Bloomsbury intellectuals were despondent. Lytton Strachey was an exception. 'God has put us on an island and Winston has given us a navy,' he said. 'It would be absurd to neglect those advantages.' The most prescient remark, oddly, came from Grey, that elegant, childless widower who had done more than anyone else to commit Britain's youth. Standing at a window with a friend that evening, watching the streetlamps being lit, he said: 'The lamps are going out all over Europe. We shall not see them lit again in our lifetime.' It was an epitaph with special application to 750,000 English boys, children only yesterday, soon to be slain in battle:[219]

> *For we are very lucky, with a lamp before the door*
> *And Leerie stops to light it as he lights so many more;*
> *And O! before you hurry by with ladder and with light,*
> *O Leerie, see a little child and nod to him tonight!*

Thus the rush of cataclysmic events came down to Tuesday, August 4, 1914, when at midnight Berlin time – 11:00 P.M. in London – Grey's ultimatum to Germany would expire. In Pear Tree Cottage, Clementine, troubled by the peremptory retiring of Admiral Callaghan, was writing to her husband, begging him to consider 'the deep wound in an old man's heart . . . *Please* see him yourself & take him by the hand and (additional) offer him a seat on the Board, or if this is impossible give him *some* advisory position at the Admiralty . . . Don't think this is a trivial matter. At this moment you want everyone's heart & soul.' It was excellent advice; Winston had made altogether too many enemies, some on matters of principle but others through sheer thoughtlessness, and the moment was rapidly approaching when he would need every friend he could find. That Tuesday was not the day to start making them, however. There wasn't time. He was alerting the captains of all British merchant ships, which flew the red ensign, and he was engrossed in the movements of the *Goeben*. Two British warships had sighted her at 9:30 A.M. He wired: 'Very good. Hold her. War imminent.' He wanted to attack at once. 'Winston with all his war paint on,' Asquith wrote to Clementine's cousin, the beautiful, worldly young Venetia Stanley, with whom he was infatuated, 'is longing for a sea fight to sink the *Goeben*.' The prime minister had no objection, but the cabinet vetoed the firing of a single shot before the expiration of Grey's deadline. Prince Louis pleaded with Churchill to give the British gunners a green light before dusk, but the first lord felt he had been insubordinate enough. Night fell and the enemy battle cruiser escaped.[220]

Winston dined at Admiralty House with his mother and brother. Heavy fighting was reported in Belgium. Berlin had ignored Grey's note. The largest human event since the French Revolution was now imminent. The last minutes of peace were ticking away, and vanishing with them, though no one knew it, was England's century of security and supremacy – its 'intolerable hegemony' in world affairs, as the German Matthias Erzberger called it. Churchill left the table to give a council of admirals and captains their final instructions. Big Ben struck the fatal hour. The message went out:[221]

Admiralty to all HM ships and Naval
Establishments
Signal

4 August 1914
11 pm
                                                                    Admiralty

COMMENCE HOSTILITIES AGAINST GERMANY

It was a warm night. Through open windows Churchill could hear a throng outside Buckingham Palace, cheering and singing 'God Save the King.' Custom required that he now report to the prime minister. All the other ministers were already there, sitting in a glum circle around the green baize of the cabinet table. Margot Asquith had been waiting with them. She had just decided to retire, and was pausing at the foot of the stairs, when she saw Winston entering No. 10 and, 'with a happy face, striding towards the double doors of the Cabinet room.'[222]

FOUR

CATARACT
1914 – 1918

In that first week of the war six million European soldiers sprang to arms with medieval ardour, and a month passed before anyone knew what had happened to them. The void was quickly filled by wild rumours, especially in Britain, which was spending less of its revenues on the army, proportionately, than in 1901. Other belligerent nations had military objectives, conscription, programmes for mobilizing civilian efforts. England had only the 'War-Book' of 1911, prepared by the Committee of Imperial Defence at Haldane's insistence. It was inadequate, and so the country was particularly vulnerable to sensational talebearers. The most extraordinary story, almost universally accepted at the time, described a force of between 70,000 and 100,000 Russians who were said to have landed in Scotland on their way to reinforce the Allies in France. An Edinburgh railway porter told of sweeping the snow from their boots. No one seems to have reminded him that they were in the middle of an August heat wave. Instead, otherwise responsible people chimed in; a laird swore that the czar's soldiers had marched across his estate, and an Oxford scholar declared that one of his colleagues was acting as their interpreter.

Spy stories flourished on the Norfolk coast. 'Foreign-looking' men were reported almost every day. Clementine wrote to Winston about them. She said that Goonie had seen a British soldier corner a suspect and 'give him a small prod with his bayonette,' which, 'tho' very exhilarating to the pursuers had the effect of making the "spy" run so fast that Goonie fears he got away.' Another time 'one of the cottager's wives' saw two men walking along a cliff with odd bulges in their coats. They gave her evil glances '& spoke to each other in a foreign tongue.' Following furtively, she watched them 'open their jackets & let fly 4 carrier pigeons!' Policemen, alerted, 'pursued the men & caught them.' Clementine learned that a decoded message retrieved from one of the pigeons revealed details of a plan to kidnap her and fly her on a German plane to Berlin, where she would remain until her husband had paid a ransom of several dreadnoughts. She wasn't intimidated: 'If I *am* kidnapped I beg of you not to sacrifice the smallest or cheapest submarine or even the oldest ship . . . I could not face the subsequent unpopularity whereas I should be quite a heroine & you a Spartan if I died bravely & unransomed.' Winston was alarmed, and his concern deepened when he learned that their car had broken down. 'It makes me a little anxious,' he wrote to her on August 9, 'that you should be on the coast. It is 100 to one against a raid – but still there is the chance, and Cromer has a good landing place near. I wish you would get the motor repaired and keep it so that you can whisk away at the first sign of trouble.'[1]

Churchill himself caught the spy fever. Driving to the Loch Ewe anchorage of the Grand Fleet with two admirals and two commodores, he spotted a searchlight on the roof of a large private house. There were no Admiralty spotlights in the neighbourhood. Conceivably, he reasoned, this one was being used to send the Germans information about fleet movements. They drove on, but when they arrived and Jellicoe told them an unidentified flying aircraft had been seen in the vicinity, Winston returned to the house at the head of a party armed with pistols and ammunition from HMS *Iron Duke*. He was now convinced that he had discovered a nest of secret agents. At the door the butler told him that this was the home of Sir Arthur Bignold, a founder of the Kennel Club and former Tory MP. Sir Arthur himself appeared, was questioned, and gave an unlikely explanation for the searchlight; he used it, he said, to catch the gleaming eyes of deer on a nearby hillside so he would know where to stalk them in the morning. To his indignation, Churchill ordered the light dismantled and its vital parts taken away. Back at the Admiralty, Winston demanded that 'the fullest report be made on the circumstances in which this searchlight came to be placed into position, together with all other facts about Sir Arthur Bignold, his guests, friends and servants.'[2] The improbable deer-stalking story proved to be true. Apart from its revelation of England's preoccupation with intrigue, even on the highest levels, this incident, like the Sidney Street siege, adds further testimony to Churchill's affinity to danger. The light might have aroused the suspicions of other ministers, but they would have sent subordinates to the scene. Only the first lord of the Admiralty would have arrived in person, gun in hand.

'I am writing in the Cabinet room, at the beginning of twilight,' Asquith wrote Venetia Stanley, 'and thro' the opposite window across the Parade I see the Admiralty flag flying & the lights "beginning to twinkle" from the rooms where Winston and his two familiars (Eddie and Masterton) are beating out their plans.' Winston had already established the routine which would become part of the Churchill legend in World War II. Adopting the Cuban siesta, he worked until 2:00 A.M. each day, woke at 8:00 A.M., and went through correspondence without rising. To Vice Admiral Sir Douglas Brownrigg he presented 'a most extraordinary spectacle, perched up in a huge bed, with the whole of the counterpane littered with dispatch boxes, red and all colours, and a stenographer sitting at the foot – Mr Churchill himself with an enormous Corona Corona in his mouth.'[3]

He was invigorated with immense gusto, enjoying his awesome responsibilities and volunteering to take over any that other ministers found burdensome. As many as twenty major Admiralty enterprises, all of them entirely dependent on sea power, were, he noted, 'proceeding simultaneously in different parts of the globe.' Under his direction, the 70,000 men of Field Marshal Sir John French's first British Expeditionary Force (BEF) were virtually secure from invasion because British warships were patrolling the

200,000 square miles of sea between Scotland and Norway, and both sides of the Straits of Dover had been mined. German and Austrian merchants ports were blockaded. Fast cruiser squadrons hunted down German sea raiders. The kaiser's colonies overseas were seized or besieged with almost larcenous zest – 'A month ago,' he remarked to the cabinet, 'with what horror and disgust would most of those present have averted their minds from such ideas!' The body of a drowned German signalman yielded a secret cipher book; as a consequence, Winston and his staff in Room 40 at the Admiralty could track the movements of German ships. But the sea wasn't large enough for him. Land and air warfare must also feel the Churchillian presence. He established a Royal Naval division of infantry. ('A band must be provided,' he minuted in a typical touch. 'The quality is not important.') His seaplanes hunted U-boats. The pilots who had been his flight instructors were directed, on August 27, to establish their own air base on the Continent at Dunkirk. Other naval fliers carried out, on his orders, a series of stunning raids on zeppelin sheds at Cologne, Cuxhaven, Düsseldorf, and Friedrichsafen and shot down six of the German airships. When Kitchener became minister for war on August 5, he asked Churchill to take over the air defence of Britain, and Winston instantly agreed. He even found time for wartime diplomacy. At Asquith's request, the first lord served on a war council whose other cabinet members were the prime minister, the foreign secretary, the chancellor, and the war minister. He secretly bargained with Italy and Japan over the terms under which they would join the Allies. 'What should we do to bring the Japanese into the war?' he was asked. He replied grandly: 'They can have China.' Grey said: 'Winston very soon will become incapable, from sheer activity of mind, of being anything in the Cabinet but Prime Minister.' At a birthday party featuring a band and a magician, Churchill's son, Randolph, the Chumbolly, shouted at the magician: 'Man, stop! Band, play!' A relative sighed: 'Just like Winston.'[4]

The new secretary of state for war was the man of the hour. He had just been raised to earldom, and on August 7 the blazing eyes, broad guardsman's moustache, and pointing finger of Kitchener of Khartoum – 'K of K,' the people called him now – appeared everywhere on a recruiting poster above the riveting message: YOUR COUNTRY NEEDS YOU! Some colleagues worried about the relationship between this hard, enigmatic man and the ebullient Churchill. Kitchener was twenty-five years older than the first lord and at one time had regarded him as an insubordinate pest. But Winston was another man now, and K of K, recognizing it, dropped him a note: 'My dear Churchill . . . Please do not address me as Lord as I am only yours, Kitchener.' Winston later wrote: 'I found him much more affable than I had been led to expect . . . In those early days we worked together on close and cordial terms. He consulted me constantly on political aspects of his work, and increasingly gave me his confidence in military matters. Admiralty and War Office business were so interlaced that . . . we were in almost daily personal consultation.' Later, after everything had gone wrong, it was Kitchener who gave Churchill the consolation he would treasure during the bleakest years of his life: 'There is one thing at any rate they cannot take from you. The fleet was ready.'[5]

Churchill's pace was exhausting. On August 9 he wrote to Clementine: 'I am over head & ears in work & am much behindhand.' Two days later he wrote her: 'This is only a line from a vy exhausted Winston . . . I wish I cd whisk down to you & dig a little on the beach. My work here is vy heavy & so interesting that I cannot leave it.' In her reply she warned of fatigue and urged him to remember: '1) Never missing your morning ride. 2) Going to bed well *before* midnight & sleeping well & *not* allowing yourself to be woken up every time a Belgian kills a German. (You *must* have 8 hours sleep every night to be your best self.) 3) Not smoking too much & not having indigestion. Now shall I come up for a day or two next Monday & tease you partly into doing these things?'[6]

The fact is that she was dying for an excuse to be in the thick of it. Understanding that, and anxious to appease her appetite for news, Churchill took what was, under the circumstances, a remarkable risk. He sent her classified information by post. 'My darling one,' he wrote. 'The enclosed will tell you what is known officially. It is a good summary. You must *not* fail to burn it at once . . . Kiss the Kittens for me. Tender love to you all. Your fondest & devoted W.' She consigned it to the flames and begged for more. Over the phone – in the Speyers' cottage – she elicited his consent to put more in the mail. After hanging up she wrote to him: 'I am longing to get your letter with the secret news. It shall be destroyed at once. I hope that in it, you tell me about the expeditionary force. Do I guess right that some have gone already? Be a good one and write again & feed me with tit-bits. I am being so wise & good & sitting on the Beach & playing with my kittens, & doing my little housekeeping, but how I long to dash up & be near you and the pulse of things.' Apparently the letter, when it arrived, was a letdown. 'It was most interesting,' she wrote him on August 10, 'but I was disappointed because I hoped you were going to tell me about the Expeditionary Force. Do send me news of it. When it is going, where it will land, which regiments are in the first batch, etc. I long for it to arrive in time to save the Liège citizens from being massacred in their houses.'[7]

Even Winston couldn't tell her that. And until the BEF saw action, the public couldn't even be told of its existence. If the Germans knew of its presence in France, they would alter their plans accordingly. It was indeed inherent in most of the Admiralty's accomplishments that everything known about them had to be highly restricted. The transport of troops, the charting of courses for warship patrols, negotiations with the Japanese and Italians, Room 40 – all these would have been compromised if revealed. Information about engagements at sea could be disclosed, but in the first phase of the war most of this news was bad. The *Goeben* and the *Breslau* entered the Dardanelles, and the sequel was worse than anything Churchill had imagined. The kaiser grandly announced that he was selling both vessels to Turkey as replacements for the two Winston had virtually buccaneered. The crews, however, remained German. They led the Turkish fleet across the Black Sea to bombard the Russian Black Sea ports of Odessa, Nikolayev, and Sevastopol. Russia, in retaliation, declared war on Turkey; England and France were then obliged to do the same. That was the price the Allies paid for Churchill's high-handed 'requisition' of July 28. If he had let the Turks have their ships their country might have remained neutral or even come in on England's side.

In late August the sky briefly brightened. Beatty entered German home waters and won the war's first naval battle, sinking three of Tirpitz's cruisers, damaging three more, and killing or capturing a thousand men at a cost of one damaged ship and thirty-five British bluejackets. Clementine, back in Admiralty House with the children, sent Kitchener the news while Churchill dressed for dinner. 'Winston,' she wrote, 'thinks this is rather a "Coup." ' Then the Germans went underwater. Churchill, addressing an all-party recruiting rally in Liverpool, said he hoped 'the navy will have a chance of settling the question of the German Fleet,' then added, 'if they do not come out and fight in time of war they will be dug out like rats in a hole.' That was tempting fate. The British cruisers *Aboukir*, *Hogue*, and *Cressy* were patrolling the Dutch coast. Feeling 'constant, gnawing anxieties about the safety of the Fleet from submarine attack,' he had ordered them withdrawn, but they were still there when, the morning after his Liverpool speech, a U-boat sank all three in less than an hour, taking 1,459 tars with them.[8] And that was only the beginning. Another U-boat entered Loch Ewe and torpedoed the cruiser *Hawke*. Next the dreadnought *Audacious* went down, followed by the *Formidable*. Clearly Scapa Flow was insecure; Churchill ordered the Grand Fleet to sea while the Orkney defences were strengthened. During their absence, three battle cruisers of the German High Seas Fleet under the command of Franz von Hipper emerged from their Baltic Sea sanctuary, bombarded the British ports of Hartlepool, Whitby, and Scarborough, and sailed away without a scratch. Overseas, a squadron of fast cruisers under Maximilian von Spee roamed the Pacific Ocean, sinking British freighters almost at will. The cruiser *Emden* steamed into the Bay of Bengal, shelled Madras, prowled around the approaches to Ceylon, and destroyed fifteen Allied merchantmen. When a British force under Sir Christopher Cradock attacked von Spee off the Chilean coast, the Germans wiped out the British in a sensational battle and drowned Cradock.

In time all these would be avenged. Von Hipper would be intercepted on his next sortie and so badly mauled that he would never reappear on the high seas. Von Spee and his entire squadron would be sunk in the waters off the Falkland Islands. An Australian cruiser would annihilate the *Emden*. Only the U-boats would venture to take the offensive after that, and while their toll was spectacular, their torpedoing of American merchantmen trading with England would eventually bring the United States into the war. But in late 1914 all that lay in the future. The Admiralty's initial defeats shocked Britons.

395

They had thought their navy invincible. The shelling of their coast, the threat to transports bringing Indian troops back to fight in France, the sinking of their proud warships, evoked cries of pain and anger. Inevitably the Admiralty's first lord, the most visible member of the government, paid a price for his flamboyance.

The lord mayors of Hartlepool, Whitby, and Scarborough demanded coastal artillery and dreadnoughts anchored off their beaches. The Indian government telegraphed that Madras must be protected. The *Morning Post* found that 'grave doubt is expressed on every hand' about Churchill's competence: 'In the War Office we have a soldier in whom the Army and the nation have confidence. In the Admiralty, upon the other hand, there is a First Lord who is a civilian, and cannot be expected to have any grasp of the principles and practice of naval warfare.' Thomas Bowles, a former Tory MP, published a pamphlet charging that the three cruisers had been lost off the Netherlands 'because, despite the warnings of admirals, commodores and captains, Mr Churchill refused, until it was too late, to recall them from a patrol so carried on as to make them certain to fall victims to the torpedoes of an active enemy.' The House was hostile; when he triumphantly announced the naval fliers' air raids on Germany, he was castigated for violating Swiss airspace. 'What's the navy doing?' hecklers cried, and he could not reply without jeopardizing missions and men. 'In spite of being accustomed to years of abuse,' he later wrote, 'I could not but feel the adverse and hostile currents that flowed about me.'[9]

Some flowed very close. Lloyd George told his secretary and mistress, Frances Stevenson, who kept a diary, 'Churchill is too busy trying to get a flashy success to attend to the real business of the Admiralty. Churchill blames Admiral Cradock for the defeat in South America – the Admiral presumably having gone down with his ship & so unable to clear himself. This is characteristic of Churchill.' Asquith wrote to the King that the cabinet felt the naval losses were 'not creditable.' The King, who already regarded Churchill as unreliable and irresponsible, was disgusted with his Liverpool speech. After the loss of the three cruisers, His Majesty's private secretary, Lord Stamfordham, wrote: 'Indeed seeing what alas! happened today when the rats came out of their own accord and to our cost, the threat was unfortunate and the King feels it was hardly dignified for a Cabinet Minister.' Even Kitchener, usually steadfast, despaired during one cabinet meeting, saying that a German invasion was not only possible, but that England would not be able to stop it. Churchill challenged him to have the brightest experts in the War Office pick any British beach, any day, and work out the logistics of landing 150,000 men. The Admiralty would then show how they could hurl those men back into the sea.[10]

Nevertheless, someone's head had to roll. It was scapegoating time again, and the choice of the victim reflects ill upon all who participated in his undoing. Since the outbreak of the war the first sea lord had been the target of a vicious witch-hunt. The press had hounded him, and every minister had been inundated with anonymous letters questioning his loyalty. Lord Charles Beresford, Fisher's bête noire, told the House that while Prince Louis was an 'exceedingly able officer,' nothing could alter the fact that he was a German, had German servants, owned property in Germany, 'and as such should not be occupying his present position.' Churchill warned Beresford not to repeat those remarks: 'The interests of the country do not permit the spreading of such wicked allegations by an officer of your rank, even though retired.' Violet Asquith wrote that her father's reaction to the smear campaign was one of 'disgust.' That is not the impression left by his letters to Venetia Stanley, however. He wrote to her that he was not, 'entre nous, very trustful of the capacity of Prince Louis.' Then; 'Or poor blue-eyed German will have to go.' And then: 'He *must* go.'[11]

He went. Churchill told the King that the attacks on the first sea lord's 'name and parentage' had subjected Louis to an intolerable strain: 'The exacting duties and heavy responsibilities of his office have no doubt affected his general health and nerves, so that for the good of the service a change has become necessary.' Back at the Admiralty, he wrote Louis that he and Asquith agreed that 'a letter from you to me indicating that you felt in some respects yr usefulness was impaired & that patriotic considerations wh at this junction must be supreme in yr mind wd be the best form of giving effect to yr decision. To this letter I wd on behalf of the Govt write an answer.' There was more of this, all of it lamentable. He closed: 'No incident in my public life has caused me so much sorrow.' Their parting interview may have caused him more. The prince had just learned that his elder son, Maurice, a grandson of Queen Victoria and an infantry lieutenant, had been killed in France. With great dignity the grieving father said that 'as a loyal subject of His Majesty' he was leaving 'the great service to which I have devoted my life' to ease 'the burden laid on His Majesty's Ministers.' Thus Louis Alexander of Battenberg, GCB, GCVO, KCMB, PC, was evicted from office on shabby charges of disloyalty to which a Liberal government capitulated. At the King's request Louis changed his name to Mountbatten. One day his other son, Dickie, then fourteen, would vindicate him.[12]

The question of his successor was a momentous one. Haldane had written Churchill that if Lord Fisher were returned to active duty, it would 'make our country feel that our old spirit of the Navy was alive and come back.' Violet Asquith had 'not a shadow of doubt that Winston would wish to appoint Lord Fisher . . . There was a magnetic mutual attraction between these two and they could not keep away from one another for long.' The old salt had been bombarding Churchill with advice, sometimes on profound matters, sometimes on trivia: 'Why is standard of recruits raised 3 inches to 5 feet 6? . . . What d—d folly to discard supreme enthusiasm because it's under 5 feet 6. *We are a wonderful nation!* astounding how we muddle through! There's only one explanation – We are the lost 10 Tribes!' He was now seventy-four. On his frequent visits to the Admiralty, Winston, in his words, 'watched him narrowly to judge his physical strength and mental alertness' and had 'the impression of a terrific engine of mental and physical power burning and throbbing in that aged frame.' He sounded him out 'and soon saw he was fiercely eager to lay his grasp on power.' No one else would do, Winston told Asquith. When the prime minister agreed, the first lord was elated. Violet, seeing him immediately afterwards, said: 'No one knows his weather better than you do – and you are no doubt prepared for squalls ahead.' Winston said: 'I know him – and I know that I can manage him.'[13]

The difficulty was that Fisher felt the same way about Churchill. And there were doubters even then. Clementine was apprehensive; she was afraid the old admiral would be 'like the curate's egg.' Beatty wrote to his wife: 'The situation is curious; two very strong and clever men, one old, wily, and of vast experience, one young, self-assertive . . . but unstable.' Aitken believed that Churchill had 'co-opted Fisher to relieve the pressure against himself,' but had no 'intention of letting anyone else rule the roost.' He foresaw a duel between a first lord and a first sea lord 'both bent on an autocracy.' Admiral Rosslyn Wemyss predicted: 'They will be as thick as thieves at first until they differ on some subject, probably as to who is to be Number 1, when they will begin to intrigue against each other.' The most determined opponent of the appointment was George V. The 'Sailor King' had served fifteen years before the mast, and he distrusted Jacky Fisher. He summoned Churchill to Buckingham Palace, where, according to Stamfordham's account of their conversation, the King said that Winston's choice was 'a great surprise.' His Majesty thought that 'Lord Fisher has not the confidence of the Navy; he is over 73 years of age. When First Sea Lord . . . he created a state of unrest and bad feeling among the officers of the service.' Churchill replied that no other admiral was fit for the job. The King ended the audience by saying that he could not approve until he had seen Asquith. Stamfordham bore the sovereign's message to No. 10: 'The proposed appointment would give a shock to the Navy which no one could wish to cause in the middle of this great War.' Lord Fisher, the royal message continued, had become aged; he talked and wrote a great deal, but his opinions changed 'from day to day.' Asquith himself was troubled by Fisher's 'strangely un-English' face, with its 'twisted mouth' and round eyes, 'suggesting the legend (which I believe quite untrue) that he had a Cingalese mother,' but he replied that he supported Churchill's decision. The King, having done all a constitutional monarch could do, signed the appointment but wrote to the prime minister: 'I do so with some reluctance and misgivings.'[14]

He then sent for the appointee. Churchill had coached Fisher carefully. The meeting lasted an hour, and afterwards the King wrote in his diary: 'He seems as young as ever.' The two agreed to meet once a week. Winston wrote to Asquith and Grey that the old admiral 'is already a Court Favourite.' The choice seemed inspired. It was immensely popular with the country. Since the old admiral usually awoke at 4:00 A.M., between them he and Churchill could keep an almost unsleeping watch at the Admiralty. Winston loved Fisher's wit, his contempt for pomp, his devotion to the service. He wrote to him;

'Contact with you is like ozone to me.' To Clementine he wrote: 'Tomorrow old Fisher comes down to the yacht with me. This always has a salutary effect.' Certainly Fisher's energy was astounding. He wrote to a friend: 'Thanks for your dear letter! Isn't it fun being back? Some d—d fools thought I was dead and buried! I am busy getting even with some of them! I did 22 hours work yesterday but 2 hours sleep not enough so I shall slow down! SECRET. The King said to Winston (I suppose dissuading) that the job would kill me. Winston was perfectly lovely in his instant reply: "Sir, I cannot imagine a more glorious death"! Wasn't that delicious? But burn please!' He wrote to Jellicoe: 'Let everyone be optimistic, and shoot the *pessimists!*' To Beatty he said: 'It's not numbers that tell, but GUNNERY! *Gunnery, gunnery, gunnery!* All else is twaddle. Hit the target!'[15]

At the outset the first sea lord's relationship with the first lord was as Wemyss had predicted: superb. In Churchill's words, 'As long as the port and starboard lights shone together all went well.' The old man proposed a daring plan to force an entry into the Baltic Sea and secure command of it, cutting Germany off from its Scandinavian supplies and freeing Russian troops for an amphibious assault on Berlin. Winston, with his love of adventure, was delighted. He authorized the building of landing craft. Then he questioned Fisher about details. Before the Baltic could be entered, the Elbe River must be blocked. How could this be done? Could British warships enter the Baltic while Tirpitz's fleet was free to sortie from the Kiel Canal and attack the ships left behind in Scapa Flow? How could the Baltic islands be seized while barring the Elbe? The admiral was vague; clearly he hadn't thought it through. Slowly Churchill began to realize that the King had been right, that the aged first sea lord 'was very old. In all matters where naval fighting was concerned he was more than usually cautious. He could not bear the idea of risking ships in battle.' Winston had trapped himself. Fisher was his man, confirmed despite the protests of, among others, the sovereign. If the old salt turned on him, Churchill would be alone. And they were bound to find themselves on a collision course eventually, for Winston believed in taking chances – 'It is not right to condemn operations of war simply because they involve risk and uncertainty,' he told the cabinet – while his first sea lord, so audacious in conversation and letters, was transformed into an archconservative when the prospect of action loomed. 'He settled,' Churchill wrote bleakly, 'upon a doctrine widely inculcated among our senior naval officers, that the Navy's task was to keep open our communications, blockade those of the enemy, and to wait for the Armies to do their proper job.'[16]

But the armies were not doing their proper job. The assumption had been that Belgium would be the battleground. That was the gist of the War Office summary Winston had sent Clementine on August 9. Three days later *Punch* had run its first wartime cartoon, showing a brave little Belgian boy in wooden shoes barring the way to a fat German trespasser, with the caption 'No

Thoroughfare!' Heavy casualties had not been expected. When Winston learned that his young cousin Norman Leslie had been killed in action he thought it bad luck. Even in South Africa death had come to relatively few. He had no way of knowing that fifteen thousand British soldiers had fallen in five days – and that their losses had been light compared to those of the French. On the morning of August 24, three weeks after Germany declared war on France, he looked up from his desk and saw Kitchener standing in the doorway. K of K's face was peculiar. Winston had 'the subconscious feeling that it was distorted and discoloured as if it had been punched with a fist. His eyes rolled more than ever.' Wordlessly he held out a telegram from the commander of the BEF, Sir John French. The Belgian fortress of Namur had fallen to the enemy. At the time this was considered a disaster. Namur was fifty-seven miles from the German frontier and the gateway to France. Neither Kitchener nor Churchill could have envisioned what lay ahead: a further BEF retreat of 157 miles, putting the Tommies just outside the suburbs of Paris before they rallied. To cheer up the war minister, Winston took him to the Other Club and proposed, after dinner, his intention to break the club rule forbidding any toast but that to the King; with a flourish he raised his glass to 'success to the British arms.' He beamed at Kitchener, who drank but still looked pummelled.[17]

Five days later another member of the club suffered a similar shock. That Saturday afternoon F.E. Smith, the official press censor, was handed a dispatch from Arthur Moore, the war correspondent of *The Times*. Moore had written that the Allied forces had virtually disintegrated under an 'immediate, relentless, unresting' enemy advance. He was awed by the 'irresistible vehemence' of the Germans, whose numerical superiority was so great that 'they could no more be stopped than the waves of the sea.' The BEF, a 'retreating, broken army,' was being 'forced backwards, ever backwards,' suffering 'very great losses' reducing it to 'bits of broken regiments' that were 'grievously injured' and some divisions which had 'lost nearly all their officers.' F.E. suspected that the correspondent was simply windy. Nevertheless, he passed what became known as 'the Amiens dispatch' in the shrewd belief that it would make excellent recruiting propaganda. Thus it was that members of the English establishment sat down to breakfast on Sunday morning and found themselves confronting a front-page headline, FIERCEST FIGHT IN HISTORY, followed by the subheads *Heavy Losses of British Troops – Mons and Cambrai – Fight Against Severe Odds – Need for Reinforcements*. In a box the editor explained that the story was being run to alert the country to the 'extreme gravity of the task before us.' H.G. Wells thought: 'It was as if David had flung his pebble – and missed!' Asquith indignantly scolded the paper, but F.E. had been right; on Monday morning recruiting posts were packed with young men eager to rescue their brothers in France. 'Kitchener's Army' had begun to form.[18]

What had happened? Part of the explanation is Gallic stupidity. There is a theory that the last competent French general lies in Napoleon's tomb, and nothing that happened on the fluid front that summer refutes it. Ever since Louis Napoleon's defeat at the hands of the Prussians a generation earlier, cadets at Saint-Cyr-l'École had been imbued with the belief that, as General Ferdinand Foch put it, 'There is only way to defend ourselves – to attack as soon as we are ready.' This was the doctrine of the *offensive à outrance*, of *cran*, of charging mindlessly while shouting: *'Vite, vite! Allez, allez!'* Field regulations stipulated that 'the French Army henceforth admits no law but the offensive . . . the offensive alone leads to positive results.' The bible of this faith was the general staff's Plan XVII, its blueprint for an irresistible march to the Rhine. The instant war was declared, they would invade German-occupied Lorraine with their right wing and advance through Alsace. As the Germans met the threat by transferring troops from their centre, the French would hit the centre with everything they had. *Voilà:* a quick, decisive victory.[19]

Plan XVII was hopelessly flawed. It assumed parity in the populations of the two countries, and there was none. Since 1871 German Fraus had been conceiving far more frequently than Frenchwomen; despite the Reich's commitment in the east, against Russia, the kaiser had mobilized over 1.5 million men in the west, enough to guarantee superiority in the first clash. The French plan's total commitment to massed attacks overlooked the changes in warfare wrought by modern technology – the machine gun, heavy artillery, barbed wire – all of which had been obvious to European observers of the Russo-Japanese War ten years earlier. Most grievous of all, the French generals were guilty of what Napoleon had called the cardinal sin of commanders: 'forming a picture' – assuming that the enemy will act in a certain way in a given situation when in fact his behaviour may be very different. It seems never to have occurred to them that the Germans, too, might have a plan. But they did. It was the Schlieffen Plan, completed in 1906 by Count Alfred von Schlieffen, then the kaiser's chief of staff. The count had anticipated Plan XVII. He intended to draw the French right into Lorraine in a 'sack manoeuvre' while his own right wing, a million *Soldaten*, swept down through Belgium like a swinging scythe, cutting a swath seventy-five miles wide and enveloping France's extreme left flank.

Germany's enemies should have been aware of this. In 1912 Henry Wilson, cycling through the Low Countries, saw that all new German railroad construction in the area converged on Aachen and the Belgian frontier. But Joseph Jacques Césaire Joffre, constable of France and the French commander in chief, was blind to it. Immediately after the declaration of war he marched triumphantly into Lorraine, not suspecting that the slowly retreating enemy was luring him into a trap. Meanwhile, Alexander von Kluck, commanding the German right, wheeled down through Belgium, overwhelming the fortresses of Liège and Namur. His men, their *feldgrau* uniforms coated with white dust from shattered buildings, advanced across Belgium almost unopposed, burning villages and shooting hostages as they went. General Charles Lanrezac commanded the French left wing, lying in Kluck's path. As early as August 8 Lanrezac warned Joffre's headquarters, *Grand Quartier Général* (GQG), that he might be flanked. His concern, he was told, was 'premature.' GQG informed him that a flanking manoeuvre was 'out of proportion to the means at the enemy's disposal,' that the enemy columns his scouts had sighted must be on some 'special mission,' probably serving as a screen. As evidence of their strength accumulated, Joffre actually rejoiced. It meant, he said, that they were thinning their ranks in the centre, where he was about to strike.[20]

He struck on August 21 in the wilderness of the Ardennes. As American GIs discovered thirty years later, the Ardennes is ill-suited to fighting. Thickly forested, slashed with deep ravines, and fogged with mists from peat bogs, it resembles a scene in a Hans Christian Andersen tale. Caesar, who took ten days to cross it, called it a 'place of terrors.' Moreover, its slopes were such that the French would be charging uphill. They found the Germans dug in and ready. Bayonets fixed, Joffre's men lunged upward in an *attaque brusque*. Machine gunners slaughtered them. During the four-day battle of the Frontiers, of which this was a part, 140,000 Frenchmen fell. Yet even this massacre failed to discourage Joffre. The British, who had lost only 1,600 at Mons, were defeatist, but the word from GQG was that although Joffre's drive in the centre had been 'momentarily checked,' he would 'make every effort to renew the offensive.'[21] That was fantasy. The German right, outnumbering the defenders two to one, was about to roll up Joffre's left, and if he didn't know it, Lanrezac did. Learning that the French attackers in the Ardennes not only had failed but were actually retreating, Lanrezac saw himself facing encirclement. On the evening of August 23 he ordered a general retreat. It spread along the entire Allied line. Plan XVII had crumbled. The last chance for a short, victorious war had vanished. Urgency, even panic, was in the air. The French fell back and back. The German advance was relentless. The Allies would be lucky to save Paris. Actually, they didn't; it was Kluck who saved it for them. He blundered, swinging east of the capital on September 3 and thereby offering his flank to Joseph-Simon Gallieni, the retired officer charged with the city's defence. After the first skirmishes there the exhausted German infantrymen gave ground. The French rallied on the Marne, and after a seven-day battle involving more than 2,000,000 men, Kluck recoiled and dug in. Then the sidestepping began, the lines of the opposing armies extending westward and then northward as each tried to outflank the other in a 'race to the sea.' The possibility that eventually they might run out of land seems never to have occurred to them. The sacrifices in the opening battles had been so great on both sides – in August the French alone had lost 206,515 men – that the thought of stalemate was unbearable.

The Germans were masters of northern France, but the Belgians still held out. In Brussels on August 17 their premier, Count de Broqueville, had reported to King Albert that the enemy, outnumbering his forces four or five to one, were attacking across the Gette River, fifteen miles away. Liège had fallen; Namur was doomed. During the night of August 18 the king, executing a skilful disengagement manoeuvre, withdrew his five divisions from Brussels and the Gette and retreated into the great port of Antwerp, Belgium's strongest fortress. They reached there, intact, two days later. The disappointed Kluck reported to *Oberste Heeresleitung*, the kaiser's headquarters, that Albert's army had 'managed to escape our grasp.' He was forced to leave two corps – 60,000 men, badly needed on the Marne – to invest Antwerp. Even so, on August 25 the Belgians sortied and fell on the rear of Kluck's army, driving it back on Louvain. Shots were fired, and Kluck's men shouted: *'Die Engländer sind da!' 'Die Franzosen sind da!'* General von Luttwitz, the military governor of Brussels, summoned the American minister and told him that Louvain civilians had either fired on the Reich's troops or signalled the attackers. 'And now of course,' he explained, 'we have to destroy the city.' It was burned to the ground as an example for those who felt tempted to defy German might.[22]

Zeppelins bombed Antwerp, but until the second month of the war the fortified city faced no serious threat. On September 5, however, de Broqueville warned the British Foreign Office that the enemy troops besieging the port were being heavily reinforced. He asked for weightier artillery, aircraft, and anti-aircraft guns. Four days later the kaiser ordered the capture of the city whatever the cost, and on September 28, 420-millimetre Krupp howitzers began pounding the outworks with 2,000-pound shells. The question of Antwerp's value to the Allies now arose. Was its defence vital? The cabinet was indecisive. In 1911 Fisher, then in full possession of his faculties, had written that in the event of war between Germany and an Anglo-French alliance, the 'overwhelming superiority' of the British navy, not Britain's army, would 'keep the German Army out of Paris . . . It is Antwerp we shall seize,' he concluded, 'and not go fooling on the Vosges frontier.' But provisioning Antwerp was a logistical nightmare. The port's link with the North Sea was the Scheldt River, which belonged to the Netherlands, and the frightened Dutch, determined to remain neutral, were turning back all incoming ships except those bearing food and medicine. With Antwerp's sea approach barred, the only other route open was a thin, exposed, fifty-mile-long land corridor. Kitchener, replying to the September 5 note, said he had no munitions to spare and even doubted the port was in danger. 'I expect they will hang on to Antwerp,' he wrote. On the second day of the war Churchill had vetoed sending an expeditionary force there on the ground that while he could guarantee a safe passage across the Straits of Dover, he couldn't protect troop transports taking the longer route across the North Sea to the Scheldt, then still open.[23]

Winston had not yet grasped the connection between Antwerp's resistance and holding the Channel ports – Dunkirk, Calais, Boulogne – but he was alert to the necessity of denying the ports to Kluck. So was Joffre. Early in September the constable had asked that British infantry be landed at Dunkirk, to make a demonstration on the Germans' right flank. Churchill's naval fliers were already based there, and Kitchener asked him to supervise the

The Western Front
August 25 to September 1, 1914

0 | 25 | 50 | 75 | 100
Miles

'0 | 25 | 50 | 75 | 100
Kilometers

● Allies, Aug 28 ■ Allies, Sept 1
German advance

G W HARD

landing party. His departure was kept secret; even the cabinet wasn't told. Asquith wrote to Venetia on September 9: 'Winston is just off to Dunkirk . . . he will be back by lunch tomorrow. Don't say anything of this, as he doesn't want the colleagues to know.' He commanded a detachment of marines and the Oxfordshire Hussars, his reserve regiment, of which Sunny was colonel in chief. The episode reflects little credit on Churchill. He requisitioned several naval vehicles and eight three-ton trucks to provide Sunny and his officers with all the comforts of their Blenheim manoeuvres. 'Probably no other regiment,' wrote Adrian Keith-Falconer in *The Oxfordshire Hussars in the Great War*, 'went to France accompanied by such a fleet of motor transport solely for its own personal use.' Winston's orders were: 'Select your point and hit hard.' His men were joyously received by villagers, but their feint left no impression on the enemy; Kluck wasn't even aware of their existence. The Tommies called them the 'Dunkirk Circus.' And Churchill, with his incorrigible love of panoply, lent the ineffective foray a touch of opéra bouffe by appearing in the full-dress regalia of an Elder Brother of Trinity House. A French officer asked him what uniform he wore. '*Je suis*

404

un Frère Aîné de la Trinité,' he replied. '*Mon dieu!*' gasped the Frenchman. '*La Trinité!*'[24]

The moth could not resist the flame. Less than a week later Winston was back in France, driving from Calais to British GHQ in Fère-en-Tardenois with the Duke of Westminster. To avoid being swept up by Kluck's advance, they had to take a wide detour, traversing the entire British front. Near Soissons, Churchill had a long talk on a haystack with a major general, Sir Henry Rawlinson. Winston wrote afterwards: 'I saw the big black German shells, "the coal boxes" and "Jack Johnsons" as they were then called, bursting in Paissy village . . . When darkness fell I saw the horizon lighted with the quick flashing of the cannonade. Such scenes were afterwards to become commonplace: but their first aspect was thrilling.' Four days later he returned to Dunkirk, kibitzing at air-raid briefings. He had scarcely returned to London when he alerted the light cruiser *Adventure* to take him over again. The cabinet was beginning to mutter about his absences. Clementine warned him: 'Now please don't think me tiresome; but I want you to tell the PM of your projected visit to Sir John French. It would be very bad manners if you do not & he will be displeased and hurt . . . Of course you will consult K. Otherwise the journey will savour of a week-end escapade & not a mission. You would be surprised & incensed if K slipped off to see Jellicoe on his own.' He took her advice, and K of K, more tolerant than his colleagues, replied: 'No objection – I hope you will counteract any wild talk.' Nevertheless, Churchill was trifling with fate. Having made so many unnecessary appearances at the front, he would be hard pressed later to defend trips which were essential.[25]

By now he saw the strategic significance of Antwerp. Grey had sent identical notes to the Admiralty and the War Office: 'Time presses for the Belgians. I am afraid we can do very little if anything, but if we can do nothing the Belgians may surrender Antwerp very soon.' Kitchener was as yet unalarmed. Churchill, however, drew up a list of equipment he could dispatch at once and ended: 'WE MUST HOLD ANTWERP.' Even though the Germans were retreating from the Marne to the Aisne, the release of their two corps, still tied down by the entrenched camp at Antwerp, would permit Kluck to dash to the Channel ports and seize them before English troops were dug in. By September 29 Winston had converted Kitchener. The war secretary was ready to send men and field guns. 'We had a long Cabinet this morning,' Asquith wrote to his beloved the following afternoon. 'The Belgians are rather out of "morale," & are alarmed at the bombardment of Antwerp . . . They are sending their archives & treasure over here, & talk of moving the seat of Government to Ostend. Kitchener has given them some good advice . . . to entrench themselves with barbed wire &c in the intervening spaces, & challenge the Germans to come on.'[26]

The following morning de Broqueville described his situation as 'very grave'; only Allied troops could 'save Antwerp from falling.' Asquith sent

Venetia a note: 'The fall of Antwerp would be a great moral blow to the Allies, for it would leave the whole of Belgium at the mercy of the Germans. The French telegraph that they are willing to send a division (of 15,000 to 20,000) & put it under a British general . . . We resolved at the Cabinet to-day that, if the French cooperation is satisfactory, we would divert our 7th Division (of the finest troops) wh was just going to join Sir J. French.' The next day, Friday, October 2, he wrote to her: 'The news from Antwerp this morning is far from good & gives me some anxiety. The Germans battered down 2 of the forts, and what is worse got in between them & drove a lot of Belgians out of their entrenchments.' He was pessimistic: 'It is a very difficult situation – particularly as our officer reports that it is the morale of the Belgian commanders rather than of the men wh shows signs of collapse.' He wanted to boost their spirits. 'But it is no good to lure them with false hopes.' With that, he left for Cardiff to make a speech at a recruiting rally. Thus he was absent when the crisis came.[27]

The Belgian government, despairing, had resolved to pack up and leave for Ostend on Saturday morning. They predicted that their troops in Antwerp would hold out for another five or six days, but the British ambassador there, Sir Francis Villiers, thought it 'unlikely that when the Court and Government are gone resistance will be much prolonged.' Antwerp was the only Allied fortress left between Kluck and the Channel. If the enemy reached Calais, Kitchener thought, an invasion of England would be feasible. That evening he and Grey conferred at Kitchener's house in Carlton Gardens, between Pall Mall and St James's Park. With the prime minister away, they needed the opinion of another senior minister, so they decided to consult Churchill. He was aboard a train, bound for Dover. On their orders, the engineer reversed direction, and from Victoria Station a waiting car drove Winston to Carlton Gardens. After listening to their analysis he recommended sending the Admiralty's marine brigade to the city. Then he volunteered to go to the beleaguered city himself and report to them by telephone and telegraph. They agreed, and shortly after midnight he was off again. Grey wired Sir Francis: 'First Lord of the Admiralty will be at Antwerp between 9 and 10 tomorrow. He is fully acquainted with our views, and it is hoped he may have the honour of an audience with the King before a final decision as to the departure of the Government is taken.' Sir Francis wired back that the evacuation had already begun, but de Broqueville would summon an emergency cabinet meeting now to reconsider that decision. As a result of the meeting, all Belgian troops were ordered to remain at their posts. In London that morning Asquith, returning to the fait accompli, wrote to Venetia that he was 'anxiously awaiting Winston's report. I don't know how fluent he is in French, but if he was able to do himself justice in a foreign language, the Belges will have listened to a discourse the like of which they have never heard before. I cannot but think that he will stiffen them up to the sticking point.'[28]

Churchill's car, roaring up to Antwerp's hôtel de ville in a cloud of dust, reminded one observer 'for all the world of a scene in a melodrama where the hero dashes up bare-headed on a foam-flecked horse, and saves the heroine, or the old homestead, or the family fortune, as the case may be.' In undress uniform – no epaulets, no cocked hat – he conferred with de Broqueville and assured him that, in addition to the two thousand seasoned marines who would arrive that evening, he was sending for his two naval brigades, two million rounds of ammunition, and five days' rations. Albert and the Belgian premier, much moved, promised to defend the city for at least ten more days provided the Allies launched a major relief operation within seventy-two hours. Winston cabled Kitchener and Grey: 'I must impress on you the necessity of making these worn and weary men throw their souls into it, or the whole thing will go with a run.' Sunday morning he toured the city's outer forts in a Rolls-Royce. Henry Stevens, the naval rating who drove him, later recalled that although he was out of earshot most of the time, he could see that 'Mr Churchill was energetic and imperative. He discussed the situation with his own Staff and some of the Belgian officers, emphasising his points with his walking stick . . . His actions were emphatic. He appeared on occasions to criticise the siting and construction of the trenches . . . Mr Churchill dominated the proceedings and the impression formed that he was by no means satisfied with the position generally. He put forward his ideas forcefully, waving his stick and thumping the ground with it . . . At one line of trenches he found the line very thinly held and asked where "the bloody men were." He certainly was not mollified when he was told that was all that were available at that point.' Winston was in fact deeply disappointed. Back at the hôtel de ville he telegraphed Kitchener that the defenders were 'weary and disheartened,' that because many of the outworks had been flooded to thwart the Germans, only shallow trenches could be scooped out of the waterlogged earth, furnishing little shelter 'to their worn out and in many cases inexperienced troops.'[29]

The marines landed and were greeted by ecstatic Belgian citizens. Kitchener cabled that the cabinet approved of the immediate dispatch of the naval brigades. He had formed these units, first called 'Churchill's pets' and then 'Churchill's innocent victims,' just before the war. They were green and largely untrained. The officers lacked revolver ammunition. Many of the men had neither fired rifles nor dug trenches. Among their officers were Asquith's son Arthur ('Oc') and the young poet Rupert Brooke, whom Eddie Marsh had introduced to Winston in quieter days. Churchill had been unwise to ask for them and his colleagues had been unwise to agree, but it was a heady moment; the prime minister wrote to Venetia: 'I have a telegram from Oc sent off from Dover pier on Sunday evening: "Embarking to-night: love." I suppose most of the territorials & recruits would envy him, being sent off after 3 days to the front! I am sure he will do well, but it is a hazardous adventure.' It was also an uncomfortable one. Brooke, who had assumed that after crossing the Channel they would spend a month 'quietly training,' wrote home that they bivouacked their first night under shellfire in the deserted garden of a château and were awakened at 2:00 A.M. 'So up we got – frozen and sleepy – and toiled off through the night. By dawn we got into trenches –

very good ones – and relieved Belgians.'[30]

By sheer force of will, Churchill had taken charge of Antwerp's defence. He was rounding up men, searching for weapons and ammunition, directing troops, siting guns, and telegraphing the Admiralty for high-explosive shells, shell fuses, fire-control balloons, steel rope, entrenching tools, field telephone sets, and '30 Maxim guns on tripod mountings, with establishment of proportionate ammunition.' Excited, aroused, even elated, he sent Asquith a remarkable wire early Monday, suggesting that he quit the cabinet and lead troops: 'If it is thought by HM Government that I can be of service here, I am willing to resign my office and undertake command of relieving and defensive forces assigned to Antwerp in conjunction with Belgian Army, provided that I am given necessary military rank and authority, and full powers of a commander of a detached force in the field.'[31]

. The prime minister was astounded. At the end of a letter to King George, in which he reported that 'Mr Churchill has been in Antwerp since Saturday afternoon & has successfully dissuaded the King & his Ministers from retiring to Ostend,' he noted that he had 'this morning received from Mr Churchill a patriotic offer to resign his office & take command of the forces at Antwerp,' but, while appreciating the first lord's 'zeal and skill,' he had replied that 'his services could not be dispensed with at home.' To Venetia, Asquith was more frank. He thought the proposition 'a real bit of tragi-comedy.' His response to Winston had been 'a *most decided* negative.' When he read it to the cabinet, 'it was received with a Homeric laugh.' Kitchener, the only soldier in the cabinet, did not join in the laughter. He thought the idea sound and was prepared to commission Winston a lieutenant general.[32]

Asquith wouldn't hear of it. The command would go to General Rawlinson, now in Dunkirk. Rawlinson was having difficulty getting through, however, and Winston telegraphed Kitchener: 'In view of the situation and the developing German attack, it is my duty to remain here and continue my direction of affairs unless relieved by some person of consequence.' The British marines went into action that Monday afternoon and threw back an enemy attack. Early in the evening Churchill inspected their lines. They were, he told Kitchener, 'cheerful and well dug in.' Gino Calza Bedolo, war correspondent for the *Giornale d'Italia,* was visiting a position near Lier, southeast of Antwerp, when he saw a striking figure standing in the midst of a group of officers. 'He was still young,' Bedolo told the London Lyceum Club several weeks later, 'and was enveloped in a cloak, and on his head wore a yachtsman's cap. He was tranquilly smoking a large cigar and looking at the progress of the battle under a rain of shrapnel, which I can only call fearful. It was Mr Churchill, who had come to view the situation himself. It must be confessed that it is not easy to find in the whole of Europe a Minister who would be capable of smoking peacefully under that shellfire. He smiled, and looked quite satisfied.'[33]

That night Rawlinson couldn't get closer than Bruges, fifty-one miles away. The Belgians and the Royal Marines were exhausted. Churchill's only reserves were the six thousand inexperienced men in the naval brigades. He didn't want to use them now, and was determined not to expose them to the ferocity of the enemy's storm troops, so he assigned them to a defensive position between the front and the city. At 1:00 A.M. he wired London: 'All well. I have met Ministers in Council, who resolved to fight it out here, whatever happens.' In the early hours of Tuesday, October 6, the weary Belgians actually counterattacked, but were quickly beaten off. Asquith wrote that 'under Winston's stimulus the Belgians are making a resolute stand. I have just seen a telegram which shews that this morning both the Belgians & our Marines were pushed back. The inner forts (it says) are being held by our naval brigade [sic] – which shows that Oc & his companions have arrived & are already within range.' Rawlinson was 'expected shortly.' Presumably the British '7th Division & Cavalry & the French Marines' were on their way. 'It is to be hoped that they will arrive in time, but it is an anxious situation. Winston persists in remaining there, which leaves the Admiralty here without a head . . . I think that Winston ought to return now that a capable General is arriving. He has done good service in the way of starching & ironing the Belges.'[34]

At 5:00 P.M. Rawlinson finally arrived. But he was alone, and his forty thousand men had not even come ashore. For the king and his ministers, that was the last straw. Already the Germans were close enough to pulverize the city with their howitzers. Because of the Belgians' 'complete exhaustion and imminent demoralisation,' Churchill wired, they were evacuating Antwerp. The eight thousand British troops would hold the inner line of defence as long as possible and then follow. Churchill toured the three brigades, one marine and two naval, for the last time. His reception was mixed. Green troops are always shocked by the primitive conditions of life in the field and usually blame those who put them there. These boys had shivered all night in thin oilskins, and one wrote to his father: 'We cursed a car containing Churchill who came out to see what was going on & we were glad when he departed.' After hearing from his son, Asquith wrote to Venetia: 'Strictly between ourselves, I can't tell you what I feel of the *wicked* folly of it all. The Marines of course are splendid troops & can go anywhere & do anything: but nothing can excuse Winston (who knew all the facts) from [sic] sending in the other two Naval Brigades.'[35]

Churchill reached Dover Tuesday night. There he learned that all three brigades of the naval division were fighting in the front line, that Rawlinson had moved his headquarters back to Bruges, and that Clementine had given birth to a daughter. Thursday morning, when he reported to the cabinet, Asquith thought him 'in great form & I think he has thoroughly enjoyed his adventure. He is certainly one of the people one would choose to go tiger-hunting with . . . He was quite ready to take over in Belgium, and did so in fact for a couple of days, the army the navy & the civil government.' Grey wrote to Clementine; 'I can't tell you how much I admire his courage & gallant spirit & genius for war. It inspires us all.' Haldane called the journey 'a great and heroic episode.' Lloyd George told him it was a 'brilliant effort' and then asked: 'What are the prospects?'[36]

The prospects were wretched. Kluck's bombardment was shattering the centre of Antwerp. The French had decided not to send reinforcements. The marine brigade commander was preparing to abandon his trenches. On Saturday the Belgians surrendered while the British troops escaped along the narrow land corridor. Some wandered over the Dutch border and were interned. For the others, Rupert Brooke wrote, the flight 'was like several different kinds of Hell – the broken houses and dead horses lit by an infernal glare. The refugees were the worst sight. The German policy of frightfulness had succeeded so well that out of that city of half a million, when it was decided to surrender, not ten thousand would stay . . . I'll never forget that white-faced endless procession in the night, pressed aside to let the military – us – pass, crawling forward at some hundred yards an hour, quite hopeless, the old men crying and the women with hard drawn faces. What a crime!' Asquith wrote: 'Poor Winston is very depressed, as he feels that his mission has been in vain.'[37]

Others put it much more strongly. The previous Sunday, when prospects seemed relatively bright, Captain Herbert Richmond, the navy's assistant director of operations and a venomous critic of the first lord, had written in his diary at the Admiralty: 'The siege of Antwerp looks ugly. The 1st Lord is sending *his* army there; I don't mind his tuppenny untrained rabble going' – he meant men like Brooke and young Asquith – 'but I do strongly object to 2000 invaluable marines being sent . . . It is a tragedy that the Navy should be in such lunatic hands at this time.' Now, after the capitulation, the Tory press was in full cry, led by H.A. Gwynne, the editor of the *Morning Post*. A *Post* leader called the stand at Antwerp 'a costly blunder, for which Mr W. Churchill must be held responsible . . . We suggest to Mr Churchill's colleagues that they should, quite firmly and definitely, tell the First Lord that on no account are the military and naval operations to be conducted or directed by him.' Gwynne wrote to six members of the cabinet that Antwerp was proof 'that Mr Churchill is unfitted for the office which he now holds,' excoriating him as 'a man who has shown most signally his incompetence at least in time of war.' There were vehement denunciations in *The Times*, and the *Daily Mail*, reprinting the *Post* attack, described the operation as 'a gross example of mal-organization which has cost valuable lives and sacrificed the services during the continuance of the war not only of a considerable number of gallant young Englishmen but also of a considerable section of the Belgian Army.'[38]

Extraordinary stories were circulated. Sir Francis Hopwood, a civil lord of the Admiralty, wrote to Lord Stamfordham that Winston had been aboard a train Friday evening when 'somewhere along the way he heard that the Belgian Government intended to evacuate Antwerp. He rushed back to London and saw K and E. Grey in the small hours of the morning. Then in spite of their remonstrances he left for Antwerp.' Stamfordham, believing it, replied: 'Our friend must be quite off his head.' Beatty wrote to his wife: 'The man must have been mad to have thought he could relieve [Antwerp] . . . by putting 8,000 half-trained troops into it.' The next day he wrote to her again, prophesying that 'this flying about and putting his fingers into pies which do not concern him is bound to lead to disaster.' Bonar Law called Antwerp 'an utterly stupid business'; the first lord, he believed, had 'an entirely unbalanced mind, which is a real danger at a time like this.' Even Churchill's cabinet colleagues were critical. After reflecting upon the expedition, Lloyd George told Frances he felt 'rather disgusted' with Winston. 'Having taken untrained men over there, he left them in the lurch. He behaved in rather a swaggering way when over there, standing for photographers and cinematographers with shells bursting near him.' Asquith, smarting over his son's discomfort, told his wife that the first lord was 'by far the most disliked man in my Cabinet by his colleagues.' Margot wondered why. 'He is rather lovable I think,' she said, 'and though he often bored me before the war I've liked him very much since. I *love* his spirit of adventure – it suits me – and I love his suggestiveness.' Asquith replied irritably: 'Oh! He is intolerable! *Noisy*, longwinded and full of perorations. We don't want suggestion – we want wisdom.'[39]

Because the strategic consequences of Antwerp were being worked out in high secrecy, Churchill could not defend himself in public or in the House. In private letters he pointed out that he had acted with the fullest authority and could hardly be held responsible for the French failure to reinforce the garrison. Welcoming home the brigades on October 18, he pointed out that untrained troops had been used because the need 'was urgent and bitter' and they 'could be embarked the quickest' – an explanation that Asquith, in a letter to the King, had endorsed at the time. The real justification for Antwerp, however, was that, far from being an exercise in futility, it had provided an invaluable contribution to the Allied cause. Asquith knew it, and once his private grievance had healed, he wrote that Churchill, by delaying the fall of the city by at least a week, had 'prevented the Germans from linking up their forces.' On October 29 he added: 'The week at Antwerp was well spent, & had a real effect on the general campaign.' Afterwards the British *Official History of the War* found that while 'the British effort to save Antwerp had failed' it had 'a lasting influence on operations. Until Antwerp had fallen the troops of the investing force were not available to move forward on Ypres and the coast . . . they were too late to secure Nieuport and Dunkirk and turn the northern flank of the Allies as was intended.' And in March 1918 King Albert told a British officer: 'You are wrong in considering the RND [Royal Naval Division] Expedition as a forlorn hope. In my opinion it rendered great service to us and those who deprecate it simply do not understand the history of the War in its early days. Only one man of all your people had the prevision of what the loss of Antwerp would entail and that was Mr Churchill.' The delay, the king continued, 'allowed the French and British Armies to move northwest. Otherwise our whole army might have been captured and the Northern

French Ports secured by the enemy.'[40]

In the autumn of 1914 this was unknown. The British public wasn't even aware that Rawlinson had brought the Belgian army out intact, covering their escape along the Flanders coast, to fight beside the Allies for the next four years. They only knew that the first lord was acquiring a reputation for designing madcap schemes and interfering with the duties of other ministers. Winston himself later concluded that he had erred in taking the field: 'Those who are charged with the direction of supreme affairs must sit on the mountain-tops of control; they must never descend into the valleys of direct physical and personal action.' But at the time the fight for the city had merely whetted his appetite. Believing that the enemy was most vulnerable on his northern flank, he drew up plans for assaults on Borkum and Amesland in the North Sea and a proposal to 'attack with explosives the locks of the Kiel canal or vessels in the canal.' His imagination ranged elsewhere, however; he envisioned campaigns on the Danube or amphibious landings at the Austrian seaport of Kotor on the Adriatic. He even contemplated violations of Dutch neutrality.[41]

Asquith described a long session with Winston, 'who, after dilating in great detail on the actual situation, became suddenly very confidential, and implored me not to take a "conventional" view of his future. Having, as he says, "tasted blood" these last few days, he is beginning like a tiger to raven for more, and begs that sooner or later, & the sooner the better, he may be relieved of his present office & put in some kind of military command. I told him he could not be spared from the Admiralty, but . . . his mouth waters at the sight & thought of K's new armies. Are these "glittering commands" to be entrusted to "dugout trash," bred on obsolete tactics of 25 years ago – "mediocrities, who have led a sheltered life mouldering in military routine" &c &c. For about ¼ of an hour he poured forth a ceaseless cataract of invective and appeal, & I much regretted that there was no short-hand writer within hearing . . . He is a wonderful creature, with a curious dash of schoolboy simplicity (quite unlike Edward Grey's), and what someone said of genius – "a zigzag streak of lightning in the brain." '[42]

In assuming that statesmen could conduct the war, Winston was dwelling in a world of illusion. The politicians having lost control of events and precipitated a general war, the professional militarists of every belligerent nation were in the saddle. The officer classes were declaring that no one should have a voice in the war unless he had spent forty years in uniform – which, as B.H. Liddell Hart acidly observed, would have disqualified Alexander, Hannibal, Caesar, Cromwell, Marlborough, and Napoleon. Antwerp, they said smugly, was an example of what you might expect if civilians were in command. The British public believed them. It was generally assumed in England that Churchill had been responsible for a pointless bloodletting in Belgium. The casualty lists told another story: 57 Englishmen had died at Antwerp; 158 had been wounded. In France, by the end of 1914, the cost was 95,654 British soldiers killed in action.

* * *

The race to the sea was over and no one had won it. A week after the Germans seized Antwerp, they reached the Channel coast and overran Ostend. There they pivoted, to turn the Allied flank. Joffre, however, asked the British to thwart them, and Churchill, in response, ordered heavy shelling from English warships offshore. It worked. Now the Allies attempted to turn the Germans, but by the end of the month it was obvious that the enemy could not be dislodged either. The front was deadlocked. A wavering seam of trenches, within which troops huddled, began on the Swiss border and ended 466 miles away on the shore at Nieuport, just below Ostend. Because the armies on both sides were enormous, the density of human concentration was unprecedented: there was one soldier for every four inches of front. Mobility, and the opportunity for manoeuvre, were gone. The deadlock was as obvious as it was intolerable. Surely, people thought, with the expensive and ingenious arsenals available to general staffs, an early breakthrough was inevitable. It wasn't. It wasn't even possible, because offensive weapons were no match for the weapons available to defenders. And whenever a position was in peril it could be swiftly reinforced; troop trains could rocket to the tottering sector, while the attacking infantrymen could plod no faster than soldiers in the Napoleonic wars.* The British Tommies, bewildered and increasingly fatalistic, turned a gay song into a dirge:

> It's a long way to Tipperary,
> It's a long way to go

They were the first men to be exposed to poison gas, massed machine-gun fire and strafing aeroplanes, and they lived with rats and lice, amid the stench of urine, faeces, and decaying flesh, staring up at the sky by day and venturing out only by night. Separated by the junk of no-man's-land, the great, impotent armies squatted month after month, living troglodytic lives in candle-lit dugouts and trenches hewn from Fricourt chalk or La Bassée clay, or ladled from the porridge of swampy Flanders. In the north the efficient Germans tacked up propaganda signs (*Gott strafe England; Frankreich, du bist betrügen*) and settled down to teach their language to French and Belgian children while the Allies counterattacked furiously. These titanic struggles were called battles, but although they were fought on fantastic scales, strategically they were only siege assaults. Every Allied wave found the kaiser's defences stronger. The poilus and Tommies crawled over their parapets, lay down in front of the jump-off tapes, and waited while their officers studied the

---

* Astonishingly, all this had been predicted in 1899 by a Polish financier named Jean de Bloch. He published a book, *Is War Impossible?* prophesying that war, 'instead of being a hand-to-hand contest . . . will be a kind of stalemate . . . Everybody will be entrenched in the next war. It will be a great war of entrenchments. The spade will be as indispensable to the soldier as his rifle . . . All wars will of necessity partake of the character of siege operations . . . Your soldiers may fight as they please; the ultimate decision is in the hands of famine . . . That is the future of war . . . the bankruptcy of millions and the break-up of the whole social organization' (Wolff, page ix).

new gadgets called wristwatches before blowing their zero-hour whistles. Then the men arose and hurtled towards as many as ten aprons of ropy wire, with barbs thick as a man's thumb, backed by the pullulating Boche. *Morituri te salutamus.* A few trenches would be taken at shocking cost – the price of seven hundred mutilated yards in one attack was twenty-six thousand men – and then the beleaguerment would start again. In London, newspapers spoke of 'hammer blows' and 'the big push,' but the men knew better; a soldiers' mot had it that the war would last a hundred years, five years of fighting and ninety-five of winding up the barbed wire.

> *Keep the home fires burning*
> *Though the hearts are yearning*

It was a weird, grimy life, unlike anything in their Victorian upbringing except, perhaps, the stories of Jules Verne. There were a few poignant reminders of prewar days – the birds that carolled over the lunar landscape each grey dawn; the big yellow poplar forests behind the lines – but most sounds and colours were unearthly. Bullets cracked and ricochets sang with an iron ring; overhead, shells warbled endlessly. There were spectacular red Very flares, saffron shrapnel puffs, and snaky yellowish mists of mustard gas souring the ground. Little foliage survived here. Trees splintered to match-wood stood in silhouette against the sky. Newcomers arriving from Blighty ('The necessary supply of heroes must be maintained at all costs,' said Carson) were shipped up in box-cars built for *hommes* 40 or *chevaux* 8 and marched over duckboards to their new homes in the earth, where everything revolved around the trench – you had a trench knife, a trench cane, a rod-shaped trench periscope, a trench coat if you were an officer, and, if you were unlucky, trench foot, trench mouth, or trench fever.[43] In the course of an average day on the western front, there were 2,533 men on both sides killed in action, 9,121 wounded, and 1,164 missing.

> *Domine Deus, Agnus Dei, Filius Patris:*
> *qui tollis peccata mundi, miserere noblis.*

Even in quiet sectors there was a steady toll of shellfire casualties – the methodical War Office called it 'normal wastage.' The survivors were those who developed quick reactions to danger. An alert youth learned to sort out the whines that threatened him, though after a few close ones, when his ears buzzed and everything turned scarlet, he also realized that the time might come when ducking would do no good. If he was a machine gunner he knew that his life expectancy in combat had been reckoned at about thirty minutes, and in time he became detached towards death and casual with its appliances: enemy lines would be sprayed with belt after belt from water-cooled machine guns to heat the water for soup. Hopes for victory diminished and then vanished. After one savage attempt at a breakthrough Edmund Blunden wrote that 'by the end of the day both sides had seen, in a sad scrawl of broken earth and murdered men, the answer to the question. No road. No thoroughfare. Neither race had won, nor could win, the War. The War had won, and would go on winning.'[44]

> *There's a long, long trail a-winding*
> *Into the land of my dreams*

A month after Antwerp, Churchill received a letter from Valentine Fleming, an MP and fellow officer in the QOOH, now serving in France: 'First and most impressive,' Fleming wrote, were 'the absolutely indescribable ravages of modern artillery fire, not only upon all men, animals, and buildings within its zone, but upon the very face of nature itself. Imagine a broad belt, ten miles or so in width, stretching from the Channel to the German frontier near Basle, which is positively littered with the bodies of men and scarified with their rude graves . . . Day and night in this area are made hideous by the incessant crash and whistle and roar of every sort of projectile, by sinister columns of smoke and flame, by the cries of wounded men . . . Along this terrain of death stretch more or less parallel to each other lines of trenches, some 200, some 1,000 yards apart . . . In these trenches crouch lines of men, in brown or grey or blue, coated with mud, unshaven, hollow-eyed with the continual strain and unable to reply to the everlasting run of shells hurled at them from 3, 4, 5 or more miles away and positively welcoming an infantry attack from one side or the other as a chance of meeting and matching themselves against *human* assailants and not against invisible, irresistible machines . . .' Winston sent this to Clementine with a note: 'What wd happen I wonder if the armies suddenly & simultaneously went on strike and said some other method must be found of settling the dispute! Meanwhile however new avalanches of men are preparing to mingle in the conflict and it widens and deepens every hour.'[45]

Asquith felt desperate. 'I am profoundly dissatisfied with the immediate prospect,' he wrote to his beloved on December 30. He saw the war as 'an enormous waste of life and money day after day with no appreciable progress.' Over the holidays Lloyd George drew up a memorandum predicting that a few more months of trench warfare 'will inevitably destroy the *morale* of the best of troops' and 'any attempt to force the carefully-prepared German lines in the west would end in failure and in appalling loss of life.' Under these conditions, Churchill believed, victory would be 'bought so dear as to be almost indistinguishable from defeat.' There was, however, a difference between his mood and that of the rest of the cabinet. They felt desperate; he felt challenged. The answer to immovable defence, he reasoned, was irresistible assault employing new tactics. He suggested what he described as 'the attack by the spade' – some three hundred interconnected tunnels dug over a two-mile front towards the enemy's lines and emerging within sixty yards of his trenches, where they would be inaccessible to his artillery. Then he proposed a collective metal shield, 'pushed along either on a wheel or still better on a Caterpillar,' behind which several men could hide while crossing no-man's-land.[46]

The War Office dismissed these as absurd, and in fact they were impractical. But he was groping towards something effective. His search had begun on September 23, before the Antwerp crisis, when he had been looking for a way to protect his airmen at Dunkirk. Buying up all available Rolls-Royces, he had ordered them clad in improvised armour. 'It is most important,' he wrote, 'that the . . . armed motor-cars should be provided to a certain extent with cars carrying the means of bridging small cuts in the road, and an arrangement of planks capable of bridging a ten- or twelve-feet span quickly and easily should be carried with every ten or twelve machines.' The bridging apparatus didn't work; it couldn't reach across a double line of trenches. But an army colonel attached to GHQ in France believed it could be made to work. He approached Sir Maurice Hankey, secretary to the cabinet. Hankey approached Churchill, and on January 5, 1915, Winston sent Asquith a memorandum. It would be simple, he wrote, to quickly 'fit up a number of steam tractors with small armoured shelters, in which men and machine guns could be placed, which would be bullet-proof.' A 'caterpillar system would enable trenches to be crossed quite easily, and the weight of the machine would destroy all wire entanglements.' A fleet of them could make 'many *points d'appui* for the British supporting infantry to rush forward and rally on them. They can then move forward to attack the second line of trenches.' The cost would be slight. 'If the experiment did not answer, what harm would be done? It should certainly be done now.'[47]

The idea was not new. H.G. Wells had conceived it in 1903. But it had been science fiction then. Now, with superior steel plating, improved internal-combustion engines, and caterpillar tracks, it was practical. Asquith forwarded Winston's memo to Kitchener, who passed it along to his ordnance general, who pigeonholed it. In February, however, the matter came up again. Dining at the home of the Duke of Westminster, Churchill met Colonel Ernest Swinton, an officer fresh from the BEF who believed a large cross-country armoured car could scale almost any object. The following morning Winston summoned Captain Eustace Tennyson D'Eyncourt, an Admiralty designer, and asked him to devise a 'land ship' using caterpillar treads. Secrecy was urgent; to mislead the Germans, everyone connected with the project would tell the others in the Admiralty that they were making 'water carriers for Russia' – vessels to carry large vats of drinking water into the czar's front lines. Colonel Swinton predicted that the War Office would designate them 'WCs for Russia.' He suggested they be called 'tanks' and Churchill agreed.[48]

On February 20 Winston had the flu, so the first meeting of the 'Land Ship Committee' was held in his Admiralty House bedroom. Four days later he initialled its recommendation 'as proposed & with all dispatch.' An order for a prototype was placed with Messrs Fosters of Lincoln, which suggested using a tractor as a model. By the end of the month Churchill had persuaded Asquith to earmark £70,000 for the committee. On March 9 Winston was shown the first designs. He minuted: 'Press on.' Eleven days later D'Eyncourt asked him to approve manufacture of eighteen tanks. Churchill wrote to him: 'Most urgent. Special report to me in case of delay.' His one fear was that the invention would be disclosed prematurely, before enough of them were ready, thereby destroying the element of surprise and alerting the enemy to the new weapon. But when the first one clanked weirdly across the Horse Guards Parade under his eager eyes, observers from the War Office said tanks weren't wanted at all; they would be unable to cope with mud. Even in the Admiralty the project was called 'Winston's Folly.'[49]

Meanwhile, the insensate killing in France continued. By the end of November, 1914, Britain and France had suffered almost a million casualties. Their leaders were trapped by geography and the sheer mass of the men mobilized. What was needed, *The Times* suggested, was strategy with a 'touch of imagination.'[50] *Vision*, perhaps, would have been a better word. Certainly the cabinet, preferring another battleground, almost *any* other battleground, was straining to look in all directions. Visible and close at hand was the North Sea island of Borkum, which, if seized, could be used in a variant of Fisher's suggestion – as a staging area for an amphibious invasion of the German coast, twelve miles away. Violations of Dutch and Danish neutrality, regarded as unconscionable earlier, were now debated. The only other possibilities lay in the eastern Mediterranean, on the vulnerable edges of the tottering Turkish empire: Salonika in northeastern Greece, Syria, Gallipoli, and the Dardanelles, the strait separating Europe from Asia. Here in southeastern Europe, England might find new allies. Greece, Bulgaria, Rumania, and Montenegro shared a common hatred of the oppressive Turks. Farsighted British imperialists had long dreamed of a Balkan league, a union of Christian states federated with the Empire. Now it seemed to be within reach. In the second week of the war Eleutherios Venizelos, an anglophilic Liberal Greek premier, had proposed an Anglo-Greek alliance and volunteered to send sixty thousand men to occupy Gallipoli. The War Office was enthusiastic; in peacetime, Britain's general staff, like Greece's, had studied the peninsula and concluded that it was ripe for plucking. But Grey, wary of extending England's commitments, and believing he could change his mind later, rejected Venizelos's overture.

If one conceives of the waters in that part of the world as a listing stack of irregular glass globes – the kind of weird, bubbling apparatus Dr Franken-stein used in infusing life into his monster – the vessel on top would be the Black Sea. The Black Sea empties through a bottleneck, the nineteen-mile-long Bosporus, into the Sea of Marmara. Constantinople stands on both banks of the Bosporus strait. The Sea of Marmara, continuing downward, drains through a second channel, the thirty-eight-mile-long Dardanelles, into the Aegean Sea, an arm of the Mediterranean. Until the end of 1914, over 90 per cent of Russia's grain and half its exports had passed through the Bosporus and the Dardanelles, also known as the Hellespont. For ships approaching from the south, the Dardanelles is the key to Constantinople. It is astonishingly slim. Viewed from a height, it looks more like a river, and is in fact no wider than the Hudson at Ossining. At its mouth, by Cape Helles on the

AUSTRIA-HUNGARY

Belgrade

MONTE-
NEGRO

SERBIA

ALBANIA

R U M A N I A

Bucharest

Danube River

BULGARIA

RUSSIA

Odessa

CRIMEA

Sevastopol

B L A C K
S E A

THRACE

Kavalla
Salonika

LEMNOS

LESBOS

AEGEAN
SEA

G R E E C E

M
E
D
I
T
E
R
R
A

RHODES

CRETE

N
E
A
N

S
E
A

CYPRUS

BOSPORUS

Constantinople Uskudar

SEA OF
MARMARA

DARDANELLES

Bursa

Sakarya R

Eskişehir

Angora

Smyrna

OTTOMAN EMPIRE
(TURKEY)

AEGEAN
SEA

GALLIPOLI

Kilid Bahr

The Narrows

Chanak

Sedd-el-Bahr

Kephez
Point

Cape
Helles

DARDANELLES

Kum
Kale

Eren Keui

ASIA
MINOR

0   5000
YARDS

G.W.WARD

The Turkish Theater
1915

0   50   100   200   300
MILES

0   50 100   200   300
KILOMETERS

A F R I C A

418

Aegean, on the tip of the Gallipoli peninsula, it is four thousand yards wide. The banks open up as you proceed upward but then close again at the Narrows, where the channel is less than a mile across. Byron swam it easily in March 1810. Gallipoli forms the western shore of the strait. A military force holding the peninsula would dominate the Dardanelles. In the autumn of 1914 it was defended by a skeletal garrison of Turks.

Churchill was keenly aware of the position's military significance. On August 17, when Turkey was neutral, Asquith had written to his wife: 'The Turk threatens to give trouble in Egypt and elsewhere, and the Germans are doing all they can to get hold of him. Winston is quite prepared to send a swarm of flotillas into the Dardanelles to torpedo the "Goeben" if necessary.' Two weeks later, before the battle of the Marne had even begun and with Turkey still a nonbelligerent, Churchill had persuaded Kitchener to send him two generals, who, with two admirals, would 'examine and work out a plan for the seizure by means of a Greek army of adequate strength of the Gallipoli peninsula, with a view to admitting a British Fleet into the Sea of Marmara.' The following day, with Turkey still neutral, the cabinet had agreed to help Serbia and Rumania and, in Asquith's words, 'to sink Turkish ships if they issue from the Dardanelles.' The prime minister wanted to frighten the Turks out of the war. His first lord expected them to come in. At the same meeting, according to the diary of Joseph Pease, a fellow minister, Churchill proposed that once the first shots had been fired the Admiralty should concentrate on 'landing Greek forces on isthmus on west side of Dardanelles [Gallipoli] & controlling Sea of Marmara.' Grey, troubled, wrote to him four days later: 'I don't like the prospect in the Mediterranean at all, unless there is some turn of the tide in France.' Churchill replied: 'There is no need for British or Russian anxiety abt a war with Turkey . . . The price to be paid in taking Gallipoli wd no doubt be heavy, but there wd be no more war with Turkey. A good army of 50,000 & sea-power – that is the end of the Turkish menace.'[51]

In the last week of September 1914 a British squadron lying off Cape Helles had stopped a Turkish torpedo boat and, finding German soldiers aboard, turned it back. Learning of this, the German officer who had assumed command of the strait had mined the Dardanelles, ordered that all lighthouses be darkened, and erected signs on precipices declaring that the channel was closed. This had been a flagrant violation of an international convention guaranteeing free passage of the strait. Its sequel, the attack on the czar's Black Sea ports by German cruisers flying the Turkish colours, had brought Turkey in as a formal belligerent. Worried about the security of Egypt, Churchill asked Fisher to investigate 'the possibility & advisability of a bombardment of the sea face forts of the Dardanelles.'[52] Fisher found the prospects excellent, and during a ten-minute shelling by British warships, a lucky shot hit the magazine of the enemy position at Sedd-el-Bahr, destroying the fort and most of its guns. The wisdom of this strike is doubtful, however. The Turks, warned, withdrew their big guns to the two ancient, crenellated fortresses guarding the channel's Narrows at Chanak. Later in this campaign

419

the same sin would be repeated again and again. The British would strike a heavy blow. It would be effective but indecisive. They would return to find the enemy alerted and strengthened.

In London the War Council met for the first time on November 25.* Churchill, according to Hankey's notes, urged 'an attack on Gallipoli peninsula. This, if successful, would give us control of the Dardanelles, and we could dictate terms at Constantinople.' Fisher spoke up, asking 'whether Greece might not perhaps undertake an attack on Gallipoli on behalf of the Allies.' Grey then delivered a rueful report. King Constantine, nagged by his German wife, unwilling to fight his cousin the kaiser, and worried about Bulgarian intentions, had vetoed Premier Venizelos's troop offer. Winston, undiscouraged, pointed out that Constantine's throne was wobbly. Surely he could be subverted. They must not give up. Before them lay a chance to execute the greatest flanking movement in history. He felt military greatness stirring within him. 'I have it in me,' he had confided to a friend, 'to be a successful soldier. I can visualize great movements and combinations.' In private he repeated his arguments to Asquith, pressing him to open a new front in the Balkans. On December 5 Asquith wrote to Venetia, 'His volatile mind is at present set on Turkey & Bulgaria, & he wants to organise a heroic adventure against Gallipoli and the Dardanelles: to wh I am altogether opposed.'[53]

By Christmas Winston had reluctantly changed his mind. The troops were unavailable, and he assumed the strait couldn't be taken until they held the peninsula. To be sure, the Dardanelles had been forced by ships alone in 1807, when Napoleon was advancing eastward. Seven British men-of-war under Admiral John T. Duckworth had run the gauntlet, reached the Sea of Marmara, and returned through the channel a week later without losing a single vessel. But twentieth-century fortifications were more imposing. In his early years as first sea lord, Fisher had pondered the Dardanelles problem twice and concluded that it would be 'mightily hazardous.' On March 15, 1911, Winston himself had written to the cabinet: 'It is no longer possible to force the Dardanelles . . . nobody would expose a modern fleet to such perils.' Now, on December 22, 1914, he wrote to Fisher: 'The Baltic is the only theatre in wh naval action can appreciably shorten the war.' The old admiral continued to look eastward. 'I CONSIDER THE ATTACK ON TURKEY HOLDS THE FIELD!' he replied, 'but ONLY if it's IMMEDIATE.' However, his plan called for 75,000 British soldiers now in French trenches, plus the Indian and Egyptian garrisons, none of which were available. Similarly, when Lloyd George wanted to land 100,000 men in Syria or Salonika, the men were not to be had. On December 30 Asquith noted that he had received 'two very interesting

* The War Council had succeeded the Committee of Imperial Defence. In May 1915 the council was dissolved and then replaced, a month later, by the Dardanelles Committee. The committee, in turn, was supplanted by the War Cabinet, which held its first meeting on December 9, 1916. In October 1919 the War Cabinet went the way of the others, and the peacetime cabinet was restored to full authority.

memoranda' from Hankey and Churchill. Both wanted to end the senseless slaughter in the trenches. Hankey pointed out that the BEF was not advancing in France and the British were losing more men than the Germans. He proposed a broad flanking movement through the Balkans. Churchill's minute opened with a ringing cry that the new armies Kitchener was forming ought not to be sent to 'chew barbed wire.' He then renewed his proposal to storm Schleswig-Holstein via Borkum. In his diary Captain Richmond wrote: 'It is *quite mad* . . . It remains with the army, who I hope will refuse to throw away 12000 troops in this manner for the self-glorification of an ignorant and impulsive man.' Refuse they did, and the ministers' frantic search for a better battlefield continued. On New Year's Day the prime minister found two more propositions on his desk, from Lloyd George and, again, from Winston. He noted: 'They are both keen on a new objective & theatre as soon as our troops are ready. W., of course, for Borkum and the Baltic: LG for Salonica to join in with the Serbians, and for Syria!'[54]

The Russians forced their hand. They, too, had lost a million men, and had suffered crushing defeats at Tannenberg and the Masurian Lakes. Their rifles and ammunition were in short supply. Now the Turks were threatening the Caucasus. Grand Duke Nicholas summoned the chief British observer accompanying his army and told him that if the Turkish drive continued, he would have to wheel southward to meet it, reducing his commitment to the German front. This was grave. If the Russians fell back, German troops now fighting in the east could be moved into France. The threat brought Kitchener, until now obsessed with the trenches, into the debate over grand strategy. He came to the Admiralty to suggest a naval 'demonstration at the Dardanelles.' Winston replied that if any such move were to be effective, an infantry commitment would be necessary. When Kitchener returned to the War Office, his staff told him that every English soldier who could be mustered was required on the western front – another standoff. On January 4 Churchill expressed reservations about any attack on Turkey; he still favoured the Baltic. The War Council met repeatedly, pondering plans to relieve the pressure on their harried Russian ally. Kitchener opened the January 8 session with a depressing report: a new German drive in France was imminent. Lloyd George interrupted to say heatedly that trench fighting would never lead to victory. Was there, he asked, no alternative theatre 'in which we might employ our surplus armies to produce a decisive effect?'[55]

Kitchener could think of only one, and he asked the others to support him in backing it. 'The Dardanelles,' he said, 'appear to be the most suitable objective, as an attack here could be made in co-operation with the Fleet. If successful, it would re-establish communications with Russia; settle the Near Eastern question; draw in Greece and, perhaps, Bulgaria and Rumania; and release wheat and shipping now locked up in the Black Sea.' Hankey added that a Dardanelles victory 'would give us the Danube as a line of communication for an army penetrating into the heart of Austria and bring our sea power to bear in the middle of Europe.' The first lord was sceptical. When he asked about troops, the minister for war was evasive. The attack, it seemed, would have to be by ships alone. Churchill therefore rejected it. As late as January 11 he was still pressing for action in the North Sea. The following day, however, events took a sudden, unexpected turn.[56]

Napoleon had written: 'Essentially the great question remains: Who will hold Constantinople?' It does not seem essential today, but before the advent of air power the lovely, decaying, sprawling, 2,600-year-old capital of Byzantium was as vital to control of the world's trade routes as it had been in 85 B.C., when the Roman general Sulla signed a famous treaty with Mithridates VI, king of Pontus, in the ancient city of Dardanus, thereby giving the nearby strait its name. As recently as 1886, Lord Salisbury, when he was successfully negotiating free passage to Constantinople for British ships of the line, had written to Winston's father: 'You are naturally sarcastic about my Dardanelles, and I hope the matter will not come up in our time . . . I consider the loss of Constantinople would be the ruin of our party and a heavy blow to the country.'[57]

Exotic, vaguely sinister with its skyline of onion-domed mosques and slender minarets, its ornate Topkapi Palace housing the sultan's seraglio, its noisome Haydarpasar stews, the luxury hotels overlooking the Bosporus, the Golden Horn separating the city from its wealthy suburbs, Constantinople had seen Saracens and Crusaders eviscerate one another, had watched red-bearded Sultan 'Abdul the Damned' butcher his subjects in the streets, and seemed stained by its memories. Abdul's successors, the Young Turks, were a small improvement on him. Their leader, Enver Pasha, was a vain, shallow, cruel megalomaniac who strutted around in a dandy's uniform, fingering his sword hilt. He and his fellow pashas didn't even treasure their own past; if the British approached, they planned to demolish Constantinople out of spite. Saint Sophia, Hagia Sophia, the Blue Mosque, and other priceless buildings were primed with dynamite. Henry Morgenthau, the American ambassador, begged them to save Saint Sophia at least, but a Young Turk told him: 'There are not six men in the Committee of Union and Progress who care for anything that is old. We all like new things.'[58] They thought of themselves as modern politicians, but they were politically inept. The people mistrusted them deeply; every neutral diplomat believed that at the first sight of a British warship off the Golden Horn, the masses would rise. The Young Turks were proud of their militarism. Yet the country's defences were in wretched shape – obsolete, undermanned, badly led. Actually, the army's officers included a military genius: thirty-three-year-old Mustapha Kemal. But Kemal despised the Germans. Therefore he was banished from Constantinople. As a sign of his low station he was ordered to defend remote Gallipoli.

'I *loathe* the Turk,' Margot Asquith wrote in her diary on November 9, 'and really hope that he will be wiped out of Europe.' Young men of her class saw it rather differently. They held no brief for the country's present rulers, but Asia

Minor fascinated them. Classically educated in England's public schools, they had an almost mystical regard for the heroes who had dominated it in its days of greatness. The city of Troy had stood not four miles from the southern entrance to the Dardanelles. Around it lay the once embattled Troad, now called the Troas Plain. And high above loomed Mount Ida, from whose 5,800-foot peak the gods were said to have witnessed the Trojan War. Upon learning that he was bound for the Bosporus, Rupert Brooke wrote: 'It's too wonderful for belief. I had not imagined Fate could be so benign. . . . Will Hero's Tower crumble under the 15-inch guns? Will the sea be polyphloisbic and wine-dark and unvintageable? Shall I loot mosaics from St Sophia, and Turkish Delight and carpets? Shall we be a Turning Point in History? Oh God! I've never been quite so happy in my life I think. Never quite so pervasively happy; like a stream flowing entirely to one end. I suddenly realise that the ambition of my life has been – since I was two – to go on a military expedition against Constantinople.' It was Brooke, the symbol of the idealistic generation now being fed to the guns, who had just written:[59]

> If I should die, think only this of me:
> That there's some corner of a foreign field
> That is forever England.

Even Churchill, who had despised his Greek classes at Harrow, confronted the Turkish challenge with a quickening pulse; at the climax of his novel, *Savrola,* an admiral had led his ships past a gauntlet of blazing forts. That, however, had been fiction. To the Admiralty, Kitchener's insistence upon a naval attack, unsupported by infantry on Gallipoli, seemed futile. Nevertheless, Churchill summoned his senior admirals and asked their opinion. As he expected, they were pessimistic. Yet he was reluctant to leave the issue there. It was crucial, and not only because of the need for Grand Duke Nicholas to keep Germany's eastern armies tied down. Russia's grain was wanted to feed the Allies; 350,000 tons of it were piled up in the Black Sea ports. Any action in Asia Minor would have to be confined to old battleships not needed by Jellicoe in the North Sea. England's security could not be compromised. As it happened, old battleships were available; in his last naval estimates Winston had provided funds to keep such vessels in commission. There was another factor. 'Like most people,' he testified before a commission investigating the campaign in 1916, 'I had held the opinion that the days of forcing the Dardanelles were over . . . But this war had brought many surprises. We had seen fortresses reputed throughout Europe to be impregnable collapsing after a few days' attack by field armies without a regular siege.' Before he broke the bad news to Kitchener, he decided, he would send a query to Vice Admiral Sackville Carden, commanding the blockading squadron off Cape Helles. He wired him: 'Do you consider the forcing of the Dardanelles by ships alone a practicable operation. It is assumed that older battleships fitted with minebumpers would be used preceded by colliers or other merchant craft as bumpers and sweepers. Importance of results would justify severe loss. Let me know your views.'[60]

Admiral Carden's reply reached the Admiralty on the morning of January 5, 1915, and it was electrifying. 'With reference to your telegram of 3rd instant,' it began, 'I do not consider that the Dardanelles can be rushed. They might be forced by extended operations with large number of ships.' He outlined four phases of action: levelling defences at the entrance, clearing the channel up to the Narrows, reducing the Narrows forts, and the 'final advance to Marmara.' As Churchill later testified, this was '*the* most important telegram. Here was the Admiral, who had been for weeks sitting off the Dardanelles, who presumably had been turning this thing over in his mind again and again, wondering on the possibilities of action there, who produced a plan, and a detailed plan and a novel plan.' He showed it to the sea lords, who were as startled as he was; Fisher enthusiastically volunteered to send Carden his newest superdreadnought, the *Queen Elizabeth*, whose fifteen-inch guns had not even been fired yet. Churchill testified: 'We all felt ourselves in the presence of a "new fact." Moreover, the *Queen Elizabeth* came into the argument with a cumulative effect.' He replied to Carden: 'Your view is agreed with by high authorities here. Please telegraph in detail what you think could be done by extended operations, what force would be needed, and how you would consider it should be used.' In his answer, which arrived in London on January 11, the admiral asked for twelve battleships, three heavy cruisers, three light cruisers, sixteen destroyers, six submarines, four seaplanes, twelve minesweepers, and a score of miscellaneous vessels. He planned to open with a long-range bombardment of the forts; then, with minesweepers leading the way, to sail close and destroy them seriatim. At the same time, the Turks would be misled by diversionary shelling on both coasts of Gallipoli. He wanted a great deal of ammunition, and once he had broken through to the Sea of Marmara, he intended to keep the Dardanelles clear by constant patrolling. 'Time required for operations,' he concluded, 'depends greatly on morale of enemy under bombardment; garrison largely stiffened by the Germans; also on weather conditions. Gales now frequent. Might do it all in a month about.' He proposed to start the operation on February 1 with hull-down fire from the *Queen Elizabeth*.[61]

Churchill laid all this before Asquith and Kitchener early in the afternoon on January 12. He had been particularly pleased with Fisher's response, writing him how glad he was that, as a result of the first sea lord's initiative, the mighty new ship would be 'firing all her ammunition at the Dardanelles forts instead of uselessly into the sea.' At noon the next day he put the War Council in the picture. Sir John French was there. After discussing the progress of plans for an amphibious attack on the German U-boat pens in Zeebrugge, Belgium, which he favoured, Winston stepped up to a map and described Carden's proposal, arguing, as Lloyd George put it, 'with all the inexorable force and pertinacity, together with the mastery of detail he always commands when he is really interested in a subject.' He said the Admiralty could spare the twelve old battleships Carden wanted and add three modern dreadnoughts 'without reducing our strength in the main theatre of war.' Then he said:

'Once the forts are reduced, the minefields will be cleared and the Fleet will proceed up to Constantinople and destroy the *Goeben*.' According to Hankey's memoirs, *The Supreme Command*, 'The idea caught on at once . . . The War Council turned eagerly from the dreary vista of a "slogging match" on the Western Front to brighter prospects, as they seemed, in the Mediterranean.' Asquith liked it now. Lloyd George agreed, and so did Kitchener. Arthur Balfour, present as a senior statesman, thought it would be hard to imagine a more useful operation. K of K said that if the bombardment proved ineffective, they could cancel the rest of the operation. The decision was unanimous: 'That the Admiralty should prepare for a naval expedition and take Gallipoli with Constantinople as its objective.'[62]

Fisher said nothing. The sea lords made a point of never speaking up at these meetings. As he once explained: 'When sailors get round a Council Board they are almost invariably mute. The politicians who are round the Board are never mute; they would never have got there if they had been mute.' Yet even when he was silent his presence was felt, and an understanding of him and the minister for war, the two professionals on the War Council, is essential to a grasp of what was happening and, more important, to what lay ahead. Both were immensely popular with the British public, so much so that the cabinet members, their nominal superiors, would go to almost any lengths to avoid antagonizing them. Erratic and peppery, the old admiral seemed the very personification of English sea traditions, a dauntless figure who ranked with Drake and Nelson. Churchill compared him to 'a great castle, which has long contended with time; the mighty central mass of the donjon towered up intact and seemingly everlasting.' But the mightiest castle crumbles in time, and probably no septuagenarian could have borne the strain of serving as first sea lord in 1915. Moreover, Fisher's temperament was ill-suited to working in harness with Churchill through an endless series of crises. Violet Asquith wrote of the admiral: 'He lived by instincts, hunches, flashes, which he was unable to justify or sustain in argument. Though words poured from his lips and from his pen he was no match for Winston as a dialectician. In trying to defend his own position he trumped up reasons and pretexts of no substance which Winston easily demolished . . . His personal intimacy with Winston and affection for him increased his sense of helplessness in standing up to him.'[63]

Kitchener was underrated by the rest of the cabinet. Like Fisher, he had predicted the year of the war's outbreak, and he had been among the first to see the possibilities of the Dardanelles. It was his tragedy, and England's, that no one dared say no to him. As Churchill testified a year later, 'His prestige and authority were immense. He was the sole mouthpiece of War Office opinion in the War Council . . . He was never, to my belief, overruled by the War Council or the Cabinet, in any military matter, great or small . . . Respect for the man, sympathy for his immense labours, confidence in his professional judgement, and the belief that he had plans deeper and wider than any we could see, silenced misgivings and disputes, whether in the

Council or at the War Office. All-powerful, imperturbable, reserved, he dominated absolutely our counsels at this time.' Sir Osbert Sitwell thought he knew why. Six months earlier, at the time of Sarajevo, Sitwell had written that Kitchener 'plainly belonged to some different order of creation from those around him . . . he could claim kinship to the old race of gigantic German generals, spawned by Wotan in the Prussian plains, and born with spiked helmets ready on their heads . . . he sat there with the same suggestion of immense strength and even of latent fury.'[64]

Kitchener was caught in a bloody debate between the 'Westerners,' as they were called – those who believed the war could be won only in France – and the 'Easterners,' who were convinced that the solution lay in Asia Minor, the Balkans, Italy, or the Baltic. Almost without exception, the Westerners were crusty, stubborn, conservative regular army officers who had been posted to France because that was where the fighting had begun, and whose professional reputations could be made only there. If France became a dead end, their sacrifice of all the lives there would have been made in vain. Haig said the key to victory was 'attrition,' which, his general staff explained, meant 'wearing down the Boches.' But this assumed that more Germans were dying than Englishmen. And it wasn't true. In the struggle for Flanders, three British soldiers fell for every two Germans. In the battle of the Somme, the figures were two British to one German. Incessant shelling back and forth across no-man's-land meant that even in the quietest sector more than a thousand Britons died every week. Sir John French admitted to the War Council that 'complete success against the Germans in the Western theatre of war, though possible is not probable.' When his subordinates heard of this they turned mutinous and began to plot against him. Henry Wilson was alarmed by the news of the Daranelles preparations. He wrote to Bonar Law that 'the way to end this war is to kill Germans, not Turks. The place where we can kill most Germans is here, and therefore every man and every round of ammunition we have got in the world ought to come here. All history shows that operations in a secondary and ineffectual theatre have no bearing on major operations – except to weaken the force there engaged. History, no doubt, will repeat her lesson once more for our benefit.'[65]

This was poppycock. The way to end a war is to win it – defeating the enemy by superior strategy, not by counting his dead, especially when, as in this case, his count is lower than yours. And history refutes Wilson. Day by day, in World War I English losses in France were triple those in World War II, when, with Churchill as prime minister, British armies were fighting all over the world. Between 1914 and 1918 Britain's generals slaughtered the most idealistic generation of young leaders in the history of England, and all to no purpose. Never in the field of human conflict have so many suffered so much to gratify the pride of so few. And this was clear to some men at the time. Those not blinded by chauvinism were shocked and incredulous. Siegfried Sassoon, a decorated hero of the trenches, threw his medal away and wrote: 'Pray God that you may never know / The hell where youth and laughter go.'

'How long,' D.H. Lawrence wrote to Asquith's daughter-in-law Cynthia, 'will the nations continue to empty the future?'[66]

Lord Salisbury had warned the generation of parliamentarians who would succeed him: 'No lesson seems to be so deeply inculcated by experience of life as that you should never trust experts. If you believe doctors, nothing is wholesome; if you believe theologians, nothing is innocent; if you believe soldiers, nothing is safe.' They hadn't forgotten, but they were bullied by the military experts' doctrine of attrition. Thus cowed, they writhed and protested. Lloyd George wept over the millions of youths who did 'their intrepid best to obey the fatuous orders,' advancing 'against the most terrible machine-gun fire directed against troops.' Churchill pointed out: 'A policy of pure attrition between armies so evenly balanced cannot lead to a decision . . . Unless this problem can be solved satisfactorily, we shall simply be wearing each other out on a gigantic scale and with fearful sacrifices without ever reaping the reward.'[67]

These civilian ministers knew the military hierarchy didn't have the answers. But neither did they. Like animals trapped in a maze they scurried this way and that, so confused that they wouldn't have recognised a way out if they had stumbled upon it. In that same War Council meeting which adopted the Dardanelles plan, orders were issued to draw up plans for operations in Salonika, the Netherlands, Rumania, and the Gulf of Kotor on the Adriatic. Lloyd George wanted rolling stock built for the Salonika railroad 'and perhaps barges built for the Danube.' Churchill agreed. 'At the worst,' he said, 'they would be a good feint.' Then he himself, who had just delivered a brilliant presentation of the flanking movement through Turkey, said: 'We ought not to go South until we can do nothing in the North. Is there, for example, no possibility of action in Holland?'[68] Grey replied that there was none. Nothing could be done there until the War Office could provide at least 300,000 soldiers for an expedition. Winston said no more. Calls for troops stopped every ministerial discussion. Troops had to come from Kitchener. Kitchener would have to get them from the BEF, and there would be hell to pay in France. He would have paid if he were sure an operation would succeed. But in this new war, with its machines and gas and mines and land ships that sailed underwater, nothing could guarantee success. Inertia bound him; he sided with his brother officers across the Channel while Fisher, similarly torn, fell back on the peacetime axiom that a good naval commander doesn't risk the vessels entrusted to him.

Actually, Fisher was more confused than Kitchener. Later his conduct would raise questions about his sanity, but his bewilderment on January 13 is understandable. The council had decided that the Dardanelles task force should 'take Gallipoli with Constantinople as its objective.' How could a fleet 'take' a peninsula? How could it occupy a great city? As we know now, the occupation of Constantinople would have been unnecessary; the dissident Turkish mobs would have done the job for them. At the time, however, no one in London could have guessed that. Nevertheless, the plan pleased everyone.

Grey saw neutral states lining up to join the Allies. Arthur Balfour, who had been invited to join the council, not as a member of the Opposition, but as an elder statesman, thought everything about the Dardanelles sounded splendid. The French, similarly enchanted, offered four battleships. The Russians hinted that they might send troops, which was impractical. Kitchener, who did not know that, was delighted.

Churchill now set aside all thoughts of a Baltic campaign and concentrated on the Dardanelles. He believed the battle was as good as won, always a dangerous assumption in war. By coincidence January 13 was the Russian New Year, and he had sent an extravagant holiday message to Saint Petersburg: 'Our resources are within reach and inexhaustible; our minds are made up. We have only to bend forward together laying aside every hindrance, keeping nothing back, and the downfall of the German ambition is sure.' For the next week he and an ad hoc Admiralty war group examined every particular detail of the coming attack, sending and receiving telegrams from Carden almost hourly. Each instruction, each technical problem, was read, endorsed, and initialled by the first sea lord with the famous scrawled green F. Yet the old admiral was seething. Like a tumour, an irrational terror was growing in him – the fear that the Aegean expedition would weaken the Home Fleet, encouraging Tirpitz to steam into Scapa Flow with a superior force, sink every British warship left there, and win the war. In that case Jellicoe would become the defeated admiral. But he did not share the first sea lord's doubts. He kept sending him reassurances. Fisher was unconsoled. On January 19, six days after the decision, he wrote to Jellicoe that the ships sailing to the eastern Mediterranean were '*all urgently required at the decisive theatre at home!* There is only one way out, and that is to resign! But you say "*no,*" which simply means I am a consenting party to what I absolutely disapprove. *I don't agree with one single step taken,* so it is fearfully against the grain that I remain on in deference to your wishes.' The next day he wept on Hankey's shoulder. Hankey told Asquith, who wrote to Venetia that the old man was 'in a very unhappy frame of mind,' that he 'likes Winston personally' but was frequently overruled ('he out-argues me') on purely technical naval matters.'[69]

The Dardanelles assault had been approved, not by Churchill, but by the entire War Council. Fisher had participated in every step taken since then. Winston had no inkling of his anxiety until, eight days after the arrival of Carden's plan of attack, the first sea lord urged the recall of the destroyer flotilla and an Australian submarine which had been sent to the Aegean from Scapa Flow. He himself had suggested the dispatch of the *Queen Elizabeth,* but on January 21, in another letter to Jellicoe, he wrote that its transfer was 'a serious interference with our imperative needs in Home waters, and I've fought against it "tooth and nail." . . . I just abominate the Dardanelles operation, unless a great change is made and it is settled to be a military operation, with 200,000 men in conjunction with the Fleet. I believe that

Kitchener is coming now to this view of the matter.' But Kitchener wasn't, at least not yet. Thus far the War Office had not been drawn in. Churchill would have been elated had K of K offered 200,000 men, or even a fraction of that. Lacking troops, Winston was moving forward on the strength of Carden's professional opinion. All of them had endorsed it, including Fisher. Yet the old salt continued to have second thoughts. His blaming Churchill was a consequence of senility. Matters had come to a head; even he recognized that, and so, on January 25, he submitted a rebellious memorandum to the first lord, with a request that it be printed and circulated among members of the War Council before their next meeting, scheduled three days hence. His paper was a flat renunciation of the entire Dardanelles plan. 'We play into Germany's hand,' he wrote, 'if we risk fighting ships in any subsidiary operations such as coastal bombardments or the attack of fortified places without military co-operation, for we thereby increase the possibility that the Germans may be able to engage our Fleet with some approach to equality of strength. The sole justification of coastal bombardments . . . is to force a decision at sea, and so far and no further can they be justified.' Therefore, the Admiralty should be satisfied with blockading the enemy: 'Being already in possession of all that a powerful fleet can give a country we should continue quietly to enjoy the advantage without dissipating our strength in operations that cannot improve the position.'[70]

Churchill was stunned. He immediately drew up a table comparing the naval strengths of Britain and Germany, pointing out that England's domination of the North Sea would be unweakened by the Dardanelles task force. Jellicoe concurred. Fisher wouldn't budge. Asquith refused to circulate either his memorandum or Winston's table. On the morning of the next War Council meeting Churchill found Fisher's resignation on his desk. 'I entreat you to believe,' he said in part, 'that if as I think really desirable for a complete *"unity of purpose"* in the War that I should gracefully disappear and revert to roses at Richmond (*"The heart untravelled fondly turns to home"*) that there will not be in my heart the least lingering thought of anything but regard and affection and *indeed much admiration* towards yourself.'[71]

Winston hurried across the Horse Guards Parade to No. 10. Asquith, furious, summoned Fisher to his upstairs study, heard his version and Churchill's, and told them his decision. As a sop to Fisher, the Zeebrugge operation was shelved. The Dardanelles plan would stand unchanged. The three men then descended to the Cabinet Room to join the council. Fisher remained taciturn as usual until Churchill mentioned French and Russian reactions to Carden's coming campaign in Turkey. At that he spoke up, saying he had 'understood that this question would not be raised today, and the Prime Minister is well aware of my views in regard to it.' With that, he rose, left the table, and stood at a window with his back to the others. Kitchener went to him. Fisher, tight-lipped, said he was leaving the Admiralty. Kitchener pointed out that everyone else believed in the plan, that the prime minister had issued the directive, and that it was the first sea lord's duty to follow orders. Reluctantly the old admiral returned to his seat. As he himself said later, 'Naval opinion was unanimous. Mr Churchill had them all on his side. I was the only rebel.' Asquith told the meeting that Churchill was anxious to have everyone's views on the importance of the coming campaign. Kitchener considered the naval attack to be 'vitally important. If successful, its effect would be the equivalent of a successful campaign fought with the new armies.' Grey said it would settle the situation in the Balkans, particularly in Bulgaria. Balfour was rhapsodic. He thought it would cut Turkey in half, turn Constantinople into an Allied base, provide them with Russian wheat, and open a passage to the Danube. 'It is difficult,' he said, to 'imagine a more helpful operation.'[72]

During these cheerful forecasts, Asquith scribbled a note to Venetia: 'A personal matter which rather worries me is the growing friction between Winston and Fisher.' As the council broke for lunch, the prime minister called the old salt to his study, and, after a turbulent hour, persuaded him to support it. Fisher, indeed, seemed to have been transformed into an enthusiast. He even suggested – and the offer was accepted – that Carden be reinforced by two 1908 battleships from Scapa Flow, the *Lord Nelson* and the *Agamemnon*. 'When I finally decided to come in,' he later testified, 'I went the whole hog, totus porcus.' Churchill sprang a surprise during that afternoon's session. He announced that he didn't want troops even if Kitchener offered them. 'A landing in force under fire on the Gallipoli peninsula' once the Turks were 'fully awakened,' he argued, would involve 'a greater stake.' A successful naval action could produce 'revolutionary effects at Constantinople and throughout the Balkans.' The prospects for success were so bright that he believed it worthwhile 'to try the naval plan' even though, if it failed, 'a subsequent military operation' would be rendered 'more difficult.' If a brigade of Tommies was available, he suggested, it should be sent to Salonika, where, he believed, the appearance of no more than 10,000 British soldiers would bring Greece's 180,000 troops into the war. As the dinner hour approached, he conferred with Fisher and Vice Admiral Henry Oliver, chief of the Admiralty War Staff, then told the council, with Fisher's approval, that the Admiralty was united in its determination to 'make a naval attack on the Dardanelles.' Oliver said: 'The first shot will be fired in about a fortnight.'[73]

Actually, it would not be fired for over three weeks. Meanwhile, misunderstandings and disagreements, inherent in war by committee, multiplied. 'No single man,' Robert Rhodes James has observed, 'can, or should, bear responsibility for the series of decisions, half-decisions, and evasions of decisions that marked the initiation of the Gallipoli campaign. The manner in which the Asquith Government drifted into this vast commitment of men and resources . . . condemns not any individual but rather the system of war government practised by the Administration.' Churchill, however, had become the operation's most visible advocate and its most eloquent spokesman. As he saw the situation in early 1915, France had become an abattoir, the Russians were bogged down, the German fleet refused to come out and fight, and the world's finest military instrument, the Royal Navy, was idle. There-fore, as Asquith noted, 'Winston is for the moment as keen as mustard about his Dardanelles adventure.' It had become *his* Dardanelles adventure. Even the prime minister now thought of it that way. As such, it would become a cross he bore for years. Later it was seen as a monument to his genius. In *Through the Fog of War*, Liddell Hart wrote: 'Everyone realizes that, in the words of the German official account, "Churchill's bold idea was not a finespun fantasy of the brain." We too now know, as the Germans did in the War, how feasible was the Dardanelles project, and how vital its effect would have been.' Another writer, Edward, Grigg, declared that had Churchill's advice been followed – had he had the power of the prime minister – 'not only the entire development of the First World War but also the fate of Britain, and Europe, too, would have been different.'[74]

But he was *not* prime minister. In attempting to reshape the entire direction of the war from the Admiralty, he was headed for rocks and shoals. It was Antwerp again – in spades. As he recalled in 1949: 'I was ruined for the time being over the Dardanelles, and a supreme enterprise cast away, through my trying to carry out a major and combined enterprise of war from a subordinate position.' Ian Hamilton described him as 'one who has it in him to revive the part of Pitt, had he but Pitt's place.' Lacking it, he was unable to force, not the Dardanelles, but Britain's naval and military commanders. Moreover, being wholly competent himself, he assumed that they were, too. They weren't. Hindenburg called the British soldiers of that war 'lions led by donkeys.'[75] Some were stupid; others were devious. Haig told the War Office that the Germans being taken prisoner were in wretched condition, proof that the enemy was scraping the bottom of the barrel; when the prime minister crossed the Channel to see for himself, Haig packed a POW camp with sick, scrawny captives. Able politicians should see through such scams. They are, or ought to be, shrewd judges of men, and Churchill's continuing misjudgement of Fisher, his failure to realize that his first sea lord was a Judas, spelled trouble ahead. So did his puzzling claim that he didn't need troops on Gallipoli.

At first it passed unnoticed. At the next meeting of the War Council, on February 9, Churchill informed them of a dazzling *coup de maître*. Venizelos had been persuaded to defy his king and turn the Greek island of Lemnos over to the British as a base for operations against Turkey. It was a masterstroke, accomplished with tact and restraint – Winston had overruled Fisher's pre-posterous proposal that they annex Lemnos and Lesbos – and the ministers were too elated to question this intrusion into Grey's domain. It was four days later, when the warships detailed to shell the Dardanelles had assembled off Cape Helles, and Carden was awaiting the last minesweepers before attacking, that Hankey became the first to challenge Winston's position on troops. He approached Asquith, who wrote to Venetia that Hankey 'thinks very strongly that the naval operations of which you know should be supported by landing a fairly strong military force. I have been for some time coming to the same opinion, and I think we ought to be able without denuding [Sir John] French to scrape together from Egypt, Malta & elsewhere a sufficiently large contingent.' Others were reaching the same conclusion independently. The next day Richmond sent Hankey a memorandum arguing that 'the bombardment of the Dardanelles, even if all the forts are destroyed, can be nothing but a local success, which without an army to carry it on can have no further effect.' Hankey replied, 'Your Memo. is absolutely A.1 . . . I am sending it to Jacky.' Fisher wrote to Richmond: 'YOUR PAPER IS EXCELLENT.' That same day Admiral Sir Henry Jackson submitted a minute to the first lord: 'The naval bombardment is not recommended as a sound military operation unless a strong military force is ready to assist in the operation, or, at least, follow it up immediately the forts are silenced.'[76]

All this gave Churchill pause. In first broaching the subject of the Dardanelles, he had specified the need for infantry; his switch had been based on Carden's assurance that warships could do the job alone. Now, a month later, he belatedly roused himself and cast about for sources of troops. As it happened, the very day he received Jackson's opinion, the Greeks rejected Grey's offer of a Salonika expedition. That meant a first-class division, the Twenty-ninth, was available for assignment elsewhere. Asquith called an emergency meeting of the War Council. Kitchener agreed that the Twenty-ninth should sail to Lemnos 'at the earliest possible date.' There they would be joined by a marine brigade and the Australian and New Zealand troops now in Egypt, all of which would be available 'in case of necessity to support the naval attack on the Dardanelles.' The first lord was directed to assemble sufficient transports to carry 'a force of 50,000 men at any point where they might be required.' The attempt on the strait was now imminent. K of K passed Winston a note: 'You get through! I will find the men.'[77]

The bond between Churchill and Kitchener was vital to the campaign, and at this very unfortunate moment it was cut. The origins of the dispute are unclear. Apparently Winston, on one of his visits to France, had told Sir John French that he might be in a position to lend him some Admiralty troops and equipment. It had been an informal remark. It was also ill-advised. K of K was sensitive about his prerogatives. When French sent the War Office a written request for the men and the matériel Churchill had so unwisely dangled before him, the war minister went straight to the prime minister. Asquith wrote to Winston: 'Kitchener has just been to see me in a state of some perturbation. He has just received two official letters from French, in which he announces that you have offered him a Brigade of the Naval Division, and 2 squadrons of armoured cars. Kitchener is strongly of the opinion that French has no need of either. But, apart from that, he feels (& I think rightly) that he ought to have been told of, & consulted about, the offer before it was made.' That evening Margot Asquith wrote in her diary: 'Of course Winston is intolerable. It is all *vanity* – he is devoured by vanity . . . It's most trying as K and he had got a modus vivendi.' Churchill explained that it was all a misunderstanding, but in the morning Asquith wrote to Venetia: 'I am rather vexed with Winston who has been tactless enough to offer Sir John F (behind K's back & without his knowledge) a brigade of his Naval Division, and 2 squadrons of his famous Armoured Cars which are being hawked about from pillar to post.'[78]

On such petty quarrels did the fate of millions hang. Winston wrote Kitchener on February 19, attempting a reconciliation. It wasn't enough. The war minister's rage was still glowing when the War Council met that afternoon to confirm its decision, made three days earlier, to send the Twenty-ninth Division to Lemnos. K of K bluntly told the dismayed ministers that he had changed his mind. He had decided to withhold, not only the nineteen thousand trained men of the Twenty-ninth Division, but also the thirty thousand Australians and New Zealanders in Egypt. Asquith, Churchill, and Lloyd George protested – Lloyd George thought even these wouldn't be enough; he wanted to reinforce them with the ten-thousand-man Royal Naval Division, fifteen thousand Frenchmen, and ten thousand Russians. Grey's support was tepid; Lemnos rankled, after all. Kitchener said he would think it over. But four days later when Winston repeated his request for men – it was 'not a question of sending them immediately to the Dardanelles,' he explained, 'but merely of having them within reach' – K of K replied that the Twenty-ninth still could not be spared. The Russian front was fluid, he had said; if disaster struck there, the men of the Twenty-ninth were 'the only troops we have available as a reserve to send over to France.' It was his impression that the Dardanelles had been conceived as a naval attack; did Churchill plan to lead an army, too? Not at all, said Winston. He could, however, imagine a situation in which victory was within reach 'but where a military force would just make the difference between success and failure.' One senses his frustration when Lloyd George, his strongest supporter in the last discussion, now warned against using troops 'to pull the chestnuts out of the fire for the Navy,' suggesting that if the Dardanelles miscarried, 'we ought to be immediately ready to try something else' in the Middle East – presumably Syria, his pet idea. Kitchener was immovable. He doubted the Turks would try to defend Gallipoli. Churchill said they might have forty thousand men there already. If so, Kitchener predicted, they would evacuate the peninsula after the bombardment.[79]

The War Council voted to postpone further discussion of the division's destiny until the next meeting. Winston, appalled and angry, demanded that his objection be entered in the council's minutes, and so it was: 'MR CHURCHILL said that the XXIX Division would not make the difference between failure and success in France, but might well make the difference in the East. He wished it to be placed on record that he dissented altogether from the retention of the XXIX Division in this country. If a disaster occurred in Turkey owing to the insufficiency of troops, he must disclaim all responsibility.' That evening he wrote to his brother that this 'was vy vexatious to me, & hard to bear . . . The capacity to run risks is at famine prices. All play for safety. The war is certainly settling on to a grim basis, & it is evident that long vistas of pain & struggle lie ahead. The limited fund of life & energy wh I possess is not much use in trying to influence these tremendous moments. I toil away.'[80]

Asquith shared his chagrin, but such was Kitchener's power to intimidate that even the prime minister wasn't prepared to risk offending him. Of this pivotal meeting he wrote to Venetia: 'We are all agreed (except K) that the naval adventure in the Dardanelles shd be backed up by a strong military force.' Kitchener was being 'very sticky,' he thought, because 'he wants to have something in hand, in case the Germans are so far successful against Russia for the moment, as to be able to despatch Westwards a huge army – perhaps of a million – to try & force Joffre & French's lines.' Asquith himself felt that 'one must take a lot of risks in war, & I am strongly of the opinion that the chance of forcing the Dardanelles, & occupying Constantinople . . . presents such a unique opportunity that we ought to hazard a lot elsewhere rather than forgo it. If K can be convinced, well & good: but to discard his advice & overrule his judgement on a military question is to take a great responsibility. So I am rather anxious.'[81]

Churchill at any rate could send the Royal Naval Division, survivors of Antwerp. For the first time in his life he joined a royal entourage; he and the prime minister accompanied George V to Blandford, where the King reviewed the men before they shipped out. Oc Asquith was there, and Rupert Brooke. Margot wrote in her diary: 'The whole 9,000 men were drawn up on the glorious downs and Winston walked round and inspected them before the King arrived. I felt quite a thrill when I saw Oc and Rupert with walking sticks standing in front of their men looking quite wonderful! Rupert is a beautiful young man and we get on well, he has so much intellectual temperament and nature about him. He told Oc he was quite *certain* he would never come back but would be killed – it didn't depress him at all but he was just *convinced* – I shall be curious to see if this turns out to be a true instinct . . . *They marched past perfectly.* I saw the silver band (given to the Hood Division by Winston's constituents) coming up the hill and the bayonets flashing – I saw the uneven ground and the straight backs – 'Eyessssss RIGHT!' – and the darling boy had passed. The King was pleased and told me they all marched wonderfully.' Brooke wrote:[82]

> Now, God be thanked, Who has matched us
>   with His hour,
> And caught our youth, and wakened us from
>   sleeping.

His instinct turned out to be true. In two months he was dead. He had been twenty-seven years old. Winston wrote his obituary in *The Times*: 'This life has closed at the moment when it seemed to have reached its springtime. A voice had become audible, a note had been struck, more true, more thrilling, more able to do justice to the nobility of our youth in arms engaged in this present war, than any other – more able to express their thoughts of self-surrender, and with a power to carry comfort to those who watched them so intently from afar. The voice has been swiftly stilled. Only the echoes and the memory remain.'[83]

It wasn't much. His father, a housemaster at Rugby, where Rupert had been so popular, drew small comfort from it. His dons at King's College, Cambridge, wondered instead what he would have become. Oc grieved for a year. Then he himself, having survived the Dardanelles, was killed in France.

But they had marched well at Blandford. Even the King had remarked on it.

Sackville Hamilton Carden was not the ideal commander for the Aegean squadron. Approaching sixty, he had been superintendent of the Malta dockyards until the outbreak of the war and lacked the temperament of a fighter. Churchill's candidate for the appointment had been Sir Arthur Limpus, a younger, more aggressive admiral who had studied the Dardanelles for years, but in early September, when Turkey had still been neutral, Grey had felt that naming Limpus would provoke the Turks. Carden was an able strategist. His plan to rush the Dardanelles was sound. But he was a worrier. He worried about the heavy concentration of enemy guns on the banks of the strait and was uncomforted by assurances that they were small, obsolete, and poorly sited. Driftage in the channel troubled him; although there was no tide in the strait, tributaries and melting snows produced a five-knot current, and chunks of floating ice could be expected at this time of the year. Vessels which could navigate the Orkney Islands, however, would have no problems here. The danger of minefields preyed on his mind. This was a real hazard, but the Admiralty had judged the risk acceptable and provided him with sufficient minesweepers. None of these objections mattered in themselves. Carden's weakness was that, faced with an operation requiring exceptional daring, he was unsure of himself. It was a disease among military leaders in that war, and it was catching. Confronted by so many martial innovations, most senior officers had by 1915 become excessively cautious and easily discouraged. Bravery had nothing to do with it. Carden's second in command, Vice Admiral John de Robeck, was brave in battle, but faced with crucial decisions, he would prove to be of the same stripe.

Their long-awaited attack opened at 9:51 on the blustery morning of Friday, February 19, 1915. The Allied task force – eight British battleships, four French – approached the mouth of the strait and opened fire on the Turkish forts guarding its lips, Kum Kale and Cape Helles. It was no contest. The range of the defensive batteries was so short that their shells couldn't even reach the ships. At two o'clock that afternoon the warships closed to six thousand yards; at 4:45 P.M. de Robeck led *Vengeance, Cornwallis,* and *Suffren* closer still. Most of the blockhouses, shrouded in smoke, appeared deserted. Then night fell. High seas, snow, and sleet prevented further action until the following Thursday. But in the interim Carden, encouraged by the one-sided duel, telegraphed the Admiralty: 'I do not intend to commence in bad weather leaving result undecided as from experience on first day I am convinced given favourable weather conditions that the reduction of the forts at the entrance can be completed in one day.'[84] When the weather cleared, de Robeck carried the assault up to the very muzzles of the blockhouses. The remaining Turkish and German gunners fled northward. Royal Marines landed on Gallipoli, spiking guns and destroying searchlights. Another party went ashore at Kum Kale. Minesweepers penetrated the strait six miles upstream, to within three thousand yards of Kephez Point, without meeting significant resistance. Carden wired London that he expected to reach Constantinople in two weeks.

The War Council was ecstatic. Fisher wanted to hurry to the Aegean and lead the next assault, on the Narrows. The export of Russian wheat seemed imminent; in Chicago the price of grain fell sharply. Churchill, meanwhile, was counting all his unhatched chickens. At the end of February he cabled Grand Duke Nicholas: 'The progress of an attack on Dlles is encouraging & good & we think the Russian Black Sea Fleet shd now get ready at Sebastopol to come to the entrance of the Bosporus at the right moment, of wh we will send notice.' Asquith wrote to Venetia: 'Winston is breast high about the Dardanelles.' The same evening the political climate in Athens went through yet another transformation. King Constantine was having second thoughts. Like the rest of the Balkan rulers, he wanted to be on the winning side. Violet Asquith was 'sitting with Clemmie at the Admiralty when Winston came in in a state of wild excitement and joy. He showed us, under many pledges of secrecy, a telegram from Venizelos promising help from the Greeks . . . Our joy knew no bounds.' Violet asked if Constantine knew of this. 'Yes,' said Churchill, 'our Minister said Venizelos had already approached the King and he was in favour of war.' Moreover, he went on, Bulgaria, Rumania, and Italy were all 'waiting – ready to pounce – all determined to play a part in the fall of Constantinople.' Violet recrossed the Horse Guards 'treading on air. Turkey, encircled by a host of enemies, was doomed, the German flank was turned, the Balkans for once united and on our side, the war shortened perhaps by years, and Winston's vision and persistence vindicated.'[85]

He was already contemplating peace terms. To Grey he wrote two days later: 'We must not disinterest ourselves in the final settlement of this region . . . I am having an Admy paper prepared abt the effect of a Russian control of the Straits and Cple. I hope you will not settle anything further until you can read it. English history will not end with this war.' Others were also looking to the future. Fisher wrote Winston: '*Moral: – Carden to press on!* and Kitchener to occupy the deserted Forts at extremity of Gallipoli and mount howitzers there! . . . Invite Bulgaria by telegram (direct from Sir E. Grey) to take Kavalla and Salonica provided she *at once* attacks Turkey and tell Greece "*Too late*"! and seize the Greek Fleet by a "coup" later on. They wd probably join us now *if bribed!* All the kings are against all the peoples! Greece, Bulgaria, Rumania! *What an opportunity for Democracy!*' Asquith told Venetia that one of his ministers had written 'an almost dithyrambic memorandum urging that in the carving up of the Turks' Asiatic dominions, we should take Palestine, into which the scattered Jews cd in time swarm back from all the quarters of the globe, and in due course obtain Home Rule. (What an attractive community!)' Hankey had prepared a seven-page paper: 'After the Dardanelles: The Next Steps.' He advocated a broad drive by British, Serbian, Greek, Rumanian, and Russian troops, targeted on the Carpathian Mountains between what are now Czechoslovakia and Poland. Others wanted to follow the Danube from the Black Sea through Austria-Hungary, into Germany's Black Forest. Churchill, to whom the War Council now listened with great respect, disagreed. 'We ought not to make the main lines of advance up the Danube,' he said on March 3. 'We ought not to employ more troops in this theatre of war than are absolutely essential in order to induce the Balkan states to march.' He still believed that the proper strategy was an 'advance in the north through Holland and the Baltic.'[86]

During this euphoric interlude, Kitchener's Twenty-ninth Division shrank in significance. Churchill told the War Council that in exploiting Constantinople's capitulation they could count on 140,000 men: the British troops in Egypt, the Royal Naval Division now at sea, 2,000 Royal Marines already on Lemnos, a French division, the three Greek divisions Venizelos had promised, and a Russian corps preparing to embark at Batum, the Black Sea port near the Russo-Turkish border. He hadn't even counted the Rumanians, Bulgarians, and Italians waiting in the wings. Greece's 60,000 troops alone could seize and fortify Gallipoli. But speed, as Fisher had noted, was essential. On March 4 Winston wrote to Grey: 'Mr Venizelos shd be told *now* that the Admiralty believe it in their power to force the Dardanelles without military assistance, destroying all the forts as they go. If so, Gallipoli Peninsula cannot be held by Turks, who wd be cut off & reduced at leisure. By the 20th inst 40,000 British Infantry will be available to go to C'nople, if the Straits have been forced, either by crossing the Bulair Isthmus, or going up the Dardanelles. A French Divn will be on the spot at the same time. M. Venizelos shd consider Greek military movements in relation to these facts.'[87]

It was at this point that what he later called 'the terrible Ifs' began to accumulate. If Greece had entered the war then, everything would not have hinged on Carden's conquest of the Narrows. The forts there could have been taken from the rear, by land. Churchill warned Grey two days later: 'If you don't back up *this* Greece – the Greece of Venizelos – you will have another wh will cleave to Germany.'[88] Precisely that happened. It wasn't Grey's fault. The blame lay in Saint Petersburg. Both London and Paris agreed that King Constantine should receive Constantinople's surrender. The czar, who more than anyone else needed a victory on this front – whose very life depended on it – refused even to discuss the idea. The Bosporus was *his*, he told the incredulous British ambassador on March 3; once Constantine entered it in triumph he would never leave. When word of this reached Athens three days later, the Venizelos government fell and was replaced by German sympathizers led by M. Zaimis, who held that Greece must remain neutral

437

because it was threatened by an invasion of Bulgarians. The first domino had failed to topple. The others awaited events in the Dardanelles.

That same day Carden began to encounter difficulties – nothing serious, but enough to exasperate him and temper the enthusiasm at home. Turkish riflemen appeared at Cape Helles and Kum Kale and drove off the British landing parties. Gales and another storm developed on March 8, and when the sky cleared the admiral's battleship captains, ordered to silence the land batteries between Kephez Point and Chanak, reported that they couldn't get within range of them. Minefields barred the way. It was then that the admiral discovered his Achilles' heel. By tradition, British trawlers used for minesweepers were manned by civilians, fishermen recruited in England's commercial ports. The Turkish guns couldn't reach the warships, but they were raking the trawlers, which backed away. One trawler officer told Commodore Roger Keyes, Carden's chief of staff, that his men 'recognize sweeping risks and don't mind getting blown up, but they hate the gunfire, and point out that they aren't supposed to sweep under fire, they didn't join for that.'[89]

Keyes, the ablest officer in the operation, called for volunteers from his Royal Navy tars. Meanwhile, he offered the fishermen bonuses. That night the trawlers tried again. The enemy surprised them with huge searchlights from Germany, uncrated that very afternoon. Blinded by their glare, the sweeper crews turned tail. Keyes pointed out that the enemy fire, though deafening, was wild. He persuaded them to try again the following night. Again they fled. As he wrote afterwards: 'I was furious and told the officers in charge that they had had their opportunity . . . It did not matter if we lost all seven sweepers, there were twenty-eight more, and the mines had got to be swept up. How could they talk of being stopped by heavy fire if they were not hit? The Admiralty were prepared for losses, but we had chucked our hand in and started squealing before we had any.'[90]

In London, Churchill agreed. That same day – March 11 – he wired Carden: 'Your original instructions laid stress on caution and deliberate methods, and we approve highly the skill and patience with which you have advanced hitherto without loss. The results to be gained are, however, great enough to justify loss of ships and men . . . We do not wish to hurry you or urge you beyond your judgement, but we recognize clearly that at a certain period in your operations you will have to press hard for a decision, and we desire to know whether you consider that point has now been reached.' There was no reply – Winston terrified Carden – but in forty-eight hours the bluejacket volunteers were ready, and despite the arrival of new German searchlights and more accurate fire, the sweepers persevered. In the morning shoals of mines, cut adrift by the trawlers' kites, floated southward with the current. In four or five days, Carden's staff believed, they would be ready to assault the Narrows. But Churchill was impatient. And his query was still unanswered. He telegraphed again: 'I do not understand why minesweeping should be interfered with by firing which causes no casualties. Two or three hundred casualties would be a moderate price to pay for sweeping up as far as the Narrows . . . This work has to be done whatever the loss of life and small craft and the sooner it is done the better. Secondly, we have information that the Turkish forts are short of ammunition, that German officers have made desponding reports and have appealed to Germany for more. Every conceivable effort is being made to supply ammunition. It is being seriously considered to send a German or Austrian submarine, but apparently they have not yet started. Above is absolutely secret. All this makes it clear that the operations should now be pressed forward methodically and resolutely by night and day. The unavoidable losses must be accepted. The enemy is harassed and anxious now. The time is precious as the interference of submarines would be a very serious complication."[91]

The first lord's information about the enemy's ammunition shortage was accurate. German messages had been intercepted and decoded. As he testified the following year, it was this intelligence coup 'that led Lord Fisher and me, with the assent of those whom we were consulting over it, to change the methodical advance and the step-by-step bombardment . . . into a more decided and vehement attempt to quell and smash up the fortresses at the Narrows and force them to use their ammunition.' At the time, however, security precautions prevented him from revealing his source to Carden. The strain and suspense were too much for the admiral. He replied that he expected to lunge at the Narrows on March 17, but he was exhausted. On the morning of March 15, after two sleepless nights, he told Keyes that he could not survive more pressure from Churchill. He had decided to resign his commission. His staff tried to argue him out of it, but a Harley Street neurologist serving with the fleet examined him and said the admiral was near collapse; his nerves were shot; he must be sent home immediately. Thus, less than two days before the critical attempt on the Narrows, the command devolved on de Robeck. The Admiralty telegraphed him: 'Personal and Secret from First Lord. In entrusting to you with great confidence the command of the Mediterranean Detached Fleet I presume . . . that you consider, after separate and independent judgement, that the immediate operations proposed are wise and practicable. If not, do not hesitate to say so. If so, execute them without delay and without further reference at the first favourable opportunity . . . All good fortune attend you.'[92]

The date was Wednesday, March 17, 1915. De Robeck replied that he would attack in the morning,

It was a day out of season: pleasant, warm, with bright sunshine and a flawless overarching sky. De Robeck's attacking fleet, the mightiest ever seen in the Mediterranean, was spearheaded by four dreadnoughts, flanked by two battleships. A mile behind them came the four French men-of-war, also flanked by British battleships. Six more battleships, surrounded by destroyers and trawlers, were held in reserve; they were to clear away the last obstacles, sail through the Narrows, and enter the Sea of Marmara the following morning. Twelve hours later the Union Jack and the French tricolour would fly over Constantinople.

A morning fog rose at 10:30, revealing the enemy forts, and the first six warships, taking the bone in their teeth, sailed towards them. After twenty-five minutes of manoeuvring, each captain picked his target, half of them facing the Chanak, or Asian, side of the Narrows, and the other half facing the Kilid Bahr, or European, side. Once more the warships were beyond the range of the frustrated Turkish and German gunners. Howitzers on the cliffs downstream could hit the ships, but their shells bounced harmlessly off the thick steel armour. Meanwhile, the forts were being systematically demolished. Ten minutes before noon a British gunner hit the magazine of a key Chanak blockhouse; it erupted in a single sheet of flame. It was the turn of the French. At eight bells, noon, de Robeck signalled Admiral Emile-Paul-Aimable Guépratte to come forward. The *Suffren*, *Bouvet*, *Charlemagne*, and *Gaulois* fanned out and continued the terrific bombardment for another forty-five minutes. Both banks now resembled a tortured Dantean vision: billowing clouds of dense, roiling smoke, stabbing spurts of flame from the howitzers; roars of bursting shells; debris that heaved and shifted with each hit, dismembered corpses flying upward and into the channel, where ineffectual little fountains of water marked the failure of the fortress guns still in action to reach the towering warships. Occasionally a howitzer shell struck a French or British superstructure, but fewer than a dozen seamen had been wounded. The enemy was approaching extremity. Fort 13 on the European shore had also blown up. The forts' fire-control communications had been destroyed. Batteries were covered with rubble and the dead. Breechblocks were jammed. De Robeck was now ready to sweep up the last mines and pass his fleet through to the Sea of Marmara. At 1:30 he ordered the French to move aside and signalled the last six battleships and their escorts to move forward past the defeated enemy, and it was then, at 1:45 in the afternoon, a hairbreadth from victory, that the trouble began. *Bouvet*, pivoting in *Suffren*'s wake close to the strait's Asian bank, was rocked by a tremendous explosion. In less than two minutes she heeled over and sank, taking with her the captain and 639 seamen.

Officers on other ships assumed that a lucky howitzer gunner had hit *Bouvet*'s magazine. The six newly arrived battleships bombarded the banks; by four o'clock enemy fortress fire had ceased altogether and the British minesweepers advanced. They were working skilfully, cutting mine cables with their kites, when a howitzer shell landed among them; then they panicked and turned about. Another line of trawlers advanced; the same thing happened. This was irritating, but hardly worrisome. Graver by far was the misadventure of *Inflexible*, which was mysteriously hit at 4:41 P.M. not far from the place where *Bouvet* had gone down. Listing heavily to starboard, *Inflexible* left the battle line. De Robeck suspected a mine. Less than five minutes later a third battleship, *Irresistible*, was struck near the same spot. She, too, was out of action. Now senior officers were both alarmed and

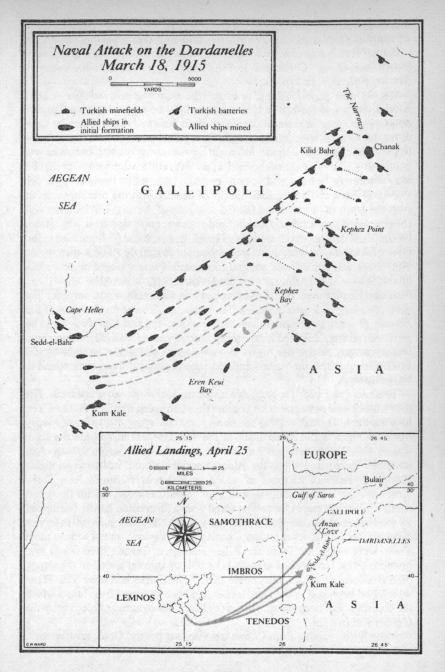

Naval Attack on the Dardanelles
March 18, 1915

0   5000
YARDS

- 🪨 Turkish minefields
- 🚢 Allied ships in initial formation
- 🐟 Turkish batteries
- ⚓ Allied ships mined

AEGEAN

SEA

G A L L I P O L I

The Narrows

Kilid Bahr   Chanak

Kephez Point

Kephez Bay

Cape Helles

Sedd-el-Bahr

A S I A

Eren Keui Bay

Kum Kale

Allied Landings, April 25

0   MILES   25

0   KILOMETERS   25

25 15

26

26 45

EUROPE

Bulair

40
30'

Gulf of Saros

40
30'

AEGEAN

SEA

SAMOTHRACE

N

GALLIPOLI

Anzac Cove

Sedd-el-Bahr

DARDANELLES

40

IMBROS

Kum Kale

40

LEMNOS

A S I A

TENEDOS

G W WARD

25 15'

26

26 45'

mystified. The trawlers had swept these waters. De Robeck believed there was only one explanation: the enemy was floating mines down the current. He broke off action and ordered a general retirement. During the withdrawal a fourth man-of-war, *Ocean,* was lost the same way and in the same waters as *Bouvet, Inflexible,* and *Irresistible.*

Keyes, who stayed behind to direct the rescue of the stricken vessels, moving back and forth in a cutter by the light of a few surviving Turkish searchlights, was far from discouraged. Both banks of the Dardanelles were quiet. He had, he wrote afterwards, 'a most indelible impression that we were in the presence of a beaten foe. I thought he was beaten at 2 P.M. I knew he was beaten at 4 P.M. – and at midnight I knew with still greater certainty that he was absolutely beaten; and it only remained for us to organize a proper sweeping force and devise some means of dealing with the drifting mines to reap the fruits of our efforts. I felt that the guns of the forts and batteries and the concealed howitzers and mobile field guns were no longer a menace. Mines moored and drifting about could, and must, be overcome.'[93] Returning to the *Queen Elizabeth,* he was, therefore, astounded to find de Robeck distraught. His career was ruined, the admiral moaned; his losses would never be forgiven; as soon as the Admiralty saw his action report, he would be relieved and dismissed from the service. Keyes replied that Churchill would never act like that. The day had been anything but a disaster. Except for the crew of the *Bouvet,* fewer than seventy sailors had been hit. The disabled ships could be repaired; all were destined for the scrap heap anyway. Obviously the next step was to convert British destroyers into sweepers – the tackle, wire mesh, and kites were available on Malta – and continue the attack. They were bound to break through.

The enemy agreed. De Robeck's misfortune, they knew, was a freak. His four unlucky ships had been hit because they had sailed too close to shore. Ten days earlier a Turkish colonel had supervised the laying of a string of twenty mines parallel to the Asian bank of the Dardanelles, just inside the slack water. The British sweepers had missed them, but they weren't much of an obstacle; in skirting them the Allied warships would still have an eight-thousand-yard-wide channel in which to manoeuvre. Surely, the Turks reasoned, the English admiral would not repeat his error. British fleets had ruled the world's waves for two hundred years. They could hardly be stopped by the shattered defences left at the Narrows. The Turkish guns still in service were almost out of ammunition – some were *completely* out – and no more shells were available. Once the Allies were past Chanak they would face nothing but a few ancient smooth-bore bronze cannon aimed in the wrong direction. Mines would not trouble them. The Turks had none left. Those which had been laid in the Dardanelles had been collected from mines which the Russians had been floating down the Black Sea in hopes of blowing up the *Goeben* and *Breslau.*

Already the exodus from Constantinople had begun. Gold, art treasures, and official archives had been moved to Eskişehir, in western Turkey. Two special trains, their fires banked, stood ready in the station at Uskudar, just across the Bosporus, to carry the sultan, his harem, his suite, foreign ambassadors, and wealthy pashas and beys into the interior. There was an air of panic in the streets. The city's two arsenals, visible from the water, could be easily destroyed by naval gunfire. After the war the Turkish general staff declared that 'a naval attack executed with rapidity and vigour' would have found the capital's garrison 'impotent to defend it,' and Enver Pasha, Turkey's wartime military dictator, added: 'If the English had only had the courage to rush more ships through the Dardanelles they could have got to Constantinople.' The *Goeben* and *Breslau* had weighed anchor and were preparing to steam away across the Black Sea. Otto Liman von Sanders, the senior German general on this front, said afterwards that if de Robeck had ordered a renewal of his attack on March 19, he would have found the city undefended. 'The course of the World War,' he said, 'would have been given such a turn in the spring of 1915 that Germany and Austria would have had to continue the struggle without Turkey.' Keyes steamed through the strait in 1925. His eyes filled. He said: 'My God, it would have been even easier than I thought. We simply *couldn't* have failed . . . and because we didn't try, another million lives were thrown away and the war went on for another three years.'[94]

He had sensed this at the time. So had Churchill. Far from recalling de Robeck, when Winston read his report of the March 18 action he immediately dispatched four more battleships to his command. The French similarly replaced the *Bouvet* with the *Henry IV*. The French admiral, unlike the British, was eager to return to the Narrows. Jacky Fisher was not. He had waxed hot and cold on the operation, and Winston never knew, from one day to the next, what stand his first sea lord was going to take. Before the struggle in the Narrows he had grumbled, 'The more I consider the Dardanelles, the less I like it.' Yet after the battle it was Fisher, not Churchill, who first proposed to make good the British losses with new battleships. 'De Robeck is really better than Carden,' he said, 'so Providence is with us.' On the afternoon of March 19, when the Admiralty's director of naval intelligence brought them newly intercepted German messages, providing details of the shell shortage in the Narrows forts, Fisher read the report aloud, waved it over his head, and shouted: 'By God, I'll go through tomorrow!' Winston scanned it and said: 'That means they've come to the end of their ammunition.' Fisher danced a jig and cried again: 'Tomorrow! We shall probably lose six ships, but I'm going through!' Yet a few hours later, at a sombre meeting of the War Council, he declared that it was impossible to 'explain away' the losses of such great vessels, that he had always feared that the price of forcing the Dardanelles would be twelve sunken battleships, and that he would prefer to lose them elsewhere.[95]

What troubled him? It was Gallipoli. He cried to Lloyd George: 'The

Dardanelles! Futile without soldiers!' And he said: 'Somebody will have to land on Gallipoli sooner or later.' Before the attack he had sent Churchill a memorandum: *'Are we going to Constantinople or are we not?'* If NOT – then don't send half a dozen battleships to the bottom which would be better applied at Cuxhaven or Borkum. If YES – then push the military co-operation with all speed & make the demonstration with all possible despatch at *both* extremities of the *Gallipoli* Peninsula.' Admiral Jackson concurred and set forth his reasons: 'To advance further with a rush over unswept minefields and in waters commanded at short range by heavy guns, howitzers, and torpedo-tubes, must involve serious losses in ships and men, and will not achieve the object of making the Straits a safe waterway for the transports. The Gallipoli peninsula must be cleared of the enemy's artillery before this is achieved . . . The time has now arrived to make use of military forces to occupy the Gallipoli peninsula, and clear away the enemy on that side. With the peninsula in our possession, the concealed batteries on the Asiatic side, which are less formid-able, could be dealt with more easily . . . and the troops should be of great assistance in the demolition of the fortress's guns.'[96]

This was, of course, a gross distortion of the situation. No one had sug-gested rushing over unswept minefields, the battleships were invulnerable to the shore batteries in the Narrows, and the artillery at the mouth of the strait, which had been cast in the days of sailing ships, was useless even against trawlers, whose helmsmen could steer beyond their range. Nevertheless, Fisher had a point. Eventually someone *would* have to occupy Gallipoli. That was why Churchill, supported by a majority of the cabinet, had wanted to send out the Twenty-ninth Division and the Australians and New Zealanders (Anzacs) in February. After Kitchener had vetoed that, the operation became what Winston called 'a legitimate war gamble.' It was a good gamble. Liddell Hart has described it as a 'sound and far-sighted conception, marred by a chain of errors in execution almost unrivalled even in British history.' Once Constantinople fell, the Turks would have been unable to fortify the penin-sula. Russians – and, almost certainly, new Balkan armies – would have been lunging across their frontiers. Had the czar not been a dolt, the conquest of Gallipoli would by now have been complete. Peter Wright, a member of the War Council, later wrote: 'Our navy was in command of the sea; the Greeks were eager to join us and attack in the peninsula with their whole army. The Gallipoli campaign should have succeeded without the loss of a single British soldier.'[97]

Before the year was out it would cost over a quarter-million Allied casualties, counting 47,000 Frenchmen sacrificed in support operations. All were lost in vain; every inch of the peninsula would remain in enemy hands. The lion's share of the blame must be laid at the door of Lord Kitchener. Unlike French, Haig, and Wilson, mesmerized by the butchery in France, K of K grasped the possibilities in the east. He had told the War Council that if the fleet could not 'get through the straits unaided, the Army ought to see the business through.'[98] Yet he had been evasive when Churchill argued passionately for a combined military and naval operation, and, at a time when a relatively small British expedition could have done the job, he had mulishly refused to release th idle Twenty-ninth Division. Gallipoli was no natural fortress. Except for a series of jutting heights known as Sari Bair, it was relatively flat and largely barren, covered with stony soil, coarse scrub, a few olive trees, and scattered flocks of sheep and goats. Thinly held, as it was before the tumult in the Narrows alerted the Turks, Gallipoli could have been seized in a few days, almost without bloodshed.

Now that England was committed in the Mediterranean, with Grey telling the council that failure there 'would be morally equivalent to a great defeat,' Kitchener, speaking as secretary for war, told the startled cabinet that 'the military situation is now sufficiently secure to justify the despatch of the XXIX Division.' The trench fighting at Neuve Chapelle was at its height; barring unexpected developments there, nineteen thousand Tommies could embark five days hence. The war minister, a firm believer in locking the barn door after the horse has escaped, had also decided to commit the Anzacs to Gallipoli. Altogether, counting the Egyptian garrison and the Royal Marines, the 'Mediterranean Expeditionary Force,' as he called it, would number over seventy thousand. The council was excited; as Churchill wrote afterwards, 'Everybody's blood was up.' The commanding general would be Kitchener's protégé and Winston's old friend, Ian Hamilton. K of K told Hamilton: 'If the Fleets get through, Constantinople will fall of itself and you will have won, not a battle, but the war.'[99]

Asquith thought Hamilton 'a sanguine enthusiastic person, with a good deal of *superficial* charm . . . but there is too much feather in his brain.' His performance in small wars had been superb. He had fought well at Majuba, on India's North-West Frontier, and in South Africa, and had been a keen military observer in Manchuria during the Russo-Japanese War in 1904. None of this was evident in his appearance. He was scrawny, bowlegged, and birdlike in his movements, and his manner was almost effeminate. He also wrote poetry and kept a voluminous, gossipy diary, which diminished him in the eyes of bluff officer types. Clementine disliked him, but Winston regarded him as dashing and chivalrous; he wrote to Kitchener of the appointment: 'No choice could be more agreeable to the Admiralty, and to the Navy.'[100] Churchill wanted him in the eastern Mediterranean, and he wanted him there fast; on the first lord's orders, a special train would take the general to Dover, he would cross the Channel on HMS *Foresight*, another special train would rush him from Calais to Marseilles, and there HMS *Phaeton*, a fast cruiser, would pick him up and carry him to his command. Churchill saw him off at Charing Cross Station, whence Chinese Gordon had left on his own fateful journey to Egypt over thirty years earlier. Because of Kitchener's touchiness, Hamilton explained, there would be no communication between him and the Admiralty. Winston said nothing, but it was a deplorable decision. The train pulled away amid gay shouts, and the dainty general settled down to study a prewar report on the Dardanelles, an out-of-date Turkish army handbook, and a highly inaccurate map of Gallipoli.

Heavy seas kept de Robeck's fleet idle on March 19, but he and Keyes put the time to good use; on the following day the admiral reported to Churchill that sixty-two destroyers were being converted into minesweepers, all to be crewed by bluejacket volunteers, and steel nets would soon be laid across the strait to catch any loose mines. The French, de Robeck reported to London, had been 'quite undismayed by their loss.' On all Allied warships 'officers and men are only anxious to re-engage the enemy.' He ended: 'It is hoped to be in a position to commence operations in three or four days.' Keyes wrote to his wife from the *Queen Elizabeth:* 'I am spoiling to have at it again.' The War Council had authorized Churchill to tell de Robeck that he could 'continue the operations against the Dardanelles' provided he thought it 'fit.' Clearly he did, but the first lord goaded him just the same: '*Queen* and *Implacable* should join you very soon; and *London* and *Prince of Wales* sail tonight . . . It appears important not to let the forts be repaired or to encourage enemy by an apparent suspension of the operations. Ample supplies of 15-inch ammunition are available for indirect fire of *Queen Elizabeth* across the peninsula.'[101]

Everything was proceeding smoothly until Hamilton sailed up on the *Phaeton,* studied the Gallipoli shore through field glasses, ventured into the mouth of the Dardanelles, and then sailed off to establish his headquarters on Lemnos. De Robeck wrote to him there: 'We are all ready for another go, and not the least beaten or down-hearted.' The general took another view. He inspected the crippled *Inflexible,* talked to several army officers on the island, and telegraphed Kitchener: 'I am most reluctantly driven to the conclusion that the straits are not likely to be forced by battleships, as at one time seemed probable, and that, if my troops are to take part, it will not take the subsidiary form anticipated. The Army's part will be more than mere landing parties to destroy forts; it must be a deliberate and prepared military operation, carried out at full strength, so as to open a passage for the Navy.' This was an extraordinary rush to judgement. He hadn't seen the Narrows, was unaware of the devastation there, and knew almost nothing about the capabilities of huge naval guns. Kitchener replied immediately: 'You know my views, that the Dardanelles must be forced.' If troops were needed 'to clear the way,' such operations, he said, 'must be carried through.' On March 22, four days after the ship-to-shore fight in the Narrows, de Robeck anchored off the island to confer with the Mediterranean Expeditionary Force's commander in chief, who at this point had no army, no plan, but a strong distrust of swift action. Afterwards they disagreed on who said what. According to the general: 'The moment he sat down de Robeck told us that he was now quite clear *he could not get through without the help of all my troops.'* According to the admiral, Hamilton spoke first, and having 'heard his proposals, I now considered a combined operation essential to obtain great results and object of campaign . . . To attack Narrows now with Fleet would be a mistake, as it would jeopardize the execution of a bigger and better scheme.'[102]

De Robeck's account is more convincing – until now he had never considered discontinuing his assault – but doubtless he was easily seduced. To naval officers who had risen to flag rank during the long peace, losing ships was a crime, and he had already blurted out to Keyes that he felt guilty. Moreover, he knew that Fisher, the very symbol of the Royal Navy, disapproved of the Dardanelles operation. Churchill backed it, but Churchill was a politician; politicians moved from one ministerial post to another, or dropped out of the cabinet altogether. At the Admiralty, first lords came and went, while the Royal Navy lasted forever. If the army wanted to take over here, de Robeck could only feel a sense of deliverance. He asked Hamilton if the troops would be put ashore on Bulair Isthmus at the top of the peninsula. No, said Hamilton, he would land on the southern tip and fight his way up from there. De Robeck asked when. Hamilton said he needed a little over three weeks. In that case, the admiral said, he would suspend his own drive until the fighting began on Gallipoli. He telegraphed the Admiralty that the army 'will not be in a position to undertake any military operations before 14th April . . . It appears better to prepare a decisive effort about the middle of April rather than risk a great deal for what may possibly be only a partial solution.'[103]

Keyes felt 'fearfully disappointed and unhappy.' Churchill was dumbfounded. As he later testified, he believed 'that we were separated by very little from success. Although at the outset I should have rejoiced at the provision of an army, I saw the disadvantages which would attend its employment after what had happened . . . Landing and storming the Gallipoli Peninsula, now that the Turks were fully alarmed, seemed a formidable business. It seemed to me a far more serious undertaking than the naval attack. It would commit us irrevocably if it failed, in a way no naval attack could have done. The risk was greater. The stakes were far higher . . . and above all I feared the inevitable delay.' Fisher, backed by Admirals Sir Arthur Wilson and Sir Henry Jackson, disagreed. Up to this point, they said, they had supported the attempt to force the strait because the commander on the spot had recommended it. But now that de Robeck and Hamilton had agreed on a joint effort, the Admiralty, in Fisher's words, was 'bound to accept their view.' Churchill later recalled: 'For the first time since the war began, high words were used around the octagonal table.' He drafted a telegram to de Robeck, ordering him to break through to the Sea of Marmara, but it was never sent, because he had to consult the War Council first, and although Asquith – and Kitchener – agreed with him, the prime minister refused to overrule three distinguished admirals.[104]

The next day Winston drafted a personal telegram to de Robeck. Fisher wrote to him: *'Send no more telegrams! Let it alone!'* It went out anyway. 'What has happened since the 21st,' he asked, 'to make you alter your intention of renewing the attack as soon as the weather is favourable?' The answer was ambiguous. Churchill lowered his sights, hoping that the delay would be temporary. Then events conspired against him. Word reached London from Constantinople that 'during the last fortnight about 150 mines, any amount of ammunition, guns, &c, have been coming through Roumania from Germany . . . The ammunition comes through quite openly, and there is nothing to prevent the Germans from bringing in even big guns.' To Winston this was a spur to instant action. The admirals, on the other hand, argued that it meant greater danger for their ships in the Dardanelles. Churchill urged Grey to protest this abuse of Rumanian neutrality. Grey said it would be useless. Then, on Friday, March 26, the British consul general cabled from Rotterdam that Dutch troops were massing on their frontiers; a German invasion was expected hourly. It was a false alarm, but it triggered anxiety about the strength of the Home Fleet. The second, third, and fourth sea lords took the extraordinary step of demanding written assurance from Fisher that the force in Scapa Flow was adequate to meet all challenges. Captain Richmond was spreading his poison in the Admiralty. The first lord's 'personal vanity,' he wrote typically, 'occupies so large a place in the arrangements that the operation is either a fiasco or is most wasteful in lives or matériel – or both.' Finally, Grey urged caution. Italy was on the verge of declaring war on Germany. An unsuccessful attempt to break through the Narrows might discourage it.[105]

Shortly before dawn on Saturday a long message from de Robeck reached the Admiralty. As a study in stagnation it is a remarkable document. Silencing the forts, he said, would require 'an excessive expenditure of ammunition,' which 'cannot be spared.' Complete conquest of the blockhouses on either side of the strait would require 'demolishing parties. To cover these parties at the Narrows is a task General Hamilton is not prepared to undertake and I fully concur with his view.' The 'mine menace' was 'even greater than anticipated.' As he saw it, 'the result of a Naval action alone might in my opinion be a brilliant success or quite indecisive.' It was a risk, and he wasn't prepared to take it when the army could 'occupy the Peninsula which would open up the Strait as guns on Asiatic side can be dominated from the European shore sufficiently to permit ships to pass through.' He concluded: 'With Gallipoli Peninsula held by our Army and Squadron through Dardanelles our success would be assured. The delay possibly of a fortnight will allow co-operation which would really prove factor that will reduce length of time necessary to complete the campaign in Sea of Marmara and occupy Constantinople.'[106]

When Kitchener told the War Council that the army was now prepared to take over the job of opening the Dardanelles, Winston knew he was beaten. Though he felt, as he said, 'grief-stricken,' he gracefully replied to de Robeck: 'I had hoped that it would be possible to achieve the result according to original plan without involving the Army, but the reasons you give make it clear that a combined operation is now indispensable . . . All your proposals will therefore be approved.' De Robeck now became Hamilton's subordinate, providing naval support when and where requested. Every subsequent decision in the theatre was made by either Kitchener or Hamilton. The navy never again tried to sweep mines, reduce forts, or break through the Narrows to the Sea of Marmara. Day by day the vision of victory receded, though Churchill was slow to abandon hope. On April 29 Sir George Riddell found him studying a map. In his diary Riddell set down Winston's remarks. 'This,' Churchill had said, 'is one of the great campaigns of history. Think what Constantinople is to the East. It is more than London, Paris, and Berlin rolled into one are to the West. Think how it has dominated the East. Think what its fall will mean. Think how it will affect Bulgaria, Greece, Rumania, and Italy, who have already been affected by what has taken place. You cannot win this war by sitting still. We are merely using our surplus ships in the Dardanelles. Most of them are old vessels. The ammunition, even the rifle ammunition, is different from that which we are using in France – an older type – so there is no loss of power there.' Then he said: 'I am not responsible for the Expedition . . . I do not shirk responsibility, but it is untrue to say that I have done this off my own bat.'[107]

Nevertheless, the British public believed he had done it all off his own bat. Most of them think so today.

Silence descended upon the strait. As the weeks passed, the Turks realized that they had been granted a reprieve. In time they persuaded themselves that they had triumphed. The Westerners, to whom they had felt inferior, had been routed. Islamic xenophobia stirred in them; they wanted to express their savage new strength on any available enemy. The Armenians were available. They were Christians, they were clever, they prospered as moneylenders in cities and villages, and they were suspected of sympathizing with the Russians. Rumours spread. They were sending information to the czar's troops, it was said: they were smuggling in arms and plotting a revolt. So a pogrom began. The men were tortured and shot; the women were recruited for harems; the very young and very old were sent down the roads to Syria, Persia, and Mesopotamia, where robbers stripped them naked and left them to die of hunger and exposure. Before it was over, 750,000 Armenians were dead.

Barbarism was one expression of the new Turkish mood. Another, which boded ill for Hamilton's troops, was the soaring morale of the *askar*, or private soldier. The *askari* were in a fighting temper, and they knew where they were going to fight; Turkish spies were active in Cairo, watching British officers scour shops for Gallipoli guidebooks. British soldiers cruising in the waters off the peninsula watched the entrenchment grow there. Every morning found them higher and wider. By the middle of April – Hamilton had set his landing date back eleven days – Von Sanders had sixty thousand men behind barbed wire and machine guns, backed by heavy Skoda artillery from Bohemia. His field general would be Mustapha Kemal. Von Sanders was aware of Kemal's Germanophobia, but he also knew he was fiercely patriotic and the best combat commander in the country. Both leaders were exceptionally talented. Their troops were ready. And they had plenty of time; five precious weeks intervened between the break-off of de Robeck's naval attack and the arrival of Hamilton's transports off the peninsula.

Gallipoli offers the invader four beaches: Bulair, at the neck, where de Robeck wanted Hamilton to land; Suvla Bay, halfway down the peninsula; Ari Burnu, south of there; and at Cape Helles, on the toe, where Royal Marines had walked in complete safety a month earlier. Five major landings were made on the cape, near the village of Sedd-el-Bahr. Casualties were heavy. A naval aviator flying overhead looked down on the Aegean, usually a brilliant shade of blue. He saw a strip 'absolutely red with blood . . . a horrible sight to see' between the beach and fifty yards out.[108] The Anzacs were supposed to come ashore at Gaba Tepe, in the vicinity of Ari Burnu. A navigation error put them a mile to the north, where they faced precipitous cliffs from whose scrub-covered ridges the Turks could deliver a murderous, scything fire. Ian Hamilton remained at sea, riding around in the conning tower of the *Queen Elizabeth*, out of touch with his shore commanders and his staff. He refused to intervene, even when it became apparent that everything had gone wrong; officers on the spot, he said, were better qualified to make decisions. They, playing for safety, tried to establish beachheads – venturing inland was considered either impossible or too hazardous – while each evening their commander in chief, before retiring to his bunk on the battleship, wrote five-thousand-word entries in his diary, reflecting upon the mysteries and ironies of life.

Later another landing was made at Suvla. It was the same story. The force commander was an elderly, ailing officer who had made his reputation as a teacher of military history and had never commanded troops in war. Coming ashore, he sprained his knee. He sent word to Hamilton that 'if the enemy proves to be holding a strong line of continuous entrenchments I shall be unable to dislodge them till more guns are landed. All the teaching of the campaign in France proves that continuous trenches cannot be attacked without the assistance of large numbers of howitzers.'[109] There were no trenches and very few Turks. He had twenty thousand men ashore. Still, he was reluctant to advance. Following his commander in chief's example, he returned to his ship and spent a safe, comfortable night aboard. Meanwhile, Mustapha Kemal arrived and occupied the heights overlooking the beach.

Winston's brother, Jack, who had seen action as a major at Ypres and was now serving on Hamilton's staff, wrote him from Helles that Gallipoli was 'siege warfare again as in France. Trenches and wire beautifully covered by machine gun fire are the order of the day. Terrific artillery fire against invulnerable trenches and then attempts to make frontal attacks in the face of awful musketry fire, are the only tactics that can be employed.' In the first month Hamilton lost forty-five thousand men. The pattern continued. It was over-the-top carnage, with no gains of consequence. Jack wrote: 'I don't think another big push will be attempted until reinforcements arrive. We shall have to dig in and await the Turks' attacks.' Gallipoli had become a mere extension of the deadlock on the western front. Hamilton knew it. He telegraphed

Kitchener that he was watching his attack 'degenerate into trench warfare with its resultant slowness.'[110]

'Damn the Dardanelles,' said Fisher. 'They will be our grave.' Churchill had told Riddell that 'Fisher and I have a perfect understanding.' In fact, they had no such thing. The old admiral had raised no objections to Hamilton's landings, but the general's subsequent frustration had depressed him. Winston kept trying to stir Fisher's fighting spirit. 'It is clear,' he wrote to him on May 3, 'that the favourable turn to our affairs in S.E. Europe arose from the initial success of our attack on the Dardanelles, was checked by the repulse of the 18th, & can only be restored by the general success of the operation. It is thus necessary to fight a battle, (a thing wh has often happened before in war) & abide the consequences whatever they may be.' The old salt was unconvinced. And he was beginning to recite his litany of complaints to outsiders. One afternoon at No. 10 Margot Asquith faced him down. She bluntly told him: 'You know you have talked too much – all London knows you are against the Dardanelles expedition. Why didn't you resign?' He muttered: 'It's a lie – I've seen no one, been nowhere, I'm far too busy.' But it was true. Word of the rift at the Admiralty had reached back-benchers in the House. An MP asked 'whether Lord Fisher was consulted with regard to the March action on the Dardanelles by the Fleet; and whether he expressed the opinion that the attack ought not to be made in the circumstances in which it was made.' Winston replied: 'If the insinuation contained in the question were correct Lord Fisher would not now be at the Admiralty.' Asquith had asked Churchill to carry on secret negotiations with the Italians on the terms under which they would enter the war against Germany. This entailed commuting to Paris, and during one of his absences Clementine, hoping to perk up the old salt, invited him to lunch at Admiralty House. It went well until, after Clementine thought he had left, she found him lurking in a corridor. She asked: 'What is it?' He said: 'You are a foolish woman. All this time you think Winston's with Sir John French he is in Paris with his mistress.' Clementine was speechless. She was convinced Fisher was losing his mind. When Churchill returned, she told him what had happened. Fisher, she said, had been 'as nervous as a kitten.'[111]

In Hamilton's failure Roger Keyes saw opportunity. Four days after this remarkable scene in London, the commodore persuaded de Robeck to convene all his admirals in the *Queen Elizabeth*'s wardroom. There he unveiled a new plan of naval attack. Leaving older battleships to shield the army's beachheads, the destroyers which had been refitted as minesweepers would lead the Allies' most powerful dreadnoughts through the Narrows. It would be accomplished in a single day. All those present, including de Robeck, enthusiastically endorsed the operation; Guépratte telegraphed his minister of marine: '*A fin d'assister l'Armée dans son action énergique et rude, nous méditons vive action flotte dans détroit avec attaque des forts. Dans ces conditions il me faut mes cuirassés* Suffren, Charlemagne, Gaulois *dans le plus bref délai possible.*'[112] The plan was forwarded to London for approval, which they took for granted. Fisher didn't like it, of course; he wanted no part of any further action in the

451

strait. And Churchill, from whom one would expect support, had a problem. Assuming that all hopes of forcing the Dardanelles had been abandoned, he had agreed to provide Italy with four battleships and four cruisers from de Robeck's fleet. Yet the idea of reaching Constantinople was still exciting. He believed something could be worked out. He was arguing the issue with Fisher when an aide brought them word that a daring Turkish submarine commander had sunk HMS *Goliath* south of the Narrows.

The loss could be borne. *Goliath* was no Goliath. She was a small, senectuous battleship which had been launched when Victoria was still Queen. But the presence of an enemy submarine in these waters frightened Fisher. There might be others. (There weren't.) He insisted that *Queen Elizabeth* leave the Mediterranean at once. To appease him, Winston agreed. The meeting of the War Council the next day, on Friday, May 14, was, in Churchill's word, 'sulphurous.' Kitchener was infuriated. He had sent an army to Gallipoli with the understanding that the navy would force the Dardanelles, he raged; the first lord had enticed him by dwelling upon 'the marvellous potentialities of the *Queen Elizabeth*,' and now Hamilton was being left in the lurch. K of K's 'habitual composure in trying ordeals left him,' Winston wrote. 'He protested vehemently against what he considered the desertion of the army at its most critical moment.' At this, Fisher flared up. The ship 'will come home,' he declared; 'she will come home at once; she will come home tonight or I shall walk out of the Admiralty then and there.' He added that he was 'against the Dardanelles and have been all along.' That enraged Churchill. 'The First Sea Lord,' he retorted, 'has agreed to every executive telegram on which the operations have been conducted.' Sending out the *Elizabeth*, indeed, had been his idea. The wounding words flew back and forth, and Asquith couldn't stem them. To calm Fisher, the prime minister, on Hankey's advice, had promised the old admiral on Tuesday that no action would be taken in the eastern Mediterranean without his consent. The *Elizabeth* would be recalled; two battleships, *Exmouth* and *Venerable*, would replace her.[113]

Back at the Admiralty that evening Winston went over the details with Fisher in the first sea lord's office. They reviewed the entire operation. New orders would be drawn up for de Robeck. Churchill confined his recommendations to matters he knew the old admiral would accept. As he left, an aide heard him say: 'Well, good night, Fisher. We have settled everything, and you must go home and have a good night's rest. Things will look brighter in the morning and we'll put the thing through together.' Working later, as was his custom, he put everything in writing. At the last moment he added two submarines, which de Robeck had requested, to the Dardanelles naval reinforcements. He left the papers for the first sea lord with a note: 'I send this to you before marking it to others in order that if any point arises we can discuss it. I hope you will agree.'[114]

At nine Saturday morning, May 15, he called at the Foreign Office to put the final touches on the Italian treaty. He was returning across the Horse Guards when his private naval secretary hurried up and said: 'Fisher has resigned, and I think he means it this time.' He handed him the brief note from the first sea lord: 'After further anxious reflection,' it began, 'I have come to the regretted conclusion I am unable to remain any more as your colleague . . . As you truly said yesterday I am in the position of constantly veto-ing your proposals. This is not fair to you besides being extremely distasteful to me. I am off to Scotland to avoid all questionings.' Churchill wasn't perturbed; Fisher had submitted eight previous resignations. But when he discovered that he was nowhere to be found – that he had literally deserted – Winston took the letter to No. 10. Angered, Asquith instantly wrote Fisher: 'In the King's name, I order you to return to your post.' Delivering this command was another matter. That afternoon the old admiral was run to ground in a dingy Charing Cross hotel room. After a long argument, he agreed to see the prime minister. Lloyd George, encountering him in the No. 10 waiting room, was struck by the 'dour change in him . . . A combative grimness had taken the place of his usual genial greeting; the lower lip of his set mouth was thrust forward, and the droop at the corner was more marked than usual. His curiously oriental features were more than ever those in an Eastern temple, with a sinister frown. "I have resigned!" was his greeting, and on my inquiring the reason he replied, "I can stand it no longer."' He had made up his mind, he said, 'to take no further part in the Dardanelles foolishness.' Lloyd George begged him to wait until Monday, when he could put his grievances before the War Council. Fisher refused to wait 'another hour.' He told the prime minister the same thing. After a long argument, Asquith wrung from him a promise to remain in London, but the old man flatly refused to withdraw his resignation, to return to the Admiralty, or to see Churchill.[115]

He went back into hiding. At 10:00 P.M. a mutual friend brought him a letter from Winston, who was trying to find out what this was all about. The answer, in Fisher's reply through the intermediary, was the two submarines. He wrote that 'the series of fresh naval arrangements you sent me yesterday morning convinced me that the time had arrived for me to make a final decision – there being much more in these proposals than had occurred to me the previous evening when you suggested some of them.' This was absurd, of course; the vessels were insignificant, and Churchill had offered to talk it over. But Fisher had been looking for an excuse, and his hand shook as he scrawled on: 'YOU ARE BENT ON FORCING THE DARDANELLES AND NOTHING WILL TURN YOU FROM IT – NOTHING – I know you so well! . . . *You will remain* and I SHALL GO – It is better so . . . You say with much feeling that *"it will be a very great grief to you to part from me."* I am certain you know in your heart no one has ever been more faithful to you than I have since I joined you last October. *I have worked my very hardest.*' He moved to the Ritz and wrote to Reginald McKenna, Winston's predecessor at the Admiralty, that while he wouldn't quote Churchill's letter, 'it absolutely CONVINCES me that I am right in my UNALTERABLE DECISION to resign! *In fact I have resigned!* . . . At every turn he will be thinking of the military and not the naval side – *he never has done otherwise.* His heart is ashore, not afloat! *The joy of his life is to be 50 yards from a German trench! . . .* I am no longer First Sea Lord. *There is no compromise possible!'*[116]

Well, there was, and he was angling for it. He very much wanted to be back at the Admiralty, but with dictatorial powers. This surfaced in his subsequent attempts to negotiate with Asquith. He would serve under McKenna or Grey, he said, but not Churchill or Balfour. Admiral Wilson must leave the Admiralty, Fisher must be empowered to appoint his own Admiralty Board, the first lord would 'be absolutely restricted to policy and parliamentary procedure,' and 'I shall have complete professional charge of the war at sea, together with the absolute sole disposition of the Fleet and the appointment of all officers of all ranks whatsoever, and absolutely untrammelled sole command of all the sea forces whatsoever.' In a postscript he added that these conditions 'must be published verbatim so that the Fleet may know my position.' Hankey, to whom he delivered these terms, told him they were impossible. Asquith said the old man was either 'traitorous' or 'unhinged.' Fisher then sent word of his resignation to Bonar Law. That was malicious. His sole motive now was to ruin Churchill.[117]

After nine years in power the Liberal government was shaky, and frustration over the bloody, interminable war was at the root of it. Fisher wasn't the only officer playing politics. Sir John French needed an excuse for the failure, the previous Sunday, of his offensive against Aubers Ridge, where 11,000 men fell without gaining a single yard. The newly knighted Henry Wilson had noted in his diary: 'Sir J told me he thought it quite likely that K's second army would go to Gallipoli. This *must* be stopped.' Churchill's strongest argument for strengthening the drive against Turkey was that of the 644,000 Englishmen in uniform, 560,000, or 87 per cent, were fighting in France, and, as he had told the War Council, he could not see 'the smallest reason for believing' that there would be any change in 'either the British or French lines.' To keep its flow of reinforcements coming from home, the BEF badly needed an alibi. Therefore French told Colonel Charles à Court Repington, the haughty military correspondent for the Northcliffe newspapers, that the politicians in London were mismanaging their end of the war. It was a lack of high-explosive shells, he said, which had prevented him from breaking through. On Friday *The Times* carried scare headlines: NEED FOR SHELLS. BRITISH ATTACK CHECKED. LIMITED SUPPLIES THE CAUSE. A LESSON FROM FRANCE. The problem, according to this line of reasoning, was that inadequate munitions were being sent to the western front. 'British soldiers,' said *The Times*, 'died in vain on Aubers Ridge on Sunday because more shells were needed. The Government, who have so seriously failed to organize our national resources, must bear their share of the grave responsibility.' Their error, it was argued, had been compounded by the creation of a second, pointless front. Of Gallipoli *The Times* declared: 'The novel interests of that enterprise cannot be allowed to distract us from what is, and will remain, the decisive theatre of operations. Our first thoughts must be for the bent but unbroken line of battle in the West.' The Liberal editor of the *Westminster Gazette* agreed that 'the war will be ended by killing Germans and in no other way.'[118]

Churchill was slow to grasp the threat to him. Gallipoli, after all, was Kitchener's responsibility. But he was being held responsible for the entire campaign, land as well as sea. 'Mr Churchill's characteristics,' said the *Morning Post*, 'make him in his present position a danger and an anxiety to the nation,' and, in another editorial, 'Mr Churchill's instincts for the melodramatic have blossomed into megalomania.' *The Times* charged that 'the First Lord of the Admiralty has been assuming responsibilities and overriding his expert advisers to a degree which might at any time endanger the national safety . . . When a civilian Minister in charge of a fighting service persistently seeks to grasp the power which should not pass into his unguided hands, and attempts to use that power in perilous ways, it is time for his colleagues in the Cabinet to take some definite action.' His absences from the Admiralty were noted and criticized. The government could not reveal that he was negotiating Italy's entrance into the war, and when Tories in the House asked why he wasn't at his desk, and Asquith evaded the question, they shouted: 'Joy ride!' Rumours spread that he was intriguing against Kitchener. Lord Esher's son wrote to his father from Paris: 'Why can't he stick to his own job? He is becoming an object of amusement and some scorn here. The French are beginning to shrug their shoulders when he is mentioned – a bad sign.' Esher passed this letter along to the King. Winston continued to be unpopular among Liberal back-benchers, who now, according to *The Times's* parliamentary correspondent, considered him to be 'the author of all their ills.' Even in the cabinet and the War Council he had become a controversial figure. That Saturday evening when Fisher resigned, Lloyd George told his mistress that if the resignation were accepted, Winston would have to surrender his office. After George had left her, Frances rose from bed and committed his hard words to her diary. Political ruin, Lloyd George had said, would be 'the Nemesis of the man who has fought for this war for years. When the war came he saw in it the chance of glory for himself, & has accordingly entered on a risky campaign without caring a straw for the misery and hardship it would bring to thousands, in the hope that he would prove to be the outstanding man in this war.'[119]

Lloyd George did not speak for the prime minister. But Asquith's emotional stability, unknown to his colleagues or even his family, had just been dealt a cruel blow. All these months he had been sustained by his love for Venetia Stanley. It was a sign of his dependence upon this sophisticated but shallow young woman that he disclosed every state secret to her; indeed, it is arguable that she had become England's greatest security risk. And Venetia, unlike Lloyd George's Frances, was not constant. She had finally decided that the disparity between her age and Asquith's – thirty-five years – was too great. That Friday, May 14, she had told him that their relationship was over. She intended to marry Edwin Montagu, a future cabinet minister. Only the week before he had written to her, 'You give me the life blood of all that I do, or can ever hope to do,' and that if anyone wanted to destroy him, he could do it 'effectively, & without a moment's delay, when any veil is dropped between me & you – soul of my life.' Now, after reading her crushing letter, he wrote to her brokenly: 'This is too terrible; no hell could be so bad.' When Bonar Law confirmed Fisher's elopement and threatened a major debate in the House, Asquith refused to pick up the gauntlet. He lacked the strength. Afterwards he wrote to the young woman he still adored: 'You alone of all the world – to whom I have always gone in every moment of trial & trouble, & from whom I have always come back solaced and healed & inspired – were the one person who could do nothing, & from whom I could ask nothing. To my dying day, that will be the most bitter memory of my life . . . I am on the eve of the most astounding and world-shaking decisions – such as I wd never have taken without your counsel & consent. It seems so strange & empty & unnatural: yet there is nowhere else that I can go, nor would I, if I could.'[120] Bonar Law proposed a coalition, and Asquith listlessly agreed. Ironically, Churchill had been advocating this new step for several weeks. It never occurred to him that he might not be a part of a new cabinet. But the Tories had eyed his scalp too long. The exclusion of Churchill was Bonar Law's price for Conservative participation in the government; Balfour must become first lord.

Winston, who knew none of this, had realized that Fisher's departure would precipitate an uproar in the House. He had prepared a stout defence of his Dardanelles record; he meant to deliver it from the front bench, presenting, at the same time, his nominees for a new Admiralty Board. 'I had,' he later recalled, 'prepared for a Parliamentary enquiry of the most searching character.' He meant to summarize the navy's record of achievement, of which 'I shall always be proud to have had a share,' declaring: 'The terrible dangers of the beginning of the war are over, the seas have been swept clear; the submarine menace has been fixed within definite limits; the personal ascendancy of our men, the superior quality of our ships on the high seas, have been established beyond doubt or question; our strength has greatly increased, actually and relatively from what it was in the beginning of the war, and it grows continually every day by leaps and bounds . . . On the whole surface of the seas of the world no hostile flag is flown.'[121]

Although exhausted by the Italian negotiations – Sir Henry Wilson had noted in his diary on May 7 that he 'looked ill and unhealthy' – Churchill polished this speech all day Sunday, May 16. Monday morning, as a matter of form, he went to the prime minister for clearance. It was then that he learned he would not be permitted to speak. There would be no debate. Asquith, reading it, slowly shook his head. 'No,' he said, 'this will not do. I have decided to form a National Government, and a very much larger construction will be required.' He looked up and asked: 'What are we to do for you?' This was Churchill's first inkling that his reign as first lord of the Admiralty was over. He was thunderstruck. He had assumed that the prime minister, who had shared all his decisions, would stand by him. Asquith asked him whether he wanted another post in the cabinet or would 'prefer a command in France.' Before Winston could answer, Lloyd George entered the room. George, who had been deeply involved in the negotiations with Law – 'LG,' Sunny wrote to Winston, 'has done you in' – asked the prime minister: 'Why do you not send him to the Colonial Office? There is great work to be done there.' Winston said numbly that he would refuse any office which cut him off from the conduct of the war. That evening he put it in writing, sending a note to No. 10: 'So far as I am concerned if you find it necessary to make a change here, I shd be glad – assuming it was thought fitting – to be *offered* a position in the new Government. But I will not *take* any office except a military department, & if that is not convenient I hope I may be found employment in the field.'[122]

By Tuesday morning, however, the prospect of leaving the Admiralty had become unbearable to him. That evening F.E. Smith and Max Aitken called, and Aitken wrote later that Winston 'was clinging to the desire of retaining the Admiralty as if the salvation of England depended upon it,' that he would 'even have made it up with Lord Fisher' if he could have remained as first lord. He talked wildly of soliciting support among the Tories. Aitken bluntly told him he had no hope there. Nevertheless, on Wednesday, Churchill sent Bonar Law documents to justify his pride in his record as first lord. 'Now that there is I rejoice to think good prospect of our becoming colleagues,' he wrote to his most implacable political enemy, 'I feel entitled to send you the enclosed papers.' In a postscript he added that 'this great event of a National Government must be made lasting.'[123]

If only the facts were known, he believed, he would be kept on. He prepared a long statement for the press, defending his Dardanelles role, and showed it to Lloyd George. George, minister of munitions in the new government, was appalled. This material was classified, he said; if it appeared, the troops on Gallipoli would be compromised. Both he and Grey, Churchill suddenly realized, were treating him as though he had already left the government. He lost his temper. Turning on Lloyd George, he snapped: 'You don't care. You don't care if I am trampled underfoot by my enemies. You don't care for my personal reputation.' His old ally broke in: 'No, I don't. I don't care for my own at the present time. The only thing I care about now is that we win in this war.' That was cant. He, too, was a political animal. Had he been in Winston's plight he would have been at his wits' end. George is a key figure in the history of that time, but his position during that turbulent week is murky. He cynically told his mistress, 'The situation for Churchill has no meaning but his own prospects,' and she, who always reflected his views, wrote in her diary of Winston's fall: 'I am rather sorry for him, as it must be a terrible experience for one who has had so much power in his hands. But all the same I think he deserves it.' It was the chancellor who, upon learning of Fisher's departure for Scotland, had told Asquith: 'Of course, we must have a coalition, for the alternative is impossible.' Clementine regarded that as a piece of 'Welsh trickiness.' She told Winston she thought Lloyd George a Judas. Yet afterwards George called Churchill's dismissal 'a cruel and unjust degradation.

The Dardanelles failure,' he said later, 'was due not so much to Mr Churchill's precipitancy as to Lord Kitchener's and Mr Asquith's procrastination.'[124]

Churchill set his jaw. He wouldn't quit. He was ready to pay almost any price rather than surrender the Admiralty. 'In the evening,' Hankey wrote in his diary that Wednesday, 'Churchill offered Fisher any terms he liked including a seat in the Cabinet, if he would stay with him at the Admiralty.' An intermediary carried the message, as before, and Fisher again played the informer, sending the letter to Bonar Law and scribbling across it: 'I rejected the 30 pieces of silver to betray my country.' It seems never to have occurred to him that he was betraying the friend who had brought him back from retirement. Sir Arthur Wilson, who had succeeded Fisher as first sea lord, said he would refuse to serve under any first lord except Churchill. 'This,' Winston wrote Asquith, 'is the greatest compliment I have ever been paid.' Heartened, he wrote to Law again. 'The rule to follow,' he began, 'is what is best calculated to beat the enemy, and not what is most likely to please the newspapers.' The conduct of the Dardanelles operation 'should be reviewed by the new Cabinet. Every fact should be laid before them.' He himself bore 'a tremendous responsibility' for the campaign against the Turks. 'With Sir Arthur Wilson's professional aid I am sure I can discharge that responsibility fully. In view of his statement to the Prime Minister and to the naval Lords that he will serve as First Sea Lord under me, and under no one else, I feel entitled to say that no other personal combination will give so good a chance.' At stake was 'the safety of an Army now battling its way forward under many difficulties.' For nearly four years Churchill had been, 'according to my patent, "solely responsible to Crown and Parliament" and have borne the blame for any failure: and now I present to you an absolutely secure naval position . . . Therefore I ask to be judged fairly . . . I do not ask for anything else.'[125]

He wrote that 'if the Admiralty were in uninstructed or unfriendly hands' it might 'lead to the abandonment of the Dardanelles operation' which 'otherwise is a certainty,' and asked Asquith to 'fancy my feelings if, at this critical moment – on mere uninformed newspaper hostility – the whole intricate affair is to be taken out of my hands & put in the hands of a deadly foe of the plan.' He was 'clinging to my *task* & to my *duty*.' He could not defend himself without putting England's security at hazard. The Conservatives knew only what they had read in the press. 'But *you* know. You alone know the whole situation and that it is my duty to carry this burden safely: and that I can do it. Let me stand or fall by the Dardanelles – but do not take it from my hands.' Clementine also took the remarkable step of writing to the prime minister. Her husband, she told him, had mastered 'every detail of naval science. There is no man in this country who possesses equal knowledge capacity & vigour. If he goes, the injury to Admiralty business will not be repairable for many months – if indeed it is ever made good during the war. Why do you part with Winston? unless indeed you have lost confidence in his work and ability? But I know that cannot be the reason. Is not the reason expediency – "to restore public confidence." I suggest to you that public confidence will be restored in

458

Germany by Winston's downfall . . . If you send him to another place he will no longer be fighting. If you waste this valuable war material you will be doing an injury to this country.'[126]

To swallow pride and crawl thus must have been excruciating for both Winston and Clementine. And it was all for nothing. Asquite wrote to Venetia that he had received 'the letter of a maniac' from her cousin Clementine. Bonar Law – who said privately that Winston 'seems to have an entirely unbalanced mind' – replied to Churchill that his removal as first lord was 'inevitable.' Asquith wrote to Winston: 'You must take is as settled that you are not to remain at the Admiralty.' There could be no appeal from that. Winston, who like other critics of Asquith had taken to calling him 'The Block' in private, replied: 'All right, I accept your decision. I shall not look back . . . I must wait for the march of events at the Dlles.' On the next Saturday, May 22, Winston saw the prime minister briefly. Asquith called it 'a most painful interview to me: but he was good & in his best mood. And it ended all right.' Yet there was still no place for him in the new cabinet. Two days later Margot wrote in her diary: 'What a satire if the coming Coalition Government of which Winston has gassed so much should not contain him! I know Henry [Asquith] too well to suppose this but there is no doubt if Henry wanted to make himself supremely popular with every party *ours and the others* he would exclude Winston. I would not wish this, there is something lovable in Winston and he is a real pal but I should not be surprised if he wrecked the new Government.'[127]

How unpopular *was* Churchill in the spring of 1915? He was controversial, of course; he always had been. But he himself believed he was now friendless. Asquith's daughter, who had loved him as her father loved Venetia, came to him in tears. They 'slipped away' together, she wrote, and he 'took me into his room,' whereupon he collapsed in a chair, 'silent, despairing – as I had never seen him. He seemed to have no rebellion or even anger left. He did not even abuse Fisher, but simply said, "I'm finished." ' She protested; he said, 'No – I'm done.' Yet the day after his final dismissal Italy had entered the war, and he more than anyone else had been responsible for England's new ally. His most loyal supporters remained steadfast. Virtually all the younger flag officers went on record as supporting him. At Gallipoli, Hamilton discovered 'in the Air Service the profound conviction that, if they could only get in touch with Winston Churchill, all would be well. Their faith in the First Lord is, in every sense, *touching.*'[128]

But Englishmen demanded a whipping boy. If they couldn't beat the Germans, they could turn on one of their own, and Churchill, the ostentatious poseur, was the obvious choice. Sir Henry Wilson wrote to Bonar Law:'a man who can plot the Ulster Pogrom, plan Antwerp, & carry out the Dardanelles fiasco is worth watching.' In some vague way Winston was held accountable for everything that had gone wrong, from the shell crisis to the hopeless seesaw in the trenches. He had lost ships. He had frequently been away from his desk – on urgent missions, though they didn't know what. He had ignored expert advice – even the counsel of Fisher, England's greatest admiral. He was a reckless adventurer, a man loyal only to his own ambition. The Dundee *Advertiser* reported that many of his Liberal constituents believed that he 'should be excluded altogether from the Cabinet on the ground, as they contend, that he is in large measure responsible for precipitating the present state of affairs.' Admiralty diehards, impotent during his early naval reforms, now struck out savagely. Captain Richmond called him 'ignorant.' Admiral Sir Henry Jackson, who was appointed first sea lord when Balfour replaced Churchill, described the attempt to force the Dardanelles as 'a mad thing to do.' The naval correspondent of *The Times* reported: 'The news that Mr Churchill is leaving the Admiralty has been received with a feeling of relief in the Service, both afloat and ashore,' and commented that while he had brought a 'breezy atmosphere' with him, he had also created 'a sense of uneasiness lest those very qualities of his which might be of advantage to the State in other circumstances, should lead him into making some false step, which, in the case of the Fleet, upon which our all depends, would be irretrievable.' On May 24 Frances Stevenson wrote in her diary: 'There is no section of the country, so far as I can see, that wishes him to stay at the Admiralty.' According to her, Winston's private naval secretary had advised the prime minister 'that on no account ought Churchill to be allowed to remain at the Admiralty – he was most dangerous there.' Even Asquith, whose punishment Winston was taking, joined the posse. Churchill, he complained, 'is impulsive & borne along on the flood of his all too copious tongue,' and, further, 'it is a pity that Winston has not got a better sense of proportion. I am really fond of him, but I regard his future with many misgivings. I do not think he will ever get to the top in English politics with all his wonderful gifts.' In war, losers, even more than winners, need to create martyrs. Churchill was England's Armenian.[129]

He suffered. His Black Dog had never been so bad; he was in the pit of the worst depression of his life. After he had said his goodbyes at the Admiralty on Saturday and sent a farewell telegram to the Royal Naval Division, Eddie Marsh wrote to Violet Asquith: 'I am miserably sorry for Winston. You can imagine what a horrible wound and mutilation it is for him to be torn away from his work there . . . it's like Beethoven deaf.' Sir George Riddell called on him and wrote in his *War Diary*: 'He looked very worn out and harassed. He greeted me . . . and said, "I am the victim of a political intrigue. I am finished!" ' Lloyd George later said that it was 'the brutality of the fall' that 'stunned' Winston, and Churchill himself wrote afterwards: 'Like a sea-beast fished up from the depths, or a diver too suddenly hoisted, my veins threatened to burst from the fall in pressure . . . At a moment when every fibre of my being was inflamed to action, I was forced to remain a spectator of the tragedy, placed cruelly in a front seat.' Clementine later told Martin Gilbert: 'The Dardanelles haunted him for the rest of his life. He always believed in it. When he left the Admiralty he thought he was finished . . . I thought he would never get over the Dardanelles; I thought he would die of grief.'[130]

At the time she, too, was distraught. After calling at Admiralty House, Edwin Montagu wrote to Venetia, now his fiancée: 'I went by request to see poor Mrs Winston. She was so sweet but so miserable and crying all the time. I was very inarticulate, but how I feel for her and him.' Back in his Treasury Office he wrote to Clementine that 'Winston is far too great to be more than pulled up for a period . . . Have no misgivings as to the future; I have none, I'm sure he has none.' But Winston had many, and what cut deepest were the lost chances which had gone up in the smoke rising from British ineptitude in Turkey. One of his dinner guests at this time was Ellis Ashmead-Bartlett, a war correspondent who had just returned from Gallipoli. Unlike young Churchill in India, the Sudan, and South Africa, journalists covering this campaign had been heavily censored – a full month had passed before the *Illustrated London News* had been permitted to publish photographs of the fighting – and an uninformed public, susceptible to rumour, had contributed to Churchill's ruin. Ashmead-Bartlett wanted to talk to him about that. But his host wouldn't listen to anyone. Ashmead-Bartlett noted in his diary: 'I am much surprised at the change in Winston Churchill. He looks years older, his face is pale, he seems very depressed and to feel keenly his retirement from the Admiralty . . . At dinner the conversation was more or less general, nothing was said about the Dardanelles, and Winston was very quiet. It was only towards the very end that he suddenly burst forth into a tremendous discourse on the Expedition and what might have been, addressed directly across the table in the form of a lecture to his mother, who listened most attentively. Winston seemed unconscious of the limited number of his audience, and continued quite heedless of those around him. He insisted over and over again that the battle of March 18th had never been fought to a finish, and, had it been, the Fleet must have got through the Narrows. This is the great obsession of his mind, and will ever remain so.' Jennie wrote Leonie: 'If they had made the Dardanelles policy a certainty, Constantinople would have been in our hands ages ago. *In confidence*, it is astounding how Winston foresaw it all.'[131]

His obsession with what might have been kept him in civilian clothes for six months. Asquith promised him a seat on the War Council, now renamed the Dardanelles Committee, if he would accept the lowest of cabinet posts, chancellor of the duchy of Lancaster. 'Where is Lancaster?' jeered the *Bystander*. 'And what is a Duchy?' The position was a sinecure, which, as Lloyd George put it, was 'generally reserved either for beginners in the Cabinet or for distinguished politicians who had reached the final stages of unmistakable decrepitude.' The chancellor's only duty was to appoint county magistrates. In false cheeriness Winston wrote to Jack Seely: 'The Duchy of Lancaster has been mobilized. A strong flotilla of magistrates for the 1915 programme will shortly be laid down.' His salary was immediately cut from £4,500 to £2,000 a year. Asquith offered to let the Churchills stay on in Admiralty House, but

461

Clementine refused to accept charity from the man who, as she saw it, had sacrificed her husband to save his own office. Ivor Guest gave his cousin the temporary use of his house at 21 Arlington Street, behind the Ritz; then they would move in with Goonie in Jack Churchill's South Kensington house at 41 Cromwell Road, opposite the Natural History Museum. On May 23, eight days after the crisis over Fisher's resignation had erupted, Winston turned the Admiralty over to Balfour. One of the new first lord's first decisions was to scrap the tank project. According to Captain D'Eyncourt's memoirs, *A Shipbuilder's Yarn*, the new first lord called him in and asked: 'Have not you and your department got enough to do looking after the design and construction of ships without concerning yourself about material for the Army?' Appropriations already in the pipeline produced a small number of tanks in 1916. To Churchill's dismay, Lloyd George told him that the army planned to use them immediately. Winston went to Asquith, pleading against untimely use of the trench weapon which, he believed, could be decisive. He was ignored. On September 15 a handful of tanks went into action on the Somme. The British infantry was unprepared to consolidate their quick gains, and the element of surprise was squandered. 'My poor "land battleships," ' Churchill wrote, 'have been let off prematurely and on a petty scale. In that idea resided one real victory.' Here he, too, was premature. The tank's time would come again, and yet again.[132]

In the weeks after he cleared out his Admiralty desk his depression deepened. 'It is odious to me,' he wrote to Seely, 'to remain here watching sloth and folly with full knowledge & no occupation.' To Jack on Gallipoli he wrote: 'The war is terrible: the carnage grows apace, & the certainty that no result will be reached this year fills my mind with melancholy thoughts. The youth of Europe – almost a whole generation – will be shorn away. I find it vy painful to be deprived of any direct means of action.' Beginning in late May, he took his and his brother's families to a rental property in Surrey each weekend. 'I am off to Hoe Farm,' he wrote to Jack on June 19. 'How I wish you cd be there. It really is a delightful valley and the garden gleams with summery jewellery. We live vy simply – but with all the essentials of life well understood & provided for – hot baths, cold champagne, new peas, & old brandy.' Yet even here he drew apart from the others and paced endlessly between the garden and a small wooden summerhouse. He tried golf again and again and hated it; it was, he said, 'like chasing a quinine pill around a cow pasture.' Then, in a flash of inspiration, his sister-in-law introduced him to painting. Goonie painted herself; she set up her easel in the garden one Sunday, and when she noticed Winston watching her with interest, she suggested he try it, using some of the children's watercolours. There was plenty to paint, she pointed out: the garden, the woods, the house, a nearby pond. He tried, liked it, and did it well. He had a natural visual eye, and knew it; during the Boer War he had supplemented his dispatches with sketches drawn in the field; touched up by newspaper illustrators, they had been published. Obviously, he could be good if he applied himself. It struck him that in this dark hour of life the 'Muse of

Painting' might have come to his rescue – 'out of charity and out of chivalry, because after all she had nothing to do with me – and said, "Are these toys any good to you? They amuse some people." '[133]

But watercolours would not do. Being Churchill, whatever he did had to be done for the ages. He told Clementine: *'La peinture à l'huile est bien difficile, mais c'est beaucoup plus beau que la peinture à l'eau.'* She needed only that hint; she was off and running, and when she returned she brought a palette, canvasses, an easel, a smock, and tubes. Unfortunately she had neglected to bring turpentine, and that aborted his first venture. Finally he was ready. Later he described his sensations on the threshold of that first attempt. With everything assembled, 'the next step was to *begin*. But what a step to take! The palette gleamed with beads of colour; fair and white rose the canvas; the empty brush hung poised, heavy with destiny, irresolute in the air. My hand seemed arrested by a silent veto. But after all the sky on this occasion was unquestionably blue, and a pale blue at that. There could be no doubt that blue paint mixed with white should be put on the top of the canvas. One really does not need to have had an artist's training to see that. It is a starting-point open to all. So very gingerly I mixed a little blue paint on the palette with a very small brush, and then with infinite precaution made a mark about as big as a pea upon the affronted snow-white shield. It was a challenge, a deliberate challenge; but so subdued, so halting, indeed so cataleptic, that it deserved no response.'[134]

At that most appropriate moment an automobile was heard in the drive, and out stepped Hazel Lavery, a neighbour, the wife of an artist, and a gifted painter herself. Her appearance was not a coincidence. Clementine was making up for the turpentine. Hazel strode up and said: 'What are you hesitating about? Let me have a brush – the big one.' She splashed it into turpentine, socked it into the blue and white, thrashed it about on the palette, and delivered several huge, savage strokes on what Winston called 'the absolutely cowering canvas.' Anyone could see, he wrote, 'that it could not hit back. No evil fate avenged the jaunty violence. The canvas grinned in helplessness before me. The spell was broken.' He was delighted. This was his style; this was how he lived. It was inevitable that he should become an audacious painter, and a gaudy one; nothing that he ever touched was done by halves. 'I cannot pretend to be impartial about the colours,' he wrote. 'I rejoice with the brilliant ones, and am genuinely sorry for the poor browns.' When he reached heaven he would 'require a still gayer palette than I get here below. I expect orange and vermilion will be the darkest, dullest colours upon it, and beyond them there will be a whole range of wonderful new colours which will delight the celestial eye.'[135]

Eddie Marsh, who watched his first efforts, thought that 'the new enthusiasm . . . was a distraction and a sedative that brought a measure of ease to his frustrated spirit.' In fact, it would be a solace to him for the next fifty years. He had, he believed, discovered the solution to anxiety and tension. Exercise, travel, retreat, solitude, forced gaiety – he had tried these and none had worked. 'Change,' he now wrote, 'is the master key. A man can wear out a particular part of his mind by continually using it and tiring it . . . the tired parts of the mind can be rested and strengthened, not merely by rest, but by using other parts . . . It is only when new cells are called into activity, when new stars become lords of the ascendant, that relief, repose, refreshment are afforded.'[136]

He painted landscapes and still lifes; never people. For one of his studies of bottles he coined a word: *bottlescape*. The dazzling hues were always there, a kind of signature. He knew desperation, but never a grey day. Once, painting in a drab, monochrome countryside, he introduced a dramatic range of mountains which were not there. A puzzled companion asked if he had seen a mirage. No, said Churchill; he just 'couldn't leave it quite as dull as that.' In time he became very good. An art critic scrutinized his work at a Royal Academy exhibition and wrote: 'I was bound to recognize that their creator is a real artist. His canvasses bear the mark of the spontaneity of a sincere and exuberant, but undisciplined vocation. His landscapes are vigorous and sometimes sensitive. His use of colour is often happy . . . I think his fame as a statesman has prejudiced his reputation as an artist.'[137]

At Hoe Farm he also rejoiced in the company of small children. Sarah was still an infant, but Diana was six and Randolph four, and his two nephews, Johnny and Peregrine, were also there. Long afterwards Johnny would recall how, when he and his brother were given a box of Meccano – a kind of Erector Set – they started building a cantilever crane in the farmhouse dining room. Their uncle appeared, puffing on a cigar. He watched thoughtfully for a while, and then murmured: 'Hm. A bascule bridge would be better, you know.' Johnny explained that they hadn't enough pieces. Churchill waved his hand impatiently, summoned a servant, and sent her out to buy several Meccano boxes. Then, Johnny remembers, he 'took off his coat and began preparing the largest model bascule bridge ever . . . The final construction was a gigantic piece of engineering some fifteen feet long and eight feet high, with a roadway which could be lifted by means of wheels, pulleys and yards of string.' It was so big that the dining room became unusable. The family had to eat elsewhere.[138]

He also played 'gorilla' with the children. Donning his oldest clothes, he would lurk behind shrubbery, waiting for one of them to appear. When one did, he would leap out roaring 'Grr! Grr!' and advance menacingly, his arms swinging limply at his sides. 'The realism was alarming,' Johnny recalls, 'but we squealed with delight and enjoyed this exclusive performance hugely. Few people can say that they have seen an ex-First Lord of the Admiralty crouching in the branches of an oak, baring his teeth and pounding his chest with his fists.' Winston's son remembered that when his father dropped from a limb, 'we would all scatter in various directions. He would pursue us and the one he caught would be the loser.'[139]

In the Dardanelles Committee the ex-first lord was less effective, but he had lost none of his persuasive powers, and in the beginning most of his recommendations were adopted. On June 1 he circulated a paper among the members, arguing that while a decision in France had proved impossible, a relatively small expansion of Hamilton's army could bring victory. 'It seems most urgent,' he wrote, 'to try to obtain a decision here and wind up the enterprise in a satisfactory manner as soon as possible.' Bonar Law and Sir Edward Carson, another old Churchill adversary, disagreed, but the committee voted to send five more divisions to Gallipoli. In France, Sir Henry Wilson raged: 'That makes 9 there and 22 here, and not a single Boche facing the 9. How they will laugh in Berlin.' In any event there was no doubt that Britain was betting heavily on Gallipoli. Hamilton's army now numbered 120,000 troops. Surely he could break through.[140]

He didn't. An old military maxim runs: 'Never reinforce failure.' That is how Hamilton used his fresh troops. Churchill telegraphed him, urging a landing on the Bulair Isthmus. Hamilton, obsessed with logistics and matériel, replied that he doubted his troops were capable of the effort, or that it could succeed under the best of conditions. His troops, bogged down, fought, not only Turks, but also summer flies. Discipline grew lax; the men grumbled that they were victims of 'the politicians.' Hamilton wired the War Office that he needed ninety-five thousand more men to provide 'the necessary superiority.'[141] Kitchener told him that Gallipoli had had its chance, and the Dardanelles Committee, to Winston's alarm, began to consider evacuating the peninsula. Whatever the problems in the east, Churchill said, the west was not the answer. In September the first troops of Kitchener's army went over the top in France to capture the village of Loos and the high ground a mile beyond. After two days fifteen thousand English and Scottish soldiers had been killed and the German wire was intact. Churchill searched the map again, and, the following month, when Bulgaria entered the war as a German ally, drew up a four-point plan of attack to open a broad Balkan front from the Aegean, offering opportunities for movement and thrusts.

It was rejected. Churchill's theories of war, Aitken concluded, were 'so hare-brained that it would be humorous if the lives of men were things to joke about, or, I might add, to trifle with.' Even Violet Asquith, who defended him passionately, rated him 'a guided gambler.' In fact, his military thought was on a plane so extraordinary that others simply could not grasp it. In his multivolume history of the Great War he dwelt upon the significance of manoeuvre, which, he wrote, may assume many forms, 'in time, in diplomacy, in mechanics, in psychology.' Only when military and political thought were joined could leaders discover 'easier ways, other than sheer slaughter, of achieving the main purpose.' As he conceived of it, the 'distinction between politics and strategy diminishes as the point of view is raised. At the summit true politics and strategy are one.'[142] Thus the internal political complexes of the Balkan states, in his mind, were linked to events on all European battlefields. Because these states were politically weak, the opportunities were there and should be seized. Others, lacking his imaginative grasp, dismissed him as superficial. Actually, he was plumbing depths whose very existence was unsuspected by them.

And so the achievements his genius might have wrought were irrevocably lost. His credibility had shrunk as Hamilton's prospects for victory faded. Once more he was being blamed for a plan that had not been his. Accustomed to respect and even deference, he now had to endure slights which, less than a year ago, would have been unthinkable. Balfour recalled Fisher from Scotland and appointed him chairman of the Admiralty's Committee on Inventions and Research. Churchill angrily wrote to Asquith: 'Fisher resigned his office without warning or parley . . . You ordered Fisher to return to his post in the name of the King. He paid no attention to yr order. You declared that he had deserted his post in time of war; & the facts are not open to any other construction. For ten days or more the country was without a First Sea Lord as Fisher did not even do his duty till his successor was appointed.' To Balfour he added: 'All this must be viewed in relation to a very old man.' He decided not to send the letter, but made his views known to the prime minister through a mutual friend. It didn't matter. His protest was ignored. The next week Kitchener suggested that he make an official trip to the Dardanelles and Gallipoli. Winston was delighted. Since all British positions on the peninsula were within range of Turkish artillery, he took out a new insurance policy, giving him £10,300 coverage. In addition he held £1,000 in Witbank Collieries stock. He explained all this in a letter to Clementine, to be delivered in the event of his death, and told her where she could find the 'complete' Admiralty papers documenting his record. 'There is no hurry,' he wrote, 'but some day I shd like the truth to be known. Randolph will carry on the lamp. Do not grieve for me too much. I am a spirit confident of my rights. Death is only an incident, & not the most important wh happens to us in this state of being. On the whole, especially since I met you my darling one I have been happy, & you have taught me how noble a woman's heart can be. If there is anywhere else I shall be on the look out for you. Meanwhile, look forward, feel free, rejoice in life, cherish the children, guard my memory. God bless you. Good bye. W.'[143]

Kitchener suggested that Hankey accompany him, and it was agreed. The King sent word to him that he was 'glad to hear' of his mission. A warm note arrived from Grey. Winston spent a final Sunday with the family at Hoe Farm. Then, after the cabinet meeting had broken up on Monday morning, Asquith, Kitchener, and Grey gathered around to wish him a fond farewell. At that point a Tory minister unexpectedly returned and asked where Churchill was going. Told, he made a beeline for Bonar Law. The upshot was that the Conservatives opposed the trip. Asquith again caved in rather than, as he told Churchill, face 'any serious division of opinion.' Lord Curzon, one of the Tories who had protested, wrote to Winston that 'we shared a doubt as to the reception that public opinion might give to such an act, for which the Govt would be held collectively responsible.' The unkindest cut came from Kitchener. The reason he had asked Hankey to go along, he said, was that he thought someone should watch Churchill. After discussing the Tory veto with K of K, Lord Esher wrote in his diary: 'He laughed over it a good deal and admitted that he would not have been sorry to get rid of Winston for a while.' News of this reached Churchill. The message to him was clear. He wasn't wanted. He wasn't even trusted.[144]

If others had doubts about forcing the Narrows, British submarine commanders didn't. They slipped in and out, roaming the Sea of Marmara and the Black Sea and sinking Turkish ships within sight of Constantinople. Because of them, enemy troops were chronically short of ammunition. Nevertheless, the British learned from prisoners, aerial reconnaissance, and agents in Constantinople that Turkish reinforcements were pouring into Gallipoli. Hamilton wrung his hands. On October 16 he was sacked and General Sir Charles Monro, who had been fighting in France, replaced him. One of Monro's first duties, the War Office told him, would be to determine whether or not the peninsula should be abandoned. Since he was an ardent Westerner, scornful of this theatre, there could be little doubt about his decision. Churchill later called him 'an officer of quick decision. He came, he saw, he capitulated.' Before he could take over, however, Roger Keyes made a last plea for a naval assault on the Narrows. He arrived in London on October 28 and converted Balfour and the sea lords. Churchill saw a sparkle of hope. 'I believe,' he wrote, 'we have been all these months in the position of the Spanish prisoner who languished for twenty years in a dungeon until one morning the idea struck him to push the door which had been open all the time.'[145]

When Kitchener joined his proselytes, Keyes seemed to have won. Asquith, Balfour, and Kitchener gathered to plan 'an abrupt naval coup de main upon the Straits.' But Balfour, hedging his bet, said the navy would act only if the army also attacked – which would require Monro's approval – and Law threatened to resign unless the whole Turkish theatre was shut down. After a communications breakdown between London and the Aegean, Kitchener personally visited the peninsula. He met Keyes aboard the *Dartmouth*. 'Well, I have seen the place,' he said. 'It is an awful place, and you will never get through.' Keyes asked what had changed his mind. K of K was vague, but it is a fair guess that Monro had decided him. Hamilton's successor was on the scene now, spreading defeatism. Kitchener wired London that the Suvla and Anzac beachheads should be evacuated. Cape Helles would be held 'for the time being.'[146]

On November 6 the Dardanelles Committee was renamed the War Cabinet and Winston was excluded from it. It was time for him to go; past time. He had known it for weeks. Early in September he had asked Asquith for a field command, suggesting that a major general's commission with the command of an army corps would be appropriate for someone with his knowledge and experience. The prime minister approached Kitchener, who said that he 'would like to get rid of Churchill, but could not offend the Army.' Winston then proposed that he be appointed 'Governor-General and Military

Commander-in-Chief of British East Africa.' He felt sure he could raise an army of Africans. Balfour told Hankey and James Masterton-Smith, a veteran civil servant at the Admiralty, a version of this. Hankey entered it in his diary. Churchill, according to Balfour, had given Asquith 'a scheme for attacking the Germans' in their African colonies 'with armoured cars.' He added that perhaps if he succeeded in this, the 'military objections to his [assuming] a high post of command would disappear. All this tickled Mr Balfour so much that he positively pirouetted on one foot, looking very odd in his long frock coat, so that Masterton-Smith and I fairly roared with laughter.'[147]

The laughingstock of the cabinet submitted his resignation on November 11. Asquith accepted it the next day. Not many mourned his departure. The *Manchester Guardian* was one; an editorial described it as 'a great national loss, for in our opinion – though we dare say there are few who share it – he had the best strategic sense in the Government . . . There have been two opportunities of winning the war. One was last October before the fall of Antwerp, the other was this spring when a great effort by land and sea would have won through to Constantinople and saved us all of our troubles in the East now. Mr Churchill saw them both at the time and though his ideas were adopted, neither in Flanders nor in the East did they have anything like a fair chance.'[148]

Churchill was without political office for the first time in ten years, and as was customary when ministers stepped down, he made a personal statement in the House of Commons – a privilege which had been withheld from him when he left the Admiralty. Later he expanded his remarks before the commission investigating the Turkish campaign. He denied that he had 'foisted' a civilian plan upon 'reluctant officers and experts.' He said: 'You may condemn the men who tried to force the Dardanelles, but your children will keep their condemnation for those who did not rally to their aid.' In his peroration he cried: 'Undertake no operation in the West which is more costly to us in life than to the enemy. In the East, take Constantinople. Take it by ships if you can. Take it by soldiers if you must. Take it by whichever plan, military or naval, commends itself to your military experts. But take it; take it soon; take it while time remains.' Asquith rose from the Treasury Bench to acknowledge his departure briefly. He praised him as 'a wise counsellor, a brilliant colleague, and a faithful friend,' but did not mention his own role in the Dardanelles decisions. His daughter, who had watched from the gallery, wrote to Winston 'one line to say I thought your speech *quite* flawless – I have seldom been more moved . . . Is there anything you *haven't* got for the Front? Compass? Luminous wristwatch? Muffler & Tinderlighter? If there is any lacuna in your equipment let me fill it.'[149]

There was one, but she could do nothing about it. He needed a command. At the very least, he thought, he should be given a brigade, preferably in a division fighting Turks. He didn't get one. It was fashionable that fall, in Parliament and the War Office, to deride him as an attitudinarian who had been a 'mere subaltern.' In fact, his military qualifications were more substantial than that. He was a reserve major who had commanded the defence of Antwerp. As a young officer he had seen fighting in Cuba, India, the Sudan, and South Africa. Twice he had witnessed German war manoeuvres, an advantage no one on the general staff shared. He had made a thorough study of the arts of war and had published five books on military subjects. His years as first lord ought to have counted for a great deal. 'Instead,' as Max Aitken wrote afterwards, 'he was extruded from the centre of action by men of lesser ability and initiative, and his knowledge and inventiveness of mind – all were wasted.'[150] Asquith and Kitchener ignored his every appeal. In the end he had only his commission in the Queen's Own Oxfordshire Hussars – that and his acquaintances among the redtabs in France, which, because of his genteel birth and public career, were several. He decided to join his regiment in France. There, at least, he would be among friends. He would see what else he could manage along the way.

On Tuesday, November 16, he held a farewell luncheon at 41 Cromwell Road, inviting Goonie, Nellie Hozier, Eddie Marsh, and Margot and Violet Asquith. Violet would later remember that 'Clemmie was admirably calm and brave, the rest of us trying to "play up" and hide our leaden hearts. Winston alone was at his gayest and his best and he and Margot held the table between them. They had always been an uneasy combination, as neither of them really enjoyed the other's society and she could not forbear from rubbing in the evils which had followed in the wake of the coalition and reminding him that he had always wanted one. He made his stock reply, that we should have sought one, not in our hour of weakness but at a time of strength.' For the rest of the group, Violet thought, the lunch 'was a kind of wake.'[151]

Wednesday, Aitken arrived, bursting with energy, as always, and found 'the whole household was upside down while the soldier-statesman was buckling on his sword.' He was also supervising the packing of cigars, port, vermouth, whisky, camping equipment, and assorted creature comforts. 'Downstairs,' Aitken saw, 'Mr "Eddie" Marsh, his faithful secretary, was in tears . . . Upstairs, Lady Randolph was in a state of despair at the idea of her brilliant son being relegated to the trenches. Mrs Churchill seemed to be the only person who remained calm, collected and efficient.' On Thursday, Major Churchill crossed the Channel aboard a regular steamer to Boulogne, where, to his surprise, a car had been sent by Sir John French to meet him. After reporting to his regiment, he joined the BEF's commander in chief for dinner at Saint-Omer 'in a fine château,' he wrote home, 'with hot baths, beds, champagne & all the conveniences.' French received him warmly; his own position had become highly precarious, and he could empathize with the fallen Churchill. More generous than Asquith or the War Office, he offered him a choice between serving here as an ADC or commanding a brigade. 'The brigade,' Winston instantly replied. It was settled that he would first spend a training period with the Grenadier Guards. He wrote home: 'Midnight. My dearest soul – (this is what the gt d of Marlborough used to write from the low countries to his cat) All is vy well arranged . . . but as I do not know to wh

The Western Front
Late 1915

•••••••• Front line

battalion I am to be sent, I cannot tell the rota in wh we shall go into the trenches.'[152]

Approaching the front in that war was a shocking experience. Winston hadn't been in the field for fifteen years, and he had never seen anything like this. He was a middle-aged man, accustomed to indulgence, whose skin felt unchafed only when caressed by silk. There would be none of that here. On Saturday he lunched at La Gorgue and learned that he had been attached to the grenadiers' Second Battalion, commanded by Lieutenant Colonel George 'Ma' Jeffreys, the only surviving officer of the original battalion which had gone into action here in 1914. They would be reentering the line that night in front of Merville, near Neuve Chappelle, one of the many villages, like Ypres, Bullecourt, and Messines, whose very names had become symbols for the suffering here. He was driven part of the way towards the thundering artillery and then proceeded on foot with Jeffrey's sweating, heavy-laden, sleepy-eyed headquarters staff. 'It was a dull November afternoon,' he would write in the March 1924 issue of *Nash's Pall Mall*. An icy drizzle fell over the darkening plain. As we approached the line, the red flashes of the guns stabbed the sombre landscape on either side of the road, to the sound of an intermittent

470

cannonade.' After nearly four hours they reached battalion headquarters, 'a pulverized ruin called Ebenezer Farm,' where they were provided with rations and 'strong tea with condensed milk' – not his idea of liquid refreshment.[153]

Jeffreys greeted him coldly: 'I think I ought to tell you that we were not at all consulted in the matter of your coming to us.' Winston respectfully replied that the decision had not been his; he ventured to say it would work; in any case they must make the best of it. After a long, hostile silence, the adjutant said: 'I am afraid we have had to cut down your kit rather, Major. There are no communication trenches here. We are doing all our reliefs over the top. The men have little more than what they stand up in. We have found a servant for you, who is carrying a spare pair of socks and your shaving gear. We have had to leave the rest behind.' Churchill said that was 'quite all right'; he was sure he would be 'very comfortable.'[154]

No one spoke to him again as they moved up. He felt, he said afterwards, 'like a new boy at school in charge of the Headmaster, the monitors, and the senior scholars.' He knew why; every British soldier in France was bitter about the reinforcements which had been sent to Gallipoli, and he, of course, was to blame for that. At length they leapt over a parapet and rushed into the front-line trenches. There he was given his choice of sleeping quarters for the night, a signal office eight feet square, stiflingly hot, and occupied by four busy Morse signallers, and a dugout two hundred yards away. Having 'surveyed' the signal room, he asked for directions to the dugout and was led there. It turned out, he later recalled, to be 'a sort of pit four feet deep containing about one foot of water.' It was there, in the mud of Flanders, trapped in a deadlock he had tried so hard to break, that he learned the outcome of his hopes in the east. It came in a scrawled postscript to a letter from Clementine: 'Large posters just out: – TROOPS WITHDRAWN FROM DARDANELLES – OFFICIAL.' After 213,980 British casualties, the evacuation of Gallipoli had begun. It would continue through December into January. Not a man fell in winding down the operation. Virtually all future losses would be here on the western front, where no end was in sight.[155]

So frosty a reception by fellow officers would have daunted almost any other newcomer, but Winston was too proud, and his ego too strong, to be scarred by petty slights. He was, he later wrote, 'infinitely amused at the elaborate pains they took to put me in my place and to make me realize that nothing counted at the front except military rank and behaviour.' Here they were wrong. He expected special treatment and he got it. Soldiers' mail was notoriously slow; letters to and from Cromwell Road, carried by a King's messenger from the Admiralty, were delivered overnight. No other fighting man could speak to his wife over a telephone. Churchill did; he rode back to French's GHQ and heard her over a special Admiralty line. After hanging up he wrote to Clementine that because another officer had been in the room, 'I cd not say much & even feared you might think I was abrupt.' She wrote that the conversation had been 'very tantalizing, as there is so much I want to say to you which cannot be shouted into an unsympathetic receiver!' But millions of husbands and wives would have given much to be so constrained, and so tantalized.[156]

August visitors traipsed up to the trenches to see him: Lord Curzon, General Seely, and F.E. Smith, now attorney general, who, to his fury, was arrested by a sentry for want of a proper pass. At Saint-Omer, Winston had encountered another acquaintance, Edward Louis Spiers. They had met before the war in the home of Venetia Stanley's sister Sylvia. Spiers, now a young cavalry captain, was serving as a liaison officer between the BEF and Joffre's staff. He invited Winston to join him in a tour of the French lines. Churchill was confident that he was immune to AWOL charges – he was right – and off they went. A French general insisted on being photographed with Winston. Churchill wrote home: 'I was received with much attention, more so in fact than when I went as 1st Lord.' As a parting gift he was crowned with a poilu's steel helmet, 'wh I am going to wear,' he told Clementine, 'as it looks so nice & will perhaps protect my valuable cranium.'[157]

The battalion adjutant could not limit him to spare socks and a razor. He was entitled to his kit; he got it, and more. If he had to live in such conditions, he intended to be properly equipped. His wife sent him a pillow. That was a start. Somehow he acquired a tin bathtub, a pocket Shakespeare, then brandy – Jeffreys kept a 'dry' mess – and a stock of fine cigars. Clementine wrote: 'I wake up in the night & think of you shivering in the trenches; it makes me so miserable (You know how warm the Kat has to be before she can sleep).' Like Violet Asquith, she wanted to know if she could send him anything to make his life more endurable. As a matter of fact, he replied, she could. He wanted a leather waistcoat, a pair of wading boots ('water proof canvas tops coming right up to the thigh'), a periscope ('most important'), a sheepskin sleeping bag, two pairs of khaki trousers, a pair of brown buttoned boots, and three small face towels. 'Voilà tout!' he wrote at the end. 'Your little pillow is a boon & a pet.'[158]

How did the other officers feel about this? Astonishingly, they not only tolerated him; he became genuinely popular. He invited them to share his brandy, cigars, tub, and the groaning hampers of food from Cromwell Road. 'I never saw such dainties & such profusion,' he wrote to Clementine of one which arrived when the battalion was in a rear area. 'We shall eat them sparingly keeping the best for the trenches.' He volunteered to join Jeffreys on his daily rounds of the lines, and thereafter, as he put it, he and the colonel 'slid or splashed or plodded together through snow or mud . . . for two or three hours at a time each day and night; and bit by bit he forgot that I was a "politician" and that he "had not been consulted in the matter of my coming to his battalion." ' Presently the second in command went on leave; Winston was asked to take his place. He accepted, solemnly declaring this 'one of the greatest honours I have ever received.' Then he startled Jeffreys by suggesting that he could learn more about trench warfare if he lived, not in the comparative comfort of battalion headquarters, but up with one of the line companies, on the edge of no-man's-land.[159]

Amazingly, he learned to like it. 'It is,' he admitted, 'a vy curious life to live.' But after the humble, fettered duchy of Lancaster, after being blamed for what went wrong when he lacked the power to make it right, he felt free. 'I do not feel any prick of conscience at being out here,' he wrote to Curzon. 'I was and am sure that for the time being my usefulness was exhausted and that I could only recover it by a definite and perhaps a prolonged withdrawal . . . I do not know when I have passed a more joyous three weeks: . . . I share the fortunes of a company of Grenadiers. It is a jolly life with nice people; and one does not mind the cold and wet and general discomfort.' The 'indomitable good temper' and 'inflexible discipline' of the grenadiers impressed him. He in turn charmed them by referring to himself as 'the escaped scapegoat' and saying: 'Perhaps it is better to be irresponsible and right than responsible and wrong.' Major General the Lord Cavan, the commander of the Guards Division, proposed that he wait at brigade headquarters, away from the slime of the front, until a suitable command could be found for him. He declined, writing to Clementine: 'I said I wouldn't miss a day of it. Nor did I.' He wrote again: 'I am vy happy here. I did not know what release from care meant. It is a blessed peace. How I ever cd have wasted so many months in impotent misery, wh I might have spent in war, I cannot tell.'[160]

He won the affection of the men by his easy manner with them. He wrote: 'I keep watch during part of the night so that others may sleep. Last night I found a sentry asleep on his post. I frightened him dreadfully but did not charge him with the crime. He was only a lad, & I am not an officer of the regiment. The penalty is death or at least 2 years.' The troops also delighted in his treatment of visiting officers from Saint-Omer; he insisted they join him in inspection of the front line, where their highly polished boots became spattered with mud and their elegant whipcord breeches torn on the barbed wire. One pompous brigadier, arriving after the battalion's position had been damaged by a heavy barrage, told him that *this really would not do*, that the place must be made *safe*: 'You know, it's dangerous – positively *dangerous*.' Churchill replied: 'Yes, sir. But this is a very dangerous war.' No major British offensives were launched during his six months in Flanders, but it was a wretched existence, and why he should have looked forward to his spells on the brink of no-man's-land so eagerly is difficult to grasp. As he later wrote, 'cannonade and fusillade were unceasing' and 'no one was ever dry or warm.' Part of the reason lay in his remarkable gift for romanticizing squalor. In a letter to his wife he wrote: 'Last night . . . after dinner, I had a splendid walk with Archie [Archibald Sinclair, his second in command and later a political colleague] all over the top of the ground. We left the trenches altogether and made a thorough examination of all the fields, tracks, ruins etc immediately behind our line. You cannot show yourself here by day, but in the bright moonlight it is possible to move about without danger (except from random bullets) & to gain a vy clear impression. Archie was a vy good guide. We also went in front of our parapet into the No man's land & prowled about looking at our wire & visiting our listening posts. This is always exciting.' On November 30 the Germans celebrated his forty-first birthday by shelling him for three hours – which is how he, the ultimate egoist, regarded it. Then the battalion left the line for a rest, and he exulted in telling Clementine how they marched 'while the men sang "Tipperary" and the "Farmer's Boy" and the guns boomed applause. It is like getting to a jolly good tavern after a long day's hunting, wet & cold & hungry, but not without having had sport.' He was, he confessed, dazzled by 'the bright eyes of danger.'[161]

Undoubtedly he enjoyed isolation from the abuse and intrigues of London. But the essence of his Flanders mood – finding profound satisfaction where others saw only horror – lay deeper. It derived from a hard, medieval streak, a capacity for viewing bestiality and senseless brutality with a clear, untroubled gaze, responding in kind, even glorying in it. He was fascinated by scenes which revolted others. Few men, whatever their peacetime pursuits, could bear the sight of bloated rats feeding on corpses. In one stretch of earthworks abandoned by the Germans, Edward Spiers later recalled, the rodents 'were appalling things; they were huge . . . Had you fallen in a trench you would never have got out alive. They would have devoured you. One heard them at night running about in the barbed wire.' Churchill thought them immensely interesting. 'Winston,' Spiers remembered, 'pointed out that they had played a very useful role in eating human bodies.' In a letter to Clementine, he described a patrol of Tommies returning from no-man's-land with a captured German: 'Such men you never saw. The scene in the little dugout when the prisoner was brought in surrounded by these terrific warriors, in jerkins & steel helmets with their bloody clubs in hand – looking pictures of ruthless war – was one to stay in the memory. *C'est très bon.*'[162]

And yet . . .

The mind-set of the warrior is rigid, inflexible, fiercely intolerant. He cannot think kindly of the enemy; cannot, usually, regard him as human. And any suggestion that his own view of war may be even slightly flawed is both provocative and profoundly resented. Churchill did not fit that mould at all. He was, in fact, its obverse. In World War II he would shock Britain by praising the generalship of Erwin Rommel. In this war he became captivated by the poetry of England's most eloquent pacifist, an officer spared by a court-martial solely because of his valiant combat record. One of Winston's acquaintances wrote to a friend: 'By the way, *who* is Siegfried Sassoon? . . . Winston knows his last volume of poems by heart, and rolls them out on every possible occasion.' A lieutenant, recalling such a recitation, wrote: 'I had never heard of Sassoon or his poems and we were soon told something of his history . . . We quickly realized that the main theme of the poems was anti-war, the futility of war and the misery war brought. We heard that the Generals were seriously worried at the damage to morale these poems might inflict on the troops.' An officer said to Churchill: 'I should leave that man alone if I were you. He might start writing a poem about *you*.' Churchill instantly replied: 'I am not a bit afraid of Siegfried Sassoon. That man can think. I am afraid only of people who cannot think.'[163]

Later in the war, when Winston was back in London, Eddie Marsh introduced the two men. Sassoon's recollection of the meeting survives. He found Winston 'leisurely, informal, and friendly. Almost at once I began to feel a liking for him . . . He broached – in a good-humoured way – the subject of my attitude to the War, about which – to my surprise – he seemed interested to hear my point of view.' Churchill, Sassoon recalled, 'was making me feel that I should like to have him as my company commander.' There came a point, however, when the conversation developed into a monologue: 'Pacing the room, with a big cigar in the corner of his mouth, he gave me an emphatic vindication of militarism as an instrument of policy and stimulator of glorious individual achievements . . . Transfixed and submissive in my chair, I realized that what had begun as a persuasive confutation of my anti-war convictions was now addressed, in pauseful and perorating prose, to no one in particular.' As the dazed poet left, Winston offered him a civilian appointment. 'Had he,' Sassoon wondered, 'been entirely serious . . . when he said that "war is the normal occupation of man"? He had indeed qualified the statement by adding "war – and gardening." But it had been unmistakable that for him war was the finest activity on earth.'[164]

Certainly it stimulated *him*. On December 28, 1915, *The Times* carried an interview with a corporal, an Orangeman, who was quoted as saying of Churchill, 'A cooler and braver officer never wore the King's uniform . . . During the Ulster business before the war there was no man more detested in Belfast, but after what we have seen of him here we are willing to let bygones be bygones – and that is a big concession for Ulstermen to make . . . His coolness is the subject of much discussion among us, and everybody admires him.' Repeatedly, when he was elsewhere on the line, his frail sandbagged shelter was demolished by direct hits. Like Douglas MacArthur, who also defied enemy fire here two years later, he felt shielded by mysterious intervention, believing that 'Chance, Fortune, Luck, Destiny, Fate, Providence seem to me only different ways of expressing the same thing, to wit, that a man's own contribution to his life story is continually dominated by an external superior power.' One experience, as he saw it, seemed to confirm him. At the end of his first week at the front he received word that the corps commander wanted to see him in Merville; a car would meet him at the Rouge Croix crossroads. It was a muddy, three-mile hike, under German observation most of the time; he would write afterwards that 'the shriek of [enemy] shells' was constant, but he and his batman 'toiled and sweated on,' until, on arrival, they were dumbfounded to learn that the general had changed his mind. What, Churchill asked a staff officer, was the point of the rendezvous? 'Oh, it was nothing in particular,' the staff officer replied. 'He thought as he was coming up this way he would like to have a talk with you.' Winston was furious. He began 'another long, sliding, slippery, splashing waddle back to the trenches . . . The sedentary life of a Cabinet Minister, which I had quitted scarcely a month before, had not left me much opportunity to keep fit.' Back with the grenadiers, someone shouted to him: 'You're in luck today.' Five minutes after he had left, his dugout had been blown up. The officer with whom he shared it had been annihilated. 'Suddenly,' Churchill wrote afterwards, 'I felt my irritation against General — pass completely from my mind. All sense of grievance departed in a flash . . . How thoughtful it had been of him to wish to see me again, and to show courtesy to a subordinate . . . And then upon these quaint reflections there came the strong sensation that a hand had been stretched out to move me in the nick of time from a fatal spot.'[165]

His mother begged him to 'be sensible' and 'take the trenches in small doses' – as though he could manage that. Jennie felt close to him now; like his father at about the same age, he had quit the cabinet in disgrace. But Winston was unresponsive to her; his daily missives went to Clementine. In a typical letter from a rear area he began: 'I sit in a battered wicker chair within this shell scarred dwelling by the glowing coals of a brazier in the light of an acetylene lamp.' The grenadiers had been 'hunted by shells during these last two days in "rest billets." ' His bedroom had been pierced by shells three times; a nearby church steeple, which had withstood sixteen months of fighting, had been obliterated. 'One lives calmly on the brink of an abyss,' he wrote. He had come to understand how the unremitting strain transformed men, their first ebullience fading and leaving only 'dull resentment.' The infantrymen he had spoken to during his trench tours sensed the 'utter inability to take a decision on the part of the Government . . . Some urge me to return and try to break them up. I reply no – I will not go back unless I am wounded; or unless I have effective control.' Clementine was the one constant, indispensable figure in his squalid trench life. He endorsed virtually all of her political judgements; she was his 'vy wise & sagacious pussy cat.' Once several days passed with no mail from Cromwell Road; he signed himself 'your vilely neglected pig.' His letters to her often read like those of a child writing home from camp, and like a camper he made many small demands: 'I want 2 more pairs of thick Jaeger draws [sic] vests & socks (soft), 2 more pairs of brown leather gloves (warm) 1 more pair of field boots (like those I had from Fortnum & Mason) only from the fourth hole from the bottom instead of holes there shd be good strong tags for lacing quicker. One size larger than the last. Also one more pair of Fortnum & M's ankle boots . . . With these continual wettings and no means of drying one must have plenty of spares . . . Also send me a big bath towel. I now have to wipe myself all over with things that resemble pocket handkerchiefs.'[166]

She eagerly complied. Her need was as great as his, her worry greater. When he wrote to her of his aborted rendezvous with the corps commander, she replied in anguish: 'It is horrible to sit here in warmth & luxury while danger & suffering are so close to you. That dreadful walk across the fields there & back among falling shells was on Nov 24th & now it is 10 days later & Heaven knows what narrow escapes you may have had since.' One of Winston's cousins – his aunt Clara's daughter Clare, who, like Venetia Stanley, had been

476

a bridesmaid at their wedding – had just learned that her husband had been killed in France. Clementine wrote: 'My darling, I don't know how one bears such things. I feel I could not weather such a blow. She has a beautiful little son 8 weeks old, but now her poor "black puss" sleeps in Flanders. You *must* come back to me my dear one.' She prayed that he wore 'a steel helmet always & not the Glengarry.' She had 'ceased to have ambitions for you. Just come back to me alive that's all.' She loved him 'very much more even than I thought I did – for Seven years you have filled my whole life & now I feel more than half my life has vanished across the channel.' She wondered: 'If I came to Dieppe could you get 2 days' leave? I'm very very lonely.' Dieppe proved impossible, but later he slipped home from time to time. Like all wartime couples they desperately sought privacy during their brief hours together, once in Dover Pier's dreary Lord Walden Hotel and once in Cromwell Road, after which they had to cut it rather fine at Victoria Station. In her note to him that evening one recognizes the powerful tug between the shadow of death and the light of desire: 'I could not tell you how much I wanted you at the station. I was so out of breath with running for the train.'[167]

Love letters should not be taken literally. Their very language is hyperbole. Winston did not really mean that he was determined to stay at the front until either wounded or recalled to high office. Nor had Clementine forsaken her hopes for his career. Both saw future greatness for him on a far shore; the problem was to navigate the bewildering currents between here and there. Sir John French's promise of a brigade – four thousand men – might provide a way. A brilliant stroke in the field could bring acclaim, a reversal of his political fortunes, and, conceivably, a chance to change the direction of the war. 'The hour of Asquith's punishment and K's exposure draws nearer,' he wrote to his wife. These 'wretched men,' he went on, 'have nearly wrecked our chances. It may fall to me to strike the blow. I shall do it without compunction.'[168]

'I long for you to have a Brigade,' she wrote back. But she had misgivings. The leap from major to brigadier general was a mighty one. Lord Cavan counselled caution. Lead a battalion first, he advised Winston; get the feel of handling troops and then take on the greater responsibility. Clementine thought that wise: 'I am absolutely certain that whoever is C in C, you will rise to high commands . . . But everyone who *really* loves you & has your interest at heart wants you to go step by step whereas I notice the Downing Street tone is "of course Winston will have a brigade in a fortnight." Thus do they hope to ease their conscience from the wrong they have done you, and then hope to hear no more of you . . . Do get a battalion *now* & a brigade later.'[169]

Upon reflection, he agreed. The field marshal, however, wouldn't hear of it. Churchill wrote: 'I proposed to French that I shd take a battalion; but he rejected it, & said "no a brigade at once" & that he wd settle it quickly in case any accident shd happen to him. I have acquiesced.' One doubts he had been hard to persuade. He was dreaming of glory on the battlefield. On December 2 Edward Grigg, a grenadier officer, wrote to his mother: 'Winston was attached to the Company again for all the last period in the firing line. It was very cold and very wet – first a bitter frost, and then rain, sleet and thaw, which puts us up to the calf in mud and slime. That part of the line is in bad order, too, and we had nothing but a small dug-out about 2 ft 6 high with a wet mud floor to live and sleep in, and we all got kinks in our spines getting in and out of the beastly thing. But Winston accepted the situation with great cheerfulness and we had quite a good time. He has forgotten his political legacy from Lord Randolph, and thinks much more, I am sure, of the military instincts which have descended to him from the great Duke of Marlborough.'[170]

Later in the month he was summoned to GHQ. French was in England, he was told, but his appointment as brigadier general was definite. He would command the Fifty-sixth Brigade in the Nineteenth Division, which, he wrote home, 'is a regular Division in the second new army, & the Bde I shall command comprises 4 Lancashire Battalions . . . Altogether it is a vy satisfactory arrangement.' He anticipated some 'criticism & carping' at home, but no more than if he had taken a battalion for a few weeks, in which case it would have been said that he had used it 'merely as a stepping stone etc.' He was 'satisfied this is the right thing to do in the circumstances, & for the rest my attention will concentrate upon the Germans.' Spiers would be his brigade major; Eddie Marsh, he hoped, would be brought over in one capacity or another. He asked Clementine to order a new tunic bearing a brigadier's insignia. She, for her part, forgot her qualms, and wrote back that she was 'thrilled.'[171]

Not everyone in London was thrilled. Over lunch, in the crowded grillroom of the Berkeley Hotel in Piccadilly, Lord Esher, just back from Saint-Omer, told her: 'Of course you know Winston is taking a Brigade & as a personal friend of his I am very sorry about it; as I think he is making a great mistake. Of course it's not his fault, Sir John forced it upon him.' She put all this in a letter to her husband, adding: 'He then launched forth again, saying that you had been in the greatest danger, in more than was necessary etc & that French had determined to give you this Brigade as he was convinced you wd otherwise be killed. After this I crawled home quite stunned & heart-broken.' Churchill himself was unsurprised; he had begun to appreciate the unpopularity of the appointment. At GHQ Sir Henry Wilson wrote in his diary: 'Winston came up this morning to my room & had a long talk. I advised him *not* to take a Brigade as it would be bad for Sir John, Winston and the Brigade, but I did not convince him.'[172]

Sir Henry was dissembling – a complex man, he couldn't even be candid in his diary – for by then he surely knew that Sir John was beyond help or harm. At that moment the commander in chief was facing the music in Downing Street, the victim of bad strategy, worse tactics, an impossible war, and, to some extent, the disloyal intrigues of his senior subordinate, Sir Douglas Haig. Asquith wrote that he 'had for some time felt past fears and growing doubts as to Sir John French's capacity to stand the strain of his task with its ever-increasing and unforeseeable responsibilities.' So he dismissed him. Before they parted, French mentioned that he had given Churchill a brigade, and, according to him, 'Asquith said he was delighted.' But the prime minister was also a political weather vane, and he shortly learned that rumours of Churchill's promotion had already aroused hostility in Parliament. Sir Charles Hunter, a Tory MP with a military background, rose at Question Time to ask 'if Major Winston Churchill has been promised the command of an Infantry brigade; if this officer has ever commanded a battalion of Infantry; and for how many weeks he has served at the front as an Infantry Officer.' After an interval the under secretary of state for war deftly replied: 'I have no knowledge myself, and have not been able to obtain any, of a promise of command of an Infantry brigade having been made to my right hon[ourable] and gallant Friend referred to in the question.' Having 'consulted books of reference and other authentic sources of information,' he had found that his gallant Friend had never commanded a battalion. As to the time he had been in combat, 'the answer to the last part of the question would be about four weeks.' The House laughed. Hunter then demanded to know if Churchill had been assured of a battalion command. Several of Winston's friends cried, 'Why not?' Sir Charles Robertson, a former India army officer and an admirer of Churchill's, inquired sarcastically: 'Is not the question absurd on the face of it, Major Winston Churchill being under sixty years of age?' But another Tory MP, Evelyn Cecil, ended the exchange on a venomous note, asking: 'Is the right hon[ourable] Gentleman aware that if this appointment were made it would be thought by very many persons both inside and outside this House a grave scandal'[173]

Aitken had the impression that this 'apparently frightened The Block.' He also heard that Bonar Law had expressed 'unswerving antagonism to Churchill,' arguing that 'to give Churchill an influence on the conduct of affairs in France would be a disaster,' and that Lloyd George 'would not give any countenance to projects for Churchill's preferment.' If true – Aitken was a prodigious gossip – this is puzzling, for when Law and George visited Haig at GHQ a month later, they told the new commander in chief that if he saw fit to give Winston a brigade there would be 'no difficulty at home.' Whatever the pressures, Asquith swiftly buckled. He sent a note to French, who had not yet been formally relieved, saying that on reflection, far from being delighted, he feared that 'with regard to our conversation about our friend – the appointment might cause some criticism' and was therefore inadvisable. 'Perhaps,' he added, 'you might give him a battalion.' Dismayed and embarrassed, French phoned Churchill at GHQ. 'I have something extremely unpleasant to say,' he began, and then he read the prime minister's veto. Winston was astonished. If he had wanted a battalion, he could have had it long ago; six months earlier, when the Dardanelles was winding down, he had been offered one in the QOOH. Churchill had just finished a letter to Clementine when the field marshal's call had been put through. He unsealed the envelope and added on a slip marked 'later': 'I reopen my letter to say that French has telephoned me from London that the PM has written to him that I am not to have a Brigade but a Battalion. I hope however to secure one that is going into the line. You will cancel the order for the tunic! Do not allow the PM to discuss my affairs with you. Be vy cool & detached and avoid any sign of acquiescence in anything he may say.' She instantly replied: 'My Dear – your letter has just come telling me that your hopes of a Brigade have vanished. I do trust that Haig will give you one later. If he does it may be all for the best – but if not it is cruel that the change at GHQ came before all was fixed . . . My own Darling I feel such absolute confidence in your future – it is your present which causes me agony – I feel as if I had a tight band of pain round my heart.'[174]

Winston's resentment deepened. 'I am awfully bitter and so is French,' he wrote F.E. Smith; 'what ill-fortune.' Brooding, he wrote to Clementine: 'To measure Asquith's performance one has to remember that on my leaving the Admiralty he offered me a Brigade: & that when I told him three months ago of the offers French had made to me if I came out to the front, he advised me to go and assured me that any advancement wh was thought fitting by the C in C would have his hearty concurrence. One has to remember all the rest too of a long story of my work & connexion with him. Altogether I am inclined to think that his conduct reaches the limit of meanness & ungenerousness. Sentiments of friendship expressed in extravagant terms; coupled with a resolve not to incur the slightest criticism or encounter the smallest opposition – even from the most unworthy quarter. Personally I feel that every link is severed: & while I do not wish to decide in a hurry – my feeling is that all relationship should cease.' Clementine loved and honoured her husband, but she did not always obey him. 'You know I'm not good at pretending,' she wrote him, 'but I am going to put my pride in my pocket and reconnoitre Downing Street.' Nothing came of it. Winston was unsurprised. The prime minister was a 'weak and disloyal chief,' he said; 'Asquith will throw anyone to the wolves to keep himself in office.' During a winter thaw, she accepted an invitation to join the Asquiths at Walmer Castle and wrote to Winston of how they could 'distinctly hear the rumble of heavy guns' across the Channel. She played golf with 'the Prime who was feeling very pleasant & mellow . . . at one moment [I] thought I was going to give the boy a good beating (which I shd have relished) but Alas! I fell off towards the end & he won by a short length.' Winston reproached her mildly for going and asked what Asquith had said. She replied: 'You know what the PM is – He loathes talking about the War or work of any sort – He asked anxiously if you were happy.'[175]

The Block could be left to the mercies of Lloyd George, who began his intricate campaign to dethrone the prime minister and then replace him. Churchill, meanwhile, had to deal with a new commander in chief. His wife wrote to him: 'Do you know Sir Douglas Haig? Did he agree to your appointment or was it finally settled before he supervened? He looks a superior man, but his expression is cold and prejudiced, & I fear he is narrow.' Actually, he and Winston had been acquainted in the early Edwardian years, when he was a major and Winston a young MP, but that had been long ago, and Haig, a dour Scot, was elusive even to those who were close to him. At Oxford he had been regarded as 'headstrong, bad-tempered, and intractable.' In the army he had learned to control his temper, and he brought valuable qualities to Saint-Omer: a remarkable grasp of detail, tranquillity under pressure, and absolute self-confidence. He was blindly loyal to military tradition, however. 'The role of the Cavalry on the battlefield,' he wrote, 'will always go on increasing'; bullets, he believed, had 'little stopping power against a horse.' One has the distinct feeling that to him, machine guns, tanks, and aircraft were, if not contemptible, at least bad form. His greatest assets in his rise had been his powerful social connections. His wife had been a member of the royal household, and he knew the King well enough to write to him that French, his immediate superior, 'is quite unfit for his command at a time of crisis in our nation's history.'[176]

The way to break through the German trench line, Haig thought, was to use horses in 'mass tactics' – a theory which, as Leon Wolff points out, had been abandoned by even the most ardent cavalry officers. The official British history of the war would tactfully conclude that he was 'not swift of thought.' Bernard Shaw, who visited GHQ shortly after Haig took over, wrote: 'He was, I should say, a man of chivalrous and scrupulous character. He made me feel that the war would last thirty years, and that he would carry on irreproachably until he was superannuated.' Haig and Sir William ('Wully') Robertson, the new chief of the Imperial General Staff, were exponents of attrition. Churchill, attrition's heretic, could expect little from them. No compromise was possible between his concept of war and theirs. After reading a Churchill memorandum on the use of tanks and mortar, Leo Amery wrote in his diary: 'Whatever his defects may be, there is all the difference in the world between the tackling of a big problem like this by a man of real brain and imagination, and its handling by good second-rate men like Robertson and Haig, who still live in the intellectual trench in which they have been fighting.' On arriving in France, Winston had headed straight for the front to see for himself what it was like. In the whole course of the war, Haig never visited the trenches. Scenes of carnage, he said, might influence his judgement. Afterwards Churchill etched him in acid. Haig, he wrote, reminded him of 'a great surgeon before the days of anaesthetic, versed in every detail of such science as was known to him: sure of himself, steady of poise, knife in hand, intent upon the operation; entirely removed in his professional capacity from the agony of the patient, the anguish of relations, or the doctrines of rival schools, the devices of quacks, or the first-fruits of new learning. He would operate without excitement, or he would depart without being affronted; and if the patient died, he would not reproach himself.'[177]

This judgement lay in the future on December 18, 1915, Sir John French's last day as commander in chief, when, after picnicking in the countryside with Winston, French returned to GHQ and approached Haig on what he called 'a delicate personal matter.' He explained the broken promise to Churchill –

481

broken by Asquith – and then, according to Haig's diary, said he was 'anxious that Winston should have a Battalion. I replied that I had no objection because Winston had done good work in the trenches, and we were short of Battalion CO's.' The new commander in chief then sent for Churchill, who wrote to Clementine that evening: 'He treated me with the utmost kindness & consideration, assured me that nothing would give him greater pleasure than to give me a Brigade, that his only wish was that able men shd come to the front, & that I might count on his sympathy in every way.' Beaming, Winston asked whether Haig would like to read 'Variants of the Offensive,' a memorandum on trench warfare he had written while the grenadiers were in the rear area. He wrote home that Haig replied that 'he wd be "honoured" – ! So I am back on my perch again with my feathers stroked down.' Spiers wrote: 'WC has Douglas Haig to heel. DH is ready to do anything for him.'[178]

He was ready to do nothing of the sort. It is doubtful that Haig read 'Variants of the Offensive.' If he had, he probably wouldn't have understood it. And had he understood it, he would certainly have felt affronted. Churchill proposed flamethrowers, improvised infantry shields, wire-cutting torches fuelled by gas cylinders, and massive tunnelling operations. And he looked beyond the siege warfare in France and Belgium to fluid movements in other theatres of action. 'He was probably the only member of Asquith's Cabinet,' Clement Attlee would later write, 'who had a grasp of strategy.' Certainly he seemed to be the only British officer in Flanders who grasped the desperate need for innovations. Civilization was bleeding to death. 'The chaos of the first explosions,' he wrote, 'has given place to the slow fire of trench warfare: the wild turbulence of the incalculable, the terrible sense of adventure have passed . . . A sombre mood prevails in Britain. The faculty of wonder has been dulled; emotion and enthusiasm have been given place to endurance; excitement is bankrupt, death is familiar, and sorrow numbs. The world is in twilight; and from beyond the dim flickering horizons comes tirelessly the thudding of the guns.'[179]

On New Year's Day, 1916, Haig appointed Churchill a lieutenant colonel and gave him an infantry battalion, the Sixth Royal Scots Fusiliers, consisting largely of Lowland Scots, many of them miners from the Ayrshire coalfields. Winston wrote home that he would be glad to see the last of Saint-Omer, 'a desert' since French had left. He was now responsible for thirty officers and seven hundred men, and that evening he dined with the divisional commander at his headquarters in Merris. The grenadier colonel's welcome had been cold, but here, he wrote, 'they evidently will like vy much to have me. The general – Furse – is extremely well thought of here and is a thoroughly frank & broadminded man . . . Most of the staff had met me soldiering somewhere or other, & we had a pleasant evening.'[80]

His assurance was premature. Cheery greetings from the general and his staff were one thing; the battalion was another. The Sixth Royal Scots had been badly mauled at Loos and were deeply attached to their commanding officer, whom Churchill was replacing. The switch was therefore unpopular with them. Hakewill Smith, the battalion's only regular officer, later recalled that he heard of it with 'horror.' 'When the news spread,' wrote Andrew Gibb, the young adjutant, 'a mutinous spirit grew . . . Why could not Churchill have gone to the Argylls if he must have a Scottish regiment! We should all have been greatly interested to see him in a kilt . . . Indeed, any position at all in the Expeditionary Force seemed not too exalted for Winston if only he had left us our own CO and refrained from disturbing the peace of the pastures of Moolenacker.' Winston arrived there mounted, at the head of a cavalcade bearing his luggage, bathtub, and a boiler for heating the bath water. Moolenacker Farm, the battalion's reserve billet, consisted, in his words, of 'squalid little French farms rising from a sea of soppy field and muddy lanes.' The farm wives were awed. They whispered: *'Monsieur le Ministre! Monsieur le Colonel!' 'Ah, c'est lui?' 'C'est votre Ministre?'* The soldiers were less impressed. His first parade, after lunch, was a farce. The men were standing at slope arms when their new CO rode up on a black charger and cried: 'Royal Scots Fusiliers! Fix bayonets!' As a cavalryman he did not know that this order could not be carried out from the slope. A few men put their rifles on the ground and yanked their bayonets from their scabbards; the rest stood immobile, baffled. Gibb whispered to him that 'Order arms' must intervene, and Churchill growled the command. He inspected his troops and then barked another cavalry order: 'Sections right!' This meant nothing to the Jocks. They didn't budge. Gibb had to rescue him again.[181]

But he was determined to learn. He got the drill down, enrolled in nearby machine-gun and bomb-throwing schools, and patrolled the battalion area each night with Archie Sinclair. His batman found warm, dry quarters for him in one of the farmhouses, where, he wrote home, 'the guns boom away in the distance, & at night the sky to the Northward blinks & flickers with the wicked lights of war.' It never entered his mind that he was not entitled to every available comfort; nor, in that day, before the rise of the egalitarian passion, did it occur to his men. But he was not an insensitive officer. To boost morale, he organized a concert and games. He wrote: 'Poor fellows – nothing like this has been done for them before. They do not get much to brighten their lives – short though they might be.' He decided to brighten each of their days with a lecture from their CO. One day he struck a dogged pose and announced sonorously: 'War is declared, gentlemen – on lice!' There followed, in Gibb's words, 'such a discourse on *pulex Europaeua*, its origin, growth, and nature, its habit and its importance as a factor in wars ancient and modern, as left one agape at the force of its author.' And then the Sixth Royal Scots Fusiliers were thoroughly deloused.[182]

Sometimes he was preposterous. The outline of one speech he made to his junior officers survives. He sensibly began: 'Keep a special pair of boots to sleep in & only get them muddy in a real emergency. Use alcohol in moderation but don't have a great parade of bottles in yr dugouts. Live well but do not flaunt it.' Then he said: 'Laugh a little, & teach your men to laugh – gt good humour under fire – war is a game that is played with a smile. If you can't smile grin. If you can't grin keep out of the way till you can.' In Churchill, G.A. Henty still lived. On the other hand, he was a source of invaluable advice on master masonry and the handling of sandbags, all of which would be immensely useful when they moved up on the line. He devised clever plans for shelters, scarps, counterscarps, half-moon dugouts, and ravelins. These might save their lives; they appreciated that. But when he announced that batmen must serve as bodyguards, sacrificing their lives, if necessary, for their officers, laughter drowned him out. Some of his schemes, said Gibb, were 'too recherchés, too subtle to stand the practical test of everyday fighting.' If a parapet was hit during the day, he ordered, it must not be repaired until nightfall; that way, the Germans would not know what damage they had done. Later, under fire, bullets passed through the gaps and men were hit. The order was quietly countermanded.[183]

On January 24 they were ready. At eight o'clock that morning, with Churchill riding on his horse at the head of the column, they marched from Moolenacker Farm into the Belgian village of Ploegsteert, or 'Plug Street,' as the Tommies called it – the jump-off point for a maze of paths and shallow communications trenches which led soldiers eastward to and from the front – taking casualties from the German shellfire along the way. Churchill lodged that night in a battered convent (the 'Hospice,' he called it) belonging to the Sisters of Charity. It was the twenty-first anniversary of Lord Randolph's death. He wrote to his mother: 'I thought of my father on Jan 24 & wondered what he would think of it all. I am sure I am doing right.' To his wife he wrote: 'I am extremely well-lodged here – with a fine bedroom looking out across the fields to the German lines 3,000 yards away. Two nuns remain here and keep up the little chapel which is part of the building . . . On the right & left the guns are booming; & behind us a British field piece barks like a spaniel at frequent intervals.' He contrasted the view from his Admiralty office, from which he had been able to see the Horse Guards Parade and the windows of the Cabinet Room at No. 10, to the prospect here: '2 bright red pigs rooting about among the shellholes.'[184]

In the darkness the battalion moved up to the front-line trenches. Churchill established his headquarters in a shattered building known as Lawrence Farm – he called it his 'Conning Tower' – about five hundred yards behind no-man's-land. He was responsible for a thousand yards of trenches. Following deep, winding, sandbagged gullies, he could move up to the British wire and then check the entire position. 'It takes nearly 2 hours to traverse this labyrinth of mud,' he wrote. 'On the average,' wrote Gibb, 'he went around three times a day, which was no mean task in itself, as he had plenty of other work to do. At least one of these visits was after dark, usually about 1 A.M. In wet weather he would appear in a complete outfit of waterproof stuff, including trousers and overalls, and with his French light-blue helmet he presented a remarkable and unusual figure.' Lieutenant Jock McDavid saw him 'stand on the first step in broad daylight, to encourage the Jocks, and to prove . . . how little danger there was of being hit.' He was undismayed when, from time to time, his experiments demonstrated that the danger was very great indeed. Once he and his adjutant were in an advance trench when Winston suggested they peer over the parapet, to get a better look at the German fortifications. They drew small-arms fire, and then shellfire. 'Do you like war?' Churchill asked dreamily. 'At that moment,' Gibb wrote, 'I profoundly hated war. But at that and every moment I believe Winston Churchill revelled in it.'[185]

On February 3, he and Archie were lunching with several other officers at Lawrence Farm when, he wrote to Clementine, 'there was a tremendous crash, dust & splinters came flying through the room, plates were smashed, chairs broken. Everyone was covered with debris and the Adjutant (he is only 18) hit on the finger. A shell had struck the roof and burst in the next room – mine and Archie's . . . The wonderful good luck is that the shell (a 4.2) did not – & cd not have – burst properly. Otherwise we shd have had the wall thrown in on us – & some wd surely have been hurt.' Probably it disturbed her more than him. 'I slept peacefully in my tiny war-scarred room last night,' he added, 'after a prolonged tour of the trenches.' He even found time to acquire an easel and oils and paint shell holes. She wrote frantically: '*Please* leave that wretched farm and find a safer place.' She wanted to join him: 'It wd be so easy & I cd live with the poor French women in a ruined cottage & hoe turnips.' The sensible course for him would have been to omit such alarming accounts from his letters, but Churchill was never sensible about taking risks, or thoughtful about the impact his vivid details would have on those who loved him. Since peril never upset him, it may never have occurred to him that it might distress others. 'It is one long holiday for me,' he wrote to her, '. . . like my African journey.'[186]

By now all distrust of the new CO had vanished. 'I am firmly convinced,' wrote Gibb, 'that no more popular officer ever commanded troops. As a soldier he was hard-working, persevering and tough . . . He lived soldiering: it lay near his heart and I think he could have been a very great soldier.' Winston was touched and pleased to find that the battalion's junior officers 'put up my photograph in the trenches, & I am sure they would make an effort if I asked them and some big test came upon us.' He was asking a lot of them as it was. McDavid later remembered Winston's first venture into no-man's-land: 'Clad in his long trench waterproof, shining knee-high trench boots and his blue steel helmet, with his revolver and powerful flash-lamp attached to his web-belt, he preceded me on the journey through the wire. All went well until we were within a few yards of the first post. Then enemy machine-gun fire swept the sphere of operations.' They dove into a shell crater. Abruptly a blinding ray of light appeared in the hole. Churchill roared: 'Put out that bloody light!' It was his own flashlight. As he crouched he had pressed the switch. 'Corrective action,' McDavid recalled, 'swiftly followed.' Thereafter, according to Hakewell Smith, he 'would often go into no-man's-land. It was a nerve-racking experience to go with him. He would call out in his loud, gruff voice – far too loud it seemed to us – "You go that way, I will go this . . . Come here, I have found a gap in the German wire. Come over here at once!" ' By now he 'never fell when a shell went off; he never ducked when a bullet went past with its loud crack.' Lieutenant Francis Napier Clavering was with him when Winston decided that they should climb over the top of the parapet and walk along the entire thousand-yard length of the Royal Scots' line. 'Up went a Verey [sic] light,' he recalled. 'Churchill was on his knees at the time, measuring the depth of the earth' with a yardstick. Under the flare they were clearly visible to the enemy. 'The Hun machine guns opened up, belly high. Why the hell we weren't killed I just don't understand. I didn't want to die . . . "For God's sake keep still, Sir," I hissed. But he didn't take the slightest notice. He was a man who had no physical fear of dying.'[178]

He abandoned Lawrence Farm, as Clementine had asked, only to establish himself in what he called his 'Advance Headquarters,' a hundred yards closer to the wire. Here, as in India nearly twenty years earlier, he hoped to win recognition, mention in dispatches, possibly a medal or two – some distinction which would attract attention in London. Back in reserve at the convent for two days he wrote to Clementine: 'If I come through all right my strength will be greater than it ever was. I wd much rather go back to the trenches tonight, than go home in any position of mediocre authority. But I *shd* like to see my beloved pussy cat.' Actually, the time was approaching when he would prefer even mediocre authority to Flanders, not because of the discomfort and jeopardy at the front, but because in Parliament he could at least hope to exert greater influence on the conduct of the war. His disclaimer to his mother – 'All I hear confirms me in my satisfaction to be freed from my share in the present [parliamentary] proceedings' – cannot be taken seriously. In the same letter he urged her to 'keep in good touch with all my friends.' But here again, it was his wife who had his real eyes and ears – and tongue. There was talk of creating a minister for air. She invited Curzon to lunch and suggested that Winston would be ideal for the job. 'Oh my darling I long so for it to happen, & feel that it would except for the competition for the post inside the Cabinet,' she wrote. Nothing came of it. In early February she and Goonie lunched with Curzon at his mansion, and he raised the possibility that Churchill would 'be made a Brigadier almost at once' – he even gave Clementine three bottles of brandy as a token of congratulation – yet this, too, was vain.[188]

Lloyd George lunched in Cromwell Road, but this was a great strain on his hostess. He said all the right things, expressing 'great distress at you not being in the Government,' she wrote, and saying repeatedly, 'We must get Winston back.' She didn't believe him. In her view he, not Asquith, was her husband's nemesis. 'I don't trust him one bit,' she wrote, characterizing him as 'fair of speech, shifty of eye, treacherous of heart.' Again: 'I get on so well with him & I know he likes me, but he is a sneak . . . He is a barometer, but not really a useful one as he is always measuring his own temperature [sic] not yours!' And again: 'Before taking LlG's [hand] I would have to safeguard myself with charms, touch-woods, exorcisms & by crossing myself. I can always get along with him & yesterday I had a good talk, but you can't hold his eyes, they shift away.' She thought her husband had been too hard on the prime minister: 'I think my Darling you will have to be very patient – Do not burn any boats – The PM has not treated you worse than Ll G has done . . . I feel that if the choice were equal you would prefer to work with the PM than with Ll G.' She lunched with Asquith in Downing Street. 'He talked a great deal about you and asked a great many questions. I was perfectly natural (except perhaps that I was a little too buoyant) & he tried to be natural too, but it was an effort.' She said she would take *his* hand, 'tho' I would give it a nasty twist.' Winston replied that while Lloyd George was 'no doubt all you say,' he had been opposed to the Dardanelles and not, like the prime minister, a 'co-adventurer' who had destroyed the plan by his own incompetence. Still, Churchill wanted to know more about her hour with Asquith: 'I shd like a *verbatim* report of the Kat's conversation with the old ruffian.' Unfortunately, there was little to tell. Most of the talk at No. 10 had been trivial. 'The chief topic of social gossip,' she told him, 'is who is going to India as Viceroy . . . It seems incredible.'[189]

All this was very hard on her. Clementine did not carry her husband's weight. She was admired and respected, but there could be no substitute for Churchill's presence. And she found it disagreeable to pass along his messages to political allies and confidants, particularly those she distrusted. She wrote: 'Oh Winston I do not like all these letters I have to forward – I prefer Charlotte Corday – Shall I do it for you?' The unavoidable fact was that he could not be an effective parliamentary force while prowling near the enemy wire in Flanders. Nor was the army always considerate towards officers who were also MPs, particularly when they lacked political muscle. Learning of a secret session of the House of Commons, Churchill applied for leave to attend it. Permission was granted with the understanding that he would return the moment debate ended. When an open session followed, and he asked for an extension of his leave, the appeal was denied in a War Office telegram informing him that no exception could be made 'while you are commanding R Scots Fus and your battalion is in trenches.' Clementine was furious. He could have altered policy during the session, she wrote him afterwards when he was back at the front, 'if only you had been here and spoken.' She could not blame this on Lloyd George. Asquith was responsible, and she acknowledged it. 'The Government,' she wrote, 'are in a shameful position.'[190]

Actually, he would have been wise to have stayed in Flanders that spring. It was while in Parliament on another leave that he delivered one of the most unfortunate speeches of his life. Late in the afternoon on Tuesday, March 7, 1916, he rose from the front Opposition bench to offer a closely reasoned critique of governmental blunders in the prosecution of the war. 'I shall have to strike a jarring note,' he began. He indicted Balfour's tenure at the Admiralty in the strongest language the House had heard since the outbreak of the war, charging 'slackness, indifference, want of push and drive.' The U-boat challenge was not being met, he said; there was strong evidence that German shipyards were outbuilding Britain's. The zeppelins were getting through; mismanagement of the navy could lead to defeat. It was an exceptionally impressive speech. He had the complete attention of every man there. And then, at the very end, he destroyed his message, and dealt a savage blow to his credibility, in a single sentence: 'I urge the First Lord of the Admiralty without delay to fortify himself, to vitalise and animate his Board of Admiralty by recalling Lord Fisher to his post as First Sea Lord.'[191]

It was unbelievable. He was actually advocating a return to power of the old man who had ruined his Dardanelles strategy and evicted him from the Admiralty. The House sat stunned. Asquith confessed that he was 'speechless at the time'; afterwards, he called Winston's bombshell 'suicidal' and 'a piece of the grossest effrontery.' In the Strangers' Gallery, Eddie Marsh wept. Clementine, aghast, concluded that her husband had demolished his last parliamentary support. Lloyd George simply gasped: 'A great error!' The only congratulatory note came from a predictable source, the last man with any right to expect praise from Churchill. Fisher wrote him: 'SPLENDID!!! You'll have your Reward! All I entreat you now is to entrench yourself as Leader of the Opposition! and wait for the Big thing to come to you! . . . Your attitude so excellent – a helpful *(not a hostile)* critic. *Anyhow my heart is very full!* I feel the good old times are back!'[192]

Churchill left Parliament unaware of the ridicule about to envelop him. Violet Asquith, finding him in his mother's house, asked: 'What possessed you? *Why* did you do it?' All London was asking the same question, but she was the first to be answered. He said he had conceived his proposal, she wrote, 'as a great gesture of magnanimity – the forgiveness of the wrongs Fisher had done to him, for the sake of a greater aim, our naval supremacy.' Gently she dissolved his illusion. It would not be so interpreted, she said; rather, others would see it 'as a clumsy gambler's throw for his own ends.' By noon on Wednesday he, too, saw this. The question was now whether to stay in London and carry on the debate, or take the next boat back to Flanders. Wednesday morning Fisher appeared gaily in Cromwell Road, insisting that Churchill speak again, pressing on; other MPs, the old admiral was confident, would rally around him. Clementine vehemently disagreed. After some hesitation Winston went to the House that afternoon, thereby exposing himself to the full force of Balfour's withering reply.[193]

Balfour ignored Churchill's closely reasoned arguments, even though he knew them to be unimpeachable – knew, for example, that the German submarine campaign would soon threaten England with starvation. Instead, he humiliated him. He did not imagine 'that there was a single person who heard my right hon[ourable] Friend's speech who did not listen to the latter part of it with profound stupefaction.' Churchill had 'never made the smallest concealment, either in public or in private, of what he thought of Lord Fisher.' What, AJB asked, had Winston said in delivering his 'farewell speech' the previous autumn, 'when he exchanged a political for a military career? He told us that the First Sea Lord, Lord Fisher, did not give him, when he was serving in the same Admiralty with him, either the clear guidance before the event or the firm support after it which he was entitled to expect.' The essence of the matter was 'that the right hon[ourable] Gentleman, who could not get along with Lord Fisher – I will not say that, but with whom Lord Fisher could not get on – says that Lord Fisher, who according to my right hon[ourable] Friend neither supported him nor guided him, is nevertheless the man who ought to be given as a supporter and a guide to anybody who happens to hold at this moment the responsible position of First Lord of the Admiralty. It is a paradox of the wildest and most extravagant kind.' It was more – 'the most amazing proposition that has ever been laid before the House of Commons.' In a final turn of the knife, Balfour said slowly: 'I should regard myself as contemptible beyond the power of expression if I were to yield an inch to a demand of such a kind, made in such a way.'[194]

Stung, Churchill replied that Balfour, 'a master of parliamentary sword play and every dialectical art,' had mocked a member 'who is so much younger than himself' – this was absurd, and unworthy of Winston – to evade 'a note of warning' which 'should be sounded, and sounded in time.' As to Fisher: 'The real fact is that if we could associate in some way or another the driving power and energy of Lord Fisher, with the carrying out of Lord Fisher's programme at the highest possible speed, there is no reason to believe that great public advantage would not result from that.' It was a weak defence of what would have been a strong case, had he left the old admiral out of it the day before. No one's mind was changed. All those who had been bruised by his invective in the past, who had distrusted his interlocking brilliance and instability, the inevitable handmaidens of genius, were now after him in full cry. Once more the growing frustration over the insatiable war left a residue of bitterness. Considering who they were, their breeding and their gentility, the backlashes of some were startling. Margot Asquith wrote to Balfour: 'I hope & believe that Winston will never be forgiven for his yesterday's speech. Henry & I were thunderstruck at the *meanness* & the gigantic folly of it. I've never varied in my opinion of Winston I am glad to say.' (This was flagrantly untrue.) 'He is a hound of the lowest sense of political honour, a fool of the lowest judgement & contemptible . . . Henry & I thought you admirable and if H had not had a deputation he said he wd have given Winston 10 of the nastiest minutes of his life he was so *disgusted*.'[195]

Violet Asquith, who took the other side, nevertheless wrote that 'whatever his motive, he realized that he had hopelessly failed to accomplish what he had set out to do.' Back in Cromwell Road he pondered his next move. Fisher wanted him to quit the army and lead a full-fledged attack on the government: 'Write at once and resign! *I beg you to do this!* . . . I assure you that I am not so much thinking of your personal interests (*immense as they are! because you have the Prime Ministership in your grasp!*) but of saving the country! *Now now now* is the time to save the country NOT 3 months ahead!' Had Winston's stock stood at its pre-war level, this might have been sensible. With each passing day it became clearer that Asquith's war policy was a failure. He could not remain at No. 10 much longer. Tempted, Churchill secured a written promise from

Asquith on Saturday that 'if hereafter you should find your sense of public duty called upon you to return to political life here, no obstacle will be put in your way, and your relief will be arranged for, as soon as it can be effected without detriment to the Service.' Monday, on the train to Dover, Winston argued the point with his wife. At the port he wrote to Asquith holding him to his word, scribbled a press release announcing his return to civilian life, and left it in Clementine's hands.[196]

Late that afternoon, back in Belgium, he changed his mind and dispatched telegrams from Ploegsteert withdrawing the letter and the release. But then he switched back, and for good. He was preoccupied now, not with the Germans on the other side of no-man's-land, but with his former colleagues who had taunted him from the Treasury Bench. Ten days after his return to his battalion he wrote to Clementine that he had resolved to leave the army at the first opportunity. He had served in the trenches since November, 'almost always in the front line, certainly without discredit.' Over the past fifteen years he had built a strong political reputation, 'enabling me to command the attention . . . of my fellow countrymen in a manner not exceeded by 3 or 4 living men.' England's fate was at stake, 'and almost every question both affecting war & peace conditions, with wh I have always been formostly [sic] connected, is now raised.' To remain in Flanders would be irresponsible. 'Surely,' he wrote, 'these facts may stand by themselves in answer to sneers & cavillings. At any rate I feel I can rest upon them with a sure & easy conscience. Do not my darling one underrate the contribution I have made to the public cause, or the solidarity of a political position acquired by so many years of work & power.'[197]

Clementine was unconvinced. The misjudgement, she knew, was his; he simply did not understand the transformation of his reputation wrought by the Dardanelles, or the depth of his self-inflicted wound in the exchange with Balfour. His reasons were 'weighty & well expressed,' she tactfully replied, 'but it would be better if they were stated by others than yourself.' Actually, he had put her in a ghastly position. She wrote to him: 'My Darling own Dear Winston I am so torn and lacerated over you. If I say "stay where you are" a wicked bullet may find you which you might but for me escape,' but if he left his troops the consequences might be 'a lifelong rankling regret which you might never admit even to yourself & on which you would brood & spend much time in arguing to yourself that it *was* the right thing to do – And you would rehearse all the past events over & over again & gradually live in the past instead of in the present and in the great future.' Six days later she wrote: 'The present Government may not be strong enough to beat the Germans, but I think they are powerful enough to do you in & I pray to God you do not give the heartless brutes the chance –. '[198]

Nevertheless, the yeast of revolt continued to work in him. He knew he was not needed here, nor even particularly wanted. Haig had summoned him to Saint-Omer. Back at Lawrence Farm, Winston told Hakewell Smith that the BEF commander in chief had offered him a brigade but suggested that he could be more useful by returning to London and guiding a conscription bill through the House. At the same time, GHQ informed him that his battalion would be merged with another, the Seventh Royal Scots Fusiliers, and the CO of the Seventh, being senior to Churchill, would assume command of the hybrid. Thus, as he happily put it, 'I am not leaving my battalion; my battalion is leaving me.' Ignoring Asquith this time, he sent his resignation to Kitchener, who accepted it with the proviso that he did not reapply for active service for the duration of the war. The *London Gazette* reported that he was relinquishing his lieutenant colonelcy. On April 28 he led his troops into the front line for the last time. Clementine, reconciled, wrote to him from Blenheim: 'Let me hear that you are coming home for *good* to take up your *real* work.' He sent her his last letter from Lawrence Farm on May 2. He intended to relax before plunging into politics again: 'Wd it not be vy nice to go to Blenheim for the Sunday. If you arrange this, please get me 3 large tubes of *thin* White (not stiff) from Robersons: also 3 more canvasses: and a bottle of that poisonous solution wh cleans the paint off the old canvasses . . . The Germans have just fired 30 shells at our farm hitting it 4 times: but no one has been hurt. This is I trust a parting salute.'[199]

The next morning he and his troops left Ploegsteert for reassignment, and three days later, in Armentières, he entertained his officers at a farewell luncheon. In toasting them he said he had learned that the young Scot 'is a formidable fighting animal.' Gibb remembered afterwards: 'I believe every man in the room felt Winston Churchill's leaving us a real personal loss.' The following day Winston received a highly political note from General W.T. Furse: 'It seems to me peculiarly up to you and Lloyd George to concentrate all your efforts on breaking such a futile Govt – and that, immediately. How can anyone suppose that the same men in the same flat bottomed tub can do any better in the future than they have done in the past?' Churchill optimistically wrote to his wife: 'The Government is moribund. I only trust they will not die too soon.' It was characteristic of him that he regarded himself as the obvious alternative to Asquith. Clementine had warned him that such optimism was unrealistic, but he had not believed her. Now he would learn the lesson from other, harsher critics.[200]

Churchill was never a complete outcast. During each of the several political exiles in his life his solitude was tempered by friends willing to compromise their own futures for his sake, or allies who found common cause with him. Three MPs now invited him to join them in a patriotic Opposition: Arthur Markham, George Lambert, and – Ireland forgotten – Sir Edward Carson. The *Manchester Guardian* rejoiced that Winston was back; the *Observer* wanted to see him in a ministry. F.E. Smith was a source (though his only source) of goings-on in the cabinet. Lloyd George, though bland, was at least willing to be seen with him. The unfilial Violet reported events in the Asquith household. And although Winston's popularity with the people was greatly diminished, he retained a national constituency. Max Aitken later recalled accompanying him into a railway station and passing a train crowded with British tars returning from leave. As Winston 'walked up the platform,' Aitken wrote, 'the bluejackets gave him an immense reception, cheering him with enthusiasm. Churchill was deeply moved and declared that he was encouraged to believe that he was not after all the Forgotten Man.'[201]

He would never be forgotten; he was unforgettable. But he could be ignored, mortified, and taunted, and all these would be his miserable lot throughout the year ahead. In Parliament, Bonar Law, now colonial secretary, baited him mercilessly. He was told that resignation of his command proved that he was a cheap opportunist. He learned that the Conservative Lord Derby, writing to Lloyd George, had vowed that, whatever the truce between the parties, 'Winston could not possibly be in it. Our party will not work with him and as far as I am concerned personally nothing would induce me to support any Government of which he is a member . . . He is absolutely untrustworthy as was his father before him, and he has got to learn that just as his father had to disappear from politics so must he, or at all events from official life.'[202] The patriotic Opposition grew shaky when Lord Milner, a prospective member of it, refused to be reconciled with Churchill. It then collapsed after Asquith deprived it of its chief issue, conscription, by accepting compulsory military service. Inductions began on May 25, 1916. During the previous twenty-two months two and a half million Britons had voluntarily joined the colours – a testament to the extraordinary patriotism of their generation.

Winston tried to reopen parliamentary discussion of diversionary attacks in the Baltic and the Middle East. His speeches were followed by studied silence. The U-boat threat, he said, could be met by convoys. The Admiralty said, and did, nothing. (When at his insistence convoys were introduced the following year, the monthly loss of merchant ship tonnage dropped from 874,576 to 351,105.) Kitchener's appeal for men, he pointed out, had attracted volunteers from key jobs in shipyards, mines, and munitions factories. They should be discharged from the army and put back to work: 'We hear a great deal . . . about "comb this industry," or "comb that," but I say to the War Office, "Physician, comb thyself." ' Nothing was done. His experience in the trenches led him to make practical suggestions about the front. A network of light railways behind the lines would improve logistics. British trench lights, inferior to the enemy's, should be improved immediately. The supply of steel helmets was inadequate. Staff officers safely beyond the range of the German artillery were pinning medals on one another, and that was outrageous: 'It is the privates, the non-commissioned officers, and the regimental officers whose case requires the sympathetic attention of the House and of the Secretary of State. Honour should go where death and danger go.' Logistics, trench lights, the helmet shortage, and the pernicious decorations policy went unchanged.[203]

He felt that the troops comfortably stationed in England and the safe ports of the Empire should be rotated in combat. At the front, he told inattentive MPs, he had witnessed 'one of the clearest and grimmest class distinctions in the world – the distinction between the trench and the non-trench population.' Under the present system, 'the trench population lives almost continuously under the fire of the enemy. It returns again and again, after being wounded twice and sometimes three times, and it is continually subject, without respite, to the hardest tests that men have ever been called upon to bear, while all the time the non-trench population scarcely suffers at all . . . I wish to point out to the House this afternoon that the part of the army that really counts for ending the war is this killing, fighting, suffering part.' He described red-tabbed officers in warm, safe châteaux confidently moving pins on maps, forgetting that each pin represented a multitude of human beings whose outlook was very different from their own. 'The hopes of decisive victory' grew 'with every step away from the front line,' reaching 'absolute conviction in the Intelligence Department.' The result – doomed offensives – troubled him more than any other aspect of the government's war policy. Victory would not be gained, he wrote in the *Sunday Pictorial*, 'simply by throwing in masses of men on the western front.' In the days after his return from Flanders he was particularly worried about Haig's attack, now imminent, north of the Somme River. He begged for restraint. But the cabinet agreed that as an 'amateur' he could hardly match the army's expertise. Indeed, no minister deigned to reply to him. Instead, Harold Tennant, an under secretary at the War Office, rose and followed Balfour's example by saying contemptuously: 'There is one thing which I envy my right hon[ourable] and gallant Friend, and that is the time he had in order to prepare his carefully thought-out speeches. I wish I had the same opportunity.'[204]

On July 1, 1916, after a prolonged bombardment, the British infantry went over the top, and by nightfall eighty thousand Englishmen had fallen, twenty thousand of them dead. The Ulster Volunteer Force, brave beyond belief, had been cut to pieces in the swampy valley of the Ancre. It was the bloodiest day in the history of combat. Yet Haig refused to break off the Somme action. Churchill prepared a memorandum marshalling the arguments for disengagement. 'So long as an army possesses a strong offensive power,' he wrote, 'it rivets its adversary's attention. But when the kick is out of it, when the long-saved-up effort has been expended, the enemy's anxiety is relieved, and he recovers his freedom of movement. This is the danger into which we are now drifting. We are using up division after division – not only those originally concentrated for the attack, but many taken from all parts of the line.' It would take months, he pointed out, for 'these shattered divisions' to recover. In the interval the Germans could withdraw troops from this front and send them against Russia.[205]

F.E. Smith wrote an introduction for this analysis and had it printed for the cabinet. Everyone else discounted it. Even before it had gone to press Hankey wrote in his diary that Sir William Robertson had 'told me that F.E. Smith was

The Western Front
June 1916

Front lines
▲▲▲▲▲ Belgian ━━━ British ⋯⋯⋯ French

MILES
0 — 25 — 50 — 75 — 100

KILOMETERS
0 — 25 — 50 — 75 — 100

G H WARD

writing a paper to show that the big offensive in France had failed. I suspect that Ll George & Winston Churchill are at the back of it. Personally I think it is true but it is a mistake to admit it yet.' A copy of the memo reached Saint-Omer. To Lord Northcliffe, who was visiting him there, Haig insisted that the drive must continue, and Northcliffe, convinced, wrote to the editor of the *Times:* 'Let me once more say and urge you that what is taking place on the Somme must not be measured in metres. It is the first time we have had a proper scientific attack. There are no complaints of bad Staff work . . . If we wrote communiqués as well as the Germans, we would lay much more stress on the German losses, which are *known* to be immense.' In fact, the campaign, when it finally petered out, had cost the British 481,842 men to the enemy's 236,194 – and the only gain was a few square miles of worthless mud. The *Times*, however, never mentioned Churchill's warning.[206]

The *Daily Mail* accused him of conspiring against Haig and Robertson, and therefore against England. 'The country,' it reported when the Somme bloodletting was at its height, had 'seen a Cabinet minister who had just enough intelligence to know that Antwerp and Constantinople were places of importance and yet was mad enough to embark on adventures in both places . . . In the Dardanelles affair in particular a megalomaniac politician risked the fate of our Army in France and sacrificed thousands of lives to no purpose.' He had dragged 'too pliant officers' with him 'into these reckless and hopeless "gambles" ' at a time when his sole duty 'was simply to supply the Navy with men and material.' Tragedy would have been averted if the admirals had been 'men of the stamp of Sir Douglas Haig and Sir William Robertson.' The lesson was: *'Ministerial meddling means military muddling.'* Churchill was put on notice: 'No politician who remembers the contemptible fiasco of Antwerp and the ghastly blunder of Gallipoli need expect either patience or forgiveness from the British public if he interferes with the soldiers in charge of our operations.' H.A. Gwynne of the *Morning Post* wrote to Asquith of 'a sort of plot whose ramifications I am not altogether able to trace'; its purpose was 'to get rid of DH,' and its ringleader, he believed, was the former first lord. The *Spectator* accused Churchill of playing 'the part of a political adventurer . . . with a want of scruple and want of consideration for public interests, and with a reckless selfishness, to which our political history affords no parallel.'[207]

After reading this Lloyd George told Sir George Riddell that it was 'on the whole part true.' He and Asquith had become convinced, in the words of Martin Gilbert, that 'the imaginative, constructive, hard-working colleague of prewar years was being eaten up by personal ambition, and that his judgement had been impaired.' Winston learned of this and thought it incomprehensible. It was one thing to be slandered by Balfour, Bonar Law, and Lord Derby. That was politics. The Tories were only giving as good as they had got from him. But to be distrusted, suspected, and even condemned by men who had long been friends as well as colleagues was beyond his understanding. It was not, however, beyond Clementine's. Others fawned on him and then cut him behind his back. She told him, and wrote him, that he was sometimes curt, insensitive, and inconsiderate; that he was too given to extravagant overstatement; that his manner was dictatorial and often insulting. It was not enough to be right. His assumption that he alone should stand at the centre of events, she said, offended men whose own achievements entitled them to share the stage and disagree. He lacked patience and tolerance. He was often strident and scornful, and because this had alienated first-rate men, he was driven to seek the company of others, who, as she saw it, could do him no good and might bring harm. When they had left Admiralty House, Clementine thought she had seen the last of Lord Fisher. To her horror, Winston continued to correspond with him, sent him birthday greetings, and even invited him to Cromwell Road as an honoured guest. There she could not contain herself. F.E. Smith heard her tell the old admiral: 'Keep your hands off my husband. You have all but ruined him once. Leave him alone now.' Sometimes Churchill himself realized that he had fallen among companions who were, if not evil, at least unworthy. At one function he approached a fellow guest and said shakily: 'Get me a stiff whisky and soda, and get it quick. I have just done something I hoped I would never have to do again. I have shaken hands with de Robeck.'[208]

Max Aitken, who remained constant, later wrote of Churchill in this dark time: 'He cared for the Empire profoundly, and he was honestly convinced that only by his advice and methods could it be saved. His ambition was in essence disinterested. He suffered tortures when he thought that lesser men were mismanaging the business.' Another friend described him as 'a character depressed beyond the limits of description . . . When the Government was deprived of his guidance he could see no hope anywhere.' He told Riddell: 'I am finished. I am banished from the scene of action.' On July 5 he wrote to Archie Sinclair: 'I do not want office, but only war direction . . . I am profoundly unsettled: & cannot use my gift. Of that last I have no doubts. I do not feel that my judgements have been falsified, or that the determined pursuance of my policy through all the necessary risks was wrong. I wd do it all again if the circumstances were repeated.But I am faced with the problem of living through days of 24 hours each: & averting my mind from the intricate business I had in hand – wh was my life.' In his anguish he sent his brother a long, tormented letter on July 15. 'Is it not damnable,' he asked, 'that I should be denied all real scope to serve this country, in this tremendous hour?' Asquith, he wrote, 'reigns supine, sodden and supreme.' Then: 'Tho' my life is full of comfort, pleasure and prosperity I writhe hourly not to be able to get my teeth effectively into the Boche. But to plunge as a battalion commander unless ordered – into this mistaken welter – when a turn of the wheel may enable me to do 10,000 times as much would not be the path of patriotism or of sense . . . Jack my dear I am learning to hate.'[209]

The western front haunted him – both its futility and the thought that there, at least, he might be contributing something, if only a mite, to the war effort. 'I look back a gt deal to our Plugstreet days,' he wrote to Sinclair later in the year, '& wish I cd have cut myself more adrift from London & its whirlpools and been more content with the simple animal life (& death) wh the trenches offered.' Forgetting his pledge to Kitchener, he declared: 'When I am *absolutely* sure there is no prospect of regaining control or part of it here, I shall return again to that resort & refuge.' He was struck by a bitter irony. Volunteering to fight had been 'a costly excursion' for him; in doing so he had sacrificed the power he now craved. 'If I had stayed Chancellor of the Duchy and shut my mouth & drawn my salary, I shd today be one of the principal personages in direction of affairs . . . Under a fair pretence of fine words,

496

there is a gt *déconsideration* of all who wear uniform. Not one of these gallant MPs who has fought through the Somme at the head of their battalions, stands a chance agst less clever men who have stopped & chattered at home. This to me is the most curious phenomenon of all. It is quite inexplicable to me.'[210]

He seldom addressed the House now. C.P. Scott of the *Guardian*, calling on him in South Kensington, urged him to keep his flag flying in Parliament. Eventually, he predicted, recruits would rally to him. Winston shook his head. Except in Scott's paper, his remarks were unreported. Indeed, they were largely unheard; few members came in to hear him – 'what a contrast with the old days, when my rising was the signal for the House to fill!'[211] He preferred to reach his public through the *Sunday Pictorial*. Writing an article took no longer than preparing a speech; every word was printed, and he was paid £250, about five shillings a word, for each piece. That was important. He needed every penny he could make. His brother, now fighting under Haig, had only his officer's salary. Jennie, who had let her own house and moved into 41 Cromwell Road while Winston was in the trenches, contributed £40 a month, but with three adults, and five children in the nursery under a nanny, they had to run a tight ship. The Christmas holidays were another matter. Sunny invited them all to Blenheim – his political quarrels with Winston and Clementine had been long forgotten – and they welcomed the new year with an enormous bonfire. Winston tossed an effigy of the kaiser on the flames. Across the Channel, at the stroke of midnight, the Germans filled the sky with brilliant green flares. A British battery fired ten shells, paused, and fired seven more. It was 1917.

Clementine had seen the way to sever his knot of agony nearly a year earlier, while he was still in Flanders. Once the facts about the Dardanelles were made public, she believed, her husband would be absolved of all blame, for both the failure to force the strait and the subsequent tragedy of the peninsula. On January 11 she had written to Winston: 'If you ask the PM to publish the Dardanelles papers let me know what happens. If he refuses or delays I beg you not to do anything without telling me first & giving me time to give you my valuable (!) opinion on it . . . If he dissents I fear you will have to wait. If you insisted on publication against his wish you would have against you all the forces of cohesion & stability including every member of the Cabinet. On the other hand when the papers are eventually published his refusal to do so earlier will have a very bad effect for him . . . I am very anxious that you should not blunt this precious weapon prematurely.'[212]

That same day, Churchill had read in *The Times*, Carson had said in the House that the expedition against Turkey had been 'admirably conceived.' From Lawrence Farm, Winston had written to his wife: 'Gradually people will see what I saw so vividly this time last year, but alas too late forever.' It was never too late to correct the record, she replied, and when he returned to Parliament as a civilian he found that in this case it was imperative. During a debate over conscription Asquith had proposed that Ireland be exempt. The Easter rebellion in Dublin the previous April had been followed by executions; feeling ran high there. Winston, disagreeing with the exclusion, said: 'This is a time for trying to overcome difficulties and not for being discouraged or too readily deterred by them.' An Irish Nationalist shouted: 'What about the Dardanelles?' It was a cry he was to hear again and again, in the House, in meeting halls, and on the streets. Clementine had been right. He had to clear his name. And only the truth – in the documents – would do it.[213]

On June 1, 1916, in what was surely one of the most ill-advised political decisions of his life, the prime minister agreed. The decision was reported in the next day's *Times*. Bonar Law, speaking for Asquith, told the House that all papers relevant to the campaign would be assembled and laid before the country. Churchill wrote to the prime minister the next morning, offering to help sort them out. Ian Hamilton's reputation was also at stake, and although his hopes for exoneration were less realistic than Winston's, he nonetheless cherished them. Three days later he and Churchill dined at the general's home in Hyde Park Gardens. Afterwards they reviewed Hamilton's copies of twenty telegrams he had sent to the War Office from Gallipoli. Not one of them, Churchill realized, had been laid before the cabinet. This was powerful evidence of negligence on Kitchener's part. There seemed to be no way he could explain it away. While they talked, a voice became audible in the street outside. Someone was shouting K of K's name. As Hamilton told in his memoirs: 'We jumped up and Winston threw the window open. As he did so an apparition passed beneath us. I can use no other word to describe the strange looks of this newsvendor of wild and uncouth aspect. He had his bundle of newspapers under his arm and as we opened the window was crying out "Kitchener drowned! No survivors!" ' The war minister, on a mission to Saint Petersburg, had been aboard HMS *Hampshire* when she hit a mine. Hamilton wrote: 'The fact that he should have vanished at the very moment Winston and I were making out an unanswerable case against him was one of those *coups* with which his career was crowded – he was not going to answer!'[214]

Kitchener having joined the Glorious Dead, the K of K myth was strengthened tenfold. Blaming him was impolitic now; the number of those who shared the Dardanelles guilt had been diminished by one. Asquith then had second thoughts about a full disclosure of the documents. Two weeks later Hankey wrote to Churchill that the prime minister had resolved not to open the minutes of the War Council on the ground that ministers, fearing that their remarks might be 'liable to publication,' would be hesitant to speak out in future meetings, and that 'it would be very difficult to resist a pressure to publish proceedings in regard to other aspects of the war which might not be in the public interest.' Winston protested to Asquith that only the council's archive could show, among other things, 'the strong support of the naval project given by you, Grey, Kitchener & A. Balfour' and his own 'disclaimer of responsibility if a military disaster occurred through inadequate troops not being sent in time,' which 'was not an ordinary incident of discussion, but that I asked formally & at that time that my dissent shd be placed on record.' It was inconceivable to him that the prime minister could not appreciate 'that this fact is vy important for a true judgement on the event.' Asquith, replying, repeated the argument that 'the public interest' might suffer. To Lloyd George, who had succeeded Kitchener at the War Office, Winston bitterly remonstrated that the promise to release the minutes had been given to the House 'after prolonged consideration & with full knowledge both of the facts and of the suitability of the documents for publication at this juncture.' Surely the country had a right to know the role played by the prime minister, 'who alone cd have co-ordinated the naval and military action & given to the war-policy of the country the necessary guidance & leadership.' That, of course, was precisely what the prime minister did not want the country to know. His ruling stood. Winston wrote to his brother: 'The Govt have decided to repudiate their pledge to publish the D'lles papers. My dossier was more than they could face. There will be a row, but there are many good arguments in the public interest against publishing: and many more good arguments in the Government interest!'[215]

But Parliament was not so easily gulled. There was a tremendous row in the middle of July, when Asquith informed the House that 'the presentation of these papers must be postponed,' that his commitment to release them 'cannot for the moment . . . be fulfilled' because it would entail 'omissions so numerous and so important that the papers actually presented would be incomplete and misleading.' Carson led the attack on this position, and he had great support; Bonar Law's assurance had been given, not to Churchill, but to the entire House, and the MPs' curiosity was immense. Lloyd George proposed that a secret committee of MPs investigate the Turkish campaign. Asquith accepted the compromise. He announced the appointment of a select commission, comprising eight distinguished Englishmen headed by Lord Cromer, 'to inquire into the conduct of the Dardanelles operations.' This Royal Commission of Inquiry into the Dardanelles did not satisfy Churchill. He told the House that it was a poor substitute for opening the books, 'as was originally intended and promised by the Prime Minister, in the name of the Government.' But at least it would not be a whitewash. Cromer couldn't be bought. And Winston would be allowed to testify and submit evidence.'[216]

The commission's hearings opened on August 17. Winston devoted five months to his defence. 'I am hopeful that the truth may be published,' he wrote Seely. 'But failure & tragedy are all that are left to divide.' It was hard to reconstruct the past, key evidence was unavailable to him, he had to skirt the issue of Kitchener's incompetence, and since the commissioners included a field marshal, an admiral, and a captain, it was difficult to criticize the conduct of officers in the strait and on Gallipoli. In one of his appearances, on September 28, he declared that the facts proved five points: there had been full authority for the assault, a reasonable chance of success, 'all possible care and forethought exercised' in preparing for the attacks, 'vigour and determination, in the execution, and no compromise of military interests elsewhere. 'Everything I hear about the D'lles Commission encourages me,' he wrote to Sinclair at the end of November. 'The interim report cannot now be long delayed and I have good hopes that there will be a fair judgement. I sh'd like to have it out as soon as possible. But the days slip away.'[217]

They were slipping away from Asquith, too. Less than a week later he was manoeuvred into resigning, undone by Lloyd George and widespread Tory dissatisfaction with his conduct of affairs. George had finally made it. On December 7, 1916, he 'set out,' in Winston's words, 'upon his march as High Constable of the British Empire,' with Balfour moving from the Admiralty to the Foreign Office and Bonar Law becoming chancellor of the Exchequer, leader of the House, and the government's second in command. Since most of the Liberal ministers, offended by George's coup, had resigned with Asquith, the old Welsh radical's government was dominated by Conservatives. There was no place in it for Churchill. He had assumed there would be. But he was still widely regarded as a discredited adventurer. The *World*, a weekly journal which carried a popular column on politics, had commented on November 14: 'Mr Churchill, in his frantic effort to reinstate himself in public esteem, is enlisting the support of some powerful newspaper interest . . . But if a serious attempt is being made to foist Winston once more on the British public the matter would assume a different aspect . . . Winston Churchill is responsible for the *opéra bouffe* Antwerp expedition which made the British nation ridiculous in the eyes of the world . . . He was responsible for the disastrous Dardanelles expedition which ranks with Walcheren as one of the greatest military disasters of our time.'* There was still a spark of defiance in Lloyd George. He toyed with the idea of appointing Churchill and then bent to the storm. In his memoirs he recalled asking Bonar Law, 'Is he more dangerous *for* you than when he is *against* you?' Law answered: 'I would rather have him against us every time.' A colleague had drawn up a list of possible ministers. Churchill was not on it. George wrote in the margin: '? Air Winston.' But there was still no air ministry and he did not create one. The last blow to Churchill's chances of office came on December 7, when four members of the new cabinet – Lord Curzon, Lord Robert Cecil, Austen Chamberlain, and Walter Long – told Lloyd George that they would serve only on the condition that Churchill be excluded.[218]

The Lloyd George Winston had once known would have bridled at a Tory veto. He didn't now, but at the time Churchill knew of neither the challenge nor the submission to it. Discussing the political future with Scott of the *Manchester Guardian*, he said, according to Scott, that 'Lloyd George, "with all his faults," was the only possible alternative Prime Minister. I asked if in case George formed a ministry he could count on being included. He said he thought so – that George would desire it and that it would be in his interest.' In

---

* Walcheren was the scene of an attempt, conceived by the second Earl of Chatham in 1909 during the Napoleonic Wars, to capture Antwerp. It was a catastrophe.

fact, he believed he would be offered a choice of posts. All things considered, he rather preferred a return to the Admiralty. The brutal fact that he would have nothing was revealed to him after a dinner in F.E. Smith's Belgravia house. The new prime minister was there; the purpose of the meeting was to discuss the makeup of the new government. Incredibly, Lloyd George had suggested that Churchill be invited. Winston naturally took this to mean that he would be offered a seat on the Treasury Bench. Early in the conversation the guest of honour was summoned to Buckingham Palace. He asked Max Aitken to join him for the taxi ride. In the cab, George said that there would be no office for Winston and, Aitken later wrote, 'asked me to convey a hint of this on my return to the party . . . He thought Churchill too confident of high office in the new regime. It would be better if Churchill were dashed a bit at first.' Back at the table Aitken found the unsuspecting Winston in a jovial mood. Choosing his words carefully, Aitken said: 'The new Government will be very well disposed towards you. All your friends will be there. You will have a great field of common action with them.' Aitken's account continues: 'Something in the very restraint of my language carried conviction to Churchill's mind. He suddenly felt he had been duped by his invitation to the dinner, and he blazed: "Smith, this man knows that I am not to be included in the new Government." ' According to Aitken, an 'almost ludicrous' scene followed: 'Churchill changed from complete optimism to violent anger and depression. He abused me most violently, and when I got tired of it and replied in kind he picked up his hat and coat and, without even putting them on, dashed into the street. Smith ran out after him and tried to calm him, but in vain.' In the morning Winston telephoned to apologize. 'It was really quite unnecessary on his part,' Aitken wrote. 'It is impossible to feel hurt at anything Churchill says in this vein, for he is always so willing to take as good as he gives, and makes no complaint about the counter-blow.' Aitken himself was feeling resentful, but for another reason. He, too, had hoped for office. Instead, the new prime minister offered him a peerage. He reluctantly agreed. Thus he became – and spent the rest of his life regretting it – Lord Beaverbrook.[219]

Reconciled, Churchill wrote to Sinclair: 'It will be odd now on the direct opposition Bench with all the furious ex Ministers arriving. I expect they will be vy anxious to be civil to me. But I intend to sit in the corner seat in a kind of isolation.' He seemed puzzled at being passed over. Clementine's shrewd eye saw the transformation in Lloyd George, however. 'At one time he abused the Dukes to please the working-men,' she wrote. 'Now he has abused the working-men to please the soldiers.' He had deposed Asquith by insisting that he would prosecute the war more vigorously, providing the generals with everything they needed. This tactic had been effective because the politicians and the press, to keep civilian morale at fever pitch, had glorified the military hierarchy, endowing it with an almost ecclesiastical aura. After the appalling Somme and Verdun casualty lists, the sensible move for the Allies would have been the pursuit of a negotiated peace. Lord Lansdowne recommended just that. A meaningful victory, he suggested in a cabinet memorandum, was clearly impossible. He asked: 'Can we afford to go on paying the same sort of price for the same sort of gains?' Haig, responding, assessed the outlook for 1917 as 'excellent.' Robertson wrote: 'Quite frankly, and at the same time respectfully, I can only say that I am surprised that the question should be asked. The idea had not before entered my head that any member of His Majesty's Government has a doubt on the matter.' Lloyd George called Lansdowne's letter 'a terrible paper.'*[220]

What made this gifted statesman climb into bed with Douglas Haig and Wully Robertson? There is only one possible explanation. He had been twisted by his yearning for power. He profoundly disagreed with Robertson's western strategy, but he had been unable to change it because of the ennoblement of the general staff by an adoring country. Privately he said that the War Office kept 'three sets of figures, one to mislead the public, another to mislead the Cabinet, and the third to mislead itself.' He also said: 'If people really knew, the war would be stopped tomorrow, but of course they don't – and can't know. The correspondents don't write and the censorship wouldn't pass the truth. The thing is horrible, and beyond human nature to bear, and I feel I can't go on any longer with the bloody business.' But of course he did go on, as men in high office always have, justifying themselves to themselves, by making little adjustments in their reasoning. Haig held him in contempt. When he heard that Lloyd George had asked Foch's opinion of British strategy, he said tightly: 'I could not have believed that a British minister could have been so ungentlemanly.' Later, when 1917 had become even madder than 1916, he wrote in his diary: 'LG is feeling that his position as PM is shaky and means to try and vindicate his conduct of the war' – as though it had been Lloyd George's, not Haig's and Robertson's – 'in the eyes of the public and try to put the people against the soldiers.' He added a patronizing note: 'Quite a nice little man when one had him alone, but I should think most unreliable.' Robertson agreed. He wrote of George: 'I can't believe that a man such as he is can remain for long head of the government. Surely *some* honesty and truth are required.'[221]

Churchill, who could have been invaluable to his old colleague when the 1917 campaign was being planned, remained in purgatory. But the end of his personal martyrdom was in sight. In January the Royal Commission of Inquiry issued an interim report. Its only criticism of Churchill was that he had been 'carried away by his sanguine temperament and his firm belief in the success of the operation which he had advocated.' The heavy losers were

---

* Churchill also disapproved of it. He did not believe that the main effort should be made on the western front, but the only solution acceptable to him was a German surrender. Commenting on Lansdowne's proposal, he asked: 'What is the contrary view? It is in a sentence that *this war has got to be won & that it is not won yet.*' He added, in a phrase which would become familiar to Americans when President Truman dismissed General MacArthur in 1951: 'Let us not delude ourselves by thinking that there is any substitute for victory.'

Asquith and Kitchener. Asquith was faulted for failing to keep his colleagues informed and for 'the atmosphere of vagueness and want of precision which seem to have characterized the proceedings of the War Council.' Kitchener's failure to consult his general staff, the commissioners concluded, had created 'confusion and want of efficiency,' and his delays in sending troops – delays Winston had protested at the time – had been ruinous. Three months later the commission's final report disposed of all accusations against Churchill. He had always acted with the full support of his naval advisers, it found, and had been blameless of any 'incorrect' behaviour. In the commissioners' view his plans had been right; others had been responsible for the flaws of execution. Asquith was again condemned, even more severely. Winston was not completely satisfied – the findings, he said, omitted 'proof that when we stopped the naval operations the Turks had only three rounds of ammunition' – but he thought they were 'at any rate an instalment of fair play' and he told the House that the commissioners had 'swept away directly, or by implication, many serious and reckless charges which have passed . . . throughout the land during the long months of the last two years.' By telling their 'long, tangled, complicated story,' they had relieved him of the burdens 'which have been thrown on me and under which I have greatly suffered.' Now 'the current of public opinion and the weight of popular displeasure' which had been 'directed upon me' could recede.[222]

They didn't; not yet. He had been cleared in the House, but acquittal in the public's view was another matter. Hatred of Churchill, like the later hatred of Franklin Roosevelt, satisfied the emotional needs of too many people. As a politician Lloyd George had to reckon with their feelings. He thought he understood one reason for their distrust of Winston. 'Here is the explanation,' he later wrote. Churchill's 'mind was a powerful machine, but there lay hidden in its material or make-up some obscure defect which prevented it from always running true. They could not tell what it was. When the mechanism went wrong, its very power made the action disastrous, not only to himself but to the causes in which he was engaged and the men with whom he was co-operating . . . He had in their opinion revealed some tragic flaw in the metal.' Such people ignored the commission's report, or discounted it, or found him objectionable for other reasons. No. 10 extended no invitation to him through the remainder of April and May. It was June 18 before Lloyd George summoned him, and then it was to say that he would 'try' to get him back the Duchy of Lancaster. Winston felt insulted. He declined it on the spot. Frances Stevenson, a reliable guide to George's moods, described Winston as 'very sulky' when the two men met at a Guildhall function, and noted in her diary that everyone 'remarked how surly he was looking.'[223]

But the prime minister could no longer dismiss him from his thoughts. Churchill cut a different figure in the House now. Vindicated in the eyes of Parliament, he was once again heard with respect, and, Bonar Law's views to the contrary, Churchill against you was formidable. The *Nation,* which refused to join in the press choir deifying the military hierarchy, had prepared a series of articles demonstrating how the British had been outmanoeuvred by an enemy tactical withdrawal. The first piece had already appeared in London and was being widely reprinted in Germany. The general staff demanded that the rest of the series be suppressed. Lloyd George did it, defended the action in a highly emotional speech, and then left the floor as Winston rose to reply – an exit Winston noted with biting wit. The *Nation*'s disclosures were 'absolutely immaterial and innocent,' Churchill said; they made 'mild reading compared with the Dardanelles Report from the point of view of public confidence.' Gagging editors would only bring 'a universal harmonious chorus of adulation from morning to night about whatever was done, until some frightful disaster took place.' The prime minister's move demonstrated 'an undue love of the assertion of arbitrary power.' In George's absence, Winston asked Bonar Law to consider the uneasiness of the House. Law interrupted to say that that would be reflected in parliamentary votes – the weakest of replies. Churchill sprang: 'Do not look for quarrels, do not make them; make it easy for every party, every force in this country, to give you its aid and support, and remove barriers and obstructions and misunderstandings that tend to be superficial and apparent divergence among men whose aim is all directed to our common object of victory, on which all our futures depend.' It was the government's duty to treat Opposition concern 'fairly and justly' – not to answer with 'the kind of rhetoric or argument which might do very well on public platforms but is entirely unsuitable to the cool discussion in the House of Commons.'[224]

This was the kind of appeal which could rally Liberal, Labour, and Irish Nationalist MPs behind him, and if they united, Lloyd George could be unseated. But Churchill saw a looming issue far greater than the silencing of the press. The United States had just declared war on Germany. Churchill suspected that Haig wanted to win the war before US soldiers could reach France in strength. (He was right; on June 10 Haig wrote in his diary: 'There must be no thought of staying our hand until America puts an Army in the field next year.') Winston asked his cousin Freddie, the government's chief whip, to propose a secret session of the House. Lloyd George scheduled it for May 10. Asquith's seniority permitted him to speak first, but he was unprepared; so was everyone else in the Opposition except Churchill, who began by asking: 'Is it not obvious that we ought not to squander the remaining armies of France and Britain in precipitate offensives before the American power begins to be felt on the battlefields?' The logic, to him, was inescapable: 'We have not got the numerical superiority necessary for a successful offensive. We have no marked artillery preponderance over the enemy. We have not got the numbers of tanks which we need. We have not established superiority in the air. We have discovered neither the mechanical nor the tactical methods of piercing an indefinite succession of fortified lines defended by German troops.' The exigent question, therefore, was: 'Shall we then in such circumstances cast away our remaining manpower in desperate efforts on the Western Front before large American forces are marshalled in France? Let the

House implore the Prime Minister to use the authority which he wields, and all his personal weight, to prevent the French and British High Commands from dragging each other into fresh bloody and disastrous adventures. Master the U-boat attack. Bring over the American millions, so as to economize French and British lives, and so as to train, increase and perfect our armies and our methods for a decisive effort in a later year.' George's reply, when he appeared, was evasive – he was already committed to a new attack in Flanders – but Churchill had preyed on doubts already in the prime minister's mind. As the session ended, the two met fortuitously behind the Speaker's chair. Churchill later recalled: 'In his satisfaction at the course the Debate had taken, he assured me of his determination to have me at his side. From that day, although holding no office, I became to a large extent his colleague. He repeatedly discussed with me every aspect of the war and many of his secret hopes and fears.'[225]

How deep, Lloyd George asked Beaverbrook in June, did the Tory animosity towards Winston really go? It was still there, Beaverbrook replied, but he thought it could be defied. Office therefore came to Churchill once more on July 17, 1917, when the prime minister appointed him minister of munitions. 'Not allowed to make the plans,' he later wrote wryly, 'I was set to make the weapons.' The prime minister had confided in no one; everyone, including his closest colleagues, learned of his decision from the newspapers. The reaction was sharp. The secretary for war threatened to resign. The colonial secretary wrote to No. 10 that the prospect of facing Winston across the cabinet table made it 'extremely difficult for many of my friends to continue their support.' Leo Amery wrote in his diary that bringing Churchill 'into the Government has shaken its prestige and reputation seriously,' and Lloyd George agreed; the antagonism, he said in his memoirs, 'swelled to the dimensions of a grave ministerial crisis which threatened the life of the Government.' It peaked when forty Tory MPs sailed into Bonar Law's office to protest. Law, though angry himself, told them that the issue was not strong enough to topple the coalition. Thereafter the danger receded, though resentment remained. Nothing in recent memory had created 'such widespread bitterness,' said the *Morning Post*, which, as usual, led the Fleet Street pack, commenting that the appointment 'proves that although we have not yet invented the unsinkable ship, we have discovered the unsinkable politician.' The Dardanelles was exhumed, as though the commission had never existed. That debacle, said the *Post*, was 'managed more or less personally by Mr Churchill, whose overwhelming conceit led him to imagine he was a Nelson at sea and a Napoleon on land.' More calamities would ensue, the paper predicted: 'We confidently anticipate that he will continue to make colossal blunders at the cost of the nation.' The Tory minister Walter Long wrote on July 29, 1917: 'The real effect has been to destroy all confidence in Ll G. It is widely held that for purposes of his own quite apart from the war he has deceived and jockeyed us. The complaints come from our very best supporters, quiet, steady staunch men, and WC has made matters worse by stating at Dundee that the opposition comes from his political opponents.'[226]

It is hard to conceive of where else it could have come from; Churchill, as a new minister, was fighting a by-election in Dundee. But if the uproar in London startled him, as it must have, he showed no scars. C. à C. Repington, the military writer, described him as 'looking a different man . . . I never saw anyone so changed, and to such an advantage, in so short a time.' The return to office was largely responsible for this, but since the spring he had also presided over a happier family. The lease on 33 Eccleston Square having expired, they moved back there. They had also acquired a second home. Clementine had always dreamed of living in 'a little country basket,' and Winston had bought a grey-stone cottage in Lullenden in Kent, near East Grinstead for £6,000, cashing in £5,000 of Pennsylvania Railroad stock and a £1,000 Exchequer war bond. The property had many attractions: a large barn nearby where the children could play, a pony and light carriage for transportation when Churchill had the car in London, landscapes he could paint, and a large high room downstairs where Clementine, pregnant for the fourth time, could nap on lazy summer afternoons and still be within earshot of the nanny. At first they only went down for weekends, but after German air raids on the capital increased, they were there all the time. Winston loved Kent and during his first summer as proprietor he was often in Lullenden, leaving it to campaign fitfully in Dundee. On July 29 he was reelected with a majority 5,266 votes. Two days later he took his seat on the front bench and was greeted, according to *The Times*, 'with some cheers.' It was twenty months since he had held office. During the interval 340,973 British soldiers had been killed in action and 804,457 wounded. The missing, mutilated beyond recognition, would be remembered in annual memorial ceremonies as the 'unknown.'[117]

The Ministry of Munitions, a small empire employing over twelve thousand civil servants divided into fifty departments, was directed from the fashionable Hotel Metropole in Northumberland Avenue, abutting on Trafalgar Square. Churchill had convened its staff before the votes had been counted in Dundee, and one member, Harold Bellman, later described the meeting in his memoirs. Like everyone else in England, Bellman's colleagues had decided views about Churchill. They were nervous, they were worried, and many were hostile. 'Those who attended from the secretariat,' Bellman wrote, 'fully expected a stormy scene.' Winston, he said, 'was received rather coldly, and opened by saying that he had perceived that "he started at scratch in the popularity stakes." He went on boldly to indicate his policy and to outline his proposals for an even swifter production of munitions. As he elaborated his plans the atmosphere changed perceptibly. This was not an apology. It was a challenge. Those who came to curse remained to cheer. The courage and eloquence of the new minister dispelled disaffection and the minister took up his task with a willing staff. It was a personal triumph at a critical juncture.'[228]

His responsibilities were not limited to guns and ammunition. They included the railways aeroplanes, and tanks. Nor was the mandate confined to British needs. The Americans were building a 'bridge of ships' across the Atlantic to transport six US armies – forty-eight divisions – to France. They would need, among other weapons, 12,000 artillery pieces. Churchill quickly established contact with his American counterpart, Bernard Baruch, the chairman of the US War Industries Board, who, when they met later at the peace conference, would become his lifelong friend. Winston signed a £100,000,000 contract and entered into a gentleman's agreement with Baruch under which Britain agreed to make no profit and the United States promised to make good any loss. In the ministry itself, Winston undertook a massive reorganization. The fifty departments were reduced to twelve, and in conversation and correspondence he referred to each by a letter: finance became 'F,' design 'D,' projectiles 'P,' explosives 'X,' and so on. British businessmen were recruited and then governed by what he called a ' "Clamping" committee.' He surveyed his new realm with pride. 'Instead of struggling through the jungle on foot,' he later wrote, 'I rode comfortably on an elephant, whose trunk could pick up a pin or uproot a tree with equal ease, and from whose back a wide scene lay open.'[229]

In a speech at Bedford he identified his primary objective: the production of 'masses of guns, mountains of shells, clouds of aeroplanes.' Always the total warrior, he was indignant when told that the International Red Cross had proposed outlawing poison gas and that the French were sympathetic. He sharply pointed out that it was after all the Germans who had introduced gas to the battlefield, at Ypres in April 1915. To Louis Loucheur, France's under secretary of state for munitions, he wrote: 'Apparently France is strongly in favour of us offering to give up this form of warfare, or at any rate of accepting a German offer. I do not believe this is to our advantage . . . Anyhow I would not trust the German word.' He predicted that the enemy would let the Allies 'fall into desuetude' and then break the agreement. Far from banning it, he favoured 'the greatest possible development of gas-warfare, and of the fullest utilisation of the winds, which favour us so much more than the enemy.' His view prevailed, and he doubled the British output of gas shells; by 1918 one out of every three shells fired by Haig's artillerymen contained gas. The Red Cross protested that it was inhumane. So, Winston replied, was the rest of the war. No principle was exempt from sacrifice. The Allied Aeroplane Works was strikebound. Churchill simply took over its factories in the name of the government and ignored the *Times*'s comment that there was 'no precedent for such a measure.' Munitions workers walked out in Coventry, Manchester, and Birmingham. Lloyd George temporized. Christopher Addison, the previous munitions minister, was among those who breakfasted with Winston to discuss the crisis, and he noted in his diary that Churchill came 'out hotfoot against the strikers, his prescription being a simple one, viz, that their exemptions should be withdrawn and that they should be called up for military service. There was considerable demur, with which I agreed, to using the Military Service Act as an agent in an industrial dispute.' But when 300,000 munitions workers threatened to strike in Leeds, Winston persuaded the prime minister to threaten them with conscription. The warning worked, though British labour, which has a long memory and had not forgotten Tonypandy, put another black mark against his name.[230]

It was Churchill's energy, efficiency, and imagination which had brought him back to office, and with Eddie Marsh at his elbow, he invigorated a ministry which until now had been grim and dull. Presently countless new projects were flourishing under his direction, and he kept himself informed about all of them by ordering that all reports submitted to him must be 'on a single sheet of paper.' During his first eight months in the Metropole he visited France four times, questioning generals on their munitions needs. Often he slept in his office. This, he wrote to a friend, 'has many conveniences from the point of view of getting work done. It enables me to work up to dinner, and to begin with shorthand assistance as early as I choose in the morning.' He invested his tasks with drama and colour. He was, he boasted, 'the Nitrate King.' Writing in the *Sunday Pictorial* while still a back-bencher, he had argued that technological innovations could be used as 'a substitute for men.' Now he ordered a thousand warplanes, assigned a task force of engineers to improve trench mortars, and, in his spare time, sketched extraordinary Leonardoesque machines of war. Most were absurd. Two weren't: prototypes of the amphibious landing craft and man-made 'Mulberry' moorings of World War II. As the father of the tank he gave it priority.* This, he said, was the surest way to 'beat the trench,' to 'augment the power of the human hand and shield the sacred chalice of human life.' Its present role was 'miniature and experimental,' he wrote, but 'the resources are available, the knowledge is available, the result is certain: nothing is lacking except the will.' On the afternoon of January 3, 1916, one of his darker days at Ploegsteert, he had been summoned to Haig's GHQ, told that the Operations Division of the War Office wanted to explore his concept of a 'caterpillar,' and asked 'who to apply to in England about them.' Churchill, furious, had written to Clementine that evening: 'This after 9 months of actual manufacture and committees unending. God, for a month of power & a good shorthand writer.' He had the authority and the staff now, and he set two goals: 4,459 tanks by the spring of 1919 and twice that by the following September. Not everyone approved. The military hierarchy were sceptical. Haig in particular took a jaundiced view of Churchill's emphasis on armour. 'This is done,' he complained in his diary, 'without any consideration of the manpower situation and the cews likely to

---

* After the war a royal commission investigating the claims of inventors reported that it was 'due to the receptivity, courage, and driving force of the Rt Hon Winston Spencer-Churchill that the general idea of the use of such an instrument of war as the tank was converted into practical shape, but Mr Churchill has very properly taken the view that all his thought and time belonged to the State and that he was not entitled to make any claim for an award, even if he had liked to do so. But it seems proper that the above view should be recorded by way of tribute to Mr Winston Churchill.'

be available to put into them.' But the grumbling in GHQ was predictable. The relationship between the commander in chief and the munitions minister had become dissonant even before Churchill took office, borne only because neither could survive without the other. Even Haig could not ignore Winston's accomplishments. In another diary entry he wrote warily: 'For the time being he is most friendly and is doing all he can to help the Army. He has certainly improved the output of the munitions factories very greatly, and is full of energy in trying to release men for the Army, and replace them by substitutes.' The key phrase, however, is 'for the time being.' In the long run, Haig knew, he could expect nothing but trouble from Winston. The new minister had, in fact, become his savage critic.[231]

Churchill had joined the cabinet too late, and with too small a power base, to influence Haig's Flanders offensive of 1917. He had known it was coming. On May 10, still a political outcast, he had begged the House, in secret session, not to permit 'fresh, bloody and disastrous adventures' on the western front. Parliament was unresponsive. Thus the stage was set for the terrible, heart-breaking struggle known to historians as the third battle of Ypres and to the men who fought there as the battle of Passchendaele, Passchendaele being the Belgian crossroads village which the BEF hoped to reach in its first lunge. By any name it was Haig's masterpiece and should never be forgotten. He was convinced that he could break through the German wire, take the ridges overlooking the British position, and then recapture the vital Channel ports of Ostend, Zeebrugge, and Antwerp. On May 1 he wrote in his diary: 'Success seems reasonably possible. It will give valuable results on land and sea. If full measure of success is not gained, we shall be attacking the enemy on a front where he cannot refuse to fight, and our purpose of wearing him down will be given effect to.'[232]

'Our purpose of wearing him down will be given effect to.' That syntactical atrocity sums up the scripture of attrition. Its high priest was Haig's chief of staff, Lieutenant General Launcelot Kiggell, a tall, morose professional soldier who had been commandant of the Staff College in 1914. J.F.C. Fuller, who later became a tank commander, was one of his students there. Fuller recalled afterwards that 'the only thing I distinctly remember his saying was, "In the next war we must be prepared for very heavy casualties." His theory of war was to mass every available man, horse, and gun on a single battlefield, and . . . wear down the enemy until his last reserves were exhausted, and then annihilate him.' In one of those small collapses of prewar integrity which increased as the desperate war wore on, Jellicoe was persuaded to lie to Lloyd George, solemnly predicting: 'If the Army cannot get the Belgian ports, the Navy cannot hold the channel and the war is as good as lost.' Brigadier General John Charteris, Haig's chief of intelligence and a co-conspirator, later wrote: 'No one really believed this amazing view, but it had sufficient weight to make the Cabinet agree to our attack.'[233]

The balloon went up, as they said then, on July 31. Nine days earlier Churchill, newly appointed and still facing his by-election in Dundee, had written to the prime minister of his apprehensions over any 'renewed offensive in the west and begged him to 'limit the consequences' of any drive which had already been approved. This merely justified the Tories' fears. They saw it as proof that he had no intention of confining himself to his ministry. Hankey, who came to tea at Lullenden, noted in his diary: 'Lloyd George had given him [Churchill] my War Policy report & he was already well up in the whole situation and knew exactly what our military plans were, which I thought quite wrong.' Soon Winston was taking an active interest in the Admiralty and the War Office, transferring some of Haig's howitzers to the Russian front, advocating anti-submarine techniques, and urging that heavy battleship guns be moved ashore. The secretary for war protested and the first lord threatened to resign. Lloyd George soothed their ruffled feelings and reminded Winston that he was not a member of the War Cabinet. Churchill, unchastened, crossed to Flanders for a firsthand look at such tiny villages as Bullecourt and Messines, where so much British blood had been spilled. One of Haig's generals barred him from the trenches. Haig himself was more cordial – 'quite genial and cracked several jokes,' Marsh wrote – but inflexible about his objectives. That evening the commander in chief observed in his diary that Churchill 'means to do his utmost to provide the army with all it requires, but at the same time he can hardly stop meddling in the larger questions of strategy and tactics; for the solution of the latter he has no real training, and his agile mind only makes him a danger because he can persuade Lloyd George to adopt and carry out the most idiotic policy.'[234]

George later wished that had been true. Actually, the prime minister had been among those gulled by the high command. Marsh had noted that 'the tone of GHQ is tremendously optimistic.' The servile press served as GHQ's megaphone. *Punch* was running cartoons of cringing Germans whimpering '*Kamerad!*' to insouciant Tommies. The *Spectator* reported: 'Our Staff work in the field seems to be irreproachable . . . The infantry, whose losses are said to be comparatively light, march behind the moving curtain of shells and bless the gunners as they go.' German newspapers were carrying accurate accounts of the fighting, but *The Times* headlined a summary of them ENEMY LIES EXPOSED: *What the Germans are told – Falsification of Battle News – The Lie as a Buttress of Morale*. Communiqués from across the Channel reported that the enemy was 'visibly cracking,' that patrols found enemy troops 'preparing for emergencies,' and that there were signs which could be interpreted as being 'preliminary to withdrawal.' The War Cabinet questioned none of this. 'It naturally pleased Haig,' Lloyd George would bitterly recall, 'to have carefully chosen and nicely cooked little tidbits of "intelligence" about broken German divisions, heavy German casualties, and diminishing German morale served up to him . . . He beamed satisfaction and confidence. His great plan was prospering. The whole atmosphere of this secluded little community reeked of that sycophantic optimism which is the curse of autocratic power . . . As for General Kiggell, the Chief of Staff, he had the air of a silent craftsman, whose plans, worked out by his art in the seclusion of his workshop, were turning out well and proceeding inexorably without a hitch to the destined end.'[235]

The reality was horrible beyond imagining. Here, as on every front in the war, including Gallipoli, defensive strengths had spiked the attackers' guns, sheathed their bayonets, broken their swords, and left the once proud war-horse to forage behind the lines, entangling communications. The British infantry never had a chance. Haig's long preliminary bombardment had deprived them of surprise and, at the same time, destroyed the Flemish drainage system. The water, having nowhere else to go, flooded the trenches, and to make the field soggier, the rains were among the worst in thirty years. After three and a half months in this dismal sinkhole, the British army had barely taken Passchendaele village. The filthy, bleeding, battered men were exhausted. Many, burdened by their heavy packs, fell into brimming shell holes and drowned. In London the ambulance trains unloaded at night, smuggling casualties home out of consideration for civilian morale. Siegfried Sassoon wrote of those who fought on: 'Shoulder by aching shoulder, side by side / They trudged away from life's broad wealds of light.'

British casualties were 448,614. In Flanders fields the poppies grew between the crosses, row on uncompromising row, that marked more than 150,000 fresh British graves. The offensive had gained less than six miles of wasteland. Yet the red-tabbed generals of the high command were exultant. Against all evidence, Charteris reported that the German losses had been enormous. They congratulated one another, pinned new decorations on one another's tunics, and agreed that it would all have been over long ago if only the politicians had left the fighting to the professionals. Robertson, whose job it was to deal with the government, actually held it in contempt. He wrote to Haig that Lloyd George 'is a real bad 'un. The other members of the War Cabinet seem afraid of him. Milner is a tired, dyspeptic old man. Curzon is a gas-bag. Bonar Law equals Bonar Law.' Churchill, not being a member of the War Cabinet, wasn't even mentioned. Yet he was the one public figure who saw precisely what was happening. Gaining access to the casualty lists, he asked: 'If we lose three or four times as many officers and nearly twice as many men in our attack as the enemy in his defence, how are we wearing him down?' Haig insisted that, whatever the result, he had saved the French arms by distracting the enemy. This, as Churchill later pointed out, was mythical: 'The French Army was no doubt saving its strength as much as possible, but the casualty tables show that during 1917 they inflicted nearly as many losses on the Germans as did our own troops.' He continued: 'Accusing as I do without exception all the great ally offensives of 1915, 1916, and 1917, as needless and wrongly conceived operations of infinite cost, I am bound to reply to the question, What else could be done? And I answer it, pointing to the Battle of Cambrai, "*This* could have been done."' At Cambrai, launched as the Passchendaele drive petered out, 381 of Churchill's tanks, lurching forward with an artillery bombardment, broke through the enemy defences on a six-mile front, gained over forty-two square miles, and captured ten thousand Germans at a cost of fifteen hundred British soldiers. 'This in many

The Western Front, July 1917

Front line

MILES

KILOMETERS

G.W.WARD

variants, this in larger and better forms,' he wrote, 'ought to have been done, and would have been done if only the Generals had not been content to fight machine-gun bullets with the breasts of gallant men, and think that that was waging war.'[236]

To see for himself, he crossed the Channel and visited a sector in which, after a tank thrust, the enemy position had been overrun by British infantry. In his report to Lloyd George he wrote that he 'went on up to the extreme high watermark of the attack.' The German trench was deep, defended by a belt of wire nearly a hundred yards broad. 'This wire was practically uncut and had only little passages through it, all presumably swept by machine guns. Yet the troops walked over these terrific obstacles, without the wire being cut, with very little loss, killed many Germans, took thousands of prisoners and hundreds of machine guns.' The same was true of the enemy's second trench line, which was 'almost as strong and more deceptive.' Farther on, however, Germans in 'just a few little pits and holes' had inflicted heavy losses on the British infantry. Here, he concluded, 'the troops had got beyond the support of the Tanks, and the bare open ground gave no shelter.' He felt vindicated. He had, he believed, found the way to beat the trench.[237]

Lloyd George was uncomforted. He knew now that the Flanders campaign had been a criminal blunder. At the end of 1916 he had said gloomily: 'We are going to lose this war.' Nearly a year had passed, and the prospect now was far bleaker. Yet it was part of his tragedy, and England's, that he himself had become a strut in the web of deceit. He wrote: 'The people are not ready to pay any heed to good counsel. They still cherish illusions of a complete victory.' And he encouraged them. He felt that the mood of the country left him no alternative. Here, again, British journalists bore much of the blame. In October, when Haig lost nearly twenty-six thousand men in taking an insignificant ridge, Lloyd George had bitterly called it 'still another smashing triumph a few hundred yards ahead.' But the *Times* correspondent had described it as 'the most important British victory of the war' and applauded the commander in chief's 'calm, unhurried persistence' which compelled 'the admiration of the world' because 'with each successive stride the arrangements grow more exact, the results more certain, the losses lighter.' Philip Gibbs of the *Daily Chronicle* interviewed a German prisoner, 'a professor,' who told him: 'It will not be long before Germany makes a great bid for peace by offering to give up Belgium. By mid-winter she will yield Alsace-Lorraine; Russia will remain as before the war, except for an autonomous Poland; Italy will have what she has captured; and Germany will get back some of her colonies.' In the climate of public opinion created by such dispatches, Lloyd George did not dare break openly with his high command. Instead, he promoted Haig to field marshal and doggedly said, in an impromptu speech at Birkenhead: 'We shall just win.' The irrepressible *Nation* inquired: 'Win What?'[238]

After the Germans' titanic attempt to take Verdun in 1916, this had become a quiet theatre for the kaiser's assault troops. Their communiqués routinely reported '*Im Westen nichts Neues*' – 'All quiet on the western front.' Elsewhere their fighting men had provided plenty of news, however, nearly all of it good for them. Blessed with interior lines, they could strike anywhere by rescheduling trains, and as the deadlock continued in the west they crushed a weak eastern ally each autumn, thus releasing more troops for Belgium and France. In 1914 they mauled the Russians in East Prussia at Tannenberg and the Masurian Lakes, where Paul von Hindenburg and Erich Ludendorff made their reputations. In 1915, after de Robeck's failure to force the Dardanelles, Bulgaria joined them to knock Serbia out of the war. In 1916 Rumania, encouraged by temporary Russian gains and hungry for land, threw in its lot with the Allies. The result was a fiasco. Rumania had doubled its army over the preceding two years, but was strategically isolated, and its officer corps danced in Bucharest while spies blew up a dump of nine million shells outside the city and a dozen enemy divisions, drawn from the western front, swarmed up the Carpathians. Just before winter snows sealed the passes the Germans broke through and Rumania quit. In 1917, with a succession of revolutionary governments sidestepping to the left in Russia, it was Italy's turn. Germany sent a phalanx of picked divisions, with young Lieutenant Erwin Rommel among them, to reinforce Austria's Caporetto sector in Italy. On October 24, two weeks before Passchendaele fell, they attacked out of the Julian Alps in a thick fog. In twelve hours General Luigi Cardona's defenders were on the run. By November terrified Venetians were hiding the bronze horses of Saint Mark's and preparing to flee.

Churchill was at Lullenden, playing with his children, when Lloyd George telephoned from Riddell's country home at Walden Heath, where he was staying, and asked him to drive there at once. Arriving, Winston was shown the shocking telegrams from Rome. The prime minister was badly shaken. An attack on Caporetto had been expected, but Haig had assured them only a few days earlier that Italy would 'be able to hold her ground unaided.' Asked on October 27 if he could send two British divisions there, the field marshal now replied that the best way to help England's embattled ally was to keep 'Ludendorff busy' in Flanders. That evening Haig meticulously wrote in his diary: 'If the Italian Army is demoralized we cannot spare enough troops to fight their battles for them.' But this time he stood alone. Even Robertson understood the need to reinforce Italy. Sir Henry Wilson, after a talk with Churchill, also began to see the light. 'We may lose this war yet if we try,' his diary entry began that evening. He compared 'the different strategies – ours and the Boches': 1, We take Bullecourt, they take Rumania; 2, we take Messines, they take Russia; 3, we don't take Passchendaele, they take Italy.' To Haig's indignation, the War Cabinet ordered five BEF divisions out of the trenches and through the tunnels under the Alps to rally the Italians on the Piave. Cardona was fired. He had lost 800,000 men. Italy, unmanned, was unable to mount a counterattack.[239]

Nor was that the worst. Russia, cut off from its allies since the sealing of the Dardanelles, was collapsing within. On November 6, in the middle of the Caporetto rout, Bolshevik mobs, soldiers of the Petrograd garrison, sailors from Kronstadt, and the workers' Red Guards stormed the czar's Winter Palace. Chaos followed, but all parties reached agreement on one point. Nine million Russian soldiers had been lost in the war, and every leftist politician wanted peace – at any price. Trotsky accepted the kaiser's brutal terms at Brest-Litovsk, a railway junction on the Bug River. The implications for Britain, France, and the United States were vast. Russia was no longer an ally. Overnight it was a new war. The Central Powers were now confident of victory, and with good reason. Brest-Litovsk freed three thousand German guns and a million men – enough to give Ludendorff the whip hand on the western front provided he struck before America's waxing strength eclipsed his edge. The German strategist had designed a brilliant new assault technique, stressing stealth, surprise bombardment, gas, and infiltration, and encoded his coming operation in the west *Kaiserschlacht* (kaiser's battle). This entailed a complex of thrusts in France. By April 1, Hindenburg promised the kaiser, they would be in Paris. The Allies dug in and waited numbly. They couldn't tell where or when or how the enemy was coming, but they knew the storm was imminent. And there was almost nothing they could do about it. They were spent. Even Haig yearned for US troops now. Robertson said, 'Our only hope lies in American reserves,' and France's Pétain said, *'J'attends les américains et les tanks.'* Publicly and privately Churchill had anticipated them by several months. In Paris the previous September 17, Eddie Marsh had written in his diary: 'Winston very eloquent on the necessity of bringing every possible American soldier over to France as soon as possible, and training them here or in England instead of in America – so as not to waste transport during the time of training.' His tanks would not be available in significant numbers for another year, but he could, and did, stockpile other munitions. Convinced that the Germans would bag enormous quantities of equipment in their first drive, he redoubled his efforts at the Metropole, often working through the night. He expected the enemy's great offensive to open in the third week of February. Actually, it came a month later, on March 21, 1918. And he was there when it started.[240]

Although he was not in the War Cabinet, Lloyd George sought his advice with increasing frequency. He respected Churchill's judgement, valued his experience in the trenches, and wanted him to serve as his eyes and ears at the front. On Monday, March 18, at the prime minister's request, Churchill crossed the Channel and was driven to Saint-Omer. Unlike George, he believed that Haig would be the right man in the coming crisis. He wasn't very good at advancing, but he would be a poor retreater, too. The very stubbornness and lack of imagination which had handicapped him on the offensive would steady him when the waves of *feldgrau* came rolling across no-man's-land. Haig had many complaints that Monday, mostly about the French, yet Churchill felt he anticipated the approaching struggle 'with an anxious but resolute eye.' Together they studied the map. The immediate threat was not in Flanders but south of the Ypres salient, on a fifty-mile stretch of front which the War Cabinet, at the insistence of Premier Georges Clemenceau, had just taken over from the French. Here, north of the Oise River, 57 British divisions were confronted by 110 German divisions – over five times the German strength when they had attacked Verdun two years earlier. Haig, Winston reported, was 'daily expecting an attack of the first magnitude.'[241] He was far more vulnerable than the French and the newly arrived Americans, both of whom, at the moment, outnumbered the enemy concentrations facing them. Part of Haig's problem was that Lloyd George, after Passchendaele, had deliberately kept him short of troops to prevent him from renewing his attack. The enemy was aware of this weakness. It was logical to anticipate the first German attack of 1918 on the British front in the sector between Arras and Fère-en-Tardenois. And Ludendorff was logical.

Leaving Haig at three o'clock in the afternoon, Churchill decided to visit the Ninth Division, commanded by Major General Henry Tudor, who had been a fellow subaltern in India. Tudor's headquarters were in the ruined village of Nurlu. 'When do you think it will come?' Winston asked him. Tudor replied: 'Perhaps tomorrow morning, perhaps the day after, perhaps the week after.' The next day they toured the trenches together, and Churchill was still in Nurlu Wednesday night. As they turned in, Tudor said: 'It's certainly coming now. Trench raids this evening have identified no less than eight enemy battalions on a single half-mile of front.' Churchill woke at four o'clock Thursday morning and lay awake for thirty minutes, listening in the quiet. The silence ended at 4:40 A.M., when he heard several explosions in the distance. They were enemy mines, sapped beneath British positions. 'And then,' Churchill later wrote, 'exactly as a pianist runs his hands across the keyboard from treble to bass, there rose in less than one minute the most tremendous cannonade I shall ever hear.' In a matter of minutes all British communications were destroyed. Gas was spreading over artillery parks and machine-gun nests. 'The flame of the bombardment,' he wrote, 'lit like flickering firelight my tiny cabin.' He found Tudor on the duckboards outside. The general said: 'This is *it*. I have ordered all our batteries to open fire. You will hear them in a minute.' Churchill didn't: 'The crash of the German shells bursting on our trench lines eight thousand yards away was so overpowering that the accession to the tumult of nearly two hundred guns firing from much nearer could not even be distinguished.' A few minutes after six o'clock over 500,000 Germans, outnumbering the defenders three or four to one, loomed out of a dense fog. Winston left 'with mingled emotions' and 'motored without misadventure to Peronne.' The road to Peronne was cut behind him. By dusk he was in Saint-Omer. The British were reeling backwards. Ludendorff had hoped to split the weak seam between the British and the French at Amiens, but although Amiens didn't fall on Friday, when the Germans advanced ten miles, all contact between the two allies was broken.[242]

Churchill reached London on Saturday. At No. 10 he reviewed the situation with Lloyd George and Sir Henry Wilson, who, having outwitted all his rivals, had succeeded Robertson as chief of the Imperial General Staff. Then the prime minister took Winston aside and asked how, with its intricate trench system destroyed and troops falling back, the BEF could remain intact. Churchill answered that 'every offensive loses its force as it proceeds. It is like throwing a bucket of water over the floor. It first rushes forward, then soaks forward, and finally stops altogether until another bucket can be brought. After thirty or forty miles there will certainly come a considerable breathing space, when the front can be reconstituted if every effort is made.' Lloyd George invited him to meet with the War Cabinet at 4:00 P.M. They broke up after two hours, and Hankey recorded the dismal conclusion: 'Our casualties are going to be huge.' Lloyd George and Hankey dined with the Churchills at Eccleston Square on Sunday. The news was all bad; the fury of the enemy drive was unabated. Monday evening Winston was one of several ministers who gathered at Downing Street. Hankey wrote: 'Balfour & Churchill whom I found in company with the PM were ridiculously optimistic.' Sir John

French, now Viscount French, arrived and said bitterly that Haig had 'badly let down the army in shattering it in the hopeless Flanders offensive.'[243] During the next three days the reports from France grew blacker and blacker. Lloyd George, badly frightened, wondered how much the poor bloody infantry could stand. On Thursday he asked Churchill whether he could 'get away for a few days to France.' The day before, Foch had become generalissimo of all forces fighting the Germans, 'charged by the British and French Governments to co-ordinate the action of the Allied Armies on the Western Front.' To relieve the pressure on the faltering British, the prime minister wanted Winston to request a 'vigorous' French attack on Ludendorff's southern flank. Churchill would take with him the Duke of Westminster ('Bender'), an old foxhunting friend and the brother-in-law of Jennie's second husband. Meanwhile, Bonar Law and Sir Henry Wilson were conspiring to thwart him. His task, they felt, was an affront to Lord Milner, the new war minister. They were actually planning to prevent Churchill from reaching the French leaders when Lloyd George got wind of their intrigue and broke it up. He wired that after calling on Haig, Churchill should 'go straight to Clemenceau' in Paris. Reaching the new BEF headquarters in Montreuil, Winston and Bender were astonished to learn that the British field marshal was off taking his afternoon horseback ride. Certainly this was no weather for riding; the rain, Churchill later recalled, 'streamed down in torrents in the silent, empty streets of this peaceful little old-world town.' Nor did this seem a propitious time for Haig to be unavailable. Telephones were ringing constantly with news of troop movements. His new chief of staff told his visitors that the fighting was 'devouring' their reserves, that the enemy was still 'pouring through the gap,' and that during the past week the BEF had lost 1,000 guns and 100,000 men. The need for a French diversion was desperate.[244]

Driving through Amiens, which was already being shelled by the Germans, Churchill and the duke arrived in Paris and headed for what Winston called 'the luxuries of an almost empty Ritz.' Leo Amery found him there and wrote: 'We had a good talk while he wallowed in a hot bath and then went to bed. (Winston is in extraordinary shape and wears a long nightgown!) . . . His only preoccupation was whether the French were only counter-attacking piecemeal or were getting everything together for a really big stroke.' He sent word of his mission to the premier through the head of the British military mission at 37, rue Faubourg-Saint-Honoré. Clemenceau grandly replied: 'Not only shall Mr Winston Churchill see everything, but I will myself take him tomorrow to the battle and we will visit all the Commanders of Corps and Armies engaged.' The seventy-six-year-old 'Tiger' – he really looked like a tiger – was quite serious. Churchill thought the premier ought to stay away from the battlefield. Clemenceau said: '*C'est mon grand plaisir.*' He pointed out that danger was everywhere now; even the capital wasn't safe. It was quite true. Shells had been landing in Paris since Saturday, fired by Krupp's remarkable *Pariskanone,* whose range was eighty-one miles. In a striking example of Teutonic *Schrecklichkeit*, one shell had crashed through the roof of Saint-Gervais-l'Eglise on Good Friday and exploded in the transept during Mass, killing ninety-one worshippers. London newspapers had carried accounts of this, and Clementine wrote to Winston: 'I do hope that when the long range guns start firing you take cover.'*[245]

Their motorcade set out at ten o'clock in the morning. At Beauvais they mounted a stone staircase, passed through double doors which were opened at their approach, and were welcomed by the diminutive, moustachioed Foch. He led them into a huge, elegant conference room. Pinned to a wall before him was an enormous map of the front. 'General Foch seized a pencil,' Churchill recalled in the *Strand Magazine* of December 1930, 'as if it were a weapon, and without the slightest preliminary advanced upon the map and proceeded to describe the situation.' Everything about his method of delivery impressed Winston: 'his animation, his gestures, his habit of using his whole body to emphasize and illustrate as far as possible the action which he was describing or the argument which he was evolving, his vivid descriptiveness, his violence and vehemence of utterance.' Most of the time he spoke in French, and his tongue was so quick that Churchill missed phrases and sometimes whole sentences, but the generalissimo's meaning was quite clear. He pointed to the German gains on the offensive's first day and cried: 'Oh! Oh! Oh! How big!' Then his pencil sketched the second stage of the drive, also huge: *'Deuxième journée d'invasion. Ah! Ah!'* The third lunge, again enormous: *'Troisième journée. Aie! Aie!'* But as he progressed it became clear that each day's conquests grew steadily smaller. It was Churchill's water-bucket metaphor translated into geography. Finally he said: *'Hier, dernière journée d'invasion,'* and 'his whole attitude and manner,' wrote Winston, 'flowed out in pity for this poor, weak, miserable little zone of invasion which was all that had been achieved by the enemy on the last day . . . The hostile effort was exhausted. The mighty onset was coming to a standstill. The impulse which had sustained it was dying away. The worst was over.' Abruptly Foch cried: 'Stabilization. Sure, certain, soon. And afterwards. Ah, afterwards. That is my affair.' There was a silence. Then the premier moved towards him, murmuring: *'Alors, Général, il faut que je vous embrasse.'*[246]

It was spectacular, but it did not, of course, answer the question Churchill had brought from London. When were the French going to lance the German canker? Leaving Foch, the motorcade proceeded to the closest British head-quarters, in Drury, twelve miles south of Amiens. It was rough driving. The road was rutted with new shell holes. Obviously Ludendorff was close. At their destination, as in Montreuil, telephones never stopped ringing. Haig was there. One by one his officers described their emergency. The BEF had been stumbling backward for ten days. Churchill asked one British general if his

---

* Most people, including Churchill, called (and still call) this weapon 'Big Bertha.' *Die dicke Bertha,* literally 'fat Bertha' – named for a member of the Krupp family – was actually a huge howitzer which flung a projectile weighing a ton nine miles. These guns had been used in the siege of Liège and, later, at Verdun.

men could regroup and form a new line. 'No one can tell,' the general said. 'We have hardly anything between us and the enemy except utterly exhausted, disorganized troops . . . dead from want of sleep and rest.' The presentation ended. It was, all agreed, the worst show any of them had seen – perhaps the worst in history. Finally Clemenceau, who had been feasting on chicken and sandwiches as he heard them out, sat back contented and raised his voice above the phones. He said in English: 'Very well, then, it is all right . . . Never mind what has been arranged before. If your men are tired, and we have fresh men, our men shall come up at once and help you.' But instead of attacking the German flank, poilus would be fed into the line where the British were weakest.[247]

Churchill relayed Clemenceau's decision to Lloyd George over one of the telephones. The French premier then rose from his lunch and said: 'I claim my reward. I wish to pass the river and see the battle.' The British remonstrated, but the Tiger waved them off. He pointed to his military aide and said: 'A few shells will do [him] good.' Back at the cars he said: 'Mr Winston Churchill, we are in the British lines. Will you take charge of us? We will do what you say.' Winston, delighted, asked: 'Where do you want to go?' The premier replied: 'As far as is possible. But you shall judge.' Winston sat beside the driver in the lead car, map in hand, and off they went, across the bridge and towards the battlefield. He saw streams of Tommies, many of whom 'walked as if they were in a dream, and gave no notice of our file of brightly flagged cars. Others again, recognizing me, gave me a wave or a grin, as they would no doubt have done to George Robey or Harry Lauder' – music hall stars – 'or any other well known figure which carried their minds back to vanished England and the dear days of peace and party politics.' Presently they heard shells moaning and rumbling overhead. Some burst in the fields on either side of the road. Next small-arms fire became audible. A heavy rain was falling, and mists of evening began to gather. If they followed the map much farther, they would encounter Germans. 'On our left towards the enemy,' Churchill wrote, 'was a low ridge crowned with trees about three hundred yards away. Among these trees a few dark figures moved about . . . I thought on the whole that we had gone about far enough.'[248]

Another guide would have turned back, but if the Tiger found danger beguiling, so did Winston. The two of them left the motorcade and proceeded on foot among stragglers and bursts of shrapnel. They stood together on a small rise, surveying the disorderly scene. Several weary British officers recognized them, saluted them, and came over. Clemenceau and Churchill gave them the contents of their cigar cases. As they were leaving, a shell burst among a group of horses. One, wounded and riderless, 'came in a staggering trot towards us. The poor animal was streaming with blood.' The old premier advanced towards it and quickly seized its bridle, bringing it to a halt. His aide hurried up and said they really must leave *tout de suite*. 'Clemenceau,' Churchill wrote, 'turned reluctantly towards his car. As he did so, he gave me a sidelong glance and observed in an undertone, *"Quel moment délicieux!"* '[249]

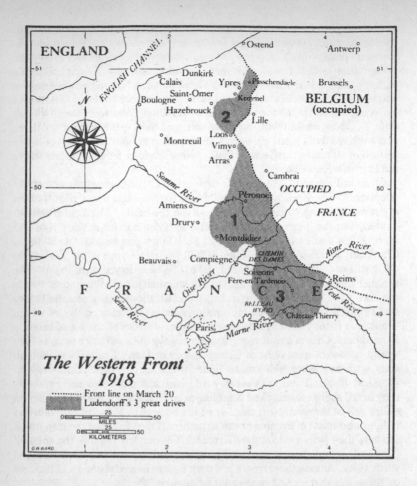

ENGLAND

ENGLISH CHANNEL

Ostend Antwerp

Dunkirk
Calais Ypres Passchendaele Brussels
Saint-Omer Kemmel
Boulogne **2** BELGIUM
Hazebrouck Lille (occupied)

Loos
Montreuil Vimy
Arras

Cambrai
OCCUPIED
Péronne
Somme River **1** *FRANCE*
Amiens

Drury Montdidier
Aisne River
Beauvais Compiègne *CHEMIN DES DAMES*
Soissons Reims
F R A N C Fère-en-Tardenois E *Vesle River*
Oise River *BELLEAU WOOD* **3**
Seine River Château-Thierry
Paris *Marne River*

*The Western Front
1918*

.... Front line on March 20
░░░░░ Ludendorff's 3 great drives
0 ┣━━━━━━┫ 25 ┣━━━━━━┫ 50
MILES
0 ┣━━━━━━┫ 25 ┣━━━━━━┫ 50
KILOMETERS

G W WARD

After calling on General Henri Pétain, the commander of all French ground troops and therefore Haig's counterpart, and dining with him in what Winston called his 'travelling military palace,' they returned to Paris. At the Ritz in the small hours of the next morning Churchill wrote to Clementine that it had been 1:00 A.M. when 'Clemenceau, alert and fresh as when we started, dismissed me. The old man is vy gracious to me & talks in the most confidential way. He is younger even than I am!' Then Winston wired Lloyd George a full account of the day. The British divisions, he reported, were 'in many cases only skeletons,' but French reinforcements would soon be arriving 'as fast as they can come up . . . Nothing more can be done than what we are doing.' At 4:00 A.M. his report went to London in cipher; it was decoded at the War Office and delivered to No. 10 at 8:30. Churchill saw the premier again at noon, and together they drafted an appeal to Woodrow Wilson for the speedy arrival of heavy American contingents. Winston telegraphed a copy of this to Lloyd George and, after lunching at the Ritz with Bender and Amery, set out alone for another tour of the front. Everything he saw convinced him that the war was approaching its climax. He wondered if this was appreciated at No. 10. Clemenceau could hardly have been more courteous, and Winston was never one to underrate his own importance, but premiers, he felt, should talk to premiers. Back at the Ritz he wired this to Lloyd George, adding: 'It is considered certain here that the Germans will pursue this struggle to a final decision all through the summer and their resources are at present larger than ours . . . Every effort must be made if we are to escape destruction.'[250]

The prime minister was handed this message when he awoke the next morning in Downing Street. He told his valet to start packing. Sir Henry Wilson joined him, and Churchill met their destroyer at Boulogne. Winston accompanied them as far as Montreuil, but the general staff insisted that he be excluded from the military talks. The council of war, held in Beauvais, included Clemenceau, Foch, Spiers (who acted as interpreter), and two American generals: John 'Black Jack' Pershing and Tasker Bliss. The meeting formally endorsed the understanding Churchill had reached with the premier. In addition, Pershing brought President Wilson's reply to the plea from Clemenceau and Churchill: 480,000 doughboys were on their way.

Lloyd George's party, including Churchill, was back in London at 2:30 the following morning. Winston went straight to his desk at the Metropole. By the weekend the situation in France was reasonably clear. Montreuil had fallen, and one of the railways between Amiens and the capital had been cut. At that point, however, Teutonic discipline had collapsed. The starved German troops – starved by the Admiralty blockade Churchill had organized in 1914 – had turned to pillage. By the time they re-formed, the hollow-eyed Tommies, their ranks thickened by French reserves from the south, had turned, anchored their lines, and were grimly holding on. Ludendorff had driven them back thirty-five miles, inflicted over 300,000 casualties, and created a huge bulge in the middle of the Allied line, but he hadn't broken through. The first crisis was over. Churchill wrote on April 6: 'I have been able to replace everything in the munitions sphere without difficulty. Guns, tanks, aeroplanes will all be ahead of personnel. We have succeeded in pulling the gun position round so completely since last summer that we can deliver 2000 guns as fast as they can be shipped. It has been touch & go on the front. We stood for some days within an ace of destruction.'[251]

As he sealed the envelope the second crisis was rising 136 miles to the east of him, in Flanders.

By early April Ludendorff had moved his 'battering ram' (*Sturmbock*) opposite the old Ypres salient. A few minutes after midnight on Sunday, April 7, some twenty-five hundred muzzles roared in unison, sending the first of what would be thirty thousand shells towards Armentières and fouling the air with mustard gas. The German storm troops had fog again, and just before dawn on Monday morning they buckled on their coal-scuttle helmets, climbed over their parapets, and lurched across no-man's-land. Once again they ruptured the British trench line, this time on a thirty-mile front along the river Lys. Everything Haig had won in his Passchendaele drive was lost in a few days. By Wednesday evening Armentières had fallen; the loss of Ploegsteert, which Churchill had fortified as a battalion commander, swiftly followed. Spiers wrote in his diary: 'Situation very critical . . . British foresee severance with French & German objective gained.'[252]

On April 18, with the outlook obscure, Winston sent the prime minister an analysis of their strategic choices. If worst came to worst, there would be only two: 'whether we should let go our left hand or our right: abandon the Channel ports, or abandon all contact with the French front line.' Loss of the ports would mean German dominance in the Straits of Dover, bottling up the port of London, the shutdown of England's key naval bases, and bombardment of 'a large part of Kent and Sussex.' But the Allied line would be intact, with 'the whole of France open for dilatory retirement or manoeuvre.' The alternative was worse. They could 'wire in' and wait. Ludendorff would undoubtedly pivot southward towards the French. But after the Germans had crushed the poilus, 'the British army would be at their disposal. They could deal with it at their convenience.' This, clearly, was the line Ludendorff hoped Britain would take. He appeared to be following an elementary principle: 'Divide your enemy's forces into two parts: hold off the weaker part while you beat the stronger: the weaker is then at your mercy.'[253]

A week later Churchill told the House that the Ministry of Munitions was in a position to deliver 'a fairly good report.' Since the opening of the first German offensive five weeks earlier the BEF had lost about a thousand artillery pieces and some five thousand machine guns. Yet the troops now had 'more serviceable guns as a whole, and more of practically every calibre, than there were when the battle began.' He crossed the Channel three days later to talk to Haig about shell supplies. Most of his time was now spent meeting the needs of the arriving Americans. Ludendorff, meanwhile, was battering his way towards the sea. On April 25 he took Mount Kemmel – a 'mountain,' on the flat Flanders plain, being a peak 350 feet high – as his men, toiling up the slope, sang the gunners' fighting song: *'Wenn einer wüsste, Wie einem ist!'* In the House, Churchill paid tribute to the British spirit: 'No demand is too novel or too sudden to be met. No need is too unexpected to be supplied. No strain is too prolonged for the patience of our people. No suffering or peril daunts their hearts.'[254]

The enemy was now within five miles of Hazebrouck, a vital railway junction and Ludendorff's chief objective. If it fell the British would face Churchill's alternatives. In London the general staff had already reached his conclusion: they must not allow the enemy to drive a wedge between them and the French. But if Hazebrouck fell, Haig would have to withdraw his entire

Churchill and Lord Fisher, 1913

Churchill in pilot's gear for a practice flight

Churchill and Asquith at Camberwell Green

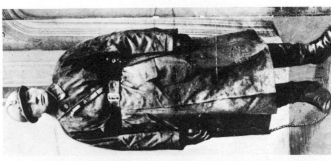

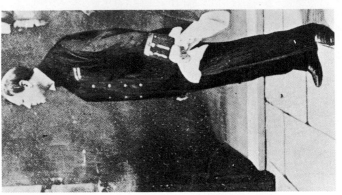

far left:
Churchill at Antwerp, October 1914

Lieutenant Colonel Churchill, 1916

'Winston's Folly'

above:
Roger Keyes, John de Robeck,
and Ian Hamilton

far left:
Sir Douglas Haig

Churchill in the summer of 1916

Churchill and
Sir Henry Wilson,
February 1919

opposite:
Churchill and a friend
in Egypt with
T. E. Lawrence (right)

Austen Chamberlain,
Stanley Baldwin and
Churchill in 1924

Churchill playing polo with
the Prince of Wales, 1924

below left:
Winston having fun
at the beach

The Duke of Sutherland
rescues a sunburned Churchill
at Deauville

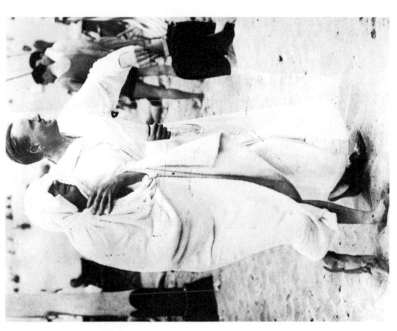

Churchill with Mary, aged two, at Chartwell

Chartwell

Work: In London
Play: At Chartwell

Churchill in the garden
at Chartwell

Churchill entering the
political wilderness
over the India issue

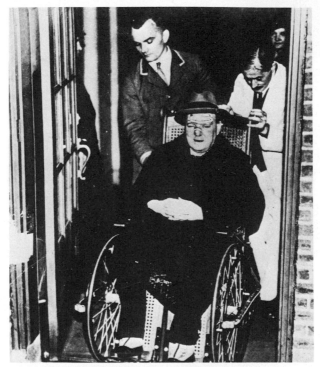

Churchill leaving Lenox Hill Hospital

left wing, abandoning Dunkirk and putting the Channel at risk. Haig, stepping entirely out of character, was stirred to eloquence. He issued an 'order of the day' to all ranks: 'There is no other course open to us but to fight it out! Every position must be held to the last man: there must be no retirement. With our backs to the wall, and believing in the justice of our cause, each one of us must fight on to the end. The safety of our homes and the freedom of mankind alike depend on the conduct of each one of us at this critical moment.' The situation was not really as bad as it seemed. The German divisions accustomed to fighting Russians were finding the British unexpectedly tough. And at this crucial point Ludendorff also behaved uncharacteristically. He hesitated. He couldn't decide which way to attack, and by the time he had made up his mind the obstinate Tommies had dug in. Foch studied his situation map and told Haig: '*La bataille d'Hazebrouck est finie.*' Ludendorff had driven in another huge bulge. Yet he still faced an unbroken Allied front. He had again achieved a tactical victory but a strategic defeat. Afterwards German military historians agreed that the battle had been a *Misserfolg* – a failure.[255]

As the spring wore on, Churchill's trips to France increased. He had established munition plants on the Continent, and he needed proximity to military headquarters for coordinating the demands of all Allied forces. Haig therefore provided him with quarters of his own, the Château Verchocq. There, Winston wrote to Clementine, he was 'very comfortable . . . I have a charming room filled with the sort of ancient wood-carved furniture that you admire and which seems to me to be very fine and old. The grounds contain avenues of the most beautiful trees, beech and pine, grown to an enormous height and making broad walks like the aisles of cathedrals. One of these must be nearly half a mile long.'[256] He was here, going over reports, when Ludendorff's third blow fell. Despite his two failures, none of the Allied leaders doubted that the kaiser's military prodigy would strike again. He had the men and he was fighting the calendar; the blockade was crippling his homeland and the American menace grew daily. Foch, ever alert, called for a 'foot-by-foot' defence of the Allied ground, and in Chaumont, General John Pershing, who had been reluctant to commit his troops piecemeal, now put all doughboys at the generalissimo's disposal. Foch and Haig had agreed that Ludendorff would pounce upon the British again. In the larger view, they were right. His ultimate objective was, not seizure of the Channel ports or splitting the Allies, but the complete destruction of the British army. First, however, there would be a massive feint, an intermezzo, in the south. He meant to maul the French so savagely that they would be incapable of supporting their ally to the north.

Pétain's troops were weaker than they appeared. They, too, had bled needlessly in 1917. Their Passchendaele had been the Nivelle campaign, named for General Georges Nivelle, who had replaced the bovine Joffre and whose star had seemed ascendant in the spring of that year. His answer to the trench had been 'the unlimited offensive.' Nivelle was handsome, swashbuckling, and popular. Even the English liked him (his mother had been

British), and in the châteaux far behind the lines where staff officers moved pins on maps, Allied generals had thrilled to his battle cry: 'One and a half million Frenchmen cannot fail!'[257] Unfortunately the excitement, the cry, and even the plan of attack had reached Ludendorff. The drive had been predicted in French newspapers and in orders circulated as low as company level, which meant that the Germans picked up prisoners carrying them. Nivelle had known this. He had also known that the enemy, as a result, were riposting with a strategic withdrawal called *Alberich* (after the evil dwarf in the Nibelungenlied), poisoning wells and sowing booby traps as they went. Nivelle had insisted that this hadn't changed a thing. In fact, it had changed everything. The new Hindenburg line was a defender's dream. It had turned Nivelle's drive into a welter of slaughter. He had made no real gains, and the moment he stopped, revolt had spread among French troops. At the height of their mutiny, fourteen out of sixteen divisions on the Champagne front had been disabled. Even troops who didn't rebel had marched into the trenches bleating in unison, demonstrating that they regarded themselves as sheep being led to the slaughter. Had the enemy known all this, Germany would have won the war with a single bold stroke. As it was, France's army had been severely crippled. The French had lost nearly 300,000 men in 1914 and now, with Nivelle's losses, they lacked the time and the resources to build a new striking force. The poilus had huddled sullenly in their trenches, and to redress their grievances the government had replaced Nivelle with Pétain, who was known to be cautious and receptive to demands from resentful troops. Even so, Clemenceau was worried about the possibility of a civilian uprising against the war. Although Churchill didn't know it, at the time of their tour of the front the premier was keeping four crack divisions in the interior of France to deal with any insurrection. The threat was real. The dissidents weren't called Bolsheviks, but France had subversive firebrands, too.

Curiously, it was the Americans, the newcomers, who picked the spot where the third German onslaught would come. The Chemin des Dames ridge, north of the Aisne, was so formidable a natural stronghold that the French had manned it with four divisions of their least reliable troops and three exhausted British divisions sent south for a rest. It happened that this was the sector closest to Paris. Ludendorff's plan was to hit it so hard that every French reserve would be committed to the defence of the capital, and when that happened he was going to wheel and drive Haig into the sea. His preparations were superb. The American prediction that a great assault on the ridge was imminent was dismissed by Foch because there wasn't a trace of activity in the German lines in that sector. Observation posts reported nothing, aerial photographs were a blank. Apparently there weren't even any enemy batteries. Actually, there were nearly four thousand heavy Krupp guns there. You just couldn't see them. Moving at night and hiding in woods during the day, with horses' hooves wrapped in rags and the sounds of creaking gun carriages masked by cages of croaking frogs, Ludendorff had massed forty-one crack divisions in a wild weald of giant trees opposite the ridge and entrusted the command to Crown Prince Rupprecht. At one o'clock in the morning of Thursday, April 25, the war's heaviest bombardment opened up and continued for nearly three hours. Before it ended, at 3:40 A.M., some of the defenders were raving, literally out of their minds. Pétain's local commander had erred in stationing his men too far forward, where they were naked to the artillery cannonade, and in failing to establish defences in depth. The Germans swarming up the slope behind a tornado of gas and shrapnel found that the Allied forces had virtually disintegrated. And there appeared to be nothing behind them but open country. The Germans were stupefied. The Allied centre was a void. Nothing like this had been seen in four years of trench warfare. Ludendorff, receiving their almost incredible report, sensed that what he had meant to be a feint could lead to swift victory. He shifted his gaze from Flanders to Paris.

The Allied reserve in this part of the line comprised seven French and two other tired British divisions. It was pitifully inadequate. The Germans, with their vast superiority in numbers and morale, overran them. To the further astonishment of the attackers, the bridges over the Aisne were intact. On their flank, near Soissons, some French resistance was developing, but the centre continued to gape wide open. By dusk that Thursday they had advanced ten miles and were on the Vesle. The French capital was eighty miles away. In the morning they crossed the Vesle, whose fine bridges were also undamaged, and surged onward, hobnail boots thumping and *feldgrau* trousers swishing weirdly in the sunshine. By May 30, when Soissons fell, they had overrun five French lines. On June 3 they were back on the Marne for the first time in nearly four years, the tip of their salient at a place called Château-Thierry. Churchill wrote to Clementine: 'The fate of the capital hangs in the balance – only 45 miles away.'[258]

At this point, writes Cyril Falls, the British military historian, 'something astonishing happened. Up the Marne came marching new men. They were two divisions only, but they strode proudly through the flotsam and jetsam always present on the fringe of a stricken battlefield . . . They were fine-looking men and even the rawest had a soldierly air.' The first Americans had arrived. Their vanguard was a brigade of US Marines, an odd mix of tough professionals and Ivy League students who, like their Oxford and Cambridge counterparts of 1914 – most of whom were now dead or maimed – had enlisted the week after their country entered the war. As they formed their line of battle an elderly French peasant shouted at them: *'La guerre est finie!'* *'Pas finie!'* a Harvard undergraduate shouted back, giving the sector its name.[259] For five days the marines held five miles of Pas Finie against the grey enemy columns which came hurtling across the wheat field. Then they counterattacked, driving five divisions of Germans back through a boulder-strewn, gully-laced forest called Belleau Wood. Only one in four survived unscratched. More than a hundred were decorated for heroism. The French renamed the wood for them. Six days later doughboys recaptured the village of

Vaux, on the other side of Château-Thierry. The crown prince ordered a halt and then a general withdrawal.

Thus ended the last of Ludendorff's sledgehammer blows. Early in July he launched a *Friedensturm*, or peace offensive, sending fifty-six divisions in a pincer movement around Reims. But Foch had developed new defensive tactics, posting thinly held forward positions to confuse the enemy and then decimating the advancing German infantry with precise artillery strikes. Moreover, ten thousand American soldiers were now disembarking every day. They reached Reims in strength, and the Germans, after initial successes, were thrown back. Returning from the front, Churchill told an audience at the Central Hall, Westminster: 'When I have seen during the past few weeks the splendour of American manhood striding forward on all the roads of France and Flanders, I have experienced emotions which words cannot describe.' Britain would claim no fruits of victory, he said, no 'territorial or commercial advantage,' only the 'supreme reconciliation' of Englishmen and Americans. 'That is the reward of Britain,' he said. 'That is the lion's share.' He wrote to Sinclair the following week: 'If all goes well, England and US may act permanently together. We are living 50 years in one at this rate.'[260]

His American mother chose this extraordinary moment to remarry. Her fiancé was Montagu Porch, a member of the Colonial Service who was three years younger than Winston. Jennie was sixty-four but she continued to be interested in men and they in her. 'I can still remember the first time I saw her,' Porch told a reporter from the *Daily Express*. It had been just before the war; 'she was sitting with some friends. She wore a green dress. Was it long or short? Don't remember. But she was very beautiful.' He had asked her to dance, and she had replied with a smile: 'I think you'd better go and dance with some of the younger girls.' He thought otherwise, and their remarkable courtship began. Porch was slender, he wore an elegant moustache, and his hair was prematurely white. Jennie had been dying her hair black; now she stopped. Porch was stationed in Nigeria, and after the war broke out he was commissioned in the Cameroons Expeditionary Force. Home on leave, he visited Jennie. Later he said he didn't remember proposing, but somehow, by the time he departed, he had the definite impression that they were engaged. On May 31, at the height of the Chemin des Dames crisis, Repington wrote in his diary: 'Lady R charming about her future. Mr Porch quite good-looking and intelligent. They get married tomorrow and go to Windsor for the weekend. Winston says he hopes marriage won't become the vogue among ladies of his mother's age.'[261]

The ceremony was held in the Harrow Road Register Office. On its eve, Porch wrote to Winston from the Connaught Hotel, thanking him in advance for attending the wedding and adding discreetly: 'I have carefully considered the position from every point of view – your mother's financial affairs are understood.' Jennie was, in fact, finally in the money. Under these improbable

526

circumstances, in the autumn of her life, she became the bride of a man of means. The Porch wealth came from Australian sheep and was substantial. Although she told the press that she would continue to be known as Lady Randolph Churchill, she was clearly in love with her new husband. When his leave expired and he returned to Africa, she assumed that she would accompany him. It seemed incredible to her that, after so many men, she would be deprived of her legal lover. Yet that was the case. 'She took steps to get a passport to Nigeria,' the newspaper *West Africa* later reported, 'but Downing Street refused because of the submarine peril . . . She pleaded over and over again, but permission was withheld.' To her sister Clara she wrote: 'Poor Porchey is very lonely.' So was poor Jennie. But peace seemed near, and she was confident that the marriage would work. 'He has a future and I have a past,' she told Lady Essex, 'so we should be all right.' Meanwhile, she sought amusement in the frantic parties of the time, learning to dance the turkey trot, patronizing the new nightclubs which had mushroomed in the West End, and finding solace in wine. Lady Diana Cooper remembers the evening a home in her neighbourhood was hit in a zeppelin raid; the wounded were being treated in her basement and the kitchen maids screaming when there 'arrived Jennie Churchill and Maud Cunard, both a little tipsy, dancing and talking wildly. They had been walking and got scared, and had stopped for a drink.' Now they planned to attend the opera, explaining, 'it being a raid night, the public required example.'[262]

Churchill's homelife was erratic that year, chiefly because of his frequent and prolonged absences, but also because they had to move again. Income from leasing the Eccleston Square house was indispensable, so they found a tenant and moved into Winston's aunt Cornelia's house at 3 Tenterden Street, just off Hanover Square. Here Clementine gave birth to another redheaded daughter, Marigold, who promptly became 'the Duckadilly.' Except during her confinement Clementine was busy with war work, running canteens, though she made sure she was always home when Winston could be there. And wherever he was, she was always in his thoughts. Writing from the Ritz when the crown prince was advancing on Paris, he told her: 'Weather permitting & the rest of it I propose to fly to Kenley Aerodrome Wed or Thursday. I will send you notice. Try to be at Lullenden so that we can be together.' The zeppelins over England worried him far more than the Krupp shells bursting near him: 'This vy clear weather & the state of the moon will certainly expose you to danger,' he wrote, urging her to stay in the country. 'I do not like to think of you & the kittens in London.' On June 3, the day after he had introduced a regular, scheduled air service between England and France, he wrote to her of the maiden flight: 'My darling, I had a touching vision of you & yr kittens growing rapidly smaller and the aerodrome & its sheds dwindling into distant perspective as I whirled away.'[263]

The love letters of statesmen rarely stand the test of time. They tend to be mawkish, fatuous, and distorted by the egocentricity which usually fuels great political achievement. Lloyd George was a man of intellect and vision. The war diminished him, as it attenuated the leaders of all belligerent powers, but what remained was still impressive. His mistress was a charming, cultivated Irishwoman. His missives to her ought to be moving. They aren't. Typically he wrote to her, in that summer of 1918: 'When I woke up at 6 my first thought was of the loving little face engraved on my heart & I had a fierce thought to go there & then to cover it with kisses. But darling I am jealous once more. I know your thoughts are on roast mutton & partridge & chicken & potatoes & that you are longing to pass them through the lips which are mine & to bite them with luscious joy with the dazzling white teeth that I love to press. I know that today I am a little out of it & that your heart is throbbing for other thrills . . . Your very jealous old Lover.' Frances had told him she was hungry, and that had inspired this.[264]

Churchill, who in public had far less control over his emotions than Lloyd George, sent Clementine notes that are stirring even now. This year marked their tenth wedding anniversary. 'Ten years ago my beautiful white pussy cat you came to me,' he wrote to her from the Château Verchocq. 'They have certainly been the happiest years of my life, & never at any moment did I feel more profoundly & eternally attached to you. I do hope & pray that looking back you will not feel regrets. If you do it [is] my fault & the fault of those that made me. I am grateful beyond words to you for all you have given me. My sweet darling I love you dearly.' Then, in a second letter: 'I reproach myself vy much for not having been more to you. But at any rate in these ten years the sun has never yet gone down on our wrath. Never once have we closed our eyes in slumber with an unappeased difference. My dearest sweet I hope & pray that future years may bring you serene & smiling days, & full & fruitful occupation. I think that you will find real scope in the new world opening out to women, & find interests wh will enrich yr life. And always at yr side in true & tender friendship as long as he breathes will be your ever devoted, if only partially satisfactory, W.'[265]

He was, as he acknowledged, an imperfect husband, less considerate of her than the tone of his letters to her suggests. To abide by his wishes constantly, as she did, was a sign of strength and forbearance not found in all wives. In following his star he sometimes hurt her deeply. She shared his mortification when he was in political eclipse. That could not be helped. But he could have spared her much. When he needlessly courted death she writhed in her bed, dreaming him dead. He could have commuted to France by sea. Instead, he flew at every opportunity. She shouldn't worry, he told her: 'It gives me a feeling of tremendous conquest over space, & I know you wd love it yourself.'[266] If he really believed he was not taking risks, he was deceiving himself. Her anxiety was fully justified. In the aircraft of 1918 eventual mishaps were inevitable. He was defying the law of averages, flying to the front every morning and returning to work at the Metropole through the evening. Once his plane caught fire over the Channel. Another of his planes somersaulted after takeoff; the pilot made a forced landing. Later, when he was piloting himself in a dual-control aircraft over Croydon airfield, the guiding stick failed. Their speed was about sixty miles per hour and they were seventy or eighty feet above the ground. The plane nose-dived and crashed. Winston's copilot was badly injured; he himself was bleeding and badly bruised. Nevertheless, he insisted on driving off and delivering a speech. Those who urged him to see a doctor were curtly dismissed.

He did not like to be told what to do. He was climbing into a cockpit, puffing on a cigar, when his flier reminded him that when they became airborne the cigar would be extremely dangerous. He scrambled down, flung the butt on the airstrip, and stamped on it. One evening in France he and Eddie Marsh were driving to his château in a Rolls-Royce. It was a trying journey, as Marsh described it in his diary: 'First a tyre burst with one of those loud bursts which make one think one has been assassinated – and then . . . Winston gave a wrong direction, left instead of right, at a crossroad.' The chauffeur protested, Churchill abruptly put him in his place, 'and on he went in the dark, on and on literally for kilometres between the close hedges of the roadside, it must be the original "long lane that has no turning." It's impossible to imagine anything more comical and provoking.' Eventually they turned around and got on the right road. Churchill accepted none of the blame. Eddie wrote: 'The climax of Winston's cursing was, "Well, it's the most absolutely f—ing thing in the whole of my bloody life." '[267]

He expected to live as he pleased, doing exactly what he wanted to do when he wanted to do it, assuming that others would alter their plans to suit his. He couldn't get away with it when dealing with, say, Lloyd George or Clemenceau, but that was only because their authority exceeded his. When he was top man, which was most of the time, he exercised his prerogatives. On another automobile trip, this time near the front, Marsh wrote: 'Winston was attracted by the sight of shells bursting in the distance – irresistible! Out we got, put on our steel helmets, hung our gas-masks round our necks, and walked for half-an-hour towards the firing. There was a great deal of noise, shells whistling over our heads, and some fine bursts in the distance – but we seemed to get no nearer, and the firing died down, so went back after another hour's delay. Winston's disregard of time, when there's anything he wants to do, is sublime – he firmly believes that it waits for him.'[268]

Visiting him after the uproar over his return to the cabinet, Hankey had noted in his diary: 'On the whole he was in a chastened mood. He admitted to me that he had been "a bit above himself" at the Admiralty, and surprised me by saying that he had no idea of the depth of public opinion against his return to public life, until the appointment was made.' But humility was foreign to him, and it didn't last. In the spring of 1918 he made a naked attempt to widen his domain. At present, he wrote Lloyd George, 'the War Cabinet alone have the power of decision & the right of regular & continuous consultation.' Moreover, most of the great offices 'are filled by Tories.' He proposed that the prime minister 'fortify' himself by appointing 'a proper Cabinet of responsible Ministers,' independent of the War Cabinet, to determine policy. He wrote: 'I do not seek this power.' But that is precisely what he *was* seeking. He declared: 'Certainly I will never accept political responsibility without

529

recognized regular power.' He was not only accepting it, but seizing it, at every opportunity. He sent Lloyd George several memoranda appealing for responsibilities and prerogatives which would have increased his authority. The prime minister didn't even reply.[269]

Despite his small significance and slight influence at the Ministry of Munitions, at least one of his fellow ministers regarded him as 'a dangerously ambitious man.' Everyone recognized his enormous potential. Like Krakatau, he was capable of erupting at any moment. But he was also curiously inconsistent. More than any other man he had recognized the folly of the trench deadlock on the western front. His proposed solutions, the Dardanelles and then the tank, had revealed an imaginative genius unique among the belligerent parties on both sides. He sensed that the terrible slaughter of the rising generation could destroy Europe's world hegemony and undo the bonds of the British Empire. Yet he still believed in military glory, still thrilled to the sound of bugles and drums. In the summer of 1918 he could tell a meeting of the Anglo-Saxon Fellowship in London: 'I am persuaded that the finest moment in the history of Britain was reached on that August night, now nearly four years ago, when we declared war on Germany.'[270]

John Squire of the *New Statesman*, a friend of Marsh's, wanted to meet him, and Eddie introduced them in the lounge of the Savoy. Later Squire set down his impressions of Churchill: 'He has enormous qualities, especially the primary quality of courage; one defect – the defect of romanticism – or rather, since romanticism may be good, of *sentimentalism*. You don't sum up Russia by calling Lenin a traitor, or by calling munitions workers well-fed malcontents. That is melodrama.' Yet, he added, 'I have met many politicians; this is the first one who was alive.' Squire, a poet and literary critic, had missed the one source of Churchill's political strength which, one feels, he should have identified immediately. It wasn't courage; bravery is common. What distinguished Winston was his remarkable mastery of the language. As he used it, the English tongue was a weapon and a benediction. It fascinated him; he adored it, and could spend hours musing over its charms and the ways to employ it with maximum effect. Gilbert Hall, one of Winston's young pilots, later recalled a dinner at the château: 'One could never predict what Mr Churchill would come up with next. During a lull he suddenly, without any warning, uttered the word "stunt." "Stunt," he repeated. "That's a remarkable word, and it has come to stay." ' He asked each of his guests to define it while he rolled his cigar across the top of his coffee cup. 'The cigar,' Hall remembered, 'was held between the first finger and thumb of each hand and he practised this untiringly and I think unconsciously for long periods, meanwhile commenting on our efforts to define this wonderful new word "stunt" that had come over to us from America.'[271]

Ludendorff had not abandoned his Flanders dream. He was manoeuvring for position, hoping for a *Siegessturm*, a stroke of victory, while Foch, on the other side of no-man's-land, was planning a general offensive. Haig, resentful of being subordinate to a French generalissimo, schemed alone. His relationship with Churchill had improved. Winston's conduct during Ludendorff's March offensive had, in Haig's opinion, proved that he was 'a real gun in a crisis.' The general intended to use 456 of Churchill's newly arrived tanks east of Amiens on Thursday, August 8, and Winston decided to go over and watch. 'We had a very pleasant fly over,' he wrote Clementine, 'and passed fairly close to Lullenden. I could follow the road through Croydon and Caterham quite easily.'[272]

Thick morning mist veiled the tanks, and the British advanced six miles, a spectacular achievement. But the infantry and cavalry – Haig had insisted on sending in horsemen – couldn't keep up with the machines. Here, as on the Somme in 1916 and at Cambrai in 1917, German resistance to the clanking new weapon stiffened and the line re-formed. Churchill, however, was elated. He wrote to Lloyd George that the assault had been 'a very great success which may well be the precursor of further extremely important events . . . It seems to me that this is the greatest British victory that has been won in the whole war, and the worst defeat that the German army has yet sustained.' He thought Haig should be congratulated. The prime minister disagreed. George believed that the general had lost a golden opportunity: 'Had Haig flung his army into the gap created and pursued the broken and demoralized Germans without respite, an even greater victory was within his grasp. When the enemy was scattered and unnerved, and their reserves were not yet up, Haig did not press forward with relentless drive and the Germans were given time to recover and reform their lines.'[273]

Both Lloyd George and Churchill were right. Haig had bungled; he wasn't prepared for a breakthrough. Nevertheless, the significance of the tanks' brief breakthrough was profound. 'It is a commonplace in military history,' writes Isaac Deutscher, Trotsky's biographer, 'that there exists a continuity between the closing phase of one war and the opening phase of the next: the weapons and the ideas invented or formed towards the end of one armed conflict dominate the first stage of the next conflict.' And the tank attack of August 8, 1918, we now know, was the turning point in the war's last convulsion. Ludendorff later called it 'the black day of the German army.' It meant that the sacred Hindenburg line had been breached – only briefly, to be sure, but what had happened once could happen again. When the news was brought to Ludendorff's headquarters (situated, ironically, in the Hôtel Britannique), he leapt to his feet and began cursing, not the Allies, but the kaiser, the Reichstag, the German navy, and the civilians on the home front. A.J.P. Taylor notes that the tank assault that Thursday deprived the German strategist of nothing 'vital from a strategical point of view.' His position was intact, some useless salients had been abandoned, the new trench complex was stronger, and Allied casualties had, as usual, been heavier than those of the defenders. 'The real effect,' Taylor writes, 'was psychological. It shattered the faith in victory which, until that moment, carried the Germans forward. The German soldiers had been told they were fighting the decisive battle. Now they realized that the decision had gone against them. They no longer wanted to win. They wanted only to end the war.' In their great 1918 offensives the Germans had lost 688,000 men. 'They were worn down,' Churchill said later, 'not by Joffre, Nivelle and Haig, but by Ludendorff.'[274]

Thus the momentum shifted to the Allies. Slowly their line crept forward. By August 26 the British forces on the Somme had regained all the ground lost in the spring and were back where they had been in Flanders. Churchill, after two weeks in London, flew back to follow the Allied armies. In Ploegsteert, he wrote to Clementine, 'all my old farms are mere heaps of brick & mouldering sandbags . . . I missed Ploegsteert's church. We ran past the place where it had stood without recognizing it! My strong dugout however wh I built at Lawrence farm has stood out the whole two years of battering, & is still in use . . . Otherwise utter ruin.' In early September he drove from the Château Verchocq to Paris. 'I was alone,' he wrote to her, '& took the road by Montdidier in order to see the ruin the war has brought on this unlucky town.' He drove for an hour 'through devastated, shell pitted facias – scraggy shreds of woods – along the road where Clemenceau & I had stood on that melancholy April day when the whole front was quivering & buckling back. Montdidier is a heap of ruins. But bad as it is, it does not reach the utter destruction of Bailleul & Meteren in the North. There the British artillery has been at work – regardless of expense – & nothing but red smears of brickbats mark the site of what was [sic] in the spring thriving townships.'[275]

Foch was charting an 'arpeggio' of drives against the Hindenburg line. 'Everyone is to attack as soon as they can, as strong as they can, for as long as they can,' he said, and: *L'Edifice commence à craquer. Tout le monde à la bataille!'* Actually, it was better organized than that. There was a master plan, and the American army was its fulcrum. Pershing's troops now held ninety-four miles on the extreme right of the Allied line. In the centre were the French, with the British to their left and King Albert of Belgium on the sea, leading a combined group which included two American divisions. The main American force, 1.2 million doughboys, would join in the tattoo of attacks, advancing through the deeply fortified Forêt d'Argonne, but their chief strategic task would be to crack the whip, with the Belgians swinging free on the other end. Six weeks of rain, fog, and heavy fighting followed. Then, abruptly, the weather cleared, revealing the trees in their autumnal splendour – coppery, golden, purplish, deep scarlet. The Allies surged forward. 'There is no hope,' Ludendorff concluded. 'All is lost.' On the first day of November, the enemy's last scribbly ditches caved in, and four days later the Germans had no front at all. Their rear guard, Sergeant Alexander Woollcott wrote in the *Stars and Stripes*, resembled an escaping man who 'twitches down a chair behind him for his pursuers to stumble over.'[276] Apart from the stolid German machine gunners, who kept their murderous barrels hot to the end, the Second Reich's soldiers had become a disorderly mob of refugees. Reports from their fatherland were appalling. Ludendorff had been sacked, there was revolution in the streets, and the fleet had mutinied when ordered off on a death-or-glory ride against the British. Each chill dawn the doughboys, Tommies, and poilus went over the top in fighting kit, driving the frail wraiths in *feldgrau* up against the hills of Belgium and Luxembourg.

Bulgaria had surrendered on September 28 and Turkey on October 21. Austria was next. 'A drizzle of empires,' Churchill said, was 'falling through the air.' On October 28 he had been invited to review British soldiers parading in Lille's Grande Place – among the party in the reviewing stand was one Lieutenant Colonel Bernard Law Montgomery, the Forty-second London Division's chief of staff – and he was at his desk in the Metropole on November 10, when Hindenburg advised Berlin that he could no longer guarantee the loyalty of the army and the kaiser fled into Holland. The Eiffel Tower in Paris beamed directions to the enemy's peace envoys, telling them which trenches to approach and where to pick up their guides. That evening Lloyd George invited Churchill to join a special cabinet which would study the implications of the peace. At five o'clock the next morning the German envoys signed Foch's dictated terms in his railway carriage at Compiègne. All firing was to cease six hours later. Churchill would recall that full moment: 'It was a few minutes before the eleventh hour of the eleventh day of the eleventh month: I stood at the window of my room looking up Northumberland Avenue towards Trafalgar Square, waiting for Big Ben to tell that the War was over.' It struck, and he could hear the baying of the crowds outside, but he felt no jubilation. 'Scarcely anything which I was taught to believe had lasted,' he wrote. 'And everything I was taught to believe impossible had happened.' Since 1914 Britain had lost 908,371 dead, 2,090,212 wounded, and 191,652 missing. Victory had indeed been 'bought so dear as to be indistinguishable from defeat.' Then Clementine arrived and proposed that they go to Downing Street and congratulate Lloyd George. Twenty excited revellers, cheering wildly, jumped on their car as it moved slowly through the rejoicing mass. F.E. Smith and Sir Henry Wilson were already with the prime minister. Others joined them. They discussed the advantage of calling an election now, whether or not to intervene in the civil war raging between Red and White Russians, and what peace terms should be presented to Germany. The 'fallen foe,' Churchill pointed out, was close to starvation. He proposed rushing 'a dozen great ships crammed with provisions' to Hamburg. His colleagues eyed him coldly. (That evening Wilson would write in his diary: 'LG wants to shoot the Kaiser. Winston does not.')* Outside, the rapturous demonstrations continued through the afternoon, frolickers romping over the Mall, throwing firecrackers and confetti. Suddenly the weather took an ominous turn. The sky darkened. Rain began to fall, hard. Some Londoners sought refuge in the lap of Queen Victoria's statue, but after huddling there a few minutes they

---

* To assure German compliance with the peace terms, the Allied blockade was not lifted until April 1919. Thus Germans continued to starve for five months after Armistice Day.

climbed down. They had found little shelter there, and less comfort. The arms were stone cold.[277]

In a Pomeranian military hospital a twice-decorated German noncommissioned dispatch runner, who had been temporarily blinded during a heavy gas attack on the night of October 13, learned of the capitulation from a sobbing pastor. The invalided noncom was still ready to fight, still throbbing with patriotic fervour, but now there would be no more fighting. Six years later the future Führer of the Third Reich set down a description of his reaction in November 1918. Night after night he lay awake, blazing with hatred for those whom he believed responsible for what he considered a betrayal:

Ich wusste, dass alles verloren war. Auf die Gnade des Feindes zu hoffen, konnten höchstens Narren fertigbringen – oder Lügner und Verbrecher. In diesen Nächten wuchs mir der Hass, der Hass gegen die Urheber dieser Tat . . . Elende und verkommene Verbrecher! Je mehr ich mir in dieser Stunde über das ungeheuer Ereignis klarzuwerden versuchte, um so mehr brannte mir die Scham der Empörung und der Schande in der Stirn. Was war der ganze Schmerz [meiner] Augen gegen diesen Jammer? Was in den Tagen darauf wurde mir auch mein Schicksal bewusst . . . Ich aber beschloss, Politiker zu werden.

[I knew that all was lost. Only fools, liars, and criminals could hope for mercy from the enemy. In these nights hatred grew in me, hatred for those responsible for this deed . . . Miserable and degenerate criminals! The more I tried to achieve clarity on the monstrous event in this hour, the more the shame of indignation and disgrace burned my brow. What was all the pain in my eyes compared to this misery? In the days that followed, my own fate became known to me . . . I resolved to go into politics.][278]

FIVE

OXBOW
1918 – 1932

'It was with feelings which do not lend themselves to words,' Churchill recalled afterwards, 'that I heard the cheers of the brave people who had borne so much and given all, who had never wavered, who had never lost faith in their country or its destiny, and who could be indulgent to the faults of their servants when the hour of deliverance had come.' One simple cheer, a curious eight-word antiphon now locked in the memory of history, was heard that Monday night and throughout the following day wherever London crowds gathered, in Mayfair and Whitechapel, Leicester Square and Regent's Park, Streatham and Harrow-on-the-Hill. It echoed and reechoed, repeated by beaming, tearful, proud, grieving, exultant Britons who rejoiced in the irrefutable evidence that their sacrifices had been redeemed and the Glorious Dead had not, after all, died in vain. Someone in a throng would chant, 'Who won the war?' and the rest would roar back, '*We* won the war!' Then once more: 'Who won the war?' Again a thundering: '*WE* won the war!' And so it went. Eventually they grew hoarse, and the tedium of it drove them away one by one, until at last all had fallen silent. Nevertheless, everyone of them believed it. They actually thought that Britain had won the war.[1]

At dawn's first light on November 21, ten days after the Armistice, the light cruiser HMS *Cardiff* steamed out of Scottish waters flying an enormous blue ensign. Twenty miles out, as prearranged, she rendezvoused with the German High Seas Fleet – the kaiser's titanic armada, most of whose guns hadn't been fired since 1914: 179 battleships, cruisers, destroyers, submarines, and other vessels, now commanded by Admiral Ludwig von Reuter, who was, that day, the most wretched seaman in Europe. Von Reuter had prayed for cloudy skies to mask his shame, but this was *Kaiserwetter*, clear, if blustery, and very bright. *Cardiff* led the humiliated enemy vessels back to May Island, in the mouth of the Firth of Forth, where Admiral Sir David Beatty, nineteen subordinate admirals, and 90,000 bluejackets awaited them on the decks of England's Grand Fleet, the greatest concentration of sea power in history. Beatty presided over 370 warships, all of whose crews were at battle stations, their guns trained on their recent foe, their battle flags snapping angrily in the rising wind. The British warships formed two parallel lines, the classic Spithead formation. Thirteen squadrons of capital ships (among them the *Queen Elizabeth*, her role in the Dardanelles forgotten) escorted the defeated fleet into the Firth and then ordered it to anchor. 'The German flag,' Beatty signalled von Reuter, 'will be hauled down at sunset today, Thursday, and will not be hoisted again without permission.'[2] By dusk swarms of English pleasure boats were festively cruising around the wretched ships of the vanquished *hohe Herr,* hooting and beating buckets with bilge pumps.

Of all the belligerents who had lunged at one another's throats four years earlier, only Britain, it seemed, had emerged strengthened. France's loveliest provinces were a wasteland of denuded earth, barbed wire, and rotting corpses. The Austro-Hungarian dual monarchy was disintegrating. Czarist Russia had ceased to exist. The fallen Second Reich, founded by Bismarck, was racked by strife and a proliferation of *Femen,* or political assassins – Hans Kohn called this frightening new phenomenon 'the sudden brutalization of German political life' – and for the next quarter century its menace would darken all Europe.[3] England's enormous prewar wealth was gone, but its factories were intact, its armed forces had never been mightier, and although England owed the United States five billion dollars in war debts, its continental allies were indebted to it for more than that. At the Versailles peace conference Britain could, in effect, cast six votes because Canada, South Africa, Australia, New Zealand, and India, all separately represented, sup-

ported the Mother Country on most issues. Woodrow Wilson's resistance to territorial acquisitions, and his insistence upon self-determination, was ingeniously met by the creation of the League of Nations mandates. Allied flags flew over these possessions, but, diplomats told the President with straight faces, they were not really annexations because ultimately – no one knew just when – they would become independent. Thus the Empire emerged from the Hall of Mirrors swollen by 988,000 square miles of new territory, inhabited by 13,000,000 people, many of whom had not even known a war was being fought. The Union Jack now flew over German New Guinea, South-West Africa, Tanganyika, parts of Togoland and Cameroon, more than a hundred German islands wrenched from the kaiser, and the Middle Eastern lands which later became Iraq, Iran, Jordan, and Israel. Rhodes's dream of a Cape-to-Cairo corridor had been achieved at last.

Best of all, for those who cherished old customs, the King-Emperor's expansion could be attributed to his Royal Navy, which, as the 'Senior Service,' had been England's original instrument of imperial growth. The army had done the dying, but even before the Versailles treaty (or *Diktat,* as the resentful Germans called it) Britons knew that trench warfare had been futile. It was the Grand Fleet which had blockaded the enemy, starving them into surrender. So tradition had triumphed after all. Englishmen liked that. They were proud of their eccentricities, even the dowdiness of their women's fashions and the odd customs of taking long hikes in the wet, bathing in cold water, flinging open windows in winter, deferring to bowler-hatted retired officers with bristling white moustaches, and driving on what was, for most of the world's motorists, the wrong side of the street. As R.H. Tawney put it, ' "Back to 1914" became a common cry.' Some wanted to go even farther back. On the eve of the war sophisticated Englishmen had felt uneasy about Britain's hegemony. But as Churchill's Harrow schoolmate Leo Amery told Lloyd George after Armistice Day, if the Empire grew mightier after the valour of its youth, 'Who has the right to complain?'[4]

The Empire had flourished on certitude and myth. 'It is the virtue of the Englishman,' Goldsworthy Lowes Dickinson had written in 1913, 'that he never doubts. That is what the system does for him.' Englishmen treasured chivalric legends. In 1912 London children, and many who were no longer children, had packed the Savoy Theatre to see *Where the Rainbow Ends,* an improbable play about two innocents, brother and sister. They are threatened by a Dragon King. Enter Saint George. He seems inadequate: silver-haired and obscured by a billowing cloak. Then the girl says tremulously: 'I am an English maiden in danger, and I ask for your aid.' Instantly, the cloak disappears and we behold a knight in dazzling armour, a great red cross on his breastplate and his hand on the hilt of a glittering Excalibur. The Dragon King boasts of degrading the British ('I flung my gold dust in the people's eyes and lulled them into false security'), but Saint George reminds Britons of their duty to 'fight aggression and foul tyranny.' As the end of the last act approaches he cries to the playgoers: 'Rise, Youth of England, let your voices ring / For God, for Britain, and for Britain's King!' They then stand and join the cast in singing 'God Save the King.'[5]

The pull of such lore retained its power, on the home front at least, while the men in the trenches were fighting a very different struggle. At Mons, it was said, an angel had led lost Tommies to safety. The *Evening News* of September 29, 1914, had carried a poem by Arthur Machen, 'The Bowmen.' In it an embattled British soldier about to be overwhelmed by waves of enemy infantry remembers and repeats Saint George's motto: *Adsit Anglis Sanctus Georgius,* which he once saw on a plate in a London restaurant. Suddenly he hears 'a great voice' calling: 'St George! St George! . . . St George for Merrie England!' Simultaneously, the attacking 'grey men' begin 'falling by thousands.' They have been shot by Agincourt bowmen in the sky. No sooner had Machen's poem appeared than dispatches from France and Belgium began reporting dead Germans slain by arrows. As late as 1917, when, one would think, the truth about the war ought to have been evident to everyone, Henry Newbolt ('Play up! Play up! and play the game!') published his *Book of the Happy Warrior,* full of chivalric fables about the events across the Channel, and E. B. Osborn brought out *The Muse in Arms,* in which he explained the gaiety of British soldiers going into action: 'The Germans, and even our Allies, cannot understand why this stout old nation persists in thinking of war as sport; they do not know that sportsmanship is our new homely name, derived from a racial predilection for comparing great things with small, for the *chevaleries* of the Middle Ages.' Today this sounds inane, but it had some basis in fact. In at least two offensives British soldiers went over the top dribbling soccer balls across no-man's-land. One occurred on July 11, 1916, when Captain W. P. Nevill and his company of the East Surrey Regiment booted a ball back and forth as they advanced along the Somme. Nevill and most of his men were killed in less than an hour. Ineluctably they inspired a poem:[6]

> On through the heat of slaughter
> Where gallant comrades fall
> Where blood is poured like water
> They drive the trickling ball
> The fear of death before them
> Is but an empty name
> True to the land that bore them
> The Surreys play the game.

It is outrageous, it is preposterous, and to a later generation it is completely baffling. What *game,* in the name of God, were the Surreys playing? Ah, but they knew, and that was enough for them. Being mythical, that knowledge was imperishable, and its vitality was still strong on that sunlit morning when Beatty received the surrender of von Reuter's fleet. As the German warships approached the Firth of Forth, the British crew on the battleship *Royal Oak* heard a mysterious drumbeat coming from the lower decks. It was audible on the bridge. Twice officers dispatched bluejackets to investigate. They found nothing, but the drum continued to roll until the enemy's anchor chains ran out. The next day's newspapers carried Newbolt's old poem *Drake's Drum:*

> *Take my drum to England, hang et by the shore,*
> *Strike et when your powder's runnin' low;*
> *If the Dons sight Devon, I'll quit the port o' Heaven,*
> *And drum them up the Channel as we drummed them long ago.*

Seven months later, on a prearranged signal from Admiral von Reuter, German crews pulled the sea cocks of his 10 battleships, 9 armoured cruisers, 8 large cruisers, 50 torpedo boats, and 102 submarines, sending them to the bottom while the horrified, helpless British officers and ratings looked on. Among those witnessing this extraordinary event was a party of school-children on an excursion from Stromness in the Orkneys. Being children, they thought the show was for them. It was. It was for everybody – a defiant gesture declaring that Germany had surrendered but had not quit. In Berlin, Luden-dorff, dining with Major General Sir Neill Malcolm, the chief of Britain's military mission in Berlin, explained in his tumescent, inarticulate way that his home front had let him down. 'Do you mean,' asked Malcolm, 'that you were stabbed in the back?' Ludendorff pounced. 'Stabbed in the back?' he repeated. 'Yes, that's exactly it. We were stabbed in the back [*Dolchstoss in den Rücken*].' Hindenburg heard the phrase from him and testified before a political committee of inquiry: 'As an English general has very truly said, the German Army was stabbed in the back.' Stabbed by whom? Presently an answer emerged: the hilt of the dagger had been held by the Jews.[7]

The British were very cross with von Reuter. His conduct, they felt, had been most unsportsmanlike, and doubtless there were those who expected retri-bution from the angel of Mons, Saint George, the Agincourt bowmen, or the footballers of the Somme. If they felt chagrined, so, for very different reasons, did His Majesty's diplomats in Versailles, the following week, when the peace treaty was signed. They were satisfied with their spoils of war but departed feeling somehow diminished in the eyes of the civilized world. Lloyd George, they had assumed, would dominate the conference. In the words of a contem-porary, he was regarded as the 'one statesman in England who counted.' And Winston was almost as familiar to the British public as his chief. Robert Rhodes James has left us a vivid portrait of Churchill at this time: 'Much of the early aggressiveness has been softened by age and experience. In manner he remains alert, thrusting, eager, or in sharp contrast fitting his mood, sombre, portentous, and scowling with leaden responsibility . . . His dedication to his career is total, even obsessive. Experience has not dimmed the originality of his mind, nor the intensity of his emotions, nor the volubility of his conver-sation.'[8]

Churchill saw Versailles as 'grimly polished and trellised with live wires' over which the British prime minister repeatedly tripped. He tried, but failed, to dilute Clemenceau's draconian demands upon the Germans. Lloyd George's support of President Wilson's proposal for a League of Nations was –

to Churchill's deep disappointment – uncharacteristically tepid. The fact is that George was jealous of Wilson. The austere President was upstaging him. A weary Europe found the American's earnest idealism fresh and stirring. The centre of Sir William Orpen's painting of the signing ceremony features Lloyd George, surrounded by an Australian, a Canadian, an Afrikaner, a turbaned Indian, Balfour, Curzon, and Milner. 'But somehow the eye strays,' wrote James Morris, to 'the stiff ascetic person of President Wilson: for he is looking directly, deliberately, at the artist, with an almost accusatory expression, as though he is staring hard into the future, and willing it his way.' Lloyd George distrusted the President, and with good reason, for the Wilsonian doctrine of self-determination – the right of a people to decide their own political status – was a threat to the very survival of imperialism. Indeed, the Empire delegations, led by Australia's mercurial Prime Minister W. M. Hughes, narrowly defeated a clause in the League Covenant, proposed by Japan, which would have declared that all races were inherently equal. Hughes, a fellow Welshman, was Lloyd George's natural ally. Besides, Australia had its eye on German archipelagos in the Pacific. Wilson, offended, asked Hughes if he really meant to defy world opinion by a naked grab for colonies. The feisty Australian replied: 'That's about the size of it, Mr President.' Thus the emergence of the Third World debuted on the international stage as a moral issue. It would be crowded into the wings again and again, only to reappear cast in ever larger roles, to the exasperation and dismay of, among others, Winston Churchill.[9]

Almost unnoticed among the miles of Union Jacks in the Firth of Forth on the day of von Reuter's surrender had been a little squadron of six warships flying the Stars and Stripes. When the Admiralty signalled Beatty that morning, affirming that the enemy's capitulation 'will remain for all time the example of the wonderful silence and sureness with which sea power attains its end,' it meant *British* sea power.[10] The Royal Navy's treatment of its American cousins had been patronizing and at times even rude, but one of the first signs that England's *belle époque* was ending appeared in a naval agreement, reached in Washington after the Versailles signing, which would have been unthinkable before the war. At the turn of the century England had been spending almost twice as much on its navy as any other country. Its policy, followed by both parties, had kept its fleet strength at a level greater than that of any other two nations combined. Now England consented to observe the ratio of 5 (Great Britain), 5 (United States), 3 (Japan), 1.75 (France), and 1.75 (Italy). Imperial warship designs were discarded; the agreement stipulated the size and type of every vessel. There would never be another *Queen Elizabeth*. After the pact, the Royal Navy was required to scrap 657 ships, including dreadnoughts, battleships, and cruisers – much of the Grand Fleet's backbone. The Admiralty pledged itself never to build a naval base at Hong Kong. England's absolute command of the seas, so vital to the Empire, was over. Britannia no longer ruled the waves, not because world opinion objected, but because, having spent £5,000,000 a day during the war, it simply couldn't afford to.

It is impossible to pinpoint the beginning of imperial decline. In a sense eventual freedom became inevitable the moment a British possession was conquered, because Britain selectively extended its institutions into its colonies with the establishment of legislative councils, later to become parliaments. In the beginning this happened only in colonies dominated by white settlers. Canada became a self-governing federation in 1867 and imposed a tariff on British imports the following year. Gladstone's cabinet was outraged, but the GOM pointed out that if you grant people rights, you must expect them to flex their new muscles, however disagreeable the consequences. Self-government then came to Australia in 1901, to New Zealand in 1907, and, in 1910, to South Africa.

As early as the 1880s, farsighted members of England's ruling class, seeing where all this would lead, expressed alarm that Free Trade and self-government would end in the 'dismemberment' of the Empire. To stop it, they founded the Imperial Federation League in 1884. Rhodes, Milner, Rosebery, and Joseph Chamberlain gave the league their heartiest support. Chamberlain, who had admired Bismarck's skill in uniting the former German states for commercial and military ends without sacrificing the autonomy of the Second Reich, proposed a British imperial defence league, patterned on the Reich's Kriegsverein, and a customs union along the lines of Bismarck's Zollverein. However, the Empire's self-governing colonies – now coming to be called Dominions – were not interested. They came to London for imperial conferences and loyally knelt before the throne, but when they declared war on the Central Powers in 1914, each of their prime ministers was careful to point out that his government was making its own decisions, not following London's instructions, whatever constitutional theorists might say. After the war, thoughtful men in Whitehall realized that the United States and the USSR would eventually dominate *Weltpolitik*. They tried to press the cause of imperial federation, in the hope that all countries flying the Union Jack might combine to form a third superpower.

Gradually, however, they realized they were playing upon a losing wicket. The Washington treaty was but one of several omens. India having supported the war effort, India's politicians now demanded a quid pro quo. Their leaders, some of them educated in English public schools, infuriated the British establishment by quoting Burke and Macaulay in support of the demands for immediate parliamentary self-government. They didn't get it, but their contribution of a million men and £500,000,000 to the war effort could not go unrecognized. A resolution introduced by Lloyd George in 1917, and then passed by Parliament in 1919, proved to be the first step towards Indian independence. Before 1914 both the resolution and the Washington naval treaty would have meant the fall of the government. Now press and public seemed indifferent. H. G. Wells, estimated that 95 per cent of England's population was as ignorant of the Empire as of the Italian Renaissance. Both the Colonial Office and the Indian Civil Service marked a sharp drop in the number and quality of their applicants. In large measure this was a consequence of the recent slaughter. The war had left 160,000 young English widows and 300,000 fatherless children. The flower of England's youth, its university students and recent graduates, had joined Kitchener's armies and crossed to France, most of them as infantry lieutenants. The number of those who fell is incalculable, but some figures are suggestive. In his mindless Passchendaele offensive, Haig lost 22,316 junior officers, compared to only 6,913 Germans of similar rank. We shall never know how many potential prime ministers, cabinet ministers, poets, scientists, physicians, lawyers, professors, and distinguished civil servants perished in the mud of France and Belgium, but the conclusion is inescapable: an entire generation had lost most of its ablest men. Those who survived, like Anthony Eden, of the King's Royal Rifle Corps, gassed on the Somme, and thrice-wounded Harold Macmillan of the Grenadier Guards, who had studied Horace by candlelight in his dugout, emerged with a weltanschauung which was incomprehensible to their fathers.

Part of the loss of brio may be attributed to the lack of heroes. Chivalric myth required heroic leaders. The reading public now had to settle for the thin fictional gruel of Bulldog Drummond and Richard Hannay. The war had produced no Marlboroughs, Wellingtons, Nelsons, or Gordons. Kitchener was a tarnished legend. Only the young archaeologist T. E. Lawrence, whose achievements as a colonel in the Middle East were genuine, had a postwar following. Victory had eluded Jellicoe at Jutland, the war's only major naval engagement, because, out of excessive caution, he had evaded three crucial decisions. All the British generals had been discredited, with consequences which reached far beyond the British Isles. Before the war, the Empire's overseas subjects had regarded England with affection and respect. Young Mahatma Gandhi, who had struggled up Spion Kop as a stretcher-bearer that night when Churchill was frantically rushing from colonel to colonel, trying to save the hill from the Boers – Gandhi had been decorated for his bravery afterwards – later wrote of his anglophilia then: 'Hardly ever have I known anyone to cherish such loyalty as I did to the British Constitution . . . I vied with Englishmen in loyalty to the throne.' In 1914, James Morris wrote, 'the white colonials had gone to war trustingly, innocently almost, satisfied for the most part to be loyal assistants to the Mother Country. They had been inexperienced still, as soldiers and as statesmen, and they were as indoctrinated as the British at home in their ingenuous respect for British traditions and achievements. Though they often made fun of the British, their toffs, their drawls and their domesticity, they still looked up to the Old Country, and believed as the British did themselves in the value of its systems and the skill of its leaders.'[11]

At the time of the Somme, when the fate of civilization seemed to hang in the balance, Australian boys at Melbourne's Scotch College wept when they sang the stanzas of 'Bugles of England.' The legend of Saint George was as revered in Durban and Ottawa as in London. Proud of their membership in the Empire, the colonials assumed that the graduates of Sandhurst were the finest officers in the world. In the trenches they learned otherwise. The Australians learned to despise both Major General Alexander Godley, who at Gallipoli had led them ashore, not to a beach, but to the base of a cliff, and Ian Hamilton, who, when they asked to be evacuated, had replied: 'You have got through the difficult business, now you have only to dig, dig, dig, until you are safe.' In self-mockery the survivors called themselves 'diggers' and made ribald jokes about British redtabs. Godley, they said, 'couldn't find the balls on a bull.' Some of the wittiest wartime scatology ever written was inspired by Louisa Godley, the general's wife, who visited wounded New Zealanders in an Egyptian hospital and complained that they had insulted her by not lying at attention.[12]

The Canadians were also disillusioned. On Easter Sunday, 1917, on Vimy Ridge, they had won the reputation of being the finest soldiers on the western front. Haig wasted them, of course; his lethal hand struck down everything it touched. But he also slighted them. He described a delegation of visiting Canadians, including their minister of war, as a 'well-meaning but second-rate sort of people.' Indeed, he let it be known that in his judgement all 'colonial generals' were 'ignorant and conceited.' Australians and New Zealanders, he said, were likely to desert at the first opportunity. He made it a point to keep them separated from British divisions, explaining to his staff that they would exert 'a bad influence.' It was probably impossible to deepen the contempt of Irish Catholics for the British, but Kitchener had a try at it, issuing orders that under no circumstances would Catholics be permitted to fight under their own officers.[13]

By Armistice Day the image of the Mother Country in its greatest possessions had been irretrievably altered, although there was little understanding of this in London. Someone in the royal household – it is impossible to trace the source – thought it a splendid idea for the King's four sons to reign over the four Dominions. The question was raised in Ottawa, Canberra, Wellington, and Cape Town; then quietly shelved. The Empire's five additional votes at Versailles had been misunderstood. They were a sign, not of imperial unity, but of the Dominions' independence. As early as 1917 their four prime ministers, meeting in London, had resolved that when the fighting ended they must have an 'adequate voice in [imperial] foreign policy and in foreign relations.' Jan Christiaan Smuts, South Africa's next premier, even called them 'autonomous nations.' British omniscience had been exposed as a fraud. They were less willing to accept decisions made in Whitehall and Westminster, though the tug was still strong; when the first summons came, they wavered, awed by the momentous decision to defy parental authority. The test came shortly over an incident in Turkey, and here, as so often in the making of British history during his life, Churchill, then at the Colonial Office, was right in the middle of it. He sent an 'inquiry' to the Dominions, asking whether they were prepared, if the need arose, to send troops to the troubled area. *The Times* was offended. This, said its editorial, was a typical example of Winston's lack of good judgement; imperial possessions weren't asked, they were *told*. 'Although the Dominions may speak with many voices for themselves as individuals,' its leader declared, 'they speak as one when the time comes to speak for the Empire.' But they didn't. They spoke as many. Only New Zealand and Newfoundland meekly complied. The Australians agreed under protest. The South Africans refused. 'Very important questions of policy would be involved as far as the Union is concerned,' Smuts cabled, 'by any decision of the Union Government to take part in military operations in Eastern Europe and it is felt by the Union Government that such a step should not be taken without calling Parliament together.' The Canadian prime minister, Mackenzie King, took the same stand. King fully understood the implications of his response, but in his diary he wrote: 'If membership in the British Empire means participation by the Dominions in any and every war in which Great Britain becomes involved, I can see no hope for an enduring relationship.'[14]

As it turned out, the men weren't needed, but the precedent had been set. The King's statesmen brooded. Most of his British subjects, however, gave the issue neither first nor second thought. Imperialism, so thrilling a creed only a few years earlier, had lost its charisma. They simply didn't care. The young in particular were more concerned with finding a home and a steady job. Labour, now the most exciting of the parties, was either indifferent towards the Empire or downright hostile. Newspapers found that events in England's far-flung possessions bored their readers. 'Back to 1914'? They wanted no part of it. The chairman of the Empire Day Committee acknowledged that Britons were simply incurious about the 'many dark corners where the rays of our Empire sun have not been able to penetrate.' Philip Guedalla discovered that in the early 1920s the doctrine of Imperialism attracted merely 'a dim interest [among] research students.'[15] Intellectuals jeered at values *fin de siècle* Britain had held sacred. Lytton Strachey's sardonic, sniggering *Eminent Victorians* was an immediate success when it appeared in 1918. His next book, *Queen Victoria*, which presented its subject as a trivial, quirky woman, became required reading in universities between the wars. And the generals, who had seemed mighty only yesterday, were left to the merciless pens of cartoonists.

Sometimes a social event, wholly divorced from political considerations and affairs of state, can illumine the mood of a time. In this sense, the British Empire Exhibition at Wembley is immensely instructive about the temper of postwar England. Assembled at the terminus of the London underground railway at a cost of £4,000,000, it dwarfed Britain's last great fair, the Crystal Palace. Pavilions celebrated the genius of the imperial peoples, the fair managers enlisted Kipling to acclaim imperial glory, and Edward Elgar provided the music, which largely comprised various renditions of his 'Land of Hope and Glory.' Tibetan trumpeters blew bugle calls. The tomb of Tutankhamen was reconstructed, he being, as W.S. Gilbert would have put it, a sort of British ancestor by purchase. Visitors travelling on the exhibition's Never-Stop Railway passed beneath thousands of massed Union Jacks, and Lord Milner expressed the conviction that Wembley would prove a 'powerful bulwark' against subversives who would undermine the Empire. The King himself went on the radio to hawk its attractions. ('This great achievement reveals to us the whole Empire in little . . .') The exhibition, solemnly conceived, should have reaffirmed Britain's confidence in its imperial destiny.[16]

It didn't. It became a joke. The most popular feature had been lifted from an American carnival. 'I've brought you here to see the wonders of the Empire,' a Noël Coward character told his children, 'and all you want to do is go to the Dodgems.' P.G. Wodehouse's Bertie Wooster drawled: 'I mean to say, millions of people, no doubt, are so constituted that they scream with joy and excitement at the spectacle of a stuffed porcupine fish or a glass jar of seeds from Western Australia – but not Bertram . . . By the time we had tottered out of the Gold Coast Village and were looking towards the Palace of Machinery, everything pointed to my shortly executing a quiet sneak in the direction of that rather jolly Planters' Bar in the West Indies section.' The intellectuals of Bloomsbury and Hampstead, solidly anti-imperialist, organized a group called the WGTW, the Won't Go To Wembleys. Mayfair's Bright Young Things, soon to find their minstrel in Evelyn Waugh, treated it, James Morris wrote, 'as a spree.' They performed naughty acts in the Nigerian Handicrafts Exhibition – 'Did you Wemble?' they slyly asked one another, and if you nodded it meant you had performed a lewd act under the eyes of the wogs – after which the bobbies usually released them, because the boys bore patrician names and so many of the naked girls turned out to be widows of the Glorious Dead. 'A great empire and little minds,' Edmund Burke had said in 1775, 'go ill together.' Now T.S. Eliot wrote: 'I had not thought death had undone so many.'[17]

Churchill watched all this and grieved. In the notes for a speech to his constituents he wrote: 'What a disappointment the twentieth century has been. How terrible and how melancholy is long series of disastrous events wh have darkened its first 20 years. We have seen in ev country a dissolution, a weakening of those bonds, a challenge to those principles, a decay of faith, a abridgement of hope on wh structure & ultimate existence of civilized society depends . . . Can you doubt, my faithful friends, as you survey this sombre panorama, that mankind is passing through a period marked not only by an enormous destruction & abridgement of human species, not only by a vast impoverishment & reduction in means of existence but also that destructive tendencies have not yet run their course?'[18]

Honour, as he understood it, seemed dead in England, and gone with it were innocence, rationalism, optimism, and the very concept of an ordered society. He asked almost pathetically: 'Why should war be the only purpose capable of uniting us? All for war – nothing is too good for war. Why cannot we have some of it for peace?' An age, the age he had adored, appeared to have reached journey's end, and journeys no longer ended in lovers meeting. The government seemed to need, not diplomats, but economists, of whom he knew almost nothing. The disposition of the British public was a backlash against everything he cherished, and he found that hard to bear. 'I was,' he wrote, 'a child of the Victorian era, when the structure of our country seemed firmly set, when its position in trade and on the seas was unrivalled, and when the realisation of the greatness of our Empire and of our duty to preserve it was growing ever stronger.' Now that was threatened, and threatened from within. He reflected that the 'shadow of victory is disillusion. The reaction from extreme effort is prostration. The aftermath even of successful war is long and bitter.' These, he realized, would be years of 'turbulence and depression.' But he would soldier on. Surely the great imperial strengths, tradition and continuity, could not long be denied. Eventually the tide would turn. He was certain of it. It never crossed his mind that the ebb might be permanent – that he and all he cherished would, in the end, be stranded forever.[19]

He continued to think of the Empire as an 'old lion, with her lion cubs by her side,' and while he could shrug off the Stracheys and the Wodehouses and the WGTW as temporary abhorrences – he could never have accepted the Wembley circus as a metaphor for imperial majesty anyhow – he was deeply angered by any retreat from the distant frontiers of what he regarded as Britain's rightful realms. When Curzon supported Milner's recommendations for Egyptian sovereignty, Winston passed him a note: 'It leaves me absolutely baffled why you shd be on this side, or why you shd have insisted on keeping Egyptian affairs in yr hands' – Curzon had been an able imperial administrator as viceroy of India (1898-1905) and foreign secretary (1919-1921) – 'only to lead to this melancholy conclusion. It grieves me profoundly to see what is unfolding.' In a City of London speech on November 4, 1920, he sounded paranoid, hinting at a sinister 'world-wide conspiracy against our country, designed to deprive us of our place in the world and rob us of victory.' He did not see how, in the long run, such a plot could succeed: 'Having beaten the most powerful military empire in the world, having emerged triumphantly from the fearful struggle of Armageddon, we should not allow ourselves to be pulled down and have our Empire disrupted by a malevolent and subversive force, the rascals and rapscallions of mankind . . . now on the move against us. Whether it be the Irish murder gang, or the arch-traitors we had at home, they should feel the weight of the British arm. It was strong enough to break the Hindenburg line; it will be strong enough to defend the main interests of the British people.'[20]

Confronted by foes, he was always like this: galloping, mud-spattered, high in oath. But once a foe was down, he sprang from his saddle and extended a helping hand. Had Arthur reappeared in modern Britain, Churchill would have been his Galahad. It is not without significance that he loved round tables and always had at least one in each of his several homes. His faith in gallantry ran deep. Years later he told his physician how, at the end of an engagement on the western front, when one of his tank crews had to surrender to the enemy, the Germans saluted them and complimented them on their valiant fight. He smiled. He said: 'That is how I like war to be conducted.' Even in the last weeks of 1918, when the popular slogans were 'Hang the Kaiser!' and 'Squeeze them till the pips squeak!' he repeated his watchwords: 'In victory, magnanimity; in peace, goodwill.' He agreed with the Germans that the Versailles terms had been dictated by the victors; he would have preferred a negotiated settlement. 'I was all for war,' he told Bernard Baruch when they met. 'Now I'm all for peace.' In a long memorandum to himself he concluded that both sides had been guilty of atrocities unprecedented in war between civilized states. Germany had been 'in the van,' but had been 'followed step by step' by Britain, France, and their allies. 'Every outrage against humanity or international law,' he wrote, 'was repaid by reprisals – often of a greater scale and of longer duration' than Germany's. 'No truce or parley mitigated the strife of the armies. The wounded died between the lines: the dead mouldered into the soil. Merchant ships and neutral ships and hospital ships were sunk on the seas and all on board left to their fate, or killed as they swam. Every effort was made to starve whole nations into submission without regard to age or sex. Cities and monuments were smashed by artillery. Bombs from the air were cast down indiscriminately. Poison gas in many forms stifled or seared the soldiers. Liquid fire was projected upon their bodies. Men fell from the air in flames, or were smothered often slowly in the dark recesses of the sea. The fighting strength of armies was limited only by the manhood of their countries . . . Torture and Cannibalism were the only two expedients that the civilised scientific Christian States had been able to deny themselves: and these were of doubtful utility.' Nor had the Armistice ended it. Relief for the prostrate nations was wholly inadequate. All they were accomplishing, he told a friend, was the return of victims 'again and again to the shambles. Nothing is wasted that can contribute to the process of waste.'[21]

It is a sign of Churchill's stature as a politician that what he wrote in private, and said to friends, he repeated from the platform when campaigning for office. Immediately after the Armistice, Lloyd George called England's second khaki election of the century. Winston told his constituents that the Germans must be clothed, sheltered, and fed, that the triumphant Allies ought not 'to be drawn into extravagances by the fullness of their victory.' He particularly deplored staggering reparations. Immediately James K. Foggie, a leading Dundee Liberal, wrote to him: 'I think the great card to play & the one which will give you a huge victory, is that you declare, "that Germany must pay this country & the other allied Nations, all expenses caused by the War." Germany started the War, & has been defeated, therefore it stands to reason she must pay. Had Germany beaten our Empire she certainly without doubt, would have made us pay all expenses. Dundee will stand for nothing else. Dundee has given over 30,000 soldiers. Almost 20% . . . have been killed.'

Doubtless Foggie spoke for an overwhelming majority of the Dundee electorate, but Churchill wouldn't budge. As it happened, it didn't matter. Lloyd George's timing had been precise. The coalition was swept back into office – though the Tories had outpolled the Liberals for the first time in thirteen years, and Labour strength was growing.[22]

Winston had been reelected by what his bitterest adversary in the constituency, the Tory Dundee *Advertiser,* called the 'immense majority' of 15,365. Clearly he was entitled to a more prestigious cabinet post. His stubborn courage in adversity since Gallipoli, his capacity for taxing work, his brilliance and force – all argued strongly against extending his exclusion from the government's highest councils. He wanted to return to the Admiralty but realized that was impolitic. The War Office was available, however; Milner was moving to the Colonial Office. Winston's critics trembled at the thought of entrusting military decisions to him again. Leo Amery wrote to the prime minister: 'Don't put Churchill in the War Office. I hear from all sorts of quarters that the Army are terrified at the idea.' The *Daily Mail* and *Morning Post* echoed Amery's warning, but nothing could have given Lloyd George greater pleasure than dismaying the men responsible for the Somme and Passchendaele. On January 9, 1919, he relieved his minister of munitions, whose desk at the Metropole had long been cleared anyway, and invested him with twin portfolios. Churchill was now secretary of state for war and air.[23]

He inherited an army crisis. The vast mass of the troops were civilians who had signed up for the duration. They wanted their discharges as soon as possible. Of the 3.5 million men under arms, fewer than a third would be needed for armies of occupation in Germany and the Middle East. A majority, therefore, were eligible to return home as soon as transport could be arranged. The difficulty lay in deciding who should go first. Senior officers, whose temporary rank depended upon the size of their commands, were in no hurry to expedite the process. Milner had established a system under which priority was assigned to 'key men' in industry. But these blue-collar workers, by the very fact of their indispensability, had been among the last to be called up; many had not been drafted until the manpower crisis of the previous March. Now they were being released from the service while volunteers who had fought in the trenches for four years remained there. In the week before Churchill moved into Whitehall, soldiers had rioted in Dover and Folkestone, demanding immediate demobilization. Two days later Milner had issued new regulations under which only men with job offers could be discharged. This left three million Tommies with no prospect of an early return to civilian life, and their mood was ugly. On Winston's first day in his new office he was handed a telegram from Haig, reporting a rapid deterioration of army morale under the latest rules. Proof of it lay in London, within earshot of the War Office. A mob of insubordinate Tommies had gathered on the Horse Guards Parade, waving seditious signs. Had they but known it, that was the last way to win concessions from Churchill. He called in a group of anxious officers and asked them: 'How many troops have we got to deal with them?' A battalion of guards, he was told, and three squadrons of the Household Cavalry. 'Are they loyal?' he inquired. The officers replied that they hoped so. He asked: 'Can you arrest the mutineers?' They were uncertain but had no other suggestions. He said: 'Then arrest the mutineers.' He watched from his window while the demonstrators, deflated, permitted the guards to surround them and then lead them away.[24]

By now reports of barracks disturbances were arriving from commanding officers in France, Flanders, Mesopotamia, Palestine, Greece, and Italy. Haig warned that unless the stampede was stopped, 'the Germans will be in a position to negotiate another kind of peace.' Churchill was more worried about the impact upon the Bolsheviks, in Moscow and Saint Petersburg, who were calling for uprisings by soldiers all over the world. There were Communist agitators in Britain, too, particularly around military and air bases. Sir Henry Wilson noted in his diary that the new war minister directed him to bring home 'all reliable troops, i.e. Household & other Cavalry, Yeomanry, Home County Rgts: etc.' At the same time Winston decided that no men would be mustered out who had fought less than two years in France; eligibility for discharge would be determined by age, length of service, and wounds. But young conscripts would still be needed to police the new territories being absorbed by the Empire. No one liked compulsory service – until three years earlier the country had never known any form of conscription, even in wartime – but there was no alternative. Since Lloyd George was at Versailles, the cabinet had to act in his absence. After consulting Austen Chamberlain, the new chancellor of the Exchequer, Churchill drew up plans for an army to garrison the British Zone in occupied Germany. The War Cabinet approved and advised George of its action. An announcement was prepared. By the time it was released to the press, Winston wrote in his diary, 'the great adventure of "compulsing" a million men in time of peace to serve abroad will have begun.' In his view it came in the nick of time, because 'all our power over the Army is slipping away.'[25]

Britons accustomed to wartime regimentation accepted the extension of conscription, partly because the new demobilization scheme seemed fair. In the meantime, however, Milner's old regulations had kindled a major revolt in Calais, where five thousand Tommies, newly arrived from England, demanded that they be returned home immediately. Haig reported to Winston that their attitude was 'threatening, insubordinate, and mutinous.' At his direction, he said, General Henry G. Sandilands sent a brigade with fixed bayonets into their camp and arrested the three ringleaders. He wanted them executed; otherwise, he believed, 'the discipline of the whole Army will suffer, both immediately & for many years to come.' Churchill disagreed. Execution, Winston wrote, 'should be used only under what may be called life and death conditions, and public opinion will only support it when other men's lives are endangered by criminal or cowardly conduct.' The field marshal spared the three men, but he was incensed by what he regarded as civilian meddling. He noted in his diary that he had the 'power by Warrant' to put men before firing squads without consulting the War Office. His days of wielding such power were numbered, however. Parliament awarded him £100,000 and made him an earl, but the historians were beginning to catch up with Douglas Haig. Lesser generals were appointed to lofty civilian roles: governor-general of Canada, high commissioner for Egypt, high commissioner for Palestine, governor of Malta, offices in the Indian Empire. London never summoned Haig from his retirement in Scotland. Forgotten and ignored, he died of a heart attack in 1928.[26]

By the end of January, 1919, some 980,000 soldiers had been repatriated, and eight months after assuming office, Churchill had reduced Britain's military expenditures by nearly 70 per cent. Britian's army, he said, had 'melted away.' The demobilization had been a triumph of organization, but it left him uneasy. England, he believed, now needed a large standing army. Postwar Europe had become dangerous. In the spring some 70,000 of Ludendorff's former troops, marching under the banner of the Rote Soldatenbund (Red Soldiers' League), had seized a cache of arms in Bochum, defeated a right-wing *Freikorps* in a pitched battle, and occupied six Ruhr cities, proclaiming workers' republics in each. Under Versailles the Ruhr was out-of-bounds to German and Allied troops, but Berlin sent in troops of the Reichswehr, the Weimar Republic's army, and suppressed the revolt; rebels were tried before *Freikorpskämpfer* military courts and shot. Britain, Italy, and the United States approved the Reichswehr action, but the French, infuriated by this invasion of the 'neutral' Ruhr, countered by occupying four German towns. In Paris, Winston discussed the incident with André Lefevre, the French minister of war. He told him that France had 'committed a grave error in tactics and had lost far more prestige and authority than they had gained.' The present threat to Western civilization, he said, was not German militarism; it was bolshevism. By now the Ruhr was quiet. The Rote Soldatenbund having been shattered, both Berlin and Paris withdrew their troops. Churchill's anxiety over the spread of communism did not fade, however. Years later Bernard Baruch wrote to him recalling one day in Paris, when the Versailles talks were in progress and the two of them 'were walking through the Bois de Boulogne, talking of the problems which burdened a world exhausted by war and groping for peace.' A wind had risen; the sky was darkening; Baruch expressed concern about the weather. His letter continued: 'Suddenly you broke your brisk stride, paused and, lifting your walking stick, pointed to the East. Your voice rumbled ominously: "Russia! Russia! That's where the weather is coming from!" '[27]

In the spring of 1918, when Ludendorff was plunging his bloody fists into the Allied line in France and Belgium, the Bolsheviks in central Russia stood naked to invasion. And no regime, not even Napoleon's, had ever been threatened by more formidable enemies. Led by the czar's professional officers, over 300,000 'White' Russians, loyal to the Romanovs, were forming armies on the Reds' five-thousand-mile front – over ten times the length of the western front. On December 30, 1917, Japan had become the first foreign country to intervene in Russia's internal struggle, landing troops at Vladivostok in Siberia. Two battalions of Tommies from Hong Kong occupied Murmansk next, and, six weeks later, with Frenchmen at their side, Archangel. American doughboys joined them. Meanwhile, British soldiers from Salonika and Persia seized the Baku-Batum railroad while British warships blockaded Russia's Black Sea and Baltic ports. National motives varied. All felt vindictive towards an ally who, as they saw it, had betrayed them by signing a separate peace, and they were determined to recover vast stores of munitions they had shipped to Russia – arms which the Germans, in the last crisis of the war, were bent on capturing. Japan also wanted to annex Russian territory. The Americans were determined to prevent that and, at the same time, to free beleaguered Czechoslovaks.

The Allies were united in their resolve to crush bolshevism, though in those months it appeared to be disintegrating without their help. The Ukraine had proclaimed its independence on January 28. In April and May similar declarations followed in the Caucasian states of Georgia, Armenia, and Azerbaijan. Lenin had agreed to the Germans' terms at Brest-Litovsk in order to gain some 'breathing space,' but every day the Bolsheviks had less space in which to breathe. By signing the treaty they had yielded Poland, the Baltic provinces, and Finland. Now the Whites and the Allies vowed to take the rest. The Red Army was in a pitiful state. Some troops were approaching starvation. Few had coats; half of them lacked boots and underwear. Rifles were in short supply. So was ammunition. Weapons rusted because oil was unavailable. Horses died; there was no fodder. The logistical situation was appalling. Coal mines had been flooded. Factories had been demolished. The sources of fuel, steel, and iron were in White hands. Lenin had spoken grandly of riding to triumph on a wildly careening 'locomotive of history,' but on Russia's railway tracks his trains laboured forward at a speed of one mile an hour. His only two military assets were interior lines and the ingenuity of his commissar of war, Leib Davydovich Bronstein, who had taken the name of Leon Trotsky and who, over the next two years, was to prove himself a commander of genius.[28]

Even with Trotsky the Reds would have been doomed had they been forced to fight during the first winter of their revolution. But the White counterrevolutionaries were still gathering their forces, and the Allies were pinned down by the Germans. It was typical of this confused, tumultuous war that the first shots were fired by soldiers who were neither Reds, Whites, nor Allies. Before the overthrow of the czar, his officers had organized a Czechoslovakian legion comprising seventy thousand prisoners of war eager to fight the Austrians. These were the men who concerned Woodrow Wilson. Brest-Litovsk had stipulated they be disarmed by the Bolsheviks, but it wasn't done, and the Allies had been unable to spare the shipping to evacuate them. They were being marched and countermarched aimlessly across the Urals and Siberia when they learned that the Reds were planning to disarm them. In

June 1918 they revolted and seized a section of the Trans-Siberian Railway. That feat attracted the attention of the counterrevolutionary Admiral Aleksandr Kolchak. He recruited them under his banner and opened the civil war's first great offensive, capturing Omsk, Ekaterinburg, and, against negligible opposition, most of the country between the Volga and the Pacific. In Omsk the Siberians announced that they were now an autonomous nation – another territorial loss for the Bolsheviks. Among the casualties during this drive had been the czar, his family, their doctor, and three servants. They had been imprisoned in Ekaterinburg; when Czech troops approached in July, their guards shot them. They would have been killed anyway. The Reds had read Marat: 'Woe to the revolution which has not enough courage to behead the symbol of the ancien régime.' But Trotsky was disappointed. He had looked forward to prosecuting Nicholas in a public trial, and had designated himself as public prosecutor.

By the summer of 1918 it seemed likely that Trotsky himself would stand in the dock, with Kolchak as his hanging judge. On August 6 the Red Army broke and fled from Kazan on the east bank of the upper Volga, over four hundred miles west of Ekaterinburg and the last important strongpoint between the Whites and central Russia. If Kolchak and his Czechs crossed the river there, they could pour across the open plain – that muddy okra-sown countryside grazed by brown, low-slung cows – and take undefended Moscow, which had become the seat of the new government in March. Nothing could stop them; the villages were completely indefensible. The Central Executive of the Soviets declared the regime to be in danger. Trotsky ordered conscription and left for the front aboard a train which would serve as his mobile headquarters for the better part of three years. Arriving in Svyazhsk, a village on the west bank of the Volga, opposite Kazan, he rallied his panicked soldiers with fiery eloquence and led them back to the front. There he boarded a rusty boat and summoned the sailors of Kronstadt to swell his ranks. Leaders who had joined their men in the rout were brought before him and sentenced to death. He issued a proclamation: 'If any detachment retreats without orders, the first to be shot will be the commissar, the next the commander . . . Cowards, scoundrels, and traitors will not escape the bullet – for this I vouch before the whole Red Army.'[29] Heavy fighting continued throughout that month and into the next, until, on September 10, the Bolsheviks recaptured Kazan. By the end of the month the entire Volga basin was back in their hands. Moscow had been saved. Trotsky celebrated the victory by executing hostages and launching his first Red Terror against civilians who had not actively supported his troops.

Meanwhile, the White general Anton Denikin was planning an attack with thirty thousand counterrevolutionaries from his base on the Don while a third counterrevolutionary army, under General Nickolay Yudenich, was bearing down on Petrograd, whose Red defenders were led by the Ossetian Joseph Stalin. It was at this point, in mid-1918, that Churchill's participation in the Russian struggle began to be felt. He was still a junior minister then, and his role was severely limited, but he was the revolution's most vehement British foe. He had been the first to grasp the strategic significance of the Czechs. At his urging, the cabinet voted to remain in Murmansk and Archangel, recognize the Omsk regime, send munitions to Denikin and the rebels in the Baltic states, occupy the Baku-Batum railway in the Caucasus, and establish a strong British expeditionary force in Siberia.

Winston then set out to warn the British public against what he called the 'poison peril' in the East. In Dundee, he said: 'Russia is being rapidly reduced by the Bolsheviks to an animal form of barbarism . . . The Bolsheviks maintain themselves by bloody and wholesale butcheries and murders . . . Civilisation is being completely extinguished over gigantic areas, while Bolsheviks hop and caper like troops of ferocious baboons amid the ruins of cities and the corpses of their victims.' In a memorandum he wrote: 'Nobody wants to intervene in Russian affairs. Russia is a vy large country, a vy old country, a vy disagreeable country inhabited by immense numbers of ignorant people largely possessed of lethal weapons & in a state of extreme disorder. Also Russia is a long way off.' He understood England's yearning for peace. 'Unhappily,' he continued, 'events are driving in a different direction, and nowadays events are vy powerful things. There never was a time when events were so much stronger than human beings. We may abandon Russia: but Russia will not abandon us. We shall retire & she will follow. The bear is padding on bloody paws across the snows to the Peace Conference.'[30]

He conferred with the War Cabinet again on December 31 to discuss the government's Russian policy, but Lloyd George was becoming critical of his hawkish stand. George told Riddell: 'Winston . . . wants to conduct a war against the Bolsheviks. That *would* cause a revolution!' The prime minister toyed with the idea of opening talks with the Reds. Churchill, hearing of it, rushed to Downing Street and, according to the diary of Mary Borden, Edward Spiers's wife, 'Winston told LG one might as well legalize sodomy as recognize the Bolsheviks.' Nevertheless, on the eve of Churchill's appointment to the War Office, the cabinet, supporting the prime minister, voted against any attempt to topple the Reds by force; British troops already in Russia would be eventually withdrawn. When the *Daily Express* reported 'ominous signs' of a 'gigantic campaign' against Russia – and commented that the 'frozen plains of Eastern Europe are not worth the bones of a single British Grenadier' – it misread the government's mood. Backing the counter-revolutionaries in other ways was still possible, however, and the new war minister meant to do it, ignoring, if necessary, the views of his colleagues.[31]

The immensity of Russia determined the strategy of the civil war. As a theatre of military operations it was the antipode of the western front: deep White thrusts into the interior would be followed by Red thrusts, equally deep, towards the country's outer fringes. Where Haig had measured gains and losses in yards, Trotsky and his enemies thought in terms of hundreds of miles. The conflict was fought out in three theatres bearing the names of their counterrevolutionary commanders, Kolchak, Denikin, and Yudenich, and

Map labels: G W HARD · BARENTS SEA · NORWAY · SWEDEN · Murmansk · FINLAND · Archangel · SIBERIA · URAL MOUNTAINS · *Bolshevik* · Petrograd · *Russia* · BALTIC SEA · YUDENICH (1919) · Perm · Ekaterinburg · Omsk · Petropavlovsk · LATVIA · EAST PRUSSIA · Volga River · Kazan · Ufa · POLAND · Vilna · Moscow · Warsaw · Brest-Litovsk (1920) · Orel · Kursk · Voronezh · *Anti-Bolshevik-Occupied Territories 1919 and 1920* · Kiev · Kharkov · Don River · DENIKIN (1919) · Poltava · RUMANIA · UKRAINE · Nikolayev · — Anti-Bolshevik fronts · Odessa · Rostov-on-Don · MILES · SEA OF AZOV · KILOMETERS · BULGARIA · BLACK SEA · Constantinople · GEORGIA · Tiflis · Batum · ARMENIA · Baku · AZERBAIJAN · CASPIAN SEA · KOLCHAK (1919) · T U R K E Y · PERSIA · AEGEAN SEA

was followed by a Polish invasion, which must be considered separately. As of New Year's Day, 1919, the Whites were being supported by over 180,000 troops from Britain, France, Italy, Greece, Serbia, Japan, the United States, and the Czechoslovaks. Germany's capitulation had left them with no excuse for intervention, but bolshevism was not a Russian movement; Lenin said again and again that his objective was a world revolution. Moreover, the Reds were committing acts which, even after the horrors of the war just ended, were regarded as unprecedented atrocities. Photographs had been smuggled out; the victims were of both sexes and all ages, and the evidence of extraordinary torture and obscene mutilation was unmistakable. The Red Cross wanted to bring food to the afflicted. Lenin approved. Trotsky refused. 'Fools and charlatans' would misunderstand his tactics, he said; he wanted no outsiders to witness what they described as 'the burning and scorching' of the 'bour-

556

geois.'[32] Churchill had acquired copies of the pictures and was trying, without success, to get them published in England.

The defeat of the Germans and Austro-Hungarians also meant the withdrawal of their armies westward. That left a vacuum in central Europe. Trotsky wanted to fill it with the Red Army, but the defence of the homeland came first. His troops were tied down by Kolchak in the Urals and Denikin in the south. Petrograd was Stalin's problem; Trotsky was in no hurry to solve it for him. Lenin could not be ignored, however. Now that Kolchak had been stopped in his tracks, Lenin wanted to clear the Don and the northern Caucasus of the enemy. Trotsky thought the Ukraine more tempting; he believed new foreign expeditions would soon land on the Black Sea beaches. The debate became academic when Kolchak, reinforced by peasant farmers who revered the czar's memory, broke through the Red defences and captured Ufa and Perm. This was a crisis; a linkup of Kolchak and Denikin on the Volga seemed imminent. Red counterattacks flung Kolchak back. Then twelve thousand French poilus – Clemenceau's antibolshevism was far more ardent than Lloyd George's or President Wilson's – arrived from the Black Sea, as Trotsky had feared, and took Odessa and Nikolayev. Unfortunately Clemenceau had forgotten the Nivelle disaster and its impact upon the morale of French soldiers. The poilus resented their mission. Bolshevik agitators infiltrated their ranks and found them receptive. They rebelled, and the entire French expeditionary force had to be evacuated. Simultaneously, Bolshevik guerrillas and the Red Guards in the Ukraine, who had been scorned by Lenin and Trotsky, surprised them by seizing Kharkov, in the eastern Ukraine, on February 3. Everything had happened and nothing had happened. Neither side was strong enough to subdue the other. But leaders on both sides were discouraged. Clemenceau and Foch began assembling a new force of French infantry. And in Whitehall, Winston Churchill had moved into the War Office with the authority and determination to deal the Bolsheviks savage blows.

Churchill did not rejoin the inner cabinet until November 1919, but as secretary of state for war and air he frequently appeared before it, and there, six weeks after the Armistice, he first raised the Bolshevik issue with the government's highest council. England had two options, he said; it could either permit Russians 'to murder each other without let or hindrance' or intervene 'thoroughly with large forces, abundantly supplied with mechanical appliances.' He proposed to reinforce the troops already there with as many as thirty divisions. The prime minister wanted no part of it. Sir Henry Wilson wrote in his diary: 'Winston all against Bolshevism and therefore, in this, against Lloyd George.' A week later the two clashed again. Churchill urged the dispatch of an Allied army 'to restore the situation and set up a democratic government'; the Reds, he believed, 'represent a mere fraction of the population, and would be exposed and swept away by a General Election held under

Allied auspices.' George vehemently disagreed; he was 'definitely opposed to military intervention.' Yet he was equally reluctant to abandon Kolchak, Denikin, and Yudenich. He said he thought it best that the Russians settle their differences among themselves, but he agreed to keep the British battalions in Murmansk and Archangel until the dust had settled. The fact is that the old champion of social reform had never felt comfortable with foreign affairs. He was vacillating, always an alarming symptom in a national leader and one which, in this case, threatened the very survival of the Liberal party. The coalition still ruled, but Tories dominated it. They were siding with Churchill. Balfour told Winston: 'I admire the exaggerated way you tell the truth.' When Churchill attacked Lenin and Trotsky in the House, the loudest cheers came from the Conservative benches.[33]

Squaring off against his party's prime minister was not, however, good politics. Neither was it wise. He was repeating his mistakes of 1914 and 1915. He had been right about Antwerp and the Dardanelles, but wrong in trying to direct the campaigns from the Admiralty. Only the man at No. 10 Downing Street could make policy. Churchill had lacked the power to override doubters then, and he lacked it now. And now, as then, his high profile guaranteed that, should the attempt to destroy the new masters of the Kremlin fail, he would be blamed. Nevertheless, he persevered. The emergence of Communists as leaders of a great nation aroused his powerful aggressive instincts. Not until Hitler showed his fist would Winston again be so vehement. As a monarchist he had been shocked by the brutal murder of the Romanovs; Lloyd George said that 'his ducal blood revolted against the wholesale elimination of Grand Dukes.' Yet he never advocated a restoration of the Russian monarchy. Instead, he proposed a social democratic regime in Moscow. It was the Red dictatorship which outraged him. Its atrocities and pogroms were, he believed, the inevitable consequence of Marxism in action. To him they represented a new barbarism. As a conservative in the purest sense – a defender of freedom, justice, and the great achievements of the past – he saw civilization gravely endangered. Bolshevism, he said, was 'a ghoul descending from a pile of skulls.' He told the House: 'It is not a policy; it is a disease. It is not a creed; it is a pestilence.' The Red Executive Committee was 'subhuman.' Lenin 'was sent into Russia by the Germans in the same way that you might send a phial containing a culture of typhoid or of cholera to be poured into the water supply of a great city, and it worked with amazing accuracy.'*[34]

When President Wilson proposed a Russian armistice and the withdrawal of all Allied forces, Churchill replied that this would mean 'the destruction of all non-Bolshevik armies in Russia' and 'an interminable vista of violence and misery.' He said: 'The theories of Lenin and Trotsky . . . have driven man

---

* Later, in *The World Crisis: The Aftermath*, he rephrased this: 'They transported Lenin in a sealed truck like a pleague becillus from Switzerland into Russia.' If this rhetoric sounds extravagant, it should be remembered that the Bolshevik holocaust – five years of fighting, pestilence, and famine – cost fifteen million lives.

from the civilization of the twentieth century into a condition of barbarism worse than the Stone Age and left him the most awful and pitiable spectacle in human experience, devoured by vermin, racked by pestilence, and deprived of hope.' Allied intervention was only temporary, he said: 'There are now good reasons for believing that the tyranny will soon be overthrown by the Russian nation. We have steadfastly adhered to our principles that Russia must be saved by Russian manhood.' No conscripts would be sent to Murmansk and Archangel, he assured the House, and the families of British soldiers killed there would be told 'what purpose these men are serving,' but the effort must be made. If Lloyd George recognized the Soviet regime, he hinted, he would resign. The repatriation of Russian prisoners of war from German camps angered him; instead of being returned to Moscow, he said, they should have been recruited by the counterrevolutionary armies. 'Of all tyrannies in history,' he declared in April 1919, 'the Bolshevik tyranny is the worst, the most destructive, and the most degrading.' In his view it was far viler than the kaiser's Second Reich. His nightmare was a military alliance between a hostile Russia and a vengeful Germany. Instead, he suggested the Germans be encouraged to invade Russia – or, as he put it to Violet Asquith, to 'Kill the Bolshie and Kiss the Hun.' Exceeding his authority, he sent howitzers to Kolchak and Denikin and appealed to British volunteers who would join a 'Slavo-British Legion,' serving as a rear guard when Murmansk and Archangel were evacuated. A whole generation of Englishmen knew nothing but fighting, and over eight thousand actually enlisted.[35]

'Churchill's eloquence, enthusiasm, and personality,' Hankey noted, produced 'an electrical effect.' They also triggered a reaction. Even in the War Cabinet his supporters were a minority. Sir Henry Wilson wrote in his diary that 'neither LG nor the Cabinet would throw their hearts into beating the Bolsheviks . . . I am all in favour of declaring war on the Bolsheviks, but the others, except Winston, won't.' Curzon, the foreign secretary, described the White Russian situation as one of 'complete failure.' Austen Chamberlain at the Exchequer was doubtful of 'any good results' because the Whites were 'completely untrustworthy,' the British forces were 'very tired,' and even the Czechs were 'less willing to fight.' All in all, he concluded, the intervention was 'hopeless.' Lloyd George came down on one side, then the other. He observed enigmatically that although England was 'at war' with the Bolsheviks, the country had decided 'not to make war.' Then he strengthened the naval blockade of Petrograd. Swinging back again, he complained that the first six months of intervention had cost the government £73,000,000 'for our military forces alone, including transport,' and if naval expenditures were included the figure would be twice that – for what, he said, 'were after all very insignificant operations.' Next he raised the figure of £100,000,000 but wrote to Churchill: 'If Russia were anxious to overthrow Bolshevik rule, the help we have given her would have provided her with a full opportunity. We have discharged faithfully our honourable obligations to Denikin and to Kolchak. We have never entered into any with Yudenitch and I hope we shall not do so.

The British public will not tolerate the throwing away of more millions on foolish military enterprises . . . Let us therefore attend to our own business and leave Russia to look after hers.' The prime minister's thinking, Winston observed, stopped 'short of a definite character on which a policy, or even a provisional policy,' could be based.[36]

Readers of British newspapers had the impression that Churchill was acting alone. The press headlined the fighting in Russia as 'Mr Churchill's Private War.' The *Daily Express* declared: 'The country is absolutely unwilling to make a great war in Russia . . . Let us have done with the megalomania of Mr Winston Churchill, the military gamester. Let us bring our men back – if we can.' The strongest opposition, however, came from the Labour party, which in these months was quietly making converts of thousands of Liberals disillusioned with Lloyd George's postwar drifting, and thereby reshaping Britain's political future. Lenin and Trotsky had assumed that the Russian revolution would be followed by a 'German October,' a 'French October,' and an 'English October.' Although they were to be disappointed, the war had thickened socialist ranks everywhere, and the new left did not share Churchill's hatred of the Soviet Union. Sir David Shackleton, a civil servant, warned the government that British socialists deeply resented the intervention in Siberia. In June 1919 a Labour party conference at Southport unanimously passed a resolution condemning 'the war in the interests of financial capitalism' and calling for 'the unreserved use . . . of political and industrial power' to end all British opposition to the Communists 'whether by force of arms, by supply of munitions, by financial subsidies, or by commercial blockade.' At the London docks dock-workers refused to load munitions on the *Jolly George* when they learned that the cargo was destined for White enemies of the Bolsheviks. Ramsay MacDonald, the Labour party leader, wrote in the *Socialist Review:* 'Churchill pursues his mad adventure as though he were Emperor of these Isles . . . delighting his militarists and capitalists.' MacDonald predicted 'new offensives, new bogus governments, new military captains as allies.' In the Albert Hall one Colonel C. J. L'Estrange Malone, a disillusioned officer, spoke glowingly of the Red achievements and urged his audience to overthrow Parliament. 'What are a few Churchills and Curzons on lamp posts,' he asked, 'compared to the massacre of thousands of human beings?'[37]

Malone was sentenced to six months in prison for inciting revolt. The British left regarded him as a martyr. Churchill, speaking to his Dundee constituents, said of the Bolsheviks, 'I know they have got a few friends here, but it is very lucky for those people that the great mass of the British nation is sensible, solid, and sound, because when it comes to revolutions the revolutionaries are the first to suffer, and when the revolution has come to an end all the most excitable people have been put out of the way, and you have got a great period of reaction, with probably a military dictator as the head of state.' Replying to MacDonald in the *Weekly Review* of June 22 he wrote: 'Bolshevism means in every country a civil war of the most merciless kind between the discontented, criminal, and mutinous classes on one hand and the contented or law-abiding on the other . . . Bolshevism, wherever it manifests itself openly and in concrete form, means war of the most ruthless character, the slaughter of men, women, and children, the burning of homes, and the inviting in of tyranny, pestilence, and famine.' He then wrote a provocative piece for the London *Evening News* urging Germany and Poland to build a dyke against Bolshevism. A Labour spokesman called him 'sinister and dangerous,' and added: 'We repudiate him and his works.' The leftist Robert Smillie sardonically thanked 'our comrade Winston Churchill for uniting the British democracy. We could not do it: the people would not believe us. But Winston and his friends have done it.' Ernest Bevin declared that Winston had damaged himself by 'appealing to the old enemy – with whom we were never going to speak or trade – to rise to the occasion and defeat Soviet Russia.' Churchill replied that Labour was 'quite unfitted for the responsibility of Government.' The spread of bolshevism, he solemnly warned the House, might threaten Britain's imperial possessions, including India. This was greeted with laughter, but it wasn't as farfetched as it seemed; Trotsky, according to Isaac Deutscher, had suggested that 'the Red Army might find the road to India much shorter and easier than the road to Soviet Hungary . . . The revolution's road to Paris and London might lead through Kabal, Calcutta, and Bombay.'[38]

Nothing came of it, because Lenin recognized Trotsky's proposal for what it was: a cry of anguish, an attempt to sound a note of hope at a time when Communist fortunes were at one of their low points. On the battlefronts the seesaw continued. In the spring of 1919 Kolchak renewed his broad advance towards the Volga, and Moscow once more held its breath. Trotsky now had 500,000 men under arms, but his most reliable troops were fighting elsewhere. Then, in late April, one of his officers, a former colonel on the czar's general staff, outflanked Kolchak, cut his supply lines, and sent him reeling back towards the Urals. Before the Red Army could celebrate its victory, however, Denikin lunged back into the Ukraine. He met negligible resistance. The peasants greeted his troops as heroes; bolshevism was unpopular here, and it grew more so when bands of defeated Reds crisscrossed the countryside looting, raping, and pillaging. On May 29 Churchill told the House that Denikin 'has advanced his whole front, in some places, to a distance of eighty miles, and in this he has been aided by rebellions which have broken out among the people.'[39] In Siberia, Kolchak dug in after a 180-mile retreat and threw back Red Army attacks. Meanwhile, the French had evacuated Odessa, the American and Italian expeditionary forces sailed away, and soviets were proclaimed in Hungary and Bavaria. The spring campaigns, in short, were indecisive.

So was Lloyd George. On this issue he had lost control of his ministers. British warships, he suggested, should be withdrawn from Petrograd waters, and Curzon, supporting him, urged his colleagues to 'proceed with caution' because there was 'a strong element in the House of Commons that is opposed to intervention.' Nevertheless, the War Cabinet, after hearing Churchill, resolved that 'a state of war' existed 'between Great Britain and the Bolshevik Government of Russia' and, therefore, that 'our Naval forces in Russian waters should be authorized to engage enemy forces by land and sea, when necessary.' Winston wanted supplies and munitions rushed to Denikin. He even proposed building a railway for him. Yet his support was far from blind. He demanded that the White general adopt a land-reform programme, establish 'a constituent assembly on a democratic franchise to decide the future form of Russian Government,' and recognize the independence of Poland, Finland, and the Baltic states. Later he also asked for a written promise to suppress anti-Semitism. Six million Jews lived in Russia. Reports of Ukrainian pogroms had reached London, and British Jews were furious. But Denikin, confident of imminent triumph, ignored all of Churchill's conditions.[40]

Events in the early fall of 1919 seemed to confirm Denikin. Kiev, the capital city of the Ukraine, had fallen to him on the last day of August. He swiftly retook Kharkov, took Odessa and Rostov-on-Don, and was pressing the Reds' weak centre, towards Kursk and Voronezh, along the shortest line to Moscow. Simultaneously, Yudenich, armed by Churchill and supported by the Royal Navy, fought his way into the outskirts of Petrograd. Lenin, telegraphing that 'the fate of the entire Revolution is in question,' ordered that positions be defended 'to the last drop of blood.' Trotsky retorted that weapons and ammunition which he had been promised had not yet arrived, and attempts to suppress White marauders roaming behind Red Army lines had 'up to now yielded almost no result.' Lenin proposed abandonment of the city and withdrawal of all Red Army units from all fronts for a circle-the-wagons defence of Moscow. If that were lost, he said, they would retreat to the Urals. Trotsky protested. Petrograd, he told the Politburo, was 'the cradle of the Revolution.'[41] Stalin agreed; the loss of Russia's two great cities, he said, could not be borne. Boarding a train to take personal command of Petrograd's defences, Trotsky was handed a copy of a Churchill statement claiming that troops from fourteen nations would soon join in an anti-soviet crusade. He dismissed it with a scornful laugh and said he would defend the beleaguered city house by house and, if necessary, room by room. Bad news awaited him on arrival. Yudenich had seized Krasnoe Selo, the last strongpoint between him and the centre of the city. His drive was spearheaded by British tanks, newly arrived from Churchill. Their appearance had panicked the defenders.

This was Trotsky's hour. Improvising armoured cars in Petrograd factories, he inspired the Red troops, and, in a week, threw the Whites back. Lenin wired him: 'It is damnably important to us to finish off Yudenich . . . If the offensive is to be launched, cannot a further 20 thousand or so Petrograd workers be mobilized, plus 10 thousand or so of the bourgeoisie, machine guns to be posted to the rear of them, a few hundred shot and a real mass assault on Yudenich assured?' His commissar of war had anticipated him; it had been done. Trotsky then turned to the southern theatre. Believing the Whites there were overextended, he ordered a counterattack, and Denikin fell back in confusion on Kiev, Poltava, and Kharkov. Then Kolchak's army was crushed in Siberia. The three great counterrevolutionary armies had been defeated in just three weeks – this time for good. By December the Red Army was back in Petropavlovsk and Omsk. Denikin had been beaten back to Kursk, eighty miles south of Orel. Yudenich was retreating towards the Estonian border. Kolchak's headquarters were in remote Irkutsk, fifteen hundred miles east of Omsk. The British expedition had been evacuated. Sir Henry Wilson wrote in his diary: 'So ends in practical disaster another of Winston's military attempts. Antwerp, Dardanelles, Denikin. His judgement is always at fault, & he is hopeless when in power.' Churchill himself wrote: 'There seems to be very little doubt of the complete victory of the Bolsheviks in the near future. The Japanese will no doubt hold up to Lake Baikal . . . Everywhere else we must look for a complete smash up.' Lloyd George's vacillation was over. On the day Kharkov fell, he and Clemenceau met at No. 10 and agreed not to 'enter into any further commitments as to furnishing assistance to the anti-Bolshevik elements in Russia, whether in the form of troops, war material or financial aid.' They added that 'a strong Poland' was 'in the interests of the Entente powers.'[42]

The blunt truth is that a strong Poland was in the interests of Poland and no one else. Since the split of its ancient kingdom in 1138 the country had been partitioned and repartitioned by Russia, Prussia, and Austria-Hungary, and between 1795 and the proclamation of a Polish republic by General Józef Pilsudski in 1918, it could be found on no map. Pilsudski was the archetypal Polish patriot. He had been exiled to Siberia by the czar and jailed by the Germans, and he had fought with the Austrians between 1914 and 1916, when he had left the field to nurse his dream of an independent nation. Now that dream had been realized, but, like most of his countrymen, he was less interested in peace than in acquiring adjacent territories occupied by Russians. In September 1919 Ignace Paderewski, the republic's premier, asked the Allies to finance a drive towards the Soviet capital by 500,000 Poles. Churchill disapproved, as did Wilson, and for the same reason: 'I quite agree with you that it would be madness for us to advise Paderewski, and to support him in any attempt to occupy Moscow. If anything could combine all Russia into a whole, it would be a march of the Poles on Moscow. I can almost conceive Denikin and Lenin joining hands to defeat such an object.'[43]

Pilsudski struck in the first week of March, seized Kiev and Vilna, and occupied most of the Ukraine. But his triumph was a brief, doomed flicker. As Churchill and Wilson had foretold, the invasion of Mother Russia deeply stirred her masses. To followers of the Greek Orthodox faith this was a struggle with Roman Catholic heretics, and to men who still cherished loyalty to the Romanovs, a fight with a hereditary enemy – 'a truly Russian war,' as Deutscher put it, 'even though waged by Bolshevik internationalists.' Aleksei Brusilov, the late czar's commander in chief, put his sword at Trotsky's disposal. Ukrainians found the Poles even more lawless than the Reds and Whites and expelled them. On June 12 Kiev was retaken. By August 14 the Red Army, now five million strong, had reached the outskirts of Warsaw. 'Nothing can save Poland now,' Churchill wrote gloomily and left London to play polo at Rugby.[44] Curzon offered to mediate the dispute; Lloyd George gave both sides ultimata, but the days were past when British statesmen could settle foreign quarrels by fiat. Salvation reached Warsaw in the form of General Maxime Weygand and a force of French troops. The Poles and poilus rallied on the Vistula. The Reds retreated; Pilsudski, unchastened by his rout, invaded the Caucasus. A provisional peace was signed on October 12 at Riga, though fighting between Russians and Poles, supported by Rumanian allies, continued until late in the 1920s.

Disaster having been averted, Winston, relieved, wrote: 'Poland has saved herself by her exertions & will I trust save Europe by her example.' Yet in some obscure way the Polish adventure had damaged him. The British press depicted the Bolsheviks as victims of aggression – worse, aggression that failed – and Churchill was England's most vigorous anti-Bolshevik. Every Red victory was a blow to his prestige, and, now that the tide had turned, the pins representing counterrevolutionary forces on the War Office's map of Russia were being plucked out one by one. By February 7 Kolchak had been captured and executed by Bolsheviks in Irkutsk. Yudenich had fled to England. On March 27 Denikin, abandoning hope, turned his command over to Baron Pëtr von Wrangel and sailed for France. Because the Red Army was busy fighting Poles, Wrangel, driving north from his base on the Sea of Azov, overran much of southern Russia, but after Riga the Reds wheeled and hurled him back into the Crimea. Churchill begged the inner cabinet to support Wrangel. Their response was icy. One minister wrote in his diary: 'At the Cabinet this morning the PM gave Winston a dressing down about Russia. Winston had been complaining that we have no policy. This the PM described as ridiculous. Our policy was to try to escape the results of the evil policy which Winston had persuaded the Cabinet to adopt.' Another diarist wrote: 'Churchill bumbles on about Russia.' On November 1 Wrangel evacuated his army to Constantinople, and tens of thousands of White refugees boarded French ships and vanished into permanent exile.[45]

Churchill wouldn't quit. His defiance in defeat, which would thrill England twenty years later, embarrassed his colleagues now. British officers in Berlin informed London that Ludendorff wanted to confer with Churchill about the Bolshevik menace. To the astonishment of his fellow cabinet members, Winston expressed interest. H. A. L. Fisher, minister for education, wrote to Lloyd George that he was 'alarmed.' He was convinced that Ludendorff's goals were sinister. Churchill didn't see it that way. 'In my view,' he wrote in a minute, 'the objective wh we shd pursue at the present time is the building up of a strong but peaceful Germany wh will not attack our French allies, but will at the same time act as a moral bulwark against the Bolshevism of Russia.' He added that 'the advice of the WO throughout the last 15 months has constantly tended to that recovery, stability, & tranquillisation of Europe, wh wd enable Britain to enjoy the fruits of victory. It is a pity it has fallen on deaf ears.'[46]

Certainly the cabinet was deaf to his proposals that he confer with the Second Reich's discredited warlord, and after reflection he dropped the idea. Thus the Russian epic was played out without further British intrusions. The Bolsheviks still faced obstacles. Japanese troops remained in Vladivostok after all the other Allies had left, drove off a Soviet attack, inflicting heavy losses, and did not leave Russian soil until the autumn of 1922. The Baltic states of Estonia, Latvia, and Lithuania retained their freedom until 1940. Extending Red control over the Caucasus was a slow, exasperating business. Long after Wrangel had left, Georgia continued to be ruled by Mensheviks. Trotsky had agreed to leave the Georgians alone, but in 1921, while he was absent on an inspection tour of the Urals, the Red Army invaded the republic and, after severe fighting, seized Tiflis, its capital. The man who had done this, sabotaging Trotsky's promise to Georgia, was himself a native Georgian. He hated Trotsky even more than he hated Churchill for intervening, and he was Joseph Stalin.

Winston had one arrow left in his anti-Bolshevik quiver. Lloyd George had been a radical young parliamentarian, but now, like all British prime ministers, he was dedicated to expansion of British trade, and when a Soviet trade mission arrived in London after the counterrevolutionaries had been overwhelmed, the prime minister saw to it that they were provided with every comfort. There was no alternative to peaceful coexistence with them, George told the House; it had become 'perfectly clear now to every unprejudiced observer that you cannot rush Bolshevism by force of arms.' But Churchill was not an unprejudiced observer. He refused to 'grasp the hairy paw of the baboon.' Commercial ties with England would strengthen Lenin's regime, he said, and 'as long as any portion of this nest of vipers is left intact, it will continue to breed and swarm.' Besides, he asked Lloyd George, how would the Reds pay for British goods? The answer outraged him. The Russians planned to barter with gold and precious stones taken from the czarist nobility. 'This treasure does not belong to the Russian Bolshevik Government,' he said at a cabinet meeting. 'It has been forcibly seized by these usurpers . . . The jewels have been stolen from their owners in Russia and in many cases from their corpses.' The gold was similarly 'bloodstained.' England would be giving the Reds 'a special title to this plundered gold in order that with it they may make purchases in the British market. It seems to me that this is a very serious step to take.'[47]

Nevertheless, the government took it a few minutes later. Winston almost resigned on the spot. He was 'so upset by the decision,' Hankey noted in his diary, 'that he declared himself unequal to discussing other items on the Agenda affecting the army. He was quite pale and did not speak again during the meeting.' As it broke up he glowered at the prime minister and inquired heavily whether any minister would now be 'fettered' if he wished to deliver anti-Communist speeches. Assured that he was free to say what he pleased, he drove to Oxford that evening and addressed the Oxford Union. Flaying the Lenin government, he said he believed 'that all the harm and misery in Russia has arisen out of the wickedness and folly of the Bolshevists and that there will be no recovery of any kind in Russia or in Eastern Europe while these wicked men, this vile group of cosmopolitan fanatics, hold the Russian nation by the hair of its head and tyrannize over its great population . . . The policy I will always advocate is the overthrow and destruction of that criminal regime.'[48]

He had been candid, he had been prophetic, and he paid a price. Men who had forgotten the Dardanelles remembered it now and felt their earlier assessment of him confirmed. A new rift had opened between him and Lloyd George. The growing delegation of Labour MPs marked him as their chief enemy. In some instances their enmity did him honour; it was later found, for example, that the *Daily Herald,* a Labour newspaper, was subsidized by Russian money. But his bitterness and his isolation from old friends were curiously at variance with his usual generosity of spirit. H. G. Wells, returning from Russia, declared that Red excesses had been necessary to 'establish a new social order' and that the British naval blockade had been partly responsible for Russian starvation. Churchill, replying in the *Sunday Express,* wrote: 'We see the Bolshevik cancer eating into the flesh of the wretched being; we see the monstrous growth swelling and thriving upon the emaciated body of his victim. And now Mr Wells, that philosophical romancer, comes forward with the proposition that the cancer is the only thing that can pull the body round; that we must feed and cultivate that. After all, it is another form of life. It is "a new social order." Why be so narrow-minded as to draw the line between death and disease, still less between right and wrong? Adopt an impartial attitude. Put your money on the disease if you think it is going to win.' Wells struck back with asperity. He had known Churchill for years, he wrote in the next week's *Sunday Express.* He liked him and admired him. 'But,' he said, 'I will confess that it distresses me that he should hold any public office at this time . . . I want to see him out of any position of public responsibility whatever.' Winston's retirement and his return to private life, he suggested, would not 'be a tragic fall . . . Mr Churchill has many resources. He would, for instance, be a brilliant painter.'[49]

On Lloyd George's fifty-seventh birthday, Churchill lunched with the prime minister, and Frances Stevenson noted that he 'waxed very eloquent on the old world & the new, taking up arms in defence of the former.' He was, she wrote, 'simply *raving*' about 'trading with Russia' which 'absolutely & finally ruins his hopes of a possible war in the East.' When another guest chided him, she wrote, 'Winston glared at him, & almost shouted "You are trying to make mischief!" ' That evening Lloyd George, Frances, and Churchill dined at Ciro's. Winston, she noted, was still 'ragging D[avid] about the New World. "Don't you make any mistake," he said to D. "You're not going to get your new world. The old world is a good enough place for me, & there's life in the old dog yet. It's going to sit up & wag its tail." ' The prime minister remarked that Winston was 'the only remaining specimen of a real Tory.' That, too, was prophetic.[50]

It is a striking fact that Churchill, the acmic warrior, left a colourless record at the Ministry of War and Air, and not only because his Russian policy was a complete failure. The postwar demobilization was his only real accomplishment at the War Office. Otherwise, his military policies were cautious and stingy. Wherever he found fat he cut it, but he cut a great deal that was lean, too. He preserved the separate identity of the Royal Air Force yet left it little but its name. On Armistice Day, Britain had been the world's greatest air power; two years later England was reduced to three home squadrons, as against France's forty-seven. And three months after that, when Churchill resigned from the ministry to become colonial secretary, *The Times* observed: 'He leaves the body of British flying well nigh at that last gasp when a military funeral would be all that would be left for it.' His management of the army had been equally disappointing. Young career officers, appreciative of his role in tank development, expected that he would refashion their services along modern lines. Unaware of his sentimental yearning for his golden days with the Fourth Hussars and the Twenty-first Lancers, they were stunned when he sided with the red-tabbed diehards and shared their yearning for a return to 1914. His most shortsighted policy was his acceptance of Lloyd George's guiding principle, endorsed by the War Cabinet in August 1919, that 'the British Empire will not be engaged in any great war during the next ten years and that no Expeditionary Force will be required.' At times Winston even echoed the litany of the Little Englanders. On June 18, 1920, he told the cabinet that 'the military forces at the disposal of Great Britain' were 'insufficient to meet the requirements of the policies now being pursued in the various theatres.' One would have expected Churchill, the tribune of Empire, to call for an increase in those forces. Instead, he argued that a cutback in imperial commitments was 'indispensable if grave risk of disaster is not to be incurred.' Otherwise, he said, 'the possibility of disaster occurring in any or all of these theatres must be faced, and the likelihood of this will increase every day.'[51]

He was always readier to defy public opinion than most public men, but here he was trimming his sails to meet the prevailing political winds. After the survivors of the western front came home, Britons wanted nothing more to do with war; most of them hoped never again to lay eyes on an Englishman in uniform, and they were losing their taste for Empire. Privately he worried about that. A bellicose war minister and a pacifistic electorate would not work comfortably in harness, however, and though he would later reconcile himself to such an incompatibility, in those early postwar years he did not feel the risk justifiable. As Liddell Hart wrote, Churchill 'was eager to make a fresh mark in current political affairs, and the best chance lay in the postwar retrenchment of expenditure.'[52] It was expedient to cut taxes and he did it ruthlessly. His objectives, however, were unchanged. He freely entered into agreements in which the eventual use of force, or threat of it, was implicit, confident that if he had to show the flag, Englishmen would support him.

By now it was clear that he was too strong and too able to be confined to a single ministry. As home secretary he had often appeared at the Treasury; at the Admiralty he had led Irish policy; as lowly minister of munitions he had managed to influence the conduct of the war. Now he freely crossed ministerial lines of authority and assumed responsibilities which rightfully belonged in the India Office, the Colonial Office, and the Foreign Office. Naturally, his colleagues resented this, but the offended minister almost always found himself a minority of one. The others recognized Churchill's gifts. Even the prime minister, who frequently discovered himself at loggerheads with him now, tolerated what, in another man, would have been called meddling and might even have merited dismissal. Churchill had become the most powerful speaker in Parliament. No one, not even the gifted Lloyd George, could hold the House as Winston did. Indeed, on one memorable occasion he accomplished a rare feat. Eloquence, wit, and charm have not been uncommon in that body, but seldom in its six centuries has a speech actually changed the opinion of the majority, transforming imminent defeat into triumph. Churchill did it on July 8, 1920, thereby vindicating England's honour.

The origins of that day's controversy lay in a shocking episode. A few months after the war an Englishwoman, a missionary, had reported that she had been molested on a street in the Punjab city of Amritsar. The Raj's local commander, Brigadier General Reginald Dyer, had issued an order requiring all Indians using that street to crawl its length on their hands and knees. He had also authorized the indiscriminate, public whipping of natives who came within lathi length of British policemen. On April 13, 1919, a multitude of Punjabis had gathered in Amritsar's Jallianwallah Bagh to protest these extraordinary measures. The throng, penned in a narrow space smaller than Trafalgar Square, had been peacefully listening to the testimony of victims when Dyer appeared at the head of a contingent of British troops. Without warning, he ordered his machine gunners to open fire.The Indians, in Churchill's words, were 'packed together so that one bullet would drive through three or four bodies'; the people 'ran madly this way and the other. When the fire was directed upon the centre, they ran to the sides. The fire was then directed upon the sides. Many threw themselves down on the ground, and the fire was then directed on the ground. This was continued for eight or ten minutes, and it stopped only when the ammunition had reached the point of exhaustion.' Dyer then marched away, leaving 379 dead and over 1,500 wounded. Back in his headquarters, he reported to his superiors that he had been 'confronted by a revolutionary army,' and had been obliged 'to teach a moral lesson to the Punjab.' In the storm of outrage which followed, the brigadier was promoted to major general, retired, and placed on the inactive list. This, incredibly, made him a martyr to millions of Englishmen. Senior British officers applauded his suppression of 'another Indian Mutiny.' The Guardians of the Golden Temple enrolled him in the Brotherhood of Sikhs. The House of Lords passed a measure commending him. Readers of the Tory *Morning Post*, Churchill's old scourge, subscribed £2,500 for a testimonial. Leading Conservative MPs took up his cause, and Lloyd George reluctantly agreed to a full-dress debate. Venetia Montagu's husband, Edwin, now the secretary of state for India, would open for the government, with Churchill scheduled at the end.[53]

Montagu's speech was a calamity. He was a Jew and there were anti-Semites in the House. He had been warned to be quiet and judicial. Instead, he was sarcastic; he called Dyer a terrorist; he worried about foreign opinion; he 'thoroughly roused most of the latent passions of the stodgy Tories,' as one MP noted, and 'got excited . . . and became more racial and more Yiddish in screaming tone and gesture,' with the consequence that 'a strong anti-Jewish sentiment was shown by shouts . . . Altogether it was a very astonishing exhibition of anti-Jewish feeling.' The Ulster MPs had decided to vote against Dyer. After Montagu's speech they conferred and reversed themselves. Sir Edward Carson rose to praise the general – who was watching from the Strangers' Gallery – as 'a gallant officer of thirty-four years service . . . without a blemish on his record' who had 'no right to be broken on the *ipse dixit* of any Commission or Committee, however great, unless he has been fairly tried – and he has not been tried.' Carson ended: 'I say, to break a man under the circumstances of this case is un-English.' 'Un-English,' in the context of the time, was anti-Semitic – roughly the equivalent of 'kike.' MPs roared their approval. The government was in trouble. Lloyd George being absent, Bonar Law, the leader of the House, asked Churchill to speak immediately.[54]

Churchill's approach was entirely unlike Montagu's. He called for 'a calm spirit, avoiding passion and avoiding attempts to excite prejudice.' Dyer, he said, had not been dismissed in disgrace; 'he had simply been informed that there was no further employment for him under the Government of India.' But the incident in Jallianwallah Bagh was 'an extraordinary event, a monstrous event, an event which stands in singular and sinister isolation.' He quietly observed that the number of Indians killed was almost identical with the number of MPs now sitting within range of his voice. An officer in such a situation as Dyer's, he said, should ask himself whether the crowd is either armed or about to mount an attack. 'Men who take up arms against the State must expect at any moment to be fired upon . . . At Amritsar the crowd was neither armed nor attacking.' Thus the general had not, as he claimed, faced a 'revolutionary army.' Another useful military guide, Churchill continued, was the maxim that 'no more force should be used than is necessary to secure compliance with the law.' In the Great War, he and many other members of the House had been British soldiers 'exerting themselves to show pity and to help, even at their own peril, the wounded.' Dyer had failed to follow their example; after the massacre, his troops had simply swung around and marched away. Churchill knew, and many members of Parliament knew, of many instances in which officers, in 'infinitely more trying' situations than the one in Bagh, had, unlike the general, displayed an ability to arrive 'at the right decision.' Then, as if with a stiletto, Churchill knifed Dyer: 'Frightfulness is not a remedy known to the British pharmacopoeia.'[55]

He twisted the blade. Dyer's most vocal champions agreed with Churchill's stand in Russia. It was compassion and its absence, he said, which marked the difference between Englishmen and Bolsheviks. His own hatred of Lenin's regime was 'not founded on their silly system of economics, or their absurd doctrine of an impossible equality.' It arose from 'the bloody and devastating terrorism which they practise . . . and by which alone their criminal regime can be maintained.' It was intolerable in Russia; it was intolerable in Amritsar. 'I do not think,' he said, 'that it is in the interests of the British Empire or of the British Army for us to take a load of that sort for all time upon our backs. We have to make it absolutely clear, some way or another, that this is not the British way of doing business.' He quoted Macaulay: 'The most frightful of all spectacles [is] the strength of civilisation without its mercy.' England's 'reign in India, or anywhere else,' Churchill continued, 'has never stood on the basis of physical force alone, and it would be fatal to the British Empire if we were to try to base ourselves only upon it. The British way of doing things . . . has always meant and implied close and effectual cooperation with the people. In every part of the British Empire that has been our aim.' As for Dyer, Churchill himself would have preferred to see the general disciplined. Instead, he had been allowed to resign with no plan for further punishment, 'and to those moderate and considered conclusions we confidently invite the assent of the House.'[56]

He sat and they rose crying, 'Hear, hear.' After five more hours of debate they voted for the government, 247 to 37. Carson's motion for mild approval of Dyer was defeated 230 to 129. The Archbishop of Canterbury wrote Curzon that Churchill's speech had been 'unanswerable.' *The Times* called it 'amazingly skilful' and declared that it had 'turned the House (or so it seemed) completely round . . . It was not only a brilliant speech, but one that persuaded and made the result certain.' Winston, the editorial concluded, had 'never been heard to greater advantage.'[57]

Late in 1920 Churchill told Lloyd George that he wanted to move to another cabinet post – the Foreign Office, the Colonial Office, or, preferably, the Exchequer. He was tired of wringing half crowns from frugal military budgets, presiding over troop withdrawals, and trying to suppress terrorism in southern Ireland with responsibility for order but no power to negotiate a political solution. Moreover, the prime minister shared few of his views about the army and the RAF. On January 23 of the new year Winston told Sir Henry Wilson that he could not last 'much longer in the WO owing to differences with

LG.' He bluntly wrote George: 'I am vy sorry to see how far we are drifting apart . . . When one has reached the summit of power & surmounted so many obstacles, there is danger of becoming convinced that one can do anything one likes, & that any strong personal view is necessarily acceptable to the nation & can be enforced upon one's subordinates.' He understood that. 'No doubt I in my time of important affairs was led astray like this. I suddenly found a very different world around me: though of course all my fortunes were on a petty scale compared with yours . . . But is yr policy going to be successful? I fear it is going wrong.' Churchill thought it a mistake to negotiate with the new Russian leaders, thought George underestimated the returning popularity of the Conservative party, and believed that 'one of the main causes of trouble throughout the Middle East is *your* quarrel with the remnants of Turkey . . . All the soldiers continually say they disapprove of the policy against Turkey . . . This soaks in.' On February 14, 1921, the prime minister, unwilling to lose the most talented member of his cabinet, appointed him colonial secretary. That evening Churchill received his new seals from George V. He wrote to Clementine that his room at the Colonial Office 'is very fine and sedate . . . at least twice as big as the old one – an enormous square, but well warmed. It is like working in the saloon at Blenheim.'[58]

His immediate concerns were Ireland and the Middle East, which was in chaos. Because Turkey had been on the losing side in the war, the old Ottoman Empire had disintegrated. In the peace settlements Turkey had been reduced to a shadow of its former self, a small Asiatic state in the Anatolian uplands around Ankara. During the fighting in the desert against the Turks, France's and England's most powerful ally had been the army of Husein ibn-Ali, sharif of Mecca and ruler of the ancient kingdom of Hejaz (now part of Saudi Arabia). In October 1918 forces led by the sharif's son Faisal had entered Damascus in triumph. Faisal had appeared at Versailles, registered at the Hotel Metropole, and emerged dressed in immaculate Hashemite robes and attended by two enormous Nubians carrying glittering swords. But when he had appealed for Arabian self-determination, speaking as the emissary of 'my father, who, by request of Britain and France, led the Arab rebellion against the Turks' and asking that 'the Arabic-speaking peoples of Asia . . . be recognized as independent sovereign peoples, under the guarantee of the League of Nations,' he was ignored.[59] Afterwards diplomats from Whitehall and the Quai d'Orsay met quietly in San Remo, Italy, and divided up the Middle East in a muffled version of their nineteenth-century scramble for African possessions. Husein remained as sovereign of Hejaz, but France got Syria and Lebanon; Persia (Iran) was under British protection; and Mesopotamia (Iraq) and Palestine came within Britain's sphere of influence, providing the Empire with a direct overland route between imperial troops in Egypt and the Persian Gulf.

But Arabs were not docile Punjabis. Back in Damascus, Faisal was proclaimed king of Syria. Neither France nor England would recognize him; indeed, French troops arrived, dethroned him, and forced him to flee. Then his brother Abdullah recruited a private army in Mecca, capital of Hejaz, and announced that he would march on Damascus and drive the poilus into the sea. Next the Iraqis rose and besieged several British garrisons. Arabs rioted in Jerusalem, and, most ominous of all, Bolshevik forces were reported crossing into Iran. A British infantry division, transferred from India to Baghdad by Churchill, pacified Iraq. Persian cossacks drove the Bolsheviks across the border. Then as now, however, the knottiest problem of all lay in Palestine. The Balfour declaration, promulgated in 1917 when Arthur Balfour was the coalition's foreign secretary and Jewish political power was at its zenith in London, had proclaimed that the British government favoured 'the establishment of a national home for the Jewish people and will use their best endeavours to facilitate the achievement of that object, it being clearly understood that nothing shall be done which may prejudice the civil and religious rights of existing non-Jewish communities in Palestine.'[60]

When Churchill took over at the Colonial Office, this declaration was part of his legacy. His feelings about Balfour's largesse appear to have been mixed. Of Zionism he had written in 1908: 'Jerusalem must be the ultimate goal. When it will be achieved it is vain to prophesy; but that it will some day be achieved is one of the few certainties of the future.' But after the declaration he peevishly wrote that the Jews 'take it for granted that the local population will be cleared out to suit [their] convenience.' Later, in the *Illustrated Sunday Herald*, he hailed Chaim Weizmann's 'inspiring movement' to build a new nation 'by the banks of the Jordan' as a 'simpler, a truer, and a far more attainable goal' than the 'absolutely destructive' Bolshevik conspiracy to establish 'a world wide communistic state under Jewish domination.' This backhanded endorsement carried a sour tang of anti-Semitism, and it surfaced again in 1920, when, opposing economic aid to Russia, he said he saw 'the gravest objections to giving all this help to the tyrannic Government of these Jew commissars.' That same year he expressed fresh reservations about the creation of a Zionist state, writing to Lloyd George on June 13, 1920, that 'Palestine is costing us 6 millions a year to hold. The Zionist movement will cause continued friction with the Arabs. The French ensconced in Syria with 4 divisions (paid for by not paying us what they owe us) are opposed to the Zionist movement & will try to cushion the Arabs off on us as the real enemy. The Palestine venture is the most difficult to withdraw from & one wh certainly will never yield any profit of a material kind.'[61]

Nevertheless, by the time he entered the Colonial Office he was committed to it. The more he pondered the issue, the more his enthusiasm for a Jewish homeland grew, and he reaffirmed the declaration at a time when a majority of the British officials in the Middle East were urging that it be repudiated. Lieutenant General Sir Walter Congreve, commander in chief of His Majesty's forces in the Middle East, typically predicted that the Arabs would not return to tranquillity until their 'aspirations are attended to,' which 'means Zionist aspirations being greatly curbed.' He continued: 'As long as we persist in our Zionist policy we have got to maintain our present forces in

The Palestine Mandate

SYRIA

LEBANON

° Damascus

IRAQ

Haifa

Jordan River

Tel Aviv
Jaffa
Jerusalem

MEDITERRANEAN
SEA

Gaza

DEAD SEA

SAUDI
ARABIA

PALESTINE

NEGEV
DESERT

TRANSJORDAN

EGYPT

SINAI DESERT

Akaba

Gulf of Akaba

G.W.WARD

Palestine to enforce a policy hateful to the great majority – a majority which means to fight & to continue to fight and has right on its side.' Walter Smart, a senior civil servant in Egypt, wrote bitterly of 'Anglo-French bargaining about other people's property, the deliberate bribing of international Jewry at the expense of the Arabs who were already our Allies in the field, the immature political juggleries of amateur Oriental experts, the stultification·of Arab independence and unity . . . all the immorality and incompetence inevitable in the stress of a great war.'[62]

Churchill decided to sail out to the eastern Mediterranean on the French steamship *Sphinx* and see for himself, taking with him Colonel T. E. Lawrence, Air Marshal Sir Hugh Trenchard, and Archie Sinclair, now Winston's private secretary. The Arabs could not have chosen a more passionate spokesman than Lawrence – 'Lawrence of Arabia,' who spoke fluent Arabic, had led them against the Turks, had suffered several grave wounds, and, after surviving capture and torture, had emerged as a shining figure. His shyness was legendary. Privately Winston wondered about that. Lawrence, he said wryly, 'has a way·of backing into the limelight.' But including him in the delegation was a brilliant political stroke. Outraged by the betrayal at San

Remo, he had begun writing his great *Seven Pillars of Wisdom*, the leitmotiv of which would be British shame. When George V had received him at a royal audience and attempted to award him the DSO and a Companionship in the Order of the Bath, Lawrence had politely refused the decorations, leaving the shocked monarch, in the King's own words, 'holding the box in my hand.' If this man of honour supported a Middle Eastern settlement, the sheikhs of Araby would hesitate to reject it.[63]

The *Sphinx* would stop at Marseilles to pick up Clementine, who had been visiting friends in France. From the Hotel Bristol in Beaulieu she wrote to Winston: 'I am thrilled by the idea & so so longing to see you.' Replying, he told her to pack the proper clothing for sight-seeing trips and tennis – 'Do not forget your racquet.' In a second letter he wrote: 'We shall have a beautiful cabin together. If only it is not rough – then I shall hide in any old dog hole far from yr sight . . . If it is fine, it will be lovely & I shall write & paint & we will talk over all our affairs.' His mother, now living in Berkeley Square, dropped him 'a line to wish you bon voyage – & a speedy return – Give my love to Clemmie . . . I will look after the children & give you news of them. They are great darlings & do you both great credit!'[64]

Meanwhile, Weizmann had told the Political Committee of the Zionist Organization that he was worried about Churchill's mission. The new colonial secretary was 'of a highly impressionable temperament,' he said, and he expected the Arabs to 'organize an agitation to greet him on his arrival in the East.' On March 1, Winston's last day in London before the six-day voyage, Weizmann sent him a long letter, demanding that the Jewish state's eastern boundary be extended east of the Jordan River to include all of Transjordan (now Jordan). Transjordan, he wrote, 'has from the earliest time been an integral and vital part of Palestine.' Here the tribes of Manasseh, Gad, and Reuben 'first pitched their tents and pastured their flocks.' The climate was 'invigorating,' the soil 'rich,' irrigation would be 'easy,' and the hills were 'covered with forests.' There 'Jewish settlement could proceed on a large scale without friction with the local population.' How friction with the Arab inhabitants could be avoided he did not say. Nor was that all. Weizmann also wanted Palestine's southern frontier pushed southward. Churchill was non-committal. He favoured including the triangular wedge of the Negev Desert in the Palestine Mandate, but not the east bank of the Jordan. Two days later, when the ship paused at Marseilles, a newspaperman came aboard and asked him the purpose of his trip. He replied disingenuously: 'I am endeavouring to realise French and British unity in the East. My journey to Egypt and Asia Minor is proof of this. We must at any price coordinate our actions to the extent of uniting them. It is by those means only that we shall be able to arrive at lasting quiet, and diminish the enormous expenditure we are both making.' Privately he was more entertaining. He told his party: 'What the horn is to the rhinoceros, what the sting is to the wasp, the Mohammedan faith is to the Arabs – a faculty of offence or defence.'[65]

As Weizmann had predicted, Churchill's arrival in Cairo was a tumultuous event. A few weeks earlier he had publicly described Egypt as part of the British Empire, and newspapers here had carried the story. El Azhar University students were staging a one-day protest strike. Thousands of spectators, many carrying rocks, awaited his appearance in Station Square. The bridge leading into Shubra Road was packed to capacity. 'Various notables,' the *Palestine Weekly* reported, 'waited patiently in the station, which had been cleared of all unauthorised persons, and Bristol Fighters and huge Handley Pages circled overhead. The train steamed in to the station half an hour late and amid intense excitement disgorged five boxes and other baggage.' But where was Churchill, the great Satan? Prudently, he and his party had detrained at the suburban terminal of Shubra, whence they had motored unseen and undisturbed to their destination. The newspaper noted that 'a disorderly rabble gathered outside Shepheard's crying "Down with Churchill!" but they were dispersed speedily and without casualty.' Being students, they had picked the wrong hotel. He was staying at the Semiramis.[66]

The Semiramis, another newspaper reported, was 'a scene of feverish bustle,' as high commissioners, generals, governors, and civil servants checked in from the Persian Gulf, Iraq, Palestine, and British Somaliland. His Marseilles interview to the contrary, Winston's real purpose in Cairo was, not the knitting together of Allied unity, frayed though it had become, but the choosing of two kings, protégés of the British, to rule over Iraq and Transjordan. As Lawrence later wrote frankly, he and Winston had already reviewed the aspirants 'over dinner at the Ship Restaurant in Whitehall.' The two likeliest candidates were Husein's sons, *amir* Faisal and *amir* Abdullah. On March 12, 1921, the Cairo conference opened at the Mena House. 'Practically all the experts and authorities on the Middle East were summoned,' Churchill wrote afterwards, a singular description of a meeting at which, of the thirty-eight participants, thirty-six were British. Lawrence suggested that Faisal be crowned head of Iraq, 'not only,' the minutes read, 'because of his personal knowledge and friendship for the individual, but also on the ground that in order to counteract the claims of rival candidates and to pull together the scattered elements of a backward and half-civilized country, it was essential that the first ruler should be an active and inspiring personality.' His motion, with Churchill's approval, carried without dissent. Abdullah, in Lawrence's opinion, was 'lazy and by no means dominating,' but though unfit to rule Iraq he would be permitted to reign over Transjordan under the watchful eye of a British high commissioner. Churchill announced his intention to appoint Abdullah in Palestine, and in later years he would say: 'The Emir Abdullah is in Transjordania, where I put him one Sunday afternoon in Jerusalem.' Zionism's hopes were honoured; Sir Herbert Samuel, the Empire's high commissioner in Palestine, was instructed to foster a Jewish homeland. It was all very insular – Faisal and Abdullah would send their sons to public schools in England – and it was also rather medieval. Churchill enjoyed this feudal role immensely. And Lawrence was delighted. He continued to hold other politicians in contempt, but in the *Seven Pillars* he would write enthusiastically of Winston's accomplishments, concluding that, as a result of them, 'I must put on record my conviction that England is out of the Arab affair with clean hands.' When at long last the book was published he sent an inscribed copy to 'Winston Churchill, who made a happy ending to this show . . . And eleven years after we set our hands to making an honest settlement, all our work still stands; the countries have gone forward, our interests having been saved, and nobody having been killed, either on one side or the other. To have planned for eleven years is statesmanship. I ought to have given you two copies of this work!' James Morris wrote: 'The routes to India were safe as never before, the oil wells of Iran and the Persian Gulf, the Abadan refinery, all were securely in British possession.'[67]

Other matters lay before the conference, notably the occupation of Iraq by British troops. Churchill decided to withdraw them, and, in a grand if absurd gesture, declared that the entire country – 116,600 square miles – would be defended by the emaciated RAF, thereby saving the Exchequer £25,000,000 a year. Then he left the details to subordinates in Mena House and departed to enjoy leisure outside. The Egyptian climate is at its most pleasant in March, and he sprawled happily beneath its sun. He knew he was unpopular with the Egyptians – many vehicles carried stickers reading '*à bas Churchill*' – 'but,' as Jessie Crosland, the wife of a civil servant, recalled half a century later, 'he didn't care. He took his easel out and sat in the road painting – he also talked so loudly in the street that the generals got quite nervous.' Cordons of police held back furious mobs who had come to stone him. Carried to and fro in an armoured car, he painted the Sphinx and the Pyramids while Clementine admired them, and he even held a one-man show of his canvasses. On an expedition in the desert he was careening forward on a loping camel when his saddle slipped, dashing him off. Several colourfully dressed bedouins galloped up and offered one of their horses, but he rose, dusted himself off, and growled: 'I started on a camel and I shall finish on a camel.' An Englishwoman who attended the conference remembers: 'When things were boring in the hotel everyone would cheer up when Winston came in, followed by an Arab carrying a pail and a bottle of wine.' On their last day in Egypt, Winston and Clementine were driven to a Nile dam, which he painted. Returning, they crashed into another car. Churchill, a journalist observed, was 'far more concerned about the safety of his painting than about himself.' According to the *Egyptian Gazette*, no one was hurt. Indeed, at a farewell ball given by Lord Allenby, the country's high commissioner, Clemmie was reported to have danced until 'close on midnight.'[68]

Her husband had left the dance floor earlier in the evening, when Sir Herbert Samuel arrived from Jerusalem. The *Palestine Weekly* noted that 'Mr Churchill at once went upstairs with him and was seen no more.' The discussion of the river Jordan, its banks, and its people, had begun. At midnight on March 23, Winston, Clementine, Sir Herbert, and Lawrence boarded a train in Cairo Station for their first Palestinian stop, Gaza. There, early the following morning, they confronted a mob of 150,000 Arabs, whose 'chief cry,' according to a British officer, 'over which they waxed quite frenzied, was: "Down with the Jews! Cut their throats!" ' This, incredibly, was unexpected. Winston's Arabists had assured him that there was no incongruity in England's separate pledges to the Jews and to the Arabs. Even Lawrence had believed that Palestinian hostility to Zionism had been over-rated and could easily be contained; he had endorsed Abdullah, despite his reservations about him, because he thought Abdullah could persuade his people to accept a Jewish homeland. But when he heard the shouting crowds at Gaza and successive stops, he realized his error. Churchill, misunder-standing their fervour, thought they were acclaiming him and waved back cheerfully. Lawrence then translated their chants, and Winston muttered that he was at least grateful they weren't stoning him. Actually, they were plotting violence, but against the Jews, not him. Abdullah's appeals for calm were ignored. So was a government ban on all demonstrations during Churchill's tour. In Haifa ten Jews and five policemen were wounded by missiles and knives, and two innocent bystanders, a young boy and a Moslem woman, were killed. The Executive Committee of the Haifa Congress of Palestinian Arabs, calling on Winston, handed him a twelve-thousand-word statement denoun-cing the Balfour declaration and the concept of Palestine as a Jewish home-land. Jews, they said, had been scattered over the earth for thousands of years, 'and have become nationals of the various nations amongst whom they settled. They have no separate political or lingual existence . . . Hebrew is a dead language.' If there was such a thing as Jewish power and a Jewish nation, what was the status 'of those high Jewish officials who are serving England to-day? Are they Jewish nationals or English nationals? . . . It is obvious they cannot be both at the same time.'[69]

This was debatable, but reasonable – very different from the throngs that screamed 'Palestine for the Arabs! Down with the Zionists!' – and Churchill was attentive. But then they made a mistake. They threatened him. 'If England does not take up the cause of the Arabs,' they declared, 'other Powers will . . . If she does not listen, then perhaps Russia will take up their call some day, or perhaps even Germany.' Now his temper rose. As Lawrence wrote to a friend, 'The man's as brave as six, as good-humoured, shrewd, self-confident & considerate as a statesman can be: & several times I've seen him chuck the statesmanlike course & do the honest thing instead.' The political response to such an overture would be equivocation. Winston bluntly told them that it had been Englishmen, not Palestinian Arabs, who had overthrown their Turkish oppressors: 'The position of Great Britain in Palestine is one of trust, but it is also one of right.' Nearby, he reminded them, more than two thousand British soldiers were buried, 'and there are many other graveyards, some even larger, scattered about in this land.' To fulfil that trust, 'and for the high purposes we have in view, supreme sacrifices were made by all these soldiers of the British Empire, who gave up their lives and blood.'[70]

Whatever his previous doubts about the justice of creating a Zionist state, they were gone now. He knew that it would be expensive. He said: 'In Africa the population is docile and the country fruitful; in Mesopotamia the country is arid and the population ferocious. A little money goes a long way in Africa and a lot of money goes a very little way in Arabia.' But he believed the price must be paid. At the same time, however, he urged the Jews to be realistic. After trying to speak at the Mosque of Omar, where he was shouted down by Arabs, he visited the Hebrew University, still under construction, to plant a symbolic tree. 'Personally,' he told his audience, 'my heart is full of sympathy for Zionism.' He believed 'that the establishment of a Jewish National Home in Palestine will be a blessing to . . . Great Britain.' Then he reminded them that when the British promised to support Zionism, they also 'assured the non-Jewish inhabitants that they should not suffer in consequence. Every step you take should therefore be also for the moral and material benefit of all Palestinians.' He said: 'I am now going to plant a tree, and I hope that in its shadow peace and prosperity may return once more to Palestine.'[71]

It will surprise no one who has lived in the Middle East that the tree broke as it was handed to him, that there was no backup, and that they had to settle for a scrawny palm which wouldn't even grow in that soil. Harry Sacher, an English Zionist who was practising law in Palestine, wrote to a friend that 'Churchill spoke very plainly in reaffirming the Balfour Declaration, both to the Jews and the Arabs. But he also told the Jews that they must do their bit, and he enlarged upon the pressures on the [British] taxpayer, and the anti-Zionist critics in Parliament. The Arabs are angry, and there was a bit of trouble in Haifa, where a crowd was dispersed by force, perhaps too much force. I am not happy about the Arab position.' He wondered 'whether the British Government may not finish by dropping the whole thing and clearing out – for financial reasons. I really don't know whether England today can afford such a luxury as a foreign policy, with or without mandates.'[72]

Back in England the House discovered that Winston's commitment to the Palestine problem was absolute. At times it seemed a thankless task. Some English Zionists regarded the creation of Transjordan as a betrayal of Balfour's pledge; one of them, Richard Meinertzhagen, wrote to a friend that he had confronted Winston and 'told him it was grossly unfair to the Jews, that it was another promise broken and that it was a most dishonest act, that the Balfour Declaration was being torn up by degrees and that the official policy of HMG to establish a Home for the Jews in Biblical Palestine was being sabotaged; that I found the Middle East Department whose business it was to implement the Mandate almost one hundred per cent hebraphobe and could not the duration of Abdullah's Emirate in Transjordan be of a temporary nature, say for seven years . . . Churchill listened and said he saw the force of my argument and would consider the question. He thought it was too late to alter but a time limit to Abdullah's Emirate in Transjordan might work.'[73] It wouldn't have worked, and he must have known that, but on this very delicate issue he had to listen to all sides and, however great the strain, exercise an uncharacteristic restraint.

On May 31, 1921, he reported to the cabinet that the 'pronounced suspicion of Zionism' among Palestinian Arabs was unjustified. There was no validity in 'current accounts of the inferior quality of recent Jewish immigrants.' Indeed, they had 'created a standard of living far superior to that of the indigenous Arabs.' But they would need protection. The rioting in Haifa had spread to Jaffa; Jews were dying. 'Zionist battalions,' he believed, were not the solution. He recommended 'a strong local gendarmerie.' Nor did he favour elections; the Arab majority 'would undoubtedly prohibit further immigration of Jews.' But how many Jews? At present Palestine was inhabited by over 500,000 Moslems and fewer than 80,000 Jews. Two weeks later he assured the House that Arab fears that 'in the next few years they are going to be swamped by scores of thousands of immigrants from Central Europe, who will push them off the land,' were 'illusory.' Jewish immigration would be 'a very slow process, and the rights of the existing non-Jewish population would be strictly preserved.' Here he was dissembling. His private papers show that he anticipated a Zionist state of between three and four million – Israel's population today.[74]

Arab violence in Palestine was growing. On the fourth anniversary of the Balfour declaration Samuel cabled Churchill that a gang of 'roughs' had invaded Jerusalem's Jewish quarter; gunfire had been exchanged and policemen had found four corpses, three of them Jews. Meanwhile, Winston had delivered a major speech in the House on Middle Eastern developments. Arabs had fought with the Allies during the war, he reminded them, and Allied 'pledges were given that the Turkish rule should not be reintroduced in these regions.' At the same time, a promise 'of a very important character' had been given to the Jews – that Britain would do its best 'to establish a Jewish national home in Palestine.' England was 'at this moment in possession of these countries,' providing 'the only form of Government existing there.' To redeem these assurances he had created Iraq and Transjordan, which had given 'satisfaction to Arab nationality.' Now he promised to move towards a political solution in Palestine. If the Arabs were provided with a democratic form of government, they would 'veto any further Jewish immigration,' and this would violate England's pledge, which would mean 'that the word of Britain no longer counts throughout the East and the Middle East.' He believed the riddle could be solved. He could not guarantee 'complete success, but I do believe that the measures which we are taking are well calculated to that end.' He had 'great confidence in the experts and high authorities' working on the problem, and he asked Parliament to give them 'support in the difficult and delicate process of reduction and conciliation which lies before us, and on which we are already embarking.'[75]

Applause was prolonged. 'Winston has had a great success,' Austen Chamberlain wrote to Lloyd George, 'both as to his speech & his policy, & has changed the whole atmosphere of the House on the Middle East question.'

But many were unconvinced. Churchill was not the only English politician to believe that there was a predominance of Jews in Red Moscow, and hebraphobia, as Meinertzhagen called it, was still quite respectable then. Lord Winterton warned Winston that 'once you begin to buy land for the purpose of settling Jewish cultivators you will find yourself up against the hereditary antipathy, which exists all over the world, to the Jewish race.' The Zionists were alarmed, but Churchill, undiscouraged, proceeded to draft a Palestinian constitution which would prevent the Arab majority from barring Jewish investment and immigration. He assured the nervous Zionist leaders that 'His Majesty's Government have no intention of repudiating the obligations into which they have entered towards the Jewish people.' A House referendum on the declaration and the constitution was scheduled for June, and anti-Zionists in both the Commons and the Lords began to hold strategy meetings. In the upper house they were a heavy majority; despite an appeal from Balfour, a newly created earl, the peers voted down his declaration, 60 to 29. Churchill told the House that it couldn't be renounced, that it was 'an integral part of the whole mandatory system, as inaugurated by agreement between the victorious Powers and by the Treaty of Versailles.' To those who argued that the Arabs could develop Palestine's economic wealth by themselves, he said: 'Who is going to believe that? Left to themselves, the Arabs of Palestine would not in a thousand years have taken effective steps towards the irrigation and electrification of Palestine. They would have been quite content to dwell – a handful of philosophic people – in the wasted sun-drenched plains, letting the waters of the Jordan continue to flow unbridled and unharnessed into the Dead Sea.' An Arab delegation called at the Colonial Office. He told them bluntly: 'The British Government mean to carry out the Balfour Declaration. I have told you so again and again. I told you so at Jerusalem. I told you so at the House of Commons the other day.' The House backed him, 292 to 35, rendering the Lords' vote meaningless. On July 22 the League of Nations approved. All legal hurdles for the birth of Israel had been cleared.[76]

Yet it remained in gestation for another quarter century. British Arabists remained militant. On August 19, 1922, Lord Sydenham wrote to *The Times* that in Palestine the British had adopted 'a policy of forcing by British bayonets a horde of aliens, some of them eminently undesirable, upon the original owners of the country.' Later that year, when Churchill was all but immersed in the bogs of Ireland, the government issued a White Paper affirming the declaration but adding that this did not mean 'the imposition of a Jewish nationality upon the inhabitants of Palestine as a whole.' This bland concession to the Arabs infuriated Weizmann without placating the Arabs. The only alternative seemed to be a continuance of British rule. In 1928 the Zionists, with British encouragement, established the Jewish Agency for Palestine to manage their interests there. The immediate response of the Arabs was a pogrom. A succession of British commissions studied the Palestine dilemma in 1929, 1936, 1938, and 1939. Some suggested restrictions on Jewish immigration; one proposed partition. The Arabs struck back with violence, terrorism, and boycotts of British goods. With the outbreak of World War II, England once more needed the Arabs as allies, and nothing was done until the postwar years, when Jewish terrorists took matters into their own hands. Robert Rhodes James, who is perhaps Churchill's most astute critic, believes that his failure 'to produce a workable solution in the area cannot be held against him. It was a task beyond his capacities, but it is probably true to say that it was beyond the capacities of any individual to accomplish. At the time it seemed as though he had skilfully reconciled the conflicting wartime assurances made by the British to the Arabs and the Jews.' His successors in the Colonial Office were either lacking his determination, intimidated by the Arabs, or infected by racial prejudice. Poring over the old documents, one has the feeling that they themselves did not know.[77]

In his speech of June 14, 1921, Churchill had told the House that any successful Middle Eastern policy would eventually depend upon 'a peaceful and lasting settlement with Turkey.'[78] That was precisely what Britain lacked, and it is a supreme irony that the most damaging blow to Winston's prestige during his two years as colonial secretary came from – of all places – the Dardanelles. Moreover, the man who dealt it was the victor of Gallipoli, General Mustapha Kemal, now Kemal Atatürk ('the Great Turk'), who had become an enlightened dictator consecrated to the transformation of his homeland into a modern state. At San Remo and in the Treaty of Sèvres, imposed on the weak sultan by the Allies, Turkey had been stripped, not only of its Arab possessions, but of many lands inhabited by Turkish people. The Bosporus and the Dardanelles were internationalized and the shores of both straits demilitarized. Moreover, Greece, Turkey's ancient enemy, had been awarded Smyrna, Thrace, and the sultan's Aegean islands.

Lloyd George was responsible for this. A passionate philhellenist, under the spell of Premier Venizelos, he believed the Greeks were completely justified in their determination to regain what they regarded as their lost territories in Asia Minor, including areas not awarded them at Sèvres. Churchill vehemently disagreed. For eight months he urged Lloyd George to negotiate with Kemal. The prime minister replied that Kemal was a rebel and an outcast. At a cabinet meeting in the first week of 1920, Winston recommended that British troops be withdrawn from Constantinople. George said they would leave only when Greek soldiers were ready to replace them. Curzon, the foreign secretary, agreed with Winston; so did the foreign ministers of France and Italy. Churchill pointed out that since England was not prepared to field an army against the Turks, its support of Greece's adventurism was dangerous. Championing Kemal's revolution as vigorously as he opposed Lenin's, he wrote to George that an attempt to force new terms on him 'wd require great & powerful armies & long costly operations. On this world so torn with strife I dread to see you let loose the Greek armies.' He received no reply. He sent feelers to the Turks and learned that 'Mustapha Kemal is willing to negotiate.' Again he wrote to the prime minister: 'No doubt my opinions seem a vy unimportant thing. But are you sure that about Turkey the line wh you are forcing us to pursue wd commend itself to the present H of C?' In a war, he predicted, the Turks would defeat the Greeks, and 'to let the Greeks collapse at Smyrna will leave us confronted with a Turkish triumph and the Turks will have got back Smyrna by their own efforts instead of as the result of a bargain with us.' To Lord Derby he wrote: 'I think we should use Kemal and a reconciled Turkey as a barrier against the Bolsheviks and to smooth down our affairs in the Middle East and in India.'[79]

To Lloyd George's embarrassment, the Venizelos government fell. George still wouldn't budge, however. Greek friendship, he told the House, was essential for England, and he was unwilling 'to purchase a way out of our difficulties by betraying others.' He also reported that his ministers were in 'unanimous agreement' that Smyrna should not be returned to Turkey. That was untrue, and Churchill angrily reminded Hankey, who had drafted the minutes of the meeting, that he had expressed his conviction that 'the restoration of Turkish sovereignty or suzerainty over the Smyrna Province is an indispensable step to the pacification of the Middle East.' It was also his impression that these views had been shared by the lord privy seal, the chancellor of the Exchequer, and the secretary of state for India.[80]

As Lloyd George climbed farther and farther out on his limb, Kemal completed his ruthless suppression of his Turkish rivals and united the country behind him. The caliphate had been abolished, ending fourteen centuries of Islamic rule. Elected president and appointed commander in chief of the armed forces, Kemal vowed to reconquer all Turkish territories occupied by foreign forces. In defiance of the Allies, he had kept the sultan's army intact, and his *askari*, with their preference for the bayonet and their fearsome war cry – '*Uhra, Uhra!*' ('Kill, Kill!') – routed the Armenians and Georgians in the east and then the French in the south. While he was preoccupied with these theatres, the Greek army invaded Turkey. At first their advance was virtually unopposed. Riddell wrote in his diary: 'LG is still very pro-Greek and much elated at the Greek military successes. He said we always regarded the Turk as a first-class fighting man but even here he had broken down. LG told me he believes the Greeks will capture Constantinople, and he evidently hopes they will.' Frances Stevenson wrote: 'D. very interested in the Greek advance. He has had a great fight in the Cabinet to back the Greeks (not only in the field but morally) & he & Balfour are the only pro-Greeks there. All the others have done their best to obstruct & the WO have behaved abominably. However D. has got his way, but he is much afraid lest the Greek attack should be a failure, & he should be proved to have been wrong. He says his political reputation depends a great deal on what happens in Asia Minor.' He kept such doubts from his colleagues, jubilantly telling the House: 'Turkey is no more!'[81]

He was wrong. In the summer of 1921, when the Greek invaders were within thirty miles of Angora (now Ankara), Kemal turned and defeated them on the Sakarya River. The Allies, alarmed, tried appeasing him by forbidding the Greeks to approach Constantinople and offering unspecified revisions of the Sèvres treaty. Kemal, who had already denounced its provisions, ignored them. Mounting a counteroffensive, he crushed the Greeks in the battles of Afyon Karahisar and Bursa. They broke and fled in confusion across the Dumlu Pinar plateau, towards the coast. In the second week of August he was within a day's march of Smyrna. By now he had become a terrible myth – '*le mangeur d'homme*,' the French called him – and his frantic enemies, unable to stand against him, turned on the civilian population. Every Turkish village in the path of their flight was burned to the ground. Inside Smyrna, Turkish women and children were put to the sword. But Smyrna was home to thousands of Armenians and Greeks, too. When the Greek soldiers escaped by sea, and Armenians unwisely resisted the onrushing *askari*, the Turks ran amok. Moving systematically from street to street, they dragged all civilians who weren't Turks from their hiding places and butchered them on their own thresholds. Those who sought refuge in Smyrna's wooden churches faced an even ghastlier fate. The church walls were drenched with benzine and then fired. Refugees who attempted escape from cremation were bayoneted as they leapt out. The flames spread. Kemal's men sealed off the Turkish quarter, encircled the rest of the city, and cheered as it was reduced to ashes. The few civilians still alive were then massacred. Except for the homes of the Turkish natives and a few buildings near the Kassambra railway station, Smyrna was destoyed.

These appalling events were unknown to the outside world for several weeks. Royal Marines had evacuated British subjects from Smyrna before the atrocities began. It was the consensus of European statesmen – with the exception of Lloyd George, who stubbornly doubted the Greeks had suffered 'a complete debacle' – that the invaders had asked for it. Paris urged Athens to sue for an armistice, and Sir Horace Rumbold, the British high commissioner in Constantinople, agreed, cabling Curzon that any such truce must be followed by 'the immediate and orderly evacuation of Asia Minor by Greeks.'[82] But by now the situation was beyond the control of anyone except Kemal, whose momentum kept growing. Soon the straits and even the Gallipoli peninsula were in danger. Here the Turks faced, not Greeks, but British, French, and Italian soldiers. At Sèvres the Allies had established 'neutral zones,' including the Dardanelles, the Sea of Marmara, and the Bosporus, which were proclaimed international waters to be guarded by Allied infantry. Kemal, however, recognized no neutrals in his struggle. On Turkish soil anyone not for him was against him, and putting Smyrna behind him, he wheeled towards the Sea of Marmara, on whose shores a force of demoralized Greek soldiers had taken refuge. But they were not his main objective. The horrified maritime powers – chiefly England – realized that he meant to close the straits.

Now, as in 1915, the key position there was Chanak, the Dardanelles' port of entry, a seedy waterfront town of crooked streets and high walls still pocked and pitted from de Robeck's shelling. Once it became clear that Kemal had designs upon it, the French and Italian contingents stationed there withdrew, leaving a few thousand British troops to confront fifty-two thousand Turks. Churchill suggested that the Tommies be boated across to the European shore, thereby yielding everything on the Asian side to Kemal. If this were done, the first lord of the Admiralty assured the cabinet, the Royal Navy could still keep the channel open. The War Office forwarded the proposal to General Sir Charles Harington, the commander of the occupation force in Constantinople, but Harington insisted that his men remain in the town as a rear guard. Lloyd George was against Winston's idea anyway. He said that if they were to 'scuttle' from the threat, 'our credit would entirely disappear.'[83] Colonel Digby Shuttleworth, a tactful officer, was dispatched to Chanak. At his request, the Admiralty sent the battleships *Ajax*, *Iron Duke*, and *Marlborough* and the seaplane carrier *Pegasus* to anchor between Chanak and Gallipoli and train their guns on the approaches to the town.

Churchill had a sickening feeling of déjà vu. The ghosts of de Robeck, Fisher, and Kitchener rose before him. He told the cabinet that he felt 'very uncomfortable' about the weakness of Shuttleworth's position and recommended that not only Chanak but also Constantinople be abandoned, drawing 'the whole of the British forces' into Gallipoli. This, he said, would involve 'no serious risk,' and had 'the very great merit that it would mystify, confuse, and hold up the enemy.' Lloyd George shook his head. To take that line, he said, 'would be the greatest loss of prestige which could possibly be inflicted on the British Empire.' Churchill withdrew his motion and switched course. 'The line of deep water separating Asia from Europe,' he said, was 'a line of great significance, and we must make that line very secure by every means within our power. If the Turks take the Gallipoli Peninsula . . . we shall have lost the whole fruits of our victory, and another Balkan war would be inevitable.' He then joined Lloyd George, Balfour, Sir Laming Worthington-Evans, and F.E. Smith – who had become Lord Birkenhead in 1919 – in a hard-line bloc. 'We made common cause,' Winston later wrote. 'The Government might break up, and we might be relieved of our burden. The nation might not support us; they could find others to advise them. The Press might howl; the Allies might bolt. We intended to force the Turk to a negotiated peace before he set foot in Europe.'[84]

On September 15, 1922, they sent Kemal an ultimatum. He was told that he remained in the neutral zones at his peril: 'It is the intention of His Majesty's Government to reinforce immediately . . . the troops at the disposal of Sir Charles Harington, the Allied Commander-in-Chief at Constantinople, and orders have been given to the British Fleet in the Mediterranean to oppose by every means any infraction of the neutral zones by the Turks or any attempt by them to cross the European shores.' But where were Harington's reinforcements coming from? Not from Italy or France; their men were gone. Raymond Poincaré had announced in Paris that the French 'would not consider themselves bound by any responsibility for any development that might result from the action which General Harington had been authorized to take.' And not from the Empire, either; it was on this occasion that Churchill, on instructions from Lloyd George, asked the Dominions for troops and was turned down by all except New Zealand and Newfoundland. Winston was dining at Sir Philip Sassoon's Park Lane home on September 25 when word arrived that Kemal had finally responded to the British note. He had rejected it. Churchill was furious. Hankey, a fellow guest, wrote in his diary: 'We talked late into the night. Winston, hitherto a strong Turko-phile, had swung round at the threat to his beloved Dardanelles and become violently Turko-phobe and even Phil-Hellene.'[85]

Actually, the crisis had come and gone four days earlier, after some two hundred *askari* had occupied the village of Eren Keui, less than ten miles from Chanak, and moved towards the British outposts. Told to retire, they halted but stood their ground. Then eight hundred Turkish horsemen rode closer. The British retreated towards prepared positions. The horsemen, to their relief, did not pursue them. Shuttleworth wired Harington: 'Peaceful penetration by armed men who did not wish to fight, and yet refused either to withdraw or to halt, had not been foreseen.' Harington cautioned him to avoid any 'unnecessary' exchanges of fire.[86] The tension continued for two weeks, and at one point Harington seriously considered ordering an attempt to drive the Turks off, but early in October they marched away on Kemal's orders. After reflection Atatürk announced that he would respect the neutral zones; the Greek soldiers on the Sea of Marmara were permitted to retire unmolested into Thrace. An armistice was signed, and the following year, in the Treaty of Lausanne, the straits, Eastern Thrace, and Constantinople – which Kemal renamed Istanbul in 1930 – were peaceably awarded to Turkey.

In his biography of Curzon, Harold Nicolson writes: 'To Mr Lloyd George, and above all to Mr Churchill, is due our gratitude for having at this juncture defied not the whole world merely, but the full hysterical force of British public opinion.' Yet they paid a price, George deservedly, Winston less so. No one outside the cabinet knew of Churchill's wise counsel during the months before the highly charged name of Chanak suddenly reappeared on front pages, reminding readers of his earlier misfortune there. The *Daily Mail* then screamed 'STOP THIS NEW WAR!' and cried that not a single British soldier should fall 'in order that Mr Winston Churchill may make a new Gallipoli.' To some extent, however, he was responsible for his loss in stature. He had been genuinely affronted by what he regarded as Kemal's insolence in defying a British demand. And then he learned of the destruction of Smyrna, described in a belated report to Curzon from Sir Harry Lamb, the British consul general in the ruined city. The sack of the city outraged Winston even as Bolshevik savagery had. It was an account of 'pillage, rape and massacre,' he wrote. 'Sir Harry Lamb counted 20 corpses in 50 yards during the infernal orgy' which found 'few parallels in the history of crime.' His reaction to barbarism would always be unrestrained, and often misunderstood. Mrs Keppel wrote that

Winston was 'longing to drop the paint brush for the sword,' and Hankey noted in his diary: 'I walked across the Park with Churchill one evening towards the end of the crisis and he quite frankly regretted that the Turks had not attacked us at Chanak, as he felt that the surrender of Eastern Thrace to them was humiliating, and that the return of the Turks to Europe meant an infinity of troubles.'[87]

The British, alternately baffled and amused by the incompatibility of Arabs and Jews, never saw the parallel between the running canker in the Middle East and their own ancient quarrel with the Irish. Yet the two were not unlike, and the second, among people presumed to be more civilized, is the more perplexing. It is a source of endless wonder that these two islands, lying side by side off the coast of Europe, should have been the fount of so much anguish, each for the other. One spawned the mightiest empire in history, and its arrogant overlords were loathed by their repressed neighbours across the Irish Sea. The other, small, poor, with virtually no valuable natural resources, supported a people conspicuously lacking in political gifts and afflicted with an extraordinary incidence of alcoholism ('It is a very moist climate,' Churchill once observed), yet endowed with immense charm, romantic vision, and remarkable genius – it was the homeland of Swift, Shaw, Yeats, Joyce, Millington Synge, O'Casey, O'Faolain, and Dublin's Abbey Theatre.[88]

Ireland's impact on British public life ought to have been slight. In fact, it had been enormous. The Irish question had been a primordial parliamentary issue for generations. It had driven Pitt from office, defeated Gladstone at the height of his powers, toppled the Tories in 1885, and held the balance in the House between 1910 and 1914. When the issue of Home Rule made its periodic appearances, London newspaper accounts of it were so dense you could hardly find the non sequiturs; Churchill told his Dundee constituents: '*The Times* is speechless, and takes three columns to express its speechlessness.'[89] On the eve of the Great War, the British cabinet had been absorbed in drawing a temporary border between Ulster and Eire, narrowing it down first to the counties of Fermanagh and Tyrone, next to parishes and groups of parishes inside Fermanagh and Tyrone – and even then was unable to reach a solution which would satisfy either side. Irish hearts and English hearts beat to a different rhythm. The Irish hated the English, and Englishmen who did not return the hatred were fascinated by the Irish. Nietzsche had warned against staring too long into an abyss because eventually, he said, it would stare back. Ireland was England's abyss and it never blinked.

Like many British politicians, Winston had personal ties to Ireland. Dublin's Sackville Street, since renamed O'Connell Street, had been familiar to his grandfather, his father, and, in his childhood, to Winston himself. Yet although he could never conceive of its secession from the United Kingdom, he had never been, and never would be, accused of publicly taking sides in its draining religious feud. To him it was 'the Empire's ailing child,' which he also compared to a forest in which friends were indistinguishable from foes. 'My views,' he said once, when asked how he stood on the question, 'are a harmonious process, which keeps them in relation to the current movement of events.' He never broke completely with North or South. History's verdict, he then believed, would be clear: 'Ireland will be revealed to have been strong only in her grievance, and England weak only in the assertion of her power in interior Irish affairs.' Since Ireland, unlike the Dominions, lacked self-government, its problems had become part of his responsibilities when he entered the Colonial Office. In the opinion of the British public it was, indeed, the largest part. As Alan Moorehead observes, 'in the early 1920s it seemed at times that this issue eclipsed every other and that there could be no solution of it.' Churchill himself saw 'the dreary steeples of Fermanagh and Tyrone emerging once again.'[90]

Actually, they had been there all the time. Though he and the rest of England had been looking eastward towards the Continent between 1914 and 1918, the abyss had continued to stare at their backs. Frustrated by the prewar failures of John Redmond's Irish Nationalists, the people of southern Ireland, or Eire, as we now know it, turned increasingly, during the war years, to the leaders of the Sinn Féin. The Sinn Féiners were unwilling to settle for a parliament in Dublin. They wanted a republic like the United States, independent of England. The Easter rebellion of the Irish Republican Brotherhood (IRB) in 1916, planned in conjunction with German agents, was doomed before the first shot was fired, but the British execution of Patrick Pearse and several other rebel leaders – Eamon de Valera was spared because he had been born in America – invested them with martyrdom, an attribute highly valued in a country which cherishes the maxim that 'grass soon grows over a battlefield but never over a scaffold.' In the summer of the following year most of the survivors were belatedly amnestied, De Valera being released on July 11. Early in 1918 Redmond died, and the British then delivered two further blows to Anglo-Irish friendship. They rearrested De Valera and the rest of the Sinn Féin leadership for subversion. And then they attempted to induct Eire's men into the British army. This was a fiasco. Inducted, the men immediately deserted en masse. 'Irish conscription,' Churchill said, 'was handled in such a fashion . . . that we had the worst of both worlds, all the resentment against compulsion and in the end no law and no men.'[91] Meanwhile, Orangemen had been fighting gallantly on the western front – Kitchener had asked them for a brigade of volunteers, and they had given him a complete division – assuring Ulster status as a privileged Protestant sanctuary when Home Rule came.

Ulster excepted, Sinn Féin candidates swept Ireland in the parliamentary elections of 1918. Like Churchill in the Boer War, they had successfully exploited imprisonment as a political asset. But instead of crossing to London and taking the House of Commons' oath to a King they scorned, they met in Dublin, adopted the Easter rebellion programme, formed a Dáil Eireann ('Irish Assembly'), and elected De Valera president of it. The Dáil (pronounced 'Doyle') was suppressed by the British. De Valera went back behind

587

bars, but in February 1919 he was rescued from Lincoln Jail – and smuggled, disguised, into New York – by the daring Michael Collins, a veteran of the Easter Rising, adjutant general of the Irish Republican Army, and leader of the IRA guerrilla warfare which now began. The British put a price of £5,000 on Collins's head, but like the rest of the desperate measures adopted that year it accomplished nothing. Except in the northeastern Protestant counties civil order was disintegrating. The IRA held Eire in a thralldom of loyalty or, where that was lacking, of terror. The British authorities in Dublin Castle were under virtual siege.

In August 1919, when the Dáil was proclaimed an illegal organization, Churchill, then still minister of war, told the cabinet that the time was not propitious for an Irish solution. Yet something had to be done. Violence had become the official policy of Eire's real leaders. The relationship between their 'Irish Republic' and Great Britain amounted to a state of war. In the United States – where he had raised over five million dollars from Irish Americans – De Valera, describing negotiations between Dublin and London, said that 'the hand of Irishmen held out in good faith was spurned and spat upon.' Eire's hands now held grenades or revolvers. That year the IRA was responsible for eighteen murders of Englishmen, seventy-seven armed attacks, and an attempt to ambush the viceroy. In 1920 it grew worse. On March 26 the resident magistrate in Dublin was dragged from a streetcar and slain on the spot. Clementine wrote to Winston: 'This new Irish murder is very terrible.' He replied that Irish terrorism was 'really getting very serious . . . What a diabolical streak they have in their character! I expect it is that treacherous, assassinating, conspiring trait which has done them in in bygone ages of history and prevented them from being a great responsible nation with stability and prosperity. It is shocking that we have not been able to bring the murderers to justice.' By April, British constables were being shot down daily, five of them in one burst of gunfire in county Galway. Four British staff officers were killed in broad daylight aboard a train between Cork and Bandon. Sir Henry Wilson, now chief of the Imperial General Staff, wrote in his diary: 'Tonight Winston insinuated that the murdered officers were careless, useless fellows & ought to have taken precautions. This fairly roused me & I let fly about the Cabinet being cowards and not governing Ireland.' Winston felt the torment of frustration So did the cabinet. Exasperated during a parliamentary inquiry, Churchill asked the attorney general for Ireland: 'Why not make life intolerable in a particular area?' This had already been tried, he was told: 'We made ten thousand raids in six months. We did not get hold of the revolvers. They bury them in bogs.'[92]

Not all Eire patriots were killers. Terence McSwiney, lord mayor of Cork, went on a hunger strike and died two months later. And some terrorists favoured abduction. Scotland Yard reported: 'At a Sinn Féin meeting in a private house in Glasgow last Saturday night it was decided that the best form of reprisals against the British Government would be the kidnapping of any of the following Ministers: – the Prime Minister, Mr Bonar Law, Lord French,

Mr Winston Churchill, Sir Hamar Greenwood.' Six members of the Sinn Féin executive had been appointed to this mission and provided with £250 to carry it out. The Yard warned cabinet members to avoid Scotland 'for the next few days or weeks.' Detective Sergeant W.H. Thompson was assigned to Churchill as a bodyguard; he would be at Churchill's side, off and on, for the rest of Winston's political life. Churchill, characteristically, overreacted to challenge. His early responses to the Irish crisis were unrealistic. He proposed rewards for the capture of Sinn Féiners, blind to the bloody fate which would await any Irish informer. In Dundee he opposed consideration of Home Rule while 'the murder gang in Ireland' went unpunished. No settlement could be reached by 'surrender to treacherous murder, but only on the basis of justice and generosity,' he said, unaware that it was the lack of justice and generosity which had sown the seeds of terrorism. In the *Illustrated Sunday Herald* he wrote inaccurately: 'No nation has ever established its title-deeds by a campaign of assassination. The British nation, having come grimly through the slaughter of Armageddon, are certainly not going to be scared by the squalid scenes of sporadic warfare which are being enacted across the Irish Channel.' Clementine, troubled, cautioned him: 'Do my darling use your influence now for some sort of moderation or at any rate justice in Ireland. Put yourself in the place of the Irish. If you were ever leader you would not be cowed by severity & certainly not by reprisals which fall like rain from Heaven upon the Just & upon the Unjust . . . It always makes me unhappy & disappointed when I see you inclined to take for granted that the rough, iron-fisted, "Hunnish" way will prevail.'[93]

But he was determined that the ironfisted way should be tried first. The impulse to fight fire with fire, always plausible and always barren, was too strong to be suppressed. From the outset it raised problems, however, among them the question of who should provide the retaliatory fire. Greenwood, the new chief secretary for Ireland, told a committee of ministers: 'The Dublin police cannot be relied upon, nor the Post Office, nor the Civil Service.' Churchill observed: 'It is monstrous that we have some two hundred murders and no one hung.' Turning to the prime minister, he reminded him that 'you agreed six or seven months ago that there should be hanging.' Lloyd George confirmed it and asked Denis Henry, the attorney general: 'I feel certain you must hang. Can you get convictions from Catholics?' Henry replied: 'Substantially, no.' The possibility of martial law was raised. Churchill wrote to Sir Henry Wilson, as chief of the general staff, asking him how many men he could spare. The answer was discouraging. Of England's forty-six peacetime battalions, ten were of the guards needed for defence of the homeland and eight more were unsuitable because they were Irish. That left only twenty-eight. 'If 8 were sent to Ireland,' Wilson wrote, 'we should have very little for our own internal troubles & nothing for India, Egypt, C-ople, etc.' Sir Nevil Macready, chief commissioner of Scotland Yard, had crossed to embattled Dublin Castle with broad powers and reported that the Royal Irish Constabulary was inadequate for the job. Churchill felt it imperative to snuff out the uprising before 'flames of orange and green flashed out of the Irish furnace.' Unfortunately the extinguisher he chose contained petrol. He proposed the establishment of a temporary RIC branch, to be called the 'Special Emergency Gendarmerie.' The cabinet approved it on May 11, stipulating that the force be raised, paid, and 'administered' by Churchill's ministry. Eight thousand recruits were to be sought in England, chiefly among former soldiers. In addition, another thousand ex-officers would serve in an 'Auxiliary Division' of the RIC. The 'Auxis,' as they came to be known, received a pound a day. Members of the Gendarmerie, who were paid ten shillings a day, were issued army surplus khaki uniforms and the black belts of the RIC. They became infamous as the 'Black and Tans,' or, more simply, the 'Tans.'[94]

All over Europe the hardened dregs of disbanded armies were distorting postwar politics – in Germany the former Corporal Hitler was organizing veterans into *Ordnertruppe*, or strong-arm squads – and eight thousand British survivors of the trenches were now set loose in Eire. In his diary Wilson called this 'a panic measure,' predicting that 'raising 8000 scallawags' would 'give us no military value but great anxieties.' But he did not know the worst. He assumed that they, like the RIC, would serve as policemen. Instead, they were trained to use IRA methods against the IRA, which, in practice, meant against the people of southern Ireland. Churchill wrote to Lloyd George: 'I am prepared to support and to defend in Parliament a policy of reprisals within strict limits and under strict control in certain districts in which it should be declared that conditions approximating a state of war exist. I believe that such a policy would be less discreditable and more effective than what is going on.' He went farther. The Tans, he argued, should not be disciplined for excesses: 'I cannot feel it right to punish the troops when, goaded in the most brutal manner and finding no redress, they take action on their own account.' It was becoming increasingly difficult to pin George down on the Irish question – one day he would speak of the need to 'hunt down' the killers and the next of hopes for 'lasting reconciliation' – but he supported Winston's Tans publicly, declaring: 'We have murder by the throat . . . we had to reorganize the police, and when the Government was ready we struck the terrorists and now the terrorists are complaining of terror.'[95]

But others were complaining, too. Greenwood, the Westmorland of his day, told the press that the countryside was being pacified by the Tans, and that they were innocent of atrocities. That was untrue. The extent of their guilt is unclear; self-serving claims were made by both sides. Robert Rhodes James writes that 'no doubt their record has been excessively besmirched,' yet adds: 'After every allowance has been made, theirs is a record of squalor that was, unhappily, not without precedent, but which increasingly nauseated civilized opinion in Britain and abroad.' One notorious incident was the razing of Cork on December 11, 1920. Greenwood denied that the Tans had started the fire. Nevertheless, the cabinet authorized an investigation and then suppressed the subsequent report on the ground that 'the effects of publishing' it 'would be disastrous to the Government's whole policy in Ireland.' In 1974 Henry Pelling wrote that the savagery of the fighting between the Sinn Féin and the Tans 'is still a bitter memory.'[96]

After Cork critics arose on all sides. The Labour party's Commission on Ireland charged: 'Things are being done in the name of Britain which make her name stink in the nostrils of the world.' Sir Henry Wilson noted: 'I told Winston that I thought this a scandal & Winston was very angry. He said these "Black & Tans" were honourable & gallant officers, etc, etc & talked much nonsense . . . It is an amazing & scandalous thing.' Later he wrote: 'At Balbriggan, Thurles & Galway yesterday the local police marked down certain SFs as in their opinion actual murderers or instigators & then coolly went & shot them without question or trial. Winston saw very little harm in this but it horrifies me.' Austen Chamberlain asked for reassurance that the law-enforcement officers were not proceeding 'without control.' Greenwood was instructed 'to endeavour to limit reprisals,' but a majority of the cabinet approved a resolution 'that it would be a mistake for the Government to take the initiative in any suspension of military activities in Ireland, and that the present policy in that country should be pursued.' In public, Churchill weakly argued that the Tans merely enjoyed 'the same freedom as the Chicago or New York police in dealing with armed gangs.' After martial law had been declared in the counties of Kilkenny, Limerick, Kerry, and Cork he wrote to an archbishop who had protested, that the government had had no choice because 'no body is in corporate and continuous existence which has the power or even the constitutional right to speak for Ireland,' that both 'well-meaning individuals' and 'the Irish people' were 'paralysed by the terroristic action of a violent and desperate body of men,' and, the ultimate reason: 'Britain will never consent, while life and strength remain, to the destruction of the integrity of the British Empire. Was it not [Thomas Colley] Grattan who said "The Channel forbids union; the ocean forbids separation"? "[97]

Privately, however, his view was changing. The Tans had been given a free hand and nothing had been accomplished. England and Eire were farther apart than ever. Churchill the warrior was being transformed into Churchill the peacemaker. On November 3, 1920, he told the cabinet: 'I do not consider that the present Government attitude on reprisals can be maintained much longer. It is not fair on the troops, it is not fair on the officers who command them.' In a subsequent meeting the question of an armistice was raised. Thomas Jones, first assistant secretary (later deputy secretary) to the cabinet, noted: 'All through the recent discussions of the Irish problem the most irreconcilable Minister has been Balfour. Churchill has frankly acknowledged the failure of force.' Strongly supported by Churchill, Lloyd George approved of a truce offer, and the Sinn Féin accepted a respite in the killing. The quixotic Sir Henry Wilson was indignant. He had changed course 180 degrees. In his diary he wrote: 'So the murderers have won & the coward LG has gone down on his knees, & all his miserable Cabinet on their hunkers behind him.'[98]

Churchill had transferred his faith to a new Home Rule bill which he and Birkenhead had steered through Parliament. On December 23, 1920, the Government of Ireland Act became law, dividing Ireland into two states, the twenty-six counties of Eire and the six counties of Ulster, each of which would elect its own legislature. Eire's powers were to be greater than those provided in the 1914 bill, but defence, foreign affairs, and customs would remain in British hands. Winston, ever striving to unify the House, acclaimed the act as a 'gift,' not of one English political party, but 'the achievement of a coalition.' He considered it a turning point. So did the Orangemen. Eire did not. Southern Ireland went to the polls in May 1921, and of the 128 legislative candidates elected, 124 belonged to the Sinn Féin. They met in June, swore never to accept partition of Ireland, took a republican oath, elected Dé Valera president, and then voted themselves out of office. At this point a deus ex machina appeared in the form of George V. Opening Belfast's new parliament on June 22, the King appealed for an end to fratricidal strife. His sovereign's initiative forced Lloyd George to send De Valera a message via courier, suggesting negotiations. The leader of the Sinn Féin replied that they could meet only if it were agreed in advance that he, as a 'President,' was senior to Lloyd George, who was only a 'Prime Minister.' George indignantly refused, thereby dropping into De Valera's trap. The truce broke down and the killing resumed. Eire's people were weary, however. Even IRA members demanded an end to the bloodshed. The Tans had thinned the ranks of their battalions, and the survivors begged for at least a glimmer of relief. When Lloyd George offered again in October to negotiate, therefore, De Valera yielded slightly. The message had invited him to discuss how 'the British Empire can be best reconciled with Irish National aspirations.' He answered: 'The Irish Republic would be glad to discuss this question with the Community of Nations known as the British Empire.' Himself would never go to London, but he agreed to send his two most trusted lieutenants, Arthur Griffith, founder of the Sinn Féin, and Michael Collins, until then known in England only as a notorious IRA gunman.[99]

Churchill also yielded a little. Speaking in Dundee on September 24, he said that the establishment of 'a separate foreign Republic in Ireland' was out of the question; it would bring 'certain war – real war, not mere bushranging' between Eire and England, which would mean that 'every Irishman in the British Empire would become an alien enemy, and would be in exactly the same position as the unfortunate Germans who were in this country during the Great War.' The threat of Armageddon was his stick. His carrot was something Eire had never been offered before: partial dominion status, putting Eire almost on a par with Canada, Australia, New Zealand, and South Africa. Britain, he said, could do no more. The Irish delegates must realize that. 'Squander this conference,' he said, 'and peace is bankrupt.' *The Times* commented: 'The country will be grateful to MR CHURCHILL for the breadth and lucidity of his speech . . . whether men agree with him or not, MR CHURCHILL's able and calm review of the situation helps to restore confidence.'[100]

On the morning of October 11, Collins and Griffith were cordially welcomed at No. 10 and introduced to the cabinet across an unusually wide table – Lloyd George had anticipated that some of his ministers would refuse to shake hands with men they regarded as murderers. Churchill did not share that view. He knew the Irish delegates were brave men, and to him courage was admirable in itself. Collins in particular attracted him. He and Winston were, in fact, alike in many ways: fearless, charismatic, fiercely patriotic, ready to sacrifice everything for principle. Both had cherubic features but bulldog expressions, and they shared a ready wit. 'Winston and Michael Collins appear to fascinate each other and are bosom friends,' wrote the amazed Stanley Salvidge. Their friendship grew; after a day of exhausting deliberations, Winston would take his recent enemy home and sit up late, talking, arguing, drinking, even singing. Later he recalled one evening when Lloyd George and Griffith were also there. 'It was at a crisis,' he wrote, 'and the negotiations seemed to hang only by a thread. Griffith went upstairs to parley with Mr Lloyd George alone. Lord Birkenhead and I were left with Michael Collins meanwhile. He was in his most difficult mood, full of reproaches and defiances, and it was very easy for everyone to lose his temper. "You hunted me day and night!" he exclaimed. "You put a price on my head!" "Wait a minute," I said. "You are not the only one." And I took from my wall the framed copy of the reward offered for my recapture by the Boers. "At any rate it was a good price – £5,000. Look at me – £25 dead or alive. How would you like that?" ' Another time he slyly produced a thumbnail appraisal of himself which Collins had written: 'Will sacrifice all for political gain . . . Inclined to be bombastic. Full of ex-officer jingo or similar outlook. Don't actually trust him.' There was a moment of silence; then both men burst into laughter.[101]

Collins trusted him now, but it was Churchillian charm which kept them together, for Winston had no intention of giving much more ground. He still believed that eventually 'Ulster will join herself with Southern Ireland . . . the national unity of Ireland within the British Empire will be attained,' and he would make no concession which might jeopardize that dream, although, of course, he could not repeal the 1920 act. England, he insisted, must keep its two naval bases in the south, at Queenstown and Berehaven. Eire would be permitted no navy. Neither could it remain neutral in any future war: 'The position of absolute neutrality would have been a great difficulty to Britain in the late war. We could not have used your ports as bases from which to defend ourselves against submarine attack.' All men elected to Eire's parliament must take an oath to the King. He told Collins, and then the House: 'We do not recognize the Irish Republic.' Instead, southern Ireland would be known as the Irish Free State, or, in Gaelic, Saorstát Eireann. The Crown would be represented by an officer 'to be appointed in like manner as the Governor General of Canada,' and the Free State would assume responsibility for a share of Britain's national debt. Collins and Griffith won some points – Eire could raise an army and arm vessels to protect Irish fishermen – but they were few. Nevertheless, the Irishmen signed the treaty in the first week of December. Churchill had warned them that if they didn't, England would invade Eire, and Lloyd George had backed him up. Both sides were taking risks. As he put down his pen, Birkenhead said: 'I may have signed my political death warrant tonight.' But for once FE did not have the last word. Collins said softly: 'I may have signed my actual death warrant.' There was a long moment of silence. They realized that he had meant it. To ease Collins's reception in Dublin, Churchill raised a sensitive issue with the cabinet the following morning. He pointed out that several Sinn Féiners had been convicted of murder and sentenced to hang. 'Winston,' Jones noted, 'suggested that the Irish should be informed privately that the extreme sentence will not be carried out.' It was approved; officials were instructed to quietly assure 'prisoners now lying under sentence of death that the death penalty will not be enforced.'[102]

None of this reconciled De Valera, who immediately repudiated the pact, or die-hard Tories, particularly the Orangemen, to whom the Free State was anathema. Ulster's Unionists were furious at the government for even holding conversations with the men from Eire. Carson charged that Northern Ireland had been used as a 'puppet' in a 'political game.' He denounced each of the ministers in turn, coming down particularly hard on Curzon, who, he felt, had betrayed him. Churchill rose the following day to defend the treaty. He pointed to 'a remarkable phenomenon.' Yesterday Curzon, who had signed it, had been damned by Carson 'with brilliant and corrosive invective' as a traitor to Britain. In Dublin, at that hour, De Valera had been excoriating Collins 'for a similar offence.' Churchill asked: 'Are we not getting a little tired of all this? These absolutely sincere, consistent, unswerving gentlemen, faithful in all circumstances to their implacable quarrels, seek to mount their respective national war horses, in person or by proxy, and to drive at full tilt at one another, shattering and splintering down the lists, to the indescribable misery of the common people and to the utter confusion of our Imperial affairs.' The rest of the United Kingdom was ready, if they were not, to close the door on the 'grim, grave, and in many cases, shocking realities' of the past. 'Ireland,' he said, 'is not a daughter State. She is a parent nation. The Irish are an ancient race. Intermingled with the whole life of the Empire,' they were needed to sustain it, particularly in its new acquisitions. The time had come, indeed it was past time, to resolve the island's internal quarrel: 'If we can free ourselves from it, if we can to some extent reconcile the spirit of the Irish nation to the British Empire in the same way that Scotland and Wales have been reconciled, then indeed we shall have secured advantages which may well repay the trouble and the uncertainties of the present time.'[103]

The House, convinced, swiftly ratified the agreement. Across St George's Channel, however, De Valera remained intractable. Dominion status and, particularly, taking the hated oath were unacceptable to him. He would settle for nothing less than a republic. The Sinn Féin split on the issue – a schism mirrored today in Eire's two major parties, the Fianna Fáil and the Fine Gael – but the men elected to the Dáil took their seats. Griffith and Collins persuaded a majority that these were the best terms they could get, and on January 9, 1922, they approved the Free State treaty by a slim margin, 64 to 57. De Valera resigned, sought reelection, and lost by an even thinner margin, 60 to 58. Griffith replaced him, with Collins elected chairman of a provisional government which would serve until the next general election, to be held as soon as possible. 'So Ireland has decided!' a friend in Cairo wrote to Churchill. 'Now I hope we shall not leave a soldier or penny there & we shall see some pretty doings!' Winston could not be so gay. At Lloyd George's request, he now moved to stage centre, guiding legislation transferring powers to Dublin through the House, and becoming 'a principal,' in his words, 'in British-Irish affairs.' During the interim he would be responsible to three constituencies, in Parliament Square, O'Connell Street, and Ulster Hall. He assured the House: 'We have not given complete Dominion Home Rule. There are special reservations in this Treaty.' The situation across St George's Channel was even more delicate. At Christmas he had said: 'Should the Dáil ratify, the first step should be to get an Irish delegation . . . over here at the earliest moment.' But priorities had shifted. The overriding question now was the survival of the Griffith-Collins government. De Valera had gone underground again and plunged the Free State into civil war. Homes were again being burned, trucks hijacked, warehouses emptied, trains destroyed, and bridges and viaducts blown up. 'Traitors to the republic' were being 'executed' by IRA veterans whom De Valera had christened his 'Irregulars.' On the last day of March, when the Free State bill became law, a column of Irregulars swept through Dublin, killing a Protestant policeman and four Catholics and wounding three Catholic children. De Valera declared that both the Dublin and Belfast governments were illegitimate. Thugs prevented Collins from addressing a crowd in county Mayo. Sir Henry Wilson wrote on April 3: 'Valera is daily strengthening, & Collins daily weakening. Collins at Castlebar was ordered to stop speaking and obeyed! We are coming near the Republic.'[104]

In the House, Wilson, who was retiring as chief of the general staff to become Northern Ireland's chief defence adviser, had become the new spokesman of Ulster's MPs. He and Churchill duelled hotly. Winston ridiculed the very idea of self-government in southern Ireland. Winston said: 'It is, I think, too soon to mock or jeer. Two months ago it was too soon to rejoice. It is still too soon to lament.' Macready wrote from Dublin Castle: 'The optimistic imagination of Mr Winston Churchill, that the acceptance of the treaty would result in cessation of disturbance and a loyal interpretation of its terms, is by no means shared by the Crown forces in Ireland.' Actually, Winston's private thoughts were far from optimistic. He told Clementine: 'The Irish position seems very dark and troubled.' He wrote to Collins and Griffith, complimenting them on 'the spirit and personal courage which you have constantly shown in confronting the enemies of free speech and fair play,' and he began shipping guns and ammunition to Free State forces in Clare, Sligo, Athlone, and Dublin. Collins, crossing to London, submitted grievances about trouble-makers entering the Free State from Ulster. Churchill was already negotiating countless questions of border demarcation with Belfast, trying, as he told the House, to free England 'from the terrible curse of this long internal Irish quarrel.' In a confidential note to Alfred Cope, the assistant under secretary for Ireland, he asked: 'Do you think there is any fighting quality in the Free State Government? Will anybody die for it or kill for it?' In dealing with Irish politicians, he had learned, tact was a prerequisite. His customary broadsword would not do. The cabinet instructed him to send Collins a formal note expressing its concern over the confusion in Eire. 'Instead of this,' he wrote to Collins, knowing that formality would strike the wrong note, 'I write to you man to man.' Again and again Wilson and his followers tried to shake his confidence in the Irish signers of the treaty. In the House one of them asked him 'whether the British authorities in Ireland have evidence of some forty-one orders for assassination which were signed by Mr Michael Collins.' Winston snapped: 'No sir, and I regret that the hon[ourable] Gentleman should have placed such a question.' Trust in Collins and Griffith was an absolute necessity; it was that or land a British army, which at the moment did not exist, on Free State soil. Winston knew his political situation was shaky. The Conservatives, out of power for sixteen years, had become reckless and irresponsible. Liberals and Labour MPs, as he wrote in *The Aftermath*, 'watched with tender solicitude' while he fought for implementing legislation, trying to 'nurse into being' a strong Belfast government.[105]

He pushed Collins as hard as he could. Learning that IRA men of all convictions were planning to meet, and that they would consider renunciation of the treaty, he put him on notice: 'An adverse decision by the convention of the Irish Republican Army (so-called) would . . . be a very grave event at the present juncture. I presume that you are quite sure there is no danger of this.' In reality Collins could be quite sure of very little. A band of Irregulars had occupied Dublin's Four Courts – its law buildings – and he hadn't ordered them evicted because he wasn't certain he would be obeyed. On May 20 startling news reached the Colonial Office from one of Winston's friends in Dublin. Collins and De Valera had met on neutral ground and signed a pact, agreeing that Free State men would have sixty-four seats in the new Dáil and the Irregulars fifty-seven, thus preserving the existing ratio, and that after the election Eire would be governed by a coalition of five Free Staters and four Irregulars. 'The Irish masses,' Churchill tartly wrote afterwards, 'just like the Russians two or three years before, were not to be allowed a voice in their fate.' Churchill's informant had told him that Collins was beginning to have doubts about the agreement, however, and a confrontation might 'make him break down.' Winston wrote to Collins: 'I had better let you know at once . . . that as far as we are concerned in this country, we should certainly not be able to regard any such arrangement as a basis on which we could build.'[106] Half abashed and half mutinous, Collins arrived in London with Griffith and

William Cosgrave, another Free State leader, and tried to explain the inexplicable: that in Ireland's present chaos, any measure, however makeshift, was preferable to ravagement and slaughter. But Churchill had no time for them just then. He was rushing to the House to battle their real English adversaries. At No. 10 the three Irishmen were given tickets to the Strangers' Gallery, and they watched his fight from there.

Hardly had he reached the Treasury Bench when Sir Henry Wilson challenged him. What, he asked angrily, were the British troops in Dublin doing? 'They are not there to keep order,' he answered himself, 'because they are not allowed to keep order.' Winston tried to speak, but Wilson overrode him, shouting another question: Were not the colonial secretary's reports to the House 'from end to end an admission that every single development of the Irish problem has been miscalculated?' In replying, Churchill reassumed a fighting stance. His militant moves to suppress the Curragh mutiny eight years earlier were, he knew, remembered by almost all the MPs present. Now he had to convince them that he could be as stern with Eire as he had been with Ulster then. He said: 'We shall not under any circumstances agree to deviate from the Treaty either in the strict letter or the honest spirit.' Should an Irish coalition attempt to destroy it 'by setting up a Republic, it would be the intention of the Government to hold Dublin as one of the preliminary and essential steps in military operations.' He was confident he could mobilize enough veterans of the trenches to hold the city. Shipments of munitions to the provisional government had been stopped, he said, to avoid the possibility that they might be used later against Englishmen. The outcome of the election, now scheduled for June 16, would go far towards clarifying the situation. Wilson, unreassured, lashed back: 'The Colonial Secretary says we can wait. Can we? All this time murders are going on at the rate of . . . six or seven a day.' Winston demurred: 'I think there were only three or four murders in southern Ireland in the last ten days. The number has been larger in Northern Ireland.' Wilson pressed him again: 'My point is, can you wait while men are murdered like that?'[107]

It was not only men, of course. After the House rose Collins showed Winston a photograph of an entire family of Catholics, the McMahons, who had just been massacred in Ulster. According to Frank O'Connor, Collins's biographer, 'Churchill wept.' The Troubles were worsening. The Free State's provisional government was losing control of the country. Collins acknowledged it, and said he understood Churchill's threat to draw England's sword. De Valera was defiant: 'Mr Churchill's threats do not affect us. We deny the right of any English authority to prescribe what an Irishman shall or shall not do.' But Churchill wrote to Clementine: 'Our position is a vy strong one, so long as we adhere to the Treaty. And Ulster's position is a vy strong one so long as she respects the law. I have made it clear I will defend or conceal no irregularities of any kind. I will expose them coldly to Parliament whoever is guilty. We must not get back into that hideous bog of reprisals, from which we have saved ourselves.'[108]

All through that spring the horrors of internecine strife clotted in suffering Eire. Haemorrhaging within as IRA Irregulars fought the Free State, its battered people faced the growing possibility of intervention by Britons and Orangemen. The frontier disputes loomed ever larger. Lloyd George wrote to Churchill that he had conducted the negotiations with 'skill and patience,' but he was 'profoundly disquieted by the developments on the Ulster border. We are not merely being rushed into a conflict, but we are gradually being manoeuvred into giving battle on the very worst grounds which could possibly be chosen for the struggle. I cannot say whether Henry Wilson and De Valera are behind this but if they are their strategy is very skilful.' He suspected the Orangemen of planning to incite violence and warned against encouraging them to believe they might be reinforced by Englishmen: 'We have surely done everything that Ulster can possibly expect to ensure its security.' Churchill agreed, but he pointed out that Belfast's fears were not entirely unjustified. He could not discount the danger that the factions in southern Ireland might unite to invade the smaller state in the north. During one of Collins's calls at the Colonial Office, Winston told him that 'if any part of the Irish Republican Army, either pro-Treaty or anti-Treaty, invaded Northern soil, we would throw them out.' In point of fact he contemplated the use, not of troops, but of warships. In a memorandum he wrote: 'The effect of a blockade would not starve the Irish people, but it would at a stroke ruin their prosperity. Out of 205 millions exported from Ireland last year, 203 were purchased by Great Britain. This fact alone is decisive.'[109]

Once more he was captivated by the possibilities of force: deep within him lurked the imaginative child who had played with toy soldiers in his Mayfair nursery. If he meant to stiffen Collins's spine, however, it was unnecessary. The man was a paradigm of valour. And in the end Winston knew it, knew that Collins was not only the best but the only alternative to De Valera, who, in Winston's words, had 'come to personify not a cause but a catastrophe.' Reversing the policy he had presented to the House, he instructed Cope to resume consignments of weapons to Dublin, drawing 'arms from the British Government, which has a large surplus.' He added: 'I am quite ready to continue the steady flow of arms to trustworthy Free State troops.' Collins was constantly commuting between Ireland and England, sleeping in deck chairs, electioneering at home and drawing up Eire's constitution with Churchill and Colonial Office advisers. Confirming Winston's faith in him, he agreed to constitutional changes which could only sharpen the conviction of IRA hard-liners that he had turned his coat. The King would be invested with the formalities of executive power in the Free State; judges would be nominated by the governor-general; any constitutional amendment conflicting with the treaty would be void. These provisions would not, however, be published until the early hours of election day. Shaking Churchill's hand as he left

London, Collins said, 'I shall not last long. My life's forfeit, but I'll do my best. After I'm gone it will be easier for the others. You'll find they will be able to do more than I can do.' It was his valediction. Winston, profoundly moved, stammered a quotation from Johannes Brand, a pro-British Boer who had helped him hammer out the terms of peace in South Africa: '*Alles zal regt kom*' – 'All will come right.' Collins said he doubted it. He was right.[110]

But on Friday, June 16, he won a great victory. That morning De Valera, fulminating against the constitution's final draft, told reporters: 'As it stands it will exclude from public service, and practically disenfranchise, every honest Republican. Its test code is as comprehensive against Republicans as the test acts of the Clarendon and Shaftesbury code against Catholics and dissenters in the reign of Charles II.' But most of southern Ireland's voters had never heard of Clarendon or Shaftesbury, and, more important, Irish republicanism, in the eyes of many, had been discredited by the crimes of the Irish Republican Army. When the ballots were counted that evening they showed that the people of Eire had elected 93 candidates committed to the treaty and only 35 Irregulars. The *New York Times* called the results 'a triumph for imperial methods of pacification.' De Valera, whose terrorism had nullified his pact with Collins, described it to a *Times* correspondent as a victory of 'outrage, murder, and massacre' and said ominously, 'England's gain is for the moment only.' Once his people discovered that they had chosen lackeys of 'Churchill's hate,' who dared 'blacken forever the fair name of this fair nation,' he said, Ireland would 'rise up and fling them from the positions they have usurped and dishonoured.'[111] One of his gunmen, Reginald Dunne, a member of the IRA's London branch, received orders to wreak vengeance for the lost election by striking at the heart of the British establishment. On Thursday, June 22, six days after the Free Staters had gone to the polls, Sir Henry Wilson donned his field marshal's uniform and unveiled a memorial to Britain's war dead in London's Liverpool Street Station. Returning to his Eaton Place home by the tube and then by taxi, he was mounting his steps when Dunne and another IRA man opened fire from behind a nearby hedge. Sir Henry's hand instinctively flew to his sword hilt, but they emptied their pistols into his chest and left him sprawled on the pavement, dying.

The killers were caught before they could escape Belgravia. Within an hour Churchill was standing beside Lloyd George at No. 10, staring down dumbly at the two pistols which, in his words, had 'drunk this loyal man's blood.' Scotland Yard collared an IRA Irregular carrying a list of prominent Englishmen marked for death. Churchill's name led it. All were assigned bodyguards and the public gallery in the House was closed. As young Randolph recalled later, he and his sister Diana returned from roller-skating in Holland Park that Thursday afternoon and 'found the house surrounded by policemen. Indoors all sorts of tough-looking men were running up and down the stairs, looking in cupboards, attics and cellars.' That night Winston told Clementine he would sleep in the attic. Erecting a metal shield between himself and the attic door, he waited till dawn, gripping a Colt revolver. After breakfast he ordered an armchair reinforced with steel, and for months he slept in it, the pistol in his lap. He was, he told his wife, ready to 'fight it out.' Norman Harding, an estate agent with whom he had made an appointment to see country properties, afterwards recalled joining him in the backseat of his automobile and remarking that it was 'the darkest car I have ever been in.' Churchill explained: 'Well, you see, it is armoured, and the windows are bullet resisting, and I have a loaded revolver.' Detective Thompson sat in the front seat. Introducing him, Winston said, 'He also has a revolver.' He then turned around, the agent later remembered, and 'slid back a small shutter and asked, "You see that car behind us?" Harding did, and counted three men in it. Churchill said, 'That car will accompany us ten miles out of town, and, on our return, will pick us up again and escort us back to the Colonial Office or to my home. I have had a number of threatening letters each week, some telling me the actual time and method of my death, and I don't like it.'[112]

After the assassination of Sir Henry a wave of rage against the Irish swept England. It scalded Churchill; Lady Wilson let it be known that no one who had negotiated the Free State treaty would be welcome at her husband's funeral. Bonar Law demanded that the government act. Churchill had to respond. On the Monday after the crime he stood in the well of the House and observed that IRA Irregulars, calling their post 'Headquarters of the Republican Executive,' still held out in Dublin's Four Courts. 'Their presence is a gross breach of the Treaty,' he said. 'If it does not come to an end . . . then it is my duty to say, on behalf of His Majesty's Government, that we shall regard the Treaty as having been formally violated, that we shall take no further steps to carry out or legalize its further stages, and that we shall resume full liberty of action in any direction that may seem proper and to any extent that may be necessary to defend the interests and the rights that are entrusted to our care.' In that gentler time this was the strongest diplomatic language he could use to goad the provisional government into action. Collins realized it. During the early hours of Wednesday morning he ordered the law buildings shelled. De Valera protested that 'soldiers of the Army of the Republic have been attacked by forces of the Provisional Government at the instigation of English politicians . . . in order to avert from themselves political consequences which they feared,' and Rory O'Connor, the leader of the embattled Irregulars inside the buildings, sent out a statement to the press charging that 'the enemy is the old enemy, England . . . Mr Churchill cracked the whip in his speech . . . when he ordered the Provisional Government to attack the Four Courts.' English soldiers, he said, were preparing to rush his position. Collins and Griffith scoffed at this: 'Statements that British troops are cooperating . . . are false and malicious. None but Irish forces, with the cooperation of citizens, who are loyally and enthusiastically supporting the Government, are engaged in putting down the disorderly element who attempt to tyrannize over the people and defy their will.' In London, Churchill announced: 'The Provisional Government is solely responsible for the operations . . . They have declined assistance except so far as equipment is concerned.'[113]

The operative sentence was the last one, and it gave the lie to the rest. Macready had secretly lent Collins a battery of fieldpieces and ammunition for them. Griffith later acknowledged that he and Collins had taken their cue from Winston; they knew he would move if they did not, and so 'finally we went on.' But the real significance of the cannonade, and the subsequent storming of the position by Collins's volunteers, was much larger than that. It was an answer to Winston's earlier question. Men *were* ready to fight for the Free State. On Friday they captured a corner of the Four Courts. The defenders, abandoning hope, set the buildings ablaze and then surrendered. O'Connor subsequently became the first of seventy-seven IRA men to be executed by Free State firing squads. Churchill cheered the Free Staters' militancy, their uncompromising justice, and the implications of their readiness to raze the law buildings: 'They have not even hesitated, in order to stamp out the armed resistance to the Treaty, to invade by force of arms, and to destroy as a result of their assault, even their own property.' Privately he wrote to Collins that he understood that this had been a 'terrible ordeal for you and your colleagues' but believed it 'indispensable if Ireland is to be saved from anarchy and the Treaty from destruction. We had reached the end of our tether over here at the same time as you had in Ireland. I could not have sustained another debate in the House of Commons on the old lines without fatal consequences to . . . the Treaty . . . Now all is changed. Ireland will be mistress in her own house, and we over here in a position to safeguard your Treaty rights and further your legitimate interests effectually.'[114]

Yet it was far from over. Indeed, the Irish tragedy was approaching another crisis. On August 12 the quiet Griffith, exhausted by the accumulated strain of the past two years and privately appalled by Collins's belligerence, dropped dead of a heart attack. 'How sad for Ireland,' Clementine wrote to Winston, 'is Arthur Griffith's death.' IRA Irregulars captured Dundalk that same day, but before the week was out they had been driven back. The Free State, backed by the population, was winning everywhere now. Then, at 7:30 P.M. on August 22, a band of De Valera's gunmen ambushed Collins and his convoy on a back road in county Cork, in a gulley called Bealnamblath, between Macroos and Bandon, and Collins was slain. He was thirty years old. Almost his last words were: 'Tell Winston we could never have done it without him.' The martyred hero was wrapped in the green flag for which he had sacrificed his life, and his keening mourners sang, to the tune of the 'Londonderry Air,' that most haunting of Irish songs, now, for him, a dirge:

> *Oh, darlin' boy, the pipes, the pipes are calling*
> *From glen to glen, and down the mountain side,*
> *The summer's gone and all the roses falling,*
> *It's you, it's you must go and I must bide.*
>
> *But come ye back when summer's in the meadow,*
> *Or when the valley's hushed and white with snow,*
> *It's I'll be here in sunshine and in shadow,*
> *Oh, darlin' boy, I love you, love you so!*

Ireland after Partition

ATLANTIC OCEAN

ULSTER

Londonderry

TYRONE Belfast

FERMANAGH

Dundalk

CONNACHT

IRISH

Galway

FREE

Dublin

LEINSTER

STATE

IRISH SEA

MUNSTER

Cork

Bandon

ST. GEORGE'S CHANNEL

G.W.WARD

Churchill wrote: 'The presentiment of death had been strong upon him for some days, and he only narrowly escaped several murderous traps . . . His funeral was dignified by the solemn ritual of the Roman Catholic Church and every manifestation of public sorrow. Then Silence. But his work was done. Successor to a sinister inheritance, reared among fierce conditions and moving through ferocious times, he supplied those qualities of action and personality without which the foundation of Irish nationhood would not have been reestablished.' Cosgrave became president, with Kevin O'Higgins as his field commander. Ireland, said O'Higgins, presented 'the spectacle of a country bleeding to death, of a country steering straight for anarchy, futility, and chaos.' Then O'Higgins, too, was trapped and slain by IRA gunmen.[115]

It was a scowling year in Eire's history, but the Irish have a genius for transforming squalor into nobility. Early in the treaty negotiations Churchill had come to know, and dislike, Erskine Childers, a fervent nationalist now remembered for his classic suspense story *The Riddle of the Sands*. Childers threw in his lot with De Valera's Irregulars and became a killer of Free Staters. When he was caught and sentenced to die, Winston, in a rare moment of vindictiveness, publicly expressed satisfaction over the fate of this 'mischief-making, murderous renegade and malicious hater.' On the eve of his death Childers wrote, 'I feel what Churchill said about my "hatred" and "malice" against England is untrue . . . I die loving England, and praying that she may change completely, and finally towards Ireland.' Learning later that Childers had fought gallantly against the Germans in the Cuxhaven raid of New Year's Day, 1915, Winston issued a retraction, calling him a man of 'distinction, ability, and courage' who had died 'with the utmost composure.'[116]

In October the Dáil adopted the constitution, as drafted by Collins, Griffith, and Churchill. The Free State was then admitted to the League of Nations. After protracted deliberations, the boundary with Ulster was settled. The IRA was outlawed by the men who had served in it. De Valera was captured, imprisoned, freed; agreed to take the oath, lost election after election, and finally, ten years after Collins's murder, striking a deal with Labour deputies, became president. Ultimately his pitiless will prevailed; seeing his chance when the Empire was transformed into the Commonwealth, he proclaimed the Free State's sovereignty, the penultimate step towards republicanism, in 1937. That year Churchill, remembering Collins, Griffith, and their bright dreams of an enduring bond between Britain and the Free State, wrote sadly that 'Ireland, by paths eventually far more disastrous than those which then seemed open, has gained the power to manage or mismanage her own affairs, and lost the power to manage or mismanage those of the Empire.'[117] In 1922 he had dared hope for more, though even then he knew that he and his party would pay a political price for the tumultuous events of that summer. Before the year was out he had found it higher than he had expected.

Other political reverses were the collapse of Britain's postwar boom, the triumph of the Bolsheviks, and dismay over what was regarded as recklessness in the Dardanelles. Martin Gilbert writes that 'in the public mind it was widely believed, not only that both Churchill and Lloyd George had hoped for war with Turkey, but also that they had been disappointed when it was averted.' They had also offended the coalition's Tories, who had been shocked by Churchill's failure to consult Curzon, the foreign secretary, before appealing for Empire troops to fight for Chanak. This slight had in fact been a grave breach of decorum, and for many it was the last straw. Two senior statesmen, one from each of the two major parties, came out of retirement to register their disapproval. Asquith complained of slipshod diplomacy by 'amateurs in Downing Street.' Then Bonar Law denounced the entire Turkish affair in a letter to *The Times*. It was wrong, he wrote, 'to show any hostility or unfairness' towards the leading Moslem power, and irresponsible to do so without French support. 'We cannot act alone,' he said, 'as the policeman of the world.' In those ten words Law wrote an epitaph for the Empire's golden era, and it says much about the 1920s that no one saw it as such.[118]

In the opinion of many, Lloyd George and his cabinet had won the war but lost the peace. It was remarked upon that the prime minister's role at Versailles had been lacklustre, and he was blamed for the fact that the membership of the League of Nations, in which so much hope had been invested, did not include the United States, Germany, and Russia. A few Conservative ministers – notably Birkenhead and Austen Chamberlain – remained loyal to George. The others were restless. Critics of the prime minister were appearing on all sides, partly because he had unwisely abandoned the custom of consulting Parliament before taking action. Harold Laski wrote: 'He seems determined to sacrifice upon the altar of his private ambition the whole spirit of our public life.' *The Times* declared that the word of England had 'lost currency throughout the greater part of the world as the word of an upright land.' Francis Williams observed that the coalition had 'produced at the centre an atmosphere more like an oriental court at which favourites struggled unceasingly for position than anything seen in Britain for a century or more.' It moved Sir Edward Grey 'to indignation and despair such as I have never felt about any other British Government.' After a weekend with Lloyd George, Austen Chamberlain, and Birkenhead, Arnold Bennett noted: 'I never heard principles or the welfare of the country mentioned.' Leo Amery later recalled that Conservatives 'felt that they no longer had any policy of their own, but were being dragged along in the wake of an erratic Prime Minister whom they once again profoundly distrusted, by a little group of their own leaders who had lost, not only their principles, but their heads.'[119]

It was Churchill's fellow Harrovian Amery, then parliamentary and financial secretary to the Admiralty, who organized what came to be known as the 'Revolt of the Under Secretaries,' inviting all Tory MPs to meet at the Carlton Club on October 19, 1922. The annual conference of the National Union of Conservative Associations was just a month away, and Tory back-benchers felt their seats were in jeopardy. Austen Chamberlain, then regarded as the party's emerging leader, thought it wrong to appease them; he said he intended 'to tell them bluntly that they must either follow our advice or do without us, in which case they must find their own Chief, and form a Government *at once*. They would be in a d—d fix.' He and Birkenhead counted heavily on the results, to be announced that day, of a by-election in Newport. The Tory candidate, running against the coalition, was expected to come in last. Bonar Law, opening the meeting, was contemptuous of Lloyd George's record. His old colleagues nodded in agreement, though only one cabinet minister rose to echo him. This was the shrewd, stolid, pipe-smoking Stanley Baldwin, president of the Board of Trade, who, at that time, was largely unknown to the general public. Baldwin introduced a resolution which would dissolve the coalition. His biographer writes that he had discovered 'a new eloquence; direct, conversational, monosyllabic: rising and falling without strain or effort between the homeliest humour and the most moving appeal.' It was the voice of the new England: uncomfortable with greatness, wary of excellence, indifferent to challenges abroad. Baldwin argued that although Lloyd George was a dynamic force, 'a dynamic force is a very terrible thing' – an appropriate debut for this evangelist of political mediocrity.[120] Then the stunning tally from Newport was announced. The Tory had won by 2,090 votes; the coalitions' man had come in a bad third. Upon learning this, the MPs in the Carlton Club voted, and to everyone's surprise the result was lopsided: 87 for the coalition, 187 against. Informed of the result, Lloyd George submitted his resignation at Buckingham Palace that same afternoon. Law formed a government and a general election was scheduled for November 15, 1922.

Churchill was flat on his back in a Dorset Square nursing home, undergoing an emergency appendectomy. He was widely blamed for the coalition's fall, and not only because of his controversial policies. His loyalty to Lloyd George was suspect. Seven months earlier George had received several letters suggesting that Winston was conspiring against him. Charles McCurdy, the coalition whip, wrote to him that 'Liberals are commencing to canvass the situation that would arise' if Churchill defected to the Tories. Another correspondent told him that Winston was plotting the formation of a new coalition, to be headed by Austen Chamberlain, with himself at the Exchequer. Max Beaverbrook warned him that Winston's 'tendency is all to the Right, and his principles are becoming more Tory. I am sure he would not fancy being shut up in a coop with you even for a short time because such collocation within a narrow circle would cloud his own brilliance in the light of your superiority.' If this sounds strange coming from one of Winston's friends, it can only be added that Beaverbrook was always a strange friend. His virtue was that when Winston was in desperate trouble, he rallied to his aid. He was a fair-weather adversary, a foul-weather ally.[121]

Winston's relationship with Lloyd George was more complicated, and had changed often. In their early days together, as radical reformers they had worked splendidly in tandem. After Winston's eviction from the Admiralty in 1915 he believed that George had betrayed him; on June 9 that year he had written to Archie Sinclair that between him and George 'tout est fini.' When George moved into No. 10, Winston had fumed because no place had been found for him in the coalition cabinet; and in the spring of 1917 he had assailed the prime minister for his 'undue love of the assertion of arbitrary power' – an odd charge from one whose own thirst for authority was unslakable. Installed as minister of munitions, he had put this enmity behind him. By 1921 he believed that George would make him the next chancellor of the Exchequer. Then, during his absence in Palestine, George had bypassed him. Austen Chamberlain had written to his sister: 'Winston has come back from the Middle East as cross as a bear with a sore head & thinks that all the world is out of joint since he is not C/E.' Beaverbrook believed he had 'just grounds for his hostility.' The editor of the *Daily Mail* reported to Lord Northcliffe: 'Winston is fed up with Lloyd George. He wanted to be Chancellor but Ll G refused to give him the job. Winston holds it is not compatible with his seniority . . . when he wants a little money.' Frances Stevenson noted that Churchill now wrote to her lover as ' "Dear Prime Minister" whereas it used to be "Dear Ll G," or "My dear David." ' Winston himself thought George's attitude towards him revealed 'a certain vein of amiable malice,' and he was infuriated when, in a November 1921 cabinet meeting, the prime minister taunted him about Gallipoli. Nevertheless, the old Welsh spellbinder could still work feats of magic on him. Lord Boothby recalls waiting in a hall while the two men were closeted for about an hour. Afterwards he asked Winston: 'How did it go?' Churchill said slowly: 'Within five minutes the old relationship between us was completely re-established. The relationship between Master and Servant. And I was the Servant.' He wrote to George: 'My interests as well as inclinations march with yours, & in addition there is our long friendship wh I so greatly value . . . I wd gladly at your side face political misfortune.'[122]

Churchill faced it now, though he was slow to grasp his peril. He proudly wrote that 'the session of 1922 was the most prosperous I have ever had as a Minister in the House of Commons.' And others agreed. Clement Attlee later recalled: 'I learned in that Parliament of 1922 what a master he was in the art of answering Parliamentary Questions. He could deliver a knock-out blow or give the retort courteous with equal facility . . . One never could anticipate just what line he would take, except that it would generally be effective.' After the Irish debate of May 31, Austen Chamberlain had written to the King of 'Mr Churchill's great and growing parliamentary qualities,' commending 'to Your Majesty's particular attention a speech faultless in manner and wording, profoundly impressive in its delivery and of the first consequence as a statement of policy. It gripped the attention of the House from the opening sentences and held it, breathlessly intent, to the end.' On February 8 Winston had decided to address the House extemporaneously about Iraq – he had not tried speaking without notes in eighteen years – and afterwards he wrote to Clementine: 'It was really a great success: no worry, nor work, but quite an agreeable experience . . . I think I have really got my full freedom now in debate, and I propose to make far less use of notes than ever before.' He had learned to be savage in the attack and, in the next moment, completely disarming. When the teetotal, American-born Lady Astor became the House's first woman MP, he paused in his address to refresh himself, saying, 'I think it is a great pleasure for the noble lady, the member for the Sutton division of Plymouth, to see me drinking water.' Afterwards in the smoking room he said: 'Nancy, when you first entered the House, I felt you had come upon me in my bath and I had nothing to protect me but my sponge.'[123]

But wit and oratorical pyrotechnics, though dazzling in Parliament, could not be readily translated into votes in a general election. Preoccupied with imperial and foreign issues, he had lost touch with the new, growing forces on the left. Churchill had not entirely lost his reforming zeal; he had wanted to see social legislation introduced. So had Lloyd George. But they had been

606

thwarted by the Tory dominance in the coalition. As a consequence, the Liberal party was being devoured by Labour, which, lacking membership in the coalition, had become its most effective opposition. British socialism brought out the worst in Churchill. When he saw red at public meetings – literally saw it, for hecklers waved red flags and drowned him out by stridently singing 'The Red Flag' – his instincts overcame his good judgement. In his view, the Labour party was a sinister strand in a Bolshevik rope braided to lynch England's political and social institutions. Therefore he stalked it, declaring that 'the enthronement in office of a Socialist Government would be a serious national misfortune such as has usually befallen great states on the morrow of their defeat in war.' It would, he predicted, turn all Britain into a 'bear garden.' He thought Labour's proposal to lend the Russians money confirmed him. Socialism, he said, would bring 'Government of the duds, by the duds, for the duds.' If England survived its misrule Labour would vanish 'unwept, unhonoured, unsung and unhung.' Behind its movement 'crouched the shadow of Communist folly and Bolshevik crime.'[124]

This was superb as obloquy. It was an effective antidote for his Black Dog. And it is arguable that he foresaw socialist egalitarianism – from the few who are rich to the many who are poor – as the decisive blow to leadership by a talented, privileged elite. Yet he recruited only a handful of converts. Even his wife urged him to take 'a less hostile and negative attitude' towards the socialists. When he insisted that they were mounting 'a great vehement, deliberate attack upon the foundations of society,' Baldwin replied that he simply didn't believe it. Asquith thought the socialist leaders should be given posts of responsibility, that excluding their party from power would only embitter them. Winston told Violet Asquith that he passionately disagreed. As a consequence, he became the bogeyman of the British left. Emmanuel Shinwell, a Labour MP, recalls: 'The mention of his name at Labour gatherings was the signal for derisive cheers; when a Labour speaker found himself short of arguments, he had only to say, "Down with Winston Churchill." This never failed to draw thunderous applause. Undoubtedly, he was our most valuable propaganda asset.' They distributed pamphlets describing 'Winston's Black Record.' Considered the chief obstacle to Labour's ambitions, he was, Shinwell recalls, 'the target for every epithet in the English language.' A Labour spokesman charged: 'Mr Churchill did all he could to maintain militarism in Europe and to march armies against Russia.' The *Daily Herald* denounced him for sending 'munitions which cost us over twenty million pounds sterling to produce' to Russian counterrevolutionaries, 'all of which has gone down the drain.' In another issue, the *Herald* declared that 'Churchill cannot see that the revolt in far-off costly and reactionary adventures grows into "turbulence" at home,' that he was 'utterly out of touch with public opinion, here as everywhere else.'[125]

It was true, and it was especially true in Dundee. Now, as in 1908 – when he

607

had jubilantly claimed it as his 'life seat' – Dundee was a two-member, working-class constituency of shipbuilding craftsmen, linen weavers, jute sackers, marmalade bottlers, and commercial bakers. But he had changed since then, and so had they. After four years of disillusionment and Labour blandishments the voters saw their most illustrious MP in a new light. Unemployment was high; they were concerned with bread-and-butter issues. Winston knew that. Earlier in the year he had advised the National Liberal Council that the party must back 'better social and industrial conditions for the people.' Workers, he said, 'must know that earnest effort will reap its own reward, that the cost of living will fall.' In a statement to the Dundee electorate, written in the nursing home bed where he was convalescing from his appendectomy, he vowed to provide improved public services, increases in unemployment compensation, and better housing. The Tories, he said, represented the antithesis of this: 'Mr Bonar Law has described his policy as one of negation. Such a message . . . will strike despair in the heart of every striver after social justice. It cannot be accepted by any generous-hearted man or woman . . . Over the portals of 10 Downing Street the new Prime Minister has inscribed his words: "Abandon hope ye who enter here." '126

Yet he had to temper his attacks on Tories. He had asked Dundee's Conservatives to support him as 'a Free Trader,' writing to them that 'the formidable socialist attack which is gathering' demonstrated 'the need for patriotic men and women of sincere goodwill to stand together.' He singled out his leftist opponents: 'A predatory and confiscatory programme fatal to the reviving prosperity of the country, inspired by class jealousy and the doctrines of envy, hatred and malice, is appropriately championed in Dundee by two candidates both of whom had to be shut up during the late war to prevent them from hampering the national defence.' The Labour vote, he warned those around him, 'will be a very heavy one.' The local Tories agreed to put up no candidate against him, and he ran on the coalition's record, charging that the Carlton Club rebellion was attributable to 'the fury of the Die-Hards at the Irish Treaty,' a settlement which nevertheless would 'live and prosper.' The Chanak crisis had been admirably resolved; 'I regard my association with it as one of the greatest honours in my long official life.' He supported Lloyd George, though his praise was oddly phrased: 'I am sure that among the broad masses of faithful, valiant, toiling, Britain-loving men and women whom he led to victory, there will still be found a few to wish him well.' But he turned again and again to his radical adversaries, Georges Morel-de-Ville, who had been endorsed by Labour, and William Gallacher, a Communist. Each had been a wartime pacifist; both were meat for Churchill. Morel-de-Ville, he declared, was a member of 'that band of degenerate international intellectuals who regard the greatness of Britain and the stability and prosperity of the British Empire as a fatal obstacle to their subversive sickness.' Of Gallacher, who had organized strikes in defence industries when Winston was minister of munitions, he said that he would be remembered for his 'crazy and ferocious outpourings' and 'long record of malignant if ineffectual blows' at the integrity and safety of England, though on the whole the 'crudity' of his speeches 'renders them less pernicious and certainly less harmful than the more slimy and insidious propaganda of his companion and comrade Mr Morel,' by which, of course, he meant that Morel was more popular in Dundee and therefore a greater threat at the polls.[127]

This was vintage Churchill, but though the words were the words of Winston, the voice was the voice of a party representative in Dundee. The incumbent was still confined to his bed in Dorset Square. His being hors de combat, a supporter wrote to him, 'has really been a disaster . . . in these critical days.' The press, here and throughout the country, was hostile to the coalition. Beaverbrook, an admirer of Bonar Law, was bankrolling Tory candidates in many constituencies where Lloyd George men were unopposed, thus splitting the anti-Labour vote and boosting the socialists' chances. In Dundee the two local newspapers, owned by D.C. Thompson, had come out against Churchill. Moreover, he was not the only Liberal candidate. Ever since Lloyd George's eviction of Asquith in 1916 the party had been divided into Asquithians and Georgians, and Asquith was fielding his own national slate. To Churchill's dismay and indignation, his old ally C.P. Scott of the *Manchester Guardian* supported Asquith's man in Dundee. Winston wrote to Scott, protesting 'wrecking and splitting candidatures between Liberals' and 'the pursuance of personal vendettas,' adding: 'I expect you are pretty well ashamed in your heart of hearts at the line your caucus is taking in its bitter malevolence.' But the *Guardian* continued to trumpet the virtues of the 'Independent Liberal,' although it became increasingly clear that he had no chance of winning.[128]

Winston asked his wife to stump the district for him during the last ten days of the campaign, and off she went, carrying her last baby – an 'unbaptized infant' as the Dundee *Courier* maliciously put it. Among the Churchill friends who had come to do their part was the former Edward Spiers, now Spears; he had changed the spelling of his surname in 1918. Spears watched women spit on Clementine and wrote: 'Clemmie's bearing was magnificent – like an aristocrat going to the guillotine in a tumbril.' Her first meeting was bedlam. In an unusual dirty trick, rival partisans filled the hall with sneezing powder, and both speaker and audience were convulsed. 'The meeting,' the delighted *Courier* reported, 'was in a state of uproar almost from the beginning to end.' Outside, as Clementine fled, a taunting mob waved red flags and green IRA banners. Putting a bright face on it, she wrote to Winston, 'Every rowdy meeting rouses sympathy & brings votes & will especially as you have been so ill. Even in the rowdiest foulest place all of the people tho' abusive were really good-natured.' The newspapers, she said, were '*vile*.' He was being called a warmonger, 'but I am exhibiting you as a Cherub Peace Maker with little fluffy wings round your chubby face.' She thought 'Smash the Socialists' was the wrong line to take. The Labour line was very convincing in Dundee, especially among the destitute, who were many: 'My darling, the misery here is appalling. Some of the people look absolutely starving. Morel's Election address just out *very moderate* & in favour of only constitutional methods. So one cannot compare him with Gallacher.' She felt 'the minute you arrive the atmosphere will change & the people will be roused . . . I am longing to see you & so is Dundee – I shall be heartbroken if you don't get in.' Clemmie gamely remounted the stump, was hissed, heard her husband described as the head of England's 'Fascisti party' – Mussolini had seized power in Rome the week before – and left, head high, a reporter wrote, when a meeting 'broke up in disorder.' Birkenhead arrived to help. She wished he hadn't. He assailed Morel on the peculiar ground that he was French. 'France is a very great country,' he said, 'and, on the whole, I like a man to stick to the country, particularly if it is a great one, in which he was born.' Clementine commented tartly: 'He was no use at all. He was drunk.'[129]

A very shaky Churchill arrived four days before the election and checked into Dundee's Royal Hotel. Sitting in a padded chair, he spoke that evening at the Caird Hall, defending the coalition, the Irish Free State, and Britain's 'unshaken and unshakable' position in the world. At the end he rose painfully and asked the voters to send 'a message which will resound far beyond the limits of this small island and carry its good cheer to the suffering, struggling, baffled humanity the wide world o'er.' This, according to one journalist, was followed by 'loud cheers.' But the Caird Hall audience was friendly; it had been carefully picked. Two days later his reception was very different. 'As I was carried through the yelling crowd of Socialists at the Drill Hall to the platform,' he later wrote, 'I was struck by the looks of passionate hatred on the faces of some of the younger men and women. Indeed, but for my helpless condition I am sure they would have attacked me.' They booed, hissed, and refused to let him speak. He managed to say: 'The electors will know how to deal with a party whose only weapon is idiotic clamour'; then, according to the *Courier*, 'pandemonium broke out anew.' His voice rose in brief snatches: '. . . if about a hundred young men and women in the audience choose to spoil the meeting – if about a hundred of these young reptiles . . . We will not submit to the bullying of the featherheads, we will not be ruled by a mob . . .' But in the end he did submit, telling the appalled platform party: 'I am finished.' Detective Thompson slept by his hotel door that night, pistol in hand. A champagne party was in progress across the hall. Spears later remembered that each time a cork popped, 'We thought it was Winston being shot.'[130]

In the morning Churchill was grim. Only a desperate candidate attacks the press, and it is a measure of his plight that he lashed out at the Dundee publisher, holding him up 'here in the district where he lives to the reprobation of his fellow citizens.' D.C. Thompson, he said, had subjected him to 'ceaseless detraction, spiteful, malicious detraction' and was 'narrow, bitter, unreasonable, eaten up with his own conceit, consumed with his own petty arrogance.' The poll was held on November 15, 1922. That morning Thompson managed, as publishers always do, to have the last word. His editorial described Winston as a man 'in a vile temper. He takes no pains to conceal the fact. Like the disappointed man on the station platform he kicks out at anybody who happens to be near him. He has sprayed Labour with invective, has sprinkled many doses of it upon his fellow candidates . . . and now he has turned the full blast of his vituperation upon the Dundee newspapers. Whose turn it will be tomorrow God only knows.'[131]

Dundee elected Morel-de-Ville and a Prohibitionist. Of 151,701 votes cast, Churchill received 20,466 – less than 14 per cent of the total. For the first time in twenty-two years, nearly thirteen of which had been spent in the cabinet, he was out of Parliament. He left Dundee at once, explaining that he 'was far from well.' In London he found himself, as he put it, 'without an office, without a seat, without a party, and without an appendix.' Replying to Stamfordham, who conveyed the King's regrets, he wrote: 'It was very trying, having to do three days of electioneering with a wound so newly healed: It was quite impossible for me to defend myself in so short a time. I have always held Dundee by speeches and argument and at least three weeks are required to deal with such a large number of electors.' T.E. Lawrence wrote to Eddie Marsh: 'I'm more sorry about Winston than I can say.' Lord Esher wrote to Sir Philip Sassoon: 'The women put Winston out. When he loses his temper, he looks so damned ugly.' A fellow guest at a dinner party, Lloyd George's former private secretary, noted that 'Winston was so down in the dumps he could scarcely speak the whole evening. He thought his world had come to an end – at least his political world. I thought his career was over.' The *Daily Mail* crowed: 'Mr Churchill has had as many lives as the proverbial cat, but the indictment against him is a long one.' The *Daily Telegraph*, although never his admirer, had a more charitable word: 'The House of Commons loses, for a time, its most brilliant and dazzling speaker . . . His is perhaps the most sensational defeat of the whole election.'[132]

That was saying a great deal. Nationally, the repudiation of the coalition had been overwhelming; 81 per cent of the electorate had gone to the polls, most of them to register disapproval of the government. The Tories had swept the country, winning 345 seats. Labour, with 142, was now the principal Opposition party. Lloyd George's 'National' Liberals had carried only 62; Asquith's Liberals, a mere 54. Neither man would ever hold office again. Asquith wrote to Venetia Montagu that he was 'inclined to gloat over the corpses on the battlefield,' but five-sixths of his candidates had gone down to defeat. Churchill was far from through; on the morrow after the returns he was offered a dozen seats, among them that of Spears, who had just been elected member for Loughborough. Winston replied that he was 'greatly touched by the extreme kindness of yr offer & the willing sacrifice that it involves. It is a splendid proof of yr friendship. I cd not accept it from you. I want you to enjoy yr seat in Parliament & I shall like to feel I have one or two friends there . . . The Whips will find me a seat if I want one; but what I want now is a rest.' Margot Asquith advised him to 'lie low' for a while, to 'do nothing in politics, go on writing all the time & painting; do not join yr former colleagues who are making prodigious asses of themselves in every possible manner: Keep friends in every port – lose *no* one . . . If you have the patience of Disraeli with your fine temper glowing mind & real kind unvindictive nature you cd still command a great future.' It was sensible advice, and Churchill took it. He decided to recuperate on the Riviera, renting a villa, Le Rêve d'Or, near Cannes, for the winter. The whole family joined him there for Christmas and New Year. He worked on his Admiralty memoirs. Paul Maze, the painter, encountered him on a beach and said: 'Well, Winston, I'm painting hard, trying to forget all about the war. What are you doing?' Churchill said he was writing a book on the war. Maze said that was 'like digging up a cemetery.' Winston replied: 'Yes, but with a resurrection.'[133]

His political resurrection was to be delayed again and again. But Margot had been right: This was a good time to be publicly invisible. Two years later he would write in the *Weekly Dispatch* that when the coalition government was dismembered 'it was already perfectly clear to many of us that a period of political chaos would ensue. To the best of my ability, I warned the public of what was in store. But nobody would listen. Everyone was delighted to get back to party politics. Dear to the hearts of all the small politicians were the party flags, the party platforms, the party catchwords. How gleefully they clapped their hands and sang aloud for joy that the good pre-war days of faction had returned!' He was glad to be out of it. In February 1923 he wrote: 'The weather here has been indifferent, but I am getting much better in myself.' His friends in the House missed him. One advised him the following month: 'Don't lie low too long. Things are in the "melting pot." LG is playing what *looks* like a good game but it isn't. Nobody trusts him . . . There can only be *two* parties. That is the line of country to ride. There are hundreds of thousands who won't vote at all at present. They have *no* party. But they are anti-labour . . . The passivity of the present Govt is beyond belief. They *settle* nothing.'[134]

Bonar Law, who had waited so long for power, was proving inept at No. 10. He had become prime minister, Philip Guedalla wrote caustically, 'for the simple and satisfying reason that he was not Mr Lloyd George. At an open competition in the somewhat negative exercise of not being Lloyd George that was held in November 1922, Mr Law was found to be more indubitably not Mr Lloyd George than any of the other competitors; and in consequence, by the mysterious operation of the British Constitution, he reigned in his stead.' Ill, he resigned after less than six months in office. After the fall of Austen Chamberlain, Curzon had been the favourite to succeed Law, but Baldwin, who was emerging as a master of intrigue, outmanoeuvred Curzon's supporters and moved into Downing Street in May 1923. The country's chief domestic problem was a million jobless Englishmen. The solution, Baldwin believed, was Joe Chamberlain's old nostrum – high tariffs. Law, however, had campaigned against them; his pledge could not be dishonoured. Therefore Baldwin dissolved Parliament and went to the country again in

November. Free Trade was the one issue which could reconcile the two wings of the Liberal party. It also brought Churchill back into public life. *The Times* had observed that he 'has latterly become more conservative, less from conviction than from a hardening of his political arteries. His early Liberal velleities have dried up, the generous impulses of youth throb more slowly, and apart from some intellectual gristle his only connections with Liberalism are personal.' That was close to the mark, but for Churchill a call for Free Trade was a summons to the colours, to the blazing idealism of his early years in the House. In a statement to the press he called it 'vital to the British people and indispensable to the recovery of their prosperity.' The future of a reunited party, he said, would know 'no limits.' On November 19 he accepted an invitation from the West Leicester Liberal Association to run as their candidate. The National Liberal Club removed his portrait from its cellar, dusted it off, and restored it to its place of prominence upstairs.[135]

West Leicester, east of Birmingham, was known for its manufacture of hosiery, boots, and shoes, and his Labour opponent, F.W. Pethick-Lawrence, was formidable. Pethick-Lawrence had proposed a 'Capital Levy,' a surtax on all Britons worth more than £5,000. Workmen thought it an excellent idea. Clementine was anxious; Winston had been offered several safe seats and – unwisely, she thought – had turned them down. Equally unwise, in her opinion, was any affiliation with Lloyd George. Churchill had accepted an invitation to dine with George at Beaverbrook's home. On the morning of the dinner she left a note on his dresser: 'I want to appeal to you again before you go to Max's this evening. Ll G is not in the same position as you – He is in not out & he shares or practically shares the throne with Asquith.' Word might get around, she wrote, that Winston was working towards a new coalition. She also wished he weren't running against a Labour aspirant. It would be much better, in her view, 'to be beaten by a Tory (which would rouse Liberal sympathy) than by a Socialist. My Darling it is important – I shall say *nothing* if you go, but consider the imprudence of losing the offer of a good Wee Free Seat (as opposed to extinct Nat[ional] Liberal) for the sake of a pleasant evening.' He went. Also, to his subsequent sorrow, he lunched with Beaverbrook at London's Embassy Club, where he wagered that Labour would not reach power within a year and that Asquith would move back into No 10. The club menu survives, with their handwriting: 'I bet £5 against Winston's £4 that Labour forms a government in 1924. M.B.' and 'I bet £15 against Winston's £5 that Asquith is NOT P.M. in 1924. W. Churchill. M.B.'[136]

In West Leicester, Churchill again faced a hostile press and wild, disorderly meetings. At one of them, the *Leicester Mail* reported, Winston and Clementine were 'greeted by groans and hoots, not a single cheer being heard in the building.' A gang of hecklers accompanied him wherever he went; he christened them the 'Socialist travelling circus.' One of Churchill's recent acquaintances, young, redheaded Brendan Bracken, scouted halls in advance and told him what to expect. The expectations were almost always the same – more trouble. Cecil Roberts, the prolific writer, afterwards remembered how 'hatred of him [Churchill] was aflame. No insults were too gross to hurl at him. One, of course, the Dardanelles fiasco, regarded as his particular crime, was always brought up.' Towards the end of a frustrating evening he shouted back: 'What do you know about that? The Dardanelles might have saved millions of lives. Don't imagine I am running away from the Dardanelles. I glory in it.' Douglas Jerrold, the official historian of the Royal Naval Division, arrived in Leicester on his own initiative to confirm him. Jerrold told a mocking mob: 'I venture to say that had the campaign been prosecuted as it should have been, with enthusiasm, courage, and energy, in the same spirit in which it was begun by Mr Churchill, the war would have ended in 1917.' Few listened; fewer believed him. It seemed Winston would wear that albatross around his neck for the rest of his life. An American publicist wrote that it was 'doubtful if even Great Britain could survive another world war and another Churchill,' and an English critic declared: 'The ghosts of the Gallipoli dead will always rise up to damn him anew in time of national emergency. Neither official historians, nor military hack writers, will explain away or wipe out the memories of the Dardanelles.'[137]

New bullyraggers appeared when he spoke in London. As he left one rally, a newspaperman reported, a 'vast crowd closed round the car hooting and jeering. Despite the vigilance of the police, one man broke through and smashed one of the windows of Mr Churchill's car. The police took him into custody. When this fact became known more booing ensued, and many people spat upon the car as it drove away.' At another meeting, in Walthamstow, 'What about the Dardanelles?' was joined by 'What about Antwerp?' A youth eluded mounted police and threw a brick at Winston. Others stood shaking their fists in impotent rage. Winston told an *Evening News* reporter that the Walthamstow mob was 'the worst crowd I have ever seen in twenty-five years of public life. They were more like Russian wolves than British workmen – howling, foaming and spitting, and generally behaving in a way absolutely foreign to the British working classes.' Meanwhile, Clementine, keeping the flame alight in West Leicester, answered a pest who shouted that her husband was unqualified to represent workmen. Except for Lloyd George, she said, Churchill had done more 'for the benefit of the working classes than any other statesman,' and she cited his Shop Hours Act, Coal Mines Regulation Act, Unemployment Insurance Act, and Sweated Industries Act. She added for good measure: 'A great many people think he is essentially a military man, but I know him very well, and I know he is not like that at all. In fact one of his greatest talents is the talent of peacemaking.'[138]

In his final Leicester speech he damned tariffs and the capital levy. Churchill, never comfortable on the defensive, kept trying to make the issue, not himself, but Tory protectionism and Baldwin's claim that he had called this election to avoid breaking Bonar Law's election promise. Winston cried: 'Who is Mr Baldwin to acclaim himself such a singularly honest man? He is a man whom we only know in the last few months through the eulogies of the newspapers. He has no achievements to his record. He is an unknown man.'

Unfortunately Labour, too, was against tariffs. And Labour now had a firm grip on this constituency. Pethick-Lawrence trounced Churchill, 13,634 to 9,236; the Tory, running third, polled 7,696. In Parliament the balance had shifted once more; Baldwin's Conservative strength had been reduced by 87 seats. The Tories now held 258, as against Labour's 191 and the Liberals' 158. Lloyd George deferred to Asquith, who declared that under no circumstances would he unite with the Tories to exclude Ramsay MacDonald, Labour's leader, from office. Alarmed, Churchill wrote to Violet Asquith that her father's position meant that there was 'no possibility of averting the great misfortune of a Socialist Government being formed.' On January 17, 1924, he issued a statement predicting that 'strife and tumults, deepening and darkening, will be the only consequence of minority Socialist rule.'[139] That was hardly fair, since Labour's chief objective at the time, the defence of Free Trade, was also his. His warning was unheeded anyhow; four days later, when Baldwin lost a motion of confidence, Asquith threw his support to MacDonald, who thereby rode off to the palace to become Labour's first prime minister. Beaverbrook had been right. The alliance was too unstable to last, but Winston felt betrayed by his party. Resuming his rightward march, he resigned from it, and the National Liberal Club put his portrait back in its basement.

Less than five weeks after MacDonald moved into No. 10, Churchill dined with Beaverbrook and Rothermere, Britain's two greatest press lords. They offered him, as he wrote to Clementine the following day, their 'full support' should he contest an imminent by-election in the Abbey division of Westminster. Westminster, the Conservatives' choicest preserve, included the Houses of Parliament, Buckingham Palace, the homes of at least a hundred MPs, the greatest concentration of celebrities in England, and, as he reminded her, Pall Mall, the Victoria Palace, 'Drury Lane theatre & Covent Garden!' There was a distinct possibility that the Conservative Association might endorse him. His wife, again wary, wrote back: 'Do not . . . let the Tories get you too cheap. They have treated you so badly in the past & they ought to be made to pay.' It seemed unlikely. After his Leicester defeat Austen Chamberlain had written to him: 'I am very sorry you are still out of Parl,' but welcoming him back into the Conservative party was another matter; according to Beaverbrook, Austen was now 'very frigid and said he would not support Churchill for Westminster until he repented in sackcloth and ashes for his Liberal past, and joined the Tories openly as a penitent convert.' That, of course, was even unlikelier. In the end the Association backed Captain Otho Nicholson, a nephew of the previous member. The *Evening Standard* found strong sentiment in the district for Winston to run as an independent, however, and on March 4 he announced that he would do just that, though he expanded his label to 'independent Anti-Socialist.' Significantly, he declared: 'My candidature is in no way hostile to the Conservative Party and its leaders. On the contrary, I recognize that the party must now become the main rallying ground for opponents of the Socialist Party.' Sir Philip Sassoon wrote to him:

'I am so glad you are standing. You are BOUND to get in.' Others were less pleased. Leo Amery declared: 'The menace of Socialism is not to be fought by negatives, however brilliantly phrased.' And Labour could not be counted out, even here. Its candidate charged that as war minister 'Mr Churchill did all he could to maintain militarism in Europe and to march armies against Russia. He wasted £100,000,000 of the taxpayers' money of this country – money sorely needed to deal with unemployment, housing etc – in mad, stupid, wicked and suicidal adventures.'[140]

A wealthy friend, James Rankin, converted his London home into Churchill's headquarters, and presently eminent canvassers were seen hurrying in and out: Sir Philip, Lord Darling, Sir Eric Geddes, Lord Rothermere's sole surviving son – the other two had been killed in France – and Winston's cousin the duke. Sunny went into Westminster's shabbier neighbourhoods, unselfconsciously tapping on dilapidated doors with his gold-headed stick. Bracken solicited support in nightclubs and brokers' offices, and even recruited campaigners among the girls at the Gaiety. Presently, as Churchill recalled afterwards, 'I began to receive all kinds of support. Dukes, jockeys, prize-fighters, courtiers, actors and businessmen, all developed a keen partisanship. The chorus girls of Daly's Theatre sat up all night addressing the envelopes and despatching the election address.' Arthur Balfour told Baldwin (who remained sphinxlike throughout the campaign) that he thought Amery's intervention had been unsportsmanlike. Balfour himself was seriously considering an endorsement of Churchill. H.A. Gwynne of the *Morning Post*, still Winston's sworn enemy, heard of this and rushed to Baldwin, urging him to forbid support of Churchill by ex-ministers – to be 'strong and ruthless, if necessary.' That enraged Balfour, who promptly wrote Winston an open letter expressing his 'strong desire' to see him win and use his 'brilliant gifts' in Parliament. 'Your absence from the House of Commons,' he concluded, 'is greatly to be deplored.' Two dozen other Tories then declared for Winston. Inevitably, all this drew fire from the socialists, with the odd result that the Tory favourite in a Tory district was largely ignored. Fenner Brockway, the Labour aspirant, concentrated all his fire on Churchill, who, he said, had 'previously charged Labour with setting class against class. It is he who is now the chief exponent of a class war. He raised the bogy of Socialism, and seeks to combine all the selfish and vested interests who fear the onward march of Labour . . . Of all the politicians Mr Churchill has shown himself most unfit for the responsibility of government. His forte is to be a disturber of the peace, whether at home or abroad. He is a political adventurer, with a genius for acts of mischievous irresponsibility. He is militant to his finger-tips . . . Mr Churchill's record shows him to be a public danger and a menace to the peace of the world.' But as a polemicist Brockway was no match for Winston, who scorned Ramsay MacDonald's indifference towards the Dominions, particularly his proposal to abandon Singapore, which Australia and New Zealand regarded as essential to their defence, while dealing generously with the Russians. Churchill cried: 'Our bread for the Bolshevik serpent; our aid for foreigners of every country; our favours for Socialists all over the world who have no country; but for our own daughter States across the oceans, on whom the future of the British island and nation depends, only the cold stones of indifference, aversion, and neglect. That is the policy with which the Socialist Government confronts us, and against that policy we will strive to marshal the unconquerable might of Britain.'[141]

Churchill's public appearances were marked by the usual commotion. Winifred Holtby, a critical observer who had never seen him before, wrote to a friend of how he dealt with it. His solution was confrontation: 'He really and truly points an accusatory finger at the crowd, and cries in sepulchral tones, "I say that if another war is fought, civilization will perish." (Laughter. A sweeping gesture.) "A man laughs," (out goes the finger). "That man dares to laugh. He dares to think the destruction of civilization a matter for humour!" Indeed, he is such a preposterous little fellow, with his folded arms and tufted forelock and his Lyceum Theatre voice, that if one did not detest him one might love him from sheer perversity.' Set speeches, however, were a greater problem. Here, as when he had been challenged by prewar suffragettes, he was vulnerable. During his final address, in the Victoria Palace, *The Times* reported that 'the candidate was subjected to much interruption, the main burden of which consisted of remarks on Gallipoli and taunts by women about "murder in Ireland."'[142]

Churchill closed on an elegiac note, describing how the British Empire, 'so powerful and splendid but a few years ago,' was now, under a Labour government, 'almost ready to apologize for our very existence, ready to lay down our burden in any one of the great Oriental countries if a stick be shaken by any irresponsible chatterbox.' The constituency voted the following day, March 10. After the first hurried tally someone shouted to Winston: 'You're in by a hundred.' His followers cheered. But the shouter was premature. The official results gave him 8,114 against Nicholson's 8,187 – a difference of exactly 73 – with Brockway a close third. The Labour candidate was watching Churchill at this moment of chagrin. 'He began to tramp the length of the hall,' Brockway later wrote in *Inside the Left*, 'head down, body lurching, like a despairing animal.'[143]

In writing of Jellicoe's three lost opportunities to destroy the German fleet at Jutland, Churchill said: 'Three times is a lot.' That is equally true of three lost elections. At *The Times*, Geoffrey Dawson, later to become an archpriest of appeasement, sourly wrote of Winston's Westminster checkmate: 'The features of his late campaign that attracted legitimate criticism were his ill-timed insistence on sheer anti-Socialism as the paramount claim on the electors at this moment, and the impulse that drove him, holding these views, to jeopardize a seat which without him was at least anti-Socialist. It is no new thing, after all, to discover that judgement is not the most conspicuous of Mr Churchill's remarkable gifts.' House wags talked of organizing a dinner for the MPs who had beaten him at the polls. He had lacked a seat for nearly a year and a half now. His principal achievement had been the alienation of the socialists, in whose eyes, according to Shinwell, his 'crowning sin was the fatuous declaration that Labour was unfit to govern, an accusation that gave the greatest offence to members of the Labour party.'[144]

Churchill's refusal to accept the socialists as legitimate heirs to the fading Liberals was undoubtedly crippling; so was his scorn for the second-rate politicians, led by Baldwin, who had seized the leadership of the Conservative party. Yet in neither case could he have done otherwise and remained true to himself. He had always despised socialism, supporting welfare legislation which would deprive Labour candidates of social issues, and he would do so again. On a more profound level, as the tribune of excellence he was baffled by the hostility to brilliance which was, perhaps, the most striking feature of Britain's public life between the two world wars. How, he wondered, could the House endure year after year of what he called Baldwin's 'very mediocre intellect'? He could not grasp how lesser men were mollified, comforted, and flattered by Baldwin's bland manner and tolerance of conduct which any other prime minister would have regarded as inexcusable. If you voted for Baldwin's legislation, nothing else you did would offend him. After an MP had delivered an unforgivable personal attack on him, Amery later wrote, 'SB would meet him presently in the Lobby and would greet him genially with, "Well, old chap, I expect you feel better after that." ' Beaverbrook observed that Churchill 'resents an assault on his public policy as much as Lloyd George does an attack on his private life.' Baldwin, a political placebo, resented neither. He was content to squat on the Treasury Bench as a benign abacist, counting votes and beaming at the results.[145]

Yet Churchill, for whom no accommodation with Labour was possible, slowly came to realize that he would have to come to terms with this insipid man. Winston's position was stronger than it seemed. At the time, his setback in Westminster was generally regarded as a blunder, another example of his impetuosity. Actually, for reasons he could not have anticipated, it advanced his prospects. Had he routed the Tories' candidate, they would have found it hard to forgive him. As it was, his impressive showing as an independent, with neither a local organization nor a following in the district, was a remarkable demonstration of his personal appeal and skill as a campaigner. After the vote, Monteith Erskin, an influential Conservative, wrote to Baldwin: 'My conviction was and is that Winston Churchill would have done more to strengthen the Conservative Party than would his opponent. It seems a pity that the best interests of the country should often be at the mercy of a local Association divided in its own Councils . . . The 25 or 30 MPs who came out in the open for Winston in no way measure the actual feeling in the House. Any number told me they wanted him to win & were quietly working for his return.' The following day Lord Londonderry, a Churchill cousin who had been among his campaigners in Westminster, urged him to rejoin the Tories, writing: 'Please Winston reflect – a half way house is no use to anyone, least of all to you.' Sunny advised caution: 'I personally think you are wise to preserve a detached position from the Tory party – till you can command your terms, and get hold of the title deeds.' Eight days later, however, Churchill received a 'unanimous invitation' from the Liverpool Conservatives, asking him to address their annual convention early in the following month. Now he had to decide. He hesitated. Once before he had switched parties, and he still bore scars of the wounds inflicted then. Abuse would be unavoidable. He wondered if he could survive with his credibility intact. 'Anyone can rat,' he told a friend, 'but it takes a certain amount of ingenuity to re-rat.'[146]

In the autumn of that year Churchill turned fifty, and he looked it: portly, bald, stooped, his face lined with wrinkles accumulated during countless crises, any one of which would have aged most men overnight. Yet the overall effect was pleasant. He had begun to resemble the cartoonist's conception of John Bull, hearty and prosperous, with an ovoid torso and a low centre of gravity, good-humoured if you let him have his way but stubborn and even refractory if you didn't. His height was just under five feet, seven inches, which would have surprised those who knew him only through newspaper photographs, because his massive shoulders led one to expect a taller man. His manner was always forthright, never devious; no one ever called him enigmatic. As unsubtle as the rare roast beef he (and John Bull) loved, his expression invariably reflected his mood. He beamed, looked puckish, frowned, wept, or brooded, but of the thousands of Churchill photographs, none shows him bored. When with him it was impossible to forget one was in the presence of a great original. By now his props – the cigar, the blue polka-dot bow tie, the elegant malacca gold-topped walking stick he had inherited when Clementine's brother Bill committed suicide in a Paris hotel room – were familiar throughout England. Controversy accompanied him everywhere. Had George Gallup been conducting his polls then, and had Britons been asked their judgement of Churchill, there would have been very few No Opinions. Nearly everyone had decided views about him, which he relished, though he was ever alert to the possibilities of slander and libel. On December 10, 1923, he appeared in the Old Bailey to testify against Lord Alfred Douglas, Oscar Wilde's faithless lover. This noisome peer had distributed 30,000 pamphlets accusing Churchill of having accepted a £40,000 bribe to issue a false communiqué about the battle of Jutland, thereby enabling 'a group of Jewish financiers' to manipulate the stock market.* Had he chosen to take civil action, Winston would have won a large reward, but he believed scandalmongers belonged behind bars. He put this one there; a jury took just eight minutes to find Douglas guilty of criminal libel, and he was sentenced to six months in prison. Douglas's performance was inexcusable, but it is barely possible that he had been confused by the fact that Winston did

---

* After the Battle of Jutland on May 31, 1916, Churchill had drafted a communiqué on the action at Balfour's request, to bolster public confidence. It had merely served to identify him with public frustration over Jutland's inconclusive results.

pick up sums in the City from time to time when out of office; in 1923 he earned £5,000 as a lobbyist for Royal Dutch Shell and the Burmah Oil Company.

Though no longer in Parliament, he was always busy, always doing *something*. He had abandoned a second attempt to master flying after a postwar crash at Croydon – dusting himself off, he presided at a dinner honouring General Pershing two hours later, although, Lord Riddell noted in his diary, 'Winston's forehead was scratched and his legs were black and blue' – and he was seen less often on polo fields, particularly after two bad falls, the first at Eaton Hall, the Duke of Westminster's home near Chester, and the second at Hurlingham, where he broke his collarbone. He was reluctant to give up the game altogether, however. 'I do dumbbells every day,' he had written to the Prince of Wales, 'trying to get my elbow right for next year: not many more polo years at 47!' In fact, he was the star of a game between the House of Commons and the House of Lords. (The Commons won.) As a private citizen he followed public affairs as closely as he had in the cabinet, and was in the public eye almost as often, rebuking the French for their occupation of the Ruhr, criticizing the Harding administration ('so many hard things are said about us over there and . . . they are wringing the last penny out of their unfortunate allies'), and unveiling statues of wartime leaders, two of whom, Jellicoe and Beatty, had been appointed to their commands by him. Alone, he wrote, corrected galleys, carried on an enormous correspondence, and painted. Anything from his pen commanded an instant audience. The slightest of his articles is worth rereading today. In the early 1920s he wrote: 'May there not be methods of using exploding energy incomparably more intense than anything heretofore discovered? Might not a bomb no bigger than an orange be found to possess a secret power to destroy a whole block of buildings – nay, to concentrate a force of a thousand tons of cordite and blast a township at a stroke?'[147]

Of all his roles, the warmest, and most endearing, was that of paterfamilias. Winston adored children, and saw to it that his own would never suffer the starvation of parental affection which had made his childhood, even now, a painful memory. He built them hideouts in the woods; played 'Bear,' 'Gorilla,' charades, and other games; read to them, spun them yarns at the fireside, gave them new nicknames. In 1921 Diana, 'the gold-cream kitten,' was twelve; Randolph, 'the Rabbit,' was ten ('He looks such a thin shrimp in trousers and Eton collar!' Clementine wrote to Winston); and Sarah, 'the Bumblebee,' seven. Marigold, a two-year-old, would never be three. Her birth had been difficult for her mother, but by the time she could talk she was a treasure, one of those irresistible little heartbreakers of fey charm and manic energy whose very presence in a room endows everyone there with a fresh joy. Her father called her 'the Duckadilly.' She would race pell-mell around the dining room table while her parents entertained guests at lunch; her mother, afraid she might crack her head on one of the table's sharp corners, padded them. The Duckadilly had 'a sweet, true little voice,' as one member of the family later recalled, and her signature tune was the 1921 hit:[148]

> *I'm forever blowing bubbles,*
> *Pretty bubbles in the air.*
> *They fly so high, nearly reach the sky,*
> *Then like my dreams they fade and die.*
> *Oh, fortune's always hiding,*
> *I've looked everywhere.*
> *I'm forever blowing bubbles,*
> *Pretty bubbles in the air.*

It had been a hard winter of hacking coughs and sore throats; Marigold had fallen ill twice, and once it had become necessary to summon a physician. The family rented a seaside cottage at Broadstairs for that summer of 1921. Clementine, leaving there, and Winston, boarding a train in London, would travel by separate routes to the remote Scotland estate of the Duke of Westminster. The elder children would later entrain to join them, Marigold being left at Broadstairs with a young French governess. The Duckadilly's sickness returned. Before leaving the sea, Randolph wrote to his mother on August 2: 'Marigold has been rather ill, but is ever so much better today.' The improvement was only temporary. Alone with the young governess, after her brother and sisters had departed, she sickened again. Her throat grew worse; by August 14 she had contracted septicaemia. The governess was slow to call the doctor and slower to telegraph Clementine. By the time her mother reached her bedside, the Duckadilly's condition was grave. Clementine telegraphed Winston, who arrived on the next train from London. On Monday, August 22, he wrote to Curzon: 'The child is a little better than she was, but we are still dreadfully anxious about her.' On Wednesday evening she began to sink. Clementine was sitting beside her. Suddenly the little girl asked: 'Sing me "Bubbles." ' Her mother tried. She struggled. She tried again. Marigold put out her hand. She whispered: 'Not tonight . . . finish it tomorrow.' But Clementine never finished it. On Thursday the child died. She was two years and nine months old. Her mother and father were at her bedside when life fled from her, and long afterwards Winston told Mary, now grown, that Clementine shrieked in agony, 'like an animal in mortal pain.' He could not speak of his own agony. On Saturday they buried Marigold in London's Kensal Green cemetery. Press photographers arrived, but Winston appealed to them to leave, and they did. He wrote to Lord Crewe the following week: 'We have suffered a vy heavy & painful loss. It also seems so pitiful that this little life sh'd have been extinguished just when it was so beautiful & so happy – just when it was beginning.' The governess was dismissed, but dismissing the grief was impossible. 'Alas,' he wrote to Clementine when he was next separated from her, 'I keep on feeling the hurt of the Duckadilly.' She wrote back: 'I took the children on Sunday to Marigold's grave and as we knelt round it – would you believe that a little white butterfly . . . fluttered down & settled on the flowers which are now growing on it. We took some little bunches. The children were very silent all the way home.' And seven months later, on April 4, 1922, he wrote to her: 'I pass through again those sad scenes of last year when we lost our dear Duckadilly. Poor lamb – it is a gaping wound, whenever one touches it & removes the bandages & plasters of daily life.' To the end of her life Clementine could never speak of her lost child. Mary, the last of the Churchills' children, was born that autumn. She grew up puzzled by the identity of the little girl whose framed picture stood on her mother's dressing table, wondering who she could be.[149]

Marigold's death was one of three to sadden the family that year, though the other two, coming after fruitful lives, were easier to bear. The Countess of Airlie, Clementine's austere grandmother, expired at the age of ninety, and Winston's mother died of complications after an accident caused, appropriately, by a pair of fashionable but impractical Italian shoes. At sixty-seven Jennie was a Bright Old Thing, the greyest flapper in postwar Mayfair. She was still on the watch for new experiences. Meeting a jovial, monocled RAF officer at a party, she persuaded him to take her up, sitting in the wickerwork of his little passenger cockpit and soaring over Kent at ninety miles an hour. 'An extraordinary experience,' she told her friends. 'Right above the clouds in a little coupe.' She played a part in a film. She was forty years older than the rest of the cast, but one of the other actresses said, 'She was just one of us.' She scorned a Philadelphia clergyman who denounced short skirts, saying that people, not clothes, were moral or immoral. Long dresses, said she, speaking with the voice of experience, were no insurance against sexual licence.[150]

Returning from a lively trip to Rome, Jennie was on her way to a tea party, hurrying down a staircase in her new shoes when, three steps from a landing, she tripped, fell, and broke her left leg. It was a simple fracture; the bone was quickly set. She was convalescing in her new home in Westbourne Street, just around the corner from Sussex Square, when, two weeks after the fall, gangrene set in. Winston, informed, sent for a surgeon. Immediate amputation was necessary. Jennie calmly said she would learn 'to put my best foot forward' and added: 'Be sure you cut high enough.' The cut was above the knee. Over the next two weeks she appeared to be healing. Suddenly, after a hearty breakfast, the femoral artery in her left thigh haemorrhaged; she passed into a coma, and was dead before noon. Winston had hurried over in his pyjamas; he was with her at the end. DEATH OF LADY RANDOLPH, said the news posters; LADY RANDY GONE. Asquith told a reporter, 'She lived every inch of her life up to the edge,' and Churchill wrote to a family friend: 'She suffers no more pain; nor will she ever know old age, decrepitude, loneliness . . . I wish you could have seen her as she lay at rest – after all the sunshine & storm of life was over. Very beautiful & splendid she looked. Since the morning with its pangs, thirty years have fallen from her brow. She recalled to me the countenance I had admired as a child when she was in her heyday and the old brilliant world of the eighties & nineties seemed to come back.' Her last husband was hurrying home from Nigeria, but before he could reach England she had been buried in Bladon churchyard beside Lord Randolph. Shane

Leslie wrote: 'The feeling shewn was very considerable.' After the others had left, Winston stood alone by the open grave. He wept; and threw in a spray of crimson roses. But he was mourning his own lost youth, and the imperial glory of those years, as much as his mother. To Lord Crewe he wrote that the England 'in wh you met her is a long way off now, & we do not see its like today. I feel a vy great sense of deprivation.'[151]

Jennie herself had never given him a sense of fulfilment. There had been a time when he had needed her help, or rather the help of her powerful admirers, but that had long since passed. Since 1908 the overarching figure in his life had been his wife, and none of his other relationships, not even his love for his children, held him as closely as the matrimonial bond. It was not seamless. An oddity of the triumphant Churchill marriage, and possibly one reason for its success, is that Winston and Clementine usually took separate vacations. In 1919 they toured occupied Germany, and she accompanied him to the Cairo conference, but those were official occasions, offering no moments of intimacy. It was not until 1921 that they left England for their first joint holiday since before the war. Even then they shared their Nice beach with Sir Ernest Cassel and his niece Edwina, the future Lady Mountbatten, and they had hardly settled in when Winston was recalled to London. He wrote to Clementine that he hoped she would continue to enjoy the sunshine in his absence '& preen yr poor feathers in it,' adding, in another letter, when she was competing in an Eaton racket tournament: 'I hope you are having fun & tennis & *above all* recharging yr accumulators.' In 1925 and 1927 they would visit Venice together, but usually one of them remained in London while the other relaxed in this spa or that lodge. In most instances the vacationer was Winston. Clementine stayed at Saint-Jean-Cap-Ferrat in February 1921, participated in a tennis tournament later in the year, and spent subsequent summers at Frinton-on-Sea, Cromer, or Broadstairs with the children, but that was the extent of her recreation in the early 1920s. Winston was always urging her to cut loose: 'I strongly recommend yr going to the Ritz & pigging it there while passing thro London.' She never did. Her Spartan sense of duty kept her home.[152]

That was one reason. She had another reason. Their taste in playgrounds was, literally, miles apart. Clementine, unlike her husband, had been raised in a thrifty home and taught to distrust the voluptuous. If abroad, she instinctively sought to justify the trip by improving her mind. She enjoyed brisk sight-seeing when she did cross the Channel, preferred British seaside resorts if she needed relaxation, and disliked the exotic Riviera. Winston detested galleries and museums. He liked to hunt, play polo, and, eager for lush surroundings and colourful scenes he might paint, sought, to use his word, 'paintatious' locales bathed in bright, continual sunshine. Each tried to convert the other. Neither succeeded. If wealthy friends lured them to villas on the Mediterranean, she would decline or make only a brief *acte de présence*. Winston would reluctantly appear at a cottage she had rented on an English beach, play with the children for a day or two, and depart muttering excuses.

Occasionally she resented his absences. Early in 1922, when he was staying in southern France, first with Lady Essex and then with Beaverbrook, she had been nursing Diana, Randolph, and a maid through bouts of flu. Winston wasn't there to catch it, and she was glad for that, but she sent him a long letter describing her 'deep misery & depression.' She wished 'I were with you basking in the sun.' The only letter she had received from him had been typed, which was 'piling Pelium on Ossa coming after one of the most dreary & haunted weeks I have ever lived through' with 'all the sad events of last year, culminating in Marigold, passing & repassing . . . thro my sad heart.' After posting it, she wired him, asking him to destroy it unread. He wrote: 'My darling, I cd not bear not opening yr letter in the cream coloured envelope, in spite of yr telegram. In law it was my property once it was delivered to me, & any letter from you is better than none at all. My poor sweet . . . I am so sorry you had such a churlish message. I do so love & value yr being pleased to hear from me, & even the shadow cast by that pleasure when disappointed is dear to me.' He had, in fact, written to her at length, in his own hand. The letter had been delayed in the mail, which perhaps was just as well, for it bore alarming news: 'I must confess to you that I have lost some money here; though nothing like as much as last year. It excites me so much to play – foolish moth.' Clementine always worried about his gambling, but once it brought her a pleasant surprise. On one of those rare occasions when she accompanied him to Monte Carlo, she left the tables early, finding the play and the players tiresome, and retired to bed. He stayed with the green baize and hit a lucky streak. When she awoke next morning she found every inch of her bedspread covered with bank notes.[153]

Despite her anxiety and periodic threats of mutiny, she approved of his trips, pleased that he had 'Painting for your leisure and Polo for excitement,' and he kept her fully informed of all his activities. September of that year found him at Dunrobin, the Duke of Sutherland's castle in Scotland, writing: 'In the afternoon I went out and painted a beautiful river in the afternoon light with crimson and golden hills in the background.' That same year he reported from the Riviera: 'Yesterday Monday & today I have painted or am about to paint at Consuelo's villa. I have done a beautiful picture of Eze which I know you will want, but wh I cannot give you because Consuelo & Balzan praised it so much I gave it to them. Now I am doing one of the workmen building their house – all in shimmering sunshine & violet shades . . . A big beastly gt cloud has just come over the mountains & threatens to spoil my sunshine. Isn't it cruel! And these tiresome stupid inhabitants actually say: they *want* rain. It is too much.' Ever alert for choice gossip or the misbehaviour of the eminent, he added a postscript to one letter describing Asquith's arrival at a party given by Sir Philip Sassoon: 'The old boy turned up at Philip's party vy heavily loaded. The PM accompanied him up the stairs & was chivalrous enough to cede him the banister. It was a wounding sight. He kissed a great many people affectionately. I presume they were all relations.'[154]

'No gambling – I lost only 500 francs & was frankly bored by it,' he wrote cheerfully from Deauville a few months later. Thence he proceeded to Paris, took the night sleeper to Bordeaux, crossed to Mimizan by boat, and continued on to Biarritz by train. The Duke of Westminster's stables excited him: '24 magnificent steeds & any number of hounds. I am going to ride every morning to try to get myself fit.' Clementine was expecting Mary then, and he added: 'I think a gt deal about the coming kitten & about you my sweet pet. I feel it will enrich yr life and brighten our home to have the nursery started again. I pray God to watch over us all.' She replied from Frinton: 'I love to think of you resting & painting and riding in that lovely forest.' She was 'getting very stationary & crawl even to the beach with difficulty. I long for it to be over. It has seemed a very long nine months.' Later he wrote: 'Your own adventure is vy near now & I look forward so much to seeing you safe & well with a new darling kitten to cherish.' Late in August he joined the family at Frinton, where he promptly organized the children, their nanny, and his bodyguard – this was only two months after the assassination of Sir Henry Wilson – to join in the construction of a gigantic sand fortress, which then made a brave if hopeless stand against the rising tide. In September they were back in London for Clementine's last confinement. The sorrow of the lost Duckadilly would never fade completely, but 'Mary the Mouse' was doubly cherished for the void left by the sister she would never know.[155]

Churchill was not dawdling abroad while Clementine raised the family at home. He swam, he rode, he painted, he gambled, he cruised on Beaverbrook's yacht. But he also worked furiously on manuscripts, and no one knew better than his wife that this toil was absolutely necessary for their financial survival. After acknowledging a gambling loss he noted: 'But I have earned many times what I have lost by the work I have done here on my book.' Usually he worked in bed from breakfast until noon, but writing from Mimizan he described an altered regimen: 'I ride from 7:30 to 9, work at my book till lunch, 12:30.' Unless the skies were overcast – in which case he kept writing – afternoons were spent at his easel. After dinner he resumed work, continuing until the early hours of the following morning. Clementine prayed that the manuscripts would sell. The children were unaware, as Mary recalls, of 'how fragile was the raft which supported our seemingly so solid way of life.' From time to time they were told, 'Papa and Mummie are economizing,' were lectured about the need to turn off lights and reprimanded for long telephone conversations, yet, in Mary's words, the manner of the life her parents led 'belied the insecurity and fragility of their financial situation. They lived and entertained elegantly; they travelled; they brought up and educated their four surviving children handsomely. But had Winston's diligence, health, or genius failed, the whole fabric of their life would have crashed, for they literally lived from book to book, and from one article to the next.'[156]

Like most writers he derived his income from various sources: newspaper and magazine sales, publishers' advances, royalties from books sold in

England and other countries, and the sale of first serial rights – selections from books which appear in periodicals before publication date. And, like every other ink-stained wretch, he could never be certain of future income. During his two years out of Parliament he supported his life-style by writing, apart from books and edited collections of his speeches, thirty-three articles for the *Empire Review, Pearson's Magazine*, the *Daily Chronicle*, the *Strand Magazine, Nash's Pall Mall, English Life*, the *Sunday Chronicle, John Bull*, the *Weekly Dispatch*, the *Daily Mail*, and, in the United States, *Cosmopolitan*. His earnings from these alone were about £13,200. It made him unique among upper-class British politicians, most of whom had private incomes or lived on parliamentary salaries, and Clementine worried about that. She recognized the absolute necessity of his free-lancing, but was afraid it might be considered beneath his dignity and therefore an obstacle to high office. Her eye was on No. 10. Eventually, she believed, Winston's moment would come. She thought it might arrive in the near future. Once returned to the House, his gifts would carry him straight into the cabinet, where his chief rival – Stanley Baldwin not yet having consolidated his strength – would be Curzon, or, as she called him, the 'All Highest.' She wrote to Winston: 'I have a sort of feeling that the "All Highest" rejoices every time you write an Article & thinks it brings *him* nearer the Premiership, tho' I think that a man who had had to bolster himself up with two rich wives to keep himself going is not so likely to keep the Empire going as you who for 12 years have been a Cabinet Minister & have besides kept a fortuneless Cat & four hungry Kittens.'[157]

At that time he was considering a piece on his painting. She thought it a bad idea; to her it smacked of hackwork. What, she asked him, was he going to write about? 'Art in general? I expect the professionals would be vexed & say you do not yet know enough about Art . . . Your own pictures in particular? The danger there seems to me that it may be thought naif or conceited.' The *Strand* had offered him £1,000 for two articles, to be illustrated by four-colour and monochrome reproductions of his landscapes. She was 'as anxious as you are to snooker that £1,000 & as proud as you can be that you have had the offer; but just now I do not think it would be wise to do anything which would cause you to be discussed trivially, as it were.' Nevertheless, he went ahead. The result was his charming essay 'Painting as a Pastime,' which was later republished in *Thoughts and Adventures*, a collection of his pieces, and, later still, combined with an article on 'Hobbies' he had written for *Pall Mall*, was issued as a slender volume which sold 5,000 copies in Great Britain, was published in the United States, translated into French, German, Finnish, and Japanese, and ultimately appeared as a Penguin paperback. Among the pieces he ground out during his exile from Parliament between 1922 and 1924 were 'Who Rules Britain?,' 'The Case for Singapore,' 'Plugstreet,' 'Socialism and Sham,' 'The Danger Ahead in Europe,' 'Should Strategists Veto the Channel Tunnel?,' 'My Dramatic Days with the Kaiser,' 'If We Could Look into the Future,' 'My Own True Spy Story,' 'When I Risked Court Martial in Search of War,' 'A Hand-to-Hand Fight with Desert Fanatics,' and profiles of

Kitchener, MacDonald, Birkenhead, and Lloyd George. It occurred neither to him nor to Clementine that a time would come when, once more in political Coventry and with the survival of England at stake, he would arouse the nation with powerful articles in the press. During the 1920s he wrote for newspapers and magazines with money as his chief object. In a typical note to his wife on August 14, 1923, he reported: 'I have 8 articles to write as soon as the book is finished: £500, £400, & £200. We shall not starve.'[158]

'The book' was not to be completed for eight more years; it would run to five thick volumes, 2,517 pages, and would never be described as a potboiler. As originally conceived, it was to be a two-volume memoir of his years at the Admiralty. During the war he had carefully filed memoranda, documents, and letters, explaining, in a letter to Clementine on July 17, 1915, 'Someday I shd like the truth to be known,' and in March 1920 Sir Frederick Macmillan, at his request, set these in type so they would be readily usable. He began organizing them when Lord Esher published a distorted account of the Antwerp operation in *The Tragedy of Lord Kitchener*, charging that Churchill had 'slipped away' to Belgium on his own while Kitchener was 'in bed asleep.' By October, Winston was hard at work, singling out quotations from other men's memoirs, pasting the passages Macmillan had set on large sheets of blank paper, writing commentary in the margins, and drafting transitions. Admiral Jackson checked his facts; Eddie Marsh, his grammar, punctuation, and style. An exchange between Eddie and Winston survives:

CHURCHILL TO MARSH: Eddie. You are very free with your commas. I always reduce them to a minimum: and use 'and' or an 'or' as a substitute not as an addition. Let us argue it out. W.

MARSH TO CHURCHILL: I look on myself as a bitter enemy of superfluous commas, and I think I could make a good case for any I have put in – but I won't do it any more! E.

CHURCHILL TO MARSH: No do continue. I am adopting provisionally. But I want to argue with you. W.[159]

Soon the news that Winston was writing about the war was all over London. It was unnerving for some and exciting for others, if only because of the money involved. Late in November, Thornton Butterworth, working through Winston's agent, Curtis Brown, advanced him £9,000; Scribner's paid £5,000 as an advance for American publication. The magazine *Metropolitan* had offered nearly £8,000 for first serial rights, but he chose *The Times* instead. His deadline for both volumes was December 31, 1922, which subjected him to an unremitting pressure, but he liked it that way. On January 1, 1921, he attended another Sassoon party, at Lympne, in Kent. Riddell, a fellow guest, noted in his diary: 'I had a long talk with Winston about his book. He says he has written a great part of the first volume. He proposed to dictate 300,000 words, and then cut down the matter and polish it up. He added that it was very exhilarating to feel that one was writing for half a crown a word! He went upstairs to put in two or three hours' work on the book. When he came down, I said to LG, with whom I had been talking, "It is a horrible thought that while we have been frittering away our time, Winston has been piling up words at a half a crown each." This much amused LG.'[160]

It did not amuse Bonar Law, who said that if Churchill was quoting government documents, which he was, he was violating his privy councillor's oath. The problem of copyright torments every writer who uses contemporary sources, and Winston was no exception. He pointed out that Fisher, Jellicoe, and one of Kitchener's biographers had used confidential material. Hankey told Law that Churchill's point was a good one, but the matter was raised again and again as the several volumes appeared. Later, when he himself was back in the cabinet, Churchill learned that Birkenhead was working on a book about Woodrow Wilson. Dismayed that it might come out before the appearance of Winston's next volume and provoke an embargo on ministers publishing while still in office, he unreasonably begged FE to drop the idea. It was a false alarm; the issue was never raised. Most of his former colleagues had nothing to fear from an accurate account of the past, but all were immensely curious. They wondered, among other things, about the title. So did the author. In the last throes of the first volume, on January 30, 1922, he wrote to Clementine, 'I am so busy that I hardly ever leave the Ritz except for meals,' adding that Dawson of *The Times* had called 'and suggested himself the title "The Great Amphibian," but I cannot get either Butterworth or Scribner . . . to fancy it. They want "The World Crisis" or possibly "Sea Power and the World Crisis." We have to settle tomorrow for certain.'[161]

They settled on *The World Crisis*. 'Winston has written an enormous book about himself,' a colleague remarked, 'and called it *The World Crisis*.' Balfour said he was reading Churchill's 'autobiography disguised as a history of the universe.' A volume appeared in 1927, *The World Crisis: A Criticism*, comprising essays quarrelling with some of his statistics and minor points of strategy and tactics. They didn't amount to much. Beaverbrook was offended by the treatment of Law, whose friend he was, and the *Times* reviewer observed: 'Serious students will not need, and others will not heed, the warning that an apologia may be first-class material for history but cannot be history itself.'[162] The reviewer was absolutely wrong. It is indeed the precise strength of the work – which covers events from the prewar 'Vials of Wrath' to the aftershocks of 1922 – that the historian was either in the thick of events or had special access to many who were. He was a cabinet minister before the war, during the early and latter parts of it, and after the Armistice. In this regard *The World Crisis* is perhaps unique. Many statesmen have published memoirs; few have attempted a comprehensive account of their times. Caesar's *De Bello Gallico* and *De Bello Civili* are dry and unimaginative; Frederick the Great had a first-class mind, but his *Histoire de mon temps* was written in a language he had not mastered; Talleyrand's *Mémoires* is largely based on letters he himself did not write; Metternich is characteristically vain and obscure; Bismarck's three-volume *Gedanken und Erinnerungen* is insular, confusing, and inchoate. Thucydides' *History of the Peloponnesian War*, Clarendon's *History of the Rebellion and Civil Wars in England*, and the memoirs of Grant and Henry Kissinger, though immensely valuable, lack the breadth of *The World Crisis*. Churchill's perspective is amazingly broad. Even in describing the activities of Lenin and Trotsky, whom he loathed, he is scrupulous of facts and objective in examining the social matrix which made their rise possible.

But his achievement is greater than that. T.E. Lawrence described the second volume as 'far and away the best war-book I've yet read in any language.' John Maynard Keynes, finishing the fourth, wrote in the *Nation*: 'With what feelings does one lay down Mr Churchill's two-thousandth page? Gratitude to one who can write with so much eloquence and feeling of things which are part of the lives of all of us of the war generation, but which he saw and knew much closer and clearer. Admiration for his energies of mind and his intense absorption of intellectual interest and elemental emotion on what is for the moment the matter in hand – which is his best quality. A little envy, perhaps, for his undoubting conviction that frontiers, races, patriotisms, even wars if need be, are ultimate verities for mankind, which lends for him a kind of dignity and even nobility to events, which for others are only a nightmare interlude, something to be permanently avoided.' Keynes had touched on the work's deepest theme: its re-creation of the past, the illusion of immediacy created by the author's powerful presence. Keynes had also identified the reasons for Bloomsbury's reservations about it: the author's certitude and his lack of curiosity about subconscious motivation. Malcolm Muggeridge points out that Churchill, as a historian and biographer, 'remained obstinately Victorian and pre-Lytton Strachey' – interested in public events, that is, not in private lives. Writers like Strachey, literary beneficiaries of a decade in which irony and understatement were fashionable, dismissed Churchill's style as outmoded. In reality its essence is timeless; it found its greatest audience in 1940, when it moved an entire nation, but it lives today in allusion and everyday speech.[163]

Here he writes about the eve of Britain's 1916 offensive:

A sense of the inevitable broods over the battlefields of the Somme. The British armies were so ardent, their leaders so confident, the need and appeals of our Allies so clamant, and decisive results seemingly so near, that no human power could have prevented the attempt. All the spring the French had been battling and dying at Verdun, immolating their manhood upon that anvil-altar; and every chivalrous instinct in the new British armies called them to the succour of France, and inspired them with sacrifice and daring . . . The British Generals . . . were quite sure they were going to break their enemy and rupture his invading lines in France. They trusted to the devotion of their troops, which they knew was boundless; they trusted to masses of artillery and shells never before accumulated in war; and they launched their attack in the highest sense of duty and the strongest conviction of success.

And after the Somme:

> A young army, but the finest we have ever marshalled; improvised at the sound of the cannonade, every man a volunteer, inspired not only by love of country but by a widespread conviction that human freedom was challenged by military and Imperial tyranny, they grudged no sacrifice however unfruitful and shrank from no ordeal however destructive. Struggling forward through the mire and filth of the trenches, across the corpse-strewn crater fields, amid the flaring, crashing, blasting barrages and murderous machine-gun fire, conscious of their race, proud of their cause, they seized the most formidable soldiery in Europe by the throat, slew them and hurled them unceasingly backward. If two lives or ten lives were required by their commanders to kill one German, no word of complaint ever rose from the fighting troops. No attack however forlorn, however fatal, found them without ardour. No slaughter however desolating prevented them from returning to the charge. No physical conditions however severe deprived their commanders of their obedience and loyalty. Martyrs not less than soldiers, they fulfilled the high purpose of duty with which they were imbued. The battlefields of the Somme were the graveyards of Kitchener's Army. The flower of that generous manhood which quitted peaceful civilian life in every kind of workaday occupation, which came at the call of Britain, and as we may still hope, at the call of humanity, and came from the most remote parts of her Empire, was shorn away for ever in 1916. Unconquerable except by death, which they had conquered, they have set up a monument of native virtue which will command the wonder, the reverence and the gratitude of our island people as long as we endure as a nation among men.[164]

Churchill had received the first payment of his American advance, a cheque for £3,000, in July 1921, and on August 19 he paid £2,550 for a new Rolls-Royce. It was a token of his faith in the work's popularity, and it was more than justified. The British editions alone sold 80,551 copies. Since his British royalties ranged between 30 and 33 per cent, this brought him £58,846. Moreover, *The Times* serialized four of the five volumes. Further excerpts appeared in the *Sunday Chronicle*. An indefatigable worker, he produced the last three volumes of *The World Crisis* when serving as the cabinest's busiest minister. Considered in their entirety, his achievements as an author in that decade were prodigious, though he was not the most successful political author of those years. Five days before Christmas, 1924, when he was writing his version of the Somme, a former German soldier who had been wounded in that battle left Landsberg Prison in southern Bavaria, where he had been serving time for attempting to overthrow the government, with the rough draft of a very different account under his arm. Like Churchill, Adolf Hitler had a problem with his title. He wanted to call it *Viereinhalb Jahre Kampf gegen Lüge, Dummheit und Feigheit* ('Four and a Half Years of Struggle against Lies, Stupidity and Cowardice'), but his publisher persuaded him to settle for *Mein Kampf* ('My Struggle'). Within a few years, when its writer came to power, *Mein Kampf*'s presence would be almost obligatory in the homes of respectable burghers, and it led the list of his country's most popular graduation and wedding gifts through the 1930s. How many actually read it – ploughing through those desperate Teutonic sentences to find the verb at the end – is unknown, but its sales eventually exceeded six million copies, making it Germany's number-one best-seller and bringing Hitler $1.8 million in royalties. Unlike Churchill, he paid no taxes on this income after 1933, having declared himself exempt from them. His prose, however, has not borne the test of time.

Late in 1919, pressed for cash and not yet a wealthy writer, Churchill had sold his Lullenden estate to Ian Hamilton and moved his family in with the Freddie Guests, sharing expenses with his cousin while Clementine hunted for a new London home. A tall, handsome house at 2 Sussex Square, a block from Hyde Park's Victoria Gate and adjoined by a mews which would serve as Winston's studio, proved highly suitable, but he still yearned for a country home. Early in 1922 this became possible. On January 26 his first cousin once removed, Lord Herbert Vane-Tempest, died in a train accident. Lord Herbert had been a bachelor; Winston, as his heir, came into several thousand pounds. Clementine felt 'like a cork bobbing on a sunny sea,' while her husband sought out real-estate agents. He looked at several properties and found the one he wanted near Westerham, in Kent, some twenty-five miles from London and just a mile north of Lullenden. The house itself was ugly. Built of pleasant red brick during the reign of Henry VII, the original structure had been charming, but during the nineteenth century its owners had added ponderous bays and oriels, two ungainly wings, stifling clots of ivy, and heavy flora: rhododendrons, laurels, and conifers. Its view, however, was magnificent. Sited on eighty acres above a combe, it overlooked the great Kentish Weald, with its smooth meadows, suave green slopes, and sheltering woods of oak, beech, and chestnut, watered here by a clear spring, the Chart Well, which gave the manor its name. Years later, looking down on it, Churchill said: 'I bought Chartwell for that view.' At the time, however, he wondered if he could afford it. Clementine was in Scotland then, so he drove Diana, Randolph, and Sarah there, telling them he wanted to show them an estate he might buy. They adored it. Sarah recalled: 'We did a complete tour of the house and grounds, my father asking anxiously – it is still clear in my mind – "Do you like it?" Did we like it? We were delirious. "Oh, do buy it! Do buy it!" we exclaimed.' The asking price was £5,500. On September 15 Winston offered £4,800, explaining: 'The house will have to be very largely rebuilt, and the presence of dry rot in the northern wing is I am advised a very serious adverse factor.' Norman Harding, the agent, told him his offer was unacceptable. 'He strode up and down,' Harding recalled afterwards, 'using every argument he could think of . . . Eventually, with very bad grace, he gave way.' They compromised on £5,000.[165]

Churchill had been right; the rot was advanced, and the mansion had to be reconstructed from the ground up. An architect was engaged, a friend of his aunt Leonie's who had just finished a country place at Churt for Lloyd George. The ivy and Victorian trimmings were stripped away, high crow-stepped gables were added, and also a new wing for a drawing room, dining room, and Clementine's bedroom. The job took more than two years. Winston grew impatient. Clementine didn't. Her husband had committed a grave error. He had made the purchase without consulting her. And when she saw it, she disliked it. 'At first,' she told Martin Gilbert, 'I did not want to go to Chartwell at all. But Winston had his heart set on it.' Mary remembers that her mother 'tried very hard to love the place which so enthralled Winston. She worked like a Trojan to make it the home and haven for us all that he dreamed of. But it never acquired for her the nature of a venture shared; rather, it was an extra duty, gallantly undertaken, and doggedly carried through.' Among other things, she was concerned about the expense. The cost of rebuilding the house rose to £13,000, then £15,000, and finally £18,000. Winston wrote to her: 'My beloved, I do beg you not to worry about money, or to feel insecure. On the contrary the policy we are pursuing aims above all at *stability* (like Bonar Law!). Chartwell is to be our *home*. It will have cost us £20,000 and will be worth at least £15,000 apart from a fancy price. We must endeavour to live there for many years & hand it on to Randolph afterwards. We must make it in every way possible economically self contained. It will be cheaper than London.' He contemplated selling the house in Sussex Square: 'Then with the motor we shall be well equipped for business or pleasure. If we go into office we will live in Downing Street!'[166]

During the reconstruction of 'Cosy Pig,' as he called it, he leased Hosey Rigg, a nearby house where, he was delighted to learn, Lewis Carroll had written *Alice in Wonderland*. At weekends he would prowl around his new property, the children tagging along. He wrote to his wife: 'I am going to amuse them on Saturday and Sunday by making them an aerial house in the lime tree. You may be sure I will take the greatest precautions to guard against their tumbling down.' Sarah would remember the tree house as 'a two-storeyed affair; it was a good twenty feet high, and was reached by first shinning up a rope and then climbing on carefully placed struts between the four stems of the tree.' During the Easter holiday of 1924 he and the children began sleeping at the manor in what Mary calls 'camping' style. To Clementine, who was laid up, he wrote: 'This is the first letter I have ever written from this place, & it is right that it shd be to you. I am in bed in your bedroom (wh I have annexed temporarily) & wh is sparsely but comfortably furnished with the pick of yr two van loads . . . You cannot imagine the size of these rooms till you put furniture in them. This bedroom of yours is a magnificent aerial bower. Come as soon as you feel well enough to share it.' The children, he said, had 'worked like blacks.' He added a couplet: 'Only one thing lack these banks of green – / The Pussy Cat who is their queen.'[167]

Under his supervision – and his straining muscles – the grounds began to take shape. To Cosy Pig's natural setting he added three hundred asparagus plants, two hundred strawberry runners, and a large consignment of fruit trees: apple, pear, plum, damson, and quince. For Clementine he created a water garden, and, beyond it, a fragrant azalea glade. White foxglove was planted, then blue anchusa. Carp swam in a warm pond. Black swans, a gift from the Australian government, cruised across a large, pleasant lake which a previous owner had created by damming the spring. 'Why only one dam?' Winston asked. He wanted a place to swim. Another site was excavated and water diverted into it. Sir Samuel Hoare, in the neighbourhood, wrote to Beaverbrook: 'I had never seen Winston in the role of landed proprietor,' and described him as engaged in 'engineering works' which 'consist of making a series of ponds in the valley.' He added: 'Winston appeared to be a great deal more interested in them than in anything else in the world.' But both lakes, Churchill decided, were too weedy and muddy for swimming, so he decided to abandon one to wildfowl, drain the other, scoop out a third, waterproof its bottom, and build another dyke, hiring a crew of workmen and pressing Detective Thompson into service. Thomas Jones arrived and found Churchill 'attired in dungarees and high Wellington boots superintending the building of a dam by a dozen navvies. This is the third lake, and the children are wondering what their father will do next year, as there is room for no more lakes.' Writing to Clementine on August 19 of his first Chartwell summer, Winston mentioned – fleetingly, almost impatiently – that Conservatives in the Epping constituency, 'one of the safest seats in the country,' were actively courting him, and then hurried on to what was, for him, more exciting news: 'Work on the dam is progressing . . . The water has been rising steadily. We have this evening seven feet. It will be finished by next Tuesday, or eight weeks from its initiation. I am at it all day and every day.' A foot of mud remained in the old lake, and he was clearing it out: 'Thompson and I have been wallowing in the most filthy black mud you ever saw, with the vilest odour, getting the beastly stuff to drain away. The moor hens and dab chicks have migrated in a body to the new lake and taken up their quarters in the bushes at the upper end.' Thompson recalls pulling on rubber waders each morning before going out to 'the dig' with Winston, shovelling, patching, lining the bottom of the new excavation with bitumen, 'thick slimy mud everywhere,' and one occasion of rare mirth when 'I dropped a dollop of mud on his pate.'[168]

It was all in vain. The bitumen leaked, and the new dam, though built of cement, threatened to slide down the hill. Undaunted, Churchill built a circular pool by the house, fed by the Chart Well, whose waters came purling down through fern-fringed channels and rocks fetched by train from Cumberland. The spring was supplemented by an electric pump, which sent water to and from the ponds 'rather like a stage army,' in Sarah's phrase, or, in Winston's, 'filtered to limpidity.' It was a heated pool, then a novelty; a visiting engineer assured him that the boilers were big enough to heat the Ritz. The uselessness of the dams was frustrating, but erecting them had not been a complete waste; the lakes were comely, and the work, like his landscaping and gardening, had been a diversion from politics. Thompson believes it was good for Churchill 'to get close to the ground and the fine smell of it, and to work it and plant it and make it bloom and yield.' After the voters of Westminster had rejected him Winston wrote to a friend: 'I am content for the first time in my life to look after my own affairs, build my house and cultivate my garden.' Once the mansion was completely finished and the family had spent two strenuous days moving in, he continued to toil outside, devising rookeries, miniature waterfalls in the water garden, elaborate waterworks for the golden carp, and planting bamboo, wisteria, and acers on the banks of the carps' pool. Then, after putting up a garden wall of Kentish ragstone, he decided to become a bricklayer. Returning from London one evening, he paused in Westerham to visit Quebec House, General James Wolfe's birthplace. After examining the wall, with its dentils surmounted by a sloping top, he said: 'That's what I want.' Shortly thereafter James Scrymgeour-Wedderburn, an early Chartwell guest, scribbled in his diary: 'Winston is building with his own hands a house for his butler, and also a garden wall!'[169]

He built much more than that. Altogether he finished two cottages, several walls, and a playhouse for Mary. Scrymgeour-Wedderburn wrote: 'He works at bricklaying for hours a day, and lays 90 bricks an hour, which is a very high output.' He himself never claimed more than one a minute, but his craftsmanship was admirable; the sturdy results stand today. He wrote to Baldwin: 'I have had a delightful month building a cottage and dictating a book: 200 bricks and 2,000 words a day.' Stories about his skill reached James F. Lane, an official of the Amalgamated Union of Building Trade Workers. Lane wrote to Winston, proposing that he join the union. Winston replied: 'Would you mind letting me know whether there is any rule regulating the number of bricks which a man may lay in a day; also, is there any rule that a trade unionist may not work with one who is not a trade unionist; and what are the restrictions on overtime? I may say that I shall be very pleased to join the union if that would not be unwelcome to your members.' As it turned out, he was unwelcome. Lane sent him a union card and a certificate of membership, and addressed him as 'Brother Churchill,' but a Manchester local protested that his recruitment invited 'public contempt and ridicule.' The executive committee voted that Churchill was ineligible. He kept the certificate, however, and framed it.[170]

Like many another country gentleman, admiring his new estate, Winston decided to 'live off the land' – to make Cosy Pig pay. The consequences were uniformly disappointing. Poultry, sheep, cattle, and pigs arrived healthy and then languished. He kept hoping for success; in the summer of 1924 he wrote to Clementine: 'The 9 elder swine are sold for £31. They have eaten less than £1 a week for 18 weeks of life – so there is a profit of £13. Not bad on so small a capital.' But he really knew nothing of livestock, and his wife regarded the creatures with great apprehension. He liked them; he remarked: 'The world would be better off if it were inhabited only by animals.' Yet he resisted modern techniques of scientific farming, and was indignant when a prosperous breeder suggested artificial insemination. Churchill growled: 'The beasts will not be deprived – not while I'm alive!' The fact is that he couldn't bear to think of livestock exploited and then slaughtered. To him they were all pets, to be cherished and pampered: the golden orfe, a marmalade cat, Carolina ducks, chickens, sheldrakes, the swans, polo ponies, Canada geese, cygnets, assorted dogs, and bottle-fed lambs. One day Sarah and Mary came to him in tears. Mary's pug, they cried, was desperately ill. Their father, almost as upset as they were, dashed off an incantation to be chanted whenever the dog fell sick: [171]

> *Oh, what is the matter with poor puggy-wug?*
> *Pet him and kiss him and give him a hug.*
> *Run and fetch him a suitable drug,*
> *Wrap him up tenderly all in a rug,*
> *That is the way to cure Puggy-wug.*

Once he had said good morning to it, almost any creature at Chartwell was safe. An exception was a goose; his wife had it cooked for dinner. At the table he picked up the knife, hesitated, and handed it to Clementine. 'You carve him, Clemmie,' he said. 'He was a friend of mine.' The only animal to fall from grace was a ram named Charmayne. Winston had nursed Charmayne as a lamb, but when it grew up it turned vicious and butted everyone. A veterinarian was summoned. He performed an operation. If anything, the beast grew worse. The children were afraid of it; Clementine begged Winston to get rid of it. He scoffed at the idea. 'How ridiculous. You don't have to be frightened. It is very nice and knows me.' However, one day, to the secret delight of the children, Charmayne got behind Churchill, charged, butted the back of his knees, and knocked him flat. Before the sun set, the ram had vanished. How he had disposed of it he would not say, but Clementine hoped it had been sold, and for a good price; she wanted to see something at Chartwell pay for itself. [172]

Clementine was frequently absent from her husband's Cosy Pig in those early years. The children always missed her terribly. 'DARLING, DARLING Mummy,' Sarah wrote. 'Don't forget to come home sometime. Papa is miserable and frightfully naughty without you!' But she had other obligations. Lady Blanche was dying in Dieppe and needed her daughter by her side. Churchill, ever anxious if Clementine was unhappy, wrote to her: 'Yr mother is a gt woman: & her life has been a noble life. When I think of all the courage & tenacity & self denial that she showed . . . I feel what a true mother & grand woman she proved herself, & I am more glad & proud to think her blood flows in the veins of our children. My darling I grieve for you.' Back in London after the funeral, shopping in the Brompton Road, Clementine was hit by a bus, and although she took a taxi home without assistance, her doctor prescribed six weeks of rest in Venice. She wanted Winston to join her, but he declined to leave Kent. 'Every day away from Chartwell,' he said, 'is a day wasted.' He told her that 'every minute of my day here passes delightfully. There are an enormous amount of things I want to do – and there is of course also the expense to consider.' Clementine was well aware of their expenses. It was one of her worries about Chartwell. The payroll alone was staggering: a cook, a farmhand, a groom for the ponies, three gardeners, a nanny, a nursery maid, an 'odd-man' (dustbins, boilers, boots), two housemaids, two kitchen maids, two more in the pantry, Clementine's lady's maid, who also did the family sewing, and Winston's two secretaries.[173]

Occasionally Churchill himself became alarmed. He sent his wife one long memorandum on economy covering fourteen points. Trips were to be curtailed, their only winter visits to Chartwell would be 'picnics with hampers,' all livestock except two polo ponies would be sold, few guests would be invited 'other than Jack and Goonie,' and 'Item 14,' headed 'BILLS,' was a detailed analysis of savings to be made in the consumption of cigars and wines, the number of dress shirts he should wear for dinner each week, and even a reduction in the boot-polish inventory. He also considered renting Chartwell for the following summer for eighty guineas a week, though he wasn't really serious, and quickly backed off when Clementine took him up on it. She suggested they 'establish the children in a comfortable but economical hotel near Dinard, go there ourselves for part of the time & travel about painting for you, sight seeing for me, or we could go to Tours & do the "Chateaux" again – and we could go to Florence & Venice.' Churchill had an alternative. He thought he could put them in the black by 'going into milk.' Dismayed, she sent him a seven-page letter pointing out that all his adventures in husbandry had been disastrous: 'You will remember that the chickens and chicken houses got full of red mite and vermin; and you will also remember that one sow was covered with lice.'[174]

Invariably he became bored with issues of thrift and airily dismissed them. His wife couldn't. She had to deal with the thickening backlog of unpaid bills and the local tradesmen who called for their money. It was mortifying and, at times, infuriating. Clementine aroused was formidable, and not just within the family. Their guests crossed her at their peril. Afterwards Winston, rueful but proud of her, would say, 'Clemmie gave poor Smith a most fearful mauling,' or 'She dropped on him like a jaguar out of a tree!' Yet she was never a match for her own husband. He was too verbal, too skilful in debate, so she usually wrote to him, even when they were in the same room. Occasionally, however, she lashed out at him in exasperation; Mary recalls that 'on one occasion she became so enraged that she hurled a dish of spinach at Winston's head. She missed, and the dish hit the wall, leaving a telltale mark.'[175] But that was unlike her. She usually pursued her objectives quietly, letting servants go and cutting household costs in ways Winston would not notice until it was too late to undo what she had done. In time she left her own imprint on their country home, if only because she couldn't afford an interior decorator. Chartwell today reflects her simple, excellent taste: the clean colours – pale cream, pale blue, cerulean blue – bright moire on her four-poster bed, chintzes with bold floral designs, rush carpets, unstained oak chairs and tables, and other graceful furniture, inherited or picked up at auctions.

Hospitality was a constant source of joy to Churchill. He loved to show Chartwell off. Cyril Connolly wrote: 'A man with a will to power can have no friends.' Winston was an exception. No man yearned for dominion more than

Cosy Pig's owner, and few have had more friends. They came to Kent in a constant stream: Lloyd George, Bernard Baruch, the Birkenheads, the Duff Coopers, Eddie Marsh, Bob Boothby, the Archie Sinclairs, Brendan Bracken, the Bonham Carters, cabinet members, publishers, writers – men and women who often shared but one trait: they were gifted, and therefore worthy foils for their host. Brendan Bracken, with his quaint spectacles and carrot-red hair flaming in a tousled mop, was particularly striking. Churchill had been amused when he heard that Bracken was rumoured to be his illegitimate son; even more amused when he learned that Bracken wouldn't deny it; and delighted when Bracken took to addressing him as 'Father.' At Chartwell, Margot Asquith wrote, 'every ploy became "a matter of pith and moment."' Lord Rawlinson would come to discuss hunting and painting. Beaverbrook arrived with an enormous gift for Churchill's fifty-first birthday, a refrigerator, so Winston could drink champagne without ice. T.E. Lawrence descended the stairs to dinner wearing – to the enchantment of the children – the robes of a prince of Arabia. Professor F.A. Lindemann, 'the Prof,' looked dull in his bowler hat, but in his way he was more wonderful than Lawrence. In 1916 RAF pilots were dying daily in nose dives. At the Royal Aircraft Establishment in Farnborough, Lindemann had worked out, with mathematical precision, a manoeuvre which, he said, would bring any aircraft out of a tailspin. The pilots said it wouldn't work. The Prof taught himself to fly, took off without a parachute, deliberately sent the aircraft down in a spin, and brought it out so successfully that mastering his solution became required of every beginning flier. One evening at Chartwell, Winston said: 'Prof, tell us in words of one syllable, and in no longer than five minutes, what is the Quantum Theory.' He produced his gold watch. Lindemann did it – and at the end the entire family burst into applause. But the children's greatest thrill was provided by Charlie Chaplin. On first meeting Chaplin, Winston had written to Clementine: 'You cd not help liking him . . . He is a marvellous comedian – bolshy in politics & delightful in conversation.' His evening at Chartwell began badly. He wanted to discuss the gold standard. Churchill lapsed into a moody silence. Suddenly his guest snatched up two rolls of bread, thrust two forks in them, and did the famous dance from his 1925 film *The Gold Rush*. 'Immediately the atmosphere relaxed,' recalls Boothby, who was there, 'and thereafter we spent a happy evening, with both Churchill and Chaplin at the top of their form.'[176]

Of these years Churchill would later write: 'I never had a dull or idle moment from morning till midnight.' Even today one senses the Churchillian presence at Chartwell, in the vast study, by the dining room's round table, in the solid brick walls, the seat by the fishpond where he liked to meditate, and the studio in which his stunning paintings stand row on row, awaiting eventual public display. Perhaps, as Mary says, his painting, writing, and manual labour 'were sovereign antidotes to the depressive element in his nature.' If so, never was depression so thoroughly routed by activity and wit. One can almost hear the merry rumble of his voice when, introduced to a young man on the eve of his twenty-fifth birthday, Winston said: 'Napoleon took Toulon before his twenty-fifth birthday,' and, whipping out the gold watch, cried: 'Quick, quick! You have just time to take Toulon before you are twenty-five – go and take Toulon!'[177]

In fantasy one envisages long-ago summer afternoons here, with young voices calling scores from the tennis court, the middle-aged basking by the pool, and couples discussing imperial issues over tea and strawberries in the loggia. But if those who knew the Churchills could choose one moment of the year to relive, it would be Christmas. For them, in a nostalgic chamber of the mind, it will always be that magical eve when the entire family has gathered here, including Jack and Goonie and their young, with Randolph home from Eton, the girls rehearsing an amateur theatrical, Clementine helping the servants build a snowman, and Churchill upstairs writing one of his extraordinary love letters to her. '(The most precious thing in my life is yr love for me. I reproach myself for many shortcomings. You are a rock & I depend on you & rest on you.') Presents, hidden all week in an out-of-bounds closet, the 'Genii's cupboard', are about to appear. Fires crackle; the house is hung with holly, ivy, laurel, and yew; the Christ child gazes down lovingly from a large Della Robbia plaque. Now the double doors between the library and the drawing room are flung open and the Christmas tree is revealed in all its splendour, a hundred white wax candles gleaming, the scent of pine and wax like a breath of rapture, and Churchill, the benign sovereign in this absolutely English castle, leads the way across the threshold towards his annual festival of joy 'with my happy family around me,' as he would later write, 'at peace within my habitation.'[178]

The prickly marriage of convenience between Asquith's Liberals and Ramsay MacDonald's Labour government lasted less than a year. In the suit for divorce, bolshevism was named as co-respondent. MacDonald had recognized Lenin's regime, lent it money, and dropped charges against a Communist editor who had incited mutiny among British troops. Asquith thereupon withdrew his support, and Labour lost a vote of confidence, 364 to 198. The campaign which followed became known as the 'Red Letter Election' because a few days before the polling the Foreign Office published a letter allegedly written by Grigori Zinoviev, president of the Third International, calling on British socialists to organize an armed rebellion. Labour bitterly renounced it as a fake. Churchill shed crocodile tears. Many Labour MPs, he said, were politicians 'of high reputation' who 'stood by their country in the war' but whose position now was 'pathetic. They have been unable to keep their feet upon the slippery slopes on which they have tried to stand.' Down they slid, the way greased by the Red Letter; in October 1924 the Conservatives won 419 seats, Labour 151, and the fading Liberals a mere 40.[179]

Among the triumphant candidates was Churchill, who became the member for Epping, a seat he was to hold for the rest of his public life, although in 1945 the constituency boundary was changed and it became the Woodford constituency. He was once more a supporter of Tory policies. In May, accompanied by Clementine, he had entrained to Liverpool and, for the first time in twenty years, addressed a Conservative party rally. Afterwards he introduced his wife to their hosts. She was somewhat subdued, and he said: 'She's a Liberal, and always has been. It's all very strange for her. But to me, of course, it's just like coming home.' Presently the party's chief parliamentary whip sent him congratulations 'upon your brilliant speech.' He had spoken to a public meeting in Epping, coming down hard on MacDonald's friendly overtures to Russia, 'unquestionably one of the worst and meanest tyrannies in the history of the world.' Nominally he was a 'Constitutionalist,' but the local Conservatives had adopted him as their nominee, and he won by nearly ten thousand, polling almost 60 per cent of the votes cast, whereupon he accepted the Tory label. The *Sunday Times* reported that in Trafalgar Square 'the great cheer of the day was reserved for Mr Winston Churchill's victory at Epping.' T.E. Lawrence wrote to him, 'This isn't congratulations, it's just the hiss of excess delight rushing out,' and Ivor Guest, now Lord Wimborne, wrote: 'I hope to goodness the Tories have the good sense to offer you high office. It will be reassuring to think of a progressive mind among their counsels, as a majority such as theirs is hardly conducive to a programme of social reforms.' But Churchill doubted there would be a ministry for him: 'I think it very likely that I shall not be invited to join the Government, as owing to the size of its majority it will probably be composed only of impeccable conservatives.'[180]

He was wrong. Baldwin, a shrewder politician than Churchill, very much wanted him in the cabinet. Despite the size of his party's majority, he was afraid that Churchill and Lloyd George might form a centre party and persuade Birkenhead to back them in the Lords, thus pitting the prime minister against Parliament's three most eloquent speakers. Therefore he decided to separate Winston and George. Opportunity unexpectedly presented itself when Austen Chamberlain's half brother Neville, who had only recently entered politics at the age of forty-nine but shared old Joe's political legacy, declined the chancellorship of the Exchequer. Tory indifference to tariff reform had soured him; he preferred the Ministry of Health. Actually, it was Neville who suggested that Winston run the Treasury. Baldwin replied that the party would 'howl.' Neville said that the howl would be louder if Churchill were returned to the Admiralty. Upon reflection the prime minister agreed; summoning the Epping turncoat he asked him if he would serve as 'Chancellor.' Winston asked: 'Of the Duchy?' 'No,' said Baldwin, 'of the Exchequer.' Churchill later wrote that he had been tempted to ask: 'Will the bloody duck swim?' Instead, he replied: 'This fulfils my ambition. I still have my father's robes as Chancellor. I shall be proud to serve you in this splendid office.' He also pledged his loyalty to Baldwin and said: 'You have done more for me than Lloyd George ever did.'[181]

When Winston told Clementine, he wrote afterwards, he had 'the greatest difficulty in convincing my wife that I was not merely teasing her.' Convinced, she made him vow he would keep it from the press, letting the announcement come from No. 10. That was asking too much, however– it was like his pledge to keep their engagement a secret. That evening Winston dined at Beaverbrook's home with Freddie Guest and Birkenhead, who had been appointed secretary of state for India. They all asked Churchill: 'Are you in?' He said he was, but when pressed to name the ministry, he said: 'I am sorry, but I would prefer not to disclose that just now.' He was obviously bursting to tell them, and they were indignant that he wouldn't, but he didn't want Beaverbrook to turn it into headlines. Finally he cried: 'I am Chancellor of the Exchequer!' The phone rang; another source confirmed him; Beaverbrook decided to break the story. Birkenhead thought Winston had behaved badly by not sharing the tidings at once. According to Beaverbrook: 'Suddenly a kind of flash of intuition came to me and I made a wild but shrewd guess. "I don't believe Churchill is really to blame. He promised somebody he wouldn't tell me before he came – yes – he promised his wife." Churchill said, "You are right. She drove me to the door of your house." '[182]

The howl Baldwin had predicted followed. The *Morning Post* sourly observed that 'the idea of scrapping the Conservative Party in order to make a home for lost Liberals and returning prodigals does not appear to us to promise success.' *The Times* agreed. At the Admiralty Sir William Bridgeman, the new first lord, wrote to his wife: 'I am afraid that turbulent pushing busybody Winston is going to split the party. I can't understand how anybody can want him or put any faith in a man who changes sides, just when he thinks it is to his own personal advantage to do so.' Austen Chamberlain, unaware of Neville's role, wrote to his wife: 'Beloved: SB is mad! . . . I feel that this particular appointment will be a great shock to the party.' Sir John Simon told an amused audience: 'There is a new piece of jazz music now being played which has been called "the Winston Constitution." You take a step forward, two steps backward, a side step to the right, and then reverse. You can see that the piece is well named.' His faithful old Liberal ally, the *Guardian*, commented mournfully: 'Mr Churchill for the second time has – shall we say? – quitted the sinking ship and for the second time the reward of this fine instinct has been not safety only but high promotion.'[183]

The Exchequer was the highest gift a prime minister could bestow. Keeping the Sussex Square house was no longer an issue; it was sold, and the family moved into No. 11 Downing Street, sharing the garden behind it with the Baldwins at No. 10. Gladstone's famous red dispatch case was entrusted to Winston. Lord Randolph's Exchequer robes, put away in tissue paper and camphor by Winston's mother on Christmas Day, 1886, were aired and donned by him for his first official function, the 'Pricking [selection] of the Sheriffs' on November 13, 1924. Afterwards he lunched with Reginald McKenna, who wrote to Beaverbrook: 'He tells me he means to master the intricacies of finance and I think he will succeed, though he will find it more difficult than he imagines.' Actually, he appears to have had no concept of the challenge. Lord Boothby recalls that Churchill 'soon discovered that the Treasury was not congenial to him, and that he was basically uninterested in the problems of high finance.' After a meeting with Treasury officials, economists, and bankers, Winston told Boothby: 'I wish they were admirals or generals. I speak their language, and can beat them. But after a while these fellows start talking Persian. And then I am sunk.' As an MP, Boothby became Winston's parliamentary private secretary. After it had become clear that Churchill was having difficulties in his new office, Boothby asked P.J. Grigg, a senior civil servant at the Exchequer, why that should be. Grigg replied: 'There is only one man who has ever made the Treasury do what it didn't want to do. That was Lloyd George. There will never be another.'[184]

Certainly Winston wasn't one. Late in life he remarked: 'Everyone said I was the worst Chancellor of the Exchequer that ever was, and now I am inclined to agree with them.' But that was going too far. To be sure, he had no economic convictions apart from his blind faith in Free Trade, and it was disconcerting to hear the seigneur of British finance say loftily: 'The higher mind has no need to concern itself with the meticulous regimentation of figures.' He was far from being the worst chancellor, however, or even one of the worst; unlike his father, he knew what 'those damned dots' meant, and he had a vision, a revival of the social strategy he and Lloyd George had conceived in the first decade of the century. Welfare legislation was very much on his mind. He envied Neville Chamberlain at the Ministry of Health, telling him: 'You are in the van. You can raise a monument. You can leave a name in history.' Drafting his first budget at Chartwell, he wrote to Clementine: 'I have been working all day (Sunday) at pensions & am vy tired.' In a Treasury minute two days later he wrote: 'It is when misfortune comes upon the household, when prolonged unemployment, or old age, or sickness, or the death of the breadwinner comes upon this household, that you see how narrow was the margin on which it was apparently living so prosperously, and in a few months the result of the thrift of years may be swept away, and the house broken up.' Addressing a sceptical audience – the British Bankers' Association – he said that economic aid for 'every class and every section . . . is our aim: the appeasement of class bitterness, the promotion of a spirit of co-operation, the stabilisation of our national life, the building of the financial and social plans upon a three or four years' basis instead of a few months' basis, an earnest effort to give the country some period of recuperation after the vicissitudes to which it has been subjected.'*[185]

It was Churchill's misfortune, and Britain's, that he came to the Treasury with the right ideas at the wrong time. The country's economists were torn between, on the one hand, those who regarded the classical law of supply and

---

* Ironically, Churchill may have been the first public figure to use *appeasement* in a modern political context. As a foreign policy proposal it first appeared on May 9, 1934, in a letter to *The Times* from Lord Lothian, who suggested 'a limitation of armaments by political appeasement.'

demand as an article of absolute faith and, on the other hand, the followers, still few in numbers, of John Maynard Keynes's concept of a managed economy. A heavy parliamentary majority believed that the budget must be balanced, whatever the cost. Given the plight of the Treasury in the mid-1920s, this was wildly unrealistic. England's great prewar assets were gone, spent, like the blood of its youth, in the trenches and no-man's-land across the Channel. After the brief boom in the years immediately following the Armistice, management's prewar troubles with organized labour returned, redoubled by a huge hard core of jobless men, refugees from giant industries – coal, cotton, shipbuilding, and steel and iron – which had once thrived on exports and could no longer find markets abroad. The miners' union, exasperated with the coalfields' shortsighted, reactionary, incompetent proprietors, turned to the government. An official inquiry recommended nationalization of the mines, but nothing was done. In 1921 a mine lockout was followed by competition from the revived German coal industry, which led to wage cuts in the British coalfields. Unrest was growing there.

Another of Winston's unwelcome legacies was the servicing of England's war debt to America. Great Britain owed the United States the preposterous sum of $4,933,701,642. Interest on this exceeded £35,000,000 a year. Again and again Churchill explained to England's former ally, now its creditor, that Britain couldn't repay the principal until France had paid Britain *its* war debt. Sometimes he thought he was succeeding. On January 10, 1925, he wrote to Clementine: 'I have had tremendous battles with the Yanks, & have beaten them down inch by inch to a reasonable figure. In the end we are fighting over tripe like £100,000!' But agreement after agreement collapsed, President Coolidge saying inanely: 'They hired the money, didn't they?' A Chartwell guest noted in his diary: 'Winston talked very freely about the USA. He thinks they are arrogant, fundamentally hostile to us, and that they want to dominate world politics.'[186]

In the House of Commons annual calendar, Budget Day belongs to the chancellor of the Exchequer. Churchill's first such occasion was April 28, 1925. A large crowd awaited him outside No. 11 as he emerged smiling, the dispatch case in his hand. 'Let me take the box, sir,' said Detective Thompson, and Winston recoiled in horror, saying: 'No, no! There's but one person to guard this box and it's me!' The spectators tagged along as he proceeded down Parliament Street and into the crowded House, where Clementine, Diana, and Randolph were seated in the Strangers' Gallery. His two-and-a-half-hour speech was lucid and witty; at one point he produced a pint of whisky, poured some in a glass, and said: 'It is imperative that I should fortify the revenue and I shall now, with the permission of the Commons, proceed to do so.' Everyone cheered as he sipped except Lady Astor, who had urged Britain to follow America's example and adopt Prohibition. Bowing to her, he noted that she was 'noble' but added: 'I do not think we are likely to learn much from the liquor legislation of the United States.'[187]

Like all budgets, this one required careful scrutiny, and those who studied it line by line realized that in many ways it was an abrupt departure from the traditional Tory approach to ways and means. Churchill believed that the key to fiscal health was productivity, that the leisure class was 'but the glittering scum on the deep river of production.' He wanted to lower taxes on the poor and raise them on unearned income: 'The process of the creation of new wealth is beneficial to the whole community. The process of squatting on old wealth though valuable is a far less lively agent.' At the same time, the Treasury must assume responsibility for the victims of industrial distress. His proposals included a reduction in the pensionable age from seventy to sixty-five, immediate payment of benefits to over 200,000 widows and 350,000 orphans, and abolition of what he called 'restrictions, inquisitions and means tests' for welfare applicants – 'it would be nobody's business what they had or how they employed their time.' He believed that 'by giving a far greater measure of security to the mass of wage-earners, their wives and children, it may promote contentment and stability, and make our Island more truly a home for all these people.' Funds would be set aside to provide health insurance for thirty million Britons; it was here, he argued, that 'the State, with its long and stable finance, can march in and fill the immense gap.' A special sense of urgency, he felt, should spur the government's obligation to help those rendered helpless by circumstances over which they had had no control, adding passionately: 'It is the stragglers, the exhausted, the weak, the wounded, the veterans, the widows and orphans to whom the ambulances of State aid should be directed.'[188]

Winston had stolen Neville Chamberlain's thunder, and Chamberlain resented it. The chancellor's mandate did not include the needy. But rustling was an old Churchillian habit, and few Tories would object if he could find the funds and balance the budget without raising taxes. He could and did. He had searched the files and minds of the Treasury's senior civil servants, and had reached two momentous decisions. The first was a return to the gold standard, of which more presently; the second, a £10,000,000 cut in the service estimates, with the Admiralty as the heavy loser. Only the RAF had emerged unshorn. His reasons were various. One, perhaps, was a tribute to his father's failed crusade. But others were stronger. If he were to win pensions, health insurance, and help for the helpless, he had to wield his scalpel somewhere, and the public mood would support drastic reductions in expensive armaments. Clementine spoke for millions of Britons when she wrote urging him to 'stand up to the Admiralty . . . don't be fascinated or flattered or cajoled by Beatty.' Now that the kaiser's fleet lay on the bottom of the Firth of Forth, Winston reasoned, Britain was secure at sea. The only foreign fleets of any size were those of the United States, which was hardly likely to declare war on England, even over debts, and Japan, whose military establishment, despite its successes against the Bolsheviks, was considered laughable. Churchill assumed that the Germans would keep their word and refrain from building another fleet to challenge British sea power, though later he described this supposition as 'the acme of gullibility.'[189]

The Royal Navy felt betrayed. Here was a former first lord, whose memory was still cherished in wardrooms, 'committed,' as Admiral Sir William James puts it, 'to fight the Admiralty inch by inch for every penny of their estimates.' His chief adversary, the first sea lord, was David Beatty, a Churchill friend since Omdurman. Winston argued that battleships had been obsolescent for some time and were now obsolete. They had been torpedoed at the Yalu River in 1894, at Port Arthur in 1904, and, repeatedly, in the Great War; the American air power evangelist Billy Mitchell had just proved that they could be sunk by Martin MB-2 twin-engined bombers. At the height of the controversy Beatty wrote to his wife: 'Yesterday I was vigorously engaged with Winston and I think on the whole got the better of him. I must say, although I had to say some pretty strong things, he never bears any malice and was good-humoured through the engagement.' Later he joined those who thought Winston had lost his sense of proportion, writing to her heatedly: 'That extraordinary fellow Winston has gone mad. Economically mad, and no sacrifice is too great to achieve what in his shortsightedness is the panacea for all evils – to take 1s off the Income Tax. Nobody outside a lunatic asylum expects a shilling off the Income Tax this Budget . . . As we at the Admiralty are the principal Spending Department, he attacks us with virulence.' And again: 'I have to tackle Winston and had 2½ hours with him this evening. It takes a good deal out of me when dealing with a man of his calibre with a very quick brain. A false step, remark, or even gesture is immediately fastened upon, so I have to keep my wits about me. We of course arrived at nothing . . . We are working up a case for the Prime Minister to adjudicate on the differences which exist between us.'[190]

Baldwin, with his great skill at compromise, restored some of the Admiralty estimates, but Churchill won in the long run; during each of his five years as chancellor, every service except the RAF saw its appropriations dwindle. Even so, the public temper was such that he was frequently attacked as a military spendthrift; the *Economist* faulted him on the ground that 3 per cent of the national income was being allocated to defence, compared with 2 per cent in the later years of Victoria's reign. Perhaps any other chancellor would have done the same. But one expects more from Churchill, and the saddest page in this record is his repeated insistence that the ten-year rule adopted in August 1919 be extended from year to year.* He convinced the Committee of Imperial Defence that it was sound policy, though there was one demurrer. The minutes of the committee's two hundred and thirty-sixth meeting record that: 'LORD BALFOUR was of the opinion that nobody could say that from any one moment war was an impossibility for the next ten years and that we could not rest in a state of unpreparedness on such an assumption by anybody. To

---

* It remained in effect until 1932, 'by which time,' Telford Taylor dryly observes, 'it was a very bad forecast indeed' (in *Munich: The Price of Peace* [New York, 1979], page 201).

suggest that we could be 9½ years away from preparedness would be a most dangerous suggestion.'[191]

Churchill was to oppose rearmament as late as 1929, when B.H. Liddell Hart wrote in the *Daily Telegraph* that 'every important foreign Power has made startling, indeed ominous, increases of expenditure on its army . . . Our Government, which has to keep watch for storm signals, would be false to its duty to this nation if it reduced our slender military strength more drastically until other nations imitate the lead which we have so repeatedly given.' In one instance Churchill was false to himself. He had inveighed against MacDonald for suggesting that the naval base at Singapore be abandoned. Now he argued that Singapore, like Iraq, could be defended by the RAF. He objected to 'measuring our naval strength' against a 'fancied' threat from Dai Nippon, commenting that the Admiralty was 'unduly stressing the Japanese danger.' Indeed, he had been in No 11 less than a month when he asked the Foreign Office to declare that war with Nippon would be impossible for the next twenty years. Austen Chamberlain hesitated, but the decision was made. Early in 1924 the Admiralty recommended the establishment of a submarine base at Hong Kong and the installation 'as fast as possible' of new naval guns at Singapore. 'For what?' asked Winston, who only a few months earlier had been Singapore's staunchest champion. 'A war with Japan! But why should there be a war with Japan? I do not believe there is the slightest chance of it in our lifetime.' He was convinced that 'war with Japan is not a possibility any reasonable government need take into account.' Beatty thought otherwise. Later, with an eye on history, Winston claimed that he had been at a disadvantage because Beatty had not told him of secret telegrams bearing evidence of Japan's aggressive designs. Still, one feels that this was not Churchill's finest hour.[192]

The most sensational moment in Churchill's first budget was his dramatic disclosure that Britain, which had left the gold standard during the war, was back on it. *The Times* reported that this announcement was greeted with 'tremendous cheers.' After the applause had died down he said: 'No responsible authority has advocated any other policy. It has always been a matter of course that we should return to it.' This was simply untrue. Beaverbrook had been against it; on the evening of Budget Day he wrote to Bracken: 'My opinion of Winston has not altered. I knew from the beginning that he would give in to the bankers on the Gold Standard, which, I think, is the biggest sin in this budget.' Half a century later Boothby, looking back on a long public life, said of the return to gold that 'with the exception of the unilateral guarantee to Poland without Russian support, this was the most fatal step taken by the country.'[193]

Beaverbrook and Boothby were among the few Jeremiahs on the issue then; others, and they were almost the only others, were Winston's old colleague Reginald McKenna, a former chancellor; John Maynard Keynes; and Vincent

Vickers, who protested the move by resigning from the board of the Bank of England. Churchill has been blamed for it, and rightly so, because as chancellor he made the decision. The step was not taken lightly, however, or without learned advice. Responsibility was collective and bipartisan. In 1918 the step had been recommended by a standing committee of experts appointed by Lloyd George; a majority of Conservatives, Liberals, and Labourites had then endorsed it. Churchill regarded that endorsement as binding. According to Grigg, the new chancellor invited gold's advocates and adversaries to dinner. Sir Otto Niemeyer of the Bank of England stated the case for gold; McKenna and Keynes argued against it. Winston thought some of the points made by McKenna and Keynes were valid. 'But,' he added, staying off gold 'isn't entirely an economic matter; it [would be] a political decision, for it involves proclaiming that we cannot, for the time being at any rate, complete the undertaking which we all acclaimed was necessary in 1918, and introducing legislation accordingly.'[194]

The roster of men who supported it on economic grounds alone was formidable; they included Austen Chamberlain, another ex-chancellor; Montague Norman, the governor of the Bank of England; and Labour's Philip Snowden, Churchill's immediate predecessor at No. 11, who had intended to put Britain back on gold himself had he remained chancellor. After yielding his seals of office Snowden had eloquently set forth the case for gold in the *Observer*. One Labour MP, Hugh Dalton, a Keynes disciple, challenged Winston's decision: 'We on these benches will hold the Chancellor of the Exchequer strictly to account, and strictly responsible, if, as we fear, there should be a further aggravation of unemployment and of the present trade depression as a result of his action, and should it work out that men who are employed lose their jobs as a result of this deflation. Should that be so we will explain who is to blame.' But Dalton was almost alone in his own party. Labour's leaders didn't even put the issue to a vote. Indeed, years passed before they grasped what had happened. In 1946 Ernest Bevin told the House that Churchill had acted impulsively and 'like a bolt from the blue we were suddenly met with the complete upset of the wage structure in this country.' Bevin neglected to mention that in 1929, four years after Winston had brought England back to the prewar parity of gold, Ramsay MacDonald became Labour's prime minister for the second time while vowing to 'save the pound' – to keep the British economy belted in its twenty-four-carat straitjacket.[195]

Why did they do it, and what did it mean? British financiers, in the Treasury and in the City, were convinced that England's future prosperity could be assured only if London were reestablished as the financial centre of the globe. This, they held, would be impossible until 'the pound can look the dollar in the face.' Churchill told the House: 'We have entered a period on both sides of the Atlantic when political and economic stability seems to be more assured than it has for some years. If this opportunity were missed, it might not recur soon, and the whole finance of the country would be clouded over for an indefinite period by the fact of uncertainty. "Now is the appointed time." ' Niemeyer asked doubters: 'How are we, a great exporting and importing country, to live with an exchange fluctuating with gold, when the United States of America, Germany, Austria, Sweden, Holland, Switzerland, the Dominions . . . and Japan have a stable gold exchange?'[196] To bankers, reestablishing the credit of the pound was worth any risk. In reality, any precious metal or even a flourishing economy can serve as well as gold, and many do today. The Niemeyers, Normans, and Snowdens were living in the past, when Britannia ruled the waves and the pound was regarded with respect and awe in all the world's money markets. They assumed that the restoration of the pound's parity with the American dollar would reestablish Britain's prewar prosperity. None seemed to realize that England had squandered its wealth between Sarajevo and Versailles, or that the country's shrunken export trade could no longer provide the surplus needed to reestablish London's fiscal ascendancy over the rest of the world.

Keynes now emerged. In the *Nation*, the *Evening Standard*, and finally in a pamphlet, 'The Economic Consequences of Mr Churchill,' he went for Winston's jugular, declaring that the chancellor had acted 'partly, perhaps, because he has no instinctive judgement to prevent him from making mistakes; partly, because, lacking this instinctive judgement, he was defeated by the clamorous voice of conventional finance; and most of all, because he was gravely misled by the experts.' The return to gold, Keynes said, 'shackled' and 'enslaved' the country. 'The whole object is to link *rigidly* the City and Wall Street,' and this alarmed him because America, with its rapidly expanding economy, 'lives in a vast and unceasing crescendo. Wide fluctuations, which spell unemployment and misery for us, are swamped for them in the general upward movement.' The United States could afford 'temporary maladjustments' because its productivity was growing 'by several per cent per annum.' Once, when Victoria reigned, that had been true of Britain. 'This, however, is not our state now. Our rate of progress is slow at best,' and flaws which could have been dismissed in the nineteenth century 'are now fatal. The slump of 1921 was even more violent in the United States than here, but by the end of 1922 recovery was practically complete. We still, in 1925, drag on with a million unemployed.'[197]

The effect of going back to gold, said Beaverbrook, was 'making yet more difficult the selling of British goods abroad and so aggravating unemployment at home.' Events soon proved Keynes and Beaverbrook right. English goods which had been priced at eighteen shillings in foreign markets now cost twenty – a full pound. This handicapped all British exporters; some became hopelessly crippled. The owners of British collieries could not compete with German and American coal if they charged higher rates. Their only alternative was to cut their miners' wages. That was ominous. Coal mining, Britain's basic industry, was also the most highly organized and politicized; Keir Hardie, the founder of the Labour party, had been a Scottish miner. The miners' union protested the drop in pay. The Trade Union Congress, or TUC, the English equivalent of America's AFL-CIO, promised to back the miners all the way, and Labour MPs declared their solidarity with them. In July 1925, two days before the cuts were to go into effect, Baldwin temporized. The Treasury, he said, would subsidize the mine owners while a commission headed by Sir Herbert Samuel investigated the situation. The prime minister bought nine months of labour peace, but the cost – first estimated at £10,000,000 but ultimately £23,000,000 – was exorbitant. Churchill had agreed to the stopgap, but he protested, with the rest of the cabinet, when the prime minister proposed to extend it. Keynes was in the thick of things. He asked: 'Why should coal miners suffer a lower standard of life than other classes of labour? They may be lazy, good-for-nothing fellows who do not work so hard or so long as they ought to. But is there any evidence that they are more lazy or more good-for-nothing than other people?' They were, he said, 'victims of the economic juggernaut,' pawns being sacrificed to bridge the gap, required by the return to gold, between $4.40 and $4.86. 'The plight of coal miners,' he concluded, 'is the first – but not, unless we are very lucky, the last – of the Economic Consequences of Mr Churchill.'[198]

Winston retorted angrily: 'I have never heard of any argument more strange and so ill-founded, as that the Gold Standard is responsible for the condition of affairs in the coal industry. The Gold Standard is no more responsible than is the Gulf Stream.'[199] But evidence to the contrary was accumulating; week by week the tension in the mines grew. On March 1, 1926, the Samuel Report was released. It was a thoughtful, practical document, the result of profound research, and its conclusions were an indictment of the coal owners. Over the years, Samuel and his colleagues found, the proprietors had reaped enormous profits while bleeding the industry, refusing to replace obsolete equipment. As a consequence, theirs had become a losing business. Unless the government continued its subsidy, or nationalized the collieries, the miners would have to accept lower wages now. Later, after modern equipment had been installed, their pay would rise. No one could tell when that would be. The report gave the owners and the union six weeks to reach an agreement.

At this point the prime minister should have taken a strong stand. That is what leaders are for. The owners, with their accumulated wealth, could have been pressed to a settlement. But Baldwin had recently compromised himself, declaring publicly: 'All the workers of this country have got to take reductions in wages in order to help put industry on its feet.' So he temporized again. The commission's findings, he said, were disappointing, but if both parties could live with them, the government would not object. This encouraged extremists on each side; they shredded the report with technical arguments and then rejected it outright. Up to this point, Churchill's sympathies had been with the miners. Labour didn't appreciate that; when the coal subsidy forced him to cut health and unemployment insurance appropriations, there were cries of 'Robber!' from the Opposition benches, to which he replied that for one who had frequently been called a 'murderer,' this was 'a sort of promotion.' Unknown to them, he had sent young Harold Macmillan to Newcastle, asking him to report on the situation there, and on April 10 Macmillan – who felt it 'a great honour to be taken into your confidence' – wrote describing 'the appalling conditions in this area.' He thought that 'the patience and the endurance of the workers as a whole is really remarkable. Certainly adversity brings out greater virtues than prosperity in all classes, but peculiarly so among the working people.' Churchill was optimistic; he felt certain that a way to reward these virtues would be found. After all, those on both sides were Englishmen. Speaking to the Belfast Chamber of Commerce he said that he did not share the opinion, so widespread abroad, particularly in the United States, 'that Britain is down and out, that the foundations of our commerce and industrial greatness have been sapped; that the stamina of our people is impaired; that the workmen are lazy; that our employers are indolent; that our Empire is falling to pieces. I have never been able to take that view.' He assured his audience that the justifiable grievances of 'our much-abused coal miners' would be peacefully resolved.[200]

They weren't. Strife was now inevitable, and before it ended the conflict would cost over £800,000,000. The crisis began on May Day, 1926. That Saturday morning miners who had assembled for the day's first seven-hour shift were notified that their future pay envelopes would be thinner. They protested and the owners locked them out. At noon the TUC General Council, meeting in London, unanimously agreed that unless wage levels were restored at once, a nationwide general strike would begin on Monday at one minute before midnight. The general strike is labour's ultimate weapon. If prolonged, it can destroy society. English legal scholars then and since have agreed that to call one, or even threaten one, is a violation of the British constitution. The prospect made the entire country tremble. Yet grave as the situation was, the TUC decision was followed by forty-eight hours of chaos more appropriate in a Marx Brothers film than in the British establishment. The General Council, after alerting affiliates to its decision, sent the prime minister a letter, formally setting the deadline and offering to negotiate. Baldwin asked for two weeks' grace, 'confident that a settlement can be reached on the basis of the Samuel Report.' Since that implied a temporary acceptance of the wage cut, and since the miners had developed the slogan 'Not a penny off the pay, not a minute on the day,' the TUC replied that its membership must be consulted. It was then discovered that the miners had left London and gone home. Telegrams were dispatched recalling them, but it was late on Sunday before a TUC delegation was ready to approach the government. That evening the union men called at No. 10. Nobody was home. The cabinet was meeting next door in Churchill's house. After a long, confused delay, while the delegates waited on the pavement, Baldwin emerged with Birkenhead and said: 'Gentlemen, I am sorry to say that our efforts for peace are unavailing. Something has happened at the *Daily Mail* and the Cabinet has empowered me to hand you this letter.' They shook hands and he said: 'Goodbye; this is the end.' Gathering under a Downing Street lamp, they opened the envelope and learned that compositors at Lord Rothermere's *Daily Mail*, members of the National Society of Operative Printers and Assistants, had refused to set type for a vehemently antilabour editorial titled 'For King and Country.' Printers at the *Express* and other papers had indicated that they were prepared to do the same.[201]

It has become part of Labour myth that Churchill exploited this incident to force a showdown with the unions. Ernest Bevin repeated the accusation again and again; the cabinet was within 'five minutes' of reaching terms for a settlement, he said, when Winston learned what was happening at the *Daily Mail*, 'dashed up to Downing Street, ordered a meeting of the Cabinet, rushed Baldwin off his feet . . . and in a few minutes the ultimatum was given to us.' Stories that Churchill was hostile towards organized labour had, of course, been in circulation since Tonypandy in 1909. The misunderstanding had grown, in part, because of his diatribes on socialism, which, under Labour's banner, had become the political voice of the working class. But he himself drew a distinction. 'When all is said and done,' he wrote, 'there are very few well-informed persons in Great Britain, and not many employers of labour on a large scale, who would not sooner have to deal with the British trade unions as we know them, than with the wide vagaries of communist-agitated and totally disorganized discontent.' As he had written to James Lane of the bricklayers: 'I take a high view of the dignity both of craftsmanship and manual labour.' Bevin's account is absurd anyhow. Since the cabinet had gathered in Churchill's Downing Street home, he would hardly have 'dashed up to Downing Street' to reach it. The conference had already begun when Baldwin and his ministers learned of the *Mail* wildcatters. And the news came, not from Winston, but by telephone.[202]

After the *Mail* bombshell, Churchill was among the most vehement ministers – the others were Amery, Neville Chamberlain, and 'Jix' Joynson-Hicks, the home secretary – in vowing not to capitulate. But there were no dissenters. The vote to break off talks was unanimous. Baldwin later told the House that the cabinet interpreted the phone call as a sign that 'the first overt move in the General Strike was being actually made, by trying to suppress the press. We felt that in those circumstances the whole situation was changed.' One wonders why. It would have been easy to learn the truth by placing a few more calls. The fact was that the printers' action had been impulsive and in no way reflected a larger strategy. The TUC leaders had been unaware of it and disowned it the moment they read Baldwin's letter. The attempt to intimidate a free press outraged as many Labour MPs as Tories; more, perhaps, because some Tory back-benchers had been praying for a casus belli. Nevertheless, at 1:00 A.M. on Monday reporters in Downing Street were given a brief announcement that negotiations had been discontinued. A few hours later a TUC delegation arrived at No. 10, bearing a written repudiation of the *Mail* printers. Ramsay MacDonald told the House 'they found the door locked and the whole place in darkness.'[203] That was inexcusable, but so was the TUC's action on Saturday in raising the spectre of a general strike – for which the unions were completely unprepared – and the cloudy understanding between the miners and the TUC. The miners had authorized the unions' national leadership to negotiate for them, but not to bargain. Thus, though sporadic attempts to resume talks continued through Monday, the TUC's inability to compromise without the miners' sanction hardened the cabinet's position. And as the evening wore on Churchill, facing the imminent rupture of British order, grew increasingly defiant. He would be the most visible leader on one side; Bevin, on the other.

Bevin at that time was general secretary of the Transport and General Workers' Union, a merger of twenty-two unions, and at 11:59 P.M., as commander in chief of the general strike, he pushed the button. Six million Britons were thereby committed to walking off the job. Iron and steel foundries closed down. Bus drivers abandoned their buses. Newspapers ceased publication. No trains moved, no trucks; the tubes were silent. Building-trade workers, dockworkers, workers in the chemical industry, stayed home. Gas, sanitary, health, and food services deemed 'essential' were supposed to be spared, but many gas and electricity works came to a standstill. The government was not unprepared, however. In 1920 Churchill had devised a plan against just such a contingency. The country was divided into nine areas, each with a central controller and staff. Troops would be dispatched to convoy vehicles carrying food and fuel. The police were fully mobilized; Hyde Park became a military post; the Welsh Guards were billeted on the Victoria Embankment. Joynson-Hicks appealed for volunteers, and thousands of Englishmen and Englishwomen of the upper and middle classes drove trucks, trams, taxis, and even locomotives. Some members of the House of Lords served as railway porters. It was a peculiarly British emergency; there was little or no violence, and in many places volunteers, strikers, and policemen mingled with civility and even gaiety. Churchill, however, was not among the skylarkers. He felt grim. The miners' strike had been legitimate, even admirable, he said, 'but that is an entirely different thing from the concerted, deliberate organized menace of a General Strike in order to compel Parliament to do something which otherwise it would not do.' He wanted to intimidate the strikers with a show of force; at his suggestion, territorials were encouraged to enlist as civil constabulary reserves, and only after a long argument did his colleagues persuade him that the recruits should wear, not military uniforms, but mufti with armbands, and their weapons be limited to truncheons. Some ministers worried about costs. Churchill rumbled: 'The Exchequer will pay! If we start arguing about petty details, we'll have a tired-out police force, a dissipated army and bloody revolution.' He was embattled, and wondered why the country didn't share his mood. He said: 'One of the great difficulties of the situation is that large numbers of working people feel quite detached from the conflict; and they are waiting, as if they were spectators at a football match, to see whether the Government or the Trade Union is the stronger.' His provocative comments, friends warned him, were deepening labour's resentment of him. He replied that he rejoiced in their hostility: 'People who are not prepared to do unpopular things and to defy clamour are not fit to be Ministers in times of stress.'[204]

* * *

651

That would have ruled out the prime minister. 'Baldwin,' in the words of one British historian, now 'adopted a policy of masterly inactivity.' Churchill's delight in battle puzzled him; essentially gentle, he himself shrank from discord almost as a matter of principle. Yet he snorted when told that Beaverbrook had remarked: 'Churchill is the real power in the Government.' He knew this to be quite untrue. Beyond casting his vote, Winston had played no role in the severance of negotiations after the *Mail* episode. Later, Baldwin had excluded him from the select cabinet council which met daily to discuss supervising strikebreaking tactics. But Winston kept trying to intervene, and his combative stance loomed ever larger in the public view. Baldwin didn't want to offend him – Churchill was now next in line for the prime ministership, and his militancy was winning grudging converts among some Tory diehards – but he did want him out of his hair. Then a solution presented itself. H.A. Gwynne of the *Morning Post* approached John Davidson, a senior civil servant. If his premises were protected, he said, he would put his presses at the disposal of the government. The Tories could have their own newspaper. In a week, he predicted, he could build a circulation as high as 400,000 copies. Sir Samuel Hoare, told of the offer, proposed publishing a government paper to be called the *British Gazette*. The prime minister agreed but did not want Gwynne as its director. Instead, he appointed Churchill editor in chief. It was, Baldwin later said, 'the cleverest thing I ever did.'[205]

He may have been right. In his long career Baldwin did few clever things, and this decision prevented the chancellor from playing a major role in determining the outcome of the strike. Winston himself savoured a delicious irony. For twenty years Gwynne had been his most savage press critic, and now the *Morning Post*'s perennial target would be running the *Post*'s shop. He announced that the paper would be written, edited, and published by volunteers. Printers were a problem. On instructions from their union, Gwynne's compositors stayed out. Beaverbrook said he could send a printer's foreman at once. Given time, he could find other willing hands among his idle *Daily Express* employees, and the *Daily Mail* thought some of their men might pitch in. Winston wouldn't wait. Beric Holt, who had agreed to serve as one of the *Gazette*'s editorial assistants, recalls joining a small procession of men who, in the early hours of Tuesday, May 4, 'filed up the narrow back stairs of the *Morning Post* building just off the Strand.' In the composing room Sydney Long, night superintendent of the *Daily Express*, was already sitting at a Linotype machine, setting copy. Irish Guards and bobbies restrained an angry crowd of strikers on the street below. Churchill, in shirt sleeves, was peering down at large enamel mugs on the floor. He asked their purpose. Holt, who had been there before, replied: 'Beer, sir.' 'Have they got enough?' asked Winston. A man answered: 'Oh yes, sir, plenty.' 'Nonsense!' boomed Churchill, producing a pound note. 'There is no such thing! Send out for some more.'[206]

The presses ran all night, and by 6:00 A.M. they had printed 232,000 copies, all of which were sold within an hour. The entire issue had been set single-handedly by Long. The lead article, unsigned but written by Churchill, set the tone: 'This great nation, on the whole the strongest community which civilisation can show, is for the moment reduced in this respect to the level of African natives dependent only on the rumours which are carried from place to place. In a few days if this were allowed to continue, rumours would poison the air, raise panics and disorders, inflame fears and passions together, and carry us all to the depths which no sane man of any party or class would care even to contemplate.' On the second day the circulation rose to 507,000. A week later, on the last day of the general strike, it soared to 2,209,000. The cabinet had been under the impression that the *Gazette*'s contents would be limited to public notices, official statements, and indispensable information. Winston had assured British newspaper publishers: 'I do not contemplate violent partisanship, but fair, strong encouragement to the great mass of loyal people.' No one who knew him believed that – Beaverbrook had burst into laughter when told of it – for he was incapable of impartiality. When push came to shove, as it now had in England, he believed that the standards of traditional journalism were anaemic. 'The field of battle,' he now wrote grandly, 'is no longer transport but news.' Then: 'The State cannot be impartial between itself and that section of subjects with whom it is contending.' And, most memorably, when reproached in the House for his ringing editorial denunciations of the strike: 'I decline utterly to be impartial between the fire brigade and the fire.' [207]

That was defensible. The paper's pretence of objectivity in its news columns was not. Under the heading FALSE NEWS appeared the notice: 'Many false rumours are current. Believe nothing until you see it in an authoritative journal like the *British Gazette*.' Yet readers of the *Gazette* were led to believe that the country was in the grip, not of an industrial dispute, but of incipient revolution. The strike was described as 'a direct challenge to ordered government.' Strikers were 'the enemy.' A specious claim from a French paper that Bolsheviks were behind the TUC was reprinted in full. *Gazette* accounts of House debates were outrageously distorted, one Labour MP being described as 'a wild Socialist, passionate and shouting.' An MP's conviction that a settlement was at hand was denied by an unidentified 'Cabinet Minister.' Heavy coverage was given to Sir John Simon's irresponsible statement that each TUC leader could be successfully sued to 'the utmost farthing of his personal possessions.' At a time when the walkout had virtually paralysed Britain a headline reported that the strike was NOT SO COMPLETE AS HOPED BY ITS PROMOTERS. All Englishmen were 'calm and confident' that it would fail – the six million strikers, apparently, were no longer regarded as English. Strikebreakers were reassured: 'No man who does his duty loyally to the country in the present crisis will be left unprotected by the State from subsequent reprisals' – a pledge, involving forces of the Crown, to which the King took strong exception. Patriotic poetry appeared frequently: Kipling, and, in three issues, Tennyson's 'Soul of England.' While Baldwin's speeches and statements were bland, offensive to no one, the *Gazette* repeatedly blared that until the TUC surrendered unconditionally, 'there can be no question of compromise of any kind.'[208]

The *Gazette*'s belligerence troubled many of Churchill's old friends and allies. Lloyd George disapproved of the strike, but, as he told the House, 'I know a great many of the people responsible. They are as little revolutionaries as any men in this House. They have fought the rebellious ones in their own Party.' He accused Winston of sabotaging a TUC attempt to reach an agreement and called his paper 'a first-class indiscretion, clothed in the tawdry garb of third-rate journalism.' Churchill replied: 'It is not the duty of the *British Gazette* to publish a lot of defeatist trash.' Gwynne, of course, was sharply critical. Thomas Jones noted in his diary that the *Morning Post* editor 'has sent several messages begging that Winston should be kept away from that office where the "British Gazette" is being printed. He butts in at the busiest hours and insists on changing commas and full stops until the staff is furious.' But the heaviest protests naturally came from the strike leaders. They countered with a paper of their own, the *British Worker*. Winston was its chief target; the idea of calling an industrial dispute a revolutionary movement, the *Worker* declared, 'was mainly Mr Churchill's. It is a melodramatic "stunt" on Sydney [sic] Street lines . . . The nation has kept its head in spite of the alarming tricks played upon it. Mr Churchill has failed again, and everybody knows . . . that "revolution" exists nowhere save in Mr Churchill's heated and disorderly imagination.' The following day the *Worker* observed that 'day by day in the Cabinet's newspaper, Mr Churchill, acting as its super-editor, publishes articles by prominent men. These are suspiciously like one another . . . The reference to the Strike being directed by a "relatively small body of extremists" again betrays Mr Churchill's hand. It is mere violent, headlong, foolish propaganda – foolish because no sensible person will believe it.' They only wished that were true. Winston's articles *were* believed; his flaming prose was being read in millions of upper- and middle-class homes, which was why the unions, too, had turned to journalism. They failed. Their editorials were dense and dull. Their greatest circulation was 713,000 for a single edition. In desperation, one firebrand slipped into the *Post* building and threw a steel bar into a press. Holt recalls: 'Suddenly there was a horrible shattering jar. Power was turned off.' Workers at the Hoe Company, makers of the machine, refused to repair it. Churchill called the Chatham Dockyard, and Royal Navy ratings arrived in an impressive convoy, departed, and returned with mended parts wrapped in a Union Jack. Winston then issued each member of the staff a mauve pass. Nobody could enter the building without one.[209]

Not all *Gazette* critics lay outside the Establishment. The British Broadcasting Company was struggling to keep its news reports impartial, but Winston, according to John Reith, then its managing director, tried to treat the BBC as 'an offshoot of the *British Gazette*.' Reith appealed to Davidson, Joynson-Hicks, and Baldwin, and when Churchill asked the cabinet to let him run the BBC he was turned down. Reith did permit him to address the radio audience, however, and Beatrice Webb, perhaps the first to appreciate his mastery of this medium, described the talk as 'a vividly rhetorical representation of his own case . . . Except that his voice is harsh, he is a first rate broadcaster.' He vexed London's press lords that week, though not over a matter of principle. As the *Gazette*'s popularity rocketed, he began commandeering all the newsprint in London. Dawson remonstrated, then Rothermere, and finally Beaverbrook wrote to him that the two hundred tons of paper at the *Daily Express* would be needed the moment the strike ended. Impossible, Winston replied: 'We are expecting to publish over three millions tonight, and we shall probably have to requisition every scrap of newsprint which is available and suitable.' They met. Beaverbrook liked to tell friends that Winston had two moods, 'Winston Up' and 'Winston Down.' Down, facing defeat, he was magnificent, but 'in a position of uncontrolled power and authority,' as he was at this point, he could be frightening. Of the newsprint confrontation Beaverbrook later recalled: 'If any other man living had used such outrageous language to me as he did on that occasion I should never have forgiven him. Churchill on top of the wave has in him the stuff of which tyrants are made.' [210]

This 'terrible scene,' as Beaverbrook thereafter called it, turned out to be unnecessary. Early the following morning – Wednesday, May 12, the ninth day of the crisis – the unions capitulated. Their treasury was empty, the government's attrition policy was working, and public opinion, fired by the *Gazette*, was hostile. Arthur Pugh, the TUC chairman, called at No. 10 to surrender. Accompanying him was the TUC's general secretary, who wrote in his diary that evening: 'While we were talking, Churchill, Baldwin, and Sir Arthur Steel-Maitland [minister of labour] were pacing rapidly up and down the garden, talking animatedly. There was no sign of jubilation amongst them, and Pugh muttered to me: "I saw Churchill a few minutes ago, and he said, 'Thank God it's over, Mr Pugh.' " ' That afternoon Winston announced that the next issue of the *Gazette* would be the last. Its final headline was unfortunate. It gloated: SURRENDER RECEIVED BY PREMIER IN DOWNING STREET. In an envoi Churchill told his readers: 'The *British Gazette* may have had a short life, but it has fulfilled the purpose of living. It becomes a memory; but it remains a monument.' That evening he took a large party to see Adele and Fred Astaire in *Lady Be Good*, then playing at the old Empire Theatre. As he entered, the audience rose and gave him a standing ovation. [211]

Labour's intellectuals now singled him out for attack. Kingsley Martin, a young leftist writer, studied the columns of the *Gazette*, noted its incendiary style, found certain striking omissions – Churchill had suppressed an appeal from the Church which had blamed both sides – and concluded that Winston had been 'discredited.' The *New Statesman*, then as now a journal of eccentric opinion, perpetrated a fraud. On the night of May 10, it reported, Churchill had led a 'war party' of ministers who threatened to resign at once unless talks with the union leaders were broken off. The Churchill faction, it continued, had been 'in favour of war at all costs.' This piece of outright fiction declared: 'Mr Churchill was the villain of the piece. He is reported to have remarked that he thought "a little blood-letting" would be all to the good.' Winston considered pressing charges of criminal libel against the editors. Sir Douglas Hogg, the government's attorney general, advised against it. He would certainly win, Hogg said, but in court the defendants could discuss cabinet deliberations 'in detail,' which would offend Baldwin Tories. Winston reluctantly let the matter drop, though it was already clear to him that run-of-the-mill Conservatives viewed him with little more favour than the Labourites. Dawson of *The Times*, in a widely read account of the strike, concluded that 'Winston seems to have been the only minister who rather lost his head. He was excitable, provocative, and a great trial to his colleagues. They tried to divert his energies at an early stage to the editing of the *British Gazette*, an official propagandist organ, in which he became a similar trial to us.' [212]

Curiously, one journalist who commended Churchill's editorial performance was the irascible Gwynne. He wrote to him: 'May I lay at your feet my tribute of admiration at your wonderful energy and your marvellous powers of seeing things through?' In time Winston recalled his *Gazette* experience with nostalgia. On June 10, 1927, he wrote to Gwynne: 'I shall always look back to that extraordinary ten days. They form one of the most vivid experiences of my somewhat variegated life, and were utterly different from every other episode. I am glad to think they have left behind them a better understanding between us.' He even exploited the episode in one of his quick turns of parliamentary wit. In a tense debate he faced the Opposition and said solemnly: 'I have no wish to make threats or use language which would disturb the House and cause bad blood. But this I must say: make your minds perfectly clear that if ever you loose upon us again a General Strike, we will loose upon you' – angry shouts were on Labour lips – 'another *British Gazette*.' The expected storm, Baldwin wrote to the King, 'gave way to an outburst of unrestrained laughter in which the House was convulsed.' [213]

In a long public life clouded with misunderstandings, none was more tragic than the inexpiable enmity between Churchill and Labour. He had been a progressive home secretary; he was a humane chancellor. His record on liberal issues in many ways resembled that of Bismarck, another farsighted conservative. It was far more impressive than that of, say, Ramsay Macdonald, who waffled again and again when in power. But Winston's visceral reaction against socialism – he was always mistaking pink for red – led him into one rhetorical excess after another. It was Churchillian bombast which had touched off the Labourites' antagonism towards him. They took him at his word, despite the fact that his word, however prickly, was often conspicuously at odds with his deeds. The Dawsons of the Conservative party distrusted him for an altogether different reason. When the strikers had unsheathed their sword, he had lunged for his; he could never back away from a challenge. But at heart he still believed that the miners were right and the mineowners wrong. When the TUC collapsed he had written to Baldwin: 'To-night surrender.

656

Tomorrow magnanimity.' He had been moved to pity by Macmillan's descriptions of the hovels in which the miners lived, their brutish working conditions, and their sickly children. Now that members of the other unions had gone back to work, ending the threat to domestic tranquillity, he was eager to settle the grievances in the coalfields, which were still idle. To his dismay, the strike there dragged on for more than five months, and he and Amery were the only members of the cabinet who urged action. 'I'm all on the miners' side now,' he told Boothby after closing down the *Gazette*. Baldwin, departing for an extended holiday at Aix-les-Bains, left the matter in Winston's hands.[214]

It was a delicate, heartbreaking – and, in the end, doomed – task. The Tory ministers' hostility towards the coal strikers was unabated. By the sheer force of will, intellect, and volubility, Winston preserved the workers' right to picket peacefully; he throttled legislation to outlaw strikes when, in his words, 'a majority of those affected are in favour of it'; he used Treasury funds, not to subsidize the mines' proprietors, but to build miners' homes and fund 'training schemes and other forms of assistance for displaced miners'; and he saved the workers' right to the secret ballot – the owners argued that this would increase the number of strikes – because he was 'convinced that the majority of working men would adopt sound and sensible attitudes,' and because private polling, in his view, restricted the influence of the unions' 'extremist members.'[215]

MacDonald, he knew, was close to Herbert Smith, the president of the miners' union. On Winston's initiative, Churchill and MacDonald held two long, secret meetings, first at Chartwell and then in Sir Abe Bailey's London home in Bryanston Square, near Marble Arch. Smith had authorized MacDonald to speak for him, and the two men forged an agreement. Winston then drew up an ultimatum to be delivered to the colliery proprietors, omitting the strikers' most extravagant demands but including those terms which were minimal for them and the Labour Party. Keeping Baldwin informed, he laid this compromise before the cabinet: 'Do not, I beg you, throw this chance upon the rubbish heap of so many others.' His colleagues disapproved of this proposal – they thought it gave the workers too much – but, as one said afterwards, 'We couldn't repudiate Winston.' The real question, as he had told MacDonald, was whether the coal barons would bow to the ultimatum. It was 'quite likely,' he had said, that they 'might refuse to come, or, if they did come, might take a line that would make progress impossible.' In that event, the government 'would make no secret of their opinion that they were in the wrong,' but 'the powers of actual coercion that the Government possesses are very limited.' The miners now believed that Churchill was their best hope; the *Evening Standard* reported that both they and the TUC, asked to choose between Winston and any other member of the government, had expressed 'a marked preference for Mr Churchill as mediator.'[216]

It proved an impossible task. The owners, speaking through Evan Williams, the president of the Mining Association of Great Britain, refused to make any concession whatever. They knew the men were desperate, growing hungrier every day, with winter dead ahead. Thomas Jones described one meeting between Williams and Churchill as 'acute and at times acrimonious,' but Williams wouldn't budge. He fought every attempt at reconciliation. They met again at No. 10; Jones called it 'a ding-dong debate' which accomplished nothing. Winston's anger at the owners grew. He poured it out in letters to Clementine. She replied: 'I fear you are having a very anxious and difficult time'; the proprietors' position, she said, seemed 'hard and cruel.' He wrote to her that the talks were leading towards a 'serious collision.' She hoped he wasn't shouldering the other ministers aside and thus alienating them: 'You are having an anxious but a thrilling and engrossing time with power & scope which is what the Pig likes – I suppose Steel-Maitland and George Lane-Fox [secretary for mines] are not often allowed near the trough? If the cat were Minister of Labour or Mines she would not give up her place there without a few "miaows." '[217]

But Steel-Maitland and Lane-Fox would cede the miners nothing. And Baldwin, when he returned to London, agreed with them. Churchill proposed statutory intervention. Other wealthy contributors to Tory coffers had taken an interest in the talks, however, and when Winston wrote to Baldwin, 'I do hope that a little employers' agitation will not prevent HMG from advancing with courage & conviction against . . . detractors of the public interest,' he found that the agitation of Williams's clients had done just that. The most the prime minister would promise was a toothless appeal tribunal. After Churchill scorned 'the greedy appetites of the coal trade,' two of his closest friends, Birkenhead and Lord Londonderry, reproached him. Londonderry, a mine-owner and one of Winston's cousins, argued that the owners were fighting bolshevism. Winston replied: 'With those parts of your letter which deal with the necessity for combating Bolshevism I am in entire accord. But there could be no worse way of combating Bolshevism than to identify the Conservative Party and His Majesty's Government with the employers, and particularly with a body of employers like those headed by Mr Evan Williams . . . The duty of the Government is to occupy an impartial position in the interests of the State and of the whole community . . . You say that the Owners are fighting Socialism. It is not the business of Coal Owners as Coal Owners to fight Socialism. If they declare it their duty, how can they blame the Miners' Federation for pursuing political ends? The business of the Coal Owners is to manage their industry successfully, to insist upon sound economic conditions as regards hours and wages, and to fight Socialism as citizens and not as owners of a particular class of property.'[218]

It was hopeless. He wanted to warn the owners that if they continued to be 'unreasonable,' the government would appoint arbitrators and fix a national minimum wage. It seemed clear to him that a few rich Englishmen, and they alone, were blocking a settlement. When they refused even to participate in tripartite talks with the government and the union, he told the cabinet that their position was 'wholly wrong and unreasonable, an attitude without precedent in recent times,' and charged that they had even influenced Tory whips in the House, who had 'been at some of the Ministers, urging them to do nothing.' Certainly the cabinet's reluctance to subject the owners to any pressure whatever is singular; the impasse, after all, was eroding the national economy. Harold Laski, after accompanying miner delegates to one meeting, wrote to a friend that he thought Baldwin 'quite tragic . . . hard and a little cynical and impatient of all criticism . . . Churchill who was there was bigger and more skilful in every way – he knew how to negotiate. Baldwin merely blundering uncouthly.' Of the 1,250,000 union members, 100,000 demoralized men had returned to work by early October. Boothby, like Macmillan, went into the coalfields to talk to strikers. On October 9 he wrote to Churchill from the Carlton Club: 'It is the impression, growing every day, that the Government has now divested itself of all responsibility for the conduct of our national industries . . . that despite the promise of the first months it has become . . . a Government of reaction.' It would, he continued, 'be difficult to exaggerate the effect of your vigorous intervention in the mining dispute last month' or 'the disappointment which attended the failure of your efforts.' In the end the owners' obduracy was triumphant. As Leo Amery wrote later: 'The miners straggled back to the pits on the owners' terms, including longer hours, a beaten and resentful army.'[219]

Worse followed. In the wake of the broken strike, the parliamentary Conservatives passed a wave of antilabour legislation. All the gains Churchill had achieved for the unions were abolished. Picketing was outlawed; no worker could be disciplined for refusing to join a strike deemed 'illegal'; the attorney general was authorized to seize union funds; the Trades Dispute Act of 1906, which exempted unions from legal suit, was repealed. In a blow at the Labour party, unions were prohibited from collecting money from their members for political purposes unless they had secured their written consent. For Churchill, the low point came when a delegation of miners arrived at the Treasury and charged him with betraying them. Jones wrote in his diary that this was grossly unfair; that Winston had tried 'to go to great lengths in the way of legislation on hours, wages and conditions – which terrified his colleagues.' But all the workmen knew was that he had failed them. Smith, their leader, stood before Winston, trembling with rage. Gaunt and pale, he was a symbol of their deprivation; born in a Lancashire workhouse, the posthumous son of a miner killed in a mine accident, he himself had begun working in the pits on his tenth birthday. Later he would write of this meeting: 'We said to Churchill: "We understand you were a man of courage, but you have broken down at the first fence. You have dismounted. Have you been doing wrong while the masters have been away; and got reprimanded?" He did not like it.'[220]

He hated it, and could not reply; he understood their bitterness, for he shared it. In less than two years he would grasp the magnitude of his error in putting England back on the gold standard. Writing Grigg on July 2, 1928, he dealt savagely with the financial experts who had urged him to do it: 'They have caused an immense amount of misery and impoverishment by their rough and pedantic handling of the problem. In ruined homes, in demoralised workmen, in discouraged industry, in embarrassed finances, in inflated debt and cruel taxation we have paid the price.' Eleven years after the tumult of 1926 he wrote that industrial strife 'has introduced a narrowing element into our public life. It has been a keenly felt impediment to our productive and competitive power. It has become the main foundation of a socialist political party which has ruled the State greatly to its disadvantage, and will assuredly do so again.'²²¹ Churchill was not the only statesman to be baffled by twentieth-century economics. He was, however, among the very few British Conservatives who had seen the justice of the workers' cause. It is not the least of the ironies in his career that within twenty years, when he was at the peak of his achievements, their resentment would coalesce to drive him from office.

Today's Europeans and Americans who reached the age of awareness after mid-century, when the communications revolution led to expectations of instantaneity, are exasperated by the slow toils of history. They assume that the lightning of cause will be swiftly followed by the thunderclap of effect. Great political sea changes move at a testudinal pace, however. Change is preceded by reappraisals, false starts, and frequent setbacks. William Lloyd Garrison founded the *Liberator* in 1831, yet over thirty years passed before Lincoln freed the slaves. The big Swede christened Joseph Hagglund and remembered as Joe Hill was executed by a firing squad on November 19, 1915. It would be another generation before organized labour was ready to test its strength. Alexander Fleming discovered penicillin at St Mary's Hospital, London, in 1928. Not until the later stages of World War II would it become available to physicians, and then in limited supply. The American Equal Rights Association was founded by New York feminists on May 10, 1866, but their great-great-granddaughters are still struggling to realize their dream. Even so cataclysmic an event as the First World War did not reach its maximum impact until more than ten years after the Armistice, when Remarque's *All Quiet on the Western Front*, Hemingway's *Farewell to Arms*, Graves's *Goodbye to All That*, and Sassoon's *Memoirs of an Infantry Officer* reached audiences ready, at last, to believe what, until then, had been thought unbelievable.

So it was with the general strike of 1926 and the career of Winston Churchill. During the three years which followed, he rode a crest of acclaim in the middle and upper classes, unbruised by the grievances of those at both ends of the political spectrum who had been angered by his performance during the nine days and the long aftermath. The strike had been broken, the government had won, the miners were back in the pits, and he had been the cabinet's most colourful cheerleader. His mistakes were unobserved; hardly anyone understood economics anyway. But he certainly sounded as though *he* did. Each budget speech was more brilliant than the last. Altogether he presided over five Budget Days, a record matched only by Walpole, Pitt, Peel, and Gladstone, each of whom became prime minister. Bets were made on when Churchill would move into No. 10. His only rival was the rising star Neville Chamberlain, and even Chamberlain wrote of him in 1928: 'One doesn't often come across a real man of genius or, perhaps, appreciate him when one does. Winston is such a man.' It was generally agreed that Churchill was mellowing. Lord Winterton wrote: 'The remarkable thing about him is the way he has suddenly acquired, quite late in Parliamentary life, an immense fund of tact, patience, good humour and banter on almost all occasions; no one used to "suffer fools ungladly" more fully than Winston; now he is friendly and accessible to everyone, both in the House, and in the lobbies, with the result that he has become what he never was before the war, very popular in the House generally – a great accretion to his already formidable Parliamentary power.'[222]

His wit could still wound – 'Politics are very much like war,' he said; 'we even use poison gas at times' – and once he devastated a hostile woman MP who berated him during a dinner party, ending her diatribe by observing with scorn: 'Mr. Churchill, you are drunk.' 'And you, madam,' Churchill replied, 'are ugly. But I shall be sober tomorrow.' Yet his humour now was often gentle, even self-deprecating. After a small dinner at Pratt's Club in London, FE proposed that Lord Melchett, the richest man in the party, should pay the bill. Winston demurred: 'My dear Freddie, surely you would not deprive me of the pride and pleasure of giving a crust to Croesus?' After he had switched parties and Baldwin had made him chancellor, Churchill said: 'You know, the family motto of the House of Marlborough from which I descend is "Faithful but Unfortunate." ' A gushing woman asked him: 'Doesn't it thrill you, Mr Churchill, to know that every time you speak the hall is packed to overflowing?' Winston said: 'It is quite flattering, but whenever I feel this way I always remember that, if instead of making a political speech, I was being hanged, the crowd would be twice as big.'[223]

Baldwin was dazzled by him, and during these years, when there was no threat to it, their relationship approached genuine friendship. On the evening of each Budget Day the prime minister sent the King an appraisal of the chancellor's presentation. Each was giddier than the last. In one he wrote that Churchill 'has a power of attraction which nobody in the House of Commons can excel.' Another spoke of Churchill's 'masterpiece of cleverness and ingenuity.' In a third, reporting on a speech which had lasted three and a half hours, he wrote: 'The House became intensely interested in watching a master in the art of oratory and tantalizing the imagination unfold his ideas in a speech packed with ideas, yet so simple and clear that there could be no possible misunderstanding.' Then he sent Winston himself a note: 'I hate to use the word "brilliant": it has been worked to death and is too suggestive of brilliantine: but, if I may use it in its pristine virginity, so to speak, it is the right one. I congratulate you with both hands.' Some veteran MPs across the aisle were also impressed. Lloyd George called him 'the merriest tax collector since the days of Robin Hood.' And the press, for once, was on his side. Cartoonists

661

depicted him as the 'Smiling Chancellor,' and 'Winsome Winston.' The *Times of India* commented: 'In appearance Mr Churchill is almost jovial; one can imagine him, dressed in a cowl, the incarnation of the jolly monks and friars of centuries ago.'[224]

Of course, there were those who saw him very differently. Ardent Labour MPs attacked him relentlessly, Snowden crying after one budget speech: 'There is not one penny of relief for the wage-earning classes. Shorn of all the glamour of the Right Honourable Gentleman's eloquence, this is his Budget. No more of a rich man's Budget has ever been presented. It will not take long for the glamour to disappear, and then the great toiling masses will realize the true character of this Budget, and will realize, too, that the Tory Party is still more than ever what Lord George Hamilton declared many years ago: "A party that looks after its own friends, whether it be in office or out of office." '

On Churchill's own side of the House, Conservative back-benchers had not forgotten his stands on Home Rule and Free Trade, and their wrath was rekindled in 1928, when, led by Leo Amery, they made a fresh attempt to follow the American example and introduce protective tariffs, arguing that they would put a million Englishmen back to work. Churchill blocked them; Baldwin supported him. Amery wrote angrily in his diary of 'the whole attitude of the Cabinet under Winston's influence, and the PM's decision not to do anything'; Lane-Fox noted that the protectionists were 'now very angry and a lot is going on. It is the first sign of a real party fissure that I have yet seen.' The storm was small and it passed quickly. Winston wrote to Clementine: 'Really I feel vy independent of them all.'[225]

That was precisely his problem. His independence had become a point of political vulnerability. Of all the major prewar public men, he alone had survived; as A. G. Gardiner put it, 'Like the camomile, the more he is trodden on, the more he flourishes.' Yet after nearly three decades in public life he still floated free of any power base. Epping was a mere convenience. Unlike most senior members of the House, he had no national following, controlled no political hierarchy. Party discipline has always been taken more seriously in Britain than in the United States, and Churchill had been a disciplinary problem all his life. Beaverbrook noted that he 'neither tied the Liberals to him nor conciliated the Tories.' Gardiner wrote in 1926: 'If he changes parties with the facility of partners at a dance, he has always been true to the only Party he really believes in – that which is assembled under the hat of Mr Winston Churchill.' Gwynne's *Morning Post*, now more generous in tone, observed: 'Mr Churchill is still his own Party, and the chief of the partisans. He still sees himself as the only digit in the sum of things, all other men as mere cyphers, whose function it is to follow after and multiply his personal value a million-fold.' Harold Nicolson saw him as 'the most interesting man in London. He is more than interesting: he is a phenomenon, an enigma. How can a man so versatile and so brilliant avoid being considered volatile and unsound?' Arthur Ponsonby, who had switched allegiance from the Liberals to Labour, wrote to Eddie Marsh that Winston was 'far and away the most talented man in political life . . . But that does not prevent me from feeling politically he is a great danger, largely because of his love of crises and faulty judgement. He once said to me years ago, "I like things to happen, and if they don't happen I like to make them happen." '[226]

The Conservative party's rank and file didn't want anything to happen, ever. They could identify with Neville Chamberlain, not with Churchill. Winston could have won their loyalty at the Treasury had he pursued traditional Conservative fiscal policies. Instead, he had alienated them by introducing welfare legislation. In Parliament he was not Scottish, Welsh, or a representative of the Midlands; he was known only as a Londoner who had been elected by none of London's constituencies. That was a grave weakness in a man who hoped to beome No 10's next occupant. He seemed completely unaware of the danger inherent in an eminence acquired solely by ministerial talents, parliamentary skills, and Baldwin's fosterage. The *Weekly Dispatch* of July 10, 1927, reported that during the past week the chancellor had filled more pages in *Hansard* than any other six MPs put together; that he, not Baldwin, was leading the party, and doing it adroitly; and that he 'also has a way of dealing with the Socialists which, while it never lacks anything in force or directness, yet appeals to their sense of fair play and good humour. "Winston is up!" empties the smoking room quicker than any other announcement.' The piece ended: 'Yet with all his talents and his force of character, the main body of conservatives would never follow him as Prime Minister.' Even Baldwin doubted that the Tories would choose Churchill as his successor. 'Our people like him,' he wrote to a friend in September 1927. 'They love listening to him in the House, look on him as a star turn, and settle down in the stalls with anticipatory grins. But for leadership, they would turn him down every time.'[227]

The real complaint about Churchill's years at the Exchequer is that for the only time in his life he ignored his instincts. Intuition had warned him to shun the goldmongers, but, uncharacteristically unsure of himself, he learned the rules of fiscal orthodoxy and, for the most part, followed them. His policies were not wholly unimaginative; he established a reparations pool, whereby the Treasury would be enriched by German goods sold in Britain, and – over the strong objections of Neville Chamberlain – he introduced the rating apportionment bill of 1928 (actually young Harold Macmillan's idea), under which industry and agriculture were provided with local tax relief, the gap in income being plugged by cuts in defence and a petrol tax which brought in £15,000,000 a year. Because England's economy had been crippled by the general strike, he had little room for manoeuvre in the two budgets following it. The deficits were met by a temporary tax on rubber tyres and increased levies on wines, matches, and tobacco; by taking £12,000,000 from the Road Fund; by reducing the brewers' credit period by a month; and by rescheduling property taxes. But it was all legerdemain – 'jugglery and deceit,' as Snowden called it. Winston himself acknowledged that he had drawn on his 'adventitious resources.' Grigg pointed out that 'in spite of all the Keynesian gibes, his main object was always the reduction of unemployment.' Tinkering wouldn't do the job, however, and Churchill shied away from the deficits and bold governmental intervention Roosevelt would introduce within a few years in the depressed United States. Amery summed up Winston's financial programme in a letter to Baldwin: 'A few hand-to-mouth dodges for picking up odd windfalls, a hope that better trade and a few millions saved by cheeseparing here and there may ride matters over the next year: that is the beginning and end of it.'[228]

It was certainly the end of it. Churchill's last budget, presented on April 15, 1929, after the Tories had lost nine safe seats in by-elections over the past two months, offered little to calm their growing anxieties. His delivery, as always, was masterly. Taxpayers were to be allowed deductions for each child ('Another example of our general policy of helping the producer'). Labour's demand for deficit spending was 'the policy of buying a biscuit early in the morning and walking about all day looking for a dog to give it to.' The *Sunday Times* called his performance 'the most brilliantly entertaining of modern Budget speeches,' and Harold Macmillan would write of the Churchillian style in his *Winds of Change* that none of the new generation of MPs 'had ever heard anything of the kind . . . such mastery of language, such careful deployment of the arguments, such dexterous covering of any weak point.' But as political nourishment it was poor fare. He abolished taxes on tea, gambling, and railway passage; reduced taxes on motorcycles and bicycles; raised them on telephone service; and introduced new duties on tobacco, beer, and liquor. It was a swan song in falsetto. Grigg thought it not inappropriate. As chancellor, he said, Winston had 'tended to overestimate revenue and underestimate expenditure,' had 'convinced himself that there was a good deal to be said at that time for respectability . . . in economic affairs,' was 'apt to spoil a brilliant project by not assuring himself in advance of sufficient resources to carry it through to the end,' and was 'therefore reduced to all sorts of shifts and expedients in order to avoid having to go back on the policies on which he had perhaps too confidently embarked.'[229] Yet it's fair to add that during Churchill's Exchequer tenure state benefits had been extended to 344,800 children, 236,800 widows, 450,000 Britons over sixty-five years old, and 227,000 over seventy. He may have been no better at handling Britain's finances than his family's but here, as at home, he had established the right priorities.

In retrospect there is an air of foreboding about the English upper classes' late 1920s, a feeling that everyone of consequence is wearing tennis whites, gabbling manically, and emptying magnums of Dom Perignon in a Rolls-Royce racing headlong towards the edge of a towering precipice. It is illusion, of course, a vision of hindsight. At the time these years seemed fruitful and teeming with hope. One pictures a typical country weekend, with the Duke of York striding off the eighteenth green, Sir Samuel Hoare immaculate and not even perspiring after winning three straight sets six–love, Rex Whistler absorbed in his painting, Balfour dozing in a leather armchair, Osbert Sitwell laughing his infectious laugh as the Prof describes his recent trip to India, and Churchill and Bernard Shaw arguing over teacups about Shaw's newly published *Intelligent Woman's Guide to Socialism and Capitalism*. In other homes Sir Jacob Epstein is sculpting his *Madonna and Child*; Viginia Woolf is writing *To the Lighthouse*; D. H. Lawrence, *Lady Chatterley's Lover*; Trevelyan, his *History of England*; Evelyn Waugh, *Decline and Fall*; and A. A. Milne, to the delight of a much larger if less discriminating audience, *Winnie-the-Pooh*. In Washington, Andrew W. Mellon, 'the best Secretary of the Treasury since Hamilton,' is spreading his gospel, an echo of Sackville-West, that ostentatious consumption by the rich is a source of great pleasure for the poor. At No. 11 Downing Street a buoyant chancellor of the Exchequer is supplementing his ministerial salary by writing 'The United States of Europe' for the *Saturday Evening Post*, and, for the *Daily Telegraph*, a series of articles exposing welfare cheats called 'The Abuse of the "Dole." ' T.S. Eliot has become a British citizen. England is preparing to launch an experimental public television service. Bernard Shaw has concluded that in the absence of a world government, the British Empire is best qualified to rule the world. That world is at peace; Britain still dominates world politics. A disarmament conference, with the United States participating, is convening in Geneva. Germany has been admitted to the League of Nations. The Kellogg-Briand Pact, sponsored by the US secretary of state, has outlawed war and provided for a pacific settlement of disputes. Italy has just signed a twenty-year friendship treaty with Ethiopia.

Among those gulled by the Italian dictator, now in his fifth year of power, was Winston Churchill. Once the coal strike had ended he had plunged into his third *Crisis* volume and accepted an invitation from Roger Keyes, now an admiral, to join a week-long cruise on the Mediterranean. 'On leaving you,' he wrote to the admiral, 'I am going to stay in Rome for a few days to see Mussolini (while he lasts), and I am taking with me my brother Jack, whom you know, and my boy Randolph.' After Christmas at Chartwell they departed aboard the *Esperia*. On January 4, 1927, he wrote to Clementine from Genoa that he was greatly taken by the Fascist society: 'This country gives the impression of discipline, order, smiling faces. A happy strict school – no talking among the pupils. Great changes have taken place since you & I disembarked [here] nearly 6 years ago.' The local Fascists and the employees at his hotel were particularly attentive: 'They have been saluting in their impressive manner all over the place, & . . . gave us a most cordial welcome.'[230]

Correcting proofs until 2:30 A.M. in his hotel room, he sent them off to his publisher 'under threats of vengeance from Mussolini if anything goes wrong.' In Rome he saw the Duce twice and then held what can only be described as an unfortunate press conference. It was perfectly clear, he said, that his host 'thought of nothing but the lasting good, as he understands it, of the Italian people.' Indeed: 'If I had been an Italian, I am sure I should have been whole-heartedly with you from the start to finish in your triumphant struggle against the bestial appetites and passions of Leninism.' Englishmen had 'not yet had to face this danger in the same deadly form,' but when the time came 'we shall succeed in grappling with Communism and choking the life out of it – of that I am absolutely sure.' In his opinion the Duce had 'provided the necessary antidote to the Russian poison. Here after, no great nation will be unprovided with an ultimate means of protection against cancerous growths, and every responsible labour leader in the country ought to feel his feet more firmly planted in resisting levelling and reckless doctrines.' As a consequence, 'Externally, your movement has rendered a service to the whole world.'[231]

The text of these remarks was published in *The Times* of January 21, 1927. Liberals and Labourites were choleric. The *New Leader* stormed: 'We have always suspected that Mr Winston Churchill was a Fascist at heart. Now he has openly avowed it.' C. P. Scott of the *Manchester Guardian* was so incensed that he all but lay down and drummed his heels on the floor. Clementine wrote to Winston: 'Scott is I see vexed over your partiality to "Pussolini." ' Her husband was unruffled. He took the classic view of British foreign policy: England should support any continental regime which was hostile to England's greatest enemy – in this case, at that time, Soviet Russia. Later, when the Duce became a piratical adventurer, Churchill would scorn him as 'Mussolini the swine', and 'Mussolini the jackal.'[232]

Vesuvius obligingly erupted when Winston, Jack, and young Randolph visited Naples. Churchill played his last polo game on Malta ('It is dreadful giving it up for ever,' he wrote), reported to Clementine on their son ('The Rabbit is a very good travelling companion,' he disclosed, adding with relish: 'We have played a great deal of chess in which I give him either a Queen or two castles, or even castle, bishop and knight – and still wallop him'), and, with Randolph, was received by Pope Pius XI. The audience was preceded by much wrangling over protocol. As an important minister serving under a Protestant monarch, Winston absolutely refused to kneel. They compromised on three bows as he entered the pontiff's reception hall. Randolph later wrote in his memoirs: 'The early past of the conversation was a little sticky. Then my father and the Pope got on to the subject of the Bolsheviks and had a jolly half hour saying what they thought of them.' After stops at Athens, Paris, Dieppe, and Consuelo's villa at Eze, Churchill and his party arrived at Newhaven aboard the night ferry on January 29. A box of Treasury papers from Grigg awaited him in his car; he studied them on the way to Chartwell.[233]

Between the Exchequer and his publishers' deadlines, nearly all his holidays were working holidays. He meant to take most of the summer of 1927 off, painting at Chartwell, entertaining friends there, and sweating over walls, dams, and ponds, but then he decided to start writing an account of his youth. It is his most delightful book. Subsequently serialized in the *News Chronicle* and published by Thornton Butterworth as *My Early Life*, it sold 13,753 copies in Britain, was issued by Scribner's in the United States under the title of *A Roving Commission*, appeared, condensed, in the *Reader's Digest*, and was translated into thirteen languages and Braille. Not all his conceptions reached full term. He planned a book on socialism with the working title *The Creed of Failure* but abandoned it after outlining the first five chapters. Then T. E. Lawrence, now 338171 Aircraftman Shaw, suggested Churchill's major biographical work, writing to him from his RAF base: 'If the Gods give you a rest, some day, won't you write a life of the great Duke of Marlborough? About our only international general . . . and so few people seem to see it.'[234]

Winston's immense output – he was still writing regularly for magazines and newspapers – was possible because of his extraordinary methods of work. Like Dr Johnson producing his dictionary, he assembled a committee of researchers and secretaries and guided them as they tackled one topic after another. Asked about the thread of narrative, he said, 'Oh, I have all that in my head.' And he continued to work all hours. However late his Chartwell guests had retired, he would pace his study, dictating; one visitor recalls wakening to hear 'the sounds of footfalls on the boards and his familiar voice clearly audible.' In one month, he told Clementine, he had banked the equivalent of $72,414: a £6,000 advance for the Marlborough, £5,200 in stock dividends, £1,700 in *World Crisis* royalties, and nearly £2,000 from magazines – 'a small fortune,' he wrote, of which he was 'trying to keep 2,000 fluid for investment & speculation with Vickers & McGowan. This "mass of manoeuvre" is of the utmost importance & must not be frittered away.' It seemed sound. But most of his investments were in the New York stock market. And the year was 1929.[235]

A few months earlier, during a finance bill debate, he had been stricken by influenza, and his slow recovery suggested a weakened constitution. Those around him were worried; they were afraid he was driving himself towards a nervous collapse. The only way to divert him from public or private work was to put him on a ship or a hunt, in front of an easel, or in the midst of a crowd. Beaverbrook persuaded him to spend five days sailing to Amsterdam and back on his private yacht; the Duke of Westminster induced him to fish and hunt stags in Scotland; by royal command he hunted grouse with George V at Balmoral and painted the Highland scene from his window there. (The painting was subsequently auctioned for £120.) He wrote to a friend: 'I had a particularly pleasant luncheon with the King when we went out deer-driving, and a very good talk about all sorts of things. I am very glad that he did not disapprove of my using the Ministerial room as a studio, and I took particular care to leave no spots on the Victorian tartans.'[236] Especially sweet was a return trip to Belfast, where, on his last visit, he and Clementine had narrowly escaped a lynch mob. This time Queen's University awarded him an honorary degree, and cheering students, after presenting him with a shillelagh and a 'paddy hat,' rode him around on their shoulders.

The older Churchill children were in boarding school now, with only Mary at home, but Chartwell was never lonely. As a host he was as affable as ever. Convoys of friends arrived, some as early as Thursday, for long weekends. He greeted them eagerly and was genuinely sorry to see them leave. One guest wrote in his diary: 'He was in a marvellous mood and just would not let us go. I played the piano and we talked on cricket, on music and politics.' The toys of war still fascinated him. James Lees-Milne, a friend of young Randolph's, told Martin Gilbert of one evening when 'we remained at that round table till after midnight. The table cloth had long ago been removed. Mr Churchill spent a blissful two hours demonstrating with decanters and wine glasses how the Battle of Jutland was fought . . . He got all worked up like a schoolboy, making barking noises in imitation of gunfire and blowing cigar smoke across the battle scene in imitation of gun smoke.'[237]

His closest friend was still Birkenhead – FE – with the Prof a close second. He and Beaverbrook became somewhat less intimate. The publisher wanted Winston filmed by the American Telephone and Telegraph Company, which was gathering a celluloid history of the period using what he called 'the new process of talking pictures.' The cameramen had already shot reels of Coolidge, Mussolini, and Poincaré. Churchill declined on the ground that 'I am in a far humbler class than the individuals you mention, and have no right to such prominence.' This humility is suspicious, and, in fact, he had another motive. In 1928 Beaverbrook had asked permission to print the letter Winston had sent Bonar Law in 1915, begging Law not to dismiss him from the Admiralty. As one who often earned his living by quoting the correspondence of others, Churchill could hardly refuse, but his reply was curt: 'You make me tear open old wounds and their sting returns. Certainly publish the letter as you propose, not as a thing thrust into publicity by me but on your own responsibility.'[238] In addition, the flag of Free Trade was under fire again, and Beaverbrook was sponsoring the United Empire League, a lobby for tariffs. Now in 1929 the Conservatives had been in office for five years; Baldwin had to call for a general election. United Empire candidates were running well in by-elections. Free Trade had lost its great popularity, and the prime minister committed himself to tariff reform. It was the first of several issues which were to estrange Baldwin and Churchill. England's political climate had changed, and once again, as in 1915 and 1922, Winston felt the chill of isolation gathering round, found that MPs of all parties were beginning to avoid him.

Any party in power tries to take the public's pulse from time to time, and on September 2, 1928, Churchill had written to the prime minister at Aux-les-Bains: 'I cannot feel that there is any decisive drift agst us. But Labour will have a heavy class vote; & the Liberals will queer the pitch – (what else *can* they do?).' They could continue to join Labour in droves, and that is what they were doing. That winter the Tory sky darkened; of nine by-elections in what had been considered safe Conservative constituencies, Labour had won three and the Liberals two, and the four surviving Tories had narrowly escaped defeat. Party morale was deteriorating, the cabinet was apathetic, the number of jobless growing. Beaverbrook thought that 'unemployment will be the one and only issue which counts.' Churchill, with whom he conferred, though their manner towards one another had become distant, disagreed with him, arguing that it was 'confined to certain areas which will go against the Government anyhow.' Yet within a week Winston's optimism had evaporated. He now despaired; the Conservatives were vulnerable on too many other issues. 'He accepts electoral defeat in advance,' wrote Beaverbrook, though he added that 'his judgement on such matters is worse than any prominent man I know.'[239]

In January, five months before the country went to the polls, Churchill told Baldwin that the voters should be warned that they faced a choice between socialism, which had been responsible for the general strike, and 'modern' conservatism. The trend in all countries, he said, was towards cooperation between nations and a continuum of national policy; 'women can feel these tide movements by instinct.' A graver, more delicate matter was dissension within the cabinet. Baldwin's successor would be either Winston or Neville Chamberlain, minister of health, and several ministers shared Lord Derby's view: 'I believe in Winston's capability if only he were a bit more steady. But you never know what kite he is going to fly next.' The first step for Chamberlain's supporters was to get Churchill out of the Exchequer. Amery wrote to the prime minister in March: 'The essential thing is to move Winston . . . In spite of all his brilliancy and verbal originality, he is entirely lacking in constructive thought and imagination . . . He has been, in every direction, a paralysing negative influence, and the Party knows it and would breathe a profound sigh of relief if he were shifted.' The force behind the manoeuvring was the man who stood to benefit from it. Chamberlain, who had suggested Winston's appointment as chancellor, had resolved to evict the Churchills from No. 11. Baldwin, susceptible to pressure, contemplated appointing Churchill secretary of state for India, even though the viceroy thought Winston unsuitable because he was 'out of sympathy' with Indian political aspirations and was even 'rather disposed to despise' them. The prime minister made the offer anyway and Churchill flatly turned it down. Birkenhead was doing a good job at the India Office, he said, and he shared FE's 'deep misgivings about that vast sub-continent.' Nevertheless, determined to avoid friction with Chamberlain if possible, he wrote to Baldwin that he wanted to 'associate Neville' with major Treasury decisions. Neville declined. His objective hadn't changed; he was turning to intrigue. Anticipating the possibility that the coming election might leave the Liberals holding the balance of power between the Tories and Labour, as in 1924, Churchill sounded out Lloyd George on his terms for a Conservative-Liberal alliance. This, Chamberlain told Baldwin, was disloyal. Baldwin disagreed, though he said that if the voting ended in a stalemate, he couldn't possibly share responsibility with Lloyd George. Neville wrote in his diary: 'SB said in that case he supposed the leadership would go to Winston.' Yet by spring it was obvious that Chamberlain had become Baldwin's favourite minister. Churchill realized that making common cause with his Tory critics was impossible. He wrote Clementine: 'I have made up my mind that if N Ch is made leader of the

CP or anyone else of that kind, I clear out of politics & see if I cannot make you & the kittens a little more comfortable before I die. Only one goal still attracts me, & if that were barred I shd quit the dreary field for pastures new.'[240]

Polling was set for May 30. As a national figure Churchill was expected to canvass for Conservative candidates, but he faced a strong Liberal challenger in Epping, so while he was speaking elsewhere, Clementine took soundings among the voters there. 'Darling,' she hastily scrawled, 'I do hope you enjoy your Scotch Meetings – I wish I were coming with you. But I think it is wise for me to be here & start the ball rolling.' She rented an Epping cottage – 'I think you will find this house a snug retreat,' she wrote to him, 'from which to sally forth on the constituency' – and, because there were no large halls in the town, ordered the erection of two huge tents in which Winston might address his constituents. Speaking in one of them he suggested that state insurance might be available, not just to wage earners, but to all Britons. It was his one positive note in an otherwise deplorable campaign. In Liverpool he denounced Ramsay MacDonald's wartime pacifism: 'I do not forget that, nor ought it to be forgotten.' The scientist Sir John Boyd-Orr had a surer sense of the country's mood: 'A ruling class living on dividends, masses of the people on the dole, and a Government trying to maintain an uneasy *status quo* is a picture which fills thinking people with despair.' Churchill meanwhile was calling for a vote of confidence in Baldwin's 'capable, sedate Government.' If MacDonald were returned to office, he predicted, Labour would 'bring back the Russian Bolsheviks, who will immediately get busy in the mines and factories, as well as among the armed forces, planning another general strike.' On April 30, 1929, he addressed the nation by radio. Conservatives, he said, had given England peace abroad, stable government at home, honest administration, goodwill, public and private thrift, and relief from 'the burden of galling rates.' He said: 'Avoid chops and changes of policy; avoid thimble-riggers and three-card trick men; avoid all needless borrowing; and above all avoid, as you would the smallpox, class warfare and violent political strife.' The message wasn't much, but the delivery was remarkable, and this time Beatrice Webb wasn't the only one to remark on it. The next morning's *Daily Express* commented on its effectiveness. Churchill's performance, the editorial said, 'knocked the six preceding broadcasts into a cocked hat . . . as an exhibition of polemical oratory it was superb. His voice was edged alternately with sarcasm and warning. There was a note in it of extraordinary intimacy with his audience. He began with statistics . . . and ended high on the pinnacle of perfervid patriotism.'[241]

It is singular how the brightest of politicians can convince themselves, against all evidence, that they are going to win. On May 28 Winston told his constituents: 'Victory is in the air.' It wasn't. Two evenings later he joined Baldwin at No. 10 to follow the returns. Thomas Jones recalls that at one desk 'sat the PM with narrow slips of paper on which he inscribed the . . . lists as they arrived.' At another 'sat Winston doing similar lists in red ink, sipping whisky and soda, getting redder and redder, rising and going out often to glare at the machine himself, hunching his shoulders, bowing his head like a bull about to charge. As Labour gain after Labour gain was announced, Winston became more and more flushed with anger, left his seat and confronted the machine in the passage; with his shoulders hunched he glared at the figures, tore the sheets and behaved as though if any more Labour gains came he would smash the whole apparatus. His ejaculations to the surrounding staff were quite unprintable.'[242]

By the following afternoon the final results were in: Labour, 288 seats; Conservatives, 260; Liberals, 59. Churchill himself had been reelected, but with only 48 per cent of the vote. Among the losers were two of his young protégés, Macmillan and Alfred Duff Cooper. The Liberals once more held the balance of power. Churchill and Austen Chamberlain urged the prime minister to strike a bargain with Lloyd George. That was easy for them to say; they were old friends of George's. But Baldwin who had been the architect of George's ruin in 1922, had decided that such an alliance was out of the question. After spending a weekend at Chequers thinking it over, he informed the cabinet he was going to resign. Ramsay MacDonald could take over again. All the Tory ministers then donned frock coats and boarded the Windsor train to hand the King their seals of office. Being a civil servant, Eddie Marsh could not continue as Churchill's secretary; they parted tearfully. T. E. Lawrence wrote to Eddie: 'The General election means that Winston goes out, I suppose. For himself I'm glad. He's a good fighter, and will do better out than in, and will come back in a stronger position than before. I want him to be PM somehow.' That view was not shared by the man now moving out of No. 10. According to Beaverbrook, Winston visited Baldwin in the prime minister's House office – 'the PM's room' – and told him of a strong movement to oust William Henry Davison, the party manager. Davison, said Winston, had become a focus of unpopularity. 'Baldwin told Churchill,' Beaverbrook wrote, 'that there was nobody more unpopular than himself. The difficulty of carrying Churchill, said Baldwin, was one of the main reasons for losing the election.' If true, this was the first real break between the two men.[243]

Evicted from No. 11, the Churchills rented the London home of Venetia Montagu, Asquith's old inamorata. Winston was planning a trip through Canada and the United States, to promote his books and line up editors and publishers for future writing assignments, and he left the details to Clementine. As a member of the Conservative Business Committee, or shadow cabinet, he expected to be an active Tory strategist and policymaker. 'Do not hesitate to engage one or two extra servants,' he wrote to her. 'Now that we are in opposition we must gather colleagues & MPs together a little at lunch & dinner. Also I have now a few business people who are of importance. We ought to be able to have lunches of 8-10 often, & dinners of the same size about twice a week. You should have a staff equal to this.' But his assumption that he would be in the thick of things was unjustified. Baldwin had been right; many senior members of the party held him responsible for their defeat. This was revealed to him when Ramsay MacDonald had been in power less than a week.

671

The new prime minister announced his intention to evacuate all British troops from Egypt except those in the canal zone. Winston objected vehemently, but 'when I rose in my place on the Front Opposition Bench to interrogate the Government,' he wrote in a note long afterwards, Baldwin 'sat silent and disapproving. I immediately perceived that the . . . honoured leader did not think this was a good point to press. Murmurs and even cries of dissent from the Conservative benches were added to the hostile Government interruptions, and it was evident that I was almost alone in the House.'[244]

On August 3, 1929, the *Empress of Australia* steamed out of Southampton, bound for Quebec. Among its first-class passengers were Churchill; his brother, Jack; Randolph, now eighteen; and Jack's young son Johnny. Winston spent most of the voyage working or attending to his personal exchequer. He wrote two pieces, 'Will the British Empire Survive?' for *Answers*, and a profile of a peer for *Nash's Pall Mall*. *John Bull* had already paid him for a piece on the election, 'Why We Lost.' The *Daily Telegraph* had agreed to pay him £2,500 for ten articles on this trip. In addition, £1,000 in *World Crisis* royalties had arrived before he left London, and a sale of utility shares had brought him another £2,000. He invested every shilling he could spare in the New York stock market. Financial security, he wrote to Clementine from the ship, was 'a wonderful thing.'[245]

The warmth of his Canadian welcome was also wonderful. 'The workmen in the streets,' he wrote to her, 'the girls who work the lifts, the ex-service men, the farmers, up to the highest functionaries have shewn such unaffected pleasure to see me & shake hands that I am profoundly touched.' The Canadian Pacific had put a stenographer-typist at his disposal for the journey across the continent, and Bernard Baruch had persuaded Charles Schwab to lend Churchill his private railway car, with double beds, private bathrooms, a parlour, a dining room (which Winston converted into an office), a kitchen, servants' quarters, a refrigerator, fans, and a radio. The radio, he wrote to Clementine, was especially useful: 'The wireless is a great boon, and we hear regularly from [Horace] Vickers [his broker] about the stock markets. His news has, so far, been entirely satisfactory.' The passing scenery fascinated him. He wrote that he wanted 'to see the country at close quarters, and nibble the grass and champ the branches.' To Randolph he said, 'Fancy cutting down all those beautiful trees to make pulp for those bloody newspapers and calling it civilization.'[246]

Along the way he paused to open exhibitions, dedicate memorials, consult with officials, and deliver speeches, in one of which he deplored proposals to reduce France's army, reminding his audience that Germany had twice as many youths of military age as France, which had been invaded by Germans twice within living memory. After driving across the Rockies, which he painted, a sombrero shielding him from the sun, they visited Vancouver and took the ferry to Victoria, their last Canadian stop. The next day Randolph wrote in his diary: 'We are now on the ship bound to Seattle, American soil and Prohibition. But we are well-equipped. My big flask is full of whisky and the little one contains brandy. I have reserves of both in medicine bottles. It is almost certain that we shall have no trouble. Still if we do, Papa pays the fine and I get the publicity.' Papa would have been hit by both; *he* had a case of brandy in stone hot-water bottles. In San Francisco the British consul general met their train and drove them southward through the redwoods. Winston wrote to his wife that the greater part of their six-hundred-mile journey 'lay through the woods with these enormous trees. They are really astonishing. One we saw, the biggest, 380 foot high, was three thousand or four thousand or even five thousand years old and it took fourteen of us to join our arms around its stem.'[247]

The high point of their California trip was a four-day visit with their chief California host, William Randolph Hearst, a fervent anglophobe who nevertheless wanted Churchill's by-line in his papers. Winston was willing, though he drove a hard bargain: £40,000 for twenty-two pieces. He was dumbfounded by San Simeon, Hearst's thirty-million-dollar castle. Blenheim pales beside San Simeon, a composite of all the European palaces and cathedrals the owner had admired, with tapestries, sarcophagi, stained glass, corbels, choir stalls, Gothic rooms, carved staircases, fretwork-ornamented towers, stables, swimming pools, and tennis courts. The entire property was surrounded by a transplanted forest. The man of the house dwelt in a third-floor 'Celestial Suite,' from which he descended in an elevator whose walls were hung with priceless paintings. Winston was charmed by Hearst's mistress, Marion Davies, formerly an MGM star, and enchanted when they all went off on a picnic accompanied by sixteen pack mules loaded with caviar, champagne, and a hillbilly band. Of Hearst himself, Churchill wrote home that he was 'most interesting to meet, & I got to like him – a grave simple child – with no doubt a nasty temper – playing with the most costly toys. A vast income always overspent: ceaseless building & collecting not vy discriminatingly works of art: two magnificent establishments, two charming wives [Mrs Hearst and Marion]; complete indifference to public opinion, a strong liberal and democratic outlook, a 15 million daily circulation, oriental hospitalities, extreme personal courtesy (to us at any rate) & the appearance of a Quaker elder – or perhaps better Mormon elder.' One afternoon the householder was conferring with his attorney when a maid rushed in. 'Mr Churchill is fainting!' she cried. 'He wants some turpentine!' Hearst rushed out to a terrace, where he found Winston painting, not fainting, awaiting a thinner for his oils and placidly puffing a fat cigar.[248]

Churchill and his party moved on to Santa Barbara and then, for five nights, to the Biltmore in Los Angeles – their hotel bills, Winston wrote, were paid by 'a hearty Banker' – where they toured the Hollywood studios and were Hearst's guests once again, at the Montmartre Club. That evening they dined with sixty guests, including Charlie Chaplin. Winston wrote his wife that Chaplin had 'acted his new film for us in a wonderful way. It is to be his gt attempt to prove that the silent drama or pantomime is superior to the new talkies.'* Randolph noted in his diary: 'Papa wants him to act the young Napoleon and has promised to write the Scenario.' Instead, said Chaplin, he intended to play Jesus Christ. Churchill thought a moment and then asked: 'Have you cleared the rights?'[249]

After a fishing expedition off Catalina Island (Winston caught a 188-pound swordfish in twenty minutes), his party proceeded eastward, again in Schwab's private rail car, across the Mojave Desert, by the Grand Canyon, to Chicago. Baruch met him at the station there and introduced him to the Commercial Club. Asked about Ramsay MacDonald, who was also in the United States at the time, negotiating naval disarmament, Churchill replied that England was fortunate to be represented 'by so experienced a statesman and so distinguished a man' – and then called for more British *and* American warships. On the Atlantic coast he paid a courtesy call on Herbert Hoover; toured Civil War battlefields, to pick up material for a series of *Collier's* pieces; and was in New York, staying at the Savoy-Plaza Hotel, when the market crashed. On the evening of 'Black Tuesday,' when the stock market, honeycombed with credit, collapsed of its own weight, sixteen million shares changing hands, he dined at Bernard Baruch's Fifth Avenue mansion. The other guests were bankers and financiers. When one rose to toast their British visitor, he addressed the company as 'friends and former millionaires.'[250]

The next morning Churchill heard shouts below the Savoy-Plaza apartment and looked out, he wrote, to find that 'under my window a gentleman [had] cast himself down fifteen storeys and was dashed to pieces, causing a wild commotion and the arrival of the fire brigade.' Ever the curious journalist, he made his way to Wall Street. There, recognized by a stranger, he was invited inside the Stock Exchange. 'I had expected to see pandemonium,' he wrote, 'but the spectacle that met my eyes was one of calm and orderliness.' No wonder; apparently he hadn't been told that brokers are forbidden to run on the floor of the exchange, and the big sellout was over anyhow, stocks now being offered for a fraction of their value. Churchill concluded: 'No one who has gazed on such a scene could doubt that this financial disaster, huge as it is, cruel as it is to thousands, is only a passing episode in the march of a valiant and serviceable people who by fierce experiment are hewing new paths for man, and showing to all nations much that they should attempt and much that they should avoid.'[251]

He still hadn't made the connection, still didn't grasp that since September 3, when he had left Vancouver, Wall Street investors had lost over thirty billion dollars, almost as much as the United States had spent on World War I. Later he would realize that this 'Economical Blizzard,' as he came to call it, was responsible for turning all England into 'one vast soup kitchen,' driving the country back off the gold standard, doubling the number of British unemployed, and radicalizing politics throughout Europe, especially in

* *City Lights* (1931)

Germany. In California, coming under the spell of a local stockbroker, he had been persuaded to speculate heavily. The Wall Street fever of that autumn had afflicted him; he had written to his wife: 'Since my last letter from Santa Barbara I have made another £1,000 by speculating in a stock called Simmons. It is a domestic furniture business. They say, "You can't go wrong on a Simmons mattress." There is a stock exchange [ticker] in every big hotel. You go & watch the figures being marked up on slates every few minutes. Mr Van Antwerp advises me. He is a stockbroker & one of the leading firms. I think he is a vy good man. This powerful firm watch my small interests like a cat a mouse.' William Van Antwerp was a member of E. F. Hutton, a reliable company, but the most stable brokers were impotent in the panic selling of Winston's last week in New York. Though he had not been wiped out, his financial independence had disappeared in the reams of ticker tape. Throughout the coming decade he would have to write furiously to keep his family and style of living afloat. This bleak dawn was just beginning to break upon him when he sailed from New York on October 30. But when he reached Southampton he momentarily forgot it. A more immediate threat hung over the world he loved. Lord Irwin,* the new viceroy in New Delhi, had recommended 'the attainment of Dominion status' as Britain's goal for its Indian Empire, Labour had endorsed Irwin's proposal, and so, without consulting other leaders of the Conservative party, had Stanley Baldwin.[252]

Describing his new Hollywood acquaintances to Clementine, Winston had written that he had entertained 'the leading men I like best, mostly British born, & all keenly pro-England.' Among the English expatriates there was a craggy-faced, forty-six-year-old ex-soldier named Victor McLaglen who had served three years in the Life Guards, commanded a company of the Irish Fusiliers in the Middle East during the war, and, during the months which followed the Armistice, policed Baghdad as provost marshal. After touring the Empire as a boxer, wrestler, and vaudeville stunt man, McLaglen had arrived in Hollywood and found employment on the Fox lot, where he was now rehearsing *The Black Watch* under the direction of John Ford. A few blocks away, MGM was shooting two other motion pictures: *Trader Horn*, with W. S. Van Dyne, Harry Carey, and C. Aubrey Smith, and, simultaneously, *Son of India*, starring Smith. These three were the first in a series of films which, for the next several years, would provide millions of moviegoers with images of the glory, legends, and myths of the British Empire. They included *The Lost Patrol* (McLaglen, Gary Cooper, Boris Karloff), *Lives of a Bengal Lancer* (Cooper, Franchot Tone), *Clive of India* (Ronald Colman and Loretta Young), *Rhodes of Africa* (Walter Huston), *The Charge of the Light Brigade* (Errol Flynn), *Gunga Din* (Douglas Fairbanks, Jr, Sam Jaffe, Joan Fontaine, Cary Grant, McLaglen), *Wee Willie Winkie* (Shirley Temple, McLaglen,

* In 1934 he would become Lord Halifax, and is best remembered by that title.

Smith), and *Stanley and Livingstone*, which tugged at many a heart when Spencer Tracy, courteously removing his hat, approached Sir Cedric Hardwicke and said: 'Dr Livingstone, I presume?'[253]

It was great entertainment, if poor history – Colman and Huston were not in the least like the ruthless Clive and Rhodes – and the lush California countryside was far more romantic than the stark Khyber and the African bush. But it was presented as history, something over and done with, and therein lies its real significance. No one outside England, not even Hollywood's dream merchants, could pretend that the Empire was still like that. Inside England was another matter. Opinion was divided there. Imperial destiny still had its rapt congregations in Britain, even in the Labour party; they believed that Britain's position in the world, even its self-confidence, depended upon its far-flung realms. The faithful joined the Victoria League, the United Empire League, the British Empire Union, the League of Britons Overseas, and the Empire Day movement, whose only achievement was securing a half-holiday once a year for England's schoolchildren. The Tory press, notably the *Daily Express*, remained fiercely chauvinistic. Boy Scouts, then at the height of their popularity, wore the broad-brimmed hats of the Boer War and shared their motto 'Be Prepared' with the South African police. British soldiers continued to fight colonial wars in Iraq, Afghanistan, Yemen, and Palestine, battling first the Mad Mullah of Somaliland and then a Burmese monk whose followers believed he could fly if he chose, though to their disappointment he never so chose. Indeed, imperial possessions were still being acquired; the Empire reached its territorial peak in 1933 with the conquest of the Hadhramaut, a remote (and worthless) tract in southern Arabia. When a battle cruiser bearing the Prince of Wales passed through the Suez Canal and sailed down the Red Sea, with RAF biplanes forming a ceremonial umbrella overhead, native troops on both banks cheered, and in Aden the prince was greeted by massed Union Jacks and an enormous streamer: TELL DADDY WE ARE VERY HAPPY UNDER BRITISH RULE. In Buckingham Palace, Daddy addressed all his global subjects by radio every Christmas. Imperial conferences, determining policies vital to the Dominions, were still held regularly in London. So enlightened a parliamentarian as Boothby, visiting Jamaica, was reassured to see four Royal Navy battle cruisers anchored off Kingston, 'one of them waving the flag of the Commander-in-Chief, West Indies Station . . . The British Empire still existed.' At No. 10 Stanley Baldwin proclaimed: 'The British Empire stands firm as a great force for good. It stands in a sweep of every wind, by the wash of every sea.' No public event in England was complete without a passionate chorus of 'Land of Hope and Glory' or 'Soldiers of the Queen', with its affirmation that 'England is master' and:[254]

> *We're not forgetting it*
> *We're not letting it*
> *Fade away and gradually die*

Yet Baldwin was now preparing to let the Indian Raj do just that. He wasn't moved by principle. If Churchill's symbol is the hand forming a *V* for victory, Baldwin's was the wetted forefinger held up to test the wind. He did it very well. In England, he knew, ardent imperialists were a minority. Labourites were at best indifferent to the Empire; the billion pounds invested in India wasn't theirs. The passion of the new age was egalitarian. Even among the aristocracy one found young patricians who felt guilty about their member-ship in a privileged class. For most postwar Britons, it seemed, imperial songs and slogans had become empty rituals; in their hearts they didn't much care. 'The British were losing interest in their Empire,' James Morris wrote, 'and there was a falling-off of recruitment for the Indian services.' By the early 1930s the Indian Civil Service had shrunk to five hundred men. In England news from remote colonies interested the older generation; their children, including Oxbridge graduates, found it rather tiresome. As late as February 9, 1933, with Hitler in power, the Oxford Union debated the resolution 'that this House will in no circumstances fight for its King and Country' – and then approved it, 275 to 153. The King himself, still Emperor of India and the British Dominions beyond the Seas, wrote sombrely, if awkwardly: 'I cannot look into the future without feeling no little anxiety about the continued unity of the Empire.' Walter Lippmann, echoing Burke while pondering the indif-ference or even hostility of young aristocrats to imperial strength, reminded them that no empire in history has long survived without a devoted, steadfast ruling class.[255]

The fashionable – and fashionable Englishmen have far greater influence than their counterparts in, say, the United States – rejected every symbol of the Victorian era, from oratorios and organs to antimacassars. Kipling was mocked. The Prince of Wales was popular because he himself was rebelling against the Establishment he soon would lead, it was then assumed, for the rest of his life. When abroad he flirted with unsuitable young colonial women, fox-trotted until long after midnight, and rode bucking broncos. He didn't even dress properly. Tieless, in trousers too short to cover his ankles, his cap on the back of his head, he looked far more like one of Mayfair's Bright Young Things than the royal family's heir apparent. This was not only conduct unbecoming to England's future sovereign; it was downright 'un-British.' His critics didn't actually mean he seemed Jewish. The term had been expanded during the 1920s. In the past, English dignity had been stiffened by the intangible concept of British national character. Even Ireland had been awed by it. The Dominions and Crown Colonies were expected, not only to admire it, but to imitate it. As the 1920s were succeeded by the 1930s it became evident that they were letting the side down, were becoming un-British. Canadians were aping the Americans; Toronto was indistinguishable from Buffalo. The Australians talked like cockneys, and loud cockneys at that. English settlers in South Africa, it was said, had become effete, unlike the robust Afrikaners. Worst of all, for those loyal to the Empire, was the mockery of imperial solemnity at home – the braying, irreverent laughter of their own intellectuals. The image of the traditional, fatherly British colonel, once exemplified by men like C. Aubrey Smith, was being replaced by David Low's Colonel Blimp, who told tedious barracks tales to obese chums in a Turkish bath. P. G. Wodehouse depicted sons of the aristocracy as weak, incompetent, dipsomaniacal clowns, and J. B. Morton – a Harrovian and an Oxonian who had led troops in France – ran mocking little pieces in the *Daily Express*: 'ADVERTISEMENT CORNER: Will the gentleman who threw an onion at the Union Jack and repeatedly and noisily tore cloth during the singing of "Land of Hope and Glory" at the Orphans' Outing on Thursday, write to Colonel Sir George Jarvis Delamaine Spooner, late of Poona, telling him what right he has to the Old Cartbusian braces which burst when he was arrested?'[256]

The Raj was the chief target of the English literati. Aldous Huxley, grandson of the great Thomas Henry, was another traitor to his class; India, he wrote, reminded him of the old man of Thermopylae, who never did anything right. 'All over India,' wrote George Orwell, 'there are Englishmen who secretly loathe the system of which they are part.' E. M. Forster's *Passage to India*, perhaps the finest English novel of the 1920s, written by a Bloomsbury author who had been private secretary to a maharaja, was a devastating, though perhaps unjust, portrayal of Indian Civil Service racism. In the eyes of such men all imperial achievements were dross. Burma was part of the Indian Empire; Orwell had served there as a policeman, and he dismissed the sum of British efforts there as 'second-rate.' Bombay was, in Huxley's opinion, 'one of the most appalling cities in either hemisphere.' The architecture of rebuilt Kuala Lumpur, the capital of British Malaya, was similarly derided, and so was New Delhi, the work of Edwin Lutyens and Sir Herbert Baker, though here the critics may have had a point. The only city expressly designed to intimidate a people, New Delhi was begun in 1911, when George V travelled there during the Coronation Durbar to lay the foundation stone, and it was finished just in time for the British to move out, an ambiguity vaguely preserved in its disconcerting Secretariat. But what dismayed traditionalists most was the intellectuals' total renunciation of every value, every standard, every icon which had been cherished in the imperial past. Nothing was sacred, not even the Crown. When George V died his last words were: 'How is the Empire?' The story got around London drawing rooms and the common rooms in Oxford and Cambridge that he had actually said: 'What's on at the Empire?'[257]

All this was threatening to the defenders of a rich national legacy, and it was a new experience for them. Their fathers had snorted and had ignored the Ruskins and Paters and Wildes because British supremacy, in those days, had been unquestioned. No more; since the Armistice, England had steadily lost ground to competitors abroad in virtually every field of endeavour. Yet Englishmen could not rid themselves of the old complacency. Cunarders, they told one another, were the world's finest ocean liners, and RMS *Queen Mary*, now about to be launched, would set a standard none could surpass.* They

* Originally she was to have been christened the *Queen Victoria*. A Cunard executive told George V that the company wanted to name her after 'the greatest of all English queens.' The King was delighted. 'Oh,' he said, 'my wife *will* be pleased.'

were right, but steamships, like locomotives, in the construction of which the Victorians had also excelled, were not the transport of the future. Britannia had ruled the waves and the railway tracks, but was far from indomitable on highways and in the air – especially the air. Imperial Airways, Morris wrote, 'enjoyed semi-official privileges,' yet its management was inefficient and its schedules ridiculous; a person flying from London to Cape Town had to change planes six times.[258] Seasoned British travellers preferred KLM. But Britain's greatest aerial fiasco was the maiden voyage of the R 101, the costliest airship ever built in England, a few months after Churchill's return from the United States. Great hopes were reposed in the R 101. A pet project of Ramsay MacDonald's, it was expected to demonstrate Britain's enduring dominance in technology and provide mail and passenger service between Canada, South Africa, Australia, and India. This superzeppelin, powered by diesel engines, took off from Cardington in Bedfordshire on October 4, 1930, bound for Karachi, 3,652 miles away. It had travelled 300 miles when it struck a low hill on the outskirts of Beauvais, northwest of Paris, and collapsed in flames. The Empire's prime ministers, assembled in London to draft the Statute of Westminster, observed a minute of silent prayer. It should have been longer. They were mourning the passing of something far more momentous than a dirigible.

But the Dominion leaders had much to celebrate, too. In 1926 England and its white possessions had become 'autonomous communities within the British Empire, equal in status, in no way subordinate to each other in any aspect of their domestic or foreign affairs, though united by a common allegiance to the Crown, and freely associated as members of the British Commonwealth of Nations.' Now came the Statute of Westminster, which was just beginning its two-year progress through the parliamentary process. It was a historic measure, international in its implications, perhaps the vastest piece of legislation ever to pass through this or any other legislative body. Arthur Balfour called it 'the most novel and greatest experiment in Empire-building the world has ever seen.'[259] Jan Christiaan Smuts, its author, knew better. The statute was in fact a blue-print for the dismantling of the Empire. Under its terms, the Mother Country relinquished all authority over the white Dominions; laws passed by the House of Commons were inapplicable in them, and the House could not overrule acts of Dominion parliaments, which, indeed, were granted veto power over the succession to the British throne.

The Statute of Westminster was not only flexible; it was equivocal. Its language might be interpreted any way you liked. *Civis Britannicus Sum* could be translated to mean everything or nothing. A New Zealand lawyer could cite a precedent in Britain's elaborate imperial judicial system; the New Zealand judge could defer to the precedent or laugh it out of court. Ireland could and did quote the statute as justifying its complete secession from the Commonwealth, converting itself into 'a sovereign, independent and democratic State.'[260] While the imperial conference was deliberating over the phrasing of the statute, and the R 101 was disappearing in a bellying sheet of flame, taking forty-eight British lives with it, Mohandas Gandhi was observing his sixty-first birthday in a Poona jail. Since the statute in this early draft excluded possessions inhabited by men with pigmented skin, Gandhi and his cause, it would seem, gained nothing from it. But the language of Lord Irwin's presentation defined the Commonwealth as colour-blind – if it hadn't, the pressure of twentieth-century history would have made the discrimination indefensible anyhow. Even as Victor McLaglen, Ronald Colman, and C. Aubrey Smith held audiences enthralled, the Empire they were celebrating was fading with the credits.

In every age there are certain articles of faith which society accepts unquestioningly, with or without evidence; often, indeed, in the face of inconvenient facts. The faith may be religious, moral, or political. During the last quarter of the twentieth century it has become political. Creeds, like streams, gather strength as they narrow, thriving on bigotry – at present, liberal bigotry. In our time the institution of European colonialism is condemned as an abomination. No defence of it is admissible. The transformation of former colonies into emerging nations is regarded as inherently benign, one of the few great achievements in a troubled century. Africa, we are told, is free. Certainly it is free of foreign administration, but the question of whether the people of Libya, Uganda, Angola, or Katanga enjoy political freedom – not to mention the four freedoms, from fear and want and of religion and speech, proclaimed by Churchill and Roosevelt in 1941 – is so provocative that raising it is bad taste. Yet despite the hopes raised by Gandhi and his gifted successor, Jawaharlal Nehru, the results of their statecraft are rather different from those they anticipated. The old Indian Empire is now split into five nations. In all of them the beneficence which was expected to replace the departed Raj is, if present, extremely well camouflaged. This is not an argument against the rise of national pride in what we have come to call the Third World. To disapprove of what Macmillan called 'the winds of change' would be like passing judgement on the decline of Rome, the Reformation, the Renaissance, or the Industrial Revolution. History can never be put in the dock. But before examining it, one should clear the mind of cant.

In 1885 a clique of upper-class Indians established, as an annual custom, a three-day Christmas-week picnic. They called it the Indian National Congress. Except in 1906, when its members approved a mild resolution favouring some form of Indian self-government in domestic affairs, the congress had no political overtones until 1920. Nevertheless, the damage to imperial authority had been done long before that. It is obvious now that the ultimate failure of the Raj was social, not political. Lord Willingdon told Boothby he once invited a distinguished Indian prince, a friend of his, to lunch at Bombay's Yacht Club. When they were ordering drinks, a porter came over and told Willingdon: 'I am sorry, your Excellency, but the secretary has asked me to tell you that niggers are not allowed in this club.' Boothby himself agreed with Clemenceau's observation that Englishmen and Indians in the Raj 'do not

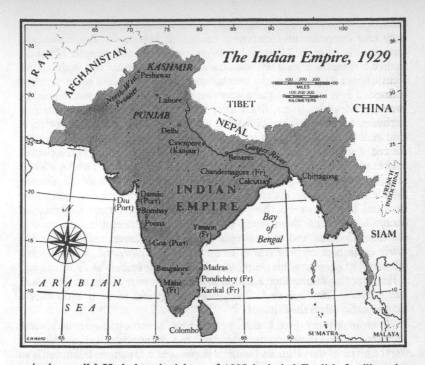

mingle at all.' Had the picnickers of 1885 included English families, the congress might have remained a frolic. Like Gandhi, who conceived of England as 'a land of philosophers and poets, the very centre of civilization,' the original congressmen were fervent anglophiles.[261] But this, from the British point of view, was less a blessing than it seemed. The most sophisticated of them spent several years in the Mother Country – Gandhi was admitted to the Inner Temple, one of London's four law colleges ('inns of court') – or sent their sons there: Jawaharlal Nehru, like Churchill, attended Harrow. Inspired by the liberal idealism of their English teachers, they returned home with a new sense of purpose, which grew, after the Armistice, when they followed the events in Ireland with intense interest. Under Gandhi's guidance the congress became a mass movement, with Indian freedom as its objective. Motilal Nehru, Jawaharlal's father, became co-founder of the Swarajya party. *Hind Swaraj* is a subtle Hindi phrase; under Motilal it was translated as 'Indian home rule,' or the achievement of dominion status; later, when his son rose to power, it came to mean independence – a socialist republic.

In either case, the task confronting the congress was almost beyond imagining. Ireland was difficult, but in India the problems of nationhood were increased a thousandfold. The Raj wasn't even entirely British; France ruled five small colonies there and Portugal three. The subcontinent's vast population, which increased by some thirty-four million each decade, was divided into four dominant ethnic strains: Caucasoid, Mongoloid, Australoid, and Negroid. They spoke 225 main languages; each of the most popular 12 was the native tongue for at least ten million Indians. The illiteracy rate in the Indian Empire was 88 per cent; the average diet, between six and seven hundred calories a day. Idols, and there were thousands of them, were worshipped by Hindus, Moslems, Jains, Buddhists, Sikhs, and Zoroastrians, and the possibilities for religious conflict were limitless. Moslems regarded swine as unclean. To Hindus, cows, monkeys, and the waters of the Ganges were sacred. Assam headhunters knelt before the skulls of their victims and chewed their fathers' bones, regarding the marrow as an aphrodisiac. To offer a Sikh a cigarette, or to light up near one of his shrines, could be suicidal. Hindus and Moslems were forever stalking one another with daggers, swords, spears, and torches. The followers of these warring faiths did not live apart; they mingled daily. Segregating them, even roughly, would require the relocation of between fourteen and sixteen million people. Moreover, native rulers and their subjects often prayed at different altars. The nawab of Junadagh was a Moslem; 81 per cent of his people were Hindus. The maharaja of Kashmir was a Hindu; of his four million Kashmiris, 80 per cent were Moslems. 'India is an abstraction,' Churchill said. 'India is a geographical term. It is no more a united nation than the Equator.'[262]

Two out of every three Indians were Hindus. Because of their beliefs, seven hundred million cattle roamed unharmed in a country which always teetered on the brink of starvation and sometimes plunged into famine. Hinduism is an exquisite maze of twistings and circlings and doublings-back, of poetry and philosophy and taboos, of hauntingly lovely corridors and frightening tunnels into the darker places in the human mind, and many pilgrims from the West, having studied it, have emerged the better for the journey. One of them, Frank Lloyd Wright, once told a group of fellow architects that Hindu thought takes a longer route on its way to reach a conclusion and 'gathers more richness along the way.' In an illustration which would almost certainly have baffled Churchill, Wright drew a diagram:[263]

To those who have not mastered it, the reasoning in the Bhagavad-Gita or the more complex Upanishads can be immensely frustrating. A single idea sets off a series of cerebral reactions so complex that one may become quickly, and hopelessly, entangled – as in the Dharma Chakra, or Wheel of Asoka, now displayed on the Indian flag. The wheel dates from 228 BC, and its hub, rim, and spokes blend concepts of light, truth, simplicity, compassion, renunciation, humility, faith, strength, fellowship, and interdependence, all entwined in an image which links, reinforces, and merges them. You do not have to understand it to feel its conceptual power, but the learned Hindu will pity you for your ignorance. He will also feel superior to you in other ways. High Brahmins, for example, seem to their Western friends to bathe incessantly. They are probably the cleanest people in the world. To them, Englishmen and Americans are coarse and crude, with unspeakable personal habits.

But the social expression of Hinduism is the doctrine, or, more accurately, the practice, of caste, and though its scholars find the subject distasteful, the historical origins of this pernicious system lie in a racism starker than any bigotry found in the veld of South Africa or the red clay of northern Georgia. Over a thousand years before the birth of Christ, Aryans of uncertain origins conquered the black Dravidian and Munda natives and imposed a hierarchical structure on the entire subcontinent. Brahmanism and its major gods – Siva, Vishnu, Krishna, Rama, and the creator Brahma – evolved through successive generations, but the basic principle, or lack of it, endured: the lighter your skin, the higher your caste. Historically, the four great castes are the Brahmins, scholars and priests; Kshatriyas, soldiers and administrators; Vaishyas, merchants; and Sudras, servants and manual labourers. Gandhi was a Vaishya; Nehru, a Kashmiri Brahmin. But there are countless subcastes, including one for prostitution: if a girl is born into it, she spends her life as a whore; if the child is a boy, he will be a pimp until, having raised another generation of whores and pimps, he dies. You can see his sisters and daughters today, locked in the Cages of Bombay.* One caste makes beds, another washes dishes, a third dries them – which is why every British household in the Raj required swarms of servants. Any member of any caste would perish before moving his own garbage, which is the duty of those who have no caste at all – the Untouchables. There were between sixty and seventy million Untouchables in Gandhi's day. He called them *harijans* ('beloved of God') and worked hard to better their lot, but even Mahatma ('great-souled') Gandhi never suggested the abolition of caste, a reform which, Churchill held, would be absolutely necessary before India could be considered civilized.

Vaishyaism was not the only theological influence in Gandhi's childhood home. Jainism was also esteemed there, and his respect for it was to shape the destiny of the subcontinent. Jains believe in tolerance, vegetarianism, fasting for self-purification, and ahimsa, the doctrine of the sanctity of every living creature. A devout Jain will not even swat a mosquito. Gandhi never went that far, but his belief in nonviolence was absolute. That was why he had become a stretcher-bearer, not a soldier, in the Boer War, and *satyagraha*, Hindi for

---

* The cages are for display purposes. They are there, not to lock the girls *in*, but to lock the customers *out* – until rupees have changed hands.

'nonviolence,' was to be his most effective tactic in the struggle for Indian independence; among its subsequent converts were American civil rights workers, who adopted it in the 1960s. Punishing a man who keeps turning the other cheek is frustrating and, eventually, pointless. Beginning in the 1920s, Raj policemen arrested thousands of the Mahatma's *satyāgrahis*, who cheerfully lined up outside prisons, waiting to be escorted to their cells. Unfortunately, the tension between Hindus and Moslems mounted as their enthusiasm for the movement grew; and the possibilities of violence multiplied. The Mahatma sought to overcome it by calling for national unity, coining the slogan '*Hindu-Muslim ek hai!*' ('Hindu and Moslem are one!') Few accepted it, however, and after a series of sinister ritualistic murders a congress mob stormed a police station in the United Provinces and slew the constables. Gandhi called off his campaign. His people, he said, had failed to grasp his message. But the British, who had been itching to get their hands on him, arrested him just the same, and on March 18, 1922, he was tried for sedition in what the docket called 'Case No. 45 of the Ahmedabad Sessions, *Rex Imperator v Gandhi*.' The evidence was a series of articles he had written in his political journal, *Young India*. He pleaded guilty and asked for penal servitude: 'To preach disaffection towards the existing system of Government has become almost a passion with me . . . I am here therefore to submit to the highest penalty that can be inflicted upon me, for what in law is a deliberate crime, and what appears to me to be the highest duty of a citizen.' The puzzled young English magistrate paid tribute to his sincerity and sentenced him to six years, adding: 'I should like to say in doing so that if the course of events in India should make it possible to reduce the period and release you, no one would be better pleased than I.'[264]

Gandhi was out in two years. He found his movement was in disarray. It had split into two factions over whether or not to accept a British invitation to join local legislatures. More depressing, the enmity between Hindu and Moslem members was deepening. Gandhi fasted for three weeks; it solved nothing. In London, Birkenhead, adamantly against any concessions to congress demands, was winning every skirmish. Immediately after the war Parliament had authorized an investigation of the Indian political scene by a royal commission. Appointing the members was FE's job. In 1927, after a long series of delaying actions, he named a panel of undistinguished British backbenchers – not a single Indian – under the chairmanship of Sir John Simon, of whom Birkenhead said patronizingly: 'How much better in life and how much more paying it is to be blameless rather than brilliant.'[265] By the fall of 1929 Simon and his colleagues (who included the still unknown Clement Attlee) were completing a ponderous document which, when published the following year, would omit any mention of dominion status, the key issue in India. Then Lord Irwin surprised everyone by facing the issue squarely. He asked Labour's William Wedgwood Benn, father of the future Tony Benn and later Birkenhead's successor at the India Office, to summon a conference which would include, not only Britons, but also members of the congress and representatives of the maharajas ruling India's princely states. Wedgwood Benn was delighted. Depressed by the stodgy Simon Commission, Labour had been searching for some way to mollify the Indian nationalists. Here, clearly, was a superb opportunity. Notice of the conference was published in the *Indian Gazette* of October 31, 1929. The same issue carried Irwin's declaration that granting dominionhood was implicit in the humane, enlightened tradition of the Raj, and Baldwin's endorsement of this position.

Uproar followed. Birkenhead furiously attacked Irwin in the House of Lords. Lord Reading, following him, said flatly: 'It is frankly inconceivable that India will ever be fit for Dominion self-government.' In the House of Commons, Baldwin was facing a revolt. Tories were questioning, not only his wisdom, but also his integrity. On October 23, when Winston was visiting the War Museum in Richmond, examining a tattered Confederate flag, the Conservative leader had informed the shadow cabinet of Irwin's coming statement and added that he approved of it. Churchill would disagree, of course, and so would the City, with its massive investments in the subcontinent, but Baldwin believed that the voters, weary of India, would be glad to shuck off the burden. With the exception of Sir Samuel Hoare, the prime minister's senior colleagues had told him they thought it would be a mistake to support the viceroy. They thought they had convinced him. And now he had done it anyway. Three of them threatened to resign. Faced with the possibility of a party split, he offered lame excuses. He had acted in his 'personal capacity,' he said, not as leader. They weren't having any of that. Then he told them he had been under the impression that Irwin had spoken out at the urging of the Simon Commission. But the commission hadn't completed its inquiries, and friends of its members knew the report would be weak. The shadow cabinet meeting broke up in confusion. To make sure his views were understood, the fourth Marquess of Salisbury, son of the great prime minister, wrote to Baldwin: '*I need not say what a shock* it was to learn that the declaration was to be made before anything had been laid before the country, though we had appointed a Commission for this very purpose.' He felt mortified: 'What a dislocation! Poor Conservative Party!' Salisbury regarded Indian self-government as an 'extreme absurdity' and hoped 'you will be able to stop it, to convince the Gvt and to convince Edward Irwin that the Party will be shaken to its centre' if this line were not abandoned. He ended: 'We must resist it.' George Lane-Fox sent Irwin word that the Tories were 'not very comfortable' with his position. Geoffrey Dawson, who thought the viceroy was right, nevertheless wrote to him: 'The tide here is running pretty strongly against your ideas, and you cannot hope to carry them out by depending on the Labour Party alone.'[266]

politician, he had resources stronger than his party critics', even though they constituted, at that time, a majority. The whips belonged to him, and also the party machine, including the constituency committees and associations. He could count on the support of *The Times* and of Reith at the BBC. Most of his MPs were indebted to him in one way or another. He called in these IOUs and had just about suppressed the rebellion when, on Tuesday, November 5, Winston Churchill returned from the United States.

Earlier, Irwin had urged Churchill to update his views on India by talking to some members of the congress. Winston had replied: 'I am quite satisfied with my views on India, and I don't want them disturbed by any bloody Indians.' Since leaving Bangalore in 1899 he had taken little interest in the subcontinent. He seems to have been unaware that the Simon Commission and all that followed were the consequences of a pledge made by Lloyd George in 1917, defining England's aim in India as 'the granting of self-governing institutions with a view to the progressive realisation of responsible Government in India as an integral part of the British Empire.' But although Winston had seldom thought of the Raj, his feelings about it were strong. No Englishman was more persuaded of Queen Victoria's wisdom in saying, 'I think it very unwise to give up what we hold.' Indeed, that summed up his attitude towards the entire Empire. He considered it, among other things, a matter of national self-interest. To Churchill, Amery observed, 'England is still the starting point and the ultimate object of policy.' The Empire gave Britain its prestige; it made Britain the world's most powerful nation. Without its imperial possessions the country would be merely an obscure island lying off the European continent. England deprived of its imperial possessions would, for him, be like Samson shorn of his hair or Antaeus without his feet on earth. Moreover, his vision of India, in particular, was crowned by a romantic nimbus. It was the magic land he had known as an impressionable young cavalry officer, a realm of rajas' palaces, the Taj, shikar, bazaars, fakirs, temples, shrines, and howdahs, a symbol of imperial splendour and proud glory, Britain's most priceless possession. To yield it, he said, would be 'a hideous act of self-mutilation.'[267]

Many, including some who were close to him, concluded that he lived in the past, a 'mid-Victorian,' as Amery called him in August 1929, 'steeped in the politics of his father's period, and unable ever to get the modern view.' Certainly Churchill often quoted pronouncements about the subcontinent made long ago by men now deep in their graves. One of them, indeed, was Lord Randolph: 'Our rule in India is, as it were, a sheet of oil spread out over and keeping free from storms a vast and profound ocean of humanity.' Another was Lord Morley: 'There is a school of thought who say that we might wisely walk out of India and that the Indians could manage their own affairs better than we can. Anybody who pictures to himself the anarchy, the bloody chaos that would follow from any such deplorable step might shrink from that sinister decision.' And, from J. R. Seeley's *Expansion of England*, published in 1883, when Winston was an Ascot schoolboy, he remembered the judgement that British withdrawal from the subcontinent would be 'the most inexcusable of all conceivable crimes and might possibly cause the most stupendous of all conceivable calamities.'[268]

There was another side to this, and it should be examined thoughtfully. As a boy at the Crystal Palace Winston had described the ruffian who accosted Count Kinsky as a 'sort of Kaffir' and a 'Mulatto.' In Cuba, fresh out of Sandhurst, he had distrusted 'the negro element among the insurgents.' He never outgrew this prejudice. Late in life he was asked if he had seen the film *Carmen Jones*. He had walked out on it, he replied, because he didn't like 'blackamoors.' His physician was present, and Winston asked what happened when blacks got measles. Could the rash be spotted? The doctor replied that blacks suffered a high mortality rate from measles. Churchill said lightly, 'Well, there are plenty left. They've got a high rate of production.'[269] He could greet Louis Botha and Michael Collins as equals, but his relationship with any Indian, even an accomplished barrister like Gandhi or a fellow Harrovian like Nehru, could never be as between compeers. It followed, therefore, that their country must remain a vassal state. This was the underside of his position in the great debates over India's future which began in 1929. Today it would be called an expression of racism, and he, as its exponent, a racist. But neither word had been coined then; they would not appear in the Oxford English dictionary or Webster's for another generation. Until recently – beginning in the late 1940s – racial intolerance was not only acceptable in polite society; it was fashionable, even assumed.

The popularity of prejudice when Parliament was pondering the India question is demonstrated by the extraordinary success of Katherine Mayo's *Mother India*, which went through forty printings in the 1920s. Churchill read it in 1927, as two notes by Chartwell visitors attest. On August 10 Victor Cazalet reported that his host 'admires the book *Mother India* very much,' and on September 27 Lord Lloyd wrote: 'I was staying a weekend recently with Winston who was immediately struck with Mother India – Miss Mayo's book. It's all true.' Viewed from the 1980s, her work seems almost comparable to the *Protocols of Zion*. Vile in its insinuations, wildly inaccurate, and above all hypocritical, this single volume by an elderly prig poisoned the minds of millions who might otherwise have reflected thoughtfully on Gandhi's movement. Her case against the Hindu custom of child marriage is indisputable, but she did not stop there. Hindu mothers, she said, taught their sons and daughters to masturbate. Citing 'highest medical authority,' she charged that every child practising onanism 'bears on its body the signs of this habit,' and that 'when constantly practised during mature life,' which she declared was the case in India, 'its devastation of body and nerves will scarcely be questioned.' This chapter ends: 'Given men who enter the world physical bankrupts out of bankrupt stock, rear them through childhood in influences and practices that devour their vitality; launch them at the dawn of maturity on an unrestrained outpouring of their whole provision of creative energy in one single direction; find them, at an age when the Anglo-Saxon is just coming into full glory of manhood, broken-nerved, low-spirited, petulant ancients; and need you, while this remains unchanged, seek for other reasons why they are poor and sick and dying and why their hands are too weak, too fluttering, to seize the reins of Government?' 'Miss Mayo has dropped a brick,' Irwin wrote to Neville Chamberlain. 'It will make the Hindus of course see red.' Winston Churchill, being a larger figure than Katherine Mayo, dropped a bigger brick by sanctioning it. The same can be said of liberal men and women on both sides of the Atlantic who accepted her vicious fantasy without demur. The *Spectator* observed that 'the evils which Miss Mayo attacks are widespread and deep-rooted,' and that until they had been expunged, 'India can hardly take the place that she ought to occupy in the family of nations.' *Survey's* reviewer called the book 'challenging, prickly with facts and neglected angles of approach . . . I confess I learned more from this book on the inner Indian and why the East is East than I ever knew before.' The leftist *New Statesman* described it as 'the most important and truthful book that has been written about India for a good deal more than a generation.' Across the Atlantic, the *New Republic* welcomed it. *Outlook* found it 'free from sentimentalism, artisanship, and preconceived notions. It is a straight-forward account.' *Catholic World* commented: 'There is no gainsaying her statements.' To the *New York Herald Tribune, Mother India* was 'calm, hard-headed – though not hard-hearted.' The *New York Times* reported: 'Her detachment is obvious. If she quotes, she gives her authority. If she describes, it is an eyewitness. The facts that she states are not likely to be disputed.'[270]

Churchill, however, always had second and third thoughts, and they usually improved as he went along. It was part of his pattern of response to any political issue that while his early reactions were often emotional, and even unworthy of him, they were usually succeeded by reason and generosity. Given time, he could devise imaginative solutions. Russia had been more than he could handle – though it should be remembered that he would have been content to see a socialist regime there provided it renounced wholesale slaughter – but his record had been impressive in South Africa, the Middle East, and Ireland. He was prepared to accept provincial self-government in India provided Britain retained certain rights of 'paramountcy,' including control of foreign affairs, communications, and defence. What he could not overlook was that India, Gandhian *satāgraha* notwithstanding, was a land of violence. Even as Churchill was binding up his loins to confront Baldwin in the House, Indian terrorists tried to assassinate Irwin, of all people, as the viceregal train entered Delhi. (Churchill cabled Irwin congratulations on his escape; the viceroy, who himself was not untainted by racial condescension, replied that, luckily for him, Indians 'seem to be less efficient in their execution than in their design.') Bengalis then raided an arsenal in Chittagong, killing eight British guards. An uprising in Peshawar left thirty dead. After a terrorist had been executed in Cawnpore (now Kanpur), Hindus rioted and murdered over three hundred Moslems. Churchill said: 'Wednesday's massacres at Cawnpore, a name of evil import' – in June 1857 the British community there had been wiped out by mutineers who, legend has it, threw their corpses down a well – 'are a portent. Because it is believed that we are about to leave the country, the struggle for power is now beginning

688

between the Moslems and Hindus . . . The British troops are now pacifying and calming the terrified and infuriated populace. But the feud is only at its beginning.' His dire warning outraged leaders of the congress, and was discounted by Wedgwood Benn and Baldwin. Today it is discredited; in 1967 Professor Arno J. Mayer of Princeton wrote that the freeing of India 'never produced any of the dire consequences predicted by Churchill.' But it did. Eighteen years after his warning, when the Raj ended and the last British soldiers sailed from Bombay, over two million Hindus and Moslems were slain during six months of savagery. Like Turkey's slaughter of the Armenians, the Russian civil war, and the destruction of the European Jews in the early 1940s, it was a great human disaster; in a word, a holocaust.[271]

Back in England with Hearst and Wall Street behind him, Churchill took the boat train from Southampton, reaching Venetia Montagu's house on the evening of Tuesday, November 5. Clementine had told him that a half-dozen worried Tories awaited him in the drawing room. They thought Baldwin wrong about India but were concerned about party reprisals. Not to worry, Winston told them cheerfully; he would stand alone, if necessary, and speak for all of them. As it happened, he had company. Lloyd George, though his powers were waning, was still effective and beyond Baldwin's reach. The debate on the Irwin declaration opened on Friday. MacDonald spoke for it; Baldwin announced that the Conservatives supported him. George then rose to reply. Davidson wrote that Churchill had 'sat through SB's speech glowering and unhappy' but he leaned 'forward during the "Goat's" speech cheering every mischievous passage in it.' Davidson estimated that at least a third of the Tory MPs would vote against the declaration. They had listened glumly to their leader; their applause for him had been perfunctory. Dawson wrote to Irwin: 'The naked truth is that his speech, to which I listened, was heard in almost icy silence by the House.' Hoare wrote: 'It is certainly true that scarcely anyone in the party liked it. The diehards were much upset and . . . Austin, FE, Winston and Worthy [Sir Laming Worthington-Evans] were violently opposed to it.' Hoare thought he himself had been 'the only supporter of Stanley's attitude.' It was his impression that 'Winston was almost demented with fury.' Lane-Fox observed that 'There were several people such as Winston and Worthy whom I saw and heard crying "No." ' Had there been a vote, he thought, half the Tory MPs would have defected, but he felt confident that 'since they have had time to think, the vast majority of the Conservatives have returned to their loyalty to SB.'[272]

Churchill's first attack on the declaration came, not on the floor of the House, but in the columns of the *Daily Mail*. It appeared on November 16, establishing a position on the issue from which he never wavered. Britain's 'rescue of India from ages of barbarism, internecine war, and tyranny,' he wrote, 'and its slow but ceaseless forward march to civilisation' constituted 'upon the whole the finest achievement of our history.' Now it was 'the duty of public men and women to make it plain without delay that the extension of Dominion Status to India is not practicable at the present time and that any attempt to secure it will encounter the earnest resistance of the British nation.' Self-government was unthinkable for a community which 'treats sixty millions of its members, toiling at their side, as "Untouchables," whose approach is an affront and whose very presence is a pollution,' and it was absurd to contemplate it 'while India is a prey to fierce racial and religious dissensions and when the withdrawal of British protection would mean the immediate resumption of medieval ways.' If the viceregal proposal were adopted the British Raj would be replaced by a 'Gandhi Raj' because 'the political classes in India represent only an insignificant fraction of the three hundred and fifty millions for whose welfare we are responsible.' England could not, and indeed should not, 'close the long avenue of the future.' But the idea that 'Home Rule for India or Dominion Status or full responsible status for India can emerge from anything that is now being done is not only fantastic in itself but criminally mischievous in its effects.'²⁷³

The struggle over Indian self-government mounted throughout 1930 and was fought against a background of tumultuous events. The Cawnpore riots resumed and the death toll passed one thousand, Afridi tribesmen emerged from the hills and attacked a strong British garrison in Peshawar, and Gandhi delivered his most brilliant political stroke, his Salt March to the Indian Ocean. He had been searching for some way to make his movement comprehensible to the masses. The Raj held a monopoly on the production and sale of salt. But salt should be free, said the Mahatma; the seas alone held enough to satisfy the world's population a thousand times over. So he began his trek on March 12, scooping a spoonful of salt from brackish earth along the way. He never reached the seaside. While sleeping by a river, he was arrested by nervous British policemen; they had arrived stealthily in the middle of night to avoid a riot. But the Salt March continued without him. His original spoonful was sold for sixteen hundred rupees. Professors led their students to the shore. The Raj banned newpapers congratulating them. Indian youths raided a Raj salt depot. The British police responded with brutality and mass arrest; by the end of May, 100,000 Gandhi followers were behind bars, Nehru among them. He wrote to his leader, who was cheerfully spinning cotton in another prison: 'May I congratulate you on the new India you have created by your magic touch?'²⁷⁴

Churchill's response to all this was that the viceroy had asked for it. His declaration had displayed weakness; enemies of the Raj were exploiting it. The Afridis had stormed Peshawar because they had been encouraged to believe that 'Lord Irwin's Government was clearing out of India, and that rich spoils lay open to their raids.' During his service on the frontier, before the turn of the century, the fathers of these tribesmen had hidden in the hills. To hunt them had been 'like going into the water to fight a shark.' Now they were witnessing 'the shark coming out to the beach.' To Boothby he wrote that it would be 'easy . . . to crush Gandhi and the Congress.' The party should be broken up and its leaders exiled to another British possession. The difficulty, as he saw it, was the indecisiveness of MacDonald's government and the lack of leadership on either side of the House. 'When eagles are silent,' he said, 'the parrots begin to jabber.' On September 28 he distributed a brief statement to the press declaring that he would remain in public life until the India issue was settled. Lord Burnham, owner of the *Daily Telegraph* and a Tory ally, wrote to him that 'the scales are most unfairly weighted against such of us as believe that our betrayal of India would be a crime against civilisation . . . The real tragedy is that India is crying out to be governed and we refuse to govern.' Burnham added: 'FE's illness is a great blow.'[275]

FE's death, which swiftly followed, was a far greater blow. He was relatively young – still in his fifties – and to Churchill he had almost been a member of the family. On October 1 Clementine wrote Margaret Smith, Lady Birkenhead: 'Last night Winston wept for his friend. He said several times "I feel so lonely." ' FE, secure in the House of Lords, had confidently led the defenders of the Raj; now they turned to Winston. Churchill's position in the Commons, very different from his lost friend's, was growing more difficult every week. Yet he could see no alternative. He wrote: 'When I think of the way in which we poured out blood and money to take Contalmaison or to hold Ypres, I cannot understand why it is that we should now throw away our conquests and our inheritance with both hands, through helplessness and pusillanimity.' On September 24 he had written to Baldwin: 'What times we live in! The most serious of all our problems is India. I am now receiving, in consequence of my speeches, streams of letters from our people in India and the feeling of anxiety that we are being let down . . . I do earnestly hope that you will not allow your friendship with Irwin to affect your judgement or the action of your party upon what, since the War, is probably the greatest question Englishmen have had to settle. Very strong currents of feeling and even passion are moving under the stagnant surface of our affairs, and I must confess myself to care more about this business than anything else in public life.'[276]

Baldwin was unmoved. He had already confided to a friend that if he formed another government, Churchill would not be part of it. Winston's incapacity for teamwork, he said, far outweighed his talents. Clementine saw what was coming. Politics, she wrote to their son, 'have taken an orientation not favourable to Papa.' India was the main issue, but Baldwin, strongly supported by the shadow cabinet in this instance, endorsed high tariffs. Churchill protested. On October 14 the two men held a long private talk and agreed that there was a definite breach between them. That evening Baldwin wrote to Churchill of his 'profound regret that there is a real parting of the ways and a friendship towards you which had grown up through six years of loyal and strenuous work together.' He insisted that he continued to 'cherish the hope that you may yet see your way to stay with us,' but by his actions he was sabotaging that hope, if indeed it existed. The Tory tariff policy remained unchanged, and Winston contemplated resignation from the shadow cabinet.

He was nudged again when Lord Lloyd, the strong British high commissioner in Cairo, was recalled with Baldwin's approval as the first step in the evacuation of all British troops, except those in the canal zone, from Egypt. 'During the last forty years,' a furious Churchill told the House, 'everything has turned upon the British garrison in Cairo. With its departure the once glorious episode of England in Egypt comes to an end. It is not without a bitter pang that I contemplate this.' He observed that 'there is a sombre philosophy nowadays which I hear in some quarters about Egypt and India. It is said: "Give them all they ask for! Clear out and let things go to smash, and then there will be a case for us to come back again!"' 'Such a doctrine, he said, 'is no foundation for the continuance of British fame and power. Once we lose our confidence in our mission in the East . . . it will be a presence which cannot long endure.'[277]

Baldwin wrote to a friend that Churchill wanted 'to go back to pre-war and govern with a strong hand. He has become once more the subaltern of hussars of '96.' But Winston was far from alone. The very die-hard members of the party to whom he had once been anathema founded the Indian Empire Society and invited him to address their first meeting. It was held in London's Cannon Street Hotel, hard by St Paul's, on December 12, 1930. They wanted powerful political medicine, and he believed he knew the prescription. In Lahore, Kipling's beloved citadel in the Punjab, members of the congress had burned the Union Jack. Their meeting, said Winston, should have been 'broken up and its leaders deported.' Gandhi had been treated far too leniently in the beginning; he should have been arrested and tried 'as soon as he broke the law.' Even now, firm measures, demonstrating Parliament's resolve 'to govern and guide the destinies of the Indian people in faithful loyalty to Indian interest,' could, perhaps within a few months, 'bring this period of tantalized turmoil to an end.' Each Indian province should be given 'more real, more intimate, more representative organs of self-government,' leaving the central authority in the hands of the Raj. But there could be no compromise with 'the forces of sedition and outrage,' because 'the truth is that Gandhi-ism and all it stands for will, sooner or later, have to be grappled with and finally crushed. It is no use trying to satisfy a tiger by feeding him with cat's meat. The sooner this is realised, the less trouble and misfortune will there be for all concerned.'[278]

'What a monstrous speech Winston has just made,' Irwin wrote to Geoffrey Dawson at *The Times*. Dawson, agreeing, ran an editorial declaring that Churchill was 'no more representative of the Conservative Party' than 'the assassins of Calcutta' were of the Indian Congress, and his speech would 'have just as little influence.' Dawson and his fellow lords of the British media were doing something about this last. Churchill wanted to address the nation on the issue. He offered Sir John Reith £100 for ten minutes on the BBC. Reith, like any trapped civil servant, scurried to higher authority, in this case Wedgwood Benn, who replied that he felt 'most apprehensive' at the prospect of Winston on the air; he was afraid the consequence would do 'immense harm to India.'

Reith thereupon rejected Churchill's proposal, explaining that he opposed 'American' broadcasting methods. This, Winston said, was an 'oppressive decision.' He thought 'the American plan would be better than the present British methods of debarring public men from access to a public who wish to hear'; when 'an Imperial issue like the discharge of our mission in India is being debated, it seems to me that at least an equal solicitude for impartiality is required from you.' The Establishment was closing ranks against him. News accounts of his speeches in Parliament shrank and appeared deeper and deeper in newspapers' inside pages. He protested to Rothermere of the *Daily Mail* that they were 'the only weapon I have for fighting this battle.' If the *Mail* buried its accounts of them, 'Baldwin with the Times at his back is master of the fate of India.' Gagged, he struggled on, addressing the Indian Empire Society twice more, always assailing Gandhi, whose cause and dedication were incomprehensible to him. In his view the Mahatma was 'a malignant and subversive fanatic,' a cynical manipulator of 'Brahmins who mouth and patter principles of Western Liberalism and pose as philosophic and democratic politicians.' And all the time he continued to attend meetings of the shadow cabinet. If his colleagues felt awkward, he was not in the least embarrassed. As he saw it he was true to the widow's uniform he had once worn:[279]

> *Dear-bought and clear, a thousand year,*
> *Our fathers' title runs.*
> *Make we likewise their sacrifice,*
> *Defrauding not our sons.*

As the rift grew between Baldwin and Churchill, Conservative MPs were faced with the nightmare of every workaday politician: the obligation to choose sides in an intramural quarrel. Some found it relatively easy. Lord Weir thought Britain needed 'inspiration' and Winston could provide it. Lord Knutsford wrote to him: 'Some day you must lead the whole country. I look for this.' But others were more vulnerable. Neville Chamberlain privately wrote to a young MP on November 29: 'I, myself, would very much prefer to go more slowly in the matter of Indian reform, and try a series of cautious experiments, which might perhaps last for fifty years or more, before culminating in a complete system of Central and Provincial self-government.' Publicly, however, Chamberlain was among Baldwin's most enthusiastic backers. Lane-Fox wrote to Irwin that the party was 'not very comfortable' with his declaration, and in another letter told him: 'The average Conservative was of course rather shocked by the way in which Gandhi was originally allowed to break the law in the matter of his salt campaign and march to the sea.' A clear majority of the Tory MPs thought Churchill right, but most of them had too much to lose to say so. Despite their convictions, men like Chamberlain persuaded themselves that they were bound by a higher loyalty to oppose, in his words, those who were 'either hostile' to their leaders 'or disposed to join cliques led by men whose motives are much more complicated.' This last referred to the possibility that Winston was planning a revolt, deliberately dividing the party, as his father had, hoping to reach No. 10 through a coup. Davidson put it bluntly in a letter to Irwin: 'Winston's game, of course, has been obvious, as it always is. He is not the son of Randolph for nothing.' Beaverbrook thought Churchill's stand revealed 'a defect of character' and a willingness 'to take up anything as long as it leads to power'; that he had changed 'party, political friends and political dogmas so often' that his credibility was 'nearly gone.' At present, said Beaverbrook, he was 'trying to make a corner for himself in Indian affairs. He is now taking up the stand of a veritable die-hard. But,' he concluded, 'he does not carry conviction . . . His voice lacks that note of sincerity for which the country looks.' Irwin disagreed. To him, Churchill presented a real threat. Irwin noted that at least twenty times between March and December Winston had challenged the leadership's position on India, and, on each occasion, Baldwin had barely mustered a majority of Tories.[280]

Winston go? In 1904 he had crossed to the Liberals; in 1924, back to the Conservatives. But Labour was now the Opposition, and he and they glared at one another from opposite ends of the parliamentary spectrum. Therefore his only choice was what political journalists call 'the wilderness' – the cold, bleak, barren limbo of discredited or incompetent MPs whom no party wants. Nevertheless, no one can doubt that he was moved by a genuine conviction. That cannot be said of those with whom he was parting company. The Tory leaders were uninspired by Indian nationalism. One searches in vain for ringing affirmations of freedom or admiration for Gandhian saintliness in their speeches, letters, and diaries. What comes through, like the pounding on a wall of a man who wants the party in the next apartment to quiet down so he can sleep, is a determination to avoid discord, unpleasantness, or any rude interruption of long serene weekends in the country. England's ruling class, or those of them in power, had lost their fathers' inflexible determination. A. G. Gardiner had described the English patrician as 'a personality that is entirely fearless,' belonging to 'a caste that never doubts itself.' A. L. Rowse, fellow of All Souls College, Oxford, quotes Gardiner and then adds: 'Never till 1931, we may say; for in that year the caste lost confidence in itself and, undermined by fear, it lost not only confidence but conscience. Confused in mind about everything, except the main chance – its own preservation – it survived from year to year, from month to month, from day to day, by blurring the clarity of all issues, even the most dangerous – that of the nation's safety; it maintained its enormous majority by electoral trickery, it spoke and perhaps thought in the language of humbug, it hoped to stave off conflict . . . by offering appeasement.'[281]

By January 8, 1931, Churchill had made his decision. He foresaw MacDonald's fall and the formation of a new government, but, he wrote to his son, 'I have no desire to join such an administration and be saddled with all the burden of whole-hog Protection, plus unlimited doses of Irwinism for India. I shall be much more able to help the country from outside.' The 'breaking-point in my relation with Mr Baldwin,' as he later called it, came less than three weeks later. Irwin wanted to lay the foundations for his 'round-table' conference with the congress leaders, to be held in London. To clear the air he planned to release Gandhi from jail, and on January 23 he cabled Baldwin: 'My immediate fear is lest, in the forthcoming debate in Parliament, Winston should make mischief. Do, if you can, get some helpful and cordial speeches made from our side to discount possible bad effect of what he may say. Best of all, speak yourself and send him to Epping for the day.'[282]

Gandhi was freed forty-eight hours later. Outraged Raj officials in India and Conservative associations throughout England were speechless. Churchill, of course, was not. On the evening of Monday, January 26, he rose in the House and – his other remarks on India having been delivered elsewhere, 'out of doors,' in the parliamentary expression, and therefore being forgivable – took his first fateful step into the wilderness. 'I must of course first of all make it clear,' he said at the outset, 'that I do not speak for the official Opposition nor for my right hon[ourable] friend the Leader of the Opposition.' He spoke, he said, 'solely as a Member of Parliament, of some service in this House,' whose views ought not to go 'unrepresented in this discussion.' He then laced into the viceroy's declaration, deplored the tabling of the Simon Report, and criticized the government's decision to bar Simon and his fellow commissioners from the round table. 'Our trusted friends and lawful, formal authoritative advisers are set aside,' he charged, 'in order to placate those who are the bitterest opponents of British rule in India.' The promise of dominion status was to be laid before 'the gleaming eyes of excitable millions' while sixty thousand Indian agitators were locked up, a situation virtually without precedent, at least since the Mutiny. To imagine that these resentful men would emerge docile was, he thought, absurd. Britons should not permit themselves 'to be edged, pushed, talked and cozened out of India.' After two hundred years of fidelity and achievement, and thousands of British soldiers' lives sacrificed 'on a hundred fields,' Englishmen had earned 'rights of our own in India.' Public opinion in the United Kingdom would not tolerate the spectacle of British women and children 'in hourly peril amidst the Indian multitudes,' yet this was the future to which, 'step by step and day by day, we are being remorselessly and fatuously conducted.'[283]

By custom, either MacDonald or Wedgwood Benn should have replied to him. Baldwin did it instead. His decision was unwise; he answered Winston's rolling, cadenced rhetoric with a meandering, legalistic defence of the round table. Lane-Fox reported to Irwin that 'while SB was vigorously cheered by the Socialists, there was an ominous silence on our benches. And I am afraid this represents the position in our party on many things.' Nevertheless, it was Churchill who had sinned, and now he must pay the forfeit for flagrant disobedience of his party's leader. On Tuesday morning Lord Hailes approached him, like a summons server, with the formal request for his resignation from the shadow cabinet. Afterwards Hailes set down Winston's reaction. 'Face reddened then went white. Pouted furiously. Walked to a corner of the room, picked up his silver knobbed cane, came back and brought the cane down full force on the table. As he looked at me, I imagined that I might be the next victim. Then his face suddenly puckered into a smile. "So the Conservative P. wants to get rid of me, does it? All right, I'll go quietly now." ' He scrawled a paragraph to Baldwin: 'Now that our divergences of view upon India policy have become public' – persisting in the quaint conceit that nothing in British politics becomes public until uttered in the House – 'I feel that I ought not any longer to attend the meetings of your "Business Committee" to which you have hitherto so kindly invited me.' Baldwin replied on Wednesday: 'I am grateful to you for your kind letter of yesterday and much as I regret your decision not to attend the meetings of your old colleagues, I am convinced that your decision is correct in the circumstances.'[284]

Churchill's departure left the shadow chancellorship vacant. To fill the void, Baldwin appointed Neville Chamberlain.

Churchill's parliamentary career had come to resemble the Greek legend of Sisyphus, who was condemned to toil up a steep hill pushing a huge stone which, just before he reached the top, always rolled back to the bottom. Twice he had been regarded as England's next prime minister, first as a Liberal, then as a Conservative. Now he was once more cut off from all inner political councils. But during those first months in the wilderness he felt unfettered, exhilarated, free to loose verbal thunderbolts whenever so moved. Young MPs who thought they had heard Churchillian philippics at their most venomous now learned otherwise. When Gandhi arrived in Delhi to meet Irwin, Winston thundered: 'It is alarming and also nauseating to see Mr Gandhi, a seditious Middle Temple lawyer, now posing as a fakir of a type well-known in the East, striding half-naked up the steps of the Vice-regal palace, while he is still organising and conducting a defiant campaign of civil disobedience, to parley on equal terms with the representative of the King-Emperor.' And even as die-hard back-benchers howled with appreciative laughter, they were shocked at the cruel attack on MacDonald, the titular prime minister, who was permitting Baldwin to run his government. Winston told the House: 'I spoke the other day, after he had been defeated in an important division, about his wonderful skill in falling without hurting himself. He falls, but he comes up again smiling, a little dishevelled but still smiling.' Then, staring at MacDonald across the well, he continued: 'I remember when I was a child being taken to the celebrated Barnum's Circus which contained an exhibition of freaks and monstrosities, but the exhibit on the programme which I most desired to see was the one described as "The Boneless Wonder." My parents judged that the spectacle would be too revolting and demoralizing for my youthful eyes, and I have waited fifty years to see the Boneless Wonder sitting on the Treasury Bench.'[285]

Epping staunchly supported its member. His constituents, he wrote Clementine, were 'loving, ardent, and unanimous.' Indeed, he believed there was 'no doubt that the whole spirit of the Conservative party is with me, and that much of their dissatisfaction with SB turns itself into favour with me.' This was no illusion; that same week the party's principal agent wrote to Neville Chamberlain: 'Many of our supporters are worried about the question of India. They lean much more towards the views of Mr Churchill than to those expressed by Mr Baldwin in the House of Commons.' Nevertheless, when a Gandhi–Irwin pact was signed in early March – the Mahatma agreed to call off all *satyāgraha* and attend the round-table conference in London to discuss India's future – Baldwin endorsed it. He opened the House debate on March 12 and was followed by Wedgwood Benn, who accused Winston of advocating a policy of 'the lathi, the bayonet, the machine-gun and artillery.' Churchill reminded the House of his speech in the Dyer debate and his repeated opposition to 'brutal force in India,' and pointed out that most of the Indians who had died over the past year had been killed, not by British troops, but in 'religious fights' between Moslems and Hindus. It was all true. Yet the feeling persisted that he was scheming for power. Leo Amery wrote in his diary that upon leaving Parliament he had 'heard Winston haranguing a press correspondent in the Lobby to the effect that he was not going to let India be betrayed without telling England all about it. I am afraid we are in for some difficulties over the India business. Winston has chosen his moment and his excuse for separating with the Party very adroitly.'[286]

He enjoyed frequent successes. At his urging Lord Lloyd agreed to challenge Baldwin in the party's India Committee, and at one point Lloyd mustered a majority of diehards against the round table. 'Winston has done a good deal to corrupt them,' Dawson wrote to Irwin. Churchill's eloquent plea for the Untouchables was particularly effective. ('A multitude as big as a nation, men, women and children deprived of hope and of the status of humanity. Their plight is worse than that of slaves, because they have been taught to consent not only to a physical but to a psychic servitude and prostration.') The *Daily Mail* and the *Daily Express* provided him with such full coverage that Baldwin, like virtually all leaders stung by a free press, protested. 'What the proprietorship of the papers is aiming at,' he charged, 'is power and power without responsibility – the prerogative of the harlot.' At the Albert Hall, Tory back-benchers heard Churchill describe how dissent was being suppressed by the alliance of political chieftains now sharing the same nest. Baldwin had 'decided that we are to work with the Socialists, and that we must make our action conform with theirs. We therefore have against us at the present time the official machinery of all the three great parties in the State. We meet under a ban. Every Member of Parliament or Peer who comes here must face the displeasure of the party Whips.' In the House, despite jeers, hostile interruptions, and outbursts, he roared until he was heard: 'By your actions you have produced misery such as India has not seen for half a century. You have poisoned relations between the Mohammedans and the Hindus.' Then he flourished photographs of Indian corpses mutilated in the communal killings, pictures taken on the spot which were, he cried, 'so revolting that no paper would be able to publish them.' All spring and throughout the summer he kept his drumfire, and in the *Daily Mail* of September 7, when Gandhi was on his way to London – no other Indian politician accompanied him; he alone would speak for India's 350 million – Churchill warned that the round table would lead to 'nothing but further surrenders of British authority.' Without the 'guidance and control' of the Raj, he wrote, such 'pure savagery' as the Cawnpore killings would be repeated all over the sub-continent, an inevitable consequence of unchecked Hinduism and its 'whole apparatus,' as represented at Benares on the Ganges, 'with its palaces and temples, its shrines and its burning ghats, its priests and ascetics, its mysterious practices and multiform ritual . . . unchanged through the centuries, untouched by the West.'[287]

This was Churchill at his most effective. His prose soared. His commitment was total. At that time, on that issue, he was speaking for most Englishmen. And yet . . .

It was all as sounding brass or a tinkling cymbal. The public was distracted by the growing financial crisis. The House had wearied of India. Lloyd George had to enter hospital for a major operation; Churchill, ostracized, left for Chartwell. Britain therefore was deprived of the two authentic geniuses in its public life; 'as we have said several times in the last few days,' Hoare wrote to Neville Chamberlain on August 31, 'we have had some great good luck in the absence of Winston and LG.' Thus Baldwin and MacDonald were free to pursue their separate grails: business as usual for Baldwin; disarmament for MacDonald. Winston returned and spent six months trying to pry them apart, but Baldwin ignored him, attending the round-table talks and accepting Labour's lead in the conferences with Gandhi, while MacDonald – who never forgave him for the Boneless Wonder gibe – lost his poise but once. Baited by Brendan Bracken, who was quoting Churchill, the prime minister glared at Bracken and shouted, 'You swine!' – an indiscretion which, Dawson being away for the time, appeared in *The Times*, to Winston's delight. Some senior Tories worried about their restless back-benchers. Sir Malcolm Hailey wrote of the round-table discussion that he was 'beginning to feel' that Baldwin 'may not have been quite correct in believing that he could carry the whole of the Conservative Party in any decision at which he might arrive.' He concluded, however, that 'the general block' of Tory MPs wers likelier to follow the leader than be 'swayed by the very extreme views of Winston Churchill.' Seeing Winston isolated, others were reluctant to join him in Coventry. Churchill, their elders told them, was a rogue elephant, an opportunist; his pleas for Indian minorities, his support of Indian self-government on the local level, and his prediction of a bloodbath should the Raj leave were dismissed as wily diversions or hyperbole. He wrote to Boothby: 'Politics are very interesting. My late colleagues are more interested in doing me in than in any trifling questions connected with India or tariffs.'[288]

They were careful not to accost him in the House, where he was at his most dangerous. After one of his most effective speeches, Wedgwood Benn completely ignored his arguments and evasively replied that although Winston had 'entered the Irish Conference with a dripping sword, he emerged with a dripping pen, and I am not without hope that even here, as he did in the Irish case, he will come in this matter to a better judgement.' Baldwin blunted his thrusts with sweeping generalizations. Ignoring the issue of Indian independence, he said that it was England's aim to introduce 'self-governing institutions' to the subcontinent 'with a view to the progressive realisation of responsible Government in India as an integral part of the British Empire' – an Empire which, although he did not say so, the Statute of Westminster, not to mention future events, would eventually dismantle. He said: 'We have impregnated India ourselves with Western ideas, and, for good or ill, we are reaping the fruits of our own work.' But only a fraction of the subcontinent's population had been exposed to Western thought, and it was this elite which would rule India when the Raj pulled out.* Baldwin thought the House should agree 'to keep India out of party politics.' It had been in party politics for three centuries; if Parliament couldn't determine the future of the Raj, who should? He was 'firmly convinced that such articles as Churchill's pieces in the *Daily Mail* 'will do more to lose India for the British Empire, will do more to cause a revolutionary spirit, than anything that can be done in any way by anyone else.' Even though 'the rank and file refuse to face facts,' he said. 'the leader has to look at them, and he has to warn his people.' It was 'the supreme duty of a political figure to tell the people of the country the truth, because truth is greater than tactics.' The question which stumped Pontius Pilate held no mysteries for Stanley Baldwin, and in his gentlest, most civil manner he advised his colleagues to keep their opinions in this matter to themselves and leave all decisions to him, the prime minister, and the secretary of state for India.[289]

But Churchill had the bone in his teeth, and wouldn't yield it until events wrenched it from him. Intricate efforts to resolve the Indian question continued on what he called their 'downward slurge,' ending in the Government of India Act of 1935, the longest single piece of legislation ever to emerge from the House of Commons – 'a gigantic split,' said Churchill, 'of jumbled crochet work.' He had fought it for three years in what was probably the most brilliant parliamentary performance of his life. He lost, but so did everyone else; the act's ultimate objective, an all-India federation which would weave together all the provinces and states on the subcontinent, was rejected by the congress, the Moslems, and the Indian princes. Nevertheless, it was a long step towards dissolution of the Raj. British India was destined to vanish in Winston's own lifetime. A harbinger was the welcome England extended to Gandhi when he arrived in the fall of 1931, clad only in his homespun shawl and swaddling dhoti, a long loincloth worn by Indian men at home but never, until now, seen

* During the early 1950s, when this writer was living in Delhi as a foreign correspondent, social scientists began a comprehensive poll of Indian villages to determine how many natives knew British rule had ended in 1947. The survey was aborted when it was discovered that a majority didn't know the British had even arrived. England's East India Company was chartered in 1600.

in Britain. Had the phrase Radical Chic existed then, it would have described the Mahatma's reception. He planted trees, gave unsolicited advice on a thousand topics, was extolled by Anglican clergymen, entered the goat which supplied his milk in an English dairy show and was awarded first place, had lunch with Lady Astor, and was invited to tea with the King and Queen. Everyone of consequence clamoured to meet Gandhi, with one exception. Churchill refused to see him. Winston was roundly criticized for this, though he had company outside Britain. On December 13 the Mahatma called at the Vatican for an audience with the pope and was turned away. The reason, he was told, was his 'inadequate clothing.'[290]

The Crash of '29, like the Blizzard of '88, is identified with a specific year. Even more is it associated with an American city and a particular street. But it wasn't confined to Wall Street – the first European quake had come in Vienna, when the Credit-Anstalt, Austria's largest bank, closed its doors – and the repercussions were international. Wall Street's significance derived from the new role of the American financial community as successor to London's City. It was the linchpin of the world's economic system, and when it snapped the whole structure came tumbling down. The New York Stock Exchange, more familiarly known as the Big Board, was the trading centre for Churchill's securities, and he was among those who discovered to their dismay that the Crash was only the beginning; price levels sank lower and lower throughout 1930, and by the summer of 1931 they made the ticker readings of the '29 panic look lofty. Britain, in trouble since the return to gold, was mired in its worst fiscal crisis since the bursting of the South Sea Bubble in 1720. Indeed, this was worse. South Sea stock had plunged to 13.5 per cent of its highest quotation, but then it had rallied; the company had continued to do business for eighty years and paid dividends. By the end of 1931, however, the average securities in New York and London were worth 11 per cent of their pre-Crash value. Investors in the Big Board had lost seventy-four billion dollars. The panic was spinning in vicious circles. Retail sales ebbed, so costs were cut by laying off workers. The workers laid off could not buy the goods of other industries. Therefore sales dropped further, leading to more layoffs and a general shrinkage of purchasing power, until farmers were pauperized by the poverty of industrial workers. In forming his second government, Ramsay MacDonald had hoped to break this cycle. Instead, the lines of jobless Britons grew longer. The TUC declared that it would accept no cuts in unemployment benefits. England having left the gold standard, the pound dropped from $4.86 to $3.49. The King called MacDonald to Buckingham Palace and asked him to remain in power as head of an all-party national government. Two Labour ministers, Snowden and J. H. Thomas, agreed to serve with him; the rest of the Labour party called them traitors and withdrew their support. Baldwin went along, however, and with Lloyd George still ill, Simon and Sir Herbert Samuel committed the Liberals.

Churchill was the last man in Parliament entitled to criticize any government's Treasury policy, but, never conspicuous for lack of gall, he did so anyhow, describing Snowden's management of the Exchequer as 'incompetent.' He agreed that all parties should 'come to the rescue of a Socialist Government reduced to impotence.' At the same time, he warned that he would remember his 'grievous complaints' against those he held responsible for the plight of the economy. The dole was reduced despite the unions, and after £25,000,000 had been withdrawn from the Bank of England in a single day –a record – the Old Lady of Threadneedle Street was saved from bankruptcy by credits from Washington. But so many makeshift decisions trembled in the balance that the House required a national referendum. Before the general election, Hoare wrote that he was 'very nervous' about the outcome. He needn't have been. The results were an astonishing triumph for the national government, which won 554 of the 615 seats in the House. It was a landslide, but there was more to it than that; the largest part of the avalanche was a historic Tory sweep. The Conservative party was now represented by 473 MPs, over three-fourths of the House, while Labour had dropped from 236 to 52 – the bitter fruit of MacDonald's split with mainstream Labourites. So huge was the Conservative majority that Baldwin was expected to form a new government. He declined; they had campaigned as a coalition, he said, and should so rule. He knew he could oust MacDonald whenever he chose, but this was not the moment. Instead, he installed himself as lord president of the council and picked the new cabinet: eleven Tories, including Hoare at the India Office; five National Liberals; and four National Labourites. Under any other circumstances, Churchill, with his seniority and achievements, would have received a major ministry. His own reelection had been spectacular. Although MacDonald had disparaged him on the stump, and one government minister, Samuel, had actually appeared in Epping to call for his defeat, Winston's margin of victory had exceeded twenty thousand votes, nearly two out of every three. He nursed a faint hope that a summons might arrive from No. 10. None did. His popularity in the country remained high, but his cause had been repudiated; only twenty candidates endorsed by the Indian Empire Society had been elected, and even before polling Baldwin and MacDonald had agreed that there would be no place for Churchill. 'Like many others,' he wryly wrote afterwards, 'I had felt the need of a national concentration. But I was neither surprised nor unhappy when I was left out of it . . . What I should have done if I had been asked to join I cannot tell. It is superfluous to discuss doubtful temptations that have never existed.' Snowden was elevated to the peerage and Neville Chamberlain robed as chancellor of the Exchequer. To Winston, England's political future seemed hopeless. MacDonald, Baldwin, Chamberlain – the reign of mediocrities stretched over the horizon and beyond. In all Parliament he could count on the absolute support of just two MPs, Boothby and Bracken. His isolation was virtually complete. 'Now, truly,' writes Kenneth Young, Beaverbrook's biographer, 'Churchill was out in the cold.'[291]

He accepted it, 'defiant,' by his maxim, 'in defeat.' In the House he sat on the front bench, on the government's side, just below the aisle. 'What a gap there is,' wrote Guy Eden, 'what a vast, terrific chasm, between the Treasury Bench, seat of power, and that seat just two feet, six inches away, below the gangway!' Clement Attlee later recalled: 'Here he was well placed to fire on both parties. I remember describing him as a heavily armed tank cruising in No Man's Land.' What intrigued Eden 'above all else was the manner of his treatment by the Tory members. I have watched him, accompanied by a sole companion, walking broodingly through the corridors of the House or conversing in the Smoking Room with a few admirers like Brendan Bracken and Robert Boothby. But generally, Tory members gave him a wide berth.' In opposition he adopted a technique of maintaining constant streams of objections, some audible and to the point, others quite unintelligible. One afternoon a minister in the middle of a speech was distracted by Churchill. Winston was making movements of disagreement. The irritated minister said: 'I see my right honourable friend shakes his head, but I am only expressing my own opinion.' 'And I,' said Winston, without looking up, 'am only shaking my own head.'[292]

That was clever and gentle, but his tongue had a much rougher side, and many who had been slashed by it, inside the House and out, now descended upon him like vultures homing in on carrion, believing, as Beaverbrook did, that he had 'finally shot his bolt.' Churchill had accused all MPs who favoured dominion status for India, whatever their party allegiance, of defeatism and inadequate patriotism. Samuel now flung this back at him: 'If indeed the truest patriot is a man who breathes hatred, who lays the seeds of war, and stirs up the greatest number of enemies against his country, then Mr Churchill is a great patriot.' Now that he was down, many MPs, hitherto silent, reached the conclusion that Churchill was obsessed by a relentless *besoin de faire* which had expressed itself in such adventures as Gallipoli, the Russian civil war, and the breaking of the general strike. Publicists wrote of him as an outcast, as untouchable as the *harijans* he had championed. 'The tragedy of Mr Churchill,' one commented in 1931, 'is that whilst in reality he has nothing to *offer* the genuine Labour man, he fails to command the confidence of the Conservative. For the ghosts of Gallipoli will always rise up to damn him anew . . . What sensible man is going to place confidence in Mr Churchill in any situation which needs cool-headedness, moderation, or tact?'[293]

In the rooms and halls of Parliament he was humiliated and subjected to sneers, snubs, patronizing nudging, and indifferent shruggings from those who saw him coming and turned their backs. Detective Thompson, still assigned to him – Winston had told the Yard he no longer needed a bodyguard, but the Yard, intercepting threats on his life from Indian nationalists, decided otherwise – was angry and puzzled. A rough, brusque man, unintimidated by rank, Thompson questioned some who had slighted Churchill. 'He's like a weather-vane,' explained one. Another said: 'His life is one long speech. He does not talk. He orates . . . He does not want to hear your views.

He does not want to disturb the beautiful clarity of his thoughts by the tiresome reminders of the other side.' Baldwin told friends and even casual acquaintances how pleasant it was to attend meetings without Winston there to ignore the agenda and introduce 'some extremely clever memorandum submitted by him on the work of some department other than his own.' Churchill's critics called him rash, impetuous, tactless, contentious, inconsistent, unsound, an amusing parliamentary celebrity who was forever out of step. 'We just don't know what to make of him,' a troubled Tory MP told Lady Astor. She asked brightly: 'How about a nice rug?'[294]

He was hurt and baffled. Long afterwards a legend arose that he had endured these slights philosophically. 'In the midst of so many outward upheavals,' Alan Moorehead wrote, Churchill was 'the least displaced person one could possibly imagine.' He himself lent credence to the myth. 'There was much mocking in the press about my exclusion,' he said later, 'but now one can see how lucky I was. Over me beat the invisible wings.' At the time they were both invisible and inaudible. Guy Eden has recalled: 'He clearly hated it and a bitterness crept into his speeches which had not been there before and which has not been there since . . . Political life is a merciless affair, and the man who has been at the top of the tree is most ruthlessly "clawed" – to use one of Churchill's own favourite words – when he falls, or even slips.' Bewildered, Winston said: 'I have never joined in an intrigue. Everything I have got I have fought for. And yet I am more hated than anybody.' In a rare moment of self-pity he told a friend: 'Here I am, after almost thirty years in the House of Commons, after holding many of the highest offices of state. Here I am, discarded, cast away, marooned, rejected, and disliked.' There seemed no way out. He saw little to choose between Baldwin and MacDonald – 'two nurses,' he called them, 'fit to keep silence in a darkened room.'[295]

He missed Birkenhead terribly and found solace in one of FE's old speeches: 'The world still has its glittering prizes for those who have stout hearts and sharp swords.' But this, he realized, was not the time for either. No glittering prizes awaited Britons like him in 1931 or for long thereafter; stout hearts were suspect in the early 1930s, and sharp swords scorned, even by those whose lives would depend upon them in a crisis. It was time to hibernate. He let the lease on Venetia Montagu's house lapse and made Chartwell his family's year-round residence. The Churchills had no London home now. Winston kept a pied-à-terre in Morpeth Mansions, near Parliament, but the House seldom saw him. He was toiling on Chartwell's outside grounds, driving his Black Dog away by hard manual labour and, inside, writing his way out of debt. If he were to survive his political wilderness, he would need much more than the £500 stipend of a back-bencher. He intended to make a new fortune and invest it wisely, relying on Baruch's advice, avoiding speculation, and turning away from all the fiscal totems he had deified at the Treasury. 'I have gone whole hog against gold,' he wrote Boothby. 'To hell with it! It has been used as a vile trap to destroy us. I would pay the rest of the American debt in gold as long as the gold lasted, and then say – "Henceforward, we will only pay in goods. Pray specify what goods you desire." '296

Less than two weeks after surrendering his chancellor's seals at Windsor he had begun research on his Marlborough biography, working in Blenheim's archives with two assistants: Maurice Ashley, a young scholar whom he hired at £300 a year, and Colonel Charles Holdern, at £500. His literary approach, he wrote to Ashley, 'will probably not be to "defend" or "vindicate" my subject, but to tell the tale with close adherence to chronology in such a way and in such proportions and with such emphasis as will produce upon the mind of the reader the impersonation I wish to give. I have first of all to visualize this extraordinary personality. This I can only do gradually as my knowledge increases.' He was one of those authors – this writer is another – who believe that the past should not be judged by the standards of the present. He wrote: 'One has got to find out what the rules of the age were – there certainly were rules. Murder plots, for instance, were treated quite differently from treason even in its grossest form.' To the proprietor of the *Daily Telegraph*, who was dickering for the Marlborough serial rights, he wrote: 'I have no doubt that I shall be able to tell this famous tale from a modern point of view that will rivet attention.'297

At Chartwell several pots were always boiling on his stove; while researching Marlborough he was finishing *My Early Life*, correcting galleys for an additional *World Crisis* volume, on the war's eastern front, and pouring out a flood of magazine articles. At one point he was contracting to write twelve pieces for a British magazine, contributing regularly to *Collier's* and the Hearst Syndicate, and denouncing abuse of wealth in the *Daily Mail*. Editors were bombarded with his suggestions for topics: '*Women and the future*. To what heights will the ascendancy of women go? Will there be a woman prime minister? *Women and finance*. A world controlled by women? *If they had lived long ago*. Take a number of the world's most prominent men and imagine their careers in past eras. Henry Ford in Cromwellian days . . . Mussolini with Henry VIII, Ramsay MacDonald in the French Revolution, Bernard Shaw with the ancient Greeks, and so on.' In a note to his son he wrote: 'I have got a good crop of articles for 1931, and indeed am quite weighed down with work. But that is much better than being unemployed.' And while absent on a research trip he sent Clementine a hasty scrawl: 'Am vy remiss writing. Much pressed business. Everything continues satisfactory. Arranged twenty-two new articles in weeklies, all maturing before June and usual terms, monthly in advance, all involving heavy work in return.'298 During the two years between his eviction from No. 11 and the end of 1931 he published 104 pieces including excerpts from his books, in, among other periodicals, *Scribner's*, *The Times*, the *Strand*, the *Saturday Review*, the *Sunday John Bull*, *Nash's Pall Mall*, the *News Chronicle*, and the *Daily Telegraph*. His topics ranged from 'Government of the / by the / for the Dole-Drawers' to (from him, of all people) 'Back to the Spartan Life in Our Public Schools.' He dashed off twelve profiles of famous public figures – MacDonald, Nancy Astor, Bernard Shaw, Baden-Powell, Lloyd George, and Arthur Balfour among them – for which the *Sunday*

Pictorial paid him £200 each. Then he published these sketches in a volume, *Great Contemporaries*. Another collection of pieces appeared in book form as *Thoughts and Adventures* in Britain, and in the United States as *Amid These Storms*. In addition, eight collections of his speeches appeared in the book-stores, including one volume dealing with India and the Raj. Few professional writers, who devote their working lives to their trade, produce as much over entire lifetimes as he turned out during this brief span.

In protesting the slack press coverage of his parliamentary speeches on India, he had written Rothermere that each of them required 'an effort which is equal to that which would enable me to earn £3/400 by writing one of the numerous articles I have on my books.' [299] This was no exaggeration. Churchill wrote superb copy, and eager editors on both sides of the Atlantic knew it. As a consequence, he was one of the world's most highly paid writers. In America his *World Crisis* volumes had earned him, after Curtis Brown's commissions, $20,633.10. In one month book royalties, publishers' advances, and magazine cheques brought in £3,750. The *Sunday Pictorial* paid £2,400 for a series of character studies. A single piece in the *Daily Mail* sold for £600, and a series for the *Mail* brought £7,800. George Harrap, the publisher, advanced him £10,000 for the Marlborough; Scribner's paid £5,000 for the American rights. And his impressions of the United States, set down in twenty-two articles and widely reprinted abroad, eventually earned £40,000. By the end of 1931 his writing income for that year had reached £33,500, and his peak years lay ahead; in less than five years his magazine sales in the United States alone, after commissions, would bring him $35,379.78.

At fifty-seven he was a skilful literary craftsman, knew it, and rejoiced in his mastery of the language. 'I have been reading a good deal on "Marlborough," ' he wrote Clementine. 'It is a wonderful thing to have all these contracts satisfactorily settled, and to feel that two or three years agreeable work is mapped out and, if completed, will certainly be rewarded. In order to make sure of completing the task within three years instead of leaving it to drag on indefinitely, I am going to spend money with some freedom upon expert assistance.' Ashley, who was providing some of that assistance – though £300 a year does not suggest that his employer's expenditures for expertise were particularly free – had found, as had others, that Winston's method of composition was beguiling and unorthodox. He remembers how Churchill 'would walk up and down the room (and when I worked for him it was usually his bedroom), puffing a cigar while a secretary took it down as best she could in Pitman. Occasionally he would say "Scrub that and start again." At times he would stop . . . at others he would be entirely swept on by the stimulus of his imagination.' [300]

Like a battlefield veteran who avoids any mention of combat, Winston seldom mentioned politics during his early days in the wilderness. Lloyd George and Bracken were fellow guests at a country weekend in Coombe. So was Harold Nicolson, who wrote in his diary: 'LlG begins at once: "Now, what about this National Government? We here must form a National

Opposition." ' George was 'throwing out little sparks of compliments to right and left, drawing Winston in,' Nicolson noted. 'The impression was that of a master-at-drawing sketching in a fig leaf, not in outline, but by means of shadows around it.' Nevertheless, Churchill, who had always found talk of political manoeuvring irresistible, refused to be drawn. He was vivacious, but on other topics. Nicolson concluded: 'Winston is very brilliant and amusing but not constructive.'[301] However, he continued to follow developing situations at home and abroad. Each morning he and Clementine carefully read newspapers and sent notes to each other, via servants, on significant items. One consequence of this was that Churchill became the first statesman in England to discover that, for the second time in a generation, a strange light had appeared and was growing upon the map of Europe.

Germany's Nationalsozialistische Deutsche Arbeiterpartei (National Socialist Workers' party), which became famous and then infamous as the Nazi party, began in Munich as one of hundreds of splinter movements spawned in the wake of Versailles. Adolf Hitler, then a police spy, attended a meeting – since only two dozen people were present, it could hardly be called a rally – in September 1919. Hitler came to observe, but, seeing possibilities invisible to almost everyone else, he enrolled as the workers' party's seventh member. After the country's inflationary panic of 1923, he thought he saw his chance to lunge for power, but his attempted coup that November, which turned into a fiasco, was ridiculed throughout the Republic of Germany as the *'Bürgerbräu-Putsch'* ('Beer Hall Riot') and his storm troopers' public tantrums were dismissed as an example of postwar Germany's black humour. The Nazis were to have the last, mad laugh, but not then; the 1920s were desperate years for Hitler and his movement. Prosperity means thin gruel for revolutionaries, and as long as the boom lasted, life in the Weimar Republic was, on the whole, calm, pleasant, and amusing. American bankers had lent the country seven billion dollars, on terms so generous as to make it almost a gift. Fuelled by these loans, Weimar's economy seemed stable. German business was good; unemployment dropped to 650,000, an irreducible figure which meant that just about everyone in the country who wanted a job had one.

The Nazis' hopes had risen at the end of 1924, when their leader was released from Landsberg. Ludendorff had repudiated them, and Göring was in exile, but they believed Hitler's gifts as a spellbinder would put things right. They forgot that he was only on parole. The judge had warned him against disruptive activities, which was like King Canute instructing the tides. In his first public appearance after leaving prison, the parolee told a crowd that Weimar, like Marxists and Jews, was Germany's 'enemy.' He cried: 'In this struggle of ours there are only two possible outcomes – either the enemy passes over our bodies or we pass over theirs.' He was confident the Nazis would win because they would not shrink from wielding 'weapons of spiritual and physical terror [*geistigen und körperlichen terrors*].' The judge decided he had violated his parole and enjoined him from public speaking for the next two years.[302]

But Hitler was more than an orator. He was also an excellent administrator. At that time there were fewer than 27,000 Nazis in the country. His recruiting drives slowly lengthened the rolls: 49,000 in 1923; 72,000 in 1927; 108,000 in 1928. Subgroups were organized; the Deutsches Jungvolk for children, the Bund Deutscher Mädel for girls, the N.S. Frauenschaften for women, and the Kulturbund for intellectuals. The most visible Nazis were the brawling brownshirts of the Sturmabteilung (SA), but while their leader spoke affectionately of these *'alten Kämpfern'* ('old fighters'), he relied more heavily on his Schutzstaffel (SS), who swore personal loyalty to him, wore black uniforms in frank imitation of the Italian Fascisti, and were led by a deceptively mild-mannered Waldtrudering chicken farmer, Heinrich Himmler. Hermann Göring (already known throughout Germany as the Fat One) was soliciting contributions from his family's wealthy friends. And a crippled, twenty-eight-year-old Rhinelander with journalistic aspirations, whose applications for a reporter's job had been repeatedly rejected by the *Berliner Tageblatt*, joined the small staff of the party's fortnightly newsletter, the *N.S. Briefe*. This was Joseph Goebbels, who would become the Nazi megaphone. As chief of this tightly knit political conspiracy, Hitler invested himself with the title *Partei-und Oberster-Sturmabteilung, Führer Vorsitzender der Nationalsozialistische Deutsche Arbeiter Kerband.* One word survived: *Führer.* It means 'leader.' History would remember him by it. Later the mere mention of the German Führer would terrify Europe and countries beyond the seas, but during those lean years the Nazis were only impressing one another. In the national election of May 20, 1928, they polled some 810,000 votes – 2.6 per cent of the 31,000,000 cast. Hitler, now in his fortieth year, found diversion from defeat that summer by falling in love with his blonde, beautiful, twenty-year-old niece, Geli Raubal, the daughter of his widowed half sister. Royalties from sales of *Mein Kampf* – the book had already earned 59,058 reichsmarks – permitted him to keep Geli, Geli's mother, and Geli's sister in the Villa Wachenfelt, on the Obersalzberg, overlooking Berchtesgaden. All three women acquiesced in the establishment of this strange household. His niece's feelings seem to have been ambivalent. She admired her powerful uncle and was flattered by his attentions. Yet she slowly came to resent his tyrannical manner towards her, and she was, and was to remain, sexually passive. Hitler's infatuation, on the other hand, was absolute. The following year he sent the mother and the sister packing and moved his niece into his nine-room luxury flat on Munich's Prinzregentenstrasse. There was talk. Several party members suggested to him that this was unwise; the party might pay a heavy political price for it. Infuriated, he forbade them even to mention her name in his presence. His intentions were probably honourable; he gave every sign of preparing for marriage. In retrospect his love for Geli seems to have been the one humane emotion in his life, though it was, of course, incestuous.

Nazi political prospects brightened after the Crash. The Republic of

Germany was a victim of the Crash – the principal victim. No other country was hit so hard. All sources of American largesse dried up; every scheduled loan was cancelled. Lacking markets for Germany's export trade, Weimar could not afford imports; not even essentials, including food. The republic's most prestigious financial institution was the Darmstäder und Nationalbank. When it failed, all other Berlin banks closed, too. Thousands of businesses went bankrupt. The world's longest breadline stretched down the Kurfürstendamm. Hitler, rejoicing in the *Völkischer Beobachter*, the Nazi newspaper, wrote: 'Never in my life have I been so well disposed and inwardly contented as in these days, for hard reality has opened the eyes of millions of Germans to the unprecedented swindles, lies and betrayals of the Marxist deceivers of the people.'[303] Demoralization in the Reichstag led to legislative paralysis, which was succeeded, in turn, by new elections on September 14, 1930. Hitler furiously crisscrossed the country, promising jobs and bread for all, exposure of bureaucratic corruption, the rebuilding of a strong Germany, ruthless punishment of the Jewish financiers who had precipitated this crisis, and repudiation of the Versailles *Diktat*.

The election returns startled everyone, including Hitler. All extremist parties had gained. The Communist vote had risen 25 per cent. But 6,409,600 Germans had cast their ballots for Nazi candidates – a gain of over 690 per cent. In twenty-eight months, they had vaulted from the smallest party in the Reichstag to the second largest, second only to the Social Democrats. Until now their leader had been regarded as a wild-eyed, seedy man in a dirty trench coat, consigned to the lunatic fringe of Weimar politics, constantly in trouble with the tax authorities, too humble to enter the halls of the great and powerful. Now he was courting industrialists and senior generals of the Reichswehr, and all of them were listening very carefully. In one of those flashes which demonstrated his political genius, he decided to testify at the trial of three Leipzig lieutenants who, in defiance of a standing order, had smuggled copies of the *Völkischer Beobachter* into their barracks. Those who expected him to defend the young officers did not yet know their Führer. In the witness box he disowned them and recommended that they be punished. Spectators gasped; they didn't realize that he was wooing the defendants' superiors. Using the trial as a forum, he promised that Nazis would 'see to it, when we come to power, that out of the present Reichswehr a great Army of the German people shall arise.' The judge asked if the Nazis would reach power through constitutional means. Hitler affirmed it; knowing how the German mind worked, he had abandoned any thought of a coup and meant, instead, to become head of state by legal means, with a formal mandate from the Reichstag. But he was also aware of the Teutonic love for inflammatory phrases. Shifting in his chair, he added: 'I can assure you that when the National Socialist movement is victorious in this struggle, there will be a National Socialist Court of Justice, too. Then the November 1918 revolution will be avenged and heads will roll [*Köpfe rollen*]!'[304]

Köpfe rollen! A delicious shudder passed through Germany. Here was the imperious voice they had missed since the kaiser had fled. By now the entire country was familiar with the Nazis' symbol, their *Hakenkreuz*, or swastika – a black crooked cross imprinted on a white circle against a red background – and their party anthem, 'Die Fahne Hoch' ('Raise the Banner'), written by Horst Wessel, a clergyman's son who had abandoned his family and university classrooms to live in a slum with a retired prostitute, work for the party, and roam Berlin's streets fighting Communists. In February 1931 the Communists murdered Wessel, making him an instant martyr. Over 100,000 men were now enrolled in the SA and SS, forming a private army larger than Weimar's Reichswehr, whose senior officers, studying the transcript of the Leipzig trial, decided that they had found their man. Soldiers were no longer disciplined for reading the *Völkischer Beobachter*. The country's millionaires conferred with Hitler, Göring, and the financial wizard Hjalmar Schacht, a recent Nazi convert. A majority of them decided that although the Nazi leader was a vulgar demagogue, he had an extraordinary gift for rousing latent patriotism in the people and might be able to suppress Weimar's weak democracy, stubborn trade unions, and the Socialists and Communists. Contributions from big business, which had been distributed among other conservative parties in the past, were channelled into the Nazi coffers. Gustav Krupp, the munitions tycoon, became, in the word of a fellow industrialist, '*ein Obernazi*' – 'a super Nazi.' As 1931 approached its end, Germany seemed sickened by a disease without a cure. Over five million men were out of work. Crippled veterans of the war were begging on street corners. Farmers' mortgages were being foreclosed. Inflation had all but wiped out the middle classes. The Reichstag foundered in confusion; its 107 Nazi deputies were using fists and clubs to break up debates and drown out parliamentary motions. President Hindenburg, now eighty-four, was withdrawing into the stupor of senility. Gregor Strasser, who had led the party while Hitler was in prison, told a reporter: '*Alles, was dazu dient, die Katastrophe zu beschleunigen . . . ist gut, sehr gut, für uns und unsere deutsche Revolution* [All that serves to precipitate the catastrophe . . . is good, very good for us and our German revolution].'[305]

At this historic moment Hitler was struck by a personal tragedy. Before their affair Geli had been taking voice lessons in Vienna, which she adored; now she wanted to return and resume them. Her uncle absolutely refused to consider it. They quarrelled bitterly. On the morning of September 17, after he had descended the stairs from their apartment and was entering his car, she thrust her head out of a window. Neighbours heard her cry: 'Then you won't let me go to Vienna?' He shouted back, 'No!' and drove off.[306] The next morning her body was found in the flat. She had shot herself through the heart. Hitler was incoherent with grief. In death she achieved what he had denied her in life; she was buried in the family's Viennese plot. Hitler could not attend the funeral. Six years earlier, to avoid deportation while paroled, he had renounced his Austrian citizenship. Since his application for German citizenship had not been approved, he was *staatenlos*, stateless – a man without

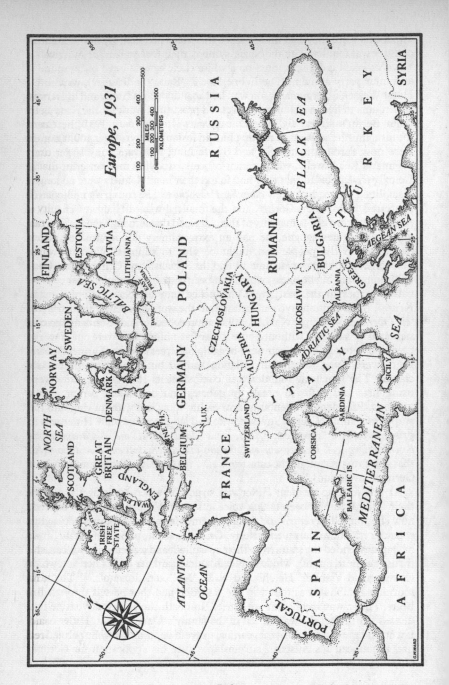

Europe, 1931

a country. Under these circustances foreigners, who could not fathom his growing mystique in central Europe, found it difficult to take him seriously.

Churchill took him seriously. Germany had worried Winston since the Armistice. On September 24, 1924, when Hitler was still in Landsberg, dictating his book to Rudolf Hess, Winston had warned that 'the soul of Germany smoulders with dreams of a War of Liberation or Revenge.' It could not, he wrote, 'be kept in permanent subjugation.' He read *Mein Kampf* in its entirety as soon as E. J. Dugdale's translation became available, but long before that he had studied translated excerpts, and, perhaps because of his own aggressive instincts, he grasped Hitler's message. The book's 'main thesis,' he wrote, 'is simple. Man is a fighting animal; therefore the nation, being a community of fighters, is a fighting unit.' It was Hitler's argument that the ferocity 'of a race depends on its purity. Hence the need for ridding it of foreign defilements. The Jewish race, owing to its universality, is of necessity pacifist and internationalist.' Hitler believed that only 'brute force' could assure Germany's survival. As Churchill understood it, *Mein Kampf* proposed a sweeping Teutonic political strategy, proposing that 'the new Reich . . . gather within its fold all the scattered German elements in Europe. A race which has suffered defeat can be rescued by restoring its self-confidence. Above all things the Army must be taught to believe in its own invincibility.'[307]

Charisma and patriotism were qualities Churchill greatly admired. They had formed his first impression of Mussolini, and he did not, at first, find Hitler completely beyond the pale. He respected him, Guy Eden writes, 'as a man of vision, even if it was distorted vision, and drive, even if it was a drive to evil.' Hitler's early life had been a catalogue of failures, Churchill observed, but 'these misfortunes did not lead him into Communist ranks. By an honourable inversion he cherished all the more an abnormal sense of racial loyalty and fervent and mystic admiration for Germany and the German people.' Afterwards, when Hitler had become Führer of the entire nation, a prophet of outrageous dogmas, Winston said that while he despised Nazism, he hoped that, should England ever lose a war, it would 'find a champion as indomitable to restore our courage and lead us back to our place among the nations.' Nevertheless, he had realized, while Hitler was still in his own wilderness, that sooner or later the man must be destroyed. It is arguable that Churchill was one of the first to comprehend Hitler's menace because each man was a mirror image of the other. Hitler, with his own remarkable instincts, seems to have sensed that Churchill, though a political outcast then, would ultimately be his archenemy. He told a British diplomat in Berlin that he regarded Churchill as a '*Deutschenfresser*' – a 'devourer of Germans.' 'I naturally cannot prevent the possibility of this *Herr* entering the Government in a couple of years,' he said, adding that he foresaw difficulties 'if Churchill comes to power in Great Britain instead of Chamberlain.'[308]

Long before his countrymen understood the Nazi challenge, Winston

711

realized that Hitler was the very embodiment of evil, but even when they were locked in the most desperate war Europe had ever known, Churchill referred to him as 'this monstrous product of former wrongs and shame.' He meant Versailles. He agreed with Hitler; the treaty had, he believed, been a humiliating *Diktat*. This was not entirely reasonable. The Allied terms had been far less harsh than those Germany had imposed on Russia at Brest-Litovsk in 1918. German pride had been mortified at Versailles, however; the subsequent resentment was not rational but emotional, and Winston, emotional himself, grasped it because, had their roles been reversed, he, too, would have been enraged. That rage was a political reality, and, he believed, ugly consequences were inevitable. In 1925 he wrote that 'from one end of Germany to the other an intense hatred of France unifies the whole population,' and he suggested the establishment of neutral zones on German frontiers. He also urged 'a substantial rectification' of Weimar's eastern border, consistent with ethnic realities. Sooner or later, he warned, 'Germany will be rearmed'; steps should be taken to prevent 'aggression against Poland,' which could draw both France and England into another European conflict. He saw them preparing to do it again and felt premonitions of 'future catastrophe.' By 1928 he realized that the ten-year rule had been 'a grievous error.' The United States was urging Britain and France to reduce their defence establishments and reduce German reparations payments. Churchill disagreed. Writing to a friend about 'these stupid disarmament manoeuvres,' he commented that 'personally I deprecate all these premature agreements on disarmament.' In a cabinet meeting he opposed any reparations cuts as long as Washington remained adamant on the issue of Britain's war debts; 'we have given everything, and paid everything,' he argued, 'and we cannot make any new sacrifice.' A strong French army, he maintained, would shield England from the 'most probable danger' of being drawn into another conflict on the Continent.[309]

Few were convinced, or even interested. His stand on India was popular among die-hard Tory back-benchers, but even they turned away when he raised the question of another war. The last one had been so ghastly that any resumption of it was unthinkable. And men in public life dreaded the charge of 'warmonger,' with its attendant possibility that one day they might be held answerable for mass slaughter. H. G. Wells had warned them: 'We must put ourselves and our rulers and our fellow men on trial. We must ask: "What have you done, and what are you doing, to help or hinder the peace and order of mankind?" A time will come when a politician who has wilfully made war and promoted international dissension will be as sure of the dock and much surer of the noose than a private homicide. It is not reasonable that those who gamble with men's lives should not stake their own.' Throughout 1930 Churchill fought almost alone, and always unsuccessfully, against the Labour government's decision to accept a reduction of naval power below the Admiralty's specifications of Britain's minimal requirements. He rose in the House to warn against emasculation of the navy, and for the first time found support in the *Morning Post*. 'I think this naval business is going to carry us a long way,' he wrote to H.A. Gwynne in response. 'It may become part of a definite movement to a strong assertion of the life-strength of the British Empire.' It didn't; Baldwin supported Labour, and Tory MPs refused to sign Winston's petition of protest. Walter Lippmann wrote: 'The people are tired, tired of noise, tired of inconvenience, tired of greatness and longing for a place where the world is quiet and where all trouble seems dead leaves, and spent waves riot in doubtful dreams of dreams.' Churchill himself thought England had entered a 'period of exhaustion which has been described as Peace.'[310]

By June of 1931 even MacDonald felt that disarmament had gone 'pretty near the limit of example.' Churchill believed the limit had been passed, and called for rearmament. 'England's hour of weakness is Europe's hour of danger,' he told the House. Britain was now 'extremely vulnerable,' he said; its army, 'cut to the bone,' was little more than a 'glorified police force,' and the RAF's strength was an eighth of that of France's air arm. On August 10 he wrote in the Hearst papers: 'German youth mounting in its broad swelling flood will never accept the conditions and implications of the Treaty of Versailles.' Germany and Austria announced the creation of a customs union, and he was alarmed. 'Beneath the Customs Union,' he wrote, 'lurks the "Anschluss" or union between the German mass and the remains of Austria.' The consequence of such a combination would be a 'solid German block of seventy millions' threatening two nations: France, with its dwindling population, and Czechoslovakia. The Czechs had 'three million five hundred' Austrian-Germans in their midst. 'These unwilling subjects are a care. But the *Anschluss* means that Czechoslovakia will not only have the indigestible morsel in its interior, but will be surrounded on three sides by other Germans. They will become almost a Bohemian island in a boisterous fierce-lapping ocean of Teutonic manhood and efficiency.'[311]

The French and the Italians, after reading his speech, objected to the customs union – on economic, not military, grounds – and Weimar, ever unsure of itself, dissolved it, demonstrating that even out of office Churchill was still a force in European politics. Prince Otto von Bismarck-Schönhausen, grandson of the great chancellor and himself a diplomat posted to Germany's London embassy, had sought an interview with him the year before. The two men had met on Saturday, October 18, 1930. In a secret memorandum Bismarck had reported to Berlin that Churchill had been following newspaper accounts of German political developments 'in detail,' and had spoken of the Nazis in 'cutting terms.' Hitler, he had held, had 'contributed towards a considerable deterioration of Germany's external position.' The Nazi leader was now insisting that he would never wage aggressive war, but Winston didn't believe him. By his own admission, the man was untrustworthy; Churchill quoted *Mein Kampf*: 'The great masses of the people . . . will more easily fall victims to a great lie than to a small one.' He was 'convinced,' Bismarck wrote, 'that Hitler or his followers will seize the first available opportunity to resort to armed force.' In their discussion Bismarck had referred to the 'unsuitability' of the Polish Corridor – a strip of territory which gave Poland, otherwise landlocked, access to the free port of Danzig and the Baltic. Winston had replied that 'Poland must have an outlet to the sea.' He pointed out that German freight and railway traffic passed through the corridor every day to enter East Prussia. Bismarck delivered his report to Albrecht Bernstorff, the embassy's senior counsellor. Bernstorff, in turn, forwarded it to the Wilhelmstrasse. In a covering note he commented: 'Although one should always bear in mind Winston Churchill's very temperamental personality when considering his remarks, they nevertheless deserve particular attention,' on the ground that 'as far as can be humanly foreseen he will play an influential role in any Conservative government in years to come – however difficult his personal position may be in the Conservative party, where he is mistrusted as an erstwhile Liberal and free-trader.'[312]

It was at this point that Churchill decided to monitor Britain's preparedness. He asked the prime minister for access to figures on the strength of the country's armed forces. MacDonald found military matters tiresome, even trivial. He casually approved his request, and then, apparently, forgot about it. The consequence of this exchange of notes was one of those bureaucratic decisions which are self-perpetuating, remaining in effect unless or until withdrawn. Future prime ministers, unaware of it, would brood over the source of Churchill's detailed information about service developments. The answer lay, undiscovered, in their own files at No. 10.

Geli Raubal had lain long in her grave when the Austrian government finally approved Hitler's request to cross the border. He spent an entire evening in the cemetery, on his knees, weeping over her tombstone.

That same week Charles de Gaulle, a French major recently returned from a military mission in the Middle East, was working quietly at his desk in his home at 110, boulevard Raspail, in the sixth arrondissement of Paris, writing *Le Fil de l'épée* (The Edge of the Sword), a short book on the essence of leadership. Francisco Franco was also in Paris; having defeated Abd-el Krim's Riff army in Morocco and sworn allegiance to the new Spanish republic, he was studying at l'Ecole Militaire, France still being considered proficient in military science.

On the other side of the world, Hideki Tojo was serving on the staff of Japan's Kwangtung army, which, using the Mukden incident of September 19 as an excuse, had invaded Manchuria and was now investing the Chinese city of Harbin. Chiang Kai-shek, the new generalissimo of the Chinese Nationalist forces, the Kuomintang, was prevented from launching a counter-offensive by a Yangtze flood and flank skirmishes with Mao Tse-tung's Chinese Communist guerrillas.

Benito Mussolini had survived an assassination attempt the week before only to be thrown by his horse, forcing him to cancel plans for a Berlin visit. His pride had been restored by a *New York Times* feature article describing the tremendous 'force of his personality' and a statement from Boston's William

Cardinal O'Connell calling him 'a genius given to Italy by God.'[313]

In Moscow a Kremlin spokesman informed foreign correspondents that Joseph Stalin, general secretary of the Central Committee of the Communist party, was writing a book 'dealing with Soviet challenges.'[314] Actually, Stalin was no writer and not much of a reader. He usually spent his evenings reading junk fiction; his favourite novel was a translation of Edgar Rice Burroughs's *Tarzan of the Apes*, and he was looking forward to an early screening of MGM's film *Tarzan, the Ape Man*, starring Johnny Weissmuller, Maureen O'Sullivan, and C. Aubrey Smith. Stalin had just expelled an American woman, Mrs E. G. Grady, for telling a joke about his crudity. He was extremely sensitive about his image, and though he cultivated the myth that he enjoyed anonymity, he was constantly in the news, congratulating factory workers who had met their quota of tractor production, for example, and demonstrating the success of his agricultural collectivization policy by exporting grain. This was specious. Because of his agricultural policy, ten million peasants were starving to death. Stalin's wife, Nadezhda Alliluyeva, begged him to relent; having failed to persuade him, she, like Hitler's Geli, would take her own life within a year.

The most interesting politician in the United States was Governor Franklin D. Roosevelt of New York. Reelected by a thundering plurality of 725,000 votes, he had persuaded his legislature, a few weeks earlier, to establish the state's Temporary Emergency Relief Administration, thus making his the first state to assume responsibility for victims of the Depression. In Albany his wife was packing for Warm Springs, the date of their departure depending on his mother's health.

None of these men knew any of the others, but Franklin Roosevelt and Winston Churchill passed within hailing distance of each other on the evening of Saturday, December 12, 1931. The governor was in his Manhattan town house at 49 East Sixty-fifth Street, conferring with J. H. McCooey, a Tammany politician, and Winston was in a taxi between the Waldorf-Astoria and Bernard Baruch's mansion at 1055 Fifth Avenue. Churchill, accompanied by Clementine and Diana, was in New York on business. Early in November he had signed a contract which would bring him £10,000 for forty lectures in the United States. In addition, Esmond Harmsworth of the *Daily Mail* had agreed to pay him £8,000 for a series of pieces on America's situation, prospects, and mood.

The Churchills had planned to leave England earlier, but parliamentary matters had detained him. The House was rewording the final clauses of the Statute of Westminster, which meant another debate on India. Kay Halle, an American journalist and an early flame of Randolph's, was staying at Chartwell the evening before he spoke, and she remembers him 'rehearsing that speech all night.' The statute, he told the House the following evening, set forth the Raj's new permissiveness in 'cold legal language.' Indian agitators would be emboldened by the limitations on British power now inherent in dominion status. He was troubled by the transfer of defence, finance, and police powers to native leaders, and the lack of safeguards for minorities. The front bench was tense; Hoare had written to Irwin that he was 'very nervous' about the new House – needlessly, it turned out, for when Churchill introduced an amendment rephrasing the statute, Sir John Simon, Sir Austen Chamberlain, and Baldwin spoke against it, and it was defeated overwhelmingly, 369 to 43. Having affronted the Conservatives, Winston then gratuitously offended Labour by saying that MacDonald had performed an 'inestimable service' for Britain: 'He has destroyed the Socialist Party as a Parliamentary force.'[315] With that, he was off. Everything he did was contentious now. The morning of his departure from Southampton, newspapers ran editorials castigating him on another issue. They had been promoting a 'Buy Britain' campaign. Churchill, the staunch Free Trader, had ignored the Cunard line and booked passage on the German steamship *Europa*.

His first lecture, in Worcester, Massachusetts, on December 11, was an appeal for Anglo-American unity: 'We shall travel more securely if we do it like good companions.' Most of the next day was spent in his Waldorf Tower apartment, 39 A, preparing future lectures and writing for the *Daily Mail*. Baruch had invited him to dine that evening with mutual friends, but after climbing into the taxi Winston discovered that he could not remember the address of the mansion. The driver was of little help; he was new to Manhattan. They cruised around for an hour, Winston growing increasingly exasperated with the traffic lights which were new to him; they had not yet been introduced in England. Finally he told the driver to let him out on the Central Park side of Fifth Avenue. He believed he could recognize the house from the sidewalk. Turning to cross the street, he made two mistakes. The light was against him, and he had forgotten that Americans drive on the right. He glanced in the other direction, saw nothing coming, and stepped off the curb. Immediately he was hit by a car driving at over thirty miles an hour. Mauled, he was dragged several yards by the car, and then flung into the street. He later wrote: 'There was a moment of a world aglare, of a man aghast . . . I do not understand why I was not broken like an eggshell, or squashed like a gooseberry.' In fact, he was gravely injured, bleeding heavily from his head and both thighs. A small crowd gathered. The driver, an unemployed mechanic named Mario Constasino, was distraught. Though in shock and great pain, Winston wiped the streaming blood from his face and assured the mechanic that he had been blameless. The fault was entirely his own; he had looked the wrong way. Churchill was cold; the temperature was in the low forties, and a wind was rising. Another taxi stopped, and he was helped into it. At Lenox Hill Hospital he was moved into a wheelchair. He thought he had reached sanctuary, but inside he learned that even hospitals have bureaucrats. A receptionist asked him to identify himself. 'I am Winston Churchill,' he said, 'a British statesman.' He added: 'I do not wish to be hurt any more. Give me chloroform or something.' It wasn't that easy. How was he going to pay for this? Lenox Hill was a private hospital, and these were hard times. He had only a few dollars in his pocket. He asked them to call the Waldorf, and after what seemed an eternity, Clementine and Detective Thompson hurried in. Churchill said faintly, 'They almost got me that time, Thompson.' Clementine having produced the cash, chloroform was administered. 'A few breaths,' he wrote afterwards, 'and one has no longer the power to speak to the world.'[316]

Otto C. Pickardt was the physician who examined him. Clementine cabled Pickardt's finding to Randolph: 'Temperature 100.6 Pulse normal. Head scalp wound severe.' (It had, in fact, been cut to the bone.) 'Two cracked ribs. Simple slight pleural irritation of right side. Generally much bruised. Progress satisfactory.' If the hospital had any doubts about the eminence of its new patient, they were resolved when King George telephoned to inquire about his condition. In the beginning Winston's recovery was swift. He quickly made friends with Pickardt, and then with Constasino, who appeared during visitors' hours to apologize again. Churchill cabled Lindemann, asking him to calculate the shock, to a stationary body weighing two hundred pounds, of a car weighing twenty-four hundred pounds and travelling between thirty and thirty-five miles an hour, bearing in mind that he had been 'carried forward on the cowcatcher until brakes eventually stopped car, when I dropped off' and that 'brakes did not operate till car hit me.' He needed the information as quickly as possible, he said, adding: 'Think it must be impressive. Kindly cable weekend letter at my expense.' The Prof replied: 'Collision equivalent falling thirty feet on pavement. Equal six thousand foot pounds energy. Equivalent stopping ten-pound brick dropped six hundred feet or two charges buckshot point-blank range. Rate inversely proportional thickness cushion surrounding skeleton and give of frame. If assume average one inch your body transferred during impact at rate eight thousand horsepower. Congratulations on preparing suitable cushion and skill in bump.'[317]

Churchill wanted the figures for a piece he was scribbling, propped up in bed, on 'My New York Adventures.' In it he wrote: 'I certainly suffered every pang, physical and mental, that a street accident or, I suppose, a shell wound can produce. None is unendurable. There is neither the time nor the strength for self-pity. There is no room for remorse or fears. If at any moment in the long series of sensations a grey veil deepening into blackness had descended upon the sanctum I should have felt or feared nothing additional. Nature is merciful and does not try her children, man or beast, beyond their compass. It is only where the cruelty of man intervenes that hellish torments appear. For the rest – live dangerously; take things as they come, dread naught; all will be well.' He telegraphed this to the *Daily Mail* three days after Christmas with a note to the editor: 'Am now able to crawl around fairly well . . . Good wishes for New Year and love to your pets Ramsay and Baldwin.' Harmsworth cabled back £600.[318]

Pickardt prescribed a rest, and back at the Waldorf, Clementine packed for Nassau. On their return he would need a secretary, and she hired Phyllis Moir, a young Englishwoman who had worked in the British Foreign Office.

Thompson met Miss Moir at the door of Apartment 39 A and said softly: 'You'll find him pretty weak and tired. That accident gave him a nasty jolt and he only came out of the hospital a few days ago.' She recalls that her first impression of Churchill was of 'a humpty-dumpty sort of figure reading a letter.' He was wearing a brown pin-striped suit, a matching polka-dot bow tie, and 'black buttoned boots with odd-looking cloth tops.' She was particularly impressed by 'his small, delicate, beautifully shaped hands – the hands of an artist.' He was smoking 'a huge cigar,' which he laid aside to say, rather distantly: 'I understand you are willing to accompany me in my peregrinations.' Miss Moir confirmed it, and when the Churchills sailed for the Bahamas on New Year's Eve, she set about converting a maid's room in the apartment into an office for herself. It had been her impression that he would soon be fit and ready to work. That had been his, too, and his American lecture agent urged him to be back by January 15, 1932, pointing out that every week's delay meant the loss of engagements and thousands of dollars.[319]

It proved impossible. In Nassau he suffered from severe aftershock and depression. 'Vitality only returning slowly,' he wired the agent on January 3. Five days later a nervous reaction struck. He wrote Pickardt that he had experienced 'a great and sudden lack of power of concentration, and a strong sense of being unequal to the task which lay so soon ahead of me.' Clementine and the physician dealt with the agent while Winston, attended by a night nurse, fought insomnia with nightly sedation, and forced himself to exercise a few minutes each day. His easel was there, but did not attract him. He wrote to his son: 'I have not felt like opening the paint box, although the seas around these islands are luminous with the most lovely tints of blue and green and purple.' Clementine wrote to Randolph: 'Last night he was very sad & said that he had now in the last 2 years had 3 very heavy blows. First the loss of all that money in the crash, then the loss of his political position in the Conservative Party and now this terrible injury – He said he did not think he would ever recover completely from the three events.'[320]

On January 15 his spirits began to return. He outlined two lectures: another call for closer ties between Washington and London and an analysis of the Depression's impact on Europe. But he warned his agent that he was still 'astonishingly feeble' and that 'you will find me, I am afraid, a much weaker man than the one you welcomed on December 11. I walk about five hundred yards every day and swim perhaps one hundred and fifty. But I tire so quickly and have very little reserve.' A few days later, reporting that he was 'steadily improving and gaining strength,' he agreed to a formidable schedule: fourteen lectures, moving to a different city almost every day. Pickardt had rescued him from the hardship of Prohibition with a note on his stationery: 'This is to certify that the post-accident convalescence of the Hon Winston S. Churchill necessitates the use of alcoholic spirits especially at meal times. The quantity is naturally indefinite but the minimum requirements would be 250 cubic centimetres [slightly over eight ounces].'[321]

Thus fortified, and accompanied by Miss Moir, to whom he dictated a constant stream of notes and observations – she had yet to master his lisp, and was disconcerted by 'his curious habit of whispering each phrase to himself before he said it aloud' – he spoke to two thousand people in the Brooklyn Academy of Music on January 28, picking up momentum as the evening progressed. They were enthusiastic, and so was Churchill. He was all business now, granting interviews, writing to Boothby to suggest that they both attend the American political conventions in the summer, and visiting Washington for long talks with key senators and a short one with Hoover. In the capital he stayed with the British ambassador, Sir Ronald Lindsay. Miss Moir remembers that 'these two made the oddest contrast, the immensely dignified diplomat standing ill at ease at the foot of the old-fashioned four-poster and the Peter Pan of British politics sitting up in bed, a cigar in his mouth, his tufts of red hair as yet uncombed, scanning the morning newspapers.' Diana used the embassy for a party, inviting all her young American acquaintances. One morning Winston approached his new secretary, grinning mischievously. 'I've done something really dreadful, Miss Moir. I've just asked the Washington exchange operator for a glass of sherry, thinking I was speaking on the house telephone. I'm afraid I gave her rather a shock.'[322]

His lecture tour was a success; the *Daily Telegraph* called it 'a triumphal progress.' He liked Americans, and they sensed it. As a foreign politician he could not support any presidential candidate, but his admiration for Roosevelt was obvious, and that, too, was popular that year. During a radio interview the announcer told his audience that, next to the King, Churchill was 'probably the best-liked man under the Union Jack.' Winston solemnly told them: 'War, today, is bare – bare of profit and stripped of all its glamour. The old pomp and circumstance are gone. War now is nothing but toil, blood, death, and lying propaganda.' Peace would be assured, he continued, provided France kept a strong army and England and the United States remained masters of the seas. The interviewer asked: 'I take it that you haven't a high opinion of these disarmament conferences?' Churchill said vehemently: 'No, I have not! I think that since the Great War they have done more harm than good.'[323]

Before sailing home on the *Majestic* – he had Bought British after all – Winston conferred with Charles Scribner over future books, planned an investment programme with Baruch, and visited the *Collier's* office to discuss further ideas for magazine pieces. Outwardly he seemed to have recovered from his accident. It was an illusion. His euphoric spells alternated with periods of weakness and gloom. The trip was 'drawing wearily' to a close, he wrote to Randolph, and he had missed his *Daily Mail* deadlines. 'I have been terribly remiss in my articles,' he wrote to Harmsworth, 'but, although I have got several very good ones in my head, I have not had the margin of life and strength to do them while travelling and speaking so many nights in succession.' To Thornton Butterworth, his British publisher, he wrote: 'I am much better, but I feel I need to rest and not to have to drive myself as hard. You have no idea what I have been through.' His friends realized he had suffered an ordeal, however. While he was still in Nassau, Brendan Bracken had approached them, suggesting that they show their affection by buying him a new car. Among the contributors were Harold Macmillan, John Maynard Keynes, Lindemann, Lord Lloyd, Austen Chamberlain, Charlie Chaplin, Beaverbrook, Rothermere, the architect Sir Edwin Lutyens, the painter Sir John Lavery, and the Prince of Wales, whose romantic involvement would presently become interwoven, and then knotted, with Churchill's political future. The gift – a £2,000 Daimler – awaited him at Waterloo Station. Several of the donors were there, and they sang: 'For he's a Jolly Good Fellow.' Winston tried to smile, then bowed his head and wept.[324]

At Chartwell he toiled on the grounds, roughed out articles, and slowly worked his way back into the Marlborough material with the help of F. W. D. Deakin, a young don from Christ Church, Oxford. Like all Chartwell guests, Bill Deakin was expected to work with his hands from time to time. One day, in the middle of building a wall, Churchill looked up and gloomily asked him: 'Do you suppose that in five hundred years these bricks will be excavated as a relic of Stanley Baldwin's England?'[325]

His life, Virginia Cowles wrote, had 'apparently ended in a quagmire from which there seemed to be no rescue.' Reith of the BBC, believing his fangs drawn, at least on fiscal issues, permitted him to discuss monetary policy in his first radio broadcast to the United States. 'Believe me,' Winston told the Americans, 'no one country, however powerful, can combat this evil alone.' The audience listening at their Philcos and Atwater Kents was estimated at thirty million, but in Britain the event passed almost unnoticed. In Moscow, Stalin was receiving a British delegation led by Lady Astor. He inquired about politicians in England. 'Chamberlain,' she said, 'is the coming man.' Stalin asked: 'What about Churchill?' Her eyes widened. *'Churchill?'* she said. She gave a scornful little laugh and replied, 'Oh, he's *finished.*'[326]

ACKNOWLEDGEMENTS

David (now Sir David) Pitblado introduced me to Winston Churchill (himself still unknighted) in the Verandah Grill of the *Queen Mary*, that greatest of Cunarders, on January 24, 1953. The prime minister, or 'PM,' as his entourage called him, was returning home with his family after a holiday and a series of meetings in Washington. As a young foreign correspondent on my way to the Middle East and India, I was delighted to discover that my cabin, M 101, was adjacent to Churchill's suite. Even better, Pitblado, then the prime minister's principal private secretary, had read the British edition of my first book and thought it commendable. He graciously arranged for me to see the PM from time to time during our five-day voyage to Southampton. It would be inaccurate to say that Churchill and I conversed. Alone with him I was mute, having, in fact, nothing to say. He had everything to say, and like Gladstone speaking to Victoria, he addressed me as though I were a one-man House of Commons. It was superb. I was enthralled, and eagerly accepted an invitation to tour the rooms of No. 10 Downing Street, with a Scotland Yard inspector as my guide, during my layover in London.

Thus began my accumulating debt to British hospitality. It is now immense. While researching this work I took a flat in Mayfair, but I seldom dined there alone. The 'Churchillians,' as Sir John Colville calls them, entertained me in their homes, answered all my questions, suggested other sources, and provided me with valuable introductions. Lady Soames, DBE (Mary Churchill), packed a picnic lunch and drove me to Chartwell, where we spent the day wandering through the mansion and its grounds and examining scores of her father's canvasses. It was in the flat of Jane Williams, who is triply qualified as an observer of the English patriciate – she worked with Churchill and is the niece of both Lord Butler ('Rab') and Lord Portal of the RAF – that I first found myself at a table with 'Jock' Colville, Churchill's assistant private secretary during the PM's second premiership in the early 1950s. Butler himself received me in his country home shortly before his death. So did Lord Head at Throope Manor; General Sir Ian Jacob, military assistant secretary to the War Cabinet from 1939 to 1945, at Woodridge; and Harold Macmillan at Birch Grove House in Sussex. It was typical of Macmillan's gallantry that although he felt too ill to eat, he had laid out a champagne lunch for me.

Such graciousness can lead to pleasant embarrassment. When my London hack drew up outside the Oxford studio of Oscar Nemon, sculptor of Churchill, Nemon raced out of the house, his smock flying behind him, and insisted, to the point of physical pummelling, on paying the cabby. At No 1 Eaton Square, Lord Boothby broke out a shining bottle of prime bourbon although it was only 2:00 P.M. Sir John Martin in Watlingham, Martin Gilbert on Oxford's Harcourt Hill, and R. L. James on Oxford's Blenheim Drive clearly assumed that I would arrive with an enormous appetite. Sir William Hawthorne, Master of Churchill College, Cambridge, expected me to be both

721

omnivorous and omnibibulous; when we rose from his high table and left the room I felt sheathed in an alcoholic mist. But as it cleared, I met two meticulous Churchill scholars: Captain Stephen Roskill, RN, and Correlli Barnett, keeper of the Churchill Archives. Remarkable shortcuts were disclosed in social situations. Over biscuits in Twisden Road, for instance, A. J. P. Taylor guided me towards Lloyd George, Bonar Law, and Beaverbrook papers. Churchill himself was never a clubman, but in exploring the web of his friendships I found those last bastions of male chauvinism invaluable. Holding honorary membership in three London clubs, I could entertain and then interview, sotto voce, men who would have been reticent in other surroundings. But here, once again, I was guest more often than host – of Sir David Hunt at the Athenaeum, for example, and Sir William Deakin at the Oxford and Cambridge, and George Malcolm Thompson at the Garrick. It was from the Reform Club that Graham Norton and I sallied forth one glistening evening for a nightlong exploration of Victorian London's architectural relics, winding up near Covent Garden.

Others who welcomed me or visited me for taped sessions were Cecily 'Chips' Gemmell, Lord Soames, Lady Diana Cooper, Lord Selkirk, Lord Hailsham, John Griggs, Malcolm MacDonald (son of Ramsay and himself an MP), Lord Strauss, Sir Fitzroy MacLean, Mark Bonham Carter, Mrs Kathleen Hill, Grace Hamlin, A. A. Montague Browne, Richard Hill, Velma Salmon, Lady Avon, Noel Mander, Lord Geoffrey Lloyd, Julian Amery, Denis Kelly, Sir Charles Martin, Lord Southborough, and, in his delightful Sussex cottage outside Robertsbridge, Malcolm Muggeridge. Not all my respondents were British. Virginia Cowles is undeniably American, though in her Belgravia home she evokes the presence of Mrs. Miniver. Averell Harriman is a triumph of the English-Speaking Union; he seems at home in either London or New York, provided the background is expensive and in exquisite taste. His wife, Pamela, though active in US politics, will never pass as American. She was born a Digby in Dorset, Thomas Hardy country, and you know it from her every gesture. Her first husband was Randolph Churchill; their son, born during the Battle of Britain, is the second Winston Spencer Churchill, MP, who was my thoughtful host at lunch in the House of Commons.

Documents of contemporary history are less accessible in the United Kingdom than in the United States. Britain has no Freedom of Information Act. All Churchill papers in the Royal Archives are reserved for the official biography. The seal cannot be broken on other sensitive government documents – Cabinet, War Office, Foreign Office, Admiralty, Colonial Office, and Air Ministry – until fifty years after the event. Moreover, the papers of prominent public men are more scattered than those in US presidential libraries. By far the largest single source of evidence for this volume is in the Churchill College Archives Centre at Cambridge University, the repository of 215 collections of private papers, including those of McKenna, Bridgeman, P. J. Grigg, Bevin, Bracken, Carson, de Robeck, Fisher, Crewe, Keyes,

Rawlinson, Shane Leslie, E. L. Spears (partial), Beatty (partial), and Hankey (partial).

Documents left by other public men are frequently found beneath different roofs. Balfour's papers are in Scotland's National Register of Archives, the Public Record Office, the Reference Division of the British Library (formerly the British Museum Library), and in the private collection of Lord Rayleigh. Asquith's are in Oxford's Bodleian Library ('Bodley'), in the Smuts Archive, and in the collection of Mark Bonham Carter. Halifax's are filed in the India Office Library, the Public Record Office, and the estate of his heir. Some of Lord Esher's are in the Bodleian and some at Churchill College. Northcliffe's are dispersed among *The Times* Archive, the British Library, and the Bodleian. T. E. Lawrence's may be found in the Bodleian, the British Library, the Houghton Library at Harvard University, and the University of Texas Library. One would expect all of Beaverbrook's to be in the Beaverbrook Library, but no; some are there and some in the House of Lords Record Office. Because Lloyd George decided to take a peerage in the last weeks of World War II, some of his papers are in the House of Lords. (At about the same time he married his mistress, who became the Countess Lloyd George of Dwyfor; *her* extraordinary diaries, covering the years 1912 to 1949, are in the Beaverbrook Library.) Other valuable Lloyd George material is on the shelves of the Lloyd George Archive in Great Missenden, Buckinghamshire; the National Library of Wales; and the Beaverbrook Library. Bonar Law's papers are in the Bodleian, the Beaverbrook Library, and the Lords. Hankey's war diary (1912–1938) is in the Public Record Office, the diaries of Prince Louis of Battenberg in the Milford Haven Collection. Samuel's papers are in the Lords, as are Churchill documents on the founding of Iraq and his anti-Bolshevik years after Versailles. The Cecil, Jellicoe, and C. P. Scott papers are in the British Library. Milner's and H. A. L. Fisher's are housed in the Bodleian; Haldane's, Rosebery's, Haig's, and Margot Asquith's in the National Library of Scotland, Edinburgh; Hamilton's and Robertson's at King's College, London; Cockran's and some of Marsh's in the New York Public Library; Joseph and Austen Chamberlain's in the Birmingham University Library; most of Sir Henry Wilson's, including his microfilmed diaries, in the Imperial War Museum; those of Mottistone and Cherwell ('the Prof') in the Library of Nuffield College, Oxford; Curzon's in the India Office Library; Derby's at Liverpool University; and Baldwin's in the Cambridge University Library. Amery's, some of Spears's, Philip Sassoon's, some of Marsh's, Ponsonby's, and Asquith's letters to Venetia Stanley Montagu – probably the most valuable single source for the government's prosecution of the war between 1914 and 1916 – remain in private possession. The cabinet and War Council minutes, the Dardanelles Commission evidence, and imperial conference minutes are filed in the Public Record Office. Verbatim accounts of all proceedings in the House of Commons and the House of Lords between 1881 and 1932 may be found in the *Parliamentary Debates (Hansard)*.

Tracing all these would have been impossible without the original research, generosity, and encouragement of Martin Gilbert. As he wrote me, 'our work goes in tandem.' My gratitude toward him is profound.

On my own behalf and that of my archival research assistant in England, Deborah Baker, whose task it was to sift and sort out documents, I should like to thank D. G. Vaisey (Department of Western Manuscripts, the Bodleian Library), Diana Grimwood Jones and Gillian Grant (Middle East Centre, St Anthony's College, Oxford), Mrs P. Piper and N. A. M. Rodger (Public Record Office, Kew, Richmond, Surrey), G. J. Slater (Public Record Office of Northern Ireland), Marion Stewart (Churchill College, Cambridge), H. S. Cobb and F. Johnson (Record Office, House of Lords), A.N.E.D. Schofield and D.H. Bourke (British Library), D.M. Smith and C.C. Webb (Borthwick Institute of Historical Research, University of York), Wing Commander R. Martin Sparkes (Annexe), Wayne Furman (New York Public Library), A.E. Cormack and R.F. Barker (Royal Air Force Museum, Hendon), Gordon Phillips (*Times* Archive), Patricia Methven (Liddell Hart Centre of Military Archives, King's College, University of London), D.A. Clarke and G.E.A. Raspin (British Library of Political and Economic Science), R.A.W. Suddaby (Imperial War Museum), B.C. Bloomfield (India Office Library and Records), J.K. Bates (National Register of Archives, Scotland), Dr B.S. Benedikz (Special Collections, University of Birmingham), Henry James Scrymgeour-Wedderburn (Dundee Archives), E. P. Scott (Hove Area Library, East Sussex), Kay Chapman and R.J.B. Knight (National Maritime Museum), Christine Kennedy (Nuffield College Library, Oxford), Peter McNiven (University of Manchester), Ralph Malbon and W. Wilcox (City Library of Liverpool), D.M. Griffiths and R. Geraint Gruffydd (National Library of Wales, Aberystwyth, Dyfed), L. R. Day (Science Museum Library, South Kensington), V. E. Knight (Library of the University of Liverpool), E. C. Blayney (Foreign and Commonwealth Office), A. D. Maclean, Mrs Diane Nutting, the second Viscount Trenchard, and John Spencer-Churchill, eleventh Duke of Marlborough, who gave me the freedom of Blenheim Palace.

Once again I express my deep appreciation to the staff of Wesleyan University's Olin Library, in particular to J. Robert Adams, Caleb T. Winchester Librarian; and to Joan Jurale, head reference librarian; Edmund A. Rubacha and Susanne Javorski, reference librarians; Margaret Halstead, reference secretary; Erhard F. Konerding, documents librarian; Steven Lebergott, chief of interlibrary loans; and Alice Henry, circulation assistant. Other members of the staff who were especially helpful were Suzanne Fall; Ann Frances Wakefield; Dale Lee; and Alan Nathanson, bibliographer.

I am immensely indebted to Dr Robert Byck, professor of psychiatry at Yale Medical School, for his observations on depression, Carl Jung, and Dr Anthony Storr's analysis of Churchill's 'Black Dog'; and to my friend and colleague Jeffrey Butler, professor of history at Wesleyan, for his meticulous review of the completed manuscript in the interests of historical accuracy, a vital service which was also provided – and provided superbly – by two British readers, Peter Day and Nigel Viney.

I am most appreciative of assistance furnished by Adoreen M. McCormick and Marilyn Dekker of the Library of Congress, who were helpful in verifying the lyrics of popular songs quoted in the text; Perry Knowlton, Adam Deixel, and Iam Gonzalez at the Curtis Brown literary agency, who provided access to Churchill's American royalty statements; and Mrs J. A. Openshaw of North Kingston, R.I., for generously sharing the recollections and memorabilia of her father, William J. Harvest, who, as a lance corporal in the Fourth Hussars, served under Lieutenant Winston Churchill in Bangalore between 1896 and 1899.

My inestimable assistant, Margaret Kennedy Rider, has, as always, proved to be understanding, perceptive, loyal, and tireless. Deborah Baker was as reliable as the sturdiest English oak. Virgina Creeden and Diana Scott were invaluable in securing permission to quote from letters, diaries, documents, and published works, as was Ellen Panarese in the matter of photo research. Finally, I once more offer deepest thanks to Don Congdon, my literary agent; Roger Donald, my editor; and Melissa Clemence, my tireless, gifted copy editor – three dedicated professionals without whose patience and counsel the publication of this work would have been literally impossible.

W.M.

Wesleyan University
February 1983

SOURCE NOTES

In these notes on sources of quoted material, works have generally been cited by author's last name only, or, in the case of an author of multiple works, by author's name and brief title; for full listings, see the bibliography.

Works by Churchill, which include collections of his writings or remarks compiled by others, are cited by abbreviated title only, but are also listed in full in the bibliography. Please note the following forms of citation:

Aftermath	*The World Crisis: The Aftermath*
Crisis I–V	*The World Crisis*, Volumes I to V
RC	*A Roving Commission*
Wars	*Young Winston's Wars*

The Official Biography of Winston Spencer Churchill and its companion volumes are cited as follows:

WSC I–V	The five biographical volumes
CV I/1–V/2	The companion volumes, from Volume I, Part 1, to Volume V, Part 2

Complete listings of this work appear at the beginning of the bibliography.

In addition, the following forms of citation are used:

NYT	*New York Times*
Times	*The Times* (London)
WM	Author's interviews

A discussion of the author's interview subjects and of various document collections may be found in the author's acknowledgments.

Preamble: The Lion at Bay

1. *Hansard* 28/5/40
2. Berlin 15
3. WM / Lady Soames 27/10/80; Laurence Thompson 96
4. *Irrepressible* 218; Laurence Thompson 148, 169
5. Moran 833; Laurence Thompson 133; *Hansard* 13/5/40; Herbert in Marchant 105; *Hansard* 4/6/40
6. Berlin 5; *Churchill Years* 102; WM / Pamela Harriman 22/8/80; Berlin 6; Longford *Churchill* 127; Nel 53, 54
7. *NYT* 30/5/40; Moran 655
8. CV I/2 1004; Harriman 205
9. *Wars* 112; CV I/2 974; Sarah Churchill 71; *RC* 65
10. *Wars* xxvi; Stevenson 38; WSC III 31; CV II/3 1989; Gardner 254, 285
11. *RC* 64; *Irrepressible* 286; McGowan 47; *Irrepressible* 300; Moran 674, 595; WSC V 837-838
12. WM / Jane Williams 7/10/80; McGowan 163; Howells 70; *Irrepressible* 224, 222, 318, 160; Moran 722
13. *Churchill Years* 22; Moran 717; *Irrepressible* 167
14. *Irrepressible* 225; Attlee in Stansky 197
15. Boothby *Rebel* 63
16. *RC* 10; WM / Sir John Martin 23/10/80; Martin in Wheeler-Bennett 143; WM / Richard Hill 7/11/80
17. Attlee in Stansky 189
18. *Observer* 20/12/51; *Hansard* 18/6/40, 4/6/40; Berlin 8
19. *RC* 5, 73

727

20. Storr in A.J.P. Taylor et al. 237
21. CV I/1 414; *Irrepressible* 265
22. Storr in A.J.P. Taylor et al. 238-239; Bryant 12-13; Moran 57; H.H. Asquith *Letters* 267
23. *Times* 21/1/27; *Step by Step* 57, 170; Moran 835
24. Liddell Hart in Stansky 95; *Irrepressible* 234; Moran 834
25. Moran 835; Rhodes James *Failure* 349; W.H. Thompson 87; Bonham Carter 9; Moran 776; Gardiner in Stansky 52; W.H. Thompson 44
26. *Churchill Years* 21; CV II/1 104; *Churchill Years* 237
27. *RC* 330-331; *Hansard* 12/11/40
28. CV I/1 584; *Savrola* 31-32, 234; Sarah Churchill 17
29. Beaverbrook *War* I 128; Moran 179; Storr in A.J.P. Taylor et al. 262
30. Storr in A.J.P. Taylor et al. 262; Ridell *War Diary* 49; Nel 139; CV I/2 862; Storr in A.J.P. Taylor et al. 270; Moran 796
31. Storr in A.J.P. Taylor et al. 259
32. Attlee in Stansky 198; Moran 827; Moir 203; Howells 61; *Irrepressible* 263, 6; *Wit* 45-46
33. *Wit* 65; Cowles *Churchill* 93
34. *Irrepressible* 263; Moran 460; Storr in A.J.P. Taylor et al. 254; Cowles *Churchill* 10
35. Moran 576; Hunt 65
36. *River War* II 110; Stansky xi
37. WSC V 1106
38. Moran 453; Hunt 67, 68
39. Berlin 2; *Great Contemporaries* 342, 372; Bonham Carter 119
40. Bonham Carter 4; Moran 457, 511; McGowan 161; Herbert in Marchant 110; *Irrepressible* 154
41. Coote in Eade 181; Chandos 166; *Irrepressible* 69, 159
42. *Amid These Storms* 300; Moran 746; *Irrepressible* 166; Chandos 184; Brooks in Eade 363
43. Moran 456; Eden in Eade 84; McGowan 24; *Irrepressible* 122
44. Rhodes James *Failure* 27; WM / Jane Williams 7/10/80; Hunt 70; Nel 50
45. Cowles *Churchill* 5; *Churchill Years* 206
46. *Irrepressible* 195, 204-205; McGowan 145; *Irrepressible* 340
47. *Irrepressible* 85, 325, 255, 272, 181; WM / Sir David Pitblado 21/10/80
48. Attlee in Stansky 206; Shaw in Eade 463
49. *Irrepressible* 63
50. *Irrepressible* 203; Howells 110; McGowan 93; Gardner 169
51. Moran 472; *Churchill Years* 14; Cowles *Churchill* 336; McGowan 39; Martin in Wheeler-Bennett 141
52. Howells 85; WM / Viscount Head 17/11/80
53. Howells 85; *Irrepressible* 186
54. Mary Soames to Virgil Johnston 13/6/72; Hunt 65

Prologue: Land of Hope and Glory

1. WM / Lord Boothby 16/10/80
2. Cross 143; Morris *Pax* 177; *Wars* 139-140
3. Morris *Pax* 109
4. Edmund Taylor 22; WM / Virginia Cowles 25/10/80
5. Morris in Perry and Mason 153
6. Collier 94-95; Morris *Pax* 133; Morris in Perry and Mason 146
7. Morris *Pax* 51
8. Morris *Pax* 132, 137
9. Moorehead *Nile* 290
10. Morris *Pax* 465
11. Morris *Pax* 187; Nicholson in Perry and Mason 207, 209; Morris *Pax* 188
12. Cross 89
13. Morris *Pax* 119
14. CV I/2 690, 684
15. CV I/2 688
16. Henry James 1-6
17. Coleman in Perry and Mason 60
18. McGregor in Perry and Mason 180, 181
19. Bailey 44
20. Davis *Cousins* 149-150
21. Norton 105
22. Best 75-76
23. Norton in Perry and Mason 171, 172; G.M. Young *England* 24

24. Phillips 197
25. Phillips 87
26. Best 75, 74, 117, 119
27. G.M. Young *England* 2; Phillips 62;
    G.M. Young *England* 7
28. Best 233, 212
29. Konig 'Eleventh Edition'
30. Best 281; McGregor in Perry and
    Mason 178
31. Frost and Jay 39; Oxford English
    Dictionary definition of *weekend*
32. Edmund Taylor 31; Martin I 40;
    Collier 96, 104-105; Phillips 42;
    Martin I 164, 54
33. *Crisis* I 199; Gardner 31n; Best 243-
    244
34. Frost and Jay 39
35. Best 240; *Little Dorrit* ch. 34
36. Best 230; Cowles *Churchill* 71-72
37. *Times* 20/7/1863
38. Reader 20, 22; Best 165
39. Cross 32; *Last Chronicle of Barset* ch.
    83
40. *Blenheim* 2
41. *Lord Randolph* I 1
42. Longford *Wellington* 399
43. McGregor in Perry and Mason 178;
    Martin I 278; WM / Graham
    Norton 8/10/80; Martin II 140

44. Martin II 360; Edmund Taylor 24
45. McGregor in Perry and Mason 178;
    WM / Pamela Harriman 22/8/80;
    Tuchman *Proud* 20
46. Martin I 44-45
47. Sackville-West 17
48. WM / Graham Norton 8/10/80
49. WSC I 6, 7
50. WSC I 13-14
51. WSC I 15
52. Blake *Disraeli* 692
53. Harris 485-486, 483
54. Harris 483
55. CV I/1 8; Howard 77
56. Howard 77
57. Eliot *Heiresses* 63; Moran 636; Eliot
    Heiresses 62
58. Moran 636-637
59. Martin I 99
60. Martin I 50, 52
61. CV I/1 8-9, 14
62. Martin I 53; CV I/1 11; *Lord
    Randolph* I 41, 42
63. CV I/1 12
64. CV I/1 15, 19, 21
65. CV I/1 20; Martin I 91; *Blenheim* 2
66. CV I/1 1-2; Martin I 107
67. CV I/1 2
68. Martin I 108; Pelling 19; *Blenheim* 16

Part One: Headwaters, 1874–1895

1. Longford *Churchill* 17; CV I/1 6
2. *RC* 5; Bonham Carter 12; Eliot
   Heiresses 67-68; *Lord Randolph* I
   72-73
3. Eliot *Heiresses* 69-70
4. *Lord Randolph* I 74
5. CV I/1 26-27, 28
6. CV I/1 29; WSC I 29; CV I/1 31, 57,
   39; *Lord Randolph* I 74
7. WSC I 31; *RC* 8; CV I/1 48
8. *RC* 4
9. WSC I 35-36; Margot Asquith *Autobiography* I 64
10. *RC* 5, 111; *Savrola* 33
11. Storr in A.J.P. Taylor et al. 248;
    WSC I 43; *RC* 4, 8; Martin I 138;
    Wit 32
12. *RC* 1, 2
13. *Lord Randolph* I 92; WSC I 39; CV
    I/1 77

14. *Great Contemporaries* 55
15. Goertzel and Goertzel 262; *RC* 8
16. CV I/1 79; *RC* 3
17. *RC* 10, 11
18. *RC* 12; CV I/1 82, 88, 84, 83
19. CV I/1 84, 83, 86, 89, 87, 88, 83n
20. CV I/1 86; *RC* 13
21. WSC I 51
22. WSC I 48, 47; CV I/1 92, 93, 94, 95,
    96
23. CV I/1 98; Cowles *Churchill* 30; CV
    I/1 154
24. CV I/1 98, 99, 125, 136, 143, 146,
    149, 115; *RC* 13
25. CV I/1 131, 108; Cowles *Churchill* 31
26. CV I/1 152, 135, 136
27. CV I/1 111; Cowles *Churchill* 32; *RC*
    19
28. *RC* 112
29. CV I/1 150, 151

30. CV I/1 152
31. CV I/1 160, 116, 117, 118, 119
32. CV I/1 120
33. *RC* 13; CV I/1 120, 121
34. Eliot *Heiresses* 72
35. CV I/1 111, 101, 142, 133, 103, 126, 227, 128
36. CV I/1 105, 127, 113
37. Harris 485
38. Pelling 28
39. Martin I 249, 250, 277, 299, 177
40. Martin I 227, 176, 319
41. Martin II 9
42. CV I/1 256; *Savrola* 157
43. Cowles *Churchill* 33; CV I/1 106
44. *RC* 46; Cowles *Churchill* 33
45. CV I/1 100, 304, 305, 143-144
46. CV I/1 100, 103
47. CV I/1 103, 122, 125, 133
48. Margot Asquith *Autobiography* II 65; Harris 472, 478
49. *Lord Randolph* I 283-284
50. *RC* 8; *Lord Randolph* I 120, 121, 209-210
51. CV I/1 88, 89; *Lord Randolph* I 295; Harris 474
52. WSC I 65
53. *Lord Randolph* II 65
54. WSC I 73; Harris 478; Margot Asquith *Autobiography* I 140
55. Rhodes James *Lord Randolph* 203; Martin I 219
56. Harris 478
57. Harris 660; WSC I 74; Harris 480; WSC I 79
58. *RC* 47; WSC I 81
59. Rhodes James *Lord Randolph* 295; Martin I 230; Harris 479
60. Eliot *Heiresses* 72; Martin I 230; Harris 481
61. CV I/1 144, 108, 137, 143
62. CV I/1 102; *RC* 15
63. CV I/1 156, 157, 158; *RC* 15
64. CV I/1 157, 158
65. CV I/1 162; *RC* 16
66. Tomlin in Chaplin 30
67. WSC I 108; Chaplin 84-87
68. CV I/1 161; Wollaston in Eade 20; *RC* 39; Tomlin in Chaplin 28
69. Wollaston in Eade 19; Siddons in Chaplin 18; Cowles *Churchill* 36; Wollaston in Eade 21
70. *RC* 30, 34-35; Bromage 3

71. *RC* 31; Tomlin in Chaplin 28; Martin I 217, 255
72. CV I/1 161; Mottistone in Chaplin 33, 34; Amery in Chaplin 21, 22
73. CV I/1 311; Cowles *Churchill* 36
74. *RC* 27, 22
75. CV I/1 192, 193-194
76. CV I/1 168-169
77. Siddons in Chaplin 11-12
78. CV I/1 204, 205; *RC* 25
79. *RC* 16-17
80. CV I/1 152, 159, 162; Chaplin 87-88
81. Mottistone in Chaplin 34
82. Siddons in Chaplin 17; Chaplin 57
83. WSC I 115; CV I/1 176, 177, 178
84. CV I/1 179, 180, 185, 186, 292, 300, 198
85. CV I/1 275-276, 292
86. CV I/1 292, 218
87. *Spectator* 7/25/91; *Review of Reviews* 4/1892
88. CV I/1 204, 182, 187, 185, 274, 275, 254
89. CV I/1 254, 247
90. CV I/1 250-251, 253
91. CV I/1 256
92. CV I/1 257-258, 256
93. CV I/1 256, 257
94. CV I/1 257
95. CV I/1 257
96. CV I/1 204, 323, 268, 256
97. CV I/1 284, 287, 259, 290
98. CV I/1 291-292
99. CV I/1 293, 294, 295, 296
100. CV I/1 297, 299, 301, 304, 303
101. CV I/1 301, 299, 300, 303
102. CV I/1 299, 301, 302, 304, 306
103. CV I/1 301, 305-306
104. CV I/1 306-307, 295; Rhodes James *Failure* 10
105. CV I/1 197; *RC* 19; CV I/1 222, 223; WSC I 130
106. CV I/1 259; *RC* 27, 113-114; McGowan 96; WSC I 151
107. CV I/1 337; *RC* 110, 111; CV I/1 338, 347-348
108. CV I/1 339, 325, 326; WSC I 171
109. Farwell *Kipling* 144; CV I/1 353, 359
110. Goertzel and Goertzel 273; *RC* 30; CV I/1 365
111. *RC* 28, 29
112. *RC* 26-27; CV I/1 371

730

113. CV I/1 376
114. CV I/1 380, 387
115. CV I/1 388
116. CV I/1 390-391
117. CV I/1 397, 393, 394
118. *RC* 37; CV I/1 402, 404
119. CV I/1 414
120. CV I/1 386, 413, 414
121. *RC* 31, 32
122. CV I/1 378; *RC* 33
123. *Spectator* 5/8/93
124. *RC* 33, 46
125. CV I/1 386
126. CV I/1 423; Cowles *Churchill* 33; *RC* 38-39; Bonham Carter 15; McGowan 44; *RC* 31, 32
127. Bonham Carter 14; Harris 471; Martin I 312; *River War* I 37; WSC I 232
128. CV I/1 468, 469
129. CV I/1 470, 471, 478
130. CV I/1 419
131. CV I/1 424, 425
132. *RC* 59, 38, 43, 44
133. *RC* 43, 44
134. 'The Royal Military College'
135. 'The Royal Military College'; *RC* 45
136. Farwell *Kipling* 145
137. CV I/1 439, 433n; *RC* 59
138. *RC* 60
139. Farwell *Kipling* 68
140. *RC* 52, 54
141. *RC* 55; Martin I 334; Cowles *Churchill* 40
142. CV I/1 532, 530, 528, 527; *Irrepressible* 24
143. WM / R.A. Butler 5/11/80
144. CV I/1 540
145. *RC* 61-62
146. CV I/1 478, 433; *RC* 59-60
147. Foster 217
148. Foster 378; WSC I 226
149. Blunt *Diaries* I 142; Harris 487, 488
150. Harris 489, 490, 491
151. WSC I 226; Martin I 326, 327; *Harper's Weekly* 5/1/95; Harris 491
152. CV I/1 535
153. CV I/1 540
154. CV I/1 531
155. CV I/1 533; *Lord Randolph* II 484; *RC* 49, 62
156. *Review of Reviews* 3/1895; *Outlook* 2/2/95; Martin I 228; *Harper's Weekly* 5/1/95; CV I/1 545
157. Marchant 20; *RC* 62, 74
158. *RC* 62; CV I/1 557
159. CV I/1 555-556; *RC* 63; CV I/1 559
160. CV I/1 562, 565, 567
161. CV I/1 635, 625
162. CV I/1 627, 626
163. Farwell *Kipling* 68; CV I/1 556, 559, 562
164. *RC* 65, 66
165. *RC* 64; CV I/1 577; *RC* 89, 90
166. *RC* 72
167. CV I/1 566
168. *RC* 73
169. CV I/1 579; WSC I 246; CV I/1 578

Part Two: Stream, 1895–1901

1. Farwell *Kipling* 49; Norton in Perry and Mason 132; Farwell *Kipling* 70, 72
2. Norton in Perry and Mason 131, 132
3. Farwell *Kipling* 62, 110
4. Bond 'Why the Thin Red Line Was So Thin'
5. Farwell *Kipling* 116, 119
6. *RC* 75
7. CV I/1 590, 592, 593
8. CV I/1 595
9. CV I/1 596, 597
10. CV I/1 599, 598, 600, 597
11. CV I/1 597; Martin II 68, 69; *Amid These Storms* 52
12. *RC* 77; CV I/1 604
13. CV I/1 606
14. CV I/1 606
15. CV I/1 604, 611-612
16. CV I/1 612; *RC* 80; CV I/1 613; *Wit* 64
17. CV I/1 614, 615
18. WSC I 266; CV I/1 620
19. CV I/1 621, 622
20. WSC I 267; CV I/1 666; WSC I 269
21. *RC* 99-100; CV I/2 723-724; WSC I 270
22. *RC* 89; Martin II 61; CV I/1 579; *RC* 93, 94
23. *RC* 89; CV I/1 672

24. CV I/2 743, 747, 922
25. CV I/2 742; CV I/1 673, 674
26. CV I/1 676
27. CV I/2 680, 682-683
28. Wollaston in Perry and Mason 67
29. RC 101-102
30. RC 102, 101, 103, 104; Lockhart in Stansky 12
31. CV I/2 688
32. RC 107
33. WSC I 314; RC 103, 105-106
34. CV I/2 697, 684, 702, 753-754, 705, 722
35. Churchill Years 70
36. CV I/2 685, 686-687, 692
37. RC 109, 110
38. RC 111; CV I/2 724, 742, 726, 730
39. CV I/2 746, 730
40. CV I/2 767, 768, 765
41. RC 115-116, 117
42. CV I/2 746, 779
43. CV I/2 779, 702, 716, 704, 731, 729
44. CV I/2 734, 748, 750
45. CV I/2 754, 755, 756; Martin II 105; CV I/2 768
46. RC 120-121
47. CV I/2 770, 771
48. CV I/2 772, 773, 774
49. CV I/2 807n
50. CV I/2 775; RC 123
51. RC 124
52. RC 126-127; CV I/2 781, 784
53. Wars 19
54. CV I/2 787-788, 797; RC 132; CV I/2 797
55. CV I/2 792, 793, 796-797, 800
56. CV I/2 788; RC 132; CV I/2 792; RC 137
57. Wars 22; RC 137, 139
58. RC 140, 141, 142; CV I/2 799
59. CV I/2 799; RC 142, 143
60. CV I/2 799; RC 147
61. WSC I 349; CV I/2 830; Wars 60; Cowles Churchill 50
62. CV I/2 804, 805, 809, 811, 814
63. CV I/2 808, 839, 835
64. Moorehead Churchill Trial 10; Cowles Churchill 49; CV I/2 883, 806; RC 158-159
65. CV I/2 922, 869, 912, 889; RC 211; Wit 45; CV I/2 839, 840
66. CV I/2 841, 913, 895
67. Athenaeum 16/3/98; RC 154-155

68. CV I/2 930, 931; RC 155; CV I/2 855, 813, 856
69. Crisis I 251; RC 151-152; CV I/2 949, 948, 837, 882, 883; Martin II 129
70. RC 164
71. WSC I 378, 379
72. CV I/2 951; RC 167, 170; CV I/2 964
73. CV I/2 949-950
74. CV I/2 952; RC 167; CV I/2 956; Wars 71; RC 168; Wars 75
75. Wars 122, 123
76. River War II 40, 59; Wars 89
77. Wars 96; CV I/2 969; RC 169; CV I/2 971; River War II 73
78. Wars 85, 86, 87, 88
79. RC 173; Wars 99; RC 174
80. Wars 100, 101
81. RC 174, 175, 177
82. RC 178, 180
83. RC 183; CV I/2 977, 972; RC 184, 185; River War II 112, 111
84. River War II 130, 132
85. RC 188; CV I/2 978
86. CV I/2 978
87. CV I/2 978; RC 192, 191
88. CV I/2 973; RC 192; CV I/2 978; RC 193, 102
89. RC 193
90. CV I/2 979, 973; Wars 133
91. Wars 131-132, 133
92. Wars 122; CV I/2 979; River War II 44; Wars 123; RC 196
93. Girouard 'When Chivalry Died'
94. River War II 212
95. CV I/2 1004; River War II 195; CV I/2 979, 999, 984
96. Wars 130; CV I/2 974, 995
97. RC 197, 198
98. River War II 128; Wars 111, 113
99. Wars 126, 128
100. CV I/2 984
101. WSC I 408, 409; CV I/2 990
102. CV I/2 697, 989
103. CV I/2 1003; RC 201, 199; CV I/2 1015
104. WSC I 295; CV I/2 1011
105. WSC I 422; RC 211; CV I/2 996
106. Steevens in Eade 64, 65-66
107. CV I/2 1016-1017, 1020
108. CV I/2 1023; RC 228
109. CV I/2 1028, 1033, 1035, 1036
110. RC 224, 226

111. Martin II 183; *Manchester Courier* 7/7/99; *RC* 225-226
112. CV I/2 1038; *RC* 227
113. CV I/2 1051; Pakenham 171
114. *RC* 231
115. *Irrepressible* 36
116. Pakenham 32, 7; WSC I 435; Pakenham 113
117. Pakenham 110; Margot Asquith *Autobiography* II 85
118. *RC* 234; *London to Ladysmith* 3; CV I/2 1055-1056; WSC I 441; *RC* 236
119. *RC* 237; *London to Ladysmith* 16; CV I/2 1058
120. *RC* 234, 241
121. *London to Ladysmith* 42; *Wars* 158
122. WSC I 447
123. Pakenham 177; *Wars* 158; *RC* 244; *Wars* 172
124. *RC* 245
125. *Wars* 172; *RC* 248; *Wars* 169; WSC I 450, 452
126. *RC* 250, 252
127. WSC I 460; *RC* 253; *Wars* 269
128. *RC* 258
129. *RC* 259
130. CV I/2 1077-1078, 1063-1064, 1075, 1074, 1084
131. CV I/2 1086
132. CV I/2 1102
133. CV I/2 1085, 1085n
134. Cowles *Churchill* 64
135. *Wars* 183, 184
136. *Wars* 185
137. *RC* 281, 282
138. *RC* 282, 283, 284
139. *RC* 285, 283
140. CV I/2 1090; WSC I 481
141. *RC* 290, 299; CV I/2 1091; WSC I 481
142. *RC* 290
143. WSC I 489; *Johannesburg Star* 22/12/23; *RC* 295
144. *RC* 296; CV I/2 1131; Martin II 210; CV I/2 1093

145. *RC* 303, 301; CV I/2 1093; *RC* 304
146. *RC* 304, 305
147. *London to Ladysmith* 364; CV I/2 1144; *Wars* 231
148. Pakenham 307
149. Pakenham 308, 310
150. *London to Ladysmith* 307; CV I/2 1147, 1146
151. *London to Ladysmith* 309, 310, 311; *Wars* xxi
152. Eliot *Heiresses* 74
153. WSC I 495; CV I/2 1151, 1149-1150
154. *RC* 325-326; *Wars* 265
155. CV I/2 1167; *Irrepressible* 3; CV I/2 1164; *RC* 329; CV I/2 1161
156. CV I/2 1143, 1151, 1144, 1147
157. *RC* 327; *London to Ladysmith* 345, 346; CV I/2 1168
158. CV I/2 1172
159. CV I/2 1145; *Wars* 290, 291-292
160. *Wars* 292
161. *Ian Hamilton's March* 262; Moran 203
162. *RC* 349
163. *RC* 350; WSC I 512
164. WSC I 513; *Wars* 288
165. CV I/2 1178
166. CV I/2 1199
167. Cowles *Churchill* 67; *RC* 355
168. CV I/2 1201; *RC* 355; Pakenham 492; *Daily Mail* 27/9/1900; WSC to Oldham Conservative Club 29/9/1900; Oldham Conservative Club to WSC 30/9/1900
169. CV I/2 1196; *RC* 357; Bonham Carter 53; *RC* 356; CV I/2 1206
170. WSC I 282; Bonham Carter 56
171. *RC* 360; CV I/2 1222n, 1222; *Irrepressible* 42
172. CV I/2 1225, 1224
173. *RC* 361; CV I/2 1225
174. CV I/2 1231
175. Steevens in Eade 66

Part Three: Rier, 1901-1914

1. *NYT* 15/2/01
2. *NYT* 15/2/01
3. WSC II 6
4. *RC* 362, 363; *Hansard* 18/2/01; *RC* 364

5. *Hansard* 18/2/01; *RC* 364
6. *RC* 364, 365; *Daily Chronicle* 19/2/01; *Daily Express* 19/2/01; *Daily Telegraph* 19/2/01; *Morning Post* 19/2/01; *Daily News* 19/2/01; *RC* 366,

367

7. *Daily Mail* 7/6/01; Moir 205-206; *Irrepressible* 50, 49
8. Webb *Partnership* 269; Rhodes James *Failure* 16, 15, 20; Blunt *Diaries* II 74-75
9. *Daily Mail* 7/6/01; *Punch* 8/6/04; *RC* 366; *Amid These Storms* 55; WSC II 17
10. *Hansard* 13/5/01
11. Cowles *Churchill* 87; WSC II 20; Cowles *Churchill* 88; Bonham Carter 72
12. *RC* 367; CV II/1 49; Coote in Marchant 39; *Wit* 29; Cowles *Churchill* 92, 94
13. Bonham Carter 5, 6; Rhodes James *Failure* 29
14. CV II/1 62, 64; *Hansard* 18/3/03
15. Cowles *Churchill* 94; *RC* 369
16. *RC* 369-370
17. Cowles *Churchill* 95; Bonham Carter 81
18. *Hansard* 31/7/02; CV II/1 162; Bonham Carter 77; CV II/1 174
19. WSC II 54; *Hansard* 28/5/03; *Review of Reviews* 10/1903
20. WSC II 58; CV II/1 185
21. Coote in Marchant 38; Cowles *Churchill* 96
22. *Times* 7/3/05
23. *RC* 367; CV II/1 188; Bonham Carter 93
24. Cowles *Churchill* 89-90; CV I/2 751; CV II/1 239
25. *Irrepressible* 51; WSC II 63; CV II/1 218; Cowles *Churchill* 98
26. CV II/1 225, 243, 244
27. CV II/1 266; Cowles *Churchill* 98; CV II/1 269, 288, 289
28. *Daily Mail* 30/3/04; *Monthly Review* 11/1903; *Irrepressible* 52; *Hansard* 28/3/05; Rhodes James *Failure* 23; *Hansard* 24/7/05; WSC II 63; *Hansard* 24/3/04
29. *Hansard* 24/7/05, 27/7/05
30. CV II/1 225; WSC II 72; Rhodes James *Failure* 32; Brooks in Eade 359; Winterton in Eade 86-87; *Irrepressible* 50
31. Cowles *Churchill* 99; Brooks in Eade 359; Marchant 47; *Punch* 8/6/04; Moorehead *Churchill Trial* 25;

Bonham Carter 85

32. *Daily Mail* 30/3/04; WSC II 76; *Pall Mall Gazette* 31/3/04
33. *Daily Mail* 23/4/04; WSC II 77; Bonham Carter 88
34. Cowles *Churchill* 102; *Hansard* 16/5/04; Bonham Carter 89
35. *Punch* 8/6/04; Cowles *Churchill* 103
36. WSC II 79; *Punch* 8/6/04
37. Margot Asquith *Autobiography* II 134; *Sunday Times* 27/5/24; *Wit* 24
38. Cowles *Churchill* 99; WSC II 71
39. Pelling 87; WSC I 527; CV I/2 1229
40. WSC II 244; CV II/1 587
41. Boothby *Rebel* 24; *Wit* 84; Moir 79
42. Soames 118; Longford *Churchill* 37; WSC II 241; Bonham Carter 3-4
43. Bonham Carter 117-118; CV II/2 800; CV I/2 1232
44. Paul Thompson 71, 72
45. Sackville-West 86, 52
46. Martin II 275; Sackville-West 193-194
47. Martin II 276
48. Tuchman *Proud* 20
49. WSC II 89, 88
50. Anita Leslie *Lady Randolph* 308; WSC II 120
51. Rhodes James *Failure* 16; *Harper's Weekly* 6/8/04
52. Blunt *Diaries* II 74; Hore-Belisha in Eade 393, 394; Bonham Carter 6-7; Anita Leslie *Lady Randolph* 303; *Wit* 43; *Great Contemporaries* 176; *Wit* 42
53. Rhodes James *Failure* 17
54. Cowles *Churchill* 91
55. CV II/1 164-165, 587
56. Bonham Carter 172-173; Marsh 166
57. CV II/2 798; Rhodes James *Failure* 60
58. *Crisis* I 199
59. *Crisis* I 199
60. Ensor 551
61. *Irrepressible* 116
62. Cowles *Churchill* 104; *Punch* 22/3/05; Cowles *Churchill* 103
63. Moorehead *Churchill Trial* 26; Samuel in Marchant 49
64. Bonham Carter 120; Marsh 149
65. CV II/1 421; Marsh 152, 153; Martin II 304
66. WSC II 111; *Churchill Years* 36;

WSC II 427; Bonham Carter 101-102; WSC II 120

67. *Daily Mail* 5/1/06; *Manchester Guardian* 11/1/06
68. Bonham Carter 102; WSC II 119-120
69. *Amid These Storms* 207-208
70. *Hansard* 27/2/06
71. *Hansard* 28/2/06, 14/3/06, 21/3/06
72. Margot Asquith *Autobiography* II 86; Marsh 151; Hyam in Stansky 30; CV II/1 534; WSC II 180
73. Marsh 150; CV II/2 797; Hyam in Stansky 22; Pelling 98, 99; Hyam in Stansky 23, 30
74. Hyam in Stansky 24
75. Hyam in Stansky 24-25, 29
76. *Wit* 37; Memorandum of 8/2/07 concerning Aliens Act, Home Office Papers
77. CV II/1 530; Hyam in Stansky 34; *Hansard* 30/6/06; Bonham Carter 110; *Daily Mail* 1/7/06
78. *Liberalism* 98; CV II/2 684
79. WSC II 221; CV II/2 692, 693
80. CV II/2 693, 732; *Outlook* 2/5/08
81. CV II/2 765; Cowles *Churchill* 115; Marsh 163; McGowan 153; Eden in Eade 110
82. *Amid These Storms* 208-209; WSC II 254-255; *Times* 24/4/08
83. WSC II 250; *Morning Post* 25/4/08; CV II/2 789, 787
84. Bonham Carter 171
85. *Irrepressible* 62; WSC II 242
86. Soames 50; CV II/2 781; Soames 54-55
87. CV II/2 798, 800-801; Soames 55
88. *Irrepressible* 17
89. CV II/2 801, 803
90. Soames 67; Blunt *Diaries* II 214
91. *RC* 370; CV II/2 820; Bonham Carter 173
92. McGowan 39; Blunt *Diaries* II 271; Soames 71
93. WSC II 284-285, 339; Soames 91
94. *Irrepressible* 264; CV II/2 918
95. *Savrola* 57; Soames 127, 128
96. Pelling 174; *Great Contemporaries* 174; WSC II 339-340; Soames 110
97. CV II/2 765; Soames 117
98. WSC II 386; CV II/3 1715; Soames 79
99. Cowles *Churchill* 122; *Nation* 7/3/08;

100. Webb *Partnership* 417; Moorehead *Churchill Trial* 31; Bonham Carter 107
101. Cowles *Churchill* 106
102. Cowles *Churchill* 107
103. WSC II 272, 273
104. WSC II 499; CV II/2 938; Cowles *Churchill* 126; *Crisis* I 33
105. WSC II 299
106. WSC II 305-306, 311
107. CV II/2 887; Soames 73; *Hansard* 29/4/09; Cowles *Churchill* 128; Bonham Carter 146
108. *Hansard* 25/6/07
109. Cowles *Churchill* 129; *Daily Express* 6/9/09; *Times* 6/9/09
110. *Daily Express* 6/9/09; Cowles *Churchill* 132; WSC II 315; Soames 109
111. Pelling 109; CV II/2 967; *Irrepressible* 64; WSC II 316, 315, 320
112. CV II/2 909, 968; WSC II 321
113. Margot Asquith *Autobiography* II 138; Soames 129; Tuchman *August* 1
114. WSC III 87
115. WSC II 347; Cowles *Churchill* 127; WSC II 442, 463
116. Moran 472; WSC II 352, 351, 349
117. *Wit* 29
118. Bonham Carter 151, 174
119. CV II/2 1141; Memorandum 'Imprisonment for Debt' 23/8/10, Home Office Papers; WSC II 375, 373; *Yale Review* 2/1911
120. *Times* 23/7/10; WSC II 377; CV II/2 1034, 1094
121. WSC II 329; WSC III 179; Rhodes James *Failure* 42, 60; Bonham Carter 107; Rhodes James *Failure* 39; Webb *Partnership* 404
122. WSC II 419-420
123. Cowles *Churchill* 144
124. Cowles *Churchill* 143n; *Hansard* 24/11/10; *Daily Mail* 9/2/50; Cowles *Churchill* 144
125. *Times* 9/11/10; *Daily Express* 9/11/10; CV II/2 1207
126. *Amid These Storms* 68
127. *Amid These Storms* 69-70
128. WSC II 394; *Daily News* 4/1/11
129. WSC II 395; *Amid These Storms* 72;

Rhodes James *Failure* 43; Pelling 138

130. WSC II 365; CV II/2 1274
131. WSC II 370; CV II/2 1282
132. CV II/2 1285; WSC II 371; CV II/2 1290
133. Rhodes James *Failure* 43, 44; *Hansard* 22/8/11; Isaacs in Eade 371
134. *Wit* 28
135. *Great Contemporaries* 37; CV II/1 582; WSC II 191
136. CV II/2 723, 903, 911, 913, 910
137. CV II/2 911-912
138. CV II/2 1079
139. Cowles *Churchill* 153; *Crisis* I 44
140. CV II/2 1105, 1116
141. *Crisis* I 49
142. *Crisis* I 60-61; Cowles *Churchill* 154
143. Soames 97, 98
144. Cowles *Churchill* 157; Bonham Carter 188
145. *Crisis* I 68
146. Soames 99; *Crisis* I 122; Soames 124, 121
147. Soames 126, 101
148. Soames 84; CV II/3 1723; Soames 123; Bonham Carter 190
149. Pelling 147; *Crisis* I 71; WSC II 558
150. *Crisis* I 123-124
151. Cowles *Churchill* 157; CV II/3 1595, 1504, 1597
152. Tuchman *August* 50; *Crisis* I 101, 102
153. *Crisis* I 103; *Daily News* 10/2/12; Bonham Carter 197; WSC II 546
154. Tuchman *August* 53, 326
155. Tuchman *August* 326, 330
156. CV II/3 1517, 1518
157. CV II/2 1316; Tuchman *August* 195, 203; *Crisis* I 81
158. Cowles *Churchill* 158; *Crisis* I 72
159. WSC II 527-528
160. *Crisis* I 76; Bacon *Fisher* II 138
161. *Crisis* I 90, 146-147; Marder II 416
162. Marder II 430; *Crisis* I 78; Bacon *Fisher* II 148; WSC II 565; Marder II 459, 461; WSC II 566
163. Bonham Carter 202-203; Marder II 467
164. *Crisis* I 123; *Irrepressible* 71
165. *Fleet* 10/1912; Pelling 149; *Wit* 57
166. Tuchman *August* 422; Manchester

'Great War' 110; *Crisis* I 338; Low in Eade 444

167. Tuchman *August* 239; CV II/3 1874; Wrench in Eade 291; *Crisis* I 337
168. Joubert in Eade 160; CV II/3 1883-1884; Soames 130
169. WSC II 681, 682
170. WSC II 682; Joubert in Eade 161; Pelling 168
171. CV II/3 1889, 1890; Soames 131
172. CV II/3 1893; Cowles *Churchill* 7; Soames 131; CV II/3 1920
173. Soames 132, 133, 134
174. CV II/3 1921-1922
175. *Crisis* I 111; WSC II 552; Churchill to Viscount Grey 20/1/12, quoting letter from Berlin, Grey Papers; CV II/3 1492; Churchill to Grey 24/10/13, Grey Papers
176. WSC II 636-637
177. Tuchman *August* 91
178. *Daily Chronicle* 3/1/14; Pelling 153; WSC II 662; CV II/3 1872
179. WSC II 663
180. *Great Contemporaries* 345; Blunt *Diaries* II 289; Eden in Eade 110; *Lord Randolph* II 59
181. Morris *Trumpets* 222; *Great Contemporaries* 82; WSC II 444; *Review of Reviews* 3/1912
182. Bonham Carter 228; *Times* 7/2/12
183. Bonham Carter 228; *Times* 9/2/12; Soames 104
184. Bonham Carter 228; Bromage 21-22
185. Bonham Carter 230; *Irrepressible* 70; WSC II 484
186. WSC II 484; Cowles *Churchill* 168; WSC II 456; Bromage 31-32, 30
187. *Great Contemporaries* 347; Bromage 37, 31
188. WSC II 454; Bromage 35; Pelling 158; *Times* 9/10/13; Bonham Carter 236
189. WSC II 463-464
190. Morris *Trumpets* 225; Bromage 39, 36, 31; Bonham Carter 230
191. Cowles *Churchill* 169
192. Morris *Trumpets* 227
193. Bromage 43
194. Bonham Carter 237; *Times* 15/3/14; Bromage 42; WSC II 474

195. CV II/3 1414
196. Bromage 47
197. Cowles *Churchill* 170; Bonham Carter 239; Rhodes James *Failure* 54
198. *Hansard* 28/4/14; *Crisis* I 195
199. *Hansard* 28/4/14; Bonham Carter 243; CV II/3 1418
200. Bromage 38; WSC II 488
201. *Crisis* I 205
202. *Crisis* I 201, 210; CV II/3 1421; WSC III 3
203. CV II/3 1987-1988
204. WSC III 4; CV II/3 1987; Tuchman *August* 71; *Crisis* I 209
205. WSC III 6
206. WSC III 8; Soames 137; CV II/3 1988
207. Tuchman *August* 93; *Crisis* I 225; *Great Contemporaries* 148; *Crisis* I 226
208. WSC III 5; CV II/3 1989
209. Tuchman *August* 96; H.H. Asquith *Letters* 138; WSC III 22; CV II/3 1991, 1995-1996
210. *Crisis* I 236, 238
211. CV II/3 1993-1994
212. *Crisis* I 524; CV II/3 1992; Tuchman *August* 140; *Crisis* I 37
213. Tuchman *August* 72, 95, 90; H.H. Asquith *Memories* II 10
214. Martin II 365; Rhodes James *Failure* 65-66; H.H. Asquith *Memories* II 11; Tuchman *August* 96
215. Tuchman *August* 96, 92; WSC II 24, 23
216. Beaverbrook *War* I 22, 23
217. Kenneth Young 34; *Crisis* I 231; CV II/3 1997-1998
218. Kenneth Young 34; H.H. Asquith *Letters* 146
219. Tuchman *August* 143; *Crisis* I 239; Tuchman *August* 94, 118; *Crisis* I 235; Edel 200, 202; Tuchman *August* 122
220. Soames 140; *Crisis* I 239; H.H. Asquith *Letters* 150-151
221. Tuchman *August* 323; CV II/3 1999
222. Margot Asquith *Autobiography* II 196

Part Four: Cataract, 1914–1918

1. WSC III 44; Soames 145; CV III/1 28
2. WSC III 83
3. H.H. Asquith *Letters* 334; Pelling 188
4. *Crisis* I 306, 305; WSC III 50, 43; Rhodes James *Failure* 45; Martin II 370
5. WSC III 35; *Crisis* I 252; *Crisis* II 391
6. CV III/1 28, 31; Soames 144
7. CV III/1 28; Soames 143
8. WSC III 59, 84; *Crisis* I 432
9. *Morning Post* 10/21/14; WSC III 86; Bonham Carter 280; *Crisis* I 432
10. Stevenson 10; CV III/1 250, 128
11. CV III/1 70, 66; Bonham Carter 280; CV III/1 173; H.H. Asquith *Letters* 287, 290
12. CV III/1 220, 221, 225-226
13. CV III/1 203; Bonham Carter 280; CV III/1 118-119; *Crisis* I 436-437; Bonham Carter 281
14. WSC III 187; Beaverbrook *War* I 105; Rhodes James *Failure* 68; CV III/1 221, 224-225; H.H. Asquith *Letters* 305; CV III/1 232
15. WSC III 153; CV III/1 243; WSC III 154
16. *Crisis* I 441; *Great Contemporaries* 339; WSC III 262
17. *Crisis* I 289; WSC III 35
18. Tuchman *August* 387, 388; *Times* 30/8/14
19. Tuchman *August* 33, 34
20. Tuchman *August* 190
21. Tuchman *August* 235, 243
22. Tuchman *August* 224, 319
23. Tuchman *August* 52; CV III/1 97
24. H.H. Asquith *Letters* 227-228; WSC III 73-74; CV III/1 135; *Irrepressible* 75
25. *Crisis* I 303; Soames 141; CV III/1 141
26. CV III/1 96, 97; WSC III 101
27. WSC III 101; H.H. Asquith *Letters* 258, 259
28. *Crisis* I 367; CV III/1 157; H.H. Asquith *Letters* 260
29. Rhodes James *Failure* 71; CV III/1 161; WSC III 109, 108

30. WSC III 48; H.H. Asquith *Letters* 262; Bonham Carter 276-277
31. CV III/1 163
32. CV III/1 167-168; H.H. Asquith *Letters* 262, 263
33. CV III/1 167, 170; WSC III 115
34. CV III/1 172, 173
35. CV III/1 173; WSC III 119; H.H. Asquith *Letters* 275
36. CV III/1 177, 173, 178
37. Bonham Carter 277; H.H. Asquith *Letters* 268
38. WSC III 110; *Morning Post* 13/10/14; CV III/1 195; *Daily Mail* 14/10/14
39. CV III/1 174, 175; WSC III 133-134, 132; CV III/1 191; Stevenson 6; WSC III 329, 330
40. WSC III 129; H.H. Asquith *Letters* 271, 296; Bonham Carter 278-279; WSC III 125
41. Rhodes James *Failure* 71-72; CV III/1 26
42. H.H. Asquith *Letters* 266-267
43. Manchester 'Great War' 111
44. Blunden *Mind's Eye* 38
45. CV III/1 272-273, 274
46. H.H. Asquith *Letters* 346; CV IH/1 350, 351; *Crisis* II 2; CV III/2 1306; *Crisis* II 79
47. CV III/1 132, 377-378
48. WSC III 536
49. WSC III 536, 537; *Churchill Years* 62
50. Higgins 144
51. Margot Asquith *Autobiography* II 203; CV III/1 75, 76; WSC III 205; CV III/1 95
52. CV III/1 236
53. CV III/1 278, 279; Higgins 75; CV III/1 297
54. Moorehead *Gallipoli* 37; WSC III 220n; CV III/1 326, 367; H.H. Asquith *Letters* 345; CV III/1 344; WSC III 236-237; H.H. Asquith *Letters* 357-358
55. WSC III 232; CV III/1 391
56. CV III/1 393
57. Higgins 1
58. Moorehead *Gallipoli* 73
59. WSC III 219; Bonham Carter 296
60. WSC III 220; CV III/1 367
61. CV III/1 380; WSC III 248, 250; CV III/1 381, 406
62. CV III/1 406-407; Moorehead *Gallipoli* 40; CV III/1 409, 410; WSC III 252; CV III/1 411
63. Higgins 117; *Crisis* I 438; Bonham Carter 290
64. WSC III 313; Higgins 65
65. Cowles *Churchill* 214; Moorehead *Churchill Trial* 48; CV III/1 410; Higgins 174-175
66. Higgins 224
67. Higgins 117; Wolff 190
68. CV III/1 411, 410
69. CV III/1 414, 429-430; H.H. Asquith *Letters* 387
70. CV III/1 436, 453, 454
71. CV III/1 460
72. CV III/1 463; *Crisis* II 164; CV III/1 464
73. H.H. Asquith *Letters* 405; WSC III 273, 274; CV III/1 469
74. Rhodes James *Failure* 85; Higgins 136; Liddell Hart *Fog of War* 288
75. Higgins 49; Rowse in Eade 495
76. H.H. Asquith *Letters* 429; CV III/1 513; WSC III 287
77. CV III/1 516
78. CV III/1 517-518, 525; H.H. Asquith *Letters* 436
79. CV III/1 557, 569, 558
80. CV III/1 573-574, 580
81. CV III/1 554-555
82. WSC III 305-306
83. *Times* 26/4/15
84. Moorehead *Gallipoli* 56
85. CV III/1 584; H.H. Asquith *Letters* 456; Bonham Carter 302
86. CV III/1 605-606, 680, 690, 617-618
87. CV III/1 634
88. *Crisis* I 274; CV III/1 645
89. Moorehead *Gallipoli* 57
90. Moorehead *Gallipoli* 58
91. CV III/1 677-678, 687-688
92. WSC III 337; CV III/1 706
93. Moorehead *Gallipoli* 69
94. Moorehead *Churchill Trial* 45; Moorehead *Gallipoli* 74; *World's Work* 12/1929
95. CV III/1 636, 730; WSC III 357, 358; CV III/1 712
96. Moorehead *Gallipoli* 79; CV III/1 698, 677

738

97. Rhodes James *Failure* 87
98. CV III/1 559
99. CV III/1 560, 664; Moorehead *Gallipoli* 80, 83
100. H.H. Asquith *Letters* 257; CV III/1 629
101. WSC III 358; Moorehead *Gallipoli* 86; WSC III 363; CV III/1 711, 718-719
102. Moorehead *Gallipoli* 86, 87, 88
103. CV III/1 723-724
104. Moorehead *Gallipoli* 91; WSC III 364-365; Rhodes James *Failure* 84
105. CV III/1 732, 729; *Morning Post* 25/3/15; Higgins 171
106. CV III/1 752, 753
107. CV III/1 753; WSC III 411
108. Moorehead *Gallipoli* 143
109. Moorehead *Gallipoli* 257
110. CV III/2 852, 855; Moorehead *Gallipoli* 165
111. CV III/1 770; WSC III 411-412; Bonham Carter 310; WSC III 419
112. Moorehead *Gallipoli* 166
113. *Crisis* II 364; Moorehead *Gallipoli* 168; *Crisis* II 361; CV III/2 884-885
114. WSC III 345; CV III/2 885
115. *Crisis* II 373-374; Bacon *Fisher* II 256; CV III/2 888; Moorehead *Gallipoli* 170; WSC III 439
116. *Crisis* II 377; CV III/2 892; WSC III 442
117. CV III/2 906, 907, 911
118. WSC III 430; CV III/2 880; *Times* 14/5/15; Moorehead *Gallipoli* 157; WSC III 555
119. Rhodes James *Failure* 88; *Times* 18/5/15; WSC III 424, 425; Stevenson 50
120. H.H. Asquith *Letters* 585, 586, 596; WSC III 447
121. *Crisis* II 385; WSC III 488-489
122. WSC III 414; *Crisis* II 381; CV III/2 940; WSC III 448; CV III/2 898
123. WSC III 445; CV III/2 908
124. Stevenson 52, 74; Cowles *Churchill* 201; WSC III 476; Moorehead *Gallipoli* 171
125. CV III/2 914, 915, 920, 922, 923-924
126. CV III/2 925, 926, 921
127. CV III/2 932; Kenneth Young 37; CV III/2 924, 926, 927, 932; WSC III 466
128. Bonham Carter 330; Moorehead *Gallipoli* 118
129. CV III/2 894; Dundee *Advertiser* 23/5/15; WSC III 399; *Times* 22/5/15; Stevenson 52, 53; H.H. Asquith *Letters* 546, 508
130. Pelling 204-205; WSC III 457; Rhodes James *Failure* 91; *Amid These Storms* 307; WSC III 473
131. CV III/2 948, 955; Moorehead *Gallipoli* 172; Martin II 372
132. CV III/2 1017; WSC III 537; CV III/2 1559
133. CV III/2 1180, 1042; *Irrepressible* 77; *Amid These Storms* 307
134. *Amid These Storms* 307-308
135. *Amid These Storms* 308, 313-314
136. Marsh 248-249; *Amid These Storms* 297
137. *Wit* 50; Rothenstein in Marchant 150; Holliday and Pernes 18
138. J.G.S. Churchill 34
139. J.G.S. Churchill 32
140. CV III/2 982
141. Moorehead *Gallipoli* 236
142. Kenneth Young 36; Longford *Churchill* 61; *Crisis* II 6
143. CV III/2 1081, 1084, 1098
144. CV III/2 1100, 1101, 1103
145. *Crisis* II 516; Moorehead *Gallipoli* 318-319
146. Higgins 228; Moorehead *Gallipoli* 324, 326
147. CV III/2 1183; Pelling 208; WSC III 563
148. *Manchester Guardian* 13/11/15
149. *Hansard* 15/11/15; Bonham Carter 351; CV III/2 1272
150. Beaverbrook *Power* 118
151. Bonham Carter 352, 353
152. Beaverbrook *War* II 74; CV III/2 1276; WSC III 572; CV III/2 1277
153. *Amid These Storms* 101, 102
154. *Amid These Storms* 101
155. *Amid These Storms* 101, 103; Soames 196
156. *Amid These Storms* 103; CV III/2 1324; Soames 186
157. CV III/2 1314, 1318
158. Soames 173; CV III/2 1283, 1284

159. CV III/2 1370; *Amid These Storms* 103, 104
160. CV III/2 1320; *Amid These Storms* 105; CV III/2 1315; *Irrepressible* 76; CV III/2 1300, 1278
161. CV III/2 1289; Bonham Carter 364; *Amid These Storms* 105; CV III/2 1425, 1290; Bonham Carter 365
162. WSC III 625; CV III/2 1331
163. CV IV/1 373; WSC IV 140
164. Sassoon *Journey* 116-119
165. *Amid These Storms* 106, 108, 109, 110
166. CV III/2 1293, 1423, 1432, 1433, 1309-1310; WSC IV 135; CV III/2 1291, 1311
167. Soames 182; WSC III 595; Soames 211, 193, 173, 207, 197
168. CV III/2 1331
169. WSC III 583; Soames 184-185
170. CV III/2 1311, 1302-1303
171. CV III/2 1322; Soames 189
172. Soames 192, 193; CV III/2 1325
173. H.H. Asquith *Memories* 136; CV III/2 1333; *Hansard* 16/12/15
174. Beaverbrook *War* II 75, 76; WSC III 697; Soames 190; WSC III 611; CV III/2 1332; Soames 193-194
175. WSC III 615; CV III/2 1333; Soames 200; CV III/2 1352; WSC III 666; Soames 219, 220
176. Soames 192; Wolff 32, 35
177. Wolff 35, 36; WSC IV 51; *Great Contemporaries* 227
178. WSC III 614; CV III/2 1334, 1335, 1336
179. Attlee in Stansky 199; 'Four Crises in the Great War' 30/7/16
180. CV III/2 1351
181. WSC III 629, 630; CV III/2 1361; WSC III 632
182. CV III/2 1365, 1377; WSC III 639
183. CV III/2 1399; Cowles *Churchill* 211
184. CV III/2 1405, 1396, 1398
185. CV III/2 1399; Cowles *Churchill* 211; WSC III 657
186. CV III/2 1412; WSC III 661; CV III/2 1410
187. Pelling 217; CV III/2 1482; WSC III 657, 658, 672
188. CV III/2 1405; WSC III 604; Soames 218

189. WSC III 622, 698; Soames 209, 200, 199, 202; CV III/2 1352, 1363, 1369-1370; WSC III 683
190. Soames 238; WSC III 758
191. *Hansard* 7/3/16
192. Bonham Carter 369; WSC III 725; CV III/2 1443
193. Bonham Carter 371
194. *Hansard* 8/3/16
195. *Hansard* 8/3/16; CV III/2 1443, 1444
196. Bonham Carter 371; CV III/2 1444, 1450
197. CV III/2 1460, 1461
198. Soames 234, 236, 238
199. Pelling 216; WSC III 759; CV III/2 1498
200. WSC III 760; CV III/2 1501, 1498
201. Kenneth Young 41
202. CV III/2 1545
203. *Hansard* 23/5/16, 24/7/16
204. *Hansard* 23/5/16; WSC IV 14; Pelling 222; WSC III 774
205. CV III/2 1538
206. CV III/2 1534
207. *Daily Mail* 13/10/16; WSC III 811; *Spectator* 11/3/16
208. Pelling 216; WSC III 825; Bonham Carter 368-369; Boothby *Rebel* 50
209. Cowles *Churchill* 214; CV IV/1 5; CV III/2 1530, 1531
210. CV IV/1 37-38
211. WSC III 816
212. Soames 204
213. WSC III 685; CV III/2 1372; WSC III 762
214. WSC III 780
215. CV III/2 1518, 1520, 1529, 1530
216. WSC III 789, 790
217. CV III/2 1533, 1570; CV IV/1 34
218. Boothby *Rebel* 19; WSC III 822
219. CV III/2 1584; Kenneth Young 44-45
220. CV IV/1 36; WSC III 681; Wolff 28
221. Wolff 25, 271, 157, 48
222. *New Republic* 14/6/17; WSC IV 9; *Hansard* 20/3/17
223. Cowles *Churchill* 221; WSC IV 26; Stevenson 157
224. *Hansard* 17/4/17
225. Wolff 205; WSC IV 17; *Crisis* III 262
226. *Crisis* IV 2; CV IV/1 102, 103; Pell-

ing 229; *Morning Post* 19/7/17;
WSC IV 29; CV IV/1 118
227. Pelling 230; Soames 220; WSC IV
35
228. WSC IV 32
229. *Crisis* IV 7, 9
230. WSC IV 61; CV IV/1 300, 301;
Times 11/7/18; WSC IV 127-128
231. WSC IV 38; *Crisis* IV 199; WSC IV
72; CV III/2 1354
232. WSC IV 17; Wolff 72
233. Wolff x
234. WSC IV 33; CV IV/1 108; WSC IV
47
235. WSC IV 47; Wolff 155-157; *Times*
18/8/17
236. Wolff 157, 263; *Crisis* IV 43, 61
237. CV IV/1 390-391
238. Wolff 24, 204, 162
239. Wolff 240, 241
240. Manchester 'Great War' 114; WSC
IV 48
241. *Crisis* IV 128
242. *Crisis* IV 129, 130, 131
243. *Crisis* IV 144; WSC IV 81; CV IV/1
278, 279
244. *Amid These Storms* 165; WSC IV 85;
CV IV/1 282; *Amid These Storms*
166, 167
245. *Amid These Storms* 168; CV IV/1
282; WSC IV 89; *Amid These Storms*
177; CV IV/1 288
246. *Amid These Storms* 170, 171
247. WSC IV 95; *Amid These Storms* 173
248. *Amid These Storms* 173, 174, 175
249. *Amid These Storms* 176

250. *Amid These Storms* 177; CV IV/1
291, 288, 289, 294
251. CV IV/1 300
252. WSC IV 106
253. WSC IV 107, 108
254. *Hansard* 25/4/18
255. Toland 156; Falls 345
256. CV IV/1 368
257. Manchester *Krupp* 300
258. CV IV/1 324
259. Falls 345; Manchester 'Great War'
121
260. WSC IV 122; CV IV/1 343
261. Martin II 364; WSC IV 115
262. WSC IV 115; Martin II 390, 389,
385; WM / Lady Diana Cooper 20/
10/80
263. CV IV/1 324, 249, 323
264. Toland 374
265. CV IV/1 393, 395
266. CV IV/1 387
267. WSC IV 154
268. WSC IV 48
269. CV IV/1 108, 309, 315, 302, 310
270. WSC III 23; WSC IV 123
271. WSC IV 149-150, 139
272. *Churchill Years* 64; CV IV/1 368
273. CV IV/1 370
274. Deutscher 476; *Crisis* IV 231-232;
A.J.P. Taylor *First World War* 152;
Wolff 271
275. CV IV/1 251, 394
276. Manchester 'Great War' 123, 127
277. WSC IV 158; *Crisis* IV 273; Moir
215; WSC IV 166
278. Shirer 48

Part Five: Oxbow, 1918–1932

1. *Crisis* IV 275; *NYT* 17/11/18
2. Morris *Trumpets* 206
3. Kohn 308
4. Rhodes James *Failure* 109; Morris
Trumpets 205
5. Girouard *Camelot* 2
6. Girouard *Camelot* 284-285; Osborn
viii-ix
7. Shirer 51n-52n
8. Cowles *Churchill* 229; Rhodes James
Failure 106
9. *Wit* 24; Morris *Trumpets* 211, 209n
10. Morris *Trumpets* 206
11. Gandhi 212; Morris *Trumpets* 212

12. Moorehead *Gallipoli* 155
13. Morris *Trumpets* 213
14. Morris *Trumpets* 212, 215; CV IV/3
2029
15. Morris *Trumpets* 304
16. Morris *Trumpets* 300-301
17. Morris *Trumpets* 302
18. WSC IV 915
19. WSC IV 171; *RC* vii
20. CV IV /3 1736; *Daily Telegraph* 5/11/
20
21. Moran 443; Soames 247; WSC IV
913-914
22. CV IV/1 422-423

23. Dundee *Advertiser* 29/12/18; CV IV /1 448
24. *Crisis* V 63
25. WSC IV 182; CV IV/1 451, 479
26. CV IV/1 501, 502; WSC IV 193
27. WSC IV 196; CV IV/2 1069; Baruch in Marchant 164
28. Deutscher 388
29. Deutscher 421
30. *Evening News* 28/7/20; *Times* 27/11/ 18; WSC IV 228
31. WSC IV 229; Riddell *Intimate* 21; WSC IV 235; *Daily Express* 3/1/19
32. Deutscher 421
33. Rhodes James *Failure* 117-118; CV IV/1 471; WSC IV 356
34. Lloyd George *Treaties* 325; *Irrepressible* 78, 80, 79
35. Rhodes James *Failure* 122; WSC IV 365, 244; *Times* 12/4/19; WSC IV 278
36. Hankey *Control* 70; CV IV/1 525; WSC IV 240; Rhodes James *Failure* 125; WSC IV 324-325; Beaverbrook *Power* 406
37. WSC IV 349; *Daily Express* 3/1/19; 'The Red Fever'; Rhodes James *Failure* 134; WSC IV 305; Rhodes James *Failure* 136; WSC IV 433-434
38. WSC IV 290; *Weekly Review* 22/6/ 19; WSC IV 365-366; Deutscher 457
39. *Hansard* 29/5/19
40. CV IV/2 729; CV IV/1 660
41. WSC IV 325; Deutscher 442
42. WSC IV 352; CV IV/2 1059, 987; WSC IV 362
43. WSC IV 329
44. Deutscher 460; CV IV/2 1190
45. CV IV/2 1190n, 1035
46. CV IV/2 1048, 1049
47. *Hansard* 10/2/20; CV IV/2 1111, 1238
48. CV IV/2 1246; WSC IV 440
49. WSC IV 441; *Sunday Express* 5/12/ 20, 12/12/20
50. Stevenson 196-197
51. Liddell Hart 'Churchill in War'; Rhodes James *Failure* 139; CV IV/2 1123
52. Liddell Hart 'Churchill in War'
53. *Hansard* 8/7/20

54. CV IV/2 1140, 1141; *Hansard* 8/7/20
55. *Hansard* 8/7/20
56. *Hansard* 8/7/20
57. WSC IV 411; *Times* 9/7/20
58. CV IV/2 1319, 1260-1261, 1262, 1354-1355
59. Morris *Trumpets* 257-258
60. Pelling 261-262
61. WSC IV 484; 'Zionism vs. Bolshevism'; CV IV/2 1120
62. WSC IV 615; Morris *Trumpets* 258
63. Sarah Churchill 35
64. Soames 259; CV IV/2 1368, 1380, 1384
65. WSC IV 540, 541, 543; *Irrepressible* 44
66. WSC IV 544
67. *Times* 4/3/21; Morris *Trumpets* 260, 259; WSC IV 545; *Irrepressible* 132; *Great Contemporaries* 163
68. WSC IV 557; W.H. Thompson 33; *Egyptian Gazette* 24/3/21
69. WSC IV 552, 558, 563
70. WSC IV 562, 895, 565
71. *Times* 8/6/21, 31/3/21
72. CV IV/2 1423
73. WSC IV 583
74. CV IV/3 1484; WSC IV 597; 'Zionism vs. Bolshevism'
75. WSC IV 637, 594, 596, 597, 598
76. CV IV/3 1505; WSC IV 599; *Hansard* 4/7/22; WSC IV 628
77. Rhodes James *Failure* 149
78. *Hansard* 14/6/21
79. CV IV/2 1054-1055, 1260, 1268, 1272
80. *Hansard* 22/12/20; CV IV/2 1264
81. WSC IV 611; Stevenson 230; *Hansard* 21/7/20
82. CV IV/3 1980; WSC IV 820
83. CV IV/3 2043
84. CV IV/3 2040, 1241, 2043, 1980; *Aftermath* 449
85. CV IV/3 1995, 2057; WSC IV 841
86. WSC IV 835
87. Cowles *Churchill* 239; *Daily Mail* 18/ 9/21; *Aftermath* 464-465; WSC IV 862
88. WSC IV 467
89. *Irrepressible* 61
90. *NYT* 12/12/18; Coote in Marchant 40; Moorehead *Churchill Trial* 60-61; *Aftermath* 335-336

91. *Aftermath* 294
92. Bromage 62; WSC IV 449; CV IV/2 1062, 1248; WSC IV 453
93. CV IV/2 1232; *Aftermath* 303; 'The Murder Campaign in Ireland'; Soames 270
94. WSC IV 452, 453; CV IV/2 1090; Hansard 23/2/20; *Aftermath* 287
95. WSC IV 451, 463-464; Rhodes James *Failure* 143
96. Rhodes James *Failure* 141, 142; Pelling 268
97. Rhodes James *Failure* 144; CV IV/2 1195, 1214; WSC IV 466; Rhodes James *Failure* 142; *Hansard* 23/2/20; CV IV/2 1274, 1275
98. Rhodes James *Failure* 142; *Aftermath* 301-302; WSC IV 666
99. Bromage 63; WSC IV 667, 668
100. Dundee *Advertiser* 24/9/21; WSC IV 669
101. Bromage 66; *Crisis* V 305
102. *Hansard* 15/12/21; Bromage 69; *Hansard* 16/2/22; *Gathering Storm* 276; WSC IV 677
103. Bromage 71; *Hansard* 15/12/21
104. *Aftermath* 324-325; *Hansard* 2/3/22; *Aftermath* 329; WSC IV 703
105. WSC IV 707; Bromage 75-76; WSC IV 688, 711; *Aftermath* 355, 338; WSC IV 708; *Hansard* 16/2/22; *Aftermath* 328
106. *Aftermath* 340, 349, 348
107. Bromage 83; *Hansard* 31/5/22
108. O'Connor 251; *NYT* 2/6/22; CV IV/3 1768
109. Macardle 966; *Aftermath* 355; CV IV/3 1849-1850
110. *Aftermath* 342; CV IV/3 1881; *Aftermath* 355
111. *NYT* 22/6/22, 18/6/22; *Aftermath* 359-360
112. *Crisis* IV 111; Soames 312; WSC IV 739
113. *Hansard* 26/6/22; *NYT* 7/7/22, 29/6/22; *Aftermath* 364
114. Bromage 91; Macardle 757; *Aftermath* 367
115. WSC IV 745; *Aftermath* 369, 370
116. *Times* 13/11/22; Bromage 96-97; *Aftermath* 370
117. *Great Contemporaries* 322
118. WSC IV 861; *Times* 7/10/22

119. *Nation* 10-11/1919; Rhodes James *Failure* 154, 155
120. WSC IV 864; G.M. Young *Baldwin* 40
121. WSC IV 773; Kenneth Young 60
122. WSC IV 907, 581; Stevenson 210; Boothby *Rebel* 52; CV IV/2 1055, 1054
123. *Amid These Storms* 213; Attlee in Marchant 74; WSC IV 901; CV IV/3 1766; *Irrepressible* 243, 85
124. CV IV/1 94; WSC IV 883; *Wit* 68; WSC IV 774
125. Shinwell in Eade 122, 121; *Daily Herald* 7/6/19, 1/8/19
126. *Times* 7/11/22
127. *Times* 28/10/22; WSC IV 874
128. CV IV/3 2097, 2116-2117
129. WSC IV 878; Dundee *Courier* 7/11/22; Soames 272, 273; WSC IV 879, 878, 880
130. Dundee *Courier* 12/11/22; *Amid These Storms* 212; Dundee *Courier* 14/11/22; WSC IV 885
131. WSC IV 886; Dundee *Courier* 15/11/22
132. WSC IV 887; *Amid These Storms* 213; CV IV/3 2128, 2125, 2126; WSC IV 892, 888; *Daily Telegraph* 17/11/22
133. CV V/1 3, 47; *Irrepressible* 93
134. 'The Future of Mr Lloyd George'; CV V/1 29, 41
135. Rhodes James *Failure* 164; *Times* 15/11/20; WSC V 15
136. WSC V 18; Kenneth Young 67
137. WSC V 19, 19n; *Review of Reviews* 1/1924; Rhodes James *Failure* 98
138. WSC V 20; Rhodes James *Failure* 166; Cowles *Churchill* 251
139. WSC V 20; CV V/1 92-93, 96
140. CV V/1 112, 113; Soames 274; CV V/1 83; Cowles *Churchill* 253; CV V/1 116; WSC V 35, 34
141. *Amid These Storms* 214-215; Rhodes James *Memoirs* 194-195; WSC V 35; Rhodes James *Failure* 169
142. Rhodes James *Failure* 169-170; *Times* 19/3/24
143. WSC V 36, 37; Pelling 291
144. *Times* 21/3/24; Shinwell in Eade 121
145. Telford Taylor 551; Beaverbrook

Press 108
146. CV V/1 132, 133, 40; *Wit* 70
147. WSC IV 210; CV IV/3 1710; CV IV/2 1353; *Gathering Storm* 41
148. WSC IV 387; Soames 255
149. Soames 263; CV IV/3 1618; Soames 264; CV IV/3 1623, 1957
150. Martin II 394
151. *London Evening News* 18/6/21; Martin II 398, 399, 401; CV IV/3 1532; WSC IV 604; CV IV/3 1536
152. Soames 253; CV IV/3 1934
153. WSC IV 763; Soames 266; CV IV/3 1713
154. Soames 284; WSC IV 613; CV IV/3 1712, 1933
155. CV IV/3 1952, 1956; WSC III 791; CV IV/3 1958
156. CV IV/3 1713, 1957; Soames 306, 305
157. Soames 257-258
158. Soames 257; CV V/1 55
159. CV III/2 1098; WSC IV 757, 758-759
160. WSC IV 752
161. WSC V 4
162. Cowles *Churchill* 246; *Times* 10/4/23
163. CV V/1 86; *Nation* 3/9/29; Muggeridge in Eade 347
164. *Crisis* III 170, 197
165. Soames 257; Fedden 14; Sarah Churchill 22; WSC IV 793, 794
166. WSC IV 11; Soames 287-288; CV V/1 58
167. CV V/1 56; Sarah Churchill 29-30; Soames 292; CV V/1 144, 145
168. Sarah Churchill 25; CV V/1 655, 746, 179, 178; W.H. Thompson 123
169. Sarah Churchill 25, 24; W.H. Thompson 88; Fedden 21; CV V/1 1340
170. CV V/1 1340, 1333, 1347-1348; Pelling 316; CV V/1 1348n
171. CV V/1 179; *Irrepressible* 261, 262; Sarah Churchill 28
172. Cowles *Churchill* 274; Sarah Churchill 27
173. Soames 347; WSC V 107; WM / Lady Soames 9/10/80; CV V/1 1055
174. Soames 296, 297
175. Soames 303; WM / Lady Soames 9/10/80
176. Rhodes James *Failure* 336; WM / Lady Soames 27/10/80; Longford *Churchill* 79; CV V/2 97; Boothby *Rebel* 51
177. Rhodes James *Failure* 337-338; WM / Lady Soames 27/10/80; WSC V 302
178. Soames 306; Fedden 9
179. CV V/1 215
180. Pelling 292; CV V/1 152; WSC V 53; *Sunday Times* 31/10/24; CV V/1 226, 232, 233
181. WSC V 59, 60
182. WSC V 60; Kenneth Young 71, 72, 73
183. Rhodes James *Failure* 170; WSC V 60; *Times* 9/12/24; *Manchester Guardian* 7/10/24
184. WSC V 62; Boothby *Rebel* 46
185. *Wit* 69; *Irrepressible* 98; CV V/1 264, 445, 448-449; *Current Opinion* 2/1925
186. CV V/1 337, 1342
187. W.H. Thompson 70; *Irrepressible* 99; W.H. Thompson 71
188. *Hansard* 28/4/25
189. Soames 277; James in Eade 149
190. James in Eade 148; WSC V 78; CV V/1 356, 376
191. Rhodes James *Failure* 184
192. Rhodes James *Failure* 185; CV V/1 306, 307
193. *Times* 29/4/25; *Hansard* 28/4/25; Kenneth Young 74; Boothby *Rebel* 39
194. WSC V 100
195. *Hansard* 4/5/25, 13/2/46
196. Rhodes James *Failure* 176; WSC V 97
197. Cowles *Churchill* 260; *Nation* 21/2/25
198. *Sunday Express* 12/7/25; Keynes 23
199. *Times* 13/7/25
200. *Hansard* 5/5/26, 22/4/26; WSC V 147-148, 146
201. Cowles *Churchill* 264; *Hansard* 5/5/26; Cowles *Churchill* 265
202. *Hansard* 13/2/46; *Great Contemporaries* 375; WSC V 300n
203. *Hansard* 5/5/26
204. *Hansard* 3/5/26; WSC V 164, 165;

Churchill Years 79
205. Rhodes James *Failure* 191, 188
206. Holt in Eade 187, 189
207. WSC V 158; Liddell Hart *Memoirs* II 144; Holt in Eade 191; Pelling 314
208. Rhodes James *Failure* 189, 190
209. *Hansard* 3/5/26; CV V/1 713; Rhodes James *Failure* 192; WSC V 168; Holt in Eade 189
210. Webb *Diaries* 166; CV V/1 718; Kenneth Young 71, 84
211. Kenneth Young 84; CV V/1 721; WSC V 172
212. Pelling 315; *New Statesman* 22/5/26; CV V/1 727; *Times* 8/6/26
213. WSC V 172; CV V/1 1014; *Hansard* 7/7/26; CV V/1 740
214. CV V/1 717; Boothby *Rebel* 44
215. CV V/1 728, 730, 733
216. WSC V 212, 189; CV V/1 765; *Evening Standard* 19/10/26
217. CV V/1 807; WSC V 193; CV V/1 820, 823, 824
218. WSC V 202; CV V/1 866
219. CV V/1 760; WSC V 208, 219; CV V/1 851, 852; Rhodes James *Failure* 193
220. WM / Harold Macmillan 4/11/80; WM / Lord Boothby 16/10/80
221. CV V/1 1307; *Great Contemporaries* 375
222. CV V/1 1328, 1006
223. *Wit* 23, 13; *Irrepressible* 104, 6; McGowan 138
224. CV V/1 985, 1272, 1464; *Hansard* 11/4/27; WSC V 235; *Times of India* 11/4/27
225. *Hansard* 29/4/25; WSC V 292; CV V/1 1316, 1326
226. Rhodes James *Failure* 207, 206, 205; CV V/1 1443-1444
227. CV V/1 1050
228. *Hansard* 11/4/27; CV V/1 984
229. WSC V 324; Macmillan 176; Rhodes James *Failure* 196
230. CV V/1 878, 908, 907
231. CV V/1 908; *Times* 21/1/27
232. *New Leader* 28/1/27; WSC V 226
233. CV V/1 909
234. CV V/1 1448
235. CV V/2 87
236. CV V/1 1052
237. WSC V 265
238. Kenneth Young 100; CV V/1 1052, 1236
239. CV V/1 1332; Kenneth Young 104; CV V/1 1375; Kenneth Young 105
240. CV V/1 1412; Rhodes James *Failure* 205; CV V/1 1444; Gilbert *Churchill Wilderness* 18, 19; WSC V 317; CV V/2 61
241. WSC V 327, 328; Rhodes James *Failure* 201; WSC V 313, 325; *Daily Express* 1/5/29
242. WSC V 328
243. CV V/1 1474; Kenneth Young 118n
244. CV V/2 85-86; WSC V 337
245. CV V/2 40
246. CV V/2 61, 40; WSC V 340; CV V/2 42
247. WSC V 345; CV V/2 82
248. CV V/2 96-97; Swanberg 494
249. CV V/2 97; WSC V 348; Sarah Churchill 35
250. WSC V 349, 350
251. WSC V 350; *Gathering Storm* 34; 'The American Mind and Ours' *Irrepressible* 106; CV V/2 95; WSC V 353
252. *Irrepressible* 106; CV V/2 95; WSC V 353
253. CV V/2 98; Smith and Cawkwell 173, 318-438 passim
254. Morris *Trumpets* 334; Boothby *Rebel* 37; Morris *Trumpets* 311
255. Morris *Trumpets* 278; Telford Taylor 197-199; Morris *Trumpets* 335
256. Morris *Trumpets* 305
257. Morris *Trumpets* 307, 364, 337n
258. Morris *Trumpets* 357
259. Morris *Trumpets* 335, 337
260. Morris *Trumpets* 337
261. Boothby *Rebel* 54; Gandhi 278-279
262. *Wit* 27
263. Day 65
264. Morris *Trumpets* 283-285
265. Rhodes James *Failure* 216
266. Rhodes James *Failure* 215; CV V/2 107, 108; WSC V 367
267. Morris *Trumpets* 298; Rhodes James *Failure* 221, 222
268. Rhodes James *Failure* 206, 222
269. Moran 692
270. CV V/1 1042, 1054; Mayo 26, 32; WSC V 243n; *Spectator* 16/7/27; *Survey* 1/8/27; *New Statesman* 16/7/

27; *Catholic World* 27/10/27; *New York Herald Tribune* 12/6/27; *NYT* 5/6/27

271. CV V/2 126; WSC V 401-402; Mayer in Stansky 183

272. WSC V 354-355; CV V/2 111

273. *Daily Mail* 16/11/29

274. Morris *Trumpets* 290

275. WSC V 368; Boothby *Rebel* 53; *Wit* 29; WSC V 370

276. Soames 331; CV V/2 186

277. CV V/2 226, 193; WSC V 338; Rhodes James *Failure* 218

278. CV V/2 222; WSC V 376, 377

279. WSC V 377; *Times* 13/12/30; WSC V 358; CV V/2 287; WSC V 359; CV V/2 258; Rhodes James *Failure* 219

280. WSC V 373, 375n2, 367; CV V/2 290, 293; Kenneth Young 116

281. Rowse in Eade 499

282. CV V/2 243; *Gathering Storm* 33; CV V/2 250

283. *Hansard* 26/1/31

284. CV V/2 252, 250-251

285. *India* 94; Moorehead *Churchill Trial* 74

286. CV V/2 280, 279; *Hansard* 12/3/31; CV V/2 265

287. CV V/2 291; WSC V 400, 398; *Hansard* 13/5/31; *Daily Mail* 7/9/31

288. Boothby *Rebel* 83; WSC V 377; Boothby *Rebel* 54

289. WSC V 404-405; *Hansard* 12/3/31

290. Morris *Trumpets* 297; *NYT* 14/12/31

291. *Hansard* 8/9/31; Gilbert *Churchill Wilderness* 39; Kenneth Young 118

292. Eden in Eade 107; Attlee in Marchant 74-75; Shinwell in Eade 124; W.H. Thompson 71

293. Gardner 2, 1

294. *Daily Telegraph* 15/11/40; WM / Lord Butler 5/11/80

295. Moorehead *Churchill Trial* 71; Longford *Churchill* 84; Eden in Eade 106, 107; Rhodes James *Failure* 205; *Irrepressible* 6, 117

296. Birkenhead *Professor* 135; CV V/2 399

297. CV V/2 18, 26-27

298. Birkenhead *Professor* 133; CV V/2 244, 105

299. CV V/2 258

300. CV V/2 38; Pelling 414

301. CV V/2 334

302. Payne 212; Shirer 119

303. Shirer 136

304. *Frankfurter Zeitung* 26/9/30

305. Shirer 149

306. Shirer 132

307. 'Shall We All Commit Suicide?'; *Gathering Storm* 55-56

308. Eden in Eade 116; *Step by Step* 144; WM / Lord Butler 5/11/80; Hitler in Eade 210

309. *Amid These Storms* 249; WSC V 123; CV V/1 1335; WSC V 304-305

310. Rhodes James *Failure* 241n

311. *Hansard* 29/6/31; *New York American* 10/8/31; *New York Journal* 31/3/31

312. WSC V 406, 407

313. *NYT* 25/1/31

314. *NYT* 11/6/31

315. WM / Kay Halle 6/8/80; WSC V 418, 417

316. *Worcester Telegram* 13/12/31; 'My New York Adventures'; W.H. Thompson 108

317. CV V/2 382; Birkenhead *Professor* 134-135

318. 'My New York Adventures'; CV V/2 386

319. Moir 30, 31, 32

320. CV V/2 396, 393

321. Gilbert *Churchill Wilderness* 43-44

322. Moir 36, 82-83

323. WSC V 426; Gilbert *Churchill Wilderness* 45

324. CV V/2 406, 410; Gilbert *Churchill Wilderness* 46

325. *Wit* 83

326. Cowles *Churchill* 285; WSC V 431; Moran 65

SELECT BIBLIOGRAPHY

In most books it is impossible for a scholar to single out one source which towers above all others. In this case, however, it is not only possible; it is essential. The Official Biography of Winston Spencer Churchill, which has been in preparation, under the supervision of the Chartwell Trust, for eighteen years, is the definitive work on his life. Indeed, some documents, including those in the Royal Archives, Windsor Castle, are closed to other researchers until the official biography is complete.

Thus far the work – which has reached the year 1939 – comprises eighteen volumes totalling 20,827 pages. And World War II is yet to come. At this writing, Martin Gilbert, the official biographer, has just completed a manuscript covering the years 1939 to 1941. It is, he says, as long as this volume of mine. In its entirety, the official work is grouped into five biographical volumes and thirteen companion volumes. The biographical works have been issued under five major headings:

Volume I: *Youth, 1874-1900*, by Randolph S. Churchill. London, 1966.
Volume II: *Young Statesman, 1901-1914*, by Randolph S. Churchill. London, 1967.
Volume III: *The Challenge of War, 1914-1916*, by Martin Gilbert. London, 1971.
Volume IV: *The Stricken World, 1916-1922*, by Martin Gilbert. London, 1975.
Volume V: *The Prophet of Truth, 1922-1939*, by Martin Gilbert. London, 1977.

The companion volumes, 16,359 pages, are similarly grouped and consist of reproduced documents:

Companion Volume I, Part 1, 1874-1896, edited by Randolph S. Churchill. London, 1967.
Companion Volume I, Part 2, 1896-1900, edited by Randolph S. Churchill. London, 1967.
Companion Volume II, Part 1, 1901-1907, edited by Randolph S. Churchill. London, 1969.
Companion Volume II, Part 2, 1907-1911, edited by Randolph S. Churchill. London, 1969.
Companion Volume II, Part 3, 1911-1914, edited by Randolph S. Churchill. London, 1969.
Companion Volume III, Part 1, July 1914-April 1915, edited by Martin Gilbert. London, 1973.
Companion Volume III, Part 2, May 1915-December 1916, edited by Martin Gilbert. London, 1973.
Companion Volume IV, Part 1, January 1917-June 1919, edited by Martin Gilbert. London, 1978.
Companion Volume IV, Part 2, July 1919-March 1921, edited by Martin Gilbert. London, 1978.
Companion Volume IV, Part 3, April 1921-November 1922, edited by Martin Gilbert. London, 1978.
Companion Volume V, Part 1, The Exchequer Years, 1922-1929, edited by Martin Gilbert. London, 1981.
Companion Volume V, Part 2, The Wilderness Years, 1929-1935, edited by Martin Gilbert. London, 1981.

Companion Volume V, Part 3, 1936-1939, edited by Martin Gilbert. Forthcoming.

The liveliest biographer of Winston Churchill is Winston Churchill. He led a fascinating life, he knew it, and he exploited it. Like most journalists, he told his choicest stories over and over. He wrote no fewer than nine versions of his dramatic escape from the Boer prisoner-of-war camp in 1899. One, 'How I Escaped from the Boers,' was published in the Johannesburg *Standard and Diggers' News* on December 23, 1899. Three others appeared in the *Morning Post*, on December 27 and 28, 1899, and January 24, 1900. Later came 'How I Escaped from Pretoria' (*War Pictures*, March 3, 1900), 'My Escape from the Boers' (*Strand*, December 1923 and January 1924), 'My Escape from Pretoria' (*News of the World*, February 10, 1935), 'How I Escaped' (*Sunday Chronicle*, January 2, 1938), and the version in chapters 21 and 22 of his book *A Roving Commission*. This last account has appeared in several anthologies, and Churchill lectured on this feat innumerable times. There are no significant discrepancies among the many versions. He told this tale, and others, over and over simply because he had a family – and an expensive life-style – to support.

I. By Winston Spencer Churchill

1. BOOKS

Thoughts and Adventures. London 1932.

The Gathering Storm. Vol. I of *The Second World War*. London, 1948.

Great Contemporaries. London, 1937.

Ian Hamilton's March. London, New York, and Bombay, 1900.

Immortal Jester: A Treasury of the Great Good Humour of Sir Winston Churchill. Compiled by Lester Frewen. London, 1973.

India. Speeches and introduction. London, 1931.

Irish Home Rule: A Speech . . . at Belfast on February 8th, 1912. London, 1912.

Irrepressible Churchill: A Treasury of Winston Churchill's Wit. Selected and compiled with historical commentary by Kay Halle. New York, 1966.

Liberalism and the Social Problem. London, 1909.

London to Ladysmith: Via Pretoria. London, New York, and Bombay, 1900.

Lord Randolph Churchill. 2 vols. London and New York, 1906.

Maxims and Reflections. Selected by Colin Coote and Denzil Batchelor. London, 1947.

My African Journey. London, 1908.

On Naval Armaments: From a Speech on the Naval Estimate in the House of Commons, March 26, 1913. London, 1913.

Painting as a Pastime. London, 1948.

The River War: An Historical Account of the Reconquest of the Soudan. 2 vols. London, New York, and Bombay, 1899.

My Early Life. London, 1930.

Savrola: A Tale of the Revolution in Laurania. Reprinted New York, 1956.

Step by Step: 1936-1939. Articles. London, 1939.

The Story of the Malakand Field Force: An Episode of Frontier War. London, New York, and Bombay, 1898.

The Wit of Sir Winston. Edited by Adam Sykes and Icia Sproat. London, 1965.

The World Crisis, Vol. I (1911-1914). London, 1968.

The World Crisis, Vol. II (1915). London, 1968.

The World Crisis, Vol. III (1916-1918, part 1). New York, 1927.

The World Crisis, Vol. IV (1916-1918, part 2). New York, 1927.

The World Crisis: The Aftermath (1918-1928). New York, 1929.

The World Crisis, Vol. V: *The Eastern Front*. New York, 1931.

Young Winston's Wars: The Original Despatches of Winston S. Churchill, War Correspondent, 1897-1900. Edited by Frederick Woods. New York, 1972.

2. ARTICLES

'The Abuse of the "Dole." ' *Daily Telegraph*, March 26 and 27, 1930.

'The American Mind and Ours.' *Strand*, August 1931.

'Antwerp: The Story of Its Siege and Fall.' *Sunday Pictorial*, November 9, 1916.

'Arthur James Balfour.' *Strand*, April 1931.

'Asquith.' *News of the World*, February 16, 1936.

'Astor and G. Bernard Shaw.' *Sunday Pictorial*, August 16, 1931.

'Back to the Spartan Life in Our Public Schools.' *Daily Mail*, December 1, 1931.

'Back to the Wild Tumult of Peace.' *News of the World*, March 24, 1935.

'Balfour.' *News of the World*, March 22, 1936.

'Battle of Sidney Street.' *Pall Mall*, February 1924.

'Birkenhead.' *News of the World*, March 1, 1936.

'The Blunder That Beat Germany.' *Sunday Chronicle*, January 9, 1938.

The Boer War: sixty-six telegrams and thirty-five letters to the *Morning Post*, dated November 16, 1899, to July 25, 1900.

'B.-P.' *Sunday Pictorial*, August 30, 1931.

'British Cavalry.' *Anglo-Saxon Review*, March 1901.

'The British Officer.' *Pall Mall Magazine*, January 1901.

'Cartoons and Cartoonists.' *Strand*, June 1931.

'The Case for Singapore.' *Sunday Chronicle*, March 30, 1924.

'Chamberlain.' *News of the World*, March 29, 1936.

'Chamberlain.' *Pall Mall*, February 1930.

'Changing the Political Camp.' *News of the World*, February 24, 1935.

'Charge!' *Sunday Chronicle*, December 19, 1937.

'Charge of the Twenty-first Lancers.' *News of the World*, January 27, 1935.

'Clemenceau.' *News of the World*, March 15, 1936.

'Clemenceau: The Man and the Tiger.' *Strand*, December 1930.

'Consistency in Politics.' *Pall Mall*, July 1927.

'Could Labour Govern the Country?' *Illustrated Sunday Herald*, November 16, 1919.

'Crucial Events in the Great War.' Thirteen essays in the *Daily Telegraph*, May 5 to July 15, 1930.

The Cuban Insurrection: five dispatches to the *Daily Graphic* published in December 1895 and January 1896, and three essays in the *Saturday Review*, dated February 15, March 7, and August 29, 1896.

'Curzon.' *News of the World*, March 8, 1936.

'The Dangers Ahead in Europe.' *Weekly Dispatch*, June 15, 1924.

'The Dardanelles Held the Key to Peace.' *News of the World*, March 17, 1935.

'A Day with Clemenceau.' *Strand*, December 1930.

'The Decisive Factor in the Allied Victory.' *News of the World*, June 13, 1937.

'A Difference with Kitchener.' *Cosmopolitan*, November 1924.

'Douglas Haig.' *Pall Mall*, November 1928.

'The Dover Barrage.' *Daily Telegraph*, November 30, 1931.

'Dreadnoughts at Bay.' *Collier's*, July 5, 1930.

'The Dream.' *Sunday Telegraph*, January 31, 1966.

'The Election.' *Daily Chronicle*, November 6, 1922.

'Election Memories.' *Strand*, September 1931.

'The Ethics of Foreign Policy.' *United Services Magazine*, August 1898.

'False Security.' *Sunday Chronicle*, February 17, 1924.

'Fashoda Incident.' *North American Review*, December 1898.

'Fifty Years Hence.' *Strand*, December 1931.

'Fisher.' *News of the World*, January 19, 1936.

'Foch the Indomitable.' *Pall Mall*, July 1929.

'Four Crises in the Great War.' *Sunday Pictorial*, July 9, July 16, July 23, and July 30,

1916.

'French.' *News of the World*, February 2, 1936.

'Frontier Days in India.' *News of the World*, January 20, 1935.

'The Future of Mr Lloyd George.' *Weekly Dispatch*, June 29, 1924.

'The Gentle Art of Losing.' *The Times*, April 4, 1930.

'George Curzon.' *Pall Mall*, January 1929.

'The German Splendour.' *Cosmopolitan*, August 1924.

'Government of the / by the / for the Dole-Drawers.' *Daily Mail*, June 18, 1931.

'Great Events.' Articles in *News of the World*, May 30 to July 4, 1937, and October 10 to November 21, 1937.

'Great Men of the Times.' Twelve sketches in *News of the World*, January 12 to April 5, 1936.

'The Great War by Land and Sea.' Six instalments in *London Magazine*, October 1916 to March 1917.

'Haig.' *News of the World*, February 9, 1936.

'Haig . . . the Man They Trusted.' *Daily Mail*, October 3, 1935.

'A Hand-to-Hand Fight with Desert Fanatics.' *Cosmopolitan*, December 1924.

'Have We Done with Germany?' *Illustrated Sunday Herald*, November 23, 1919.

'Herbert Henry Asquith.' *Pall Mall*, August 1928.

'Hindenburg in War and Peace.' *Daily Mail*, August 2, 1934.

'Hobbies.' *Pall Mall*, December 1925.

'Homage to Kipling.' *John O'London's*, November 26, 1937.

'The House of Commons and Its Business.' *World*, July 13, 1909.

'How Antwerp Saved the Channel Ports.' *Sunday Pictorial*, November 26, 1916.

'How I Escaped.' *Sunday Chronicle*, January 2, 1938.

'How I Escaped from Pretoria.' *War Pictures*, March 3, 1900.

'How I Escaped from the Boers.' *Standard and Diggers' News* (Johannesburg), December 23, 1899.

'How I Placated Lord Roberts.' *Pall Mall*, October 1927.

'How the Grand Fleet Went to War.' *News of the World*, March 10, 1935.

'How We Made the Irish Treaty.' *Pictorial Weekly*, January 20, 1934.

'If I Were a Boer, I Hope I Should Be Fighting in the Field.' *Westminster Gazette*, March 18, 1901.

'In an Indian Valley.' *Pall Mall*, September 1927.

'India: The Coming Clash.' *Daily Mail*, October 14, 1933.

'India and Dominion Status.' *The Times*, November 25, 1931.

'The India Bill.' *The Times*, March 5, 1935.

'India in 1917.' *The Times*, February 14, 1935.

'India Insistent.' *Daily Mail*, September 7, 1931.

'The Influenza.' A poem written in 1890 and published for the first time in the *Harrovian* of December 10, 1940.

'In the Air.' *Pall Mall*, June 1924.

'The Irish Treaty.' *Pall Mall*, January 1924.

'Is Parliament Played Out?' *Illustrated Sunday Herald*, May 30, 1920.

'I Was a Prisoner of War.' *Sunday Chronicle*, December 26, 1937.

'I Was Conscious Through It All.' *Daily Mail*, January 5, 1932.

'Jellicoe.' *Sunday Chronicle*, October 24, 1937.

'Joseph Chamberlain.' *Daily Mail*, December 1, 1932.

'Kitchener.' *News of the World*, January 12, 1936.

'Kitchener.' *Sunday Chronicle*, October 31, 1937.

'Lawrence of Arabia's Name Will Live!' *News of the World*, May 26, 1935.

Letter to the Editor concerning the School Display and Gymnasium, signed 'Junius Junior.' *Harrovian*, March 17, 1892.

'Liberalism.' *English Life*, January 1924.
'Lloyd George.' *News of the World*, February 16, 1936.
'Lloyd George.' *Sunday Pictorial*, September 6, 1931.
'Lloyd George's Memoirs.' *Daily Mail*, September 7, 1933.
'Lord Birkenhead: The Man and His Career.' *Weekly Dispatch*, August 31, 1924.
'Lord Kitchener.' *The Times*, October 16, 1923.
'Lord Oxford as I Knew Him.' *Daily Mail*, October 18, 1932.
'Lord Roberts.' *World's Work*, June 1901; reprinted in *Windsor Magazine*, July 1901.
'Lord Rosebery.' *Pall Mall*, October 1929.
'Lord Ypres.' *Pall Mall*, January 1930.
'Ludendorff at Tannenberg.' *Collier's*, May 17, 1930.
'Ludendorff's "All or Nothing." ' *Daily Telegraph*, July 14, 1930.
'Ludendorff's Last Card.' *Collier's*, July 12, 1930.
'Man Overboard.' A short story. *Harmsworth Magazine*, January 1899.
'Man Power Problem: Wanted – a Policy.' *Sunday Pictorial*, April 8, 1917.
'The Man Who Saved Paris.' *Collier's*, May 31, 1930.
'Mass Effects in Modern Life.' *Strand*, May 1931.
'The Meaning of Verdun.' *Collier's*, November 18, 1916.
'Memoirs of the House of Commons.' *Pearson's Magazine*, December 1923-January
    1924.
'Men Who Have Influenced or Impressed Me.' *Strand*, February 1931.
'Mesopotamia and the New Government.' *Empire Review*, July 1923.
'Methods of Barbarism.' *The Times*, June 28, 1901.
'Mobilization in 1914.' *The Times*, April 9, 1936.
'Monarchy vs. Autocracy.' *Illustrated Sunday Herald*, February 1, 1920.
'Moses.' *Sunday Chronicle*, November 11, 1931.
'Mr Asquith and Lord Kitchener.' *The Times*, November 1, 1923.
'Mr H.G. Wells and the British Empire.' *Empire Review*, November 1923.
'Mr Snowden's Horoscope.' *Weekly Dispatch*, August 10, 1924.
'Mr Wells and Bolshevism: A Reply.' *Sunday Express*, December 5, 1920.
'The Murder Campaign in Ireland.' *Illustrated Sunday Herald*, June 13, 1920.
'My African Journey.' *Strand*, March to November 1908.
'My Budget Forecast.' *Sunday Pictorial*, April 19, 1931.
'My Dramatic Days with the Kaiser.' *Cosmopolitan*, August 1924.
'My Entry into Politics.' *News of the World*, February 17, 1935.
'My Escape from Pretoria.' *News of the World*, February 10, 1935.
'My Escape from the Boers.' *Strand*, December 1923 and January 1924.
'My Happy Days in the West Indies.' *Daily Mail*, March 23, 1932.
'My New York Adventures.' *Daily Mail*, January 4, 1932.
'My Spy Story.' *Cosmopolitan*, September 1934.
'The Mystery of the Marne.' *Collier's*, June 14, 1930.
'The 1921 Speech: Meaning of Dominion Status.' *The Times*, February 16, 1935.
The Northwest Frontier: five telegrams to the Allahabad *Pioneer Mail* dated September
    9 to December 15, 1897; five letters to the *Pioneer Mail* dated September 24 to
    November 5, 1897; and fifteen dispatches to the London *Daily Telegraph*, dated
    October 6 to December 6, 1897.
'Observations of the United States.' Twelve letters to the *Daily Telegraph*, November
    18, 1929, to February 3, 1930.
'Officers and Gentlemen.' *Saturday Evening Post*, December 29, 1900.
'On the Flank of the Army.' A short story. *Youth's Companion*, December 18, 1902.
'Our Task for Peace in Palestine.' *Glasgow Evening News*, February 28, 1930.
'Painting as a Pastime.' *Strand*, December 1921 and January 1922.
'The Palestine Crisis.' *Sunday Times*, September 22, 1929.

'Panic in the East.' *Collier's,* May 3, 1930.
'The "Panther" Affair.' *Saturday Review,* October 3, 1931.
'Partition Perils in Palestine.' *Evening Standard,* July 23, 1937.
'The Peril in India.' *Daily Mail,* November 16, 1929.
'Personal Contacts.' *Strand,* February 1931.
'Philip Snowden.' *Sunday Pictorial,* August 2, 1931.
'Plugstreet.' *Pall Mall,* March 1924.
'The Poison Peril from the East.' *Evening News,* July 28, 1920.
'The Profound Abyss.' *Evening News,* March 19, 1920.
'Proposal for a New Political Party.' *Living Age,* September 13, 1919.
'Ramsay MacDonald.' *Sunday Pictorial,* July 26, 1931.
'Ramsay MacDonald: The Man and the Politician.' *Weekly Dispatch,* May 25, 1924.
'The Real Kitchener.' *Illustrated Sunday Herald,* April 25, 1920.
'The Real Need of the British Navy.' *Sunday Pictorial,* June 24, 1917.
'The Red Fever.' *Illustrated Sunday Herald,* January 25, 1920.
'The Red Plot – and After.' *Weekly Dispatch,* November 2, 1924.
'Reflections on the Strategy of the Allies.' *Century,* May 1917.
'A Review of T.E. Lawrence's *Seven Pillars of Wisdom.*' *Daily Mail,* July 29, 1935.
'The Right to Strike.' *Illustrated Sunday Herald,* December 7, 1919.
'Rise and Fall of Parties and Politicians.' *News of the World,* March 31, 1935.
'The Royal Military College, Sandhurst.' *Pall Mall Magazine,* December 1896.
'Russia: Is It the Turning Point?' *Sunday Pictorial,* July 8, 1917.
'Savrola: A Military and Political Romance.' Serialization of Churchill's novel in *Macmillan's Magazine,* May to December 1899.
'Shall We All Commit Suicide?' *Pall Mall,* September 1924.
'Ships Could Have Forced the Dardanelles.' *Daily Mail,* October 2, 1934.
'Should Strategists Veto the Channel Tunnel?' *Weekly Dispatch,* July 27, 1924.
'Sidney Street and "Peter the Painter." ' *News of the World,* March 3, 1935.
'Singapore: Key to the Pacific.' *Pictorial Weekly,* March 24, 1934.
'Sir Edward Marsh's Death: Mr Churchill's Tribute.' *The Times,* January 14, 1953.
'Sir Herbert Samuel.' *Sunday Pictorial,* November 15, 1931.
'Sir John Simon.' *Sunday Pictorial,* November 8, 1931.
'Sketches of Twelve Key Figures.' *Sunday Pictorial,* July 26 to November 15, 1931.
'A Smooth Way with the Peers.' *Nation,* March 9, 1907.
'Socialism and Sham.' *Sunday Chronicle,* April 6, 1924.
'Socialist Quackery.' *Daily Mail,* May 8, 1929.
'Some Impressions of the War in South Africa.' *Journal of the Royal United Services Institution,* July 1901.
'Stark Truths about India.' *Daily Mail,* December 12, 1930.
'State Insurance.' *People's Journal* (Dundee), June 19, 1909.
'Taken Prisoner by the Boers.' *News of the World,* February 3, 1935.
'The Three Cruisers.' *The Times,* February 26, 1923.
'Three-Party Confusion.' *Sunday Chronicle,* March 2, 1924.
'Tragedy of the Torpedoed *Lusitania.*' *News of the World,* June 6, 1937.
'A Trapped Armored Train.' *Cosmopolitan,* January 1925.
'Tribute to Lord Birkenhead.' *The Times,* October 1, 1930.
'Tribute to Rupert Brooke.' *The Times,* April 26, 1915.
'Trotsky: The Ogre of Europe.' *Pall Mall,* December 1929.
'The True Story of the Tank.' *Sunday Chronicle,* January 16, 1938.
'The Truth about "Jix." ' *Sunday Pictorial,* August 9, 1931.
'The Truth about the Navy.' *Illustrated Sunday Herald,* November 9, 1919.
'The Truth about War Debts.' *Answers,* March 17, 1934.
'Twenty-one Years Ago Today: The Inside Story of the War.' *Sunday Chronicle,*

August 4, 1935.
'The U-Boat War.' *Daily Telegraph*, November 1931.
'Under Fire.' *Sunday Chronicle*, December 12, 1937.
'The United States of Europe.' *Saturday Evening Post*, February 15, 1930.
'The Victim of Sarajevo.' *Saturday Review*, September 26, 1931.
'The War by Land and Sea.' *Collier's Weekly*, September 30, 1916.
'The War on the Nile.' Thirteen letters to the London *Morning Post*, dated August 31 to
   October 13, 1898.
'What I Heard and Saw In America.' *Daily Telegraph*, November 18, 1929, to February
   1930.
'When Britain Nearly Starved.' *Sunday Chronicle*, January 23, 1938.
'When I Risked Court Martial in Search of War.' *Cosmopolitan*, October 1924.
'When I Was Young.' *Strand*, December 1924.
'When the Crash Came to the United States.' *News of the World*, June 20, 1937.
'Who Rules Britain?' *John Bull*, March 22, 1924.
'Why I Gave Up Flying.' *Pall Mall*, July 1924.
'Why More Taxes?' *John Bull*, April 12, 1930.
'Why We Lost.' *John Bull*, June 15, 1929.
'Will America Fail Us?' *Illustrated Sunday Herald*, November 30, 1919.
'Will the British Empire Last?' *Answers*, October 26, 1929.
'With Buller to the Cape.' *Pall Mall*, November 1927.
'Zionism vs. Bolshevism.' *Illustrated Sunday Herald*, February 8, 1920.

II. About Winston Spencer Churchill
1. BOOKS

Ashley, M. *Churchill as Historian*. London, 1968.
Bardens, Dennis. *Churchill in Parliament*. London, 1967.
Bonham Carter, Violet. *Winston Churchill: An Intimate Portrait*. New York, 1965.
Cawthorne, Graham, ed. *The Churchill Legend: An Anthology*. London, 1965.
Chaplin, E.D.W., ed. *Winston Churchill and Harrow*. London, 1941.
Churchill, Randolph, and Helmut Gernsheim, eds. *Churchill: His Life in Photographs*.
   New York, 1955.
Churchill, Sarah. *A Thread in the Tapestry*. New York, 1967.
The Churchill Years: 1874-1965. By the editors of the Viking Press, text by *The Times* of
   London, with a foreword by Lord Butler of Saffron Walden. New York, 1965.
Coombs, D. *Churchill: His Paintings*. Cleveland, 1967.
Cowles, Virginia. *Winston Churchill: The Era and the Man*. New York, 1953.
D'Abernon, Viscount. *Portraits and Appreciations*. London, 1930.
Dawson, R. MacGregor. *Winston Churchill at the Admiralty, 1911-1915*. Toronto, 1940.
Eade, Charles, ed. *Churchill by His Contemporaries*. London, 1953.
Eden, Guy. *Portrait of Churchill*. New York, 1945.
Fedden, Robin. *Churchill and Chartwell*. Westerham, Kent, 1968.
Gardner, Brian. *Churchill in Power: As Seen by His Contemporaries*. Boston, 1970.
Gibb, Captain A.D. *With Winston Churchill at the Front*. Glasgow, 1924.
Gilbert, Martin. *Churchill's Political Philosophy*. Oxford, 1981.
—. *Winston Churchill: The Wilderness Years*. London, 1981.
Gilbert, Martin, ed. *Churchill*. Englewood Cliffs, N.J., 1967.
—. *Churchill: A Photographic Portrait*. Boston, 1974.
Graubard, Stephen Richards. *Burke, Disraeli, and Churchill: The Policies of Per-
   severance*. Cambridge, USA, 1961.
Gretton, Admiral Sir Peter. *Former Naval Person: Winston Churchill and the Royal
   Navy*. London, 1968.
Guedalla, Philip. *Mr Churchill: A Portrait*. London, 1941.

Holliday, Frank F., and P. Sousa Pernes. *The Statesman and the Writer*. London, 1957.

Howells, R. *Simply Churchill*. New York, 1965.

Kraus, René. *Winston Churchill in the Mirror: His Life in Pictures and Story*. New York, 1944.

Longford, Elizabeth. *Winston Churchill*. Chicago, 1974.

McGowan, Norman. *My Years with Churchill*. New York, 1958.

Marchant, J., ed. *Winston Spencer Churchill: Servant of Crown and Commonwealth*. London, 1954.

Moir, Phyllis. *I Was Winston Churchill's Private Secretary*. New York, 1941.

Moorehead, Alan. *Churchill: A Pictorial Biography*. London, 1960.

—. *Winston Churchill in Trial and Triumph*. Boston, 1955.

Moran, Lord. *Churchill, Taken from the Diaries of Lord Moran: The Struggle for Survival, 1940-1965*. Boston, 1966.

Nel, Elizabeth. *Mr. Churchill's Secretary*. New York, 1958.

Nott, Stanley. *The Young Churchill: A Biography*. New York, 1941.

Observer, ed. *Churchill by His Contemporaries: An Observer Appreciation*. London, 1965.

Paterson, Tony. *A Seat for Life*. Dundee, 1980.

Pelling, Henry. *Winston Churchill*. London, 1974.

Reid, Percy G. *Churchill: Townsman of Westerham*. London, 1969.

Rhodes James, Robert. *Churchill: A Study in Failure, 1900-1939*. New York, 1970.

Scott, Alexander MacCallum. *Winston Churchill in Peace and War*. London, 1916.

—. *Winston Spencer Churchill*. London, 1905.

Sencourt, R., ed. *Winston Churchill*. London, 1940.

Snow, C.P. *Variety of Men*. New York, 1967.

Stansky, Peter, ed. *Churchill: A Profile*. New York, 1973.

Taylor, A.J.P. *Churchill: Four Faces and the Man*. London, 1969.

Taylor, A.J.P., et al. *Churchill Revised: A Critical Assessment*. New York, 1969.

Thompson, Malcolm. *The Life and Times of Winston Churchill*. London, 1945.

Thompson, Walter Henry. *Assignment: Churchill*. New York, 1955.

Urquhart, Fred, ed. *WSC: A Cartoon Biography*. London, 1955.

Wheeler-Bennett, Sir John, ed. *Action This Day: Working with Churchill*. New York, 1969.

Young, Kenneth. *Churchill and Beaverbrook: A Study in Friendship and Politics*. New York, 1966.

2. ARTICLES

Attlee, Clement. 'Churchill on Balance,' in *Churchill by His Contemporaries: An Observer Appreciation*. London, 1965.

Bacon, R.H. 'Tragedy of the Dardanelles: Conflicting Views of Winston Churchill and Lord Fisher.' *World's Work*, December 1929.

'Balfour and Churchill.' *Commonweal*, February 18, 1931.

Beaverbrook, Lord. 'Political Battles of the World War: The Fisher-Churchill Row and the Fall of Asquith.' *World's Work*, September 1928.

Berlin, Sir Isaiah. 'Winston Churchill in 1940,' in *Personal Impressions*. London, 1980.

'Bravery of Winston Churchill.' *Current Literature*, March 1900.

'Britain's Big Trio: Asquith, Lloyd-George, and Winston Churchill.' *Current Literature*, November 1912.

Buell, R.L. 'Winston Churchill's Criticism of President Hoover.' *Current History*, June 1929.

'Chamberlain and Churchill.' *Outlook*, November 19, 1924.

'Churchill in Parliament.' *Independent*, September 22, 1904.

'Churchill's Queer Position.' *Living Age*, January 24, 1914.

Colvin, Ian. 'Great Mr. Churchill.' *Atlantic*, January 3, 17, 24, and February 27, 1925.

Commager, H.S. 'Winston Churchill: An Appreciation.' *American Mercury*, August 1945.

Corbett, James. 'Winston Churchill and the Future.' *Fortnightly Review*, November 1926.

Dedijer, Vladimir. 'Participants as Historians.' *Times Literary Supplement*, May 30, 1968.

Ehrman, John. 'Lloyd George and Churchill as War Ministers,' in *Transactions of the Royal Historical Society*. London, 1961.

'England's Proposal to Germany for a Naval Holiday.' *Independent*, October 30, 1913.

Gardiner, A.G. 'Churchill and Federalism.' *Fortnightly Review*, November 1912.

—. 'Genius without Judgment: Churchill at Fifty,' in *Portraits and Portents*. New York, 1926.

Hirst, F.W. 'Churchillian Finance: The Fifth Budget.' *Contemporary Review*, June 1929.

Liddell Hart, B.H. 'Churchill in War.' *Encounter*, April 1966.

Lucy, Sir Henry. 'Arthur Balfour and Winston Churchill: A Parliamentary Duel.' *Nation*, March 30, 1916.

—. 'Lord Haldane and Winston Churchill.' *Nation*, December 9, 1915.

—. 'Mr Churchill's Resignation.' *Nation*, December 2, 1915.

—. 'Winston Churchill.' *Nation*, July 22, 1915.

—. 'Winston Churchill at the Admiralty.' *Nation*, November 19, 1914.

Marshall, D.J. 'Winston Churchill: England's Political Bad Boy.' *Living Age*, April 8, 1929.

Mayer, Arno J. 'The Power Politician and Counterrevolutionary,' in *The Critical Spirit*, edited by Kurt H. Wolff and Barrington Moore, Jr. Boston, 1967.

'Men Who Control the Destiny of Europe: Winston Spencer Churchill.' *World's Work*, September 1914.

'Mr Churchill's Failure to Stop Naval Rivalry.' *Literary Digest*, November 15, 1913.

Muggeridge, Malcolm. 'The Totemization of Sir Winston Churchill,' in *Smiling Through the Apocalypse*. New York, 1960.

Repington, C. à Court. 'Churchillian Strategy.' *Blackwood's*, November 1923.

Rowse, A.L. 'Churchill Considered Historically.' *Encounter*, January 1966.

Rusticus Expectans. 'Mr Winston Churchill and Democracy.' *Westminster Review*, January 1906.

Sidebotham, H. 'Expert or Strategist: Mr Churchill and the Dardanelles Report.' *New Republic*, May 5, 1916.

'Signal Defeat.' *Outlook*, May 2, 1908.

Stead, W.T. 'On the Eve of the Irish Home Rule Bill.' *Review of Reviews*, March 1912.

—. 'Winston Churchill's Offer.' *Independent*, April 11, 1912.

Strachey, J. St. Loe. 'Churchill's Chance: The British Chancellor and Opportunism.' *Independent*, June 27, 1925.

Sydenham of Combe. 'Mr Churchill as Historian.' *Quarterly Review*, July 1927.

Weerd, H.A. De. 'Winston Churchill: A British War Lord.' *Current History*, January 1929.

Whittemore, Reed. 'Churchill and the Limitations of Myth.' *Yale Review*, December 1954.

'Winston Churchill, MP, as a Man of Letters.' *Bookman*, July 1908.

'Winston Churchill and Irish Home Rule.' *Outlook*, October 26, 1912.

'Winston Churchill's Approval of Fascism.' *Literary Digest*, February 26, 1927.

'Winston Churchill's Versatility.' *Blackwood's*, September 1912.

'Winston Churchill's War on the War Leaders.' *Literary Digest*, February 26, 1927.

III. About the Churchills
1. BOOKS

Balsan, Consuelo Vanderbilt. *The Glitter and the Gold*. New York, 1925.

Blenheim Palace. Woodstock, Oxfordshire, 1979.

Churchill, J.G.S. *A Churchill Canvas*. Boston, 1961.

Churchill, Peregrine, and Julian Mitchell. *Jennie, Lady Randolph Churchill: A Portrait with Letters*. London, 1974.

Churchill, Lady Randolph. *Small Talks on Big Subjects*. London, 1916.

Churchill, Randolph S. *Twenty-one Years*. London, 1965.

Cornwallis-West. Mrs. George. *The Reminiscences of Lady Randolph Churchill*. London, 1908.

Eliot, Elizabeth. *Heiresses and Coronets*. New York, 1959.

—. *They All Married Well*. London, 1960.

Escott, Thomas H.S. *Randolph Spencer-Churchill as a Product of His Age: Being a Personal and Political Monography*. London, 1895.

Fishman, Jack. *My Darling Clementine*. New York, 1963.

Fleming, Kate. *The Churchills*. London, 1975.

Foster, R.F. *Lord Randolph Churchill: A Political Life*. Oxford, 1981.

Gorst, Harold. *The Fourth Party*. London, 1906.

Jennings, L.J., ed. *Speeches of the Right Honourable Lord Randolph Churchill*. London, 1889.

Leslie, Anita. *Lady Randolph Churchill: The Story of Jennie Jerome*. New York, 1969.

—. *The Remarkable Mr. Jerome*. New York, 1954.

Martin, Ralph G. *Jennie: The Life of Lady Randolph Churchill*. 2 vols. New York, 1969, 1971.

Peacock, Virginia. *Famous American Belles of the Nineteenth Century*. Philadelphia, 1901.

Rhodes James, Robert. *Lord Randolph Churchill: Winston Churchill's Father*. New York, 1960.

Roberts, Brian. *Churchills in Africa*. New York, 1970.

Rosebery, Lord. *Lord Randolph Churchill*. London, 1906.

Rowse, A.L. *The Churchills: From the Death of Marlborough to the Present*. New York, 1958.

—. *The Early Churchills*. New York, 1958.

—. *The Later Churchills*. London, 1958.

Soames, Mary. *Clementine Churchill: The Biography of a Marriage*. London, 1979.

2. ARTICLES

Cornwallis-West, Mrs. George. 'The Reminiscences of Lady Randolph Churchill: English Social Traits – Life at Blenheim.' *Century*, December 1907.

Escott, T.H.S. 'Lord Randolph Churchill.' *Fortnightly Review*, March 1895.

'Lady Randolph Churchill and Her Friends.' *Bookman*, December 1908.

'Lord Randolph Churchill.' *Harper's Weekly*, January 5, 1895.

'Lord Randolph Churchill.' *Review of Reviews*, March 11, 1895.

'Lord Randolph Churchill.' *Spectator*, August 5, 1893.

'Lord Randolph Churchill on the Descent of Woman.' *Spectator*, July 25, 1891.

'Lord Randolph's Pose.' *Spectator*, March 15, 1890.

Lucy, Henry W. 'Lord Randolph as I Knew Him.' *Blackwood's*, May-June 1907; *Putnam's*, May 1907.

Mann, J.S. 'Love Story of a Famous Statesman.' *Current Literature*, April 1906.

Maxwell, Sir Herbert. 'Lord Randolph Churchill.' *Living Age*, April 6, 1895.

Quinault, R.E. 'The Fourth Party and the Conservative Opposition to Bradlaugh.' *English Historical Review*, April 1976.

—. 'Lord Randolph Churchill and Tory Democracy.' *History* (London), April 1979.
'Reminiscences,' a review of Lady Randolph Churchill's book. *Bookman*, December 1908.
'Rosebery on Statesmanship.' *Living Age*, November 10, 1906.
'Statesmanship and Politics.' *Blackwood's*, February 1906.

IV. General Works
1. BOOKS

Adams, James Truslow. *Empire on the Seven Seas*. New York, 1940.
Amery, Julian. *Joseph Chamberlain and the Tariff Reform Campaign*, Vols. V and VI. London, 1969.
Amery, L.S. *My Political Life*. 3 vols. London, 1953.
Amery, L.S., ed. *The Times History of the War in South Africa*. 3 vols. London, 1900-1905.
Antwerp expedition: a summary of facts in the official *Military Operations: France and Belgium, 1914*, Vol. II. London, 1926.
Arnot, R. Page. *The Miners: A History of the Miners' Federation of Great Britain*. London, 1949.
Ashmead-Bartlett, E. *The Uncensored Dardanelles*. London, 1928.
Askwith, G.R. *Industrial Problems and Disputes*. London, 1920.
Aspinall-Oglander, C.F. *Roger Keyes*. London, 1951.
Asquith, Lady Cynthia. *Diaries, 1915-1918*. New York, 1969.
Asquith, H.H. *Fifty Years of Parliament*. 2 vols. London, 1926.
—. *Letters to Venetia Stanley*. Edited by Michael and Eleanor Brock. Oxford, 1982.
—. *Memories and Reflections, 1852-1927*. 2 vols. Boston, 1928.
Asquith, Margot. *The Autobiography of Margot Asquith*. 2 vols. London, 1920.
—. *More Memories*. 2 vols. London, 1922.
Atkins, J.B. *Incidents and Reflections*. London, 1947.
Bacon, Admiral Sir R.H. *The Life of Lord Fisher of Kilverstone*. 2 vols. New York, 1929.
Bagehot, Walter. *The English Constitution*. Garden City, N.Y., 1961.
Bailey, J.M. *England from a Back-Window*. Boston, 1878.
Baldwin, A.W. *My Father: The True Story*. London, 1955.
Balfour, A.J. *Chapters of Autobiography*. Edited by B. Dugdale. London, 1930.
Banks, Olive. *Prosperity and Parenthood: A Study of Family Planning among the Victorian Middle-Classes*. London, 1954.
Barnes, J. *The Great War Trek, with the British Army on the Veldt*. New York, 1901.
Barnett, Correlli. *Britain and Her Army*. New York, 1970.
—. *The Collapse of the British Power*. New York, 1972.
Barrymore, Ethel. *Memories*. New York, 1955.
Beaverbrook, Lord. *The Decline and Fall of Lloyd George*. London, 1963.
—. *Men and Power*. London, 1956.
—. *Politicians and the Press*. London, 1925.
—. *Politicians and the War: 1914-1916*. 2 vols. New York, 1928.
Begbie, Harold. *The Mirrors of Downing Street*. London, 1920.
Best, Geoffrey. *Mid-Victorian Britain, 1851-1875*. New York, 1972.
Birkenhead, Second Earl of. *'F.E.'* London, 1960.
—. *Halifax*. London, 1965.
—. *The Professor and the Prime Minister: The Official Life of Professor F.A. Lindemann, Viscount Cherwell*. Boston, 1962.
Blake, Robert. *Disraeli*. London, 1969.
Blake, Robert, ed. *Private Papers of Douglas Haig, 1914-1919*. London, 1952.
Blunden, Edmund. *Mind's Eye*. London, 1934.

—. *Undertones of War.* New York, 1929.

Blunt, W.S. *Gordon at Khartoum.* London, 1911.

—. *My Diaries: Being a Personal Narrative of Events, 1888-1914.* 2 vols. New York, 1921.

Bond, Maurice. *The Houses of Parliament: The Palace of Westminster.* London, 1973.

Boothby, Lord. *I Fight to Live.* London, 1947.

—. *Recollections of a Rebel.* London, 1978.

Boraston, J.H. *Haig's Despatches, 1915-1919.* London, 1919.

Bott, Alan, and Irene Clephane. *Our Mothers.* London, 1932.

Bowle, John. *The Imperial Achievement.* London, 1974.

—. *Viscount Samuel: A Biography.* London, 1959.

Boyle, Andrew. *Poor Dear Brendan.* London, 1974.

Brett, M.V., ed. *Journals and Letters of Reginald Viscount Esher.* London, 1934.

Briggs, A. *The Birth of Broadcasting.* London, 1961.

Brockway, A.F. *Inside the Left.* London, 1947.

Bromage, Mary C. *Churchill and Ireland.* South Bend, Ind., 1964.

Brownrigg, Sir Douglas E.R. *Indiscretions of the Naval Censor.* New York, 1920.

Bryant, Sir Arthur. *Turn of the Tide: 1939-1943.* London, 1957.

Buckley, Jerome Hamilton. *The Victorian Temper: A Study in Literary Culture.* Cambridge, 1981.

Bullough, Vern and Bonnie. *Sin, Sickness, and Sanity: A History of Sexual Attitudes.* London and New York, 1977.

Burn, W.L. *The Age of Equipoise.* London and New York, 1964.

Butler, Jeffrey. *The Liberal Party and the Jameson Raid.* Oxford, 1968.

Butler, Colonel Lewis. *Sir Redvers Buller.* London, 1909.

Callwell, Charles E. *Field-Marshal Sir Henry Wilson.* 2 vols. London, 1927.

Campion, Lord. *Parliament: A Survey.* London, 1952.

Chalmers, Rear Admiral W.S. *The Life and Letters of David, Earl Beatty.* London, 1951.

Chamberlain, Sir Austen. *Politics from Inside: An Epistolary Chronicle, 1906-1914.* New Haven, 1937.

Chandos, Viscount. *Memoirs.* London, 1962.

Charques, Richard. *The Twilight of Imperial Russia.* London, 1958.

Charteris, Brigadier General John. *At GHQ.* London, 1931.

—. *Field-Marshal Earl Haig.* New York, 1929.

Clark, G.N., ed. *The Oxford History of England.* Oxford, 1936.

Cleugh, J. *Secret Enemy: The History of a Disease.* London, 1954.

Coffey, Thomas M. *Agony at Easter.* New York, 1969.

Cole, Margaret, ed. *Beatrice Webb's Diaries, 1924-1932.* London, 1932.

Collier, Robert Laird. *British Home Life.* Boston, 1886.

Colville, Sir John. *The Churchillians.* London, 1981.

—. *Footprints in Time.* London, 1976.

Cook, Olive. *The English Country House: An Art and a Way of Life.* London, 1974.

Cooper, Lady Diana. *The Rainbow Comes and Goes.* Boston, 1958.

Cornwallis-West, George. *Edwardian Hey-Days.* New York, 1930.

Cowles, Virginia. *Edward VII and His Circle.* London, 1956.

Cowling, Maurice. *The Impact of Labour, 1920-1924.* Cambridge, 1971.

Cross, Colin. *The Fall of the British Empire.* New York and London, 1968.

Cruttwell, C.R.M.F. *History of the Great War.* Oxford, 1934.

D'Abernon, Viscount. *An Ambassador of Peace.* 3 vols. London, 1929-1930.

Dardanelles Commission. *Final Report.* London, 1919.

—. *First Report.* London, 1917.

Davis, Richard Harding *Our English Cousins.* New York, 1894.

—. *Real Soldiers of Fortune.* New York, 1906.
Dawson, Robert M. *The Development of Dominion Status, 1906-1936.* London, 1937.
Day, Price. *Experiment in Freedom.* Baltimore, 1948.
De Gaulle, Charles. *Lettres, Notes et Carnets, 1919-Juin 1940.* Paris, 1980.
Dennie, C.C. *A History of Syphilis.* Springfield, Ill., 1962.
Deutscher, Isaac. *The Prophet Armed: Trotsky, 1879-1921.* London, 1954.
Dickinson, F.A. *Lake Victoria to Khartoum.* London, 1910.
Dilke, Charles. *Greater Britain.* London, 1968.
Divine, A.D. *D.S.M. Dunkirk.* New York, 1948.
Drake, Emma. *What a Young Wife Ought to Know.* Philadelphia, 1901.
Driberg, Tom. *Beaverbrook: A Study in Power and Frustration.* London, 1956.
Duff-Cooper, Alfred. *Haig.* New York, 1936.
Dugdale, B.E.C. *Arthur James Balfour, KG, OM, FRS.* 2 vols. London, 1930.
Edel, Leon. *Bloomsbury: A House of Lions.* London, 1981.
Edmonds, J.E. *British Official History of the War.* London, 1948.
Edwards, Michael. *British India, 1772-1947.* London, 1967.
—. *High Noon of Empire.* London, 1965.
Eireann, Dáil. *Official Report: Debate on the Treaty between Great Britain and Ireland, December 1921-January 1922.* Dublin, n.d.
Elibank, Viscount. *A Man's Life.* London, 1934.
Ensor, R.C.K. *England, 1870-1914.* London, 1936.
Escott, Thomas H.S. *Great Victorians.* London, 1916.
—. *Social Transformations in the Victorian Age.* London, 1897.
—. *Society in the Country House.* London, n.d.
Esher, Viscount Reginald. *Journals and Letters.* 4 vols. London, 1934-1938.
Evans, Hilary and Mary. *The Party That Lasted 100 Days: The Late Victorian Season.* London, 1976.
Evans, Dr. Joan. *The Victorians.* Cambridge, 1966.
Falls, Cyril. *The Great War.* New York, 1959.
Farwell, Byron. *Mr. Kipling's Army.* New York, 1981.
—. *Queen Victoria's Little Wars.* New York, 1972.
Feiling, Sir Keith. *The Life of Neville Chamberlain.* London, 1946.
Fisher, Admiral of the Fleet Lord. *Memories.* London, 1919.
Fitzroy, Sir Almeric. *Memoirs.* 2 vols. London, 1926.
Florinsky, Michael F. *The End of the Russian Empire.* Collier-Macmillan, 1981.
Fortesque, Granville. *Russia, the Balkans and the Dardanelles.* Melrose, 1915.
Fraser, P. *Joseph Chamberlain.* London, 1966.
Frost, David, and Antony Jay. *The English.* New York, 1969.
Fussell, Paul. *The Great War and Modern Memory.* New York and London, 1975.
Gandhi, M.K. *Gandhi's Autobiography.* Housmans, 1952.
Gardiner, A.G. *Certain People of Importance.* London, 1926.
—. *Prophets, Priests and Kings.* London, 1908.
Garnett, David, ed. *Letters of T.E. Lawrence.* New York, 1939.
Gathorne-Hardy, Jonathan. *The Rise and Fall of the British Nanny.* London, 1972.
General Sir Ian Hamilton's Dispatches. May 20, August 26, December 11, 1915. London, 1915.
Gilbert, B.B. *The Evolution of National Insurance in Great Britain.* London, 1966.
Gilbert, Martin. *Churchill and Zionism.* London, 1974.
Girouard, Mark. *The Return to Camelot: Chivalry and the English Gentleman.* New Haven, 1981.
Goertzel, Victor, and Mildred George Goertzel. *Cradles of Eminence.* Boston, 1962.
Graubard, S.R. *British Labour and the Russian Revolution.* Boston, 1956.
Green, Martin. *Children of the Sun: A Narrative of 'Decadence' in England after 1918.*

Constable, 1977.

Grenville, J.A.S. *Lord Salisbury and Foreign Policy: The Close of the Nineteenth Century.* Oxford, 1964.

Grey of Fallodon, Viscount. *Twenty-Five Years, 1892-1916.* London, 1925.

Grierson, J.M. *The British Army.* London, 1899.

Grigg, P.J. *Prejudice and Judgment.* London, 1948.

Haig, Douglas. *Private Papers of Douglas Haig, 1914-1919.* Edited by Robert Blake. London, 1952.

Haldane, Sir James Aylmer L. *How We Escaped from Pretoria.* London, 1901.

—. *A Soldier's Saga.* Edinburgh, 1948.

Haldane, Viscount Richard B. *An Autobiography.* New York, 1929.

—. *Before the War.* New York, 1920.

Halifax, The Earl of. *Fullness of Days.* London, 1957.

Hamer, W.S. *The British Army: Civil-Military Relations, 1885-1905.* Oxford, 1970.

Hamilton, General Sir Ian. *Gallipoli Diary.* 2 vols. London, 1920.

—. *Listening for the Drums.* London, 1944.

Hamilton, W.G. *Parliamentary Reminiscences and Reflections, 1868-1885.* London, 1917.

A Handbook for Travellers in India and Pakistan, Burma and Ceylon: Including the Portuguese and French Possessions and the Indian States, 16th ed. London, 1949.

Hankey, Lord. *The Supreme Command, 1914-1918.* London, 1961.

—. *The Supreme Control at the Paris Peace Conference, 1919.* London, 1963.

Harriman, W. Averell, and Elie Abel. *Special Envoy to Churchill and Stalin, 1941-1946.* New York, 1975.

Harris, Frank. *My Life and Loves.* New York, 1963.

Hassall, Christopher. *Edward Marsh: Marsh's Letters Quoted.* London, 1959.

Healy, T.M. *Letters and Leaders of My Day.* New York, 1929.

Herbertson, A.J., and O.J.R. Howarth, eds. *The Oxford Survey of the British Empire.* Oxford, 1914.

Higgins, Trumbull. *Winston Churchill and the Dardanelles.* New York, 1963.

Hitler, Adolf. *Mein Kampf.* London, 1972.

Hobson, J.A. *Imperialism: A Study.* London, 1902.

—. *Problems of Poverty.* London, 1891.

Houghton, Walter. *The Victorian Frame of Mind, 1830-1870.* London, 1957.

Howard, Michael. *The Franco-Prussian War.* London, 1961.

Hübner, Baron von. *Through the British Empire.* London, 1886.

Hunt, Sir David. *On the Spot: An Ambassador Remembers.* London, 1975.

Hurst, M. *Joseph Chamberlain and Liberal Reunion: The Round Table Conference of 1887.* London, 1967.

Hyde, M.M. *Carson.* London, 1953.

India Defence League. *Prominent Supporters of the I.D.L.,* 3rd ed. London, 1934.

Jackson, Holdbrook. *The Eighteen Nineties.* London, 1939.

James, Henry. *English Hours.* London, 1981.

Jenkins, Roy. *Asquith.* London, 1964.

—. *Mr Balfour's Poodle.* London, 1954.

Jog, Narayan Gopal. *Churchill's Blind Spot: India.* Bombay, 1944.

Jones, Ralph E. *Fighting Tanks since 1916.* Harrisburg, Pa., 1933.

Jones, Thomas. *A Diary with Letters.* Oxford, 1954.

—. *Lloyd George.* Cambridge, Mass., 1951.

—. *Whitehall Diary.* 3 vols. Edited by K. Middlemas. London and New York, 1969-1971.

Kee, Robert. *Ireland: A History.* London, 1982.

Kennedy, A.L. *Salisbury.* London, 1953.

Kerr, M. *Prince Louis of Battenberg*. London, 1934.
Keyes, Admiral Sir Roger. *Naval Memoirs*. London, 1934.
Keynes, J.M. *Economic Consequences of Mr Churchill*. London, 1925.
Kincaid, Dennis. *British Social Life in India*. London, 1938.
Knightley, Philip, and Colin Simpson. *The Secret Lives of Lawrence of Arabia*. London, 1969.
Kohn, Hans. *The Mind of Germany*. New York, 1960.
Kruger, Rayne. *Goodbye Dolly Gray*. London, 1949.
Laver, James. *Victorian Vista*. London, 1954.
Lavery, J. *The Life of a Painter*. London, 1940.
Lawrence, A.W., ed. *T.E. Lawrence by His Friends*. London, 1937.
Lawrence, T.E. *Seven Pillars of Wisdom*. London, 1973.
Lee, Sir Sidney. *King Edward VII*, Vol II. New York and London, 1925.
Lehmann, Joseph H. *All Sir Garnet*. London, 1964.
Leslie, Anita. *Edwardians in Love*. London, 1972.
Leslie, Sir Shane. *Men Are Different*. London, 1937.
The Letters of Queen Victoria. London, 1926.
Liddell Hart, Sir Basil H. *A History of the First World War*. Boston, 1964.
—. *Memoirs*. 2 vols. London, 1965, 1966.
—. *Reputations Ten Years After*. Boston, 1928.
—. *Through the Fog of War*. New York, 1938.
—. *The War in Outline*. New York, 1936.
Limon von Sanders, Otto. *Five Years in Turkey*. Annapolis, Md., 1927.
Lloyd, T.E. *Empire to Welfare State*. New York, 1970.
Lloyd George, David. *The Truth about the Peace Treaties*. London, 1938.
—. *War Memoirs*. Boston, 1934.
Longford, Elizabeth. *Queen Victoria: Born to Succeed*. New York, 1965.
—. *The Suffragette Movement*. London, 1931.
—. *Wellington: The Years of the Sword*. London, 1969.
Lucy, H.W. *The Balfourian Parliament, 1900-1905*. London, 1906.
—. *Memories of Eight Parliaments*. London, 1908.
Ludwig, Emil. *The Nile: The Life-Story of a River*. New York, 1937.
Lunt, W.E. *History of England*. New York, 1928.
Macardle, Dorothy. *The Irish Republic*. Dublin, 1953.
Macaulay, T.B. *Critical and Historical Essays*. London, 1907.
McElwee, William. *Britain's Locust Years, 1918-1940*. London, 1962.
McGurrin, James, and Bourke Cockran. *A Free Lance in American Politics*. New York, 1948.
Mackay, Ruddock R. *Fisher of Kilverstone*. Oxford, 1973.
McKee, Alexander. *Vimy Ridge*. London, 1966.
Mackenzie, Sir Compton. *Gallipoli Memories*. London and Toronto, 1929.
McKenzie, R.T., and Allan Silver. *Angels in Marble: Working-Class Conservatives in Urban England*. London, 1968.
Macleod, Iain. *Neville Chamberlain*. London, 1961.
Macmillan, Harold. *Winds of Change*. London, 1966.
Macready, General Sir Nevil. *Annals of an Active Life*. New York, 1925.
MacVeagh, Jeremiah. *Home Rule in a Nutshell: A Pocket Book for Speakers and Electors*, 4th ed. With an introduction by Right Hon. Winston S. Churchill, MP. London, 1912.
Manchester, William. *The Arms of Krupp, 1587-1968*. Boston, 1968.
Mansfield, Peter. *The British in Egypt*. New York, 1972.
Marder, Arthur J., ed. *Fear God and Dread Nought*. 3 vols. London, 1952-1959.
Margetson, Stella. *Victorian High Society*. London, 1980.

Marlowe, John. *Milner*. London, 1976.

Marsh, Sir Edward Howard. *A Number of People: A Book of Reminiscences*. New York and London, 1939.

Massingham, H.J., and Hugh Massingham. *The Great Victorians*. New York, 1932.

Maurice, Sir F. *Haldane, 1856-1915*. 2 vols. London, 1937.

Mayo, Katherine. *Mother India*. London, 1930.

Meijer, Jan M., ed. *The Trotsky Papers, 1917-1922*. 2 vols. The Hague, 1964, 1971.

Meinertzhagen, Colonel Richard. *Middle East Diary, 1917-1956*. New York, 1959.

Melchett, A.M.M., First Baron. *The Jewish National Home and Its Critics: The Oxford Speeches, by Sir Alfred Mond and Dr. Chaim Weizmann*. London, 1922.

Middlemas, Robert Keith, and J. Barnes. *Stanley Baldwin*. London, 1969.

Milne, Admiral Sir Archibald Berkeley. *The Flight of the Goeben and the Breslau*. London, 1921.

Milner, Alfred, Viscount. *The Nation and the Empire*. London, 1913.

Moggridge, D.E. *The Return to Gold, 1925*. London, 1969.

Monroe, Elizabeth. *Britain's Moment in the Middle East*. London, 1981.

Moorehead, Alan. *Gallipoli*. New York, 1956.

—. *The Russian Revolution*. New York, 1958.

—. *The White Nile*. London, 1970.

Morgenthau, Henry. *Secrets of the Bosphorus*. London, 1918.

Morley, Lord. *Memorandum on Resignation, August, 1914*. London, 1928.

Morris, James. *Farewell the Trumpets: An Imperial Retreat*. London, 1979.

—. *Pax Britannica: The Climax of an Empire*. London, 1979.

Nevill, Lady Dorothy. *Leaves from the Notebooks of Lady Dorothy Nevill*. Edited by Ralph Nevill. London, 1907.

Nevinson, Henry W. *The Dardanelles Campaign*. New York, 1918.

Nicolson, Harold. *Curzon: The Last Phase*. London, 1934.

—. *Some People*. Boston, 1926.

Nicolson, Nigel, ed. *Harold Nicolson: Diaries and Letters, 1930-1939*. London, 1966.

Norton, Graham. *Victorian London*. London, n.d.

O'Connor, Frank. *Death in Dublin: Michael Collins and the Irish Revolution*. Garden City, N.Y., 1937.

O'Hegarty, P.S. *The Victory of Sinn Fein*. Dublin, 1924.

Osborn, E.B., ed. *The Muse in Arms*. London, 1917.

Owen, Frank. *Tempestuous Journey: Lloyd George, His Life and Times*. London, 1954.

Pakenham, Thomas. *The Boer War*. London, 1979.

Pankhurst, Sylvia. *The Home Front*. London, 1933.

Payne, Robert. *Life and Death of Adolf Hitler*. New York, 1973.

Pease, A. *Elections and Recollections*. London, 1932.

Peel, Mrs. C.S. *How We Lived Then: 1914-1918*. London, 1929.

Perry, George, and Nicholas Mason, eds. *The Victorians: A World Built to Last*. New York, 1974.

Peruginia, Mark Edward. *Victorian Days and Ways*. London, 1936.

Petrie, Sir Charles. *Life and Letters of the Right Honourable Sir Austen Chamberlain, 1939-1940*. 2 vols. London, 1940.

—. *The Victorians*. London, 1960.

Phillips, Janet and Peter. *Victorians at Home and Away*. London, 1978.

Ponsonby, Sir Frederick. *Recollections of Three Reigns*. London, 1951.

Pound, R. *The Strand Magazine, 1891-1950*. London, 1966.

Priestley, J.B. *The Edwardians*. New York, 1970.

Quennell, Peter. *Victorian Panorama*. London, 1937.

Rabinowicz, Oskar K. *Winston Churchill on Jewish Problems: A Half-Century Survey*. London, 1950.

Raymond, E.T. *Mr Lloyd George: A Biography*. London, 1922.
—. *Uncensored Celebrities*. London, 1918.
Reader, W.J. *Life in Victorian England*. New York, 1964.
Recollections of Dublin Castle and of Dublin Society by a Native. London, 1902.
Redesdale, Lord. *Memories*. London, 1915.
Redmayne, R.A.S. *Men, Mines and Memories*. London, 1942.
Reith, J.C.W. *Into the Wind*. London, 1949.
Repington, Lieutenant Colonel Charles à Court. *A Diary*. Boston and New York, 1922.
—. *The First World War, 1914-1918*, Vol. I. London, 1920.
Rhodes James, Robert. *Memoirs*. New York, 1970.
Richards, J. Brinsley. *Seven Years at Eton*. London, 1883.
Riddell, Lord. *Intimate Diary of the Peace Conference and After*. London, 1933.
—. *More Pages from My Diary, 1908-1914*. London, 1934.
—. *War Diary, 1914-1918*. London, 1933.
Robb, Janet Henderson. *The Primrose League, 1883-1906*. New York, 1942.
Roberts, Cecil. *The Bright Twenties*. London, 1970.
Robinson, Ronald, and John Gallagher, with Alice Denny. *Africa and the Victorians*. London, 1965.
Roskill, S.W. *Hankey*. 3 vols. London, 1973.
—. *Naval Policy between the Wars, 1919-1929*, Vol. I. London, 1968.
Rowse, A.L. *The English Spirit*. London, 1944.
Rumblelow, Donald. *The Siege of Sidney Street*. New York, 1973.
Ryan, A.P. *Mutiny at the Curragh*. London, 1956.
Sackville-West, V. *The Edwardians*. London, 1960.
Samuel, Lord. *Memoirs*. London, 1948.
Sassoon, Siegfried. *Memoirs of an Infantry Officer*. New York, 1930.
—. *The Poems of Siegfried Sassoon*. London, 1938.
—. *Siegfried's Journey, 1916-1920*. New York, 1946.
Seal, A. *The Emergence of Indian Nationalism: Competition and Collaboration in the Later Nineteenth Century*. Cambridge, 1971.
Searight, Sarah. *The British in the Middle East*. London, 1979.
Seeley, J.R. *The Expansion of England*. London, 1883.
Seely, Major General the Right Honourable J.E.B. *Adventure*. London, 1930.
Sheridan, Clare. *Nuda Veritas*. New York, 1928.
Shirer, William. *The Rise and Fall of the Third Reich*. London, 1960.
Slatin, R.C. *Fire and Sword in the Sudan*. London and New York, 1896.
'S.L.S.' (John St. Loe Strachey). *The Great Bread Riots, Or What Became of Fair Trade*. London, 1883.
Smalley, George. *Anglo-American Memories*. New York and London, 1911.
Smith, John M., and Tim Cawkwell. *World Encyclopedia of Film*. New York, 1972.
Somervell, D.C. *British Politics since 1900*. London, 1933.
Spears, Brigadier General Edward L. *Liaison, 1914: A Narrative of the Great Retreat*. New York, 1931.
—. *Prelude to Victory*. London, 1939.
Spender, J.A. *The Life of the Right Honourable Sir Henry Campbell-Bannerman*. 2 vols. London, 1923.
Spiers, Edward M. *The Army and Society, 1815-1914*. London, 1980.
—. *Haldane: An Army Reformer*. Edinburgh, 1980.
The Spion Kop Despatches. London, 1902.
Steevens, G.W. *Egypt in 1898*. Edinburgh, 1898.
—. *From Cape Town to Ladysmith*. Edinburgh and New York, 1900.
—. *In India*. Edinburgh, 1899.
—. *With Kitchener to Khartoum*. New York, 1898.

Stern, A. *Tanks, 1914-1918*. London, 1919.

Stevenson, Frances. *Lloyd George: A Diary by Frances Stevenson*. Edited by A.J.P. Taylor. New York, 1971.

Strike Nights in Printing House Square. London, 1926.

Sueter, M. *Evolution of the Tank*. London, 1937.

Swanberg, W.A. *Citizen Hearst*. New York, 1963.

Sydenham of Combe et al. *The World Crisis: A Criticism*. London, 1977.

Taylor, A.J.P. *A History of the First World War*. London, 1974.

Taylor, A.J.P., ed. *Lloyd George: A Diary by Frances Stevenson*. London, 1971.

——. *My Darling Pussy: The Letters of Lloyd George and Frances Stevenson*. London, 1975.

Taylor, Edmund. *The Fall of the Dynasties*. New York, 1963.

Taylor, Rex. *Michael Collins*. London, 1958.

Taylor, Telford. *Munich: The Price of Peace*. London, 1979.

Thompson, Laurence. *1940*. New York, 1966.

Thompson, Paul. *The Edwardians: The Remaking of British Society*. Bloomington and London, 1975.

Thornton, A.P. *The Imperial Idea and Its Enemies*. London, 1959.

Tillett, Ben. *History of the London Transport Workers' Strike, 1911*. Published from the offices of the National Transport Workers' Federation, West India Dock Road. London, 1911.

Toland, John. *No Man's Land: 1918, the Last Year of the Great War*. London, 1982.

Trevelyan, George Macaulay. *British History in the Nineteenth Century and After (1782-1919)*. London, 1937.

——. *History of England*. New York, 1926.

Trotsky, Leon. *The Russian Revolution*. London and New York, 1936.

Tuchman, Barbara W. *The Guns of August*. London and New York, 1962.

——. *The Proud Tower: A Portrait of the World before the War, 1890-1914*. London and New York, 1966.

Ullman, R.H. *Britain and the Russian Civil War*. Princeton, 1968.

——. *Intervention and the War: Anglo-Soviet Relations, 1917-1921*. Princeton, 1961.

Walder, David. *The Chanak Affair*. London, 1969.

Warwick, Frances, Countess of. *Discretions*. New York, 1931.

Webb, Beatrice. *Diaries, 1924-1932*. London, 1956.

——. *Our Partnership*. London, 1948.

Wemyss, V.M.A. Wester. *Life and Letters of Lord Wester Wemyss*. London, 1935.

Williams-Ellis, Clough. *The Tank Corps*. New York, 1919.

Wilson, T. *Downfall of the Liberal Party*. London, 1966.

Wilson, T., ed. *Political Diaries of C.P. Scott, 1911-1918*. London, 1970.

Winterton, Earl. *Orders of the Day*. London, 1953.

Wolff, Leon. *In Flanders Fields: The 1917 Campaign*. London, 1979.

Woodcock, George. *Who Killed the British Empire?* London, 1974.

Woodham-Smith, Cecil. *The Great Hunger*. London, 1962.

——. *Queen Victoria: Her Life and Times*. London, 1972.

Woodruff, Philip. *The Men Who Ruled India*. 2 vols. London, 1953, 1954.

Wrench, Evelyn. *Alfred, Lord Milner*. London, 1958.

Wrench, J.E. *Geoffrey Dawson and Our Times*. London, 1955.

Wright, Peter E. *Portraits and Criticisms*. London, 1925.

Young, G.M. *Stanley Baldwin*. London, 1951.

——. *Victorian England: Portrait of an Age*. London, 1936.

2. ARTICLES

'Ambassador Morgenthau's Story.' *World's Work*, August 1918.

Asquith, Herbert H. 'The Genesis of the War.' *Saturday Evening Post*, July 21, 1923.

'A Belfast Riot That Evaporated.' *Literary Digest*, February 24, 1912.

Bond, Brian. 'Why the Thin Red Line Was So Thin.' *Times Literary Supplement*, August 22, 1980.

'Britain's Meteoric and Versatile Chancellor of the Exchequer.' *Current Opinion*, February 1925.

British Officer. 'A Social Life of the British Army.' *Pall Mall Magazine*, January 1901.

'The British Sovereign Back from the War.' *Literary Digest*, May 9, 1925.

'British Statesmen Debate the London Treaty.' *Congressional Digest*, June 1930.

Gardiner, A. 'Who Will Succeed Lloyd George?' *Century*, October 1921.

Girouard, Mark. 'When Chivalry Died.' *New Republic*, September 30, 1981.

Guedalla, Philip. 'Portrait of a Buccaneer.' *Harper's*, June 1927.

Kennan, George F. 'Toward August 1914.' *New Republic*, November 3, 1979.

Konig, Hans. 'The Eleventh Edition.' *New Yorker*, March 2, 1981.

Laski, Harold. 'More Political Portraits.' *Living Age*, May 1931.

Liddell Hart, Sir Basil H. 'World War,' in *Encyclopaedia Britannica*, 14th ed., Vol. XXIII. London, 1929.

Littlefield, Walter. 'Great Britain's Literary Government.' *Critic*, May 1906.

Manchester, William. 'The Great War,' in *Controversy and Other Essays in Journalism*. Boston, 1976.

Masterman, Lucy. 'Churchill: The Liberal Phase.' *History Today*, November and December 1964.

Panter-Downes, Mollie. 'Books.' *New Yorker*, August 31, 1981.

Rosenstone, Robert A. 'The Generation of 1914.' *New Republic*, November 3, 1979.

Taylor, A.J.P. 'How a World War Began.' *Observer*, November 1958.

COPYRIGHT
ACKNOWLEDGEMENTS

The author is grateful to the following publishers, individuals, and companies for permission to reprint excerpts from selected material as noted below.

Quotations from H.H. Asquith's letters to Venetia Stanley are made by kind permission of the Hon. Mark Bonham Carter and are published in *H.H. Asquith: Letters to Venetia Stanley*, edited by Michael and Eleanor Brock (Oxford University Press, Oxford and New York, 1982).

Lord Beaverbrook from *Politicians and the War: 1914-1916*. Copyright 1928 by Doubleday & Company, Inc; copyright renewed 1956 by Lord Beaverbrook. Reprinted by permission of Methuen.

Wilfrid Scawen Blunt from *My Diaries: Being a Personal Narrative of Events, 1888-1914*. Copyright 1921 by Wilfrid Scawen Blunt. Reprinted by permission of Alfred A. Knopf, Inc., and Martin Secker & Warburg Limited.

Violet Bonham Carter from *Winston Churchill: An Intimate Portrait*. Copyright ᶜ 1965 by Violet Bonham Carter. Reprinted by permission of Harcourt Brace Jovanovich, Inc., and Eyre & Spottiswoode (Publishers) Ltd.

Mary Bromage from *Churchill and Ireland*. Copyright ᶜ 1964 by the University of Notre Dame Press. Reprinted by permission of University of Notre Dame Press.

'Peace' and 'The Soldier' by Rupert Brooke from *The Collected Poems of Rupert Brooke*. Reprinted by permission of Dodd, Mead and Company.

Winston S. Churchill from *Amid These Storms: Thoughts and Adventures*. Copyright 1932 by Charles Scribner's Sons; copyright renewed 1960 Winston S. Churchill. Reprinted by permission of Charles Scribner's Sons and the Hamlyn Publishing Group Limited. Originally published by Odhams Press Ltd.

Winston S. Churchill from *My Early Life: A Roving Commission*. Copyright 1930 by Charles Scribner's Sons; copyright renewed 1958 Winston S. Churchill. Reprinted by permission of Charles Scribner's Sons and the Hamlyn Publishing Group Limited. Originally published by Odhams Press Ltd.

Winston S. Churchill from *The World Crisis*, 1911-1914, and *The World Crisis*, 1915, copyright 1923 by Charles Scribner's Sons, copyright renewed 1951 Winston S. Churchill; from *The World Crisis*, 1916-1918 (2 vols.), copyright 1927 by Charles Scribner's Sons, copyright renewed 1955 Winston S. Churchill; from *The Aftermath*, 1918-1928, copyright 1929 by Charles Scribner's Sons, copyright renewed 1957 Winston S. Churchill. Reprinted by permission of Charles Scribner's Sons and the Hamlyn Publishing Group Limited. Originally published by Odhams Press Ltd.

Winston S. Churchill's dispatches from *Young Winston's Wars: Original Despatches of Winston Churchill, War Correspondent, 1897-1900*, edited by Frederick Woods. Reprinted by permission of Seeley, Service & Cooper.

Winston S. Churchill; Volume I, *Youth, 1874-1900*, by Randolph S. Churchill. Copyright ᶜ 1966 by C & T Publications, Ltd. *Companion Volume I, Part 1, 1874-1896*. Copyright ᶜ 1967 by C & T Publications, Ltd. *Companion Volume I, Part 2, 1896-1900*. Copyright ᶜ 1967 by C & T Publications, Ltd. Reprinted by permission of Houghton Mifflin Company and William Heinemann Ltd.

Winston S. Churchill; Volume II, *Young Statesman, 1901-1914*, by Randolph S.

The illustrations appearing in the book were supplied or reproduced by kind permission of the following:

INDEX

Abd-el Krim, 714

Abdullah ibn-Husein, 572, 575, 577, 578

Abdullah Ibn Mohammed (the Khalifa), 226-7; chosen by the Mahdi, 223; technological superiority of British troops and, 223-4; WSC's report on troop positions of, 228-9; attack led by, 228-9; British cavalry charge against, 230-2

Acton, William, 52

Addison, Christopher, 507

Admiralty. *See* Churchill, Winston Leonard Spencer: public life and political career, Admiralty

advertising in Victorian London, 57-8

Afghanistan, 676

Africa: British Empire in, 38, 41; life of British residents of, 49; WSC vacation in, 322; *see also* Egypt; South Africa

Africaans language, 321

Aftermath, The (WSC), 558n, 596

aircraft: WSC on effects of invention of, 8-9; WSC's belief in, 16, 362; WSC's flying lessons in, 362-6; in 1920s and 1930s, 679

air force, 362

Airlie, Countess of, 352, 622

Aitken, Max (later Lord Beaverbrook), 177, 609, 720; on WSC, 19, 655, 702; Clementine's dislike of, 329; German declaration of war on Russia and, 386; WSC's order for full naval mobilization and, 386; Fisher as first sea lord and, 398; on WSC after Dardanelles failure, 457; on WSC's theories of war, 465; on WSC after resignation from Dardanelles Committee, 469; service in France by WSC and, 469, 479; on WSC's reaction to being out of government service, 492, 496; Lloyd George government and, 501, 605; and WSC's growing influence after vindication, 505; MacDonald as Labour's first prime minister and, 615; on WSC's reaction to criticism of public policy,

618; social life with WSC and, 624, 637, 640, 667; on WSC's *World Crisis*, 628; and WSC as chancellor of Exchequer, 640; return to gold standard and, 645, 647; Baldwin government and, 652; *British Gazette* under WSC and, 652, 655; on WSC and party discipline, 662; 1929 election and, 668-9, 671; on India policy of WSC, 694

Alanbrooke, Viscount, 15-16

Albert, King of Belgium, 402-3, 532; Antwerp battle and, 407, 409; on WSC at Antwerp, 411-12

Albert, Prince Consort, 94, 140

Albert Edward, Prince of Wales (later Edward VII): advertising slogans and, 58; social circle around, 73, 94-5 144, 145, 165, 193; Randolph Churchill and, 82; affair between George Churchill and Lady Aylesford and, 95-6; Randolph Churchill reconciliation with, 99; WSC's childhood meetings with, 107, 110; Jennie Churchill and, 114-15, 202, 206, 220, 301; WSC in Fourth Hussars and, 177-8, 193; WSC's *Malakand Field Force* and, 219; Kitchener and, 220, 234, 236; WSC in Boer War and, 251, 266; *see also later entries under* Edward VII

Alexandra, Queen of England, 94, 95, 115, 337

Allahabad *Pioneer*, 209, 215, 218, 238

Allenby, Lord, 576

American Telephone and Telegraph Company, 668

Amery, Leo, 247; at Harrow with WSC, 130; on WSC's abilities, 481, 686; WSC as minister of munitions and, 505; WSC in France and, 517, 521; on British Empire after Armistice Day, 539; on appointment of WSC to War Office, 550; unpopularity of Lloyd

771

of, 500, 501; WSC's speech on American forces in France and, 504-5; on Turkish affair in Dardanelles, 603; WSC's views on socialist leaders and, 607; in 1922 election, 609, 611; MacDonald as Labour's first prime minister and, 613, 615; on death of Jennie Churchill, 622; MacDonald's coalition with, 638

Asquith, Margot, 8; on WSC, 17, 432, 459; on Jennie Churchill's beauty, 97; Randolph Churchill's political career and, 122; on Boer War, 245; WSC's unpopularity in House and, 296; WSC's switch to Liberal party and, 299; WSC's speech on Milner's policy in South Africa and, 318; on social reform, 336; death of Edward VII and, 337; WSC as home secretary and, 341; military appropriations requests and, 366; on WSC after declaration of war against Germany, 388; on WSC's spirit of adventure in war, 411; on Turks, 422; on troop inspections with George V and WSC, 434; Dardanelles campaign and, 451; WSC's career in government after Gallipoli failure and, 459; WSC at French front and, 469; WSC's speech requesting Fisher's recall and, 489; 1922 election and, 612; on Chartwell, 637

Asquith, Violet, 20; WSC on depressive spells to, 20; WSC on magic of words to, 24; on WSC's nanny, 93; relationship with father, 156-7; Oldham election after Boer War and, 272; WSC's lecture tour and, 273; on WSC's speaking style, 286, 287; Free Trade issue and, 289, 290; impressions of WSC at first meeting, 301, 308; on Eddie Marsh, 315; on Clementine Churchill, 324; WSC's honeymoon and, 327; economic policy and, 332, 335; WSC as home secretary and, 339; Admiralty offer to WSC and, 352; Clementine Churchill's feelings towards, 354; as neighbour to Churchills at Admiralty House, 354; on Admiral Fisher, 360, 425; Prince Louis's German background and, 397; on WSC's despair after Gallipoli, 459; on WSC's theories of war, 465; WSC's departure for French front and, 469;

on WSC's speech after resignation from Dardanelles Committee, 468; on WSC's speech requesting Fisher's recall, 488, 489; WSC's return to politics and, 491; WSC's anti-Bolshevik stand and, 558-9; WSC on socialist leaders to, 607; MacDonald as Labour's first prime minister and, 615

Astor, Lady, 28, 606, 642, 700, 703, 704, 720

Astor, William Waldorf, 114

Atatürk, Kemal. *See* Kemal, Mustapha

Athenaeum (publication), 218

Atkins, J.B., 246, 249, 262, 264, 286

Attlee, Clement, 684, 702; on WSC, 10, 21, 29; Dardanelles strategy of WSC and, 13; WSC's wit directed at, 28-9; on WSC's grasp of strategy, 482; on WSC's performance in Parliament, 606

Aubers Ridge, France, 454

Australia: in British Empire, 38, 41, 677; German possessions after Versailles given to, 542; self-government granted to, 543; World War I and, 543; disillusionment with British leadership in, 545

Austria and Credit-Anstalt failure, 700

Austro-Hungarian Empire, 275; German action in Balkans and, 349; ultimatum to Serbia from, 378-9, 381; declares war on Serbia, 382; Russian mobilization against, 384-5; surrender of, 533; after war, 538-9

Aylesford, Lady, 95-6, 100

Aylesford, Lord, 95-6

Baden-Powell, R.S.S., 266, 312, 704

Bagehot, Walter, 29, 60, 61, 68, 70

Bailey, Sir Abe, 657

Bailey, J.M., 53

Baker, Sir Herbert, 678

Balaam, John, 108, 137, 163, 203

Balaam, Mary, 108

Balcarres, Lord, 237

Baldwin, Lucy, 640

Baldwin, Stanley, 17, 626, 640, 664, 720; on WSC, 17, 703; at Harrow, 127; fall of Lloyd George coalition and, 604; WSC's view of socialism and, 607; as prime minister, 612; MacDonald as Labour's first prime minister and, 615; Westminster election with WSC and, 616; WSC's attraction to Conservative party and, 618; asks WSC to be Chancellor of Exchequer, 639-40, 661; budget proposals and, 644, 661; union strikes after return to gold standard and, 650, 652, 653-4, 655, 657, 658, 659; *British Gazette* under WSC and, 652, 656; WSC's desire to run BBC and, 654; tariffs supported by, 662; political power of, 663; 1929 election called by, 668; WSC during election and, 668-71; offers WSC secretaryship for India, 669; resignation of, 671; MacDonald's policy in Egypt and, 672; dominion status for India recommended by, 675, 676-7, 684-5, 688, 689-90; on British Empire, 676-7; rift between WSC and, 691-2, 693-6; *Times* support for, 693; Gandhi's release from prison and, 695; Gandhi-Irwin pact endorsed by, 697; anger at newspaper coverage of WSC, 697, 698, 699; MacDonald after 1929 Crash and, 700; WSC on, 703; Statute of Westminster and, 715-16;

Balfour, Arthur J. ('AJB'), 27, 119, 218, 280, 665; on WSC, 27, 241, 308; WSC's childhood introduction to, 129, 188; Oldham elections and WSC and, 241, 272; WSC's maiden speech in House and, 282; as prime minister, 289; Free Trade issue and, 289, 291-2, 293, 294; Randolph Churchill and, 291, 292, 310; WSC's antagonism for, 294-5; WSC's switch to Liberal party and, 299; defeat of government of, 299; WSC on, 309, 314, 704; reaction to WSC's publications, 310, 628; resigns as prime minister, 314; South African policy of WSC and, 321; WSC's marriage and, 326; House of Lords reforms and, 334, 338; WSC as home secretary and, 339, 344; Home Rule and, 368, 376; War Council debate on Carden's Dardanelles plan and, 424-5, 428, 429-30, 498; Fisher's resignation from Admiralty and, 453-4; WSC's career after Gallipoli failure and, 456, 460, 462; Keyes's plea for naval assault on Gallipoli and, 467; WSC's request for field command and, 468; WSC's speech on Fisher's recall and, 487, 488-9, 490; Lloyd George government and, 500; British actions

at French front and, 517; on WSC's antibolshevism, 558; Palestinian policy of, 572, 580; Greek policy of, 582, 584; WSC in Westminster election and, 616; WSC's communiqué on battle of Jutland at request of, 619n; on WSC's budget and military preparedness, 644-5; on Statute of Westminster, 679; WSC's protest of naval reductions and, 712

Balfour declaration, 572, 579; Arab denunciation of, 577; WSC's support of, 578, 580; House attempts to vote down, 580

Balkan wars of 1912 and 1913, 349

Ballin, Albert, 366, 382

Bank of England, 701

Baring, Hugo, 199, 201, 205

Baring, Maurice, 104-5

Barnes, Reginald: Cuban trip with WSC and, 186-7, 188, 189, 191-2; in India, 199-200, 201; WSC's letters to, on Pathan uprising, 211, 212-13; in Boer War, 247

Barrymore, Ethel, 300

Bartley, Sir Trout, 295

Baruch, Bernard, 549, 637, 672, 674, 715, 716; WSC as minister of munitions and, 507; spread of communism and, 552; investment advice from, 703, 719

Bath Daily Chronicle, 207

Battenberg, Prince Louis of (later Lord Mountbatten), 74; appointed second sea lord, 359; appointed first sea lord, 361; with WSC on vacation, 381; Austria's declaration of war on Serbia and, 382; British ultimatum to Germany and, 388; reactions to German background of, 397; removed from office, 397; changes name to Mountbatten, 397

Beach, Sir Michael Hicks-. *See* Hicks-Beach, Sir Michael

Beaconsfield, Earl of. *See* Disraeli, Benjamin

Beatty, David: with Kitchener expedition in Egypt, 228, 233; with WSC at the Admiralty, 359, 361, 382; wins war's first naval battle, 395; on Lord Fisher as successor to Prince Louis, 398; on WSC at Antwerp, 411; surrender of German fleet to, 537-8,

issue and, 289, 290; British neutrality and, 383; WSC's exclusion from Lloyd George government and, 500

Century (publication), 94

Chamberlain, Austen, 155, 299-300, 720; WSC in House and, 297; Home Rule and, 338-9, 372; WSC's exclusion from Lloyd George government and, 500; British Zone in occupied Germany and, 551; on civil war in Russia after revolution, 559; WSC's Middle East policy and, 579; WSC's Irish policy and, 591; fall of Lloyd George coalition and, 604, 605; on WSC's parliamentary qualities, 605-6; fall of, 612; Westminster election with WSC and, 615; on WSC's appointment to Treasury, 640; Far East military bases approved by, 645; return to gold standard and, 646; 1929 election and, 671; Indian self-government and, 689; Statute of Westminster and, 716

Chamberlain, Joseph, 13, 119, 129, 280, 612, 639; WSC on, 18, 25; on British Empire, 40, 43; Home Rule and, 154; Randolph Churchill's health and, 169; WSC's interest in South Africa and, 242; Boer crisis and, 244-5, 264, 289; Oldham election of WSC and, 272; WSC's maiden speech in the House and, 282; Brodrick's military policy criticism by WSC and, 285; young Conservatives around WSC and, 288-9; Free Trade issue and, 289-92, 293; WSC's challenge to leadership of, 292, 293, 296, 318, 367; WSC's switch to Liberal party and, 299, 367; defeat of government of, 299; Balfour as prime minister and, 314; Milner's mining policy in South Africa and, 318; WSC's wedding and, 326; self-government among Dominions and, 543

Chamberlain, Neville, 5, 300, 688, 696, 711, 720; WSC's stand against, 100, 119n; as minister of health, 639, 640, 641; WSC's introduction of health insurance and, 643; union strikes after return to gold standard and, 650; as rival of WSC, 661; on WSC as man of genius, 661; Conservative support for, 663; rating apportionment bill of 1928 and, 663; election of 1929 and, 669;

Indian self-government and, 693, 697, 698; as Chancellor of Exchequer, 701

Chamberlain, Sir Neville Bowles, 76

Chant, Mrs Ormiston, 165-6

Chaplin, Charlie, 637, 673-4, 720

Charles I, King of England, 80

Charles II, King of England, 80

Charteris, John, 509, 511

Chartwell, Kent, 30-1, 631-8; background of, 631; WSC buys, 631; renovations of, 631-2; WSC involved in work at, 632-4; animals raised at, 634-5; WSC's absence from, 635; financial matters touching, 635-6; hospitality of, 636-7, 667; WSC's later memories of, 637-8; used as year-round residence, 703

Château-Thierry, France, 525, 526

Château Verchocq, France, 523, 528

Chatterbox (magazine), 46, 47, 141

Chemin des Dames ridge, France, 524-5

Cherwell, Lord. *See* Lindemann, Frederick A.

Chiang Kai-shek, 275, 714

Chichele-Plowden, Sir Trevor John, 237

Childers, Erskine, 602-3

children, Victorian attitudes towards, 63

China, 275

Chinese immigrants in South African mines, 317-19, 321

Churchill, Charles. *See* Marlborough, Charles, ninth Duke of

Churchill, Clementine, 68, 324-31; WSC introduced to, 301; beauty of, 324, 353-4; background and personality of, 324; WSC's courtship of, 324-5; WSC's marriage proposal to, 325-6; wedding and reception of, 326-7; honeymoon of, 327; pet names used by, 327; pregnancy with first child of, 327-8; first home of, 328; birth of daughter Diana to, 328; son Randolph born to, 328; love letters between WSC and, 328-9, 528, 638; response to snubs to, 329; reaction to WSC's friends by, 329; financial matters and, 330, 626, 635-6; danger to WSC and, 330-1; effect of WSC's political life on, 331, 353-4, 360; idea of lover rejected by, 337; George V's coronation and, 338; WSC as home secretary and, 343; Asquith's offer of Admiralty to WSC and, 352-3; perquisites of Admiralty office and, 353; cruises with WSC and, 353, 360; WSC's flying lessons and, 362-5, 528; Belfast trip of WSC and, 369, 370; war dispatches received by, 394, 399; letter to Kitchener, on British winning of first naval battle of World War I, 395; on Lord Fisher, 398; daughter Sarah born to, 409; Ian Hamilton disliked by, 445; Fisher after Gallipoli failure and, 451; on Lloyd George, 457; letter to Asquith, on WSC's position at Admiralty, 458-9; WSC's departure from Admiralty and, 460-1, 463; WSC's painting and, 463; WSC's departure for fighting in France and, 469; letters and packages sent to France by, 476-7; efforts in London on behalf of WSC by, 486-7; WSC's speech in House suggesting Fisher's recall and, 488; WSC's desire to return to civilian life and, 490; New Year's 1917 with family at Blenheim, 497; desire for country home, 506; birth of daughter Marigold to, 527; married relationship of WSC and, 528, 623; celebrations at end of war and, 533; trip to Egypt with WSC, 574, 576, 577; fear of assassination attempts by Irish terrorists and, 599-600; socialists and, 607; Dundee election (1922) and, 609-10; West Leicester election (1923) and, 613, 614; death of Marigold and, 620-2, 624; birth of daughter Mary to, 622, 625; vacations taken by, 623-5; WSC's writing and, 625, 626, 706; ambition for WSC to be prime minister, 626; Chartwell and, 631, 632, 633, 634, 635-6, 638; Epping election (1924) and, 638-9, 640; WSC at Treasury and, 640; WSC's speech on Budget Day (1925) and, 642-3; Indian self-government debate and, 689; death of F.E. Smith and, 691; WSC's U.S. lecture tour and, 715, 717; WSC's injury in car accident and, 717, 718 LETTERS TO WSC: during courtship, 325-6; after birth of son Randolph, 328; about military camp, 330; on budget legislation and social reform, 334, 336; on WSC's flying lessons, 363, 364-5; on preparations for war, 381, 394; on retirement of Admiral Callaghan, 387; on stories of spies in England, 391; on projected trip to France, 405; on WSC in trenches, 472; on concern over WSC's health, 476; on promise of brigade to WSC, 477, 478, 480; to WSC as lieutenant colonel, Sixth Royal Scots Fusiliers, 485, 486-7, 490, 491; on WSC's return to political life after military service in France, 495; on WSC's need to clear name after Dardanelles campaign, 497; on Lloyd George, 501; on trip to Egypt, 574; on violence in Ireland, 588, 589, 601; while campaigning in Dundee for WSC, 609-10; on WSC's acceptance of West Leicester invitation to be candidate, 613; on son Randolph, 620; on missing WSC during his vacation, 624, 625; on her ambition for WSC to be prime minister, 626; on naval appropriations in budget, 643; on WSC's mediation in coal miners' strike, 658; on WSC's opinion of Mussolini, 666; on 1928 elections, 670 LETTERS FROM WSC: on Burley-on-the-Hill fire, 311, 325; on loss in Manchester election, 324; during courtship, 325; on birth of daughter Diana, 328; love letters, 328-9, 528, 638; from military camp, 330; on budget legislation and social reform, 334, 336, 337, 338; on meeting Kaiser Wilhelm, 348; on social affairs with his family, 353; on home and domestic expenses, 354, 384; on his flying lessons, 363, 364, 365; on Home Rule, 377-8; on spending time with his family on vacation, 381; on impending war, 379, 382, 383-4, 386, 415; on preparations for war, 381, 382; on concern over safety of family on coast, 391-2; war information sent in, 394; on Fisher, 398-9; on proposed trip to Dardanelles, 466; from French front, 469-70, 471, 472, 473-4, 476, 497, 520, 523, 527, 528, 531, 532; on promise of brigade, 477, 478, 479-80; while lieutenant colonel of Sixth Royal Scots Fusiliers, 482, 483, 484, 485, 486, 487, 491; on decision to leave army, 490; on clearing his name after Dardanelles campaign, 497; on Clemenceau, 520; on worry over zeppelin raids on England, 527; on room at Colonial

Office, 571; on Irish terrorism and
Home Rule problems, 588, 595, 597-8;
on extemporaneous speech on Iraq,
606; on offer of support in Westminster
election (1924), 615; on death of
daughter Marigold, 621, 622, 624;
while on vacation, 623, 624-5; on
Asquith, 624; on writing, 626, 627,
704, 705; on Chartwell, 632, 633; on
Lindemann explaining Quantum
Theory, 637; from Treasury, 641; on
war debt to U.S., 642; on
independence while at Treasury, 662;
on Fascist society in Italy, 665; on
cruise of Mediterranean with son
Randolph, 666; on new home rented
from Venetia Montagu, 671; on stock
market investments, 672, 674, 675; on
visit to Hearsts at San Simeon, 673; on
Hollywood actors, 675; on support
from Epping in Indian self-
government debate, 696
Churchill, Diana (daughter), 19, 620,
624, 631, 642; birth of, 328; father's
play with, 464; fear of assassination
attempts by Irish terrorists and,
599-600; with WSC on American
lecture tour, 715, 719
Churchill, George. *See* Marlborough,
George, fifth Duke of; Marlborough,
George, eighth Duke of
Churchill, Lady Gwendeline
('Goonie') (sister-in-law), 325, 353,
379, 391; social life with Churchills
and, 379-81, 469, 636, 638; German
spy seen by, 391; Churchills live with,
462; WSC introduced to painting by,
462; WSC in France and, 486
Churchill, Henry Winston
('Peregrine') (nephew), 464
Churchill, John. *See* Marlborough,
John, first Duke of; Marlborough,
John, seventh Duke of
Churchill, John ('Johnny') (nephew),
464
Churchill, John Strange Spencer
('Jack') (brother), 194, 206, 298, 322,
348; childhood of, 100, 105, 109, 116,
136; visits to WSC at St. George's by,
104; influence of WSC on, 105; as
WSC's playmate, 108, 112, 160; birth
of, 113; holidays with Mrs Everest
('Woom'), 137, 142; holidays with

WSC, 142, 148, 151; at Harrow, 148,
158; letters from Mrs Everest to, 159;
father's declining health and, 169-70,
171; Mrs Everest's funeral and, 179,
180; commission in South African
Light Horse, 263; wounding of, 264;
marriage of, 325; WSC dines with, 388;
on Gallipoli landing, in letter to WSC,
450; Churchills move in with, 462; in
war in France, 497; at Chartwell, 636,
638; vacation in Mediterranean with
Churchills, 665, 666
LETTERS FROM WSC: from India, 49;
from Thomson sisters' school,
Brighton, 106; on Crystal Palace visit,
140-1, 142; from France, while
studying language, 145; on music hall
speech, 166; from Fourth Hussars,
176; on West Point visit, 187; from
India, 204; on war, from Admiralty,
462; on being out of House and government service, 496
Churchill, Marigold (daughter), 527;
birth of, 527; death of, 620-1; reaction
of parents to death of, 621-2, 624
Churchill, Mary (daughter), 4, 31; on her
mother, 354; death of sister Marigold
and, 621, 622; birth of, 622, 625; on
economizing by parents, 625;
Chartwell and, 632, 634, 635, 636, 637,
667
Churchill, Pamela (daughter-in-law), 6;
see also Harriman, Pamela
Churchill, Randolph ('the Chumbolly')
(son), 216, 393, 466, 620, 624; war and,
6; WSC on his relationship with, 156;
birth of, 328; WSC's play with, 464;
fear of assassination attempts by Irish
terrorists and, 599; letter to mother, on
health of Marigold, 621; Chartwell
and, 631, 632, 638; WSC's Budget Day
(1925) speech and, 642; on
Mediterranean cruise with WSC, 665,
666; WSC's American lecture tour and,
718, 719
Churchill, Lady Randolph ('Jennie')
(mother), 497; South African visit of,
during Boer War, 23, 263; love affairs
of, 75, 113-15, 139, 144-5, 172, 174,
187, 193, 206, 301, 337; meets
Randolph Churchill, 83, 86;
engagement to Randolph, 87-8;
wedding of, 88-9; pregnancy and birth

of son Winston, 89-90; as independent woman after marriage, 89; on early years of marriage, 93-4; as mother to young WSC, 93, 97, 98; Prince of Wales and, 94, 114-5, 202, 301, 337; George Churchill's affair with Lady Aylesford and, 94-6; in Ireland, 96-9, 113; beauty of, 97; WSC at St. George's School and, 102-6; as hostess, 104, 111, 139, 144; WSC's health and, 109-11, 149; Randolph's political career and, 111, 155; pleas from WSC to visit him at school, 111-112; awareness of Randolph's venereal disease, 113; birth of son Jack to, 113; Randolph's reaction to love affairs of, 115; WSC's knowledge of love affairs of, 115, 144-5, 301; Randolph's resignation from cabinet and, 124; WSC visited at Harrow by, 128, 131, 138; WSC introduced to men in Parliament by, 129; WSC during school holidays and, 137, 145; Count Kinsky and, 139, 140-1, 172, 174; Randolph's declining health and, 169, 171-2; sea voyage with Randolph, 171-2; Randolph's death and burial and, 173; behaviour during Randolph's illness noted, 174; assistance to WSC's career by, 175, 206, 217, 623; beginning of WSC's military career and, 175, 176; defrauded of money, 200; books sent to WSC in India by, 203-4; publication arrangements for WSC's dispatches from India by, 209; WSC's desire to join Kitchener and, 219-20; *Anglo-Saxon Review* launched by, 239-40; WSC in election campaigns and, 241; WSC's escape from imprisonment during Boer War and, 255, 259; hospital ship *Maine* and, 263, 265; marries George Cornwallis-West, 263, 271, 309; WSC's maiden House speech and, 281; Clementine Hozier introduced to WSC by, 301; suffrage movement and, 307; on Eddie Marsh as private secretary, 316; WSC's courtship of Clementine and, 324, 325; death of Edward VII and, 337-8; divorces Cornwallis-West, 338; coronation of George V and, 338; ship launched by, with WSC in Admiralty, 353; letter to sister Leonie on

inevitability of war, 385; WSC dines with, 388; WSC's departure for fighting in France and, 469; marries Montagu Porch, 526-7; in zeppelin raid on London, 527; death of, 622
LETTERS TO RANDOLPH CHURCHILL: during engagement, 87; on George Churchill's affair with Lady Aylesford, 95-6; on young WSC, 97; on WSC's education, 105, 142; on Sandhurst entrance examination, 146-7
LETTERS TO WSC: at St. George's School, 104; on French language tutoring, 143, 146; at Sandhurst, 151-2, 158; on Mrs Everest's dismissal, 158-9; on his trip to Cuba, 186; on money matters, 194; on British blockade of Crete, 206; while he covers Pathan uprising, 215; on Pamela Plowden, 300; on his meeting the kaiser, 348; during fighting in France, 476; on his trip to Egypt, 574
LETTERS FROM WSC: first, 101; from St. George's School, 103-4; from Thomson sisters' school, Brighton, 107, 108; pleas for visit to school, 111-12; about politics, 117, 118; on his father's political career, 119, 120; from Harrow, 125, 126, 128, 130, 131-2, 133-4, 139, 142-3, 146; on his health, 136; on his need for Mrs Everest ('Woom'), 136; from France while being tutored, 142-4, 145-6; on Sandhurst entrance examination, 146; from Sandhurst, 153, 154, 168; on Mrs Everest's dismissal, 158-9; on preference for infantry appointment, 168; on his father's declining health, 173; from Fourth Hussars, 177-8, 193, 194; on polo fall, 177; on Mrs Everest's funeral, 179-80; on his father's grave, 180; on New York City visit with Bourke Cockran, 187; on money matters, 194; request for assistance to avoid being posted to India, 195; on his life in Bangalore, 200; on meeting Pamela Plowden, 200-1; request for English rose seeds, 201; on pony for horse racing in India, 202; on books for reading in history, 203-4; on writing novel *Savrola*, 205;

decision to go to Harrow, 125; on school vacation with family, 145; on Sandhurst infantry appointment, 153; on Sandhurst allowance, 153-4; on observing father in House, 154-5; on prostitution in music halls, 166

Churchill, Sarah (daughter), 8, 19, 365, 464, 620; WSC's punishment of, 30; on WSC, 93; birth of, 409; Chartwell and, 631, 633, 635

Churchill, Sir Winston (1620-1688), 80

Churchill, Winston Leonard Spencer: genealogy of, 77-81; family tree (chart) of, 78; Jerome grandparents of, 84, 85-6; mother's pregnancy and birth of, 89-90; quoted on his birth, 90; birth notice in *The Times*, 90; baptism of, 93; awareness of family background of, 109

CHILDHOOD: relationship with parents in, 93, 98; in Ireland, 96-9; fears of being abandoned in, 99; affection and devotion of nanny Mrs Everest in, 97-8; assertiveness with servants in, 98; military games in, 99, 108; study of childhood patterns of eminent men applied to, 100, 149-50; playmates in, 100; lack of sense of personal safety in, 100; interest in politics during, 101, 117; Disraeli's death and, 101; problems with arithmetic during, 102; Victoria's Golden Jubilee and, 107; as leader of childhood games, 108; relationship with father in, 112, 115, 116-17; awareness of mother's affairs in, 115, 144-5; meetings with men prominent in Parliament during, 129; House of Commons visit during, 129; as awkward and rebellious teenager, 142-3; religious attitudes in, 147; *My Early Life* written on, 666-7

EDUCATION

ST. GEORGE'S SCHOOL, ASCOT, 102-6; reaction to being sent to, 102-3; journey to, 103; Latin grammar exercises at, 103; later memories of, 103, 104; pleas to mother to visit, 104; rebelliousness at, 104-5; canings at, 104, 105; achievement at, 105

THOMSON SISTERS' SCHOOL, BRIGHTON, 106-8, 111-12; academic progress at, 106, 125; books read at,

107; later memories of, 110; pleas to mother to visit, 111-12

HARROW SCHOOL, 124-36, 159; birchings at, 14, 129; memory of books learned at, 23; flair for language at, 24; entrance examination for, 125-6; later memories of, 125, 127, 131, 134; assignment to lowest form upon arrival, 126; and patriotic songs at, 127; as disciplinary problem at, 128-9, 130-1; reaction of classmates to, 128, 130; visits of Jennie to, 128, 131; political awareness at, 129-30; hobbies at, 130; writes for school paper at, 130-1, 135; letter to school paper at, 130-1; academic achievement at, 131-4, 142-3, 155-6; ability recognized at, 133; mathematics instruction at, 133-4; Latin and Greek instruction at, 134; reading at, 134-5, 203; gifts from Randolph while at, 138; and Eton-Harrow cricket match, 139, 140; tutoring in French while on vacation from, 142-6; Sandhurst entrance examination preparations at, 146, 147, 148; last term at, 148; room with brother Jack shared at, 148; and sports at, 148; religious attendance at, 204

ROYAL MILITARY COLLEGE, SANDHURST, 153-4, 159-61, 167-9; entrance examination to, 151; infantry appointment at, 151-3; arrival at, 153; allowance from Randolph at, 153-4; Randolph's visit to, 157; gift of gold watch from Randolph at, 157-8; subjects and exercises taught at, 159-60; later memories of, 159, 160, 161, 168, 213; typical day at, 160; riding at, 160, 167; achievements at, 160-1; popularity among fellow cadets at, 161; London trips from, 161-2; newspaper reading at, 163; passes out of with honours, 168; and suit against Bruce-Pryce, 176-7

JOURNALISM: subjects for articles, 23, 626, 665, 704, 705; income from, 24, 620, 626; articles for school paper at Harrow, 130-1, 135; plan to cover British blockade of Crete, 206; Allahabad *Pioneer* offer for letters from London, 238; article on economic problems, 331; obituary for Rupert Brooke in *The Times*, 434-5; on western front battles, 493, 508, 517-18; preference for writing over speaking, 497; articles on bolshevism, 560-1; on Weizmann in Palestine, 572; on Irish terrorism, 589; on Lloyd George coalition defeat in 1922, 612; audience for articles by, 620; as editor of *British Gazette* during general strike, 652-4; on Indian self-government, 699; on being hit by an automobile in New York, 717

CUBAN INSURRECTION, 186, 189-92; decision to cover, 186; *Daily Graphic* agreement for dispatches covering, 186; permission granted for trip to, 186; departure for, 187; New York stopover in, 187-9; sighting of Havana in, 188; dispatches from, 189-91; on being under fire, 190; Spanish Red Cross awarded to, 191; press conference on, 191-2; later thoughts on Cuba based on, 192

MALAKAND FIELD FORCE, INDIA, 209-17; later memories of, 24, 211; attraction of life in India in, 49; decision to leave for India, 209; journey to join Sir Bindon Blood in, 209-11; attitude towards danger in, 210; aversion to whisky conquered in, 210; dispatches from, 211, 212, 215-16; physical discomfort in, 212; attack and counterattack in valley in, 212-15; ambition for House seat and, 212, 214, 217; Fourth Hussars rejoined after, 215; criticism of military establishment in, 215; courage and resolution praised by Jeffreys in, 215; reactions to dispatches from, 215, 216; lack of by-line from, 215-16; book written from dispatches on, 217-19

KITCHENER EXPEDITION, SUDAN, 219-36; later memories of, 24; Jennie's assistance in joining, 219-20; trip to War Office to obtain position with, 220-1; attached to Twenty-First Lancers, 221; *Morning Post* contract in, 221; arrives in Cairo, 222; dispatches from, 222, 224, 226-7, 232, 235-6; journey to join Kitchener in, 224-8; language used in dispatches from, 225, 235-6; lost on way to join, 226; sighting of Omdurman in, 226; report to Kitchener on troop positions by, 228-9; first meeting with David Beatty in,

228; attack of Khalifa's army in, 228-9; British cavalry charge in, 230-2; casualties in, 232; melodramatic and romantic tone of dispatches from, 233; brutality of British soldiers described in, 234; attitude towards war revealed in, 233; Mahdi's tomb defaced in, 234; Kitchener's reaction to dispatches in, 234; skin donated to wounded soldier in, 235; desire for medals from, 235; ambition for House seat and, 235, 236; book written from dispatches on, 236; tribute to slain Arabs in, 236; reactions to dispatches from, 238

BOER WAR, 242-70, 462; attitude during, 23; departure for South Africa in, 242-3; voyage and arrival at Cape Town in, 245-6; arrival at front in, 246-7; armoured-train mission in, 247-9; old friends encountered in, 247; dispatches from, 247, 250, 255, 260, 264-5, 266-7, 268, 269; as prisoner of war in, 249-52, 339; letter to War Office in, 248; Haldane's report on conduct in, 249; ammunition used in, 249-50; demand for release in, 250-1; response to imprisonment during, 250; Victoria Cross considered for, 251, 270; escapes from prison camp in, 252-5; hides with British miners in, 255-7; train journey to border in, 257-8; map of escape route in, 258; and British consul after escape in, 258-9; received as hero at Durban in, 259-60; South African Light Horse commission in, 260-1; Spion Kop action in, 262-3; Jennie's arrival with hospital ship in, 263; Ladysmith falls in, 264; writing of books based on, 264, 271; political ambitions and, 264; and Roberts in Cape Colony, 265-70; Prince of Wales's reaction to dispatches from, 266; interpretation in dispatches of incidents in, 266-8; Johannesburg engagement in, 268-9; prisoner-of-war camp revisited in, 269; Diamond Hill battle in, 269-70; lecture tour on, 273-5

MILITARY CAREER

FOURTH HUSSARS, 175-9, 193-207; and Randolph's preference for Sixtieth Rifles commission after Sandhurst, 151-2, 167, 168, 175; commissioned as second lieutenant in, 175; riding and drill in, 175-6, 177; suit against Bruce-Pryce for homosexual allections in, 176-7; daily life and recreation in, 177; Victoria in review of, 178; social life and, 178-9; political interest during, 178-9; financial support and debts in, 183, 193, 194, 200; trip to Cuba while on leave from, 186; party with Prince of Wales and, 193; desire not to travel to India with, 195; departure for India with, 195; shoulder injury upon arrival in India with, 198; staff and servants in, 199; opinion of India during service with, 199; typical day in, 200; rental of bungalow in, 199-200; later memories of, 200; meets Pamela Plowden, 200-1; hobbies in, 201; polo matches in, 201-2; intellectual curiosity awakened during service with, 202-3; horse racing in, 202; opinions expressed in letters from, 204; novel *Savrola* written during service with, 205; restlessness with life in, 205-6; and proposal to cover British blockade of Crete, 206; accumulated leave taken in England by, 207-9; and permission for leave to report on Pathan uprising, 209-10, 215; rejoins, after attachment to other regiments, 215, 238; reaction to dispatches of, 215-16; and Tirah expedition, 217; desire to leave, 219; Kitchener expedition and, 221, 222; Inter-Regimental Polo Tournament in, 238; resignation from, 238; lessons learned from, 238

TWENTY-FIRST LANCERS, NILE EXPEDITIONARY FORCE. *see* journalism, Kitchener expedition, Sudan, *above*

SOUTH AFRICAN LIGHT HORSE, BOER WAR, 260-4; conflict between *Morning Post* contract and, 260; commissioned in, 260-1; strategy of Boers and, 261-2; Spion Kop battle and, 262-3; Jennie's visit with hospital ship and, 263; Ladysmith entered by, 264

QUEEN's OWN OXFORDSHIRE HUSSARS, 330, 347-8, 404, 469

WESTERN FRONT, 469-91; decision to leave for, 469; arrival at front, 469-71; attached to grenadier's Second Battalion in, 469, 470; life in trenches in, 471-3; interest in and enjoyment of warfare in, 473-6; Clementine's letters and packages to, 476-7; promise of brigade in, 477-80, 482; Haig and, 481-2; appointed lieutenant colonel, Sixth Royal Scots Fusiliers, 482; first parade with Royal Scots, 483; speech to men of Royal Scots, 483-4; march to Ploegsteert, 484; popularity among men of, 485-6; Clementine's efforts in London on behalf of, 486-7; leave from, for House speech, 487-9; decision to leave, 489-91

PERSONAL LIFE AND CHARACTERISTICS

APPEARANCE: at birth, 90, 93; at Sandhurst, 153, 158; while reporting on Pathan uprising, 210; at age fifty, 619

AWARDS AND HONOURS: Nobel Prize in literature, 24; Spanish Red Cross, 191; considered for Victoria Cross, 251, 270; honorary degree, Queen's University, 667

CHARACTERISTICS: singing in House of Commons, 25; wit, 27-9, 243, 308, 314, 315, 316, 319, 320, 606, 661; cigar smoking, 30, 530; situations provoking tears, 30, 32; love of animals, 30-1, 634-5; assertiveness with servants, 98-9; fascination with war games, 99-100, 108, 668; lack of sense of personal safety, 109, 210, 310-11, 392; affection for nanny, 131; generosity to nanny, 159, 179; leadership ability, 166; reaction to authority, 166, 261; as young officer in Fourth Hussars, 177; jealousy of Curzon and other ministers, 179; as peer among distinguished men, 188; enjoyment of warfare, 190, 385, 411, 412, 473-6; disregard for time, 193, 529; cocky attitude, 199; attitude while playing polo, 201-2; interest in politics, ethics, 202-3; desire for medals, 235, 270; ambitions for House, 235, 236, 237-8, 284-5, 314-15; interest in attending university, 237; response to imprisonment, 250; grasp of strategy and tactics, and readiness to criticize senior officials, 261; scrap-books of clippings about himself, 308; capacity for work, 309; as weekend guest, 309-10; take-charge attitude, 310-11;

tendency to exaggerate, 320; silk underwear for skin sensitivity, 327; admission of self-doubt, 329; awareness of poverty, 331; national crisis while bathing, 343; love of uniforms, 347-8, 404; high drama in public role, 355; exceeding authority granted to him, 382, 386, 455, 529-30, 568; routine for working, 392-3; ability to handle major tasks simultaneously, 392-3; vanity, in arguments, 432; as husband, 528; independence, 529, 662; sympathy with the beaten, 548-9; similarities to Michael Collins, 593; fascination with possibilities of use of force, 598; hospitality, 636-7, 667-8; reaction to gift of car from friends, 720

AS SEEN BY CONTEMPORARIES: in Fourth Hussars in India, 199, 215, 216; by Kitchener, 225; Duchess Fanny on romance and, 237; Steevens on future greatness of, 239; conduct in Boer War, 248-9; in early House career, 284; unpopularity in House, before switch to Liberal party, 293-7; Violet Asquith on, at first meeting, 301; as bachelor in Mount Street rooms, 308-9; Earl of Elgin on, at Colonial Office, 319; as social reformer, 331, 332, 335-6; in Liberal party, 341; audience reaction to newsreel of, as home secretary, 344-5; as heroic leader, 345; as conservative in House, 347; and zest for war, 385; during preparations for war, 385-6; at start of World War I, 388; calmness under fire, 408; Asquith on, at Admiralty, 460; popularity among soldiers in France, 472-3, 485; after return from France, 491-2; Lloyd George on distrust of, 503-4; postwar sentimentalism of, 530; postwar portrait of, 541; Balfour on, 558; after election losses, 610-11, 617, 702-3; after flying crash, 620; Beaverbrook on moods of, 655; during recuperation from car accident, 717-18; Lady Astor on end of career of, 720

FAMILY LIFE: punishment of children, 30; on relationship to son Randolph, 156; birth of daughter Diana, 328; birth of son Randolph, 328; play with children, 381, 464, 667; worry about safety of family, 391-2;

daughter Sarah born, 409; Meccano construction sets and gorilla games, 464; New Year's 1917 with family at Blenheim, 497; at Lullenden cottage, Kent, 506, 514; birth of daughter Marigold, 527; homelife during war, 527; fear of assassination attempts by Irish terrorists, 599-600; after election defeats, 620; on death of daughter Marigold, 621, 624; birth of daughter Mary, 622; vacations with, 623; worries about financial position and, 641-2; and reenactment of battle of Jutland, 668

FINANCES: income from writing, 77, 239, 264, 322, 497, 625-6, 627, 630, 667, 672, 675, 705; Sandhurst allowance, 153-4; political ambitions and, 174-5, 238; Fourth Hussars appointment and, 193, 200; investments with Cassel, 273, 330; income from lecture tours, 274, 715; as president of Board of Trade, 330; at Admiralty, 354; Pear Tree Cottage expenses, 384; as chancellor of duchy of Lancaster, 461; after returning from military command in France, 497; and libel action against Lord Alfred Douglas, 619-20; as lobbyist, 620; need to economize, 625-6, 635-6; worries about, 641-2; stock market investments, 667, 672, 674-5, 700

HEALTH: depression, 19-21, 98, 460, 462, 606, 637, 703, 718; thrown from horse, 99; during childhood in Ireland, 100; colds at St. George's School, 103-4; canings at St. George's School, 104, 105; mumps and measles, 109; pneumonia, 109-11; at Harrow, 129; influenza, 136, 667; fall at Deepdene estate, 149-50; near-drowning in Lake Geneva, 153; polo accidents, 177, 238, 620; shoulder injury in India, 198, 238; sunburn in India, 205; while reporting on Pathan uprising, 212; skin donation to wounded soldier with Kitchener, 235; during Oldham election, 240; during sea voyage, 245; loss of memory during House speech, 297-8; assassination attempts on, 330; crashes during flying lessons, 528-9; appendectomy, 608; hit by car in New York, 716-18

786

322; death of manservant during, 322; cruises, 353, 360, 667; with family at Pear Tree Cottage, 379-81; with family after defeat in 1922 election, 612; Mediterranean cruise, including visits with Mussolini and Pope Pius XI, 665-6; in Ireland, 667; tour of Canada and U.S., 672-6; visit with William Randolph Hearst, 673; visit to Wall Street, 674; visit to Hollywood, 675-6; hit by car in New York, 716-18
PUBLIC LIFE AND POLITICAL CAREER (INCLUDING HOUSE OF COMMONS): Randolph Churchill's influence and memory in, 21, 116-17, 174-5, 240, 283, 284, 286, 292, 298, 367, 370, 686, 694; Neville Chamberlain feud with, 119n; childhood visits to House and, 129; interest in, while in Fourth Hussars, 178-9; first public speech in, 207; desire to stand for House as Conservative, 207-8; military activities and ambition for seat in, 212-13, 214, 217, 235, 264-5; money needed for seat, 238; romantic life and, 237, 240, 300; decision to stand for office, 240; first election, Oldham (1899), 240-1; loss in, 241; win in 1900 Oldham election, after return from Boer War, 271-2; nineteenth-century standards and ideals held in, 274-5; beginning of political career, 275-6; chance for greatness in, 275; assumes seat in House, 280; familiarity with customs of House, 280; maiden speech in House, 281-3; audience for maiden speech, 281; reaction to maiden speech, 283; early months in House, 283-90; military policy of Brodrick criticized by, 285-8; naval policy and, 287, 333, 350, 712-13; as leader of 'the Hooligans,' 288; Joe Chamberlain's discussion with Hooligans and, 288-9; Free Trade issues and, 289-92, 293, 296, 298, 299; Home Rule and, 292 (see also Admiralty; Colonial Office, below); considers switch to Liberal party, 292-3; Oldham reactions to speeches and policy in, 294; unpopularity of, among House members, 294-7; loss of memory during House speech, 297-8; last speech as Conservative, 298; switch to Liberal party, 298-300; social reform legislation and, 305, 331-7, 347; suffrage movement and, 307, 317; capacity for work in, 309; Balfour and, 314; Manchester election (1906) and, 314, 316-17; Eddie Marsh hired as private secretary to, 315-16; appointed under secretary of state for colonies, 314-15 (see also under secretary of state for colonies, below); wit in speeches in, 320; appointed member of Privy Council, 321; appointed president of Board of Trade, 323 (see also Board of Trade, below); loss in Manchester election (1908), 323-4; win in Dundee by-election (1908), 324; knowledge of poverty, and policies of, 332; House of Lords blocking of social reform bills and, 334-5; 'People's Budget' of 1909 and, 334-6, 338; need for reform of House of Lords and, 335-7; parliamentary reform act and, 337-8; ambition to be prime minister, 339; offered Home Office by Asquith, 339 (see also Home Office, below); regarded as conservative in politics, 347; appointed to Admiralty, 352; (see also Admiralty, below); promised seat on Dardanelles Committee by Asquith, 461; accepts post as chancellor of duchy of Lancaster, 461; advice to Dardanelles Committee, 464-5; official trip to Dardanelles suggested by Kitchener, 466-7; excluded from War Cabinet, 467; resigns from Dardanelles Committee, 467-8; request for African command, 467-8; speech to House suggesting recall of Fisher, 487-9; return to political life after service in France, 491-2; reaction in House to speeches on campaign in France, 492-3; memo on war in France prepared by, 493-5; unpopularity of war views of, 496-7; and House debate over conscription, 497-8; attempt to clear name after Dardanelles campaign failure, 497-500, 502-3; and Lloyd George as prime minister, 500-3; growing influence of, after vindication, 503-5; on American entry into war, 504-5; appointed to Ministry of Munitions, 505 (see also Ministry of Munitions,

below); return to House, after 1917 Dundee election, 506; in 1918 Dundee election, 550; appointed secretary of state for war and air, 550 (*see also* Ministry of War and Air, *below*); and Dyer incident of British troops firing on Indian civilians, 568, 569-70; appointed to Colonial Office by Lloyd George, 571 (*see also* Colonial Office, *below*); in Dundee election (1922), 607-11; out of public eye after defeat, 612-13; as West Leicester candidate in 1923, 613-15; in Westminster election (1924), 615-17; Baldwin as head of Conservative party and, 618; activities to keep in public eye after election defeats, 620; win in Epping election (1924), 638-40; appointed to Treasury by Baldwin, 639-40 (*see also* Treasury, *below*); as possible successor to Baldwin, 669; after 1928 election loss, 671-2; fall of Baldwin government and, 671; Indian self-government debate and, 687-700; attacks Irwin declaration, 689-70; on Gandhi's political activities, 690-1; rift with Baldwin, 691; Gandhi's release by Irwin and, 695; resignation from Baldwin's shadow cabinet, 695-6; isolated from other politicians, 698-9; Government of India Act of 1935 fought by, 699-700; in 1931 Dundee elections, 701; criticism of Labour party economic policy after 1929 Crash and, 701; excluded from Baldwin-MacDonald coalition government, 701-3; reactions to rise of Hitler and, 711-12; objection to customs union between Germany and Austria, 713; receives permission from MacDonald for access to military information, 714; Lady Astor to Stalin concerning end of career of, 720

UNDER SECRETARY OF STATE FOR COLONIES, 317-22; appointed to office of, 314-15; Milner's policy on Chinese immigrants in mines in South Africa and, 317-19; with Elgin at, 319-21; Transvaal constitution and, 321

BOARD OF TRADE, 323-4; appointment as president of, 323;

Manchester election loss and, 323-4; salary at, 330; social reform policy under, 332; and strikes settled by, 342; interest in aviation at, 362

HOME OFFICE, 339-53; appointed to, 339; salary and responsibilities at, 339; penal reform policies in, 339-41; reports to King George from, 341, 342, 343; strikes settled by, 342-3, 345-7 anarchists in siege of Sidney Street and, 343-5; use of army in strikes and, 346-7; regarded as conservative in policies at, 347; and meeting with Kaiser Wilhelm, 347-8; Agadir incident with Germany and, 349-50; preparations for war with Germany under, 350-2; British policy of isolationism and, 351; annual visit to King at Balmoral, 352

ADMIRALTY, 352-460; Asquith offer of, 352; perquisites of office in, 353; salary and home with, 354; high drama of public role at, 355; German sea power watched in, 354, 355-7, 383; Haldane's visit to Germany and, 356-7; pledge of British neutrality in war between France and Germany and, 357; Wilson fired as first sea lord, 358; Lord Fisher's advice sought, 358-60; War Staff organization in, 359; proposal for transporting troops to France, 360-1; inspection of ships in, 361; new weapons encouraged by, 361-2; interest in aviation at, 362; takes flying lessons, 362-6; 'Naval Holiday' proposal in, 366; military appropriations sought for, 366-8; Home Rule issues in, 368-78; and trip to Belfast, 369-70; Carson's covenant against Home Rule and, 372-4; Ulster Volunteer Force and, 373-4; German support for Belfast and, 373, 374, 377; plan to strengthen British troops in Ireland and, 376; plea to Carson for truce and, 377-8; Austrian ultimatum to Serbia and, 378; trial mobilization of, 379; war preparations at, 379-88; conference to avert war proposed by, 382; authority exceeded in, 382, 386, 455, 529; support for France from, 383, 385-6; sale of warships to Turkey refused by, 384; war on Russia declared by Germany, 386; full naval mobilization order given, 386; British ultimatum to Germany over invasion of Belgium, 387-8; war declared on Germany, 388; preparation of navy for war, 392-9; routine for work during war, 392; handling of major tasks simultaneously, 392-3; first naval battle of war won, 395; questions about competence at, 396-7, 410, 411; Prince Louis moved from Admiralty position by, 397; Lord Fisher asked to succeed Prince Louis by, 397-9; and fall of Belgian fortress Namur, 400; defence of Antwerp and, 403, 406-12; Dunkirk landing supervision by, 403-4; war in France and, 403-5, 415; visit to Antwerp, 406-9; offer to resign office and command forces at Antwerp, 408; King Albert on value of, at Antwerp, 411-12; tank warfare advocated in, 416-17, 462; Dardanelles campaign and, 419-22; and War Council meeting on Dardanelles, 420, 421; Carden's plan of attack on Gallipoli and, 424-6; preparations for Gallipoli attack and, 428-35; Fisher's threat to resign and, 429; dispute with Kitchener and, 432; reviews troops with George V, 434; British attack on Gallipoli launched, 436-7; and delays in Carden's continuation of attack, 438-9, 444-5; de Robeck's attack and, 442, 443, 446, 447; and Hamilton's appointment as commanding general, 445; delay in continuing attack and, 447, 448; responsibility for failure of campaign, 449, 455, 460; Fisher on failure of campaign, 451-2, 453; and negotiations with Italy concerning fighting Germany, 451, 452; Fisher resignation and, 453, 456; Dardanelles campaign as threat to career and, 456-61; Asquith offer of another post, 456-7; unpopularity at, 459-60; departure from, 460, 462; book planned on years at, 627

MINISTRY OF MUNITIONS, 505-33; appointed to, 505; reactions to appointment of, 505; first meeting with staff in, 506-7; and primary objectives of department, 507; and government takeover of munitions

factories after strikes, 507-8; tank warfare and, 508; Haig's Passchendaele drive and, 509-13; and trips to front, 510, 512, 515-16, 523-4, 526, 531, 532; German attack on Italy and, 513-14; fighting in France and, 514-23; and need for American soldiers in France, 515; and advice to Lloyd George, 515, 516-17; visit with Clemenceau and, 517-21; and report to House on progress of war, 522; and desire for broader power, 530; and Haig's offensive against Hindenburg line, 531-2; victory and Armistice and, 533; Versailles peace conference and, 541-2, 549; troops from Dominion countries in war and, 545-6; dismissed from office by Lloyd George, 550

MINISTRY OF WAR AND AIR, 550-70; criticism of appointment to, 550; postwar troop repatriation and, 550-2; Haig's retirement and, 552; invasion of Ruhr by Red Soldiers' League and, 552; British policy towards Bolsheviks in Russia and, 555, 557-66; reaction to anti-Bolshevik policy of, 559-60; anti-Semitism in Russia and, 562; Polish resistance to Russian advances and, 563-4; proposed meeting on bolshevism with Ludendorff, 564-5; Lloyd George's commercial policy towards Russia and, 565, 566; H.G. Wells's trip to Russia and, 566; record at, 567-8; acceptance of Lloyd George's policy on military forces and, 567

COLONIAL OFFICE, 570-612; appointed to, 571; Turkey's postwar settlements and, 571; Palestine and, 572, 576-81; legacy of Balfour declaration and, 572; commitment to build Zionist state and, 572, 578; trip to eastern Mediterranean and, 573-8, 605; boundaries of proposed state and, 574; reception in Egypt and, 574-7; meeting on occupation of Iraq, 576; trip to Palestine and, 576-8; Arabs' meeting with, 577; and tree planting, 578; and House and cabinet discussion of policy in Palestine, 578-80; and British policy towards Turkey, 581-6; Lloyd George's refusal to negotiate with Kemal and, 581-2; Turkish massacre in Smyrna and, 583; and British reaction to massacre, 583-6; Home Rule for Ireland and, 586-603; and personal ties with Ireland, 586-7; Sinn Féin leadership and, 587-8; Dáil formation and outlawing by British and, 588; reaction to terrorism in Ireland and, 588-9; branch of Royal Irish Constabulary created by, 589-90; criticism of policy in, 591; question of armistice with Ireland raised, 591; and Government of Ireland Act and division of Ireland, 592; Collins and Griffith negotiation of Free State treaty with, 592-4; and defence of treaty, 594; transfer of power to Ireland and, 594-5; and response to violence after transfer of power, 595-9, 600-1; and acceptance of Irish constitution by voters, 599; election results in Ireland and, 599; and Sir Henry Wilson assassination, 599; fears of assassination attempts and, 599-600; and Collins's death, 601; and execution of Erskine Childers, 602-3; and adoption of Irish constitution, 603; and fall of Lloyd George coalition, 604, 605; and relationship with Lloyd George, 605-6; general elections (1922) and, 607-12

TREASURY, 639-64; asked by Baldwin to accept, 639-70; reaction of press to appointment of, 640; use of Randolph's Exchequer robes in, 640; ideas at, 641-2; war debt to U.S. and, 642; budget speeches at, 642-3, 660-2, 663-4; and state obligation to those in need, 643; military appropriations and, 643-4; rearmament and, 645; MacDonald's policy on naval base at Singapore and, 645; return to gold standard and, 645-8, 659-60; coal miners' strike and, 648-9, 657-9; general strike and, 649-51, 653-5, 660; *British Gazette* during general strike and, 652-4, 656; and settlement of strike, 655; criticism of strike policy and, 655-6; enmity of Labour party and, 656-8; antilabour legislation and, 659-60; relationship with Baldwin and, 661-2; criticism of economic policy in,

662, 663; independence of political party and, 662-3; last budget in, 664; overview of accomplishments at, 664; elections of 1928 and, 668-71

SPEECHES: tempo used in, 24-5; preparation and writing of, 26-7; classical phrases used in, 26; marking and typing of text in, 26-7; critics of, 27; wit in, 27-9; childhood imitations of father's style in, 129; World War II broadcasts and, 131; first public, at Empire music hall, on prostitution, 165-6; Cockran's advice about, 188; press conference after visit to Cuba, 191-2; first political, in defence of Conservative party, 207-8; at Bradford, before leaving to join Kitchener, 221-2; speaking exercises used for, 273; lecture tours, 273-4, 715. 716; maiden House, 281-3; Violet Asquith on strengths of, 287; loss of memory during, in House, 297-8; against Milner policy in South Africa, 318-19; on social reform, 331-2; on impact of shell upon a warship, 361; on Home Rule, 368-9, 371-2, 374, 375; after resignation from Dardanelles Committee, 468; to troops in Sixth Royal Scots Fusiliers, France, 483-4; to House, suggesting recall of Fisher, 487-9; on campaign in France, 492, 493-7; mastery of language in, and political strength, 530; on danger to Empire after end of war, 548; on bolshevism, at Oxford Union, 565-6; on Dyer incident of British troops firing on Indian civilians, 568, 569-70; about Iraq, extemporaneously, 606; Budget Day, 642, 660, 664; radio broadcast during 1928 election, 670; on Indian self-government, 692, 695, 697-8; on Untouchables, 697; radio interview during American lecture tour, 719; on monetary policy in British radio broadcast to U.S., 720

WRITINGS, 625-31, 703-5; *Savrola*, 19, 98, 115, 205, 237, 239, 264, 423; *The River War*, 22-3, 239, 242, 264, 284; feeling for language in, 24-5, 530; influences on style of, 24, 208, 217, 239; criticism of style of, 24; Nobel Prize for, 24; choice of words in, 25; *Marlborough: His Life and Times*, 77,

157, 667, 704, 705, 720; income from, 77, 239, 264, 322, 497, 625-6, 627, 630, 667, 672, 675, 705; first childhood, 101-2; techniques used in, 135, 667, 705; poetry at Harrow, 135; theme of lonely childhood of great men in, 157; *Lord Randolph Churchill*, 157, 173, 308, 309, 310, 325; foreign terms explained in, 211, 225; process of, 217-18; *The Story of the Malakand Field Force*, 217-19, 220, 238, 264; response to praise for, 218-19; resignation from Fourth Hussars to continue, 238-9; *London to Ladysmith via Pretoria*, 264, 271; interpretation of incidents reported in, 267-8; *Ian Hamilton's March*, 271; social life while working on, 309-10; *The Second World War*, 315n; tendency to exaggerate in, 320; *My African Journey*, 322, 327; on honeymoon, 327; *Great Contemporaries*, 330, 705; obituary for Rupert Brooke in *The Times*, 434; memo on war in France, 493; *The Aftermath*, 558n, 596; after election defeats, 620; ambition to be prime minister and, 626; planned book on Admiralty, 627; *Thoughts and Adventures (Amid These Storms)*, 626, 705; *The World Crisis*, 627-30, 665, 667, 672, 704, 705; Eddie Marsh's role in, 627; use of government documents in, 628; poetry for family, 632, 635; depressive tendencies and, 637; *My Early Life (A Roving Commission)*, 666-7, 704; proposed book on socialism, 667; with secretary, 718-19; *see also* journalism *heading and subheadings, above*; letters *under* Churchill, Clementine; Churchill, John ('Jack'); Churchill, Lady Randolph ('Jennie'); Churchill, Lord Randolph; Cockran, Bourke; Plowden, Pamela

Church of England, 50, 60, 306
Clarence, Duke of, 145
class structure: in Victorian England, 53-4; in Indian caste system, 683
Clavering, Francis Napier, 486
Clemenceau, Georges, 515, 517, 524, 680; WSC visits with, 518-21, 532; council of war with, 521; Versailles peace conference demands of, 541-2; antibolshevism of, 557, 563

Clive, Robert, 37
clubs in India, 197-8
Coal Mines Regulation Act, 614
coal mine strikes, 648-51, 657-60
Cockran, Bourke, 114; WSC visits with, 187-8, 191; advice on speaking from, 188; affair with Jennie Churchill, 193; WSC's lecture tour on Boer War and, 273
WSC'S LETTERS TO: on Cuba, 192; on House politics, 204, 293, 296, 299; during Boer War imprisonment, 251; on Oldham election, 272
Cody, Buffalo Bill, 107
Colley, Sir George, 183n
Collier, Robert Laird, 43, 67
Collier's (magazine), 23, 674, 704, 719
Collins, Michael, 687; De Valera rescued from jail by, 588; treaty with WSC negotiated by, 592-4; De Valera's views on treaty and, 594; elected head of provisional government, 595; fighting against new government and, 595-6; in London for WSC debate over Irish problems, 597-8; shelling of IRA headquarters ordered by, 600-1; slaying of, 601; Dáil adopts constitution drafted by, 603
Colonial Office: selection of candidates for, 48; postwar applications to, 543-4; *see also* Churchill, Winston Leonard Spencer: public life and political career, Colonial Office
Committee of Imperial Defence, 350, 351, 356, 391, 420n, 644
communism: agitators in Britain and, 550-1; WSC's concern over, 552, 665-6; *see also* bolshevism
Comyns-Carr, Mrs. J., 114
Congreve, Sir Walter, 572
Connaught, Duchess of, 310
Connaught, Duke of, 178, 310, 337
Connolly, Cyril, 636
conscription: in Ireland, 498, 587; WSC's plan for, 551
Conservative Business Committee, 671
Conservative party
    LORD RANDOLPH CHURCHILL AND, 99, 117-24; Fourth Party organized by, 119; 'Tory democracy' as rallying cry of, 120; resignation from Cabinet and, 123-4; Gladstone's last government and, 155

WSC AND, 17; Marjoribanks explains working of, 155; fall of Rosebery government and, 178; Jameson Raid and, 192; WSC's desire to stand for Parliament as member of, 207-8, 240; WSC on greatest achievement of, 208; speeches for, 236-7; Oldham elections, 240-1, 271-2; WSC's maiden speech in House and, 282; Free Trade issue and, 289-91; WSC switches to Liberal party from, 292-3, 298-9, 367; WSC's last speech as member of, 298; lower-class allegiance to, 303-4; changing religious attitudes and, 306; attack on WSC as Liberal from, 314; Milner's policy in South Africa and, 317-8; WSC's loss in Manchester election and, 323; social reform legislation and, 334-6, 663; 1910 general election and, 337; parliamentary reform and, 338; WSC as home secretary and, 340-1, 344, 346; strikes and, 342-3, 346; WSC's German policy at Admiralty and, 356; Prince Louis's appointment and, 361; military appropriations request from WSC and, 336-7; Home Rule and, 370, 372, 375, 596; British neutrality and, 383; WSC on Somme campaign and, 496-7; WSC as minister of munitions and, 505; postwar election and, 549-50; unpopularity of Lloyd George coalition and, 604-5; WSC on, in Dundee election, 608; WSC as independent in Westminster election and, 615-17, 618; WSC considers switching back to, 618-19; return to gold standard and, 646; distrust of WSC in, after general strike, 656-7; tariffs and, 662; opinion of WSC within, 662, 663; 1929 general election and, 668, 669-71; WSC's opposition to MacDonald and, 671-2; Indian self-government and, 685, 689-90, 691, 692, 693-4, 695, 698-9; 1931 election and, 701; WSC's protest of naval reductions and, 712-3

Constantine, King of Greece, 420, 436, 437

Constantinople, 417, 420-3, 585; strategic importance of, 422; fascination with, 423; as objective of Dardanelles battle plan, 427; exodus from, after de Robeck's attack, 442-3; Bolsheviks in, 564; British occupation

of, 581

Constasino, Mario, 716, 717

contraception, 302

Cook, Captain James, 40

Cook, Thomas, 40, 43

Coolidge, Calvin, 642

Cooper, Alfred Duff, 637, 671

Cooper, Lady Diana, 30, 527

Cooper, Wright, 127-8

Coote, Colin, 291

Cope, Alfred, 596, 598

Cork, fire in, 590-1

Cornwallis-West, Daisy, 309

Cornwallis-West, George, 263, 303, 338

Cosgrave, William, 597, 602

Coué, Emile, 306

Courtney, Ivon, 363

Cowles, Virginia, 335, 720

Cracroft, B., 69

Cradock, Sir Christopher, 395, 396;

Craig, James, 370

Crash of '29, 674, 675, 700, 707-8

Credit-Anstalt, 700

Creighton, Mandel, 167

Crete, 194; Greek-Turkish clashes on, 206, 207

Crewe, Lady, 301

Crewe, Lord, 319, 337, 621, 623

Crippen, Dr H.H., 339-40

Cripps, Sir Stafford, 5, 28

Cromer, Lord, 206, 239; Kitchener's expedition and, 220, 221, 234; in World War I, 391; Royal Commission of Inquiry into the Dardanelles headed by, 499

Cromwell, Oliver, 67, 80

Crosland, Jessie, 576

Crowe, Eyre, 351

Crystal Palace, 140-1

Cuba, 204; WSC's visit to, 186, 189-92, 205

Cunard, Maud, 527

Currie, Sir Donald, 138

Curzon, Lady, 86, 238

Curzon, George, Lord, 113, 466, 548; WSC's first meeting with, 178-9; WSC as under secretary of state for colonies and, 320-1; WSC in France and, 471-2, 473; Clementine's letter to, on WSC in proposed ministry of air, 486; exclusion of WSC from Lloyd George government and, 500; in Lloyd George's War Cabinet, 511; on Lloyd

George's policy towards civil war in Russia after revolution, 559, 561-2, 564; British policy towards Turkey and, 581, 583, 585, 603; WSC's Irish policy and, 594; Baldwin as prime minister and, 612; WSC letter to, on Marigold Churchill, 621; Clementine on, as WSC's rival, 626

Cust, Harry, 114

Cyprus, 329, 322

Czechoslovakia, 3, 553

D'Abernon, Viscount (Sir Edgar Vincent), 97, 114

Dáil Eireann: formation of, 587; declared illegal by British, 587-8; partition of Ireland and, 592; Free State treaty accepted by, 594; constitution adopted by, 603

Daily Chronicle, 163, 194, 344, 367, 626; WSC's maiden speech in House in, 283; interview with German prisoner in, 513

Daily Express, 335, 343; WSC's speeches reported in, 283, 335; on WSC at the Admiralty, 355; Jennie Churchill's marriage to Porch in, 526; on civil war in Russia following revolution, 555, 560; newspaper strike and, 650, 652-3, 655; on WSC in 1929 election, 670; chauvinism towards Empire in, 676, 678; Indian self-government debate in, 697

Daily Graphic: Randolph Churchill's letters from South Africa in, 137, 138, 243; WSC's trip to Cuba reported in, 186, 189-91

Daily Herald, 566, 607

Daily Mail, 45, 163, 306, 307, 312, 321, 362, 605, 626; WSC's articles for, 242, 704, 705, 717; WSC's elections reported in, 272, 316, 611; on WSC, 275; WSC in House reported on by, 283, 284-5, 294-5, 297; military policy of WSC reported in, 410, 495, 550, 583; strike at, 649, 650, 652; Indian self-government debate covered in, 689-90, 693, 697-8, 699

Daily Mirror, 312

Daily News, 163, 283, 304, 344, 356-7

Daily Telegraph, 166, 291, 367, 645, 665, 691, 719; WSC's columns on Pathan uprising in India in, 209, 211, 212, 215,

217; WSC appointed permanent correspondent for, 217; Boer War reported in, 245, 255-6; WSC's House speeches in, 283, 287; on WSC's loss in 1922 election, 211; WSC's articles for, 665, 672, 704

Dalton, Hugh, 646

Dardanelles, 417-61; Attlee on WSC's strategy in, 13; rightness of WSC's policy in, 16; WSC's first hearing of, 167; military significance of, 417-19; maps of, 418, 441; German mining of, 419; War Council recommendations on, 420; WSC's recommendations on, 420-1, 530; Kitchener to War Council on, 421-2; Carden's plan of attack in, 424; War Council debate and approval of, 424-9; WSC's preparation for war in, 428-35; Carden as commander in, 435; British attack on Gallipoli in, 435-6; British public reaction to attack in, 436-8; continuation of Carden's battle in, 438-9; de Robeck's attack in, 439-43; exodus from Constantinople and, 442-3; WSC's reaction to fighting in, 443-4; Hamilton dispatched to, 445; naval delays in resuming battles in, 446-8; Gallipoli landing in, 450-1; Fisher's evaluation of situation in, 451-2; Fisher's resignation over, 452-3; newspaper reaction to situation in, 454-5; WSC's career after failure in, 456-61, 490; Keyes's plan for naval assault of, 467; WSC's speech on, after resignation from Dardanelles Committee, 468; WSC's attempt to clear name in, 497-500, 502; WSC's later career haunted by, 505, 563, 566, 614, 617; British policy towards Turkish occupation of, 583-5, 603; *see also* Gallipoli

Dardanelles Commission. *See* Royal Commission of Inquiry into the Dardanelles

Dardanelles Committee, 420n; WSC promised seat on, 461; WSC's work on, 464-5; troops sent to Gallipoli by, 465; WSC's resignation from, 467-8

Darling, Lord, 616

Dartmoor Shepherd, 340

Davidson, H.O.D., 132

Davidson, John (civil servant), 652, 654, 689, 694

Edward VII, King of England: British Empire and, 42; coronation of, 115; opens Parliament, 279; mistresses of, 115, 301, 303, 337; WSC's social life with, 310; Balfour's resignation as prime minister and, 314; WSC as under secretary of state for colonies and, 319; Asquith as prime minister and, 323; WSC's courtship and marriage and, 325, 326; social reform and, 332; WSC's demand for House of Lords changes and, 337; Jennie Churchill and, 337; death of, 337-8; *see also earlier entries under* Albert Edward, Prince of Wales

Edwardian society, 301-7; contraception in, 302; affairs outside marriage in, 302-3; lower classes in, 303-5; changing religious attitudes and, 306; technological change and, 306-7; views of Empire in, 307; suffrage movement in, 307; London and, 312; literature and writing in, 313; theatre in, 313-14

Egypt, 220-36, 548, 552; British Empire and, 39-40; Randolph Churchill against Gladstone's occupation of, 119; France in, 223, 234-5; WSC arrives in, en route to Kitchener's camp, 223-4; map of, 224; WSC visits, 239, 574-5, 576; attitude of British administrators in, 239; evacuation of British troops from, 672, 692; reception for Prince of Wales in, 676

Egyptian Gazette, 45, 576

Eleventh Hussars, 184

Elgar, Edward, 38, 313, 374, 546

Elgin, Earl of: WSC as under secretary of state for colonies under, 315, 319-20; WSC's letter to, on talk with kaiser, 348

Eliot, T.S., 547, 665

Elizabeth II, Queen of England, 30

Elliott, Maxine, 22

Empire. *See* British Empire

Empire Day movement, 546, 676

Empire music hall, London, 165-6, 678

Encyclopaedia Britannica, 63

Ensor, R.C.K., 313

Entente Cordiale, 381

Enver Pasha, 422, 443

Epping: WSC's campaigns at, 638-9, 670, 671; support for WSC in, 696-7

Erskin, Monteith, 618

Erzberger, Matthias, 388

Esher, Lord, 333, 455, 466-7, 478, 611, 627

Essex, Lady, 527, 624

Estonia, 565

ethics, WSC's interest in, 202-3

Eton, 47, 102, 139, 156

Eugene of Savoy, 80

Europe: in 1914, map, 380; November 11, 1918, map, 538; 1931, map, 710; *see also individual countries*

Evening News, 163, 614; lore of war in, 540; WSC's article against bolshevism in, 560; *Evening Standard*, Westminster election reported in, 615; Keynes against gold standard in, 647; coal miners' strike reported in, 657

Everest, Mrs Elizabeth Anne ('Woom'): as friend and confidante of WSC, 13-14; influence of, 18, 22, 205, 241; hiring of, 93; WSC's preschool years and, 93-4, 98, 99, 100-2; WSC's tributes to, 97-8; affection and devotion of, 97-8, 131; WSC encouraged in first letter by, 101-2; diphtheria of, 109; WSC's holidays with, 108, 112, 137, 142; WSC's health and, 110, 136, 149, 176; WSC at Harrow and, 131; WSC's need for, 136-7; errands done by, 136; letters to WSC from, 136-7, 138, 139, 144; letters to Jennie from, 137; WSC's trip to France and, 143, 144; dismissed as housekeeper from Duchess Fanny's household, 158-9; WSC on dismissal of, 158-9; WSC's military career and, 176; death and funeral of, 179; headstone from WSC and Jack Churchill for, 179-80

excess-profits tax, 18

Fabian Society, 107

Faisal ibn-Husein, 571, 575

Falls, Cyril, 525

Farwell, Byron, 161, 184

fascism, WSC's interest in, 16, 665-6

feminist movement. *See* suffrage movement

Fergusson, Sir James, 287

Ferté, Sir Philip Joubert de la. *See* Joubert de la Ferté, Philip

Fianna Fáil, 595

film industry, 673, 675-6

Fincastle, Lord, 218
Fine Gael, 595
Finland, 553, 562
Fisher, Cecil, 360
Fisher, H.A.L., 564
Fisher, Sir John Arbuthnot (later Lord
  Fisher): WSC's action on request for
  monies from, 333; as legendary figure,
  358; WSC at Admiralty seeks advice
  from, 358-9, 360; letters to WSC from,
  358, 359-60, 375; on WSC's Home
  Rule speech, 375; WSC's policy after
  war declared on Austria supported by,
  382; as successor to Prince Louis as
  first sea lord, 397-9; on German threat
  to Paris, 403; German coast invasion
  strategy of, 417; early views on
  Dardanelles campaign of, 419-20; War
  Council debate on Carden plan and,
  424-5, 428; WSC's preparations for
  battle and, 428-30, 431-2; on Carden at
  Gallipoli, 436, 437, 439; on de
  Robeck's attack and ship losses, 443-4;
  on delays in resuming battle, 447;
  evaluation of situation by, with WSC,
  451-2; to Clementine about WSC's
  mistress, 451; resignation of, 452-3,
  455; reactions to resignation of, 456,
  457-8; WSC's career and, 457; request
  from WSC to return to the Admiralty,
  458; appointed to Admiralty
  committee by Asquith, 466; WSC's
  recommendation for recall of, 488-9;
  Fisher's reaction to, 488; WSC's
  continuing relationship with, 496
Fitzgibbon, Lord, 149
Fitzroy, Almeric, 311, 341
Fleming, Valentine, 415
Flotte, Die (magazine), 357
Foch, Ferdinand, 401, 502; on air force in
  wartime, 362; WSC's meeting with,
  518; council of war with, 521;
  Hazebrouck defence and, 523; Chemin
  des Dames ridge and, 524;
  Château-Thierry and, 526; drive
  against Hindenburg line by, 530-1,
  532; Armistice signed by, 533;
  anti-Bolshevik forces assembled by,
  557
Foggie, James K., 549-50
Forbes, Reverend Dr Edward, 88
Forster, E.M., 678
Forster, W.E., 163

Foster, R.F., 83n
Fourth Hussars. *See* Churchill, Winston
  Leonard Spencer: military career,
  Fourth Hussars
Fourth Party, 119, 280
France, 276, 584; battle of Dunkirk and,
  3-4; Franco-Prussian War and 84;
  Dreyfus affair in, 163, 235; Egypt and,
  223, 234-5; and Triple Entente, 312;
  preparations for war with Germany by,
  350; British neutrality and, 357, 383,
  385; Austrian-Serbian dispute and,
  381; WSC watches German ship
  movements near, 383; WSC seeks
  support for, 385-6; order from WSC
  for full naval mobilization and, 386;
  Germany declares war on, 387; British
  ultimatum over German invasion of
  Belgium and, 387-8; declares war on
  Turkey, 395; fighting in, 400-2, 403-5,
  413-14; general staff Plan XVII in, 401;
  Kluck advances into, 401-3; battle at
  Ardennes in, 402; on Western Front
  maps, 404, 470, 494, 512, 520;
  Dunkirk battle and, 403-5; Germans at
  Ostend and, 413; trench warfare in,
  413-15; War Council debate over plans
  in, 426-7; casualties in, 426; WSC's
  decision to leave for, 469-70; Somme
  campaign in, 493-5, 629-30; WSC on
  need for American forces in, 504;
  WSC's proposals to outlaw poison gas
  in, 507; WSC visits, as minister of
  munitions, 508, 509; American forces
  enter fighting in, 515, 521, 525, 532;
  WSC's evaluation of British policy in,
  515; council of war held in, 521;
  Armentières falls in, 522; worry over
  loss of Channel ports in, 522;
  Hazebrouck defence in, 522-3; WSC's
  continuing trips to, 523-5, 529;
  Chemin des Dames ridge defence in,
  524-5; Château-Thierry in, 525-6;
  tanks first used in, 531; Hindenburg
  line breached in, 531-2; final battles in,
  532-3; Armistice signed with, 533;
  effects of war on, 538; postwar naval
  power of, 542; Ruhr invasion and, 552;
  civil war in Russia after revolution and,
  555-6, 557, 564; air power of, 567;
  Syria and, 571, 572; British policy
  towards Turkey in Dardanelles and,
  581-2, 583-4; WSC on Somme

campaign in, 629-30; Indian colonies of, 681

Franco, Francisco, 16, 714

Franco-Prussian War, 84, 282

Frankland, Thomas, 269

Franz Ferdinand, Archduke, 378

Franz Joseph I, emperor of Austria, 275

Frazer, Sir James, 306

Free Food League, 293

Free State. *See* Irish Free State

Free Trade: WSC's support for, 289-92, 293, 296, 298, 299, 316; WSC and Chamberlain disagree over, 289-92, 293; WSC's return to public life and, 613, 615; WSC's later career and memories of, 662

French, Sir John, 264; WSC's plan to strengthen British soldiers in Ireland and, 376; naval protection of, 392-3; fall of Namur and, 400; WSC visits at front, 405; War Council debates on Dardanelles plan and, 424, 426; WSC's preparations for Dardanelles campaign and, 431-3; Aubers Ridge offensive and, 454; WSC's arrival in France as major and, 469; WSC promised brigade by, 477, 478, 479, 480, 482; on Haig's Passchendaele offensive, 516-17; Irish kidnap plot against, 588

Freud, Sigmund, 75, 164, 306

Frewen, Clara (aunt), 107, 139, 200, 476; WSC's childhood and, 112; Jennie Churchill's letters to, 172, 527

Frewen, Clare (cousin), 108, 476-7

Frewen, Moreton (uncle): WSC's childhood and, 107, 110, 111; as editor of WSC's *Malakand Field Force*, 218

Fuller, J.F.C., 509

Furse, W.T., 482, 491

Gallacher, William, 608, 610

Gallico, Paul, 32

Gallieni, Joseph-Simon, 402

Gallipoli, 417, 419; Carden's attack on, 424-5, 435-6, 438-9; Fisher on need to take, 444; newspaper reaction to attack on, 454-5; WSC's career after failure of attack on, 456-61; Dardanelles Committee sends troops to, 465; Keyes's plan for naval assault on, 467; Hamilton's campaign on, 498; Australian troops at, 545; Turkish forces on, 583-4; WSC's later career

haunted by, 585, 606, 614, 616, 702; *see also* Dardanelles

Galsworthy, John, 127, 340

Gandhi, Mohandas (Mahatma), 195, 197, 680, 683, 684, 687; WSC on, 16, 693, 696; in Boer War, 250, 262, 683; anglophilia of, 544, 681; imprisonment of, for movement for Indian self-government, 684, 692; Salt March of, 690, 693; WSC's reaction to Irwin's freeing of, 695; pact with Irwin signed by, 697; London conference on India attended by, 698, 699, 700

Gardiner, A.G., 341, 345, 662, 694

Gardiner, S.R., 67

Garibaldi, Giuseppe, 217

Garnett, Theresa, 330

Geddes, Sir Eric, 616

general strike, 649-51, 660; background to, 649-51; beginning of, 651; *British Gazette* published in, 652-4; end of, 655

George, David Lloyd. *See* Lloyd George, David

George, Saint, legend of, 539-40, 544-5

George III, King of England, 72

George IV, King of England, 184

George V, King of England, 178, 606, 656; WSC's childhood meeting with, 107; Edward's death, and coronation of, 337-8; People's Budget and, 338; parliamentary reform and, 338; WSC as home secretary and, 341, 342, 343; industrial unrest and, 345, 346; WSC's advice on Germany to, 349; WSC's annual visit to Balmoral with, 352; WSC at Admiralty and, 360; Home Rule debate and, 368, 373, 374, 376, 377; Austrian ultimatum to Serbia and, 379; WSC's denial of warships to Turkey and, 384; South American naval losses and, 396; German background of Prince Louis and, 397; Lord Fisher as successor to Prince Louis and, 398-9; battle for Antwerp and, 408, 411; criticism of Kitchener related to, 455; WSC's trip to Dardanelles and, 466; Haig on French's abilities to, 481; British Empire Exhibition and, 547; WSC's appointment to Colonial Office and, 571; Lawrence of Arabia's refusal of decoration from, 574; appeal for end to strife by, after division of Ireland, 592; sends regrets to WSC after 1922 election loss, 611; *British Gazette* on general strike and, 653; WSC's budget proposals reported to, 661; WSC's social engagements with, 667; seals of office of ministers after 1929 election received by, 671; British Empire and, 677, 678; naming of *Queen Mary* and, 678n; Gandhi invited to tea with, 700; MacDonald asked to form government after Crash of 1929 by, 700; inquiry after WSC's health from, 717

George VI, King of England, 3, 5, 30

Georgia (Russia), 553, 565, 582

Germany, 13; battle for Dunkirk and, 3-4; WSC's attitude towards, after defeat, 18; Franco-Prussian War and, 84; as WSC begins public life, 275-6; naval power of, 306-7; Triple Entente and, 312; projected war with, 333, 348, 349, 350; WSC as home secretary and, 347-8; WSC's view of Teutonic character of, 348; Agadir incident and, 349-50; WSC's preparation for war with, 350-2; Haldane's visit to, 356-7; military appropriation requests by WSC and, 366-7; Irish collaboration with, 373, 374, 377; WSC on Mediterranean ship movements of, 383; secret agreement between Turkey and, 384; demands Russian demobilization, 384-5; declares war on Russia, 386; declares war on France, 387; British ultimatum over invasion of Belgium to, 387-8; British declaration of war against, 388, 530; warships sold to Turkey by, 394-5; first naval battle against, 395; warfare in Belgium with, 399-400, 402-3; warfare in France with, 400-2, 403-5, 413-14; and Kluck's advance into France, 401-3; battle of Ardennes with, 402; attack on Antwerp by, 403, 406-13; on Western Front maps, 404, 470, 494, 512, 520; Dunkirk battle and, 403-5; Ostend taken by, 413; mining of Dardanelles by, 419; Somme campaign and, 493-5, 629-30; United States declares war against, 504; WSC's proposal to outlaw poison gas use and, 507; Passchendaele drive by Haig and, 509-13; Italy

attacked by, 513-14; Brest-Litovsk treaty with Russia and, 514; U.S. forces enter fighting in France against, 514-15, 521, 525, 532; Armentières fall and, 522; Hazebrouck defence against, 522-3; Château-Thierry and, 526; tanks first used against, near Amiens, 531; and breach of Hindenburg line, 531-2; troops of, after fall of Hindenburg line, 532-3; final battles of war and, 532-3; Armistice signed with, 533; Hitler at close of war and, 534; surrender of fleet by, 537-8, 540-1; on map of Europe, November 11, 1918, 538; Versailles peace conference and, 538-9, 541-2, 549, 552, 712, 713; lore of war and, 540-1; reparations and, 549, 663; WSC plans to garrison British Zone in, 551; Ruhr invasion by Red Soldiers' League from, 552; civil war in Russia after revolution and, 553, 557, 558, 559, 565; Easter rebellion in Dublin and, 587; remnants of disbanded army organized by Hitler in, 590; rearmament by, 643; League of Nations admission of, 665; Hitler in, 706-14; Crash of 1929 and, 707-8; on map of Europe, 1931, 710

Gerrard, Eugene, 363

Gibb, Andrew, 483-5, 491

Gibbon, Edward, 80, 240; WSC's familiarity with works of, 24, 97, 203-4; WSC's style influenced by, 24, 204, 217, 239

Gibbs, Philip, 513

Gibraltar, 40

Gilbert, Martin, 460, 495, 603, 632, 668

Gilbert and Sullivan, 49, 58, 61, 67, 197

Girouard, Mark, 233

Gladstone, Herbert, 118, 155

Gladstone, William, 311, 367, 543; Disraeli and India and, 47; Victorian sexual attitudes and, 73-5; Randolph Churchill and, 116, 117-22, 123; Fourth Party and, 119; WSC's childhood impressions of, 129; last government of, 154-5; resignation of, 155; WSC's views on, 204; London treaty of 1884 in Boer republics and, 243; Home Rule and, 368, 586

Gladstone, Mrs William, 74

Gobineau, Count Joseph Arthur de, 12

Godley, Alexander, 545

426; German prisoners of war and, 431;
promise of brigade to WSC and, 478,
479, 481-2; replaces French in
command, 480-2; as early
acquaintance of WSC, 480-1;
military plans of, 481; WSC made
lieutenant colonel by, 482, 490;
Somme campaign and, 493, 494, 497;
outlook in 1917 from, 502; U.S. entry
into war and, 504; Passchendaele drive
by, 508-13, 517, 522, 544; on Italian
defences, 514; WSC's confidence in,
515; WSC visit to France and, 517,
518; Hazebrouck defence by, 522-3;
Chemin des Dames ridge assault by,
524; tanks used near Amiens by, 531;
Canadian soldiers under, 545;
repatriation of troops and, 550, 551;
retirement of, 552
Hailes, Lord, 695-6
Hailey, Sir Malcolm, 698
Hakewill Smith, Edmund, 483, 485-6,
490
Haldane, Aylmer, 221; armoured-train
mission of, 247, 248-9; WSC's conduct
described by, 249; as prisoner of war,
249; WSC's escape and, 251-3; escape
of, 269
Haldane, R.B. (later Lord Haldane), 281,
292, 352; on early WSC speech, 221-2;
social reform and, 332; German visit
of, 356-7; WSC at Admiralty and, 359;
war preparations and, 391; as successor
to Prince Louis, 397; on WSC during
battle for Antwerp, 409-10
Halévy, Elie, 332
Halifax, Lord. *See* Irwin, Lord
Hall, Gilbert, 530
Halle, Kay, 715
Hamel, Gustav, 365
Hamilton, Sir Edward, 290, 293
Hamilton, Lord George, 123, 662
Hamilton, Ian, 183, 228, 498, 631; with
WSC on ship to England, 207; WSC's
assignment to India and, 217; WSC's
letters from Kitchener expedition to,
228-9, 230, 231-2, 233, 234; in Boer
War, 247, 261, 264, 266, 268, 269-70;
WSC's wedding and, 326; on WSC,
431; as head of Gallipoli campaign,
446; attack on Gallipoli delayed by,
446-9; beach landings by, 450-2; on
military's faith in WSC, 459; in

France, 465-6; relieved of command,
467; attempt to clear reputation by,
498; on trench warfare, 545
Hands, Charles E., 316, 317
Hankey, Sir Maurice, 437, 452, 454, 529,
628; on WSC's enthusiasm for war,
385; WSC's advocacy of tanks and,
416; Dardanelles campaign and, 420,
421; War Council debate on Carden's
plan and, 424-5; WSC's troop plans in
Dardanelles and, 428, 431-2; Fisher
unrest and resignation and, 452, 454;
on WSC's desire to have Fisher return
to Admiralty, 458; with WSC on trip to
Dardanelles, 466; WSC's request for
field command in France and, 468; on
Smith's book on campaign in France,
493; WSC's attempt to clear name in
Dardanelles campaign and, 498;
Passchendaele report of, 510; on
casualties in France, 516; WSC's anti-
Bolshevik speeches and, 559, 565-6;
WSC's policy towards Kemal in Turkey
and, 582, 585, 586
Hansard, 663
Harcourt, Lewis, 385
Harcourt, Sir William, 113
Hardie, Keir, 163, 342, 647
Harding, Norman, 600, 631
Harding, Warren G., 620
Harington, Sir Charles, 584, 585
Harmsworth, Alfred (later Lord North-
cliffe), 163, 242, 298, 312, 494, 605
Harmsworth, Esmond, 715, 717, 719
Harper's Weekly, 172, 174
Harrap, George, 705
Harriman, Averell, 7-8
Harriman, Pamela, 75; *see also* Churchill,
Pamela
Harris, Frank, 82, 112, 118, 157;
Randolph Churchill's House career
and, 122, 124; Randolph's declining
health noted by, 170-1
Harrovian (school paper), 130, 135, 148
Harrow Gazette, 138
Harrow School, 47, 71, 124-36, 158, 681;
WSC's visit to, during World War II, 6
WSC ATTENDS: his academic achieve-
ment at, 22; his memory for facts at,
23, 24; his flair for language at, 24;
entrance examination to, 124-6; and
patriotic songs of, 127; Eton-Harrow
cricket match and, 139, 140; Sandhurst

entrance examination preparations at, 146, 147, 148; last term at, 148
Hartington, Lord, 96, 117
Hazebrouck, France, 522-3
Hazlitt, William, 26
Head, Anthony, 31
health-insurance legislation, 334, 339, 643
Healy, Timothy M., 376
Hearst, William Randolph, 187, 204, 673
Hearst, Mrs William Randolph, 673
Hearst Syndicate, 673, 704, 713
Hely-Hutchinson, Sir Walter, 260, 265
Henley, W.E., 39, 164
Henn, Thomas Rice, 47
Henry, Denis, 589
Henry II, King of England, 370
Henry VIII, King of England, 80
Henty, G.A., 60, 484
Hess, Rudolf, 31, 711
Hicks-Beach, Sir Michael, 110, 122, 290, 310
Hilferding, Rudolf, 305
Hill, Kathleen, 11
Hill, Richard, 11
Himmler, Heinrich, 707
Hindenburg, Paul von, 431, 513, 515, 533, 541, 709
Hindenburg line, 531, 532, 548
Hindlip, Lord, 168
Hinduism, 682-3
Hirsch, Baron, 114, 115, 145
history: WSC's childhood study of, 132, 133; WSC's reading in, while in India, 203-5
Hitler, Adolf, 4, 5, 32, 275, 706-14; WSC's reaction to, 16, 20, 711-13; at close of World War I, 534; remnants of disbanded army organized by, 590; *Mein Kampf* title and, 630; leadership of, 706-8; Crash of 1929 and, 707-8
Hoare, Sir Samuel, 5, 633, 652, 685, 698, 701, 716
Hobson, John Atkinson, 305
Hodder and Stoughton (publishers), 322
Hoe Farm, Surrey, 462, 464
Hogg, Sir Douglas, 656
Holdern, Charles, 704
Holland. *See* Netherlands, the
Holt, Beric, 652, 654
Holtby, Winifred, 617
homelife in Victorian society, 63-6
Home Rule for India, 690; *see also* India

Home Rule for Ireland, 120, 586-603; music hall songs on, 58; Randolph Churchill and, 121, 154, 155, 292, 368, 369, 370; Gladstone's bill (1886) for, 121; WSC's childhood exposure to House debate on, 129; WSC's support for, 292, 367, 368-78; Asquith and, 338-9; Carson's covenant against, 372-3; Kipling's poem on Ulster Volunteer Force and, 374; WSC's ties to Ireland and, 586-7; Sinn Féin leadership in Ireland and, 587-8; Dáil formation and outlawing by British and, 587-8; terrorism in Ireland and, 588-92, 595-8; Government of Ireland Act dividing Ireland and, 592; Collins and Griffith in London to negotiate Free State treaty and, 592-4; Dáil adoption of treaty and, 595; IRA violence and, 595-7; constitution drafted and adopted and, 598-9, 603; WSC's later career and memories of, 617, 662, 698-9
Hong Kong, 542, 645
Hoover, Herbert, 674, 719
Hopkins, Harry, 28
Hopwood, Sir Francis, 410
Hore-Belisha, Leslie, 308
Horrocks, Brian, 161
Household Cavalry, 551
Household Management (Beeton), 61, 65-6
House of Commons: upper-class control of, 69; Edward VII opens new session of, 279-80; customs of, 280; welfare legislation in, 305; Royal Commission of Inquiry to clear WSC's name in, 498-500, 502; anti-Jewish sentiment in, 569; Statute of Westminster and authority of, 679; *see also entries for* Churchill, Lord Randolph; Churchill, Winston Leonard Spencer: public life and political career
House of Lords, 280; social reform bills from Commons blocked in, 305, 334-5; WSC on need for reform in, 335-7; and parliamentary reform act, 337, 338; Home Rule bill in, 371
Housman, A.E., 350
Howard, John, 255, 257
Howe, Lady, 144, 281
Howe, Lord, 144
Hozier, Bill, 619
Hozier, Lady Blanche, 324, 325; marriage of daughter to WSC, 326;

802

death of, 635

Hozier, Clementine. *See* Churchill, Clementine

Hozier, Nellie, 353, 469

Hughes, W.M., 542

Hugo, Victor, 107

Hunt, Sir David, 24

Hunt, George William, 59

Hunter, Sir Charles, 479

Husein ibn-Ali, 571, 575

Ian Hamilton's March (WSC), 271

Illustrated London News, 37, 461

Illustrated Sunday Herald, 572, 589

Imperial Federation League, 543

imperialism: WSC's defence of, 208; Wilsonian doctrine of self-determination and, 541-2; postwar attitudes towards, 546-7; *see also* British Empire

India, 38, 543; British administration of, 40, 195-6; Last Stand immortality in, 46; Randolph Churchill's visit to, 117; Randolph as secretary of state for, 120-1; WSC with Fourth Hussars in, 194, 195-7, 198-9; magic of local life in, 196-7; life of British residents in, 197-8; Pathan uprising reported by WSC in, 208-17; demands for protection in war from, 396; spread of bolshevism as threat to, 561; Dyer incident of shooting by British troops in, 568-9; Baldwin considers appointing WSC secretary of state for, 669; dominion status recommended for, 675; changes in, as Empire changes, 677, 678; literary works on, 678; Indian National Congress in, 680-2; in 1929, map, 681; Hinduism in, 682-3; caste system in, articles 683; Gandhi's imprisonment for published on, 684; conference on dominion status for, 685; WSC's feelings about Empire and, 686-9; Mayo's *Mother India* influences views of, 687-8; attack by WSC on Irwin declaration on, 689-90; Gandhi's Salt March in, 690; Baldwin-WSC rift and, 691-2, 693-6; WSC's speech and articles on, 692-3, 697-8; Gandhi-Irwin pact on, 697; Government of India Act of 1935 for, 699-700; Statute of Westminster and, 715-16

Indian Civil Service, 40, 677; candidates for, 47-8, 544; life of British residents in, 49-50; Indian natives in, 196; number of men in, in 1930s, 677; literary portraits of, 678

Indian Empire Society, 692, 693

Indian Gazette, 685

Indian National Congress, 107, 680-2

India Office, 47

International Red Cross, 507, 556

IRA. *See* Irish Republican Army (IRA)

Iran, 539, 571, 576

Iraq, 539, 571, 575, 576, 579, 606, 645, 676

Ireland, 677; rightness of WSC's policy in, 16; John Churchill as viceroy of, 96; Randolph Churchill and family in, 96-9; WSC on politics in, 99, 548; WSC in Colonial Office and, 570; impact on British life of, 586; WSC's personal ties with, 586; Sinn Féin leadership in, 587-8; conscription in, 587; Dáil formed, and suppressed by British in, 587-8; terrorism in, 588-91, 595-8, 601-2; WSC on, 588-9; special branch of Irish Constabulary established in, 589-90; razing of Cork by fire in, 590-1; Government of Ireland Act dividing, 592; De Valera's representatives negotiate Free State treaty covering, 592-5; Dáil adopts treaty in, 595; violence by IRA over treaty in, 595-7; WSC's House speech on violence in, 597; constitution written by Collins and WSC for, 598-9; and slaying of Sir Henry Wilson, 599-600; and death of Griffith, 601; and death of Collins, 601; constitution adopted by Dáil in, 603; after partition, map, 602; Statute of Westminster and, 679-80; *see also* Home Rule for Ireland

Irish-Americans, 273

Irish Catholics, 303, 545

Irish Coercion Laws, 204

Irish Free State, 610; treaty establishing, 593, 594, 595; terrorism following treaty for, 595-7, 599-602; WSC's support for, 595-6; constitution framed for, 598-9; constitution ratified in, 603; after partition, map, 602

Irish Nationalists: Randolph Churchill and, 119, 120, 121; Gladstone's last government and, 155; Rosebery and, 178; WSC's maiden House speech and,

282; Home Rule and, 368-77; British ultimatum to Germany supported by, 387; WSC's policy in Dardanelles and, 498; growing influence of WSC after vindication and, 504; Sinn Féin leadership and, 587

Irish Republican Army (IRA), 99, 602, 603; power of, 588; police trained in methods against, 590; violence by, 595-8, 602; Dublin's Four Courts occupied by, 596-7, 600; constitutional provisions against, 598, 603; Free State treaty ratification and, 598-9; Sir Henry Wilson slain by member of, 599

Irregulars (members of IRA), 595; violence by, 595, 598, 599, 601; Dublin's Four Courts occupied by, 596-7, 600

Irving, Sir Henry, 156

Irwin, Lord (later Lord Halifax), 5, 675, 680, 686, 688, 716; conference on dominion status for India and, 684-5; assassination attempts on, 688; debate over declaration of, 689-90, 694-5; on WSC's speech before Indian Empire Society, 692; Gandhi released from prison by, 695; Gandhi's meeting and pact with, 696, 697

Israel. *See* Palestine

Istanbul, 585

Italy, 275, 542, 552, 665; Tripoli invaded by, 349; declaration of neutrality and, 387; WSC's negotiations with, over war with Germany, 451, 452, 456; German attacks on, 513-14; British policy towards Turkey in Dardanelles and, 581, 584; WSC's trip to, 665-6

Jackson, Sir Henry, 432, 444, 447, 460, 627

Jacobs, Aletta, 76

Jainism, 683

James, Henry, 51, 71

James, Sir Henry (later Lord James), 100, 110, 169, 170

James, Lionel, 225

James, Robert Rhodes. *See* Rhodes James, Robert

James, Walter H., 149, 150-1

James, William, 29, 306

James, Admiral Sir William, 644

James II, King of England, 80

Jameson, Leander Starr, 163, 192

Jameson Raid, 163, 192, 244, 281

Japan, 16, 275; League of Nations and, 542; postwar military power of, 542, 643; Russia and, 553, 556; WSC on possibility of war with, 645

Jeffreys, George, 470-1, 472

Jeffreys, Patrick, 212, 213, 214, 215

Jellicoe, Sir John, 362, 423, 620; appointed to war staff at Admiralty, 359; as commander in chief of Home Fleet, 382; naval preparations before World War I and, 392; Lord Fisher as first sea lord and, 399; Dardanelles plan and, 428-9; on Passchendaele drive, 509; battle of Jutland and, 544, 617

Jennings, Louis, 82, 112, 170

Jerome, Clarissa ('Clara') (grandmother): WSC on, 83; family life of, 83-5, 86; Jennie's marriage to Randolph Churchill and, 86-9, 89; letters from Randolph Churchill to, 87-8, 93; WSC's childhood impressions of, 130; Randolph Churchill's declining health and, 173; death of, 179

Jerome, Clarita. *See* Frewen, Clara

Jerome, Jeanette ('Jennie'). *See* Churchill, Lady Randolph ('Jennie')

Jerome, Leonard (grandfather): background of, 85, 86; WSC on, 85; daughter Jennie's marriage to Randolph Churchill and, 86-9

Jerome, Leonie. *See* Leslie, Leonie

Jerrold, Douglas, 614

Jeune, Mary, Lady (later Lady St. Helier), 241; WSC's desire to join Kitchener and, 219, 221; WSC's courtship and marriage and, 324-5, 327

Jewish Agency for Palestine, 580

Jews: WSC as under secretary of state for colonies and, 320; German loss in war blamed on, 541; British reactions to Ukrainian pogroms for, 562; *see also* anti-Semitism; Palestine

Jocelyn, John Strange, 113

Jocko (riding master), 175-6

Joffre, Joseph Jacques Césaire, 361, 401-2, 403, 413, 434, 472, 523

Johannesburg in Boer War, 268-9

Johannesburg *Star*, 258

Jones, Thomas, 591

Jordan, 539

Joubert, Piet, 251, 253, 256

Joubert de la Ferté, Sir Philip, 363

804

Kruger, Paul, 244-5, 246, 256, 269, 272
Krupp, Gustav, 709
Kynnersley, H.W. Sneyd-. *See*
Sneyd-Kynnersley, H.W.

labour unions. *See* strikes; unions
Labouchère, Henry du Pré, 58, 169
Labour party, 5, 32, 281; WSC on, 18,
21, 607, 608, 609; social reform policy
of WSC and, 332; strikes and, 346,
648; WSC's growing influence after
Dardanelles vindication and, 504;
views of, on British Empire, 546;
British policy towards bolshevism and,
560-1; Lloyd George and, 566; Home
Rule and, 596, 603; opinion of WSC in,
607; in 1922 elections, 608, 609, 611; in
1923 elections, 613, 615; WSC in
Westminster election and, 615-16, 617;
WSC on ability to govern of, 617-18;
return to gold standard and, 646;
WSC's enmity with, 656-8; in 1929
elections, 670-1; in 1931 elections,
700-1
Labour Representative Committee, 281
Lamb, Sir Harry, 585
Lambert, George, 491
Lancaster, duchy of, 461, 503
Lane, James F., 634, 650
Lane-Fox, George, 658, 662, 685, 689,
693, 695
Langtry, Lillie, 58, 288, 338
Lanrezac, Charles, 401-2
Lansdowne, Lord, 194, 311, 501-2
Laski, Harold, 10, 18, 27, 604
Latvia, 565
Lausanne, Treaty of, 585
Laver, James, 68
Lavery, Hazel, 463
Lavery, Sir John, 720
Law, Andrew Bonar, 569, 609, 614, 632;
WSC's wit and, 320; WSC in
Manchester election and, 338; Home
Rule and, 370-1, 372, 373, 374, 375;
WSC on, 375; WSC's plan to
strengthen British soldiers in Ireland
and, 376; German declaration of war on
Russia and, 386; on Antwerp defence,
411; Wilson letter to, on war plans,
426; Fisher's resignation from
Admiralty and, 454; WSC after
Gallipoli failure and, 456-9, 668;
Dardanelles Committee and, 465, 467;

WSC's request for brigade in France
and, 479; WSC's return to House and,
492; WSC's attempt to clear name after
Dardanelles campaign and, 498, 499,
503; Lloyd George government and,
500, 511; WSC's appointment as
minister of munitions and, 505; WSC's
policy in France and, 517; Irish kidnap
plot against, 588; IRA murder of
Wilson and, 600; on WSC's handling of
Turkish affair, 603-4; fall of Lloyd
George government and, 604, 605;
WSC on, in 1922 election, 608; as
prime minister, 612; WSC's use of
documents while writing and, 628
Lawrence, D.H., 427
Lawrence, T.E., 629; as hero after war,
544; WSC's visit to Palestine with, 573-
4, 575, 576-7; on WSC in elections,
611, 639, 671; as guest at Chartwell,
637; biography of Marlborough
suggested as subject for WSC by, 667
League of Britons Overseas, 676
League of Liberals Against Aggression
and Militarism, 333
League of Nations, 571, 580, 603, 604,
665; Versailles peace conference and,
538-9; Lloyd George supports, 541-2
Lebanon, 571
Lee, Robert E., 347
Lees-Milne, James, 668
Lefevre, André, 552
Leicester Mail, 613
Lemnos, 431, 432, 433
Lenin, V.I., 305, 581; WSC on, 530, 566,
665-6; Brest-Litovsk treaty and, 553;
civil war in Russia after revolution and,
553, 556-7, 561, 562, 563; belief in
spread of revolution beyond Russia by,
556, 558-9; attacks on theories of, 558-
9, 570; British commercial policy
towards, 565; British recognition of,
638
Leninism, 666
Leslie, Anita, 111
Leslie, Ann, 89
Leslie, Jack (uncle), 112, 324
Leslie, Leonie (aunt), 168, 315, 631;
background and childhood of, 84, 85;
WSC's childhood and, 107, 108, 109,
112; WSC's letters to, 166-7, 187, 348;
Jennie Churchill's letters to, 172, 174,
385, 461; WSC's apartment decorated

by, 271; WSC travels with, 310; meets Kaiser Wilhelm, 348

Leslie, Norman (cousin), 400

Leslie, Olive (cousin), 107

Leslie, Shane (cousin), 108, 114, 298, 622-3

le Tonnelie, Henri, 114

Lewis and Lewis (solicitors), 176

Liberal party, 613; Randolph Churchill's attacks on, 118-22; Gladstone's last government and, 154; Jameson Raid and, 192; WSC's desire to stand for Parliament as Conservative and, 207-8; Oldham election of WSC and, 271-2; WSC's switch to, 292-300; Home Rule and, 299, 368, 370, 372, 375, 596; lower-class allegiance to, 303-4; social reform legislation and, 305, 331-2, 335; Milner's mining policy and, 317-18; WSC's policy in South Africa and, 321-2; WSC's loss in Manchester election and, 323; in 1910 election, 337; parliamentary reform and, 338, 339; opinions of WSC in, 341; WSC as secretary of state and, 341, 345; WSC as home secretary and, 351; support of fighting in France in, 386; WSC's growing influence after vindication and, 504; British policy towards bolshevism and, 560; in 1922 elections, 609, 611, 612, 613; return to gold standard and, 646; in 1929 elections, 668, 669, 671

Liddell Hart, B.H., 412, 431, 444, 567, 645

Liège, Belgium, 401, 402

Liman von Sanders, Otto, 443, 449

Limpus, Sir Arthur, 435

Lindemann, Frederick A. ('the Prof'), 15, 637, 717, 720

Lindsay, Lady, 114

Lindsay, Sir Ronald, 719

Lippmann, Walter, 677, 713

Lithuania, 565

Little, J.D.G., 151, 152

Litvinov, Maxim, 343

Liverpool, 345, 346

Liverpool Conservative Association, 285

Lloyd, Lord, 687, 692, 697, 720

Lloyd George, David, 18, 21, 281, 539, 609, 628, 631, 698, 700; opinion of WSC of, 8, 24, 284; switch to Liberal party by WSC and, 298; WSC's

opinion of, 309, 627, 704-5; WSC's wedding and, 326; Clementine Churchill and, 329; social reform and, 332, 333, 334, 606; National Health Insurance Act and, 334, 339; 'People's Budget' of 1909 and, 334, 335; prison reform by WSC and, 340, 341; unions and, 342; Agadir incident and, 350; social life with Churchills and, 353, 637; new weapons bought by, 361-2; military appropriation requests from WSC and, 336-7; Home Rule and, 368, 371, 373, 376; on mediation for European disputes, 379; British neutrality and, 383, 385; support for France in war by, 385; WSC's order for full naval mobilization and, 386; ultimatum to Germany over Belgium invasion and, 387; South American naval losses and, 396; battle for Antwerp and, 410, 411; on trench warfare, 415; Dardanelles campaign and, 420-1, 443-4; War Council debate on Carden's plan and, 424-5; on Fisher, after resignation, 453; Gallipoli failure of WSC and, 455-8; on WSC after leaving Admiralty, 460, 461; tank warfare and, 462; WSC's request for brigade in France and, 479; fall of Asquith government and, 480, 491; Clementine Churchill on, 486-7, 613; WSC's return to politics and, 491, 492; Haig's Somme campaign and, 494, 495; Asquith's resignation and, 500, 501; new government formed by, 500; WSC's exclusion from new government and, 500-3; WSC's growing influence after vindication and, 503-5; WSC as minister of munitions and, 505, 507; Haig's Passchendaele drive and, 509, 510, 511, 512-13; British policy in France and, 515-17, 520-1; WSC's advice on war policy to, 515, 516-17; WSC to, on his visit to Clemenceau, 519, 520-1; love letters to Frances Stevenson from, 527-8; WSC's relationship with, 529, 639, 705-6; WSC's attempt to increase his power and, 530; WSC's letter to, on Haig's use of tanks in France, 531; Versailles peace conference and, 533, 541, 542; Indian self-government and, 543, 689; election after Armistice called by, 549-

50; bolshevism policy of, 566; postwar military policy of, 567; as speaker, 568; Dyer incident of shooting by British troops in India and, 569; WSC appointed to Colonial Office by, 571; Palestine and, 572, 579; Kemal in Turkey and, 581-5; WSC's attempt to clear name after Dardanelles campaign and, 582; Irish violence over Home Rule and, 589, 590, 592, 599; Free State treaty negotiation by, 592-3, 594; transfer of power in Ireland supervised by WSC and, 595; Irish border disputes and, 598; fall of government of, 604-5; WSC's loyalty to, 605, 608; 1922 election and, 611; Baldwin's new government and, 639; Treasury and, 641, 661; return to gold standard and, 646; general strike and, 654; on England's aim in India, 686

Lockhart, Sir William, 217

London, 44-5; as centre of British Empire, 38; in Victorian times, 51-2, 57-8, 161-7; architecture of, 57; advertising in, 57-8; WSC's trips from Sandhurst to, 161-2; in 1870s, 161-7; availability of newspapers in, 163; in Edwardian times, 312; political refugees in, 343-4; strikes in, 345; *see also* Victorian society

London, Jack, 304

Londonderry, Lord, 202, 618, 658

Londonderry, Theresa, Lady, 260, 319

London Gazette, 491

London to Ladysmith via Pretoria (WSC), 264, 271

London *World*, 113

Long, Charles, 247

Long, Sydney, 652

Long, Walter, 500, 505

Longmans (publisher), 218

Lord Randolph Churchill (WSC), 157, 325; father's illness recalled in, 173; writing of, 308, 309; publication and success of, 310

Lorraine, 401

Lothian, Lord, 641n

Loucheur, Louis, 507

Louis Napoleon, 84, 400, 401

Louis of Battenberg, Prince. *See* Battenberg, Prince Louis of

Louvain, Belgium, 403

Love, Mabel, 165

Low, David, 678

lower classes: in Victorian society, 51-2, 303-5; religious attitudes of, 60; legislative relief for, 305

Luce, Clare Boothe, 67-8

Lucy, Henry, 299

Ludendorff, Erich, 552, 706; attack in France by, 513-18, 521-2, 523, 524, 525, 526; breaching of Hindenburg line and, 530, 531, 532; on causes of loss of war, 541

Lullenden cottage, Kent, 506, 514, 631

Lumley and Lumley (solicitors), 221

Lushington, Gilbert Wildman-. *See* Wildman-Lushington, Gilbert

Luttwitz, General von, 403

Lutyens, Sir Edwin, 678, 720

Luxemburg, Rosa, 305

Lytton, Lady. *See* Plowden, Pamela

MacArthur, Douglas, 29

Macaulay, Thomas Babington, 47, 70, 240, 313, 543, 570; WSC's childhood reading and memorization of, 14, 23, 109, 133, 138, 203; WSC's style influenced by, 24, 217, 239

McCooey, J.H., 715

McCurdy, Charles, 605

McDavid, Jock, 484, 485

MacDonald, Ramsay, 346, 616, 656, 704; WSC's anti-Bolshevik policy and, 560; as Labour's first prime minister, 615, 671; Asquith coalition with, 638; WSC and policies of, 639, 671-2, 674, 696, 703, 716; Singapore policy of, 645; return to gold standard and, 646; general strike and, 650, 657; WSC's denunciation of, in 1922 election, 670; R 101 zeppelin project of, 679; question of Indian self-government and, 689, 691, 695; fall of government of, 694; new government formed by, after Crash of 1929, 700; 1931 elections and, 701; disarmament and, 713

McGowan, Norman, 26

MacGregor, O.R., 52, 75

Machen, Arthur, 540

McKenna, Reginald, 333, 352-3, 358, 453, 454, 640, 645, 646

McKinley, William, 273

McLaglen, Victor, 675, 680

McMahon family, 597

Elgin, 319; WSC's vacation with, 322; WSC's meeting with Clementine Hozier and, 325; Sidney Street newsreel report and, 344; on life at Admiralty House, 354; WSC at Admiralty and, 392, 460; on WSC's painting, 463; WSC in France and, 469, 478; WSC introduced to Sassoon by, 475; WSC's speech in House suggesting Fisher's recall and, 488; with WSC at Ministry of Munitions, 508; on Haig during Passchendaele drive, 510; WSC on need for American forces in France and, 515; on WSC's independence, 529; WSC's writing edited by, 627; loss of job by, after WSC's election loss, 671

Marshall, George C., 16
Martí, José, 186
Martin, Sir John, 7, 11
Martin, Kingsley, 655
Martin, Ralph G., 114
Martin, Rowland, 227, 232
Marxism, 558
Marxist Social Democratic Federation, 323
Mary, Queen of England, 178, 678n, 700
Massingham, Hugh, 28, 283, 286, 308, 318
Master and Servant Law, 65
Masterman, Charles, 331, 341, 345, 346
Masterman, Lucy, 334
Masterton-Smith, James, 392, 468
Masurian Lakes, 513
Maxwell, Sir Herbert, 173
Maxwell, Lady Robert, 220
Mayer, Arno J., 689
Mayhew, Christopher, 22
Mayo, C.H.P., 134
Mayo, Katherine, 687-8
Maze, Paul, 612
Meinertzhagen, Richard, 578, 580
Mein Kampf (Hitler), 630, 707, 711, 713
Melbourne, Lord, 74
Melchett, Lord, 661
merchant marine, 43
Meredith, George, 10
Metropolitan (magazine), 627
Middle East: British Empire in, 38, 39; postwar division of, 539, 571, 572; WSC's interest in, in Colonial Office, 571-2; *see also* Palestine
Middleton, Richard, 237-8, 240

Milbanke, Sir John, 130, 140
Military Service Act, 508
Mill, John Stuart, 49
Millais, Sir John, 58
Milne, Sir Berkeley, 383, 386
Milner, Sir Alfred (later Lord Milner), 13, 242, 245, 246, 492; Boer War and, 270; WSC opposes mining policy of, 317-19; WSC's South African policy and, 321; in Lloyd George's War Cabinet, 511; WSC's military policy in France and, 517; Imperial Federation League supported by, 543; on British Empire Exhibition, 547; recommendations for Egyptian sovereignty from, 548; at Colonial Office, 550; postwar troop repatriations and, 550, 551
mines: Chinese labourers in South African mines, 229, 317-18, 321; strikes in, 342-3, 648-50, 651, 656-60
minimum-wage bill, 334
Mining Association of Great Britain, 657
Minssen, M., 143-4
Minto, Lord, 274, 300
Mitchell, Billy, 644
Moir, Phyllis, 717-18, 719
Moltke, Helmuth von, 84
Monro, Sir Charles, 467
Montagu, Edwin, 455, 461, 569
Montagu, Venetia. *See* Stanley, Venetia
Montgomery, Bernard Law, 25, 28, 533
Montreuil, France, 521
Moore, Arthur, 400
Moore, George, 114
Moore, J.F., 127, 133, 134
Moore, Vera, 106
Moorehead, Alan, 587, 703
Moran, Lord, 9, 21, 22, 23
Morel-de-Ville, Georges, 608-11
Morgenthau, Henry, 422
Moriarty, L.M., 135, 146
Morley, John (later Lord Morley), 292, 297, 367, 385, 386, 387, 686
Morning Post, 495, 712; WSC's dispatches from Boer War for, 38, 242, 247, 250, 255, 260, 265, 266, 268; WSC's speeches reported in, 207, 221, 281, 283; WSC's dispatches on Kitchener for, 221, 222, 225, 226-7, 232, 233, 238; elections reported in, 324, 616; Home Rule question in, 374; WSC's ministry appointments

reported in, 396, 505, 550, 640; criticism of Antwerp operation in, 410; on WSC's leadership in Dardanelles, 455; *British Gazette* printed on presses of, 652, 653, 654; on WSC and party discipline, 662

Morocco, 312, 714; Agadir incident in, 349

Morrell, Philip, 387

Morris, James, 41, 44-5, 48, 542, 544, 547, 576, 677, 679

Morton, J.B., 678

Moscow, 554

Mother India (Mayo), 687-8

Mottistone, Lord. *See* Seely, John E.B.

Mountbatten, Dickie, 397

Mountbatten, Edwina, 74, 623

Mountbatten, Lord Louis. *See* Battenberg, Prince Louis of

movies. *See* film industry

Mowatt, Sir Francis, 285, 290

Muggeridge, Malcolm, 629

Munich agreement, 316

Murray, Janet Horowitz, 52

music and songs, 56-7, 307; WSC mentioned in, 6, 271; patriotism in, 38-9, 127, 204, 676; Gilbert and Sullivan and, 49, 58, 61, 67, 197; in music halls, 39, 58-9, 63-4, 165, 167, 307; in Victorian domestic life, 63-4; popular songs, 67, 162, 188, 620-1, 676; British soldiers in India and, 210; during Boer War, 259-60; dirge for Collins, 601; theme of Empire reflected in, 676

music halls, 31, 307; patriotism in songs of, 39; in Victorian England, 58-9; WSC's speech on prostitution in, 165-6; in Edwardian society, 313

Mussolini, Benito, 275, 610, 665; WSC on, 16, 24

My African Journey (WSC), 322, 327

My Early Life (WSC), 666, 704

Namur, Belgium, 400, 401, 402

Napoleon, 10, 37, 160, 249

Nash's Pall Mall, 626, 672, 704

Natal *Witness*, 251

Nation (journal), 331, 629, 647

National Health Insurance Act, 334, 339

National Liberal Club, 322, 613, 615

National Liberals, 611, 613, 701

National Life and Character (magazine), 164

National Observer, 164

National Review, 173

Nationalsozialistische Deutsche Arbeiterpartei (National Socialist Workers' party), 706

National Sunday League, 165

National Union of Conservative Associations, 120, 604

naval power. *See* sea power

navy: WSC's support for, in House, 287; isolationist policy and, 311; WSC on requests for monies for, 332-3, 350; WSC on importance of, 355-6; preparation for war of, 391-9; success in war and, 539; agreement with U.S. limiting, 542; WSC's budget at Treasury and, 643-4; *see also* Churchill, Winston Leonard Spencer: public life and political career, Admiralty

Nazism, 6, 706-9; WSC's mispronunciation of, 21; rise of, 706-7

Nehru, Jawaharlal, 74, 197, 680, 681, 683, 687, 690

Nehru, Motilal, 681

Netherlands, the, 417

Nevill, W.P., 540

Newbolt, Henry, 541

Newcastle Leader, 191

New Delhi, 678

Newfoundland, 546, 585

New Leader (newspaper), 666

Newnes, George, 163

New Republic (journal), 688

News Chronicle (newspaper), 666

newspapers. *See* press

New Statesman (publication), 8, 530, 655, 688

New York: Jennie and Randolph Churchill visit, 171; WSC visits, on way to Cuba, 187-8; WSC's lectures on Boer War in, 273; WSC's car accident in, 716-17

New Yorker (magazine), 54

New York Times, 6, 85, 279, 599, 688

New Zealand, 616; self-government in, 543; military backing for Great Britain from, 545, 546, 585

Nicholas, Grand Duke, of Russia, 421, 423, 436

Nicholas II, czar of Russia, 164, 552, 554; war with Turkey and, 437; shooting of, 553, 558

Nicholson, Otho, 615, 617

811

Piaktow, Peter, 343
Pickardt, Otto C., 717, 718
Pilsudski, Józef, 563
Pitt, William (the Elder), 12, 80, 160n
Pitt, William (the Younger), 80
Pius XI, Pope, 666, 700
Plowden, Pamela (later Lady Lytton):
    WSC's introduction to, 200-1; WSC's
    romance with, 237; WSC's political
    ambitions and, 237, 240; reaction to
    The River War by, 239; WSC's escape
    from prison in Boer War and, 259;
    WSC's Canadian lecture tour and, 274;
    end of WSC's romance with, 300;
    WSC's wedding and, 326
    LETTERS FROM WSC: on Oldham elec-
    tion, 240; during Boer War
    imprisonment, 251; on Boer War, 261,
    262, 264, 265
Plummer, Douglas, 316
Poincaré, Raymond, 584
poison gas, 507, 549
Poland, 713-14; German invasion of, 23;
    Russia and, 553, 562
Pond, J.B., 273, 274
Ponsonby, Arthur, 383, 662-3
Poor Law, 65, 305
Porch, Montagu, 526-7, 622
Portal, Charles, 17
Portugal, 681
Portuguese East Africa, 252, 258-9
poverty. *See* lower classes
press: in British Empire, 45; and avail-
    ability of publications, 163, 164; in
    India, 197, 205; war inflamed by, 204;
    union strikes reported in, 307; in
    Edwardian London, 312; during
    general strike, 652-4
Prevention of Poaching Act, 65
Primrose League, 105, 111, 117, 207
Prince of Wales. *See* Albert Edward,
    Prince of Wales; Edward, Prince of
    Wales
Prince of Wales (battleship), 16
prison reform, 339-41
Privy Council, WSC appointed to, 321
Prohibition, 642, 673
Prohibitionists, 611
prostitution, WSC's Empire music hall
    speech on, 165-6
protectionism. *See* Free Trade
Protestants, 303, 316
public schools, 47, 71, 183

Pugh, Arthur, 655
Pulitzer, Joseph, 187, 204
Punch (magazine), 45, 64, 197; WSC in
    House reported in, 283, 285, 286, 296;
    on WSC's switch to Liberal party, 298,
    299; Randolph Churchill in, 308; on
    Balfour, 314; wartime cartoons in, 399-
    400

Quebec conference, second (1944), 8
Queen Mary (ship), 19, 678
Queen's Own Oxfordshire Hussars
    (QOOH), 330, 348, 404, 469
Queen's University, 667

racism: in India, 45, 683; WSC's views on
    minorities and, 687
Raffles, Stamford, 37
Raglan, Lord, 183
railroad strikes, 346-7
Ralph, Julian, 284
Ramsden, Caryl John, 220
Ramsey, Lady de. *See* de Ramsey, Lady
Rand, South Africa, 268, 317
Rankin, James, 616
rationalism, 164
Raubal, Geli, 707, 709
Rawlinson, Sir Henry, 405, 408-9, 412,
    637
Read, Sir Herbert, 24
Reading, Lord, 685
Readymoney, Sir Cowasjee Jehangir, 198
Red Cross, 507, 556
Red Letter Election, 638
Redmond, John, 371, 372, 374, 375, 387,
    587
Red Soldiers' League, 552
Reith, Sir John, 654, 685, 692, 693, 720
religion: in Victorian society, 60; WSC's
    views on, 147, 204-5; changes in 1870s
    in attitudes towards, 164-5; in
    Edwardian society, 306
reparations after World War I, 549, 663,
    712
Repington, Charles à Court, 454, 506,
    526
Republican party (U.S.), 291, 293
Repulse (battleship), 16
Review of Reviews, 137, 138, 164
Rhodes (island), 16
Rhodes, Cecil, 13, 37, 163, 243, 292, 293,
    539, 543
Rhodes, Frank, 225

813

Rhodes James, Robert, 146, 284, 430, 541, 581, 590
Richmond, Herbert, 410, 421, 432, 448
Riddell, Sir George, 20, 449, 451, 460, 495, 514, 620, 627
Rideing, William H., 170
River War, The (WSC), 22-3; writing of, 239, 242; income from, 264; dedication of, 284
Robeck, John de. *See* de Robeck, John
Roberts, Lord, 178, 183, 216-17, 260; in Boer War, 263, 265-6, 267-9, 270; distrust of WSC by, 266; Diamond Hill battle and, 269-70; Ulster Volunteer Force and, 374
Roberts, Cecil, 613
Robertson, Sir Charles, 479
Robertson, Norman Forbes, 114
Robertson, Sir William ('Wully'), 481, 495, 502
Romanovs, 86, 558, 563
Rommel, Erwin, 474, 514
Roose, Dr Robson, 124-5; WSC's health and, 109-10, 136, 149, 240; Randolph Churchill's health and, 113, 169, 172, 173
Roosevelt, Franklin D., 11, 28, 275, 664, 680, 715; WSC on, 24, 30
Roosevelt, Theodore, 263, 273, 306
Rose, Dr John, 149
Rosebery, Lord, 114, 157, 281, 284, 292; on Randolph Churchill as Chancellor of Exchequer, 122; WSC's childhood meetings with, 129, 188; Randolph Churchill's declining health and, 169 170, 171; fall of government of, 178; on African expansion, 245; opinion of WSC of, 284; WSC's switch to Liberal party and, 298; Imperial Federation League supported by, 543
Ross, Alexander, 258
Rote Soldatenbund, 552
Rothermere, Lord, 615, 649, 655, 693, 705, 720
Rothschild, Lord, 158, 206, 374
Rothschild, Lionel, 300
Roving Commission, A (WSC). See *My Early Life*
Rowntree, Benjamin Seebohm, 297, 304
Rowse, A.L., 694
Royal Commission of Inquiry into the Dardanelles, 499-500, 502-3
Royal Commission on Marriage and

Divorce, 302
Royal Dutch Shell, 620
Royal Irish Constabulary, 589-90
Royal Military College, Sandhurst, 545; WSC's academic achievement at, 22, 161; entrance examination for, 146-7, 148, 151-2; WSC's tutoring for examination for, 149, 150-1; subjects and exercises at, 159-60; typical day at, 160
Royal Naval Air Service, 362
Royal Navy. *See* navy
Rufus I and II (pet dogs), 31
Ruhr, 552
Rumbold, Sir Horace, 583
Rupprecht, Crown Prince, 525
Russell, Bertrand, 387
Russia, 32, 275; WSC's views on, 13, 16, 530; war with Turkey, 59, 395, 437; Randolph Churchill's speech against, 123; Balkan presence of, 123, 349; British blockade of Crete and, 206; Triple Entente with, 312; as Serbia's ally against Austria-Hungary, 381, 384; German declaration of war against, 386; British Dardanelles campaign and, 419, 421; British postwar policy towards, 533; postwar damage in, 538; revolution in, 552-3, 559-60; Labour party policy towards, 607; MacDonald's recognition of, 638; WSC's later career haunted by, 702; *see also* Bolsheviks

Sacher, Harry, 578
Sackville-West, Vita, 77, 302, 303
St. George's School, Ascot, 102-5; WSC's reaction to being sent to, 102-3; WSC's later memories of, 103, 104; WSC's rebelliousness at, 104-5; canings at, 104, 105; WSC's achievement at, 105-6
St. Helier, Lady. *See* Jeune, Mary, Lady
Salisbury, Lord, 70, 129, 154, 178, 206, 280, 290; in Africa, 41; WSC's childhood meetings with, 110, 188; Randolph Churchill and, 119-24; Randolph Churchill appointed secretary of state for India by, 120-1; Randolph Churchill appointed Chancellor of Exchequer by, 122; Randolph Churchill's letter of resignation and, 123-4; Armenian crisis and, 167; Greek-Turkish clashes

372; German declaration of war on Russia and, 386; WSC's naval mobilization order and, 386; on war in France, 400; peace terms discussed with, 533; WSC's profile of, 627; general strike and, 649, 658; as secretary of state for India, 669; Indian self-government and, 684-5, 689; death of, 691

Smith, Hakewill. *See* Hakewill Smith, Edmund

Smith, Herbert, 657

Smith, Kinkaid, 114

Smith, Margaret (later Lady Birkenhead), 310, 325, 637, 691

Smith, W.H., 163

Smuts, Jan Christiaan, 16, 270, 679

Smyrna: awarded to Greece, 581; Turkish massacre in, 583, 585

Sneyd-Kynnersley, H.W., 104, 105-6, 129

Sneyd-Kynnersley, Mrs H.W., 119

Snow, C.P., 15

Snowden, Philip, 646, 662, 663, 700, 701

social attitudes: Pleasant Sunday Afternoon (P.S.A.) and, 305-6; technological change and, 306-7; *see also* Edwardian society; Victorian society

socialism: WSC's reaction to, 607; coal miners' strike and, 658; WSC plans book on, 667

Socialist Review, 560

socialists: WSC's loss in Manchester election and, 323; British policy towards Russian bolshevism and, 560; Indian self-government and, 695

social reform, 18; before Lloyd George and WSC, 305; WSC in House and, 331-7, 663; House of Lords changes bills on, 334; 'People's Budget' of 1909 and, 334-5; need for change in House of Lords and, 335-7; parliamentary reform act and, 337, 338; prison reform and, 339-41

Somervell, D.C., 299

Somervell, Robert, 132, 134

Somme, France, 462, 532, 544; casualties in, 426; WSC on, 429-30

songs. *See* music and songs

Sopwith, Tom, 3

'Souls, the' (social set), 113, 114

South Africa, 677; Randolph Churchill

visits, 138, 243; Chinese labourers used in mines in, 299, 317-19, 321; map of (1899), 244; WSC as under secretary of state for colonies and, 320-1; Germany in, 348; military backing for Great Britain from, 666; *see also* Boer War

South African Light Horse, 260-1, 263

Soviet Union. *See* Russia

Spain and the Cuban insurrection, 186, 189-92

Spears, Edward. *See* Spiers, Edward Louis

Spectator (newspaper), 137, 138, 155, 218, 688

Spencer-Churchill. *See* Churchill

Spencer family, 80-1

Speyer, Sir Edgar, 381, 394

Spiers, Edward Louis (later Edward Spears), 185; war in France and, 472, 474, 478, 521, 522; 1922 Dundee election and, 609, 610, 611

Spion Kop, battle of, 262-3, 267, 544

Spurgeon, C.H., 59

Squire, John, 530

Stalin, Joseph, 275, 720; in England, 343; civil war in Russia after revolution and, 554, 557, 562, 565; image of, 715; WSC and, 720

Stalin, Nadezhda Alliluyeva, 715

Stamfordham, Lord, 396, 398, 410-11, 611

Stanley, Arthur, 288

Stanley, Venetia (later Venetia Montagu), 461; marriage of, 455-6; WSC rents house from, 671, 703; ASQUITH'S LETTERS TO: on WSC's preparations for war, 388, 392; on Prince Louis, 397; on Dunkirk, 404; on battles in Belgium, 405, 406, 407, 408, 409; on warfare, 415; on Dardanelles campaign, 420, 428, 431-2, 436; on Clementine Churchill, 459; on 1922 election, 611

Statute of Westminster, 679-80, 715

Steel-Maitland, Sir Arthur, 655, 658

Steevens, G.W., 239, 275

Stevens, Henry, 407

Stevenson, Adlai, 187, 188

Stevenson, Frances: on WSC at beginning of World War I, 8; South American naval losses and, 396; WSC at Antwerp and, 411; on WSC after Gallipoli defeat, 455, 457, 460; Lloyd

and WSC, 613; WSC's elections reported in, 617; WSC's *World Crisis* in, 627, 628, 630; return to gold standard in, 645; Indian self-government debate in, 685, 692, 698

Times Literary Supplement, 313

Times of India, 218, 662

Tirpitz, Alfred von, 357, 366, 428

Tojo, Hideki, 275, 714

Tonga, 42

Torrance, E. Paul, 133

Town Topics (magazine), 113

Trades Dispute Act of 1906, 659

Trade Union Congress (TUC), 647, 649-51, 653-4, 655, 657, 700

trade unions. *See* strikes; unions

Trafford, Thomas, 114, 115, 145

Transjordan, 575, 578, 579

Transport and General Workers' Union, 651

Transport Workers' Union, 346

Travers, William R., 85

Treasury. *See* Churchill, Winston Leonard Spencer: public life and political career, Treasury

Treitschke, Heinrich von, 58

Trenchard, Hugh, 363, 573

trench warfare, 413-15; WSC's life in, 473-4; WSC on, 493; recognition of folly of, 530, 539

Triple Alliance, 312

Triple Entente, 312

Tripoli, 349

Trollope, Anthony, 51, 68, 72

Trotsky, Leon: civil war in Russia after revolution and, 553-7, 561, 563, 565; WSC attacks policy of, 558; belief in spread of revolution beyond Russia of, 560, 561

Truth (weekly review), 176-7

Tuchman, Barbara, 75

Tudor, Henry, 515-16

Turf Club, London, 202

Turkey, 40; Greek clashes with, on Crete, 206, 207; Balkan wars of 1912 and 1913 and, 349; WSC denies warships to, 384, 395; secret agreement between Germany and, 384; Russia declares war on, 395; division of, 581; Mustapha Kemal in, 581-6; Lloyd George and, 581-2, 603; Smyrna destroyed by, 583; British troops dispatched to, 583-6; *see also* Dardanelles

Turner, Joseph, 72

Twain, Mark, 273

Tweedmouth, Lady. *See* Marjoribanks, Fanny

Tweedsmuir, Lord. *See* Buchan, John

Twenty-first Lancers: WSC attached to, 221; motto of, 222; in battle of Omdurman, 228-33; cavalry charge by, at Omdurman, 230-3; casualties among, at Omdurman, 232-3

Uganda, 48-9

Ukraine, 557, 562, 564

Ulster Liberal Association, 369

Ulster Volunteer Force, 371, 376, 493; support for, 373-4; Kipling poem honouring, 374

Unemployment Insurance Act, 614

Unionists: Randolph Churchill and, 121; WSC in Manchester election and, 316; WSC's trip to Belfast and, 369, 370, 372

Union of South Africa, 321; *see also* South Africa

unions, 307; WSC's support for, 297; WSC ineligible for, as bricklayer, 634

United Empire League, 668, 676

United Press, 5

United States, 12, 32, 275; troops of, fighting in France, 515, 521, 525, 532; WSC visits, 187-8, 273-4, 715-19; Cuba and, 191, 192; WSC's lecture tour on Boer War in, 273; British isolationism and, 311; emergence as sea power of, 542; British war debt to, 642; economic conditions in, 647; disarmament and, 665, 712; Franklin D. Roosevelt in, 715

Untouchables: in Indian caste system, 683; WSC's plea for, 690, 697

upper classes: in Victorian society, 66-77; in late 1920s, 664-5

U.S. Military Academy, West Point, 159; WSC visits, 187

Vaal Krantz, battle of, 264, 266

Valdez, Juarez, 189-91

Van Antwerp, William, 675

Vanderbilt, Consuelo. *See* Marlborough, Consuelo, Duchess of

Vanderbilt, Cornelius, 187

Vane-Tempest, Lord Herbert, 631

Vanity Fair (magazine), 100, 283, 308

Venizelos, Eleutherios, 437; proposed allegiance and troop support to Britain from, 417, 420, 436; Lemnos turned over to British as base for operations by, 431; fall of government of, 437, 582; Lloyd George supports, 581

Verne, Jules, 9

Versailles peace conference, 552; British Empire gains at, 538-9; signing of treaty at, 541; Germany and, 541, 549, 552, 712, 713; WSC on, 541, 549; Turkish losses after, 571; Palestine and, 580

Vickers, Horace, 672

Vickers, Vincent, 645-6

Victoria, Empress Dowager, of Germany, 219

Victoria, Queen of England, 94; British Empire and, 38, 39, 45, 235, 686; on Chinese Gordon's death, 46; advertising slogans and, 57-8; attitude towards divorce of, 63; on class system, 70; Randolph Churchill and, 81-2, 99, 121, 122, 123; George Churchill's affair with Lady Aylesford and, 95; Golden Jubilee of, 107; Kaiser Wilhelm II visits with, 140; Gladstone's resignation and, 155; review of Fourth Hussars by, 177-8; Diamond Jubilee of, 193, 195, 208; Boer War and, 260, 263; death of, 274, 275; Edward VII on, 279; isolationist policy of, 311; Home Rule and, 368; Strachey biography of, 546

Victoria League, 676

Victorian society, 51-77; colonial life in, 48-50; in London, 51-2; sexual attitudes in, 52-3, 73-7; class structure in, 53-4; transportation in, 54-6; dress in, 54; attitudes towards death in, 56-7; music halls in, 58-9; British soldier in, 59; beliefs and attitudes held in, 60-3; work in, 60-1; attitude towards war in, 62, 233; domestic life in, 63-6; servants in, 64-5; upper-class life in, 66-77; availability of newspapers in, 163; WSC as defender of, 275; workmen in, 347; isolationist policy of, 351; rejection of symbols of, in 1920s and 1930s, 677-8

Villiers, Lady Caroline, 73

Villiers, Sir Edgar. See D'Abernon, Viscount

von der Schulenberg, Count, 347

von Hipper, Franz, 395

von Reuter, Ludwig, 537

von Sanders, Otto Liman. See Liman von Sanders, Otto

von Spee, Maximilian, 395

Walden, Thomas, 242, 249

Wales, Prince of. See Albert Edward, Prince of Wales; Edward, Prince of Wales

Wall Street, 674

Walpole, Sir Robert, 160n, 280

Wanklyn, J.L., 292

war: Victorian attitudes towards, 62, 233; newspapers and, 204; lore of, after World War I, 540; as a game, 540

War Cabinet, 420n; WSC excluded from, 467; WSC's attempt to increase power with, 529-30; Bolsheviks in Russia and, 555, 562

War Council: Dardanelles campaign debated in, 420; Carden's plan discussed and accepted in, 424-8; WSC's troop preparations for Dardanelles campaign and, 433, 437; Gallipoli attack plan and, 436, 444-5, 447, 448, 452

War Office: permission to WSC to travel to Cuba from, 186; WSC's desire to join Kitchener in Egypt and, 219, 220, 221; Boer War and, 242, 248, 260; Lloyd George on, 333; Admiral Fisher on, 358; WSC's advocacy of tank warfare and, 417; Hamilton's request for more troops from, 465

Warrender, Hugh, 114

Warwick, Lady, 67, 113, 292

Watson, James, 239

Watt, A.P., 218

Webb, Beatrice, 164, 305; opinion of WSC of, 284, 331, 332, 341, 654-5, 670; WSC on social reformers and, 323

Webb, Sidney, 164, 305, 332

Weekly Dispatch, 612, 626, 663

Weekly Review, 560

Weil, Simone, 283

Weimar Republic, 552, 706-8

Weir, Lord, 693

Weizmann, Chaim, 572, 574, 580

welfare legislation. See social reform

Welldon, J.E.C., 216; WSC's entrance examination to Harrow and, 125-6;

popularity of, 127; disciplinary problems with WSC and, 128-9, 130-1; academic achievement of WSC and, 131, 133, 135, 142; letters to Randolph and Jennie Churchill from, 138; WSC's Sandhurst entrance examination and, 146-8, 149; WSC's letters to, 204; WSC's marriage and, 326

Wellesley, Lady Charlotte, 73

Wellington, Duke of, 71, 73, 183, 184, 351

Wells, H.G., 65, 164, 313, 362, 400, 416, 543, 712; on WSC, 323, 364, 566; WSC influenced by, 332; Bolshevik revolution supported by, 566

Wemyss, Rosslyn, 398

Wessel, Horst, 709

West Leicester election, 613-15

Westminster, Duke of ('Bender'), 271, 405, 416, 521, 625, 667

Westminster, Statute of, 679-80, 715

Westminster election (1924), 615-17, 618

Westminster Gazette, 167, 455

West Point. *See* U.S. Military Academy, West Point

Weygand, Maxime, 6, 564

Weyler, Veleriano, 191

White, Sir George, 242, 246, 264

Whitehead, Alfred North, 59

White Paper on Palestine, 580

Wilde, Oscar, 111, 164, 306

Wildman-Lushington, Gilbert, 363-4

Wilhelm II, kaiser of Germany, 276, 288; WSC's childhood view of, in Crystal Palace visit, 140-2; Boer War and, 260; WSC's meetings with, 310, 347-8; Anglo-French relationship and, 312; funeral of Edward VII and, 338; Agadir incident and, 349; Haldane's visit with, 356, 357; sea power emphasized by, 357; 'Naval Holiday' proposal from WSC to, 366; Austrian-Serbian dispute and, 381; Russian demobilization demanded by, 384-5; Armistice and peace negotiations and, 533, 539

William III, King of England, 80

Williams, Evan, 657-8

Williams, Francis, 604

Willingdon, Lord, 680

Wilson, Allen, 46

Wilson, Sir Arthur, 358, 359, 447

Wilson, Sir Henry, 517, 521, 551; British strategy in World War I and, 351, 462, 514; Home Rule and, 373-4, 376; Fisher's resignation and, 454; Gallipoli campaign and, 454, 465; on WSC, 456, 459, 588, 591; on desire to serve under WSC, 458; WSC advised against taking brigade by, 478; as chief of Imperial General Staff, 516; peace terms discussed with, 533; British policy against Bolsheviks in Russia and, 557, 558-9, 563; Lloyd George and, 570; violence in Ireland over Home Rule and, 588, 589, 591, 597, 598; murder of, 599-600

Wilson, Sir Horace, 5

Wilson, John, 38

Wilson, Muriel, 300, 326

Wilson, Lady Sarah (aunt), 263, 266, 600

Wilson, Woodrow, 521, 539, 628; League of Nations proposal of, 541-2; bolshevism in Russia and, 553, 557, 558

Wimbourne, Lady. *See* Guest, Lady Cornelia

Wimbourne, Lord. *See* Guest, Ivor

Winchester (school), 47, 124-5

Wingate, Sir Reginald, 227

Winterton, Earl, 296, 580, 661

Wodehouse, P.G., 547, 678

Wolfe, James, 634

Wolff, Sir Henry Drummond, 105, 119, 123, 186

Wolff, Leon, 481

Wollaston, Sir Gerald, 128

Wollaston, Nicholas, 198

Wolseley, Sir Garnet, 37, 47, 183, 185, 186, 191

woman suffrage. *See* suffrage movement

women in Victorian society, 76-7

Women's Social and Political Union, 307

Won't Go To Wembleys (WGTW) (group), 547, 548

Wood, Sir Evelyn, 206, 219, 220, 221, 225

Wood, Sir Kingsley, 5

Woodstock, Oxfordshire, 88, 90, 99

Woollcott, Alexander, 532

workers: dangers of workplace for, 60-1; WSC's first public speech mentioning, 208

World Crisis, The (WSC): writing of, 627-31, 665, 704; reviews of, 629; selections from, 629-30; WSC's income from,

A SELECTION OF BESTSELLERS FROM SPHERE

FICTION

CHASE THE MOON	Catherine Nicolson	£1.95 □
BROTHERLY LOVE	William Blankenship	£1.95 □
FOLLOWER	Stephen Gallagher	£1.95 □
SOLITAIRE	Graham Masterton	£1.95 □
THE QUEEN'S MESSENGER	Robert L. Duncan	£1.95 □

FILM AND TV TIE-INS

THEY CALL ME BOOBER FRAGGLE	Michaela Muntean	£1.50 □
RED AND THE PUMPKINS	Jocelyn Stevenson	£1.50 □
THE RADISH DAY JUBILEE	Sheilah Bruce	£1.50 □
MINDER	Anthony Masters	£1.50 □
SCARFACE	Paul Monette	£1.75 □
THE KILLING OF KAREN SILKWOOD	Richard Rashke	£1.95 □

NON-FICTION

THE 101 BEST AND ONLY LIMERICKS OF SPIKE MILLIGAN		£1.25 □
THE MANUAL OF NUDE PHOTOGRAPHY	Jon Gray, text by Michael Busselle	£5.95 □
THE ESSENTIAL GUIDE TO LONDON	David Benedictus	£2.95 □
TWINS	Peter Watson	£1.75 □
SHADOWS ON THE GRASS	Simon Raven	£1.95 □

All Sphere books are available at your local bookshop or newsagent, or can be ordered direct from the publisher. Just tick the titles you want and fill in the form below.

Name _____

Address _____

_____

Write to Sphere Books, Cash Sales Department, P.O. Box 11, Falmouth, Cornwall TR10 9EN

Please enclose a cheque or postal order to the value of the cover price plus:

UK: 45p for the first book, 20p for the second book and 14p for each additional book ordered to a maximum charge of £1.63.

OVERSEAS: 75p for the first book and 21p per copy for each additional book.

BFPO & EIRE: 45p for the first book, 20p for the second book plus 14p per copy for the next 7 books, thereafter 8p per book.

Sphere Books reserve the right to show new retail prices on covers which may differ from those previously advertised in the text or elsewhere, and to increase postal rates in accordance with the PO.